# THE THIRTIES

# The Daily Telegraph

# THE THIRTIES

## A CHRONICLE
## OF THE DECADE

edited and introduced by
DAVID HOLLOWAY

researched by
DAVID WARD

foreword by
W. F. DEEDES

SIMON & SCHUSTER
London . Sydney . New York . Tokyo . Singapore . Toronto

First published in Great Britain by
SIMON & SCHUSTER LIMITED 1993
under the licence of Telegraph books.

A Paramount Communications Company

**Simon & Schuster Limited**
**West Garden Place**
**Kendal Street**
**London W2 2AQ**

Simon & Schuster Sydney Australia Pty Limited

A CIP catalogue record for this book is available from The British Library
ISBN 0-671 - 71259-4

Photo Credits:
Pictures on pages 25, 33, 35, 36, 43, 44, 58, 60, 72, 81, 85,
88, 91, 105, 106, 121, 122, 130, 133, 148, 152, 154, 160, 169, 171: Hulton Deutsch Collection.
Pictures on pages 59, 119, 122: Topham.

Phototypeset by SLG
Printed and bound in Great Britain by Butler & Tanner, Frome and London.

# CONTENTS

# INTRODUCTION

The 1930s were, almost certainly, the most crowded decade of the 20th century. This book, like its companion volumes for the fifties and sixties, is not an attempt to provide a systematic history of the period but more a tapestry showing how events great and small, and how life was lived, were reflected in one newspaper, *The Daily Telegraph*. The dominating themes, the rise of Hitler, the Abyssinian War, the Spanish Civil War and the final outbreak of the Second World War, can only be represented by examples of the way that they were reported and commented upon at the time.

All the extracts printed here are, though often shortened for reasons of space, exactly as they were originally printed. No hindsight has been allowed other than in the short introductions to each year which occasionally comment on how events turned out differently from the expected. Some, like the foreign correspondent who found conditions in the German concentration camp he visited tolerable might, were he alive, wish to change his mind. The obituarist of the swindler Kreuger saw his words of praise made nonsense within months. Others, too, might be surprised that their enthusiasm for or rejection of books, films and plays were not what they would show today.

Inevitably some years contained more material than others but the division of the pages between news, comment, criticism, obituaries and sports reporting has been maintained, each year being given the same space. As *The Daily Telegraph* did not begin to print news on its front page until April, 1939, specimens of the old front page have been included together with samples of the main news page which was in effect the front page. Wherever possible, the original pictures have been used.

\*

The final selections are mine. The responsibility for omissions, and I am conscious of how many there, inevitably, are, lies with me alone. Apart from that the preparation of this book has been the result of teamwork. David Ward, who has taken over the full responsibility for the research after Diana Heffer, the researcher of the earlier volumes in this series, retired to motherhood, has shown immense skill in producing both the important and the quirky stories to be found here. The smooth production of the final volume owes much to his struggles with microfiche and photocopiers which regularly broke down.

I must thank my old editor, Bill (Lord) Deedes, for writing the preface. He joined the *Morning Post* at the beginning of the decade and transferred to *The Daily Telegraph* when the papers merged in 1937. His immaculate memory has done much to shape this book. I must also thank those at Simon & Schuster, Sian Parkhouse, Fenella Smart, Catherine Reed and Jo Beerts, who have turned a soggy mass of gummy pages into such smoothness. Finally, I must thank my family for, with only mild complaints, putting up with a recitation of the more recondite details of the 1930s. Once again, Sally has been my constant support, even when the dining room table became ever stickier.

David Holloway, July 1993

# The Daily Telegraph

## FOREWORD

On the night of September 30, 1938, I came back from Downing Street to the old *Daily Telegraph* office in Fleet Street with my share of the story of Chamberlain's return from Munich and "peace in our time". In the corridor outside our sub-editors' room, I encountered our Night Editor, Bob Skelton, who (as his kind invariably do) demanded my copy instantly. Then he paused, tapped me on the midriff and, in a different tone of voice, said unexpectedly: "I think you're for it, young man. I suppose you realise that?"

I had no affection for Skelton, but thereafter I respected his judgement. On my way home that night long after midnight, I decided I had been born under the wrong stars. My working life in newspapers had begun in 1931, in the aftermath of the Wall Street crash of October '29. Now, it seemed, we were going to war again. Next day I talked with Victor Gordon Lennox, the diplomatic correspondent whom I sometimes assisted, and Helen Kirkpatrick, star of the Chicago *Daily News*, who worked with us. Skelton was right, they said.

So it is not hard to paint the 1930s in the darkest colours. The decade began by reducing men to penury. It ended by sending them to war. Looking back on it again, it strikes me that the tragedy of the 1930s lay not simply in what happened, but also in what failed to happen. It could have been a brilliant decade. New ideas were in the air. Men and women were still pioneering – on land, in the air and at sea. We were through the worst of the 1920s, when everyone was recovering from a terrible war, and half the families of England had someone to mourn.

Let nobody judge the 1930s, incidentally, Chamberlain, Munich and so on, without weighing the impact of that war. It was in human terms the most destructive war in history. Families lost fathers, women lost lovers, mothers lost sons on a scale that now transcends the imagination. "Never again!" they said. The public zeal for peace at almost any price, which contributed to the East Fulham by-election result of 1933, the Oxford Union resolution of that same year, "That this House refuses to fight for King and Country", the Peace Ballot of 1935 and on to Munich itself, sprang in great part from the years 1914—18, saturated in blood, from which we recoiled. That is not popular history's version of those times; nor Winston Churchill's – witness his chapter "The Locust Years 1931—35" in volume one of his second world war history. But a writer who passed through his impressionable years in the 1930s is entitled to give evidence. Deep-seated public feeling against war prevailed here in the early, middle and later 1930s. In Germany, it was different. There, from Versailles onwards, through the downfall of the Weimar republic, the rubbishing of the mark, and a social abyss, the prevailing sense was not of loss, but of humiliation.

Of course, with hindsight, we should have paid attention to this, its likely consequences, and then taken earlier steps. Of course we should have heeded Churchill's warnings. But that prophet was not seen then as he is now. He was a politician out of office, brilliant but erratic, who had got it wrong in the first world war at the Dardanelles and resigned office, who had taken the wrong line on Independence for India, the wrong line on the Abdication, and whose judgement was not to be taken wholly on trust. Most political historians of the 1930s will continue to assert that the people of this country were betrayed by their political leaders. My evidence is that, until the last minute, the people of this democracy made abundantly plain to their leaders that they wanted peace above all else. As we go through this decade again in this volume, it may assist the reader to approach this aspect of it with a relatively open mind.

"Black Thursday" on Wall Street, October 24, 1929, when 13 million shares changed hands, was the overture to the 1930s. In Britain, unemployment topped 1.5 million, Oswald Mosley stormed out of the Labour Government in disgust at its failure to deal with the unemployed, Hitler published *Mein Kampf* and came second in the German elections.

By July 1931, a watershed in history, unemployment had soared to 2.71 million, Mosley had formed a new party, and Ramsay Macdonald's second Labour Government was pole-axed by a report which recommended swingeing cuts in government spending. In August this brought them down, and Britain to the brink. Coaxed by King George V, Macdonald, Baldwin and the Liberal leaders, Samuel and Simon, formed a coalition, devalued the pound, and called a General Election in the name of national survival. Unsurprisingly, they scored a

rout. When the votes had been counted, 554 seats went to the Government (473 of them to the Tories) and 56 to Labour. The Navy mutinied at Invergordon, the Stock Exchange closed for two days, there were riots at Glasgow. *The Morning Post* sent me to Drury Lane to see Noel Coward's panorama of the 20th century, *Cavalcade*, an unexpectedly nostalgic offering from such an author. That and Chaplin's *City Lights* were London's prime entertainment during those fraught hours. Dance hit of the year was "Just One More Chance…"

In a totally different world, the pioneers were striking out on their own. In April 1930, Amy Johnson, 27, daughter of a Hull fish merchant, became the first British woman to fly to Australia alone. In June of that year Sir Henry Seagrave killed himself in another land speed record attempt. In October, the giant airship R101 on a maiden voyage to India crashed in France, killing almost everyone on board, including the Secretary of State for Air. In 1931, Captain Malcolm Campbell took his Bluebird at 245 mph across Daytona Sands. A brave man called Picard took a balloon to a height of 52,000 feet. Jim Mollison, later to marry Amy Johnson, flew to Australia in the record time of 214 hours. In the air, the pilot Stainforth beat his own record with a speed of 408.8 mph.

Taking this on a stage, in 1932 Amelia Earheart of America landed her plane in Ireland, after crossing the Atlantic solo in record time, and Campbell clocked up 272 mph in Bluebird at Daytona Beach — by 1935 this was 300 mph. In 1936, the *Queen Mary* sailed on her maiden voyage with 1,840 passengers, and the airship Hindenberg crossed the Atlantic in 46 hours. A month later, the Queen Mary wrested the Atlantic Blue Riband from France's Normandie in an Atlantic crossing of three minutes inside four days. Beryl Markham flew the Atlantic alone. A year later, the Normandie had won back the Atlantic Blue Riband, the Hindenburg had blown up in flames at Lakehurst, New Jersey – a story I helped to report – and Amelia Earheart had disappeared somewhere in the Pacific. In 1938, Howard Hughes, the film mogul, flew round the world in less than four days in a Lockheed averaging 208 mph, and they launched the *Queen Elizabeth.*

It is worth dwelling on the further consequences of these different ventures. With the crash of our own R101 in 1930 and the destruction by fire of Germany's Hindenburg in 1937, the passenger-bearing airship passed into history. So in a sense have the great international liners which sprinted competitively across the Atlantic. At one point they sustained the seaport of Liverpool – until Southampton was found by Americans to be closer to Cherbourg and the continent. From the then magical Adelphi Hotel, designed for the comfort of the American in transit, I witnessed the more or less simultaneous collapse of Atlantic shipping and cotton. No other city suffered twin blows like that.

The racing motorists like Malcolm Campbell, and the lone aviators, Lindbergh, Johnson, Mollison, Earheart, Batten, Markham, bore more fruit. There was nothing mysterious about Campbell; he was simply brave and very fit. But the aviators I met professionally were outside my ken, particularly the women. Yet in the longer run, their work did most for our world of today. They found a path for the Boeing 747 and 400.

In the world of light music and fiction, plays, motion pictures, the 1930s merits a chapter on its own. The talking picture had arrived by the end of 1930, and we sang "On the sunny side of the street". By 1931, television was swiftly becoming a practical reality. Radio had become wholly reliable. In 1932, Shirley Temple reached the screen, Aldous Huxley published *Brave New World*, Waugh wrote *Black Mischief* and Greene produced *Stamboul Train*. Laurel and Hardy appeared, the Marx Brothers played in *Horse Feathers*, and the best melodies came from the motion picture *Forty Second Street.*

The year 1933 gave us "Smoke gets in your eyes" and "Stormy Weather". A year later we had Astaire and Rogers in *The Gay Divorce* and "You're the Tops." John Christie's Glyndebourne first saw the light of day. The mid-1930s gave us the best of the black-and-white movies, with Garbo, Hepburn, Gable, Colman, more Astaire and Rogers, and Irving Berlin's "Cheek to Cheek".

In 1936, the BBC produced its first TV programme. Pinewood opened. We danced to "The way you look tonight". Margot Fonteyn, 18, had a triumphant debut in *Giselle* at Sadler's Wells. Orwell's *Road to Wigan Pier* came out. Jean Harlow, a symbol of Hollywood, died at 26. GEC offered a TV set for £50,

Gershwin died at 38, Anna Neagle starred in *Victoria the Great*, and New York saw Steinbeck's "Of Mice and Men".

In the gathering dusk of 1938, Disney gave us *Snow White and the Seven Dwarfs*, the BBC broadcast television's first opera, Wagner's *Tristan and Isolde*. They also mounted their first film on TV, *Man of the Moment*. Orson Welles produced H G Wells's *War of the Worlds* on radio and started a panic. "Ladies and gentlemen, I have a grave announcement to make. Incredible as it may seem, strange beings who landed in New Jersey tonight are the vanguard of an invading army from Mars." Police switchboards, roads – and churches – were immediately jammed. Many claimed they had seen the Martians. Wells had feared the show might bore people!

In the final, fatal year, we danced to "Over the Rainbow," and "When the Deep Purple Falls". The final curtain fell at the Lyceum. Gielgud's *Hamlet* ran. Ivor Novello's *The Dancing Years* had the stage at Drury Lane, until it gave way to ENSA. There was *Good-Bye Mr. Chips*, Steinbeck's *The Grapes of Wrath* and finally Jan Struther's *Mrs. Miniver*: "This is the people's war. It is our war. We are the fighters. Fight it then. Fight it with all that is in us. And may God defend the right…"

Running through some of the light music of the 1930s, which still lingers in my head, I perceive that the real revolution in this country has been fought by the song-writers. Much of the entertainment of the 1930s — the films, the plays and much of the dance music — was saccharine sweet. There were reasons for this. The entertainers, and in particular the burgeoning Hollywood industry, made escapism from the dole queues and later the shade of war part of their business. Men and women did not seek *realité* during their leisure hours. They wanted escape from it. The song writers who knew their business helped them to find it. During the war, Vera Lynn – "There'll be bluebirds over the White Cliffs of Dover" – and her kind were the Forces' favourites. Sooner or later there was bound to be a violent reaction. It came with rock and rap.

None of this was of much direct concern to those for whom the Great Depression of the 1930s spelled a lost life. When King Edward VIII, just before his Abdication, went to South Wales and said, "something must be done" he met not only young men who had not worked since leaving school, but also their fathers, who had not worked since the birth of those sons. Part of this catastrophe was universal, but it was concentrated here because world competition had caught up with Britain's basic industries, debilitated by the first war and its aftermath, by neglect and, unquestionably, by a certain failure of capitalism to adapt.

Baldwin believed part of the answer was Protection, that is, a tariff barrier to protect our manufacturers. Beaverbrook thought it lay in Empire Free Trade. Nothing decisive was done until after the crash of 1931. I travelled to Dover to report the first day of tariffs on foreign goods.

The corners of this kingdom hardest hit by the prolonged world depression were where the oldest industries had flourished. Thus Tyneside, West Cumberland and much of South Wales eventually became designated Distressed Areas. Lancashire followed. I saw a good deal of them, partly because of a small idea which the *Morning Post* had conceived in the winter of 1936, and which *The Daily Telegraph* (after absorbing the *Morning Post* in 1937) sustained that year and in 1938. In essence, it comprised sending a Christmas present by post, anonymously, to the children of every unemployed parent in the Distressed Areas.

The idea could only succeed if every school teacher in the afflicted areas proved willing to send the name, address, age and sex of the eligible children. They did this, I recall, without exception. Every department of state involved co-operated. Extra trains were run, additional postmen were found. In the first year we picked six big London stores for the gifts – initially, about 120,000 of them at an average price of 2s 6d (roughly £4 today). The girls worked voluntarily after hours to pack them. The stores threw in money of their own. King Edward VIII sent one of the last cheques of his reign. Thereafter his mother, Queen Mary, made an annual visit to our office to watch progress.

We had one mishap. I spent weekends in one of the Distressed Areas, seeking copy which would colour our daily appeal to readers. One Saturday evening at dusk in Merthyr Tydfil I came across a scrawny little girl of about six in a dirty pinafore, with a translucent face and enormous eyes staring into a toy shop window. She was clutching the hand of a much younger brother. She wrote her own profile, to which I unwisely added the imaginary name of Elizabeth. In alarming numbers, *Daily Telegraph* readers sought to adopt her, foster her, give her a home, pay for her education, endow her for life. They sent cheques, earmarked "Elizabeth". After that, we kept names out of it.

What comes back over the years is the extent to which people then in distress counted upon their neighbours. This was so in many poor districts, including where I lived in Bethnal Green, but particularly so in South Wales. There, at one point, men would cycle 20—30 miles a day and back for work; but they were reluctant to move their families to the West Midlands, where prospects were brighter. They had discovered that when one household had a loaf of bread, and the neighbouring household no bread, both households ate half a loaf.

About that time, when the dole was in question, some medical body pronounced that it was physically possible for a man to subsist on a diet of herring, oatmeal, spinach and milk (I think it was) for 7d a day. One of our reporters, a serious and abstemious South African, was chosen to try this out for a week. Towards the final day, I cheerily asked him how he felt. He said interestingly, that on viewing an approaching train at Blackfriars Underground that afternoon, he had felt suddenly that his brightest future lay under the train. I duly reported this, and was instructed to take him to the Wellington public house at Aldwych for a steak and chips, for which the newspaper would pay.

It so happened that much later, in 1944, some of us found ourselves engaged in battle alongside the renowned 50 Division, drawn from the Tyne and the Tees. They were foremost among the warriors of the second war, used (Lord Montgomery told me later) in every main assault, until there was virtually nothing left of them. These Geordies had been recruited from a predominantly Distressed Area. Most of us enjoyed more hot dinners than they did. Yet they entered and fought the war as crack troops.

The 1930s left a legacy of political bitterness, which some of us who entered post-war politics encountered. Churchill lost in 1945 partly on account of that legacy. Yet the extraordinary fact remains that, when it came to the point in September 1939, this nation of rich and poor, of Sunningdale and Tyneside, of Eaton Square and Bethnal Green, appeared to be one people. There is something here which I have never fully understood. How did it come about that, after the experiences of the 1930s, we got the response we did in East London when the bombing became really serious?

Given a majority of virtually ten to one in the House of Commons, the National Government might be supposed to have had power to do as it chose; but it ran into difficulties with its proposals to grant India independence, the first chapter in the End of Empire. Churchill, who had spent some of his early life soldiering in India, lead a spirited Tory rebellion against first the Government's White Paper and then the enormous Government of India Bill itself. It was his hand in its proceedings as Parliamentary Under Secretary which established the political reputation of Mr R A Butler. The *Morning Post* was on Mr Churchill's side, and I was required to report the mishaps and embarrassments which befell the Tory party during this dispute.

This included a by-election in the Wavertree division of Liverpool in February 1935, where Randolph Churchill (with every encouragement from his father) fought the official Tory candidate on the India issue. Campaigning with the Churchill family from the Adelphi Hotel had its attractions, but the predictable outcome was to deliver the seat to Labour. After the final week, Randolph asked me to escort his two sisters, Sarah and Diana, on the evening train back to London. They held forth on the talents of their brother Randolph, his spontaneous platform appeal, his gift of speaking off the cuff. They contrasted this with his father's more laboured style; he prepared everything, and on days of heavy preparation, it was hell for everyone else in the household. Why could not father do it like Randolph did it? I have often thought back on that conversation.

Towards the end of 1934, there were reports of border clashes between Mussolini's Italy and Abyssinia, where Emperor Haile Selassie had been crowned Emperor in 1930. This came at the end of a disturbing year. Mosley was on the rampage in this country, calling for a modern dictatorship. There had been a bloody purge of the brownshirts in Germany, in which Ernst Roehm, formerly a close associate of Hitler's, was taken from his bed and shot. Chancellor Dolfuss of Austria was assassinated by a gang of Nazis. Hindenburg of Germany, last of the old guard, died. King Alexander of Yugoslavia and France's Foreign Minister, Louis Barthou, were assassinated at Marseilles. Churchill warned us that our weak defences "could lead to us being tortured into absolute subjection".

In those circumstances, Abyssinia seemed a long way off. Early in 1935, Italian troops began to pass through the Suez canal on their way to East Africa. We increased our defence spending, Neville Chamberlain declared that Britain was "80 per cent recovered from the Depression", King George V enjoyed a heart-warming Silver Jubilee in London, and we put Abyssinia out of mind. In July, it was clear that Mussolini intended serious business. One or two newspapers began to look at the map. Sir Samuel Hoare at the Foreign Office declared it to be "The League of Nations' Greatest Test".

I was young, unmarried and easily insured. The *Morning Post* asked if I was willing to stick it out on the Abyssinian side. In those days there was no Terminal 4 at Heathrow airport for correspondents in a hurry. I travelled from Victoria station in London via Dover, Calais, Paris, Marseilles; thence by Messageries Maritime steamer through the Mediterranean, the Suez canal and the Red Sea to

Jibouti. From there, after a day or two, the railway took three days and two nights to reach Addis Ababa, roughly a fortnight in all. Bearing, as I did, about a quarter of a ton of luggage and supplies, the journey was arduous. My travelling companion from Jibouti onwards was H. R. Knickerbocker, then a Hearst International News Service correspondent, later one of the honoured contingent of American international correspondents who took post in London at the start of the war and gave a good account of us. His salary was paid in gold, wherever he happened to be. We hit it off, and his guidance proved invaluable. Communications for newspaper correspondents in the mid-1930s were primitive. At Port Said, the Chief of Police, to whom I had an introduction from England, gave me his guess for the outbreak of war, based on what was going through the Canal. He was not far out. It took me a day and a half to get this back to the newspaper through the ship's signal office.

In Addis Ababa itself, they were unprepared for us. Two men sat at the cable office, apparently tapping out telegrams to our newspaper offices in morse code. At ordinary rates, it cost 1s 6d (say £2.50) a word. Everyone filed urgent, which cost 2s 6d (say £4) a word. Even that did not guarantee arrival in London on the same day. It was a whimsical process. Newspaper offices developed grievances. I shared a German *pension* with Evelyn Waugh, who was on the *Daily Mail*'s pay roll. The combination of Waugh's notion of news and Abyssinia's system of communications maddened them. Furious cables arrived for Waugh, which found their way later into his satirical novel about it all, *Scoop*.

There was no television in those days. Nor did radio have much part to play, but there was movietone news. Fox Movietone moved a lavish unit into Addis Ababa, under the captaincy of Lawrence Stallings, author of two great Hollywood hits *What Price Glory?* and *The Big Parade*. This made our lives brighter - and some of us richer, for they paid a dollar a foot for "action film". H. R. Knickerbocker lived up to his reputation by finding a black aviator, who flew him over the battle lines. He saw virtually nothing, but in the world of the blind, the cock-eyed man is king. Knickerbocker's flight totally outclassed an illicit expedition which Waugh and I and one other contrived to reach the northern front. We were nicked, threatened with execution, returned to the capital and carpeted by the British Minister, Sir Sidney Barton.

In the context of what was going on elsewhere in the world, this was a serious war. It has always seemed to me that all of us failed to convey that. As it proceeded, I went south to the ancient city of Harar, to report the Italian drive from the South. Two young women from Spanish newspapers accompanied me. We found that a mustard gas attack by Italy had crammed the local hospital, where the conditions were unspeakable. The Spanish girls rolled up their sleeves, put their newspapers on hold, and plunged into the wards. They were among the few, I have always thought, to emerge from that war creditably.

Given today's system of communications, the Abyssinian war might have had different consequences. There was no television to report horrors instantly and in colour. There were no four-wheeled drive land cruisers for cross-country work. To put it simply, the news media occupied a much lowlier place in public affairs than it does today. This applied even more to the Spanish Civil War, which came in the following year. This was far more serious for Europe than the Abyssinian War was. The Russians were engaged on the Republican side. Italy and Germany increasingly threw their weight onto the rebels' side. The International Brigade included volunteers from all our countries.

The Spanish Civil War would today have attracted even more attention than the war in former Yugoslavia has done. It was reported, but at a distance as it were. Without television and radio as competitors, newspapers moved at an altogether more leisurely pace. At one point in the Spanish Civil War, *The Daily Telegraph* dispatched me to Lisbon. I travelled by ship from Southampton with an enviously jolly crowd bound for Madeira. Recalled urgently to the office, and with three days to wait for a boat, I decided to risk the Sud Express which ran from Lisbon to Paris, though haltingly because of the civil war.

In an altogether different realm, the pace of communications shaped events. Early in 1936, gossip circulated about the King's friendship with Mrs Ernest Simpson. Nothing was said in the British newspapers, but a certain amount of tittle-tattle appeared in overseas publications. These were heavily doctored by the wholesalers in this country, not on grounds of censorship but from fear of libel. There are various versions of why British newspapers published nothing. One version is that Lord Beaverbrook enjoined silence on his co-owners in Fleet Street. The truth was probably more complex. There was fear of libel. Newspapers exercised more discretion towards public figures – and royalty in particular - than they do today. Apart from the Simpson divorce proceedings, heard at the Ipswich Assizes on October 27, and a much-reproduced holiday picture of the King and Mrs Simpson in Yugoslavia, there was nothing firm to go

on. My editor, H. A. Gwynne, took overseas cuttings which I had collected to the Prime Minister. Baldwin said he needed more time.

Early in December, the floodgates were released - unwittingly - by the Bishop of Bradford whose relatively subdued criticism of the King was splashed in the *Yorkshire Post*. The ensuing crisis lasted no more than ten days, and I have sometimes wondered whether the outcome might have been different had the affair been openly reported from the first, as it certainly would have been today. On the whole, I doubt it. The course of events might have been different, but the outcome would have been the same.

The King had influential supporters, some of whom presented his predicament as that of a radical sovereign of whom Conservative Ministers were determined to be rid. The Archbishop of Canterbury, who inspired lines beginning - "My Lord Archbishop, what a Cantaur, And when your man is down, how bold you are …" was made to appear in similar colours. The silent majority, however, conveyed its feelings pretty clearly in a relatively short space of time. Baldwin's final speech to the Commons won a wide measure of agreement. Much later, I learned a curious fact about the speech, which had been hurriedly prepared on scraps of paper. On arrival in the House, Baldwin was dismayed to find that he had mislaid it. His parliamentary private secretary, Tommy Dugdale (later Lord Crathorne), returned to No. 10 in search of it. He found traces of the speech on the staircase and then, following the trail to an upstairs loo, was able to piece it all together.

On the lighter side, it was a decade in which popular sport became important news. It opened with graceful figure of Bobby Jones, who in 1930 won both the Amateur and Open Golf Championships of both Britain and America, a feat unlikely to be repeated. In that same year, Don Bradman arrived in this country with the Australian cricket side. He opened with an innings of 236 against Worcestershire, scored 334 in the Headingley test, 254 at Lords and 232 at the Oval, ending the season with 2,960 runs and an average of 98.66. This mastery of British bowlers by a single batsman contributed towards the ill-starred plans of Douglas Jardine, who captained the next English side to visit Australia in the winter of 1932–33. Bodyline bowling by two or three accurate fast bowlers was conceived as a counter-stroke to Bradman's dominance. It led only to an unholy row, ultimately involving the Commonwealth Secretary, echoes of which are heard today.

Another dominant figure was Helen Wills Moody who in July 1933 scored her sixth victory at Wimbledon. The following year at Wimbledon, however, attracted more attention. It was decreed that women could wear shorts, and one or two made the most of it. For British sport 1934 was a handsome year. Henry Cotton won the Open at St George's, Fred Perry won the Men's singles at Wimbledon, and Dorothy Round won the Women's singles. Jack Hobbs, in his 55th year, left the cricket field in 1935. In that year, the American Jesse Owens broke five records and equalled a sixth within the space of 45 minutes. In the following year he was the star of the Berlin Olympics in the 100 metres, 200 metres, long jump and 400 metres relay. That year, a star arose on another field when Obolensky, then 19, played a major part in England's first rugby victory over New Zealand.

In 1937, Joe Louis became the first black heavyweight champion since Jack Johnson in 1915. Mrs Miller became the first woman to win the Derby with Midday Sun. Sydney Wooderson set up a new world record for the mile in 4.60 minutes. Patsy Hendren left the cricket field, as Len Hutton and Denis Compton were seen as future stars. In 1938, Americans won all five titles at Wimbledon, Helen Wills Moody winning her 8th championship. At the Oval in August, Len Hutton fulfiled promise with an extraordinary innings of 364 out of a total of 907 for 7, which enabled England to crush Australia by an innings and 579 runs.

Thereafter, the European shadows rapidly grew longer. As Hutton was bringing in his bat, our Ambassador in Berlin, Sir Nevile Henderson, was recalled to discuss Germany's growing threat to Czechoslovakia. In September, France sent troops to the Maginot Line. On September 7 an editorial appeared in *The Times*, suggesting that the Czech Government might consider as an alternative to their present proposals the secession of the fringe of alien populations in their territory. The proposal, widely believed to have been inspired by the Government, created in Europe next day what its author and *Times* editor, Geoffrey Dawson, described in his diary as "hubbub". The episode, which a subsequent history of *The Times* makes no attempt to gloss over, is rendered important by the evidence of the late Rab Butler, then junior Minister at the Foreign Office. "I am myself convinced that Halifax knew this article was to be written: the two Yorkshiremen [Halifax and Dawson] were very close and I saw Dawson leaving the Foreign Office on the 6th after a long interview with the Foreign Secretary."

Not everyone was asleep. I was closely acquainted with Anthony Winn who, after Eton and Christ Church, Oxford, had become a *Times* lobby correspondent. He wrote a note about Duff Cooper's resignation in October 1938, for which

Dawson substituted one of his own, more critical of Duff Cooper. Winn resigned. "My distaste for what I frankly regard as a silly and dangerous policy has been hardening for weeks," he wrote to Dawson. Winn joined *The Daily Telegraph*, but only for a short time. He was killed in action in the Desert in November 1942.

Chamberlain, in fact, made three expeditions to Germany. I saw him off from Heston in his little plane for the second visit at 8.30 a.m. Tuesday, September 22. Unknown to him, I reported, the Cabinet arranged late on Monday night to be present to wish him Godspeed on his fateful journey. Just before boarding the plane he stepped to the microphones and said: "When I was a little boy, I used to repeat, if at first you don't succeed, try, try, try again. When I get back, I hope I may be able to say as Hotspur in *Henry IV* 'Out of this nettle, danger, we pluck this flower, safety.'" That conveyed very well the flavour of the month.

He had given the Cabinet an impressively candid impression of Hitler, "the commonest little dog you ever saw." The Cabinet minutes recorded, more discreetly, "On a first view, Hitler was unimpressive." After the unsuccessful second visit, all seemed lost, and they began digging trenches in the parks. Chamberlain was in course of reporting failure to the House of Commons on September 28, when a note was hurriedly passed to him. This is how Harold Nicolson described the scene:

> He adjusted his pince-nez and read the document that had been handed to him. His whole face, his whole body seemed to change. He raised his face so that the light from the ceiling fell full upon it. All the lines of anxiety and weariness seemed suddenly to have been smoothed out; he appeared ten tears younger and triumphant. "Herr Hitler," he said, "has just agreed to postpone his mobilisation for 24 hours and to meet me in conference with Signor Mussolini and M Daladier at Munich."

The fundamental reason why Ministers subscribed gratefully to Munich and, thereby appeared shamefully to betray the Czechs, was the prospect of an ill-defended civilian population being massacred by the bomber. I knew about our air defences, for I had been the newspaper's civil defence correspondent for two years. Six months before Munich, London had recruited less than one-fifth of the 126,000 ARP wardens it needed. In outer London the figure was 7,700 volunteers out of 46,000. Our other defences against the air were in similar disarray. The bomber's potential was not fully known, but some of us knew enough about the modern bomb to make it seem awesome. My estimate at the time was that our urban population would remain highly vulnerable until at least the end of 1939.

Our ill-preparedness at the time of Munich has become notorious, and almost a generation of politicians have been reviled for it. In fact, we had reluctantly accepted the need for some rearmament as early as 1933 and this proceeded, but (as Churchill constantly pointed out) we moved at a slower rate than Hitler's drive. Our rearming was *surreptitious*. Ministers feared that if the extent of it became public knowledge, it would be held against them. The subject was muted in the General Election of 1935 - notwithstanding the fact that Mussolini was by then at war with Abyssinia and we had warships standing by in the Mediterranean. They were alleged to be without shells for their guns.

In a profoundly unwise speech, Baldwin later attempted to explain why it had been muted. Speaking with "appalling frankness" in November 1936, he told the House of Commons: "Supposing I had gone to the country and said that Germany was rearming and we must rearm, does anybody think that this pacific democracy would have rallied to that cry at that moment? I cannot think of anything that would have made loss of the election [1935] more certain."

Churchill in the first volume of his war memoirs, *The Gathering Storm*, enters this in the index as: Baldwin: confesses putting party before country. The imputation of that is deadly, and it has become accepted as the true version of events. In reality, it was not as simple as that. Churchill was nearer the mark when he later described Munich as a *national* disgrace. For Baldwin was right. Had he called on the country to support a strong programme of rearmament in the General Election of 1935, there is a good chance that he would have lost it. I was temporarily out of the country, but the mood was unmistakable. Rab Butler has put on record how he was reviled in the election campaign as a warmonger and militarist.

The Peace Ballot of 1935, conducted by the League of Nations Union, set the tone. Spread over 8 months, it had produced 11,559,165 answers to five separate and somewhat ambiguous questions. There were many ways of interpreting it, but the emphasis laid on "collective security", rather than action by Britain, was unmistakable. This was in line with Labour's policy, which was to reject any programme for great armaments, but to place reliance on the League of Nations and a sharing of the burden by other nations. In other words, if the sheep huddled together into one corner of the field, they would become less vulnerable to the wolf.

There has been very little speculation by historians as to what the consequences of a Labour victory in 1935 might have been; but it has to be weighed. In reality, from the election onwards, the pace of rearmament was quickened. In the Spring of 1936 work on the big new block in Whitehall, which is now the Ministry of Defence, was halted in order to divert more resources to defence. Not all were neglectful of their duties. The Spitfires and the Hurricanes which, in the hands of our fighter pilots, defended us in the Battle of Britain, were not put on the drawing board until Churchill took office in 1940. The central question is whether in the first half of the 1930s this democracy would have supported and sustained rearmament on a scale which Hitler undertook on behalf of a humiliated Germany. The honest answer is that it almost certainly would not.

Looking back on it, it is plain that as well as failure by our own politicians to read Hitler's mind and future intentions clearly, there was grotesque failure by our newspapers fully to report what was going on in Germany. The persecution of the Jews, for example, had begun very early on. Liberals and Jews in Germany had reason to be fearful from early 1933. Early in that year, the Nazis were burning books. In June Hitler banned all opposition parties. There was a gruesome show trial of van der Lubbe for the Reichstag fire of February 1933. In June of 1934, Ernst Roehm, formerly a close associate of Hitler's, was dragged from his bed and shot. There were tales of perversity and debauchery among senior Nazis. In July, Dolfuss was assassinated by a gang of Nazis - while Hitler was listening to Wagner's *Das Rheingold* at the Bayreuth Festival. All this and more, in the first half of the 1930s.

If some of these events had been reported as they would have been today, it is not inconceivable that the public's mind vis-a-vis the threat posed by Hitler would have changed much sooner than it did. As it was, reporting of much that went on in Germany was muted. There were reasons for this. At the outset, many regarded the advent of Hitler as no bad thing for Germany. Those who saw the terms of the Versailles Treaty after the first war as insanely punitive of Germany thought they perceived a certain logic in the advent of such a man. After we had learned more of his nature, another mood prevailed. It was important not to provoke this somewhat excitable and sometimes hysterical figure. Certain of his demands, taking the excesses of Versailles into account, were not totally unreasonable. If we were not going to fight him, we had to find a way of living with him. Nobody was inclined to fight, so the second course was the only one open to us.

To a degree very hard now to explain, newspapers (with a few honourable exceptions) followed this emollient prescription. Of course correspondents in Berlin who overstepped the mark were at risk of being thrown out; every sensible correspondent tries to stay the right side of that line. Editors, on the other hand, took their line too readily from Ministers. *The Times* was not the only offender. Up to the last moment, Lord Beaverbrook's newspapers were fatuously proclaiming that there would be no war this year or next. Churchill's warnings about the state of Germany's rearmament were treated as fair copy; they seemed not to disturb the German leadership unduly. Dirty news about Germany was barely publishable.

We have reached a position today when the news media collectively and television in particular is held to excite public attitudes which, in turn, bring undue pressure on Governments to act against their judgement. Events in former Yugoslavia are a case in point. In the 1930s, it seems to me, precisely the opposite applied. The newspapers - there was no effective television news - said very little about Hitler's Germany calculated to excite public feeling. Only the Jews in this country, who knew what was happening, felt tormented.

Perhaps the best way to sum up the 1930s is to describe them as years of lost opportunity. Men who spent much of their adult lives on the breadline wasted their lives. Their womenfolk grew prematurely old. Yet there was so much promise gathering about us, rising again from the abyss of Flanders in 1914—18. Men and women seemed ready, single-handed, to test small planes and fast cars to destruction. There was a strong air of inventiveness; we saw the birth of the products of which we now take for granted. Regular recreation became a recognised part of English life. The stage sparkled with comedy as well as the works of George Bernard Shaw.

After the convalescent 1920s, it seemed we had the opportunity to rebuild a better world. Many believed that. In America, Roosevelt was proclaiming that we had nothing to fear but fear itself. We feared another war, too much perhaps for our own good. So, in Europe, it gradually fell apart. The opportunities drifted away from us. Finally we were left only with Mrs. Miniver on our stage. "This is the people's war. It is our war. We are the fighters. Fight it then. Fight it with all that is in us. And may God defend the right …"

But that belongs to the next decade.

W.F. Deedes

# 1930

The effects of the Depression which had begun in 1929 were being felt all the more keenly. In Germany and the United States the unemployment figures were over 10 million and in Britain they passed the two million mark during the year. It is not surprising that political unrest was being felt in many countries. In Germany the Nazi party, led by an Austrian citizen, Adolf Hitler, first emerged as a possible government. In Russia, Stalin continued his reign of terror, collectivising all agricultural land and killing the peasant farmers. In the United States the authorities in Chicago admitted defeat and allowed mobsters like Al Capone to run the city.

In India, the publication of the Simon Report failed to quell the civil unrest. Mr. Gandhi started off on his long march down the west coast of India and before the end of the year was in custody, as was the future first Prime Minister of an independent India, Pandit Nehru. In scenes of "barbaric splendour", the Emperor Haile Selassie acceded to the throne of Abyssinia.

In Britain the financial crisis forced the Chancellor of the Exchequer, Philip Snowdon, to raise Income Tax by 6d (2 1/2p). The old Poor Law was brought to an end. Sir Oswald Mosley resigned from the government and issued his own manifesto for solving the unemployment problem, pressaging the ideas he was to formulate when he formed the British Union of Fascists. A plan was produced to form a united body to run all London's transport. The Flying Squad was formed.

The Naval Treaty was signed in London limiting the size of fighting vessels, an accord signed by many nations, few of whom intended to keep to its terms. The French occupying troops withdrew from the Rheinland, thus ending the occupation of German territory by the allied victors of the Great War.

The crash of the giant airship R 101 in Northern France, at the start of a proving flight to India, led to the abandonment of the programme for building large lighter-than-air machines and the later breaking up of the R 101 even though it had made a successful Atlantic crossing. Amy Johnson became the first woman to fly solo from England to Australia. Sir Henry Segrave won the world land-speed record, only to lose it to Captain Malcolm Campbell and then to regain it. His efforts to achieve the water-speed record as well led to his death on Lake Windermere, close to the point where, more than 30 years later, Donald Campbell, the son of Segrave's great rival, was also to lose his life.

Among others who died during the year was the Poet Laureate, Robert Bridges. He was succeeded in office by John Masefield. Other writers to die were D.H. Lawrence and Sir Arthur Conan Doyle. The political world lost a former Prime Minister, Arthur Balfour, and a former Lord Chancellor, the Earl of Birkenhead.

Cricket was dominated by the 21-year-old Don Bradman, playing his first test series in Britain for Australia. His tally of records grew steadily during the summer. Jack Hobbs, taking part in his last test season for England, passed W.G. Grace's record for the total of first-class runs scored. The first football game played under floodlights was pronounced a success.

**GANDHI'S LIEUTENANT IMPRISONED**



# The Daily Telegraph



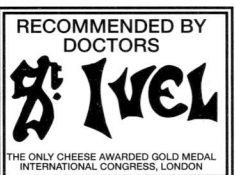

No. 23,343 POSTAGE { INLAND, CANADA AND NEWFOUNDLAND, THREE HALFPENCE / OTHER COLONIES AND PLACES ABROAD, TWOPENCE } LONDON, SATURDAY, MARCH 8, 1930 TWOPENCE

## BIRTHS, MARRIAGES, DEATHS
**(3s 6d per line)**

"IN MEMORIAM" NOTICES
**(2s 6d per line)**

For particulars of charges for annual insertion for periods of five or ten years apply to the Advertisement Manager.

*All announcements must be authenticated by the name and address of the sender. They may be handed in at the Head Office of "The Daily Telegraph," 135 Fleet-street, E.C.4, at the West-end Office, 161, Piccadilly, W.1. or at any of the Branch Offices. They may also be telephoned to Central 4242 (Extensions 7, 8 or 9), between the hours of 9 a.m. and 5 p.m. Cheques, Postal and Money Orders should be made payable to-*

*The Cashier, "The Daily Telegraph"*

## BIRTHS

**ACLAND** - On March 6, 1930, at 73, Upper Berkeley-Street, W.1. to Margaret, wife of Sir William H.D. Acland, Bt., a daughter.

**SEARS** - On March 6, 1930, at 41 Roual-avenue, Chelsea to Mary Rhodes (neé Dodge), wife of Lieut. H. P. Sears, R.N., a son. American papers, please copy.

**SPRAGGE** - On March 5, 1930, at 7, Knaresborough-place, S.W. 5, to Honor, wife of Lieut. G.J.E. Spragge, R.N., a son.

**TALBOT** - On March 6, 1930, to Cynthia, wife of Evan Talbot, a daughter.

**WARBURTON** - On March 5, 1930, at 96, Ashley-gardens, Westminster to Anne, wife of Rupert Warburton, a daughter.

## MARRIAGES

**CHAMBERS - SCOTT** - On March 6, 1930, at the Brompton Parish Church, by the Rev. Rupert Strong, Holroyd Ferris Chambers, younger son of Sir Theodore G. Chambers and Lady Chambers, to Audrey Ronald Scott, only daughter of Mr. and Mrs. Scott.

**HUNT-SURRAGE** - On March 6, 1930, Frederick J. A. Hunt, of Corrientes, Argentina, to Sylvia P.L. Surrage (neé de Gay), of Melbourne, Australia. Argentine papers, please copy.

**REES-HUGHES** - On March 5, 1930, at All Saints' Church, Bombay, Stanley Edward Rees, of Bhopal, to Kathleen Rosina Hughes (Kitty), of Epping, Essex.

## DEATHS

**CAVE** - On March 6, 1930, in London Arthur Belgrave Cave, aged 77. For about 20 years Captain in the service of the B.I.S.N. Co. Funeral at Westminster Cemetery, Hanwell, at noon, Monday, March 10.

**CHESTERMAN** - On March 5, 1930, at Exeter, Charles Frederick Chesterman, aged 80 years. Funeral on Monday at Trevalga, N. Cornwall.

**GROAGER** - On March 7, 1930, at 5, Mantague-place, Worthing, John Frederick Groager, late of Muswell Hill, in his 73rd year.

**GLENNY**, Francis Charles, on March 6, 1930, at "Kahale," Imperial-avenue, Westcliff-on-Sea, aged 53.

**HASSELL** - At 6, Warwick-crescent, W.2., Mary Louisa, widow of George Clements Hassell, of Northunberland. No mourning or flowers, by request.

**HILLIAR** - On March 6, 1930, at 8, Luke's-road, Brighton, Fanny J. Hilliar, aged 77. Funeral Monday. Service at 8, Luke's Church at two p.m., interment at the Borough Cemetery.

**HOLLAND** - On March 6, 1930, at "Glengarry," Thames Ditton, after a brief illness, Ernest Robert, beloved husband of Clara Frances Holland, aged 46. Funeral, Monday next, St. Nicholas's, Thames Ditton, 2.15.

**JONES** - On March 6, 1930, at "Selattyn," Purley Downs-road, Sanderstead, Surrey, Ronald Robert Mclan Jones, in his 83rd year. Late of Kimberley, South Africa. Funeral Sanderstead Church to-day (Saturday), at 2.30 p.m.

**LARDNER** - On March, 5, 1930, at his residence, 165 Melrose-avenue, Cricklewood, John Lardner, of The Priory Tavern, Belsize-road, Kilburn, in his 64th year. Funeral Monday, March 10, at Golders Green Crematorium, 3.30.

**LINDEMAN**, Oliver George, dear husband of Constance Ellen Lindeman, died March 6, 1930, at 151, Castlenau, Barnes.

**MILLETT** - On March 5, 1930, at Sutton-in-Ashfield, the Rev. Julian Millett, M.A., Vicar of St. Michael's, aged 48.

**MOSES** - On March 6, 1930, at Hove, Hannah, widow of Philip (Bob) Moses. Funeral at Willesden Cemetry tomorrow (Sunday) at one p.m. No flowers. Prayers at 6N, Montagu-mansions, W.1. at seven p.m.

**NOEL** - On March 5, 1930, after a short illness, at 100, Highbury-hill, N.5. Amy Sarah, widow of the late Alfred Noel, of above address, and 51 King-square, E.C.1. Interment in family grave at Islington Cemetery, on Monday, March 10, at 12.30 p.m.

**O'BRYEN** - On March 5, 1930, at 29, Ellerker-gardens, Richmond, Frances Louisa, daughter of the late Colonel J.J. O'Bryen, India Staff Corps. R.I.P.

**PIPER** - On March 5, 1930, suddenly, at King's Leigh, Whitstable, Francis Parris Piper, M.B. Lond., M.R.C.S., L.R.C.P., M.O.H., son of the late William Piper, Esq., of Ackleton Hall, Shropshire, and dearly loved husband of Heather Alleen Piper. Funeral All Saints', Whitstable, 2.30 to-day (Saturday).

**ROGERS** - On March 5, 1930, suddenly, Charles Herbert Rogers of Wimborne House, Brooksville avenue, N.W.6, dearly-loved husband of Harriet Rogers, aged 58. Funeral service at St. Jame's Church. Sussex-gardens, on Tuesday, March 11, at two o'clock; interment subsequently at Paddington Cemetery.

**TAYLOR** - On March 6, 1930, at Brooke House, 22 and 23 Warwick-lane, E.C.4. Charles Taylor, publisher and exporter. Interment Tower Hamlets Cemetery, Bow, E., Tuesday, March 11, at three p.m.

**TAYLOR** - On March 6, 1930, at 4, Florence-road, Ealing, Elizabeth Anne widow of the Hon. E.B.A. Taylor, C.M.G., late of Bahamas.

**TEMPLE** - On March 6, 1930, at Basing Lodge, Julian-road, Folkestone, Frederick Wilson Temple, F.S.I., aged 60.

## IN MEMORIAM

**BEDFORD** - In loving remembrance of Edward Bedford, C.E., who entered into rest March 8, 1929. Hove, Sussex.

**BEST** - In ever-loving memory of Alfred John Best, who entered into rest March 8, 1919 - Cial.

**BONAS** - In loving memory of our darling Harry, who departed this life on March 8, 1925, aged 15 years. Always in our thoughts.

**CANE** - In loving memory of Edward Percy, March 8, 1916 also "May," his widow, Dec. 7, 1929. Much loved - Mother.

**COXON** - In ever loving memory of my dear husband, Charles Merriman Coxon, who gently fell asleep March 8, 1929. Sadly missed.

**THOMSON** - In ever-loving memory of a dear husband and father, J.E. Thomson, who peacefully passed away March 8, 1928.

SUNDAY

**MARSH** - In ever-loving memory of Jessie Marsh, who passed away peacefully on March 9, 1925.

LONDON NECROPOLIS CO - Funerals, Cremation, Monumental Masonry. 121, Westminster Bridge-rd. S.C.1. Hop 1276. Tele. "Necropolo London"

CREMATION SOCIETY - A single payment of five guineas ensures cremation at death at any British Crematorium - Full particulars from 23, Nottingham-place, W.1. Welbeck 4168.

COOKSEY & SON. Funerals and Cremations, 266 Upper-street, Islington; 52, Amwell-street, Finsbury, Private Mortuary Chapel. No extra within 12 miles. 'Phone North 0030; Clerkenwell 2884.

DRUCE & CO. Ld., BAKER-ST., W.1. FUNERALS ARRANGED FOR and PERSONALLY CONDUCTED. MEMORIALS ERECTED IN ANY CEMETERY in ENG. or WALES. Valuations for Probate. 'Phone: Day. Welbeck 8254; Night. Epsom 239.

GREEN & EDWARDS Ld., Finchley-rd., N.W.5. FUNERALS. Efficiently arranged CREMATIONS, MODERATE CHARGES. 'Phone Hampstead 6600.

## PERSONAL

*Announcements for insertion in the Personal column are charged at the rate of 5s per line (minimum 2 lines) Trade announcements 7s 6d. per line (minimum 2 lines) Lost and Found Notices 2s. per line (minimum 2 lines). Names and addresses of advertisers must accompany all advertisements, not for publication unless desired, but as a guarantee of good faith.*

JIF. - Prevented from attending to-night. Proceed as usual - XX.

BLUTHNER BOUDOIR GRAND: perfect condition; £130 - Write E. Garat, National Liberal Club, S.W.1.

GARDEN LOVERS will find Interesting Items of Information and Advertisements on Page 20.

DO PLEASE SEND OLD CLOTHES, Toys, Books, Sports Gear, &c. Any description. Any condition. They are a tremendous help. Poorest district imaginable. Population 30,000 - Rev. S.G. Tinley, St. Luke's Vicarage, Victoria Docks. E.16.

MUSTEL ORGAN for SALE. with or without celesta, superb instrument - E.M., 34, Spencer-hill, Wimbledon.

THAT SECOND-HAND CAR you want can be obtained through the announcements in The Daily Telegraph each Wednesday.

ALCOHOLISM - An interesting Brochure on medical treatment free - Secretary, 40, Marsham-street, S.W.1.

MASSAGE AND MEDICAL ELECTRICITY - Association of Certificated Blind Masseurs. President: Sir Robert Jones, Bt,. K.B.E., C.B. CHARTERED MASSEURS and MASSEUSES undertake Massage and Electrical Treatments. London and provinces - Apply Secretary, A.C.B.M., 224, Great Portland-street, W.1. Museum 9701, 9.30 to 5.30.

£240 MORE THAN ANTICIPATED. - See Hurcomb's illustrated announcements on Page Five.

ON ARRIVAL at your CONTINENTAL DESTINATION order The Daily Telegraph to be delivered to you regularly.

BIRTH CONTROL SOCIETY and PIONEER CLINIC, founded by Dr. MARIE STOPES, 108, Whitfield-street, London W.1. Tele. Museum 9528

"I WAS VERY HAPPY at your Training Farm, and I am sure my brother, too, will learn a lot there." - from a young farmer settler in South Africa to the 1820 Memorial Settlers' Association, 199, Picadilly, London W.1.

THE ITALIAN SPAS of ACQUI, FUIGGI, MONTECATINI, RONCEGNOA, and SALSOMAGGIORE announce a MEDICAL REPRESENTATIVE will attend at COOK'S head office, Berkeley-st., W.1. daily to Mar. 12th, inclusive, to give information regarding the waters and cures to interested parties. Inquiries welcomed.

SPOTS IN THE SUN - Particulars of delightful Trips Abroad on Land and Sea can be found on Page Two under "Tours, Cruises, &c." and "Shipping and Mails"

£65 REWARD - STOLEN, on evening of 2nd inst. from house in Teignmouth-rd., Brondesbury, 2-stone Dia. and Plat. Ring. claw setting, small dia. on shoulders plat. ring set with oval shaped sap.,surrounded by dias; 2 engine-turned gold cig. cases. bearing initials M. and A.E. plat. ring set with whole pearl, surrounded with dias, 2 dias on shoulders; gold matchbox engraved M. &c. - Above reward will be paid by Toplis & Harding, 28, Old Jewry, E.C.2, to first person giving information to them leading to arrest and conviction of thieves and recovery of stolen propery or pro-rata to the value recovered.

£20 REWARD - LOST. on the 3rd instant, either in Haymarket, S.W., or between there and Devonshire-place, W. possibly in a taxicab, a Single Row DIAMOND BRACELET, set Platinum - The above reward will be paid by Messrs. Tyler & Co., 45, Holborn-viaduct, E.C.1. to anyone returning the lost bracelet to them intact.

TO Parents and Guardians - For particulars of Schools & other Educational Institutions, see under "Educational."

FOR SALE - 8-DAY TALL CLOCK by Thomas Tompion Original condition. Genuine throughout - BM/BBFX. London. W.C.

TALKIES - A CAREER OPEN to FILM ASPIRANTS with phonic voices. Consult Hollywood authority on technique and screen poise at Doreen Stone Ld., 53, Haymarket. Interviews by appointment. Regent 4353.

C.H.W. - THE COUNCIL of the CHELSEA HOSPITAL for WOMEN, S.W.3. GRATEFULLY ACKNOWLEDGE receipt of £8 from Messrs. Joseph Mears Theatres Ld., and £4 from Miss Raper. 18 beds reserved for those able to pay £5 5s. a week and small fees to the Staff for operations.

WELL-FURNISHED COTTAGE to be LET (4 bedrooms), attractive garden - Particulars from Gibson. Dutch Tea House, Boxham, nr. Chichester.

FOR A USEFUL GUIDE TO APARTMENTS, BOARD-RESIDENCE, or HOTEL ACCOMMODATION consult the Advertisements under these headings on Page 21.

SINGING - Should your voice show promise, write for free private audition, naming convenient time - Mr. Alfred North, 36, Wigmore-street, W.1.

**SHIPPING AND MAILS: TOURS, CRUISES, &c., FINANCIAL NOTICES. &c. APPEAR ON PAGE TWO.**

## CONCERTS, &c.

**ROYAL ACADEMY OF MUSIC**
YORK-GATE, MARYLEBONE-RD., LONDON, N.W.1.
Instituted 1822. Incorporated by Royal Charter, 1830.
Telephone: Welbeck 5461 (four lines)
PATRONS:
HIS MAJESTY THE KING
HER MAJESTY THE QUEEN
H.R.H. THE DUKE OF CONNAUGHT, K.G.
H.R.H. THE PRINCESS LOUISE (Duchess of Argyll),
President:
H.R.H. THE DUKE OF CONNAUGHT, K.G.
Principal:
JOHN B. McEWEN, M.A., D.Mus., F.R.A.M., F.R.C.M.

***ORCHESTRAL CONCERT**
QUEEN'S HALL
(Sole Lessees: Messrs, Chappell & Co. Ld.)
THURSDAY, 20th March at 3.
Conductor:
**SIR HENRY J. WOOD.**
The Programme will include:
BRANDENBURG CONCERTO, No 4, in G, for SOLO VIOLIN and TWO FLUTES ... ... ... ... Bach
CONCERTO for PIANOFORTE ... ... ... ... F. Delius
CONCERTINO for CLARINET ... ... ... ... Busoni

**DUKE'S REHEARSAL THEATRE**
*DRAMATIC PERFORMANCES, MARCH 19, 20, 21, 22.
* Tickets and Prospectuses, &c., can be obtained on application. A. ALGER BELL, Secretary.

QUEEN'S HALL, MARCH 20th
ELECTRIC RECORDING WITHOUT SCRATCH
**SIR HENRY J. WOOD**
Records ONLY for
**COLUMBIA 'NEW PROCESS' RECORDS**
Ask to Hear His Records at Your Dealer's.

**ROYAL COLLEGE OF MUSIC**
Prince Consort-road, South Kensington, S.W.7.
Patrons H.M. THE KING
H.M. THE QUEEN
President - H.R.H. the PRINCE of WALES, K.G.
Director - Sir Hugh P. Allen, K.C.V.O., M.A., D.Mus.
**MIDDAY RECITAL**
by ANGUS MORRISON (Hon. A.R.C.M.) (Pianoforte)
WEDNESDAY NEXT, March 12th, 1930, at 1.15 p.m.
**CHAMBER CONCERT**
WEDNESDAY NEXT, March 12th, 1930, at 8.15 p.m.
The programme will include:
VOCAL QUARTET . Gipsy Songs, Op. 133 . Brahms.

**ROYAL ALBERT HALL.**
TO-MORROW, at 3 p.m.
LIONEL POWELL presents
**CORTOT - THIBAUD - CASALS**
(By arr. with Ibbs & Tillett).
**ONLY APPEARANCE**
Pleyel Piano. H.M.V. Records
15s, 12s, 10s 6d, 7s 6d, 5s 9d, 4s 9d 3s 6d, 3s.
LIONEL POWELL, 161, NEW BOND-STREET, W.1.

**CORTOT - THIBAUD - CASALS**
Record EXCLUSIVELY for
**"HIS MASTER'S VOICE"**
**Hear their Records at your Dealer's**

**QUEEN'S HALL,**
Sole Lessees, Chappell & Co. Ld.
MONDAY NEXT, at 8.15,
**LONDON SYMPHONY ORCHESTRA**
PROGRAMME:
Overture, Romeo and Juliet Tschalkowsky
Concerto for Pianoforte Grieg
**CORTOT**
Symphony No 4 in E minor Brahms
CONDUCTOR:
**ABENDROTH**
PLEYEL PIANO H.M.V. RECORDS.
Tickets, 17s, 12s, 8s 6d, 5s 9d, 4s 9d, 3s 6d.
LIONEL POWELL, 161 New Bond-street, W.1.

**CORTOT**
**ABENDROTH**
**LONDON SYMPHONY ORCHESTRA**
Record EXCLUSIVELY for
**"HIS MASTER'S VOICE"**
Any Dealer will give you full particulars of their Latest Recordings.

**PAUL ROBESON**
TOUR in the
INTERNATIONAL CELEBRITY SUBSCRIPTION CONCERTS
EDINBURGH ........................ Mch. 8
NEWCASTLE ........................ " 10
MIDDLESBROUGH ................ " 12
SHEFFIELD ........................ " 14
MANCHESTER ........................ " 15
CARDIFF ........................ " 16
Particulars from LIONEL POWELL, 161, New Bond-street, W.1.

**PAUL ROBESON**
Records EXCLUSIVELY for
**"HIS MASTER'S VOICE"**
Hear His Latest Recordings at your Dealer's.

WIGMORE HALL, VIOLIN RECITAL.
THURSDAY, MARCH 27, at 8.15
**ALFREDO CAMPOLI**
CHAPPELL PIANO, At the Piano - IVOR NEWTON.
Tickets, 12s, 8s 6d, 5s 9d, 3s.
LIONEL POWELL, 161, New Bond-street, W.1.

WIGMORE HALL THURSDAY, APRIL 3, at 8.15
VIOLIN RECITAL
**ANTON MAASKOFF**
Bosendorfer Piano. At the Piano - REGINALD PAUL.
Tickets (incld tax) 12s, 8s 6d, 5s 9d, 3s.
LIONEL POWELL, 161, New Bond-street, W.1.

**JACQUES VAN LIER**
has returned to Europe from his successful FIFTH NORTH AFRICAN TOUR,
and has just completed a series of concert engagements in Germany. He will be in France from March 9 to 15 for further concert engagements.
**JACQUES VAN LIER**
All inquiries for dates, &c.,
LIONEL POWELL, 161, New Bond-street, W.1.

33rd CONCERT, ÆOLIAN HALL, THURS., MAR. 27, 8.15
**JACQUES VAN LIER**
SERIES of CLASSICAL and MODERN CONCERTS
JESSIE McLENNAN Soprano
JACQUES VAN LIER Solo Violoncello
Vocalion Records
MARIE WHITE Solo Pianoforte.
At the Piano - ENID BROOK BECHSTEIN PIANO
Tickets, 8s 6d, 5s 9d, 3s.
LIONEL POWELL, 161, NEW BOND-STREET, W.1.

**BECHSTEIN PIANO**
WILL BE PLAYED BY
**MARIE WHITE**
ÆOLIAN HALL, THURS., MARCH 27, at 8.15.

CONCERT DIRECTOR
TOUR MANAGER
**T. ARTHUR RUSSELL**
70, WIGMORE-STREET, W.1.
Telephone: 5913 Welbeck
Connections in America, Australia, South Africa, &c.

**PEOPLE'S PALACE, MILE-END**
In AID of QUEEN MARY'S HOSPITAL, FOR THE EAST-END (Sec.: Major Raphael Jackson), and under the Patronage of HER MAJESTY.
**KUBELIK MAR. 18, at 8.30**
FIRST APPEARANCE OF A WORLD-FAMOUS VIOLINIST IN EAST-END FOR 25 YEARS.
THE WHOLE OF THE PROCEEDS OF THIS CONCERT WILL BE DEVOTED TO THE FUNDS OF THE HOSPTIAL
POPULAR PRICES: 5s, 4s, 3s, 2s, 1s. (with a few Special Seats at 10s 6d and 7s 6d.)
TICKETS FROM: The People's Palace, and from The Secretary, Major Raphael Jackson, at the Hospital, all usual libraries, and
T. ARTHUR RUSSELL, 70, Wigmore-st., W.1. 5913 Wel.

**KUBELIK**
Records EXCLUSIVELY for
**"HIS MASTER'S VOICE"**
Hear his Records at your Dealer's

WIGMORE HALL TUES, NEXT, March 11, at 3.15
T. ARTHUR RUSSELL announces the REAPPEARANCE in LONDON of MAURICE
**EISENBERG**
At the Piano - GEORGE REEVES BLUTHNER PIANO
Tickets: 10s 6d, 7s 6d, 4s 9d, 3s. at Hall, and T. ARTHUR RUSSELL, 70, Wigmore-st., W.1. 5913 Wel.
**EISENBERG** **Will Play:**
Sonata, D Major (Beethoven), Sonata, C Major (Casella), Sonata (Valentini) and group of solos by Grazioli, Turina, De Falla, Hindemith.

ROYAL ALBERT HALL
SUNDAY, MARCH 16, at 3
LIONEL POWELL presents
**LONDON SYMPHONY ORCHESTRA IN A WAGNER PROGRAMME**
CHOSEN BY THE PUBLIC
**ODA SLOBODSKAYA**
THE FAMOUS PRIMA DONNA
CONDUCTOR:
**ALBERT COATS**
H.M.V. RECORDS
Tickets, 8s 6d, 5s 9d, 3s 6d,3s, 2s 4d.
LIONEL POWELL, 161, New Bond-street, W.1.

**ALBERT COATES**
**LONDON SYMPHONY ORCHESTRA**
Record EXCLUSIVELY for
**"HIS MASTER'S VOICE"**
Any Dealer will give you full particulars of their Latest Recordings.

**PHILIP ASHBROOKE**
20, Old Cavendish-st., W.1. Mayfair 2070.
GROTRIAN HALL, WED, NEXT, 8.30
**LLOYD POWELL**
PIANOFORTE RECITAL
Toccata and Fugue in C min BACH
Sonate-Fantasie, No 2 SCRIABIN
Polonaise Fantasie in A fl. ma. } CHOPIN
Mazurka in C sh. min
Valse in D fl. ma.
Prelude, D min.: Two Studies
La Serenade Interrompue } DEBUSSY
Hommage à Haydn, &c.
Gadabout MEDTNER
and Solos by RACHMANINOFF, GRIEG, LISZT, &c.
BLUTHNER PIANOFORTE, Tickets, 8s 6d, 5s 9d, 3s.
PHILIP ASHBROOKE, 20 Old Cavendish-st. Mayfair 2070.

INDEX TO CLASSIFIED ADVERISEMENTS APPEARS ON PAGE 30

GROTRIAN HALL, SAT, MARCH 22, at 3.15
**SAPELLNIKOFF**
ONLY RECITAL THIS SEASON
BLUTHNER PIANOFORTE, Tickets, 10s 6d, 5s 9d, 3s.
PHILIP ASHBROOKE, 20, Old Cavendish-st., Mayfair 2070

WIGMORE HALL, TUES., MARCH 25, at 8.15
**EDWARD PARKER**
PIANOFORTE RECITAL
BECHSTEIN PIANOFORTE 5s 9d, 3s 6d, 2s 4d.
PHILIP ASHBROOKE, 20, Old Cavendish-st., Mayfair 2070

**BECHSTEIN PIANO**
WILL BE PLAYED BY
**EDWARD PARKER**
WIGMORE HALL, TUESDAY, March 25th, at 8.15

**THE MICHELL DIRECTION**
(Paddington 5651.) 39, OXFORD-TERRACE, W.2.

WIGMORE HALL
**SOLOMON** **SOLOMON**
SATURDAY NEXT
**MARCH 15, at 3**
ONLY RECITAL THIS SEASON
**SOLOMON** **SOLOMON**
Choral Prelude "Sleepers, awake" ............... BACH-BUSONI
Sonata No. 7 (HAYDN): Variations ......... HANDEL-BRAHMS
Prelude, Aria and Finale ............................ CESAR-FRANCK
Six Etudes ........................................................ CHOPIN
La Cathedrale Engioutie: "L'isle Joyeuse" ........... DEBUSSY
Four Preludes ............................................ RACHMANINOFF
STEINWAY PIANO, 12s, 8s 6d, 5s 9d, (res,) 3s 6d.
THE MICHELL DIRECTION, 39, Oxford-terrace, W.2.

**FESTIVAL**
of
**CONTEMPORARY ARTS**
at
**BATH**
MARCH 29th to APRIL 5th
THE PUMP ROOM ORCHESTRA
under the direction of EDWARD DUNN.
SOLOISTS:
ALBERT SAMMONS
STEUART WILSON
CHRISTIAN CARPENTER
MAURICE COLE
JOHN IRELAND
LIONEL TERTIS

CONDUCTORS:
CONSTANT LAMBERT
ERIC COATES
DR. JOHN IVIMEV
HERBERT BEDFORD
VICTOR HELY HUTCHINSON
ALBERT KETELBY
GAVIN GORDON

MODERN DANCES by
PENELOPE SPENCER and PHYLLIS BEDELLS

VERSE SPEAKING by
PHYLLIS KEEVES
DULCIE BOWICE
WILLIAM FOX

TALES by
DESMOND McCARTHY (Literature)
W.H. DARLINGTON (The Drama)
HOWARD ROBERTSON (Architecture)
and others
Festival tickets (numbered seats) for all events, 25s., unreserved 15s.
For further particulars write to the SPA DIRECTOR, BATH.
See also Page Ten.

NATIONAL SUNDAY LEAGUE CONCERTS
**PALLADIUM** To-morrow, at **2.30**
ALL-STAR MATINEE
In AID of the CHILDREN'S COUNTRY HOLIDAY FUND, organised by Miss PEGGY O'NEIL
The following Artistes have kindly promised to appear:

| | |
|---|---|
| BILLY BENNETT | PERCY MARMONT |
| EDDIE BOUCHARD | BILLY MILTON |
| LILLIAN BURGISS | ROBERT NAYLOR |
| JESSIE BROUGHTON | PEGGY O'NEIL |
| & DENNIS CREEDON | JAMES RAGLAN |
| MADELINE CARROLL | JUDY SKINNER |
| TOM CLARE | MILDRED TELFORD |
| SELWYN DRIVER | THAT CERTAIN TRIO |
| OLIVE GOFF | SYBIL THORNDIKE |
| TOPKISS GREEN | VIOLET VANBRUGH |
| OLIVE HATHWAY | FREDERICK WHELDON |
| URSULA JEANS | GEORGIE WOOD |

Read sts., 1s 10d, to 10s 6d. Box-office open until 9 p.m. to-day and from 11 a.m. to-morrow. Gerrard 1004.

**L.G. SHARPE**
25, HAYMARKET, S.W.1. Telephone Gerrard 5564

GROTRIAN HALL, TUESDAY NEXT, 8.15
**FRANCES HATFIELD**
(Mezzo-Contralto), VOCAL RECITAL
At the Piano - GERALD MOORE.
**FRANCES HATFIELD**
BLUTHNER PIANO Tickets 8s 6d, 5s 9d,2s 4d.
L.G. SHARPE, 25, Haymarket, S.W.1. Gerrard 5564

FIRST APPEARANCE IN LONDON OF
**GUY MARRINER**
New Zealand Pianist.
TWO PIANOFORTE RECITALS
Tickets 8s. 6d., 5s. 9d., 2s. 4d. Gerrard 5564

# CALAMITOUS END TO GREAT BRITISH AIRSHIP

## EMPIRE APPALLED BY LOSS OF R101
## WITH 46 LIVES

◆

### MYSTERY OF WRECK AND EXPLOSION

---

### LORD THOMSON AND SIR SEFTON BRANCKER AMONG DEAD

---

### "SLOW DOWN" SIGNAL THAT CAME TOO LATE

---

### CRASH INTO FRENCH HILLSIDE

The attempted flight to India of the Airship R101 has ended in a disaster of a magnitude only previously paralleled in British aviation when the R38 crashed over the Humber in 1921, and forty-four lives were lost.

Eight hours after leaving Cardington, the R101 flew into a hillside in Northern France near the city of Beauvais. She was immediately wrecked by explosion and fire.

Only eight persons of the 54 aboard escaped with their lives. No officer was saved.

Lord Thomson, Secretary of State for Air, was one of the passengers who perished, the other forty-five victims including:

Sir Sefton Brancker, Director of Civil Aviation;

Major G.H. Scott, Assistant Director of Airship Development and officer in command of the flight;

Flight Lieut. H.C. Irwin, captain of the ship;

Lt.-Col. V.C. Richmond, the designer; and

Wing Commander R.B.D. Colmore, Director of Airship Development.

One of the victims was a survivor of the R38 disaster - the assistant chief coxswain, W.A. Potter.

The largest airship in the world, R101 had been built at the Royal Airship Works, Cardington, at a cost of £600,000. She was the property of the State and was not insured.

### CAUSES UNEXPLAINED

No satisfactory explanation of the cause of the disaster is available. All that emerges from the statements of survivors is that the vessel lost altitude through being beaten down by a storm.

The officer in command became aware that the ship had descended dangerously near the ground. The message "slow down" was received in the engine car. It came too late.

Within a moment, with engines running at cruising speed, the vessel crashed, nose first into the hill.

Houses in the city of Beauvais, four miles away, were shaken by the explosion which followed. Flames enveloped the R101. Within a short space she was reduced to a pitiful wreck.

### PUBLIC INQUIRY TO BE HELD

The Air Council propose to arrange for a public inquiry into the disaster, to be held in this country, subject to co-ordination with the arrangements which are being made by the French Government.

News of the catastrophe came to London as a complete surprise. From first to last no message indicative of any difficulty had been received from the airship.

She had set out from Cardington at 7.36 p.m. (Summer time) on Saturday and passed over London two hours later. She was dimly discernible from below as a phantom cigar passing beneath an overcast sky.

### PASSENGERS GONE TO BED

The British coast was crossed in the vicinity of Hastings. At 11.38 p.m. the R101 was above French soil. At midnight the following report was issued:

After an excellent supper our distinguished passengers have smoked a final cigar, and after sighting the French coast have gone to bed to rest after the excitement of leave-takings.

All essential services are functioning satisfactorily, and the crew have settled down to watch-keeping routine.

Shortly after one o'clock in the morning Croydon air station received the message. "Will not require you further to-night." Then not long before the final catastrophe the French air station at Le Bourget was asked to work out the position of the vessel. It was determined as one kilometre north of Beauvais, and the R101 was so informed. That was the last time wireless communication was held with the vessel.

At 2.16 came the laconic and dramatic report from Le Bourget:

G.F.A.A.W. a pris feu - has taken fire.

### POLICIES OF INSURANCE

It is understood that Lord Thomson, his valet, and all the officers had taken out special accident policies for substantial amounts, issued by the British Aviation Insurance Society and Lloyds.

Sir Sefton Brancker had not taken any special precaution against accident. The crew were not covered.

Major Cooper, Accidents Investigator to the Air Ministry, arrived at Beauvais yesterday afternoon to make an examination of the wreckage. He was accompanied by various experts, among whom was Squadron Leader Booth, the hero of the day when the R33 broke away from her mooring mast and was swept by a gale across the North Sea.

It is understood that the remains of the victims will be brought home for interment in this country.

THE TWISTED SKELETON OF R101, photographed while the débris was still burning.

## "TWO DANGEROUS DIPS AND THEN CAME THE CRASH"

◆

### SURVIVORS' STRUGGLE THROUGH BURNING FABRIC

**By Herbert Routh, "The Daily Telegraph" Special Correspondent**

BEAUVAIS, Sunday Night.

The giant British airship R101, which left Cardington aerodrome at 7.30 last night for Karachi, now lies a mangled wreck at Allonne, a little town four miles south of Beauvais, in the Oise Department. Of the airship's total complement of crew and passengers only eight have survived the disaster.

The wreckage lies in a hollow across a high hedge. All the cars and the forepart of the hull are twisted out of recognition. The district is a great expanse of fields interspersed with hillocks and patches of broom.

The stern of the vessel and about a third of its length, however, remain standing, with their metal-work practically undisturbed. A Union Jack, which was untouched by the fire, remained for some hours, but was removed this afternoon and handed to the British Military Attaché.

#### Airship in Difficulties

The disaster occurred shortly after two o'clock this morning. Inhabitants of Allonne had been awakened by the noise of the airship's engines. She was flying low, and was obviously in difficulties owing to the heavy wind and rain. The noise of the engines was sufficient to wake people from sleep.

Shortly afterwards there was a terrific explosion and a blinding flash, and a great yellow glare shot with tongues of flame was seen proceeding from the neighbouring Fecq Wood. The explosion was so terrific that houses for some distance were shaken.

People from Allonne and the neighbourhood hurried to the spot to find the great dirigible blazing furiously. Firemen and gendarmes were also quickly on the spot.

#### Hydrogen Gas Explosion

Just before the crash the airship had been flying at about fifty or sixty miles an hour at a height of about 1,000 feet. It has been established that it was the hydrogen gas of the vessel which exploded. The gas valves of the airship were found blown out of the wreck.

Another fact which may prove of importance in determining the cause of the disaster is that a quantity of airship fabric has been picked up some miles from the wreck.

This may help in establishing whether the airship had suffered damage in the air before she struck the hillside.

#### A TERRIBLE SIGHT
#### MOST OF VICTIMS ASLEEP

A young Frenchwoman who was one of the first to arrive said afterwards:

"Oh, what a horrible sight met our eyes! Flames leaped towards the sky; and in vain did the firemen play their hoses on the blazing ship. We could see bodies in the cabins; they seemed to be twisted like strips of burning cheese.

"However, we were able to save an

Englishman who was alone in the forward cabin. Later we extricated frightfully burned bodies from the wreckage."

Major Seurin, Commandant of the gendarmerie on the spot, said:

"Despite all my efforts, I could not get near the ashes. It was a horrible sight. The flames were shooting up very high, and the heat was terrific, especially where the oil tanks were."

When the disaster occurred twelve of the crew were on duty. The rest of those on the ship were asleep. The eight survivors were all in the cabin.

#### Survivors' Stories

The story of the disaster is best told in the words of the survivors.

One of these, Mr. J.H. Binks, engineer, of Sheffield, whom I interviewed in the Beauvais Hospital, to-day said of:

"We were travelling at about 60 knots just before the explosion occurred. The wireless was working well, for we sent out a message to Le Bourget just before the disaster.

"I know little of what really happened. We had orders to go slow, and immediately these orders were obeyed. It was just then that we seemed to strike, and the explosion followed.

"The service tank was just above us, and it burst and the water came down over us. We crouched in the bottom of the coach, with rags and anything over us, and then tried to get out.

"We could see then through the framework how most of the envelope had been burned and the framework was crumbling, but we were able to scrape through it."

#### Weighted Down By Rain

Mr. H.J. Leech, foreman engineer at the Royal Airship Works, Cardington, said that everything seemed normal until the vessel approached Beauvais.

Then it was suddenly shaken by a violent storm of wind, and he had the impression that the airship was being swung from side to side. It was flying low, and it proved very difficult to make any headway against the strong wind.

"Then," to quote Mr. Leech, "the rain suddenly came down, and so wetted the ship that she answered badly to the helm, although everything possible was being done to regain altitude.

"Twice she dipped dangerously, and then on the third occasion she ran nose first into a hill and, crashing, burst into flames with a tremendous explosion."

What Mr. Leech did not emphasise is his own part in the work of rescue, for it was largely due to his efforts that other survivors got out of the blazing mass in time.

This is Mr. Leech's third airship wreck in fourteen years. The other two were during the war.

#### Eddies In Hills

Another of the survivors said:

"We started from Cardington in fine weather, but conditions became steadily worse as we approached the Channel, and over the sea it was really bad.

"Nevertheless, the voyage was uneventful until we reached Beauvais, by which time the conditions were very rough, the wind and rain being terrific.

"It was not, however, a storm which would normally have given us cause for anxiety - I have been through much worse - but that spot beyond Beauvais has a bad reputation for air accidents, several aeroplanes having crashed there.

"I think it must be the result of eddies caused by the range of hills at that place.

"At the time of the accident there were on duty one man in each of the four forward engine-cars, and two in the after engine-car.

#### Engines Running Well

"Just after passing over Beauvais the ship was weathering the storm well and the engines were running quite normally, when without warning she dipped her nose at an angle of 45 deg. to the ground. She descended some distance, straightened out, then dipped again at the same angle, striking the side of the hill with great force. (The hill is 780 ft above sea-level.)

"The forward engine-cars were crushed under the hull, which in turn collapsed and buried the cabins in wreckage. I counted a space of about a second between the crash and the explosion, which was followed by a roar of flame. The hull caught fire from end to end.

"It was a case of getting clear as quickly as possible, and all the men in this (hospital) ward own their lives to bursting their way through the wreckage and getting to safety."

# GREAT FASCIST TRIUMPH IN GERMANY

## WILL HITLER ATTEMPT AN ARMED REVOLT?

**FROM OUR OWN CORRESPONDENT**

BERLIN, MONDAY.

Official, though still provisional, returns of the Reichstag Elections are now available. They do not differ materially from those which I was able to telephone to The Daily Telegraph at an early hour this morning.

They show definitely, indeed, the extraordinary success with which the National Socialist (Fascist) Campaign has met. Herr Hitler's 107 followers will occupy rather less than one-fifth of the 574 seats in the Reichstag when that body reassembles. They have thus increased their representation ninefold, for they had only 12 Deputies in the old Reichstag.

To-night it is understood that the Government will remain in office and face Parliament when it meets early in October.

The Stock Exchange here reacted to the elections by a very panicky mood. Leading stocks depreciated by as much as 20 points. It was stated on the Bourse that the collapse was largely due to the sale of German paper held abroad.

The meaning of the election is clear. It is discontent, often bordering on despair. This sentiment has a double origin. It arises partly from the general world-trade slump and partly from the breakdown of the Reichstag as a legislative machine.

A very similar landslide occurred in the "inflation" elections of 1924 and was due to similar causes. On that occasion the Socialists lost 32 seats, and the German Nationals returned the strongest party in the Chamber, while the Communists and National Socialists were 62 and 32 respectively. Then, as now, the German people turned from orthodox Parliamentary practitioners to political quacks. But the economic stress resulting from depreciation, plus stabilisation, passed away, and the electorate came back to its old party allegiances. A like process of reaction may take place now, but there are other and less edifying possibilities.

A MARCH ON BERLIN?

The most sinister of these is that in the intoxication of victory Herr Hitler may attempt another "march on Berlin." The fist two of that kind at Munich in 1923 was a pitiful fiasco. But his chances will seem to him infinitely more favourable at the present moment. Such a step would almost certainly mean civil war. Even if the army were to join the Fascists, the Prussian Government would undoubtedly attempt to organise a defence of the Republic with the State police, who, apart from artillery, have practically all the armaments of soldiery.

It is, however, believed by inside political circles that so long as Hindenburg is President and General Groener War Minister the army may be relied upon to stand firm against the Fascist inveiglement.

That the overthrow of the Republic by violence is in the real programme of the National Socialists there can be no doubt whatever. There are, however, reasons for supposing that they realise - at any rate, in their cooler moments - that their chances are small unless they have the support of, at any rate, a substantial section of the army.

**(September 16)**

# 2,000,000 DEAD IN CHINESE FAMINE

2,000,000 persons already dead and 2,000,000 more doomed to certain death before June.

That is the grim report brought back to Peking by the foreign investigators who have inquired into the famine situation in the Chinese provinces of Shensi and Shansi on behalf of the International Famine Relief Commission.

In these two great districts, with a joint area more than three times that of England and Wales and a population of about 42,000,000, food and fuel are alike lacking.

There are no railways and few roads, and the breakdown of local cart transport renders it practically impossible to bring in relief from outside.

The animals which drew the carts have been eaten and the carts themselves broken up and utilised as firewood.

This appalling tragedy of human misery and affliction is believed to be due primarily to the failure of the crops.

But the rapacity of the brigand-like Chinese soldiery and the civil wars are also largely responsible.

An intensely cold winter is aggravating the position.

Kansu, a province nearly as big as Shansi and Shensi combined, with a population of 6,000,000, is unapproachable except by walking. This province was last year the scene of a wholesale massacre by Moslem bandits.

**(January 14)**

# U. S. TOURIST INVASION

The van of an Atlantic fleet of thirteen vessels from New York arrived at Cherbourg yesterday. They were the Bremen, Leviathen, Majestic, Berengaria, Columbus, and Cleveland. Twelve trains, says the Exchange Telegraph, were required to convey the tourists to Paris.

**(July 23)**

# 4 ELEPHANTS IN LONDON STAMPEDE

## LORD MAYOR'S SHOW PANIC

Between thirty and forty spectators of the Lord Mayor's Show - most of them women and children - were injured yesterday when the four elephants taking part in the procession charged a red lion mascot held up by students of King's College on the Thames Embankment.

As soon as it saw the "lion" the leading elephant trumpeted loudly and dashed through the crowd straight at it, seizing it in its trunk, while the other elephants, also trumpeting, followed it.

Hundreds of people lining the pavement scattered in all directions. Women screamed and fainted, and many fell and were trampled on.

The lion is King's College mascot and is called "Reggie." He is annually "presented" to the new Lord Mayor by the students on the Embankment, but yesterday the elephants upset their calculations.

THE "LION" SEIZED

A number of students were carrying the lion - a life sized model painted scarlet and with tail rampant - on a stretcher, and for some time had been letting off fireworks and amusing the children in the crowd with it.

Immediately on seeing the lion the leading elephant trumpeted and charged, its mahout powerless to control it. The students dropped the mascot and ran into the college, but one, unable to escape, was chased by the elephant round a tree and back on to the Embankment.

After picking up the lion the elephant kicked it, and, satisfied that it was not alive, allowed its mahout to lead it back into the procession.

The other three elephants dashed into the stampeding crowd as far as the gates of King's College, and it was several minutes before their attendants were able to control them. The majority of the injured fell in the rush to escape, and were trampled on by others in the crowd.

"FOUR BIG PETS"

Mr. Race Power, of Brixton-hill, to whose wife the elephants belong, said last night: "The elephants are each about 30 years old. This is the first time that they have been involved in anything of the kind. They are four big pets and as good as little children. It is regrettable that the college students teased them in this unhappy way. That was the cause of the whole trouble.

"I shouted to the students to drop their lion, but instead of doing so they dragged it with them. Naturally the elephants followed it, and tried to reach it until it was dropped. As soon as they saw what it actually was they turned away and immediately quietened down.

"The lion is the natural enemy of the elephant and it was a shame to tease our quartette. Never at any time throughout the procession were the elephants out of control.

Statements about the elephants charging the crowd are quite ludicrous. Our little grandson was at the head of one of them, and had there been any 'charge' he would have been thrown. I am sorry about the whole incident, but I think that the elephants were absolutely harmless. The whole affair lasted no more than two minutes."

Eleven persons were treated at Charingcross Hospital for slight injuries, but none was detained.

**(November 4)**

# DISTINGUISHED INVALIDS

The following reports on the condition of distinguished invalids were received yesterday:

The Hon. Mrs. HENDERSON: A good day.
Mrs. J. B. JOEL: Improving
Lord HEWART: Progressing.
Bishop TREFUSIS: Seriously ill.
Sir FRIEDRICH ECKSTEIN: Slight improvement maintained.
Mr. WILLIAM BENNETT, MP: Much better; going home to-day.

**(May 31)**

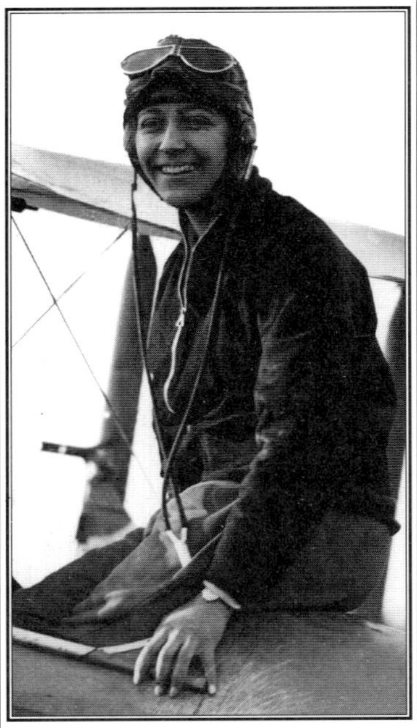

Miss Amy Johnson

# LONE GIRL FLIER ON WAY TO SYDNEY

## AUSTRALIA'S GREAT WELCOME

## KING'S MESSAGE OF CONGRATULATION

Smiling and almost immediately combing her disordered hair, Miss Amy Johnson on Saturday stepped from her second-hand aeroplane at Port Darwin, Australia, after one of the most daring lone flights in history.

In 19 ½ days she had flown - her own pilot and her own mechanic - from Croydon, covering a total of 9,495 miles, facing the terrors of desert lands and shark-infested seas.

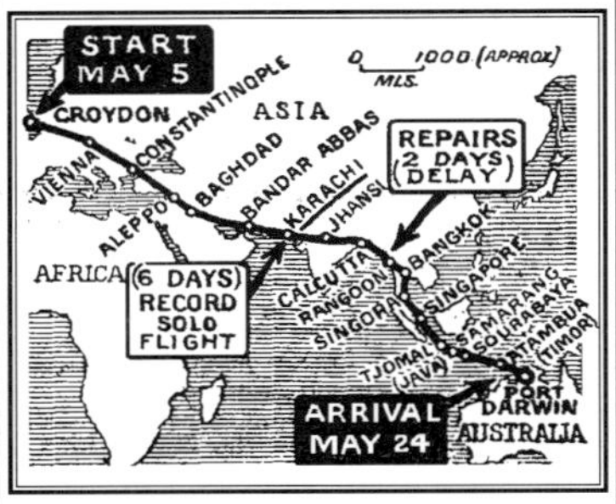


The world has acclaimed her a heroine. From all quarters congratulations have poured in upon her, and Australia has given her an almost Royal welcome.

The King and Queen were among the first to convey congratulations in the following message from Buckingham Palace:

"The Queen and I are thankful and delighted to know of Miss Johnson's safe arrival in Australia, and heartily congratulate her upon her wonderful and courageous achievement.

"GEORGE R.I."

Miss Johnson left Port Darwin on her resumed flight to Sydney at 7.30 this morning.

(May 26)

# NATIONAL CORPS OF FLYING SQUADS

## POLICE CAR PATROLS IN EVERY TOWN

The Daily Telegraph is in a position to state that an important scheme for curbing the activities of motor-car bandits throughout the country is under the consideration of the authorities and is likely shortly to be adopted.

Briefly, the scheme is to patrol all county and urban districts with Flying Squad motor-cars, all equipped with wireless and in constant touch with headquarters.

Conferences on the subject have been held between Home Office officials, New Scotland Yard chiefs, and various chief constables, and the opinion is unanimous that the great and growing menace of motor-car banditry can be checked only by the combined efforts of the country's police forces.

**(February 24)**

# FLYERS AT LISBON

Major Franco and eight companion aviators reached the outskirts of Lisbon in three aeroplanes yesterday afternoon. According to the British United Press the Portuguese Minister of War told Major Franco that the Government would compel the airmen to remain in the town until instructed further.

**(December 16)**

# STORY OF FLIGHT

## COURAGE - AND BAD LUCK

Miss Johnson left Croydon on May 5. She hoped to beat Mr. Bert Hinkler's record of flying from London to Australia in 15 ½ days, but cruel luck in the matter of bad weather and damage to her machine robbed her of that honour.

Nevertheless she has set up one new record, her six-day trip between London and Karachi (4,140 miles) being the quickest for any solo flier.

At Karachi she was two days ahead of Mr. Hinkler, but two days later, on May 13, the troubles began which put any hope of further record-breaking out of the question.

Landing by mistake at Insein, near Rangoon, instead of at Rangoon itself, her machine ran into a ditch, one of the wings and wheels and propeller being damaged. Two valuable days were lost in effecting the repairs before she left for Bangkok.

Blinding rain and strong headwinds further delayed her passage, and as conditions got worse en route from Bangkok to Singapore all hope of beating the record was abandoned.

May 19 saw Miss Johnson forced down at Thomal, in Java, many miles short of Sourabaya, which she hoped to reach that day. Bamboos pierced the wings of her Gipsy-Moth aeroplane when she landed. These were patched with sticking-plaster, and the next day she arrived at Sourabaya, being unable to fly further owing to the damage to her 'plane.

Further trouble was then discovered, and Miss Johnson was forced to remain at Sourabaya all Wednesday, instead of setting off as she had intended after the wings had been repaired.

DARING "TAKE OFF"

Over the Java Sea she was forced down to within six feet of the shark-infested waters. "I really thought it was the end," she said, "but somehow I reached the coast and followed it until I ran out of fuel and came down at Tjomal."

The only place she could find to land at Tjomal was a 240-yards-long piece of land on a sugar estate, which had been cleared as a house site. This was 80 yards too short for a normal take-off, but next morning, after her luggage had been removed, she just managed to get away, clearing the land by a few yards. She flew to a field a few miles away, where she took on her luggage again and resumed her flight.

**(May 26)**

# FREAKS OF U.S. BOYS

In New York, New Jersey, and Massachusetts the police are taking measures to stop bicycle marathons in the public streets, "tree-sitting" endurance tests, and kite-flying contests after dark.

One team of boy cyclists in the summer heat sweated through its 240th hour, and would not dismount until compelled. Peter Soriano, aged 13, to-day passed his 250th hour in the limbs of a tree near his home at Tarrytown, New York, and yesterday received a haircut aloft.

In the stern repressive measures now general the police have the support in many cases of indignant parents. The newspapers are refusing to print reports of crank endurance tests, and one of the widest circulation announces to-day that "tree-sitting is no longer news unless the competitor falls off and breaks his neck." Two such fatalities have already been reported.

**(August 4)**

# GOVERNMENT BY DICTATORS

## SIR OSWALD MOSLEY'S MANIFESTO

**By Our POLITICAL CORRESPONDENT**

Sir Oswald Mosley's manifesto advocating an emergency programme to meet the present economic crisis was issued for publication during the week-end.

The main proposals are:

An Emergency Cabinet of not more than five Ministers, with power to carry through an emergency policy.

A national planning organisation to assist in the development of industry.

Import control board for foodstuffs and guaranteed price for agricultural products.

Trade agreements with the Dominions.

Capital expenditure on an ambitious policy of constructive works.

Creation of a public utility organisation to produce houses and building materials.

Postponement of the repayment of war debt.

In addition to Sir Oswald himself, sixteen Socialist M.P.'S have signed the document, and the strength of the "Moseley group" in Parliament thus stands revealed. The number of avowed supporters of the "more drastic and determined policy" set forth in the manifesto must be a disappointment to its author.

NOT PRACTICABLE

In the course of last week many Socialist members were invited to lend their aid. The response was certainly less ready than some of Sir Oswald's friends anticipated. The Maxton section of the party - that is, the extreme Left wing - is unrepresented except for Dr. R. Forgan and Mr. John McGovern.

The trade union group has shown no enthusiasm for the new move.

**(December 8)**

# VISIT TO MOON PROPHECY

## "FEASIBLE IN 10 OR 15 YEARS"

**FROM OUR OWN CORRESPONDENT**

PARIS, Tuesday.

"I am perfectly certain that within ten or fifteen years a journey to the moon and back will be perfectly feasible."

These words were not uttered by a romancer addressing a popular audience. They sum up the considered opinion of an eminent French scientist, M. Robert Esnault-Pelterie, and they were spoken at a meeting in Paris of scientists of several nations, all students of what M. Esnault-Pelterie named "Astronautics."

Indeed, M. Esnault-Pelterie is not at all bothered by the technical problems that have to be solved. He has made an exhaustive study of the discovery of the German inventor, Hermann Oberth, that theoretically it should be possible to make a rocket from which gas would be expelled so as to drive the rocket at more than 4,000 yards a second.

**(April 10)**

# NEW ELECTRIC LAMP

A new electric hand lamp, claimed to give a continuous or intermittent illumination of consistent brilliance for eight hours without refill, was demonstrated yesterday at the Everlite works, on the Metropole Estate, Waltham Abbey.

**(February 28)**

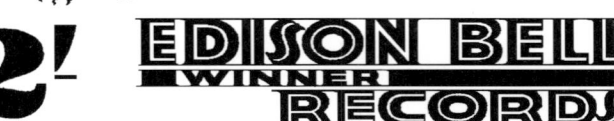

# NAVAL TREATY SIGNED IN LONDON

## FAMOUS BATTLESHIPS WHICH ARE TO BE "SCRAPPED"

**The London Naval Treaty of 1930 - the official title - containing the agreements and conclusions arrived at by the Five-Powers Naval Conference, was signed at St. James's Palace yesterday - exactly three months after the opening of the Conference by the King in the Royal Gallery of the House of Lords.**

**The salient points of the Treaty, which will be operative till 1936, are as follows:**

FIVE-POWER AGREEMENT

**Capital Ships**

A building "holiday," with 70,000 tons "reservation" by France and Italy.

The following ships to be disposed of:

| Britain | America | Japan |
|---|---|---|
| Benbow, Iron Duke, Marlborough, Emperor of India, Tiger. | Florida, Utah, Arkansas (or Wyoming). | Hiyei |

Iron Duke, Arkansas (or Wyoming) and Hiyei may, however, be retained for training purposes.

**Submarines**

Limitation to 2,000 tons and 5.1-inch guns, with the exception of three submarines for each Power not exceeding 2,800 tons and 6.1-inch. (France retains in this number a vessel already launched of 2,880 tons with 8-inch guns).

"Humanisation" rules to remain in force permanently. All Powers to be invited to subscribe to them.

THREE-POWER AGREEMENT

**Tonnage Figures**

Following are the figures for completed tonnage not to be exceeded on Dec. 31, 1936:

| | BRITAIN | AMERICA | JAPAN |
|---|---|---|---|
| Cruisers (guns more than 6.1 in.) | 146,800 | 180,000 | 108,400 |
| Cruisers (guns of 6.1 in. or less) | 192,200 | 143,500 | 100,450 |
| Destroyers | 150,000 | 150,000 | 105,500 |
| Submarines | 52,700 | 52,700 | 52,700 |
| Totals | 541,700 | 526,200 | 367,050 |
| Maximum number of cruisers with guns of more than 6.1 in. | 15 | 18 | 12 |

**Destroyers**

Limitation to 1,850 tons and 5.1-inch guns.

**"Safeguarding" Clause**

This permits, under certain conditions, new construction to meet increased programmes by Powers which have not signed the Three-Power Pact.

**(April 23)**



# AMAZING SCENE IN THE HOUSE OF COMMONS

## M.P. WALKS AWAY WITH MACE

**By A STUDENT OF POLITICS**

WESTMINSTER, Thursday Night.

An affront to the majesty of Parliament was offered to-day such as it has never suffered from any of its sons since Cromwell.

The Socialist member for Peckham, Mr. John Beckett, seized the Mace, put it under his arm, and before the House could recover from its astonishment, had carried it down the floor and crossed the bar.

There it was wrenched from his possession by the stout attendant at the door and brought back to its place on the table by the Serjeant-at-Arms.

Mr. Beckett was then expelled from the House after a vote on which there were, surprisingly, as many as four dissentients.

But the sequence of events must be told from the beginning.

At the end of questions, Mr. Fenner Brockway rose from the end of one of the back benches below the gangway and asked for the advice and help of the Speaker.

His grievance was that he wished to debate the Government's policy towards India, but was prevented by an agreement between the leaders of the three parties that nothing should be said on the floor of the House about India.

A GENUINE GRIEVANCE

No other answer was possible, but Mr. Fenner Brockway persisted in arguing his grievance even after the Speaker had risen to his feet. For a member to continue speaking after the Speaker has risen is a gross breach of order, but for quite two minutes it was persisted in, despite the protests, growing ever louder, from the Opposition benches. "Name!" "Name!" they cried as he continued to speak, though no one now could hear him through the hubbub.

The Speaker "named" the member and looked towards the Ministerial bench and Mr. MacDonald promptly rose and moved his suspension. On such a motion there is no debate and the House promptly divided.

Mr. Brockway had probably expected this ending and deliberately incurred the risk. He had (from his own point of view) a genuine grievance for these agreements between the party leaders, however wise, undoubtedly curb the liberty of debate.

The tellers against the motion were Mr. W.J. Brown and Mr. John Beckett. They were naturally back from the division lobby first, as so very few had voted on their side, and Mr. Beckett sat down on the steps of the gangway waiting for the other pair of tellers.

When the "Aye" tellers appeared, the "No" tellers joined them, but slouched up the floor of the House and ostentatiously did not bow.

The senior "Aye" teller was about to announce the figures when Mr. Beckett, who was standing at the other end of the line near the Ministerial benches, suddenly made a grab at the Mace and made off with it down the floor.

There were a group of members standing, as usual, between the bar, which is represented by a coloured strip of carpet, and the door, where they are on the floor of the House but technically outside it.

ATTENDANT'S PRESENCE OF MIND

Actually Mr. Beckett had made his way through this group before he was arrested by the attendant at the door, an old servant of the house and a big man, who alone showed presence of mind in a House where everyone else seemed to be too paralysed to do anything but shout.

It was amazing that no one on the Ministerial side jumped up and stopped Mr. Beckett, for he walked just in front of their feet.

Had the attendant, too, been affected by the general paralysis of astonishment, the sitting of the House would have been stopped. The Mace is the symbol of the authority of the Commons. It is put on the table at the beginning of every sitting, and on a ledge under the table when the House goes into Committee.

"What shall I do with the Mace?" asked a panic-stricken usher when the raging Lord General Cromwell had driven out the Long Parliament by his objurgations. It was then that he said, "Take away that bauble." and someone did take it away and it has disappeared. It was pure gold.

The present Mace is a new one, gilt, not gold, and first appeared on the table of the House of Commons in 1660.

**(July 8)**

## SENDING PICTURES BY TELEGRAPH

From next Tuesday Londoners will be able to telegraph their photographs, or any pictures or facsimiles, to Berlin.

The Postmaster-General announced last night that a direct service will be inaugurated on that day. Pictures from other places in Great Britain will be sent by post to London, and in the same way between Berlin and other places in Germany. The normal working hours for the service between London and Berlin will be seven a.m. to eleven p.m.

**(January 2)**

# AIRPORT SCHEME FOR CENTRAL LONDON

## THREE PARKS MENTIONED AS POSSIBLE SITES

"The Daily Telegraph" is able to-day to announce that a proposal is under consideration for the formation of an air port in the centre of London. Hyde Park, Regent's Park and Battersea Park have been mentioned, among other open spaces, as possible sites.

The matter is now being discussed by the Air Ministry and the London County Council, and a sub-committee has been appointed to examine the proposal in detail.

It is declared that the rapid growth of commercial and private flying make such a development imperative. It is proposed that Croydon should not be superseded in any way, but that for the passenger lines the two ports should be linked together.

"THE DAILY TELEGRAPH" is also able to announce the adoption by the Royal Air Force of a new type of "Interceptor Fighter," which will be the fastest war 'plane in the world.

The machine is the Hawker "Hornet," and it has been chosen after long and intensive tests. It is capable of more than 190 miles an hour, and can climb 20,000 feet in a very few minutes.

**(May 28)**

# 1,340 MILES OF FILMS

## YEAR'S WORK OF THE CENSORS

The British Board of Film Censors last year examined 7,063,435 feet - 1,338 miles - of film, embracing 2,155 subjects.

This fact is disclosed in the annual report of the Board, issued last night.

Of the films examined, it is stated:

923 silent films and 721 sound films were passed for universal exhibition;

280 silent films and 182 sound films were passed for exhibition to adult audiences;

293 films were referred to the publishers for amendment; and

Seven films were totally rejected.

Of the 300 films to which objection was taken, 251 were granted certificates after amendment and in some cases very drastic alteration. The remaining forty-two are still being considered by the publishers but, adds the report:

"In many cases it is the theme to which objection has been taken, and it is difficult, especially in the case of the auditory films, to see how they can be amended. Consequently there is little likelihood of these films being publicly exhibited."

REASONS FOR REJECTION

Among the reasons given for the exceptions taken to films are mentioned:

Materialisation of the conventional figure of Christ;

Ministers of religion in equivocal situations;

References to the Prince of Wales;

Inciting workers to armed conflict;

British officers and forces shown in a degrading light;

Girls and women in a state of intoxication;

"Orgy" scenes;

Reflections on the medical profession;

Suggestive and indecorous dancing;

Outrageously indecent incidents disguised under would-be morals;

Marital infidelity and collusive divorces;

Pernicious scenes in the underworld of large cities;

Executions and incidents connected therewith;

Criminals shown in affluence and apparently successful in life without retribution;

"Crook" films in which sympathy is enlisted for criminals;

"Third Degree"

Cruelty to animals;

Irreverent, blasphemous, and suggestive sub-titles;

Coarse speech; and

Unwarranted reference to well-known public characters.

Referring to the new problems raised by sound films, the report states:

Generally speaking, it is found that the dialogue far more emphasises the situation than is the case with titling.

The examination of sound films had put much greater strain on the examiners. In many cases it is extremely difficult to follow the dialogue and almost impossible to hear every word."

In a reference to "a large number of films which may be classed as 'Back Stage Drama' submitted last year, the report states:

The themes are often sordid, and the lives of the principal characters, if not actually immoral, are, at all events unsavoury.

**(March 18)**

## ELECTRICITY IN THE COUNTRY HOUSE

How electricity, both for light and power, may be introduced into the country house or cottage far from any outside supply, is described in a booklet just issued by the Chloride Electrical storage Co. Ltd. It describes the many advantages of such a supply and the simplicity of the machinery required.

**(March 11)**

# JOHN MASEFIELD AS POET LAUREATE

The King has been graciously pleased to appoint John Masefield, Esq., D. Litt., to be Poet Laureate in Ordinary to His Majesty, in the room of Robert Bridges, Esq., O.M., D. Litt., M.A., deceased.

The above announcement in the LONDON GAZETTE last night records the appointment of the eighteenth Poet Laureate in succession to Spenser, with whom the office, in its modern form, is considered to have begun.

Born fifty-five years ago, John Masefield had filled at various times the roles of

Sailor,

Bar-tender, and

Beachcomber

before gaining world-wide renown as a novelist and poet.

Among the general public Masefield's name is widely known as the author of the poem "I must go down to the sea again," which, set to music by John Ireland, has been sung the world over. This was one of the "Salt Water Ballads" with which he made his public debut as poet.

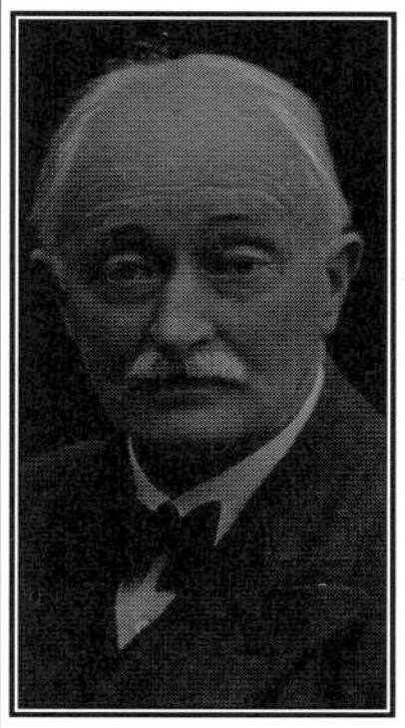

MR. JOHN MASEFIELD

Mr. Masefield was born near Ledbury, within sight of the Malvern Hills. As a boy he ran away to sea, and found the way to America. There he lived a vagrant life until he took work behind the bar in a public-house in Little Greenwich, doing sixteen hours a day for $10 a month. He also gained some sort of a living as a carpet weaver and gardener.

The chance purchase of a copy of Chaucer determined him to be a poet. Following his return home he published "Salt Water Ballads," and this was followed by nearly forty volumes, a miscellaneous collection of prose, poetry, and plays.

**(May 10)**

## GIRLS WHO "MAKE UP" IN PUBLIC

"I do wish that the young woman of to-day would not do in public parts of her dressing and toilet, which should be done in the privacy of her own room. It is very bad form and bad taste, because it is putting too much value upon mere appearance."

Dr. Winifred Cullis, Professor of Physiology, University of London, made this appeal here to-day when she spoke at the annual speech-day of the Bournemouth School for Girls.

"Whilst I like to see girls well dressed and smartly turned out," she added, "I do not think much of the mentality of people who, in all sorts of really serious circumstances, suddenly turn to their toilet.

**(February 1)**

## JUDICIAL IGNORANCE OF COCKTAILS

A reference to cocktails in the Divorce Court yesterday led to Mr. Justice Hill's confession of ignorance concerning this modern habit.

"I am ignorant about cocktails," said the judge. "I am an old duffer and know nothing about modern habits. Nobody has ever had a cocktail in my house or ever will, and I have never been to any place where people consumed cocktails."

**(July 2)**

# OVER 30 MILLIONS NEW TAXATION

## SIXPENCE ON INCOME TAX

### NO FURTHER REVENUE FROM PETROL

**ADDITIONAL TAXATION**

**Income Tax -**
Standard rate higher by 6d., but under revised system of graduation the raising of the rate will have little effect on earned incomes below £1,000.
**Surtax -**
Increases ranging from 3d. to 1s. 6d. on current rates.
**Death Duties -**
Rates increased on estates over £120,000 by amounts ranging from one to ten per cent. on present duty. Highest rate: 50 per cent.
**Beer -**
Duty increased by 3s. a barrel.

**TAXATION REMITTED**

*Bookmakers' certificates abolished.*
*Motor-cycle and motor goods vehicle duties reduced.*
*Stamp Duties - Minor remissions.*

**OTHER PROPOSALS**

Valuation of land with a view to taxation of rateable values.
Amendment in the law to provide against Budget deficits.
Legislation to prevent the avoidance of Estate Duty on landed estates through the medium of private companies.

These, briefly summarised, are the alterations in the incidence of taxation and other proposals which Mr. Snowden indicated in his Budget statement yesterday.

His plans are devised with the intention that the burden of new taxation shall in the main be borne by super tax-payers and persons with income exceeding £1,000. Three-quarters of the income tax-payers will escape the effects of the raising of the standard rate.

In the case of beer the new impost will not result in any increase in price to the consumer.

Contrary to expectation, there is no increase in the duty on petrol. No provision, Mr. Snowden expressly stated, is made for expenses of a General Election this year.

Of the £33,000,000 additional revenue expected to result this year from the new taxation, it is estimated that the principal allocations will be:

| | |
|---|---|
| Income-tax ... ... ... ... ... | £21,000,000 |
| Surtax ... ... ... ... ... | £7,500,000 |
| Death duties ... ... ... ... ... | £3,000,000 |

**(April 15)**

# The Daily Telegraph

## AT ONE PENNY

Wide interest was created yesterday by the announcement that the price of THE DAILY TELEGRAPH is to be reduced to one penny as from Monday next.

Telegrams and telephone messages were received in the morning from every quarter, and before the day was out letters were arriving in large numbers.

The change of price has been welcomed on the ground that it is bringing a newspaper of established reliability within the reach of all thinking men and women. They will now have available at a popular price a paper they can trust.

As stated yesterday, there will be no change in the form, size or policy of THE DAILY TELEGRAPH.

It will continue to present the news of the day in a full but bright and easily digested form, without bias or distortion.

**(November 28)**

## SITE OF SODOM DISCOVERED

JERUSALEM, Tuesday.

The ruins of an old city, believed to be Sodom, one ot the two so-called Cities of the Plain which, according to Genesis, were destroyed by fire and brimstone because of their great wickedness, have been discovered in the centre of the Eastern Plain of Jordan, approximately five miles to the north of the Dead Sea. The discovery is regarded as of great importance.

The dead city has been brought to light by the researches of the Pontifical Biblical Institute of Jerusalem, which has been making excavations on the site for the last five weeks. The operations have been directed by Father Alexis Mallon, assisted by M. Réné Neuville, the French Vice-Consul.

Pottery and other finds show that the city was built in the early Bronze Age, and is therefore more ancient than Jericho. It possessed an advanced type of civilisation.

The excavations prove that the city was destroyed by a great fire early in the dawn of history and has remained uninhabited ever since.

**(January 1)**

## THE CATAPULT ON TRIAL

### ROMAN BALISTA FOR MODERN FLYING

**By MAJOR C.C. TURNER**
**"Daily Telegraph" Aviation Correspondent**

For some time past experiments with aeroplane catapulting contrivances have been in progress at Farnborough, not solely for use at sea, but also definitely for land operations.

This contrivance is the twentieth-century counterpart of the ancient Roman Balista. By compressed air it launches, not a mere missile, but an aeroplane complete with pilot.

Hitherto, the catapult launching contrivance has been used only on certain warships, and for mail expediting purposes, on a few ocean liners. It will be increasingly used for both, but a vast new field for it is opened up by the experiments now in progress.

Aircraft so launched from points close to hostile troops or territory would start on their operations with all their fuel in hand, whereas starting from far at the rear they might only reach their reconnaissance or attack objective just in time to turn homewards.

£10,000 MACHINE

The balista is capable of being transported over land by "caterpillar" traction. It weighs something less than twenty tons. Its cost, considering the service it could render, is certainly not a serious matter; probably it can be built for less than £10,000.

If the alternative were the construction of an aerodrome in bad country, the balista would be economical, besides conferring the immense advantage of immediate readiness.

Warfare and mail service to ocean liners by no means exhaust the possibilities. The balista may contain the germ of a solution of the problem of aeroplane services to the centre of great cities; although at present, obviously, it is not a complete solution, for it is only a starting, not a landing contrivance.

**(October 24)**

## £1,000,000 MOTOR MERGER

One of the first schemes that will be submitted to the Bankers' Industrial Development Company for its financial support is an amalgamation of three motor manufacturing firms – Rover, Lanchester, and Standard.

A merger of these concerns has been talked of for many months. Every difficulty that was raised in the negotiations has now been settled with the exception of finance. A sum in the neighbourhood of £1,000,000 would be required for re-equipment and as working capital for the combine.

**(April 4)**

# 69 CHILDREN KILLED IN A PAISLEY CINEMA

## BURNING FILM FUMES CAUSE PANIC

The biggest and most terrible cinema fire disaster ever experienced in Britain, and one of the worst ever recorded, occurred yesterday afternoon. Sixty-nine children lost their lives and thirty-seven were injured in a panic which followed the breaking out of fire in the spool-room of the Glen Cinema, Paisley.

Terrified by dense fumes which filled the place, and acting under the natural impulse to follow each other, hundreds of children, many only a few years old, and some with babies in arms, scrambled out of their seats and made for one of the exits from which about ten steps led to the street.

Some of the children in front fell, and the staircase and exit quickly became filled with piles of bodies breast high. On the top of one pile of bodies was found lying dead a baby aged about eighteen months.

With the spread of the panic a number of the children fell beneath the seats, where they were found later by the firemen, police and civilians carrying out the work of rescue. Two were lying behind a curtain in the orchestral enclosure. Others in terror had even tried to climb the screen.

According to news received up to a late hour the majority of the deaths were due to crushing and suffocation, though it is suggested that a number may have been killed either by the fumes or by gas. One of the firemen was overcome, and it is thought that gas brackets may have been broken in the rush of children.

It is understood that a young man in the spool-room, which is quite away from the cinema hall proper, had laid a spool of film on the floor when he heard a hissing noise. He looked round and saw flames rising from the spool, which was in its metal case.

He threw it out into a passage and ran to find the manager. The latter rushed to the spot, seized the film case, and threw it out of the door on to a piece of vacant ground at the side of the cinema. But by that time the fumes had drifted into the cinema and the panic had begun.

**(January 1)**

## 48 HOURS' WEEK BY LAW

**By OUR POLITICAL CORRESPONDENT**

Miss Bondfield formally introduced in the House of Commons yesterday a bill "to regulate the hours of work in industrial undertakings."

This is the long-promised measure to ratify the Washington Convention establishing a legal 48-hours' week. The text is to be issued to-day.

Almost immediately the Government had taken office last June the announcement was made that the Convention would be ratified. The reason for the delay in bringing forward the necessary legislation has been the difficulty of applying the 48-hours' week to railway and road transport workers.

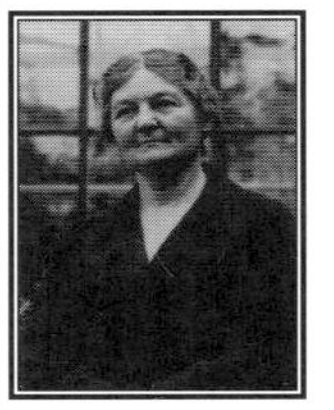
MISS MARGARET BONDFIELD

To overcome this difficulty prolonged negotiations have been required between representatives of the trade unions concerned and officials of the Ministry of Labour. A general agreement has now been reached and is embodied in the bill. I understand that it deals with the question of the maximum amount of "commercial overtime" to be permitted under the statute.

**(April 17)**

## COLOUR PROBLEM IN BRITAIN

### MENACE OF MIXED UNIONS

The present conditions under which coloured seamen from the West Coast of Africa enter Liverpool constitute a real social menace and are detrimental to the best interests of blacks and whites alike.

This passage occurs in the foreword to a report on the colour problem in British ports, which has just been issued by the Liverpool Association for the Welfare of Half-Caste Children.

Discussing the coloured man's attitude to white women, the report states that "the negro, usually well dressed, generous with what money he has, a good singer and dancer, shows to advantage and makes a good impression on the girls in the poor and overcrowded district he frequents.

"In his own country, the negro's relations with women are restricted by a rigid tribal discipline; in this country he is cut adrift from these restrictions before he has developed the restraint of Western civilisation. The negro thus tends to be promiscuous in his relations with white women."

The social menace of the position is described as being so serious that a solution is declared to be a matter for thorough reconsideration by local and national authorities.

**(June 16)**

*A new story of "Jeeves" by*

**P. G. WODEHOUSE**

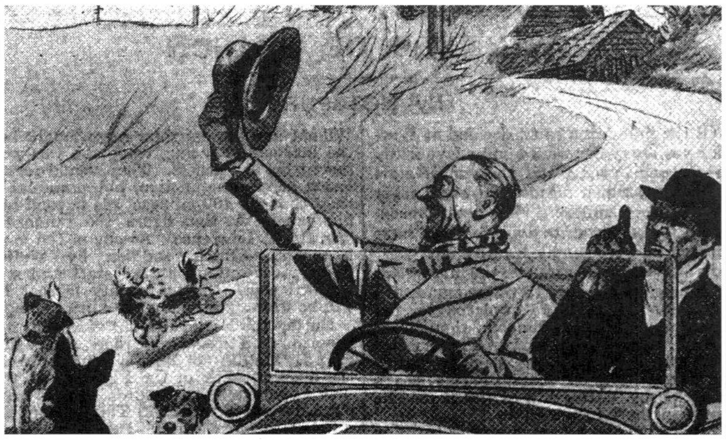

*in the April*

STRAND

MAGAZINE

*One Shilling* *On Sale Everywherre*

# THE CORONATION OF ETHIOPIA'S RULER

## SCENE OF BARBARIC SPLENDOUR

With barbaric splendour Ras Tafari Makonnen was crowned King of Kings and Emperor of Ethiopia at Addis Abeba yesterday.

A vast throng witnessed the ceremony, which took place in a specially built church in the grounds of the Cathedral of St. George. The walls were not carried up to the roof, so that those outside were able to see what took place.

The Duke of Gloucester represented King George, and almost all the important countries in the world sent missions.

Thousands of wild tribesmen, with their chiefs, had gathered in the capital for the great event, some having travelled for weeks to reach Addis Abeba. Their spears and shields and lion-skin cloaks contrasted with the brilliant uniforms of the high dignitaries and Diplomatic missions.

Ras Tafari had spent the night in prayer and meditation. But at dawn he discarded the humble robe of the suppliant, and, returning to the Palace, arrayed himself in his Coronation robes.

Half an hour before the ceremony the Emperor, a slightly-built man of medium height, but with the black-bearded profile of a Pharaoh, drove from his palace to the church in the coronation coach of the ex-Kaiser, drawn by six Austrian cream horses along a route lined with troops.

ROBE OF CRIMSON VELVET

Awaiting him were the priests, wearing gorgeous velvet vestments surmounted by capes of heavy gold embroidery, and a distinguished throng of Abyssinian and foreign notables. The Emperor was attired in a rich robe of crimson velvet trimmed with gold embroidery.

The Coronation ceremony itself was brief. After the recital of prayers - Abyssinia's religion is a primitive form of Christianity - the Archbishop of Abouna placed the richly jewelled crown on the head of the ruler, who takes the title of Selassie I.

Then came a religious ceremony in the Cathedral proper. At its close the Emperor drove back through the gaily-decorated streets and under triumphal arches erected under his own supervision for the occasion, to the palace, where at noon he received the congratulations of the Duke of Gloucester and the leaders of the other foreign missions and delegations.

In the evening a brilliant State banquet was held. This was the prelude to seven days of feasting, during which the entire Abyssinian army will be fed in relays. The priests and the populace are to be similarly entertained.

DRINK FROM HONEY

Raw and semi-cooked meat figures largely in the menu, with a native bread resembling pancakes, and for wine a compound made from honey.

Enormous quantities are consumed on account of the duration of the feasts. The Coronation banquet given by the late Empress Zauditu lasted four and a half hours, after which time the Empress retired, thereby releasing her European guests from an unaccustomed ordeal.

An important event during the festivities will be the banquet offered by the British Minister, Sir Sydney Barton, in honour of the Emperor. For this a special cake weighing about 180lb and standing over 5ft in height has been sent from London.

The Duke of Gloucester, who is understood to have taken a cine-camera with him, may well find an opportunity on this occasion for securing a series of unique pictures. On the conclusion of the festivities his Royal Highness will take up residence at the British Embassy until he leaves for his shooting expedition in British Somaliland.

**(November 3)**

## WHITE SLAVERY

### GERMAN GIRLS LURED TO SPAIN

Another scandalous instance of what is euphemistically known as the white slave traffic is reported in the Nachtausgabe. Once more the victims came from Berlin.

In this case the chief culprit is said to be a Spaniard, whose agents got together in this city some months ago a troupe of seventy-nine "dancers." The young women were engaged to go abroad under the English name of "The Sunshine Dancing Girls." Their journey took them to Barcelona, and here, to quote the report referred to, "after they had been compelled for a time to appear in the most disreputable resorts under the most disagreeable conditions, the impossible was demanded from them."

News has now been received here that Frau Schmeling, whose departure from Berlin with her "ballet" was reported in THE DAILY TELEGRAPH on April 28, has been arrested in Montevideo on a charge of carrying on illegal traffic in girls. Steps have already been taken to expel her from the big union of music-hall performers of which she was a member.

**(May 1)**

# UNITED FEDERATION OF ALL INDIA

## SIMON COMMISSION'S PROPOSALS

Volume II, of the Simon Report, embodying the Statutory Commission's recommendations for the future development of the Indian Constitution, is issued to-day.

Emphasising that the goal of British policy is the attainment of a United Federation of All India, the report, which is unanimous, reorganises British India on a Federal basis. The principal recommendations are:

BURMA - Immediate separation from India.

PROVINCIAL GOVERNMENT - Abolition of dyarchy, and maximum of autonomy consistent with the common interest. Legislatures to be enlarged on a wider franchise, and representation of Mohammedans and depressed classes to be protected.

CENTRAL GOVERNMENT - Substitution of a Federal Assembly, elected by the Provincial Councils, for the present Legislative Assembly. The Council of State to be retained.

THE ARMY - Control to be transferred to an Imperial authority, and frontier protection to become an Imperial function.

THE INDIAN STATES - A Council for Greater India to be set up to confer on "matters of common concern" between British India and the States, as a step to eventual federation.

POLICE - To be transferred to Indian control.

CIVIL SERVICES - Indian Civil Service and Indian Police Service to continue to be recruited on an All-Indian basis by the Secretary of State.

**(June 24)**

# GANDHI BEGINS HIS GREAT MARCH

## SCHEME TO DEFY THE LAW

**FROM OUR OWN CORRESPONDENT**

BOMBAY, Wednesday.

Early this morning Mr. Gandhi began his much advertised "great march," which is to end at a point on the Gulf of Cambay, near Jalalpur.

Scorning modern methods of transport, he and his followers are performing the journey on "Shank's mare."

At the start he was accompanied by seventy-nine "volunteers," drawn from various parts of India and by a large crowd of sympathisers. Most of the latter, however, soon halted and turned back.

With the exception of one Christian and two Moslems, all the "Volunteers" are Hindus. The majority belong to the teacher and student classes. Over one-third come from the Gujerat district of Bombay, of which Mr. Vallabhai Patel, Gandhi's imprisoned "Chief of Staff," has been described as the "Uncrowned King."

As already stated in THE DAILY TELEGRAPH, Gandhi's intention is to defy the Salt Act. He and his friends will manufacture salt from sea water, which is prohibited by law. They will also seize existing stocks of salt - if they are allowed to do so.

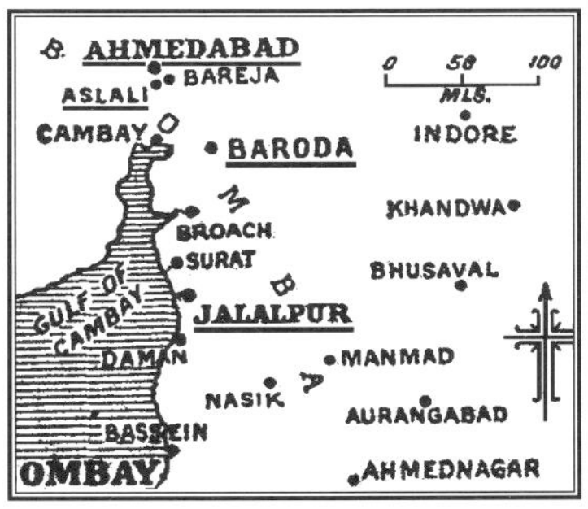


Gandhi's actual start was begun from his Ashram, or seminary, at Sabarniati, near Ahmedabad. An attempt was made to invest the enterprise with the atmosphere of the Crusades. One pamphlet distributed among the crowd in connection with the Civil Disobedience Fund demanded gifts for one who was, "soon to ascend the Cross like Jesus Christ."

APPEAL FOR MONEY

This effort to invest the Mahatma with the halo of martyrdom was accompanied by a successful monetary appeal. Gandhi had not proceeded far before his volunteers had collected 5,000 rupees (£375), while at the rear of the procession came a fine horse presented to Gandhi by a local lady.

**(March 13)**

## KING'S NEW CARS

The King and Queen have ordered five new Daimler cars. Their Majesties have intimated to Messrs. Stratton-Instone, Ltd., through whom the cars will be supplied, that the order is placed so that it may stimulate British industry, now passing through difficult times, and help unemployment during the winter months.

The cars comprise two 40-50 horsepower "double six" limousines, and one 30-40 h.p. brougham for the King, and one of each model for the Queen. All five are to be fitted with the new Daimler transmission system of "fluid flywheel" and semi-automatic gear-box. The coachwork will be carried out by Hooper and Co.

**(October 3)**

# SIX MONTHS FOR PUNDIT NEHRU

At Allahabad yesterday Pundit Motilal Nehru, president of the Congress Working Committee, and Dr. Syed Mahmud, secretary of the Committee, were sentenced to six months' simple imprisonment.

They were tried on two charges, says Reuter:

1. Of being members of an unlawful association, namely, the Working Committee of the All-India Congress Committee, an offence under Section 17 (1) of the Criminal Law Amendment Act;

2. Of having abetted the commission by the public of an offence, namely, the violation of three Ordinances, by passing the publishing resolution No. 2 at a meeting of the Congress Working Committee on June 12.

In answer to the District Magistrate, both the accused refused to produce any defence, or, indeed to answer any question.

**(July 2)**

# CARNIVAL OF CRIME IN CHICAGO

## TEN DEATHS IN EIGHT DAYS.

**FROM OUR OWN CORRESPONDENT**

CHICAGO, Thursday.

A carnival of crime in Chicago which has involved ten homicides in eight days is traced in part to official lethargy following on the financial chaos and payless days for the city's employees.

Efforts to raise the wind by the advance payment of taxes are being continued with unabated energy, but in the meantime the gangsters become more active. Murder has increased, a bank has been raided, many bombs have been thrown, and several stores have been blown up.

It is stated to-day that young women have been wielding guns and "blackjacks" to aid the criminal operations of their male confederates. Two of the gangsters' latest victims were liquor "racketeers," whose deaths are recorded nonchalantly because, in Chicago, it has become the fashion for gangsters and bootleggers to settle their quarrels amongst themselves.

In an effort to get money for Chicago's immediate wants, Mr. Wallace Caldwell, President of the Board of Education, has gone to New York to sell School Board Tax warrants to Eastern financiers and thus pay the salaries of the 13,500 school teachers and principals who have not had a pay day since Christmas.

"Chicago," said Mr. Caldwell, "the second city in the United States, is not yet broke, but we want everybody to lend a hand."

**(February 7)**

# LYNCHING ORGY IN TEXAS

One of the wildest riots in the history of the South-West resulted in an orgy of destruction in Sherman yesterday and continued far into the night.

A negro was burned alive, many prominent buildings were set on fire, and three blocks of flats in the negro section were wrecked. The militia were called out and fired on the crowd, which numbered several thousand. Only two persons, however, have been reported wounded.

The outbreak arose through the determination of the mob to lynch a 41-year-old negro, who was admittedly guilty of assaulting a white woman. In an attempt to reach the offender, the frenzied rioters burned down the courthouse.

**(May 12)**

# SYDNEY'S GREAT BRIDGE

## ITS 1,670-FOOT SPAN CLOSED

## WONDERFUL FEAT OF ENGINEERING

**FROM OUR OWN CORRESPONDENT**

SYDNEY, Tuesday.

The two halves of the huge 1,670-foot span of Sydney Harbour Bridge were closed just before midnight, some days earlier than was expected.

Thus the most important operation in the construction of the world's heaviest steel arch has been completed after six years' work, though thousands of tons of steel have still to be placed in position.

Each of the halves weighs about 14,000 tons, but so carefully was the work planned and executed that, when the tension was taken off the cables supporting them, and the two sectors lowered slightly, they met exactly.

It will be recalled that the first crossing was made on Aug. 8, when the Governor-General and Lady Stonehaven followed the engineers, walking along the planks joining up the two ends of the arch, which were then a few feet apart.

The building of this bridge is one of the greatest triumphs of British engineering and has excited world-wide interest, for never before have engineers of any nation attempted to build an arch bridge of such dimensions. Entirely new principles entered into its construction.

HUGE TRAFFIC CAPACITY

The structure, which is to be completed next year, is the strongest and most rigid long-span bridge in the world. Messrs. Dorman, Long, and Co. Ltd. were the lowest and the successful tenderers at £4,217,721.

With its five steel approach spans on either side, the bridge will have a total length of steelwork of 3,770 feet. It is about 135 feet wide, and provides for four lines of electric railways, a roadway 56 feet between the kerbs (sufficient for six lines of vehicular traffic), and two footways, each 10 feet wide. It is estimated that at maximum capacity 168 electric trains, 6,000 vehicles, and 40,000 pedestrians will be able to cross the bridge hourly.

The arch rises to a total height of 410 feet. The decking is 190 feet above mean sea level, giving a clearance of 170 feet at high water, sufficient for the safe passage of the largest steamers. It has 35 feet greater headway than the Brooklyn and 20 feet more than the Forth and Quebec bridges.

**(August 20)**

# HUNDREDS DEAD IN SOUTHERN ITALY

## EARTHQUAKE HAVOC AT NAPLES

**FROM OUR OWN CORRESPONDENT**

ROME, Wednesday.

A disastrous earthquake shook the South of Italy at one o'clock this morning. Two hundred and sixty persons are known to have been killed, but an official communiqué this evening announces that the dead will number more than 400. It is feared that over 1,000 have been injured.

The shocks lasted 45 seconds, and were felt most severely in the city of Naples and in the region immediately to the east of it, as far as the Adriatic port of Bari.

Melfi, a town of 14,000 inhabitants suffered most severely, being almost entirely destroyed. More than 160 deaths have occurred there.

A renewed outbreak again shook Melfi this afternoon, causing further loss of life. The town rocked at intervals for over an hour, the last shock being felt at 6.20. The inhabitants have deserted it for the open fields.

While the damage at Naples was not so great, the violence of the shocks, which are compared with those that destroyed Messina in 1908, was such that the people rushed pell-mell into the streets, and the city was soon in panic. To add to the confusion, the electric current failed. In the stampede a child was trampled to death and several persons were injured. The earthquake was accompanied by flashes of lightning, and the scene was lit up besides by flames from Vesuvius.

BUILDINGS COLLAPSE

Many houses were badly damaged, and ten deaths occurred amid the falling masonry. The fifth floor of one building collapsed, killing a child and injuring five other persons. In another three members of a family were rushing downstairs when the staircase gave way. The mother and daughter were killed under the debris, while the father has lost the use of speech through shock.

**(July 24)**

# MORE FOSSIL REMAINS OF EARLIEST MAN

## SKULL FOUND IN CHINESE CAVE

A discovery, which constitutes the passing of another milestone in the evaluation of the history of the human race, has rewarded the researches of the scientific investigators in China.

In the very cave at Chou Kou Tien, where a skull of Sinanthropus Pekinensis was found eighteen months ago, a second skull has been unearthed.

As is remarked in the cable from our Peking correspondent, the cave may be said to have yielded the remains of a "veritable Adam and Eve."

Whereas the first fossil remains were pronounced to be those of a woman, the new skull is regarded as being that of a man.

These creatures, members of an extinct genus of the human race, are believed to have lived about a million years ago. The second skull was unearthed some months ago, but the announcement of its discovery is now made public for the first time.

Dr. Elliot Smith, Professor of Anatomy in the University of London, who points out below the significance of the discovery, is leaving for China on Aug. 14 to take part in the investigation of these fossil remains of man.

**(July 31)**

# TUTOR'S ROOM TRAGEDY

Detective-Sergeant Willis died in hospital yesterday morning from wounds received in the shooting tragedy which occurred on Tuesday in a tutor's room at King's College.

He was the last of the three victims resulting from the action of the undergraduate, Douglas Newton Potts, who is alleged to have shot and killed his college tutor, Mr. A.F.R.. Wollaston, fired at the detective, and then turned his automatic on himself during an interview in Mr. Wollaston's room in the college.

Sergeant Willis, who was shot in the groin, was operated on, but took a sudden turn for the worse, and died early yesterday morning. He was 36, and leaves a widow. The inquest has been provisionally fixed for to-morrow.

The King's College flag flew at half-mast yesterday for the dead tutor, and the luncheon which was arranged to take place there to-day on the installation of the Chancellor and the conferring of honorary degrees will be held instead at Caius College.

Fresh light was thrown on the triple tragedy and its origins by inquiries made yesterday, showing Potts to have been a young man of erratic temperament.

It is believed that the three men were standing around the table, and that Potts suddenly jumped up, and, with his back to the door, pulled out an automatic pistol and threatened to shoot if either of the others moved.

Then, it is thought, Sergeant Willis jumped forward and tried to cover Mr. Wollaston, but at that moment Potts fired twice and rapidly and the police officer fell. He next turned the weapon on Mr. Wollaston who was killed outright, and then on himself.

**(June 5)**

# PRINCESS MARGARET ROSE OF YORK

## NEW NAME IN THE ROYAL FAMILY

The following statement was issued last night from 145, Piccadilly, W.1:

It is officially announced that the names chosen for the infant daughter of their Royal Highnesses the Duke and Duchess of York will be MARGARET ROSE.

The christening will take place in the private chapel at Buckingham Palace next month.

The name Margaret, which has figured prominently in the Royal houses of both England and Scotland, is borne in a slightly different form by the Princess's mother, the Duchess's names being Elizabeth Angela Marguerite.

The second name Rose, which is that of the Duchess's sister, Lady Rose Leveson-Gower, will be borne by a British Princess for the first time.

The christening ceremony in the private chapel at Buckingham Palace, where the little Princess's elder sister was baptised in May, 1926, will, it is understood, be entirely private. The date is likely to be some time after October 9.

**(September 23)**

## BANDITS' THREAT TO KILL MISSIONARY

Two British women missionaries, held for ransom by Communist bandits in China, are in imminent danger. Their captors threaten to kill one of them if £5,000 is not immediately forthcoming for their release.

To lend colour to their threat the bandits have had the revolting brutality to cut off a finger of one of them, an elderly women who has spent her life in the mission field, and have sent the grim token with their demand.

**(August 6)**

## INJURED AT POLO

## LORD LOUIS MOUNTBATTEN

While playing polo at Gosport on Saturday, Lieut.-Commander Lord Louis Mountbatten had a fall and broke his left collar bone.

**(May 5)**

# RAZORS IN LONDON GANG FIGHT

## WILD SCENES IN SOHO

A free fight between members of South London and West-end gangs in a Soho public-house last night resulted in

£200 damage to the public-house;

Injury to five men; and

The arrest of five men.

Razors were freely used, and tables were upset, chairs and glasses thrown and mirrors smashed. Attracted by the blowing of police whistles, a great crowd assembled and watched a big force of police attempting to separate the combatants. One man, Sydney Baxter, of Hackney, was taken to Middlesex Hospital unconscious and was detained for an operation.

Five men have been charged with causing malicious damage and one with obstructing the police.

**(February 5)**

# GRAMOPHONE IN A BELFRY

## EXPERIMENT AT STOKE POGES

### ILLUSION OF BELLS

**By A Special Correspondent**

STOKE POGES, Thursday.

A country churchyard, the setting sun casting its long shadows across the green, the music of the bells floating on the evening air. Can the conventional mind name anything more amply charged with rustic sentiment?

This evening I stood by the lych-gate of Stoke Poges church. At the end of the gravel path I could just see the tomb which I knew was that of Thomas Gray, whose Elegy was written in this very place.

From the belfry in the Norman tower came the sound of bells tumbling and crashing out their resonant notes. What was it that made the occasion strange, that had drawn little knots of critical listeners, most of whom had come from London for the sole purpose of hearing such familiar clangour?

The answer is astonishing enough — there were no bells pealing in the belfry, no team of village ringers at the rope-ends. The illusion of bells — and it was a perfect illusion — was being produced by means of gramophone records conjoined with amplifiers and loud speakers. Lately the Gramophone Company has been experimenting with the microphone recording of church bells, and now for the first time borrowed music was being flung from a silent belfry.

So we heard the bells of St. Margaret's, Westminster, the famous peal of York Minster, and the carillon of Loughborough. Even though I knew whence the sound came, the illusion was too strong for knowledge to destroy it.

There are many belfries without their rightful peal. Bells are costly and the times are hard on parish funds. But so successful did to-day's experiment seem that it should not be long before every village church can send out its proper merry din.

**(May 23)**

# "MOVIES," "TALKIES," & NOW "SMELLIES."

## NEW AMERICAN DEVICE

**From Our Own Correspondent**

NEW YORK, Thursday.

To make talking pictures more realistic a patent for a "smellie" device has been granted to Mr. John Leavell, of Los Angeles. By an ingenious process the odours of green fields and flowers and also of ham and eggs or onions can be literally projected into the atmosphere and "breathed by the audience."

This "smellie" device is described in the patent as "an apparatus for supplying an olfactory impression in conjunction with a motion-picture impression, also the means for transmitting and producing the same." Europe will be supplied in April.

**(March 15)**

# MOSCOW'S SAVAGE WAR ON RICH PEASANTS

## A DELIBERATE CAMPAIGN OF EXTERMINATION

**FROM OUR OWN CORRESPONDENT**

BERLIN, Monday.

No more staggering account of Stalin's present rule of blood and terror has yet appeared in print than that published to-day by the Sotzialisitcheski Vyestnik from its underground correspondent in Russia.

According to this writer, at least forty of the more prosperous peasants, who, as often as not, owe their comparative affluence to greater sobriety and industry, are massacred in cold blood every day.

Moreover, the diurnal tale of victims is constantly increasing, and is likely to go on doing so for some time to come.

The massacre of the "Koulaks," as the Bolsheviks call all peasants who for one reason or another they have decided to destroy or ruin, is being carried out in interpretation of a secret circular.

This document, of the existence of which the rank and file of the party has no knowledge, is itself based on the decision (published on Feb. 2) of the Central Executive Committee of the Bolshevik party to "dekoulakise" Russia.

**(February 25)**

# POPE DENOUNCES SOVIET

## "LEAGUE OF MILITANT GODLESS."

**FROM OUR OWN CORRESPONDENT**

VATICAN CITY, Sunday.

The Pope has addressed a letter to Cardinal Pompili, Vicar-General in Rome, announcing his intention to open a "crusade of prayer" against the anti-religious movement in Russia. He requests the Cardinal to make the necessary arrangements for the celebration on St. Joseph's Day (March 19) of a Mass of Supplication.

This Mass, which will be celebrated by the Pope at the tomb of St. Peter, in the Basilica, will be the central ceremony inspiring innumerable other rites of "expiation, propitiation, and atonement" throughout the world. Indeed, the actual sentence in which the Pope calls for spiritual support for his crusade is of considerable interest, and has been interpreted as an appeal extending even to those outside the Roman Catholic faith. It reads:

"We are fully convinced that not only the clergy and people of Rome, but also our venerable brethren in the Catholic Episcopale, and the whole Christian world, will join in our supplications either on the same day or such other holy day of obligation as may be set apart for the purpose."

In the course of his denunciation of the anti-religious movement of the Soviet "League of the Militant Godless," the Pope gives examples of the blasphemy and activities against which he desires the crusade of prayer to be directed.

FORCED APOSTASY

Factory workers of both sexes, he says, have been compelled to sign a formal declaration of apostasy and of hatred to God under penalty of being deprived of bread, clothing, and lodging tickets, "without which every inhabitant of that unhappy country risks perishing of hunger, cold, and destitution." He continues:

"Moreover, in every city, and in numerous villages, infamous and grotesque spectacles are being devised like the one which took place at Christmas in Moscow under the eyes of the foreign diplomatists. They witnessed the passage of carnival cars containing numbers of youths in sacred vestments, who were mocking at and spitting on the Cross, whilst on other cars large Christmas trees had been erected, from which dangled dolls, representing Catholics and orthodox bishops."

**(February 10)**

# EVACUATION OF RHINELAND

## LAST FRENCH TROOPS LEAVE

**From OUR SPECIAL CORRESPONDENT**

MAINZ, Monday.

Though the Allied occupation of German territory nominally comes to an end only at midnight to-day, the last of the French troops were on their way to the frontier early this afternoon.

The withdrawal from Wiesbaden was marked by a significant exchange of compliments. At the closing meeting of the Rhineland Commission the French Commissioner, M. Tirard, said: I am confident that the early evacuation of the Rhineland will be generally regarded as a manifestation of our common will to pursue a policy of peace between the two nations."

Baron Langwerth von Simmern replied with an expression of the wish that to-day might begin a period of complete and lasting international reconciliation.

A SILENT CROWD

The ceremony began at 9.30 a.m., and long before this hour the streets round the hotel overlooking the Kurgarten, where the Rhineland Commission conducted its business, were crowded. General Guillaumat, the French commander, and the French, British, and Belgian High Commissioners appeared on the balcony.

A few moments afterwards the band and a battalion of the 21st Infantry Regiment arrived with the colour. The Belgian, British, and French flags were hauled down to the music of the National Anthems, the ceremony being watched by the great German crowd in silence.

The Germans hoisted a big German flag immediately the French flag was taken down, although it had been agreed upon that the German flag should not be flown until the German police entered the town. When the French flag was taken down there were shouts of "Bravo" and wild cheering, and, as the French soldiers marched away, the crowd sang "Deutschland Uber Alles."

The troops entrained at noon. A huge crowd had assembled, and when the train started, many of the Germans hooted, but the soldiers merely laughed. The last French troops crossed the frontier at five p.m.

**(July 1)**

# THE PASSING OF THE OLD POOR LAW

## CARE OF SICK AND DESTITUTE

**By the Rt. Hon. NEVILLE CHAMBERLAIN, M.P., Minister of Health in the late Government.**

The Local Government Act of 1929 has been so often spoken of as the "Derating Bill" that even now it is not always remembered that the derating provisions are only one of a series of far-reaching reforms achieved by the last great measure of the late Conservative Government.

April 1, will see the end of the old Poor Law system, and it is of interest to consider what is going to take its place, and what are the advantages and improvements which the new system may be expected to bring in its train.

PRESERVING CONTINUITY

I do not propose in this article to touch upon the provisions of the Act which will have the effect of spreading the Poor Law charges over wider areas, because, important as are these provisions to the general ratepayer, I am concerned here rather with the effect of the changes on the administration of the law, and upon the welfare of those who will, in one form or other, be recipients of relief.

It is obviously desirable that, in making so far-reaching a change, we should avoid anything like a complete break of continuity, or discard the valuable experience accumulated in the course of many years by members of existing Boards of Guardians.

Turning to the subject of the assistance itself, this may be given either in an institution or by way of outdoor relief. In the rearrangement and reorganisation of institutional relief will be found one of the greatest reforms initiated under the new system. It must be remembered that the Guardians have been under a statutory obligation to relieve destitution, without regard to the cause which may have brought that destitution about.

VALUE OF SPECIALISATION

Among the inmates of their institutions, therefore, are to be found persons suffering from various diseases and disabilities, the treatment of which, had they not been destitute, would have devolved upon the municipal or county authorities. The test of treatment therefore, in the past has been, not the nature of the disability, but this has led, not only to the treatment of the same disability by two different authorities, but to a lowering of efficiency in the treatment itself. The whole tendency of modern medical practice, as of industrial practice, is towards specialisation.

In order to get the best treatment available, patients must be classified and transferred to an institution designed to deal with the disability from which they are suffering.

Such an ideal could never be achieved under the old system. In moving the second reading of the bill, I gave the House of Commons an analysis of the inmates of a rural Poor-Law institution, chosen at random, on a particular night. Out of 107 inmates, 55 were infirm and senile, 7 acutely sick, 6 epileptic, 8 certified lunatics, 18 certified mental deficients, 9 uncertified mental deficients, 1 able-bodied man, and 3 healthy infants. Such an accumulation of persons requiring such diversity of treatment, in a single institution is surely revolting to our humanity and in itself a condemnation of the system which produces it.

It would be too much to expect that a complete transformation will be effected under the new plan in the twinkling of an eye. But at least we may fairly assume that an immediate improvement will take place, and that the new Poor Law authorities will lay their plans for the ultimate provision of whatever buildings may be necessary for the proper institutional treatment of all the various cases that they will have to deal with.

There remains to be considered the treatment of the able-bodied unemployed. Certain enthusiastic reformers have complained that the Local Government Act leaves the position of this class of persons unaltered. By the operation of the Relief Regulation Order of 1911, outdoor relief cannot be given to them unless they are reduced to such a condition of destitution that in fact they are no longer able-bodied. It is argued that conditions have changed fundamentally since the principles on which this Order was founded were laid down. To-day, it is said, we are face to face with a situation in which large numbers of men are unable, in spite of all their efforts, to find work, and it can no longer be suggested that their position is due to any fault of their own.

ABLE-BODIED UNEMPLOYED

I do not think it can be denied that there is much truth in these contentions, and that there is need for a reconsideration of the whole position of the able-bodied unemployed. But the answer to my critics is

The proper treatment of the able-bodied unemployed would necessarily involve reconsideration of our system of unemployment insurance, which, under the Act recently passed by the present Government, has ceased to be a true insurance scheme, and has become a hotch-potch of insurance inextricably mixed up with out-relief divested of its proper safeguards.

**(March 31)**

# PUBLIC OWNERSHIP FOR LONDON TRANSPORT

## THE GOVERNMENTS BIG SCHEME

## TRAMS, BUSES & TUBES UNDER ONE AUTHORITY

It was officially announced yesterday that the Government propose to take immediate steps to carry out their policy of transferring to public ownership all the transport services of London.

Their proposals involve the creation of a Traffic Board to control all the manifold transport organisations - omnibuses, tramways and tubes - now conducted by municipal and private organisation. The capital involved in carrying out such a gigantic merger would exceed £110,000,000.

Mr. Herbert Morrison, who as Minister of Transport, is primarily concerned in the evolution of the Government's scheme, has already held discussions with representatives of the undertakings concerned.

A decision has yet to be reached regarding the precise constitution of the new authority. The Government's declared aim is to:

Combine business-like management with public ownership by the creation of a small Board consisting of persons of proved business capacity, under a chairman who would combine business acumen and vigour with wide knowledge and experience.

Upon their advent to office the Socialist Government were successful in securing the rejection of the merger, under private control, of the Underground Railway, the London General Omnibus Company, and the London County Council Tramways which was on the point of receiving Parliamentary sanction.

**(October 3)**

# DISCOVERY OF A NEW PLANET

## "BEYOND NEPTUNE'S ORBIT"

It is announced from Harvard Observatory that a new planet beyond Neptune's orbit has been discovered by the Lowell Observatory in Arizona.

The name of the astronomer has not yet been disclosed, but he is believed to be Professor Percival Lowell.

The discovery is characterised as the outstanding event in recent astronomical history. The announcement was made by Professor Shapley, Director of the Harvard Observatory, at Cambridge (Mass.) yesterday.

The present position of the new planet is given as "close to Delta Geminorum."

The planet can only be seen by the most powerful telescopes. Its exact distance from Neptune, its size, composition, speed, and orbit are still unknown.

Its present position for observation purposes is indicated as "between Jupiter and Neptune along the ecliptic," says an Exchange Telegraph message.

**(March 14)**

# WOMEN BATHERS IN THE SERPENTINE

## PRIZE FOR FIRST ARRIVAL

Mixed bathing will be allowed in the Serpentine from 4.30 p.m. to-day.

To mark the event the Serpentine Swimming Club will present a medal to the first woman bather.

The pavilion, which has cost £4,250, provides accommodation for 140 men and forty women. Each bather is given a locker, the key for which is held by the attendant while bathing is in progress.

Two sets of cubicles each covered with canvas, provide additional accommodation for men and women on either side of the pavilion. Additional cubicles are to be provided for children.

Contrary to expectations, no provision has been made in Hyde Park for sun bathing.

The hours for bathing for adults, as already announced in THE DAILY TELEGRAPH, are:

| | |
|---|---|
| WEEKDAYS: | 6.0 a.m. to 10.0 a.m. |
| | 4.30 p.m. to 8.30 p.m. |
| SUNDAYS | 6.0 a.m. to 10.0 a.m. only. |

**(June 16)**

# THE INVISIBLE PREACHER

## PLAN FOR WORSHIP BY WIRELESS

**Our Ecclesiastical Correspondent writes:**

The report of the Church Assembly Commission on the staffing of Parishes, which is to be considered next week, includes wireless broadcasting among the means available of supplementing the services of the clergy in places where the shortage is acute.

"We are of opinion," it states, "that the possibilities of using broadcasting in churches where there is no priest or duly authorised person to conduct the services should be more thoroughly explored.

"We know of places where the congregation of a parish church has in this way joined in the service held in some distant cathedral. It has shared in the prayers, joined in the hymns, and listened to the sermon.

"Distance has been annihilated by broadcasting and a fellowship of worship throughout the Catholic Church may become a new reality. Would it not be possible to arrange that isolated or distant churches which otherwise could have no service should have it relayed to them?"

Tribute is paid to the care which the B.B.C. has taken over the religious side of its work, and the commission says it has reason to hope that sympathetic consideration would be given to a request for a Sunday afternoon service.

**(November 13)**

# X-RAYS REVEAL A MASTERPIECE

THE DAILY TELEGRAPH is able to announce what in many quarters will be regarded as the most remarkable art "find" of the century, either in England or abroad - the discovery of a new masterpiece by Holbein.

Revealed by means of X-rays, the picture has been established to be a portrait of Sir William Butts, eldest son of Henry VIII's physician and a noted favourite of Queen Elizabeth.

Over it had been painted a portrait of the same subject later in life, and months of the most delicate work were needed to remove this.

As now revealed, however, the portrait, which has been preserved beneath its coat of protecting pigment for nearly 400 years, is declared to be a superb example of Holbein's work at its best.

**(February 27)**

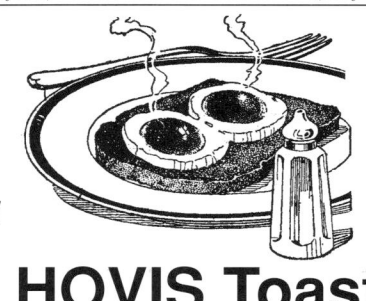

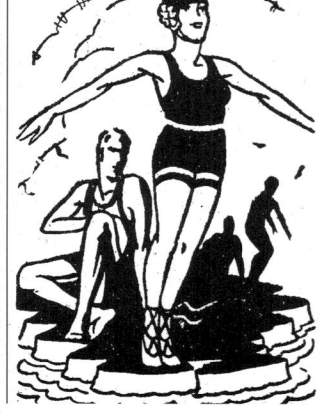

# STATE SUBSIDY FOR OPERA IN BRITAIN

## A GRANT OF £92,000 THROUGH B.B.C.

For the first time in the history of this country there is to be State supported grand opera.

Mr. Snowden announced in the House of Commons yesterday that the Government proposed to make a grant of £92,000 over a period of years towards the expense of presenting grand opera at Covent Garden and the provinces.

The grant will be paid through the British Broadcasting Corporation, and follows the announcement published in THE DAILY TELEGRAPH on Saturday last that the B.B.C. had come to an arrangement with the Covent Garden Opera Syndicate Ltd. for a "grand season" in London and a two weeks' season in at least six centres.

THE DAILY TELEGRAPH learns that the Government plans were known to the B.B.C. when they made their announcement last week, and it will in no way affect their scheme.

ADDITION TO B.B.C. INCOME

Mr. Snowden's statement, which was in reply to Mr. O. Lewis (C., Colchester) was as follows: H.M. Government has agreed, subject to the voting by Parliament of the necessary funds, to make a grant of £5,000 for the last quarter of the current calendar year and a grant of £17,500 a year for five years beginning on Jan. 1, 1931, towards the expense of presentation of grand opera, not merely at Covent Garden but also in the provinces. The remaining necessary funds will be provided by the British Broadcasting Corporation and by private investment.

**(November 21)**

# THE RETURN OF MENUHIN

## NO TRACE OF THE BOY PRODIGY

**By ROBIN H. LEGGE**

When some months ago Yehudi Menuhin, the violinist, made his first appearance in England, the musical world rose as one man in enthusiastic praise. Yesterday he reappeared again in the Albert Hall, and a mass of some 5,000 or 6,000 people acclaimed him in no uncertain manner. It was genuine enthusiasm.

And now, if one notices anything that seemed absent a year ago, it is that Menuhin appears to be almost more boyish than before. (He is still less than fourteen years of age.) Not, be it said, in his extraordinary musical mentality, but in his manner.

Since last he visited us he has continued his studies with Georges Enesco and with the redoubtable Adolf Buschin in Basle. There his natural well-being has been cared for no less diligently than his musical, and in consequence we have now a stalwart, hearty young man who plainly has lived freely in the fresh air, and is not of the hot-house breed that is here to-day but gone tomorrow, not of the kind of which prodigies used too often to be made.

As a fact Menuhin is no prodigy. He is a complete and consummate artist, equipped as not by any means all the violin virtuosi of twice his age are equipped. His tone, if slightly less forceful now than before - or so it seemed to me - is of the greatest purity, while his intonation is absolutely accurate. Moreover, his phrasing is always quite beautiful. His playing, indeed, is of the kind we call masterly, and if now and then he shows a slight inclination to hurry - as in the Preludio of Bach's Solo Partits in E major, and again in the Finale of the Mendelssohn Concerto, the notes are there, clear as any bell.

**(December 8)**

# NEW ORCHESTRA FOR THE B.B.C.

## "BEST IN ENGLAND"

The formation of a large new permanent orchestra of 112 or 114 players was announced by the B.B.C. yesterday.

Concerts are to be given every Wednesday next season at the Queen's Hall. The leading instrumentalists will be duplicated, so that the orchestra may split into two or even three separate sections when necessary.

Dr. Adrian Boult, the B.B.C.'s new musical director (formerly, director of the City of Birmingham Orchestra), who has just taken up his duties at Savoy-hill, stated last night to a representative of THE DAILY TELEGRAPH that the new orchestra is intended to be of a national character. it will be, in fact, the permanent enlarged form of the experimental orchestra of ninety-eight players which was formed about a year ago.

To some extent it will overlap Sir Henry Wood's Queen's Hall Orchestra, as some of the players will belong to both, but it will be altogether distinct from the London Symphony Orchestra.

**(May 30)**

# FIGHTS IN NEW COWARD PLAY

## HUSBAND AND WIFE COME TO BLOWS

Do people of apparent birth and breeding really do these thing? The sort of things, I mean, that they do in "Private Lives," Mr. Noel Coward's new comedy, presented by Mr. Charles B. Cochran at the new Phoenix Theatre last night before what is commonly called a brilliant audience. The brilliant audience laughed and applauded all right, though that may have been due to the often extremely witty dialogue, as well as some very excellent acting - but the question still persists: and with a corollary to it.

Do such people, man to woman, in the course of a lover's or other sort of quarrel, smack each other in the face, smash gramophone records over each other's heads, and roll on the floor together, still thumping, kicking, and possibly also biting and scratching; it was not possible to keep meticulous count of all the minor details? And even if they do, is their engagement in such pursuits a dramatic spectacle altogether calculated to please?

EXCELLENT ACTING

Apart from this man v. woman smacking business - which may be authentic in some sort of real life, but is not remarkably attractive on the stage - the piece contains much that is amusing, but the halt and slow-down after the first act is marked. The acting last night, however, was of a high standard throughout; Mr. Coward and Miss Gertrude Lawrence (acting, I believe, her first "straight" part) played the (first) husband and wife in just the right key of comedy - and if the scrap was inevitable, they certainly scrapped with agility, and even some degree of grace. Mr. Laurence Olivier and Miss Adrianne Allen, in their rather thankless parts as second-edition spouses, gave them admirable support, though they scrapped less interestingly; and Miss Lawrence's frocks were charming. M.D.

**(September 25)**

# JOHN GIELGUD AS HAMLET

## MASTERLY PIECE OF ACTING

Mr. John Gielgud, responding at last to enthusiastic calls for a speech at the conclusion of the first performance of "Hamlet" last night at the Queen's Theatre, simply expressed his gratitude and that of his colleagues in the Old Vic company to Mr. Maurice Browne for giving a chance in the West End to a team that had played together for eight months.

But I take leave to conjecture, what Mr. Gielgud could not in his modesty, that Mr. Browne would not have made this venture if it had not been for Mr. Gielgud's own magnificent performance. If it is every serious actor's ambition (as it is proverbially every comedian's) to succeed as Hamlet, then Mr. Gielgud must be a much-envied man. He has fulfilled that high ambition while he is still of hamlet's age, and his performance of this most exacting part puts him at one bound among our foremost actors.

Many qualities are needed for Hamlet. I only hesitate to say that Mr. Gielgud has them all, because praise that is too sweeping weakens itself and becomes mere indiscriminate adulation. This Hamlet has youth, grace, intelligence, emotional power, sense of poetry, and a most beautiful voice and articulation. I doubt whether any actor in our time has had all these attributes in the same degree.

Not even Forbes-Robertson's playing of the part has made a greater impression on my mind than this one; but I will not attempt to compare the two, for when I saw Sir Johnston in the part he was playing it for almost the last time. His was then an elderly Hamlet; Mr. Gielgud's is a young man. Comparison would be impossible and unfair.

Of the rest of the company I cannot speak at length. Miss Martita Hunt invested the Queen with a thick-witted good-nature which exonerated her from all suspicion of complicity with Claudius. A highly intelligent study of a stupid woman. Mr. Gylas Isham's Horatio, Mr. Francis James's Laertes, Mr. Bramber Wills's Polonius were perhaps the best of the others. Miss Adèle Dixon was appealing as Ophelia sane, but Ophelia mad was not within her compass. W.A.D.

**(May 29)**

# NEW OUTRAGE ON "RIMA."

Epstein's "Rima" in Hyde Park was again daubed with paint last night.

Shortly before ten o'clock a police constable on patrol in the Park found that the panel had been smeared with green, red and black.

Near by was an empty paint tin, but a search revealed no other clue to the perpetrators of the outrage.

**(January 22)**

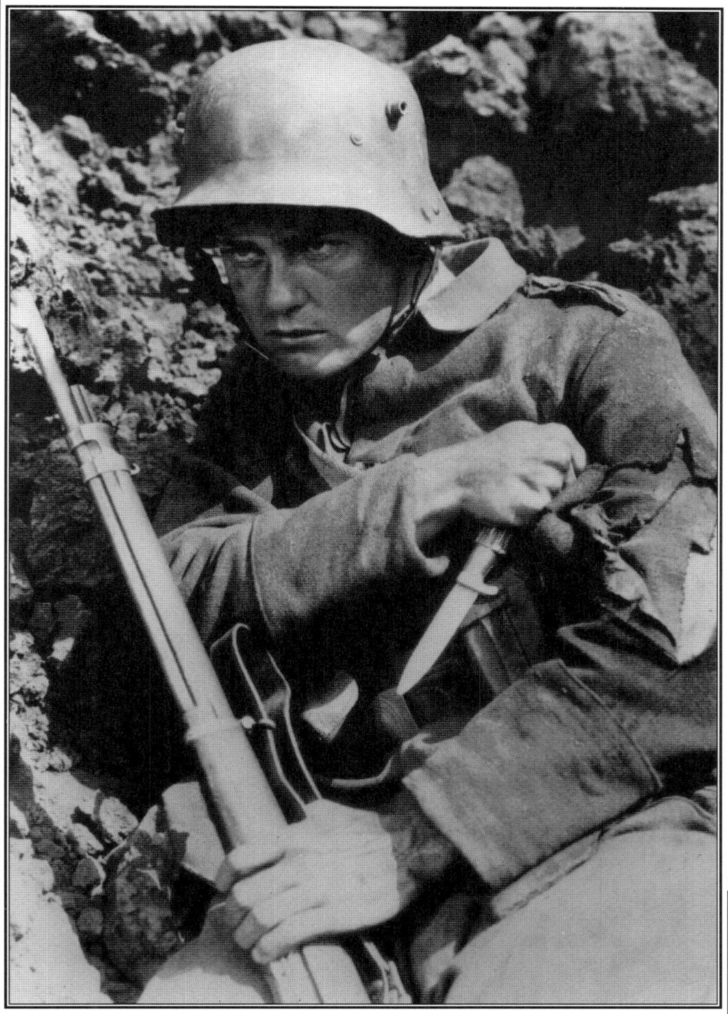

THE ANTI-WAR FILM "All Quiet on the Western Front."

# NEGRO ACTOR AS OTHELLO

Shakespeare is being well served in London this year. To Mr. Ainley's appearance as Hamlet, and Mr. John Gielgud's two big successes at the "Old Vic" there is now added Mr. Paul Robeson's eagerly awaited "Othello," which has justified expectation and is a really memorable performance.

The much-debated question whether Shakespeare meant Othello to be a negro or an Arab can be left to the professors; but it is certainly true that by reason of his race Mr. Robeson is able to surmount the difficulties which English actors generally find in the part of Othello without even seeming to notice that they are there. In Mr. Tearle's fine rendering, for instance, one felt that Othello's jealousy was aroused more suddenly and with less reason than was credible in such a man.

But that is because Mr. Tearle comes of a race which holds self-control to be almost the greatest of the virtues. Mr. Robeson, on the other hand, comes of a race whose characteristic is to keep control of its passions only to a point, and after that point to throw control to the winds. And so, when the madness of jealousy seizes this Othello under the subtle pricking of Iago's goad, we have no doubts concerning the genuineness of his passion. He is borne away helpless on the tide of that passion, and the rest follows inevitably.

For the rest, Mr. Robeson has a fine presence, a beautiful voice, which gives the poetry its best quality, and conveys the sense of nobility.

The only other performance in this production which deserves to be mentioned in the same breath with his is Miss Peggy Ashcroft's beautifully simple and sincere Desdemona. The transition from the gaiety of the young bride to the utter misery of the misused young wife shows that Miss Ashcroft has a wide range.

**(May 20)**

# MR. MAUGHAM'S NEW NOVEL

Questions of literary taste - and, it might almost be said, literary ethics - are raised by "Cakes and Ale," the latest novel, published to-day by that accomplished author and playwright, Mr. W. Somerset Maugham.

There are a number of similarities between one of the principal figures in the story, Edward Driffield, and Thomas Hardy which will suggest to many readers that the character is meant to be a portrait.

Outstanding among these is the description of Driffield as a great novelist, the last of the Victoriana, and an O.M., whose death at the age of 84 occasioned a national outburst of veneration and praise.

If Mr. Maugham meant Driffield to be a picture of Hardy the portrait is entirely unwarranted and unfair.

**(September 29)**

*RECENT FICTION*

# THE CASTLE

**By FRANZ KAFKA. (Secker. 7s 6d.)**

This superbly written German novel is a sort of religious allegory bearing certain broad points of resemblance – as Mr. Edwin Muir points out - to "The Pilgrim's Progress"; it is perhaps fated to be more discussed than read.

Struggling to disentangle the essence from the accident, one finds that the book turns on the efforts of a certain Land Surveyor, called K throughout, to gain admission to a mysterious Castle.

As to the interpretation of the allegory, it seems that K's objective is Divine Grace, and that the tale is designed to demonstrate the difficulties confronting man when he earnestly endeavours to seek a connection with the grace of the Godhead. Obviously, it is not everybody's book, but if the reader is prepared to make his way slowly and to allow himself to become completely submerged in the deep waters of the narrative he will find Kafka's dream-world an enchanting place. The translation, by that accomplished pair, Willa and Edwin Muir, merits every praise.

**(April 8)**

# CYNICISM AND WIT

Mr. Evelyn Waugh's outlook is distinctly cynical. In "VILE BODIES" he gives us a malicious but, at times, intensely funny skit on ultra-modernity, which, in parts, is good enough to be read aloud. He altogether lacks Miss Margery Sharp's geniality, which is a pity in view of the fact that they both rebel against the same thing, she more effectively in spite of less wit and less originality. He is at his happiest in his nomenclature (Lady Metroland, Lord Circumference), and in his picture of titled gossip-writers driven to invent picturesque people and novel social customs. He is less happy when he lets his saeva indignatio get the better of him. Colonel Blount, who fails to remember both faces and names, is excellent, but there is something unnecessarily nasty in the episode where his newly-married daughter takes advantage of this disability to pass Christmas under his rood in the society of her lover in the guise of her husband.

Mr. Waugh has obviously read Mr. Norman Douglas with profit, but it would do him no harm to delete some of what his Miss Runcible would call his "shock-making" tactics. The film scene of Wesley and Whitefield fighting a duel over Selina, Countess of Huntingdon is gorgeous fun, but the love-making of some of his callous bright young things is altogether too much like the Channel-crossing in the first chapter, just "sick-making."

**(January 17)**

# "ALL QUIET" AS A FILM

"All Quiet, on the Western Front" the talking picture version of Erich Maria Remarque's famous book, was presented privately yesterday at the Regal. It is no empty figure of speech to say that few, if any, pictures, certainly no war pictures, have ever created a more profound impression. For considerably over two hours the audience sat almost motionless, fascinated by the masterly fashion in which this aspect of the Great War, as seen through German spectacles, has been transferred from the printed page to the screen by Lewis Milestone, the Russo-American director, who was himself present in the theatre.

You are conscious of something exceptional immediately the picture opens, when you see and hear Kantorek, the school-master, addressing an impassioned harangue to the youths under his charge concerning patriotism and the duty of everyone to defend the Fatherland. Out of the open windows you see the long lines of field grey uniforms marching steadily through the streets of the little town to martial music, and you understand the enthusiasm with which his young auditors respond.

After that come all the horrible realities of war, which the director has done nothing to mitigate or gloss over. A brutal drill sergeant, whom the little company of youths whose fortunes you are following had known as a postman in civil life, knocks all the self-respect out of his subordinates. Continuous bombardment terrifies them, and semi-starvation, filth, and vermin make their existence one long martyrdom. Bayonet charges, in which trenches are lost and retaken; machine guns spraying out death; hospitals where operations are performed almost before your eyes, and dying men are removed from their beds in order to make room for newcomers; nothing, it seems, is omitted.

**(June 6)**

# EMIL JANNINGS' FIRST TALKIE

## "THE BLUE ANGEL"

A pitiful account of a man's moral degradation is unfolded with grim realism in "The Blue Angel," Emil Jannings' first talking picture, presented privately at the Regal. There may be a difference of opinion as to the legitimacy of utilising such a theme for popular entertainment; there can be but one opinion concerning the masterly manner in which the task has been carried out.

Jannings is first introduced to us as a professor in a German provincial gymnasium. He leads a simple, austere, carefully mapped-out existence, his sole relaxation being his morning talk with his pet bird in its cage. But from the moment of his first visit to the Blue Angel, the low café to which he has gone in order to detect some of his pupils in forbidden territory, all is changed. He himself falls under the spell of the vulgar dancer, whose photographs he had discovered in the boys' possession, and almost before he realises what has happened, he has become her slave, body and soul.

Emil Jannings gives a superb portrayal of the professor, and Marlene Dietrich, as Lola, the dancer, is almost equally good. The dialogue, which is introduced only when necessary, is spoken in English by the principals, although with a marked German accent. Certain incidents, one especially, no British or American producer would ever have dared to depict.

**(July 30)**

# A FRENCH FILM

## THE PARIS UNDERWORLD

What a small contribution audible dialogue makes to a screen play, directed and acted with vision and understanding, is strikingly exemplified in "Under the Roofs of Paris," presented yesterday at the Alhambra.

Save for a few rare occasions when one or other of the characters in this little French masterpiece spits out an expletive, and one brilliantly staged scene showing how a street ballad singer gradually infects with his own enthusiasm every member of the surrounding crowd, even the cynical, observant detective, the picture is silent. Yet so admirable is the acting that you are never in doubt for an instant as to the mental images reflected in the expressions and gestures of every one of these carefully drawn types of the Paris underworld.

**(December 12)**

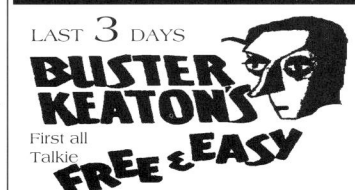

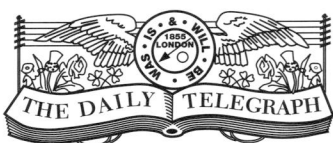

THE DAILY TELEGRAPH

135, FLEET STREET LONDON

Telephone: CENTRAL 4242

**TO-DAY'S WEATHER FORECAST**

LONDON & S.E. ENGLAND - Wind South-westerly, moderate or light. Bright intervals. Showers, perhaps thunder. Moderate or rather low temperature.

ENGLISH CHANNEL - Sea slight.

Lighting-up time. 10.6 p.m.

Sun rises 5.5 a.m. : sets 9.6 p.m.

Moon rises 12.4 a.m. : sets 2.20 p.m.to-morrow. Last quarter to-morrow.

High water at London Bridge. 7.29 a.m. and 7.26 p.m.

# A DANGER SIGNAL IN GERMANY

Germany's fifth General Election under the Republican Constitution has administered to that régime the rudest shock that any established system of government has suffered in our time without actual collapse. The principal importance of this election, as was pointed out yesterday in The Daily Telegraph, lies in the evidence that it yields as to the strength of the reaction against parliamentary democracy in a country which has had but ten years' experience of it; and, now that the results are fully known, that evidence is seen to be sufficiently impressive - much more so than the anti-Republican parties themselves ever imagined that they could make it. Communism has strengthened its position in the Reichstag, already no negligible one, by over one-third; but the far more sweeping success of the German imitation of Fascism is, in the strict sense, a political portent - a glaring danger-signal to democracy which its upholders in Germany, though still a majority, cannot dare to disregard. The National Socialists, who are Germany's disciples of the principles and methods of Fascism, and have hitherto been a fractional party in the central Legislature, had disclosed a notable increase of strength in the recent State elections in Saxony, Thuringia, and Wuerttemberg; cool observers allowed them a possible gain of fifty seats. That figure, in the result, is nearly doubled, and a party numbering twelve members in the last Reichstag will in the next be the only one approaching the strength of the solid Socialist block.

This is the worst testimonial that could be written for the political sense of the millions who have raised the party to that position. It lives upon nothing but a ranting emotional appeal to disappointment and discouragement. Its programme is a farrago of patently ruinous follies, including the non-payment of reparations, the repudiation of the peace-treaties, and the overthrow of the Republic in favour of a dictatorship of partisan ruffianism. Its leader is a foreigner - though Austria shows no anxiety to claim as a citizen the man whom German law refuses to acknowledge as a German - an accomplished mob-orator, and an utterly reckless political incendiary with one frustrated scheme of organised revolt already on his record. "Down with the Republic and all its works!" is the simple gospel of Hitler and his brown shirts. Of what they would put in place of it the one thing clear is that it would fling Germany back into the position of a State cut off from the comity of nations and from all the bitterly needed means, available now, of repairing her economic misfortunes.

**(September 16)**

# CRIME AND PUNISHMENT

The case of the unhappy man who, having been sentenced to ten years' penal servitude and fifteen strokes with the cat, committed suicide in Wandsworth Prison, has attracted much attention. It is well that the public should carefully consider the facts of his fate and the inferences as to our system of criminal punishment which may be drawn from it. Many people hastily assumed that what drove him to his death was fear of the lash, and we have suffered from a good deal of emotional argument - for there is sentimentality on both sides of the question - as to the morality and expediency of flogging.

The humanitarians who have been assuring us that it is a horrible cruelty which darkens men's lives and that the only rational way of treating the criminal is by segregation with curative discipline, should this morning be conscious of absurdity. The grim fact has given the lie to their theories. By the evidence of his wife it has been proved that what the man did fear in his punishment was not the flogging but the ten years of prison. The old brutal penalty of the lash he "did not mind."

But it would be a grave misfortune if this exposure tempted public opinion into the fallacy that corporal punishment is to be generally approved and encouraged in criminal sentences. The case is not logically to be read in favour of those stalwarts who assure us that flogging, and only flogging, is the deterrent of crimes with violence.

The rational inference is that the efficacy of the lash is far from certain. One case, arresting as it is, does not afford material for a general revision of our system of criminal penalties. But it should, if well considered, produce an effect almost equally important, distrust of universal principles and unvarying methods in the treatment of criminals.

**(April 5)**

# THE CHANNEL TUNNEL

The idea of a Channel Tunnel, which for years has exercised a singular fascination over the minds of many people in this country, is certainly brought somewhat nearer to realisation by the generally favourable report of the Committee, which is published to-day, and which is warmly greeted by the French Tunnel Committee. But how much nearer it is very difficult to say, for the Committee were only asked to examine the economic aspects of the problem; the strategic aspects will have to be submitted to quite another body for a decision, which, if hostile, would necessarily be as fatal to the project as it was before the war. It is not expected that the engineering difficulties would prove exceptionally formidable; at any rate, if they were they would be revealed during the construction of the pilot tunnel, which is estimated to cost £5,600,000. The cost of the two traffic tunnels is put at £25,000,000, but it is notorious that these preliminary estimates, especially in connection with submarine engineering, are usually largely exceeded. This has a vital bearing on the question whether a Tunnel could pay which could not hope to attract heavy goods traffic, and whether the requisite capital could be raised by private enterprise alone, for the Committee are emphatic that the scheme should "not be accorded any special financial assistance by Government." With that stipulation we entirely agree.

**(March 15)**

# FAGGING

Widespread sympathy will be felt for the parents of the unhappy Public Schoolboy who, it is asserted, was driven to take his life because he could not face the prospect of returning to a school where he would be called upon to fag. Emphasis was laid upon the fact by his parents that his was a naturally happy nature, and the evidence of the school authorities that they found him unusually quiet only goes to prove that something was preying on the boy's mind. It is generally admitted that a boy's second term at a Public School is invariably his most trying, for the freshness has worn off, and he is no longer considered immune from the apparently inevitable rough and tumble of school life, and it is peculiarly unfortunate that in this instance the boy should have had to spend five weeks, or about half of that trying term, in hospital with measles. This would of itself induce a low condition of mind, and the fact that he had never been caned for inefficient fagging is sufficient proof that he was rather fearful of unknown terrors to come than of any repetition of tortures already endured.

With the bereaved father's belief that the system of fagging could, with advantage, be altered, we are in full accord. It is a privilege which should never be extended to those who are capable of abusing it, and the fact that in this instance, as in so many others, a boy was called upon the behests of one who was in a lower form, had its obvious dangers.

On the other hand, it cannot be denied that for the great majority the fagging system has proved itself over a period of years an invaluable factor in training older boys to wield power and younger boys to obey. Though often tedious and menial, fagging is very seldom terrifying. Bullying is quite another matter, and really bears no relation to the question.

**(May 10)**

# THE TRAVELLER PRINCE

## FLAIR FOR ENJOYMENT IN WHATEVER LATITUDE OR CLIME.

**By Montagu Slater.**

*Surely the most widely travelled of Royalties of all time, the Prince of Wales leaves for Africa to-day, to resume the shooting expedition interrupted just a year ago by the illness of the King.*

The Prince of Wales seems to possess in a happy abundance the qualities of a born traveller. He has shown repeatedly his power of sensing an atmosphere, adapting himself to the local colour, not only doing what Rome does but becoming for the moment a Roman. He is a traveller with a handicap.

Receptions - like umbrellas - tend to have a strong family likeness wherever you find them. Only a traveller of the very first class would have known how to make a series of official visits travels in the best sense. And that the Prince of Wales has done.

The journey on which he is now starting is in its way an excellent example of the Prince's power to find his element in widely-separated latitudes, to make himself by his very enthusiasm and enjoyment a Freeman of the traveller's Rome to which all roads lead.

The story of the recreative half of his last visit to Africa reads with all the easy fluency of spontaneous enjoyment. On his first elephant hunt he brought down an elephant with tusks that weighed 65lb apiece, and on the way back he added to his bag a crocodile. It was then apparently that his taste for African big-game hunting began to develop rapidly. He altered his plans, and instead of returning to civilisation went off on another hunting expedition.

He came back presently to the nearest golf course - the only one in the world with the local rule that, if a ball is found to be lying in a hippopotamus's footmark, it can be lifted without penalty.

As all the world knows, in the midst of these equatorial entertainments he received the news of his father's illness, and he made the swiftest of all his journeys - a rush across two continents to the King's side. It has been reported that his father's greeting (he was then past the crisis of his illness) was, "Well! how many elephants did you shoot?"

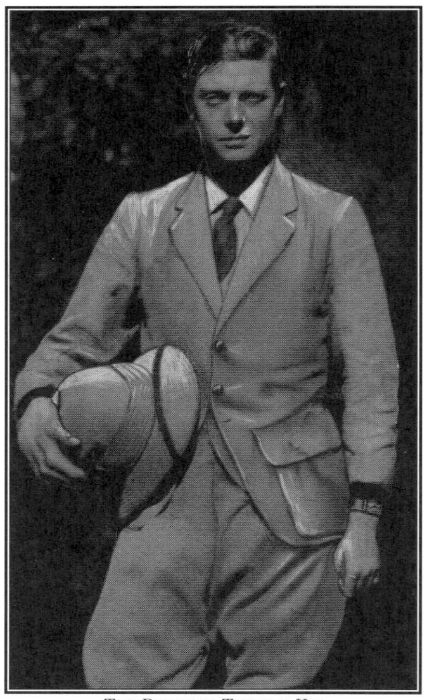

The Prince in Tropical Kit

That interrupted African holiday which he was so brilliantly enjoying is now happily resumed. It is perfectly clear that in Africa, as much as in Canada, in Australia, in America, he has demonstrated the first of the traveller's virtues. He entered into the spirit of the place completely. There is no guest so popular as one who thoroughly enjoys himself.

Here are two small pictures of this scene of meeting between the races. The first is official - the last meeting between his Royal Highness and the Maori chiefs. In the modern sitting-room of the Prince's hotel, amid the furniture and trappings of a new civilisation sit the grey-haired chiefs of the Maori tribes. In the middle of them is the Prince - the symbol of the civilisation that has triumphed over theirs. With simple dignity the chiefs present him with one of the few remaining heirlooms of their race - a battle-axe of greenstone - and then step silently out into the gathering night, back not to the wold and independent life of their traditions, but to the settlements where they are to end their days.

The second picture is unofficial. Late one night, when all the official receptions and feedings were over for the day, outside the window of his Royal Highness's bed-room came the plaintive strains of native music, throbbing through the still night air. Without a word his Royal Highness walked out into the darkness. Not far away he found the source of the music, where a group of natives were sitting round singing their traditional songs. For more than an hour the Prince sat with them, listening, and gathering an impression of his father's people alone, and without the carefully rehearsed but meretricious pageantry.

It was surely the true traveller's instinct that led the Prince, when the cow-punchers of Saskatoon were giving an exhibition of horsemanship, to enter the arena and mounting a comparatively tame broncho, head a charge of cowboys. One has known travellers of whom it might be said wherever they walk, there is Bond-street. There would, for that matter, be some excuse for supposing that wherever the Prince goes on his official visits the world becomes an endless flight of town hall steps. The fact that the real truth is just the contrary is proof enough that the Prince of Wales is a traveller by taste as well as necessity.

The sailor brings back his parrot, and the Prince of travellers is not accustomed to coming home unladen. In Australia he collected four emus, three opossums, and a small kangaroo - though the kangaroo fell into a decline and was buried at Trinidad. The opportunities for collecting pets are in Africa infinitely richer and more varied. One looks for an exciting cortège when the traveller again returns. Where will he put all those specimens? But that is another question.

**(January 3)**

# THE NEW HIGHWAY CODE

## WANTED, A STERNER NOTE

**By A.G. Throssell, Daily Telegraph Motoring Correspondent.**

It is evidence of the importance Mr. Herbert Morrison attaches to the Highway Code that he has submitted it in draft for the criticism of all interested parties, although by so doing, instead of laying it before Parliament at once, he has abandoned his expressed desire to have the code in force by the time that the speed limit ceased to be.

The criticism is not likely to be severe. It is an excellent code, entirely free from bias and prejudice, either anti-motoring or pro-pedestrian. The precepts addressed specially to motorists occupy twice as much space as those for any other section of road-users, but that is only natural since we are both the most numerous and the most dangerous when we misbehave.

If anything the code is too suave, too fatherly. For timid learners it is about as sound and complete a lesson in deportment as could be devised, but as a table of commandments, a list of things good drivers do not do, and bad drivers do and ought not, it is not precise enough.

The people who offend against the code - which after all is not a new thing, but has governed the actions of the vast majority of motorists for years past - are either thick-witted or thick-skinned. Whichever their disability, blunt do's and don'ts are better suited to them than polite maxima about obligations, and responsibilities.

I should like to see clear-cut denunciations of the practice of overtaking on bends, "chancing" cross-roads, parking or leaving cars on bends, or within white-line areas, or facing the wrong way after dark. All these aims are referred to, but only indirectly. They should be specified.

### GOOD FEATURES

On the other hand, the Morrison code contains several excellent points which have not hitherto ever had official backing. "The right-hand side of the road belongs first to on-coming traffic." English drivers, even comparatively good ones, too often forget that simple fact. Many American States emphasise it by a white line all the way down the centre of the roads.

Another good precept is that "in no circumstances can the sounding of a horn excuse a driver from taking every other precaution to avoid an accident." Perhaps the police will be less inquisitive about horn sounding in future.

Best of all is the advice to drivers of coaches and lorries not to drive head to tail, but to leave ample space for faster cars overtaking to pull in between them. That is born of a true appreciation of private motorists' difficulties, and they will bless Mr. Morrison for that if for nothing else in the code. Innumerable accidents have happened because a driver has found too late that the huge opaque vehicle he was overtaking was not alone, but one of a convoy in close formation.

This is all the more valuable since the speeds of heavy vehicles will now be limited, and so, too, is the command that they should keep on the extreme left.

### THE SLOW VEHICLE

Drivers of horse-drawn vehicles are bidden to obey the same rule, and to remember that they may be the cause of serious obstruction if they do not observe the courtesies of the road. But unless the mobile police pull them up when they transgress we cannot hope that these prehistoric survivals will notice any highway code.

**(December 18)**

# LONDON DAY BY DAY:

Hunting men in particular will be delighted with the appointment of Mr. John Masefield as Poet-Laureate, for "Reynard the Fox," perhaps his best known poem, besides being as English as Chaucer, is as full of the spirit of the chàse as anything of Surtees.

Ordinary men and women will be pleased at the appointment, because Masefield is so much the ordinary man of action made articulate, while Oxford will be happy because the Poet Laureate still lives on Boar's Hill. Here is a Laureate who is in every respect English and national, a sailor home from the sea, a hunter home from the hill. He can be trusted to interpret all our moods.

## The Development of Skating

A convincing proof of the development of skating in this country was given after yesterday's luncheon at the London Ice Club. It was announced that Miss Sonja Henie, the present Olympic Lady Skating Champion, who has won the world's championship four times, has been persuaded by the fact that we now have so many excellent rinks in England to do the bulk of her year's training here.

Miss Henie speaks excellent English and she chattered away cheerfully all the time without a trace of the "swelled head," which, after all, would be very understandable in one who, at the age of eighteen, has made such a success.

Although she says that she is very out of practice, Miss Henie went on to the ice after luncheon and gave a short demonstration. An expert who watched her performance with me said that, in his opinion, she has increased her speed and power by thirty per cent. in the last two years.

## "Luigi"

London life loses a great personality by the death of Luigi Naintre, manager of the Embassy Club in Bond street, and for twenty-five years known and well-liked in the restaurant world of the West-end.

Under his aegis the position of that club has been built up from that of a not-too-successful dance restaurant, to which admission was not difficult to obtain, to one of outstanding exclusiveness and remarkable prosperity.

To Luigi it yielded a comfortable fortune and a handsome annual income, although it ceased to be his personal property a few years ago. To all the smartest in the land, from the Prince of Wales downwards, it has been a restaurant-club above reproach, in which they might entertain and meet their friends.

The success was very largely attributable to Luigi, not solely, I think, to his personal relationship with his clients - though these were unusually intimate - but in equal degree to his genius for earning the affection of those who worked for him.

## The Brangwyn Paintings

The trustees of the late Earl of Iveagh will be faced with a difficult problem as the result of the decision reached by the Royal Fine Art Commission - that the sixteen paintings executed by Mr. Frank Brangwyn are not suited to the Royal Gallery of the House of Lords, for whose decoration they were intended.

I learned yesterday that Lord Iveagh had been prepared to expend £30,000 on a comprehensive scheme of redecoration for the Royal Gallery, to include the rejected pictures. But it was, apparently, the view of the Commission that no such scheme could be carried out which could fit the Chamber to accommodate pictures executed in such brilliant colouring as those which Mr Brangwyn has painted.

This is the problem which will shortly confront the trustees, for there is, I gather, little doubt that the House of Lords will accept the opinion of the Fine Art Commission.

## Laureate of hunting field Queen of the Ice

## Speed Boats on the Riviera

It is becoming evident that high-speed motor-boats are going to play an important part in the social life of the Riviera during the coming summer. Within the last twenty-four hours I have heard of two such craft, both of which will be arriving in the neighbourhood of Juan-les-Pins shortly.

The first is Sir Henry Segrave's Miss Alacrity, sister to Miss England, with which he captured the world's record in America last year. The other boat to which I refer is the property of Mr. Jack Coats, a wealthy young Scottish landowner and master of hounds.

**PETERBOROUGH**

# PARIS 1930-1931 COLLECTIONS FIRMLY ESTABLISH LONGER SKIRTS

## SIX INCHES BELOW KNEE FOR SPORTS AND STREET WEAR

**By Our Paris Fashion Expert: Illustrated By Scavone**

IN reviewing the 1930-31 collections, there are many characteristics in common with last season's modes . . . the general trend, for example is established on these lines, but one of the most striking points is the disappearance of uniformity.

Variety cleverly distributed by the "haute couture" promises to develop a more individual choice from each respective class. In shelving uniformity different types - rather than one - have influenced a diversity of line in modes that seem to break all fashion records in variety. What is more to the point, not one depends on the other in the pursuit of style.

The establishment of new lengths has been gradual, but this season they become immutable. We may protest, but think as we will, short skirts cease to play the light fantastic! Longer lines prescribe greater dignity. This does not imply, however, that they are going to be a drawback, as there is no question at all of sweeping up the dust along the by-ways.

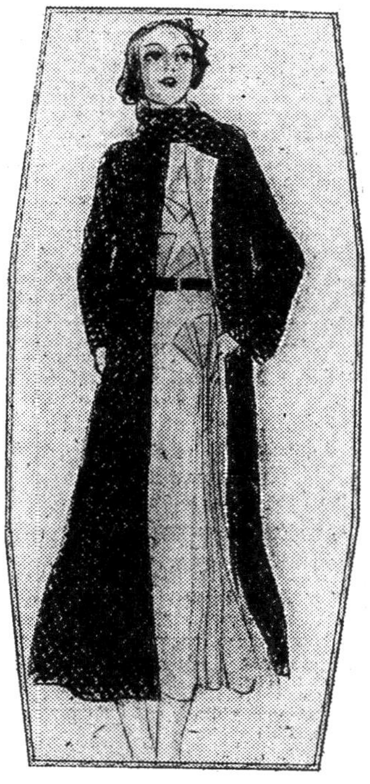

*Jersey cloth helps fashion this Premet morning ensemble, which consists of a butter yellow jersey dress, indicating interesting incrustations to tone, and a tweed belt to match the full-length overcoat. This is made in a yellow-and-brown mixture basket weave tweed, lined with yellow jersey cloth.*

Mid and below-calf lengths are distinguishing proportions for afternoon wear, but, oddly enough, both have been looking somewhat disgruntled during the heat in Paris since so many young people have discovered the secret of wearing ankle lengths.

Lines must be slim and lengths may be uneven, but not unduly so. Materials, too, should be chosen from the soft, clinging varieties, but pointed ends in every case falling over short underskirts encourage criticism. The compromise means neither one thing nor the other. This is by the way, and the little more or little less than is destined to mar or make a silhouette will be decided by good taste.

Apart from afternoon and evening modes the two-inch below knee level for sports wear is definitely taboo. The reason is obvious, for as a class they are grouped with morning ensembles and indicate a type that can be worn in town or country, also with equal ease for golfing or travelling. On the other hand, practically all winter sports modes outside golf nowadays quote trousers. In any case, the average six-inch below level will detail a brief length in comparison.

VARIETY IN TWEEDS

Since these ensembles are for sports, travel and street wear, tweed is naturally the material of first importance, but, not withstanding the general classification, it is interesting to note how all the big houses develop separate styles. This is due to the fact that variety as an individual asset develops not only one but many important changes.

In one instance, for example, three different types are evolved in tweeds for morning wear - the jersey dress, coupled with a mixture tweed overcoat, the tweed costume with jersey blouse, and the heavy tweed mixture executed on costume tailleur lines to wear with a lingerie blouse. This is a decidedly smart note which is more particularly applied for town wear, and conforms to the trend for subdued colours and blouses never veer from white or cream embroidered Georgette nor tweeds from simple mixtures in dark colours - black is an excellent example, also dark green. In the styles with long overcoats the dress is assorted in a light tone picked from the tweed mixture - like the one seen in the sketch, which is made of butter yellow jersey cloth.

Apple green in one of the new dress lainages looks excellent, too, under a dark green tweed coat lined with the same material. The line of these coats is straight, but a slight curve at the waist often varies a fuller trend treated with raglan yokes. Small fur or scarf collars develop changes, and three-quarter depths vie with full lengths for popularity.

Jacket-suits of tweed indicate the fashion for jersey or tuslic blouses in beige with navy blue, for instance, or amber with purple. These lighter coloured materials are likewise applied in a matching sense for linings and narrow bias scarves incrusted with tweed to replace collars. With this tendency for tweed suits, skirts take a subtle turn on slim semi-cloche lines and pleats in preference to godets - which are being gradually eliminated from lainage modes, as well as silken ones where "en forme" movements are more in evidence.

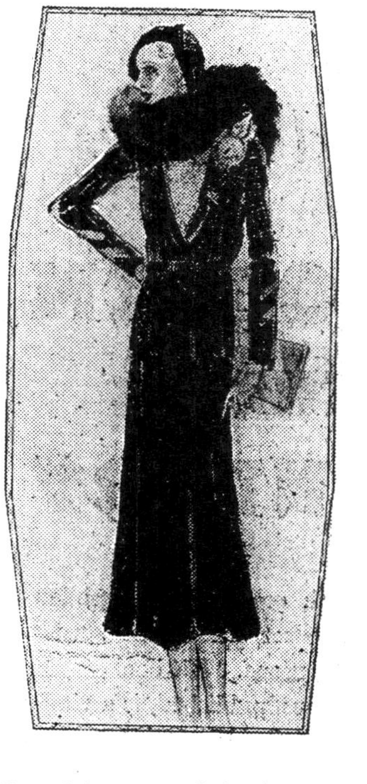

*One of the new trends for the autumn-winter season is the smartly tailored tweed morning suit, that is not to be confused with sporting modes, for it is designed by Premet, to wear with lingerie blouses of the finest quality. It is not so much a question of ruffles and jabots that give these blouses their classification, but embroidered plastrons outlined with lace.*

Variety in blouses also exercises an influence on waistlines. The tucked-in variety can be indulged by those who prefer it, but, on the whole, tunic lines are expected to win out on the new winter styles. This particular line resembles the cossack blouse, but it is gauged according to jacket or coat lengths. Longer lines, however, apply to afternoon modes, and they might break anywhere from half to three-quarter length in velvet, satins, crêpe-de-Chine or lamés.

For ordinary street wear they stop just a trifle below the waist, which is indicated by a belt that frequently tips the hipbone level.

**(September 5)**

## IN DEFENCE OF THE HUNTING WOMAN.

**By Lady Ingram**

MUCH abuse of the hunting woman has recently appeared. We have been called, amongst other uncomplimentary things, "a vacuous and voluble crowd, who indulge perpetually in small talk."

Those ignorant of hunting always "give themselves away completely" when they start discussing this sport. The hunting woman is no better or worse than any other woman in society. We drink fewer cocktails than in London, take more violent exercise, and, in winter, become perhaps obsessed with one idea, but we do no one harm, and we mind our own business.

Country people have no objections to us; they love hunting and do everything in their power to assist us, rushing to open gates, cheering us on our way and turning out in force at all the meets to enjoy a fine free pageant.

FARMER'S DAUGHTER

It is pure fallacy to think that hunting is only a sport for the rich. To-day I rode home from hunting with a girl of 18 - a farmer's daughter - mounted on a rough cob, whose long coat was plastered with mud and sweat. They had been having the time of their lives!

Many people who hunt can only afford to keep one horse, and that at the sacrifice of things that other people might regard as necessities; while I could name many girls who "strap" their own horses, after a long day in the saddle.

If hunting ceases, there will be many people in the countryside to lament our passing; the farmers, grooms, horse-breeders, saddlemakers, blacksmiths. For who, with sufficient means to go abroad, would stay in England, in the winter, when hunting ceases to be.

**(January 1)**

## *Lady Erleigh On The Weak Spot In Modern Girls' Upbringing*

THE minute one enters a well-known and spacious Kensington house, one is made aware of the personality of its chatelaine, a mother with all the modern ideas and probably the best-known leader of the infant welfare movement - Lady Erleigh.

The morning orders that were being given when I called were those of a woman who, like the women of bygone days, is a commanding personality in her own home. Yet, being the orders of a woman of 1930, they related, not to matters of the household, which, thanks to Lady Erleigh's powers of organisation and to modern labour-saving methods, runs automatically, but to the public work she has taken up, now that her children go to school and she has more time for outside interests.

During our talk this able mother of modern times and exponent of twentieth-century child care showed that some of her most important ideas on the upbringing of her two daughters and son are very old ideas indeed.

She quoted the old Jesuit saying to this effect, "Give me a child for the first seven years and do what you like with it after."

Before her children went to school there was very little time for public work, for a great deal had to be devoted to the nursery. Here she worked with her nurses, whom she chose young so that they would accept her ideas and not try to impose theirs. They came from a well-known London training college in domestic science.

"It is the first years in which you get your chief influence," she said. Always fond of history, she told her little boy, who was then 6, a story about the evolution of the world. He was so interested that she wrote it down, little dreaming that this and the other stories of the world's history she related to him would by 1930 be a standard book in P.N.E.U. schools. It is called "In the Beginning."

In the great homes of the past the mothers themselves initiated their daughters into the arts pertaining to the care of children and the household. Lady Erleigh told me that she preferred to entrust this all-important part of a daughter's education to the experts at the day nursery and the domestic science college.

INCREDIBLE!

"It is a woman's chief job." she insisted. To build up a race of great mothers is one of the principal things education should do for girls, this mother believes. "It is incredible to me," she said "that so many English girls should have no training in the handling of little children.

"I found that in France all the good families sent their daughters to crêches to learn this. The girls came-regularly, and I was surprised to see how seriously they took it."

She told me how difficult it still is in this country to arrange for young girls of 18 and 19 to have this training, and how she would like to see them coming to the day nurseries to get it. Unfortunately many of the domestic science colleges will not take girls for less than a year, and short courses are badly wanted to meet the need of the average girl.

As for other forms of housecraft, Lady Erleigh recognises that it is better to send daughters to a domestic science school. "You don't get very good results at home," she said.

**(August 18)**

# Greater Variety For Breakfast

## Country House Dishes Adapted

**By Mary Evelyn**

COUNTRY breakfasts, luncheons, and teas are not suited to town life, but they are ideal in the country, and the hostesses of our great houses see that their traditions are observed.

To-day the sideboard is still well supplied with home-cured hams, tongue, raised pies, pressed and spiced beef, potted fish and meats, cold game, boned poultry, cold salmon, according to the time of year, watercress and tomatoes.

These form the background of a well-chosen hot menu, supplemented by two or three kinds of preserves, apple and quince, as well as orange marmalades, damson cheese, black currant jelly, and apple butter, accompanied by piping hot home-made rolls (in addition to crisp toast and the modern crispbread), all made from cherished family recipes. To these may be added grapes, green figs, peaches, and nectarines at this time of year.

One or more dishes from August country breakfast tables might well serve to vary the sameness of our town menus.

Here are several from which a bill of fare can easily be selected, according to the numbers it is to serve and the resources of the neighbourhood. If, for example, trout or grayling are unobtainable, a fresh herring is excellent, split, bound, dipped in oatmeal, and grilled or broiled. (Grilling is done over the fire, broiling in front of it.)

*Tea, and coffee with milk and cream.*
*Scotch oatmeal porridge and milk.*
*Grilled or broiled trout, grayling, or fresh herring.*
*Dry curried prawns.*
*Cold roast grouse and Bradenham ham.*
*Devilled chicken.*
*Mushroom omelette.*
*Little loaves of scrambled eggs.*

**(August 20)**

# CHANGED HYDE PARK

## PASSING OF FASHION PARADE

**From Correspondent**

London has lost one of its most famous institutions. It has passed away silently, almost imperceptibly - the Sunday Church parade in Hyde Park - not a tear shed; perhaps, to mark its demise.

But is has gone, may be never to return. Once upon a time, fashion and society in all their glory were to be seen on Sundays promenading from Grosvenor Gate to Hyde Park Corner, and thence along Rotten Row.

What has happened?

The public has discovered Hyde Park as a playground. To-day the picnic (was it not the famous Lord Chesterfield who first used the word in print!) is the thing.

That was obvious to an observer who strolled through the cool shade of the pleasaunce yesterday. The Park has become the resort of those who are "out" for the day rather than the diversion of those who wish to spend a formal hour between church and luncheon.

Indeed, it savours of happy paradox that, while those who live about the heart of London go to spend the week-end in the country beyond its borders, those who dwell without should seek pleasure and recuperation in the central parks. These latter find their joy in "rus in urbe."

But custom dies hard, and if there were fewer top-hats abroad, they gathered closer about their standard by Stanhope-gate.

Even here they had been driven to a secluded retreat beneath the trees, while a "topper-less" phalanx occupied the once-sacred ground on the island of grass opposite the gate itself. This phalanx was packed as close as any theatre audience.

**(July 7)**

# A NEW MORRIS SIX

## FEATURES OF THE £215 "MAJOR"

**By Maurice Sampson, of the "Autocar"**

Although the existing series of Morris cars, from the Morris Minor to the Isis saloon, is continued for the coming season, main interest in the 1931 programme will be centred on an entirely new production.

This is the Morris Major, a six-cylinder car of 14.9 h.p., and available with three types of body, a fabric salonette which consists of a two-door, close-coupled saloon finished in black at £215, a coachbuilt coupé with a folding head in lake or black at £220, and a coach-built saloon with folding head in lake or black finish at £225.

The power unit in this interesting newcomer is substantially the same as the one which has been fitted successfully to many thousands of Morris-Oxford Sixes sold during the present season.

The engine is notable for an air cleaner which acts as a pre-heater for the mixture, thermostatically operated radiator shutters, a S.U. carburetter which may quite justly be said to be free from flat spots, a special oil-filtering device whereby impurities are removed each time the clutch pedal is depressed, coil ignition, pump water circulation, side valves, a bore and stroke of 63.5 x 102 mm. (1,938 c.c.), calling for an annual tax of £15.

An attractive feature of this power unit is its ability to run great distances without the need for decarbonising, and its willingness to accept almost any grade of fuel.

Coupled to the engine is a three-speed gear box and a plate clutch fitted with cork inserts. Thence the drive is taken through an enclosed propeller shaft to a spiral bevel-driven rear axle. Mechanically operated four-wheel brakes are used. The cars are fitted with bumpers, and electrically operated dipping and swivelling headlamps. Current is generated by a 12-volt dynamo, and the various controls are neatly grouped on the top of the steering wheel.

UP TO 65 M.P.H.

Despite the very moderate prices, the general finish is good. The chassis itself follows conventional lines, and in common with all the Morris models, the complete car provides chromium plating for bright parts. Triplex glass throughout. Bishop cam-steering, bumpers fore and aft, a calor-meter water temperature indicator, and, last but by no means least, thoroughly adequate mudguards.

This car is designed particularly to appeal to the motorist who hitherto, by reasons of initial and running costs, has been compelled to accept a four-cylinder car. Acceleration is claimed to be remarkably good, and a speed of 65 m.p.h. is stated to be within the car's ability.

**(August 30)**

# GRECIAN LINES

Hairdressers,. dressmakers, and shoemakers are all encouraging the Grecian trend.

Sandals are worn with evening and dinner gowns, and in the afternoon gowns draped effects borrowed from Grecian art are making a strong appeal.

Set to fall from either shoulder, classic draped effects give slimness to the figure.

**(March 31)**

# "BARE-LEGS" FASHION AT GOODWOOD

## VISITOR'S INNOVATION

A visitor to the paddocks at Goodwood yesterday aroused considerable interest by her unconventional holiday attire.

She wore no stockings, and her legs were burnt brown by the sun. Her frock, which was quite long, was of flowered cotton material, and she wore a white linen hat with an upturned brim, which was decorated with gaily flowered cretonne.

**(August 1)**

# CURRENT FOOD PRICES

Approximate prices of good quality food in Greater London will be found below:

FRUIT AND VEGETABLES

| | s | d | s | d | | s | d | s | d |
|---|---|---|---|---|---|---|---|---|---|
| Apples - | | | | | Plums - | | | | |
| English des. lb | 0 | 4 | 0 | 6 | Desert lb | 0 | 8 | 1 | 0 |
| English Finest | 0 | 8 | - | - | Cooking | 0 | 2 | 0 | 4 |
| English Cooking | 0 | 2 | 0 | 4 | Raspberries - | | | | |
| New Zealand | 0 | 5 | 0 | 6 | punnet | 1 | 3 | 2 | 0 |
| Blackberries - | 0 | 9 | 1 | 0 | Tomatoes - | | | | |
| Cultivated | 0 | 9 | 1 | 0 | English lb | 0 | 5 | 0 | 7 |
| Blk Currants | 0 | 6 | - | - | Imported | 0 | 4 | - | - |
| Bananas doz | 1 | 6 | 2 | 0 | Aubergines ea | 0 | 4 | 0 | 5 |
| Hothouse grapes - | | | | | Beans - | | | | |
| Black lb | 1 | 3 | 3 | 0 | Kidney lb | 0 | 3 | 0 | 4 |
| Grape fruit ea | 0 | 4 | 0 | 8 | Scarlet runners | 0 | 1½ | 0 | 2 |
| Green figs | 0 | 4 | 1 | 0 | Cabbage ea | 0 | 2 | 0 | 4 |
| Greengages lb | 0 | 6 | 0 | 10 | Celery, head | 0 | 4 | 0 | 5 |
| small box | 1 | 6 | 2 | 0 | Cauliflowers ea | 0 | 4 | 0 | 7 |
| Pineapples ea | 2 | 6 | 3 | 0 | Mushrooms - | | | | |
| Nectarines ea | 0 | 8 | 2 | 0 | Forced lb | 2 | 6 | 3 | 6 |
| Pears - | | | | | Onions | 0 | 1½ | 0 | 2 |
| Dessert ea | 0 | 2 | 0 | 4 | Peas lb | 0 | 3 | 0 | 6 |
| English lb | 0 | 3 | 0 | 4 | Potatoes - | | | | |
| Oranges doz | 1 | 0 | 2 | 0 | 18lb, 10lb | 1 | 0 | - | - |

BEEF

| | S'ch | | Ch'd | | | S'ch | | Ch'd | |
|---|---|---|---|---|---|---|---|---|---|
| | s | d | s | d | | s | d | s | d |
| Aitchdone | 0 | 11 | 0 | 7 | Brisket | 1 | 0 | 0 | 9 |
| *Topside | 1 | 8 | 1 | 3 | Sirloin | 1 | 10 | 1 | 2 |
| *Silverside | 1 | 4 | 1 | 2 | Rump steak | 2 | 8 | 1 | 10 |
| Midribs | 1 | 8 | 1 | 0 | Beef steak | 1 | 8 | 1 | 4 |

* Boneless

| | MUTTON H. K. | | MUTTON N. Z. | | LAMB H. K. | | LAMB N. Z. | |
|---|---|---|---|---|---|---|---|---|
| | s | d | s | d | s | d | s | d |
| Loin. whole | 1 | 9 | 0 | 11 | 1 | 11 | 1 | 3 |
| Legs | 1 | 8 | 1 | 1 | 1 | 8 | 1 | 4 |
| Shoulders | 1 | 2 | 0 | 10 | 1 | 6 | 1 | 1 |
| Neck. whole | 1 | 3 | 0 | 9 | 1 | 5 | 1 | 0 |

FISH

| | s | d | s | d | | s | d | s | d |
|---|---|---|---|---|---|---|---|---|---|
| Salmon lb | 4 | 0 | 4 | 6 | Lobsters ea | 1 | 0 | 6 | 0 |
| Turbot | 1 | 4 | 2 | 3 | Whiting | 0 | 4 | 1 | 0 |
| Halibut | 1 | 6 | 2 | 0 | Prawns doz | 1 | 3 | 1 | 6 |
| Brill | 1 | 4 | 1 | 6 | Cod lb | 0 | 10 | 1 | 4 |
| Soles | 2 | 6 | 2 | 9 | Hake | 0 | 10 | 1 | 4 |
| Lemon soles | 1 | 4 | 1 | 6 | Haddock | 0 | 8 | 0 | 9 |

# LAW REFORMER AND LORD CHANCELLOR

## TRIUMPH OF MAIDEN SPEECH

The Earl of Birkenhead was in a real sense what is called a "Lancashire lad," but, as a matter of fact, he was born in the town of Birkenhead, on the Cheshire side of the Mersey; and it was from his native town that he took his title.

Frederick Edwin Smith came from a strong and an ambitious stock. His father had an adventurous career as a soldier in India and real estate agent, and when he was a middle-aged man he became a member of the Bar.

After preparation at the local school in Birkenhead, Fred Smith went to Wadham College, Oxford, and there he began that series of triumphant assaults on every possible position which brilliant gifts could attain that was characteristic of his whole very prosperous and very remarkable life

AN UNFRIENDLY HOUSE

When F. E. entered the House of Commons as member for the Walton Division of Liverpool, in 1906, he came to the House a stranger even in name to most of its members.

Smith chose admirably the hour at which he rose to make his maiden speech. It was early in the sitting, when the House was full, including the Treasury Bench, and when, therefore, he had an audience larger than usually falls to the lot of the new member. And yet, to realise the full measure of success which followed, one has to add that it was about as unfriendly a House as ever a young member addressed.

Smith had not been on his legs for many minutes when he was able to prove that the House had found a man whom it could not cow; to whom it could not even refuse to listen. It might howl, and it did howl; it might be restive, and it was restive; it had to listen; it had even to laugh; it had in the end to sit dumbfounded under the Niagara tide of passionate invective which this impassive-faced and defiant boy poured out upon it.

It was perhaps the most successful maiden speech ever made in the House of Commons. From that hour "F. E." was made.

The times were exciting, for there was the historic Budget, with the land taxes of Mr. Lloyd George; there was the struggle over the Parliament Act; above all there was a fight over Home Rule for Ireland. In all these controversies Smith was a protagonist. But it was on the question of Ireland that he took the most prominent and the most daring part.

He was a man a good deal influenced by his personal associations, and one of his closest associates was Sir Edward (Lord) Carson. When that redoubtable figure announced that he was going to organise a force in the North of Ireland to resist, if needs be by arms, the application of Home Rule to the Orange districts of the province of Ulster, going into everything as he did with vehemence and the overmastering joy of life and of battle which was a chief quality of his nature, Smith made speeches quite as vehement as those of Sir Edward Carson himself.

As a Yeomanry officer he was mobilised at the outbreak of the Great War. He was then summoned at a moment's notice, on Aug. 8, by Lord Kitchener and Mr. Winston Churchill, and asked to undertake the task of establishing a Press Bureau. He put in seven weeks' work, and then, feeling that the bureau was on its feet, he resigned. He wished to undertake active service.

He was attached as Intelligence and Recording Officer to the Indian corps in France. He remained with the corps until after the battle of Neuve Chapelle, by which time he had risen to Lieut-Colonel and had been mentioned in despatches.

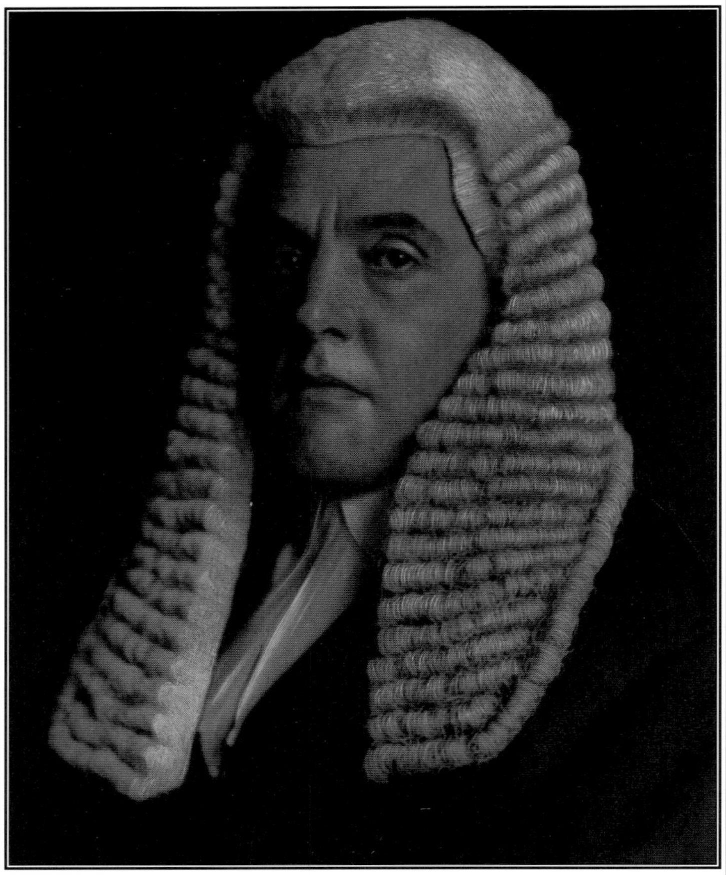

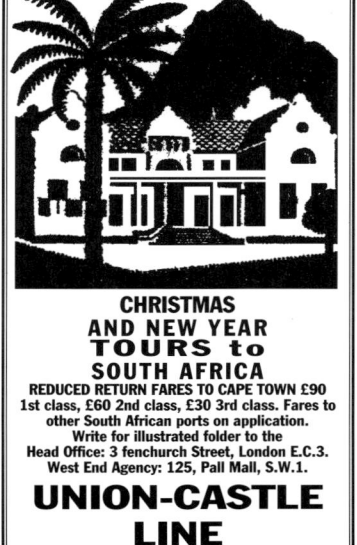

THE EARL OF BIRKENHEAD

SOLICITOR-GENERAL IN COALITION MINISTRY

In May, 1915, the first Coalition Government was formed, and Mr. Asquith recalled Smith from France and offered him the post of Solicitor-General. Thus his first Government office, long foreshadowed by his Parliamentary promise, came to him from the hands of one of his political opponents. He accepted the offer, and was knighted on appointment.

He was only 42 years of age at the time - a very early age to have reached so great a position; it was part of that triumphant progress which most of his life had been.

The next great turn in his career of dazzling fortune came when suddenly the announcement was made that F. E. had been raised to the lofty position of Lord Chancellor - the greatest legal prize not only in England, but in the whole world. It came to him most unexpectedly. Lord Finlay was dispossessed of the Chancellorship after he had held it for a short time, Smith hesitated to leave the Commons, but it was a choice between that and the Attorney-Generalship without a seat in the Cabinet. He had been given a night in which to decide. He took the title of Lord Birkenhead.

AS LORD CHANCELLOR

He was but 46 years of age when he became Lord Chancellor, the youngest man to occupy the Woolsack in modern times; younger even than Herschell and Cairns, who were both 49 when they attained that dignity.

As Lord Chancellor, he will be remembered in the future for his Law of Property Act. This, which Lord Justice Warrington described as "the greatest measure of law reform that had ever obtained the force of law," was largely the work of Lord Birkenhead. He was not the draughtsman of the bill, but it is doubtful if the measure would have passed into law without delay but for his energetic sponsorship.

Among other far-reaching results, this Act abolished the law of copyhold and went a long way towards assimilating the law relating to land ownership with that relating to private property. It remodelled the law of perpetuities, the law of primogeniture, and many minor laws. Its effect will be that the registration of title in regard to the property of land will take the place of the present complicated and expensive system of conveyancing.

Smith had such a handy and nimble mind that when the after-the-war problems presented any special difficulties he was called in, and often had to rush over to Paris to take part in the conference there with the representatives of the Allies.

The Coalition fell in 1922. In comparison with Mr. (Sir) Austen Chamberlain, Birkenhead refused to abandon Mr. Lloyd George. He declined to join the Conservative Government. At first it was said that this would be the end of his political success, but it proved very far from the truth.

When Baldwin formed his new Government Birkenhead was offered the important post of Secretary of State for India, and this he accepted.

His work at the India Office was overshadowed by an event of which we cannot yet appreciate the full importance. Mr. Baldwin's Government, with the support of all parties, determined to encroach on the ten-year period allowed for the Montagu-Chelmsford reforms by the Act of 1919. As Birkenhead put it to the House of Lords in November, 1927, "the general improvement of the relations between India and Great Britain justified the beginning of a lengthy task at once." But the Conservative Government did not remain in power long enough to control the climax of the important series of events inaugurated by the Simon Commission, and the Secretary of State for India had exchanged the Cabinet for a board of directors before the end of the Government's period of office.

The necessity of earning an income outside politics had been from the beginning a powerful force in the shaping of his career.

HIS LEGAL CAREER

The rise of the Earl of Birkenhead in the legal sphere could not so accurately be described as meteoric as his political progression. It certainly was exceptionally rapid and distinctly luminous, but so far from having the sudden and transitory qualities of a meteoric phenomenon, it was heralded over a period of strenuous years, and it left behind visible, enduring results. By common consent Lord Birkenhead was one of the most brilliant of our Lord Chancellors.

Lord Birkenhead's legal erudition has often been described as amazing. He was a man with astonishing power of assimilation.

He was the most-sought-for man when old oratory was in request. His astuteness and knowledge of men and matters was peculiarly useful in libel actions. He became a "fashionable" counsel in causes célèbre, an advocate with tremendous persuasive power over juries, not by virtue of those dramatic mannerisms sometimes employed, but by sheer force of reasoned argument. Every one of his traits of manner and style proved to be an asset. Yet these were only the more showy demonstrations of a very clever lawyer. Beneath lay a store of profound legal knowledge which was presently to serve in higher duties.

ROGER CASEMENT LEADING FOR CROWN IN PROSECUTION

Lord Birkenhead was Solicitor-General and Attorney-General under Coalition Governments during the Great War, and the largest part of his work was then concerned with matters arising out of the war. As Attorney he led for the Crown in the prosecution of Roger Casement for treason.

Finally came the offer of the Woolsack in 1919.

QUALITIES OF A GREAT JUDGE

As might be expected, in tribunals composed so largely of veteran judges as the House of Lords and the Judicial Committee, there was at first a little prejudice against the judgements of so young a recruit. But notwithstanding, Lord Birkenhead very quickly showed that he had the qualities of a great judge as well as of a great advocate, and some of the finest judgments of modern times are his. That which he delivered in the famous Archdeacon Wakeford case in 1921, lasting an hour and three quarters, stands for all time as a model of plain narration of facts, deductions to be drawn therefrom, and the application of the law to them.

**(October 1)**



# BANNED AS PAINTER AND NOVELIST

## MR. D.H. LAWRENCE

## "DAILY TELEGRAPH" CONDEMNATION

Mr. D.H. Lawrence, the English novelist, poet, and painter, died at Vence, near Nice, on sunday night, after an illness of less than a week. The news of his death was received in London from Mr. Aldous Huxley. He had been suffering from tuberculosis, but did not anticipate a fatal result, as he was considering a plan of returning to Mexico, a country for which he had conceived a great affection.

Mr. David Herbert Lawrence was born at Eastwood, Nottingham, in 1885, the son of a collier. The home was poor, and it was the mother who held it together, encouraged the boy in his literary studies, and made it possible for him to take advantage of the County Council scholarship, which he won at the age of 12. Four years later he began teaching a class of colliers' boys, while carrying on his own studies in the early morning and the evening. He came first on a list of the King's scholarship examination, but could not raise the £20 necessary for the entrance fee at the training college, but two years later he matriculated at the Nottingham Day Training College, and thenceforward the claims of teaching and literature pressed upon him, and literature eventually prevailed.

WHEN AT HIS BEST

Lawrence was at his best when writing of the people of the Midlands from whom he had sprung, and his characterisation of the miners and their class in "Sons and Lovers," his second story but his first success, is inimitable. He was impatient of what he regarded as the sham sentiment of the ordinary romantic novel, and he made his characters behave with all the inconsistencies in matters of emotion which he believed to be the usual human lot.

In 1915 his novel, "The Rainbow" was banned, following police action. In 1928 he produced a sensational story called "Lady Chatterley's Lover," in which he dealt in daring detail with incidents between "Lady Chatterley" and her lover, a gamekeeper on her estate. The book was printed in Florence, and was to have been restricted to a limited number of copies. It was later produced in America, where the manager of a Cambridge bookshop was sentenced to a month's imprisonment and fined £100 for selling a copy.

POLICEMAN AND "PANSIES"

By order of the Home Office, too, the Customs officials intercepted the manuscript of a book of poems entitled "Pansies" in the post between Italy and England and confiscated it, but an edition, with some of the more objectionable verses left out, was privately printed in London for 500 subscribers.

"When I read down the list of omitted poems," Mr. Lawrence wrote in the preface, "and recall the dozen amusing but terribly unimportant bits of pansies which have had to stay out of print for fear a policeman might put his foot on them, I can only grin once more to think of the nanny goat, nanny-goat in-a-white-petticoat silliness of it all." The royalties on the Continental sale of the book are said to have reached £10,000.

Mr. Lawrence was equally unfortunate with some of his pictures. When he displayed a number of them in a London gallery The Daily Telegraph described it as a "disgraceful exhibition," and a few days later the police made a raid and carried off some of the paintings. They were all nudes, described by such titles as "Spring," "A Boccaccio Story," and "Fight with an Amazon." The case came up at the Marlborough-street police-court, and the summons was adjourned sine die on an undertaking being given that thirteen of the pictures should not be exhibited or any reproduction of them, that two sold should be returned to the purchasers, and that some should be sent back to Mr. Lawrence.

**(March 30)**

# J.T. TYLDESLEY'S GREAT RECORD

J.T. Tyldesley, the famous England and Lancashire batsman, died with dramatic-suddenness yesterday. He was putting on his boots at his home in Manchester preparatory to going to business when he collapsed.

Born in Lancashire on Nov. 22, 1873, he reached the age of 57 last week. Tyldesley was a well-equipped batsman when he first appeared for Lancashire in 1895, and in his second match he put together a score of 152 not out against Warwickshire at Edgbaston. Two years later he made over 1,000 runs, and achieved that feat for nineteen consecutive seasons. Four times he scored over 2,000 runs, and in 1901 he secured an aggregate of 3,041, his innings including nine separate centuries and his average amounting to 55.

There were few batsmen more attractive to watch than John Tyldesley. Exceptionally quick on his feet he always appeared to have plenty of time in which to make his strokes, and, full of enterprise and dash, he scored all round the wicket in delightful style.

**(November 28)**

# SPEED KING OF THE WORLD

## SEGRAVE'S GREAT CAREER

Sir Henry O'Neal Dehane Segrave, whose death yesterday in an attempt on Windermere to achieve a world record for speed in water-craft, is reported on another page, was the most famous and most successful of the comparatively small band of specialists, colloquially known as "speed kings," evolved by the internal combustion engine. He had since March last year held the world's record for the fastest speed attained on land. He seemed certain to attain the same honour for speed on water when disaster overtook him.

Tall, slenderly built, erect, with piercing deep-set eyes and a hawk-like face, he was all that imagination called for in a speed king. He had nerves, but they were nerves of steel; a vivid imagination, controlled by a cool, alert brain.

MANY RECORDS

Sir Henry Segrave born Sept. 22, 1896, son of Mr. C.W Sergrave, of Coombe Court, Witley, Surrey, and was educated at Eton and Sandhurst, whence he was gazetted to the 2nd Royal Warwickshire Regiment during the Great War. He was transferred later to the Flying Corps, in which he spent the latter half of his military life. Being badly wounded, he was attached to the British Embassy at Washington and, while there, started to race on motor-cars in 1917. "Every race has its thrills," he once said, "and I started when I returned to England in 1919, and bought an Opel car to run on the Brooklands track. From thence I graduated as a private competitor with this 1914 Grand Prix racer, with which I won a number of races. Then Mr. Louis Coatalen offered me a car to drive in the 1921 Grand Prix race in France, and from that date I have always driven Sunbeam racers as an amateur racing driver."

In 1922 he held the 10 miles record at Brooklands at a speed of 114 miles per hour, which, though thrilling in itself, was nothing to the joy he felt in 1923, when he won the Grand Prix Race on the Sunbeam at Tours, averaging seventy-six miles per hour for the 500 miles race, being the first Englishman and the first English car to win that prize.

FIRST VISIT TO DAYTONA

By 1924 Segrave's reputation as a racing driver was thoroughly established, and soon afterwards he began his wonderful career as a maker and breaker of records as well as a winner of races.

In the summer of 1926 he was astonishing the world by driving a car at a speed of 147 miles an hour on the road, and in the following March he set out for his first visit to Daytona Beach, Florida, the stage where he won his greatest fame. That year he had a Sunbeam, fitted with two 500 h.p. Matabele aero engines. The world's record then stood at the figure of 174 m.p.h.

Segrave said when he set out that he hoped to prove that speeds in excess of 180 miles an hour were possible. On March 29 he drove the Sunbeam over the Daytona course at 203.79 m.p.h., the first man in the world to travel at over 200 m.p.h. At the end of the run the brakes failed to act. He had four miles in which to pull up, but at the end of them he still travelled at about 100 miles an hour, and to avoid being smashed up in the sad dunes he drove into the sea.

Captain Malcolm Campbell went to Daytona and raised the record to 206.96 m.p.h., and then an American driver, Ray Keech, went a fractional part of a second quicker over the measured mile and captured the honour for his country.

The record had to be regained, and Segrave set out to do it. Captain J.S. Irving, who had been in charge of the construction of his Sunbeam, designed for him a new racer, the famous Golden Arrow. This car had a Napier Lion aero engine, of twelve cylinders, arranged in three blocks of four, developing 950 b.h.p. It was the type of engine with which Lieut. Webster had won the Schneider Trophy in 1927.

THE GOLDEN ARROW

The Golden Arrow, wonderfully streamlined, and by far the most graceful racing machine ever seen, was taken to Daytona early in 1929, and on March 11, at its first serious effort, Segrave drove it to and fro over the measured mile at a mean speed for the two runs of 231.55 miles an hour. He was prepared to make another run, but two days later, Lee Bible, a young and rather inexperienced American driver, was killed driving a 36-cylinder challenger, and the meeting was closed.

On his return, Segrave received the honours of a conquering hero. He was accorded an official welcome by the Government, drove in procession through the streets of London, and later was knighted by the King at Bognor Regis, where his Majesty was convalescing.

Segrave, however, had already carried out his intention of taking to motor-boat racing. With the Golden Arrow, there travelled with him to America his first Miss England, a boat fitted with a similar Napier Lion aero engine.

With her he hoped to recapture the British International Trophy, which had been taken from us at Southampton by Commodore Gar Wood in 1922 and held by him ever since.

**(June 14)**

# DOCTOR FRIDTJOF NANSEN

## HEROIC ARCTIC EXPLORER

Dr. Fridtjof Nansen, whose death is reported on another page, was born near Christiana on Oct. 10, 1861, the son of an official, who spared no pains on his son's education. In and about his native place he, as a boy, constantly met those who had tensely struggled at the white fringe of the Arctic, and his imagination was stirred by their strange stories of adventure. Just when he had reached manhood, in 1882, he made a voyage into the Arctic region in the sealer Viking. This settled his future. With all the earnestness of his mind and heart he resolved to devote his life to the problem of the Arctic.

When he was 26 he formed a resolution to cross Greenland from east to west, and a year later, in 1888 he made the adventurous journey, accompanied by three Norwegians and two Lapps.

THE SAILING OF THE FRAM

Four years later, in 1893, Nansen set out on his greatest adventure - His valiant attempt to reach the North Pole in the Fram. His scheme, based on a long and scientific investigation, was to let his ship become frozen into the ice north of Siberia, and drift with the current setting towards Greenland.

He watched the building of his ship with great anxiety, and there was no prouder or more hopeful man in the country than Nansen when he boarded the Fram on his great adventure, and standing on the bridge took a last view of his beloved home as the good ship, fully equipped and splendidly manned, steamed slowly down the fjord.

In September the Fram reached the New Siberian Islands, and made fast to an ice-flow and drifted North to 84 deg 7 min on March 3, 1895. It was made quite clear to those on board that the current would not take the Fram across the North Pole, and that if the Pole were to be reached some of the expedition must attempt to get there over the ice. This meant leaving the ship, going North, and returning to the nearest known land, for owing to the irregularity of the ice-drift it was hopeless to think of again reaching the Fram. Nansen did not hesitate. Accompanied by Lieutenant Johansen he quitted the ship on March 14, 1895, with three sledges, two kayaks, and twenty-eight dogs, their expectation being that they would reach the Pole in about fifty days.

TOO TIRED TO EAT

It was a terrible journey. The continual toil of hauling and carrying the sledges caused extreme exhaustion, and sometimes in the evening Nansen and his companion fell asleep as they struggled along. Their clothes froze hard upon them. The sleeve of Nansen's coat rubbed deep sores in his wrist.

"How cold we were," he declared, "as we lay there shivering in the bag waiting for supper to be ready. Supper was delicious. These occasions were the supreme moments of our existence - moments to which we looked forward all day long. But sometimes we were so weary that our eyes closed, and we fell asleep with the food on the way to our mouths. Our hands would fall inanimate with the spoons in them, and the food fly out on the bag."

In the early days of April Nansen reluctantly realised that further progress was impossible, and on the memorable 7th of that month the furthest north point was reached, 86 deg 14 min, the highest latitude then attained. Here they were forced to stop. They were 128 miles from the Fram and 260 miles from the Pole. On their trudge back difficulties thickened about them, and the 100 days they had allowed themselves to complete their venture increased to more than half again. Their dogs were killed one by one to provide food for the rest, until two only remained. Each day the explorers looked death in the face.

Through storm and fog they won their way forward, sometimes by sledge, sometimes by kayak, leaping from floe to floe and ferrying back to get their baggage over. When the ice gave out they paddled to Frederick Jackson Island, in the north of Franz Josef Archipelago. The two adventurers wintered in Franz Josef Land, and again started out on the long, lone trail.

On the Windward, Nansen and Johansen sailed to Vardoe, Norway, which they reached on Aug. 13, the date, strangely enough on which the Fram, breaking loose from her ice-prison after a period of thirty-five months, passed through the last floes into open water. To Tromsoe the Fram proceeded, and there, on the afternoon of Aug, 25, 1896, the yacht Otaria, with Nansen and Johansen on board, glided alongside the famous Arctic ship. Little wonder that such a homecoming was made the occasion of great national rejoicings.

The Great War stirred him to renewed activity and to a mission which brought relief to thousands, if not millions, of his fellow-creatures. In 1919 he suggested to Mr. Lloyd George, M. Clemenceau, President Wilson, and Signor Orlando a scheme, which met with their approval, for supplying famine-stricken Russia with food, and carried it out with enormous success. For these and other humane efforts he was awarded the Nobel Peace Prize.

**(May 14)**

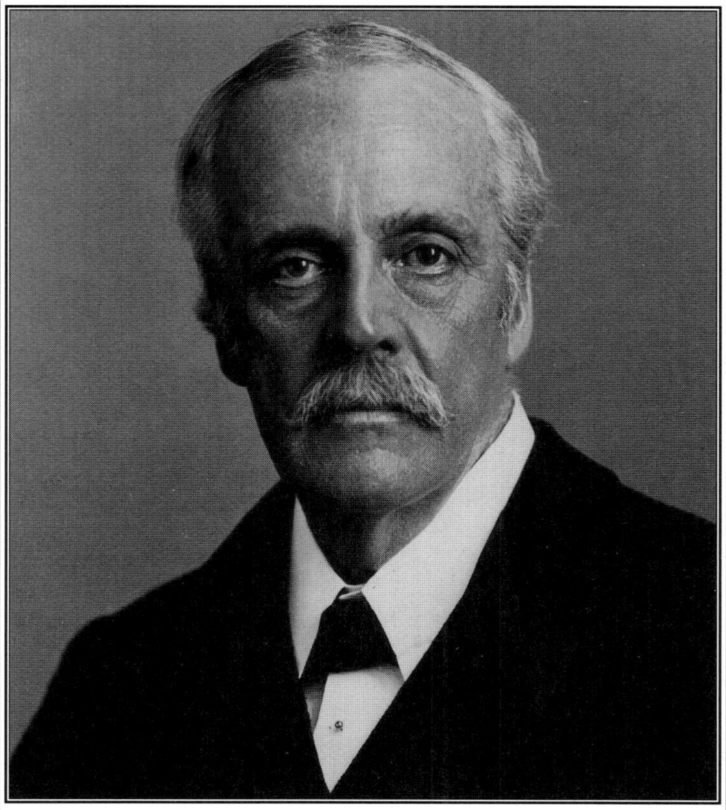

Lord Balfour

# PASSING OF A GREAT STATESMAN

## LORD BALFOUR'S LONG LIFE OF SERVICE TO THE EMPIRE

"A GREAT statesman." In these words King George in his telegram of condolence sums up what will be the verdict of history on the Earl of Balfour, whose passing the whole Empire deplores to-day. His Majesty goes on to speak of Lord Balfour as "a life-long friend, a great and charming personality, a wise and trusted counsellor." It may be said that Lord Balfour was all of these things to every one who came in touch with him, the humblest of them as well as the greatest in the land.

He enjoyed almost everything that the heart of man could desire. Fortune smiled upon him at birth, for he was heir to an ample patrimony, and among his close relatives was Queen Victoria's last and trusted Prime Minister, who, knowing his nephew's quality of brain, disdained the facile charge of nepotism when he offered an early advancement. In intellectual power he had no superiors, and though he became Prime Minister, the academician persisted to the end, contributing to his adroitness and finesse in debate, but also, as the event proved, constituting a source of weakness when he was called to rule a Cabinet.

He upheld in his day the cause of the Union with Ireland with complete conviction. He believed it practicable to wean Irish Nationalists from their devotion to Home Rule if - side by side with the redress of their grievances, which were many, the satisfaction of the popular land hunger and a wide extension of local self-government - Ireland was governed with unflinching firmness and without yielding an inch to political clamour and still less to intimidation and outrage.

The period of his career where he showed to least advantage was that during which he was First Minister of the Crown. But he succeeded Lord Salisbury as Premier when the long ascendancy of the Unionist party was drawing rapidly to a close, when the reaction from the popular excitement of the South African War had already set in, and when his most powerful and masterful colleague, Joseph Chamberlain, was about to start the Fiscal Controversy which caused such deep divisions in the Unionist party. That controversy, in fact, ruined his Premiership, though he passed the best Education Act and the fairest Licensing Act of modern times, and so, always striving to prevent disruption, he drifted on to the disastrous General Election of 1906. Dark and tempestuous days followed. It is now generally acknowledged that the rejection of the Budget of 1909, in which both Balfour and Lansdowne were agreed, was a capital political blunder, but, on the other hand, few believe that the unrestricted veto of the Lords could have long survived. Murmurings arose among the discontented against a leader who seemed to lead only to defeat, and Balfour retired from the leadership of the Unionist party in 1911 with a message of farewell which indicated that he considered his political career to be closed.

A new phase, however, was soon to begin. The outbreak of the Great War renewed his youth, and he found his true métier when, on the retirement of Sir Edward Grey, he took over the Foreign Office in the Coalition Government of Mr Lloyd George. Some of his Notes were masterpieces of incalculable value to the Allied cause.

Lord Balfour was one of a class in which this country has been singularly rich. If he showed at times the fastidious taste of the aristocratic dilettante, he was also fired by a real passion to excel, and capable of sustained effort when necessity compelled; his eager intellectual curiosity led him high into the rarefied realms of philosophy; he was a real lover of music, a zealous player of golf and tennis, and on the purely political side an ardent lover of the institutions of his country and the cause of ordered progress.

**(March 20)**

# MAN OF A THOUSAND FACES

## MR. LON CHANEY

Mr. Lon Chaney, the famous film star, and the greatest make-up expert on the screen, died at Los Angeles yesterday. He was forty-seven years old.

He was born on April 1, 1883, at Colorado Springs, Colorado. His mother, the youngest daughter of Emma Kennedy, who founded the Deaf and Blind Institute of Colorado, and his father, a barber, were both deaf and dumb from birth. Suddenly, before he reached his 'teens, Lon's mother entirely lost the use of her limbs, and Lon, the second of four normal children, had to abandon school, and become a household drudge and a nurse.

Lon Chaney's first introduction to the theatre was as "prop" boy at the Colorado Springs Opera House, where his elder brother, John, was a stage hand.

Then, when he was about 18, Lon became a dancing comedian for several years, until he came to Hollywood and tried his luck in picture studios.

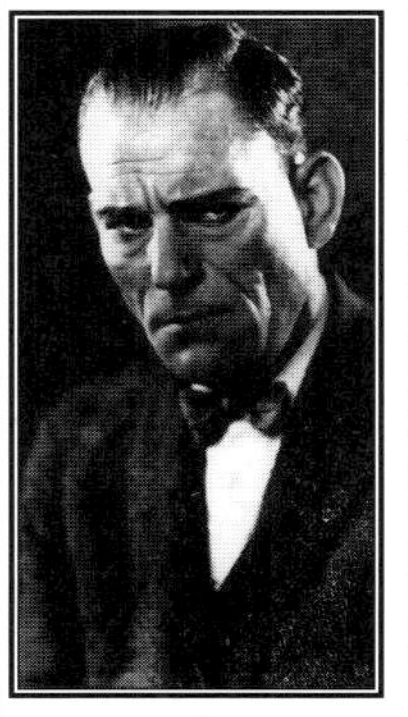

Lon Chaney

He made his first real success on the screen as a cripple in "The Miracle Man," produced about eleven years ago. In order that the personage he represented might be as true to life as possible, the actor went through all sorts of physical tortures. Not a single detail was neglected that could add another touch to the air of suffering that characterises a helpless cripple.

Chaney's greatest triumph of character portrayal and "make-up" was as the central figure in "The Hunchback of Notre Dame." The repulsive looking, hirsute dwarf, with the body of a gorilla, and the soul of a Galahad, was a creation which none, out of all the millions who must have seen it, is ever likely to forget.

**(August 27)**

# SHERLOCK HOLMES'S CREATOR

## CONAN DOYLE'S VARIED CAREER

**By the Late T.P. O'Connor**

Sir Arthur Conan Doyle (whose death is reported on another page) was famous as the creator of Sherlock Holmes, one of the few living and permanent figures in the gallery of detective fiction.

Trained for the medical profession, Sir Arthur was in turn writer of fiction, war correspondent, playwright, historian of the South African campaign, and the sturdy champion of England in the Great War, a Roman Catholic who turned agnostic and afterwards became a strenuous advocate of spiritualism, and the man who did more than anyone to secure the release, after eighteen years' imprisonment, of Oscar Slater, who had been sentenced to death for the murder of a woman in Glasgow.

He came of Irish stock, his uncle being "Dicky" Doyle, the famous artist of Punch. His father was a public official in Edinburgh, where Conan Doyle was born on May 22, 1859. The family being strictly Roman Catholic, young Doyle was sent to Stonyhurst, and then came a year in Germany, and five years as a medical student in Edinburgh. During those student days his real education as a man of letters began, by studying the characters of some of the remarkable men who were professors in the medical school. One of them, Dr. Rutherford, stood for Professor Challenger; another, Dr. Joseph Bell, was the original of Sherlock Holmes.

EARLY LITERARY EFFORTS

Conan Doyle had not long been in the medical school before the literary ferment was working in him. A friend who had been impressed by the vividness of style in Doyle's letters to him, suggested that he had a talent for writing, and under this encouragement Doyle wrote his first published tale, which was accepted by Chamber's Journal, and brought a fee of three guineas.

He got the post of medical man on a small vessel trading to West Africa, and had many wanderings and adventures. He fell a victim to a fever that nearly killed him. On his return he definitely started his career as a medical man at Southsea.

Doyle seemed in danger of settling down to the sedate and uninteresting life as a family doctor when literature began at last to hold out some brighter prospects. James Payn accepted a story for the "Cornhill," and gave him a fee of £30. Doyle also stormed the impregnable fortress of "Blackwood." But he felt that he was not getting "forrader," and that until he had produced a book he could not hope for large recognition.

He was not quite satisfied with the marvellous M. Dupin, the greatest detective in Gaboriau. He thought the type of detective in fiction could be improved on, and then he bethought himself of Dr. Bell, who became Sherlock Holmes. And so began the now famous stories.

While Doyle was awaiting the publication of the first "Sherlock Holmes" book he spent much time and labour on a historical novel, which tried to reproduce the Puritans of the Cromwellian period. It was rejected by several publishers, but Andrew Lang finally got it taken by Longmans. Then he wrote his two historical novels, "The White Company" and "Sir Nigel," both dealing with English history of the period of Edward III. In after years Sir Arthur said that these two books, in his personal judgement, constituted his best literary work.

BOXING ADEPT

A great misfortune fell upon him in the illness of his wife, which was diagnosed as consumption. He devoted years to her relief. Shut up with her in the solitude of Davos, he was enabled to devote himself entirely to literary work, and there began the "Brigadier Gerard" series. On his return from a lecture visit to America, he went to Egypt, where he became a war correspondent with the Expedition to the Soudan. He made the acquaintance of Kitchener, but turned back before the final advance to Khartoum. Returning to his literary work, Doyle found his next theme in a study of the big prize-fighters of the past; it was then he wrote "Rodney Stone" - one of his most popular works and one of his best written.

In most that he attempted Doyle succeeded but one ambition eluded him - a seat in the House of Commons.

No sketch of Doyle would be complete which did not mention his great love of sport, including riding, shooting, ski-ing, and boxing. At boxing he was something of an adept, always ready for a bout in gloves with a friend; once, indeed, he fought another man while they were both in evening dress after a party where they had both been guests.

Such then, was Conan Doyle - a manly man, a tender man, a little rough-hewn in mind and in body; the inventor of a being almost as popular as Robinson Crusoe, and the author of much innocent delight to his generation and perhaps of generations to come.

**(July 8)**

# POET LAUREATE

## DR. BRIDGES' VARIED CAREER

For years the admirers of the Poet Laureate, whose death is reported on Page Nine, have been fond of proclaiming that, no less than Spenser, Robert Bridges was the poets' poet. A cool criticism may have to point out that such enthusiasm compares a great writer with one who was not quite great; but there is no denying that the claim gives Bridges the right sort of praise.

He was not by nature - and he did not seek to be - a poet who could speak for all sorts and conditions of men. His thought and feeling were of one who dwelt apart. His expression was sedulously restrained, elaborate, and yet austere. He was incapable of vehemence either in matter or manner. He was never in ecstasies or agonies. His poetry seemed always the voice of calm reflection. The modes were subtle, highly wrought harmonies.

For such work the audience must always be the minority. But the true lovers of poetry well knew that Bridges was not merely a master of his craft, but a poet of fresh and true inspiration. His best lyrics have a spontaneity and charm which seem to belong to an earlier world. They are as sure of immortality as any of the jewels from the treasury of the seventeenth century. We may find if we please a certain aridity in a good deal of what he chose to publish, a trace of formality, the labour of the accomplished craftsman rather than the freedom of genius, and it is not likely that the bulk of his work will be long read save in the studies of scholars.

But he will live, as Donne lives, or Crashaw, by his happiest things, and they are not few or slight. He was, it has been well said, "the lover of all fine experiences of body, mind, and soul," and many of them he fashioned into lyrics which are the pure gold of poetry.

**(April 22)**

# COLLEGE WARDEN AND WIT

## DR. W.A. SPOONER

### HOW "SPOONERISMS" CAME INTO THE LANGUAGE

The Rev. William Archibald Spooner, D.D., formerly Warden of New College, Oxford, whose death is reported on another page, was famous throughout the world as the inventor of the "Spoonerism," or that transposition of the initial letters of words so as to make a ludicrous combination. Dr. Spooner strenuously denied the authorship of many of these slips of speech; Oxford undergraduates have been accused of foisting "Spoonerism" upon him; and Mr. Robert Seton, the Recorder of Devizes, once confessed to his share of responsibility in perpetuating the legend. He said that the doctor made only one "Spoonerism" in his life. That was in the early part of 1879.

He stood up in the pulpit to announce a hymn. He gave it out as "Kinkering kongs their titles take." There was a hush, and the doctor calmly repeated his slip. I am afraid that we all burst into laughter. I think the doctor then saw his mistake. It was the talk of Oxford in those days, and we used to spend hours in inventing "Spoonerisms." I collaborated with a friend who afterwards became the Rev. Arthur Sharp, and it was he who brought out a book of Spoonerisms.

THE "QUEER OLD DEAN"

The inventors of "Spoonerisms" made the Doctor say he was going from London to Oxford by the "town drain"; and to speak of a camel passing through "the knee of an idol," of a "cat occupewing his pie," of being tired of addressing "beery wenches," and of its being "kistomary to cuss the bride." Much more probable was the doctor's alleged reply to a young lady who asked him if he liked bananas. He is said to have retorted, "I'm afraid I always wear the old fashioned nightshirt."

Dr. Spooner, it is further reported, once announced a famous hymn as "Shoving leopard of Thy sheep," and referred to Queen Victoria as the "queer old dean," and to have greeted an aged relative with the remark that he was glad to see her looking as "hairless and cappy" as ever.

There is another story illustrating his absent-mindedness. He is said to have spent a whole day in looking for a public house named "The Dull Man" at Greenwich, when the place he really wanted was, "The Green Man," at Dulwich. Apart from the familiar examples, there was attributed to Dr. Spooner the invention at all events of one new word. In the course of his lectures on Greek history he used the word "mished," and on being asked afterwards what it meant, he replied that it was expressive of a certain failure, whether of body or mind - to mish" being equivalent to fail. The real word intended was "misled" but as it had been badly written in the manuscript from which the doctor was lecturing, he had formed the habit of using the word "mished," as the nearest approach to the word he wanted.

**(September 1)**

# JAMES THE HERO OF THE CUP FINAL

## LUCK OF GAME AGAINST HUDDERSFIELD IN SECOND HALF

By B. Bennison

ARSENAL … … … …2 HUDDERSFIELD TOWN … … …0

The Arsenal, for the first time in their history, won the Football Association Cup on Saturday, at Wembley, by defeating Huddersfield Town by 2 goals to nil. They triumphed not because of the superiority of their football but because they were quicker into their stride.

There were of the teams some players who were obviously affrighted by the bigness of the occasion. Others, notably James, a little, waddling Scotsman, of the Arsenal, were as men inspired. But neither side reproduced their normal game. They did infinitely better, however, than many teams I have seen at Wembley in other seasons.

Indeed, there were periods when the football was remarkable for style, cleverness, and unity of purpose. Especially was this so in the first twenty minutes, and for half an hour after the interval, when Huddersfield were fighting desperately to rob the Arsenal of the lead established by James after play had been in progress a little more than a quarter of an hour.

The hero and the most successful of all the players was James. A very ordinary line of forwards the Arsenal would have had but for him. Everything he attempted did not come off; but he had most to do with his side's success. His ball control was wonderful; his daring often amounted to impudence. There was little that he did not seem able to do. It was well, however, that he was not the incorrigible roamer he so frequently is. He had a close and greater regard for his proper position than I suspected him of, and throughout he fetched and carried with every unselfishness.

POOR MATCH FOR JACK

The great David Jack was never in a happy vein. For him he had a poor match, and had it not been for his speed Hulme would not have been specially noticed.

Lambert was a stout-hearted workman, a trier to the last gasp, without being an unusually efficient centre. Bastin, apart from the big part he played in the opening score, won little distinction.

John was by far the best of the Arsenal half-backs, though Seddon, since he made it his mission to shadow and spoil Davies, the Yorkshire centre, may be said to have pulled his weight. Baker was often sorely troubled by Smith and Raw, but, on the whole, he did his job well and creditably. Considering the enormous amount of work they had to do in the second half, Parker and Hapgood are to be warmly commended.

Huddersfield had the cleverest half-back. The victory of the Arsenal was a popular one, and when the captain, Parker, received the cup from the King there was unbounded enthusiasm.

The attendance numbered 92,488 and the gate receipts amounted to £23,365.

ARSENAL — Preedy; Parker; Hapgood; Baker; Seddon; John; Hulme; Jack; Lambert; James and Bastin.

HUDDERSFIELD TOWN — Turner; Goodall; Spence; Naylor; Wilson; Campbell; Jackson; Kelly; Davies; Raw and Smith.

Referee: T. Crew (Leicester), Linesmen: W. E. Rycroft (Lancashire) and L. B. Watson (Notts).

**(April 28)**

# ENGLAND'S GREAT VICTORY

## SCOTLAND ROUTED

England … … …5 Scotland … … … 2

No international Association football match played in this country has so stirred the people or more surely captured the imagination than that between England and Scotland at the Wembley Stadium on Saturday. And never was a result so unexpected. A victory for England by five goals to two confounded the critics. It staggered the Scots.

A crowd of 90,000 looked on. Several thousand were shut out. It was as if a considerable, a strange, excited world by some magical means had been wedged into an incredibly small space to create a scene which for colour unusualness may never be forgotten. From the moment the Duke of Gloucester arrived to shake hands with the twenty-two players enthusiasm was unbridled. It was an unexampled occasion.

Ten years have gone since England, as hosts, defeated Scotland, and not for seventeen seasons has she won the inter-country championship.

It was not that the Scots were poor or possessed of moderate skill. They encountered the finest, the best, the keenest, the cleverest combination built by the English selectors during all the years since the war.

At the interval the Scots were four goals down, three of them scored in a little more than five minutes. They had had their chances, notably when Fleming, perilously near to being offside, shot wide in an effort to give finality to a round of delightful passing.

But then Bradford might have got a goal when only a few minutes had gone had he been quicker to deal with a centre from Rimmer. We had already seen enough to be sure that England had the better balance, the greater harmony; and Crooks, after the game had been in progress twelve minutes, with no half-back to challenge him, scampered off and, having enticed Law into a false position, gave to Jack, who transferred to Watson. The West Ham player seemed likely to be crowded out, for Gray had come to the rescue, but with the smallest possible room in which to shoot, and from a most difficult angle, he took a chance, and away the ball went into the net.

Thereafter England marched to victory. Almost at once, and after Blenkinsop had headed away a shot by Morton, Rimmer, drawing greedily and to the full on his speed, rounded Gray, but a drive by Watson from his centre was saved by Harkness. In the next second the Scottish goal narrowly escaped capture; but England, playing to a roar of enthusiasm, would not be denied.

Jack and Crooks passed and re-passed in such a way that Craig was bewildered and left helpless; and it was fortunate for Scotland that Watson was adjudged to be off-side when he was provided with an excellent chance to beat Harkness.

**(April 7)**

# FOOTBALL MATCH BY ARTIFICIAL LIGHT

## EXPERIMENT IN THE MIDLANDS

From Our Own Correspondent

MANSFIELD, Saturday.

Football history was made at Mansfield to-night when a cup-tie was played with the aid of artificial light. The experiment was carried out on the Mansfield Town ground by the North Notts Football League for their senior cup final, and it proved to be entirely successful.

The ground was flooded with electric light equal to 1,000,000 candle power from four batteries of sixteen lamps each, which were installed in towers 48ft high at the corners of the ground. In addition to illuminating the playing field from end to end, the lamps shone upwards to a height of 70ft, so that the players could see the ball in the air.

The players quickly settled down to the novel conditions. They were not hampered by any shadows on the ground, and their only complaint was that they were liable to be momentarily dazzled when the ball got between their line of vision and the clear light. The referee said he was able to follow the play without difficulty.

A whitened ball was used, and had to be changed several times when it became dirty.

Among the 6,000 people present were football officials from many big clubs, including the Arsenal and Sheffield Wednesday, and they agreed that the Mansfield experiment had been amply justified.

Another night match is to be played on the same ground on Wednesday. To-night's match was between Ollerton Forest and Welbeck Athletic, the former winning, 3—0.

**(February 24)**

# WEDNESDAY LEAGUE CHAMPIONS

Victory by 6 goals to 3 over Derby County yesterday gave Sheffield Wednesday the championship of the Football League. On Monday they suffered defeat in the first meeting of the clubs, but in the match at Hillsborough they revealed their best football, scoring six goals before Derby could reply. Allen had a big share in the success, obtaining three goals, while Rimmer scored twice.

In gaining premier honours for the second year in succession Sheffield Wednesday have maintained remarkably consistent form, and the "goals against" records show that they have conceded fewer than any other member of the Championship Division.

**(April 23)**

# HOBBS'S NEW RECORD

Hobbs, recovered from the attack of neuritis which caused him to consult a doctor on Friday, opened Surrey's innings against Middlesex at the Oval on Saturday, and, scoring 40 runs, he beat W. G. Grace's record aggregate of 54,896.

**(August 11)**

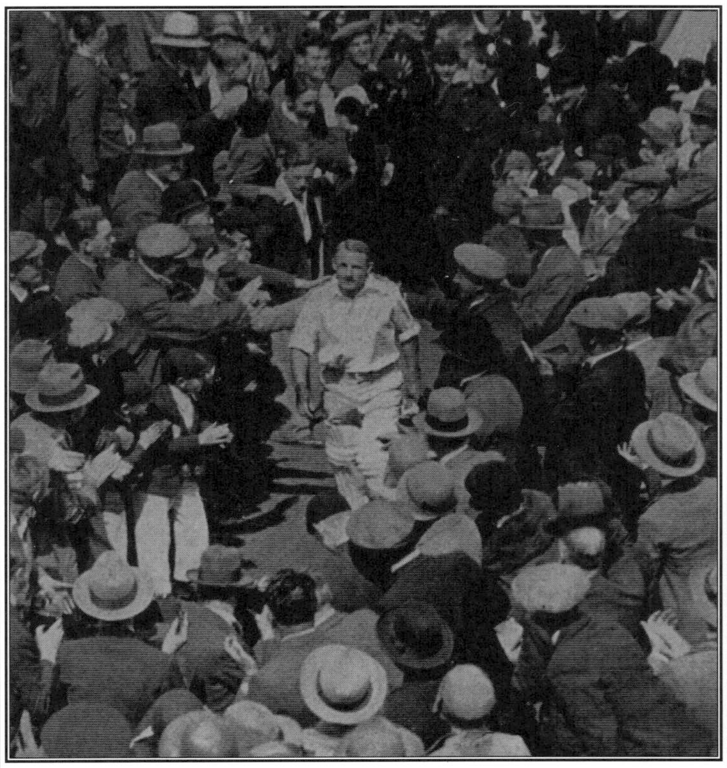

DON BRADMAN

# BRADMAN THE RECORD BREAKER

## SUPERB INNINGS OF 309 NOT OUT

Don Bradman, Australia's 21-year-old batsman, again made cricket history when the third test match opened at Leeds yesterday.

Going in when the first wicket had fallen for two runs, he completed a hundred before lunch — an achievement only equalled by V. T. Trumper and C. G. Macartney — and batting all day, reached the magnificent total of 309 not out. He was at the wicket for five hours and fifty minutes.

With this astonishing performance, following his 254 at Lord's a fortnight ago, he broke the Test match records:

Highest individual score ever made (287 by R. E. Foster at Sydney in 1903/4);

Highest aggregate made by an Australian in a full series of such matches (574 by V. T. Trumper).

Bradman has made 703 runs in the present series of Test matches. Only one batting record is now left for him to break — Hammond's aggregate of 905 in the 1928-9 series.

To-day's official weather forecast for North-Eastern England is "changeable, with some local showers."

# HOW AUSTRALIA WON THE ASHES

## FIRST VICTORY BY AN INNINGS IN THIS COUNTRY

England lost the last Test and the Ashes, Australia winning the match at the Oval yesterday afternoon by an innings and 39 runs. This is the first time in the history of Test cricket that England have been beaten by an innings in this country.

Some such result was inevitable when on Wednesday evening England, batting a second time, lost one wicket for 24 and wanted 266 to avoid an innings defeat. And after the heavy and persistant rain on Thursday, which made play on that day impossible, even an incorrigible optimist became reconciled to the defeat of England.

It was not the tremendous difference in runs, when each side had completed an innings, that threatened disaster so much as the all-round superiority of our visitors. Our batting was without consistency; it had nearly all to do with four men; our fielding was not as it should have been; and, with the solitary exception of Peebles, our bowlers failed.

England had their chances, notably that offered by Bradman when in the early 80's. If all the opportunities had been embraced Australia would not, perhaps, have got 500. But while that may be a reasonable assumption it must be confessed that, almost from the start, Australia had the ways of a winning team.

The Ashes have not been recaptured by Australia by any unusual stroke of luck, though it will be granted that the breakdown in the weather imposed conditions that were against England when they were called upon to do battle against the huge Australian total. But in the whole series the luck has been rather in favour of England, at Leeds and Manchester undoubtedly.

England would have cut a very sorry figure yesterday had it not been first for Sutcliffe and Duleep, who alone of the batsmen seemed endowed with the right temperament for the occasion, and later Hammond. Whysall, not out six on Wednesday evening, who resumed the innings in company with Sutcliffe, never looked like staying. He was caught by Hornibrook in the slips when 10 and the total 37.

**(August 23)**

ENGLAND - First Innings

| | |
|---|---|
| Hobbs, c Kippax, b Wall | 47 |
| Sutcliffe, c Oldfield b Fairfax | 161 |
| Whysail, lbw, b Wall | 13 |
| K.S. Duleopsinhjf, c Fairfax, b Grimmett | 50 |
| Hammond b McCabe | 13 |
| Leyland, b Grimmett | 3 |
| R.E.S. Wyatt, c Oldfield, b Fairfax | 64 |
| Tate, at Oldfield, b Grimmett | 10 |
| Larwood, lbw, b Grimmett | 19 |
| Duckworth, b Fairfax | 3 |
| I.A.R. Peebles, not out | 3 |
| L b 17 n b 2 | 19 |
| Total | 405 |

AUSTRALIA - First Innings

| | |
|---|---|
| W.M. Woodfull, c Duckworth, b Peebles | 54 |
| W.M. Pensford, b Peebles | 110 |
| D.G. Bradman, c Duckworth, b Larwood | 232 |
| A.F. Kippax, c Wyatt, b Peebles | 28 |
| A. Jackson, c Sutcliffe, b Wyatt | 73 |
| A. McCabe, c Duckworth, b Hammond | 54 |
| A Fairfax, not out | 53 |
| W.A. Oldfield, c Larwood, b Peebles | 34 |
| C.V. Grimmett, lbw, b Peebles | 6 |
| T. Wall, lbw, b Peebles | 0 |
| P.M. Hornibrook, c Duckworth, b Tate | 7 |
| L 22, l b 18, n b 4 | 44 |
| Total | 505 |

ENGLAND - Second Innings

| | |
|---|---|
| Hobbs, b Fairfax | 9 |
| Sutcliffe, c Fairfax, b Hornibrook | 54 |
| Whysail, c Hornibrook, b Grimmett | 10 |
| K.S. Duleopsinhjf, c Kippax, b Hornibrook | 46 |
| Hammond, c Fairfax, b Hornibrook | 60 |
| Leyland, b Hornibrook | 20 |
| R.E.S. Wyatt, b Hornibrook | 7 |
| Tate, run out | 0 |
| Larwood, c McCabe, b Hornibrook | 9 |
| Duckworth, b Hornibrook | 15 |
| I.A.R. Peebles, not out | 0 |
| L 10, lb 3, nb 2 | 21 |
| Total | 251 |

BOWLING ANALYSIS
ENGLAND - First Innings

| | 0 | M | R | W |
|---|---|---|---|---|
| Wall | 37 | 8 | 86 | 2 |
| Fairfax | 31 | 9 | 52 | 3 |
| Grimmett | 66.2 | 18 | 135 | 4 |
| Hornibrook | 31.2 | 0 | 92 | 7 |
| McCabe | 22 | 4 | 49 | 1 |
| Hornibrook | 15 | 1 | 54 | 0 |

# FIRST WOMAN TO WIN KING'S PRIZE

## HISTORIC DUEL AT BISLEY

From Our Special Correspondent

BISLEY, Sunday.

An epoch-marking event - the King's Prize at Bisley won by a woman!

So long as the crack of a rifle is to be heard over the famous common, marksmen from every corner of the British Empire will think in terms of Miss Foster's Bisley, dating events from it much as racing men do from, say, Bend Or's or Ormonde's Derby, when the years 1880 and 1886 have ceased to mean anything to them.

The King sent the following message to Earl Jellicoe, chairman of the N.R.A.:

"I most heartily congratulate Miss M.E. Foster on winning my Prize. That she should have done so is a wonderful achievement in the history of rifle shooting, and as such will be universally acclaimed."

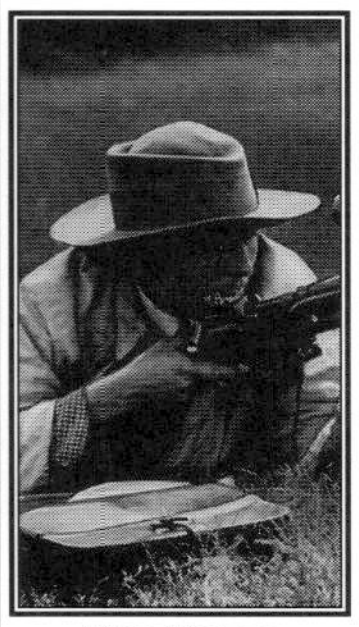

MISS FOSTER

Scenes of enormous enthusiasm were witnessed on the ranges when the result was declared.

A minute after Miss Foster's last and decisive bullet had found its mark the news of her amazing victory had been flashed to Canada, while India, Australia, South Africa, and New Zealand all heard of it in the course of the next quarter of an hour.

For long years to come those who were able to follow shot by shot the intensely dramatic duel between Lieutenant Eccles and the motor driver of the Women's Legion will thrill their comrades at the camp with stories of those hectic minutes of suspense. Neither competitor, separated by but two other marksmen, realised that the coveted prize rested between them or that the decision hung by the slenderest thread. Only those in the small group of officials behind the firing point held the secret, and they were experiencing moments charged with excitement.

THE FATAL "OUTER"

Lieutenant Eccles fired his last shot. For the second time that day he dropped to an "outer." Miss Foster still had her last shot in the breech. With it anything and everything was possible. An outer or a magpie spelt defeat, an inner involved a tie, but a bull's-eye meant victory. Those who knew held their breath as Miss Foster forced the bolt of her rifle home, brought the butt to her shoulder, and sought the alignment of foresight and target centre a thousand yards away.

**(July 21)**

# A GREAT BOAT RACE

Cambridge beat Oxford by two lengths in the University boat race on Saturday, and thus, for the first time since 1863, takes the lead in the number of victories to the credit of each University.

Cambridge has now won on forty-one occasions and Oxford on forty, one race having ended in a dead-heat. Cambridge has won seven races in succession.

The actual race will long be remembered, for Oxford, rowing better than even their supporters had hoped, went to the front at the start, and, with one momentary exception at the Crab Tree, held the lead for the better part of three miles.

The Dark Blues created a new record for the time to Hammersmith bridge. They reached this point in 7 min 10 sec, an improvement of one second on the previous best.

Brocklebank, the Cambridge stroke, did not permit himself to be flurried by his opponents' lead. Using excellent judgement, he spurted at the critical moment. The effort, well backed up by the men behind him, put Cambridge ahead, and, rowing strongly, the crew increased their advantage to two lengths.

**(April 14)**

# AMATEURISM UPHELD

## GREAT BRITAIN AND THE OLYMPIC GAMES

BERLIN, Tuesday.

Great Britain's defence of amateurism in sport triumphed at this afternoon's meeting of the International Amateur Athletic Federation, when the Swedish and Finnish motions seeking to establish the principle of "broken time" payment were rejected by 18 votes to 4, after a spirited speech by Mr. Barnard, the British delegate.

Mr. Barnard clearly indicated, says a Reuter message, that Great Britain would withdraw from the federation if the proposals to allow athletes compensation for loss of time or wages were carried. He was supported by American, French, Danish, German, and South African delegates.

**(May 21)**

# A "NATIONAL" WITH MANY THRILLS

GREAT RACE WON BY A NECK

## THIRTY-SIX HORSES FAIL TO FINISH

The Grand National can always be relied upon to provide an abundance of thrills. Yesterday's race will live in memory as one of the most exciting ever run.

History provides no parallel for the desperate finish in which the following three horses were separated only by a neck and a length and a half respectively:

1, Shaun Goilin, 100 to 8.
2, Melleray's Belle, 20 to 1.
3, Sir Lindsay, 100 to 7.

Forty-one horses started; only five finished the exacting course.

All the three placed horses had been backed heavily, and on the whole it was a bad race for the bookmakers.

Shaun Goilin, who has now made racing history, has his private romance - the horse's pedigree is unknown. Golden Day was the dam, and Shaun Goilin was born and bred in Ireland. Beyond that there is no record of his parentage. As a two-year-old he changed hands for the modest sum of twenty-two guineas.

It is literally true that this horse of uncertain ancestry won the Grand National on an apple.

Shaun Goilin has idiosyncrasies as well as great qualities, and one of them is that away from home he cannot be induced to eat normally. The horse has to be fed from the hand, and on morsels which are not the usual fare of steeplechasers.

The only food Shaun Goilin would eat yesterday before going to the post was an apple, which he took from his trainer's hand.

SCENE AT FINISH

There were extraordinary scenes of enthusiasm when Mr. W. H. Midwood, the owner, led back the winner, for Mr. Midwood has close associations with Liverpool and Cheshire, where till lately he was a Master of Foxhounds. Moreover, Shaun Goilin had been well backed.

Mr. Midwood is a well-known patron of National Hunt racing, and, naturally, it had long been his ambition to win the greatest of all steeplechases. He had tried his luck on eight previous occasions. His nearest approach to success was in 1924, when Silvo was placed third. He had paid 10,500 gns for this horse - a record for a steeplechaser.

Ireland had a big share in the victory, for both the trainer, Frank Hartigan, and the jockey, T. Cullinan, are Irish born. Neither had previously won the crown of steeplechasing. Cullinan's experience was peculiar. He had originally been engaged to ride Easter Hero. When that favourite was scratched he was given the mount on Shaun Goilin.

A record crowd - estimated at 250,000 - witnessed the race from the grandstand, omnibus tops, and every other vantage point.

Groans of disappointment and shouts of triumph followed the varying fortunes of the horses.

The whole period of the race was packed with thrills. Horses fell and broke loose; semi-stunned jockeys staggered across the course out of the way of the galloping mounts. Ambulance men were in readiness to give assistance. Several jockeys received minor cuts and bruises.

**(March 29)**

## ELECTRIC TOTE AT NEWMARKET

**By Hotspur**

NEWMARKET, Wednesday.

The Totalisator became definitely established at Newmarket as from to-day.

For the first time at the head-quarters of the turf, as also for the first time in this country, an all-electric Tote was operating.

The test to which it was subjected was a simple and straighforward one. Surprising, not to say disappointing, would have been the result had it not worked efficiently.

More serious tests await it, as, for example, on Two Thousand Guineas day a fortnight hence. These tests can be awaited without misgiving, since everything passed off well to-day.

The bookmakers have not been banished to a place behind the stands, as was at one time threatened, but they were complaining bitterly, and I think, with some fair reason, against the arrangement which was enforced for the first time.

The total takings of the Totalisator for the afternoon came to over £12,000. The amount invested in win pools was £6,838 18s and in place pools £5,913 10s.

**(April 28)**

## BETTY NUTHALL IN FINAL

Miss Betty Nuthall beat Miss Marjorie Morrill in the semi-final of the American Lawn Tennis Championship at Forest Hills yesterday. states Reuter, by 6—8, 6—4, 6—2.

**(August 23)**

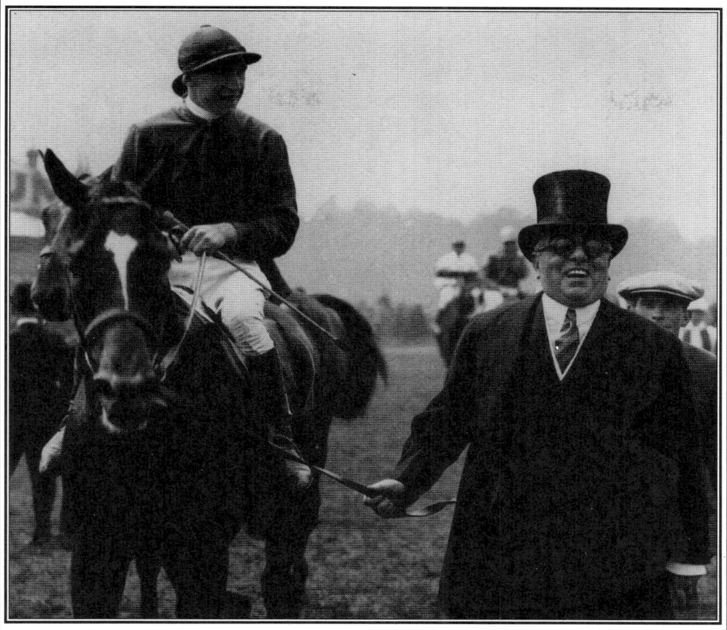

AGA KHAN'S DERBY WINNER

# THE DERBY WON BY AN 18-1 HORSE

THE AGA KHAN'S BLENHEIM

The Aga Khan's BLENHEIM (H, Wragg) 1
Mr. S. Tattersall's ILIAD (R. Jones) 2
Sir Hugo Hirst's DIOLITE (C. Ray) 3
Betting: 18 to 1 Blenheim, 23 to 1 Iliad, 11 to 4 Diolite.

The King and Queen were present at Epsom yesterday, when the Aga Khan won his first Derby with his "second string", Blenheim.

His Majesty recieved a rapturous reception, both on his arrival and when he appeared in the Royal box. After the race he sent for the owner of the winning horse and congratulated him.

The Prince of Wales, the Duke of York and the Duke of Gloucester accompanied their Majesties.

Great crowds had assembled throughout the morning. The weather remained dull, though warm and dry, till a quarter of an hour before the great race, when the sun burst through.

The favourite was beaten, but all the front rank were consistently backed, and bookmakers were, as one expressed it, "neither gainers nor losers." For the tenth time since the war, Viscount Astor was unlucky not to own the winner.

One of the Blenheim tickets in the Calcutta sweepstake is held by Mr. Percy Hogg, a Southern Railway engine-driver, of Barnstaple, Decon, and six friends, who sold half a share for £3,000. Two Coventry machinists also drew Blenheim, and sold a half-share for £2,600.

It was strongly rumoured at Westminster last night that Mr. Winston Churchill, on the advice of a political colleague, and attracted by the name of Blenheim, had backed the winner.

**(June 5)**

## KING'S CUP WON BY WOMAN AVIATOR

HUSBAND & WIFE IN FIRST FOUR

After a thrilling air race for 749 ½ miles, the King's Cup was won on Saturday by Miss Winifred Brown. The first four competitors were:

1. Miss Winifred Brown, in an Avro Avian-Cirrus 111.
2. Mr. A.S. Butler, in a D.H. Moth-Gipsy II.
3. Flight-Lieut. H.R.D. Waghorn, in a Blackburn "Bluebird" Gipsy I.
4. Mrs A.S. Butler, in a D.H. Puss Moth-Gipsy III.

Miss Brown, who on time allowance started fourteenth, took the lead between Manchester and Newcastle.

Mr. and Mrs. A.S. Butler, who were second and fourth, "spurted" with spectacular effect in the last stretch, for at Hull they were a long way behind. Mr. Butler, with a speed of 129.7 miles an hour, won the prize for the fastest time round the course.

Miss Brown received an enthusiastic welcome at Woodland, Lancashire, when she flew home yesterday.

**(July 7)**

# SHARKEY BEATEN ON A FOUL

VICTORY FOR GERMAN BOXER

## A NEW HEAVYWEIGHT WORLD CHAMPION

Jack Sharkey, the heavyweight champion of the world, was defeated last night on a foul by the German boxer, Max Schmeling, in a contest at the Yankee Stadium, New York.

The end came in the fourth round, after Sharkey had been having the better of the exchanges.

The American, who defeated the English boxer, Phil Scott, at Miami recently, after Scott had claimed "at least six fouls," received a very bad reception from the crowd when he entered the ring, and when the fight ended he was hissed and booed for a considerable time.

Schmeling thus becomes heavyweight champion of the world.

The big wooden ring was lighted by thirty gigantic arc lamps, pitched in the centre of the field. The crowd was estimated at 80,000.

THE FIGHT DESCRIBED

ROUND 1- Sharkey rushed his opponent. Both men sparred in the centre of the ring. Sharkey feinted, and a left to the jaw followed. In a clinch the German whipped over a left that missed. Schmeling landed a left to the jaw. Both were very cautious. Round even.

ROUND 2 - Sharkey forced Schmeling to the ropes, and landed with a right and left to the body. Schmeling landed an effective left to the chin. Sharkey became bolder and made his jabs harder, but the fight was fairly even.

ROUND 3 - Schmeling, with a right cross to the jaw, shook the American, who replied fiercely by whipping over a terrific right hook to the German's jaw. Schmeling was visibly shaken. Sharkey landed a series of rights and lefts. Schmeling's left eye was closing. This was Sharkey's round.

ROUND 4 - Sharkey again forced Schmeling to the ropes, but Schmeling blocked his rushes. They clinched, Sharkey getting the best of the in-fighting. The German landed a stiff right upper-cut to the jaw, and his defence was now improving somewhat. Both tried lefts to the face. Sharkey was winning on points when he delivered what was unquestionably a foul blow, and Schmeling went down.

Cries of "Foul!" came from all sides of the ring. There was considerable delay while the referee consulted the judges, and the decision was not announced for several minutes.

The crowd stood and booed Sharkey for several minutes. Sharkey, a tearful, forlorn and dejected figure, was rubbing his face with his gloves. The German, still suffering great pain, was assisted from the ring by his seconds.

**(January 13)**

## BRITISH VICTORY

FIRST FOUR PLACES AT BROOKLANDS

The "Double Twelve Hours" race at Brooklands, which was completed on Saturday, resulted in a fine British victory - the first four places all being occupied by British cars. The speeds on Saturday were lessened by the heavy rain, the racing cars at times rather resembling motorboats, with showers of spray from the track covering them. Twenty-seven competitors, including four women drivers, finished out of a field of fifty-three.

**(May 12)**

# AMERICA'S WIMBLEDON

MRS. MOODY WINS THE SINGLES

## FRENCH PAIR OUT

GREGORY AND COLLINS BEATEN

**By A. Wallis Myers**

Yesterday, at Wimbledon, the American wore his heart on his sleeve.

The wheel had turned a full circle. For nearly forty years - ever since the brothers Clarke, wearing knickerbockers, had bearded the Renshaws in their Wimbledon lair in the 'eighties - American men had laid siege in vain to the Centre Court citadel.

Ten years ago Tilden "broke through" for the first time, the same Tilden who will fight to regain the crown to-day. The breach in 1920 was revolution; to-day every event except the mixed doubles has American finalists.

It is America's Wimbledon, but her uniform domination is deserved. It is the fruit of careful preparation, conscientious training, and inspiring leadership. In Mr. Eugene Dixon, of Philadelphia, the "boys" who entered the doubles final yesterday as a solid quartette have a most capable mentor, one who is young in heart, sympathetic in manner, a student of modern tactics and relative form, himself a shrewd player.

Mrs. Moody had a good match with Miss Ryan, but never one that threatened her title. She began the tournament with the knowledge that she could give any of her opponents fifteen; she ended it with the same quiet confidence of superior skill. She had to fight for her points and was forced by Miss Ryan's drops to make several breathless excursions to the net - some of them without profit.

But Mrs. Moody's fluency of stroke, her command of length, and her accuracy of aim were such that no opponent without an open-faced drive to use when the position was prepared could hope to arrest her progress for any appreciable time.

**(July 5)**

## ENTERPRISE WINS AMERICA'S CUP

SHAMROCK LOSES AGAIN

Enterprise beat Shamrock V. in the fourth successive race yesterday. The America's Cup thus remains in the keeping of the New York Yacht Club.

The match was won in the first ten miles of the course - a beat to windward.

Enterprise on this leg established a nine minute lead. Shamrock in the next twenty miles sailed faster than the defender, and in the end lost by less than six minutes.

The yachts rounded the marks at the following times:

| | 10 miles | 20 miles | Finish |
|---|---|---|---|
| Enterprise | 1 3 15 | 1 54 0 | 2 50 0 |
| Shamrock | 1 12 14 | 2 1 53 | 2 55 54 |

**(September 19)**

## STORY OF THE SHAMROCKS

Enterprise has won by the following margins:

First race: 2min 52 sec.
Second: 9 minutes
Third: Sail over, Shamrock being disabled.
Fourth: 5min 54sec.

Sir Thomas Lipton's other Shamrocks have fared as follows:

Shamrocks I., II., and III, each beaten in three successive races.

Shamrock IV.: Lost 3 races and won 2.

Since Sir Thomas' issued his first challenge in 1899 the conditions of the contest have been varied. Formerly it was a handicap match.

**(September 19)**

## FRENCH RUGGER.

A STERN test of English manhood is soon to come. Before the month is out France will play us at Rugger. I doubt if our players, our selectors, even the Olympian wisdom of the Rugby Union itself, is awake to the perils of that encounter.

It is not necessary to have any very intimate acquaintance with the game - always a handicap in criticising players - in order to admire the heroism of men who, in the depth of winter, proceeded from France to Belfast, and defying the ravages of two channels, wore down an Irish pack. But how was the victory won? How were the physique and morale maintained? That is the question for the Rugby Union.

When Panurge wished advice on how to face the perils of life he went on a voyage to the Oracle of the Divine Bottle, and was answered in the one word, "Trinq." The priestess said it was the most gracious and intelligible rule of conduct she had ever heard. They still know their RABELAIS in France. When the French fifteen went to Belfast they took with them four kegs of wine. Of course they won.

Now they are coming to Twickenham, and it is not concealed that they are again to be accompanied by wine. I might say it is threatened. This time they have ordered six kegs. What is the policy of the Rugby Union?

**(February 5)**

# GOLF TITLE FOR BOBBY JONES

40-YEAR-OLD RECORD EQUALLED

Bobby Jones won the British Open Golf Championship at Hoylake yesterday for the third time. He was holder of the title in 1926 and 1927.

In achieving his great ambition to win the Amateur and Open Championships in the same year Mr. Jones has equalled the feat of Mr. John Ball forty years ago.

The Open Championship has gone to America for the seventh year in succession, the last British player to secure the title being A.G. Havers, in 1923.

Archie Compston, the Coombe Hill professional, had a great opportunity of regaining the championship when, at the end of the third round yesterday, he led the field by a stroke.

In the final stage, however, he collapsed badly and a round of 82 relegated him to sixth place with a total of 297.

Leo Diegel, of Mexico, and Macdonald Smith, of America, tied for second place with 293.

Yesterday's was the eleventh championship title which Bobby Jones has won. He now holds the Open Championship of America and Great Britain.

**(June 21)**

## CROWD ACCLAIMS GIRL GOLF CHAMPION

FORMBY, Friday.

One of the most brilliant achievements in women's golf was accomplished here to-day, when Miss Diana Fishwick, the 19-year-old Kentish girl, beat Miss Glenna Collett, the American champion, by 4 up with three to play, over 36 holes, and so won the British Women's Open Championship on her first appearance in the competition.

When Miss Collett had beaten in turn such distinguished representatives of British golf as Miss Molly Gourlay and Miss Enid Wilson, it was felt that the prospect of the Championship Cup - the only English trophy which has not gone to America - being held for England was very slender.

Miss Fishwick has been playing golf since she was 5, has twice won the girls' championship, and has been runner-up in the English Ladies' (Close) Championship within the last three years. She is, however inexperienced when compared with Miss Collett, who has won the American championship four times and who made such a close fight against Miss Joyce Wethered in last year's final for the open championship at St. Andrew's.

FIGHTING FINISH

The general feeling was that though the English girl would make a spirited fight and would certainly not be beaten for lack of courage, she would lack the stamina to resist Miss Collett in such a searching test.

But Miss Fishwick surprised and delighted everyone, first by so outplaying her opponent in the morning as to establish a five-holes lead, and then by holding her advantage for nine holes in the afternoon and finally winning the match three holes from home.

**(May 17)**

## GREAT T. T. FEAT

TWO SENIOR RECORDS

W. H. Handley, of Birmingham, made history yesterday when he won the senior Tourist trophy over the mountain course in the Isle of Man at an average speed of 74.24 m.p.h. He beat the record for the course by 6min 29sec, established a new record for the lap in his first circuit, and beat his own record twice in the second and third laps.

Perhaps the outstanding feature of the meeting was the fact that, despite unprecedented speeds on dangerous roads, made even more treacherous in the last two laps by heavy rain, no one was seriously injured. There were many mishaps, several riders being thrown, and eleven onlookers being slightly hurt; but a broken leg was the worst injury sustained.

British machines proved their great superiority in this test, every one of the thirteen which completed the course being of British make.

**(June 21)**

## COCHET BEATEN

SURPRISE U.S. VICTORY

Henri Cochet, holder of the Singles Championship, met with a surprising defeat yesterday at Wimbledon, in the fifth round. His conqueror, Wilmer Allison, of Texas, won in three sets — 6—4, 6—4, 6—3.

The two other Americans, W. T. Tilden and J. H. Doeg, also entered the semi-final. Fourth place fell to J. Borotra, of France.

Tilden beat Gregory with convincing ease, losing only five games; Doeg beat Mangin in a spectacular four-set match: Borotra volleyed his way through G. M. Lott.

**(July 1)**

# THE CROWNING OF ETHIOPIA'S EMPEROR

(BELOW) THE EMPEROR leaving the cathedral after the coronation. He is seen wearing his wonderful Jewelled Crown and Orb and Sceptre of Authority.

(RIGHT) THE CORONATION OF RAS TAFARI as King of Kings and Lion of Judah, at Addis Ababa.

# THE RACE FOR THE AMERICA'S CUP

SIR THOMAS LIPTON'S SHAMROCK V. (shown below) and Mr. Harold S. Vanderbilt's Enterprise, the American defender, will engage in the first of the series of seven races for the America's Cup over a course of thirty miles off Newport, Rhode Island.

## THE SILVER BULLET

SILVER BULLETT, the car in which Mr. Kaye Don is to attack Sir Henry Segrave's world land speed record of 231.31 miles per hour, at Daytona Beach, Florida.

NEEDY AND UNEMPLOYED WORKERS being offered hot soup, to assist them through the cold winter months, and to aid them in their search for work.

# 1931

In Britain, the minority Socialist government threw in its hand and a National Government was formed, a combination of Conservatives and elements from the Liberal and Labour parties. A subsequent general election produced the biggest landslide in parliamentary history. Another bad year for the Western World saw unemployment figures in the United States rise ever higher with the result that the population was on the move - to the cities or trekking to California in the hope of a better life.

The financial crisis saw a run on the Bank of England which forced the British government to leave the Gold Standard. At the time, this was thought to be a temporary measure but it proved to be a permanent one. France and Germany were in financial trouble as well. The crisis in the latter country strengthened the power of Adolf Hitler who announced his plans for the future of Germany when he succeeded as Chancellor. An equally bold and similarly authoritarian programme was put forward by Sir Oswald Mosley who proclaimed that his "New Party" would put 400 candidates in the field for the Autumn general election. In fact, none was elected.

Mr. Gandhi, released from his detention in India, came to London for the round table conference on the future of the subcontinent which issued a communiqué outlining plans for the future independence of the sub-continent. During his visit, Mr. Gandhi, dressed in his usual skimpy robe and sandals, was received by King George V in Buckingham Palace. Winston Churchill, angered by the Conservative Party's acquiescence to the plans for India, resigned from the Shadow Cabinet.

In a year of triumph in the air, Britain won the Schneider Trophy outright. So great was the superiority of British airpower, as represented by R.J. Mitchell's S6 seaplane, that no other nation was prepared to make a challenge. The British ability to provide a suitable aircraft at a time when government funds were being cut was only made possible by a donation from the eccentric Lady Houston who customarily carried patriotic slogans picked out in lights between the masts of her yacht. Sad to say, Flight Lieutenant Waghorn, who had won the 1929 race for Britain, was killed in a flying accident. In addition, Jim Mollison broke the record from Australia to Britain at the same time as his future wife, Amy Johnson, completed a successful flight to Tokyo. The air route that would eventually fly from London to South Africa was opened.

The first signs that the tide was turning against the rule of the mobsters in the United States became obvious when the most powerful of all the gangsters, Al Capone, was sent to prison. One of his great rivals, "Legs" Diamond, was shot dead.

George Bernard Shaw made a short visit to Russia and declared that the future lay with Communism, despite the reports of continuing Stalinist terror. Communists were believed to be at the bottom of the unrest in the Royal Navy at Invergordon where fleet exercises had to be cancelled because of something very like a mutiny. King Alfonso of Spain was forced to abdicate.

The great inventor Thomas Alva Edison died during the year as did the French army commander to the early years of the Great War, Marshal Joffre. Pavlova, the most popular of all ballet dancers, died, as did the best-selling novelist Arnold Bennett.

Talking pictures were firmly established although their subject matter troubled *The Daily Telegraph* film critic. In defiance of the new "talkies" Charlie Chaplin produced his most successful silent picture, *City Lights*. Noël Coward presented his most spectacular play, *Cavalcade*, a historical and patriotic chronicle of two British families which accorded oddly with the depressed mood of the times.

**BISHOP BARNES OVERRULED**

Gold Medal 7½D 7½D
DRAYTON MILL VALEO TOILET PAPER
Toilet Papers — Medicated

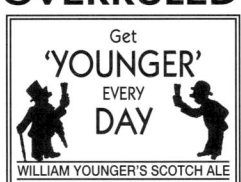

# The Daily Telegraph

Get 'YOUNGER' EVERY DAY
WILLIAM YOUNGER'S SCOTCH ALE

No. 23,725 POSTAGE { INLAND, CANADA AND NEWFOUNDLAND, THREE HALFPENCE / OTHER COLONIES AND PLACES ABROAD, TWOPENCE

LONDON, SATURDAY, JUNE 2, 1931

ONE PENNY

*The charge for announcements of BIRTHS, MARRIAGES and DEATHS is 5s per line. The charge for "IN MEMORIAM" notices is 2s 6d per line. A special rate for five or ten years' automatic insertion will be quoted on application. Announcements which must be authenticated by the name and address of the sender may be handed in to The Daily Telegraph Fleet-street, E.C.4. or to 161 Piccadilly, W.1. or telephoned to Central 4242 (Ext 7), between 9 a.m. and 5 p.m.*

## BIRTHS

BUDGE – On May 29, 1931 to Violet (née Hocking), wife of Paymaster Lieutenant-Commander L.B.H. Budge, Royal Navy, a daughter.

COLLINGWOOD – On May 30, 1931 to Anna, wife of Lawrance Collingwood, a daughter.

CRESSWELL-PRICE – On May 29 1931, at Woodcote, Beckenham, Kent, to Marjorie, wife of A.N. Cresswell-Price, a son.

ENGLAND – On May 30, 1931 at 27 Welbeck-street, W.1. to Vera (née Carter), wife of Kenneth A. England, of 5, Ladbroke-square, W.11, a daughter.

EVILL – On May 29, 1931 at 30 Curzon-street, W.1, to Wing-Commander and Mrs Strathern-Evill, a son.

GARROD – On May 29, 1931 at Whistlefield, Potters Bar, to Mollie, wife of Kenneth Garrod, a daughter.

GODFRAY – On May 28, 1931, at Louth, to Mary Dorothy, wife of Captain Terence Godfray, the gift of a son.

GOOCH – On May 28, 1931, at Stede Court, Harrietsham, Kent, to Eileen, wife of Sir Robert Gooch, Bt., a daughter.

GOSSELIN – On May 20, 1931, at Shanghai Marjorie, the wife of A.N. Gosselin, Royal Scots Fusiliers, a son.

HALL – On May 29, 1931, at Great Shefford Rectory, Newbury, to Mollie (née Dewe) wife of W.J. Hall, D.Sc. the Citrus Experimental Station, Mazoe, S. Rhodesia, a daughter.

LIVINGSTON – On May 31, 1931, at 136 Station-road, Hendon, N.W.4 to Joyce (née Snowman), wife of Dr. Lawrence Livingston, a daughter.

McINTIRE – On May 29, 1931, at Osborne House, Brunswick-square, Gloucester, to Doris (née Berkley), the wife of G.S. McIntire, B.A., LL.B. the gift of a daughter.

SHAW – On June 1, 1931, to Pixie, the wife of Cedric Shaw, M.R.C.P., M.B., at Rupert House Nursing Home, Edgware, a daughter.

STERN – On May 28, 1931 at Ashford, Kent to Joan, wife of Edward Stern, a daughter.

WEBBER – On May 30, 1931, at Stoneboro, 171 Newport-road, Cardiff, to Mr. and Mrs. Frank Webber (née Watson), 9, Cyncoed-avenue, Cardiff, a son.

ZUCCO – On May 30, 1931, at Land o'Nod. Nightingale-road. Hampton-on-Thames, to Mr. and Mrs. Zucco, a daughter (Francis Marion).

## MARRIAGES

MEREDITH-WEBSTER. – On May 30, 1931, at Christ Church, Old Southgate, by the Rev. C.F. Peploe, M.A., William Lake, youngest son of Mr. and Mrs. C.W. Meredith, of Wimbledon, to Una, only daughter of Mr. and Mrs. James Webster, of Southgate.

MILLER-PENROSE – On May 30, 1931, at St. Saviour's Highbury, John Livingstone Miller, B,Sc., A.M.I.C.E., to Ailsa Kennedy, younger daughter of Dr. and Mrs. Penrose of 69, Highbury, New Park.

MILLS-LEPETIT – On May 27, 1931, at St. Ferdinand des Ternes, Paris, Frederic Busick Woodgate Mills, of Lisbon, Portugal, youngest son of the late Mr. Henry Maynard Mills and Mrs. H.M. Mills, of Buenos Aires, to Nanie (Ann Marie), elder daughter of M. Garbriel Lepetit, of 159, Boulevard Pereire, Paris. (Argentine papers, please copy.)

NEILL-CAMPBELL – On May 26, 1931, at Temperley Scotch Church, Buenos Aires, by the Rev. Douglas Bruce, Mr. and Mrs. D.T. Neill, 8 Dudley-gardens, Edinburgh, to Annie Muriel, daughter of the late Major Wm. B. Johnston V.D., and of Mrs. Johnston 4, Hillhead-street, Glasgow, and widow of Roland Campbell, (By cable.)

## DEATHS

BISHOP – On May 30, 1931, Elizabeth Laura, widow of the Rev. J.W.G. Bishop, fell asleep, aged 87. (Tuesday), 3.30 o'clock.

BOYD – On May 28, 1931, at 13 Glencairn-crescent, Edinburgh, after a short illness, Patrick James Stirling Boyd, M.A., D.L. younger son of the late Sir Thomas J. Boyd, D.L. Lord Provost of Edinburgh, aged 80 years.

BURRELL – On May 29, 1931, at 15, Acacia-road, St. John's Wood, N.W.8. the beloved wife of Matthew Burrell. Interment St. Marylebone Cemetery, East Finchley, at three p.m. to-morrow (Wednesday, June 3). (Friends please accept this intimation.)

CHANCE – On May 30, 1031, Mary Louisa Chance, of 92 Lady Margaret-road, Tufnell Park, N. Funeral service, Camden-road, Baptist Church, N7. on Thursday, June 4, at two p.m.

COHEN – Adolph, on May 30 1931, died suddenly. Late of Shelthorpe, Elms-road, Harrow Weald, and of Basinghall-street, City. Funeral to take place, Crematorium.Golders Green, Thursday. June 4. at 2.30 p.m.

COKE – On May 30, 1931 at 42 Half Moon-street, Colonel the Hon. Wenman Coke, late Rifle Brigade. No flowers, by request.

ELLIS – On May 30, 1931, at Quarry-place House, Shrewsbury. Emily Catharine Ellis, widow of the Rev. F.R. Ellis, formerly Rector of Muchwenlock. Funeral at Shrewsbury Cemetery at two p.m., to-morrow (Wednesday, June 3).

GORDON – On May 31, 1931, at Dalwood, Lower Bourne, Farnham, Charlotte E., dearly loved wife of Albert Gordon.

HUMBLEY – On May 31, 1931, at his residence, Llais Afon, Llanddulas, Church, 11.30 to-morrow (Wednesday).

HUNT – On May 29, 1931, as the result of a motor accident. Alfred Huyshe Hunt, much beloved and only son of the Rev. and Mrs. A.E. Hunt, of Radstock Vicarage, Bath. Funeral, to-day (Tuesday), at St. Peter's Church, Marchington, Staffordshire, at noon.

## PERSONAL

*Announcements in the Personal Column (minimum 2 lines) 5s. per line. Trade, 10s per line. Lost and Found, 2s 6d per line. Names and addresses of advertisers must accompany all advertisements not for publication unless desired.*

L. – I will never forgive if there is anyone else. – THREE K'S.

WE'LL MEDITATE
Upon return-tickets for a while.
How beautifully suited to our need.
Spendthrifts like us! – John Davidson.

LEYS SCHOOL, CAMBRIDGE – Speech Day 19th June (Presentation of Prizes by Mr. John Buchan). O.L. Week 29th July to 5th August. Old Leysians wishing to attend either of the above should apply to the Bursar.

THE DERBY, FINE POSITION – Private Omnibus Party, Lunch, Tea. Refreshments £2 8s 6d – Mrs. Blair, 20 Portman-street, W.1. Mayfair 3800.

DOES YOUR SILVER NEED ATTENTION? – Write or telephone Barker's Silversmith Department. A representative will call and advise you free of charge. Firstclass work for the most moderate charges. – Apply for price list and full particulars John Barker & Co. Ld., Kensington, W.8. 'Phone Western 5432.

WRITE OF CALL AT ONE FOR DETAILS OF OUR DELIGHTFUL SPECIAL TOURS HOME AND ABROAD. – AIDES DE CAMP LIMITED, 124, WILTON-ROAD, VICTORIA, S.W.1 THE CORPS OF RETIRED OFFICERS OF HIS MAJESTY'S FORCES.

BLUTHNER PIANOS – In view of pending structural alterations to their premises, Bluthner & Co. Ld. are selling their stock of secondhand and slightly used pianos at specially low prices. Unusually favourable bargains in Player Pianos are available. Deferred payments accepted. For particulars apply to Bluthner & Co. Ld., 17-23, Wigmore-st., W.1.

300 ROOMS, 300 BATHS – THE HERMITAGE HOTEL, La Baule. The seaside of Brittany. A perfect holiday resort. Safest possible bathing. First class tennis, golf and yachting, &c. Beautiful Casino, with wonderful organisation. First among France's luxury hotels.

SEND A MITE TO SAVE A MITE – The Infants Hospital, Vincent-square, Westminster, appeals for funds to extend its work. Contributions should be sent to the Secretary.

MAPLE & CO LD. invite inspection of the finest selection of Secondhand Grand and Upright Pianos reconditioned as new by the highest-class English and Continental makers. Particulars of cash or deferred terms on application. – Maple & Co. Ld., Tottenham-court-rd., W.1.

£50,000 URGENTLY REQUIRED FOR DEVELOPMENT OF OAK-HILL JOURNALISTS' HOME. All donations large or small, gratefully received by the Chairman. Appeal Committee, or the Duchess of Richmond and Gordon (Chairman, Ladies' Appeal Committee), c.o. Institute of Journalists 2-4 Tudor-street, E.C.4.

RHEUMATISM PYRETIC TREATMENT (Dr. Wild's Method) Sister Caulfield, 9a Thistle-grove, S.W.10 Kens. 1238.

BRYANT'S CREDIT SYSTEM solves your Tailoring problems. Without inconvenience or worry you can obtain by easy monthly payments a complete wardrobe of high-class tailoring with West-end style and finish. 7s, secures a 3gn. Suit; 12s 6d a 5gn Dinner Jacket Suit 8s 6d a 3 ½ gns Overcoat. Call write or 'phone. James Bryant Ld. 4, New Bridge-st., Ludgate-circ. E.C. 4 (City 5878) or 396 Brixton-rd., S.W.9 (Bri. 3325). or 19 St. George's-street, Canterbury (tele. 651); or 7 New-rd, Brighton.

DO YOU REQUIRE A BUSINESS OF YOUR OWN? There is on Page 22 the most comprehensive list of Businesses for Sale from which you can make your choice.

"HAMPSTEAD 6447" Alanne 285 Finchley-rd., a most Fascinating Shop where expert advice on all details of dress is given without obligation. Exclusive models now showing.

AT THE WEST-END OFFICE of The Daily Telegraph, 161 Piccadilly, W.1. intending advertisers can always obtain help and advice in compiling advertisements of every description.

BOARD-RESIDENCE ONE MIN. TULSE-HILL, five min. Dulwich Stns. Lady offers board-residence for two gentlemen or ladies, or individually. Breakfast, Evening dinner, full board Sunday, 35s 6d each. Breakfast only 21s. Special terms for three friends, or individual requirements suited. – Write B., Box 6.858, Daily Telegraph. Fleet-street, E.C.4.

EXCLUSIVE CLOTHES AT MODERATE PRICES dress suits, 12 gns, dinner suits 10 gns. Carr Son & Woor Ld. 9 Savile-row, W.1. Est. 1797. 'Phone Regent 1926.

WESTCLIFF-ON-SEA IS NOW AT ITS BEST. West Cliff Hotel, only 1 hr. fr. London.

ALAN GEORGE – The most exclusive Paris Models created specially for you at one-third the usual prices. 5, Rue Lincoln (Champs Elysees).

ARE YOU NEAR RETIRING AGE? – You can settle so cheaply in South Africa. Money goes farther and gives you fuller life. Low taxes, plentiful land and labour, abundant sport, glorious sunshine. – Particulars from 1820 Memorial Settlers' Association, Dept. D.T.J. 2, 199 Piccadilly, W.1.

HOROSCOPE 5S, 10S, 20S. Birth date, time if known. Miss Bull, 11 Maddox-street, W.1. Mayfair 6578.

NEW HEARING DEVICE – The Vibraphone. Invisible, no attachments. Sold on refund basis. Unbelievable results. – Vibraphone Co., Dept. T., 235, Regent-st., W.1.

WEST-END CUTTER in an exclusive firm willing to call on clients by appointment after 7.30. Distinctive clothes at exceptionally mod. prices. – Write W., Box 9.943, Daily Telegraph, 161 Piccadilly, W.1.

FURNITURE – TO BE DISPOSED OF PRIVATELY, entire contents of exceptionally well-furnished Gentleman's residence, highest-class modern and reproduction. Any part sold separately at moiety of original cost. Also expensive carpets throughout. No dealers. – Write F., BOX 6,986. Daily Telegraph, Fleet-street, E.C.4.

## PERSONAL (CONTINUED)

IF MRS. MINNIE OGDEN, wife of Robert Ogdon, late of Red Lion Hotel, Stockport, will communicate with Freer & Co., 10 New-street, Leicester, she will hear of something to her advantage.

THE FOOL hath said in his heart: There is no God. – Px. xiv., 1

THIS GENTLEWOMAN OF 45 was destitute to the extremity of sleeping out. She has held good secretarial posts, but breakdown following severe operation has prevented her working for months, and she is still unfit. – Your cheque or order to Preb Castile, "Extremity," 55, Bryanston-st., W.1. will enable Church Army to care for her.

YOUNG MAN WANTS LODGE WITH GERMANS, summer, London. – Scott, 125 Alexandra-rd., N.W.8.

ASCOT FROCKS. Summer Ensembles, Evening Gowns. Latest Paris Creations. Wonderful selection at 5 1/2 gns. Claridge, 10 South Moulton-street, W.1.

CENTRAL LONDON THROAT, NOSE AND EAR HOSPITAL, Gray's Inn-road, W.C.1 – Derby Competition Prize winners: Actual number of donation receipts issued 22,137. 1st (22,137), E. Holloway; 2nd (22,136),A Chinnery; 3rd (22,139), Miss E Miller; 4th (22,133), H McMahon; 5th (22,131), G Barnard; 6th (22,130), Mrs. Clark; 7th (22,144), Mrs. Evans; 8th (22,129), A. Kite; 9th (22,145); M Stride; 10th (22,146), L Rice; 11th (22,126), W. Oldfield; 12th (22,149), R. Simpson; 13th (22,125), F. Green; extra (22,125), A.M. Coe. All the prize-winners have been notified by post. Grateful thanks are extended to all who participated. – John H. Young, Secretary-Superintendent.

£250 CASH COMMISSION paid to architect, builders, estate agent, or anyone introducing buyer of finely-located and Willett-built compact block of Kensington leaseholds, comprising 100 spacious and lofty rooms. Ideal for conversion into family flats. (Opposite block converted and well and fully let.) Cash £5,000 only, plus mortgage £7,500 at 6 p.c. arranged. – Write A. Box 9,920. Daily Telegraph, 161 Piccadilly, W.1.

ON ARRIVAL AT YOUR CONTINENTAL DESTINATION order The Daily Telegraph to be delivered to you regularly.

LADY WISHES TO ACQUIRE, and will pay reasonable cash price, for a small Rolls-Royce Saloon, division preferred. No canvasers. – Write, giving particulars, to Mr. Powell (Secretary), 43 Raymead-avenue, Thornton Heath.

## ARTICLES FOR SALE AND WANTED

OFFICE EQUIPMENT

FOR SALE, CODES, new, Bentley's complete phrase; A.B.C.; Marconi International; five Kalamazoo binders; Corona portable. – P., 13, The Hawthorns, Finchley, N.3.

NAT. & REM. CASH REGISTERS. 40, cond, as new. Total adders, also Burroughs adding machines. No reas. offer refused. – Deiches, 78 Long-lane, Smithfield, E.C.1.. Nat. 0674.

OFFICE FURNITURE, including kneehole mahogany desk typewriter, oak files, typists' desks, chairs &c. 'Phone for appointment, Hol. 8834, between 10 and 11. No dealers.

OFFICE FURNITURE. – Large stock secondhand desks, writing tables, revolving chairs, fire-resisting safes, all sizes. Steel cupboards, filing cabinets. Cooper, 24, Broad-st-place, Liverpool-st., E.C.2.

TAKEN IN PART PAYMENT a quantity of New Portable and Standard Typewriters. Portables, £8 10s; Standard £10 – C.O.S. Co., 8 Dyers-buildings, Holborn, E.C.1. Holborn 0221.

TYPEWRITER EXPERTS CO., 55, Little Britain, E.C. Cash or terms. Also Repairs (Nat. 8210).

MULTIGRAPH PRINTING MACHINE REQUIRED. Secondhand. Offers – Write M., Box 6,884, Daily Telegraph, Fleet-street, E.C.4.

OFFICE FURNITURE AND SAFES WANTED – Dale 146, Charing X-rd. Tem. Bar. 4801.

FURNITURE

COMPLETE HOME, 3 rooms, nicely furnished, for 35gns. cash or easy terms; sent any distance. It will pay you to write or call for full particulars. Webb's Furnishing Stores, 478 High-rd., Tottenham ('phone 1609), opp. Bruce-grove Station.

MUSICAL INSTRUMENTS
CHARLES STILES & CO.

Sale of Baby Grands. Upright and Player Pianos. – Bechstein, Steinway, Lipp. Steck &c. New and Second Hand Cash or Hire Purchase. Pianos taken in exchange – Lists 74 and 76, Southampton-row, Mus. 0439.

ARNOLD'S PIANO SALE

50 slightly USED MODELS by Steinway. Bechstein, Bluthner, Chappell, Weber &c. at about HALF CURRENT LIST PRICES. Terms from £1 monthly. Exchanges. 10 years' guarantee.
28 South Molton-street, W.1. (Bond-st. Stn.) May 3843.

STEINWAY PIANOFORTES – A few of these celebrated instruments, slightly used, for sale or on Deferred Payment. Any make of piano taken in part exchange. Secondhand Pianos by other makers also available – Steinway & Sons, 1 and 2 George-street, corner Conduit-street, W.1.

## SUNDRY

36ft. nearly new well-made OAK-FRAME PLATE-GLASS SHOWCASE COUNTERS, fitted 15 trays and sliding mirror doors, wired for electric light, Price £15 each.

128ft 6in DITTO WALL FITMENT, with centre fitted 40 sliding trays, enclosed by four sliding plate-glass doors and eight drawers under, and ends fitted with 90 divisions. Price £35.

May be seen until Monday afternoon at 13, High Holborn, W.C.1.

SCREWS – About 500 gross countersunk wood screws in packets. 1/4in to 1in. 6d per gross to clear. Dowell screws and screw eyes 5d per gross – 99 Borough High-street, S.E.1.

## CONCERTS, &C.

ROYAL ALBERT HALL

June 8th to 20th inclusive
Evenings at 8 p.m.
Saturday Matinees at 2.30 p.m.
THE ROYAL CHORAL SOCIETY
will present

"HIAWATHA"
(Coleridge-Taylor)
A DRAMATIC VERSION with SCENERY and COSTUMES.
arranged and produced by T.C. FAIRBAIRN
1,000 PERFORMERS.
The cast will include:

| | |
|---|---|
| ELISABETH AVELING | REGINAL CORTE |
| PHYLLIS EVENS | ARTHUR COX |
| OLIVE HEMINGWAY | EDWARD LEER |
| ELSIE SUDDABY | LEYLAND WHITE |
| STILES ALLEN | HORACE STEVENS |
| FLORA WOODMAN | HENRY WENDON |
| WILLIAM BOLAND | LEONARD WILLMORE |

HAROLD WILLIAMS
Chief OS-KE-NON-TON
Princess WAH-OO-AH

BALLET.

| | |
|---|---|
| PHYLLIS BEDELLS | KELLAND ESPINOSA |
| HERMIONE DARNBOROUGH | MARGIE NOEL |
| MYRTLE FARQUHARSON | AUBREY HITCHINS |
| WENDY TOYE | ELIZABETH MILLER |

Choreographist: EUPHAN MACLAREN
THE NEW SYMPHONY ORCHESTRA
Musical Director: DR. MALCOLM SARGENT

PRICES: Stalls 10s 6d; Balcony 5s 9d and 4s 9d; Gallery 2s 4d. Boxes £3 15s 0d, £ 0s 0d., and £1 17s 6d. Tickets at the Royal Albert Hall (telephone, Kensington 5360) and Agents.

WIGMORE HALL, TO-MORROW 5.30

**DORIS DOE**

SONG RECITAL
PIANOFORTE – IVOR NEWTON
BOSENDORFER PIANO. Tickets 12s, 5s 9d., 3s.
IBBS & TILLETT, 124, Wigmore-st., W.1. Welbeck 2325.

WIGMORE HALL TO-MORROW 8.30

**DONALD FRANCIS TOVEY**

HARPSICHORD RECITAL of BACH Works.
HARPSICHORD by DOLMETSCH. 12s, 5s 9d, 3s
IBBS & TILLETT, 124 Wigmore-st., W.1. Welbeck 2325.

GROTRIAN HALL TO-NIGHT at 8.30

**FRANK BRITTON**

FIANOFORTE RECITAL
GROTRIAN-STEINWEG PIANO
Tickets, 8s 6d, 5s 9d, 3s. at hall and Agents.

ADELPHI THEATRE
Charles B. Cochran presents

**ARGENTINA**

LAST PERFORMANCE TO-DAY (TUESDAY) at 3.

Prices: Stalls, 16s 6d, 12s, 8s 6d. Dress Circle 8s 6d, 5s 9d. Upper Circle 3s 6d include. tax. At all Agencies and Adelphi Box Office (Temple Bar 7611).

**TRINITY COLLEGE of MUSIC**

Mandeville-place, Manchester-square, W.1.
(Instituted 1872)
President:
E. STANLEY ROPER, M.V.O., M.A., Mus.B.
Controller of Examinations:
EDWARD D'EVRY, F.T.C.L., F.R.C.O.
On THURSDAY and FRIDAY NEXT at 7.45 p.m. and On SATURDAY NEXT, at 2.45 p.m. and 7.45 p.m.*
Performances by the College Operatic Class
at the

**NEW SCALA THEATRE**
of the Operas

**"DIDO AND ÆNEAS"**
(Purcell)
and
**"TRIAL BY JURY"**
(Gilbert and Sullivan)

Admission Free on Thursday, Friday, and Saturday afternoon. Tickets may be obtained on application to the Secretary. (Stamped addressed envelope.)
*The performance on Saturday evening will be given in AID of the
**GREAT ORMOND-STREET HOSPITAL FOR SICK CHILDREN**
Tickets from 1s 2d, to 12s 6d. including tax.
Particulars of the Teaching Department, with list of Professors, Fees, Scholarships, regulations, &c., and the Syllabuses of the Diploma and Local Examinations, free on application to the undersigned.
C.N.H. RODWELL, Secretary.

**GUILDHALL SCHOOL of MUSIC**
(Corporation of London)
JOHN CARPENTER-ST., VICTORIA-EMBANKT. E.C.1.
PRINCIPAL
**SIR LANDON RONALD**
F.R.A.M., F.R.C.M., &c.
FIRST-CLASS TUITION in any SINGLE SUBJECT from £2 a TERM.
COMPLETE MUSICAL EDUCATION
AND STAGE TRAINING
PRIVATE LESSONS in ALL MUSICAL SUBJECTS
EVENING LESSONS GIVEN up to 9 p.m.
**SPECIAL CLASSES & COURSES**
in GRAND and LIGHT OPERA, CONDUCTING
ENSEMBLE, DANCING and RUDIMENTS
LOCAL EXAMINATIONS IN ALL MUSICAL SUBJECTS
Special Training Course for Teachers, as approved by the Teachers' Registration Council.
New Students can commence at any time.
Prospectus on application from H. SAXE WYNDHAM, Secretary Telephones: Central 4459, City 5566.

## DANCING

ALL the accepted BALL-ROOM DANCES. Three strictly private Lessons ONE GUINEA – Ring Ambassador 1771 for appointment, GINA FREARSON, 131 WIGMORE-ST., W.1.

ARGENTINE TANGO by experts at "Lola's Club" 5 1/2gns. 20 lessons (1gn for 3); and all modern dances – 147a High-st, Kensington West 3004.

## LECTURES & MEETINGS

**LANTERN TALK**
showing Slides of the "Margery" Mediumship, and
DEMONSTRATION OF
**CLAIRAUDIENCE**
by the Famous American Medium
The Rev. **ARTHUR FORD**
of whom HANNEN SWAFFER writes:
"Arthur Ford's demonstration last night was either a miracle, or it was the most heartless fraud of the century."
Followed by
**DEMONSTRATION OF**
**TRUMPET VOICE**
**MEDIUMSHIP**
**IN FULL LIGHT**
by the well-known American
**MRS. MURPHY LYDY**
QUEEN'S HALL, LANGHAM-PLACE, W.1.
(Sole Lesees: Messrs Chappell & Co. Ld)
on TUESDAY, JUNE 9th at 8 p.m.
Reserved Seats. 5s and 3s; Unreserved, 2s and 1s.
Tickets can be obtained from the Queen's Hall Box Office.

SHIPPING AND MAILS

P. & O., BRITISH INDIA & NEW ZEALAND

## SHIPPING COMPANIES

**MAIL PASSENGER AND FREIGHT SERVICES**
**PENINSULAR & ORIENTAL SAILINGS**

(Under Contract with His Majesty's Government)

| Steamer | tons | L'nd'n | M'sel's | Taking pass'ng's for |
|---|---|---|---|---|
| MOOLTAN | 21,000 | - | June 5 | Bombay & Australia |
| §CHITRAL | 15,000 | June 12 | June 18 | Colombo & Australia |
| KARMALA | 9,000 | June 25 | – | Straits, China, Japan |
| MALOJA | 21,000 | June 25 | July 3 | Bombay & Australia |
| †RANCHI | 17,000 | July 3 | July 10 | Bombay & Karachi |
| *BENDIGO | 13,000 | July 10 | July 16 | Colombo & Australia |
| ¶CATHAY | 15,000 | July 10 | July 17 | Bombay & Japan |
| †MALWA | 11,000 | July 17 | July 24 | Bombay & Karachi |
| ¶KALYAN | 9,000 | July 23 | – | Straits, China, Japan |
| COMORIN | 15,000 | July 24 | July 31 | Bombay & Australia |
| †RANPURA | 17,000 | July 31 | Aug. 7 | Bombay & Karachi |
| §MONGOLIA | 17,000 | Aug. 7 | Aug. 13 | Colombo & Australia |

Taking passengers † for Malta, § for Port Sudan. ¶ Calling Southampton, * One class only at 3rd Cabin Fares.

**P & O NEW TOURIST CLASS**
**TO INDIA and AUSTRALIA**
Superior accommodation at low fares. Bombay from £30;

Return £54. Australia £39; Return £70. Available by S.S.s MOLDAVIA and MONGOLIA.

**P & O BRANCH SERVICE**
**MAIL STEAMERS TO AUSTRALIA**
Via Marseilles or Malta, Port Said, Suez, Aden and Colombo. ONE CLASS ONLY AT LOWEST FARES.

| | Tons. | London | Plymouth | Marseilles |
|---|---|---|---|---|
| BALRANALD | 13,000 | June 5 | June 6 | – |
| BALLARAT | 13,000 | July 3 | July 4 | – |
| †RENDIGO | 13,000 | July 10 | – | July 16 |
| BARADINE | 13,000 | July 31 | Aug. 1 | – |

† Not calling Malta.

**BRITISH INDIA SAILINGS**
(Under Contract with the Government of India.)
East African Steamers call outwards at Marseilles eight days. Port Sudan eighteen days after leaving London.

| Steamer | Tons | Midsbro | London | Destination |
|---|---|---|---|---|
| #MANTOLA | 9,066 | – | June 5 | East African Ports |
| c¶•†N'RB'DDA | 7.911 | June 4 | June 13 | Bombay & Karachi |
| #«MALDA | 9,066 | June 6 | June 13 | Madras & Calcutta |
| #«MASHOBRA | 8,324 | June 20 | June 27 | Madras & Calcutta |
| #MODASA | 9,070 | June 24 | July 3 | East African Ports |
| c*†§HATAR'NA | 7,522 | June 25 | July 4 | Bombay & Karachi |
| #«MANDALA | 8,281 | July 4 | July 11 | Madras & Calcutta |
| c*†§MASULA | 7,320 | July 16 | July 25 | Bombay & Karachi |
| #«MERKARA | 8,284 | July 18 | July 25 | Madras & Calcutta |
| #MADURA | 9,077 | July 22 | July 31 | East African Ports |
| *†§DURENDA | 7,241 | Aug. 6 | Aug. 15 | Bombay & Karachi |
| #MATIANA | 9,067 | Aug. 19 | Aug. 28 | East African Ports |

* Cargo Steamer. § Calling Port Okha.
† Calling at Intermediate ports if inducement offers.
« Calling at Port Sudan if inducement offers.
# Calls Tangier. ¶ Calls Navalakhi. c Calling Karachi first.

**P & O and B.I. PASSENGER OFFICES:**
P & O House, Manager: F.H. GROSVENOR
14, COCKSPUR-STREET, S.W.1.
City: 130 Leadenhall-street, E.C.3.
Strand (Passenger and Freight), Australia House, W.C.2.
**FREIGHT OR GENERAL BUSINESS**
P & O or B.I. OFFICES, 122 LEADENHALL-ST., E.C.3.
B.I. Agents: Gray, Dawes & Co. 122, Leadenhall-st., E.C.3.
Freight Brokers:
P & O Escombe, McGrath & Co., 13 Fenchurch-ave., E.C.3.; B.I.S.N. Co., Gellatly, Hankey & Co., Ltd. (Middlesbro' to Bombay and Karachi), 14 Billiter-st., E.C.3.

## NEW ZEALAND LINE

to New Zealand and through bookings to Australia
VIA PANAMA CANAL

| | | | |
|---|---|---|---|
| RANGITATA | 17,000 tons | Southampton | June 5 |
| RANGITANE | 17,000 tons | Southampton | July 3 |

and thereafter every 28 days.

Apply N.Z. S. Co. Ltd; Agents (J.B. Westray & Co. Ltd.), 138, Leadenhall-street, E.C.3. or Trans-Pacific Passgr. Agcy. (W.L. James), 14, Cockspur-street, S.W.1.

## UNION STEAMSHIP CO. OF NEW ZEALAND LTD.

To NEW ZEALAND and AUSTRALIA
By any Atlantic Line to Canada or U.S.A.
Thence via VANCOUVER or SAN FRANCISCO

| Steamer | †From Vancouver. | §From San Francisco |
|---|---|---|
| MONOWAI | June 24 | – |
| MAKURA | – | July 8 |
| NIAGRA | July 22 | – |
| MAUNGANUI | – | Aug. 5 |

†Canadian Australasian Line. via Honolulu, Fiji and Auckland to Sydney. §Union Royal Mail Line, via Tahiti, Rarotonga, Welling to to Sydney.

Apply the Trans Pacific Passenger Agency Ltd, (W.L. James. General Manager) 14, Cockspur-st., (1st floor), London, S.W.1. (Tel. Whitehall 2953), or for Vancouver Service any Office of the Canadian Railways.

# NATIONAL GOVERNMENT AND ITS TASK

## MR. MACDONALD AGAIN PRIME MINISTER

### MR. BALDWIN TO SERVE UNDER HIM IN NEW MINISTRY

### CABINET OF ELEVEN

### PARLIAMENT SUMMONED FOR SEPTEMBER 8

### SOCIALISTS PLANNING STRONG OPPOSITION

### AUTUMN ELECTION POSSIBLE

**The Socialist Government has resigned office.**

**The Ramsay MacDonald has become Prime Minister in a National Administration.**

**Mr. Baldwin has agreed to accept office under Mr. MacDonald.**

**These were the principal developments yesterday in the political crisis. It was not found possible last night to issue an announcement regarding the constitution of the new Ministry.**

THE DAILY TELEGRAPH **understands that the new Cabinet will consist of not more than eleven members, compared with the normal twenty. It will probably consist of:**

| SOCIALIST | CONSERVATIVE | LIBERAL |
|---|---|---|
| Mr. MacDonald | Mr. Baldwin | Sir Herbert Samuel |
| Mr. Snowden | Mr. Chamberlain | Sir Donald Maclean |
| Mr. Thomas | Sir Samuel Hoare | The Marquis of |
| Lord Sankey | Viscount Hailsham | Reading |

The Ministers will probably kiss hands on appointment this morning, and will immediately proceed with the task of carrying out a programme of retrenchment.

It was announced last night that Parliament will be summoned to meet on September 8.

By this date, it is expected, the economy programme will have been completed by the Cabinet. As soon as the necessary legislation has been passed the National Government will come to an end, subject to the exigencies of the Indian situation.

**Parliament will then be dissolved and a General Election on normal party lines will take place, either late in the autumn or early in the New Year.**

### THE KINGS COMMISSION

Mr. MacDonald had two audiences of the King yesterday. On the conclusion of the second, in the afternoon, the following announcement was made from Downing-street:

> **"The Prime Minister this afternoon tendered to the King the resignation of the Ministry, which was accepted by his Majesty, who entrusted Mr. Ramsay MacDonald with the task of forming a National Government on a comprehensive basis for the purpose of meeting the present financial emergency.**

> **"Mr. Ramsay MacDonald accepted the commission, and is now in conference with Mr. Stanley Baldwin and Sir Herbert Samuel, who are co-operating with him in the constitution of such an Administration."**

The discussions were continued until a late hour.

### ORGANISING OPPOSITION

Strenuous opposition to the national economy programme will be offered by dissentient members of the Socialist party. Immediately the resignation of the Socialist Ministry became an accomplished fact, steps were taken to organise a hostile campaign.

A special joint meeting of the Trades Union Congress General Council, the National Executive of the Labour party, and the Consultative Committee of the Parliamentary Labour party was summoned to meet at Transport House to-morrow afternoon for the purpose of considering the situation.

### MAJORITY ASSURED

It is already apparent that a considerable body of Socialist members of Parliament will be united in opposition. They will be led, presumably, by Mr. Arthur Henderson, and may number as many as 200.

There are 150 M.P.s who were returned as nominees of the T.U.C. In addition, there are forty-two L.L.P. members, who will vote against the Government.

In point of numbers, however, the National Government is assured of an adequate majority. It is assumed that the following votes can be relied upon:

Conservatives, 262; Liberals, 55.
MacDonald Socialists (estimate), 70. Total, 387.
Estimated Government majority, 187.

No by-elections will be necessary in the case of members of the House of Commons not now holding office who are appointed to the new Government.

## GOVERNMENT OF CO-OPERATION

### "VERY LARGE" CUT TO BE MADE

### OFFICIAL STATEMENT LAST NIGHT

The following Press communiqué was issued from No. 10 Downing-street last night:

"The Prime Minister, since kissing hands on appointment by his Majesty this afternoon, has been in consultation with Mr. Baldwin, Sir Herbert Samuel, and Mr. Snowden as to the names to be submitted to the King for inclusion as Ministers in the new Government. Considerable progress has been made.

The specific object for which the new Government is being formed is to deal with the national emergency which now exists. It will not be a Coalition Government in the

---

### DIARY OF THE DAY

**10a.m. – Party leaders received by the King at Buckingham Palace.**

**11.55 – Party leaders leave the Palace.**

**Noon. – Assembly of the Cabinet.**

**2.30 p.m. – Mr. MacDonald explains the position to junior Ministers.**

**3.0 – Mr. Baldwin at the Treasury.**

**4.12 – Mr. MacDonald again sees the King, the audience lasting twenty minutes.**

**4.50 – Officially announced that the Socialist Ministry had resigned, and that Mr. MacDonald had kissed hands on appointment as Prime Minister of a National Administration.**

**5.0 – Mr. Baldwin and Sir Herbert Samuel co-operate in the formation of the new Government.**

---

usual sense of the term, but a Government of Co-operation for this one purpose.

"When that purpose is achieved the political parties will resume their respective positions.

"In order to correct without delay the excess of national expenditure over revenue it is anticipated that Parliament will be summoned to meet on Sept. 8, and proposals will be submitted to the House of Commons for a very large reduction of expenditure and for the provision on an equitable basis of the further funds required to balance the Budget.

**"As the commerce and well-being not only of the British nation, but of a large part of the civilised world has been built up, and rests upon a well-founded confidence in sterling, the new Government will take whatever steps may be deemed to them to be necessary to justify the maintenance of that confidence unimpaired."**

### SOCIALIST ATTACK ON PREMIER

SALFORD, Monday Night.
Mr. J. Toole, Socialist M.P. for South Salford, speaking to-night, said he believed that the Socialist party, led as it would be by Mr. Arthur Henderson, would come out from the crisis stronger than ever it had been in the past. By taking up the leadership of the National Government Mr. MacDonald, he said, had left the Socialists.

## CABINET OF ECONOMY DICTATORS

### SPENDING DEPARTMENT HEADS TO BE EXCLUDED

### ELECTION IMMEDIATELY THE TASK IS ACHIEVED

**By Our Political Correspondent**

There will be, according to present indications, a General Election before the end of this year.

No one of the three political parties concerned in the formation of the National Government regards the new Administration which is in process of creation yesterday as anything more than an emergency Government.

Lest there should be any misapprehension as to the intentions underlying the political agreement which has been reached, it should be stated that the National Government must be considered as possessing little, if any, resemblance to Coalitions such as have existed in the past.

Permanent co-operation is not for a moment in the minds of those who will occupy the chief posts in the Administration which is being formed.

#### To Secure Efficiency

The position may be summarised as follows:

Mr. MacDonald, being unable to carry his Government with him, tendered his resignation to the King yesterday afternoon.

His Majesty, who had been in consultation with the leaders of the three political parties, requested Mr. MacDonald to form a Government on national lines.

Mr. MacDonald, having already assured himself of Conservative and Liberal support, has agreed to accept office again as the head of a Government composed of members of the three parties.

The Cabinet, instead of numbering about a score of Ministers, is to be limited to eleven (or twelve) members, with the object of ensuring the greatest measure of concentration and efficiency in carrying out the economy programme.

Ministers who are at the head of spending departments are to be deliberately excluded.

The Cabinet, in other words, is to be purely an Economy Cabinet, and will take arbitrary decisions which will be binding upon all departments.

It is understood that as soon as the new Government have completed the task of balancing the Budget and so re-establishing British credit abroad, there will be a Dissolution, to be followed by an appeal to the country on ordinary party lines.

#### CONSERVATIVE SUPPORT

Reasons For Mr. Baldwin's Decision

The decision of Mr. Baldwin and his colleagues, reached after prolonged consultation, to associate themselves with such of the Socialist Ministers as Mr. MacDonald can call upon to aid him is due to their conviction that the crisis is so grave that it requires all party considerations temporarily to be put aside if the situation is to be adequately met.

As soon as the programme of retrenchment, plus whatever new taxation may be necessary, has been carried through

Parliament, then it is contemplated that the members of the National Government will say good-bye to one another.

Their association, which may be a matter of only a few weeks, will come to an end, and they will go back to their respective political camps.

The date of the dissolution, which, it is apparent, has now been brought within measurable distance, may be determined by the fact that there can be no General Election until the Indian Round Table Conference has concluded its proceedings.

No one can say at the moment how long this conference will take, but it is the opinion in well-informed quarters that the Government will not "last out the year."

#### MR. MacDONALD'S COURAGE

Nine Dissentient Colleagues

There is general recognition in political circles of the fact that Mr. MacDonald has displayed great courage.

His action has meant a complete break with colleagues in the Socialist movement with whom he has worked for years. His future as a member of the socialist party must, at present, be regarded as wholly uncertain.

I understand that at the final Cabinet Council of the socialist Government, held at Downing-street, at noon yesterday, at least nine members of the Cabinet indicated definitely that they were not prepared to follow Mr. MacDonald's lead. They were:

**Mr. Arthur Henderson (Secretary for Foreign Affairs).**

**Mr. J. R. Clynes (Secretary for Home Affairs).**

**Mr. W. Adamson (Secretary for Scotland).**

**Mr. A.V. Alexander (First Lord of the Admiralty).**

**Mr. Arthur Greenwood (Minister of Health).**

**Mr. W. Graham (President of the Board of Trade).**

**Mr. George Lansbury (First Commissioner of Works).**

**Mr. T. Johnston (Lord Privy Seal).**

**Dr. Addison (Minister of Agriculture).**

The real cause of the fatal split in the Socialist Cabinet was the inability of Mr. MacDonald to carry with him a majority of his colleagues in favour of a cut of approximately 10 per cent. in the cost of unemployment insurance.

#### Possible Appointments

Considerable progress was made, yesterday, with the formation of the Government.

The precise offices to be filled by the members of the three parties forming the Cabinet have not yet been announced. They will be made known to-day, and I understand the exchange of seals, where necessary, will take place at once.

Speculation as to the posts to be given to various Ministers was freely indulged in last night.

# GREATEST POLITICAL ROUT IN HISTORY

## SOCIALIST DISASTER COMPLETE

| | |
|---|---|
| **FOR THE GOVERNMENT:** | |
| **Conservative** | **470** |
| **Liberal National** | **33** |
| **Liberal** | **30** |
| **National Labour** | **14** |
| **National** | **4** |
| **Independent** | **1** |
| **TOTAL** | **552** |
| **AGAINST THE GOVERNMENT:** | |
| **Socialists** | **52** |
| **New Party** | **-** |
| **Independent Liberals** | **4** |
| **Communists** | **-** |
| **TOTAL** | **56** |
| **Irish Nationalists** | **2** |

### GAINS AND LOSSES

| GOVERNMENT | GAINS | LOSSESS | NET GAINS |
|---|---|---|---|
| **Conservatives** | **201** | **0** | **201** |
| **Liberals** | **15** | **6** | **9** |
| **Lib. Nat.** | **11** | **0** | **11** |
| **Nat. Labour** | **2** | **2** | **0** |
| **National** | **3** | **0** | **3** |
| **Independent** | **1** | **0** | **1** |
| **TOTAL** | **233** | **8** | **225** |

Not a single seat was gained by any Opposition party.

The total electorate is approximately 30,158,967. It should be remembered that 67 members were returned to the House without a contest, 49 of them being Conservatives. Judging by the figures at the last election, the votes which would have been cast for the unopposed candidates if they had gone to the poll would be: Conservative, 967,000; Liberal, 528,000; Socialist, 319,000. These are not included in the actual totals above.

**(October 29)**

## MAJORITIES SINCE REFORM BILL

### THE 1931 RECORD

Majorities at General Elections since the Reform Bill have been:

| | | | | | |
|---|---|---|---|---|---|
| 1832 | Lib. | 370 | 1892 | Lib. | 40 |
| 1835 | Lib. | 112 | 1895 | Unionist | 152 |
| 1837 | Lib. | 18 | 1900 | Unionist | 134 |
| 1841 | Con. | 76 | 1906 | Lib. | 356 |
| 1847 | Lib. | 18 | 1910 | (Jan.) Lib. | 124 |
| 1852 | Con. | 20 | 1910 | (Dec.) Lib. | 126 |
| 1857 | Lib. | 80 | 1918 | Coalition | 263 |
| 1859 | Lib. | 50 | 1922 | Con. | 79 |
| 1865 | Lib. | 78 | 1923 | Con. over | |
| 1868 | Lib. | 116 | | Soc. | 68 |
| 1878 | Con. | 98 | 1924 | Con. over | |
| 1880 | Lib. | 115 | | Soc. | 211 |
| 1885 | Lib. | 86 | 1929 | Soc. over | |
| 1886 | Unionist | 114 | | Con. | 29 |

**(October 29)**


# Debenham & Freebody
(DEBENHAMS LIMITED)

# SALE

## Commences TO-DAY

*Typical Bargains*

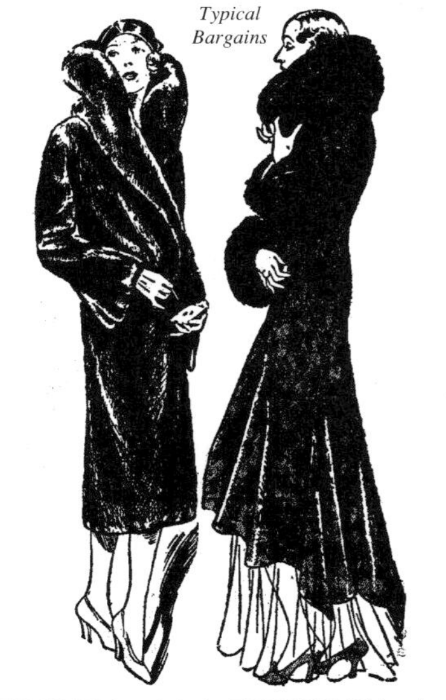

FUR COATS in seal dyed musquash and Persian lamb, &c., of which sketch in fine quality autria skins is an example.

SALE PRICE 59 gns

EVENING WRAPS in various brocades, of which sketch, copy of a Paris model in multi-coloured brocade, trimmed fur is an example.

SALE PRICE 8½ gns


## THE LAST HOUSE

The following table shows the official state of the parties in the House of Commons which was dissolved on Oct. 8:

| | |
|---|---|
| Conservatives | 252 |
| Socialists | 286 |
| Liberals | 58 |
| Ulster Unionists | 11 |
| Independents | 5 |
| Nationalists | 2 |
| Empire Crusade | 1 |
| | 615 |

**(October 29)**

## A MILLION COWS TUBERCULOUS

### HALF BRITAIN'S HERDS AFFECTED

According to an estimate given yesterday by Professor J.B. Buxton, about half the cows in England and Wales are affected to some extent with tuberculosis.

"In 1929" the professor said, "there were 2,054,073 cows and heifers in milk in England and Wales, and there are therefore over 1,000,000 tuberculous cows.

"Regardless of the question of the communicability of tuberculosis from animals to men and the bearing of animal tuberculosis on the public health, it is a well-known fact that this disease causes heavy financial loss to the livestock industry. We suffer an annual wastage of many human lives and untold suffering and misery in the case of many more."

As to eradication of the disease, Professor Buxton said that tuberculosis was no respecter of pedigree. He was often tempted to inquire of those who urged that eradication was the only solution of the problem to what extent they would be prepared to go in the case of pedigree stock.

Such a scheme would certainly involve the slaughter of at least half the breeding, the commercial cows in the country. That would not be the only cost, for there would also have to be a constant weeding-out process extending over several years.

**(July 2)**

## RADIO TUNING MADE SIMPLER

"Tuning-in" to broadcasting is reduced to the utmost simplicity in the latest production of Messrs. E.K. Cole, the makers of Ekco wireless sets.

On a circular dial are engraved the names of the principal European broadcasting stations, and the turning of a knob moves a small pointer round the dial. When the pointer indicates a particular station the set is tuned in, and the turning of the only other knob controls the volume.

**(August 27)**

## LEADERS THANK THE NATION

### GOVERNMENT'S GREAT TASK

The overwhelming evidence of national unity contained in the results of the Election is stressed in messages to the nation issued last night by the Prime Minister, Mr. Baldwin, and Mr. Philip Snowden.

**Mr. MacDonald**

### "RESPONSE BEYOND OUR DREAMS"

#### AN ASSURANCE FOR WORKING CLASSES

I venture to offer my thanks to the millions of people of all parties who have supported the appeal made by my colleagues and myself to the nation and who subordinate for the moment party feelings and issues to pressing national needs.

The majority, as unique as it is gratifying, given yesterday must convince the whole world that when this country calls for assistance willing hands and devoted minds will always respond heartily.

We appealed for a demonstration in national unity, and the response has been far beyond the dreams of the most enthusiastic of us.

To my political friends who have suffered such unusual reverses, and especially to those of them who, with splendid faith helped to sell our victory, I give the assurance that our triumph will in no way mean that either the interests or the point of view of the working classes will be overlooked in our performance of the task which is before us.

**Mr. Baldwin**

### "THIS IS NO PARTY VICTORY"

The nation has won a great and decisive victory. This is no party victory. It is an emphatic declaration by the people as a whole in favour of national co-operation in order to restore the fortunes of our country. The effect on foreign opinion cannot be overestimated. The overwhelming support given to the National Government will resound throughout the world and re-establish confidence in the stability and greatness of our country.

At home it will serve as a lesson to the political parties that the commonsense of the British people is proof against the propaganda of the demogogue. it will prove that the electors are not to be misled by specious promises or false appeals to selfish instincts. Democracy has justified itself in the most striking fashion, and the patriotic instincts of our people have been revealed in all their strength.

**Mr. Snowden**

### "LABOUR WILL RISE AGAIN"

The appeal to the electors to give a demonstration of national unity has received a response far beyond all expectations. This overwhelming majority for the National Government is not a party but a national victory.

Millions of men and women have voted for candidates with whose general political views they are not in agreement, on the sole ground of showing to the world that Britain is determined to stand four square and bring the nation through its difficulties.

I do not rejoice at the disaster which has come to the Labour Party. I regret it because the Labour leaders have brought this catastrophe upon themselves and to the party by their folly, lack of courage and leadership, and misunderstanding of the popular spirit.

**(October 29)**

## THE GRAMOPHONE COMBINE

### BALANCE SHEET SURPRISE

The combined report of the past year's results of the Gramophone Co. and Columbia Graphophone Co., now merged in Electrical and Musical Industries, is published to-day.

Profits of the combined companies only amount to £160,983, compared with £1,422,090 for the previous year. Interim dividends of 3s per share have been paid by each company, but no final distribution is forthcoming; consequently the payment of 30 p.c. for Columbias compares with 40 p.c., and that for H.M.V. 15 p.c. against 20 p.c.

Although a satisfactory amount of business was maintained at home, unfortunately, owing to various overseas difficulties, which grew worse as the year progressed, both turnover and profits suffered considerably.

**(November 30)**

# MILLIONS HUNGRY IN AMERICA

## MORE WANT & MISERY THAN IN ANY EUROPEAN COUNTRY

**From PERCY S. BULLEN**
**"The Daily Telegraph" Special Correspondent**

NEW YORK, Monday.

In all my experience I have never seen such want as exists here to-day - misery in the midst of plenty. There is more misery to the square mile to-day in the great American metropolis than in any city abroad.

American financiers and business analysts have published consoling statements indicating that the peak of the depression in the United States has been passed, that the Stock Market is scraping the bottom and that conditions generally are on the mend.

Some predict that there will be an upturn in the spring, others in the autumn, but the vast majority of responsible authorities refuse to indicate any date for that marked improvement which the public believe cannot be long delayed.

One of the most depressing factors in a situation which contrasts so vividly with the orgy of prosperity and extravagance of recent years, and which has dumbfounded the American people, is the uncertainty regarding the number of unemployed.

To-day the total is anybody's guess, and is to be found probably between a minimum of four million and six million! The claim of labour agitators and political extremists, who talk of nine millions, is undoubtedly an exaggeration, circulated for the purpose of Socialist propaganda.

It is difficult to refute, however, because the Washington Government to-day lacks the machinery for the collection of industrial statistics similar to that which European countries possess.

#### FLOCKING TO TOWNS

This uncertainty regarding the precise extent of the paralysis, measured by unemployed, which has afflicted the country in recent months accounts for much pessimism, unjustified by the facts as seen by the average observer.

That the times are hard, and probably without precedent in the memory of any person now living in the United States, most people here are convinced. The number of unemployed and the suffering they endure is reflected by the long bread lines in every big industrial city and the terrible extent to which all agencies of relief are taxed by hungry applicants.

In New York for weeks past there has been a plague of beggars, and the general conditions are almost as bad in Philadelphia, Chicago, St. Louis, and Boston.

People from small towns and agricultural districts have shown a tendency to flock to the big cities, under the impression that here wealth is most prodigal and here there is a better chance of a job.

#### No Relief, Dole or Pensions

To realise the acuteness of the situation one must understand that in America there is no Poor-law relief as in England, no dole and national system of old age pension.

Once a man loses his job he must rely upon his savings or the sale of his possessions, then upon loans from relations or friends, and finally he must apply to church and other organised agencies of charity.

The latter are swamped and are utterly unable to deal with one per cent. of the cases submitted to them. Municipal lodging-houses are crowded nightly, and in various public squares in the big cities bread lines form nightly where men wait for hours in winter weather to secure a cup of hot coffee and a meat sandwich.

One such line in the theatre district of New York has for weeks past been four deep, and the number served from an army kitchen wagon run by public subscription always exceeds 2,000. This method of relief for the most needy has become general.

**(February 3)**

## AMAZING TREK BY U.S. WORKLESS

### WHOLESALE DRIFT TO SUNNY REGIONS

The "Sun-rush" to Florida and California, where "summer spends the winter," has been augmented this year by an immense number of unemployed strangers who are going thither on foot and in goods cars on the railways but without tickets.

This influx is due to the industrial slump. The majority of the wanderers are very young men, tens of thousands of them well educated, who can find no work at home, and are resolved that, whatever happens, they shall not freeze to death.

Such armies, numbering in the aggregate hundreds of thousands of youths who are beginning life in the wrong way in idleness and uncertainty, disturb the inhabitants of America's great Riviera. The demand is therefore made that the Governors of California and Florida shall establish labour camps and make plans for the reclamation and development of waste lands.

Mr. Peter Spilsbury, one of the executive staff of the National Unemployment Relief Campaign, reports that the migration comes from the cold East and Middle West. He says that the railways cannot cope with the situation, and that "nearly all the travellers are armed, carrying pistols, knives or other weapons.

Mr. Spilsbury does not favour labour camps, which in some cases in the past have become little better than convict settlements. He suggests to the Washington authorities that the army of the United States shall take charge of these boys, clothe, feed, and train them in the military camps now existing, and provide them with certificates of training that will help them to find a place in the industrial army when times improve.

The Governors of States claim the power to establish a patrol on the boundaries to prevent these wanderers crossing. But it has been decided that the citizen of one State has the constitutional right to enter another State.

**(December 3)**

## BIGGEST HOTEL

### UNOFFICIAL PALACE OF NEW YORK

**From Our Own Correspondent**

NEW YORK, Wednesday.

The world's largest hotel, New Waldorf Astoria, was formally opened to-night with a radio address by President Hoover. Six thousand persons, including the leaders of New York's social, business, and political life, were seated at dinner.

The great structure of forty-seven storeys, with distinctive twin towers reaching to a height of 625 feet, cost £8,000,000 to build, and occupies an area of 81,000 square feet. The New Waldorf Astoria replaces the famous old structure of the same name, demolished two years ago. It is described as an exceptionally fine example of modern American sky-scraper architecture. Massive and of great height, its strong vertical lines are entirely devoid of superfluous ornament.

#### REAL LUXURY PALACE

"Unofficial Palace of New York," as the Waldorf is called, it justifies its title by the luxury of the interior decorations and furnishings of its 2,200 guest-rooms.

The great main foyer, with its classic Pompeiian atmosphere, has walls of Oregon burl maple, and columns and pilasters of black and gold marble. Spacious high-ceilinged public rooms surround the lobby and occupy the whole of the first floor.

The twin towers, which rise sheer from the centre of the structure, are occupied exclusively by 300 luxurious residential suites, designed to supply the New Yorkers' demand for private town residences, without the disadvantages of capital, cost of maintenance, and servant and management problems.

These suites, which are served by special express lifts, have their own driveway and entrance, and many are surrounded by roof gardens, beautifully landscaped, and commanding a sweeping view of the city.

Below the street level is a private railway siding, from which residents may board their private railway carriages, to be attached later to regular trains.

**(October 1)**

## CAR PARKS IN PLACE OF SLUMS

The Minister of Transport, in a circular to local authorities issued last night, urges that the provision of commodious parking places should be made a part of all town-planning schemes.

"This can be affected," he states, "either by the utilisation of convenient available spaces off the lines of traffic or by the demolition of slum areas. It is becoming an imperative need, more especially in towns which attract a large number of tourists.

**(March 5)**

# GOLD STANDARD SUSPENDED

## PROMPT MEASURES TO PROTECT FINANCIAL POSITION

**THE GOVERNMENT HAS DECIDED TEMPORARILY TO SUSPEND THE GOLD STANDARD AS FROM TO-DAY**

This prompt measure has been taken in order to prevent further withdrawals of gold from Britain, and to stop foreign speculation in the pound.

A Bill giving effect to this decision will be passed through all its stages in both Houses of Parliament to-day.

The Bank rate has been raised to 6 per cent.

Stock Exchanges throughout the country will be closed to-day.

These decisions were reached at a Cabinet meeting last night. "The Daily Telegraph" understands that the Cabinet was completely unanimous, and is confident that the country will face its difficulties calmly and with determination.

**(September 21)**

# WHY LAST NIGHT'S STEP WAS TAKEN

**By Our City Editor**

The serious financial crisis which has overwhelmed the principal money centres has forced this country off the gold standard. The announcement made by the Government last night is epoch-making.

The Bank of England is to be relieved from its obligation to sell gold at a fixed price, and while the measure is being passed through Parliament to-day the London Stock Exchange, for the second time in its history, will be closed for fresh transactions, but the arrangement of the fortnightly settlement will not be interfered with.

Thus, until there is legislation for the permission granted to the Bank by the Government to proceed in anticipation there will be no opportunity for foreign sellers to dispose of securities and withdraw bullion from the Bank.

Reluctant Decision

The decision has been taken with the greatest reluctance; but the City of London will appreciate the need for urgent measures after the experience of the concluding days of last week.

As the official statement discloses, there were very heavy withdrawals from this country by foreign institutions, mainly owing to the difficulties in other centres which have involved the repatriation of funds. One method of securing balances was by the realisation here of securities with an international market.

In normal times London welcomes the advantage accruing to an international centre, and so long as the obligations attaching to a gold standard were observed by other countries, the movement of the exchanges with the transfer of gold provided all the necessary checks and balances.

Unfortunately, for reasons which are well known, the gold standard has not functioned in accordance with its pre-war efficiency. Owing to the heavy balance of payments to France and the U.S.A. through reparations and war debts, these countries have accumulated vast stocks of bullion of no advantage to their trade and of serious disadvantage to the trade of the world. For many months this decision has been feared abroad, though the suggestion was resented in financial quarters.

Exchange Movements

What now happens is that the exchanges will move in accordance with supply and demand of currencies; but no gold will leave the Bank, as provided by the new legislation.

The steps taken by the Government to meet an urgent situation in no way affect the internal business of the country. It may, therefore, be unhesitatingly stated that banking business will be resumed to-day in a perfectly normal way.

The present situation is in no sense due to any crisis or weakness in British banking. It arises from the pressure by foreign owners to sell securities which enabled them to draw gold. The loss sustained by the Bank of England last week was a foretaste of what would have been experienced had not the Bank been relieved from its obligation.

Now that the full facts of the situation are disclosed the firm attitude of the Government should have beneficial results.

The Bank of England raised its official rate by 1 ½ per cent. to 6 per cent. to take effect from to-day. This is the first time in its history that the Bank Rate has been changed on a Sunday.

Except at the outbreak of war it is almost without precedent that the change has taken place other than at the weekly meeting on Thursday.

**(September 21)**

## SUICIDE BRIDGE OF LOS ANGELES

From the bridge which spans the deep gorge of the Arroyo Seco, in Pasadena, the beautiful garden city "millionaires suburb" of Los Angeles, no fewer than thirty-two men and women have hurled themselves to destruction on the rocks below. Pasadena police are considering a plan to install safety nets on each side.

**(July 1)**

# THE PRINCE ON "BUYING BRITISH"

## NEED FOR "HONEST TEAM WORK"

The Prince of Wales, in a broadcast last night, made an inspiring appeal to the nation and to the Empire in "buy British." The speech, which was broadcast from Birmingham, was the inauguration of the "Buy British" campaign.

In buying, said the Prince, "the first choice should be for home products, and the second for the products of the Empire overseas."

The movement "had made a remarkable advance of recent years, even of recent months." In a stirring sentence the Prince added:

"It springs from the patriotic determination of men and women of all parties that our country shall win through out of its present difficulties in prosperity, and from their belief that in order to win through we must develop to the uttermost the resources of our own country and of the Empire outside it."

**(November 17)**

# FIRST SECRETS OF THE 1931 CENSUS

Britain's population on the night of April 26 was 44,790,485, it is revealed in the preliminary census returns issued by the Registrar-General yesterday.

Although the highest total ever recorded - exceeding that of 1921 by 2,061,232 - the figures represent the lowest rate of increase (with the exception of the war decade) since census-taking began in 1801, and the lowest of any country in the world, except Sweden.

If the birth-rate remains at its present figure, the report points out, population will reach its maximum about 1950, after which it will decline at an increasing rate.

Other facts disclosed by the figures are:

The population is five times greater than in 1801, and more than treble that of 100 years ago;

Women outnumber men by 1,670,243 - compared with 1,736,221 in 1921 and 1,179,276 in 1911;

Mortality has fallen by 20 per cent. compared with 1911-21, and by 30 per cent. compared with 1901-11;

The density of population is 685 per square mile - greater than that of any other country with records, except possibly Belgium, and double that of most countries;

Eighty per cent. are living in towns - 25 per cent. in the thirteen biggest towns - and only 20 per cent. in the country.

Greater London's increase between 1921 and 1931 was at the rate of 9.7 per cent. which was three times as great as in the preceding decennium, and nearly double that for the country as a whole.

**(July 7)**

# 752 HOURS' SHUFFLING

## DANCE MARATHON ENDED

PARIS, Monday.

The Paris "Dance Marathon" ended at four o'clock this morning, the victorious couple having danced for 752 hours.

The winners are Mr. Ted Stanley, an American, of Miami, Florida, whose partner was a French girl. The reward for their efforts is a prize of 12,500f (£100).

Both had to carried off the floor when the competition ended. The girl had worn out twenty pairs of shoes and the man eight. Both, when they were capable of speech, declared "Never again."

The second prize is won by a couple who dropped out yesterday when the male partner sprained a leg while attempting fancy steps in a semi-conscious condition.

Altogether the dancers have received 200,000f (£1,600) in money given by the spectators.

**(July 21)**

# THE ROYAL SCOT

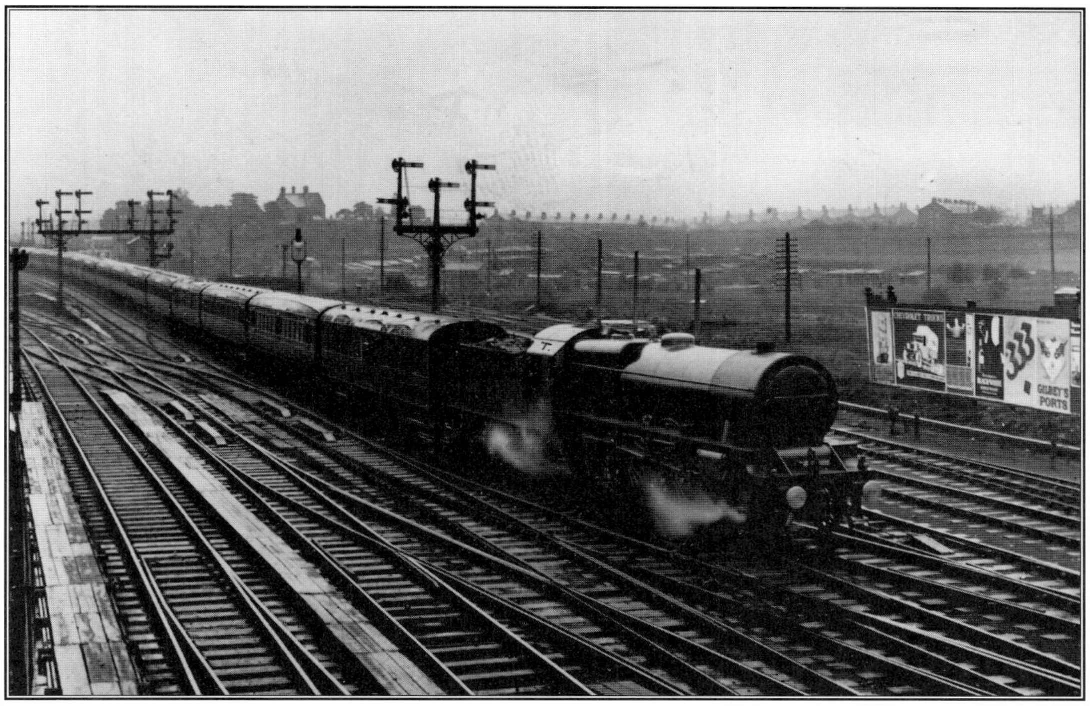

# ROYAL SCOT MEETS WITH DISASTER

## SIX PEOPLE DEAD & A NUMBER INJURED

### RESCUERS DRIVEN BACK BY STEAM

**From Our Special Representative**

LEIGHTON BUZZARD, Sunday.

It was a terrible scene which met the eyes of those who first saw the wreckage of the Royal Scot.

The great engine, thrown clear of the track, was lying on its side belching forth steam. Carriages had been thrown this way and that across four sets of metals. Four tracks were completely blocked by the wreckage.

The first coach was reduced to a mass of broken woodwork. The second coach had somehow been piled on to the top of the first. The third and fourth, swivelled around in an extra-ordinary way, had crashed through the second. A fifth had toppled over.

Of the length of that long train only four coaches in the rear were still on the metals.

From the wreckage there arose groans and cries from the passengers. Many were able to extricate themselves without difficulty, but others, and in the main they were those who were injured, were trapped in the wreckage.

Platform Dressing Station

Medical assistance from doctors and nurses was soon forthcoming, and the platform of Leighton Buzzard Station, a few hundred yards away, was transformed into a temporary dressing station.

One of the first duties of the rescue parties was to proceed to the overturned locomotive. Steam was hissing forth in scalding clouds which drove back those who sought to reach the driver and the fireman. Not until the steam had dispersed was it possible to approach, and then it was to find that Driver Hudson was dead in his cabin. Rogers, the fireman, was lying in agony beneath the engine.

He was still clasping a piece of rag which he must have been using when the crash came. Dauntless efforts were made to reach him, but death had come to put an end to his sufferings long before the engine could be moved.

The accident occurred at the very point of the main line where an express was photographed at full speed for news purposes, a few months ago. A tall gantry marks the end of a curve in the line where it approaches the station, and from this point the cross-over begins from the main line to the "down slow."

The express was being diverted to the "slow" line because of repairs to the fast line higher up. She was travelling at much below her normal main-line speed, which is about sixty miles an hour.

Panic-Stricken Women

Mr. Clare, manager of the local branch of the Westminster Bank, lives almost opposite the station. He described to me the consternation caused by the noise of the disaster as "something agonising."

Mr. Clare and his wife ran down to the line to assist in releasing passengers from the coaches. Many of them were women, and their condition was one of panic. They had to be assisted to the platform of the station and given restoratives. Members of the Scottish Association football team rendered help, as did members of the Glasgow Orpheus Choir, who had occupied the adjoining reserve coach.

Col. Hugh Sladen, Divisional Commander of the North London Division of the Salvation Army, was preparing for an afternoon service.

On hearing the crash he requisitioned the whole corps - the band included, or thirty-five men in all - and rushed to the scene to reinforce the work of the ambulance staff and the police.

**(March 23)**

# JUNGLE OUTSIDE ZOO PARK

## MOTORISTS HERDED WHILE ANIMALS LOUNGE

**From Our Special Representative**

WHIPSNADE, Sunday.

The new Zoological Park at Whipsnade presented a curious paradox to-day, for the "zoo" was a human one, and was outside the gates rather than in.

Within the 500 acres of the beautiful park the animals lounged at their secluded ease. Outside was a mechanical jungle - a mad mass of motorists mingled wheel to wheel.

All the morning in the pouring rain the cars were arriving. By midday the weather cleared, and later when the sun shone warmly the stream of cars grew rapidly thicker.

The three-acre official car park soon proved unequal to the task.

"It holds 400, and ought to hold at least 1,500," said a harassed Automobile Association official. "You see it keeps getting full, and then we have to turn motorists away.

At 4.30 another official told me: "At least 5,000 cars have been turned away. They are parking out on the common now." And, sure enough, they were. It was an amazing sight. The road up to the entrance was lined for about half a mile on either side by ranks of parked cars, bulging out at times into miniature "parks" eight or ten deep.

Once in the grounds all the turmoil was found to have been well worth while, and the large crowds wandered contentedly about, greatly enjoying the antics of the baby timber wolves, the wallabies, the bears, the beauties of Bluebell Wood and the many other attractions of a wonderful place.

It is explained that the new approach roads to the park are not yet completed, and the existing highways proved inadequate to carry the transport; but the parking ground problem has yet to be solved.

**(May 25)**

# LORD LANGFORD

MELBOURNE, Monday.

Mr. C. W. T. Rowley, who last January succeeded to the title of Lord Langford, has now, it is declared, definitely decided to assume the title, and will go to England at the end of the year

Lord Langford has for the last few years been working on a farm in Australia, and during that time his wife has been earning her living as a waitress in a London teashop.

**(March 13)**

# STALIN'S NEW DRIVE

## SECOND FIVE-YEAR PLAN

**By Our Industrial Correspondent.**

The Russian workers are being promised "a new historic stage on the way to the victory of the world proletariat."

It takes the form of a second Five-year Plan, and, like the first, will involve strenuous self-sacrifices for the workers and peasants.

Stalin has summoned a national conference in Moscow next month to consider the undertakings to be included in the programme.

One of these is an underground railway through Moscow. A Soviet Commission has been in London investigating the Underground system.

MASS OUTPUT OF CARS

Other features to be included in the second quinquennial plan are:

Mass production works for motor-cars and tractors.

New engineering, chemical, and electric equipment works.

Increased rolling stock and permanent way for the railways.

Extended land cultivation and the opening of new industrial areas.

These and other schemes are to be discussed at conference in January and June.

The first Five-Year-Plan will not be completed before the end of 1932, supposing that all the industrial sections are able to comply with the stern schedule set for them. Russian workers were promised that as a reward for abolishing the Sabbath, and concentrating intensely upon labour for five years, real wages would become twice as high as before the war, and the Workers' State would become wealthier and happier from all points of view.

**(December 15)**

# ROLLS-ROYCE BUYS BENTLEY MOTORS

## A FINAL SURPRISE

**By Our Motoring Correspondent**

Bentley Motors Ltd., its cars in stock, factory, service station and other assets has been bought by Rolls-Royce Ltd.

This new, and, it may be hoped, final surprise move in the fortunes of the famous concern was announced yesterday by Mr. A.F. Sidgreaves, managing director of Rolls-Royce. He adds that his board has under consideration the formation of a subsidiary company to carry on the Bentley business, and will in any case maintain the service arrangements for the benefit of existing Bentley owners.

Mr. F. Hill-Cole, head of the British Equitable Central Trust Ltd., which, as exclusively announced in The Daily Telegraph, acquired the assets from the liquidator last Friday, informed me yesterday evening that the negotiations which he had in view for a merger with certain steel interests having fallen through, his board decided to accept the offer of Rolls-Royce Ltd., and dispose of the whole concern to them as it stood.

This new purchase is almost as unexpected as that of a week ago, when the British Equitable Central Trust stepped in just as the sale to D. Napier and Sons Ltd. was about to be concluded. Rolls-Royce Ltd., as reported in The Daily Telegraph at the time, had considered and declined an offer of the Bentley business a week or two before a receiver was appointed for it in July.

**(November 21)**

# NEXT BRITISH STEP IN INDIA

## FEDERAL SCHEME BY CONSENT - OR COMPULSION

The Round Table Conference was brought to a close in London yesterday. There will be no intermission, however, in the work of evolving India's new Constitution.

Announcing the British policy at the final session of the Conference, the Prime Minister reaffirmed the Government's belief in an all-India Federation, and announced the next steps which are to be taken as follows:

**Three Committees will be established by the Government to deal with problems of franchise and finance.**

**They will be at work in India early in the new year. A Working Committee of the Round Table Conference will remain in being in India.**

**The North-West Frontier will be constituted a Governor's Province.**

**Sindh will be made a separate province.**

**There will be no acquiescence in the continuance of the Communal deadlock.**

**If a settlement is not arrived at by the Indians the Government will be compelled to apply a provisional scheme.**

THE DAILY TELEGRAPH learns that, as a means of keeping in touch with the negotiations in India, the Government propose to nominate members of Parliament to preside over the Committees.

**Mr. MacDonald and Parliament**

A debate on India will be opened in the Commons to-day by Mr. MacDonald, who will invite the House to endorse the Government's policy.

To-morrow Mr. Churchill will move an amendment that India shall not be given a Dominion Constitution as defined by the Statute of Westminster.

**(December 2)**

# GANDHI AT THE PALACE

## LOIN CLOTH & SANDALS

Mr. Gandhi — in loin-cloth, white blanket, and sandals — visited Buckingham Palace yesterday afternoon, and had conversations with both the King and the Queen.

He was one of the 400 guests at the tea-party given by their Majesties for the delegates to the India Round Table Conference.

The King and Queen welcomed their guests at the entrance to the famous Picture Gallery, on the first floor of the palace, and a brilliant scene was presented by the picturesque attire of the ladies- the Queen was in a lovely gown of silver shade — and the gorgeous dress of the Indians.

The first to have audience of the King was Sir Muhammed Akbar Hydari. Then followed Sir Mirza Mahommad Ismael, Rao Bahadur V. T. Krishnamacharya Avergal, Mr. Gandhi, with whom the King conversed for nearly ten minutes, Sir Tej Bahadur Sapru, Sir Muhammad Shafi, and Dr. Shafa'at Ahmed Khan.

Mr. Gandhi also had a short conversation with the Queen. He left the palace before tea was served, and drove to his headquarters at Knightsbridge.

**(November 6)**

# MOON PRIESTESS OF 500 B. C.

## GREAT PALACE DISCOVERED AT UR

A great royal palace of 500 b. c., covering an area of 1,000 square yards, is the latest discovery to be made at Ur of the Chaldees.

Following closely upon the finding of the royal tombs dating back to 2400 b.c. (announced in The Daily Telegraph last Tuesday), Mr. C. Leonard Woolley and his colleagues of the joint expedition of the British Museum and the University of Pennsylvania have laid bare the foundations of Princess Bel-shalti-nannar's palace.

It is a big and complicated building in mud brick, containing over seventy rooms and courts.

Under the brick pavement of one of the principal doorways the excavators found brick boxes containing the humble emblems of the powers that protect a house.

Chief among them was Papsugal, Messenger of the Gods, a squat and ugly mud figure girt with a copper baldric and brandishing a copper spear. With him were little mud dogs in sets of five painted in different colours. Cracked and crumbling, they were still keeping guard.

**(January 6)**

# "LAST OF SCALPERS"

## RUN DOWN BY TRAIN

EL PASO (Texas), Wednesday.

One of the last of Chief Geronimo's band of Indian scalpers, which harassed the white man's settlements of the South-West many years ago has been killed by a passenger train. Roque Molino, "Old Roque," whom friends believed to be more than 100 years of age, was struck down at a level crossing recently.

**(July 30)**

# NAVY MEN'S PAY PROTESTS

## "UNREST" IN SHIPS

## EXERCISES OF FLEET SUSPENDED

The following statement was issued by the Admiralty last night:

"The Senior Officer, Atlantic Fleet, has reported that the promulgation of the reduced rates of naval pay has led to the unrest amongst a proportion of the lower ratings.

"In consequence of this he has deemed it desirable to suspend the programme of exercises of the Fleet, and to recall the ships to harbour while investigations are being made into the representations of the hardship occasioned by certain of the cuts in pay, in order that these may be reported for the consideration of the Board of Admiralty."

A later statement announced the approval of the Admiralty to the course that had been adopted:

"Their lordships have approved of the exercises of the Atlantic Fleet being temporarily suspended while certain representations of hardship under new rates of pay are being investigated for the consideration of their lordships."

The senior officer referred to is Rear-Adml. Wilfrid Tomkinson, on whom the command devolved in consequence of the illness of Adml. Sir Michael Hodges.

**(September 16)**

# MEETINGS HELD

## SHORE INCIDENTS

**From Our Own Correspondent**

INVERGORDON, Tuesday.

Feeling over the pay reductions was known to be running high in the Atlantic Fleet, but there was no outward manifestation of unrest until Sunday.

Noisy protests where then voiced in a canteen in the town. There were then about 700 liberty men on shore, and extra pickets were landed from various ships. This action had the desired effect for a time, but in the evening, when the liberty men were waiting on the pier to return to their ships, there was a further noisy demonstration.

The protests continued on Monday. A meeting at the canteen was dispersed, and 600 ratings then adjourned to Black Park, where proposals of how to resist the cuts were discussed.

To-day no men were allowed on shore leave, but the sound of singing and cheering which reached the shore gave the impression that on board some of the ships at least the men were discussing their supposed grievances.

**(September 16)**

# DISTINGUISHED INVALIDS

The following reports on the condition of distinguished invalids were received last night:

Princess Marie Louise: Making slow progress.

Lady Chamberlain (wife of Sir Austen Chamberlain): Confined to her room with influenza.

Prebendary Gough (heart trouble): Left hospital for his London home.

**(July 4)**

# THE DOWNFALL OF CAPONE

## 11 YEARS SENTENCE & £10,000 FINE

**From Our Own Correspondent**

CHICAGO, Sunday.

Eleven years' imprisonment and a fine of £10,000— such was the sentence passed yesterday on Al Capone, gang leader and "Chicago's Public Enemy No. 1," who till now has been popularly regarded as entrenched impregnably in his underworld power and wealth— able to defy the law with complete impunity. His downfall has been brought about by convictions for evasions of the income-tax laws.

His lawyers, however, are to make a last bid.

After sentence was passed yesterday by Judge Wilkerson notice of appeal was lodged and an application was made for bail. This was refused, and Capone was taken back to Cook County Gaol, where he spent last night, after being out on bail awaiting the pronouncement of the sentence.

To-day Capone's lawyers will renew the application for bail. If this is granted it is possible that America's lord of crime might stave off prison for a year or more until the Supreme Court says the final word. But at the moment the gangster's prospects are black, and his reign seems definitely at an end.

POSSESSIONS ATTACHED

Ten years of the sentence have been imposed for three felonious violations of the income-tax law. This part will be served in the Leavenworth Penitentiary (Kansas), where good conduct may mean a reduction of almost three years. One year will then be served in the county gaol. This was imposed in respect of two convictions for not filing tax reports.

In addition to the fine, the costs of the trial are estimated at £20,000, the amount due for income-tax is estimated at £44,000 and there is an equal sum for other etceteras, bringing his total loss to almost £120,000.

To make certain of getting the money, the Government have attached Capone's palatial Florida home, his safety vaults in the banks, his gambling and vice houses, even his extensive wardrobe and personal jewellery.

The pronouncement of the sentence yesterday morning was dramatic. Judge Wilkerson's words, sharply clipped and incisive, rang clear in the hushed court — a small chamber crowded with two hundred persons.

A LAST KICK

After curtly dismissing all the legal arguments offered by defending counsel, Judge Wilkerson ordered defendant to the bar. Ponderous of body, neatly dressed in a heather-coloured suit and wearing a white silk handkerchief in the breast pocket of his coat, Capone stepped forward, his jet-black and piercing eyes fixed on the grim-faced judge and his hands clasped behind his back.

As the judge pronounced the maximum sentence for each conviction, Capone's eyes hardened and his fingers locked and unlocked. The final pronouncement hit Capone like a slap in the face.

Flushed and angry, his round, usually placid face contorted into lines of sullen hatred, he turned to be confronted by a Marshal and two deputies, who led him away.

Out in the streets the people of Chicago could talk of nothing but the Capone sentence. No one had believed "the big shot," who for six years has played the part of a modern robber baron, wiping out those who crossed his path with machine-guns, and directing with a cunning hand the beer-runners, gambling dens, and vice resorts, could be put under lock and key for such a "stretch."

Like most other people, Capone took the Federal Government's investigation into his income as a joke. Even when he was found guilty — on Oct. 18 — he merely grinned and remarked, "I am not through with fighting yet." It required three years' intensive and often dangerous investigation on the part of the Government agents to get the head of Chicago's crime syndicate safely within their net.

**(October 26)**

# TO SMASH THE ATOM

## 10,000,000-VOLT MACHINE

A huge machine capable of generating 10,000,000 volts, which, it is hoped, will point the way to the realisation of the alchemists dream of the transmutation of the elements by "smashing the atom," is being constructed at South Dartmouth, Massachusetts, under the direction of experts of the Massachusetts Institute of Technology.

The experiments by Dr. van de Graaff, it is stated, have demonstrated that the voltage is limited only by the size of the apparatus. The 10,000,000-volt generator now under construction will have brass terminals 10ft. to 15ft. in diameter, mounted on glass towers 20ft. high. The new generator, it is believed, will supply science with a new tool with which to bombard the atom. Should it fail to smash it, a larger machine capable of generating 50,000,000 volts will be constructed for the purpose.

**(November 7)**

# "A NEW PARTY OF ACTION"

## SIR OSWALD MOSLEY'S APPEAL

In a statement issued during the weekend Sir Oswald Mosley announced the formation of "a great new party of action, which shall be called 'The New Party'."

He seeks to mobilise at least 400 candidates to fight at the next election on a policy that challenges the position of all existing parties. To create such a party, he says, three things are necessary:

(1) Voluntary workers in every constituency.

(2) Candidates to fight constituencies at the next election.

(3) Finance for the work of organisation and the running of candidates.

The statement declares that sufficient support in Parliament and in the country is already assured to justify the launching of a new political organisation.

The following are other passages from the statement:

"We differ from all the old parties in our demand for a complete revision of Parliament which will change it from a talk-shop to a workshop. We challenge the fifty-year-old system of Free Trade, which exposes industry in the home market to the chaos of world conditions, such as price fluctuation, dumping, and the competition of sweated labour, which result in the lowering of wages and industrial decay.

"We challenge also the century-old system of Protection which Conservatives seek to put in the place of Free Trade, with the result that the employer alone will be protected and entrenched at the expense of both worker and consumer.

"In place of both these obsolete and ineffective systems we suggest that the worker and consumer, as well as the employer, shall be protected by modern machinery, which will maintain in this country a stable market and a high standard of life based on high wages, which alone can provide a large home market."

**(March 2)**

# LYNCHINGS DOUBLED IN A YEAR

## 24 NEGRO VICTIMS

NEW YORK, Tuesday.

During the year 1930 twenty-five lynchings occurred in America compared with twelve in 1929.

Twenty-four of the victims were negroes. Georgia had seven lynchings, Alabama and Texas four apiece, Mississippi three, Indiana and South Carolina two each, and Florida, North Carolina and Oaklahoma one each.

Mr. Walter White, acting secretary of the National Association for the Advancement of Coloured People, from whose annual report the above figures are quoted, hailed as an encouraging development "the increasing repudiation by white women of the South, of lynching as a protection of womanhood." "Of twenty-five lynchings in 1930," he said, "criminal assault was assigned as an excuse in only three cases."

**(January 21)**

# WHEN HITLER COMES INTO POWER

**From Our Own Correspondent**

BERLIN, Friday.

Herr Hitler this morning called together the English newspaper correspondents in Berlin to tell them that he expected soon to be in power, and what he intended to do when he got there.

His harangue, which lasted forty minutes, was swift and agitated. It's substance was that he would:

Acknowledge Germany's international private debts;

Refuse to pay Reparations;

Restore prosperity to Germany by shutting off imports and "developing the home-market."

He took as his text the curious document drawn up by some of his leading adherents in Hessen and given up by one of them to the Prussian police, and he repeated his already published repudiation of responsibility for this document.

"There can be no possible doubt," he said, "that we shall soon come to power by legal means, and when power is already practically within our grasp we are not likely to be such fools as to court the risk of losing it by committing illegal actions. Individual National-Socialists may commit blunders and follies, like individual members of any other party, but for the party as a whole my will and my will alone is law."

FOAMING AT THE MOUTH

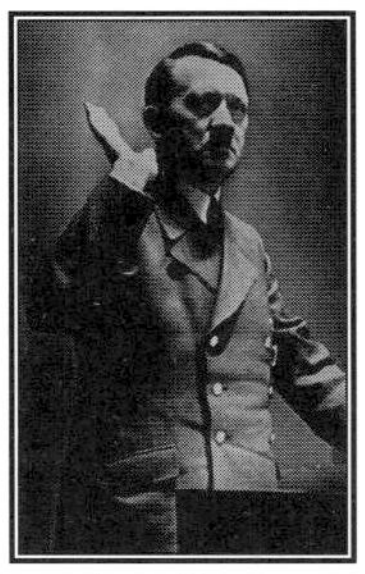

HERR HITLER

When Herr Hitler reached the subject of France and Reparations he passed into the state which is generally known as foaming at the mouth. If he lets himself go in the same way as dictator, or even merely as the dominating factor in German Government Coalition, Germany may indeed look out for squalls.

"If France is to continue her policy of blackmail," he shouted, "there will be nothing but ruin for all of us. Whatever agreements other German Governments may have made or make, we will refuse to continue political payments the demand for which is actuated by the determination to enslave us.

"And why should we pay Reparations? We of the National-Socialist party are young. We are absolutely innocent of war-guilt. Why should we be burdened with a yoke of debt for sixty years and be reduced to the rank of a second-class Power?"

**(December 5)**

# AIRWOMAN BRIDE

Miss Amelia Earhart, the first woman to fly the Atlantic, was married to-day at Noank, Connecticut, to Mr. George Palmer Putnam, one of the well-known publishing firm.

Miss Earhart is to retain her maiden name, and has decided, said Mr. Putnam's secretary, not to go away for a honeymoon.

**(February 9)**

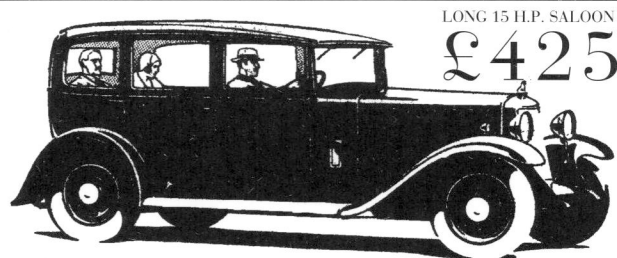

# KING ALFONSO RENOUNCES HIS THRONE

## SPAIN DECLARED A REPUBLIC

King Alfonso has abdicated and the second Spanish Republic has been proclaimed.

This swift and almost bloodless revolution was carried out in the course of a few hours yesterday.

At 3.30 p.m. King Alfonso signed the Act of Abdication. At nine p.m. he left Madrid by motor-car.

A British United Press message from Cartagena (260 miles from Madrid) early this morning stated that the King was expected there at 4 a.m. and that he would sail at once in the cruiser Principe Alfonso.

He proposes, with the other members of the Royal family, to come to London.

According to one message the Queen (who is a daughter of Princess Beatrice, aunt of King George) and her children left by special train for Paris, yesterday afternoon.

The King agreed to resign himself to the demands of the Republicans, when it was made clear to him that the only alternative to abdication was civil war. He was warned that all Republican and Socialist organisations throughout the country had been advised to revolt should he refuse to give up the Throne.

**MESSAGE TO THE NATION**

At first he offered to abdicate in favour of his eldest son, the Prince of Asturias. But Senor Zamora, the Republican leader, now Prime Minister, insisted that the Republicans would accept nothing less than complete renunciation of power into the hands of the people.

The King gave in, and at 3.30 p.m. signed the official Act of Abdication renouncing the Throne for himself and all his heirs.

**(April 15)**

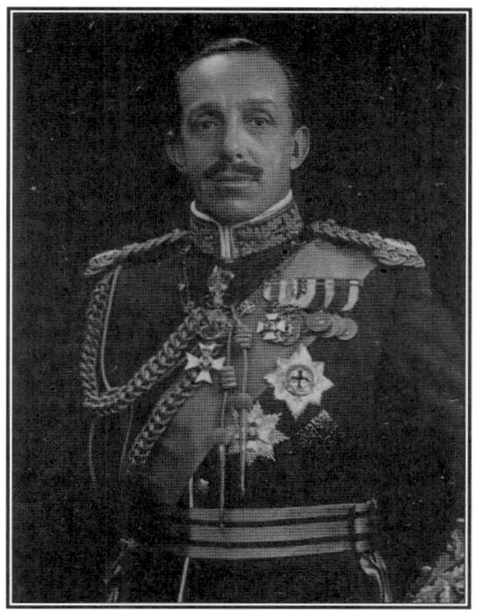

King Alfonso

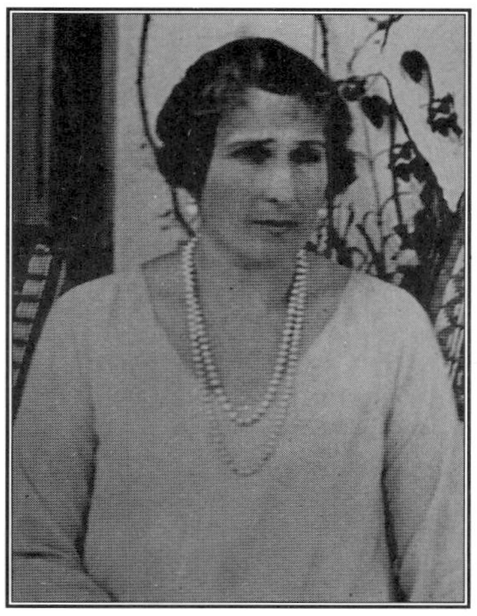

Queen Victoria

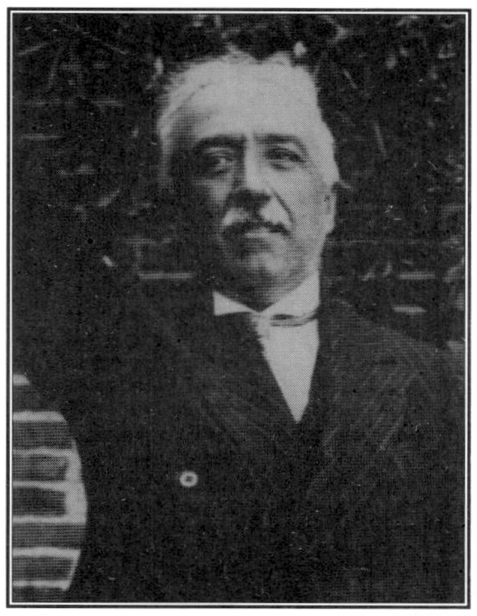

Senor Alcala Zamora

## GOVERNMENT AND BIRTH CONTROL

The Ministry of Health yesterday issued the following memorandum:

1. The Minister of Health is authorised to state that the Government have had under consideration the question of the use of institutions which are controlled by Local Authorities for the purpose of giving advice to women on contraceptive methods.

2. So far as maternity and child welfare centres (including ante-natal centres) are concerned, these centres can properly deal only with expectant mothers, nursing mothers, and young children, and it is the view of the government that it is not the function of the centres to give advice in regard to birth control and that their use for such a purpose would be likely to damage the proper work of the centres. At the same time the Government consider that, in cases where there are medical grounds for giving advice on contraceptive methods to married women in attendance at the centres, it may be given, but that such advice should be limited to cases where further pregnancy would be detrimental to health, and should be given at a separate session and under conditions such as will not disturb the normal and primary work of the centre. The Minister will accordingly be unable to sanction any proposal for the use of these centres for giving birth control advice in other cases.

QUESTION OF AUTHORITY

3. The Government are advised that Local Authorities have no general power to establish birth control clinics as such, but that under the Notification of Births (Extension) Act, 1915, which enables Local Authorities to exercise the powers of the Public Health Acts for the purpose of the care of expectant mothers and nursing mothers, it may properly be held that birth control clinics can be provided for these limited classes of women. Having regard to the acute division of public opinion on the subject of birth control, the Government have decided that no Departmental sanction which may be necessary to the establishment of such clinics for expectant and nursing mothers shall be given except on condition that contraceptive advice will be given only in cases where further pregnancy would be detrimental to health.

Advice on contraceptive methods will be given only to married women who attend the clinics for such medical advice or treatment, and in whose cases pregnancy would be detrimental to health.

**(March 26)**

## NOBEL PEACE PRIZE GOES TO AMERICA

It was announced at Oslo, Norway, yesterday that the Nobel Peace Prize had been jointly awarded to Miss Jane Addams, the American social worker, and Dr. Nicholas Murray Butler, president of Columbia University.

The prizes for chemistry and medicine were awarded to three German scientists, Profs. Warburg, Bosch and, Bergius.

**(December 1)**

## POPE'S ADDRESS TO WORLD AUDIENCE

Addressing himself to "All men and all created things," the Pope yesterday delivered his first address "urbi et orbi" through the medium of the wireless.

Throughout the world special arrangements had been made to relay the address. In the majority of cases the results were successful.

From Northern Europe to far away Australia the Pope's words were followed by listeners of many nations. Sydney reported a "most clear reception."

In the United States of America seventy-seven stations took part in the relay. The evening papers published a translation of the address.

The relay from the B.B.C. transmitters was entirely successful. The Latin words came through in a finely modulated musical voice, which spoke fast but clearly.

**(February 13)**

## HAMPSTEAD TRAGEDY

Mr. Bernard Irving, a director of A.W. Gamage Ltd, and a member of the board of Gamages (West End), was found hanging and dead at his residence in King's-gardens, West-end-lane, Hampstead, yesterday.

Mr. Irving was between 40 and 45 years of age.

The tragic incident has occurred at a time when Gamages (West End) Ltd, is in process of liquidation. The palatial new store, which this company opened in Oxford-street in September of last year, was closed a month ago.

The stock-in-trade has been sold by the receiver and the building is now in the market.

A report of the proceedings at the first statutory meeting of the creditors of Gamages (West End) appears on Page Ten.

**(June 17)**

## WAR ON CANCER WITH X-RAYS

When the Prince of Wales visited the Royal Northern Hospital, Holloway, yesterday afternoon, he watched the application of the new fluorescein ray treatment for cancer.

As he was being conducted through the X-ray department his Royal Highness saw a young man lying on a table while a powerful X-ray lamp was pouring its beams into his body. He asked Dr. Gouldesbrough, who is in charge of the department, to explain the treatment to him.

Dr. Gouldesbrough stated that it was a treatment, originated in the Royal Northern, in which the patient is first given an injection of the drug fluorescein.

"The X-ray acts upon the drug in such a way as to liberate activated fluorescein," he explained, "and this attacks and kills the cancer in the human cell. It is specially used in cases of breast and lung cancer, but in the breast treatment the fluorescein is painted on instead of being injected.

**(November 25)**

## BRITAIN'S WORST EARTHQUAKE

### LAND SHAKEN FROM THE CHANNEL TO THE HIGHLANDS

Great Britain was shaken by earthquake yesterday - the worst earthquake in which the country has been involved since official records have been kept.

Happily it was not of sufficient intensity to cause personal injury or damage to property. Widespread alarm was, however, occasioned.

MOST SEVERE ON THE EAST COAST

It is the fourth time since the beginning of the present year that an earthquake has occurred in the British Isles.

Yesterday's experience was not as severe as the tremor which shook the industrial Midlands on May 3. Its effects, however, were more extensively felt.

There is scarcely a town from the south coast to as far north as Frazerburgh, from the east coast to Wales, from which earthquake reports were not received yesterday.

It appears that the shock was most intense along the east coast, in a district nearest to the calculated centre of disturbance.

The shock was not experienced so far to the west as Penzance. Plymouth escaped without a tremor. The quake was felt in Jersey, but not in Guernsey.

There was a slight shock at Cardiff. In the Isle of Man tremors lasted about twenty seconds.

In Scotland tremors were reported from Peebles to Pitlochry and Comrie, in Perthshire, and to Frazerburgh. The disturbance was most pronounced near the Tweed.

Broken Water Main

No district of London escaped without a shaking, although the tremors were of varying degrees of intensity, being most severe in the north-east area.

Mr. Stirling Taylor, of 1, Pump-court, Temple, informed The Daily Telegraph that he was awakened by the rocking of his bed. His clock stopped at 1.25.

Half an hour after the earthquake it was discovered that a water main had burst in Great Eastern-street, Shoreditch. This fracture was unofficially attributed to the disturbance.

Explosion Feared at Sea

The intensity of the shock in East Coast towns is apparent from the following local reports:

Officers on duty at Scarborough police-station concluded that a mine had exploded off the shore.

At Driffield in the East Riding the fire brigade was called out as a precautionary measure.

Flamborough lifeboatmen, fearing that an explosion had occurred at sea, prepared for rescue work.

Several chimney stacks were brought down at Hull, and one family had a fortunate escape when heavy masonry collapsed on the roof. They concluded that the premises had been struck by lightning.

At King's Lynn the shock was so severe that it was believed that an explosion had occurred, while an engine driver feared that his locomotive would overturn.

**(June 8)**

## GREAT EXHIBITION IN PARIS

### OPENED BY PRESIDENT

**From Our Own Correspondent**

PARIS, Wednesday.

There took place this afternoon a memorable ceremony in the history of the Third Republic - the opening, by M. Gaston Doumergue, the President, of the great International Colonial Exhibition. From tomorrow it will be open to the public.

The infinite variety of the pavilions in their setting of green provided a wonderful background, and the presence of innumerable Colonial soldiers in uniforms of every design and hue made it almost impossible to believe that only a few yards away were the streets of Paris.

The President made a rapid tour of the ground before entering a spacious building which is to form a permanent Colonial Museum.

**(May 7)**

## SAFE RETURN OF TWO BALLOONISTS

News was received last evening that after being about eighteen hours in the air, and attaining a height of close on ten miles, Professor Piccard and Herr Kipfer brought their balloon down on a glacier in the Austrian Tyrol late on Wednesday night.

In a message to Madame Piccard, at Brussels, the professor says:

"We are both well. Kipfer and I. The ascent was long and difficult, but landing was made in good conditions. We reached the height we desired to attain."

The balloon, which is still lying on the glacier, and its instruments are stated to be undamaged. Patrols were sent to recover the valuable records made during this great voyage.

Professor Piccard's feat exceeds by some two miles any previous altitude reached by a balloon, and completely fulfils the plan with which he ascended from Augsburg at four a.m. on Wednesday.

King Albert has given the Professor and Herr Kipfer the Order of Leopold as acknowledgment of their achievement.

**(May 29)**

## TOSCANINI SLAPPED

### INCIDENT OVER NATIONAL ANTHEM

**From Our Own Correspondent**

Signor Toscanini's refusal to have the Italian National Anthem played during the concert which was to be given yesterday at Bologna has led to a serious incident between the conductor and some Fascists.

While Signor Toscanini was entering the theatre where the concert was to take place, he was approached and slapped on the face by a Fascist. The concert was put off and Toscanini left Bologna for Milan.

**(May 16)**

## DINNER AT THE COMMONS

Mr. Charles Chaplin dined at the House of Commons last night as the guest of Viscountess Astor, M.P., who had invited a number of other members to meet him.

**(March 14)**

## 214 HOURS FROM AUSTRALIA

### MR. MOLLISON'S GREAT FLIGHT

Two air records were set up yesterday by British pilots:

Mr. J.A. Mollison reached England from Australia in 8 days 12 hrs 25 mins, thus beating the record of Mr. C.W.A. Scott by 2 days 1h 35 min.

Miss Amy Johnson, and her mechanic, Mr. S.C. Humphreys, landed at Tokio, having completed the trans-Siberian flight from England in ten days.

Mr. Mollison, a young Scot, is a close friend of Mr. Scott, and the Gypsy Moth in which his flight was made, under the auspices of Lord Wakefield is exactly similar to that used by Mr. Scott.

"I cannot say that I enjoyed the trip," said Mr. Mollison, who had an average of only two hours' sleep a night and was so exhausted towards the end that he was unable to make any calculations at all.

His weariness was enhanced by severe eye-strain, as he lost his goggles before his journey was two-thirds done and flew thousands of miles in an open cockpit without any protection for his eyes.

This nearly led to an accident on the last lap, for he landed near Pevensey Bay, Sussex, on a beach which he took to be grassland.

**(August 7)**

## CAIRO TO CAPE BY AEROPLANE

**By Our Aviation Correspondent.**

On Saturday an Imperial Airways aeroplane with mails for various parts of Africa will leave Croydon aerodrome.

The mails will be transferred to a flying-boat at Athens.

This day week the first half of the Cape-Cairo air route will be open, and three days later the mails will have reached Mwanza, at the southern end of Lake Victoria, the terminus for the time being.

The first return journey will be begun from Mwanza on March 10. The service will be weekly.

Passengers are not at present being carried on the African route, but passengers for stations in Europe, or on the India route, or Cairo, will go by the machine which leaves Croydon on Saturday.

The present section will take the mails 2,670 miles into Africa. When the full course is complete it will be 5,750 miles in length.

Along the Cairo-Cape route twenty-seven main air stations have been provided, and in addition thirty intermediate stations are available when required. At many of the stations hotels have been built. A complete organisation has been set up.

17 WIRELESS STATIONS

There are seventeen wireless stations, and never at any point will the air liners be out of touch with the ground organisation. Both telegraphy and telephony will be employed, and by wireless direction finding a machine's exact position will be given at any moment it is needed.

The opening of the route beyond Mwanza depends on the completion of trials of the new four-engined Handley Page and the new four-engined Calcutta flying-boat, the former taking twenty-four and the latter sixteen passengers.

**(February 26)**

# BRITAIN'S GREAT SCHNEIDER TRIUMPH

## THREE NEW RECORDS SET UP: TROPHY WON OUTRIGHT

## STAINFORTH'S AMAZING 404 M.P.H.

## HIGHEST SPEED EVER ATTAINED BY MAN

**WORLD RECORD ... ... ... 386.10 m.p.h.**
**100-KILOMETRE RECORD ... ... 342.70 m.p.h.**
**COURSE RECORD ... ... ... 340.08 m.p.h.**

Such are the brilliant records set up yesterday at Calshot, when Great Britain's High Speed Flight team won the Schneider Trophy for the third time in succession, and then gave a memorable demonstration of flying speeds.

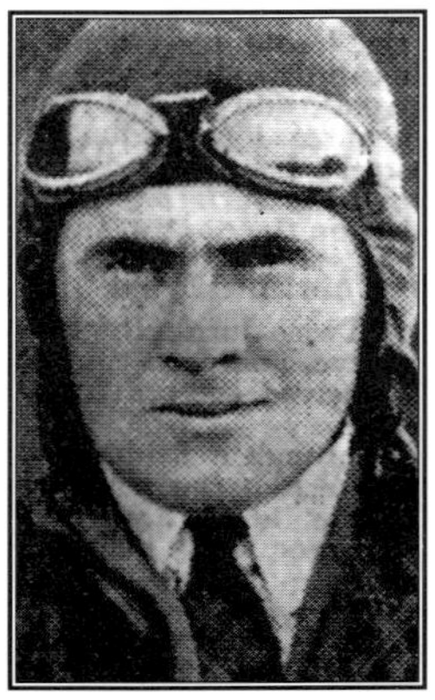

FLT.-LT. J. N. BOOTHMAN

PREVIOUS WINNERS

| | Speed per hr. |
|---|---|
| 1913- France | 45.75 |
| 1914- Gt. Britain | 86.780 |
| 1920- Italy | 107.224 |
| 1921- Italy | 117.859 |
| 1922- Gt. Britain | 145.7 |
| 1923- America | 177.38 |
| 1925- America | 232.57 |
| 1926 Italy | 246.442 |
| 1927- Gt. Britain | 281.656 |
| 1929- Gt. Britain | 328.63 |

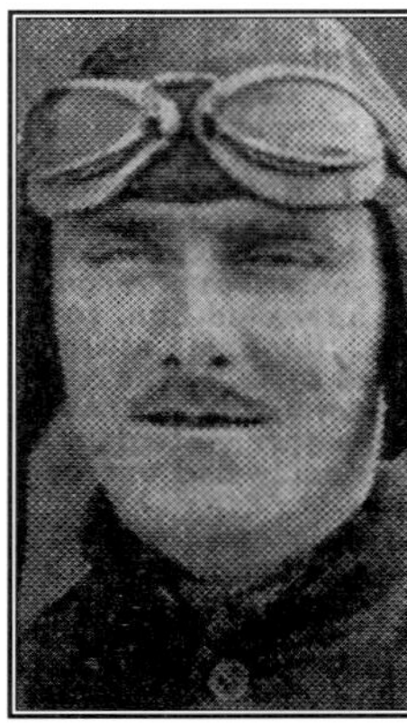

FLT.-LT. G. STAINFORTH

Yesterday's Schneider contest was the last: Britain has now won the trophy outright.

Flt.-Lt. Boothman was the winning pilot. The marvellous precision of his flight was a feature of the day. It is revealed in the following log-speed of his seven laps in miles per hour:

**343.1 342.9 341.9 341 340.6 340.5 340.08**

**A speed of over 404 miles an hour - over six and a half miles a minute - was attained at one stage by Flt.-Lt. Stainforth in setting up the new world record of 386.1 m.p.h.**

In his flight Boothman set up new course and 100 kilometres records. He and Stainforth not only added another triumphal page to the annals of British air prowess, but proved again the invincibility of British aero engines in high-speed craft.

**(September 14)**

# 6 MILES A MINUTE FOR 218 MILES

## SUPREME SCIENCE AND TECHNIQUE

**By Major C.C. Turner**

CALSHOT, Sunday.

The last Schneider Trophy contest has been held, and Great Britain has retained the trophy as a permanent possession.

This has been a great day for flying and for a demonstration of Great Britain's supremacy in the science and technique of high-speed flying.

Flt.-Lt. Stainforth, in making the world record, gave as brilliant a display of skill and mastery as I have ever seen. The speed was measured both by the electrical and the stopwatch method. Only the latter result is available at present, but it is not likely to vary by more than a mile from the other, which takes a few days to develop.

The new three-kilometre record will be surpassed when the specially-boosted engine now nearly ready at the works of the Rolls-Royce Company has been fitted into one of the two S6B seaplanes. This will be done this week and a record may be set up which would probably stand for some years.

EFFECT OF WIND

The lap times for Flt.-Lt. Stainforth's flight show that in one direction, with the wind in favour, he reached 404 miles an hour. His slowest run against the wind. was 372.8 miles an hour. In true estimates of flying speeds effect of wind, favourable or adverse, must be neutralised, hence the rules governing the record.

**AT SUCH A SPEED**

**At 404 miles an hour - Flt. Lt. Stainforth's maximum - a 'plane which started from St. Paul's Cathedral at the same moment as a man stepped off the pavement at Hyde Park Corner would pass Hyde Park Corner before the pedestrian had walked across the road.**

**At 404 miles an hour a man flying from London at noon could be at Edinburgh for lunch or New York for dinner!**

## CONGRATULATIONS!

Lady Houston, whose gift of £100,000 enabled Britain to compete in the contest, landed at Cowes last evening from her steam yacht Liberty, and at the Royal Yacht Squadron met Squadron Leader Orlebar and his colleagues of the British Schneider team.

The airmen received her congratulations and those of Lord Amulree, Minister for Air.

Lady Houston had tea with the team. Her yacht was brilliantly illuminated last night, the word "Victory" being prominently displayed amidship.

**(September 14)**

# MINISTER AT STATION IN PYJAMAS

The dignified but unconventional figure of M. Pallier, the Czechoslovak Minister to Hungary, descended this evening from an express train in Budapest central station clad only in his pyjamas. His staff, waiting to meet him were horrified, till the diplomat explained that his unorthodox attire had been forced on him by a thief who had taken his trousers through the window of the sleeping car.

The police were informed, and promptly found the trousers in a maize field beside the line. The Minister's pocket-book, which contained a considerable sum of money, was, however, missing, but various documents and keys were recovered - Reuter.

**(July 30)**

# KAYE DON BREAKS THE RECORD

## SPEED OF 110 M.P.H. IN MISS ENGLAND II.

**From Our Special Representative**
**By Telephone**

GARDONE, Thursday Night.

Mr. Kaye Don, in Miss England II., this evening on Lake Garda set up a new world's speed-boat record of 110.00 m.p.h.

He thus beat his own record of 103.49 m.p.h. (set up at Buenos Aires three months ago) by nearly 7 m.p.h.

The record was an average over a measured mile timed in both directions. The exact speeds were:

**112.06 m.p.h.**
**107.94 m.p.h.**

The triumph has come after weeks of disappointment, and after a discouraging start to-night, when, owing to the engine misfiring, the boat had to be taken back to the boathouse, and the plugs changed and other adjustments.

The surface of the lake was smooth and the light was no longer bright. Mr. Kaye Don moved off towards the north, where the grey summit of Monte Baldo was thrown into relief by the rays of the setting sun. Two miles away an occasional yellow flame from her exhaust revealed Miss England's west course along the darkening coastline.

THE FINAL DASHES

At 7.40, going at full speed, with the roar of her 4,000 horse-power engines reverberating down the lake, she tore back towards Salo, and within two minutes had disappeared into the little bay.

At 7.43 she reappeared, sending up great showers of spray. As she passed 300 yards away the launch in which I was standing trembled. Then, like a low-flying bird, she passed into the distant shadows.

A moment later a Verey light went up. She had beaten the record. At once the craft on the lake which had been hugging the shore raced to the boathouse. Friends, fellow sportsmen, photographers appeared from nowhere to crowd around Mr. Don and shake his hand.

**(July 10)**

# MORE CRASHES OF AMERICAN BANKS

**From Our Own Correspondent**

NEW YORK, Thursday.

Four small New Jersey banks, with combined deposits of more than £2,000,000, today followed yesterday's crop of failures into extinction.

Two of them were State banks, two National banks, and all were situated in Hudson County.

The rising tide of such failures throughout the United States is causing the authorities grave concern, and emphasising the need for reform of the banking laws.

The number of failures this year probably exceeds last year's record of 1,345, with liabilities of close upon £2000,000,000. In the six months ended on June 30 last 684 banks with total deposits of £91,000,000 closed their doors.

Britain, it is pointed out, has been passing through a period of post-war depression far more severe than that in the United States, and yet has been virtually free from bank failures. The simplification of State and federal banking laws and the substitution of branches of big institutions for small and weak independent banks are urged as remedies. The 24,000 banks existing here are declared to be far too many.

**(August 7)**

# BILL TO LEGALISE THE SUNDAY CINEMA

## COMMONS MAJORITY ASSURED

**By Our Parliamentary Correspondent**

The text, which was issued yesterday, of the bill to deal with the Sunday opening of places of entertainment shows that the Government, as I forecast, have decided to legislate in regard to cinemas.

Four purposes are specified for which opening on Sundays will be permitted:

Musical entertainments
Cinematograph entertainments
Exhibitions of animals or of inanimate objects
Public debates

The principle of local option is adopted.

The bill follows the practice of London County Council in allocating profits from Sunday entertainments to charitable purposes and in providing that no person shall be employed on Sundays who has worked in the place of amusement on the previous six days.

The rights of the "common informer" are abolished.

A FREE VOTE

Before proceeding with the drafting of the bill, the Government took steps to sound opinion in all three political parties. Ministers satisfied themselves that there is a substantial majority of members of the House of Commons in favour of their proposals.

That there will be opposition on the part of certain bodies has been foreseen, and there are M.P.'s who are prepared to voice it in debate.

The Government have decided that as no question of political principle is involved the matter is one that should be left to the unfettered judgment of the House.

There will be a free vote on the second reading. I understand that the same course will be pursued during the Committee and other stages of the measure.

**(April 11)**

# WOMAN MURDERER ELECTROCUTED

## THRILLING PURSUIT ACROSS U.S.

**From Our Own Correspondent.**

NEW YORK, Monday.

"Iron Irene" Schroeder, a 22-year-old bandit, paid the penalty for the murder of State Trooper Brady Paul when she was put to death in the electric chair at Bellefonte Prison, Pennsylvania, to-day. A few minutes later she was followed by Walter Glenn Dague, her lover and companion in crime.

Schroeder was the first woman to be electrocuted in the State of Pennsylvania, and every effort was exhausted by her counsel and her friends to have the sentence commuted to life imprisonment.

Both the condemned persons met death calmly. Neither required assistance in the last walk from the cells to the execution chamber.

Schroeder, whose conduct throughout the trial earned her the sobriquet "Iron Irene," maintained a smiling care-free pose to the end. Yesterday she asked for all the Sunday comic papers, which she read with apparent enjoyment, and she slept soundly until awakened at dawn this morning for the ordeal.

Dague, who was solemn and composed, declared that he was satisfied and ready. He applied himself diligently to reading the Bible.

Both the murderers had abandoned their legal mates and families in West Virginia to embark on a career of crime. Dague asserted that he was completely under the influence of the girl, who forced him into evil courses.

The man, a motor-car salesman and Sunday school teacher, had a wife and two children, while Schroeder had a husband and a 5-year-old son.

ON HER BOY'S EVIDENCE

When they fled together they engaged in a series of robberies and hold-ups. These culminated, in December, 1929, in the murder.

When two Pennsylvania troopers tried to stop their car and arrest them both the fugitives drew revolvers, opened fire, killed Paul, and severely wounded his companion. Schroeder's boy was in the car when the trooper was shot, and his evidence helped to convict her.

They then fled across the Continent in a car, pursued by the police. In Texas they were joined by a man named Wills. At one point they were fired on by the local police, while in Arizona they kidnapped a deputy sheriff and forced him to act as their guide across the desert.

Located by police, they were again fired on, and the sheriff was wounded. They callously threw him out of the car and continued their flight until they had to abandon the car on the bank of a river.

Finally they took up a defensive position behind some rocks. By this time aeroplanes had joined in the pursuit. They continued to hold off the police until the girl collapsed, whereupon they gave themselves up after a chase that had lasted for weeks.

**(February 24)**

# NEW FRIENDS OF THE MOTORIST

## ADVENT OF MOBILE POLICE

With the abolition of the speed limit of touring cars, and the imposition of a limit of 30 m.p.h. on motor-coaches, and other restrictions on the speed of commercial vehicles, which took effect yesterday, the mobile traffic control policeman becomes a very real factor in the life of the road user.

Police authorities, by the way, are particularly anxious to kill at the outset the tendency to designate these mobile patrols by the name under which they are known in the United States.

"The patrols," I was informed by a high official at Scotland Yard yesterday, "are not intended to pursue the touring motorist at high speed and inform him that he is travelling too fast."

Indeed, it is the hope of the authorities that the ordinary motorist will regard these motoring policemen as their friends.

Their duties are multitudinous, and each man has been provided with a small text book, outlining what he is expected to perform, the type of offence which he should check and the directions in which he may assist in the elimination of untoward incidents.

So far, at least, as patrols in the metropolitan district are concerned, I gather the object of the police authorities is not to obtain convictions whenever possible. The patrol who pulls up a motorist will endeavour, by pointing out in a friendly manner the nature of the offence which he has observed, to bring about a higher standard of road sense in the motoring community as a whole.

**(January 2)**

# GAITERS INSTEAD OF PUTTEES

## SUGGESTED CHANGE IN INFANTRY DRESS

**By Our Military Correspondent**

The puttee which for so many years has wrapped the British soldier's leg is now seriously threatened. It may be superseded by the gaiter.

In connection with the proposals for redesigning the infantryman's uniform and equipment that are now under consideration, a large body of military opinion seems to be inclining to a preference for some form of canvas gaiter such as the American troops wear, in place of the puttee. Several Royal Army Medical Corps authorities support this proposal. It is claimed that a suitable gaiter would be more weatherproof, and that it would be less trying for long marches.

Personally, I consider that the real fault is not with the puttee as such, but in its cut. A properly cut spiral puttee, such as officers wear, has nothing to surpass it for brightness, comfort, and weatherproofness as a calf-wear on active service. The trouble comes when a nonspiral puttee is hastily adjusted.

If a true spiral puttee was made an article of issue it would probably be better than a gaiter.

[It was reported in THE DAILY TELEGRAPH recently that the scrapping of the Army great coat in favour of an improved type of cape was contemplated.]

**(October 23)**

# £3,000,000 UNIVERSITY FOR LONDON

## BUILDING MAY BEGIN NEXT YEAR

The task of building London's great new University in Bloomsbury is to be entrusted to a single architect.

**For the past year the University authorities have been considering suitable candidates for this, one of the greatest commissions in the history of British architecture, and have viewed the work of architects throughout the country. The name of the man they have selected will probably be announced after a formal meeting of the University Court next week.**

Tentative plans, subject to the approval of the architect (who will be given a free hand) have been drawn up for developing the great site, which will extend from the British Museum to Euston-road.

**These plans include, in addition to all the necessary colleges, institutes, and schools, a University Hall to seat 2,500, a Library, a Faculty Club, chambers for the junior staff, and residential accommodation for students, the whole dominated by a huge central tower.**

**The work, which will probably begin next year, will take from twenty to thirty years to complete, and will cost between £2,000,000 and £3,000,000.**

The University, in short, will be one worthy of the capital city of the British Empire.

**(May 30)**

# WILLIAM WALTON'S "BELSHAZZAR"

## A WORK IN THE GREAT TRADITION

### THE LEEDS CHOIR

**From Our Special Representative**

LEEDS, Friday.

It is credibly reported that when William Walton's "Belshazzar's Feast" was first tried by the festival choir something like mutiny broke out in the ranks, for its difficulties appalled even singers who were not new to modern technical exigencies. With the first full rehearsal under Dr. Malcolm Sargeant came a change of heart, and as the work of preparation proceeded diffidence and suspicion gave way to appreciation and enthusiasm.

This incident is very significant, for it reveals the essential difference between the writing of Mr. Walton and that of the immense majority of modern composers. Their exorbitant demands are seldom justified by the results; Mr. Walton's demands are proportionate to the effect he secures.

#### DRAMATIC MUSIC

"Belshazzar's Feast" tells, of course, the story of the fall of Babylon and of the banquet at which the fingers of a man's hand wrote on the wall the words which spelt ruin and death. It opens with Isaiah's prophecy. "Thy sons that thou shall beget they shall be taken away," which precedes the lament, "By the Waters of Babylon." There is a barbaric hymn in praise of the God of Gold, and after the King's death the rejoicing of the Jews finds expression in a great piece of choral writing exalting the end of Jacob.

As can be gathered from this brief skeleton of the book, the telling of such a story demands a keen sense of the dramatic. Mr. Walton possesses this in a rare degree; he possesses also a more valuable skill in his ready fancy, which enables him to write music not only powerful and effective but individual. His imagination never fails him; every episode brings forth some device, some happy stroke, suggesting an inexhaustible store of resources. In the last chorus there are a few bars of less distinctive features; but, apart from this solitary instance, the choral writing, the treatment of the orchestra and the most happy declamatory episodes assigned to the soloist constitute a magnificently sustained effort of great power and marvellous ingenuity.

(October 10)

---

# SADLER'S WELLS OPERA

## "CARMEN" AS OPENING PRODUCTION

Standing room only, in pit and gallery - this was the order at Sadler's Wells Theatre last night. An historic night, moreover; for thither for the first time Miss Lilian Baylis had brought her opera company from the Old Vic to play for a fortnight and to return after a fortnight's interval.

Her plan to keep a permanent opera going in London, subsidy or no subsidy; had reached this experimental moment; and she found her audience waiting for her on the doorstep at Rosebery-avenue, as she had found them waiting in the Waterloo-road.

Carmen was the opera chosen for this opening night, and right well was it played. Lawrance Collingwood was at the conductor's desk, and kept Bizet's rhythms very much alive. It was again the turn of Enid Cruickshank (alternating with Olive Gilbert) to play the title role; Arthur Cox (alternating with Tudor Davies) to play Don José and Sumner Austin (alternating with Leslie Jones) to be the brave Toreador.

No doubt there was an extra voltage of excitement in the air, due to the important occasion. One was conscious, at any rate, of the whole company being re-vitalised, and the show was thoroughly good to see and hear. Miss Cruickshank has her Carmen well in hand; controlled yet passionate. Mr. Cox, too, does well with a part that no Englishman, I feel, can ever play perfectly, just as no Englishman can even be an authentic Toreador, well though Mr. Austin attempts it.   H.H.

(January 21)

## "POOH" WILL SING NO MORE

### MR. MILNE'S SAD DECISION

TORONTO, Tuesday.

Winnie the Pooh, Piglet, Eeyore, and a score of other characters delightfully familiar to children - and grown-ups - all over the world will have no more whimsical adventures.

This declaration by their progenitor, Mr. A.A.Milne, in an interview here, will bring regret to many firesides. The famous author said that "Christopher Robin" was now 11 years old, engrossed in games and no longer interested in the toy fancies of his childhood.

Mr. Milne added that he would not write for Hollywood producers, but he would continue to write for grown-ups.

(December 2)

---

# HOLLYWOOD'S SEX AND CRIME OBSESSION

**By G.A. Atkinson,**
**Daily Telegraph Film Critic**

NOTHING, apparently, can stop Hollywood from driving to self-destruction.

The endless procession of sex-and-crime movies has caused American cinema theatres to close down in thousands, and has caused hundreds of others to revert to variety.

Sex-and-crime movies have practically killed the picture-going habit in the States and have seriously affected box-offices in this country, despite the strength of the British film boom.

The whole world seethes with complaints about the prevalent type of talkies, and people interested in social welfare are everywhere organising to fight for cleaner films.

The effect on Hollywood of the American slump has been such that employment in the film city is at the lowest ebb in its history.

\* \* \*

Now, if ever, is the time for Hollywood producers to reform and to seek new ideas in stories and story-treatment.

*Will it be believed that they have in preparation a great flood of sex-and-crime films which, judging from advance information, are likely to be of the most outrageous type?*

I have before me the complete production schedules of two of the most important companies, and I select therefrom the following list of titles, together with extracts from the companies' own description of the proposed films:

"BAD GIRL." "The romance of a red-lipped shop-girl in a 'sleazy' dress, aching with suppressed emotions."

"THE YELLOW TICKET." "Story of a modest girl caught in the avid clutch of ignoble nobles."

"SOB SISTER." "The 'X-ray' of front page emotions and intoxicating newspaper life."

"WHILE PARIS SLEEPS." "Lovers, wastrels, and wantons are awake."

"WICKED." "Primal woman at grips with law, love, and decency."

"A TICKET TO HELL." "From stolen kisses in tenement hallways to frozen embraces in night clubs."

"LIPSTICK." "Mirror of the modern maid. A burst of flame, then crushing shame."

All the foregoing are taken from one company's list, in which the following titles also appear: "Champagne," "Sugar Daddies," "Devil's Daughter," "Honeymoon," and "Some Girls are Dangerous."

"IN HER ARMS." "Oriental pride yields to Parisian kisses."

"SURRENDER" "When pulses pound can war time hate be forgotten."

### A FILM OF HOLLYWOOD

FROM the second company's list I cull the following:

"ARE THESE OUR CHILDREN?" "Crushing indictment of the forces of evil which have betrayed our children."

"MIRACLE CITY." "The glamour, ecstasy, and heroism of Hollywood hiding its own heartbreak to inspire the world with glorious illusion."

"THE SPHINX HAS SPOKEN." "The story of a passionate adventuress who flamed across a continent."

"GLAMOUR" "The multitude in mad scramble for God-knows-what to toss at the feet of gilded woman."

"THE WOMAN BETWEEN." "Smacking with the lure of the modiste shop."

The effrontery of offering these sinister programmes to British cinema owners at a time when public opinion in this country is so much alarmed by the nature of films shown to young people, is beyond comment, though I may add that the Hays organisation, which is supposed to control American film-production, pays a Mrs. Alice Winter £1,500 a year to live in Hollywood and "protect the woman's point of view."

Mr. J.A.R. Cairns, the well-known Metropolitan magistrate, in discussing sex-and-crime movies, recently remarked: "People who are sending this stuff across the world are fouling civilisation. Our criminal courts and hospitals are left to clear up the litter, while money-bugs clear off with the money bags."

(July 13)

---

# "HENRY V" AT THE OLD VIC

## A FINE PRODUCTION

Whatever incidental weakness may sometimes be discoverable, one can always depend on tracing in a Shakespeare production at the Old Vic those qualities of "youthfulness and endeavour" which the producer, Harcourt Williams, named in a post curtain speech last night as qualities to be desired.

One may be sure, too, of finding (now that Mr. Williams has recovered from his brief lapse of grievously exceeding the elocutionary speed-limit) a worthy and thoughtful treatment of noble words. Last night's "Henry V" was finely and picturesquely done.

I would not call Ralph Richardson, admirable actor as he can be, an ideal Harry of England. A touch too much of modernism about him, perhaps, even when he assumed the part of Mars; there were times, too, when he seemed a little over-whelmed by the flood of his words. But he showed a certain sturdy dignity and power, and in some of the speeches, particularly "Upon the Kings . . ." the real note of fire.

In the dual roles of the Archbishop of Canterbury and the Dauphin, Richard Riddle added to his growing laurels for sensitive acting and beauty of diction; Robert Harris, also, for his splendidly balanced utterance as Chorus, won the well-deserved plaudits of the house.

(December 1)

## BRITISH PAINTERS IN "ABSTRACT"STYLE

**By R.R. Tatlock**

Yesterday there was opened privately an exhibition of modernist painting at the gallery of Messrs. Arthur Tooth and Sons, 155 New Bond-street.

The collection of pictures is inclined distinctly towards illustrating abstract art – that is to say, the contributions by some ten artists show us what our present-day painters have to say about form and colour as such, with little or no reference to Nature.

This movement in art, of which Cubism is the main feature, is not really typical of the English school. Its origin was French. But some of our English painters of the post-war period have undoubtedly helped towards the rationalisation (to use a modern expression) of abstract art.

One, at least, of the artists included in the catalogue, Paul Nash, has a sense of natural beauty, though his present excursions into Cubism may not appear at a first glance to support that view. Edward Burra's "Coffee" reveals imagination without constructive effectiveness.

The impression left upon the visitor is of a number of talented painters who are attempting to perpetuate a form of expression which has already become a thing of the past.

(October 2)

---

# NEW NOVEL

## RUMOUR AT NIGHTFALL

By Graham Greene. (Heinemann 7s 6d.)
**Reviewed by Howard Marshall**

THERE are writers who invest the lightest words of their characters with an oppressive significance.

They mention loyalty, let us say, and we are conscious of the sacrifices and denials which have changed history; they speak of love, and we recognise a dark passion whose sanctions lie hidden in some primeval stirring of the blood. For them each individual man walks alone among shadows; there is no escape from loneliness, no human contact possible.

Such a writer was Joseph Conrad, and such a writer is Graham Greene, whose second novel, 'RUMOUR AT NIGHTFALL," has just been published.

I would not suggest that in Mr. Greene we have yet a novelist of Conrad's calibre, though there are signs that as his work matures we may have to judge him by the same standards. At present I think his preoccupation with spiritual values and permutations leads him into unnecessary obscurity - there are times, indeed, when "Rumour at Nightfall" becomes a little irritating, so difficult is it to follow the relationships of the three chief characters. Conrad kept the current of his story running strongly, however much he emphasised the mental reactions of his protagonists, whereas Mr. Greene is apt to leave the stream for sometimes stagnant backwaters.

### REALLY ORIGINAL

For all that, "Rumour at Nightfall" is an unusual and interesting novel. The setting is Spain, and we see a journalist attempting to find Caveda, a Carlist rebel who is conducting a brilliant campaign of guerilla warfare from the mountains surrounding San Juan. Chase, the journalist, tracks down Caveda's mistress, and against his reason falls in love with her himself. So does his friend Crane, and these three are entangled in a strange emotional tragedy, with the menacing shadow of Caveda always upon them.

Mr. Greene succeeds in conveying the reality and even the importance of this tragedy, despite the atmosphere of suspense and terror which spreads through the besieged town. That alone is an achievement, and I repeat that this is an unusual novel, difficult, perhaps, but original as few novels are to-day.

(November 10)

## NOVELISTS' WAR OF WORDS

NEW YORK, Wednesday.

Mr. Sinclair Lewis crossed swords with Mr. J.B. Priestley when he landed in New York to-day from Europe.

The winner of the Nobel Prize for Literature bristled when told that Mr. Priestley had declared that Mr. Lewis was becoming a propagandist and a writer of "thesis novels" and of novels based on Press clippings. The crowning blow was a reporter's information that the English writer had described Mr. Lewis as a "has been."

(March 5)

---

# NEW TRIUMPH FOR MR. CHAPLIN

## A SHEER MASTERPIECE

**By G.A. Atkinson,**
**The Daily Telegraph Film Critic.**

Mr. Charles Chaplin bowed to a semi-delirious audience from the stage of the Dominion Theatre last evening, and said in a pleasant, easy, cultivated voice: "On an occasion like this the less said the more eloquent. It would be silly to try and tell you what I feel. I am like the young man making his maiden speech who said: "I would like to express my heartmost felt." Everyone in the United Kingdom has been simply marvellous. Some day I may try and put it all in a book.

Those were the first words spoken by Mr. Chaplin to his public. Earlier in the evening he had been brought into the theatre, at the suggestion of the police, two hours before the performance began, in order to obviate a riot round Tottenham court-road, but the rain chilled the enthusiasm of thousands who would otherwise have swarmed to see him enter the theatre.

"City Lights" has been swept into London on a tidal wave of publicity without parallel in the history of the cinema industry, but film critics are hard-boiled and are rarely affected by the occasion.

The film does not altogether justify the fuss made about it. It lacks a firm background and it lacks a strong idea. It is not so good that one wants to see it again, or at least not immediately.

The slight story of a tramp's platonic love for a blind flower-girl has to be carried over many precariously thin patches. On the other hand, it is a sheer masterpiece of comedy opportunism. There is a flash of the genius of fun or of pathos, or both, in every scene; from the opening one, which reveals Charlie sleeping in the arms of a statue that has just been unveiled, to the conclusion, which shows the girl, with her sight restored, struggling to realise that her benefactor is not a handsome young millionaire, but the shabbiest of scarecrows.

There is plenty of "sure-fire stuff" for popular audiences, especially in a boxing match in which Charlie uses the referee as a foil; in a night club scene, in which every possible misadventure happens to him, and in an extraordinarily funny episode in which he swallows a toy whistle, with the result that every intake of breath attracts dogs and taxi-cabs.

The comedian is magnificently abetted by Harry Myers, the famous "Yankee at the Court of King Arthur." Mr. Myers fills the role of a suicidal millionaire, who, when he is drunk, promises Charlie the earth, but, when sober, cannot for the life of him recollect who the little fellow is. This is the best idea in the film, and the pair make excellent use of it.

(February 28)

## "CAVALCADE" AT DRURY LANE

### MR. COWARD'S TRACT FOR THE TIMES

Excitement was in the air at Drury Lane last night. The production of Noel Coward's big spectacular play "Cavalcade" had roused high hopes. Pit and gallery were on tip-toe, and cheered the celebrities and half-celebrities in the stalls with impartial enthusiasm.

And when Mr. Coward entered his box they gave him a tremendous ovation. What a horrible anticlimax it would be, one thought, if they did not show equal enthusiasm at the end.

But all was well. After the final curtain they called him before the curtain and cheered him again and again. And certainly, "Cavalcade" should hit the modern taste for big plays and a grandiose style of production. It has twenty-two scenes, many of them conceived on a magnificent scale and carried out with the utmost lavishness. And it is acted by a company so enormous that Mr. Ramsay MacDonald's announcement of a drop in the unemployment figures seems amply accounted for.

#### THE BACKGROUND

Mr. Coward has set out to give us a pageant of English history for the past thirty-two years. And with that as background, he shows us the shifting fortunes of the Marryot family and the Bridges family - respectively employers and servants. But, as happens too often with productions of this size, the background dwarfs the figures of its protagonists till they seem puny and insignificant.

The success of this play most depends on its quality as spectacle, for dramatically it is a disappointment. The departure of the C.I.V. for South Africa, the announcement in a theatre of the relief of Mafeking, the mourners in the Park after Queen Victoria's death, the symbolic war scenes, the nerve-racking finale, with its acid comment on the insanity of modern life and its appeal to dignity and patriotism - these are the things we shall remember in "Cavalcade."

Mr. Coward, in his curtain-speech last night, paid a very gallant compliment to Mary Clare, saying that she had proved that the English stage could still give us great acting.   W.A.D.

(October 14)

---

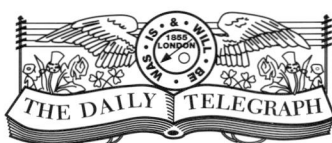

THE DAILY TELEGRAPH

OVER 250,000 DAILY

135, Fleet street., London, E. C. 4
Telephone: CENTRAL 4242

**TO-DAY'S WEATHER FORECAST**

LONDON & S.E. ENGLAND - Light N. E. wind; fair; moderate temperature.

ENGLISH CHANNEL - Light N. E. wind; fine; slight sea.

Lighting-up time. 5.13 p.m.
Sun rises 6.45 a.m. : sets 4.43 p.m.
Moon rises 4.48 a.m. : sets 9.3 a.m.to-morrow.
Last quarter on tuesday.
High water at London Bridge. 2.4 a.m.

# NO JUSTIFICATION FOR ALARM

### A Speedy Return to the Gold Standard Assured

TO-DAY the Government will ask Parliament to pass a short measure suspending the operation of the principal section of the Gold Standard Act of 1925. It will be passed by both Houses and receive the Royal Assent within a few hours. That means that Great Britain will go off the Gold Standard from today, and it is a moral certainty that she will not go off alone. This is precisely what the National Government was formed to avoid, for going off the Gold Standard means depreciation of the pound sterling. Events however, have been too strong and too hard for them, but by way of consolation we would emphasise the fact that this act of submission to the external forces and influences which rendered this decision inevitable has a very different bearing to-day from what it would have had if the Budget had still remained unbalanced. The Budget is balanced and the Budget will remain balanced. Half or more than half the sting of this enforced submission is removed now that the consequences can be faced by the British Government with fortitude and composure.

**Fundamentally Sound**

There is no need to fear a flight from the pound on the parallel of the flight from the mark or the franc. British currency is not inflated. The financial condition of the country is fundamentally sound. Nothing therefore, in the shape of a currency slide need be anticipated, though some depreciation must be expected. But it can be reduced to a minimum if the British people will keep their heads as, by their official declaration, the Prime Minister and his colleagues are resolved to keep theirs. Coolness is all. It is an opportunity for Englishmen to show that they have not lost their phlegm.

**Abnormal World Position**

We would not seem to minimise the grave importance of a step which is a blow to our national pride without precedent - in times of peace within living memory.

On Saturday, in half a day, a further ten millions were withdrawn. What would have happened to-day? What to-morrow and the day after? No artificial protection avails against an avalanche gathering new momentum in its fall.

Even if large further credits had been placed at the disposal of the British Government by friendly foreign Governments they would have been exhausted, and the position would have worsened steadily. So Great Britain goes off the Gold Standard for a time, certain that she will return when the world has become more normal. For whatever financial mistakes British Governments may have made since 1918, the present National Government are committed to the strait, narrow, and arduous path of financial rectitude, and they will brace themselves to meet and overcome whatever painful consequences may issue from the temporary depreciation of the pound.

**A Test of Citizenship**

Great Britain may have been driven to lower the proud flag of the Gold Standard, but those who have consciously helped to bring it about will be the first to regret it. Those who have taken so fractious and partisan an attitude towards the National Government may now be warned to put a greater curb upon their tongues lest worse befall. And while the people of Great Britain keep calm we hope the Government will take steps to get together with the Governments of the other Great Powers to consider what the Macmillan Committee aptly described as "The Restoration of International Trade."

In the meantime, here is an opportunity for every good citizen to refrain from carping criticism as well as from anti-social action, and so keep the depreciation of the pound within the narrowest possible limits. Foreign opinion, after the first shock, will take its colour and tone from British opinion, and that, if we know our countrymen aright, will be steady and calm, because assured of an early and speedy recovery.

**(September 21)**

# MR. SHAW'S SOCIALIST PARADISE

MR. BERNARD SHAW can give MR. KIPLING'S "Pagett, M.P." many points and a beating. His recent visit to Russia, much more fleeting than his Radical rival's to India in prewar times, occupied, all told, eleven days, during which he probably imparted more than he acquired and taught more than he learnt. As soon as he set foot in this country on his return, he said that if we wish to get over our difficulties it will only be by following the example of Russia, and yesterday, at the I.L.P. Summer School, he supplied the morning's entertainment by what we can only describe as an indecent and impudent Harlequinade. For no one knows better than Mr. SHAW that if he settled in the Socialist Paradise he so hastily left, and allowed himself a fraction of his usual licence in insulting the institutions of the country where he lives, not even his nimble wits would save him from a Soviet prison or the attentions of the Ogpu, whose gentle disciplinary methods he somehow omitted from his catalogue of Soviet attractions.

M. STALIN, his new conception of a Shavian Superman, would have no use for MR. SHAW'S critical sparklets, and he would promptly "disappear" like a swatted fly.

He may reply, perhaps, that that is because "we are all imbeciles" and that he has never had the luck to live under the rule of really good men. "The people at the heart of affairs in Russia," he said, "are not only in an enormously superior moral position, but they are nearly all intellectually superior." In fact, he found them almost worthy to talk with their august visitor on equal terms. Yet, if we remember right, even the pitiless heart of LENIN himself was almost moved to pity for Russia when he contemplated the possibility of STALIN'S succession. And under STALIN the Russian worker has lost all the ordinary human rights.

What MR. SHAW ecstatically calls the realised Socialist state is a narrow oligarchy, supported by a very small minority of the total population, who alone have any political rights, and propped by the bayonets of an immense army. Mr. SHAW left the Summer Meeting to idealise the smiling Russian peasantry enjoying the kindly fruits of the earth and their own collectivised labour, when the truth is that their harvest lies at the disposal of a Central Government harder in its exactions than any PHARAOH. The whole address was an impudent travesty of what he had left unseen and unlooked for. If we can only be saved from collapse by following the Russian lead, will Mr. SHAW say what amount of massacre he thinks would be necessary in this "imbecile" country, how long the trampling of the capitalist classes in "heavy civil war" - LENIN'S pet phrase would continue, and how he would persuade the Trades Union Congress - if it survived - under the new régime to sacrifice its standards of living and all the rights of free speech and citizenship, and all its antiherding housing regulations and submit tamely to the conscription of labour? But, perhaps, these are not fair questions to address to Harlequin after he has done his clowning and got his laugh.

**(August 6)**

# THE DUTY OF EVERY ELECTOR

EVERY elector, man and woman, knows his or her duty to-day. It is to vote. The earlier the better, so as to reduce the chance of some unexpected but imperative summons, of engagements crowding in, or the accident that may detain or prevent. If your constituency is considered a safe seat for the National candidate, make it safer! If he is fighting a forlorn hope, rally to his side! If the issue is doubtful, be among the first at the poll to start the tide swinging the right way. However small your influence, use it with tact and good humour, but in real earnest. Your word in season may be just what was wanted to convert the almost persuaded. Lend your car cheerfully, and show your good will to the cause. At the last Election the majorities ranged from single figures to tens of thousands. Your vote may be the one to decide. And always remember that the whole world is waiting for the verdict.

If the Socialists were to win the judgment of the world would be that Great Britain had decreed its own downfall by its own vote. Britain's friends would grieve, her enemies would exult.

**(October 27)**

# JACK DIAMOND

THE news of the killing of JACK DIAMOND takes a great place in the story of the day. DIAMOND had become one of the most notorious of America's "gangsters" and "racketeers," though it is said he did not rank with the wealthiest and most powerful of them.

In the great cities of America adventurous and vicious youth finds conditions which make it possible to enjoy great wealth through an exciting career of crime. No other civilised country allows such rewards to the criminal as CAPONE and DIAMOND and their like have obtained with the regularity of an income from investments.

The power of the gangster to corrupt has undoubtedly been much increased by Prohibition, which has provided enormous profits for the purveyor of drink, and enabled him to command an elaborate organisation. But it would be an exaggeration to make Prohibition responsible for all the wealth and the strength of the gangster.

DIAMOND did not limit his activities to purveying alcohol. He is charged also with dealing in drugs on a large scale. The gangs are in fact a powerful conspiracy to array the instincts of evil against a decent social order.

**(December 19)**

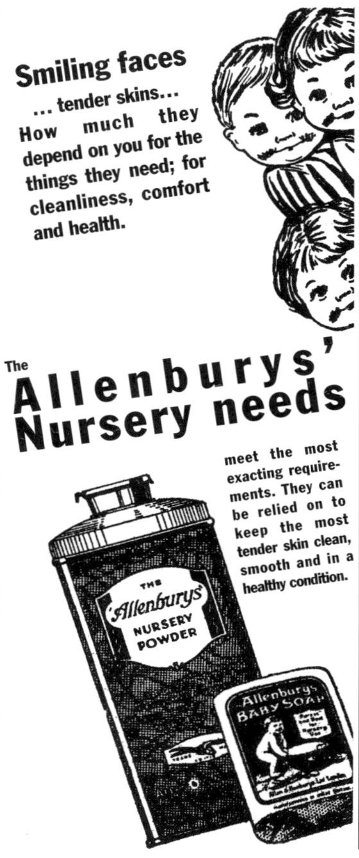
Smiling faces
... tender skins...
How much they depend on you for the things they need; for cleanliness, comfort and health.
The Allenburys' Nursery needs
meet the most exacting requirements. They can be relied on to keep the most tender skin clean, smooth and in a healthy condition.
THE Allenburys NURSERY POWDER
Allenburys BABY SOAP

# AIRCRAFT AND CRIME

## HOW TO IDENTIFY A 'PLANE

**By Major C.C. Turner**
**Daily Telegraph Aviation Correspondent.**

*The aeroplane is being used in crime and in illicit traffic. Swift and certain identification will help to hamper the air criminal. It is high time to issue to all concerned a handy book of aids to recognition, such as the Admiralty issued to air defence units during the war.*

*A few up-to-date examples are here given. In cases of doubt such guides would help to restrict the field of inquiry.*

ONE day last summer an up-river club resort was the scene of a mysterious robbery, supposed to have been committed by the pilot of an aeroplane. The club possessed a fruit machine (a slot gambling con-

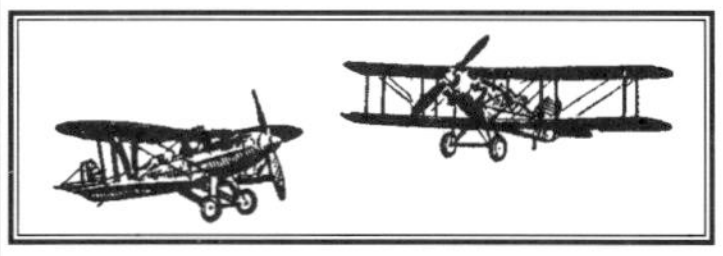

trivance) which contained nearly £20 at the time. The fruit machine stood more than two feet in height and weighed about 100lb.

On the day in question an aeroplane landed in an adjoining field often used by airmen. There were very few members and visitors present, and certainly no one noticed any suspicious occurrence. But eventually the fruit machine was missed, and almost immediately someone remarked that the aeroplane had left the field. Inquiries failed to discover anyone who had noted the identification letters on the aeroplane.

Every mechanical invention is sooner or later used by the criminal. The motor-car gives speed to the ill-doer as well as to the law-abiding, and it taxes the resources of the police. Now it is the turn of the aeroplane, which will tax the resources of the police more severely.

**A Big Bribe**

The aeroplane is being used for smuggling of small-bulk goods on which heavy duties are levied, and also drugs. In a small way it is used for those purposes throughout Europe. In the United States it is an ally of

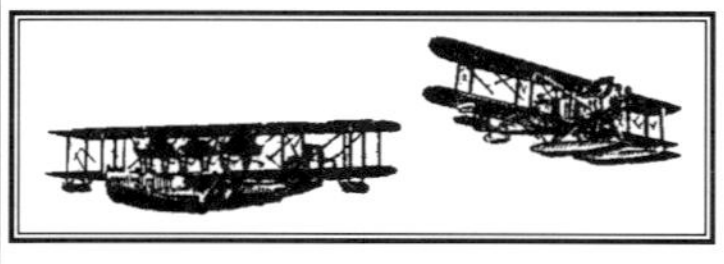

the boot-legger. Perhaps the imposition of duties on more articles coming to England will stimulate the use of aircraft.

At Customs air ports incoming travellers are closely examined, and several cases of attempted smuggling have been discovered. But the real danger lies far away from any Customs port.

There are long stretches of desolate coast and great areas of open moor where it is easy to land forbidden goods. An aeroplane crossing the coast at some other point than the regular air route near the Straits of Dover seldom arouses suspicion, and even if a doubt be felt by a look-out or a policeman, the aeroplane is out of sight in a few minutes, possibly bound for some remote destination.

**Car Confederates**

In the unlikely event of its identification letters being read and noted, and its landing subsequently being observed, the occupants have plenty of time to remove contraband before a policeman (to whom they will explain, "We lost our way") arrives on the scene.

Still more difficult to deal with is the aeroplane from which contraband is dropped by small parachutes at a spot prearranged with confederates in a fast car. The parachute may be dropped from a low altitude, so that the operation would not be observed. It can even take place at night.

The temptation is real. Dick Grace, the famous American pilot, states that at Los Angeles he was approached by men who offered him $75,000 for three nights drug-smuggling by air!

The duties levied by Great Britain on cigars, playing cards, saccharine, clocks, and watches are heavy in relation to weight, whilst the importation of certain drugs, except by authorised persons is absolutely prohibited; and unquestionably there is a market for illicit drugs in this country. The authorities are often mystified as to the manner in which such drugs in considerable quantities are imported. May not the aeroplane be the explanation?

**Air Police**

European countries have established "corridors" of air travel on their frontiers, but only a costly and thorough system of observation and air patrols could prevent aircraft passing unobserved at many places along the extensive frontiers.

An aeroplane-mounted police, seriously undertaken in America, and proposed in France, is not likely to be able to deal with the situation which will certainly arise now that the number of private aeroplanes is steadily increasing. There must be some system of observation, identification, and reporting, and the police throughout the country will have yet another duty added to their burden.

But the identification letters on aircraft are sometimes difficult to read at a great height, and the police must therefore be trained to observe typal distinctions. This is difficult sometimes even to the experienced, and too much must not be expected from the ordinary police. At the same time it should be remembered that, failing certain identification a slight indication of some typal feature will often narrow down inquiry within limits.

**Work for Air-Boy Scouts**

During the war the Air Department at the Admiralty issued throughout the service, especially with regard to defence against air attack, a little book with silhouettes of the leading British, French and German aircraft. Such a book, containing only a few leading types, might enable even an inexperienced observer to identify a type. On occasion the mere distinction between monoplane and biplane might narrow down an inquiry. But with experience and practice the police, the Boy Scouts, and others would often be able to assist in tracking down a suspicious craft.

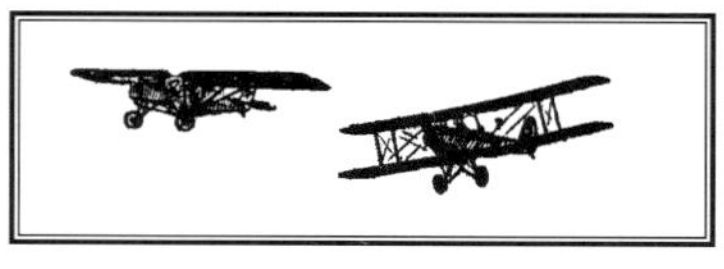

And apart from crime, there is the frequent breaking of air navigation rules, the dangerous flying, the low flying over towns, and so on, which are punishable by heavy fines. More often than not the offender escapes through failure to identify the machine and it is high time such escape should be made impossible.

**(December 1)**

# LONDON DAY BY DAY:

IN a few days the London-Paris air lines will be changing over to their more extended summer services, and with the improvement in weather conditions which it is reasonable to anticipate the steady backward and forward flow of visitors between the two capitals will, I have no doubt, show a responding increase.

Yesterday, returning from a twenty-four-hours' trip to Paris, I noticed that the French Air Union had found it necessary to duplicate their midday service, while the giant Imperial Airways machine had already left for London with its full complement.

**From the South**

WHILE I was waiting in the glorious hot sunshine at Le Bourget for the appointed hour of departure, a business-like-looking single-engined blue "liner" landed, just arrived from Marseilles.

An Englishman who was among its passengers came on to London with us. He had left Marseilles at nine a.m., and he was in London by five p.m., which, if one comes to think of it, is no more than a trifle in excess of the time occupied in travelling from Paris to London by rail and steamer.

**Catering for Women**

WOMEN appear likely to take kindly to the new policy initiated yesterday at a famous restaurant in the Haymarket by Lady Malcolm, who has recently become one of its directors.

Lady Malcolm believes that there is a demand among women for some place in the West-end where they can lunch together for about half the price usually charged at the big hotels - there the inclusive price for luncheon is seldom less than 8s - and where the cost of cocktails and other drinks is kept proportionately low.

She had also, I noticed, imported a more homely air to the place by adopting self-coloured table linen and wooden bread bowls, while giving her clients the choice of a French or an English type of cooking.

**Weather Freaks**

MY companion at luncheon yesterday has just arrived from Ireland. He reported that he had travelled in brilliant sunshine throughout the journey until within a few miles of London.

The statement seemed almost incredible, after groping one's way on an errand to the north of London and back through one of the thickest of white fogs.

Half an hour later I was hailed by Mr Gerald Portman, who will one day inherit much of the wealth derived from the Portman estate. He informed me that he had been among the unfortunates who had skidded and come to grief on the ice-bound stretch of a near-London arterial road.

**Amateur Status**

VERY many games-loving listeners will read with regret the decision of the Amateur Athletic Association that broadcasting on athletics for payment will in future involve loss of amateur status.

The argument is, of course, unanswerable. If writing and lecturing are banned broadcasting most certainly must be placed in the same category. Yet many an enthusiastic amateur has been able materially to improve his own games by reading or listening to the hints given by the proven masters, and the majority of them would prefer to take their advice from a fellow amateur to getting it from a professional.

**Chimpanzees at Play**

ZOO visitors who enjoy the chimpanzees' tea party will be interested to hear that this entertainment is now preceded by a "curtain raiser" - the chimpanzees' playtime.

At five every reasonably fine afternoon two diminutive chimpanzees, Ivy and Phoebe, are carried out on to the Fellows' lawn. There they are allowed to romp together for half an hour. Anyone may pet them, for both are docile and affectionate, and although Phoebe has a marked preference for the ladies, Ivy is impartial. She is called "Ivy" because of her clinging habits!

The chimpanzees' playtime serves a double purpose. It is good for them to run about in the fresh air, and it is also an excellent way of training them to face an audience, in readiness for the day when they join the "grown ups" at tea.

**PETERBOROUGH**

**The Popularity of Air Travel**
**Food for Women**

# WANTED, A NEW FORM OF ENTERTAINING

## EVE OF SEASON PROBLEM - DINNER PARTIES TOO COSTLY - COCKTAIL CRAZE OVER

**By Marianne Mayfayre**

THE HOSTESSES who aspire to make a name for themselves in the world of entertaining will have the opportunity of their lives during the London Season that is to begin in a few weeks' time.

Everybody is searching for a new method of entertaining. The dinner party is too costly, the cocktail party is as dead as the traditional dodo. The luncheon party is unpopular with busy modern people. There is such a dearth of ideas that hostesses have even been driven for the time being to resort to the ways of their mothers and grandmothers and give bridge and bezique parties. The world of bright young people, however, is not likely to be won by that.

### A Problem Of To-day

ON the eve of the greatest months of entertaining of the year, the social world is wondering what plans to make.

Thousands of pounds are involved in the social functions that Mayfair will organise during the next three months, and experts in the catering trade are joining hostesses in the search for a successor to the cocktail party which will be as modern in character and as inexpensive, and take place either just before or just after dinner - the only free times modern people have.

### Obsolete?

ONE thing is certain; the hostesses who want to be in the van of fashion will have nothing to do with the cocktail party this year.

The cocktail bars which have been filled up at such great expense in so many homes, and for which it was the vogue a short time ago to dress up as Cockneys or Apaches, will have to be adapted to another use.

"Cocktail parties have had their day; they are dying out," an expert who organises a great many of Mayfair's parties assured me.

### Too Expensive

THIS same authority also told me why the dinner party had lost its place in entertaining. "It is too expensive a proposition," he said. "The cocktail party only costs 4s or 5s a head, and hostesses can entertain forty or fifty people for a total cost of £10 or less. The lowest estimate for a dinner party is 15s a head, and that means not many wines. If you are going to give three or four wines the cost comes to over £1 a head.

### The Tea Cabaret

AMONG the experiments that hosts and hostesses are making is the sherry party.

I am told that the tea cabaret may prove to be the solution. This fulfils the modern condition of taking place in the late afternoon, while the cabaret appeals to modern taste. One good turn is favoured by many hostesses rather than a variety of indifferent ones.

The other possibility is the after-dinner party, a custom popular with people staying at hotels which is extending to private houses. A few friends are brought together, in this way for coffee and cognac or port.

**(April 10)**

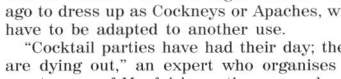

# FASHION CALLS FOR SHORTER SKIRTS FOR DAY TIME AND EVENING

**By Our Paris Fashion Expert**

AN incoming season and its pleasant changes approaches, but we are concerned for the moment with one important step - the dance step - and with visions of a shortened dance frock.

The game of prophecy is an intriguing one. If the waistline becomes easier - and it has - belts will rest on hips, even although this is but a fall of half an inch. If bodices continue to be draped - and there is evidence that summery fabrics will lend themselves to a continuance of this gracious mode - boleros and little capes will disappear. Possibly the pointed, curved and longer capes will remain, and will take over some of the bodice draperies and folds.

There is a decided move to shorten dresses, and there is every likelihood that the more stately evening dress, cut accurately to the floor, will disappear with the winter straight-pile velvets.

Lánvin has shown the shortened dance dress. Jane Régny has slit and slashed the skirts of her newer models and comes out in favour of shortened skirts and uneven hems and edges for the summer, at any rate.

We have been talking of the instep length, but now the ankle is revealed by Patou in a new skirt with V opening pointing upwards at the centre front, although this graceful gown floats backwards to a sweeping train.

Madelaine has made a dress of attractive proportions, long at the back and shortened across the front. And Mme Jenny, who is ever ready to uphold the youthful, medium measurements in the fall of skirts, says, once again, that it has taken forty years to make women young, and that therefore it is highly unlikely that she, at any rate would countenance an established full-length skirt which would consign them again to an old age. Mme Jenny has never willingly shown models for young women of dragging skirts. And all this is evidence of the shortening of the summer dance frock to instep and even to ankle length.

It is quite true that the morning and all-day dresses have been shortened to the extent of an inch. Practical women are preserving a natural line. Many elaborations still are to be found, and although fashions may be said to be evasive and complicated, it is more nearly the truth to say that they are becoming more and more individual.

The waistline, as I have said is easier. Fittings are less tight, even in models of the princess line. We are, almost certainly, entering a spring season in which the day length will be uniform, reaching a very little above the middle of the calf.

This eliminates from the summer scene the long street dress for afternoon, and settles the evening and early evening length uniformly - that is, the cocktail or bridge dress, at one with the summer dance frock, and both barely touching the instep or uneven in line and length with ankle height in favour.

Sleeves and necklines are important items. At the moment the sleeve "bells" in line with skirts that bell - the long tight sleeve promises convenience as an adjunct to the summer cocktail dress. Engagements overlap so constantly that we may expect to encounter many a long sleeved dress at the informal summer dances, following the late afternoon functions at which dressing is quite as distinguished.

**The New Scale**

Morning and "All-Day" Dresses: Shorter by one inch.

Day-time lengths generally: A little above middle of calf.

Cocktail and Bridge Frocks: Ankle length.

Dance Frocks: Barely touching instep.

**(January 2)**

# Two-In-One Rooms Make For Economy With A Modernist Air:

**By Audrey Wrangham**

EVERYONE to-day wants a house with amusing modern decorations and plenty of colour, but not everyone can afford to spend great sums on paint schemes and elaborate glass and marble panels.

Lady Cynthia Tothill, sister of Lord Bandon, has managed to make her little house in Connaught-street quite up to the minute on a small outlay with the help of the Marchese Malacrida, who has decorated some of London's most novel houses.

Perfectly plain white drawing-paper in sheets has been pasted over the walls of the dining-room, and on this has been painted a whole tribe of small green baboons, very long-tailed, climbing up and down black trees with silver-paper leaves that have been appliqué.

The curtains are casement cloth, in a deep shade of Royal purple, and the lampshades are carried out in the same scheme.

In a very few moments Lady Cynthia can turn her dining-room into a spare bedroom, for behind a screen are a wardrobe and a wash handstand, and a divan covered in a French linen with a design of green fountains upon a white ground becomes a perfectly good bed.

This system of making each room in a small house do double duty has been further carried out in Lady Cynthia's bed-room, which is also a sitting-room, and in her bath-room, which is also a dressing-room and wardrobe for all her clothes.

### GREEN BAMBOO

THE bed-sitting room has walls of the exact shade of the underpart of a mushroom, and Lady Cynthia's bed during the day-time has a sea-green moire cover and lots of cushions in buff, pink and green, while other features of the sitting-room are another big sofa covered in buff-coloured material and tall standard lamps whose shades imitate embroidery on vellum. The design is an Elizabethan one from Hampton Court.

In this case the library has been arranged all round the bed, which is in an alcove, so that the lucky owner is completely surrounded by bookshelves. Just behind is her bath-room, which is most inexpensively yet attractively done with a green rubber floor, yellow chintz curtains, and shelves with strips of glass laid over pieces of the same chintz. In big cupboards here are kept all the clothes and dressing-table accessories.

Only Bets'ann, Lady Cynthia's small daughter, whose name to the uninitiated is Elizabeth Ann, has two whole rooms for her own use, a night and day nursery, and is precisely what is best for a child, as it is light, and has no awkward corners.

The chief decorations of this room are Bets'ann's toys, which lie on shelves all round the room, so that their small owner can have them in view all the time, instead of having to shut them up in a dark cupboard.

**(January 13)**



# WHITE LINES FOR THE KERB-SHY

## TROUBLES OF HOLIDAY DRIVING

**By A.G. Throssell, Daily Telegraph Motoring Correspondent.**

A bout of motoring among holiday-makers in town and country strengthens my conviction that the most common offender against the letter and spirit of the Highway Code is the driver, who will not keep well in to his near side when others are overtaking or passing him.

Hugging the crown is only half the trouble - the worst half, no doubt, because it inflames tempers and incites even the cautious to take risks. But in a tour through the south-west I met with fewer instances of this form of selfishness than in the past. I think even the die-hards, the dangerous loiterers who like a "steady twenty-five," have realised at last that they are bound in common decency, if not in law, to give way to those who want to go faster.

What is so prevalent nowadays is the reluctance or failure to give way thoroughly and properly. Drivers of slow vehicles who travel along keeping a good five or six feet between their near wheels and the road edge and drivers who will not pull in more to their left to share the available road width equably with an oncoming vehicle - if I saw one specimen of these I saw hundreds.

### Low Average of Skill

Very often, the spirit is willing but the skill is weak. It is pitiful how many people who consider themselves capable motorists never know exactly where their near side wheels are, and cannot drive with confidence close to the kerb. From my experience this summer I should say that the standard of care, caution and considerateness is much higher than ever before, but considering how much easier to drive the modern car is I doubt whether the average of driving skill is much better, if at all.

Where the road edge is rough and irregular there is some excuse for leaving a margin, but none on these new or newly-made roads where the kerb is clearly marked and the surface smooth right up to it. A white line painted parallel to each kerb 6ft or 7ft 6in distant from it would be well worth the trouble and trifling expense. It would show the kerb-shy where they were and add about 20 per cent. to the amount of traffic the average English road accommodates.

**(August 27)**

# THE LURES OF RENO

**From Our Own Correspondent**

NEW YORK, Wednesday.

"Bigger and better divorce facilities" was the watchword which secured the re-election of Mr. Roberts as Mayor of Reno, Nevada, to-day. In his campaign, which was run to a jazzy accompaniment of music financed by the divorce colony, he defended Nevada's divorce and gambling laws, and fiercely attacked Prohibition as the climax of "national hypocrisy."

Speaking from the pulpit of Reno Methodist Church last Sunday at the invitation of the pastor, Mr. Roberts urged the placing of barrels of "good corn whisky" on the city's streets to free the community from bootleggers.

**(May 7)**

# THE SHOPGIRL'S DIALECTS

Yesterday I made a personal investigation into the justice of the accusations brought by Mr L.N. Benny, of the Portsmouth Municipal College, against the speech of shopgirls.

He had said to the Drapers' Chamber of Trade, that "saleswomen cultivate an entirely unnatural, stilted and artificial style of speech when addressing customers." And, he added, which was perhaps more cutting still, that when talking to each other, even in the presence of the customer, they "relapse into their own very slipshod English."

In visits to five West-end stores I was, on the whole, agreeably surprised. Some distortions of speech there were of course, and, in a few cases, affectations. "Wawvellous velue - quate impossible tew repate, modem"- that was actually said in my presence.

Given my data, the professor in "Pygmalion" could have tracked down at least a score of accents to their homes. I distinguished only three, the "Regent-street-Purley," the "Bond-street-Kensington" ("only naine and a hef guineas - reellah tew amusing!"), which is the most "refaned" of all.

But after all, these were exceptions. The majority spoke as naturally as people can be expected to speak when they are trying very hard to please; and scores of voices were soft and wholly charming.

"The saleswoman," said Mr A Lloyd James, adviser on phonetics to the B.B.C., "speaks no better and no worse than her sisters. She makes mistakes because she tries to imitate those she serves. The telephone girl does precisely the same thing - and is actually encouraged to do so by the Postmaster-General. The Church has its special delivery. So have many other occupations. Speech is only one form of behaviour, and must be studied in relation to all sorts of factors - professional, social, geographical, and so on."

We are left with one conclusion - that the shopgirl is not merely guiltless, but ahead of her age.

**(October 9)**

# BATHING BEACH DECENCY

An order has been issued by the Archbishop of Rouen to priests in all seaside resorts within his jurisdiction that on Assumption Day they should make an appeal in their churches for a better observance of the laws of decency on bathing beaches and in places of entertainments.

**(August 10)**

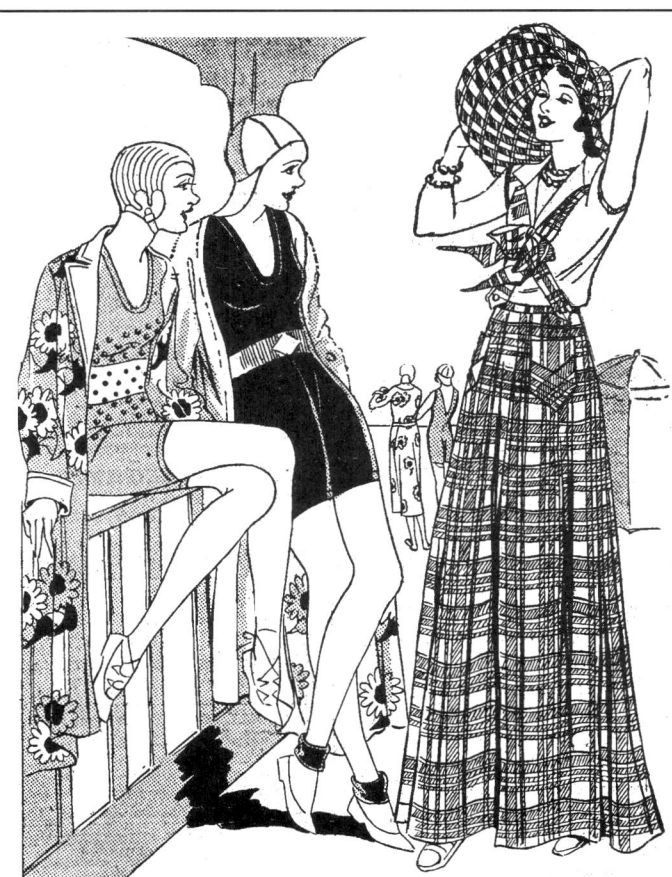

# THE ART OF MME. PAVLOVA

## PIONEER OF RUSSIAN DANCING HERE

**By Herbert Hughes**

It was in 1910 that Anna Pavlova first enslaved us by her art. She was the pioneer of Russian dancing in this country, and at the Palace Theatre, assisted by Michael Mordkin, she gave us altogether new experiences in such ballets as "Le Cygne," "Les Papillons," and "Valse Caprice."

Hitherto our knowledge of ballet had been limited to and by the conventionalised productions at the Alhambra and the old Empire - gorgeous affairs in their way, but hardly associated in our minds with the finest music or the most exquisite poetry.

Pavlova herself was rhythm incarnate, and always her dancing, whatever the subject or whatever the mood, gave one the impression of being pure improvisation.

Yet, of course, it was founded upon a technique that had been acquired through years of study and hard practice. Madame Pavlova used to relate how, when she was a child of eight in St. Petersburg, her mother took her to the Marinsky Theatre to see Tchaikovsky's ballet, "The Sleeping Beauty." "Wouldn't you like to join those people and dance with them?" her mother asked; and she had replied that she would rather dance by herself, like the lovely Sleeping Beauty. "One day I will, too," said the little Pavlova, "and in this very theatre!"

HER FIRST APPEARANCE

And actually it was at the Marinsky Theatre that the great ballerina made her first appearance. At the age of 10 she was admitted to the academy of the Imperial Ballet attached to that theatre, and remained there for six years - six years of strenuous work.

Shortly after her first London visit she appeared in Paris with the late Serge Diaghileff's Russian Ballet in "Les Sylphides," "Pavillon d'Armide" and "La Nuit Egyptienne." For some years she came regularly to the Palace Theatre, in 1920 she was at Drury Lane and in 1921 at Queen's Hall. In 1923 she brought, for the first time, her own company to Covent Garden, returning again the following year. Her touring was incessant, through every civilised quarter of the globe - America, India, Japan, China, Australia included.

In 1925 the late Theodore Stier, her conductor, gave a vivid description in the THE DAILY TELEGRAPH of one of these tours through the States. Seventy-seven towns were visited in a period of twenty-six weeks some of them being towns so small that there was actually no hotel accommodation for the company to be found. "Nobody," wrote Mr Stier, "bore the tremendous hardships of our manner of living so well, so bravely, as Madame Pavlova herself. Of the 238 performances given (this does not include Mexico) she never missed one, and at every performance, whether the town was New York or Washington or Kalamazoo, her enthusiasm for her work, and the quality of it never altered an atom; it was always superlative . . . Last Sunday (in Mexico city) we gave a performance in the Bull Ring, the Plaza de Toros.

"Imagine a place about three times the size and capacity of the Albert Hall packed with a Sunday crowd eagerly watching and enjoying 'the Fairy Doll.'

Elsewhere the writer described the habit of the men in a Mexican theatre audience of throwing their hats at the artist right on the stage as an expression of homage. "Hats kept flying about over my head," he wrote, "all the time the curtain was being taken up and down for calls."

For some years past Madame Pavlova has made her home in London, and Ivy Lodge with its delightful garden, on the heights of Hampstead, was the rendezvous of many people distinguished in the arts. She was all but unique in her own exquisite profession. A temperament so ardent, a brain so volatile, a heart so big as Anna Pavlova's will be sorely missed.

**(January 23)**

# EX-PREMIER OF JAPAN

Mr Yuko Hamaguchi, the ex-Prime Minister of Japan, who was shot at and wounded by a young Japanese student at Tokio railway station on Nov. 14, 1930, died from his injuries yesterday afternoon. He was 61 years of age.

Mr. Hamaguchi's assailant was a member of the Aikokusha, "Love of Country" Association, a reactionary patriotic organisation, and had served two sentences for blackmail and assault. Like the man who assassinated Mr. Takahashi Hara, the Prime Minister, some ten years ago, Sagoya was a weak-minded youth with a mistaken sense of patriotism.

Mr. Hamaguchi was president of the Minseito (Opposition) party in 1927. His ability as Finance Minister was widely recognised, and he did not hesitate to express decided views on the financial measures needed by Japan to restore her to complete prosperity.

**(August 21)**

# LIEUT. WAGHORN DEAD

## FIRST TO FLY 350 MILES AN HOUR

**By Major C.C. Turner**

The death yesterday of Flight-Lieut. H.R.D. Waghorn, A.F.C, winner of the Schneider Trophy in 1929, from injuries received when his aeroplane crashed at Farnborough on Tuesday, was the forty-second R.A.F. fatality this year.

Flt.-Lt. Waghorn was only 27 years of age, and his reputation as a brilliant airman had been established in the short space of nine years' membership of the Royal Air Force.

In that period also he earned the sobriquet of "Daisy" for the following telegram which he sent to his home station after making a forced landing in a march: "Forced landing at - in a nice field of daisies." Waghorn was famed for his bon mots.

He was a Londoner by birth - born at Brompton in 1904 - and was educated at Wellington College. He entered Cranwell Cadet College in 1922. Waghorn was a non-smoker, and his favourite recreation was ski-ing.

When that team of brilliant pilots, the High-speed Flight of 1929, moved from Felixstowe to Calshot for the last strenuous month's work before the Schneider Trophy contest it was at once obvious that Waghorn possessed exceptional qualities. He was a man who "flew with his head" in an uncommon degree for a pilot who also possessed amazing dash.

He was the first to fly it on a timed test, the first man to fly at 350 m.p.h.

A big, robust type, vigour expressed in every line, it was surprising to note how studious he was. He never forgot anything. His notes written on a pad strapped to his knee, together with those of the other pilots were the subject of conferences in which the leader of the team and the scientists and engine experts took part.

ALMOST IN DESPAIR

In the Schneider race he was determined there should be no silly oversight on his part, and realising the possibility of miscounting his laps, and feeling almost sure he had only done six, he carried on for the eighth! But his fuel gave out, and he alighted in a mood almost of despair. It shows how closely the thing is calculated. Half a million people knew before he did that he had won.

**(May 8)**

# SIR HALL CAINE

## MANX NOVELIST'S RISE TO FAME

Sir Hall Caine, the famous novelist, who died last night at his home, Greeba Castle, in the Isle of Man, was born in 1853. His grandfather farmed some sixty acres in the island; and his father was a blacksmith at Ramsey, who afterwards was engaged in the shipbuilding trade on the Mersey.

Before he reached the position of a great popular novelist he had to go through the mill of much drudgery and long obscurity. His first thought was to become an architect, and he was for some time in an architect's office. Afterwards he spent many years in a builder's office in Liverpool.

From the first he had the gift of making friends, and he did not hesitate while still obscure to get into communication with some of the most illustrious men of his time.

He had written to Dante Gabriel Rossetti to express his sympathy with him in an attack on his poetry and that of Swinburne under the title "The Fleshly School." This first letter led to others, with the result that Hall Caine was invited by Rossetti to come to London and be in a position which ended in that of nurse, companion, and secretary.

HIS START IN LETTERS

The long association with Rossetti came to an end with Rossetti's death at Birchington-on-Sea on Easter Day in 1882. Hall Caine once more had to face the choice of a career and of a livelihood. His first real association with literary life began with an engagement to do all kinds of work for the "Liverpool Mercury" - literary reviewing, dramatic criticism, occasional descriptive articles. His remuneration was at first only £2 a week, but this was rapidly increased. He also wrote for the "Atheneum" and the "Academy."

The idea seemed to have dawned on him slowly, and at first as an affrighting vision, that he might try his hand on a novel. It was, in fact, Rossetti who had first suggested to him the possibilities of fiction in the Isle of Man. To relieve the tedium of the painter-poet's long, wakeful nights he told him stories of the island and its strange laws and customs. "Why not write all this?" Rossetti said. But his first choice fell on a story of Cumberland life - on his mother's side he was connected with Cumberland - and thus he produced his first novel. "The Shadow of a Crime."

HIS MANX NOVELS

The book was well received, but did not achieve any popular success. That was to come with "The Deemster," "The Bondman," "The Scapegoat," and, above all, with "The Manxman."

**(September 1)**

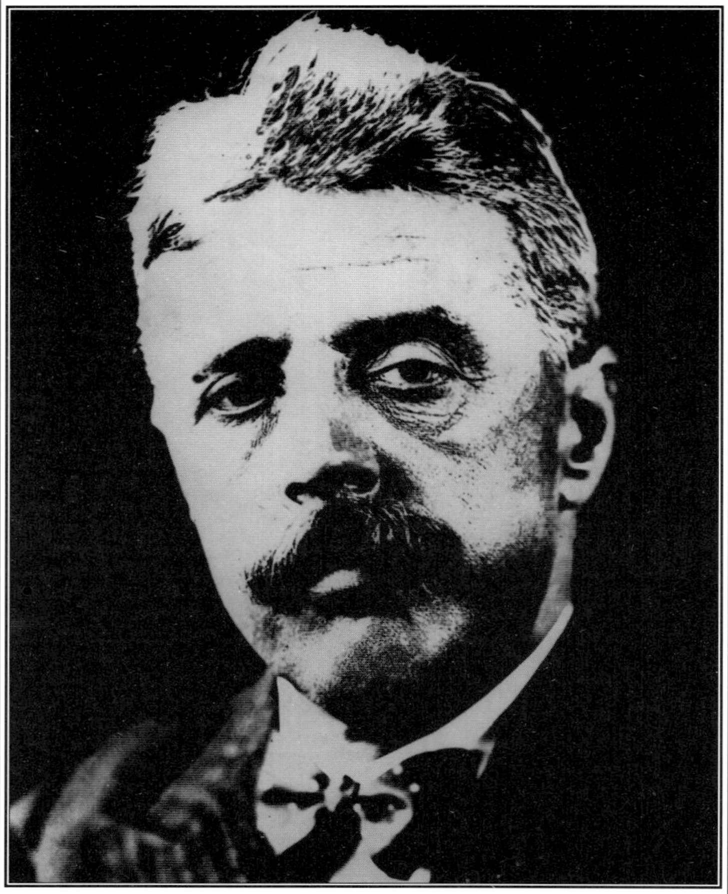

MR. ARNOLD BENNETT

# NOVELIST OF THE FIVE TOWNS

## MR. ARNOLD BENNETT

**By Rebecca West**

The tragedy of Arnold Bennett's death, which took place last night at the age of 63, is that so thoroughly did he enjoy life, the longest life would not have been too long for him. Although he affected to be stolid and blasé, he was in a continual ecstacy. He enjoyed writing. He enjoyed reading. He enjoyed going to the theatre. He enjoyed parties. he enjoyed yachting. He enjoyed staying at hotels. He enjoyed going to his tailors, to his bootmaker, even to his dentist.

It is impossible to think offhand of anything he did not enjoy. Nothing ever lost its edge for him, nothing ever became routine. It is bitter that one to whom life really was a gift should not have lived out the allotted span.

As a writer Arnold Bennett had meant much to all of us for the last twenty-five years. It is impossible to convey, to go back into the past, what his notes on "Books and Persons" in "The New Age" (a powerful and brilliant weekly under the editorship of A.R. Orage) meant to those who were in their teens and their twenties a quarter of a century ago. He stood then - and he ever went back on that attitude - for freedom and audacity.

A NECESSARY BATTLE

For one thing he claimed for English literature the right to take the whole of life for its province which had long been won by French literature. That was, at that time, a most necessary battle, for writers of the most blameless character, such as W.B. Maxwell, were then the subject of the most shameful persecution. Regarding such matters, Mr Bennett was a "bonny fechter," and was without fear, for though he enjoyed success he never moved a hair's-breadth away from any of his principles to buy it.

Even more exhilarating was his attitude to the general subject matter of literature, which inspired his criticism but found its supreme expression in "The Old Wives' Tale." This was a joyful exploitation of the possibilities of the everyday round, the common lot, as artistic material. Gissing, who had had a profound influence on late Victorian and Edwardian fiction, presented the life that was known by the vast majority of Englishmen with shudders of repulsion. To him dwellers in mean streets were human beings manqués. There had followed H.G. Wells, who insisted on these people being regarded as human beings as fully developed as any others; but he was conditioned in all his reactions to them by his sense that the mean streets must be swept away and a Utopia built in their stead.

TREMENDOUS REVELATION

But Arnold Bennett took them simply as they were, and rejoiced in the revelations of their inner beings that were evoked by the simple occasions of their daily lives. He took the Five Towns, and, refusing to blench at their lack of gentility, and refusing to take his eye off them to look at the coming dawn, celebrated them just as they were.

This was a tremendous revelation in the days of the publication of "The Old Wives' Tale." It was about the same time that he wrote that short story. "The Death of Simon Fuge," which is to some the most enchanting of all his fiction; a demonstration of how a flower of great art had its roots deep down in common earth. The sensation made by the first revelation of his quality could naturally not be repeated, but he matched the miracle time and again. It is true he compromised his own talent by publishing a vast number of works of very unequal merit, alternating full books and plays with strangely empty books and plays.

LONDON NOT THE SAME NOW

All London will miss him, and some Londoners very bitterly. For he abounded in kindliness; and it was to be noted that some of his closest friends were men who had no other friends. His rich understanding of human nature enabled him to bridge gulfs that others could not. Without a doubt, yesterday was a bad day for all of us.

**(March 28)**

# TRAGIC DEATH OF SIR WILLIAM ORPEN

## TRUE BOHEMIAN

**By a Personal Friend**

Behind the death of Sir William Orpen lies one of the saddest personal tragedies that have accompanied the passing of a great figure in the world of art.

It was only in May last that he became seriously ill, and his closest friends realised that Orpen would never paint another Academy picture. When I last saw him the one disturbing sign was that his memory was not nearly so vivid as it used to be. Latterly he could not recall events in his life which had happened the previous day.

I knew him for years, and I can truthfully describe him as the most human among successful persons I have ever met.

Unlike many of the Chelsea crowd who have achieved distinction in the artistic world, he never forgot his earlier associates, whether they failed or not. And a great many people have failed in Chelsea. In fact, he used to seek them out occasionally at some of the shabby Bohemian resorts of the neighbourhood and stand them a drink.

Before he vacated his house in Royal Hospital-road, which was recently pulled down, he walked every morning to his studio in South Bolton-gardens.

That walk was famous in Chelsea. It was a sort of progress of the great master, and he was often known on his way to distribute largesse to various people, including a certain elderly contemporary at the Slade School, who has not justified early promises of "greatness" and a crossing sweeper.

I have heard that once he was in company with the beautiful Marchioness of Cholmondeley, whom he painted, and her husband on one of these walks. The party met this redoubtable couple, who saluted Orpen and received the usual allowance they got from him when in town.

In none of his work was Orpen's generous soul more clearly revealed than in his work during the war years. One of the "official" war artists appointed by the British Government and furnished with a commission in the A.S.C. Orpen spend months at the front, and his portfolios were soon crammed with a store of sketches. Admiration for the men in the front line inspired him. Captain and private soldier alike, they were the men he took pleasure in commemorating with pencil and brush. A vein of satire was sometimes visible in the more "professional" portraits of the great, but his genial spirit loved the inhabitants of the trenches.

He was one of the first public men to publish war reminiscences of the franker sort, and it may be recalled that he followed up his serious canvas of the signing of the Peace Treaty at Versailles, which now is the property of the nation with a home in the Tate Gallery, with a grim allegory - another view of the Hall of Mirrors in which two shrapnel helmeted skeletons mount guard over a soldier's coffin.

**(October 1)**

# MR. THOMAS ALVA EDISON

## THE MOST PROLIFIC OF ALL INVENTORS

## HOPED TO WORK TILL HE WAS 150

As long as the world survives the name of Thomas Alva Edison, who died yesterday at the age of 84, will remain an outstanding symbol of astonishing genius accomplishment and public service.

"He illuminated the path of progress by his inventions," runs the inscription on the gold medal of the United States Congress presented to him in October, 1928. On the same occasion President Coolidge saluted him fittingly with the words: "Noble, kindly servant of the United States and benefactor of mankind."

These two sentences put tersely what Edison was and what he accomplished. One invention was born of his brain on the average every two weeks for fifty years, and his registration of over 1,300 patents made him the most prolific inventor of all time. The monetary value of the industries either based wholly on his inventions, or materially aided by his discoveries, has been officially estimated at the Midas-like total of £3,120,000,000.

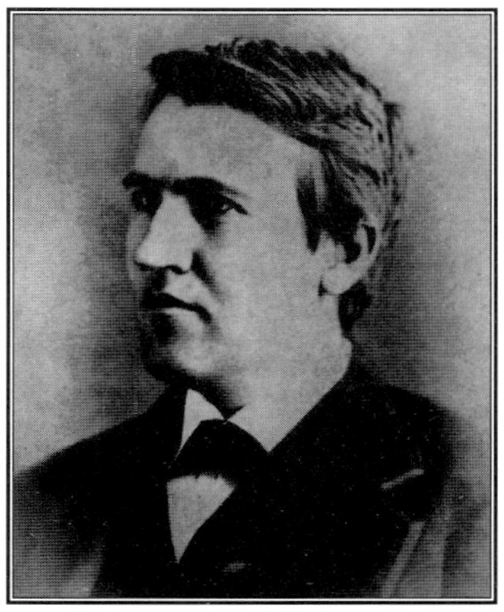

Scientist to the innermost cell of his brain, though it cannot be said that "pure science" - the search for new knowledge for its own sake - ever interested him for long - and inventor to his finger-tips, Edison was born in the little town of Milan, in the State of Ohio. His parents, though his father could point to Dutch ancestors, were really British subjects; who began in Canada.

HIS FIRST PATENT

It was a startling act of heroism that led to his true vocation. A locomotive was passing along the railway, on which a child was standing; Edison rushed forward and saved the little one's life. The child was the offspring of the stationmaster, who, out of gratitude offered to teach the boy how to operate a telegraph machine.

Edison was 21 when he resolved to try his fortunes in New York. Walking along Wall-street, he had his attention attracted by an excited crowd. The telegraphic Company had broken down, and with it the business world of the United States. Edison went boldly into the office, told the distracted proprietors that he knew something of telegraphy, was allowed to work on the apparatus, and soon had it going again. The proprietors had the intelligence to realise the value of this country boy, and Edison got the first well-paid job of his life, at what he considered then the magnificent salary of £60 a month.

His first patent was granted on July 1, 1869, for an electric vote-recorder. Since that time more than 1,300 patents for original and important work inventions have been granted to him. Their scope covers stock tickers, typewriters, telephonic and telegraphic instruments, the phonograph, many of the controlling features of central power plant construction, and operation, electric railways, motion pictures, ore milling, cement manufacture and poured cement houses, storage batteries and the transmission of electric energy without the aid of wires. His application for the latter patent was made two years before the publication of the work of Hertz. In the last year of his life he was devoting his energies to the problem of producing rubber from golden rod, a prolific weed.

THE PHONOGRAPH

The next big invention of Edison was the "phonograph" or speaking machine, for which he took out a patent in 1877. The original model was a cylinder covered with tinfoil and turned by a hand crank. He stumbled on the idea by accident.

I was engaged (said Edison) upon a machine intended to repeat Morse characters, which were recorded on paper by indentations that transferred their message to another circuit automatically when passed under a tracing-point connected with a circuit-closing apparatus. I found that when the cylinder carrying the indented paper was turned with great swiftness it gave off a humming noise from the indentations - a musical, rhythmic sound resembling that of human talk heard indistinctly. This led me to try fitting a diaphragm to the machine, which would received the vibrations or sound waves made by my voice when I talked to it, and register these vibrations upon an impressible material placed on the cylinder. The material selected was paraffined paper, and the results obtained were excellent.

In 1878 Edison paid a visit to Philadelphia, and there he saw an electric arc light for the first time. It set him tingling with anticipation of what could be done in this line; and he came to the conclusion, as the late Sir Joseph Swan, and English inventor, had done, that a filament would solve the difficulty of carrying light in an airless bulb. He examined 6,000 different vegetable growths, and spent £8,000 before he succeeded in making an incandescent lamp in which a loop of carbonised cotton thread glowed in a vacuum for over 40 hours.

The actual discovery of using a carbon filament in an exhausted glass vessel had been made as long ago as 1860 by Swan. At that time, however, he did not succeed in producing more than a red glow. In February, 1879, about the same time that Edison announced his claim in the United States, Mr Swan, as he then was, exhibited at a lecture in Newcastle a thoroughly practicable electric bulb with carbon filament. During the summer of 1880 a number of Swan lamps were shown at an exhibition in Glasgow.

In 1879 Edison's lamp was admittedly still at the laboratory stage. Later the claims of the two men came into legal conflict, and the matter was solved by a merging of their interests in the joint product known as the Ediswan lamp.

THE STORAGE BATTERY

An elaborate series of experiments enabled Edison in 1901 to introduce a storage battery to compete with the lead accumulators which had hitherto been supreme. In this the active materials were iron and nickel oxide in an alkaline solution. This battery he further improved seven years later.

Edison's inventions were the result of ceaseless energy - "one per cent. inspiration and 99 per cent. perspiration," he used to say. He was very deaf, and believed that his affliction not only helped him to think, but protected him from distraction.

Important and far-reaching as are his achievements, they become dwarfed with the man himself and his wonderful mind and charming personality. He seemed to hold the hidden things of the universe in the hollow of his hand.

**(October 19)**

# DAME NELLIE MELBA

With the passing of Dame Nellie Melba - she died at Sydney yesterday at the age of 69 - the world at large has lost a great singer and a great personality. She was not merely British, or Australian, or Scots - as she has been variously and truly claimed; she was a world figure, a woman whose art knew no frontiers, whose voice will be remembered for generations by all sorts and conditions of people.

She was in the royal line of singers, but her coming so synchronised with the advent of the gramophone that her accession to sovereignty brought with it a greater power and a wider influence than that attained by any of her illustrious predecessors.

In Paris her student career was short, for already, in 1887, Madame Marchesi pronounced her equipped for the stage, and on Oct. 12, 1887, Melba made her début at the Theatre de la Monnaie, in Brussels, as the ill-fated Gilda in "Rigoletto," she for the first time taking the pseudonym of Melba - derived from Melbourne - which name ultimately became a household word.

STAGE TRIUMPHS

In London the public received her rapturously. Sundry critics, it is true - then and later - pointed out remediable defects or inefficiencies in the singer's equipment. But the remarkable beauty of the voice, its extraordinary quality and evenness throughout a range of a full two and a half octaves, and the simplicity of its utterance completely won the public, who were quick to place the owner of the voice among their first favourites.

In 1904 she sang before King Edward at Buckingham Palace during the festivities in connection with the visit of the Archduke Francis Ferdinand, whose assassination at Sarajevo precipitated the war.

In Australia and in the United States Melba collected of £100,000 during the war at concerts she then organised on behalf of the Red Cross Fund, for which she was created a Dame of the Order of the British Empire in the first list of that Order.

One night in the summer of 1926 she stood before the footlights of Covent Garden for the last time. There, in the presence of the King and Queen, she said farewell to London, and she departed in a blaze of glory.

**(February 24)**

# JOFFRE AND THE MARNE

## VICTORY AIDED BY THE ENEMY'S MISTAKES

**By Captain B.H. Liddell Hart**

STRANGELY enough, it was not until four years before the war began that Joseph Jacques Césaire Joffre, destined to become the first Marshall of the Third Republic, was raised suddenly to a position of any real power in the French Army.

Colonel de Grandmaison, chief of the "operations" branch of the General Staff, had in 1910 opposed the existing plan of campaign in case of war against Germany, in which the French army was to be manoeuvred according to the line of invasion the enemy took. Opposed to the policy of leaving the initiative to the enemy, Grandmaison declared that there was only one mode of action - attack, which meant a headlong assault. He had the great body of military opinion with him.

General Michel, the commander-in-chief designate, almost alone stood out against the tide, and was relieved of his post. Galliéni, who had opposed his views, had the good taste to decline the succession, and when he proposed Joffre, the War Minister accepted the suggestion. He was a good Republican, devoid of political attachments, and the Government were thus induced to give him the combined functions of vice-president of the Conseil Supérieur and of chief of the General Staff, which meant control in peace and command in war. Heavy in body and intellect, he was obviously no Cassius.

The German Noose

The new plan of campaign, the new notorious Plan XVII, was based on a double miscalculation. The initial strength that the Germans could display was underestimated, and although the possibility of a German move through Belgium was recognised, the wideness of its sweep was utterly misjudged.

But in any case the French expected to nullify it, and impose their will on the enemy, by making an immediate and general offensive themselves. And it was carried out on tactical methods that blandly ignored the effects of modern fire.

Faced at length with the unmistakable news of a German advance through Belgium, Joffre and his staff were forced to readjust their plan. The trouble was that the Germans had deployed twice as many troops as they had been credited with, and for a vaster enveloping movement. The French Fifth Army and the British had, under Joffre's orders, put their heads almost into the German noose.

His Olympian Calm

It was then that Joffre realised the truth and the collapse of Plan XVII. An Olympian calm was his great asset, and with cool resolution he decided to swing back his centre and left, with Verdun as the pivot while forming a fresh Sixth Army to enable the retiring armies to return to the offensive.

It is beyond doubt that at this time of the severest trial of the war Joffre did much by his moral - rather than by his mental - influence to repair the shattered fighting power of France.

Joffre's optimism, however, might have been misplaced but for the German mistakes in the rapid advance of 1914. On Aug. 25 four German divisions were sent to the Russian front - in the belief that the decision in France had already been gained! The German command lost touch with the advancing armies and the movements of these became disjointed. The idea of a new Sedan was an obsession with the Germans, and led them to pluck the fruit before it was ripe. Von Kluck's premature wheel before Paris had been reached exposed the German right to a counter-envelopment. Thus, so much grit had worked into the German machine that a slight jar would suffice to cause its breakdown. This was delivered in the Battle of the Marne.

The immortal drama of the Marne, that battle so indecisive in its fighting, changed the whole face and issue of the war.

When Joffre's advocates say that the idea of a counter-offensive was at the back of his mind, the historian can agree; but on Sept. 3-4 Galliéni, the new Governor of Paris, realised the meaning of Von Kluck's wheel inwards, realised that he had thus exposed his flank to a stroke from Paris, and by strenuous arguments won Joffre's agreement to action.

Joffre, however, was slow to react until fresh arguments on the telephone led him, on the evening of Sept. 4, in combination with the flank thrust, to order the whole left wing to turn about and return to a general offensive from Verdun westwards, fixing the date for Sept. 6. But the delay robbed the attack of immediate British support. They created a gap in the German front - and the news of the mere approach of the British towards the gap caused the German order to retreat.

Then followed the successive and too obvious attempts of either side to envelop the other's western flank, a phase known as the "race to the sea." With their failure trench warfare settled in, and the whole front from the Swiss frontier to the sea was locked rigidly henceforth.

Joffre's long tenure of command continued, though dissatisfaction with the course of the operations was becoming widespread. It was partly due to his native shrewdness; it was due still more to the world-wide prestige he had gained in popular opinion by the "miracle of the Marne." To Chantilly, the shrine of the "Saviour of France," poured a ceaseless steam of adulation and presents from world-wide worshippers.

His hold on the public was enhanced because, although remote, he was yet so akin - the very type of the bon bourgeois. Simple in manner and tastes, he kept a strict check on his household accounts, but relished his

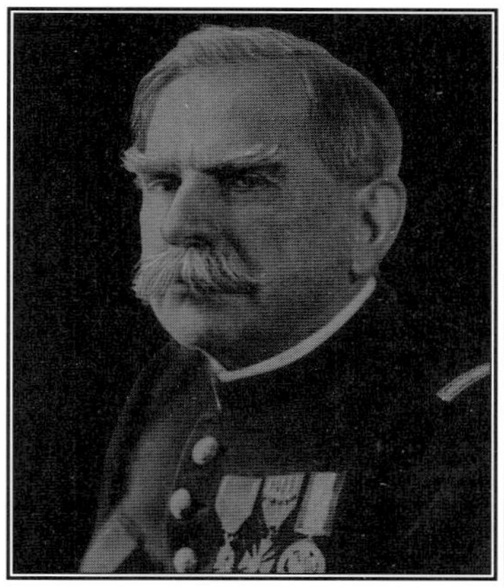

meals with all the gusto of a true French rentier, and valued his sleep. His staff learnt that it was better to sacrifice duty than to be late for meals, and only in emergency would they dare to disturb him after he had retired to bed at ten o'clock.

Incongruous as these traits may seem in a neo-Napoleonic figure, they had the value of making him a calming influence; and calm in emergency, even if it springs from insensibility, is a priceless asset. Moreover, if he was swayed by the nimbler brains of his staff officers in the technique and theory of warfare, he was indisputably master, as dominant as he was obstinate, on broad questions of policy, and jealous for his authority.

"Pauvre Joffre"

These traits, however, paved the way for disaster - at Verdun, in the spring of 1916. Joffre and Verdun became twin symbols for patient and heroic endurance. But the French defenders lost three men to the attacking Germans' two, and the drain on the French reserves almost bankrupted their share in the long-planned Allied offensive on the Somme. The bitter cost for small gain of that long-drawn-out attrition battle sealed Joffre's fate. And the failure to safeguard Verdun was now fully known. He had been retained in power through the summer mainly as a symbol to sustain the public confidence. On Dec. 27, 1916, Joffre was definitely retired, and in compensation and recognition promoted to Marshal.

**(January 5)**

# MR. A.J. COOK

## FARMER'S BOY & MINERS' SECRETARY

Few Labour leaders in the last decade have been more in the limelight than Mr. Arthur James Cook, secretary of the Miners' Federation, who died yesterday at the age of 47.

Born at Wookey, near Wells, the son of a soldier, Mr. Cook went away to start work at the age of 12, when his father proposed that he should become a drummer-boy. Finding employment with a farmer near Cheddar, he stayed there until he was nearly 16, when he migrated into South Wales.

Soon he was known as a zealous, if irresponsible, advocate of the miners' cause. He became a member of the Rhondda Miners' Unofficial Reform Committee, which in 1911 published that notorious pamphlet, "The Miners Next Step."

As miners' secretary - an appointment he obtained in 1924 - he had to witness the painful anti-climax of the teaching of "The Miners' Next Step" in the events connected with the General Strike of 1926.

But with the passing of the years came a modification of views. His change of attitude was revealed at a meeting which he addressed in South Wales in April, 1929. He had previously at a Mansion House gathering shaken hands with the Prince of Wales after his Royal Highness had toured the coalfields and made an eloquent broadcast appeal on behalf of the miners.

"I have fought," said Mr. Cook, "to protect the Communists, I have been reviled for it. I have fed them and clothed them, and I say now they are the most dishonourable set of men I have had any dealings with. This is one of the tragedies of my life.

**(November 3)**

# DEATH OF SIR THOMAS LIPTON

**By a Personal Friend**

Genuineness was the salient quality of "Tommy" Lipton's character. It entered into his dealings, his talk (which was usually racy), and his sportsmanship. No man was more candid about his humble start, as the son of an Irish couple in a Glasgow slum who never had more than a pound a week in the way of income. His "kick-off" in trade, he used to say, was at a wage of half-a-crown a week, yet he vowed to set his mother up in her own carriage-and-pair before he had done.

Sir Thomas retained the warrantable pride of the self-made man in its most amiable form.

Pride in his early experiences rarely came to his aid with more effect than once when he was dining at Kelburne Castle, and his hostess, Lady Glasgow, asked if he knew the district.

"Indeed I do, ma'am, " he replied, "and I have been to this house many times - when I was an errand boy in Largs. I have been to the back-gate many a time and delivered groceries to the maids in the kitchen. But I never thought to enter by the front gate and take a meal with its charming mistress."

When as a youth, he opened his first little grocer's shop, he was anything but certain of his future.

"I shall never be any good as a business man, and my shop will be likelier to land me in bankruptcy than to make me a fortune," he told his neighbour, from whom he often begged a cup of tea.

The last great triumph of his career was his election to the Royal Yacht Squadron at the general meeting last May. He had been a guest several times, but this attainment of membership brought him intense pride and pleasure. But ill-health prevented him from ever entering the "Castle" as a member.

"THE GAMEST LOSER"

When he sailed from New York last year he took with him a trophy, the gift of hundreds of American admirers, as a symbol of his being "the gamest loser in the world of sport."

Mr. "Jimmie" Walker, the Mayor of New York, in presenting the trophy, said that in losing the America's Cup he had captured something infinitely more important - the hearts of the American people."

## "AMBASSADOR OF FRIENDSHIP"

**From Our Own Correspondent**

NEW YORK, Friday.

Sir Thomas Lipton's fame in America far exceeded his reputation at home. For years he has been described by the American newspapers as "England's greatest ambassador of friendship."

His popularity was not restricted to sporting circles because of his persistent efforts to lift the America's Cup, but was general all over the country. Whenever he came here he attended more banquets, dinners and social functions than any other visitor. He took part in civic parades, and visited schools - where the children sang "God Save the King" in his honour - and also prisons. He was particularly popular among the convicts at Sing Sing because he induced the warden to give them a day's holiday every time he visited them.

**(October 3)**

# LAST OF THE OLD PUGILISTS

## JEM SMITH'S FIGHT OF 106 ROUNDS

The last of the famous line of the old prize ring bare-knuckled fighters, Jem Smith, has died at the Park Royal Hospital, London. Smith, who was 68 years old, had been ill since December, 1929.

Born at Cripplegate in January, 1863, Smith was a worthy successor to such giants of pugilism as Gentleman Jackson, Belcher, Cribb, and Sayers. Although only 5ft 8 ½in in height, with a fighting weight 12st-10 he had such a reserve of energy that on one occasion he fought 106 rounds with bare knuckles.

He won the English championship in 1883, when he knocked out Jack Davis in an open-air fight in Surrey in six rounds.

His most famous fight, however, was in 1887, when, as a youth of 24, he opposed Jake Kilrain, the American champion, in a fight that was styled the "world's championship" although neither of the men held the title at the time.

A "RECORD PURSE"

The purse was £2,000, a record for those days, and the contest took place in France on the banks of the Seine, as "P.R." fighting had fallen into disfavour in England. The men fought till darkness prevented their continuing, and then agreed to a draw.

Beaten in two rounds by the famous Peter Jackson at the old Pelican Club in 1888, Smith two months later drew with Frank Slavin, regarded as the greatest heavyweight of that time, in 14 rounds in Belgium.

**(September 12)**

# DERBY CROWD'S BIRTHDAY GREETING TO KING

## CAMERONIAN'S VICTORY

### SWEEPSTAKE WINNERS CHEER FAVOURITE

A crowd so vast that it is believed to have constituted a record gave the King a wonderful birthday greeting at the Derby yesterday.

The weather was fine, the racing good, and the success of Cameronian, the favourite, in the great event completed for punters a happy day. For bookmakers it was the worst Derby for some years.

Mr. J.A. Dewar had the wonderful success of winning the Derby at his first attempt, as a few weeks ago he won the Two Thousand Guineas with his first entry.

It was also the first Derby success of Fred Fox, the jockey, although he rode his first classic winner twenty years ago.

(June 3)

# A RECORD CROWD

## SUNSHINE - & WINNERS

**From Our Special Representative**

The Derby has come and gone, with the favourite safely home, to the enormous gratification of a truly enormous crowd.

Full-throated, the assembled thousands roared their welcome when the King and Queen, and all their family with them, passed into the Royal box and stood at the front.

Beyond a doubt there was added enthusiasm in the knowledge of the crowds that they were greeting his Majesty on his birthday.

Moreover, this was the King's first appearance at the Derby since his illness.

It might have happened often that June 3 and the month's first Wednesday fell together. That occurred in 1925, but that year the race was fixed in the last days of May, spoiling the "double event," and yesterday's coincidence of the race and the Sovereign's birthday is, I believe, without precedent.

The presence of the Prince of Wales, the Duke and Duchess of York, the Duke of Gloucester, Prince George, and the Earl of Harewood, besides making the Royal group an unusually large one, fitted in so well with the idea of the King and his people of all grades, from highest to lowest, united in one great family at the world's biggest carnival.

CAMERONIAN'S RACE

| | |
|---|---|
| CAMERONIAN (Mr. J. Dewar) | F. Fox 1 |
| ORPEN (Sir John Rutherford) | R.A. Jones 2 |
| SANDWICH (Lord Rosebery) | H. Wragg 3 |

Betting: 7-2; 9-1; 8-1.
Won by three-quarters of a length.

### Animated Scene

Everything combined to make this Birthday Derby outstanding in its long record. The racing was good. The day gave all that could be wanted - sunshine during the parade and the great race and for many short spells, but never hot enough to make the afternoon oppressive.

It would have taxed the Census officials to have taken the numbers of the black masses of people. Scarlet "General" buses, packed in serried ranks, made a frieze stretching from Tattenham Corner to the stands, and the bookmakers' boards, on which odds were chalked and constantly altered, a lower continuous line near by the green ribbon of the course.

On the hill, where the amusement booths and tents were packed together, the press of humanity was no less dense.

I heard many say the crowd made a new record and can well believe it.

**(June 3)**

# RACE SEEN AT HOME

## TELEVISION SUCCESS

Many people saw the thrills of the Derby on the Televisor in the comfort of their own homes.

It was the first television of the race, and was done by the Baird Television Co., in co-operation with the B.B.C.

Fifteen miles from the course, in the company's studio at Long-acre, all the Derby scenes were easily discernible - the parade of the horses, the enormous crowd, and the dramatic flash past at the winning post.

After the transmission Mr. Baird said that he was quite satisfied with the experiment.

"This marks the entry of television into the outdoor field," he said, "and should be the prelude to televising outdoor topical events."

**(June 3)**

# BRITISH GIRL'S TRIUMPH

PARIS, Sunday.

Miss Joyce Cooper, of Kingston-on-Thames, broke the 100 metres (109 yards) European swimming record for women at the international contest held by the Paris Swimmers' Club.

Her time was 1min 10 sec. The previous record was held by Mlle. Marie Braun (Holland), whose time was 1min 11 4-5sec.

**(February 9)**

# BRITAIN'S BID FOR THE DAVIS CUP

## DECISIVE MATCH WON BY FRANCE

**By A Wallis Myers**

AUTEUIL, Sunday.

The Davis Cup, symbol of the international lawn tennis team championship, will remain in French keeping for another year - the fifth in succession.

After a magnificent fight by the British team in the final stage to-day. France defeated the challengers by three matches to two.

In the first of to-day's two singles Austin beat Borotra, 7-5, 6-3, 3-6, 7-5, bringing the two countries level for the culminating match between Perry and Cochet.

The little Frenchman, coming to his best for the critical contest, beat Perry in a memorable and close encounter by three sets to one, with the score of 6-4, 1-6, 9-7, 6-3.

The dismal weather was almost forgotten in the excitement of the struggle. Frequent showers, damping and deadening the court, ever perilous to a firm foothold, could not chasten the ardour of the crowd.

### CROWD'S WILD ENTHUSIASM

Even when halts were necessary - in Perry's match the break was as much as thirty minutes - few of the thousands left their seats. Every move drew salvoes of cheers, and when with darkness falling in another burst of rain, Perry was straining, ever with cool head, to check the super-brilliant Cochet, the air was charged with excitement.

The final act was stirring. When Cochet had made the winning stroke hundreds of red seat cushions were hurled on to the court from above. Then the shouting was suddenly hushed as the strains of the "Marseillaise" came through the loudspeaker.

Players and their captains, umpires and linesmen, formed a saluting group in the centre. Cabinet Ministers and Ambassadors stood bareheaded in the rain. Next came the British National Anthem, equally honoured by the crowd.

Never before had Great Britain fought France in Paris for possession of the Davis Cup. Not since 1912 had she held it. For eleven consecutive years the United States had figured in the last stage.

### PROMISE FOR FUTURE

America's challenge had been foiled this time by Young England - and what a battle those youthful players gave the holders on their own soil! Of the five matches they won two, and during the three that were forfeited doubt over the issue was never absent.

Austin had a hard fight against Borotra in to-day's opening match. The surrounds of the court were slippery, and both men frequently stumbled as they raced for wide interceptions.

He found Borotra's service uneven and without its usual bite, and that was comforting. He was also given several points by the rigid foot-faulting of his opponent. Apparently Borotra was hopping as he delivered the ball, and the judge was not afraid to say so, even when a game was at stake and the crowd was caustically unsympathetic.

**(July 27)**

# NEW LAW FOR THE GOLFER

A point which has been the cause of many a dispute - friendly and otherwise - on the golf course, has at last been cleared up by the Rules Committee of the Royal and Ancient Club of St. Andrews, the governing body of the game.

It concerns loose impediments on the green, those irritating little obstacles, often almost imperceptible save to the man who is anxiously studying the line to the hole.

The committee has decided that forthwith Rule 28 shall read as follows:

(1) Any loose impediment may be removed from the putting green by hand or with the club, irrespective of the position of the player's ball.

(2) In removing any loose impediment the club must not be laid with more than its own weight upon the ground, nor must anything be pressed either with the club or in any other way.

**(September 30)**

# YORKSHIRE WIN CHAMPIONSHIP

## SUCCESS DUE TO FINE TEAM WORK

From White Willow
LEEDS, Tuesday.

YORKSHIRE won the cricket championship this afternoon for the first time since 1925, and it has been good to be here at their time of triumph. Even the sun smiled on them, and the only disappointing feature of the occasion is that they were unable to crown their wonderful summer with something more satisfying than the four points which have been their portion in the rain-ruined match with Middlesex.

There was no attempt by the captains to make up for the two wasted days by an immediate departure from the orthodox ceremonial. True, Middlesex closed their innings at 190 for five, and left Yorkshire a possible 2 ½ hours in which to gain a first-innings victory. By then, however, the game had lost its savour.

"I am very pleased with all of them," said F.E. Greenwood, the Yorkshire captain, when I offered him and his team the congratulations of non-Yorkshiremen on their magnificent achievement. "It is team work that has done it. Over and over again, I have called on them for an extraordinary effort, and by pulling all together we have managed to overcome not only our rivals, but, let me add, the weather."

The Yorkshire skipper is especially sensible of the fact that he has had a privilege to which other leaders of the eleven have contributed, for he is the fourth captain in six seasons, and this had been his first season at the helm. Yorks have now won the championship fifteen times.

**(August 19)**

# YORKS BOWLER'S FEAT

## VERITY'S TEN WICKETS IN AN INNINGS

At Leeds yesterday, Hedley Verity, the young Yorkshire professional, captured the cricket laurel that bowlers are for ever dreaming about and striving after.

He took all ten wickets in Warwickshire's second innings, and thus joined the distinguished band that includes only forty-two other bowlers in nearly a hundred years.

Twice last season the feat was accomplished - once by Grimmett of the Australians and once by Freeman of Kent, who had also done it a year earlier. Verity, indeed, is the thirteenth bowler to equal the record since the war, but it is doubtful if in the whole history of first-class cricket anyone has gained the distinction at such an early stage of his career.

At this time last year Verity was chiefly playing in Lancashire League cricket. Indeed, he made his début for Yorkshire on May 21, 1930, at Huddersfield, against Sussex. He figured in less than a dozen matches during the season, but he was quickly recognised as the natural successor to Wilfred Rhodes, who was on the eve of his retirement.

A slow, left-handed bowler, with command of both spin and length. Verity finished the season at the top of the Yorkshire averages, having taken 52 wickets at a cost of only 11.44 each.

Only once previously has a Yorkshire bowler taken ten wickets in an innings. Neither the great George Hirst nor Rhodes himself ever did so. The honour fell to Alonzo Drake, who was killed in the war. By a happy coincidence, Verity who hails from Rawdon, yesterday celebrated his 26th birthday.

**(May 19)**

# ROUT OF BRITISH PLAYERS IN RYDER CUP

## BEATEN BY 9 MATCHES TO 3: ALL FAIL EXCEPT HAVERS & DAVIES

**By George Greenwood**

AMERICA defeated Great Britain in the Ryder Cup contest at Scioto, Columbus, on Saturday, by a total of nine matches to three.

The United States players, who won the foursomes by three games to one, and the singles by six games to two, have thus won the rubber match. The complete results of the two days' play are:

SINGLES

W. Burke (U.S.A) bt A Compston (Britain), 7 and 6.
G. Sarazen (U.S.A) bt F. Robson (Britain), 7 and 6.
D. Shute (U.S.A) bt R. Hodson (Britain), 8 and 6.
W.H. Davies (Britain) bt J. Farrell (U.S.A), 4 and 3.
W. Hagen (U.S.A) bt C. Whitcombe (Britain), 4 and 3.
C.J. Cox (U.S.A) bt A. Mitchell (Britain), 3 and 1.
A. Havers (Britain) bt C. Wood (U.S.A), 4 and 3.
A. Espinosa (U.S.A) bt E.R. Whitcombe (Britain) 2 and 1.

FOURSOMES

Hagen and Shute bt Duncan and Havers, 10 and 9.
Sarazen and Farrell bt Compston and Davies, 8 and 7.
Mitchell and Robson bt Espinosa and Diegel, 3 and 1.
Cox and Burke bt E Whitcombe and Easterbrook, 3 and 2.
Total: U.S.A. 9; Britain 3.

The rout of the British players, following on the loss of the championship at Carnoustie, will come as a great disappointment. While the chances of victory were never substantial, there were good grounds for believing that Britain would make a more determined bid for victory than the results indicate. W.H. Davies, the sturdy little golfer from the North of England, one of the newcomers, and Havers, who had made a welcome return to form after several years of almost complete eclipse, were the only successful British players in the singles.

Others with more illustrious reputations, Compton and Robson in particular, collapsed badly, though it is only fair to say that Robson, in partnership with his old friend Mitchell, won the one foursome for Britain. Charles Whitcombe, who, I cannot help thinking committed a tactical error in standing down from the foursomes, thereby endangering the success of the side, was defeated by Hagen.

### HAGEN NOT A BACK NUMBER

The American captain has exploded the idea prevalent in the States that he is a past number. Indeed, from Reuter's account of the match, it would seem that in the department in which he has made a speciality - the rolling of three shots into two - Hagen is still the great master. Throughout the encounter, which ended on the thirty-third green Hagen was his own brilliantly eccentric self. On four occasions he almost holed out from bunkers into which he gaily sailed only to sail as gaily out again straight at the flag.

Anywhere on the course, apparently it did not seem to matter where, the pin was his magnet. Hagen, who went into luncheon with the comfortable lead of four holes, having accomplished the round in 70 as against Whitcombe's 74 held on grimly to his advantage to the end. Though the British captain made a characteristic effort to wipe out the deficit it was all to no purpose against the conjuring tricks of Hagen, who alternately exploded, hacked, and chipped the ball from doubtful places always on to the green, and generally near enough to the hole to give him a reasonable chance of holing the putt.

In explanation of his decision to drop out of the foursomes, Whitcombe said that he was not fit enough to withstand the strain of two days' play. While it is true that the terrific heat - 100 deg. in the shade on the first day - handicapped the British players, the conditions serve to illustrate the point which I have previously made, that our men, some of them at any rate, were too old for the job.

Duncan, at the age of 49, proved to be wholly unfitted for the task, and he wisely retired from participation in the singles. The glamour surrounding the name of Duncan, a form of magic which, I am afraid, was responsible for getting him into the team, has been blown away like a summer mist. Duncan has played in his last Ryder Cup match, and so, it is to be imagined, have some of the others who failed so ingloriously at Scioto.

I shall be surprised if Robson, Mitchell, Ernest, Whitcombe, and even Compton, unless he recovers the match-winning faculty, are again chosen to represent Britain in International contests. Having had their day, they must make room for younger players, who may reasonably be expected to stand the physical test of an exhausting match.

The gamble on men whose ages are nearer 50 than 40 has failed dismally, and the time has now arrived when our house, if ever we are to regain our golfing prestige, should be put in order. From the comments of the spectators at Scioto, it would seem that the American public has not been favourably impressed either with the attack or the defence of our players, a state of things which does not occasion great surprise.

**(June 29)**

# THE PRINCE WATCHES DRAMATIC FINISH

## JURADO FAILS BY ONE STROKE

The British Open Golf Championship ended at Carnoustie yesterday in a surprise win for T.D. Armour, a naturalised American, with a total for the four rounds of 296.

This is America's eighth successive victory in the championship.

In a dramatic finish, which was watched by the Prince of Wales, Jose Jurado, the Argentine professional, lost the chance of tieing with Armour by one stroke.

In the final stage Jurado required a round of 75 to win. He led Armour by no fewer than six strokes, and at the end of nine holes was still five ahead.

The fourteenth and seventeenth, however, each cost him six strokes, and at the last hole he needed a 4 to tie. Here he was left with a three-yards putt. He played the stroke with great deliberation, and the ball missed the hole by a hairsbreadth.

Armour, who is 36 years of age, was born in Edinburgh, and for many years was one of the best amateur golfers in Scotland. He went to the United States in 1924, and became a professional. His triumphs in America include the American Open Championship in 1927 and the professional title last year.

The Prince of Wales made the long journey to Carnoustie to see the last day's play; and in between his walks around the links in the wake of Jurado and the other favourites he found time for a round himself on the Barry Links, near by.

The Prince, who looked very fit and well, wore brown check plus fours. He was bareheaded and carried a beret. He was out on the course within half an hour of his arrival. A small gallery flocked towards him as he crossed over the bridge, but one of his bodyguard moved forward and said: "Please do not follow. The Prince is here to enjoy the golf."

The crowd immediately respected the request, and the Prince moved off to the fifteenth green and had his first peep at the championship through the serried ranks of the followers of Henry Cotton. He saw the leader putting disappointingly. He looked at his watch and said: "How far out is Jurado?"

The Prince's acquaintance with Jurado, the dapper little Argentine player, dates back to a number of rounds they had together in South America.

So yesterday it was Jurado whom the Prince particularly watched. He joined up with the big gallery of spectators following Jurado and Davis at the tenth tee, and went round the rest of the course with them. At the difficult "South America" hole he saw the Argentine play a brassie shot across the burn that trapped so many, lay his next shot 18 inches from the hole, and sink the putt. At this the Prince walked up, asked his score, and wished him the best of luck.

**(June 6)**

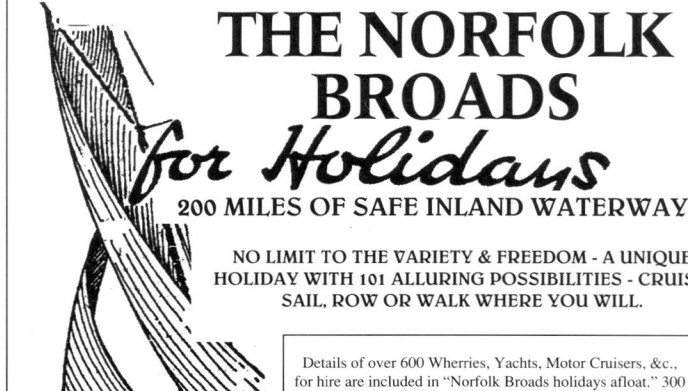

# TRIUMPH OF ALBION DASH AND CONFIDENCE

## BIRMINGHAM'S MISTAKE IN TACTICS: AN EARLY GOAL DISALLOWED

**By Frank Coles**

WEST BROMWICH ALBION .................. 2 BIRMINGHAM .................. 1

WEST BROMWICH ALBION, in winning the Cup with the youngest team that have ever appeared in the Final, have buried the bogey of Wembley "atmosphere" for all time.

Their triumph came in the most thrilling and dramatic sixty seconds of football ever witnessed at a big match, a breathless minute which will live in the memory of the 92,406 people who were at Wembley.

In the thirteenth minute of the second half Birmingham, after half-an-hour's desperate striving, deprived the Albion of a precious lead gained when the game was twenty-six minutes old. In doing so they had achieved the almost unbelievable, for no team had scored an equalising goal in a Cup Final for twenty-one years. Bradford, the scorer, overwhelmed with joy, leapt into the air, and the rest of the Birmingham players did their best to overwhelm Bradford

But it was all too good to be true - or rather, to last. Before the cheering had ended, and before many of us had made a note of Bradford's goal the ball was in the Birmingham net again!

As if goal-scoring could be made to order, the Albion's three inside forwards, straight from the re-start of play, bored a hole clean through the astonished Birmingham defence by good, old-fashioned dribbling and short passing. Liddell, the right back, half-stemmed the tide, then sliced his kick so badly that the ball rolled towards his own goalkeeper.

### Hibbs's Despairing Dash

Hibbs dashed out, slipped, and fell. He could do no more than push the ball to the feet of W.G. Richardson, who scored easily. So was the Cup won and lost.

The lasting impression I shall have of this magnificently fought Final is that, though half the Albion team were mere boys and had never played in an important cup-tie until this season, they began like veterans, and in less than a quarter of an hour were playing in a well-ordered, confident way which suggested that they had no fears about the outcome.

Birmingham, who had planned a quick offensive in the hope of forcing an early goal - and how near to success their scheme came I shall presently tell - were obviously taken by surprise. These sprightly Albion youngsters, they discovered, were capable of falling into their normal, every-day stride as though nothing more serious were at stake than a struggle for League points. And so it happened that Birmingham, in spite of their support advantage on the score of experience, and not the Albion, were the team to get rattled.

Having struck their form very early, the Albion accomplished the extraordinary feat - in a Cup Final - of never losing it.

### The Assurance of Youth

Never has the Cup been won with greater assurance and never has a team in a Final tie risen so markedly superior to the difficulties created by stormy wind, driving rain, and treacherous turf. Rain fell pitilessly and almost without cessation, but in conditions which should have favoured Birmingham it was the Albion who played the football that mattered and delighted the eye. In ball control and accuracy, in passing, short or long, the winners were incomparably the better side.

In method as well as design the Albion led the way. They realised the value on such slippery ground, of the "first-time" game, the sudden change of the point of attack by using wide, far-flung passes out to the wings. The policy paid so handsomely that, in the course of the match, they had half-a-dozen sound scoring chances.

Why were Glidden and Wood so much more menacing than Briggs and Curtis, the Birmingham wingers? Because the Albion half-backs had the skill and the brains to find their wing men with long, beautifully-controlled passes that sped over the turf at lightning pace, whereas Birmingham, making a prime error in tactics, relied on Crosbie and Gregg, their inside forwards to set their attack going.

### Speed in Tackling

Crosbie, a clever schemer, held the ball much too close and as often as not was beaten by the fine speed at which Edwards and Trentham delivered their tackles. This speed in challenging was a tremendous factor in the Albion's dominance. Their half-backs never allowed an opponent time to "work" the ball, and against such a pack of young terriers Birmingham ought to have kept the game open. It was their only possible hope.

To illustrate the point: how many chances was Bradford given either to dash through the middle or to bring his wings into action? The centre-forward, it is true, showed that he was terribly handicapped by his knee injury - he was slow in getting into top speed - but he was entitled to expect far different treatment in the matter of passes. On one of the few occasions that Morrall found him, Bradford scored a brilliant goal.

The sides changed ends with the score unaltered, and in the first minute of the second half the Albion should have increased their lead. W.G. Richardson missing an open goal and Carter heading on to the crossbar. The movement which made these chances possible - a straight-down-the-middle thrust - had far greater significance than we realised at the moment.

After thirteen minutes Bradford equalised with as good a goal as has ever been scored at Wembley. Morrall sent a lobbing pass between the backs, and Bradford, unmarked for once, took a chance with a half-volley while running at full speed. He "hit" the ball perfectly and Pearson was helpless to deal with the shot.

Birmingham, whatever their fate, had made history by scoring the first equalising goal ever registered in a Final tie at Wembley. But their joy was horribly short-lived. When the ball was set going again the Albion repeated in almost every detail the manoeuvre which had all but succeeded at the outset of the second half. This time they scored in the way I have already described.

We all felt that this meant the end of Birmingham. They fought on pluckily and in the hope of saving the match Briggs and Crosbie changed places. But it was the Albion who threatened most danger, thanks to the brilliance of Wood who, after suffering an injury, shaped like a coming International in the final quarter of an hour.

WEST BROMWICH ALBION:- Pearson; Shaw; Trentham; Magee; Richardson (W); Edwards; Glidden; Carter; Richardson (W. G.); Sandford; Wood.

BIRMINGHAM:- Hibbs; Liddell; Barkas; Cringan; Morrall; Leslie; Briggs; Crosbie; Bradford; Gregg; Curtis.

Referee: Mr. A. H. Kingscott.

**(April 27)**

# RECORD FOOTBALL CROWD

## NEARLY 130,000 SPECTATORS AT HAMPDEN PARK

In the presence of a record crowd numbering 129,810, Scotland defeated England in the Association football match at Hampden Park, Glasgow on Saturday by two goals to nothing.

The previous highest attendance was 118,115 on the same ground in 1928.

The victory enables Scotland to share the international honours with England, each country having a total of four points.

Mr. Ramsay MacDonald was present at the match, and the teams were introduced to him before play began.

**(March 30)**

# CHAMPIONS OF THE LEAGUE

## HOW ARSENAL DEFEATED LIVERPOOL

ARSENAL ... 3 LIVERPOOL ... 1

"THE whole team have pulled together with marvellous spirit all through the season - they are a big happy family." said Sir Samuel Hill-Wood, the chairman of the Arsenal, when I offered congratulations at Highbury on Saturday after Liverpool had been conquered and the League championship brought to London for the first time in football history.

I am sure those who have seen the Arsenal play frequently will agree that team spirit, which begets confidence, has been the main factor in their notable triumph. Time and again they have had an early goal scored against them, but an adverse balance never rattles them, and many a bad start has been turned into a spectacular victory.

The Arsenal started badly against Liverpool in Saturday's all-important match - in the fourth minute Roberts turned a swift centre from Barton into his own net - but their powers of recovery did not desert them. For a quarter of an hour Liverpool, especially well served by Barton and Hodgson on the right wing and by the dashing leadership of Wright, threatened to go further ahead, and then Jack levelled the scores.

A corner had been forced, Jones headed forward, and Jack, from four yards range, sent the ball into the roof of the net. Liverpool protested vigorously against the goal on the grounds of offside, and I think they were right.

Liverpool maintained their very lively challenge right up to the interval, but the Arsenal, playing with a tricky wind at their backs, seized the initiative as soon as the second half began and never loosened their grip.

**(April 20)**

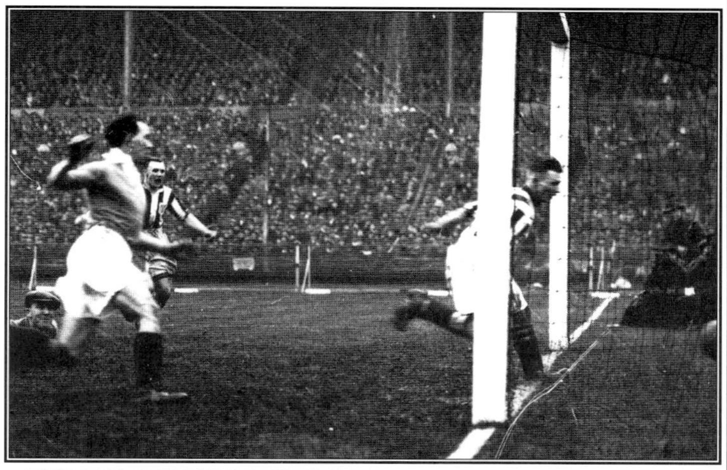

WEST BROMWICH SCORING THE WINNING GOAL against Birmingham at Wembley.

# MACPHERSON LEADS SCOTS TO BRILLIANT VICTORY

## ENGLAND GO DOWN FIGHTING: TWO FINE TRIES BY TALLENT

**By Howard Marshall**

SCOTLAND ... ... ... ... 28pts ENGLAND ... ... ... ... 19 pts.

SCOTLAND beat England at Murrayfield by five goals and a try to two goals, two tries, and a penalty goal, and I am certain no account of a Calcutta Cup match has ever opened with a more startling sentence.

Such prolific scoring seems an almost flippant outrage upon the dour traditions of this particular game, and certainly there has never been such scoring between England and Scotland before.

Nor has there ever in the history of Rugby football been so huge a crowd - 75,000 people roared and swayed and gasped through those eighty riotous minutes, and while I squeezed homewards with them I wondered if they all felt as I did, delighted and bewildered and sublimely uncritical.

Here and there I was flung against stern-faced men who growled about defence - Ford, they complained, should never have over-run Tallent so blindly, and why did the Englishmen not wallop Macpherson down before he began those twinkling runs of his?

As for the English back-row forwards, what had they to say about letting a boy like Logan go running off as he pleased to score one try himself and send Ian Smith in with another? Bad football, argued the solemn-faced men, shaking their heads in sad disapproval.

They may have been justified, though I refuse to believe that a few blemishes can in any way diminish the glory of that royal game. The purists may hug their theories, but most of us will be far happier with our memories of Tallant's superb running, and Macpherson's tactical brilliance, and the goal-kicking of Allan and Black.

The whole afternoon, indeed, takes shape in our minds as a perfect experience. First there was Murrayfield itself, and the boy pipers swaggering with such exquisite pride across that close-cropped turf, and then the menacing cloud which sent the umbrellas fluttering in the packed mounds. It had rained in the morning, but after lunch the weather held, and as Arnold and Macpherson led their men sprinting across the ground we could see that the surface was reasonably firm.

### Well-Deserved Win

Scotland deserved to win. There can be no doubt of that. Their forwards on a count had considerably the better of the tight scrummages, and at least held their own in the loose. Welsh Roughead and Crichton Miller were excellent, while Howard, and particularly Hordern, served England well. With more opportunities the Scottish outsides were always dangerous. Pope played soundly and extremely pluckily for England, but he is not yet more than a good club scrum-half.

Lind definitely outplayed Knowles, who was the weak link in the English attack, and this Scottish superiority at half-back was decisive. Then there was Macpherson, and his genius as an attacking centre was never more apparent. He did not score himself, but four tries directly followed his brilliant strokes towards gaps in the English defence.

But if England were beaten, at least they went down fighting. Their attack was better than it has been so far, and Tallent must be congratulated on his magnificent tries. Harrison again was sound, and a change at stand-off half might make this three-quarter line really formidable. Still, that is enough of criticism. This was a game which will be remembered for its general virtues rather than for the insignificant failings of individual players.

SCOTLAND- A.W. Wilson; I.S. Smith; G.P.S. Macpherson; D. St. Clair Ford; and W.M. Simmers; H. Lind; and W.R. Logan; J.W. Allan; J.H. Beattie; W.D. Welsh; H.S. Mackintosh; A.W. Walker; J.S. Wilson; W.N. Roughead; and D. Crichton Miller .

ENGLAND - E.C.P. Whiteley; J.S.R. Reeve ; J.A. Tallant; C.D. Aarvold (capt.); and A.C. Harrison; T.C.Knowles; and E.B. Pope ; R.H. Sparks; H. Rew; J.W. Forrest; B.H. Black; P.E. Dunkley; P.L. Howard; and P.C. Hordern .

**(March 23)**

# CAMBRIDGE WIN BOAT RACE FROM FIRST STROKE

**By G. C. Drinkwater**

YET again Cambridge have won the Boat Race. They have now won it eight times running, and in one more year they will have equalled Oxford's two records of nine successive wins.

From the first stroke they won their race on Saturday. This does not mean that the Oxford crew disgraced themselves. They did not, for they rowed most gallantly, but they were outpaced by just those three inches every stroke which they could not afford to give away to a man like Brocklebank.

I had thought that the crucial point of the race would come at Craven Steps, just over two minutes from the start. In fact it came when Col. Gibbon, with his stentorian voice, said "Go!"

Cambridge won by two and a half lengths, and this fairly represents the difference between the two crews. In the conditions prevailing - no bumper tide, and a head wind for the greater part of the course - their time of 19min 26sec shows that they were a crew far above the average.

University crews, for some reason, are never so good as they used to be to the old oarsmen who come to watch them at Putney in practice. I personally have no patience with that form of conceit which besets so many old Blues, and without hesitation, less than twenty-four hours after the race was rowed, I say that this year's Cambridge crew is, with the exception of their crew of 1924, the best University crew we have seen since the war, and the equal of many of the best crews that raced before the cataclysm.

It is true that they were a one-man crew, and that one man was their stroke and president, Tom Brocklebank. He conjured with the men behind him and brought them to the posts, both at Putney and at Mortlake, perfectly together.

Behind Brocklebank there was of course, the unwavering, inflexible genius of Mr. Haig Thomas, who not only coached the crew for the last six weeks of practice, but was the chooser of its personnel. How good his crew was in comparison with the best crews of to-day is shown by the result of the Head of the River race, which took place on the ebb from Mortlake to Putney a few hours after the Universities raced. Jesus College, Cambridge in this event raced second to London R.C., losing to them by 10 sec.

Oxford have no cause to be entirely discouraged by the result of the race, though at the moment there seems to be no reason why they should ever win another. They came to Putney a dispirited crew. Under Mr. Stanley Garton they improved every day in the most remarkable manner, and on his work with this crew Mr. Garton must take his place as a great finishing coach, even though he could not make them win.

**(March 23)**

# BRITISH PRESTIGE IN SPORT

## FOOTBALL DEFEATS ON THE CONTINENT

*Renewed attention has been drawn to the damage to British prestige caused by professional Association football teams who, when touring on the Continent, fail to take their games seriously and, as a result, suffer humiliating defeats.*

*Certain teams (e.g. Sheffield Wednesday and the Arsenal), have proved exceptions and by giving of their best have upheld Britain's reputation in this pre-eminently British branch of sport.*

**From A Special Representative**

I understand that strong representations are being made by members of the British colony in Rome to the authorities at home regarding the recent visit to Italy of a team sent out by the Scottish Football Association.

In a match widely advertised as "Scotland v. Italy," which was attended by 25,000 people, among whom were Signor Mussolini and a number of his Ministers, the Scottish side were beaten by three goals to none after a display on their part which was not only disappointing but deplorable.

This had followed an even heavier defeat by 5-0 at Vienna, where their victors, although an ordinary club team, completely outplayed them; and at Geneva only by the narrowest margin did "Scotland" overcome a Switzerland eleven composed wholly of amateurs.

An extraordinary outburst of adverse criticism was provoked by the match at Rome. In the Italian Press such phrases as "the decadence of British football" and "the exposure of a myth about British superiority," were used. A writer in one of the leading sporting newspapers frankly declared that although the Italians used to learn their football from Great Britain, "they can now teach the British."

It must be recognised forthwith that the time has gone past when Britain can treat other countries as novices and pupils in football. The immediate duty of the rulers of the game ought to be to resolve not to hold aloof any longer from the International Federation of Football Association - a ridiculous position in view of football's rapid progress abroad. Continental fixtures would then be automatically given real importance.

**(June 28)**

# GREAT BATTLE IN LE MANS RACE

After a thrilling race, marked by some brilliant driving, the British drivers, Sir Henry Birkin and Earl Howe, in an Italian Alfa Romeo, won the twenty-four hours Grand Prix at Le Mans, and in doing so set up a world's record.

They covered approximately 1,885 miles at at average speed of over eighty miles an hour, beating the record set up by last year's winners, Capt. Barnato and the late Cmdr. Glen Kidston, in a Bentley, who covered 1,830 miles at an average speed of over 75 m.p.h.

A Mercedes-Benz (with more than twice the power of the Alfa-Romeo) was second, a British Talbot fourth, and a British Aston-Martin fifth. Only seven out of the twenty-six starters finished, and of these three were British, two French, one Italian, and one German.

The race was marred by the worst accident in French motor-racing for ten years. One of the new Bugatti cars - a team which were racing for the first time - dashed off the road into the spectators, killing one and injuring four others, two seriously.

**(June 15)**

# SOUTH AFRICA WIN THE RUBBER

## FIFTH TEST MATCH ENDS IN DRAW

DURBAN, Wednesday.

South Africa won their third rubber of Test matches against England here to-day by virtue of their victory in the first of the five Tests at Johannesburg, on a matting wicket, last December. There have been fourteen rubbers played between the two countries - ten in South Africa and four in England - and South Africa's three victories have been won on their native soil.

The drawing of four successive Tests after the first had yielded a definite result was disappointing, but rain all but wiped out the third match, and, owing to its influence on the first day of the match just ended, the most vital game of the tour was shorn of much of its interest.

To-day's play was not desultory, but it lacked the incentive which lifts the play out of mediocrity. South Africa, who occupied the wickets for 3 ¼ hours, declared at 4.45, when their score was 219 for seven, and they were 241 runs on. England were left with only an hour's batting, during which they scored 72 for four wickets.

**(February 26)**

# 1931 CABINET – A NATIONAL CABINET

(ABOVE):THE 1931 CABINET: Back row, from left: Sir P. Cunliffe-Lister, J.H. Thomas, Marquess of Reading, Neville Chamberlain, Sir Samuel Hoare; front row: Philip Snowden, Stanley Baldwin, Ramsay MacDonald (Prime Minister), Sir Herbert Samuel and Lord Sankey.

GHANDI arriving at No. 10 Downing Street for a conference with Ramsay MacDonald.

(RIGHT): THE EMPIRE STATE BUILDING, NEW YORK CITY

(LEFT): AL CAPONE WITH US MAR-SHALL Laubenhemer.

POLICEMEN CLIMBING THE LIONS to remove the demonstrating workless.

# WORKLESS DEMONSTRATE IN IN HYDE PARK

A year of new beginnings: Franklin Delano Roosevelt defeated the tired and dispirited Herbert Hoover for the presidency of the United States. Britain followed its action of leaving the gold standard in the previous year by abandoning free trade, with the result that the chances of emerging from the depression seemed brighter. In Germany the Nazi party failed to get its expected majority in the Reichstag, causing *The Daily Telegraph* to write the over-optimistic headline, "Herr Hitler's hopes dashed for ever."

This was a sentiment as baseless as those expressed in the obituary, published in March, of Ivar Kreuger, the Swedish match king, which listed his fine qualities and successes. A month later, Kreuger was revealed as a fraudster, a blackmailer and a liar on an unprecedented scale, the Robert Maxwell of his day. Similarly, the obituarist of the popular novelist Edgar Wallace mused about the great fortune that he must have amassed. When his will was probated, he was found to be bankrupt.

The whole world waited for news of the fate of the kidnapped baby son of Charles Lindbergh, the first man to fly the Atlantic solo. Despite the payment of ransom money, the baby was found dead. In Britain, the convicts in Dartmoor Prison rioted and almost succeeded in gaining control of the prison. There was no softly-softly treatment in an effort to persuade the rioters to give up: while the army stood by; the warders fired buckshot and a force of police, armed only with truncheons, battled to restore order.

The hopes of recovery did not enthuse the millions of unemployed on both sides of the Atlantic or as far afield as New Zealand. There were hunger marches heading for both London and Washington. *The Daily Telegraph* discovered the hand of the Communist Party and the availability of "Moscow gold" in the organisation of the British marchers.

In Manchuria the Japanese confirmed their hold on the country by installing the deposed Emperor of China, the last of the Manchu dynasty, as ruler. In a spate of assassinations, the President of France and the Japanese prime minister were killed while Benito Mussolini and Herbert Hoover survived after being attacked. In India, Gandhi, imprisoned again, went on hunger strike and won his point.

The obsession with long-distance flying records continued. Amy Johnson, the heroine of the previous years' solo flight to Australia, married fellow pilot Jim Mollison and celebrated the event by beating her husband's record for a flight from England to South Africa. Amelia Earhart, who was to die a decade later in mysterious circumstances when trying to cross the Pacific, became the first woman to fly solo across the Atlantic. Malcolm Campbell added yet another land speed record and Kay Donn won back the water speed title.

The great showman Flo Ziegfeld died, as did the Bloomsbury historian Lytton Strachey. In sport, the first rumblings of the cricket bodyline controversy were heard. The veteran batsman Jack Hobbs protested at the Yorkshire leg-theory bowling, presaging the following year's controversy in Australia.

**MISS EARHART IN LONDON**



# The Daily Telegraph

To-Days Weather : Some Rain

Broadcasting: Page Seven



No. 24,027 POSTAGE { INLAND, CANADA AND NEWFOUNDLAND, THREE HALFPENCE / OTHER COLONIES AND PLACES ABROAD, TWOPENCE } LONDON, MONDAY, MAY 23, 1932 ONE PENNY

*BIRTHS, MARRIAGES and DEATHS as a line "IN MEMORIAM" notices 3s a line. (Special rate for five or ten years automatic insertion on application. Announcements authenticated by name and address of sender, may be sent to The Daily Telegraph, Fleet-st., E.C. 4 or 161 Piccadilly, E. 1 or telephoned to Central 4242.*

## BIRTHS

REGAN - On May 19, 1932 to DORIS (née McKerrow) wife of MAURICE REGAN, of 37 Chartfield-avenue, Putney, a son.

ROGERS - On May 19, 1932 in London to HAZEL, wife of FRANCIS H ROGERS, of Kabale, Uganda, a son.

SHEIL - On May 18, 1932 at 20 Charles-street, W.1. to DORRIE wife of Captain W.A. SHEIL, a son.

SMITH - On May 17, 1932 at Oaklawn Nursing Home, Sydenham to DORRIE (née Hafnmer), wife of THOMAS GREGORY SMITH, a son (Rodney).

VENNER - On May 17, 1932, at Gosfield Vicarage, Halstead, to MARJORIE, wife of Rev. R. KINGSFORD VENNER the gift of a daughter.

WALL - On May 19, 1932, to Mr. and Mrs. T WALL, Broom House, Keighley, a son.

## MARRIAGES

ALLCOCK-MILLARD - On May 14, 1932, at Woodhouse, Leicestershire, GERARD THOMAS, son of Mr. E.T. ALLCOCK, of Loughborough, to ETHEL NANCY, daughter of Dr. and Mrs. C.K. MILLARD, of Leicester.

CHIERICO-WOOD - On May 19, 1932, very quietly in London, Signor MICHAELE CHIERICO to DOROTHY, youngest daughter of the late HENRY J. WOOD, of Bilborough Court, Tunbridge Wells.

COATES-POOLE - On May 20 1932, at Holy Trinity Church, Hull by the Rev. Canon Morgan. WILLIAM RAYMOND elder son of Mr. and Mrs. WILLIAM COATES, of 20 St. Paul's-road, Bradford, to ELIZABETH ROSA (Betty), daughter of the late Captain H. GIBSON POOLE and Mrs. Poole, of Hull.

McCARTHY-McWATTERS - On May 10, 1932, at the Church of St. Philip Neri, Capt G.W. McCARTHY, Royal Irish Fusiliers, to CYNTHIA, daughter of Lt. Col. McWATTERS, I.M.S. and Mrs McWatters.

ROBINSON-BEDLINGTON - On May 19, 1932, at St. Peter's, Great Windmill-street, A.C.H. ROBINSON, of Church Close, Kensington to MARGARET BEDLINGTON, daughter of the late J.C. Bedlington, of Cardiff, and Mrs. Bedlington, of 33 Richmond-hill, Surrey.

SAVORY-LEANING - On May 19, 1932, at St. Bride's Church, E.C. CHRISTOPHER SAVORY, of Finchley, to DAPHNE THOMASIN LEANING, of Hampstead Garden Suburb.

WHITE-LLOYD - On May 14, 1932, at Great Yarmouth Parish Church, by the Rev. L. Meadows White,father of the bridegroom, BASIL MEADOWS WHITE, of Potter Heigham, to ELEANOR ADA LLOYD of Great Yarmouth.

## DEATHS

BAKER - On May 20, 1932 following an operation for meningitis, RICHARD BURTON, the very dearly loved younger son of Mr. and Mrs. H.W. Baker, of Clavering Court, Newport, Essex. aged 9 years 8 months. Funeral to-day (Monday) at Clavering Church, private.

BATTYE - On May 16, 1932, in India, as result of motor-car accident. BASIL CONDON BATTYE, D.S.O., A.M., Legion of Honour (French and Belgian), Colonel, Royal Engineers, youngest son of the late Major Leigh Richmond Battye, 5th Gurkha Rifles, and dearly loved husband of Edith Battye, at St. Agnes, Caterham, aged 49.

BRAMALL - On May 19, 1932 , at Wraxall, Bristol, MARY HARRIETT RAMALL, in her 74th year. Funeral service two p.m. to-day (Monday) at Wrexall Interment at Weston-super-Mare.

COKE - On May 19, 1932, at a nursing home, Hampstead, JULIANA DOROTHEA, last surviving daughter of the late Rev. E.P. COKE, M.A. Oxon, in her 87th year.

DEFRIES - On May 21, 1932, at 1, Grangecourt-road, Stamford Hill, N. 16 ROSE, beloved wife of HARRY DEFRIES. Funeral will leave house to-day at 2.30 for Marlow-road Cemetery.

DENNISS - On May 23, 1932, at Holmsdale, Fitzjames-avenue. Addiscombe. Surrey, ALFRED DENNISS, in his 71st year. Funeral service, Anerley Congregational Church, twelve noon Wednesday; interment Elmera End Cemetery.

GARDNER - On May 20, 1932, of pneumonia, at his residence Lytton Lodge. The Drive, South Woodford. GEORGE GARDNER, the youngest son of the late Thomas and Elizabeth Gardner, in his 97th year. Funeral at the Parish Church, Wanstead, to-morrow (Tuesday) at three o'clock. No flowers, by his own request. Cars at Scarsbrook Station to meet the 2.10 train from Liverpool-street.

GIFFARD - On May 19, 1932 at Bulkeley House, Englefield Green, GEORGE CAMPBELL GIFFARD, dearly loved husband of Jane Mary Giffard, and formerly Clerk of the Journals to the House of Commons, aged 79 years. Funeral to-day (Monday) at St. Jude's Church, Englefield Green at 2.45 p.m. Cars will meet at Egham Station 1.37 train from Waterloo.

GOTT - On May 19, 1932 at 18, Westgate-terrace, Eastcliffe-square, S.W. HILDA MARGARET BRAMLEY GOTT, eldest daughter of the late Dr. Gott, Bishop of Truro. Funeral at Tywardreath, Par. Cornwall, to-morrow (Tuesday) at eleven a.m.

HALLARAN - On May 18, 1932, at a hospital in London, RICHARD BUNBURY HALLARAN, second son of the late Venerable T.T. Hallaran, M.A. Archdeacon of Ardfert, Co. Kerry.

HARRIS - On May 17, 1932, PERCY REEVES TRAER Harris M.R.C.S., F.S.A. of 23 York House, Kensington and late of 112A Harley-street, W.1. aged 70 years, Interned at Brockwood Cemetary.

HOUGHTON - On May 21, 1932, GILBERT HOUGHTON, of Walthamstow, Essex, passed peacefully away in his 60th year. Funeral at St. Mary's Walthamstow, at 1.30 p.m. to-morrow (Tuesday, May 24).

HUDSON - On May 19, 1932 after a few days' illness, GWYNEDD MAY HUDSON, of Wick Studio, Holland-road, Hove. No flowers.

LYON - On May 19, 1932, at Silverhill, Barton-under Seedwood, EDITH JANE LYON.

## PERSONAL

*5s per line (minimum 2 lines). Trade, 10s per line. Lost and Found 2s 6d per line.*

WILLIAMS - REQUIRED, WHEREABOUTS or INFORMATION concerning ERNEST DILWYN LLEWELYN WILLIAMS born nr. Brecon 1878-9, believed killed in action at El Wadl Kut El Amarah, Apr. 1916, with 12th Iron Div. Welsh Terrs or of his issue. COMMUNICATE with McLEARY ROBSON & MENDES, Solicitors, Chancery-lane, Melbourne, Australia.

GENTLEMAN with provincial connection desires appointment. London Stock Exchange house - Write G Box 9.541 Daily Telegraph, 161 Piccadilly, W.1.

FISH is almost the only rare thing by the sea-side.
John Wilkes.

NOT QUITE FIVE - This little mite says "She can't carry her dolly far, her arms ache so" She has been ill and is still very weak, having outgrown her strength. She needs a long stay in Church Army Children's Holiday Home. - Cheques &c., to Preb. Carlile, "Betty" 55, Bryanston-street, W.1.

ABNORMALLY HIGH PRICES (maximum market price) paid for GOLD and SILVER due to rise in market. Highest prices paid for sovereigns; special rates over 500. Also urgent need of Old English Silver, Sheffield Plate, Jewellery. Diamonds, Antiques, Dental Plates (not vulcanite). Large or small quantities. Send your odd bits &c. immediately, or bring them to BENTLEY & CO., 8a and 9, New Bond-st. London W.1.

HE THAT IS WITHOUT SIN AMONG YOU let him first cast a stone at her. - St. John. vttl, 7

GENTLEMAN, undertake any legal proposition, firm or individual - Write D. Box 4.819, Daily Telegraph, E.C.4.

BEDROOM SUITE, beautiful burr walnut (40gns, Xmas), accept (6gns, Chesterfield Suite, 25gns, Xmas, take 14gns. Oak Dining Suite - Write B. Box 4.716, Daily Telegraph E.C.4.

PIANO WANTED. Brinsmead, Bechstein, or Steinway. - Write C.A., 14 King William-street, Strand, W.C.2.

SPORTS and TOYS - To LET on lease, a beautifully fitted SHOP in a very populous and high-class district. Wonderful opportunity. Lease £75 per ann. Ingoing £175. Including high-class fittings. - Write X, Y, Z. Box 4,478. Daily Telegraph E.C.4.

GUY'S HOSPITAL S.E.1. URGENTLY NEEDS HELP TOTAL ANNUAL EXPENDITURE £190,000. ENDOWED INCOME ONLY £67,000.

INTENDING ADVERTISERS can obtain help and advice in the compilation of their announcements at the West-end office of the Daily Telegraph, 161, Piccadilly, W.1.

MANAGING DIRECTOR of several companies requires PRIVATE SECRETARY, lady or gentleman. Must be thoroughly capable and possess first-class references (hotel experience an advantage), and able to invest £500 as security. Salary according to experience, and full board-residence - Write M. Box 9.523, Daily Telegraph, 161 Piccadilly, W.1.

IF YOU WOULD LIKE TO SUCCEED AS AN AUTHOR, an experienced Journalist will help you with practical tuition, both personal and correspondence. Revision of M58, undertaken also at moderate fee - Write 1, Box 7.396, Daily Telegraph, E.C.4.

THE WALTHAM WATCH DEPOT Ulster-chambers, 168, Regent-st., W.1. Reg. 3691. Sales and Repairs.

HOW TO DRESS WELL on 10s or £1 per month. Open a credit Account with Smartwear. No deposit. No references required, even from those who are not householders. Visit our magnificent show rooms, or write for Ladies Catalogue of Latest Fashions to Dept. A.38 sent gratis and post free. SMARTWEAR Ltd. 263-271, Regent-street, Oxford-circus, London. W.1. 'Phone Mayfair 6241-6.

ALCOHOLISM - An interesting Brochure on medical treatment free - Secretary, 40, Marsham-st. S.W.1.

MELOX in the Morning and MARVELS at Night keep your dogs healthy, happy, and bright"- All corn merchants, stores &c., sell Melox Dog Foods.

PIANOS - MAPLE & CO are offering the BEST possible prices for good Secondhand Pianos. - TOTTENHAM-COURT-ROAD, W.1.

THE GOLD STANDARD has been suspended, but the standard demanded by the N.S.P.C.C. for children must be maintained. Every day 300 fresh child victims of cruelty and neglect are protected by the National Society for the Prevention of Cruelty to Children. Funds urgently needed - Send your gifts to the Director. Victory House, Leicester-sq. London W.C.2.

CHOICE INDIAN and CEYLON BLEND XLNT. 1s 6d per pound, 6lb post paid 10s. Every leaf guaranteed Empire. Purchase money returned in full if satisfaction not given. - STEPHEN CARWARDINE & CO., Tea Blenders, 4-5 Victoria House, Southampton-row, London W.C.1. Established 1777.

HAMILTON-TERRACE - Beautiful detached SMALL HOUSE 10 rooms 2 bathrooms, kitchens, Garage. Good garden. Every modern convenience. Lease 60 years. G.r. £92. Price £3,950 or £10 - offer. - Stamp for particulars to E.O. case of Vickers, 24, Austin Friare, E.C.2.

LITTLE CHILDREN need our help - we need yours. Will you please send a gift to keep wards open at the East London Hospital for Children. Shadwell E.1.

HORLEY, 25 miles from London. Electric trains expected July next. HOUSE of DISTINCTION for SALE. Three receptions, six bed rooms, El light, all conveniences. Conservatory, garage. Picturesque grounds about 1 ¼ acre. Lake, island, rustic bridges, summer house, specimen trees and shrubs, kitchen garden, nut walk &c. Price £2,250 - Don't write, view Warltersville, Balcombe-road, Horley, Surrey.

INTERESTING beautiful country seat now WHITWELL HATCH HOTEL, HASLEMERE, SURREY. Central heating, gas fires, hot and cold. Squash, badminton (covered courts), riding. Wonderful views.

DO PLEASE SEND OLD CLOTHES. Toys, Books, Sports Gear, &c Any description. Any condition. They are a tremendous help. Poorest district imaginable. Rev. S.G. Tinley, St. Luke's Vicarage, Victoria Docks E.16

## CONCERTS, &c

QUEEN'S HALL, (Sole Lessees, Chappell & Co. Ltd)

### TO-NIGHT, at 8.30

HAROLD HOLT presents the

### LENER QUARTET

Quartet in G minor, Op. 10....................................DEBUSSY

Quartet in B flat major. Op 67....................................BRAHMS

Piano Quintet in E flat major Op 44....................SCHUMANN

### LENER QUARTET

At the Piano

### OLGA LOESER LEBERT

Tickets: 12s, 8s 6d, 3s 6d,3s, 2s 6d from CHAPPELL'S Box-offices. Queen's Hall, 30 New Bond-street, Steinway Piano.

ÆOLIAN HALL, TO-NIGHT, at 8.30

### AUBREY PANKEY

NEGRO BARITONE Piano - GERALD MOORE

WEBER PIANO Tickets, 9s, 5s 9d 3s

IBBS & TILLETT, 124, Wigmore-st. W.1. Welbeck 2325

GROTRIAN HALL, TO-NIGHT, at 8.15

### VICTOR BABIN

PIANOFORTE RECITAL

BECHSTEIN PIANO Tickets 12s, 8s 6d, 6s, 3s

L.G. SHARPE, 25 Haymarket, S.W.1. Whitehall 1364

### TRINITY COLLEGE of MUSIC

MANDEVILLE-PLACE, MANCHESTER-SQUARE, W.1.
(Instituted 1872)
President:
The Rt. Hon. Viscount HAILSHAM of HAILSHAM P.C.
Principal:
E. STANLEY ROPER, M.V.O. M.A. Mus. B
Controller of Examinations:
EDWARD D'EVRY F.R.C.O., F.T.C.L.
WEDNESDAY NEXT at 3 p.m.
LECTURE with ILLUSTRATIONS by
Dr. J. WARRINER
Subject: THE EVOLUTION OF THE REVOLUTIONIST
At 5.30 p.m. Students' Invitation House Concert
Lecture and Concert are open free to the public.
No tickets required.
Particulars of the Teaching Department with List of Professors Fees, Scholarships Regulations &c. Syllabuses of the Higher and Local Examinations, free on application to the undersigned.
C.N.H. RODWELL, Secretary.

## MUSIC, SINGING, ELOCUTION, &c

### THE GUILDHALL SCHOOL OF MUSIC

(Corporation of London)
JOHN CARPENTER-STREET, E.C.1.

THE BRITISH EMPIRE SOCIETY OF ARTS SCHOLARSHIP, value £50 per annum, providing complete musical education to vocalists, male or female. Candidates must be British subjects, born anywhere within the Empire, between the ages of 16 and 25 years. Candidates should apply for entry forms, which must be forwarded on or before Saturday, 4th June, 1932, to:
H. SAXE WYNDHAM, Secretary.
Telephones: Central 4459; City 5566.

## DANCING

CASANI School of Ball-room Dancing, 90 Regent-st, teach steps any dance in 3 pte. lessons, 21s Court Curtsey, 10s 6d - Regent 4438.

RUBY PEELER Eccleston Hotel (Vic. 5770) Tap and Ballroom lessons daily (Lunch hr. 5s) Court Curtsey, Dance Wed, 4.30-6.30, 2s 6d Mon 9-12, 4s

GEM MOUFLET (Miss) PARTNERS to DANCES. teaches PRIVATELY, 9.30-9.30 6 days, CURTSEY, 11 ALBEMARLE-ST, PICCADILLY, REGent 4629.

## ARTICLES FOR SALE AND WANTED

FURNITURE

AMAZING OPPORTUNITY

FOR THOSE ABOUT TO FURNISH IMPORTANT PRIVATE SALE. £75,000 OF HIGHGRADE FURNITURE MADE FOR SUPER HOTEL IN BERMUDA. This huge consignment includes BED-ROOM, DINING-ROOM and DRAWING-ROOM SUITES, Lounge, Library, Hall Furniture, and Staff rooms complete. Every article guaranteed soundly constructed and of Modern Design.

### MESSRS. DAVIS'S

FURNITURE DEPOSITORIES LTD.,

have received instruction to sell the foregoing at their spacious show rooms regardless of actual cost, and those furnishing should not fail to make an immediate inspection. We enumerate below only a few of the many bargains that may be obtained.

85 Oak Bedroom Suites complete with wardrobes, beds and springs ....................each 6 10 0
50 Double-sized ditto with triple mirror, Dressing tables, linen chests and double bedstead........................................................9 10 0
40 Double-size beautifully figured Bedroom Suites in Grey or Dark Walnut. Worth Double. Beds to match.......................................14 14 0
30 Double-size ditto with artistic Kidney Shaped or Cheval Dressing Tables ...................18 18 0
100 Complete Waxed Oak Dining Room Suites, comprising SIDEBOARD, DINING TABLE, SET OF CHAIRS, SERVICE WAGON and MIRROR, ...........................................ea. set 7 15 0

Other Complete Rooms in Walnut and Mahogany all periods equally cheap.

250 Real Cowhide Easy Chairs with loose cushions (Settees to match £5 15 0) ............each 3 3 0
50 Ditto Larger size with wings luxuriously sprung .8 15 0
350 Dining Room Chairs with loose leather seats.........9 6
50 Luxuriously sprung easy chairs in various coverings from.........................................................1 1 0
100 Writing Bureaus in Oak, Walnut and Mahogany 2 19 6

Also a vast selection of Bookcases Fitted Wardrobes, in fact, every item for Furnishing.

Any article sold separately, stored and packed free for country. ON VIEW at

DAVIS'S FURNITURE DEPOSITORIES Ltd.,

83 & 85, St. John's-rd., Clapham Junction, S.W. 11. 6 minutes Waterloo and Victoria, Estab. 1880.
'Phone Battersea 4838 Open daily 9 to 8.

## JEWELLERY

ASTOUNDING PRICES

FOR OLD GOLD, OLD-FASHIONED JEWELLERY, DIAMONDS, SILVER, PLATE, Coins, Sovereign Cases, Watches, Bangles, Chains, &c. To-day's prices may not occur again. Immediate cash to callers or post to-day for offer. Goods held over pending reply. HARRIS & CO, 37 Piccadilly, London (Regent 5523)

## MUSICAL INSTRUMENTS

ARNOLD LTD. EXCEPTIONAL BARGAINS in slightly used Pianos by all makers of repute. SPECIAL OFFER: A £300 BECHSTEIN BOUDOIR GRAND for 80gns 10 yrs' guarantee. Exchanges. Cash or terms. Open till 7 p.m. - 28 SOUTH MOLTON-ST., W.1. May 3848.

CHAS. STILES & CO.
for NEW and SECONDHAND PIANOS.
Steinway, Bechstein, Challen, Bord, &c Cash or Monthly payments. Pianos exchanged (full value). - Send for lists 74 and 76, SOUTHAMPTON-ROW, W.C.1.
Telephone Museum 0439 (2 mins. Holb. Tube).

## OFFICE EQUIPMENT

TYPEWRITER EXPERTS CO., 55 Little Britain, E.C. Cash or terms. Also repairs. (Nat. 8210)

SPECIAL OFFER: "UNDERWOOD" AS NEW, £8 8s

TYPEWRITERS. Duplicators, Adders, Calculators, Office Furn., Bought. Sold. HIRED. Repaired. - Taylor's 74, Chancery-in., W.C.2. Holb 3793.

OFFICE FURNITURE and SAFES WANTED. also job stocks of other saleable lines.- Dale, 146, Charring-cross-rd., W.C.2.

REQUIRED. cheap, reliable DICTATING DICTAPHONE MACHINE - Courtauld Institute, Middlesex Hosptial, W.1.

## WEARING APPAREL

AUCTION YOUR SURPLUS APPAREL. Thousands of private owners avail themselves of our services.A satisfied client writes: "Thanks for cheque received. I think you have done wonderfully." - SEND parcels, or write for particulars to JOHNSON, DYMOND & SON Ld., Dept. D.T. (est. 1793), 24-26 Great Queen-street, Kingsway, W.C.2. Sales daily.

## EDUCATIONAL

UNRIVALLED SUCCESSES
OF
PITMAN'S COLLEGE
IN
ROYAL SOCIETY OF ARTS EXAMINATIONS

33 SILVER AND BRONZE MEDALS IN 1931 and 201 Silver and Bronze Medals in the last ten years, with thousands of certificates in Shorthand, Bookkeeping, Typewriting, English, Commerce, Arithmetic, French, German, &c

The number of medals obtained by our candidates in 1931 is the largest number awarded to any school or group of schools in the history of the Society's Examination.

This is striking testimony to the thoroughness of the College training. Parents can be secure in entrusting their sons and daughters business training to Pitman's.

Write to-day for (a) Prospectus, (b) Evening Study Booklet, or (c) Home Study Booklet according to your requirements.

PITMAN'S COLLEGE
Advisory Governor:
The Duchess of Atholl, D.R.E., D.C.L., LL.D., M.P.
Principal: R.W. Holland, O.B.E., M.A., M.Sc. LL.D.
182 SOUTHAMPTON-ROW, W.C.1.
And Brixton, Brondesbury, City, Croydon, Ealing, Finsbury Park, Forest Gate, Lewisham, Maida-hill, Palmers-green, Wimbledon, Leeds, Manchester.

KENSINGTON COLLEGE

SPECIALISES IN SECRETARIAL TRAINING

on a thorough basis, equipping its students for responsible posts which are guaranteed on completion of Diploma Course - Prospectus and full particulars from Mr. L.E. Munford, 34 Bishop's-road, London, W.2. Telephone: *Paddington 9046.

SECRETARIAL COLLEGE
FOR EDUCATED GIRLS

Careful Modern Training culminating in FIRST CLASS POSTS
FOUR EXHIBITIONS granted annually to help clever girls. Details on application
MODERN LANGUAGES, French, German & Spanish, and the SHORTHAND of each language taught.

MISS MILDRED RANSOM

15, Great Cumberland Place, Marble Arch, W.1. Paddington 6302

BEDFORD SQUARE
SECRETARIAL COLLEGE

for educated ladies. Intensive and individual training. Moderate, inclusive fee to proficiency and a position. Foreign languages &c - 8 Bedford-sq., W.C.1. Mus. 7823.

QUEEN'S SECRETARIAL COLLEGE, 255 Cromwell-road, S.W.5. - Practical training for gentlewomen; pleasant surroundings. All subjects taught. Intensive and full courses. Two residential clubs.

PARIS ACADEMY OF DRESSMAKING AND MILLINERY,

24 OLD BOND-STREET, W.1.

Principal - Mme J. TROIS FONTAINES.
The most PRACTICAL and ACCEPTED SCHOOL in the BRITISH ISLES.
Day or Postal Courses.
Visit the Academy or write for Prospectus A.M.

THE WIGMORE SCHOOL OF DRESSMAKING
58, WIGMORE-ST., W.1.

Learn under practical conditions. Day & evening courses. Visit the School or write for terms. Fees moderate.

HATS! Learn to make your own, or as career, 12 lessons 3 gns. - THE SCHOOL OF MILLINERY, 68, WIGMORE-ST. Welbeck 9606.

AUTOMOBILE ENGINEERING
TRAINING COLLEGE

CHELSEA, S.W. 3 (DAY and RESIDENTIAL). Practical Curriculum with Modern Works Experience and Training in Administration for Entry to the Industry. Probationary Term. Syllabus from Registrar.

## EDUCATIONAL (CONTINUED)

THOMAS SCHOOL of LANGUAGES, 435-7, Oxford-st., W.1. Specially small classes. English for foreign students. Courses commencing. Write for prospectus.

HOLIDAY COACHING given by Miss Petzeche, B.A., at L'Institut des Langues, W. Ealing. 'Phone 6566.

SPANISH by young Spanish gentlemen. Experienced teacher - Write Sr. Marquez c.o. Nelson 107, Jermyn-st., S.W.1.

ARDINGLY COLLEGE SUSSEX - Inclusive fees £100 per annum Ten Entrance Scholarships, value £50-£30 for boys under 14 open for competition in June. - Apply the Headmaster.

### LEIGHTON PARK SCHOOL, READING.

An EXAMINATION for FIFTEEN OPEN SCHOLARSHIPS, value £100-£50. will take place in JUNE. Boys of all-round promise who do not reach Scholarship standard are eligible for Bursaries of similar value. Apply to the Bursar before June 1st.

WELLINGTON SCHOOL SOMERSET. A further New Wing is to be opened in September giving additional accommodation. - Prospectus and full particulars Bursar, WELLINGTON SCHOOL, SOMERSET. Last day for Entrance Scholarships, June 11th.

BOARDING SCHOOLS or TUTORS, Including BOYS PREPARATORY SCHOOLS Girls' Finishing Schools, Domestic Science or Secretarial Colleges also Nursery Schools, - Consult gratis LAVELL, BATTEN & CO. 93 Chancery-lane, W.C.2. Holborn 6105.

ADVICE on the choice of suitable
SCHOOLS and TUTORS
for Boys and Girls, with prospectuses of recommended establishments, will be given free of charge to parents stating age of pupil, district preferred range of fees and type of school required.

J & J PATON
142 Cannon-street, London E.C.4.
Telephone: Mansion House 5053.

## PRIVATE SCHOOLS & COLLEGES

JERSEY COLLEGE, (for Girls) Founded 1880, Recognised by Board of education. Chairman: The Right Hon. the Lord Gisborough.

PUPILS PREPARED for ENTRANCE and SCHOLARSHIPS to all Universities and for Domestic Science and Secretarial Diplomas. A very high standard attained in French. Excellently equipped building. Mild climate. Holiday home for children from abroad. Scholarships are available for daughters of Clergy, Missionaries, fallen Officers &c - Application for Illustrated prospectus and particulars to Head Mistress, Miss E.G. Barton (Mathematical, Tripos, Girton College, Cambridge). Jersey College, Channel Islands.

## SHIPPING & MAILS

P. & O., BRITISH INDIA & NEW ZEALAND
SHIPPING COMPANIES MAIL PASSENGER AND FREIGHT SERVICES.

P. & O. SAILINGS
(Under contract with His Majesty's Government)

| Steamer | Tons | L'nd'n. | M'sel's | Taking passng's for |
|---|---|---|---|---|
| CORFU | 15,000 | - | May 27 | Bombay & Australia |
| ¶† MANTUA | 11,000 | May 27 | June 3 | Bombay & Japan |
| MALOJA | 21,000 | June 3 | J'ne 10 | Bombay & Australia |
| ¶†RAWALPINDI | 17,000 | J'ne 10 | J'ne 17 | Bombay & Japan |
| COMORIN | 15,000 | J'ne 17 | J'ne 24 | Bombay & Australia |
| ¶†RAMPURA | 17,000 | J'ne 24 | July 1 | Bombay & Japan |
| CHITRAL | 15,000 | July 1 | July 8 | Bombay & Australia |
| ¶†MALWA | 11,000 | July 8 | July 15 | Bombay & Japan |
| NARKUNDA | 17,000 | July 15 | July 22 | Bombay & Australia |
| ¶†RANCHI | 17,000 | July 22 | July 29 | Bombay & Japan |
| CATHAY | 15,000 | July 29 | Aug. 5 | Bombay & Australia |
| ¶†CARTHAGE | 15,000 | Aug. 5 | Aug. 12 | Bombay & Japan |
| *MOLDAVIA | 17,000 | Aug. 12 | Aug. 18 | Bombay & Australia |
| KAISAR-I-HIND | 11,500 | Aug. 12 | Aug. 19 | Bombay & Karachi |
| ¶†NALDERA | 16,000 | Aug. 19 | Aug. 26 | Bombay & Japan |

Taking passengers. † for Malta. * for Port Sudan¶ Calls Southampton.

P. & O. NEW TOURIST CLASS
TO INDIA and AUSTRALIA

Superior accommodation at low fares. Available by S.S. MOLDAVIA and MONGOLIA: Bombay from £30, return £52. Australia from £39, return £70: and by the new Electric Liners STRATHNAVER and STRATHAIRD (1st and Tourist-class) Bombay £30, return £52. Australia from £40, return £72.

P. & O. BRANCH SERVICE
FAST STEAMERS TO AUSTRALIA.
Via Malta, Port Said, Suez, Aden, and Colombo
ONE CLASS ONLY. From £38 single; £58 return.

| | Tons. | London | Plymouth | Liverpool |
|---|---|---|---|---|
| *BALRANALD | 13,000 | June 10 | June 11 | - |
| *BENDIGO | 13,000 | July 8 | July 9 | - |
| *BARADINE | 13,000 | Aug. 5 | Aug. 6 | - |
| HALLARAY | 13,000 | - | - | Aug. 20 |

*Carrying H.M. Mails.

BRITISH INDIA SAILINGS
(Under Contract with the Government of India)
East African Steamers call outwards at Marseilles eight days. Port Sudan eighteen days, after leaving London.

| Steamer | Tons | Mdsbro. | London | Destination |
|---|---|---|---|---|
| #*†DALOOMA | 5,953 | May 26 | June 1 | Karachi & Bombay |
| §MASHOBRA | 8,324 | May 28 | June 3 | East African Ports |
| ¶*†MANULA | 7,326 | June 18 | June 23 | Karachi & Bombay |
| §MADURA | 9,077 | June 23 | July 1 | East African Ports |
| *†DURENDA | 7,241 | July 7 | July 16 | Karachi & Bombay |
| §MATIANA | 9,067 | July 23 | July 28 | East African Ports |
| *†NOWSHERA | 7,920 | July 28 | Aug. 6 | Karachi & Bombay |
| §MANTOLA | 9,066 | Aug. 20 | Aug. 26 | East African Ports |

* Cargo steamer; † Calling at Intermediate ports if inducement offers; § Calls Tangier. ¶ Calls Bhavnagar; # Loading at Antwerp for Bedl Bunderand Bhavnagar only.

P. & O. and B.I. JOINT SERVICE
COLOMBO, MADRAS AND CALCUTTA
(Via Malta, Port Said, Suez and Aden.)

| Steamer | Tons | M'bro | I'ham | Antwp. | Lond'n |
|---|---|---|---|---|---|
| †¶§BEHAR | 6,000 | - | - | - | May 27 |
| *MANDALA | 8,246 | June 4 | June 6 | - | June 11 |
| #§NAGPORE | 5,283 | June 16 | June 18 | June 20 | June 24 |
| *MANORA | 7,929 | July 2 | July 4 | - | July 9 |

¶ Refrigerator steamer # Not Aden † Calls Gibraltar

# LINDBERGH BABY DEAD

## SKELETON FOUND NEAR ESTATE

### CHILD BELIEVED TO HAVE BEEN MURDERED

## DEATH DUE TO FRACTURE OF SKULL

### KILLED SOON AFTER THE NIGHT IT WAS KIDNAPPED

## "HIT OR THROWN FROM CAR"

**The Lindbergh baby is dead.**

This poignant news was received just before midnight last night.

The child's remains have been found a few miles from the Lindbergh estate at Hopewell, New Jersey, from where it was kidnapped on March 1.

The following facts have emerged so far:

**The baby had been dead for some time. Only the skeleton remained.**

**It was probably deliberately murdered. There was a hole about the size of a shilling in the skull just above the forehead.**

**An autopsy revealed that death was due to a compound fracture of the skull, thought to have been caused either by being thrown out of a car or being struck by some instrument.**

**It is even suggested that the baby was murdered on the night it was stolen from the house.**

HOW REMAINS WERE FOUND

**Lying in Undergrowth**

The discovery was made at 3.15 yesterday afternoon, and the tragedy was announced to Press representatives at the Lindbergh home.

The body was found by a white man and a negro who were driving a lorry through the area.

The place is thickly wooded, and the two men came across the skeleton lying under the undergrowth.

**It was partly concealed by leaves and earth, and an attempt had evidently been made to bury the body.**

**The remains were identified by means of an undershirt or night clothes which were also found.**

The exact point where the discovery was made is reported to be five miles south-east by road of the Lindbergh estate.

The Chief of the New Jersey Police informed "THE DAILY TELEGRAPH" early to-day that steps are being taken to arrest a group of people believed to be the kidnappers.

PARENTS AT HOME

Col. and Mrs Lindbergh were at home when the discovery was made.

The discovery of the body near the home is thought to strengthen the theory that the kidnapping was done by people living in the locality.

That it was the work of "amateurs" and not professional criminals was believed to have been one of the major difficulties in the way of the parents establishing genuine contact with the kidnappers.

**23 MONTHS OLD**

The child, which was christened Charles Augustus after its father, was born on June 22, 1930 - its mother's birthday.

So interested was America in the event that all wireless programmes were interrupted on receipt of the news in order to allow songs of celebration, composed in advance, to be broadcast.

## SUSPECTED GROUP TO BE ARRESTED

### POLICE HAVE HELD THEIR HAND TILL NOW

**By Transatlantic Telephone**

Speaking early to-day to THE DAILY TELEGRAPH Col. Schwartskopf Chief of the New Jersey Police, gave the following account of the discovery.

"The body was found at 3.15 p.m. to-day by William Allen, a negro who was driving to Mount Rose, near Hopewell, along with Mr R. Orville Willson, on a truck loaded with timber.

"The truckman went into the woods on Mount Rose Hill, and, going under a bush, he lowered his head. As he raised his head he saw a skeleton on the ground. He called back to Mr Willson, and Mr Willson went into the wood to see what it was.

"He decided to go to Hopewell, and notified the police. Police investigated and found the body of a child estimated to be between 1 ½ and 2 years old, in a bad state of decomposition, with blond hair and wearing what appeared to be an undershirt and flannel band around the body.

The Identification

"Men were sent back to Hopewell to the Lindbergh estate, and received a flannel shirt similar to that the baby had on on the night of the kidnapping.

"This flannel shirt has an embroidered scalloped edge.

"This article was taken back to the scene, and compared with the clothing found on the body. They matched closely enough to afford an identification of the body as that of the Lindbergh baby.

"The body was pretty well concealed by leaves and undergrowth. The skull had a hole about the size of a shilling just above the forehead.

"The body was lying as though there had been an attempt to bury it. It was face downwards.

"It was in a bad state of decomposition, but we cannot tell how long it had been lying there.

"It was about 75 yards off the road in the woods."

On Track of Kidnappers

Co. Schwartskopf added: "As long as there was a possibility of the baby being found alive the police have been acting with a certain-about of discretion in order not to interfere with any negotiations that might result in the safety of the child.

"Now that the body has been found, every possible step will be taken to accomplish the arrest of the kidnappers and murderers.

"We have under suspicion a group of persons suspected of being the kidnappers, and immediate steps will be and are being taken to secure their arrest."

Blow from Instrument?

THE DAILY TELEGRAPH was informed by a member of the staff of the "New York Times" that the coroner had formed the opinion that death followed a compound fracture of the skull.

This may have been caused either by a blow from a blunt instrument or may have been the result of a fall as the child was thrown from a motor-car.

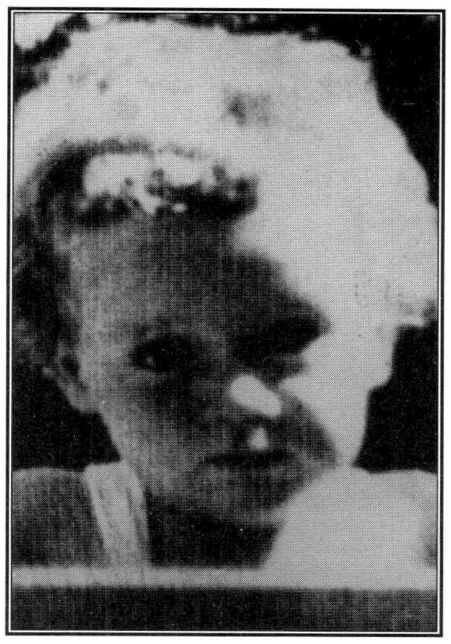

THE LINDBERGH BABY

## KILLED ON NIGHT OF KIDNAPPING?

### BODY IN BEDCLOTHES

HOPEWELL, Thursday Night.

Mr. Charles H. Mitchell, the New Jersey Country Physician, announced to-night his opinion that the baby was murdered.

It is thought that the child may have been killed actually on the night he was taken away, for the body was still wrapped in his bedclothes.

Dr. Mitchell states further that the skull was fractured either by being thrown from a motor-car or by being struck on the head.

There was no trace of a bullet or other missile.

Another theory is that the baby died some distance from Hopewell, and was brought to the estate by motor-car and deposited in the grounds unknown to any of the residents, as a crowning act of vindictiveness.

Criminals in District

The announcement that the baby has been found near Hopewell strengthens the belief that has been held in some quarters all along that the baby was kidnapped by someone who lived in the district and knew all about the Lindbergh's home life and their home. The gangsters whose services were enlisted declared that the kidnapping was the work of amateurs. hence their inability to trace the kidnappers.

As against this the whole of the country around the Hopewell estate has been so thoroughly combed that it seems difficult to conceive that the child should have been kept alive in the district without its becoming known.

MRS LINDBERGH
Bearing Up Well

Mrs. Lindbergh, who is shortly expecting another child, is reported to be bearing up well under the terrible shock. - Messages from Reuter, Central News and British United Press.

## £75,000 SPENT BY THE PARENTS

### FIERCE ANGER IN U.S.

**From Our Special Correspondent**

NEW YORK, Thursday.

News of the discovery of the remains of the Lindbergh baby when it became known in New York this evening created an intense feeling of commiseration for the Lindbergh family and fierce anger against the perpetrators.

The identification was made through a sleeping suit which the baby wore when Mrs. Lindbergh last put him to bed.

An attempt had been made to bury the body in a shallow grave, and the heavy rains recently had partly uncovered it.

The terrible discovery indicates clearly that the alleged kidnappers who had been attempting to negotiate with Col. Lindbergh and his emissaries during the last eight weeks were frauds.

The condition of the body indicated that the boy died - he was in all probability murdered - shortly after he had been stolen from the crib on March 1.

National indignation will find expression in a renewal of the demand that kidnapping of children shall be punished by death, or in the alternative, by life imprisonment.

Several States have already passed such a law, and in others similar legislation is in progress.

The Lindbergh baby was certainly the best-known baby in the world. In every home of the United States its portrait found a place alongside with the father, the famous aviator.

Since the kidnapping the quest for the child has been nation-wide, even worldwide.

It is known that at least £75,000 has been paid by the parents and Mrs. Dwight Morrow, mother of Mrs. Lindbergh, in vain efforts to find him.

A large part of this sum has been spent in special detective work, and some in payment of reward to anticipation of important evidence which was never forthcoming. The detectives in America were reinforced later by special agents in Europe.

Since the day of the kidnapping prayers have been said in churches and chapels of every denomination in the United States "imploring Divine aid," to quote the words of the Episcopal Church, "that this child of the American people may be restored to its stricken parents, and that the hearts of those who took him away may be softened and that they may repent."

Cordon Round Estate

During the first week of the kidnapping excitement tens of thousands of people from all parts of New Jersey and the adjoining States flocked to Hopewell.

The invasion assumed such alarming proportions that the militia of the State was requisitioned to reinforce the police in placing a cordon around the Lindbergh estate.

In recent days it has been stated but not confirmed that Mrs. Lindbergh, who is expected to become a mother again very soon, had made arrangements to leave for France with her husband.

Mrs. Dwight Morrow, when questioned about this plan, referred all inquirers to Col. Lindbergh, who refused to be interviewed.

Hope Abandoned

Friends in close touch with the Lindbergh family say that for six weeks past Col. Lindbergh had abandoned all hope of the child's recovery, but had never communicated this conviction to his devoted wife.

The big "shots" of the New York underworld, to whom he had applied for help in the search when police efforts proved futile, are known to have shared the father's dread apprehension.

The sensation in New York City and indeed throughout America this evening baffles description. Everywhere in the streets and in the restaurants, people were frantically eager for further news. The theatres and music-halls were in many cases almost empty, and in public squares people gathered to hear speeches voicing the anger of indignant citizens.

President Hoover was amongst the first to ask for information, and expressed his profound sorrow.

## STORY OF SEARCH

### A VISIT TO EUROPE

The discovery of the kidnapping of the baby from the second-floor nursery of the Lindbergh home was made at ten o'clock in the evening of March 1 last by Miss Betty Gow, the child's nurse. A three-section ladder lay outside. A warped wooden shutter to the baby's room was unlocked, and the police suggested that the baby had been carried through it.

Tremendous feeling was aroused throughout the country, and a widespread search was at once instituted.

A friend of Col. Lindbergh told the reporters that a ransom note was found pinned to the window-sill, generally reported to demand £10,000 for the baby's return though some doubt was later thrown on this.

Mrs. Lindbergh, stricken to the heart by her tragic loss, particularly in view of the fact that the baby was at the time suffering from a cold, published his diet through the Press with a request to the kidnappers to follow it. The diet was:

A quart of milk during the day.; three tablespoonfuls of cooked cereals morning and night; two tablespoonfuls of cooked vegetables once a day; one yolk of an egg daily; one baked potato or rice once a day; two tablespoonfuls of stewed fruit daily; half a cup of orange juice waking; half a cup of prune juice after his afternoon nap; fourteen drops of special medicine during the day.

Improvised Station

The police throughout the country at once got to work, and hundreds of persons, including the servants, were taken to an improvised police-station within the Lindbergh estate, but all were later released. There followed the detention of Henry Johnson, a sailor friend of the child's nurse, and others, but to no purpose.

After five days had passed fruitlessly, Col. and Mrs. Lindbergh turned to the underworld for help and authorised "Salvy" Spitale and Irvine Bitz, two of its well-known characters, to negotiate for them with the kidnappers. Col. Lindbergh also hired a detective from "Pinkerton's" the famous detective agency.

The churches throughout the nation were meanwhile offering up prayers for the baby's recovery.

Hope of Return

Then came the announcement that notes from the kidnappers had actually been received, and on March 27 Dr. Dobson-Peacock stated that he had definitely ascertained the baby was alive and well and would, he expected, be returned within a week.

Major Schoeffel, assistant to Col. Schwartzkopf (Chief of the New Jersey Police), paid a visit to England and the Continent "on a special mission," but nothing resulted.

Then on April 9 it transpired that after various mysterious comings and goings on the part of the child's father he had actually paid the professed kidnappers £10,000 on agreement to reveal the baby's whereabouts, but that they had not kept their word. Col. Lindbergh had either been double-crossed by them or had been a victim of an unscrupulous ruse by other criminals to obtain money.

Col. Lindbergh, deeply disappointed, thereupon announced his willingness to resume negotiations with the kidnappers and to pay them in gold instead of notes, of which the numbers would be known to the police.

£30,000 Demand

It was then declared that the kidnappers had raised their ransom demand to £30,000.

During the search Col. Lindbergh himself made numerous flights in an aeroplane to the coast and it was at one time reported that he had been in contact with the kidnappers.

Al Capone later offered a reward of £2,000 for the capture of the kidnappers or the return of the child.

# ROOSEVELT'S GREAT VICTORY IN U.S. ELECTION

## REPUBLICANS ADMIT DEFEAT OF HOOVER

**Mr. Franklin Roosevelt, the Democratic candidate for the United States Presidency, gained a decisive victory over President Hoover at the polls yesterday.**

**Early this morning it was announced that he was leading in 34 States commanding 402 electoral votes, while Mr Hoover was ahead in only eight States with a voting strength of 83. The number of votes required for election is 266.**

**The Republican campaign managers admit that President Hoover has been defeated.**

**(November 9)**

## DEMOCRATS WIN NEW YORK STATE

**From Our Own Correspondent**

NEW YORK, Tuesday Night.

To-morrow morning Mr. Franklin Roosevelt will be President-Elect of the United States, it is declared, and Government by Democrats will replace Republican rule.

With fine weather prevailing generally from the Atlantic coast to the Pacific a record rush to the polls began early and a total ballot of 40,000,000 is indicated. The voting began at six a.m. and continued until six p.m.

The certainty of Mr. Hoover's defeat is based upon trends easily discerned by analysts of the election.

A Republican victory in New York State was deemed necessary to assure President Hoover's election, and at 9.15, with 50 per cent. of the electoral districts of that State already counted, his managers frankly conceded this key territory to Mr Roosevelt.

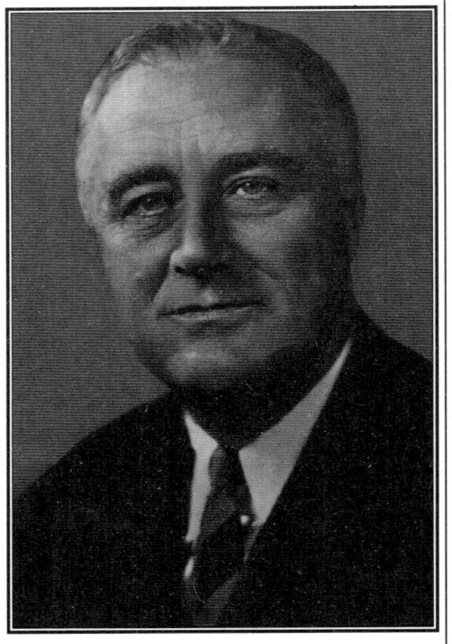

MR. FRANKLIN ROOSEVELT

Control of Congress

An overwhelming triumph for the Democratic candidate was clearly indicated on all sides, with every prospect of that party controlling the Senate and also the House of Representatives.

The Democratic headquarters claims unofficially that on the basis of the early returns the party will control the Senate by a majority of about ten and the Lower House by nearly 100.

The important Republican paper, the New York Herald-Tribune, concedes that Mr. Roosevelt has been elected and that Congress will have a Democratic majority. The candidate spent the evening at his party headquarters, where he was joined by his wife.

As the assurances of victory became steadily stronger, there were scenes of wild rejoicing both inside and outside the Democratic headquarters. Enthusiasts endeavoured to force their way in, and a strong body of police had great difficulty in holding them back.

200 RADIO STATIONS
Expert Commentators

By means of telegraphic reports furnished by Press correspondents throughout the country, and simultaneously transmitted to the newspaper offices and 200 broadcasting stations, the American public were able to follow from hour to hour and as the evening approached, almost from minute to minute, any important news from the electoral battlefield.

Commercial programmes advertising somebody's soup or chewing-gum gave way on the radio to skilled political commentaries able to analyse the results in the various States and their significance. In this way several million New Yorkers at home watched every phase of the great contest, and in a similar way audiences in noted dining-rooms and restaurants, theatres and cinema halls were kept constantly informed.

In one village the floor of a polling booth collapsed. Sixteen people fell into a cellar below and several were burnt by a furnace.

Among to-days incidents were many accusations of fraud against Tammany officials in control of the New York polling booths. The Republicans received thousands of complaints of illegal voting, and also of the "fixing" of the machine to prevent votes being recorded for Mr. James McKee in the mayoralty contest.

He took office as mayor when Mr. Walker resigned, but was not nominated by Tammany for election. But, although his name was not on the list, thousands of people voted for him. But Tammany's nominee Mr. John O'Brien (Democrat) was elected Mayor by a majority of about half a million votes.

**(November 9)**

## "JOY-RIDING" AT 6

The exploits of two children in a motor-car were described at a children's court at Weymouth yesterday when a 14-year-old boy was remanded on a charge of stealing motor rugs.

Police officers told the court that he persuaded a six-year-old girl, his cousin, to go on a joy-ride with him from London.

His mother is in America and his father is dead, and he lives with his grandmother in the Upper Norwood district of London.

Supt. Sprackling said that the boy and girl had been travelling about since Monday in a sports two-seater car, reported stolen. They had been to Brighton and spent a night in the New Forest. The little girl's home was at Walton-on-Thames.

The boy told the court that he had a few coppers and bought his child companion some milk.

It was stated there was a charge outstanding of stealing the car and petrol.

**(March 18)**

## RUBBER STAMP FORGERIES BY KREUGER

### FALSE SIGNATURES ON DOCUMENTS

**From Our Own Correspondent**

STOCKHOLM, Monday.

New sensations in the widespread criminal career of Ivar Kreuger are of almost daily occurrence. To-day, for example, a fresh search of Kreuger's private office revealed a series of rubber stamps bearing the signatures of important men.

It is now proved that Kreuger used these in many instances when he needed a vital signature, and the examination of many important and valuable documents still in his office shows the signatures to have been made with the stamps.

At his private residence the police also found a large portfolio containing many blackmailing letters. It would seem from these that Kreuger had paid large sums on many occasions, and mostly to women, as the price of silence.

The Swedish police have been in communication with the police in several foreign countries, in an endeavour to locate Kreuger's secret agents.

It is known that altogether he had formed about 200 companies, and that he had in every important town with a stock exchange at least two agents who were not know to each other. One of these sold when the prices were going up and the other bought when things were bad. In this way Kreuger earned considerable sums with which he was able to keep his affairs going.

One thing emerges clearly from the widespread inquiries, and that is that the bottom has not yet been reached. Every day new names are associated with the affair. The police investigators have already been increased.

**(April 26)**

## SENTENCE ON RECTOR OF STIFFKEY

### DEPOSED FROM HOLY ORDERS

**From Our Special Representative**

NORWICH, Friday.

This morning, in his cathedral church, the Bishop of Norwich deprived the Rev. Harold Francis Davidson of all ecclesiastical preferments and benefits in his diocese, and deposed him from Holy Orders.

Mr. Davidson was present to hear both sentences pronounced. He entered the cathedral rector of Stiffkey and Morston. He left it a clergyman no longer.

The solemn deposition of a priest is, happily, a rare occurrence in the Church of England. I doubt whether, in modern times, the terrible sentence has ever before been pronounced in the hearing of the offending clerk. In Mr. Davidson's case, however, the note of drama was maintained to the very end.

The Consistory Court of Norwich sits in the Baucun Chapel, in the south choir aisle of the cathedral. The canopied seat, in the middle of the bench, was for one hundred years the bishop's throne. Usually it is occupied by the chancellor when hearing the relatively small matters of ecclesiastical routine.

A SPIRITUAL COURT

To-day the chancellor took his rightful place as attendant on the bishop, with whom, also, was the dean, the three archdeacons, and one or two of the cathedral clergy. All were vested in the familiar choir habit, and the bishop had his pastoral staff in his left hand. The functions of lawyers were over. The bishop was acting in foro ecclesie, as a spiritual court, the origins of which are lost in the haze of antiquity.

The cathedral clock was chiming the appointed hour when the Registrar of the Diocese entered with a telegram, which he read. It was from Mr. Davidson, to say that he had motored through the night to attend, but had suffered delay.

Scarcely had the Registrar announced that the sitting would be deferred by a quarter of an hour, than there came a faint sound of hand-clapping without, and, a moment later, Mr. Davidson entered in black clerical attire and carrying a silk hat. His first act in taking his seat at the table was to pass a note to the reporters giving the name of his sister and those of the two friends who accompanied him. No man could have been more entirely self-possessed, though he occasionally betrayed emotion by picking imaginary pieces of dust from his coat.

The proceeding opened with the Bishop's repetition of the collect, "Prevent us, O Lord, in all doings, with Thy most gracious favour."

MR. DAVIDSON'S PROTEST

Before he could proceed further Mr. Davidson asked leave to speak, and on it being granted he averred, in level terms, that he was "entirely innocent in the sight of God of the graver charges" brought against him.

It was, he said, not himself but the Church authorities which were on trial. Whatever the sentence on him might be, he would devote his life to the reform of the Church courts.

He added that there was nothing that he had done that he would not do again _ "though perhaps a little more discreetly" - for he had tried to do what every clergyman ought to do.

Without other preliminary, the Bishop, standing staff in hand, immediately began to read the long and exceedingly comprehensive sentence whereby Mr. Davidson was deprived of his ecclesiastical promotions, dues, fees, emoluments, fruits of glebe, and so forth.

When all was apparently ended, prayer offered, and blessing bestowed, Mr. Davidson rose again, and said that if there were any means of appeal against the sentence he would prosecute it with all vigour to secure a fair trial before a competent judge.

But all was not over. The Bishop bade us await him at the High Altar. Standing there, it was in the great space of the medieval church, that the handful of witnesses saw the Church's extreme penalty imposed on an erring priest.

In that which followed there were signs that the Bishop was a good deal affected. At one stage his voice faded to a whisper, but he recovered and ended firmly.

The concluding prayers had been said, the blessing given, and the procession had been reformed, when in a loud voice Mr. Davidson again addressed the Bishop. He said he was glad he had deposed him, as now he could appeal to the Archbishop. Dr. Pollock did not heed, and the procession had passed on its way before Mr. Davidson had finished his speech.

**(October 22)**

## STARVING MAN HANDS OVER BIG FIND

A tramp with a halfpenny only in his possession found a large number of Treasury notes and silver coins near Burton-on-Trent to-day. Although ragged and hungry he handed over the cash intact to the police, who from their Good Samaritan Fund provided him with food and a night's lodgings.

**(July 22)**

# THE KING SPEAKS TO HIS SUBJECTS

## INTIMATE MESSAGE HEARD BY BRITONS THE WORLD OVER

The King's great message to the Empire, broadcast on the afternoon of Christmas Day, was clearly heard in most parts of the far-flung British Commonwealth.

British subjects - in every corner of the globe - sitting by English firesides, waiting up in the torrid Australian night, eating breakfast in the snowy Canadian morning, listening in Arctic wastes and tropic seas - all were linked with home by the grave and measured tones of their Sovereign.

His Majesty's message, slowly and earnestly spoken, united all his subjects in magic intimacy. It was in the following terms:

"Through one of the marvels of modern science I am enabled, this Christmas Day, to speak to all my peoples throughout the Empire. I take it as a good omen that wireless should have reached its present perfection at a time when the Empire has been linked in closer union. For it offers us immense possibilities to make that union closer still.

"It may be that our future will lay upon us more than one stern test. Our past will have taught us how to meet it unshaken.

"For the present the work to which we are all equally bound is to arrive at a reasoned tranquillity within our borders; to regain prosperity without self-seeking; and to carry with us those whom the burden of past years has disheartened or overborne.

"My life's aim has been to service as I might towards those ends. Your loyalty, your confidence in me has been my abundant reward.

"I speak now from my home and from my heart to you all. To men and women so cut off by the snows, the desert or the sea that only voices out of the air can reach them; to those cut off from fuller life by blindness, sickness, or infirmity; and to those who are celebrating this day with their children and grandchildren. To all, to each, I wish a Happy Christmas. God bless you!"

For the benefit of those who were unable to hear it at the time it was given, the message was recorded and rebroadcast in the Empire programme later in the day.

**(December 27)**

## HOW THE GREAT BROADCAST WAS MADE

### TWO MICROPHONES EMPLOYED

The King broadcast his message from a small room on the ground-floor of Sandringham House, overlooking the lovely private gardens. Normally the room is used as an office by one of the High Court-officials. For the broadcast it was empty save for a desk bearing the two special microphones in cases of Australian walnut, and the King's chair. A red lamp flashed to indicate to his Majesty that the Empire was listening.

Members of the Royal Family at Sandringham for Christmas heard the King's message on a receiving set in another room. Particularly appealing to them was the King's wish for a happy Christmas for "those who are celebrating this day with their children and grandchildren."

**(December 27)**

## "IMMORTALITY OF UGLINESS"

**From Our Own Correspondent**

OXFORD, Sunday.

A striking reference to the need for preventing unnecessary cutting down of trees and the erection of ugly houses was made by Mr. John Buchan, M.P. who presided yesterday at the annual meeting of the Oxfordshire branch of the Council for the Preservation of Rural England.

"The monstrosity of the modern jerry-builder," he declared, "is likely to last just as long as the most beautiful Tudor cottage, and if we are foolish enough to permit it we shall be saddling ourselves with an immortality of ugliness.

"In our work we must show reasonable commonsense. People must live; they must have houses; there must be means of transport; but we are apt too often to forget that the charm of rural England is the charm of its human association. That is why I believe that in the long run the preservation of rural England depends upon a revival of agriculture, and so we must not greet every reformation with a shriek like a pre-Raphaelite spinster.

"To my mind, the key-points of our work should be the prevention of unnecessary cutting down of fine timber and the building of ugly houses. I believe the community can get all the development it requires without either of these forms of disfigurement. We can have new houses built in consonance with the spirit of the countryside and at no greater cost than monstrosities.

We have awakened just in time, but I think we are in time. The Town and Country Planning Bill which will become law very shortly will do a great deal for organisations such as ours, although I have no love whatever for unnecessary State interference."

**(May 30)**

## RAMBLERS RAID A MOUNTAIN

### FIGHT WITH KEEPERS ON KINDER SCOUT

**From Our Own Correspondent.**

MANCHESTER, Sunday.

An army of 400 ramblers, men and girls, bent on gaining access to privately-owned moorland by "mass trespass" stormed the slopes of Kinder Scout, the Peakland mountain, this afternoon, and fought their way through a cordon of gamekeepers and moor wardens.

Six ramblers, all from the Manchester district, were detained for some time by the Derbyshire police, and one keeper received a severe shaking and a twisted ankle.

The ramblers, who belonged to Lancashire district branches of the British Workers' Sports Federation, marched from Hayfield to the bottom of William Clough. Here the leaders crossed a brook, and with shouts of enthusiasm, began scrambling up the boggy heather-clad slopes of Kinder Scout.

A FREE FIGHT

The "spear-head" of the army - twenty or thirty young men raced after them. Eight or ten keepers, armed with sticks, met them and trouble followed immediately.

By the time the main body of ramblers were crossing the brook a free fight was in progress. Gamekeepers' sticks were wrenched from them and others were forced to the ground.

One keeper, Mr. Edward Beaver, of Hayfield rolled some distance down the slope, twisted his ankle and was badly shaken.

One rambler fetched water for him, and after a few minutes he was able to limp away, helped by one of his colleagues.

Meanwhile the ramblers had streamed away towards Ashop Head, at the top of William Clough. A policeman seized one and took him back to Hayfield.

When almost at Ashop Head a detachment of thirty ramblers from Sheffield joined the main body, and reported a trouble-free trespass over the moors via Edale. After holding a "victory" gathering undisturbed the party returned to Hayfield, marching triumphantly towards the village, singing and laughing. But at Hayfield they were halted by a cordon of police across the road.

Gamekeepers who had taken part in the struggle on the mountain inspected the ramblers and picked out five. These were taken by the police to Hayfield police station, the rest of the party being allowed to go on through the village.

It is believed that further attempts will be made to organise "mass trespass" rambles in the Peak district.

**(April 25)**

## FLOUR PRICE INCREASE

The London Millers announce that the current price of standard grade flour in the Home Counties is now 27s per 280lb.

This is 6d more than last week's price.

**(February 23)**

# HERR HITLER'S HOPES DASHED FOR EVER

## NO CLEAR MAJORITY AT GERMAN ELECTION

**From E.H. Wilcox, Daily Telegraph Correspondent**

BERLIN, Monday Morning.

Herr Hitler's dream of ruling Germany with a purely Nazi Parliamentary majority has been dissipated for ever.

The Reichstag general elections to-day show that at last the hypnotic spell of the National Socialist propaganda has been broken.

His party appears to have won 118 new seats but there is no chance of a clear majority.

The percentages are: Hitlerites, 37.2; Social Democrats 21.5; Communists 14.4; Centre 12.6; German Nationals 5.7; Bavarian People's party 3.1; People's party, State party and Christian Socialists, 1.

From the above figures it is clear that if Herr Hitler is to form a Government, based on the new Reichstag, he can do so only by coming to terms with other groups.

His only alternative would be to drop the "legality," which he has so consistently and fervently professed during the past few years and revert to his early plans of armed revolution.

Some of his chief lieutenants are believed to have favoured such a course, even before to-day's disappointment.

The position is one of stalemate. It now seems certain that the Von Papen Cabinet will carry on the Government of the country.

**(August 1)**

# MYSTERY VOLCANIC ERUPTIONS IN THE ANDES

## VAST AREAS OF CHILE & ARGENTINE AFFECTED

VALPARAISO, Monday.

A mysterious series of volcanic eruptions and earth rumblings in the Andes has spread terror throughout the greater part of Chile and the Argentine.

The affected area stretches from Santiago to Concepcion, a distance of approximately 300 miles.

Flames, dust, and stones are being erupted from the volcano of Descabezado on the Chilean-Argentine frontier, and which was considered extinct. Ashes are falling thickly over the city of Mendoza, situated close by. This city was totally destroyed by earthquake and fire in 1861, with the loss of thousands of lives.

The giant volcano Tinguiririca and a number of minor peaks in the Central Andes have also commenced to erupt, and are belching fire and ashes.

Dense clouds of smoke and ashes are darkening many towns. Even in Buenos Aires, 800 miles away, on the other side of the continent, ashes are falling thickly.

Heavy subterranean explosions continue over the whole affected area, and huge flashes of light high up in the mountains are adding to the horror. It is feared that many have lost their lives in the remote mountain towns. Details are lacking because electric disturbances have disorganised all telegraphic communication.

By a remarkable circumstance, as though the whole Andes was in collaboration, the Dumoyo volcano in Patagonia suddenly burst into eruption. It is feared that great damage may be done in the thickly populated Chosmalal district near by. Subterranean explosions are also occurring here with remarkable rapidity, shaking the whole district.

ASHES FEET DEEP

One of the most remarkable aspects of the eruptions is that ashes have been carried right across the Continent to Buenos Aires, a distance of more than 800 miles. At first the strange visitation began to fall in a light grey cloud. It grew thicker every hour until the whole city was darkened. Decks of ships in port gathered a thick coating, and, indeed, the whole city presented a remarkable appearance.

Initial amusement in Buenos Aires at the strange visitation rapidly changed to alarm when news was received of a further eruption in the Neuquen Territory on the eastern border of Argentina.

**(April 12)**

# THREE LETTERS FOR CARS

"ALA 1" - Some time in June a motor car, registered in London, will be allotted this index number, the first of a new series.

The system which has served for twenty-nine years for the identification of motor vehicles is now in the last stage of its existence.

Established by the Motor Car Act of 1903, the arrangement of letters and figures, at first one letter and then two has provided the licensing authorities with distinguishing marks for all vehicles. Now the last possible combinations of two letters have been allotted.

In selecting one of the dozen or more different letter-and-figure arrangements that have been proposed it has been necessary to avoid, if possible, increasing the dimensions of the number plate and to keep the marks easy to read and remember. The system which will probably be adopted has three letters prefixed to numerals running up to 999 only, instead of to 9999, as at present.

UNTIL YEAR 1960

The letters will carry on the present two-letter system simply by prefixing "A."

The three-letter plan proposed will, it is calculated, meet the needs of 10,000,000 vehicles and carry the authorities on till about 1960.

(March 10)

# FIASCO OF 'RED' MARCH ON PARLIAMENT

## LIVELY SCUFFLES IN TRAFALGAR-SQ.

The attempt of the Communist-led marchers to present a petition demanding the abolition of the means test to the Prime Minister and the Speaker of the House of Commons failed completely last night.

In spite of the difficulties caused by the assembly of vast crowds of sightseers - in utter disregard of the published appeals of the Chief Commissioner of Police - none of the demonstrators reached the Houses of Parliament.

Gangs of hooligans overturned motor-cars on the Embankment, and broke windows in Whitehall and in streets off the Strand.

But after some lively skirmishes the police quickly got the crowd under control. In view of the size of the crowd the damage and the number of injuries was remarkably small.

Fifteen people were treated at Charing-cross Hospital. One police officer was injured.

Altogether between fifty and sixty persons were arrested.

MR. HANNINGTON'S ARREST

Mr. Wal Hannington, the Communist leader of the marchers, was arrested yesterday morning and charged with attempting to create disaffection in the police force.

Hannington was arrested in the course of a sudden police raid on the head-quarters of the National Unemployed Workers' Movement, of which he is organiser. he was remanded in custody for a week by Sir Chartres Biron at Bow-street.

**(November 2)**

# PASSENGER AIR LINE TO CAPE

As from to-day, for the first time since the opening of the London-Cape Town air route, the service is open for passengers as well as mails.

Aeroplanes leaving London and Cape Town to-day will each carry passengers; and use also will be made of the intermediate stations on the route.

**(April 27)**

# NEANDERTHAL SKELETONS

Three Neanderthal skeletons have been found by the Anglo-American expedition near Athlit, in Palestine. According to Mr. George MacCurdy, the well-known Yale University anthropologist, this is the greatest find in history.

**(May 4)**

# L.C.C.'S STEP TO A TALLER LONDON

## HIGHER BUILDINGS SANCTIONED

Higher buildings for London were made possible by London County Council yesterday.

Nothing approaching the skyscrapers of New York will be sanctioned. But the Council adopted regulations authorising a concession which will be welcomed by builders and property owners.

Hitherto 80 feet has been the maximum height permitted, save where dispensation was granted in exceptional circumstances.

CONTRASTS

| LONDON | Feet | NEW YORK | Feet |
|---|---|---|---|
| Thames House | 130 | Woolworth Building | 767 |
| Bush House | 120 | Bank of Manhattan | 927 |
| Broadway House | 180 | Empire State Building | 1,245 |

Under the rules adopted by the Council, yesterday, this is now increased by 20 feet to a maximum of 100 feet.

The regulations limiting the height were passed before the present methods of steel construction had reduced to a minimum the risk of fire. It is contended that the maximum could be considerably increased consistently with the requirements of safety. Building authorities are confident that in the not too distant future buildings of 150 and 200 feet will be allowed in London.

The present concession, a representative of The Daily Telegraph was informed last night, will serve as a stimulus to the development of London skywards. On important central sites the older buildings are likely to be demolished and new blocks constructed up to the new limits.

**(July 19)**

# PICTURES BY RADIO

## FIRST B.B.C. TELEVISION TRANSMISSION

**By A Special representative**

I was one of a group of guests last night at the house of Mr. Baird, to witness the first television transmission from Broadcasting House. To the several thousand "fans" who, doubtless, were looking-in — if that is the correct expression— the spectacle was fairly familiar, for the Baird Studio has been broadcasting television programmes for some time past. But most of us who were present last night were too impressed with the thing happening at all to be very critical of the results.

For us it was enough that there, before our eyes, on a frosted screen 6 inches by 4, was a diminutive Miss Louise Freear singing in her inimitable old-time manner her two great successes, "I Want to be a Lady," and "Twiddley bits." What did it matter, then, that there were dimness and flicker? It was none the less the latest modern miracle of science, with a future assured enough to make the B.B.C. feel constrained to devote half-an-hour on Monday, Tuesday, Wednesday and Friday evenings at eleven o'clock to its service.

**(August 23)**

# ZUYDER ZEE MADE A LAKE

## FISHERMEN MOURN

**From Our Own Correspondent**

The Hague, Sunday.

The historic moment of the definite cutting off of the Zuyder Zee from the North Sea was two minutes past one yesterday afternoon. The closing of the last gap in the great dyke took place in the presence of M. Colyn, chairman of the Zuyder Zee Council, M. Reyner, Minister of Waterways, and other officials.

The first load of clay was deposited on June 29, 1920, at five minutes past noon. The total time taken to separate the Zuyder Zee from the ocean was therefore 11 years, 334 days, 57 min. Queen Wilhemina was immediately informed of the completion of the task, and telegraphed her congratulations.

Although there is much rejoicing generally, the fishing folk regard the closing as a tragedy. During the ceremony flags were flown at half-mast on the boats on the Zuyder Zee fishing harbours, where there is much unemployment.

**(May 30)**

# BRITAIN'S GREAT REVIVAL

## LAST OF CRISIS MEASURES NOW REMOVED

## A STEADY RETURN TO NORMAL

Gestures by Britain of financial confidence, which are described in America as without precedent in financial history, were announced by the Chancellor of the Exchequer yesterday. They are:

1. The repayment to-morrow - six months before the money falls due - of £30,000,000 of the $40,000,000 one-year credits obtained by Britain in America on Aug. 29 last.

2. The reduction, to date, of the $40,000,000 credit obtained at the same time in France by £13,000,000. The Chancellor's statement was the first intimation that this has been done.

3. The withdrawal from to-day of the Treasury ban on dealings by British nationals in foreign exchange.

By this third step the last of the emergency measures taken at the time of the crisis last year has been removed.

The credit repayments are accepted, both at home and abroad, as the most striking demonstration of Britain's steady return to absolute financial confidence, and, as it is prophesied, financial pre-eminence.

The news created the most intense satisfaction in both financial and industrial circles, and was regarded as setting a seal on the confidence inspired by the coming of the tariff.

There was greater activity on the London Stock Exchange than has been seen for many months, industrials, as well as gilt-edged securities, benefiting. Wall Street also finished strongly after hearing the news.

**(March 3)**

# ELECTRICITY AS FARMER'S BOY

**From a Special Correspondent**

"To plough and sow
and reap and mow
And be a farmer's boy" -
such is the song of electricity in 1932.

Within three months the electricity "grid" will be completed in East Anglia, which will thus become the first area in England or Scotland to receive the full benefit of the Electricity Board's scheme.

Already, in this predominantly rural area:
Village lanes are now brightly lit by electricity;
Illuminated signs on the village green, extolling the virtues of electricity, have replaced the parish pump and the village inn as centres of meeting and gossip;
Electric lamps, cookers, irons, washing machines, and vacuum cleaners are replacing coal fires, oil lamps, and hard manual labour in farms and cottages;
Hens are being induced to lay more eggs, and tomato houses to yield more produce with the aid of electric light and heat; and
Cows are being milked, milk separated, corn threshed, hay cut, and turnips mashed, all by electricity.

In the district covered there were 884 consumers in 1927. There are now 5,400 and the number is being increased by 500 a month. This means that in many villages 80 per cent, of the houses are electrified.

**(January 22)**

# LAST HOURS OF THE FREE TRADE ERA

**1846, June 26 - Trade era ushered in with the repeal of the Corn Laws.**

**1932, March 1 - Free Trade era ends with the operation of the Ten Per Cent. general tariff on the value of non-British imports.**

**For the last time, to-day, foreign goods will pass duty free through Britain's "open door."**

The transition from the system of Free Trade to Tariffs will be swiftly and simply accomplished.

As soon as the Import Duties Bill has been accorded the Royal Assent formal notification will be made by the Treasury to the Commissioners of Customs.

All necessary preparations have been made for bringing the 10 p.c. duty into operation. The Treasury has only to "press the button" to set the machinery in motion.

**(February 29)**

# MISS SLADE SENT TO PRISON

BOMBAY, Thursday.

Miss Madeleine Slade, Mr. Gandhi's English disciple, was arrested here this morning owing to her refusal to obey the police notice to leave Bombay, and was sentenced to three months' simple imprisonment.

She is the first European to be arrested in connection with the civil disobedience campaign - Reuter.

**(February 15)**


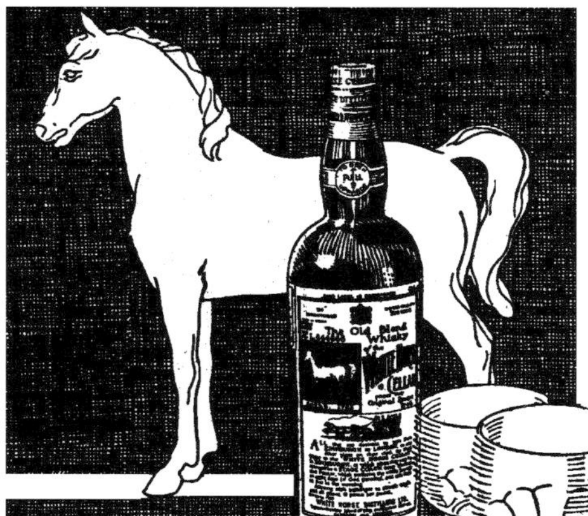

**A good prescription**

A prescription which can be thoroughly recommended to relieve weariness and loss of apetite is a small White Horse Whisky and a little water or soda. The ingredients are obtainable everywhere and making up takes only a moment. As an appetiser and aid to digestion take White Horse Whisky before or with meals; as a restorative take it at the end of the day; its beneficial effects will be felt at once.

**WHITE HORSE WHISKY**

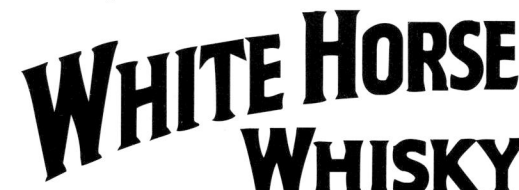

# CONVICTS MUTINY AT DARTMOOR

## 90 MINUTES' BATTLE IN PRISON

### Outbreak Starts at Parade for Service | Flames of Goal Seen for Miles Around | Troops Stand By Under Arms at Plymouth

**From Our Special Representatives**

PRINCETOWN, Sunday-Night.

A mutiny without parallel in the history of English prison life occurred at Princetown Prison, the bleak penal settlement in the heart of Dartmoor, to-day. It culminated in

A fierce fight between prisoners, police, and prison officers.

The firing of the main buildings of the prison, resulting in much damage being done.

According to one report to-night, 84 of the convicts and six warders, were injured. Twenty convicts are in hospital.

One hundred police have remained in attendance in and near the prison to-night. They had come from many towns and villages on and near Dartmoor, and had been on duty for many hours.

Trouble for a Week

Events bad apparently been working up to this climax through a series of disturbing events during the week. There was an attempted escape early in the week, and on Friday a warder was slashed about the face with a razor.

The alleged causes of discontent are:

More stringent regulations, which have been very unpopular;

A rumour that the prison was to be closed, so that men working in the quarries and on the farm would be deprived of their outdoor occupations; and

Unsatisfactory food, particularly porridge which was said to be too thin and insufficiently cooked.

The trouble came to a head this morning, when from 6 a.m. onwards convicts beat on their cell doors and shouted and booed. This went on until breakfast was taken round to the cells, and it is stated that a number of prisoners threw their porridge over the warders.

"Back to the Cells"

The uproar became so great that it was decided to allow the prisoners out for exercise. They were paraded in the yard at nine o'clock in order to be detailed for the various religious services. The parade, instead of calming the men, served to furnish the opportunity for the revolt to become more active. There were mutterings and booings as the men exercised, and instead of the call being sounded to parade for service the order was given, "Back to the cells."

This seemed to be the signal for the outburst. There are about 400 convicts at Princetown, and those taking part in the mutiny numbered between 200 and 300. The loyal ones went back to their cells, but the ringleaders of the others got together and started shouting. There was a rush for the workshops, where hammers, axes, and other tools were seized by the malcontents.

Suddenly the "Charge" rang out on a bugle which a convict had found. More men, some of them singing the "Red Flag," armed themselves with stones from a huge heap unfortunately lying handy, and launched their attack.

The warders had to retire against this onslaught behind the iron gates of the prison. They opened fire with their carbines, loaded with buckshot, but this did not prevent the attack from continuing. Within a few minutes scores of windows had been broken.

The attack was evidently concentrated on the Governor, Mr. S.N. Roberts. Both he and the Deputy Governor were actually in the office when the attack was launched. Stones crashed through the window, and as the convicts broke into the office the two officials escaped through another door, which they locked behind them as they went, and ran across to a block tenanted by prisoners who had remained loyal.

Within a few minutes of the convicts breaking into the office, smoke was seen pouring out of the windows and doors. The men had set fire to the big building, which is near the entrance and which contains all the records. This building is now practically destroyed.

The situation was at once so alarming that urgent telephone calls were sent to Plymouth, Exeter, and Tavistock for immediate police reinforcements. The trouble had apparently been anticipated on Saturday, and arrangements were all ready at Plymouth for the police to be rushed the fifteen miles across Dartmoor in the fastest motor-coaches that could be secured. The vehicles went at break-neck speed along this dangerous and world-famous road. The Chief Constable, Mr. A.K. Wilson, assisted by Chief Superintendent J.W. Lee, was in charge of this force of fifty hefty men who had been picked specially for the purpose.

Meanwhile a terrific struggle raged inside the prison. Convicts attempted to escape in all directions and over 100 of them tried to scale the high boundary wall. When the police arrived the situation was alarming in the extreme.

Armed warders were outside the gates and on the walls, making sure there should be no escapes. For over two hours the noise of carbine reports, mingling with the crackling of the flames, told of their work.

The police were quickly into action. Convicts had been shouting, "Come on in and get it," to the warders. The police slipped off their greatcoats and drew their batons. They carried no firearms.

VOLLEY OF STONES
Furious Battle with Police

As they entered the gate they were met by a volley of stones. Mr. Wilson did not mince matters. He gave the order to charge and for ten minutes there was a furious battle between them and the mutineers. Over a score of wounded lay on the ground, showing the effectiveness of the police work.

Four of the warders were attacked by a group of convicts who had isolated themselves from their comrades. The warders were in a desperate situation, but bravely fought through the crowd of convicts and regained their way to where their colleagues were fighting.

Finally the convicts scattered under the attack. One large party rushed into the store, and through the iron bars of the window signalled their surrender. They were all rounded up and thoroughly searched, the cigarettes and other goods which they had looted from the store being confiscated. Another party continued to fight, and had to be forcibly disarmed. All were then taken and locked in the cells.

Clock Tower Collapses

Meanwhile the fire in the main building was raging furiously. Inhabitants for miles around could see smoke and flames leaping up high above the prison walls. Plymouth Fire Brigade was summoned and another fast journey was made, the full equipment and motor-engine arriving shortly after the police.

But the damage had been done, and it was impossible to save the building, which is near the entrance to the prison. The familiar tower, with its clock, collapsed with a terrific crash.

**(January 25)**

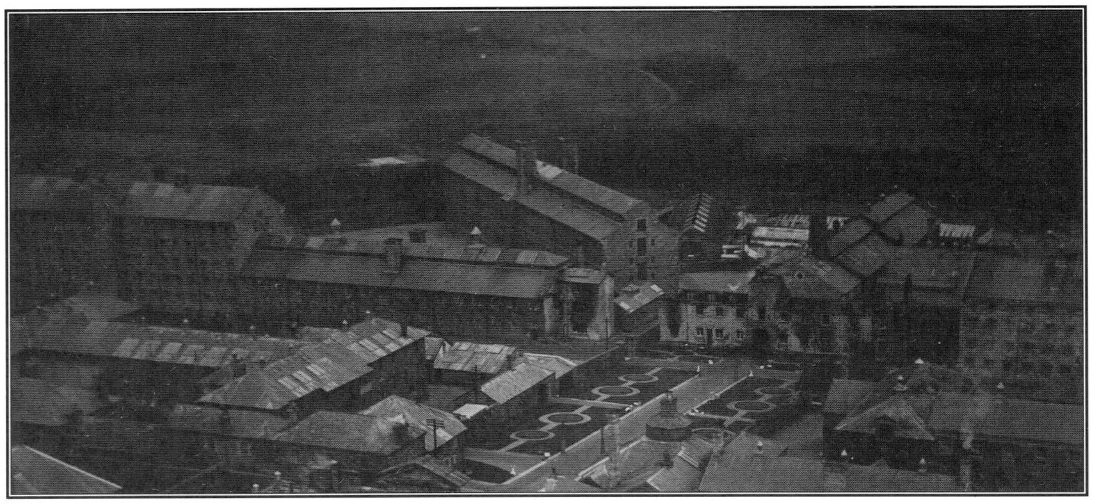

A GENERAL VIEW OF DARTMOOR PRISON before the fire.

## NO MUTINEER RETURNS TO DARTMOOR

**From Our Special Representative**

PRINCETOWN, Friday night.

Telephone wires were working late in Princetown to-night, bringing reports from prisons in all parts of the country about the safe arrival at their destinations of the men convicted of mutiny and sent away earlier in the day.

This morning twenty-three convicts left the prison to go before the judge to receive sentence. This evening they are dispersed throughout the country.

Dartmoor convict settlement had been purged of its mutineers. Never in the modern history of crime has there been such a gaol delivery.

**(May 14)**

### TOTAL OF 99 YEARS

The aggregate of the sentences passed by Mr. Justice Finlay was 99 years 8 months. The terms his lordship imposed were:

PENAL SERVITUDE

| | |
|---|---|
| Years | |
| Twelve | Davis |
| Ten | Ibbeson, Conning |
| Eight | Smith, Bullows, Mason |
| Six | Jackson |
| Four | Stoddart, Sparks |
| Three | Taylor, Muir, Dewhurst, Moore, Burgess, Garton, Roberts |

IMPRISONMENT

| | |
|---|---|
| Months | |
| Twenty-one | Horn |
| Twenty | Cosgrove |
| Eighteen | Del Mar, James |
| Fifteen | Kavanagh |
| Six | Tappenden, Gardner |

## MURDER ATTEMPT ON FRENCH PRESIDENT

### Outrage at a Book Exhibition | Police Officer and Author also Hit | Crowd's Lynching Attempt

M. Paul Doumer, President of France, was shot and seriously wounded by a would-be assassin in Paris yesterday afternoon.

At 2.30 this morning it was stated that the President had lapsed into a state of unconsciousness, and was sinking, but a further message issued at 3.15 a.m. declared that he was still fighting for his life.

A bulletin issued at 9.30 p.m., which described the wounds, said:

"The President was hit by two bullets. One traversed the region of the base of the skull and came out at the top of the right cheek. The other went in at the level of the right armpit and came out behind the shoulder, causing abundant haemorrhage.

"At six p.m., when the affects of shock had been lessened as a result of several blood transfusions, the surgeons carried out a ligature of the axillary artery, which the bullet had completely severed."

*"LINDBERGH BABY KIDNAPPER"*

The President was shot by a Russian, Paul Gorgouloff, regarding whom an official statement last night said it was an open question whether he was mad or feigning madness.

He declared that he was the leader of the Russian Fascists, and that he had committed the act because "France had helped Soviet Russia."

It has been ascertained, however, that he was at one time a member of the Communist party.

In a diary belonging to him was found the statement that he had kidnapped the Lindbergh baby, which was being brought up as "a Russian terrorist."

He was badly bruised by the crowd, who twice attempted to lynch him.

**(May 7)**

## GORGOULOFF'S DEATH ON GUILLOTINE

**From Our Own Correspondent**

PARIS, Wednesday Night.

Gorgouloff, the Russian assassin of President Doumer, was guillotined in the street outside the Sante Prison shortly after six o'clock this morning. He went to his death calmly, uttering one final cry as his body was half-flung on to the instrument of death: "Russia! Oh, my country."

The orders to erect the guillotine were given shortly after midnight, and the work was not completed until five a.m.

The spot was in the Boulevard Arago, beneath chestnut trees and in the full light of a street lamp. This lamp and others in the boulevard were, however, extinguished before the arrival of the execution party.

Measures were taken by the police to prevent sightseers approaching the guillotine, barriers being erected nearly a quarter of a mile away, and strong police cordons being posted.

Repeatedly Gorgouloff exclaimed, "My idea. My idea." "I am neither Communist nor Monarchist," he also declared. "I die for my idea like all Russian peasants oppressed by the Reds." He insisted he had no grudge against France or M. Doumer, whom he said he had killed simply to defend his "idea."

While the prison formalities were being completed his executioner bound the prisoner's hands, shaved his neck, and opened his shirt. Gorgouloff accepted two glasses of rum, but refused a cigarette. When everything was ready he was bundled into a black van drawn by two horses. His lawyer, Maître Geraud, and the priest accompanied him.

**(September 15)**



## ELECTRIC TRAIN'S 70 M.P.H.

### FIRST OF NEW EXPRESSES ON BRIGHTON LINE

**From Our Special Representative.**

THREE BRIDGES, Tuesday.

A new chapter in the book of British railway progress was opened to-day. For the first time in the transport history of the country an electric express has made a non-experimental main-line journey.

The occasion was a thirty-mile demonstration run from London Bridge to Three Bridges, in Sussex, the stage which marks the first half of the Southern Railway's London-Brighton electrification scheme.

The new service is to come into full public use on Sunday week. Early next year the electrification will cover the whole Brighton line and Worthing, and will then be extended to the Eastbourne, Seaford, and Lewes sections of the line. Soon, in the London-Brighton-Eastbourne triangle of the Southern Railway's system steam trains will be few and far between.

SPEED NOT MAIN THING

Part of the journey to-day was done at 70 miles an hour. The fastest train on the service will be capable of 75 miles an hour, and the regular expresses eventually will do the trip to Brighton in precisely 60 minutes.

But speed is not the chief object. Especial attention has been paid to the traveller's comfort, to safety and efficiency of working, and to the improvement of the service all-round.

After Sunday week there will be an increase of over 100 percent. in the number of trains between London and Three Bridges, in which every station served will share. These electric trains will run to as punctual a schedule as those on the usual suburban area, and cheap day return tickets will be issued at single fares.

**(July 6)**

## NEW WIRELESS MARVEL

### ULTRA-SHORT WAVES OVER 170 MILES

**From Our Own Correspondent.**

ROME, Sunday

A discovery of great scientific importance and commercial promise has resulted from experiments by Senatore Marconi in ultra-short wave wireless transmission.

While it was previously believed that waves of about half a metre in length had an effective radius of only about a dozen miles, adequate results both in telegraphy and telephony have now been achieved over a distance of 170 miles.

Senatore Marconi has established clear communication between Cape Figari in Sardinia and the height known as Rocca di Papa, fifteen miles south-east of Rome. The wave used was 57 centimetres, and the electrical energy consumed a few watts only - less than is required by a single electric light bulb.

Senatore Marconi has for some years been experimenting with short-wave beam transmission. On the assumption that they travel in a straight line, it was not believed that ultra-short waves could pass beyond the horizon.

The waves are equally free from fading or atmospherics; but the question whether they are suitable for broadcasting cannot be answered at present, since all tests hitherto made public have been conducted with waves concentrated into a pencil of invisible rays and "aimed" at the receiver, thus ensuring the least possible loss of energy.

**(August 15)**

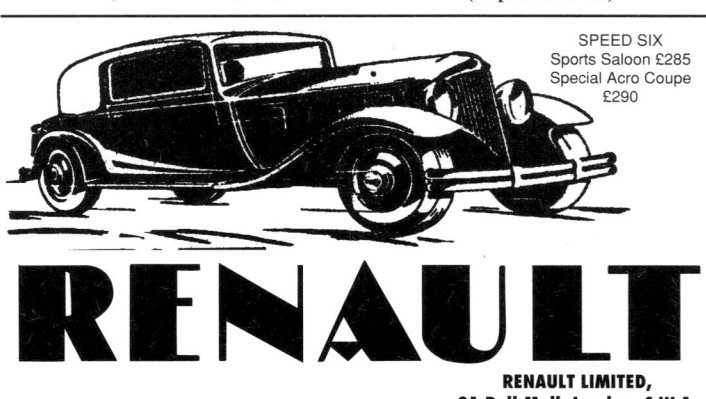

# The Daily Telegraph

## CORRESPONDENT IN LOOTED HARBIN EXPRESS

◆

## MALE PASSENGERS STRIPPED OF ALL CLOTHING

### TERRIBLE SCENES IN DARKNESS

**From J. M. Penlington, Tokio Correspondent of The Daily Telegraph**

HARBIN, Monday (delayed).

I have just arrived here after a thrilling adventure with bandits.

The express on which I was travelling left Changchun for Harbin on Sunday afternoon. All the talk was of the attack on a train on the previous day, when eleven passengers were killed. Before long we had a similar experience.

Our train was derailed during the night by raiders after a terrific fusillade. They invaded the carriages and stripped us of all our clothing and other belongings. Four soldiers were killed and many persons wounded.

The first-class passengers reached Harbin this afternoon, having lost everything. Twenty-four hours had been spent in covering a mere 150 miles.

### WILD CONFUSION
#### Lights Extinguished

We had set out from Changchun on a heavy Russian train laden with hundreds of people bound for the north. A number of Japanese soldiers who had been wounded in Saturday's engagement were also on board.

After crossing the Sungari River bridge, 30 miles south of Harbin, the first-class passengers were congratulating themselves that the danger-zone had been passed when the train was suddenly brought to a standstill by the derailment of the tender and the foremost coach, accompanied by a terrific fusillade from the darkness.

The lights were immediately extinguished. The Manchurian guard replied to the attack-

ers, who, however, soon boarded the carriages.

A scene of indescribable confusion ensued. Many shots were fired, and the savage shouts of the marauders mingled with the shrieks of the women in the compartments.

### DOORS FORCED
#### Bravery of Women

The first-class compartments were the main objective of the raiders, who swarmed into the corridors. The passengers crouched behind the closed doors of the coupés, but these were soon forced. The male inmates were violently handled. They were robbed of all their possessions and compelled to remove and hand over their clothing.

The foreign women behaved splendidly. They were deprived of all their jewellery, but, unlike the men, were not forced to surrender their clothes.

I observed that some of the raiders wore military uniforms, but the majority of them were in mufti. Among them were mere boys, armed with rifles and revolvers. These they flourished in the faces of the helpless passengers, at the same time giving vent to hysterical cries. Many acts of violence were committed by them.

I cannot speak as to what happened in the other carriages. But the interior of ours after a brief half-hour of havoc was completely wrecked.

Calm succeeded pandemonium. The bandits withdrew, laden with their booty. The long train stood dark and silent. The lights were not switched on again, and the passengers spoke only in whispers.

At last, when it seemed to be confirmed that the raiders had really gone, the train steamed slowly back to the next wayside station, where it waited until daylight. A start was then made for Harbin.

The passengers were conveyed in wagons of the breakdown train which had come to the rescue. It included an armoured car manned by Japanese troops.

#### No More Night Trains

As a result of the epidemic of railway outrages it has been decided to run trains only during the hours of daylight. They will be guarded exclusively by Japanese troops, no Manchurians being employed.

It is generally agreed that the activities of the bandits to the south of the Great Wall are inspired by political motives. In Harbin the inhabitants are on the verge of panic.

But the fact that all nationalities are not

disposed to give way to it is shown by an advertisement in to-night's Russian papers. This states that the Hong Kong and Shanghai Bank will in no circumstances pay a ransom if a member of its staff is carried off.

*(September 15)*

## KOWTOWS TO 'BOY' PRESIDENT

◆

### MANCHURIA GREETS THE EX-EMPEROR

**From G.W. Gorman**
**Daily Telegraph Special Representative**

CHANGCHUN, Tuesday.

Noticeably nervous, the former "boy" Emperor of China, Hsuan Tung, now known as Mr. Pu Yi, entered the new capital of Manchuria this afternoon amid scenes of Imperial splendour.

The Imperial yellow predominated among the flag decorations, though he came, no longer as Emperor, but to be installed to-morrow as the democratic Permanent President of the new State of Manchuria.

MR. PU YI

Former retainers of the Manchu ruling House prostrated themselves in the dust outside the railway station. Elderly men who had been mandarins under the Empress Dowager struck their foreheads on the ground in the regulation kowtow.

The oath-taking ceremony to-morrow will take place in a small chamber heavily decorated with yellow tones, but Western touches will be added by a presence of broadcasting equipment, a loud-speaker and flashlight apparatus.

Mr. Pu Yi's modestly furnished residence is completely surrounded by Chinese guards.

*(March 9)*

## MAD TRAPPER SHOT DEAD

AKLAVIK (Canada), Wednesday.

The Royal Canadian Mounted Police to-day killed Albert Johnson, the mad trapper, after a battle in which Johnson seriously wounded a staff sergeant.

Last month he shot dead one of the Mounted Police who were attemtping to capture him. He had already stood a siege on Dec. 31, when he wounded a constable.

On that occasion the police fired 700 rounds and used 30lb of dynamite in bombs. Early in February an aeroplane was sent out to bomb his cabin, but he escaped.

*(February 18)*

## SOVIETS FIND A NEW CAPITALIST PLOT

MOSCOW, Tuesday.

A clean sweep of twenty prominent Communists, including M. Zinovieff and M. Kameneff, on the ground that they were attempting to restore capitalism, is the latest action of the Communist party in its drive to purge its ranks of "undesirables."

The charges against them are that they were members or accomplices of a revolutionary group which attempted to "create by underhand methods a bourgeois and Kulak (rich peasant) organisation aiming at the restoration of capitalism, and particularly, Kulakdom, in Soviet Russia."

The majority of those expelled, it is officially stated, are persons who had previously been expelled from the party for anti-party and opposition activities.

#### "RED LETTER" RECALLED

Zinovieff, whose famous "Red letter" on the eve of a British General Election is not yet forgotten, and Kameneff, together with Riutin and Galkin, appear, according to the "Pravda" to be the ringleaders of this "class hostile" group. In addition to aiming at the restoration of Capitalism, it urged the dissolution of the State farms and the adoption of such a policy as would convert "the Socialist enterprises created by the heroic labour and enthusiasm of the working-class into concessions for capitalists."

Zinovieff and Kameneff it is recalled, have already been expelled from the party before.

The præsidium of the Executive Committee of the Communist party states that the members dealt with, although they were aware of the existence of a counter-revolutionary group and had even received documents from it, had failed to report it to the Communist party and had thus assisted its activities - Reuters.

*(October 12)*

## SON BORN TO MRS. LINDBERGH

**From Our Own Correspondent**

ENGLEWOOD (N.J.) Tuesday.

The birth of a son to Col. and Mrs. Lindbergh this morning will be some consolation for the shadow cast over their lives by the kidnapping and brutal murder of their first child.

The happy event took place here at the home of Mrs. Dwight Morrow, Mrs. Lindbergh's mother. Four specialists were in attendance, and a bulletin issued some hours later reported that Mrs. Lindbergh and the baby were doing well.

Englewood is en fête and there is great rejoicing all over the country. Messages of congratulation by cable and telegraph are being received from every part of the world. President Hoover was among those who sent words of greeting.

MRS. LINDBERGH

Col. Lindbergh has issued a statement appealing to the Press to "permit our children to lead the lives of normal Americans." He adds: "It is impossible for us to subject our second son to the publicity which we feel was in a large measure responsible for the death of our first."

Miss Betty Gow, who was nurse to the first baby, is to return to the United States on Sept. 10 to resume her duties in the Lindbergh nursery. She is at present on a visit to her mother in Scotland.

*(August 17)*

## GOVERNMENT INSIST ON CUTS IN POLICE PAY

The Government have resolved that the second instalment of the economy cut in police pay, which was decided upon a year ago, must be imposed.

A cut of 5 per cent. has been in operation during the past year; a further cut of 5 per cent. making 10 per cent. in all, is due to take effect as from the end of the present month.

Many protests against the cut have been voiced at meetings of the police organisation in different parts of the country, and the present decision follows a review of the whole position by the Home Secretary, police authorities and representatives of the Police Federation.

*(October 25)*

## POLICEWOMAN IN SERPENTINE

Hundreds of bathers in the Serpentine yesterday afternoon saw a policewoman – Miss Matthews — fall in. At the time she had been directing children to leave the water.

On getting out she detained a man who was standing on the bank. He was taken to Hyde Park Police Station and charged with obstructing the officer.

*(August 19)*

## HOW GANDHI BROKE HIS SIX-DAYS' FAST

◆

### GOVERNMENT'S MESSAGE ARRIVES JUST IN TIME
**From Our Own Correspondent**

BOMBAY, Monday.

Mr. Gandhi broke his fast at five p.m. to-day in Yeravda Gaol after having been without food for six days and five hours.

He took this course after considering for nearly an hour the British Government's message approving the agreement between the leaders of the caste Hindus and the Depressed Classes ("Untouchables") regarding the method of electing the latter's representatives.

#### ON VERGE OF DEATH

His decision came none too soon, for his physical condition had suffered seriously from his fast. Even now that he is no longer fasting, his life is still in danger.

While Indian Nationlists claim the agreement regarding the Depressed Classes and its acceptance by the Home Government as a triumph for Mr. Gandhi, English opinion here is that it is a victory for the "Untouchables."

#### PROPPED UP IN BED
#### Prayers Precede Decision

The first news of the Government's acceptance of the proposals was brought to Mr. Gandhi by his son, and soon afterwards the Inspector-General of Prisons arrived with the full statement.

Mr. Gandhi was so weak that he had to be propped up on his bed while he read the announcement. Mrs. Gandhi, Sir Rabindranath Tagore, the poet, Mr Vallabhai Patel, and a number of other friends and Indian leaders were present and discussed the situation.

Then in an almost inaudible voice he said: "My vow is fulfilled. Passive resistance has won the day." After that he sank down again on his bed.

*(September 26)*

# LONE ATLANTIC VICTOR LANDS IN STORM

## FOUR RECORDS BROKEN IN THRILLING FLIGHT

**From A Special Representative**

Miss Amelia Earhart, the 34-year-old American airwoman who on Saturday flew alone across the Atlantic in record time, arrived in London last night in a thunderstorm.

She was flown from Londonderry, where she landed, in an air-taxi, leaving her own 'plane to be sent back to America. The American Ambassador met her and, after broadcasting a message to America, she drove with him to the Embassy, where she will spend the next few days.

Miss Earhart had changed her flying kit for an orange frock, borrowed from Mrs. Bruce, the daughter of the American Ambassador, when I saw her at the Embassy last night.

Describing the flight, she said that the first four hours from Harbour Grace, Newfoundland, was perfect, in excellent weather. But after that her troubles began.

"It became terribly cold,' she said, "and I was forced to fly lower by the ice on the wings of the plane. My altimeter went out of order, and I could not tell whether I was flying at 100 or 300 feet above the sea. I could see the white breakers below me, but a thick fog rendered visibility very poor.

### "Rather Drown Than Burn"

"I was almost four hours out from Harbour Grace when exhaust trouble developed, and I saw flames coming from the exhaust, and pieces began to fall off. I was rather frightened, but I decided that there was less risk in continuing than in turning back and incurring the dangers of landing in the darkness.

"I flew close to the water, thinking that I would rather drown than burn.

"But I had no time to be really afraid. Nor had I time to eat. All I had was some tomato juice.

"Then I ran into a severe storm, and to make matters worse, I noticed that my gas was leaking. But by this time there was nothing for it but to go on.

"I was less concerned with the exhaust trouble, the leaking gasoline, and the storm than with the icy atmosphere I encountered, suggesting the presence of icebergs, which might have affected the mechanism. Later I climbed to a fairly good height.

"For hours I was flying blind through, rain and fog.

"In view of my damaged exhaust pipe and the dark I decided to try to strike Valencia.

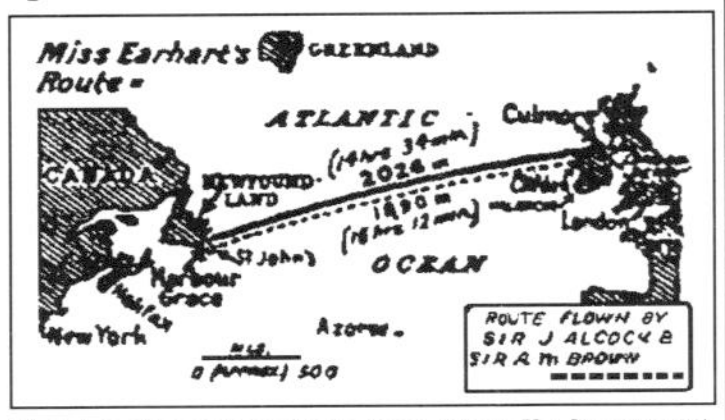


But I lost my bearings and I hardly know yet where I am.

### The Only Ship

"On nearing the coast of Ireland I sighted a vessel and circled around it. I thought they recognised me, for they whistled and sent up a rocket. I hoped that they would announce my arrival, but evidently they had no wireless. That was the only ship I sighted all the time.

"Never in my life have I greeted the dawn with such joy. The sun came out brilliantly, so much so that I was nearly blinded, and had to drop again to nearly 200ft above the water.

"I flew for a few miles in this way, and then I was glad to get to a greater height, because the Atlantic rollers are not pleasant to look upon when you are just above them. The journey went on and on, but I was so occupied with my instrument board and keeping a good control that the time did not seem quite so long as it actually was. It was a grand sight to look down on Ireland.

"I picked out a railway track, and followed it in the hope that it would lead to an aerodrome. I followed this course until I saw a town.

"Finding no aerodrome, I decided to land on the nearest suitable field. My machine is quite undamaged.

**(May 23)**

# CAMPBELL BREAKS HIS OWN RECORD

**253.968 m.p.h. In Blue Bird at Daytona**

**267.459 m.p.h. Over One of the Mile Runs**

Sir Malcolm Campbell beat his own world land speed record yesterday with 253.968 MILES PER HOUR

He thus exceeded his previous speed of 245.736 m.p.h. by over 8 m.p.h.

In one of the two-mile runs yesterday-of which the average was taken for the record-he attained the speed of

267.459 MILES PER HOUR

On the second run, in the teeth of a 20 m.p.h. wind, he reached 241.773 m.p.h.

Sir Malcolm afterwards said he was very disappointed at not having reached 265 m.p.h. for the record. If conditions were favourable he would make a further attempt to-day, and also attempts on the 10 kilometre and 10-mile figures.

Sir Malcolm also set up two other new world records: 1 kilometre—251.340 m.p.h.; 5 kilometres—241.569 m.p.h. In each case he beat his own figures, set up last year.

It is probable further that he broke the five-mile record, but no definite figures were obtained.

**(February 25)**

# "LIES PLASTERED ON GIRLS' FACES"

## BISHOP ON COSMETICS

**From Our Own Correspondent**

YORK, Sunday.

Powder and lipstick were described by the Bishop of Hull, Dr. Heywood, to-day as lies plastered over girls' faces. The Bishop was preaching to 5,000 Girl Guides in York Minster.

Commending the aim of Girl Guides to secure good health, the Bishop said:

"Do not be tempted to make yourselves ugly, as many girls are, with paint and powder and lipstick — ugly because these things are always disfiguring. You cannot hide them. They deceive nobody, and girls should not go about with a lie plastered over their faces.

"I am sorry to say some of us men tend to think the girl who thus spoils her appearance is not respectable. Throw these things away if you have any. If you have not, do not spend a penny on them.

**(May 30)**

# HATLESS WOMAN WITNESS

## WAY OUT OF DILEMMA

A young wife who applied for a separation order against her husband in Grays (Essex) Police-court yesterday had entered the witness-box and taken the oath before it was realised that she was not wearing a hat.

The Chairman (Mr. W Boatman) then said: Don't you know you are not showing proper respect to the Court by not wearing a hat?

Applicant: I haven't got one.

The Chairman: It is as bad as a man coming into court with his hat on.

Applicant said she did not read the newspapers and had not seen the references to the subject elsewhere.

At this point the probation officer came into court with a woman's hat. This was placed on the applicant's head. She blushed, and the Court smiled as the chairman said: 'It suits you very well."

The application was dismissed.

**(October 21)**

# PORTABLE SETS FOR POLICE

Government experiments with the object of fastening a wireless grip on crime were conducted on the Portsmouth-road yesterday.

High officials of the Home Office conducted a series of tests with portable wireless sets designed for police patrols.

The experiments were considered highly satisfactory on the whole, and as a result of the experts' reports it is expected that the Government will consider a scheme for equipping all the mobile police — and eventually even policemen on foot— with wireless receiving apparatus.

**(September 22)**

# SHAKESPEARE MEMORIAL THEATRE

## OPENED BY PRINCE OF WALES

**By W. A. Darlington**

The Prince of Wales, who had flown from Windsor in his own aeroplane, opened on Saturday the new Shakespeare Memorial Theatre at Stratford-on-Avon.

Mr. Baldwin (representing the Government), dramatists, poets and many distinguished Englishmen, together with the Ambassadors of the United States and France and the representatives of many other nations, were in the great gathering that took part in the day's picturesque celebrations.

The theatre has been built to replace the building which was burnt down six years ago.

THE DAILY TELEGRAPH sponsored an appeal for funds after the disaster, and the American Shakespeare Foundation, which was established with the New York representative of THE DAILY TELEGRAPH as organiser, pledged itself to raise £200,000. The balance of the cost has been contributed by England and other countries.

As I stood in the vast crowd beside the new theatre looking for the Prince of Wales to come and open the building with a silver key, I could not help reflecting sadly how utterly we of this scientific and mechanical age have lost the faculty for wonder.

For here we were - a collection of men and women drawn from every corner of the world, collected together in the heart of rural England and waiting for the King's son to lead us in an act of homage to the name of Shakespeare. And we all took it as a mere matter of course that the King's son should come swooping down to us from the clouds to perform the ceremony.

Shakespeare himself, that rare courtier, should, I felt have been there to describe this marvel. No matter how familiar he might become with modern inventions, his quick imagination could never fail to be touched by the glamour of such a scene, and to paint it in some unforgettable phrase.

**(April 25)**

# TRIUMPH FOR KAYE DON

## WATER SPEED RECORD EASILY BROKEN

Mr. Kaye Don, piloting Lord Wakefield's £40,000 speed-boat, Miss England III, yesterday, on Loch Lomond, recaptured the world's water-speed record.

The official timing of his average speed after a northward and southward run over the measured mile was 111.71 miles an hour. He thus beat the previous record of Commodore Gar Wood, the American by more than eight miles an hour.

Great Britain now holds the world's speed records on land and water and in the air. Altogether six world's speed records stand to the credit of Britain.

**(July 18)**

## GREAT ROCKET EXPERIMENT FIASCO

**From Our Own Correspondent**

BERLIN, Thursday.

Herr Winkler's rocket, which he hopes ultimately will reach the moon, was fired off amongst the sand dunes of East Prussia this afternoon. Before it had risen more than 50ft, however, the fuel chamber burst, and it fell to the ground, barely missing a shelter in which cinematograph operators were at work.

No one was hurt, but the surrounding country was covered by a dense cloud of smoke.

Herr Winkler's rocket was about 6ft high and 18in in diameter. It was propelled by a mixture of methyl and liquid oxygen.

The rocket was equipped with scientific instruments for the measurement of speed, altitude and air pressure. A parachute device was fitted to it, designed to open at the highest point reached in the stratosphere and bring it back safely to land.

**(October 7)**

# SOLIDERS' BODIES IN FRANCE

Fourteen years after the war ended that part of the old Western Front known as the "Red Zone" is still yielding up its dead. During the past months alone the bodies of 192 soliders have been recovered in the Pas de Calais Department, on the line in the Béthune and Arras region, where some of the fiercest fighting in the war took place.

The remains are those of thirty-nine identified and fifty unidentified French soliders, and sixteen known and eighty-seven unknown Germans.

**(November 10)**

# MRS. MOLLISON'S TRIUMPH

**Lympne to Cape Town in 4 Days, 6 Hours, 53 Minutes**

**Her Husband's Record Well Beaten by 10½ Hours**

## ALL KINDS OF BAD WEATHER

Such is the magnificent result of the solo flight of Mrs. J. A. Mollison (Miss Amy Johnson), who reached Cape Town yesterday at 1.30 p.m. (G.M.T.) — a result achieved after she appeared to be on the brink of failure.

Mrs. Mollison broke the record for the England-Cape Town flight— held by her husband, whose time was 4 days 17 hours 22 minutes— by

**10 hours 29 minutes.**

**She had only five hours' sleep during the whole flight;**

**She flew through every kind of bad weather;**

**She had to carry out work herself on her engine with improvised tools;**

**Through her petrol tanks being only partly filled at Gao (Sahara) she had to turn back—waisting in all 11½ hours—and only just managed to regain Gao with remaining petrol.**

The flight is a new triumph for British aircraft and British engines.

**(November 19)**

# M2 LYING IN DEEP WATER OFF CHESIL BEACH

## DIVERS' DASH TO SAVE 50 MEN ON BOARD

The British submarine,M2, disappeared after a dive in the Channel yesterday with about fifty men on board.

The first news of the accident was conveyed in a statement issued by the Admiralty at 9.30 last night. This announced that the M2 dived at 10.30 a.m. yesterday off Portland and since then no communication has been received from her.

Five destroyers, two submarines, the whole of the minesweeper flotilla of six vessels and the submarine depot ship Adamant were sent out to take up the search. Men on leave in Weymouth and Portland were summoned from cinemas and theatres to rejoin their ships.

An official at the headquarters of the Commander-in-Chief said this morning:

"A submarine of the M2 type could remain underwater in an emergency for forty-eight hours. M2 is equipped with the latest life-saving devices, including the Davis escape apparatus, which was responsible for the rescue of six men in the Poseidon disaster last June."

It is an ominous coincidence that the M2's sister-ship, M1, disappeared in similar circumstances in 1925. M1 dived off Start Point with sixty-eight men on board and was never located.

**(January 27)**

# HOPE GIVEN UP OF SAVING M2'S CREW

All hope of saving the lives of any of those on board the ill-fated submarine M2 has been abandoned. The search for the hull of the vessel will be continued.

The King has sent a message of sympathy to the bereaved relatives. A burial service will be held over the vessel if located. If she is not located, the service will be conducted over the place where the submarine was last seen

A memorial service is to be held at the Avalanche Church, Portland, to-morrow afternoon.

**(January 30)**

## DECREE FOR WOMAN NOVELIST

The hearing was concluded in the Divorce Court yesterday of the petition brought by Mrs. Mary Barbara Hamilton McCorquodale (Barbara Cartland, the novelist) and the cross-petition of her husband, Mr. Alexander George McCorquodale, company director, of Chesterfield court, London.

After an absence of a quarter of an hour the jury found misconduct on the part of Mr. Alexander McCorquodale and Mrs. Helene Ellinor Clare Curtis, wife of Major Philip Pinckney Curtis.

They found that Mrs. McCorquodale had not committed misconduct with Mr. Hugh McCorquodale, her husband's cousin.

Lord Merrivale granted a decree nisi with costs to Mrs. McCorquodale. Mr. Hugh McCorquodale was dismissed from the suit with costs.

Mr. A. G. McCorquodale and Mrs. Curtis denied on oath the allegations against them except that arising out of a cruise in the Homeric.

**(November 24)**

# FRANCE URGED TO SPEND MORE

**From Our Own Correspondent**

PARIS, Friday.

M. Landry, the Minister of Labour, has given a "spend more" New Year's message to the Freanch nation. He holds that France's proverbial thriftiness is intensifying unnecessarily the present stagnation of industry and commerce. He therefore counsels his countrymen to:

Spend, Drink champagne.

Clothe themselves in silk.

Buy hats and shoes.

Take taxis.

Go to the play, and Furnish their houses.

Frenchmen, M. Landry says, are "saving, patching and cheese-paring," even though their material situation may not have changed.

**(January 2)**

# NOEL COWARD'S NEW REVUE

## ORIGINALITY, WIT AND SATIRE

**By C.B. Mortlock**

Can it be that Mr. Noel Coward was unnerved by the crescendo of applause which rose as the curtain fell again and again at the Adelphi Theatre last night? At any rate, neither he nor Mr. Cochran appeared to round off in the traditional way the first night in London of "Words and Music."

It had been an almost magic evening - one of those brilliant audiences which from time to time assembles to assist at what everyone feels is an "occasion," and a performance which surpassed the expectation of most of us.

A REVUE WITH UNITY

Mr. Coward has given London a revue which is something much more than the usual congeries of interchangeable features. As author, composer and producer he has endowed it with a unity and rhythm which set a new artistic standard for this type of entertainment.

Once again Mr. Coward appears in the rôle of satirist, but the power of his biting commentary on the futilities of the day is so generously mixed with the jam of melody and wit that the laughter was continuous. Only once was it really stilled, and that was when Miss Ivy St. Helier, revealed in the tights and spangles of an acrobat - or rather an acrobat's wife - extracted the pathos of the ageing woman whose part it is merely to stand and fear night after night while her husband swings from hoop to hoop.

TUNEFUL MELODIES

There is melody in abundance. Two numbers, "Mad about the Boy," in which Miss Nora Howard made a particularly palpable hit, and "The Younger Generation," are the sort of tunes that you cannot get out of your head.

It is difficult to say where Mr. Coward scored most heavily. Perhaps the biggest hit was made by the skits on Russian ballet. Here was no burlesque which had lost all relation to its original, but a brilliant piece of parody. The pastiches of Rossini, de Falla, Ravel, and Chopin were startling in their fidelity and humour.

Yet, despite all the laughter, (and the absurdity of "Journey's End" done in the fashion of "White Horse Inn"), there is an underlying note of restraint and sincerity which is reflected in the décor and dresses. There are few departures from black and white and grey.

"Words and Music" is a real revue, and I have never seen a better.

**(September 17)**

# NEW RUSSIAN WORK

## A "REVOLUTIONARY" SYMPHONY

It is highly probable that we shall hear more of Dimitri Szostakovicz, the young Russian composer, whose symphony (Op. 10), written when he was seventeen, was given to-night its first performance here by the Hallé Orchestra, conducted by Sir Hamilton Harty. The symphony is by no means perfect or even mature. Indeed, the whole of the first movement betrays the youthful student's outlook - the anxious quest for originality of ideas, the tentative handling of the orchestra, and, more significant than all these, an obvious lack of staying power.

Yet this symphony, in spite of its failings, shows a remarkable degree of judgment. Though in his early works he aimed at being revolutionary, Szostakovicz, compared with the latest Schönberg, is almost a reactionary. Some of his devices can be traced directly to their source - Strauss or Liszt - and he has none of Schönberg's distaste for the natural tone of musical instruments.

It is said of Szostakovicz that he regards music as "a weapon for the struggle." It is much to his credit that his music is as unlike a weapon as could be imagined.

F.B.

**(January 22)**

# MELLOW JAZZ

## IMPRESSIONS OF THE NEW B.B.C. DANCE BAND

**By a Special Correspondent**

There was an interesting double event in broadcasting yesterday evening. From eight o'clock to half-past the first transmission was made from Broadcasting House - the palatial, new abode of the B.B.C. - and this took the form of the first programme given by the new B.B.C. dance band under Mr. Henry Hall.

Mr. Hall had prophesied that his music would be found to be "something different," and from the moment that the new band floated on to the ether with its "signature tune" - a lilting melody entitled "Dancing Time is Here Again" - the prophecy came true.

**(May 21)**

# WHAT IS MR. T.S. ELIOT'S AUTHORITY AS A CRITIC?

**By Rebecca West**

**Selected Essays. By T.S. Eliot. (Faber, 12s 6d)**
**Brave New World, By Aldous Huxley. (Chatto and Windus. 7s 6d)**

MANY who open the new volume of Mr. T.S. Eliot's "Selected Essays," put forth in such sober and seemly form by Messrs. Faber and Faber, and who recognise the sober and seemly quality of its balanced sentences, may be incredulous if told that, to my mind at least, the years this American author has spent in England have inflicted damage on our literature from which it will probably not recover for a generation.

His appointment to the Chair of Poetry at Harvard will probably inflict damage on American literature which will be only less because of the lesser time he intends to occupy it. Readers will be the more incredulous if they remember his poetry, which is indeed true and splendid poetry, and if they have read the section on Dante, which has been published separately and is of unsurpassed excellence in its field.

Yet the case against Mr. Eliot is strong. He came over here about the time of the war, when English criticism was at its low ebb, when perhaps because politics exercised such a compelling force on many able minds - it was purely arbitrary and impressionist; and he came over with a defined position.

He had been born in the Middle West where all things are new. He had been to Harvard and fallen under the influence of Professor Irving Babbitt and Professor Paul Elmer More, who have developed a movement known as Humanism, which attempts to correct the intellectual faults likely to arise in a community where all things are new.

HUMANISM

This movement very properly attempts to create as lively a respect as possible for the tradition and achievements of the past, and it is unfortunate that the limitations of its founders, which are so considerable as to counterbalance their undoubted learning, have reduced it to propaganda for a provincial conception of metropolitan gentility.

In recent years, however, Mr. Eliot's influence on English letters had been pernicious, for several reasons, which are manifest in this volume. He has made his sense of the need for authority and tradition an excuse for refraining from any work likely to establish where authority truly lies, or to hand on tradition by continuing it in vital creation.

He registers himself as fastidious by crying out against violence, confusion, and the presentation of unanalysed emotion. But he appears unable to distinguish between these vices and vigour, the attempts to find new and valid classifications in place of old ones which have proved invalid, and the pressing of the analysis of emotion to a further stage; and there seems as often as not to be no discriminative process whatsoever working behind these repetitions of his formulae.

The sober form of his sentences bears no relation to their content, which, as "Selected Essays" shows, often betrays lack of industry and flippancy, superficiality, and even vulgarity of thought.

It must be recorded that these defects are found in Mr. Eliot's work either together or not at all. When he has been industrious, as in his studies of Marlowe, Middleton, Heywood, Tourneur, Ford, and Massinger, he is serious, helpful, and sensitive. But there are a number of essays in this volume which since they are framed with an authoritative air, appear to propound meagerness as a standard of excellence.

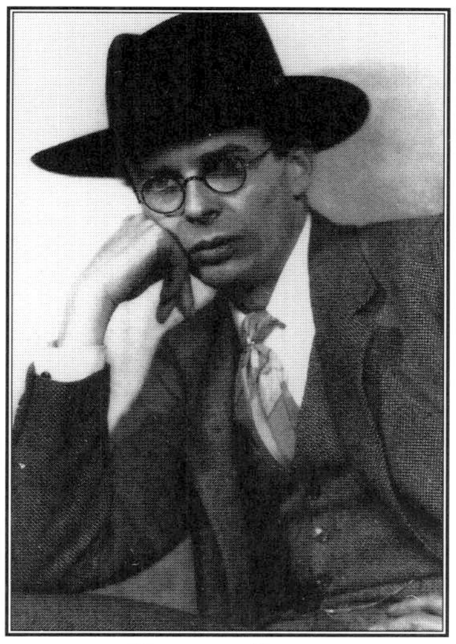

MR. ALDOUS HUXLEY

* * *

THOSE who are easily shocked had better leave Mr. Aldous Huxley's new fantasy. "Brave New World," on one side, noting as they pass, that since this is a free country they are not compelled to read it.

Those who are not easily shocked can settle down to enjoy what is not only the most accomplished novel Mr. Huxley has yet written, but also the most serious religious work written for some years. His tendency in his other novels has been to select subject matter which might fairly be described as a fuss about nothing. Even the characters in "Point Counterpoint" were carefully docketed as interesting individuals - they were, in relation to the depicted imbroglio , as lacking in allure as sexually-maladjusted cockroaches. But the argument in "Brave New World" is of major importance. One could sanely ask for nothing more than it gives.

One would say that the book was about a Utopia if it were not that a line of dreamers have given that originally non-committal term a sense of imagined perfection; for the book describes the world as Mr. Huxley sees it may become if certain modern tendencies grow dominant and its character is rather of a deduced abomination.

If one has a complaint to make against him it is that he does not explain to the reader in a preface or footnotes how much solid justification he has for his horrid visions. It would add to the reader's interest if he knew that when Mr. Huxley depicts the human race as abandoning its viviparous habits and propagating by means of germ cells surgically removed from the body and fertilised in laboratories that the embryo develops in a bottle and he is writing of a possibility that biologists are seeing not more remotely than, let us say, Leonardo da Vinci saw the aeroplane. And it would add to the reader's sympathetic horror if he realised that the society which Mr. Huxley represents as being founded on this basis is actually the kind of society that various living people, notably in America and Russia, and in connection with the Bolshevist and Behaviourist movements, have expressed a desire to establish; and that this is true even of the least pleasing details.

There is indeed, nothing at all impossible in Mr. Huxley's vision of a world where the infants are conditioned by such experiments, and by the dormitory loud speakers that whisper moral education into their sleeping ears (his pages on hypnopædia, or sleep-teaching, are among the most amusing in the book) into a lack of all characteristics save those which tend to uphold the stability of the State. Much of it is actual in America.

There is this salesmanship, which enjoins them to make a division between that which is valued and that which is preserved; they are taught to acquire an infinity of gimcrack objects, display them, throw them away. They are taught to dissipate their force on silly crowd pleasures. The talkies have become the feelies - they feel the kisses and the tears - but have not changed their fatuous essence. The chemists have found that drug they have been looking for, which intoxicates without deleterious effect on the nervous system. Leisure hours, therefore, become a blandly drunken petting-party; for promiscuity is a social duty, since it discourages far more than puritanism the growth of that disintegrating factor, love.

Mr. Huxley is attacking the new spirit which tries to induce man to divert in continual insignificant movements relating to the material framework of life all his force, and to abandon the practice of speculating about his existence and his destiny. Equally a denunciation of Capitalism and Communism so far as they discourage man from thinking freely, it is a declaration that art is a progressive revelation of the universe to man, and that those who interfere with it leave men to die miserably in the night of ignorance.

The book is many other things as well. One could cover many columns with discussion of its implications. It is, indeed, almost certainly one of the half-dozen most important books that have been published since the war.

**(February 5)**

# BOY FILM STAR'S GENIUS

## GREAT WORK IN 'SOOKY'

The youngest star of the screen; Jackie Cooper, who earns £500 a week at the age of 8, gives another astonishing performance in a picture the West-end will see in a few days.

"Sooky" is all about the friendship of two little boys, played by Jackie Cooper and Robert Coogan. How the well-to-do boy befriends his poor little friend, gets into trouble for his sake, and comforts him when his mother dies, makes one of the most human and appealing pictures ever screened.

All the acting is good, but Jackie Cooper reduces everyone else to insignificance. He is not good looking. He has a queer-shaped head from which great tufts of hair protrude. He wears the most outrageously unbecoming clothes. But through "Sooky" shines the pure genius that enabled this prodigious child to play in "The Champ" opposite one of the strongest personalities of the screen, Wallace Beery, and steal the picture.

C.D.

**(February 19)**

# NOBEL PRIZE AWARD

## GAINED BY MR. JOHN GALSWORTHY

The Nobel Trustees, cables our Stockholm Correspondent, have awarded the Nobel Prize for Literature in 1932 to Mr. John Galsworthy, O.M., in consideration of his services to literature and the drama and the cause of international and social progress.

This brings him fourth in the list of British authors thus honoured, his predecessors being Mr. Kipling (1907), Senator W.B. Yeats (1923), and Mr. G.B. Shaw (1925). The money award in each case amounts to about £8,000.

**(November 11)**

# THE BROADCAST OF "HAMLET"

## JOHN GIELGUD'S FINE ELOCUTION

Yesterday afternoon the B.B.C. gave us perhaps the most ambitious dramatic broadcast that they have yet attempted - a full performance of "Hamlet," with John Gielgud in the name-part, and a strong cast to support him.

By a "full" performance I do not, of course, mean that the whole text was used, but that the cuts were such as might reasonably have been made for a stage production of the play. As a matter of fact, the text used by Val Gielgud (the producer) was based on a script of Sir Henry Irving's in John Gielgud's possession.

Only to a man who knew the play well, and could conjure up in his mind a picture of its action, could this broadcast make its full appeal. "Hamlet" was written for the eye as much as for the ear, and it cannot be addressed to one sense only without grave loss.

How grave is that loss can be best told by comparing the tremendous effect in the theatre of John Gielgud's magnificent acting as the finest Hamlet of our time, with the faint emotions that I felt yesterday as I heard his voice borne over the ether.

Nevertheless, to those who have not had the opportunity to see his performance, it must have been deep pleasure to hear the verse of Shakespeare's masterpiece so notably well spoken.

Margaretta Scott made a gallant attempt at the impossible task of conveying the quality and pathos of Ophelia's madness by the voice alone; and Francis L. Sullivan, Martitia Hunt, Robert Donat, and others spoke the verse finely. Jack Hawkins gave Laertes a modernistic intonation that was quite out of place.

**(June 6)**

# NEW NOVEL

Cold Comfort Farm.
By Stella Gibbons. (Longmans 7s 6d)
**Reviewed by Howard Marshall**

"COLD COMFORT FARM" is Miss Gibbons' first novel, and it promises so well that I should hate to squeeze a notice of it into a final paragraph.

Possibly it will not appeal to those who take their novel-reading seriously, for it is, as the publishers admit, a distressingly frivolous story. Miss Gibbons apparently has had enough of the back-to-nature school of fiction. She is tired of emotional rustics and the passionate stirrings of the soil - so are most of us, for that matter - and she has therefore written a burlesque tale of misery and mud in Sussex.

Her plot is simple, for she achieves her satirical purpose by sending an extremely modern and sensible young woman to stay as a paying guest with some typically repressed cousins on a farm. There is a D.H. Lawrence young man and a number of T.F. Powys molecatchers and labourers, all of them suffering from sub-conscious urges and what-nots. Flora, the young woman, is not in the least intimidated, but sets about clearing up the mess in the most matter-of-fact manner.

The novel is definitely lively, intelligent, and amusing. I hope we shall hear more of Miss Gibbons.

**(September 13)**

# BEST BOOKS SINCE THE WAR

A list of the fifty best books published since the war, drawn up as a result of wide inquiry, is given in the spring issue of the "Book Window" published by W.H. Smith and Son Ltd. A sample of the books are:

"Queen Victoria," by Lytton Strachen
"Ariel," by André Maurois
"The Story of San Michele," by Alex Munthe
"The Letters of Queen Victoria."
"The Duke," by Philip Guedalla
"Napoleon," by Emil Ludwig
"The Life of Thomas Hardy,"
by Florence Hardy
"Portrait of Zelide," by Geoffrey Scott
"The Outline of History," by H.G. Wells
"A History of England," by G.H. Trevelyan
"The World Crisis," by Winston Churchill

**(April 19)**

# HORRORS ON THE SCREEN

## THE "FRANKENSTEIN" FILM

**By Campbell Dixon**

Yesterday I saw "Frankenstein" the horror film which has been the most sensational box-office success America has known for years.

If a small boy with a passion for blood and mechanics were let loose in a studio, "Frankenstein" is exactly the sort of film he would produce. Everything meaningless that perverted ingenuity could suggest - thunder and lightning, dangling skeletons, baying hounds, a mountain shack as full of dynamos as Western Electric's head station - is there to wring a gasp from the uncritical.

Everything in Mary Wollstonecraft Shelley's novel that lifted it above the level of a penny-dreadful has been omitted. "Frankestein" was published in 1817 when thinking minds were absorbed with the horrors of the new machine age. The monster stood for man's hideous creation that would eventually destroy him - or at least destroy the joy and beauty that made life worth living.

Of all this the film does not give as much as a hint. Mr. Colin Clive (Frankenstein), Mr. Boris Karloff (the monster), Miss Mae Clarke, and Mr. Frederick Kerr (the one real being in a world of robots) do their best to make the clotted nonsense convincing. Responsibility for their failure (and the jubilation at the box-office) must be divided between Mr. James Whale, the producer of "Journey's End" and the man who prepared the script.

"Frankenstein" will make a great deal of money. But it will also do more than any other film of the year to make a laughing stock of the screen.

**(January 21)**

# "MICKEY MOUSE" IN COLOUR

Mickey Mouse the world-beloved creation of Walt Disney, one of the few geniuses of the talking screen, will be seen shortly in colour.

I saw two experimental productions by Mr. Disney - not Mickey Mouse cartoons, but "Silly Symphonies," of the same school of eccentric rhythm and brilliant pantomime. These pioneer films, "Flowers and Trees," and "King Neptune," have more charm and genuine invention than ninety-nine out of a hundred full-length productions.

The colour is very effective, and the storm scenes, the sinking of the pirate ship by Neptune, and the release of the captive mermaid, will delight grown-ups and reduce children to ecstasy. As a portent, too, these colour pieces are of the first importance.

With one or two exceptions films in colour in the past have not been particularly successful, owing to the countless difficulties of lighting, clothing, and photography which have to be overcome. But no such problems confront Mr. Disney in producing colour cartoons; the colour will be perfect for the same reason that the rhythm is perfect - they are both mechanical.

**(December 9)**

# TARZAN ON THE SCREEN

**By Campbell Dixon**

Those who read "Tarzan of the Apes" will recall that an English girl in the African jungle is captured by and falls in love with a young man who has been brought up by apes.

This pleasing conception has been brought to the screen by Metro-Goldwyn-Mayer with all the resources of modern science. From the moment when Miss Maureen O'Sullivan, Mr. Neil Hamilton, and our own Mr. C. Aubrey Smith set out in search of the elephants' burial place there is never a dull moment.

The trail leads along a precipice too narrow for men, which shows again how resourceful a beast is the elephant. Then the heroine is kidnapped by a gentlemanly apeman, who hurls her into his tree hut and sleeps, knife in hand, on a most uncomfortable bough outside.

Not unnaturally she falls in love with him, and from now on the course of true love runs fairly smooth, save only for attacks by lions, tigers, hippos, crocodiles, white men, dwarfs, and rival apes.

ACROBATS AS APES

Of a distinguished cast I can mention only the artists who affixed large canvas flaps to the Indian elephants that "double" for their African kin, the specialists who built and towed crocodiles in thrilling proximity to the swimming hero; the African dwarfs (unnamed but admirably painted), supplied by all the best American sideshows; the energetic acrobats who doubled for apes; and, above all, the ingenious Mr. Dunning, who made it possible for the Ape-man (played by the former world champion swimmer, Johnny Weismuller) to grapple with lions in single combat and win every decision.

**(May 12)**

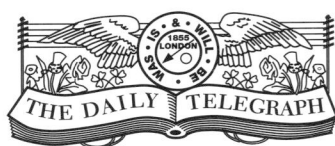

THE DAILY TELEGRAPH

135, FLEET STREET LONDON

Telephone: CENTRAL 4242

**TO-DAY'S WEATHER FORECAST**

LONDON & S.E. ENGLAND - Moderate or fresh south-westerly wind, perhaps veering later; bright intervals and showers of rain or hail, thundery at times; moderate temperature.

ENGLISH CHANNEL - Sea moderate
Lighting-up time. 6.59 p.m.
Sun rises 5.40 a.m. : sets 6.29 p.m.
Moon rises 4.11 a.m. : sets 12.51 p.m.
New Moon Wednesday.

# THE FLOOD TIDE OF CRIME

REPEATED warnings from the judges of assize should have taught the public that there has been a large increase in serious crime. How great the recent increase is, how grave the danger to society, has not yet been appreciated, and the statistics just published by the Home Office will be read with anxiety. They are, of course, belated. But in 1930, the last year recorded, the more serious crimes known to the police had risen from 134,581 to 147,031. This is quite out of proportion to the growth of the population; it follows increases in previous years but is far greater than any recently observed. We had, since the War, congratulated ourselves that the worst offence short of murder, personal violence, was declining. But in 1930 there were many more cases. The greater part of the increase in criminal activity was, however, as usual devoted to larceny, "breakings-in," and robbery of various kinds.

By far the larger number of crimes are committed by young people. Two-thirds of all those found guilty are under 30, two-fifths under 21. A middle-aged criminal is rare, an old one the exception. The official deduction is that the growth of crime is to be ascribed to two causes - first, the lawless and adventurous character of many of the generation who were without parental control in the War; and second, the industrial depression, the severity of which in the North has tempted many very young people to the less serious forms of robbery. These are no doubt true causes, though it must be remarked that 1930 is late for those who were uncontrolled boys during the War to show an increased addiction to criminality.

The official summary of the situation is not hopeful. It sees the need of a policy to "stem the tide of crime," but offers no help to one. This despair at the Home Office is not shared by the judges or by any who have given fair study to the deterrent and reformatory effects of long terms of sentence. A belief in the value of long periods of Borstal treatment used to be a cardinal principle of our dealings with crime. Under the present administration of the prisons it appears to have been abandoned. A few weeks ago, Mr. Justice HUMPHREYS was complaining that whenever judges pass the three years' sentence required for the Borstal reformatory course "perpetually the authorities liberate these young men … and the public gets the benefit of it." The adolescent offender is made into an habitual criminal, and the blame for it belongs to the prison administration. In these days no considerable body of opinion desires vindictive or cruelly punitive sentences. But there is grave anxiety over that sentimentality of the present prison administration which is displayed when an Assistant Prison Commissioner makes public speeches defending bag snatchers and car thieves as the victims of society. In such folly as this may be found one of the causes of that addiction to adventurous crime which aggrieves the Home Office. If the administration of prisons and the penal law were again in the hands of men of foresight and judgment and firmness, not much more would be heard of the growth of crime and the new criminal.

**(March 31)**

# THIS AGE OF NOISE

WHETHER this is or is not the noisiest age in history; by how much the noise of London is less ear-splitting than that of Paris or Rome; whether the combined noise of five million people shouting together will generate enough heat to boil one egg or two eggs - these are not the questions which really interest the sufferer from Noise. He is vitally concerned to know what can be done to mitigate the endless din about him. Then when he asks what is being done he finds that the net amount is very little.

Dr. KAYE, the prime authority on Noise, suggested to the British Association yesterday that many of the older motor vehicles should be relegated to some permanent home of silence. A recent law empowered interference by the police in the case of such offenders, and of the motor-cycle fiend who tears along with his silencer off. But the powers are not used. Perhaps the police have iron nerves. Nor are the horn-blowing and loud-speaking and gramophone nuisances abated. The Noise roars on.

**(September 2)**

# DISGRACE TO AMERICAN JUSTICE

THAT any new event could make the mystery of the LINDBERGH case darker and more horrible was beyond expectation. But in this the New Jersey police have succeeded. The full story of the death of the maid-servant in the LINDBERGH household, VIOLET SHARPE, has not been published, and probably never will be published. What is known is that after a series of interrogations by the police and just as she was summoned to another she was found poisoned. The first reaction of the chief of the New Jersey police, Col. SCHWARTZKOPF was to make a public statement that she had been under constant suspicion and her "suicide … tends to confirm the suspicions of the investigating authorities." Mrs. DWIGHT MORROW, Mrs. LINDBERGH's mother, is, however, of a very different opinion. She has taken care to let it be known that she "believes the poor girl was simply frightened to death." The American people, we are told, are now asking whether an innocent girl was driven to suicide by the third degree methods of the police.

They have reason. The spirit and the intelligence with which the interrogation of the girl was conducted may be judged by the statement of the Chief-Inspector in charge. "The girl was fresh and impertinent from the start until the baby was found. Then she became a bundle of nerves … Then we went to work." If the investigation of crime is entrusted to men whose minds are on that level, the only doubt is whether the result will be more gruesome or more futile.

**(June 13)**

# A HUNDRED YEARS OF THE CIGARETTE

PLANS, it is said, are in train for the celebration of the centenary of the cigarette by British firms engaged in its manufacture. To fix the actual date of origin cannot have been easy, with a number of competing legends in the field. But that which awards the honours of invention to an Egyptian soldier in 1832 has the merit of being a good story. Certainly, the makers have something to celebrate, seeing that the number of cigarettes smoked in a year in this country now runs far into the thousands of millions, with results for the trade that, despite strenuous competition, are more than satisfactory.

Since the years before the war, as the Imperial Economic Committee has shown, Great Britain has changed from a pipe-smoking to a cigarette-smoking country; and the cigarette's predominance, once achieved, has continued to grow. It is not only the entry of women into the field of consumption that accounts for the change. Men have been gradually deserting the pipe for a generation past; though not, be it hoped, for the reason suggested by RUSKIN, that cigarette-smoking "enabled a man to do nothing without being ashamed of himself."

**(October 24)**

# ALL INDIA'S PLUCKY FIGHT

DEFEAT with honour. That has been the portion of the All-India eleven in the first Test match in which their country has ever been represented at Lord's. It is very much to be doubted if the wisest of wiseacres in the pavilion anticipated that the visitors would put up such a spirited fight, let alone that they would send the wickets of England's pride flying in the first few minutes. After the Indian team's gallant showing there will be widespread regret that no further Test matches can be arranged during their present tour.

When it is remembered that the All-India team had never played together until they came to England it is evident that an important new factor has entered into the international conception of the game. The credit for the victory of the England side belongs largely to Mr. Jardine.

**(June 29)**

# MAKING OF YOUNG COMMUNISTS

## 'NURTURED ON LIES & HALF-TRUTHS

## POISONING THE MASS MIND

### ENGLAND LIBELLED IN SCHOOL BOOKS

**By Martin Moore**
**Daily Telegraph Special Representative recently in Russia.**

NO one can really understand the Russia of to-day, or form a picture of what may be the Russia of to-morrow, without some knowledge of the mental atmosphere in which the people live.

Economic facts and figures can speak for the present and the immediate future; but the mass-mind now being created must influence events for generations to come.

The creation of this mentality is a phenomenon unique in world history.

The minds of more than 160,000,000 people - few of them with any background of previous education - are being nurtured almost entirely on lies and halftruths, as far as the outside world is concerned. Communist propaganda abroad is mere purposeless talk compared with Communist propaganda at home.

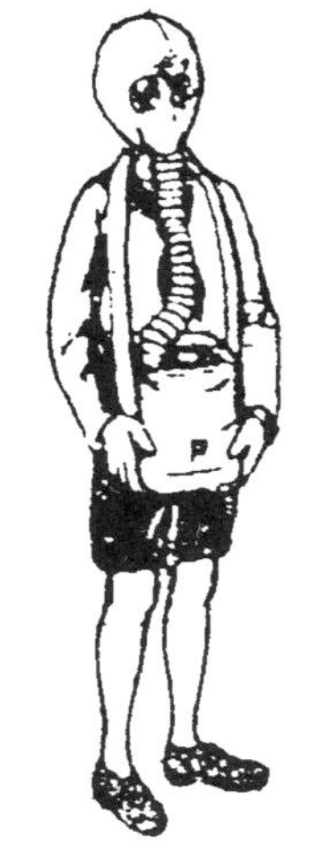

Child's Gas-Mask Drill

Do not expect to find inefficiency in this department of State activity. It is the best thing the Bolsheviks do. After all, they have had only fifteen years' experience of governing, but all the leaders have had a lifetime's training in the technique of propaganda.

From early morning until he goes to bed, in every phase of his life, the Soviet citizen is assailed by propaganda. It comes to him over the ether to the remotest villages. Propaganda shouts at the citizen from the walls of his factory, his dining-room, his club, and most of the public buildings. He reads nothing else in the newspapers. He hears propaganda from the talking screen and from the stage.

Much of this propaganda is merely designed to teach industrial and agricultural efficiency, and much of it pursues the comparatively harmless aim of glorifying the acts of the party and the Government. But whatever concerns the outside world - especially Britain and America - is based upon falsehood.

Two fundamental beliefs are drummed into the minds of even the tiniest tots at school - firstly, that the collapse of the capitalist world is imminent; secondly, that a war of aggression against the Soviet Union is in active preparation.

ENGLAND BREAKING UP

Many Russians honestly belive that the complete break-up of Western civilisation is merely a matter of months. Every item of news from abroad is designed to minister to this belief.

From a woman old enough to be a little sceptical usually came the question: "Tell me, are things really so bad in England?"

Genuine belief in the imminence of war was the original driving force behind the Five-Year Plan. Fear of "capitalist aggression" is still used as a spur to urge the people to further effort and self-denial; and it is a fear that dominates even the Kremlin to-day.

Much more serious than the propaganda by radio, poster and Press among the adult population is the distorted picture of the world presented to school-children. England is especially singled out for school-book calumny.

I reproduce without comment the following extracts from an English primer which I was fortunate enough to obtain in Moscow, despite the strict precautions taken to prevent such books from falling into foreigners' hands:

"In England and its colonies children begin to work in mines when they reach 12 years. Hundreds of children perish in accidents in the mines every year."

There followed a touching little poem, entitled "A Miner's Son in England."

"Jim is a little boy of nine
He knows no sunshine
For he must earn his daily bread
And every day with secret dread
He must go down into the mine -
A boy of nine.
"Why does he work, the little lad?
And where's his dad?
Can he not go to school instead,
And still have bread?
Jim;s father died two years ago
Killed by explosion deep below
"He was the eldest, little Jim
So there was but one way for him."

Lest it should be supposed that this schoolbook is either unofficial or dates from the earlier days of Communist propaganda, I may add that it bears the imprint of the State Publishing Department, and the date 1932.

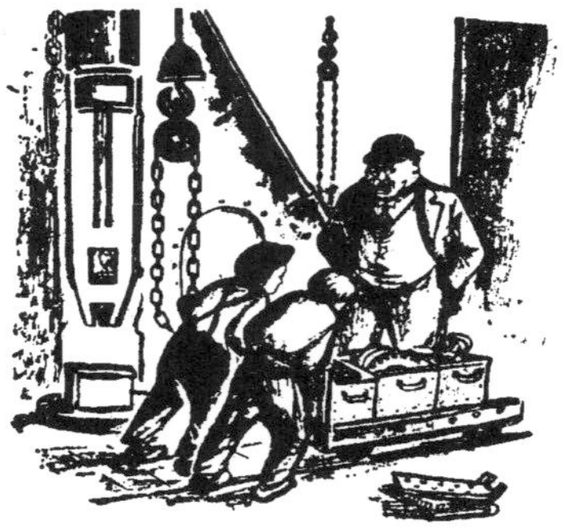

Child Labour in England.
From a Soviet School Book.

Both this primer and a companion volume for slightly older pupils contain lessons on warfare and the part children must play in it, together with profuse illustrations of military apparatus.

**(December 6)**

# New British Settlement

### ELDORADO IN THE FAR WILDS

**By Kenneth Lindsay**

I HAVE recently returned from a little-known corner of the world, on the borderland of Argentina, Brazil, and Paraguay. It is little known now, that is to say, though I think we may hear a great deal more about it in the near future.

This far north-eastern pocket of the Argentine, the "Territory of Missions" three centuries ago had a larger population than exists there to-day. But the Jesuit Missions were expelled and a dark age intervened between then and the latter part of last century. The Guarani Indians, a tribe of Mongolian origin, on the Upper Parana River, were the sole inhabitants.

When Mr. A.J. Schwelm arrived there in 1919 he found a virgin forest, a magnificent river, and the native Guarani - not an obvious place for a settlement, though a situation ripe with romance. When I arrived there a few months ago I found a thriving European colony of some 7,000 persons.

* * *

Eldorado, for that is the name of the colony, has three natural advantages - a rich virgin soil on the cleared land, cheap fuel and timber, and a plentiful water supply. But unless there had been combined with these things most careful and far-seeing organisation, and, above all, the indomitable will of a man unhampered by Government restrictions, the colony could never have achieved its present success.

Seeds and plants, like the settlers themselves, have been introduced from all over the world. Experimental farms have been set up to advise the settlers.

Climate and soil have been carefully studied. The amount and price of land have been such as to induce men to work for their own satisfaction.

The principle of free and open competition has stimulated entirely unforeseen developments. To-day, instead of one school, there are eight; instead of one shop there are twenty; there are motor agencies, a post office, a wireless station, police and justice, two churches, football teams, and a weekly cinema.

All this I saw created out of a dense virgin forest, which only twelve years ago was given up to wild and primitive life. Instead of the jaguar and the tapir, there are now cattle and poultry; instead of wild cotton and palm nuts there is cultivated yerba (the Argentine tea), tobacco, every kind of citrus fruit, vegetables and flowers; instead of semi-slave labour there is a community of peasant farmers owning their own land.

The journey is only three weeks from door to door, via Southampton, Buenos Aires, and thence by train, and finally boat to the colony.

**(April 5)**

## DISTINGUISHED INVALIDS

THE EARL OF KIMBERLEY (ill in nursing home): Much about the same.
SIR HAROLD NUTTING (operation): Condition satisfactory.
LADY DEAN PAUL: Satisfactory progress.
MISS FLORA WOODMAN (operation): Convalescent.
DR MARION PHILLIPS (operation): As well as can be expected.
MR LYTTON-STRACHEY (ulcerative colitis): Improving.

**(January 5)**

# LONDON DAY BY DAY:

THERE was pageantry on the Socialist Benches yesterday afternoon when Mr. Arthur Greenwood, the victor of Wakefield, was introduced into the House of Commons.

The small Opposition had turned up in force, and nearly every one of them wore a large red carnation in his buttonhole, which was said to have been supplied by the wife of a young peer.

Mr. Charles Edwards, the chief Socialist Whip, and Mr. Lansbury, who sponsored Mr. Greenwood, beamed as they steered their new big gun to the Speaker's table, while the Socialists roared with delight.

### Out of Practice

IT was a very ragged procession, however. There was none of the military procession which Capt. Margesson, the Chief Government Whip, instils into new Conservative members when he leads them to the Speaker's chair.

The three Socialist members scattered across the floor and seemed to be uncertain when they should bow. One could not escape the reflection that it was because they are out of practice.

### Sir Henry Wood

SIR HENRY WOOD, who brings another Promenade Season to an end this evening, is the only conductor I know who seems insensible to fatigue.

The physical and nervous strain of directing a symphony concert is much greater than most people realise, and when that recurs nightly, as it does in the Promenades, the cumulative effect of the evening performances and morning rehearsals might well tax a much younger man. But even in the torrid nights of August this summer Sir Henry Wood never faltered.

I have heard him attribute his staying power to two causes. One is that he never conducts without a score. The other that he always stands with both feet firmly planted. If you watch Sir Henry Wood carefully you will see how firm is his stance and how rarely he moves his feet.

### Connoisseurs of Eggs

HOW satisfactory it would be if we could estimate the inner worth of the breakfast egg before breaking the masking shell. This feat, I am told, is within the powers of the Zoo's latest acquisition, the egg-eating snake from South Africa, a reptile which feeds exclusively on eggs.

Presented with a dud egg, the snake, after one rapid investigation, turns away. But given a new laid egg the head, which is no larger than the top of a man's small finger, miraculously engulfs it.

### At Lord's

IT seemed as if everybody in the cricket world was present at Lord's yesterday afternoon for the second day of the match between the Gentlemen and Players. It was a field day for India, for the magnificent stand of Duleepsinhji and the Nawab of Pataudi was the talk on every hand.

Ranji, Duleepsinhji's uncle, was not present. His secretary explained to me that the prince was fishing in Ireland, for he did not anticipate any sensations in this match.

As it was, Duleep excelled himself, and the match also provided an admirable opportunity for the Nawab of Pataudi to show he is in Test match class. Ranji's box was occupied all day by half-a-dozen Indian ladies in native dress.

**The Socialsit Day of Small Mercies**
**Sir Henry Wood's Staying Power**

### A New Street Horror

I NOTICED a curious piece of crowd psychology yesterday. There was a new kind of road drill in operation in Knightsbridge which instead of making the usual machine-gun noise, made one remarkably like a dentist's drill.

Several passers-by instinctively raised their hands to their jaws.

### Devastated Coney Island

THAT a large part of Coney Island has been reduced to a state of ruin may convey very little to newspaper readers in this country. But actually it means that for the time being New York has been deprived of its playground.

In no other part of the world is there anything to compare with Coney Island. It is a sort of combination of Blackpool, and old Earl's Court, the Hamburg Menagerie, and the Vienna Prater, together with every known form of freak show and "stunt" in entertainment.

In addition to this there was the board walk and bathing beaches.

PETERBOROUGH

# What the Children Are Wearing This Winter

## THE SLIM LINE IN JUVENILE COATS

ALTHOUGH there is naturally no question of slimming in the nursery, it is a fact that modern children are much slimmer and easier to dress than they were a generation ago. Modern children take a tremendous amount of exercise, and are not, as a rule, allowed to overfeed in infancy, with the result that some very smart clothes are being fashioned for slim children in Mayfair this winter.

### TWEED AND VELVET

Princess Elizabeth and her sister have created a new vogue for the simple tweed coat, with either a velvet collar to match a velvet

béret or a stitched collar and a little stitched tweed hat. The duchess of York ordered special tweeds from the Shetlands for her two daughters some months ago. Red and white and maize and white tweeds are being woven for Lady Muriel Willoughby, who designs so many nursery outfits in Mayfair.

Prune, deep claret colour, and nigger brown are the favourite colours for frocks and coats for the girl of eight to twelve this winter. All these are practical shades - there will not be many white or pastel coloured outfits in the Park this winter - and can be combined with stitching or darning to rose beige coloured wool, and beige stockings and gloves and nigger brown shoes. A maize coloured tweed coat for a fair-haired girl, cut,

as most of them are, with a waist and a little flare below, has a velvet stock scarf of nigger brown to match the nigger-brown velvet béret. Most of the coats have little scarves that either fasten with a pin like a stock or tie into an artist's bow.

Cardigan suits are increasingly popular for indoor wear for girls, in many cases similar tweed that is used for coat and skirt being made into breeches for a smaller brother.

Raspberry red and white checked tweed makes an attractive cardigan suit, with a white crêpe de Chine blouse that buttons on to the skirt and is edged with the tweed at neck and wrists. The skirt is also mounted on a slip, so that in very cold weather a jumper can be substituted for the crêpe de Chine blouse, and there is no need to wear a top-coat as well.

In the children's department of the big stores a great feature is being made of corduroy coats and leggings fastened with the "zip" with corduroy hats to match. Fair Isle jumpers are now made in all sizes, even for the two-year-olds, and inexpensive woollen cardigans match wool taffeta shirts for small boys. These in yellow, blue, and green are worn with coloured tweed breeches, coat, and hat, all matching.

(November 17)

---

# NEW CONTRACT BRIDGE LAWS

**By Captain Lindsay Mundy**

Despite the attempt at secrecy on the part of the framers of the new laws for contract bridge, I think it will be found, when the fresh rules are made public, that there are no changes of importance which have not been foreshadowed in THE DAILY TELEGRAPH.

I am in a position to state definitely that, in cutting, the highest card will be left instead of the lowest, both for cutting in to a table and for choice of seats. The fact that the ace will now count as the highest is merely the continuation of the practice in all card games that the ace is the best card.

I think it will also be found that, in cutting, the value of the suit cut only functions in the case of a tie in the numerical value of the cards cut. This will be a great improvement on the rule at present in force in England.

The revoke penalties will, I think, be a compromise. The American practice of letting the revoker score below the line, or even go "game" will disappear, but our present law is not likely to remain quite unchanged.

There are two rumours which may be safely ignored. It would be impossible to legislate successfully against psychic bids, as they are only a question of degree and even Solomon would be unable to lay down a line beyond which bad bidding should become illegal.

Neither, I believe, will it be enacted that every hand should be played out to the bitter end. No law to that effect would ever be observed, any more than was the fine of 50 points for looking at the last trick, which I have never once seen inflicted. Bridge players would never submit to such an unnecessary and wearisome lengthening of a game which is already too long.

(October 25)

---

# MODERN GIRL & NURSING

## MAKING THE WORK ATTRACTIVE

### SMOKING SHOULD BE PERMITTED

The adaptation of the conditions of the nursing profession to meet the views of the modern girl is urged in the final report, issued to-day, of the Commission on Nursing.

The commission was appointed by "The Lancet" in December, 1930, to inquire into the reasons for the shortage of candidates, trained and untrained, for nursing the sick in special and general hospitals.

Among the suggestions put forward to attract probationers are:

Better Pay: £30 first year, £35 second year, is by no means too high.

Shorter Hours: Day's span of work should not exceed thirteen hours, including three clear hours off duty and at least an hour and a half for meals. One free day each week.

Longer Holidays: Not less than three weeks a year.

Better Cooked Food.

More Personal Liberty: Probationers should be able to go out between time of finishing duty and bedtime. Attendance at meals adjacent to off-duty time should not be compulsory.

More Opportunities for social life.

Smoking should not be unduly restricted.

Telephone Facilities.

"The change in outlook that hospital authorities have not yet recognised," says the report, "is that the modern girl does not admit the propriety of any attempt to ensure her efficiency as an employee by regulation of her private life.

(February 19)

---

# WHY THEIR DINNER PARTY WAS A FAILURE

## SIMPLICITY THE BEST POLICY FOR THE SINGLE-HANDED COOK

### By The Hon. Fenella Trefusis

"GOD sends the food, but the Devil sends the cook," according to the old proverb, and the other evening on my return from dining with some newly-married friends, I was inclined to agree with it.

We were met at the door by a smart parlourmaid, who ushered us into a really charming drawing-room, pale green walls hung with reproductions of the "Cries of London," pale apricot curtains and cretonnes, a few pieces of good furniture - not overcrowded - and some Chinese bowls filled with spring flowers were scattered about.

The company was well chosen and congenial - just a bridge four of people who were pleased meet, and an engaged pair who announced their intention of playing backgammon.

Dinner was announced, and we walked informally into a dining-room lit by candles, on the table and in sconces, which showed up the polished mahogany and shining silver and glass. Everything well thought out, even to the menu cards in old silver stands.

Everything, in fact, was perfect except the dinner. I make no pretence at being indifferent to food, and my attention was promptly engaged in reading the bill of fare: Consommé en Tasses. Sole Vin Blanc. Côtelettes d'Agneau. Pêches Melba. Sardines sur Canapé. That was what we were promised, and it seemed to me a fairly ambitious dinner to be turned out by a single-handed cook in a small household.

One does not wish to bite the hand that fed one, but, oh, that dinner! Long before the end I was wishing that my hostess had modestly confined herself to roast mutton and rice pudding.

The soup was cold, but even had it been hot the flavour would have been little different from that of hot water to which a spoonful of gravy and another of colouring matter had been added.

Sole vin blanc would have been more accurately described as fillets of plaice with a flour and water sauce poured over them.

The cutlets were undoubtedly cutlets, but mutton, not lamb, to which the mint sauce (chiefly vinegar) was an added mockery; also they were too raw to eat, as were also the green peas, large as young gooseberries, which rattled like bullets upon my plate.

The mashed potato was so stiff that it was almost impossible to persuade it to leave the spoon. I watched my fellow-guests, and admired the cunning with which knives and forks were arranged to cover as much as possible of the uneaten and uneatable food left upon their plates.

One man went as far as to put his elbows on the table and clasp his hands until his plate was removed, a form of guile which I envied but dared not imitate.

Why bottled peaches covered with jam and custard should be called Pêche Melba I have no idea. To me it appears as an inaccuracy bordering on fraud.

Sardines are excellent things when left to themselves, but when involved with a frying-pan and a bit of hard toast they seem to lose all their natural virtues, and chiefly resemble the tin from which they sprung, both in flavour and texture.

There! I have bitten the hand that fed me, and been a perfect cat, but really, that dinner!

Now it is useless to criticise without suggesting a remedy, and in this case it seems to me that the remedy is simple enough.

To start with, the menu selected was an unwise one. Consommé in a small house is always a difficulty, where there is no stock-pot or home-made glaze as a foundation. Unless one is prepared to go to the expense of buying a glass jar of consommé from some reputable firm, it is safer to stick to vegetable soups. Scotch broth, cream of spinach, peas or cauliflower, potato or carrot soup, all are excellent and easy enough to cook, provided that they are cooked long enough and slowly enough and that a spoonful of cream per person is added as the soup is removed from the fire, but oh, be sparing with the pepper that refuge of the incompetent cook!

Soles vin blanc are excellent in a restaurant, but hardly possible in a small house. The dish, though seemingly simple, is really a fairly elaborate one as regards the sauce - cream, white wine, and fish stock - and, after all, what is better and simpler than fried sole - or even plaice - provided the breadcrumbs are crumbled sufficiently fine and the fat is hot enough and deep enough!

Nothing is better than a plain grilled lamb cutlet, but let it be lamb - at this time of year - not mutton, and let it be sufficiently, but not over cooked.

If the peas are hard, don't boil them; stew them in a little milk with some chopped onion, and add some hot milk, well stirred in, to the mashed potatoes.

If you must use tinned fruit and custard, don't call it Pêche Melba; you will deceive nobody; but, anyhow, what about a rhubarb or gooseberry fool with junket? Simple, but of its kind unbeatable.

A savoury is always a difficulty with a plain cook, and is sometimes the last straw at the end of a meal which has strained all the resources of a small kitchen. A good cheese, with several kinds of biscuits, well heated in the oven before serving is generally the most popular fare and you cannot go wrong with it.

(January 27)

---

# RADIO SETS DESIGNED FOR WOMEN

### 'PRESS-THE-BUTTON' TUNING

**By a Special Correspondent.**

One of the most surprising aspects of the Radio Exhibition at Olympia is the remarkable number of women who visited the show during the first two days. Quite one-third of the total number who were passed through the turnstiles on Saturday were women.

"Women are not technically-minded," said an official of the exhibition to me, "and the manufacturers have, during the past year, gone out of their way to cater for women by two methods. First, they have reduced the operation of a radio set to the utmost simplicity; in many cases the turning of one switch only is required. There are also several automatic tuning devices which make the act of tuning purely mechanical, and require no technical knowledge.

The other way in which woman has been catered for is by constructing radio set cabinets of such design and character as to have a definite feminine appeal.

One of the best instances of automatic tuning is seen on the Zetavox stand, where that particular brand of instrument has introduced "press-the-button" tuning. On the front panel of the set are nine buttons, each of which can be set to be co-related to a different broadcasting station. Once these buttons are set into position all that is necessary is to press the button, whereupon the programme of the required station is immediately secured.

This method of tuning was designed specifically for the benefit of women. The idea is that when the husband leaves home in the morning for work he can set the buttons to plot out a day's listening for his wife, who, as each hour comes round, has only to press the appropriate button in order to be tuned straight into the station.

This particular brand of instrument has also the additional advantage of possessing high reproduction quality, and is withal a handsome piece of furniture.

### FORTY-EIGHT STATIONS

Another method of simplified tuning can be seen on the Ekco stand, where are to be found instruments fitted with a circular station indicator. Forty-eight stations are named on the indicator, and a pointer is turned round to the desired station, when its programme is immediately tuned in. The highest tribute that can be paid to this particular set is that forty-eight stations can be readily tuned in at full loud-speaker strength and natural quality of reproduction.

(August 22)

---

# RUSH TO ADOPT NEW COIFFURE

## CENTRE PARTING CRAZE

### By Marianne Mayfayre

A COIFFURE made that is certain to be seen at Little Season dances is the centre parting with a wide loose wave over each temple, and the hair carried into a shingled swathe at the back.

Two well-known sisters, one of whom has often been hostess to the Prince of Wales, have decided to adopt this hair fashion, and came to London in the middle of their holiday to have their coiffure changed. Women with broad faces who have hitherto considered this Madonna-like coiffure would not become them are now taking to it as a change from the side parting, as a hairdresser in Park-lane has discovered that by skilful thinning of the hair and with a wide loose wave, this centre parting need not widen the face at all.

One advantage of this new coiffure is that bérets and caps can be worn at any angle off the face.

(August 20)

---

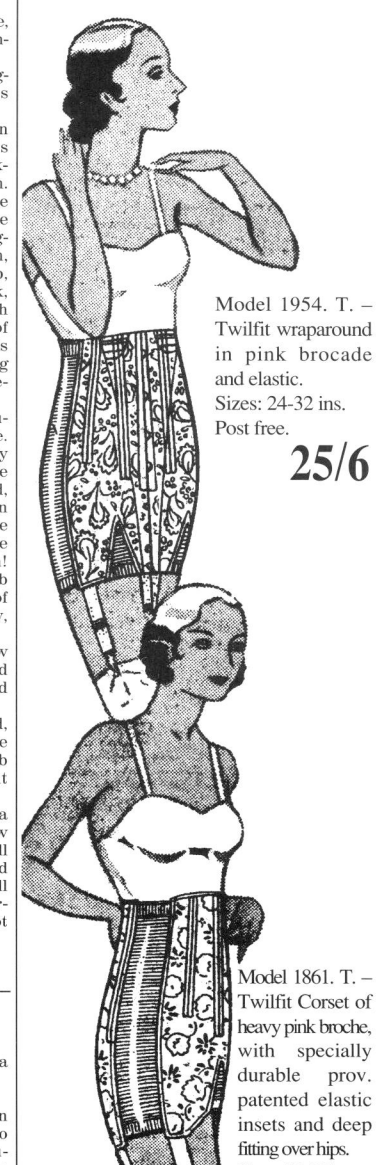
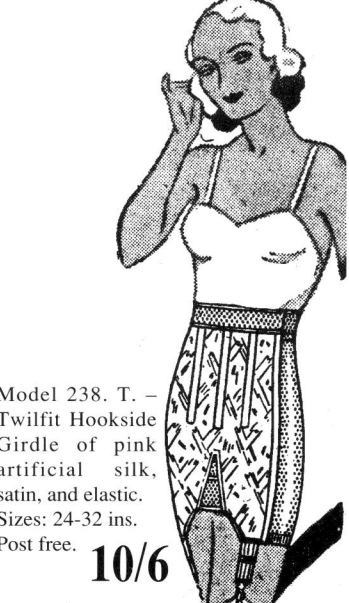

# HISTORY AS BASIS FOR ART

## GENIUS OF LYTTON STRACHEY

**By J. C. Squire**

Giles Lytton Strachey was one of the many children of Sir Richard Strachey, the famous Indian administrator. As a child he was not robust and did not go to a public school; in 1899 he went up to Trinity College, Cambridge.

Four years later, when I went to Cambridge myself, he was still haunting the place - a tall, thin, bowed figure, with an unkempt, drooping moustache and eyes that peered through moonlike magnifying spectacles. He had not set the Cam on fire. But all the best minds in the place were aware of him, and felt certain that some time so intelligent, honest, and fastidious a man must do something.

Years passed. He grew that great cushion of reddish beard, so conspicuous in the early portrait of him by Mr. Henry Lamb, now on loan to the Tate Gallery. He wrote, at rare intervals, an essay for a monthly. Delicate, in revolt against noise and vulgarity, rather indolent, and in possession of a small income, he certainly did not over tax his energies.

LITERARY DISPUTES

When, in 1912, his first book appeared - the volume on French Literature in the "Home University Library" - it was a very short book, but a very good one. Six more years elapsed, and in a day, with "Eminent Victorians" the tortoise outstripped most of the contemporary hares. "Queen Victoria" followed in 1921, "Books and Characters" in 1922, "Elizabeth and Essex" in 1928. Those, with a few odd essays, were all he wrote.

They will continue to be read, for he was an artist and a wit, a very deliberate, cunning, and selective artist, and a very ironic and penetrating wit. When his three most celebrated books appeared there were fierce disputes about his delineation of character and his interpretation of history.

A historian he was not, and did not pretend to be. He was using history as the raw material for art, as it is frequently used by playwrights. Reviewing "Queen Victoria" in 1921, I said this, and received from him a letter thanking me for responding "in so comprehending a way" to his intentions.

**(January 22)**

# FAMOUS AIR PIONEER

## FIRST 'PLANE' FLOWN IN EUROPE

**By Major C.C, Turner**
**Daily Telegraph Aviation Correspondent**

Thirty years ago the name of Santos-Dumont was as great in the airship world as that of Zeppelin himself. Twenty-two years ago his name among aeroplane designers was second only to those of the Wright Bros., the Farman Bros., and Louis Bleriot.

His small, non-rigid airships in our eyes today seem to have been mere toys, but it must not be forgotten that in the war the small class of "blimp" airship did good service.

In 1897 he made his first balloon ascent from Paris, and in the following year he began to construct dirigible airships. After many failures he built one which on Oct. 19, 1901, won a prize given by the Brazilian Government for the first flight in a given time from Saint Cloud round the Eiffel Tower and back.

Turning his attention to heavier-than-air machines, he built in 1906 a machine on the principle of a box-kite. With it he won the Deutsch-Archdeacon prize in October, 1906 while in November he flew 200 yards in 21 seconds.

FIGURE OF ROMANCE

From 1907 to 1909 Santos-Dumont designed and flew a biplane of very strange construction, with the tail first. In the latter year he designed a monoplane of the parasol type, the wing well above the engine and the cockpit with the pilot enclosed in a sort of cage. He gave this design freely to the world, and it was copied to a small extent. Its chief merit was the almost complete immunity of the pilot from injury in a crash, but the crash was almost inevitable.

This machine, the forerunner of the light 'plane was flown at the first aviation meeting at Bournemouth in 1910.

It was known as the "demoiselle" or "Flying Grasshopper," owing to its strange behaviour.

The present generation hardly realises how inspiring such men as Santos-Dumont were in the period 1900 to 1912. His was a figure of romance, and if he himself has not left us permanent traces of his work it must be admitted that his inspiration was a powerful influence in the early struggles of the pioneer flying days. He was 59 years of age.

**(July 23)**

# SUDDEN DEATH OF SOUSA

## THE "MARCH KING'S" FAREWELL

**From Our Own Correspondent**

NEW YORK, Sunday.

"God bless you, gentlemen," said Mr. John Philip Sousa in a speech delivered at a dinner given in his honour at Reading, Philadelphia, last night. Two hours later the famous "March King" suffered a heart attack, and was dead.

Of the more than 150 marches which Sousa had composed, perhaps the most celebrated was the "Washington Post." This, adapted for various forms of dance, held its own in British ball-rooms for many years. He was said "to have set more feet tapping the world over than any other living man."

Sousa created a new form of conducting with "pep" and, when his celebrated band came to England 31 years ago, his white-gloved hands and eager beard were a favourite subject for caricaturists.

His elaborate motions while conducting were unique at the time.

A "BANDSMAN" AT 13

The son of a Portuguese father and a Bavarian mother, Sousa was one of a family of ten and he was not in his teens when he began to earn his living as an orchestral violinist. At 13, he joined the U.S. Marine Corps band, and, with his soldier father, took part in a march past President Johnson and Gen. Grant.

During his first few years as a musician he mastered every instrument - even the despised E flat alto horn. He was 26 years old when he became leader of the Marine Corps Band, and held the position under five Presidents. Meanwhile the Sousa marches were being played everywhere. He composed more than 150, and in his early days had a contract with a music publisher, who paid him $35 for each march he wrote. The most famous besides the "Washington Post" was the "Stars and Stripes Forever." In addition to his marches he composed ten light operas, two overtures, twelve suites, 62 songs, six waltzes, and eleven fantasies.

**(March 7)**

# DOG'S £400 A WEEK

## RIN-TIN-TIN DIES OF OLD AGE

Rin-Tin-Tin, the world famous dog which appeared in a large number of films, has died in Hollywood of old age. He was 14, and had already outlasted the renown of many of his human rivals. He was acting in a new production called "The Pride of the Regiment" when he died.

No human star had such a fantastic life as this brown Alsatian.

He was born in Germany, captured in a German dug-out by an American officer, Lt. Lee Duncan, and taken to America. His owner trained him for the films, showing more judgment than most star-makers. Rin-Tin-Tin captured the public's imagination to such as extent that when Mrs. Duncan sued her husband for divorce in 1927, it was stated in Court that he was earning £400 a week.

Rin-Tin-Tin was starred above famous human players, stories were written specially to suit him, and audiences all over the world were thrilled when the big Alsatian broke loose in the last reel and climbed the wall in time to tear the villain from the heroine's protesting arms. In one film he had to fight and kill a vulture on the edge of a precipice. There was never a film in which he did not have to perform some feat requiring uncanny intelligence and courage.

**(August 12)**

# CHEWING GUM KING DEAD

Mr. William Wrigley the "chewing-gum king," died to-day at Phoenix, Arizona. His death at the age of 71, was the result of acute indigestion following weeks of serious illness.

At 11 he sold newspapers in New York. From waiter in a restaurant he became cashier and then travelling salesman for rubber stamps. He arrived at Chicago thirty years ago with a capital of £10 and began selling soap. Through premiums, in the shape of small packets of chewing gum, he first discovered the possibilities of making a vast fortune.

Wrigley was a business genius who relied upon advertising for success. The secret of salesmanship is, he said, to get the public's ear.

£15,000,000 A YEAR

After examining the prospects of soap and baking powder, he selected chewing gum to pave his way to fortune, with Chicago as the world's distributing centre. To popularise his wares he started national debates. "To chew or not to chew," in which leading physicians, psychologists, and business people took part.

During the war full-page advertisements drew attention to gum-chewing as a remedy for human ailments.

**(January 27)**

# IVAR KREUGER: THE LONELY GENIUS OF MAJESTIC SCHEMES

**By F.G. Lavers**

IN Paris on Saturday morning a shy, reserved young-old man of 52 died in solitude by his own hand.

The end was typical of the man and of his existence. Nothing was heard by anyone. Dead, he lay apparently for some hours undisturbed.

In a dozen of the world's capitals that day the news produced consternation and alarm. When this man, Ivar Kreuger, fired the fatal shot in the privacy of his bed-room in Paris, he stirred the world more profoundly than the whole race of spectacular suicides had done.

Yet had he chosen first to erase traces of his identity this man might have been buried as one unknown. By the world at large he was, indeed, entirely unknown.

WIELDING POWER IN SECRET

For long reputed to be one of the richest men alive, the actual controller of one of the world's biggest industrial organisations, the financier to whom Governments themselves resorted when bankruptcy stared them in the face, for whose goodwill they would risk their very existence - in secret.

The complete cosmopolitan, he was familiar with all the capitals of the world, but was known personally only to a few people in each - those who mattered.

"Silence, silence," was his motto. When he was not abroad he was at Stockholm, the headquarters of the famous Swedish Match Company which he had formed, working for the furtherance of that enormous trust, or of the equally powerful financing corporation of Kreuger and Toll, which operated in close association.

There, in a closely guarded room, he brought to fruition some of the greatest schemes of international finance the modern world has seen.

Had circumstances been different Ivar Kreuger might have spent his millions acquiring an international reputation for hospitality. He had not the time. He might have married. He had not the time. Rumour once engaged him to a young and charming member of the Swedish aristocracy. Those who knew him best dismissed the report in one word, "Impossible." They were right.

In London Kreuger was as little known as he was in other capitals - that is, outside the exclusive coteries of finance.

Every three or four months he made an appearance in London, working all day and often all night in two rooms which he occupied high up in the Savoy Hotel overlooking the Thames.

Here, within reach of the world's choicest dishes, with the finest chefs ready to obey his every behest, the thought of food never entered his head. A valet ordered his meals while the financier slaved at his desk, and, it was said, the valet eventually insisted that they should be eaten.

Until he was dead, the romance of Kreuger's life was a closed book to the man in the street.

One may look with confidence for exaggerations. It is said, for example, that he rose to affluence from obscurity, and something akin to penury. This is not strictly accurate. Kreuger's interest in the match industry was not purely fortuitous, since his family had been engaged in match manufacture for many years.

At 25 he found himself in South Africa with a respectable "pile" and he returned at length to his native land with the confidence and technical skill requisite for operations on a still larger scale. The family industry was ripe material ready at his hand. First he joined his father's concerns with eight others.

Then, boldly, he launched out into still more ambitious schemes, which brought the £10,000,000 Swedish Match Company into existence.

Kreuger showed bold strategy in going "all out" for the match monopolies which many of the States of the world had reserved for themselves. He found many of these States prepared to hand over to him the privilege of manufacture, sale, or export of matches - for a consideration.

Mr. Ivar Kreuger

**(March 14)**

# MR. C.P. SCOTT DEAD

## FIFTY SEVEN YEARS AN EDITOR

Mr. C.P. Scott, governing director of the 'Manchester Guardian,' and for 57 years editor of the paper, died early this morning. He was 85 years of age.

Though he was associated so closely with the life of Lancashire, Mr. Scott was not a Lancashire man; he was born in Bath. His father was Mr. Russell Scott, his mother was a Miss Prestwich; he was always known among his friends as "C.P." He was educated at Corpus Christi College, Oxford, where he took his M.A. degree and first-class honours in the final of the Classical School in 1869.

Shortly afterwards he joined the staff of the "Scotsman." and in 1872 became editor of the "Manchester Guardian," in succession to his cousin, Mr. J.E. Taylor, whose father, Mr. John E. Taylor, founded the paper in 1821 as a sevenpenny weekly. He was to remain editor of the "Guardian" until 1929, and from that date until his death he was governing director of the paper.

The early association of Mr. Scott with university life profoundly influenced the fortunes of the "Guardian," for he always kept a look-out on the promising young men at our chief schools of learning and constantly drew on them for additions to his staff. They came to include Mr. W.T. Arnold, grandson of Arnold of Rugby, Mr. C.E. Montague, Mr. Andrew Lang, and Mr. H.W. Massingham. It is of interest that Mr. Lloyd George was also a contributor.

Mr. Scott had a passion for pure prose. A member of the staff wrote "from whence," which his chief held to be tautological. The writer defended it on the ground that Meredith had use it. "I would not have allowed Meredith to use it twice," Mr. Scott answered, with ruthless finality.

**(January 1)**

# LIFE STORY OF FLO ZIEGFELD

## CREATOR OF FAMOUS "FOLLIES"

Mr. Florenz Ziegfeld, the creator of the famous "Follies" who has died at Los Angeles at the age of 65, might have shone as a musical conductor as his father was, had it not been for a youthful year on a ranch and the irresistible attraction of Buffalo Bill's Wild West Show.

At the age of 13 he ran away and joined Buffalo Bill. but his parents brought him back home and made him resume his schooling.

Ziegfeld discovered Sandow, the strong man, Sandow demanded £200 a week, but Ziegfeld who had no money, got him to accept 10 per cent. of the gross profits. Then Ziegfeld showed his talent for publicity, for his advertising campaign made the Trocadero receipts leap from £400 to nearly £6,000 a week.

The next step to fame was the introduction of Anna Held, the famous French actress, whom he described as "the greatest example of feminine pulchritude," and whom he married a year later. It was in her interests that he staged the famous "Milkman Suit," in which it was revealed that Miss Held bathed daily in milk.

But the charms of Anna, whom he married, did not hold him permanently, for in 1912 he divorced her. Two years later he married Billie Burke.

CHOOSING THE "FOLLIES"

Ziegfeld went everywhere to find the girls for his "Follies." They had to be blonde, 18 to 25 years of age, 5ft 6in in height 8st 6lb in weight, and intelligent. He had a mania for detail. He would examine the girls who applied for jobs with the thoroughness of a horse dealer, while he would criticise minutely every detail of the beautiful costumes which he had employed the world's greatest dressmakers to produce. His dictum for 1932 was "fuller curves - less streamlined, but, doubtless, as fast as ever."

The cost of producing his "Follies" rose from £3,000 to a sum twenty times as great, and with a weekly running cost of over £5,000 instead of a few hundred pounds.

The story is told of him that one day, two or three years ago, he borrowed a couple of thousand pounds from a friend whom he met in Fifth-avenue. Instead of applying the money to meeting a pressing emergency he spend £1,500 on jewellery for his wife, flowers for some of the leading ladies in his wonderful shows, and in making other gifts, which expressed his kindly though erratic disposition.

Mr. C.B. Cochran paid a tribute to his old friend in The Daily Telegraph a few days ago.

"Ziegfeld," said Mr. Cochran, "was a great institution in the United States. One of the loveliest women he ever engaged was an English mannequin who used to be at Lady Duff Gordon's shop in London. She is now a Mrs. Wilkinson, and lives in the South of France. Ziegfeld paid her £100 a week just to walk round a moving stage during dinners at one of his roof garden shows. She was then known as Dolores. In the same programme was Edythe Baker, now Mrs. Gerald D'Erlanger.

"Ziegfeld was always terribly bored by dialogue in a show. He had a good ear for music, and he was nearly always first to launch new dance rhythms by people such as George Gershwin and dances like the 'Bunny hug.'

The 'Show Boat' was the best thing Ziegfeld ever did; there was, however, a nigger atmosphere in the American production such as we could not get here.

**(July 25)**

# EDGAR WALLACE

## HIGH SPEED OUTPUT OF NOVELS AND PLAYS

### MILLIONS OF HIS STORIES SOLD

Mr. Edgar Wallace

For some years the name of Edgar Wallace, who died of double pneumonia at Hollywood yesterday, at the age of 57, has been one of the few which everybody in England knows, and a synonym for success. Abroad, his fame has become as nearly universal as any man's. Wherever people delight in tales of crime - and that is every civilised country - his books have had a mighty vogue.

They have been translated into almost every written language, and in foreign bookshops shelf upon shelf of Edgar Wallace takes space from the native authors. Among the English-speaking nations his plays have had still more important popularity, both materially and in esteem.

SELF-MADE MAN

One of the main elements in this triumph was clearly an abounding vitality. Not only in his swift and continuous production, but in the pervading vigour of all his work, Wallace seemed to be the embodiment of inexhaustible energy. That he should be dead at 57 is hard to believe. But certainly he had done the work of several lives in one.

If ever a man was self-made it was Edgar Wallace. Familiarity with the life of poverty has shaped the minds of many of the world's great story-tellers, but none of them came into the world so destitute of help from fortune as he.

He was born in 1875 at Deptford, to be adopted when he was nine days old by a fish-porter. In this condition of life he became early acquainted, not only with the Cockney idiom and humour, which always flowed easily from his pen, but with the reactions of the police and the recurring criminal.

The work of life began with journeys to Billingsgate at three in the morning every day, winter and summer. By the time he was 11 he was selling newspapers in Ludgate-circus. Some more formal education was obtained in Board Schools, but though there can have been little of it in duration, it had so much affect that a policeman was shocked by hearing the newsboy in vehement recitation of the quarrel scene from "Julius Caesar," thought he was light-headed, and advised him to "push-off."

The Shakespearean paper boy tried many trades before he became a private in the Royal West Kent Regiment. In that corps and in the R.A.M.C. he spend six years, and this spell in the ranks certainly made a journalist of him.

WAR CORRESPONDENT

As a war correspondent in the South African campaign he showed the inventive resource which served him later in novel and play. In the latter stages of the war Bennet Burleigh, of The Daily Telegraph, revealed that, in spite of a portentous censorship, news was being sent through uncensored. Wallace was sending much of his information through by means of a code of Stock Exchange terms addressed to a private recipient, and consisting apparently of advice on South African shares. When peace was signed it was Wallace who got the news home first.

Wallace remained a journalist to the end of his life. He was writing for newspapers to the last. One of his most conspicuous exploits, the establishment of the Press Club Derby Luncheon, happily illustrates his attachment both to his fellow-workers and to horse-racing, which was certainly, after work, the main interest of his life.

Wallace was known by the time he was approaching middle age as a writer of magazine stories and novels of incident. Still he had years to wait before he made a great success. When "Four Just Men," the first world-famous and to some tastes the best of his "shockers," was finished, "I could not," he said, "get any publisher to advance me a five-pound note on it." He published it himself, losing a good deal of money in the process, and finally being paid £75 for all rights to the book, of which 3,250,000 copies have been sold.

The most remarkable thing about his novels, the kindest critic must allow, is the exuberant fertility of the author. He is said to have written more than 150, and when against this total is set his comparatively late start in fiction and untimely death, it will be seen that his work is without parallel. Moreover, while he was turning out novels with this rapidity he was writing continuously in newspapers and latterly feeding the stage with a ceaseless flow of plays. It is a wonderful career, and no explanation but that of the amazing vigour of the man can be accepted.

The merit of three novels, which sold at the rate of 5,000,000 a year, is not to be set higher than that of a readable "shocker." Wallace was content with a plain tale plainly told, and almost the only element except swift incident which he admitted was a little straightforward humour. But the best of his plays are a very different matter.

Starting from nothing, as we have said, he became a figure of world-wide repute as dramatist, film playwright, and theatre manager. The amount and variety of work he got through was colossal; yet, though he had the reputation (which he did not discourage) of being able to turn out a full-length play between breakfast and dinnertime, he was never slipshod in his methods.

With the successful production of "The Ringer" in 1926 he established himself as our foremost writer of high-class melodrama with an atmosphere of mystery and crime - though the element of humour also was never omitted. He further proved his versatility with a musical play, "The Yellow Mask," which ran for over 200 performances at the Carlton.

Four years ago he entered into management at the Apollo, where "The Squeaker" was one of the plays produced; then he transferred to Wyndham's, and had staged several plays there, the latest being "The Green Pack," presented last Tuesday - the very day on which news of his serious illness reached London.

Wallace had busied himself a great deal with the screen during the last year or two; several of his plays were filmed, and he took a hand in the production. His visit to Hollywood was the outcome of an invitation from Radio-Keith-Orpheum to go out and write scenarios - at a (reported) salary of £800 a week. It was only part of his colossal earnings, the whole of which may be judged from the fact that twelve months ago, so he said, that he was paying the Treasury "£8,000 to £10,000 a year."

TWO SECRETS OF HIS WORK
By a Friend Who Has Watched Him

Wallace had two secrets. One was the amazing, almost mechanical, precision of his mind. He never seemed to be at a loss in the steady flow of words; he had the chess player's faculty of seeing a dozen moves ahead; and he could work in incident after incident, thrill after thrill, that would all link up in the end, with the ease of a Capablanca opening gambit.

His other secret was the ease of his style. He never tortured his brain for a startling adjective or a far-fetched simile. He wrote just as he talked, and he was one of the best talkers in London, whether in private or on a platform - crisp, broad, and humorous.

**(February 11)**

# BRIAND: THE SOUL OF FRANCE

**By David Loch**

THE death of M. Briand has not only brought to an end the career of a great European statesman, but has removed from French Parliamentary life one of its most outstanding figures.

It is true that the lawyer, as he then was, who came from his native town of Nantes to the capital in 1893, had to wait until he was 40 before journalism and the Bar opened for him his political career with a seat in the Chamber.

But between that moment and the day in January last when, at the age of 69, he handed over the Ministry of Foreign Affairs to M. Laval, M. Briand had been Prime Minister more often than any other politician under the Third Republic.

No fewer that eleven times had he been entrusted by successive Presidents with the conduct of France's Government, and in more than another dozen Cabinets he had either been Minister of Foreign Affairs or had held some other important portfolio. What, it may well be asked, was at the bottom of this phenomenal Parliamentary success, without which Briand could hardly have played the outstanding part in the world's affairs which he did?

KNOWLEDGE OF MEN

Studious Briand never was, either in boyhood or in later life, and his critics frequently accused him of never examining a question deeply.

But, on the other hand, he possessed remarkable intelligence, a great power of rapid assimilation, and a striking memory. A wide experience of men from whose conversation he said that he learned more than he did from books and documents, had given him a deep knowledge of human nature, whilst what he himself used to call his "antennæ" enabled him, as he declared, to "register the impressions of his listeners."

The result was a combination of qualities which could not fail to smooth for their possessor the path through the ambushes and quicksands of French Parliamentary life. M. Briand was, in fact, the born Parliamentarian, to whose faculties the approach of a political crisis gave a particularly keen edge.

On such an occasion he would become especially active in the lobbies of the Chamber, but outwardly, with his hands in the pockets of a short coat, and a cigarette in the corner of his mouth, the appearance of nonchalance rarely left him.

To the general public, however, it was the Briand of the Tribune who was best known, and the expectation of a speech by him would regularly fill to overflowing the public galleries of the Chamber. Broad-shouldered, with a magnificent head crowned by a mass of iron-grey hair.

**(March 8)**

# SIR RONALD ROSS

## DISCOVERED CAUSE OF MALARIA

Few men have been greater benefactors of the human race or have done more to mitigate suffering and to save life than Co. Sir Ronald Ross, K.C.B., K.C.M.G., Director-in-Chief of the Ross Institute and Hospital for Tropical Diseases, Putney Heath, whose death at the age of 75 is reported.

With rare insight Ross grasped the possibility of the mosquito theory of malaria, and with wonderful patience and pertinacity in the face of much scepticism he pursued his researches till he proved the theory to be a fact. Thus he placed in the hands of sanitarians a potent weapon, with which they have been able to cope successfully with the dread disease and to render habitable great tracts of country where previously man had only been able to live at the risk of contracting illness, which so often proved fatal.

The son of an Indian Army officer, Capt. Ross, of the 4th Gurkhas (later Gen. Sir Campbell Ross), Ronald Ross was born at Almora, in the Himalayas two days after the Indian Mutiny broke out. From Spring Hill School, Southampton, he went to St. Bartholomew's Hospital, and entered the Indian Medical Service in 1881, seeing active service in the Burmah Expedition.

In 1892 Ross began to study malaria. Laveran had discovered the malaria parasite in human blood; Ross had to discover it in the mosquito. For two and a half years, with occasional intervals, he continued his researches, and at last he secured a specimen of a species of mosquito which he had not previously seen - the species now recognised as Anopheles. He dissected it, and what followed reads like a romance.

"I could find nothing," he says, "and was just on the point of throwing up the whole thing and abandoning the inquiry, when I observed on the wall of the stomach of the mosquito what my acquaintance with the anatomy of mosquitos told me was a new object. So fagged was I with the day's work that I did not grasp the importance of the discovery. I went home and to sleep. When I awoke, my mind seemed to wake also, and it flashed upon me that I had the clue."

WORLD-WIDE BENEFITS

Ross published the results of his experiments in 1898, and the conclusion derived from microscopical work in the laboratory were confirmed by experiment. It was conclusively shown in Italy that if a mosquito of the anopheles variety bites a person suffering from malaria, and, having been kept long enough for the parasite to develop in the salivary gland, is allowed to bite a healthy person, the latter will in due time develop malaria. All that remained was for administrators to apply the knowledge gained by the scientists; and drainage of the mosquito breeding swamps and pools, or floating a film of petroleum on them to kill the insects, has proved the most feasible, and probably the cheapest method of dealing with the scourge.

The Nobel Prize for Medicine was awarded him in 1902, the Royal Society gave him its Royal medal, the African Society its gold medal, and the Royal Institute of Public Health its Harben gold medal, and many universities conferred on him their degrees. It is noteworthy that in Calcutta a Commemoration gate in honour of Sir Ronald was unveiled by the Governor in 1927.

But fortune in a material sense did not smile on him, and in 1928, stricken with illness, he announced his intention of selling all the original manuscripts relating to his discovery, because, as he said, he wanted the money for his children. Lady Houston bought the papers for £2,000 and presented them to the British Museum.

**(September 17)**

# PHAR LAP DEAD

## COST 100 GUINEAS; WON £66,450

Phar Lap, the "wonder horse" of New Zealand and Australia, has died of colic at the E.D. Perry Stock Farm, in California.

With the death of Phar Lap passes one of the greatest racehorses of all time. Bred in New Zealand from an English-bred sire, Night Raid, from a New Zealand mare, Eubreaty, Phar Lap was bought as a yearling by Mr. Davis, at Wellington for 100 guineas.

£10,000 HANDICAP VICTORY

Only last month Phar Lap carried off one of the richest prizes on the American turf, the Agua Caliente Handicap, worth £10,000. His winnings in stake money amounted to £66,450, a total which has been surpassed by only one other, the American horse, Sun Beau, who won nearly £75,000. Phar Lap's name in Senegalese means "wing of the sky" or "lightning." Phar Lap's owner issued a challenge in 1930 to race the gelding against any horse over any distance for any amount.

He was such a consistent winner that his entry for any race caused other owners to withdraw their horses. On the totalisator and with bookmakers in Australia it was impossible to back the horse.

**(April 6)**

# LORD HARRIS

## FAMOUS CRICKETER FOR NEARLY 60 YEARS

### CAPTAIN OF FIRST REAL TEST MATCH

When W.G. Grace passed away, Lord Harris, who died on Thursday at the age of 81, automatically succeeded him in the title of the "Grand Old Man," though the succession was not noted, or perhaps even admitted, at the time. The war was then in its most disheartening stage, and the most ardent cricketer was not thinking of cricket. But when at last the war came to an end and the cricket field was substituted for the battlefield, Lord Harris reminded us of his claims.

If Lord Harris was the "Grand Old Man" of cricket, he was more than that. He was administrator, business man - and even actor, for he once took part in amateur theatricals.

The son of the third Baron Harris, he had been Under-Secretary successively for India and for War, and Governor of Bombay for five years. He had been Lord-in-Waiting to Queen Victoria and aide-de-camp to King Edward and his present Majesty.

So far as cricket is concerned, Lord Harris gave early promise of the talent which later won him so many honours, and gained him a place in the Eton eleven when 17 years old. At Oxford he won his Blue as a Freshman, and took part in the Varsity match in 1872 and 1874, and he would undoubtedly have played in 1873 but for an injury to his hand. Before this he had appeared for Kent, and in 1870 he became a member of the committee of the county club, of which his father was then president, while four years later he was appointed honorary secretary. On his return from India he became president.

FIRST REAL TEST MATCH

His work for Kent did not restrict his activities, and he found time to become almost equally prominent with the M.C.C., of which he was president in 1895, and later one of the trustees and then treasurer.

Lord Harris's cricket experiences were not limited to England. Under the leadership of R.A. Fitzgerald, secretary of the M.C.C., he visited Canada in 1872, and he himself took a side out to Australia in the autumn of 1878. They played a "Test match" and lost it.

Perhaps the most memorable incident in the career of Lord Harris was when, in 1880, against the second Australian team to tour the Mother Country, he captained the eleven victorious in what was the first real Test match.

UNFAIR BOWLING

Unbounded zeal and love of the game enabled him to make the stand, which freed cricket from the once prevalent evil of unfair bowling. The crisis had come when, having taken part in a match with Lancashire, Lord Harris wrote to the Kent Committee protesting against what he termed the unfair methods of the Lancashire bowlers. His suggestion that the return engagement with that county should be scratched was carried out, and there is little doubt that if his action did not entirely remedy the evil, it did much to improve the game.

**(March 26)**

# OUR ENCOURAGING OLYMPIC GAMES RECORD

## TWO VICTORIES IN TRACK EVENTS AND BETTER TIMES THAN EVER BEFORE

**By Bevil Rudd**

THOUGH the British athletics team will bring home only two or three Olympic titles, their record in the Games at Los Angeles is far from disappointing.

T. Hampson's great victory in the 800 metres, and the success of the wonderful veteran, T.W. Green, in the long-distance walk have been duly acclaimed, but recognition has not been given to the fact that most of our athletes, though beaten, returned better times in their respective races than they have ever done before.

There is a tendency, to shrug shoulders and dismiss the showing of our team as disappointing. I think this attitude argues a lack of sense of proportion.

For instance, I am constantly hearing: "Burghley's too old now; I suppose he can't do what he did in 1928." But what are the actual facts. Burghley ran a whole second - about eight yards - faster in the final of the 400 metres hurdles than when he won and broke a record in 1928.

Tisdall, who we may claim as partly as English product, concentrated all his superb talent on his best race. He specialised and won an amazing race, defeating two superlative American hurdles who were happy in a climate and surroundings to which they were accustomed, and without a long journey behind them to disturb their finer physical and nervous adjustments.

SPLENDID HURDLERS

The Americans certainly recaptured the sprints with their famous negroes, and their hurdling prowess was equal to their record-breaking reputation. Yet Finlay was third and Burghley fourth, and but for Harper, hitting the fatal three hurdles we might have had fifth place as well. Never have our hurdlers so splendidly risen to the occasion.

We know that 10 4-5 sec for 100 metres is the best we could expect of Reid or Page. Reid's injury was most regrettable, but I doubt if he would have done much better than Page, and, with Olympic records being broken in the heats, it was too much to expect a finalist in this race. Our sprinters were good but not great.

Similarly, Rampling's alleged failure was only comparative. I should not be a bit surprised to hear that an error of judgment lost him a place in the final. Perhaps he thought he had the measure of the semi-finalists, and subconsciously took things a little too easily. But even the most devoted supporters of Rampling could not really expect him suddenly to beat 46 1-5 sec, the most astounding record of these remarkable games.

Cornes showed that Finns had no terrors for him. A fierce and unexpected tour de force by Beccali, of Italy, denied Cornes first place in the 1,500 metres, but the pace at which Cornes went was the equivalent of a 4 min 9 sec mile - and that is scarcely "disappointing." In such stern competition someone or other is going to run the race of his life - in this case it was Beccali. Just as Hampson, in the famous 800 metres, ran nearly 3 sec faster than he has ever run before.

Conditions were obviously ideal - probably track and climatic conditions will never again be of such assistance to fast times in an Olympiad. But a long journey by sea and land is not an ideal preparation for the severe nervous and physical strain of Olympic competition. We can, I think, be amply satisfied that all our men, with the possible exception of Rampling, ran faster then they have ever done before, while four of them - Hampson, Cornes, Lord Burghley, and Finlay - made the efforts of their lives.

**(August 8)**

# PAAVO NURMI

## DISQUALIFICATION OF FAMOUS ATHLETE

BERLIN, Sunday.

Paavo Nurmi, the famous Finnish athlete, was to-day disqualified by the International Amateur Athletic Federation meeting here.

Proof was put forward that Nurmi had seriously transgressed the rules governing amateurism.

The "Flying Finn" has lost his chance of achieving his greatest ambition, namely of winning the Olympic Marathon. - Reuter.

**(April 4)**

# THE DERBY WINNER

JOCKEYING FOR POSITION soon after the start of the Derby.

# LUCKY NUMBER IN THE DERBY

### 13 Letters in Name of Owner, Jockey and Mount

THE FIRST FIVE -

| | |
|---|---|
| APRIL THE FIFTH | F. Lane 1 |
| DASTUR | M. Beary 2 |
| MIRACLE | H. Wragg 3 |
| ROYAL DANCER | S. Wragg 4 |
| FIRDAUSSI | S. Donoghue 5 |

The sensation of the Derby yesterday was the complete defeat of Orwell, one of the greatest favourites for many years.

Mr. Tom Kirby Walls, the actor-manager and winning owner, has many reasons for believing in the luck of thirteen, for it entered into his victory in a remarkable way. Horse, owner, and jockey each have thirteen letters in their names.

In addition to this, "Dirty Work" is in the thirteenth week of its run under Mr. Walls's managership at the Aldwych Theatre, and his firm, Walls and Highley, was founded just thirteen years ago.

Mr. Walls disappeared after he had been congratulated by the King on his win, and was found last night at his country house at Ewell, near Epsom. Telling how he nearly gave up training for ever just before the Derby, he said:

"When I was very ill last year I should have shut up my stables entirely but for the faith I had in April the Fifth. I always thought he was a good colt. I was convinced he could do big things, so I decided to go on training for the Derby.

From the Royal box, decked with red and white flowers, a Royal family party watched the race. With the King were the Queen, in silver-grey and toque of rose and powder-blue, the Prince of Wales, the Princess Royal and the Earl of Harewood, the Duke and Duchess of York, the Duke of Gloucester, and Prince George.

## THEATRE OVATION

At the close of the performance at the Aldwych Theatre last night there was a great display of enthusiasm on the part of the audience.

Speaking from the stage, Mr. Ralph Lynn expressed regrets on behalf of Mr. Tom Walls for his absence, "but," he added, "had I been in his place I should probably have done the same.

**(June 2)**

# DISPUTED CUP FINAL GOAL

## FILM VERSION OF THE INCIDENT

# BALL ON WRONG SIDE OF LINE

**By Frank Coles**

The film version of Newcastle United's hotly-disputed equalising goal in the Cup Final on Saturday confirms the view I have expressed that it ought to have been disallowed.

The match was filmed by British Movietone News, and the "shot" is most illuminating.

It shows clearly that before Richardson (not Boyd, as was generally believed at the moment) centred into the goal mouth, for Allen to score, the ball was well over the goal-line, and, therefore, out of play.

I had a perfectly clear view of the incident, which had a vital bearing upon the result of the match, and am convinced that the ball was at least two feet over the line.

POSITION OF THE REFEREE

The "shot" is very interesting, too, as indicating the positions of the referee and linesmen. The referee is seen outside the penalty area, and it is plain that his line of vision is interrupted by at least one player. The linesman on the far side of the field, who would have been the official to be consulted in case of doubt, is some distance behind the referee.

It was rumoured in football circles yesterday that the Football Association was likely to hold an inquiry into this extraordinary happening. This rumour is denied by Sir Frederick Wall, the secretary of the Association.

The referee, when interviewed yesterday, said: "I was so certain the goal was good that I did not consider it necessary to consult the linesman. I was well up with the play, and in a position to see the incident clearly. Whatever the film may appear to show will not make me alter my opinion."

Both the King and Queen attended the match, and with their Majesties were the Princess Royal and the Earl of Harewood.

Before the match began the players and officials were presented to the King.

**(April 25)**

# SARAZEN WINS WITH LOWEST SCORE ON RECORD

## MACDONALD SMITH IN SECOND PLACE: HAVERS' GALLANT FIGHT

**By George Greenwood**

SANDWICH, Friday.

GENE SARAZEN, of New York, won the British Open Championship with the record score of 283 at Prince's Sandwich, to-day. Another American, Macdonald Smith, 5 strokes behind, was second, with 288, and A.G. Havers, of Sandy Lodge was third with 289.

American players have dominated the Championship, having won it twelve times in the last thirteen years, and nine times in succession, Havers being the only British player to break the long sequence of successes. The previous record score was held by Bobby Jones, at St. Andrews in 1927, with 285. Sarazen has beaten this figure by 2 shots, his four rounds being: 70, 69, 70 and 74.

With the exception of Havers, who with a brilliant round of 68 was within measurable distance of Sarazen, the British players failed dismally, one after another breaking down at the crucial stages of the struggle. Sarazen maintained the lead throughout the championship, playing powerful and majestic golf except in the last stretch, when the strain had begun to tell. He has succeeded in winning the title at the fifth attempt and he may be counted as worthy successor to Jones and Hager, who, between them, have won the championship seven times.

ANXIOUS TIME FOR SARAZEN

As he had expected it might turn out to be, Sarazen's last round was not a picnic; indeed, it was far from that. I suspected and the American himself confirmed the suspicion that the moment he heard of Havers' miraculous round the prospects previously so rosy become slightly clouded.

The pursuit of Sarazen by the half-a-dozen or so players within striking distance began in deadly earnest in the morning, but the chase had not long been in progress before it became plain that the task was well nigh hopeless. Indeed, with the last round to play the gap between the hunters and their quarry was widened instead of lessened.

To employ a common golfing phrase, some of the players "blew up," one of these being Alliss, who, starting only three shots in arrears, ended the next stage of the hunt eleven strokes behind. With the challenging spirit entirely absent, he played like a man with no heart for the work to be performed. He putted without confidence and with a tragic 6 at the eighth, where his spoon shot was trapped in the range of sandhills known as the Himalayas, his chances had gone.

While perhaps it is scarcely true to say that Cotton "blew up" it is correct to say that he faded peacefully out of the picture. "As the overhauling of Sarazen became an impossible business, I made no special effort," said Cotton, and so his handful of supporters gradually deserted him, and he finished the round practically alone.

HAVERS' GREAT EFFORT

Havers was the one player to rouse any enthusiasm in the British camp during the day. With a startling third round of 68, he jumped to within three strokes of the American. Because his marvellous round constitutes a new record for Prince's it may be appropriate to give his figures, which were:

Out - 4,4,2,4,3,4,4,4,4 - 33

In - 3,4,4,4,4,3,4,5,4 - 35. Total 68.

For the dignity of Prince's I dread to think what would be thought of this famous links if he had not missed a yard putt at each of the thirteenth and fourteenth, at a time when the hole, to him, at any rate, must have looked the size of a washtub. In length his driving was even more colossal than that of Sarazen. For example, at the tenth he drove well over 300 yards, and was within a small chip shot of the green. He ran the ball up to the flag and holed the putt for a 3.

**(June 11)**

# ANOTHER WIN FOR BRITANNIA

**By Major B. Heckstall-Smith**

COWES, Friday.

The third victory of Britannia to-day has surprised the experts, and to all yachting people the success of the vessel has been as unexpected as it is popular.

"Believe me sir," an old waterman said to me to-day, "that there old vessel knows when the King is aboard just as well as you or me do, and when his Majesty sets foot on her deck she goes as fast again. It were the same in his father's time, nigh forty years ago. When the Prince of Wales were aboard of her there weren't no vessel as could touch her.

**(August 6)**

# THE AGA KHAN'S ST. LEGER

## HIS FOUR HORSES IN THE FIRST FIVE

The Aga Khan made turf history yesterday. The four horses he had entered for the St. Leger finished in the first five. His colts Firdaussi (20 to 1) and Dastur (6 to 1) finished first and second respectively, and only by a narrow margin was Udaipur (9 to 1) his Oaks winner, beaten for third place. Taj Kasra was fifth.

Other owners have had two horses among the first three, but the Aga Khan's record is without parallel.

The race was remarkable also for a drama of jockeys. Michael Beary, the stable jockey, had chosen to ride Dastur, which of the four was considered to have the best chance of winning the race. Second choice was given to H. Wragg, who selected Udaipur as his mount.

**(September 8)**

# FORBRA WINS AT HIS FIRST ATTEMPT

## ONLY EIGHT FINISH IN FIELD OF 36: EGREMONT'S GALLANT BID

**By Hotspur**

LIVERPOOL, Friday.

DRAMA most vivid makes up the story of still another amazing Grand National. The great steeplechase was won by the 50 to 1 chance, Forbra, owned by Mr. W. Parsonage, who was at one time a starting price bookmaker at Ludlow. In his retirement he applies his leisure to duties as a town councillor of that town, while I believe I am right in saying he is a choirman of St. Lawrence's Church. His great triumph, therefore, should have set all the bells in Ludlow ringing.

Second was Mrs. Ireland's Egremont, ridden by Mr. E.C. Paget, beaten only three lengths, but easily at that, while third was Shaun Goilin, the hero of three years ago. He finished many lengths behind the second. Behind this brief synopsis is a story even more astonishing than usual of disaster to all the fancied horses.

Not the least astonishing thing about this National is the fact of the winner being absolutely new to the course; indeed, he is one of the season's recruits to steeplechasing. He is only seven years old, and began his jumping by fairly modest efforts over hurdles. I have no doubt he paid his way at that. Then Mr. Parsonage became his owner, and if he had a Grand National in view he can be complimented on his prescience.

The going was so firm that disasters were bound to be heavy because of the greater pace and the correspondingly greater chances of the fences taking toll when horses are going too fast to jump them if they fail to meet them properly. The big crowd of horses were assembled too soon at the start, which caused a wait, but when the signal was given they were sent tearing at the first fence as if starting in a five furlong scurry.

### Holmes Refuses at Becher's

One or two were stopped, and then at the first open ditch quite a little bunch were settled with. They included Vinicole, who was one of several that refused. Holmes was in difficulties with the fences from the start, and the sight of Becher's was altogether too much for him. He would not tackle it, neither would he when his jockey tried again.

Meanwhile things were happening in front so thick and fast as to make if difficult to keep pace with them.

At Becher's a number were left behind, but they did not include the cracks at the top of the handicap. Their supporters found relief for a few more moments. Inverse, Quite Calm, and Redlynch made their exit at the notorious jump, and Great Span had only to wait for the next fence before he joined the casualties. It was there that Pelorus Jack put himself out of it. But he was a foolish horse. Instead of quietly trotting back, he went on riderless, and was, I think, the cause of much tragedy before the race was very much older.

### Grakle's Bad Luck

Evolution found the Canal Turn fence too formidable, and at Valentine's, which follows, Coup de Chapeau disappeared, Grakle, Gregalach and heartbreak Hill were still in the race, but the last-named was beginning to labour and lose position.

So they went away on the second circuit, and here I will let Hamey, the rider of Forbra, tell the story in his own words: "I had been going well all the way," he said, "enjoying a splendid ride when once my horse had settled down. At times Egremont was driven past me, but I always gained on him at the fences. I really was having a marvellous ride, and then, at the first fence the second time round, my horse made his only mistake.

"He nearly overjumped himself, but all was well, as he made a clever recovery. Fence after fence he jumped perfectly, and no fences quite so well as the last two. He finished strongly, and that's all there was to it."

**(March 19)**

# CARNERA'S EASY WIN

PARIS, Saturday.

Primo Carnera easily won the first of the three fights which he is to have within three weeks when he completely outclassed the French champion, Maurice Griselle, in a ten-round bout at the Palais des Sports.

Griselle who was a mere human punching bag from the start, put up a plucky fight, but he was always outclassed by the Italian.

**(May 2)**

H. E. VINES (U.S.A.) on the court at Wimbledon in the final of the singles, which Vines won 6—4, 6—2, 6—0.

# H.W. AUSTIN OVERWHELMED IN THREE SETS

## BOROTRA AND BRUGNON TRIUMPH IN THRILLING DOUBLES FINAL

**By A Wallis Myers**

WIMBLEDON is over and America rules the lawn. As conclusively as Mrs. Moody won the women's championship the day before, Ellsworth Vines, also of California, won the men's on Saturday. he beat H.W. Austin in the final, 6-4, 6-2, 6-0.

Vines, the third American champion in succession, equalled the record of Tilden and Patterson by capturing the title on his first visit to England. He beat the record of H.L. Dohery, Tilden, Johnston, Lacoste, and Cochet by winning both the American and British championship under the age of 21. That feat alone makes Vines the greatest young player of all time.

Saturday's setting was impressively complete. The King and Queen were there. Just as their Majesties patronised the first Anglo-French women's final in 1919 - the equal and exciting struggle between Mrs. Lambert Chambers and Mlle. Lenglen - so, thirteen years later, they revealed their sustained interest in international lawn tennis by coming to see the first Anglo-American men's final.

The Royal visitors, as they were escorted into the committee box by Sir Herbert Wilberforce and Cmdr. Hillyard just before Vines and Austin came in, received a loyal ovation from "a capacity crowd."

THE 1932 CHAMPIONS
MEN'S SINGLES: H.E. Vines (U.S.A.)
WOMEN'S SINGLES: MRS. F.S. Moody (U.S.A.)
MEN'S DOUBLES: J. Borotra and J. Brugnon (France)
WOMEN'S DOUBLES: Mlle. D. Metaxa (France) and Mlle. J. Sigart (Belgium)
MIXED DOUBLES: E. Maier (Spain) and Miss E. Ryan (U.S.A.)

Every inch of space in the big amphitheatre girding the court was occupied. Even the roller had its camping spectators. Hundreds had queued up overnight and had slept and breakfasted before the gates. Most of these patient investors were tennis "fans", a few were tennis financiers and sold their position in the line to the highest bidder. Ring seats purchased for a few shillings were exchanged for as many pounds. It was a great day, and fine weather and perfect organisation attended it.

But if Vines played wonderful tennis, it was not a wonderful match. it was a one-sided contest. Austin did not put up the fight which was expected. He was not, as we had hoped, the David for the Goliath.

No man's knowledge can go beyond his experience. I found many observers of Saturday's final speaking as if the service of Vines was some novel and uncanny weapon impossible to counter and impossible to reproduce. The history of American and even French lawn tennis confounds that theory. At the beginning of the century Dwight Davis (who was present on Saturday) was serving nearly as fast as Vines, and finding players in his own country-ready with a reply. R.N. Williams defeated M.E. McLoughlin in the final of the American championship of 1914 by standing in and taking the Californian's thunderbolts on the rise; so did both Wilding and Parke at Wimbledon in 1913.

**(July 4)**



# FIVE CHELSEA MEN LEAVE FIELD

## BLACKPOOL SURVIVE ORDEAL

**By a Special Representative**

Blackpool ... 4 Chelsea ... 0

SEVENTEEN players, mud-covered and weary, trudged off the field after the final whistle at Blackpool to the cheers of the spectators. And well they deserved them, for it would be impossible to imagine conditions more unfavourable for football.

Even before the game had started the ground was waterlogged; what it was like at the finish, with torrential rain having fallen during play, beggars description. To add to the discomfort of the players there was a strong and icy cold wind.

Such atrocious weather was too much for some of the Chelsea players. Ferguson went off in the first half, and after the scoring of Blackpool's fourth goal fifteen minutes from the end, four more of them left the field. O'Dowd and Oakton were the first to go, but who the others were it was impossible to tell, such a bedraggled appearance did they present. Later it was learned that they were Miller and Allum.

Considering the conditions the game was contested at a fine pace, and victory went to the side that adapted themselves better to the conditions. Blackpool realised the necessity for hitting the ball hard and often; Chelsea, on the other hand, stuck steadfastly to a policy of trying to play football, and in doing this they beat themselves.

**(October 31)**

# CRICKET'S CREEPING PARALYSIS

## THE GAME INFECTED FROM TEST MATCHES DOWN TO SCHOOLS

**By Howard Marshall**

CRICKET is dying, they tell me. An exaggeration, of course, but at least it is true that countless lovers of cricket are uncomfortably aware that creeping paralysis is attacking the game.

Spectators know it, players know it, and the treasurers of county clubs know it most certainly of all.

It should be easy to diagnose the complaint and prescribe the remedy, but cricket is a complicated game.

Superficially it is possible to argue that the standard of play is as high as ever it was. Have we not our Sutcliffes and our Jardines, our Bradmans and our Woodfulls, our Grimmetts and our Freemans to prove, statistically at any rate, that this is still the golden age?

Here at once we run into controversy, for there are those who say that players like Sutcliffe, much though we admire their skill, have gone far towards draining cricket of its vitality.

### FEAR OF MISTAKES

It seems to me that imperceptibly our values have changed, and that our sense of proportion has become warped. We regard performance in Test matches as the criterion by which our great cricketers should be judged, and yet I believe that Test matches, as they are played to-day, have ceased to be games in any real sense of the word. They demand certain admirable qualities from the players who represent their countries - tenacity, courage, determination - but they produce cricket stripped of all joyousness and beauty, and to my mind the less we see of them the better.

The Test match atmosphere, moreover, is poisoning cricket and it works downwards through the counties to the schools, until we find even schoolboy batsmen playing miserably like miniature Sutcliffes

This resolves itself into a question of our mental attitude towards the game, and what is the cricketer's attitude of mind to-day? If we may judge from a great deal of the first-class cricket we see, it is a negative attitude, a fear of making mistakes, a reliance upon defence as the rock upon which success is founded.

So we find that bowling which is short of a length or over-pitched goes unpunished, while the batsman plays cramped defensive strokes, and scores only towards the on-side or by deflections behind the wicket.

### TEST PLAY RITUAL

I should like to make it clear, before we go any further, that I am not pleading for brighter cricket, for juggling with points or laws or hours of play. That side of the question can take care of itself, and we shall not need to bother about it if only we can revive the spirit of aggression, even in the Test match environment.

At present we approach Test matches as if they were solemn rituals; we almost feel, when the opening pair of batsmen emerge from the pavillion that we should stand and uncover our heads, and speak in respectful whispers.

This is all nonsense; it is high time we thought of Test match cricket as a game, and what is more, picked players to represent us who could see our point of view, men like L.G. Crawley and R.W.V. Robins, who would not be afraid to chance their arm.

I am inclined to think that there is too much coaching in our public schools, or that at least the coaching as a whole is not sufficiently imaginative.

This is where the danger lies, for instead of encouraging a boy to hit the ball, leaving the refinements of hitting to follow, there seems at present to be a tendency to insist that above all he must play the ball correctly.

This, in my opinion, is putting the cart before the horse. Our Test match cricketers may have forgotton that a ball is meant to be hit, but meant to be hit it is, and upon this elementary principle all true batsmanship is based.

It is the attacking spirit which we must foster among our young cricketers if we care for the future of the game. is it being fostered enough to-day? I doubt it.

**(July 15)**

# SOUTH AFRICAN PACK WIN NEARLY EVERY SCRUM

## LOSERS' HEROIC RESISTANCE IN THE SECOND HALF: BRAND'S GOAL

**By Howard Marshall**

ENGLAND ............ 0 pts; SOUTH AFRICA ............ 7 pts

IT is all over, the great match, and South Africa have beaten England at Twickenham by a dropped goal and a try to nil. Sitting in the stand there afterwards, while the huge crowd slowly eddied away - nearly 70,000 people watched the game - our feelings were curiously mixed. We had seen what we expected to see - the South African forwards smashing the English pack, and Osler's kicking driving England back to their line - but with our admiration was mingled a strong sense of disappointment.

The splendid South African scrummaging, the heroic English resistance in the second half, Brand's superb dropped goal, these were compensations indeed, and yet we are bound to set against them the weakness of South Africa in constructive play behind the scrummage, the collapse of the English front-row forwards, and a disturbing amount of half-hearted tackling by England.

But first let us pay tribute to South Africa. Their forwards were magnificent. They proved once and for all that hard work is the foundation of sound scrummaging. From the twenty-eight set scrums in the first half South Africa heeled twenty three times, and we shall not soon forget the way their pack walked over the ball, pushing England as they pleased.

### SCRUMMAGING THEORY

We may attribute this dominance to superior weight and physique, and it would perhaps be unjust to blame England severely for failing to hold one of the most powerful packs on record, a pack, moreover, which has played together for many weeks, and thus works like a machine. Still, it is difficult to believe that England, with so many more players to choose from than South Africa, cannot find eight forwards of equal physique and scrummaging ability.

Here we come to a fundamental difference in the theory of scrummaging. The South Africans have retained their belief in the virtue of combined shoving as the ball comes in - on the principle that the pack which then moves forward will either secure the ball or prevent its opponents from heeling it cleanly. In England, on the other hand, specialisation has gradually sapped the strength of scrummaging.

Three forwards in most English club packs - the hooker and the outside men in the back now do little or no work, and everything is left to what Arthur Budd called derisively "the forest of scraping legs." In the English pack on Saturday the front-row forwards, Norman, Carpenter and Gregory, were hooking specialists accustomed to allowing other members of the pack to push while they concentrate on heeling the ball. Is it surprising, therefore, that they buckled up against the strength of Mostert, Kipling and Boy Louw, three hard-working forwards of the highest quality?

### ENGLAND TAUGHT A LESSON

The truth is that South Africa taught us a badly needed lesson. We must return to honest scrummaging before we can hope to improve the standard of Rugby football in England. Individually the English forwards were gallant enough. They stood up to the South African onslaughts with immense courage in the loose, where Hodgson, Saxby, and Webb were particularly fine.

England's failure in the tight was all the more tragic, because the play of the English outsides suggested that with reasonable opportunities they might well have won the match. Sobey's efficiency at scrum-half, Spong's strength and resilience at stand-off half, Gerrard's thrusts in the centre - here is a most promising player - Tanner's thrust on the right wing, and Aarvold's cleverness on the left, the sum of these virtues were more dangerous than anything South Africa could produce.

**(January 4)**

# RUGBY FOOTBALL BOMBSHELL

## BOARD'S CENSURE OF MODERN TACTICS

The International Rugby Board last night issued one of the most revolutionary statements in connection with Rugby football which has appeared since the war.

It consists of a wholesale condemnation of modern scrummaging methods, and it takes the form of a plea to players, referees, and club officials to abolish specialisation among forwards in order that the spirit and standards of the game may be preserved.

The statement is highly controversial in itself, but particularly significant are the implications it contains. There can be no doubt that the International Board are most seriously concerned for the future welfare of Rugby football, for only real perturbation could have forced them to publish so sweeping an attack on present tendencies.

At first sight the manifesto seems to be making a large mountain out of a small mole-hill, though no one will deny that the board have reason for many of their conclusions. At any rate, it is certain that they have taken an unprecedented step in thus attempting to check the evolution of the game, and their action will cause widespread discussion in Rugby football circles.

**(September 3)**

# A CRICKET INCIDENT

## WAS IT SPORTING?

To the Editor of THE DAILY TELEGRAPH

Sir - One of the most curious cricket incidents I have ever seen recorded appears in your account this morning of the match at Birmingham between Yorkshire and Warwickshire.

"Layland appeared to edge a ball from Mayer into the wicketkeeper's hands, but the umpire, Woolley, gave him not out. But the batsman, expecting a contrary decision, was by then walking away. Smart threw at the stumps and missed!"

Few true sportsmen will approve Smart's action in throwing at the stumps at all in such circumstances. But what would the umpire have said had be hit them? And, apart from the question of sportsmanship, was not the ball "out of play" immediately the umpire gave his decision on the catch-at-the-wicket appeal? Yours, &c.,

London, S.E., May 20. CRICKETER.

**(August 21)**

# JACK HOBBS AND BOWLER'S TACTICS

## AN OVAL PROTEST

**By White Willow**

There was an incident at Kennington Oval on Saturday which has caused considerable controversy during the week-end.

The players concerned were Hobbs, the Surrey batsman, and Bowes, the Yorkshire bowler, and it is interesting to give the views of both players as to what happened.

Bowes, who is a fast-medium bowler, had been delivering an occasional "short" ball to Hobbs, who eventually protested against one which flew headhigh. His method of protest was to walk almost the length of the pitch and smooth down the turf, only a few yards out of the bowling crease, with his bat.

The next ball sent down was of the same kind, and Hobbs repeated his action. He also complained to Bowes during an interval that he was bowling dangerously, and "might cause some hurt which he would always regret."

### SURPRISING THE BATSMAN

Discussing the incident with me yesterday, Bowes said: "The matter is a technical one. If you grant that a fast bowler is a shock bowler, then his shortish ball is just as much a legitimate variation as the faster one sent down by a slow or medium bowler.

"Of course, if he bowled no other kind than the short ball he would be a bad bowler. So would he be if he constantly kept what is called a good length and never gave the batsman a surprise.

HOBBS

BOWES

"That is merely playing the batsman in, and the batsman would refuse to make any shots at all."

The other members of the Yorkshire team, I believe, strongly resented Hobbs' action in walking down the pitch. Hobbs, however, feels that he was justified in making a moral protest.

"Perhaps I made a mistake, especially from their point of view," he said to me, "in walking down the pitch, but after all, it was done more in a humorous spirit than anything else. The first thought that occurs to me on what Bowes has stated is also slightly humorous - that it was my brains he was nearly using!

"Seriously, though, somebody will be killed one of these days by a 'bumping' ball from some fast bowler, and then the practice will be stopped. Such a tragedy is bound to happen sooner or later."

**(August 22)**

# LAUREL AND HARDY

STAN LAUREL AND OLIVER HARDY, changing their bowlers for boaters.

## SPHERICAL CAR

INVENTOR J. A. PURVES in his spherical car "The Dynasphere'

'HORATIUS' a Handley Page airliner stands outside Croydon terminal.

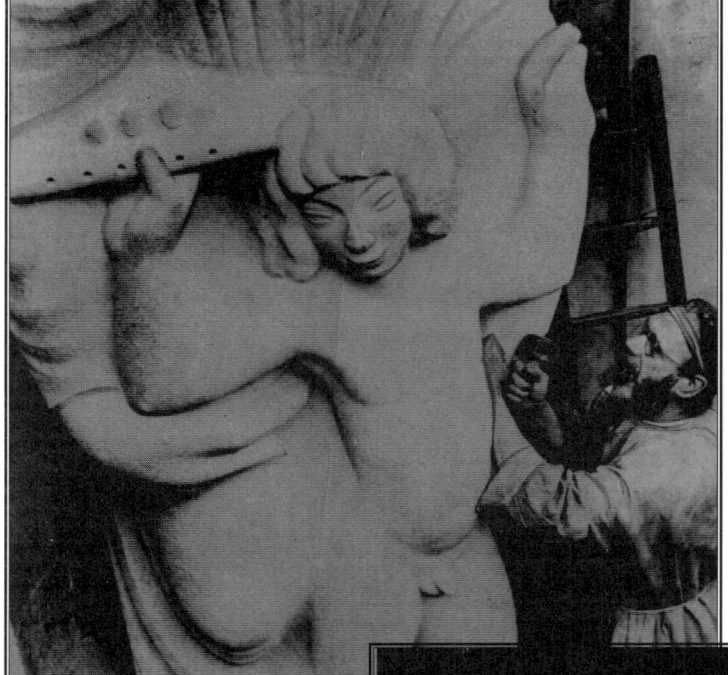

ERIC GILL at work on the figures of Prospero and Ariel, on Broadcasting House.

## THE MONTE CARLO RALLY

THE CREW OF THE HILLMAN -ECALES combination passing through London in the early hours of the morning.

Of the 116 Europeans who are competing in the Monte Carlo Rally, 35 are British. Most of the British competitiors are starting from John 'o Groats 1837 miles from Monte Carlo.

The year was dominated by the rise of Hitler. Early in the year, he was elected Chancellor and immediately the Nazi repression began. The burning of the Reichstag, which some were later to think was stage-managed by Hitler's underlings, provided an excuse to eliminate the German Communist party. The German judiciary, though, showed it still had its independence by finding most of the defendants at the trial of the supposed fire-raisers not guilty through lack of reliable evidence. The campaign against the Jews quickly got under way. Many took the drastic step of leaving their possessions behind as they fled the country. They, in the long term, were to prove the fortunate ones. The plight of the Jews was underlined by Einstein's renunciation of his German citizenship.

*The Daily Telegraph*'s correspondent in Munich, who had offended the Nazi hierarchy by his reporting of the Nuremburg rally at which Hitler had forecast a 100-year Reich, was arrested, held for some weeks and then deported, the first of several of the paper's correspondents to suffer this fate. Another *Daily Telegraph* correspondent visited the concentration camp at Dachau and found that conditions there were not too bad.

At his inauguration, President Roosevelt coined his famous phrase that his country had "nothing to fear but fear itself" as he initiated a great plan for public works to relieve the unemployment problem. His countrymen were able to celebrate this fresh start in lawful alcohol as prohibition was ended in most states.

In Britain, signs of recovery were becoming obvious as a spending spree was noted at Christmas time and income tax was reduced in the Budget. The Oxford Union by 275 to 153 passed its notorious motion that "This House would not fight for King and Country", sparking a furious response, including a leader in *The Daily Telegraph* which thundered that the Union members who had voted for the motion were "not so much red as yellow". An attempt, though, to rescind the motion failed. By contrast the British government announced a proposed increase in the number of aircraft for the RAF.

The British film industry was given a great fillip by the success of Alexander Korda's film, *The Private Lives of Henry VIII*. The technical marvels of *King Kong* left the world astounded, while on stage Fred Astaire's dancing captured many hearts.

The sporting year was dominated by the "body line" controversy. English fast bowlers concentrating on the leg stump with a semicircle of short legs caused protests from the Australian cricket authorities and a brisk exchange of messages that put Commonwealth relationships at peril. The winning of the Ashes at the beginning of the year heralded other sporting successes. Both the Ryder and Davis cups were captured for this country.

The year saw the death of Lord Grey of Falloden, the foreign secretary at the outbreak of the First World War, who spoke the immortal phrase about "lamps going out all over Europe". John Galsworthy, who had won the Nobel Prize for Literature the year before, died, as did the creator of Ruritania, Anthony Hope. The great Indian cricketer always familiarly known as "Ranji" also died.

**4 A. M. EDN. — ROUT OF ENGLAND BATSMEN: LUNCH**



# The Daily Telegraph



To-Day's Weather : Unsettled; Cooler

Broadcasting: Page Seven


No. 24,219 POSTAGE { INLAND, CANADA AND NEWFOUNDLAND, THREE HALFPENCE; OTHER COLONIES AND PLACES ABROAD, TWOPENCE

LONDON, MONDAY, JANUARY 3, 1933

ONE PENNY


*BIRTHS, MARRIAGES and DEATHS 5s a line. "IN MEMORIAM" notices 3s a line. (Special rate for five or ten years' automatic insertion on application.) Announcements authenticated by the name and address of sender, may be sent to The Daily Telegraph Fleet-st, E.C.4. or 161 Piccadilly, W.1. or telephoned to Central 4242.*

## BIRTHS

AINLEY – On Dec. 31, 1932 at 27 Westfield-avenue, Oakes, Huddersfield, to Barbara (née Walker), wife of Wilfred Hirst Ainsley, a son.

ALLAN – On Dec. 31, 1932, at 1, Linnell-drive, N.W. 11, to Mollie, wife of Alan Maurice Allan, a son.

BAINES – On Dec. 30, 1932, at Ormsby-road, Southsea, to Betty, wife of T.H. Baines, a daughter.

COWIN – On Dec. 30, 1932, at Woking, Surrey, to Leslie (née Cockshut), wife of J.H.L. Cowin, a son.

GAINSFORD– On Dec. 30, 1932, to Helen (née Fea), wife of William Gainsford, of Somersby, Spilsby, Lincs, a son.

HICHENS – On Jan 2, 1933, at 113, Eaton-square, S.W.1. to Hermione, wife of Lionel Hichens, a daughter.

LEWTY – On Dec. 30, 1932, at Alverstoke, Hants, to Lena, wife of Lieut.-Commander J.H. Lewty, a daughter.

MAY – On Dec. 28, 1932, to Evelyn Violet, wife of Frederick Stanley May, of The Bower, Heyer, Kent, a son.

MENDOZA – On Jan. 1, 1933, at 40, Belsize-grove, N.W. 3. to Daisy (née Joseph), wife of Samuel Mendoza, of Burlingham, a son.

TOMLINSON– On Dec. 28, 1932, in New York, to Elizabeth, wife of H. Charles Tomlinson, a son.

## MARRIAGES

BRAITHWAITE-LOMAX – On Dec. 31, 1932, at the Church of St. Jude-on-the-Hill, Hampstead Garden Suburb, Joseph Gurney Braithwaite, M.P., youngest son of Mr. J. Bevan Braithwaite and the late Mrs. Braithwaite, to Emily Victoria Lomax, youngest daughter of the late Mr. and Mrs. A.M. Lomax, of Edinburgh.

FARQUHARSON-LIMPENNY – On Dec. 17, 1932, at St. Patrick's Church, Fort William, Calcutta, Mr. D. A. Farquharson, 2nd Royal Garhwal Rifles, to Margaret Limpenny.

OUTRAM-LITTLEHALES – On Dec. 28, 1932, at St. James' Paddington, James Ian, elder son of the Rev. and Mrs. Arthur Outram, to Evelyn Mary, elder daughter of the Rev. C.G. and Mrs. Littlehales.

RATCLIFFE-HART – On New Year's Eve, 1932, at Northaw Church, Hertfordshire, quietly Cornwallis St. Aubyn Ratcliffe, of Kilvinton Hall, Enfield Chase, only son of the late Rev. and Mrs. C. E. Ratcliffe, to Margery Constance, younger daughter of Mr. and Mrs. Alfred H. Hart, of Hillcrest, Enfield Chase.

ROOKE-TWISLETON-WYKEHAM-FIENNES – On Dec, 31, 1932, at St. Mary's, Boltons, Noel, only son of Thomas Matthews Rooke, R.W.S. of 7 Queen Anne's-gardens, W.4. to Celia Mary, youngest daughter of the late Alberic Twisleton-Wykeham-Fiennes and Mrs. Fiennes, of 63 Redcliffe-road, S.W. 10

WAGNER-DUMMETT – On Dec. 29, 1932, at Croydon, Harold Geoffrey Wager to Elizabeth Mary Dummett.

## DEATHS

BARLOW – On Dec. 31, 1932, at The Holt, Ledbury, Lt.-Colonel Herbert S. Barlow, late the Seaforth Highlanders. Funeral Ledbury Church, to-morrow (Wednesday), two p.m. No flowers.

BIDEN – On Jan 2, 1933, at Canister House, Hampton, lately of the Mitre Hotel, Hampton Court, Rowena, in her 68th year. Service at Hampton Parish Church, Thursday, three p.m.

BODIN, William Marchant (partner of Lane, Saville & Co.) suddenly, on New Year's Eve, 1932, at 1, Bolton-road, Harrow, Funeral on Thursday, ten o'clock, at the Church of St. Joseph's, Wealdstone.

BULLING – On Jan. 2, 1933, at 18, Christchurch-avenue, Brondesbury, Charles Edward Bulling, Cremation Golders Green Crematorium on Thursday, Jan. 5, at two p.m.

BURNABY – On Dec, 30, 1932, at 30 Limes-road, Folkestone, Lt. Colonel Eustace Beaumont Burnaby, beloved husband of Alice Burnaby, aged 90.

COATES – On Dec, 31, 1932, suddenly, Charles Coates, of 4 Green-avenue, Mill Hill, N.W.7, and of the firm of Potter, Boardman and Co. Ltd. Manchester and London. Friends, please accept this intimation.

DAVIS – On Jan 2, 1933, at his residence, 30, Norfolk-street, Park-lane, W.1. Moss Davis (formerly of Nelson and Auckland. New Zealand), the much beloved and devoted husband of Leah Davis, in his 86th year. The funeral will leave the residence at two p.m. to-day (Tuesday), for Willesden Jewish Cemetery. Prayers at the New West End Synagogue, St. Petersburgh-place, Bayswater-road, at five p.m. to-day.

ERLE On Dec. 31, 1932, suddenly, at 17, Parkside, Albert Gate, S.W., Mary, widow of T.W. Erle, of Bramshott Grange, Liphook, Hants. Funeral service at St. Paul's, Knightsbridge, 11.30 a.m. to-morrow (Wednesday), before interment at Cuckfield, Sussex.

FINDLAY – On the afternoon of Saturday, Dec. 31, 1932, suddenly, at Moreton, Dorset, Sir Mansfeldt De Cardonnel Findlay, G.B.E., K.C.M.G., C.B. Funeral to-day (Tuesday) at Moreton Church.

FORESTIER WALKER – On Dec. 29, 1932, at 7 Sussex-square, W., Lieut.-Colonel Claude Edward Forester Walker, D.S.O., late R.A., of Duniston, Barham, Kent, youngest son of the late major-General G.E.L. Walker, R.E. aged 64.

FROOM – On Dec. 30, 1932, at 15, Culford-mansions, S.W.3. after a long and painful illness, Amy, wife of Lieutenant-Colonel George Froom, late of the 94th Regiment.

LEEFE – On Dec. 31, 1932, very suddenly, Drewry Octavius Leefe, of 27 Greville-road, N.W.6, in his 69th year. Funeral St. Augustine's Church, Kilburn, on Thursday, Jan 5, at 10.30 a.m.; interment Hampstead Cemetery, 11.15 a.m. Flowers and inquiries Messrs. James Crook, 259, High-rd., Kilburn, N.W.6.

## PERSONAL

*5s per line (minimum 2 lines). Trade 10s per line. Lost and Found 2s 6d. per line.*

THERE IS A LIMIT at which forbearance ceases to be virtue. Burke.

SEND A MITE TO SAVE A MITE. – The INFANTS HOSPITAL, VINCENT-SQUARE, WESTMINSTER, APPEALS for FUNDS to extend its work, – Contributions should be sent to the Secretary.

ST. AUSTELL BAY HOTEL, PAR, CORNWELL.Sunshine, Sea breezes, Hard Tennis Courts, Free Golf, Squash, Badminton, Dancing, Renowned Cuisine. Special Terms January to March.

URGENT!
TO THE PUBLIC !!
"A CUP OF HAPPINESS."
By
EDEN PHILLPOTTS.
At the Royalty Theatre.

THE ANNOUNCEMENT IN A SUNDAY PAPER THAT THE ABOVE PLAY HAS BEEN WITHDRAWN IS INACCURATE AND UNTRUE, AND WAS WHOLLY WITHOUT FOUNDATION OF ANY KIND WHATSOEVER.

S.R.L., in the Morning Post, says: "EDEN PHILLPOTTS AT HIS BEST – A BETTER PLAY THAN 'THE FARMER'S WIFE.'"

The News Chronicle says: "ON ITS MERITS SHOULD RUN AS LONG AS 'THE FARMER'S WIFE.'"

A.P. in the Daily Mail, says: "I COMMEND THIS PLAY."

TELEPHONE IMMEDIATELY, ROYALTY THEATRE, GERRARD 7331, OR ALL THE BEST LIBRARIES, FOR SEATS THIS MONTH. NIGHTLY 8.30 "A CUP OF HAPPINESS." – LEON M. LION.

PUBLIC SPEAKING. After-Dinner Speaking – See advt. of Duxbury Institute under "Education."

BOND-STREET CLOTHES on MONTHLY TERMS, SUITS, 6gns., DRESS, 8gns., OVERCOATS, 4gns. Write CALL, or 'Phone for "fairfax plan." fairfax (Tailors to Men) Ltd., Dept. C., 79, NEW BOND-ST., W. May. 1008.

THRILLS at GROSVENOR HOUSE, Fast, exciting, spectacular. ICE HOCKEY: Grosvenor House v. Stade Francais. Wednesday, Jan 4, at 8.30 p.m. Tickets. 2s 6d to 8s 6d. Combined for the Match and Dinner or Supper, from 8s 6d to 15s 6d. – Telephone Grosvenor 6363.

MOTOR-CAR HIRE SERVICE. Kens. 2477. See Col. 7, this Page, for Bargain Sale of Mileage.

THOU SHALT SHEW ME THE PATH OF LIFE; in thy presence is the fulness of joy; and at thy right hand there is pleasure for evermore (Psalm xvi. 12).

SAY "SHOO" to a cold before its says "Ahshoo" to you. PRUNOL CRYSTALLISED PASTILLES keep your system clear and so keep colds at bay. – Write to-day to PRUNOL PRODUCTS Ltd., Dept. D.T., 7, 21, Cockspur-street, London S.W.1. enclosing 1 ½d in stamps for a free sample of this delicious and effective new laxative.

SALE at FENWICK of BOND-STREET (corner of Brook-street) begins TO-DAY. Distinguished COATS, GOWNS, SUITS and SPORTSWEAR, at Fenwick's Celebrated Sale-price £3. Also Lingerie from 10s. and Hats reduced to 10s. and 15s. Come early.

HIGHEST PRICES paid for GOLD, SILVER, and Sovereigns. Cash per return. Also old English Silver, Sheffield Plate, Jewellery, Diamonds, Antiques, and Dental Plates (not Vulcanite), Large or small quantities. – BENTLEY & CO., 7a New Bond-st., London.

YOUR GOOD RESOLUTION should be to discover for yourself what a generous allowance we can make for your present FUR SHOWROOMS in PART PAYMENT of a new one from our 1933 collection. – W.B. Service, Fur Showrooms (4th floor), 235, Regent-st., W.1. (Oppos. Dickins & Jones.)

PIANO WANTED, Steinway, Bluthner, Bechstein or equivalent. – H.B. Sharp's, 4, Berkeley-square, W.

6D A MILE – Six-passenger SUNBEAM LIMOUSINE, Sloane 5121.

1,000 DOCKLAND GRANDMAS from poorest slums are to be given a New Year Tea and Entertainment. Please help to brighten their drab lives by sending a gift, 10s will pay for 20 grannies. – C. Woolmer, B.D., Supt., Victoria Dock Mission, Foster Hall, Tidal Basin, London E.16.

LATE COMPANY SECRETARY and ACCOUNTANT desires similar work, part or whole time. Audit, income-tax returns, claims, &c. Consider purchase small accountant's practice. – Write T., Box 1,574, Daily Telegraph, E.C. 4.

REQUIRED, Hove or nr., adjoining FIRST-CLASS HOTEL, detached Freehold House, 5-6 bd., sunny, pre-war, £1,000. – Write Bobbett, 58, South-rd., Weston-s-Mare.

N.Y.R. – NEW YEAR RESOLUTIONS. Please think of the orphan and destitute little ones in Dr. Barnardo's Homes in the New Year. 8,300 children always being supported. TEN SHILLINGS will feed one child for ten days. – Cheques &c., payable "Dr. Barnardo's Homes Food Fund." and crossed, addressed Dr. Barnardo's Homes, 32 Barnardo House, Stepney-causeway, E.1.

INCOME-TAX – Consult the British Taxpayers' Assn. Ltd., Grand-buildings, Trafalgar-square, W.C. 2. Inclusive Protection Service, £2 2s yearly.

SALE – Original model 10-guinea Evening Gowns, £3 3s; Fur-trimmed 12-guinea Coats. £3 13s 6d. – CLARIDGE, 10 South Molton-street, W.1.

LADY, with own CAR, WANTED, to join gentleman in profitable undertaking. – Write L., Box 3,470, Daily Telegraph, E.C.4.

PROFESSIONAL GENTLEWOMAN has quiet room for student as Sole Guest, where resident maid kept. Breakfast and optional meals. Moderate to the right person. – D. R., 15 West Cromwell-rd., S.W. 5.

INTENDING ADVERTISERS can obtain help and advice in the compilation of their announcements at the West-end Office of THE DAILY TELEGRAPH, 161, Piccadilly, W.1.

## CONCERTS, &C.

QUEEN'S HALL Sole Lessees – Chappell & Co. Ltd.
**PROMENADE CONCERTS**
CHRISTMAS SEASON (Two Weeks).
NIGHTLY, AT 8, until Jan. 14th.
**SIR HENRY WOOD**
THE B.B.C. SYMPHONY ORCHESTRA
TO-NIGHT, at 8.

| | |
|---|---|
| St. John's Eve on the Bare Mountain | Moussorsky |
| Pianoforte Concerto No. 1 in B flat minor | Tchaikovsky |
| Symphony No. 5, in E minor | Tchaikovsky |
| Carnival Overture | Glazounov |
| Overture, Russian and Ludmulla | Glinka |

Solo Pianoforte – POUISHNOFF
FULL PROGRAMMES NOW READY
Tickets 2s to 7s 6d, at
B.B.C. BROADCASTING HOUSE, W.1.
Agents & Chappell's Box-office, Queen's Hall.

## MUSIC, SINGING, ELOCUTION, &C.

**LONDON COLLEGE OF MUSIC**
Great Marlborough-street, Regent-street, W.1.
Principal – F.J. KARN, Mus.D. Toronto, Mus. B. Cantab.
Director of Examinations – G. AUGUSTUS HOLMES.
COMPLETE MUSICAL EDUCATION at moderate fees.
SPRING TERM begins MONDAY, Jan 9; 1933,
PRIVATE LESSONS DAY and EVENING, in Piano.
Singing, Violin, Organ, Elocution, &c. Also CLASSES,
Prospectus, with full details, on application to
A. GAMBIER HOLMES, Secretary.
Telephone Gerrard 6120. Telegrams 'Supertonic, London'

GERTRUDE TOMALIN gives LESSONS in ELOCUTION and DICTION. – Address c.o. Mdme. Novello Davies, 43, Aldwych, W.C.

THE BEN GREET ACADEMY OF ACTING Ltd. – Interval Club, 22 Dean-st., W.1. New Term 16th Inst.

HAROLD HOWELL. Professor of Singing.
Coach in Opera.
Weekes Studios, 14, Hanover-st., W.

## DANCING

GEM MOUFLET (Miss) PARTNERS TO DANCES teaches PRIVATELY 9.30-9.30 6 days (Near Ritz), 11, ALBERMARLE-ST., PICCADILLY. REGent 4629.

SCINTILLAS CLUB. – Informal Practice Dances for Business People. "Grub Party." Thursday 7.30 -10 p.m. Visitors 2s 6d – 9, Fisher-st., Southampton-row, W.C.1.

DAISIE BOWETT SCHOOL of BALLROOM DANCING, 58 BAKER-ST. (Wel. 3730) Four Private Lessons, 21s. Practice Class Thursdays. 8.15-10.15 2/6

MR. and MRS. RALPH MOODY. Specialists Ballroom Dancing. Latest steps, any dance, 3 pte. lessons 21s – Palace Hotel Ball Room, W.2. Padd. 8281.

CASANI School of Ballroom Dancing, 90 Regent-st., teaches steps any dance in 3 pte. lessons 21s Foxtrot, Waltz Argentine Tango. – Regent 4438.

RUBY PEELER, Eccleston Hotel (Vic. 5770). Ball Room and Tap Less, daily. Lunch hour 5s. Mondays; Dance 9-12. 4s incl. buffet. Class 8-9.

## EDUCATIONAL

**LONDON MATRICULATION**
Courses of preparation are provided by
**UNIVERSITY CORRESPONDENCE COLLEGE**
(Founder: WM BRIGGS, LL.D., D.C.L., M.A., B.Sc.)
SPECIAL ADVANTAGES offered by U.C.C. to students preparing for Matriculation include instruction by Resident Tutors. Free Loan of Textbooks, Individual Tuition, Free Re-preparation if unsuccessful, and Deferred Payments.
During the Five Years 1928-1932, 2,342 U.C.C. Students Passed London University Matriculation.
FREE GUIDE to London Matriculation, giving full particulars of U.C.C. Courses of preparation may be obtained post free on application to the Registrar.
23, BURLINGTON HOUSE, CAMBRIDGE.

**THE DUXBURY INSTITUTE**
Director of Studies: JOHN DUXBURY, (Est. 40 years) "Has taught more Members of Parliament and famous speakers than any other." (Vide Press).
PUBLIC SPEAKING – Self-confidence, fluency, persuasiveness, attained by the celebrated DUXBURY METHOD. Special course for After-Dinner Speakers.
BUSINESS MEN, SALESMEN, Special training for salesmen and representatives, through voice control and the spoken word. Intensely practical course.
Also, Spare-time Course for Teachers of Elocution.
INEXPENSIVE PRIVATE LESSONS at convenient times, day or evening.
Call or write for explanatory Booklet, stating requirements
THE DIRECTOR OF STUDIES.
THE DUXBURY INSTITUTE
41, Woburn-square, London, W.C.1. Museum 2386.

**SONS IN OR ENTERING FATHERS' BUSINESSES**
get exactly what they require in Mr. Dunlop's individual training for business management. Entirely different from the ordinary commercial course. – Full particulars from Mr. W.R. Dunlop, 57 Gordon-square, W.C.1.

**WESTONBIRT SCHOOL**
FOR GIRLS
TETBURY, GLOUCESTERSHIRE
ENTRANCE SCHOLARSHIPS value £100 to £30, and Bursaries offered to girls under 14 on May 1st. 1933. Examinations February 13th and 14th. – For full particulars apply to the Headmistress.

VICTORIA COLLEGE, WESTBURY, WILTSHIRE A Public School Education for Boys at moderate Fees. Junior and Senior Schools. Playing fields and grounds of 56 acres. Laboratory, Gymnasium. Tennis and Badminton Courts, Squash Court, Chapel. Recognised by the Board of Education. Vacancies in January Scholarships and Bursaries available. – All applications to the Headmaster.

INDIVIDUAL TRAINING in all SECRETARIAL subjects. Shorthand typewriting, bookkeeping, languages, &c. JANUARY SCHOLARSHIP, Good posts for qualified students – GROSVENOR COLLEGE (for Gentlewomen), 104, Victoria-street, S.W.1. Vic. 1301.

## EDUCATIONAL (Continued)

**PARIS ACADEMY OF DRESSMAKING AND MILINERY,**
24, OLD BOND-STREET, W.1.
Principal – Mme J TROIS FONTAINES.
The most PRACTICAL and ACCEPTED SCHOOL in the BRITISH ISLES.
Day or Postal Course.
Visit the Academy or write for Prospectus A.M.

DRESSES! – Make your own while learning. Practical tuition by principals. – Call, write for prospectus, REGENT School of DRESSMAKING, 19, Oxford-st., W. (3 doors from Tottenham-court-rd. Tube).

HATS! Learn to make your own, or as career, 12 lessons 3gns. – THE SCHOOL OF MILLINERY. 68 WIGMORE-ST., Welbeck 9606

PUBLIC SPEAKING. – Private lessons given by Mr. C. Seymour. Also Voice. Breathing, Elocution, Accent, Confidence. – 401, Strand, W.C.2. Prosp. for'd.

**KENSINGTON COLLEGE**
SECRETARIAL TRAINING.
Founded 1887.
GOOD APPOINTMENTS GUARANTEED
LANGUAGES and FOREIGN SHORTHAND.
TWO RESIDENTIAL HOUSES FOR GIRLS.
PRACTICAL EXPERIENCE in BUSY OFFICE.
MODERATE FEES.
NEXT ENTRIES, 10th JANUARY
All particulars from Mr. L.P. MUNFORD.
34, Bishop's-road, London, W.2. Paddington 9046

**AN OFFER TO PARENTS!**
The Principal of Clark's College is prepared to arrange a preliminary examination for boys and girls who are considering the opportunities available in Business, the Civil Service or the Accountancy and Secretarial Professions. This offer places parents under no obligation and enables them to have expert advice as to future prospects in any of the above appointments.
Details are obtainable from
THE PRINCIPAL
**CLARK'S COLLEGE LTD.**
126, CHANCERY-LANE, W.C.2.

CUSACK'S COLLEGE will qualify you quickly for success in commerce or examinations. –Write, call, or 'phone Bishopsgate 5172 for Prospectus. CUSACK'S COLLEGE, SUN-ST., FINSBURY-SQ., E.C.

**MARLBOROUGH GATE SECRETARIAL COLLEGE**
and
INTENSIVE BUSINESS COURSE.
For educated men and women
Director: R.W. Holland, O.B.E., M.A., M.Sc. LL.D.
Advisory Governor: The Duchess of Atholl.
SECRETARIAL TRAINING for the better business and private appointments. Foreign shorthand a speciality.
INTENSIVE BUSINESS COURSE for posts not requiring shorthand and Typewriting.
Paddington 3320 3, Marlborough-gate, W.2.

**LONDON COLLEGE OF SECRETARIES**
(Principal – Dr. E. Robert.)
Complete practical training for educated girls and women desiring to be PRIVATE SECRETARIES to professional men, politicians, or business men.
INDIVIDUAL TUITION
A suitable position found for every qualified student.
Special attention given to Foreign Shorthand.
Shorter courses in any secretarial subject. – Apply 84, REGENT-STREET, W.1. (Tel. 5538 Regent)

**SECRETARIAL COLLEGE**
FOR EDUCATED GIRLS
**MISS MILDRED RANSOM**
Careful Modern Training culminating in
FIRST-CLASS POSTS
Special INTENSIVE Course.
(seven months), with or without
MODERN LANGUAGES. Low fees.
Write or Telephone for Free Prospectus.
**15, GREAT CUMBERLAND PLACE,**
MARBLE ARCH, W.1.
Paddington 6302.

**BEDFORD SQUARE SECRETARIAL COLLEGE**
for educated ladies. Intensive and individual training. Moderate inclusive fee to proficiency and a position, Frn. Languages. Speed Classes, &c. – 8, Bedford-sq., W.C.1.

**SECRETARIAL TRAINING**
**MISS GIMSON, F.I.P.S.**
21, NETHERHALL-GARDENS, HAMPSTEAD, N.W.3.
(opposite Finchley-rd, Met. Station)
for eight years on the staff of Miss Kerr Sander's Secretarial College. Piccadilly, gives thorough modern training in all branches to educated girls.
Full course six months, shorter courses by arrangement.
Moderate fees.

**HAIRDRESSING & BEAUTY CULTURE AS A CAREER**
London's Leading Training School, day or evening tuition. Write or call for prospectus. – Walters' Hairdressing Academy, 46 Great Titchfield-street, Oxford-circus, W.1.

LATIN and GREEK. – Oral and Postal Lessons, 8 for £1, by Oxford M.A., in Honours. – W. L., la, Steele's-road, Hampstead, N.W.3.

## FINANCIAL NOTICES

CITY of WINNIPEG 4% CONSOLIDATED REGISTERED STOCK, 1940-60.
For the purpose of preparing the interest warrants, due 1st March, 1933, the BALANCES will be STRUCK on the evening of the 1st February 1933, after which date the stock will be transferred ex-dividend.
For Bank of Montreal, G.C. CASSELS, Manager.
47, Threadneedle-street, E.C.2. 2nd January, 1933.

GREATER WINNIPEG WATER DISTRICT 4 ½% STOCK, 1954.
For the purpose of preparing the interest warrants due 1st March 1933, the BALANCES will be STRUCK on the evening of the 1st February 1933, after which date the stock will be transferred ex-dividend.
For Bank of Montreal. G.C. CASSELS, Manager.
47, Threadneedle-street, E.C.2. 2nd January, 1933.

**The Daily Telegraph**
*All the Real News*

**MR. DE VALERA DISSOLVES THE DAIL**

Page 11

## TOURS, CRUISES, &C.

**COOK'S**
FOR
**TRAVEL**

**AUSTRALIA & NEW ZEALAND**
85 DAYS' TOUR TO AUSTRALIA
from
**£113 14s 6d**
Including travel tickets, hotels, sightseeing, drives, &c.

**ROUND VOYAGE TO AUSTRALIA**
(out and home by same vessel)
from
**£112.**

**98 DAYS' TOUR TO NEW ZEALAND**
from
**£211**
Including travel tickets, hotels, sightseeing drives, &c.

**ROUND VOYAGE TO NEW ZEALAND**
(out and home by same vessel).
**100 days– £112.**

**THOS. COOK & SON LTD., & WAGONS-LITS CO.,**
BERKELEY STREET, LONDON, W.1.
Offices throughout London and the Provinces.

**NORTH SPAIN** **PORTUGAL**
**MADEIRA** **MOROCCO**
**CANARY ISLANDS**
Cruises of 11 to 22 Days.
FROM £1 1S. PER DAY.
Weekly Sailings, first-class throughout.
Apply for Illustrated Brochures to:
**YEOWARD LINE**
24, James-street, Liverpool, and 60 Haymarket, London, S.W.1. or Travel Agents.

**1,000 MILES UP the AMAZON**
IN AN OCEAN LINER
s.s. HILARY, from Liverpool, February 7.
And alternate months thereafter, to PORTUGAL, MADEIRA, and BRAZIL.
CRUISE FARES, INCLUDING ALL ORGANISEED EXCURSIONS, from £75 to £100.
Apply for Illustrated Booklet of these seven weeks' cruises.
Dept. D.T.
**BOOTH LINE**
14, Adelphi-terrace, W.C. 2;
Cunard Building, Liverpool; and the usual Agents.

## ARTICLES FOR SALE AND WANTED

### FURNITURE

5FT MAHOGANY BED-ROOM SUITE, 4ft. OAK BED-ROOM SUITE, BLACK & GOLD CHINESE LACQUER CABINET, 2 WALNUT & CANE ARMCHAIRS, 2 WALNUT & CANE OCCASIONAL CHAIRS. Cost £250. What offers? Will separate. Nearly new. 28, Priestfield-road, Perry-hill, Carford.

### OFFICE EQUIPMENT

CASH REGISTERS, BACON SLICERS, AUTO SCALES, bought, sold, exchanged. Easy terms. Repairs and guaranteed overhauls. Estimates free – Deiches, 78 Long-lane, Smithfield, E.C.1. Nat. 0674.

FOR SALE, FURNITURE and FITTINGS, DRESSMAKER'S artistic SHOW ROOM and WORK ROOMS, complete £110, or offer. – Write F., Box 7,232, Daily Telegraph E.C.4.

STAFF TIME RECORDER. Urgent. – Write S., Box 7,855, Daily Telegraph, E.C.4.

TYPEWRITER EXPERTS CO., 55, Little Britain, E.C. Cash or terms. Also repairs. (Nat. 8210) SPECIAL OFFER: "UNDERWOOD." AS NEW £8 8s.

### MUSICAL INSTRUMENTS

ARNOLD LTD. SPECIAL OFFER – Slightly used. 350gns. BLUTHNER GRAND, 100gns. 50 other BARGAINS by STEINWAY, BECHSTEIN, BLUTHNER, CHAPPELL, &c. from £20. Cash or terms. Exchanges – 28, SOUTH MOLTON-ST. (Bond-st. Stn.), W.1. Open till 7.

### SUNDRY

BALDNESS – Men's looks do count. In an age when the cry, "Too old at 40," is so frequently heard, it is not mere vanity, but the bounden duty of every man to defy by all reasonable means any ageing tendency like loss of hair or premature greyness which place him at a distinct disadvantage. – Write for Booklet 14, D.T., Chaventre, 289, Oxford-street, London, W.1.

DANCE NOVELTIES – Finest show in London – GINNS 16, Red Lion-square, W.C.1. List W. free.

MICROSCOPE WANTED 1-12 oil immersion. State maker, particulars, lowest price. – Box 931, Robertson & Scott, Edinburgh.

JAFFA ORANGES DIRECT. — Case of 100 guaranteed EXTRA LARGE and choicest Jaffa Oranges 22s. 6d. carriage paid, cash with order. Ask illus. List. — H.A. GOLDNER, 63 High Holborn, W.C.1. (and at Jaffa).

A BIG PRICE PAID for metal plates and old teeth. The London Tooth Co (Dept. M.) 130, Baker-st., W.1.

# HERR HITLER PREPARES TO SUPPRESS OPPONENTS

## TWO NEWSPAPERS SEIZED IN BERLIN LAST NIGHT

## SPECIAL POLICE CHIEF WITH EXTRAORDINARY POWERS

## STORM TROOPS TO BE ARMED AND ENROLLED AS AUXILIARIES

**From Our Own Correspondent**

BERLIN, Wednesday.

Herr Hitler's determination to suppress all opposition reached a remarkable stage to-night, when the police seized all copies of two Berlin evening newspapers.

This follows a series of suppressions throughout various parts of Germany during the past week.

The rapid progress which is being made with the muzzling of the Press will virtually result in all criticism being silenced before the General Elections on March 5.

**TO CRUSH COMMUNISM**

This is not the only strong initiative which Herr Hitler is displaying. The "war against Marxism and Communism" is being carried on with unabated vigour by his Ministers, Herr von Papen and Capt. Goehring.

To-day they appointed Police-Cmdr. Stieler von Heydekamp as Special Commissioner, with extra-ordinary powers for the Rhineland and Westphalia.

This action brings all the police and gendarmes of the Rhineland under Hitler's orders, giving him power to take any action he considers necessary to crush Communism in this great industrial area.

On top of this comes a remarkable announcement that the newly-created Special Commissioner intends to arm Nazi (Hitlerite) Storm troops and use them as an auxiliary police.

**POLICE RAID KIOSKS**

**The Two Banned Papers**

The two confiscated newspapers are the "Acht-Uhr Abendblatt," which is owned by the same firm as the Liberal "Berliner Tageblatt," and the evening edition of the Socialist "Vorwaerts."

They were condemned shortly after being issued. Newspaper stalls were visited by the police, and what remained of the forbidden papers were seized.

The ground for the suppression of the papers is the account published in them of the recent shooting affray between Nazis and Communists at Eisleben.

"Vorwaerts" had collected evidence tending to discredit the official version of the affair, and the "Acht-Uhr Abendblatt" also mentioned grounds for doubting the accuracy of the police version.

I read both without noticing in them anything of an unusual character. Indeed, the opposition Press, threatened by heavy financial losses through suspension, has already become exceedingly tame.

Violent language is now confined to the Government Press, which day after day hurls unbridled insults at its political opponents, and implies that the members of the Cabinet regard their oath to the constitution as an empty form.

Orders have been issued that foreign passports are not to be given to three prominent pacifists, Herr Hellmuth von Gerlach, Herr von Ossietzky, and Herr Lehmann-Russbüldt.

**Pacificists Condemned**

Herr von Gerlach, whatever one may think of his opinions, is a man of blameless character and great courage. He has braved assassination for years in what he believes to be a holy cause.

A few days before he was forbidden to leave Germany, the Steel Helmet under the personal guidance of its candidate for the presidency, Lt-Col. Duesterberg, demanded in a formal resolution the capital punishment of Herr von Gerlach. This resolution was based on the report of a speech, which Herr von Gerlach has shown to be untrue.

In his speech at the Berlin University, the Nazi Commissary for Education in Prussia, Herr Rusts, described "the pacifist ideal" as one of the "delusive errors" which must be combated by German educational establishments.

# ESCAPED PRISONERS RECAPTURED

## ONE AGAIN CHARGED

The three prisoners who escaped from a police cell at Croydon Town Hall on Monday were recaptured yesterday.

Ernest Frederick Winter, 18 of Mitcham-road, Croydon, and Bertram Powell, 26, of High-street, Bloomsbury, were arrested last night at Thames Ditton, for alleged loitering and when taken to Kingston were recognised as two of the missing men.

The recapture of Bert Charles Mothersole, 16, of Shaftesbury-buildings, Elis David-road, Croydon, had been effected earlier in the day in Westminster.

# "RUSSIAN" OIL

## SOVIET BUYING FROM MEXICO

## FOR RESALE HERE

**By Our Motoring Correspondent**

Soviet Russia's petrol marketing organisation is purchasing motor spirit in the United States of America in order to fulfil its commitments in the United Kingdom.

I learnt yesterday from an authoritative source that a shipment of 9,000 tons (approximately 2,700,000 gallons) has been arranged by the Soviet representatives from a Gulf of Mexico port this month, and that it has been intimated that they may be in the market for a similar shipment each month for the remainder of the year.

Last year, Russian motor spirit to the amount of 76,750,000 gallons was imported into this country.

If this policy is carried out, something like 40 per cent of the "Russian" petrol delivered in Great Britain this year will come from the oilfields of Mexico and the southern States of America.

The explanation appears to be that Russia, in spite of her eagerness to export, cannot increase production fast enough to satisfy her own internal needs, and that American prices are, at the moment, so much lower than those of any European producer that buying in the "Gulf" is actually a paying proposition.

# COLOMBIA & PERU AT WAR

## GUNBOAT SHELLS TOWN

Following sharp fighting which was reported to have taken place between Peruvian and Colombian forces in the Leticia district, it is now stated that Tarapaca has been captured by the Colombians after a gunboat bombardment.

The Peruvians claim that they have inflicted considerable damage on the enemy warship Cordoba. But, according to reports from Bogota (Colombia), the attack on the Cordoba was repulsed from the air. A message from Bogota states that relations with Peru have been broken off, and that the Colombian Minister at Lima has asked for his passports.

# PRINCE SEES HIS FILM "LIFE"

When he paid a surprise visit to the Shepherd's-bush studios of the Gaumont British Picture Corporation last night, the Prince of Wales was shown a composite film in which the principal events of his life have been brought together.

He showed great interest in the film, which he has authorised himself. It is shortly to be leased to cinemas all over the world for the benefit of the funds of the National Services League.

# ENGLAND WIN BY SIX WICKETS

## 'ASHES' REGAINED AT BRISBANE

## AUSTRALIA FIGHT TO THE END

## LEYLAND'S SPLENDID INNINGS

## PAYNTER'S SIX

England won the Fourth Test Match at Brisbane to-day by 6 wickets, and so regained the Ashes, which the Australians won on their last visit to England.

**Sixth Day of Match**

**ENGLAND. – Second Innings (continued)**

| | |
|---|---|
| **Leyland, c McCabe, b O'Reilly** | **86** |
| **Hammond, c Bromley, b Ironmonger** | **14** |
| **Ames, not out** | **14** |
| **Paynter, not out** | **14** |
| **Extras** | **9** |
| **Total (4 wickets)** | **163** |

## BRISBANE CRICKET GROUND

Thursday Morning

Rain fell in the early hours of the morning, and, after a brief stoppage, more light rain began to fall at nine o'clock. It ceased at eleven o'clock, however, and play was resumed soon after noon.

A monsoon appears imminent, and it looked at first like being a race between the rain and cricket, for once the monsoon breaks one never can tell when the rain will cease.

The weather was still overcast and the skies looked threatening when Jardine inspected the wicket at 11.15 and 11.45.

Five minutes before play was due to be resumed he had the light roller put on the wicket.

The Australian and M.C.C. flags were flown at half-mast, and the umpires and fieldsmen wore black arm-bands as a mark of respect for Archie Jackson, who died yesterday.

**THE PREVIOUS TESTS**

*The three previous Test matches in Australia resulted as follows:*

**Sydney** – England, won by 10 wickets. Australia, 360 and 164; England, 524 and 1 for none.

**Melbourne** – Australia won by 111 runs. Australia, 228 and 191; England 169 and 139.

**Adelaide** – England won by 338 runs. England, 341 and 412; Australia, 222 and 193.

There were only a handful of spectators present when Leyland and Hammond came out to endeavour to hit off the 53 runs still required to win the match, rubber, and Ashes.

WALL INJURED

Tobin fielded for Wall, who injured his ankle yesterday.

The wicket did not appear to be affected by the rain when play was resumed at 12.5.

Leyland sent the English score of 107 for 2 in motion with a leg-glance off Ironmonger's first ball.

O'Reilly bowled into the wind at the other end. Both bowlers struck their length at once, and with neither batsman willing to take risks scoring was slow.

Ironmonger and O'Reilly were very accurate, and the score was increased only by a single at a time. The first half-hour yielded only nine runs.

Hammond was out at 118. His first aggressive stroke proved his downfall. He mistimed a ball from Ironmonger on the off side and Bromley at cover point made a good catch. Hammond has made the same mistake several times during the tour.

He batted 71 minutes for his 14, which was made up almost entirely of singles to the leg.

AMES IN

Ames, promoted in the batting order, was next man in and Leyland welcomed him by making a huge and lofty ondrive off Ironmonger to the boundary. Ames got off the mark with a deft single to leg.

Leyland was timing the ball well and when 76 he pulled Ironmonger for another boundary. He also scored well to the on. Woodfull sent Ponsford out to the on-side fence, but victory was now in sight.

England had made 133 of the 160 needed.

At this point Wall came limping out with drinks for the players.

Leyland continued to dominate the batting, but when he seemed likely to last out the innings he felt for a ball from O'Reilly and edged it into the slips for McCabe, at short slip, to make a fine catch. This was at 128.

Leyland made his 86 in 3 hours 42 minutes, and hit nine 4's and one 5. It was a fine innings at a crisis. Paynter made the winning stroke – a splendid hook off McCabe for 6 over the boundary. - Reuter.

# ATTEMPT ON LIFE OF MR. ROOSEVELT

## FIVE SHOTS FIRED AT U.S. PRESIDENT-ELECT

## UNINJURED

## OUTRAGE AT MIAMI RECEPTION

## MAYOR CERMAK & OTHERS HIT

MIAMI, FLORIDA, Thursday Morning.

AN ATTEMPT WAS MADE HERE LAST NIGHT TO ASSASSINATE MR. FRANKLIN ROOSEVELT, THE U.S. PRESIDENT-ELECT.

FIVE SHOTS WERE FIRED AT HIM, BUT HAPPILY HE ESCAPED INJURY.

Several persons were injured, including: Mayor Cermak, of Chicago – seriously.

Mrs. Joseph Gill, wife of the president of the Florida Power and Light Company.

A detective guarding Mr. Roosevelt and several bystanders.

The name of the assailant is given as Jose Zingara. He is said to be a Spaniard from New York City.

The assailant was seized and is now lodged in prison.

AT A RECEPTION

The shooting occurred at a public reception in the Bay Front Park at Biscayne Bay.

Mr. Roosevelt

Mr. Roosevelt had just reached Miami in the yacht Nourmahal and was standing in his touring car when the assailant opened fire.

In the car were also Mr. Dave Shots, Governor of Florida, Mr. A.G. Rennerick, of the New York City Police, and two secret service officers.

Mr. Roosevelt had just completed a brief speech to a crowd of 10,000 and was saying, "I thank you," when the shots were fired.

GRAPPLED WITH ASSAILANT

Mr. Roosevelt, according to one report, immediately sat down in the rear seat of his open touring car.

Brodnaux, a secret service agent, is credited with saving Mr. Roosevelt from injury, as he threw himself on the assailant and received a shot in the head. It is feared that his pluck and bravery may cost him his life.

The reception was a gala affair attended by fashionable holiday-makers at this favourite winter playground. There are large numbers of English people among the holiday population. The gaily-decorated city is now aghast at the attempted assassination.

One report is that Mr. Roosevelt at once drove to the station. Another says that he took Mayor Cermak to hospital early to-day.

The condition of Mayor Cermak is serious.

Mr. Cermak was standing about twenty paces from Mr. Roosevelt when the shooting began. - Reuter, Exchange, and B.U.P.

## MRS. ROOSEVELT'S COMMENT

WASHINGTON, Thursday.

"That's great," cried Mrs. Franklin Roosevelt, smiling, when she was told in New York of her husband's escape.

"You've got to expect these things," she added.

She was deeply grieved to hear of Mayor Cermak's condition and hurried to the telephone to get details from her husband himself.

The secret service chiefs have ordered the guards around Mr. Roosevelt to be doubled immediately.

The police guard round the White House has been increased.

President Hoover has cabled to Mr. Roosevelt, "I rejoice that you have not been injured."

The President states that he is shocked by the outrage. – Reuter.

# GOLD FOR BRITAIN

## £2,000,000 PURCHASE

For the fifth time since Dec. 15 the Bank of England announced yesterday a substantial purchase of bar gold.

On this occasion the amount was just over £2,000,000. This acquisition means that, out of the £19,000,000 which the Bank sold to the Treasury for the purpose of making the War Debt payment to America, nearly £12,500,000 have been replaced.

# INSULL FAMILY GAINS

## £5,000,000 PROFIT ON ALL NEW ISSUE

**From Our Own Correspondent**

WASHINGTON, Wednesday.

The Senate Banking Committee's inquiry into the collapse of the £200,000,000 Insull Utility "Empire" opened to-day.

Mr. Samuel Insull, junior, the first witness, admitted that members of the Insull family made a profit of £5,000,000 when shares of the Insull Utilities Investments, Incorporated, were offered to the public in January, 1929.

According to Mr. Insull, however, the profits were paper because the shares were now practically worthless, and so far as he knew not one of the members of the family syndicate had unloaded his holdings. "As a matter of fact," he said, "I am broke."

PUBLIC'S LOSSES

The object of the committee's inquiry was to reveal the manner in which the public lost hundreds of millions of dollars invested with the Insull concern, and to probe into Stock Exchange methods. Incidentally, the committee desires to ascertain to what extent public officials were "let in on the ground floor" – presumably for favours rendered or in prospect.

The Insull family exercised options on Utilities Investment shares at from 20s to 30s a share, according to Mr. Insull, on the day they were offered on the Chicago Stock Exchange at £6 a share.

Mr. Pecora, counsel for the Senate Committee, questioned the right of the Insull family when dealing among themselves to grab overnight a profit of more than £5,000,000. In defence Mr. Insull said the money was paid long before the public was offered them, and no one expected the shares to sell so high.

Mr. Samuel Insull, senior, his son testified, had also apparently no idea of the heights to which the shares would soar. Although he purchased 250,000 shares for the family syndicate at 48s a share, he disposed of them to others at the same price before they were listed on the exchange.

MR OWEN YOUNG A WITNESS

Mr. Owen D. Young, chairman of the Board of the General Electric, sat in the crowded committee-room smoking his pipe, and awaiting his turn as a witness. Mr. Young was listed as one of those who were given an opportunity to buy Insull stock at a low price before it was offered for public subscription.

Evidence was put before the federal Grand Jury to-day by the U.S. District Attorney in support of the indictment of Mr. Samuel Insull, senior, and Mr. Martin Insull. They are to be charged, it is said, with using the postal service with intent to defraud and concealing assets in bankruptcy.

# NEW PEERS TAKE THE OATH

## IMPRESSIVE RITUAL

**From Our Special Representative**

WESTMINSTER, Wednesday.

The picturesque brilliance of ancient ceremonial began to-day's sitting of the House of Lords. Three peers lately created, Lord Runciman, the father of the President of the Board of Trade, Lord Brocket, and Lord Milne were sworn in with that impressive ritual which the time-honoured order of the Upper House has handed down.

Black Rod came into the Chamber first, leading the way for the Earl Marshal, the young Duke of Norfolk. After them followed in their robes of scarlet and ermine Lord Runciman, between his sponsors, Lord Rhayader, still better known by his House of Commons name as the resolute Liberal, Mr. Leif Jones, and Lord Armstrong, a Conservative.

Lord Runciman took the oath in a clear voice, hesitating a little over some of the quaint, old phraseology. After signing the roll he and his sponsors proceeded to the top bench next Black Rod's box. In front of him stood Garter King of Arms, and called on him to "Sit down. Rise. Take off your hat. Bow to the Throne."

This obeisance the Lord Chancellor acknowledged, and the procession passed out of the House as it had come. But on the way, Lord Runciman, as the order of the ceremony provides, stopped and shook hands with the Chancellor, who gave him more than formal greeting. Thereafter Lord Runciman discarded his robes and took his seat on the Government side. In like manner the other peers were introduced. Lord Brocket had as his sponsors Lord Desborough and Lord Vivian. Lord Milne was accompanied by Lord Trenchard and Lord Ellenborough.

## COAL OUTPUT RECORD LOW

The Board of Trade review of the coal-mining industry during 1932, and the fourth quarter of the year, was published last night. It shows that the output of saleable coal for the whole year was 209,250,000 tons, a total which was less than the output of the previous year by 10,250,000 tons.

# GREAT FIRE IN GERMAN REICHSTAG

## ASSEMBLY HALL COMPLETELY DESTROYED

**From Our Own Correspondent**

BERLIN, Monday Night.

The German Reichstag was deliberately set on fire in no fewer than twenty places to-night, and the great hall where the Deputies actually meet was completely destroyed.

Several arrests have been made. One man, stated to be a Dutch Communist, is reported to have confessed to the outrage and to starting a fire in the Imperial Palace.

All the seats of the Deputies and the galleries of the diplomats, Press and public were destroyed. The iron pillars supporting the great golden dome are twisted, and the whole structure has been endangered.

I passed the Reichstag at 9.30 this evening. All was apparently normal. Twenty minutes later I received an urgent call that flames were bursting from the dome, which is one of the famous landmarks of Berlin.

Herr Hitler and Prince August Wilhelm, son of the ex-Kaiser, were two of the first to arrive at the Reichstag.

They were quickly followed by Capt. Goehring, President of the Reichstag, and Herr von Papen. They all entered the building to watch the firemen trying to save the lobby and the library.

THRILLING SPECTACLE
Thousands Gather

The glowing reflection of the flames could be seen through the vast glazed cupola which surmounts the building, and within an exceedingly wide radius, and tens of thousands of people flocked from all over the city to witness the thrilling spectacle.

It is understood that several fires were started in the main Session Hall of the Reichstag, which are used by the deputies.

Before midnight the fire had been so far subdued that it was possible to admit journalists into the building to inspect the damage. The woodwork was still smouldering in the central hall, which was unapproachable, and water must be poured on to it for some hours to come before the last spark is extinguished.

In the course of the investigations inside the structure it was found that the incendiaries had used for their purpose rags soaked in petroleum, and wood shavings.

HOW FIRE WAS STARTED
Suspect's Alleged Story

According to one account the foreigner who has been arrested, and who is said to be a Dutch Communist, aged 24, was actually found in the central hall.

He was dressed only in his trousers and shirt, having torn up his jacket and used it to start one of the fires.

He is said to have admitted that he found his way into the Reichstag early in the afternoon and succeeded in secreting himself until nightfall, when he proceeded to make preparations for starting the fire.

**(February 28)**

# COURTS TO TRY UNFIT

## SPECIAL TRIBUNALS

**From Our Own Correspondent**

BERLIN, Wednesday.

Special "Sterilisation Courts" are to be set up for the operation of the new law which becomes effective on Jan. 1. These will be composed of a jurist, a medical man with the dignity of an official, and a second medical man who has made a special study of eugenics.

As was reported in the later editions of The Daily Telegraph yesterday, the Bill provides for the sterilisation of persons suffering from

Congenital imbecility;
Madness;
Hereditary epilepsy;
Hereditary St. Vitus's dance;
Hereditary blindness and deafness;
Hereditary grave physical malformation; and
Chronic alcoholism.

The proposal for sterilisation may be made by the person himself (or herself), a guardian, a doctor in an official capacity, or by the head of a hospital. Every proposal must be submitted to the special Court.

If the Court decides that the person concerned shall be sterilised, this could be done against his or her will and, if the Court orders, with the application of force.

**(July 27)**

# THE REICHSTAG FIRE TRIAL JUDGMENT

**From Our Own Correspondent**

BERLIN, Tuesday.

The reasoned judgment in the Reichstag fire trial, which was read by the presiding judge, Dr. Buenger, at Leipzig on Saturday, fell into two sections. These sections were so different from one another that it seemed impossible that their authorship should be the same.

The first part of the judgment was a lucid and even ruthless analysis of the evidence.

This confirmed in full the impression which I had conveyed in my previous messages that many of the witnesses upon whom the prosecution based the brunt of their case were thoroughly unreliable. By this courageous and clear-cut judgment Dr. Buenger redeemed the promise which he made a week before that the Court would pass its sentence "undisturbed by the clash of opinion outside."

Among the points contained in the judgment were:

The acquittals are based on insufficient evidence;

Van der Lubbe is guilty of treason, the overt act being arson with intent to bring about a revolution and attempted simple arson;

Besides the death sentence Lubbe is "permanently deprived of civic rights" which in any case as a Dutch subject he does not possess in Germany;

Lubbe could not possibly have fired the Reichstag alone, but his accomplices are unknown;

Lubbe was "undoubtedly a Communist in his convictions and in his deeds."

The second portion of the judgment was more reminiscent of an election speech than a legal opinion.

A highly controversial attack on the Communist party, it was evidently intended to appease the wilder Nazis. Their views have been put forward on more than one occasion during the trial, and their spokesmen are Gen. Goering and the notorious Breslau Chief of Police Lt. Heines.

PRESS CRITICISM
ACQUITTALS "OUTRAGE"

The German Press in commenting on the trial, finds itself in a quandary. On the one hand it deplores what more extreme papers flatly denounce as a "miscarriage of justice." On the other hand, it boasts that the verdict has "left foreign traducers of Nazi justice without a leg to stand on."

Within a few hours of the verdict the official Press Bureau of the Nazi party issued a fiery statement in which the acquittals of Torgler and the Bulgarians "on formal juridical grounds" was described as an outrage "to the German nation's sense of justice."

The official Nazi organ, the "Voelkische Boebachter," adds to this manifesto the confident prediction that "National-Socialist Germany will know how to draw the necessary consequences from the Leipzig verdict, and quickly put an end to conditions which are calculated to impair the success of the Nazi revolution."

**(December 6)**



# STORM TROOPS GOOSE STEP BEFORE HITLER

## "NAZIS SAFE FOR 100 YEARS"

**From Our Special Representative**

NUREMBERG, Sunday.

To-day 120,000 troops marched past Herr Hitler, the Chancellor, during the Nazi celebrations here. Many of the squadrons broke into the "goose step."

The big rally ended this evening with a final speech by the Chancellor.

In the course of it he declared that 3,000,000 fighting men had organised themselves as champions of the "leaders of Germany."

The proceedings have proved that the Nazis, although convinced that their regime will remain triumphant for the next 100 years and more, have abandoned nothing of their extremist views.

The anti-Semitic speeches of Herr Hitler and of his propaganda Minister, Dr. Goebbels, the Pan-German theories of art and life propounded by many other speakers, and the self-glorification of the Nazi leaders in the riot of jingo patriotism expressed in terms of drums, trumpets, banners, uniforms, and tens of thousands of marching men have all shown that Hitlerite fanaticism is unabated.

If the Nuremberg rally is indeed a triumph for Herr Hitler it is a triumph organised by his leaders and celebrated by masses of his followers.

Herr Hitler, in an address, said that the German people did not desire war, because having during the last war withstood almost unaided for four and a half years the attacks of overwhelming odds, Germany had emerged with more honour than her enemies, and had no lost reputation to retrieve on the battlefield.

In an important speech outlining the Nazi Jewish policy, Dr. Goebbels claimed yesterday that the Jews were themselves responsible for their treatment in Nazi Germany. It was not Germany's fault that the Jewish race represented a constant danger to the security of the Fatherland.

They had boycotted German goods and spread atrocity reports, and they had for years monopolised positions in the professions out of all proportion to their percentage of the population. No hair of any Jew's head had, he said, been harmed in Germany "without good reason."

**(September 4)**

# FIRST VISIT TO A NAZI PRISON CAMP

**From G.E.R. Gedye**

DACHAU, Bavaria, Sunday.

By special permission of the Nazi political police I have been the first journalist allowed to visit the concentration camp for 5,000 political prisoners in the disused munition factory here. I was given a special permit and a numbered white armlet for identification, and escorted to the headquarters of Prison Commandant Wekerle.

The prison camp consists of concrete huts used by the munition workers until 1918, and now surrounded by a double high fence of barbed wire charged with electricity at a deadly high voltage. The space between this fence is patrolled day and night by armed sentries, and the prisoners are warned that any who attempt to escape will be shot without challenge.

KILLED IN DASH FOR FREEDOM

"Four made a dash for freedom last week," the Commandant told me. "They ignored the challenge to halt. They got a hundred yards before the bullets hit them; three were killed."

Entering the prison compound with the commandant, I saw 530 prisoners at work repairing huts for the use of the 3,000 or 4,000 other Bavarian political prisoners at present detained in ordinary prisons. "These men," said the commandant, "are not charged with any crime, but are under Schutzhaft– 'protective arrest.'

"They were all arrested as leaders of the Bavarian Communist party. Most of them are workmen, but there are several doctors, lawyers, writers, students and a couple of Communist deputies of the Reichstag and of the Bavarian Diet."

In the centre of each hut four tiers of wooden shelves have been put up, and on these the fifty-four inmates sleep, each on a straw sack with a blanket, separated from one another by a plank 4in high.

In one hut I saw a Jewish doctor prisoner conducting the fortnightly examination; in another a prisoner started to play a mandolin just as we entered.

Life in Dachau seems something between a severely disciplined regiment and penal servitude. The mental hardship of detention without trial by the ukase of the Nazi political department for an unknown period to be arbitrarily fixed by them, with total separation from family and friends, and the herding together of intellectual "drawing-room Communists" and degenerates, is tempered for some by the absence of solitary confinement. But the fate of those who are the victim of some private grudge in the wave of denunciations by informers is unenviable.

**(April 4)**

# BOYCOTT OF JEWS IN GERMANY IN FULL SWING

## DOCTORS & LAWYERS AFFECTED

**From Our Own Correspondent**

BERLIN, Thursday.

Only the Government papers now print details of the boycott of Jews, which officially is to begin on Saturday. In reality it is already in force in many parts of Germany.

At Breslau 28 Jewish doctors were to-day dismissed from municipal institutions. All Jews in the town are to be deprived of passports permitting them to leave the country.

The new Police Prefect Lt. Heines, declared that the Nazis would "brutally destroy whoever opposed the State or dared to tamper with the freedom and dignity of Nationalist Germany."

In some towns Jewish shops have been closed, while in others customers were prevented from entering them. At Nordhausen the offices of Jewish lawyers and the consulting rooms of Jewish doctors were also closed.

A proclamation was issued here to-night urging all Germans to avoid Jewish shops and businesses, and to consult no Jewish lawyer or doctor. The proclamation closes with the significant words: "Whoever acts contrary to the boycott proves that he is on the side of Germany's enemies."

Jewish doctors and nurses employed in Munich municipal hospitals may in future attend only Jewish patients, and Jewish doctors and students of medicine may in future dissect only Jewish corpses.

**(March 31)**

# REPRISALS PLANS

## STAFFS OF CLOSED SHOPS NOT TO BE DISMISSED

**From Our Own Correspondent**

MUNICH, Thursday.

The central committee in Munich of the anti-Jewish boycott campaign announces that all Jewish shops will be picketed by Nazis, who will "warn" would-be purchasers that the establishment is under Jewish proprietorship. The pickets are to behave "tactfully," and must not resort to force.

Jewish shops are not to be forcibly closed, nor is property to be destroyed. But Jews who may elect to close their establishments may not dismiss their employees nor enforce any wage-cuts. Multiple and single-price stores not under Jewish ownership will not be picketed.

**(March 31)**

# STORM CLOUDS IN EUROPE

## MR. CHURCHILL AND GERMAN MENACE

Three "evil and dangerous storm-clouds which either overhang us or lie on the horizon" were mentioned by Mr. Winston Churchill in a speech at a garden fête at Theydon Bois, Essex, on Saturday.

Mr. Churchill said the first of the three clouds that threatened was the state of Europe. "Nobody can watch the events which are taking place in Germany," he continued, "without increasing anxiety about what their outcome will be.

"At present Germany is only partly armed and most of her fury is turned upon herself. But already her smaller neighbours, Austria, Switzerland, Belgium and Denmark, feel a deep disquietude. There is grave reason to believe that Germany is arming herself or seeking to arm herself contrary to the solemn treaties exacted from her in her hour of defeat.

KEEPING OUR FORCES EFFICIENT

"I have always opposed this rearmament of Germany, and have criticised in the House of Commons all this foolish talk of placing her upon some kind of equality with France. The same people and the same perverse school of thought in England and the United States that have already weakened the British Navy sought to weaken the French army. But the French most prudently refused to hearken to this hazardous advice, and the fact that they refused is the main foundation of the peace of Europe to-day.

"I hope our National Government, and especially the Cabinet Ministers in charge of the Navy, the Army, and the Air Force, will make sure that the Forces of the Crown are left in a proper state of efficiency, and that they will be strong enough to enable us to count for something when we work for peace, and strong enough if war should come in Europe to maintain our effective neutrality, unless we should decide of our own free will to the contrary.

"Always remember that Britain's hour of weakness is Europe's hour of danger."

**(August 14)**

# EINSTEIN'S DECISION TO RENOUNCE GERMAN CITIZENSHIP

BRUSSELS, Thursday.

Professor Einstein, the famous scientist, has written a letter to the German Legation in Brussels asking what steps he should take to renounce his German citizenship.

He has informed the Legation that he has resigned from the German Academy of Science. The letter has been sent to the German Foreign Ministry in Berlin.

Professor Einstein is a Jew. Although he is a pacifist, his house near Berlin was recently searched for arms. – B.U.P.

# GERMAN BAN ON WORLD AUTHORS

An immense "black list" of books which the Hitlerites will remove from all public and municipal libraries has been published.

It includes some, or all, the works of the following authors known outside Germany:

| | |
|---|---|
| Schalom Asche | Arnold and |
| Henri Barbuse | Stefan Zweig |
| Ilya Ehrenburg | Adrienne Thomas |
| Lion Feuchtwanger | Eduard Bernstein |
| Heinrich Mann | Kautsky |
| Eric Remarque | Lassalle |
| Ludwig Renn | Lenin |
| Artur Schnitzler | Karl Marx |
| Richard Beer-Hofmann | Karl Liebknecht |
| | Walter Rathenau |
| Ernst Toller | Upton Sinclair |
| August Bebel | |

**(April 27)**

# The Daily Telegraph MUNICH CORRESPONDENT ARRESTED

Information was received by The Daily Telegraph last night that Mr. Noel D. Panter, the Daily Telegraph Correspondent in Munich, was arrested there yesterday by the political police.

Shortly after Mr. Panter's arrest his flat was raided and all his papers were removed.

No communication from Mr. Panter has been received by The Daily Telegraph, and it is not known on what charge he has been arrested.

The British Consul-General at Munich, Mr. D. St. C. Gainer, has applied to see Mr. Panter, but has been refused permission to do so "at the present stage."

Mr. Gainer has expressed his surprise at the refusal, and, it is understood, intends to renew his request to-day in urgent form.

Mr. Panter, who is 31 years of age, is an experienced journalist with some years' standing as foreign correspondent in European cities. Between 1925 and 1928 he acted as Rhineland correspondent for the "Times."

**(October 25)**

# MR. PANTER TO BE RELEASED

The German Foreign Office last night informed the British Embassy in Berlin that Mr. Panter, Munich correspondent of The Daily Telegraph, was to be released from prison in Munich.

According to a semi-official communiqué issued in Berlin, Mr. Panter is also to be expelled from the country.

**(November 22)**

# "PALESTINE NOT A DUMPING-GROUND"

## JEWS FROM GERMANY

Mr. Ormsby-Gore, First Commissioner of Works, declared at a meeting of the Sixth Commission of the Assembly to-day that Palestine could not be made a dumping-ground for tens of thousands of Jewish refugees escaping from Hitler persecution.

In a speech on the subject of mandates he pointed out that the present development of Palestine was largely due to the enterprise and capital of the Jewish immigrants themselves. In the first half of 1932 the number of immigrants was 5,000. In 1933 that number had increased to 15,000.

The Jews entering Palestine came from every country in the world, but it was impossible for the quota based to be changed because of the present abnormal circumstances. The process of immigration must be regulated, and the country should not be allowed to receive more immigrants than it could absorb.

**(October 3)**

# NO FROCKS FOR MISS DIETRICH

When Miss Marlene Dietrich sailed from here for a holiday in Europe late last night she admitted that her inumerable trunks did not contain one woman's dress. Attired in a well-cut dinner jacket, and trousers, she declared that her present style of dress was not universally suited to women.

Miss Dietrich was accompanied by her daughter, Maria, who was closely guarded because of threats from kidnappers.

**(May 15)**

# TOWER OFFICE IN WANDSWORTH PRISON

## CASHIERED & FIVE YEARS

Found guilty of seven of the ten charges preferred against him at the Court-martial at Chelsea last month, Lt. Norman Baillie-Stewart, the Seaforth Highlanders, the "officer in the Tower," has been sentenced to be: Cashiered, and to suffer penal servitude for the term of five years.

There is no right of appeal.

"Cashiering" is more severe than mere dismissal from the service, inasmuch as it disqualifies from entering the public service in any capacity, which dismissal does not.

The sentence will be served at Maidstone Prison. It is assumed that the prisoner, like other convicts, will be able to earn a remission of sentence, amounting to three months a year, for good conduct.

The War Office, announcing the sentence, states:

"The King, on the advice of the Secretary of State for War, has confirmed the findings of the Court on the 2nd, 4th and 9th charges laid under section 41 of the Army Act of obtaining, collecting and communicating information which might be useful to an enemy for a purpose prejudicial to the interests of the State, contrary to the provisions of the Official Secrets Acts, 1911 and 1920.

When the sentence was read to him at the Tower, where he had been detained since the close of the court-martial, Lt. Baillie-Stewart maintained the calm he showed throughout the seven days of the trial.

**(April 15)**

# POLICEMAN OF THE FUTURE

What the policeman of the future has to know – and wear — are set out with great particularity and wealth of detail in a booklet Lord Trenchard has issued for the information of those desiring to becomes candidates for the Metropolitan Police College.

The number to be taken into the college during the first year will be about sixty, divided into two groups, the first in the late spring and the second in September. Approximately two-thirds of this total will be selected (without educational examination) from those now serving in the Metropolitan Force as sergeants and constables who are still under 28 years of age (or in exceptional cases 30).

The remaining one-third will be taken in part by open competitive examination (in February) and in part (later in the year) by selection from candidates who have reached an educational standard regarded as sufficient to exempt them from any further educational test.

### THE STANDARD REQUIRED

Those who contemplate taking the competitive examination are notified in the booklet that unless they have reached at least School Certificate standard their prospects are slight. The subjects of the examination bear out this statement fully. They are:

| *Part 1 – Obligatory* | *Part 11 – Optional* |
|---|---|
| English | Latin |
| General Knowledge | Greek |
| Interview and Record | French |
| One of the following: | German |
| A Modern Language | Modern History |
| General History | Lower Mathematics |
| Elementary | Higher Mathematics |
| Mathematics | Physics plus Chemistry |
| Everyday Science | Biology |

Those appointed to the college will be provided with uniform free of charge. But the plain clothes which they will have themselves to provide is a comprehensive wardrobe. The articles required are:

| | |
|---|---|
| *3 Pairs Flannel Trousers* | *2 Suits Pyjamas* |
| *3 Tennis Shirts* | *½ doz. Collars* |
| *2 Pairs Shorts* | *Dinner Jacket Suit* |
| *1 Sweater* | *4 Dress Shirts* |
| *1 Pair Gymnastic Shoes* | *Patent Shoes* |
| *1 Overcoat* | *2 Pairs Ordinary Shoes* |
| *2 Lounge Suits* | *Suit Case* |
| *1 Hat* | *Cabin Trunk* |
| *3 Shirts* | *3 Towels* |
| *4 Vests* | *Tooth Brush* |
| *4 Pairs Drawers* | *Hair Brush and Comb* |
| *6 Pairs Half-Hose* | *Razor* |
| *3 Pairs Stockings* | *Clothes Brush* |

Handkerchiefs, curiously enough, are not mentioned.

**(November 24)**

# SPORTING BURGLAR

A unique Christmas box reached the Rev. E. L. Macassey, Vicar of St. Andrew's, Stoke Newington, yesterday.

In a neat package was a magnificent silver-gilt Communion set. The vicar thought the vessels had a familiar look, and presently recognised them as having belonged to St. Andrew's. They were stolen from the church eighteen months ago by a skilled burglar, and now they were back again for the Christmastide celebrations.

Mr. Macassey afterwards said: "I thank this burglar, and am glad that his conscience turned him into a sportsman. I wish him a happy Christmas."

**(December 22)**

# THIRD DAY OF GREAT HEATH FIRES

## BOURNEMOUTH RINGED WITH FLAME

For the third successive day big heath and woodland fires devastated large areas of the country yesterday.

The most serious outbreaks again occurred in Hampshire. One, at St. Ives, spread for miles along the Ringwood-Wimborne road, on the edge of the New Forest.

Bournemouth was ringed with fire, the flames in places leaping 50 feet in the air. Firemen fought desperately for two hours to save the Royal Naval Cordite Factory at Holton Heath, near Wareham.

Camberley brigade was called out three times in four hours to fires threatening a girls' orphanage at Hawley, the Brompton Hospital Sanatorium at Frimley and other buildings. Thousands of acres were blackened, but the buildings were saved.

Relays of soldiers from Aldershot and Bordon, stripped to the waist and wearing steel helmets and gas masks, fought further serious outbreaks in the Hartford Bridge area, the scene of Monday's big blaze, and on Slab Common, near Bordon.

Many parts of Southern England enter to-day on the fourth period of absolute drought — fifteen days with no appreciable rain — experienced this year. There is no indication yet of a break in the dry sunny conditions, and the shortage of water is causing grave concern to farmers.

**(September 7)**

# SIR O. MOSLEY AND FASCISTS STONED

**From Our Own Correspondent**

MANCHESTER, Sunday.

Sir Oswald Mosley and a London contingent of 500 Fascist "storm troops" were stoned in Manchester to-night. They were ambushed when marching to the station, after Sir Oswald had addressed the largest blackshirt demonstrations yet held in the Provinces. Several were injured.

About 3,000 Fascists attended the meeting at Belle Vue, and disorder was feared owing to the fact that another demonstration, in support of the victims of German Fascism, was being held in the Free Trade Hall.

Sir Oswald lead the procession from the local headquarters for the first mile, but then, owing to a slight back injury, withdrew.

Catcalls, boos, cries of "Down with Fascism," and "Up the Communists," were hurled at the marching ranks from the crowds who kept pace with them, but, under a strong guard of police, the marchers reached Belle Vue without incident.

### People Ejected

Trouble broke out at the meeting when a woman heckler was rebuked by the "body-guard." Members of the audience took the woman's part, and in a moment a free fight was in progress. Several of the combatants were knocked down, and several members of the audience were forcibly ejected.

"I call you to witness," said Sir Oswald, "that violence is not employed by Fascism except against those who try to make free speech impossible."

The meeting then proceeded quietly, but as the London contingent of Fascists was leaving the grounds headed by a band it was ambushed by young men who came suddenly down a side street and attacked the marching column.

The blackshirts broke their ranks and made a counter-attack. A series of fierce scrimmages broke out, blows being freely exchanged. Several of the stone-throwers were felled.

Then the police charged, and, though the crowd scattered, a number were knocked out. The Fascists were immediately recalled by bugle, and they reached the railway station without further disturbance.

**(October 16)**

# BOOTS' SHARE DEAL

After being in American ownership for thirteen years, Boots Pure Drug Co. returned to British control yesterday.

It is officially stated that 1,000,000 shares in the company have been acquired from the United Drug Co., a subsidiary of Drug Incorporated. These shares have been placed among leading insurance companies, banks, and other investment and financial institutions at a price of £6 15s per share.

**(May 9)**

# DISTINGUISHED INVALIDS

The Marquis of Lansdowne (operation); Going on very well.

Lord Irwin (influenza): Able to leave his room.

Lord Baden-Powell: Much better.

Lord Ebbisham: Going on well.

Lord Remnant (pneumonia): No weaker.

Lord Sandhurst (scarlet fever): Satisfactory.

Lord Beaverbrook: Confined to bed with a high temperature.

Countess Cave: Improving slowly.

Mr. John Galsworthy (anæmia): Condition unchanged.

Mr. F. T. Barrington-Ward, K. C. (injured in collision): Much better.

**(January 30)**

# 3 NEW THAMES BRIDGES OPEN TO-DAY

The Prince of Wales in one hour to-day will open three new bridges over the Thames, providing a system of road arteries which will make the great South-West more accessible and will simplify London's outlet to the countryside and upriver resorts.

Costing together more than £500,000, each new bridge represents one of three new ways out of London.

They are all built on the same broad lines, they bear the unmistakable imprint of their designers. The graceful spans at Hampton Court are the creation of Sir Edward Lutyens; Sir Herbert Baker is responsible for the sweeping lines of that at Richmond, and the forceful structure at Chiswick, evolved by Mr. Maxwell Ayrton, contains the longest concrete arch over the Thames, the centre span being over 150 ft long.

Chiswick and Twickenham are new bridges, but the one at Hampton Court is the fourth to be built at that spot. The third bridge was demolished recently, and the new design takes into complete consideration the historic associations of the site.

An official of the Automobile Association told a representative of The Daily Telegraph yesterday that, in his opinion, the new bridges would be used very extensively.

**(July 3)**

# THE NATIONAL GALLERY

## DIRECTOR AGED 30

It is announced from No. 10, Downing Street, that the Lords Commissioners of his Majesty's Treasury have appointed Mr. Kenneth Clark, Keeper of the Department of Fine Art in the Ashmolean Museum, Oxford, to be Director of the National Gallery, in succession to Sir Augustus Daniel, whose term of office expires on Dec. 31. The appointment is for a term of five years.

An Art Correspondent writes:

The first impression conveyed by Mr. Kenneth Clark's appointment to the Directorship of the National Gallery will be one of surprise that such a young man of 30 has been selected for such an important post, but Mr. Clark is as brilliant in his particular sphere as many headmasters who are appointed to public schools in their early manhood.

The National gallery Trustees are obviously hoping that he will have a long tenure of office. His youngest predecessor in the directorship, Sir Charles Holmes, was 48, when he was appointed in 1916.

Mr. Clark's association with that outstanding authority on Italian art, Mr. Bernhard Berenson, will be of eminent service to him in his new work. A very fine training ground, too, was provided for Mr. Clark when he succeeded Mr. Charles Francis Bell two years ago as Keeper of the Department of Fine Art in the Ashmolean Museum, which is especially rich in early Italian pictures.

**(September 2)**

# DEVIL'S ISLAND FOR U.S. GANGSTERS

WASHINGTON, Thursday.

The U.S. Department of Justice has selected a desolate island as a penal colony for gangsters.

Alcatraz Island, near San Francisco, is the spot selected. On it will be kept desperate Federal convicts, such as gangsters, racketeers, and kidnappers of the type of "Machine-gun" Kelly.

**(October 13)**

# UNITED DEFENCE POLICY FOR BRITAIN

**All Services to be Treated as One**
— Mr. Baldwin

**Air Force Equal to the Strongest**
— Lord Londonderry

## INSISTANCE ON PARITY ... BUT AT LOWEST POSSIBLE LEVEL

Two important declarations on Britain's defence policy were made yesterday.

Mr. Baldwin announced in the House of Commons that, in future, the defence of the country — Navy, Army and Air — would be examined as a whole and united estimates presented.

The Marquis of Londonderry, Minister for Air, told the House of Lords that we could no longer continue unilateral disarmament in the air. Our Air Force must be at least as strong as that of any other nation.

Declaring that we stood to-day fifth in the world's air Powers – with only 850 machines, compared with 1,650 in France, over 1,400 in Russia, and over 1,000 each in America and Italy – Lord Londonderry said:

**Our example has elicited no response;**

**We cannot continue in our present inferiority;**

**But a race in air armaments must be avoided at all costs;**

**If other countries will not reduce we must begin to build upwards – while continuing our efforts to fix parity to the lowest level to which other nations will subscribe.**

Mr. Baldwin emphasised that the Government had not lost hope of achieving regulated disarmament. "We are going on," he said, "by every means we can, to achieve an agreed result.

**(November 30)**

# THE MOTOR POSTMAN

## MECHANISING THE G.P.O. SERVICES

The days of the foot-postman and the old handcart in the Post Office are numbered. The department has decided to proceed with further schemes of mechanisation, in which the motor will play a big part.

In reply to the Union of Post Office Officials, who had protested against these schemes on the grounds that they involved the reduction of full-time jobs for postmen, the Post Office pointed out:

The services of any established postman were not to be terminated as the result of the introduction of a motor vehicle. Although there might be a smaller staff there would be definite advantages in the additional pay allowed to postmen-drivers, and in the avoidance of the physical effort involved – for instance, in propelling handcarts or carrier tricycles, particulary in hilly districts.

**(June 6)**

# FLIGHT OVER EVEREST

## BRITISH MACHINES' SUCCESS

Mount Everest, the 29,000ft Queen of the Himalayas, and the world's highest mountain, was flown over yesterday.

The Houston expedition achieved their goal when two large Westland machines passed above the peak of Everest during what was at first intended to be a trial flight.

The planes climbed to a height of 35,000ft in ninety minutes, and were in the air 3¼ hours.

The pilots in this all-British venture were the Marquis of Clydesdale and Lt.-Col. Blacker in one machine, and Flt.-Lt. Macintyre and Mr. Bennett, a photographer, in the second.

**(April 4)**

# PRISON FOR THORNTON AND MACDONALD

## GREGORY ALONE ACQUITTED

The Soviet Court which has been trying the six British employees of Metropolitan-Vickers on charges of espionage, wrecking and bribery pronounced sentence late last night as follows:

**Mr. Alan Monkhouse: Deported**
**Mr. Leslie Charles Thornton: Three Years**
**Mr. William Macdonald: Two Years**
**Mr. John Cushny: Deported**
**Mr. Charles Nordwall: Deported**
**Mr. A.W. Gregory: Acquitted**

Mr. Monkhouse, Mr. Cushny and Mr. Nordwall must leave Russia within three days. Their banishment will last for five years.

The judges found that: Thornton had been the "ringleader" in military espionage, wrecking and bribery; Monkhouse knew about these criminal activities and gave bribes to conceal defects in machinery; Macdonald organised wrecking, bribed and gathered military information; and that Cushny spied and organised wrecking.

One of the Russian prisoners, Ziebert, was acquitted. The following sentences were imposed on the others:

Gusev – Ten years
Zorin – Eight years
Krashenalnikov – Five years
Kotlyarevsky – Eight years
Kutusova – One and a half years
Lebedov – Two years
Lobanov – Ten years
Oleinik – Three years
Sukurunchkin – Ten years
Sokolov – Eight years

**CABINET'S PROMPT REPLY**

**Privy Council To Meet This Morning**

The Cabinet, at a special meeting yesterday, decided upon prompt action in reply to the sentences.

It was announced by the Foreign Office last night that a meeting of the Privy Council has been summoned for this morning at Windsor Castle for the purpose of authorising a proclamation under the Russian Goods Import Prohibition Act.

Once the powers of this Act are put into operation, by proclamation of the King, no Russian goods may come into this country except under licence.

**(April 19)**

# U.S. RECOGNISES SOVIET RUSSIA

## AMBASSADOR FOR MOSCOW

WASHINGTON, Friday.

President Roosevelt announced to-day that the United States has agreed to resume normal relations with Russia, and will exchange Ambassadors. The agreement for recognition was reached at 11.50 p.m. last night.

It is expected that Mr. William Bullit will be the first American envoy to Moscow since the advent of the Soviet régime.

The announcement followed protracted negotiations between M. Litvinoff, Soviet Commissary for Foreign Affairs, and Mr. Roosevelt and his advisers.

WHITE HOUSE TO MOSCOW

In anticipation of the resumption of diplomatic relations, an American official who has been in charge of the old Czarist Embassy here has been preparing to turn the place over to the new Russian masters.

M. Litvinoff spoke to-day with his wife and son by a two-wave radio circuit between the White House and Moscow. The conversation, which has been fully published here, commenced by M. Litvinoff with "Hello." To this Madame Litvinoff replied, "I can hear you beautifully."

"Everybody here," M. Litvinoff continued, "is sorry that you did not come with me. The President and Madame Roosevelt have also expressed their regret that you did not accompany me." "That's very kind of them," replied Madam Litvinoff.

In answer to her husband's question, Madam Litvinoff said that the weather in Moscow was beautiful and that the city was covered with clear snow.

M. Litvinoff asked, "Does the sun shine?" and his wife responded: "The sun does not shine, but there is sunshine in our hearts." After mutual "Goodbyes" the first two-wave wireless talk between the White House and Moscow was concluded.

**(November 18)**

# INDEPENDENCE FOR PHILIPPINES

**From Our Own Correspondent**

WASHINGTON, Tuesday.

The Senate to-day overrode the President's veto, and again passed the bill giving independence to the Philippine Islands after a transition period of thirteen years.

Mr. Hoover had uttered a warning that such a step would endanger American prestige in the Far East. Four cabinet Ministers had issued statements pointing out the dangers of independence both for America and the Philippines, and the probable injury to trade.

To become effective the native Legislature must accept independence within a year, and all the indications are that the island Government will reject the proposal, on the ground that it does not grant immediate freedom.

**(January 18)**

# WAR ON WORD "ALLAH"

**From Our Own Correspondent.**

CONSTANTINOPLE, Tuesday.

The President of Turkey, Mustapha Kemal Pasha, has made a new move in his war on the word "Allah" and on all Arabic speech in Moslem prayer.

As from to-day, the calling to prayer from the minaret and prayer in the interior of the mosque become obligatory in Turkish instead of Arabic throughout the Republic.

Thus, despite the reactionary incidents at Broussa and Smyrna, already reported, the Ghazi is continuing to defy the Moslem fanatics with the mailed fist.

The cry of "Let lovers of God follow us," is being raised by the reactionaries at Broussa, and Mustapha Kemal Pasha, who arrived unexpectedly in Constantinople at midnight last night, declared that the fanatics will not escape Republican justice.

Arrest of reactionaries are being made in many parts of Asia Minor. Further arrests have been made at Smyrna, and those who merely express written objection to prayers in Turkish are liable to be thrown into prison.

**(February 18)**

# TROTSKY MET BY 16 FRENCH POLICE

## SECRET COAST LANDING

**From Our Own Correspondent.**

MARSEILLES, Monday.

M. Leon Trotsky, and his wife and bodyguard made a secret landing in France to-day. They left the Italian liner Bulgaria as she approached Marseilles, and were taken in a police tug to a quiet spot some miles away from the port.

Here they entered an escorted car and departed for an unknown destination. Sixteen policemen, travelling in four fast motor-cars, had been posted at the spot where the landing was made.

M. Trotsky's three women secretaries landed in the ordinary way at Marseilles. His whereabouts are being most carefully concealed, but it is believed he will make a short stay at Royat before going to Corsica. M. Litvinoff, Soviet Foreign Minister, is at present at Royat.

**(July 25)**

# REFORMER MAYOR FOR NEW YORK

## SWEEPING VICTORY OF LA GUARDIA

Messages received from New York early this morning reported the success of the crusade, waged with bitter fierceness, to expel Tammany Hall – the Democratic machine – from control of the city's government, over which it had ruled for sixteen years.

Latest official returns in the mayoral election show that Major Fiorello LaGuardia has beaten both the Tammany candidate, the outgoing Mayor O'Brien, and Mr. McKee, the independent Democrat.

**(November 8)**

# SHADOW OF CRISIS OVER THE INAUGURATION OF MR. ROOSEVELT

## NO WILD FLARE OF ENTHUSIASM

**From Our Own Correspondent**

WASHINGTON, Sunday.

More than 150,000 people gathered on Capitol Hill yesterday to see Mr. Franklin D. Roosevelt installed as the thirty-second President of the United States.

Among this vast throng were the leading dignitaries of the nation and foreign ambassadors. It is estimated that 500,000 at least lined Pennsylvania Avenue as Mr. Roosevelt rode to the White House after taking the oath.

From the standpoint of the numbers assembled, and the national interest aroused, the ceremony will rank high, but the circumstances which lent the chief impressiveness to the great occasion were, of course, the unparalleled economic conditions.

In contrast with previous inaugurations, an air of deep solemnity pervaded the ceremony. People were curiously silent much of the time – silent, watching and listening.

The reception given the new President was warm and friendly, but there was no wild flare of enthusiasm, no mad excess of joy such as marked the coming of the new régime in the days of the great, but, as Americans now sadly recognise, artificial prosperity.

NEED FOR CANDOUR

"THE ONLY THING WE HAVE TO FEAR IS FEAR"

President Roosevelt's address was as follows:

"I am certain that my fellow Americans will expect that on my induction into the Presidency I will address them with the candour and decision which the present situation of our nation impels.

"This is pre-eminently the time to speak the truth, the whole truth, frankly and boldly, nor need we shrink from honestly facing conditions. This great nation will endure, will revive, and prosper.

"First of all let me assert my firm belief that the only thing we have to fear is fear itself – nameless, unreasoning, unjustified terror which paralyses the needed efforts to convert retreat into advance.

ONLY MATERIAL DIFFICULTIES

"In every dark hour of our national life leadership of frankness and vigour has met with that understanding and support of the people themselves which is essential to victory.

"I am convinced that you will again give that support to leadership in these critical days. Our common difficulties, thank God, concern only material things.

"Only a foolish optimist can deny the dark realities of the moment. Plenty is at our doorstep, but the general use of it languishes primarily because the rulers of the exchange of mankind's goods have failed through their own stubbornness and incompetence, have admitted their failure, and have abdicated.

"The practices of unscrupulous money-changers stand indicted in the court of public opinion, rejected by the hearts and minds of men.

THE JOY OF ACHIEVEMENT

"The money-changers having fled from their high seats in the temple of our civilisation we may now restore that temple to the ancient truths. The measure of the restoration lies in the extent to which we apply social values more noble than mere monetary profit.

"Happiness lies not in the mere possession of money – it lies in the joy of achievement, the thrill of creative effort. The dark days will be worth all they cost if they teach us that our true destiny is not to be ministered unto, but to minister to ourselves and our fellow men.

"Recognition of the falsity of the material standard of success goes hand in hand with the abandonment of the false belief that public offices are to be valued only by standards of pride of place and personal profit. There must be an end to conduct in banking and business which too often had given to a sacred trust the likeness of callous and selfish wrong-doing.

"Restoration calls not for changes in ethics alone. The nation asks for action, and action now. Our greatest task is to put the people to work. This is no unsolvable problem if we face it wisely and courageously.

"In the field of world policy I would dedicate the nation to the policy of the good neighbour who resolutely respects himself, and because he does so respects the rights of others, the neighbour who respects obligations and respects the sanctity of his agreements with world neighbours.

"If I read the temper of our people correctly, we now realise as never before our interdependence on each other; that we cannot merely take, but must give as well; that if we are to go forward we must move as a loyal army willing to accept sacrifices for common discipline, because without such discipline no leadership becomes effective.

"This leadership I propose to offer with the pledge that its purposes shall be binding upon us all as a sacred obligation and a united duty heretofore invoked only in times of armed strife. With this pledge taken I assume unhesitatingly the leadership of this great army in action. This image is feasible under the form of government we have inherited from our ancestors."

**(March 6)**

# ONE AMERICAN IN 300 A CRIMINAL

The startling estimate that one in every 300 people in the United States was concerned in crime was made to-day by Col. Moss, directing the National Crime Council.

Every year, he said, crimes averaged:
Murders, 12,000
Kidnappings 3,000
Assaults, 10,000

The murder rate had gone up by 350 per cent. in the last forty years, he added.

"The general public," Col. Moss went on, "does not realise that the most successful criminals keep an attorney on a yearly fee. The attorney telephones his client daily at a given time.

"If he fails to reach the client two days running he makes a round of the gaols. When he finds him he goes to see a 'sympathetic' judge, who helps to release the client on a habeas corpus basis.

"Our greatest difficulty lies in the alliance of corrupt judges, crooked politicians, and grafting police officers."

**(August 28)**

# INNOCENT NEGRO LYNCHED

COLUMBIA (Tennessee), Sunday.

An innocent man has now fallen to the fury of a lynching mob after a Grand Jury had set him free.

The negro had been charged with an assault on a white woman. But last Wednesday he was released by the Grand Jury, which found no true bill against him. Two days later a mob caught him, and after taking him to a spot three miles from Columbia hanged him to a tree on the roadside. – B.U.P.

**(December 18)**

# U.S. LAUNCHES HER PROSPERITY DRIVE

## IMMEDIATE RELEASE OF £175,000,000

**From Our Own Correspondent**

WASHINGTON, Monday.

President Roosevelt's vast and complex experiment of Government "partnership" in business and his campaign to create at least 5,000,000 jobs for the unemployed before the winter, was launched to-day.

The public works programme approved by Congress calls for the immediate release of approximately £175,000,000, "under recovery by legislation," in order to provide work.

For grants from this enormous sum, various cities, including New York, which is suffering severely from unemployment, are now clamouring excitedly.

It is understood that most of the public works, which are planned to meet a national emergency and to forestall "dole" legislation, which would otherwise be inevitable, are "self-liquidating" – that is to say, they will finally pay for themselves.

A great organisation, with Gen. Hugh Johnson as industrial administrator – and "commander-in-chief" under President Roosevelt – and Col. Donald Sawyer in charge of the public works programme, is being built up. Trade union co-operation has been secured.

£80,000,000 FOR ROADS

In addition to the £80,000,000 to be distributed at once for roads, the "Recovery Programme" arranges also for huge grants for
High school stadiums,
Police headquarters,
Bridges and tunnels,
City streets, and
Sewage disposal systems.

**(June 20)**

# EXECUTION BY GAS IN U.S.

**From Our Own Correspondent**

CARSON CITY, Monday.

"Humane killing" was tried out in a new form to-day in Nevada State Penitentiary.

Instead of dying in the usual electric chair, Elmer Miller, condemned for the murder of his young wife, perished in a "delicate aroma of almond blossoms," according to the official description.

A bucket of sulphuric acid was placed beneath the prisoner's chair in the condemned cell at Carson City Gaol, and at the critical moment the executioner dropped a number of sodium cyanide pellets into the fluid. Within fifteen seconds the twelve-foot-square lethal chamber was filled with sweet-smelling gas so potent that the prisoner was already unconscious.

**(May 9)**

# HOW AMERICA "DROWNED" PROHIBITION

## FIRST LEGAL DRINKS FOR 13 YEARS

**For Our Own Correspondent**

NEW YORK, Tuesday Night.

The death throes of Prohibition – which was born 13 years 10 months and 18 days ago in America, and has been slowly dying for months – ended at 5.31 this afternoon (10.31 p.m. Greenwich time).

It was then that Utah became the 36th State to ratify the vote for repeal. The message was flashed throughout the United States. Steamers in the ports, loaded with liquor, blew their sirens and bells rang.

In a short time New York was "repeal mad," Times-square and Broadway were tightly packed with people watching the electric news signs, and drinking places did a roaring trade. Noisy sightseers completely jammed the traffic in the Broadway district, and 900 good-humoured policemen were rendered practically helpless.

The weather also decided to "go wet" and it started to drizzle.

When the signal finally came that the new age had dawned, a bugler, on the steps of one leading hotel, sounded the Last Post and Reveille. Simultaneously inside the Roosevelt Hotel the lid of a coffin in which a black-robed figure of Prohibition has been "lying in state" was nailed down and its handles transformed into beer taps.

"AL SMITH" COCKTAILS

At Sherry's, one of New York's oldest and most popular restaurants, the proprietor unlocked his pre-prohibition cellar of wines when the signal came, and the waiters were dressed in the national costumes of the wine-producing countries. Innumerable "new deal" and "Al Smith" cocktails made their appearance, and in the McAlpin Hotel an 83-year-old bar-tender of former days, Hans Neumann, reappeared behind the bar.

**(December 6)**

# CHANGE OVER IN THE NIGHT

## L.P.T.B. TRAVEL TO-DAY

Londoners awoke this morning to find that the greatest transport management revolution in history has taken place quietly while they slept.

All their familiar means of travel have undergone a great, if invisible change. There are no more L.C.C. trams, or "General" omnibuses, or Tube or District trains, to mention but a few of the means of travel. They are all units in the London Passenger Transport Board.

The Board – it will soon become the L.P.T.B. to Londoners, as familiar a group of initials as L.C.C. or T.O.T. – is now the biggest passenger transport system in the world.

4,000 MILLION JOURNEYS

It will control the travel of Londoners and London visitors (who already make 4,000,000 journeys a year, and are to be encouraged to make more) over an area of 2,000 square miles.

This area embraces not only all London but:
All Hertfordshire
Parts of Essex, Bedford, Buckingham, Surrey, Sussex and Kent, including
The whole of St. Albans, Luton, Chipping, Wycombe, Guildford, Reigate and Gravesend.

The L.P.T.B. took over at midnight:
89 undertakings with a total capital of £120,000,000.
A staff of 71,000,
226 railway stations,
75 garages,
36 tramway depots,
5,350 omnibuses,
2,660 trams and trolley 'buses,
420 motor coaches,
3,000 Underground railway carriages.

But Londoners will have to look very closely to see to-day any outward and visible sign of the great change.

TODAY'S ONLY SIGN

They will pay the old fares, receive the usual tickets from men in usual uniforms, but on every fare board will appear the warning that "Tickets now issued by this undertaking will be deemed to have been issued by the board."

The task of obliterating the existing identity marks on the 'buses, trams and trains is already in hand. Vehicles will appear next week with the name of their new owners painted on the sides.

**(July 1)**

# MIXED BATHING BAN AT OSWESTRY

After an animated discussion to-day, the Oswestry Council, by eleven votes to eight, defeated an amendment to allow mixed bathing in the Corporation swimming baths.

Councillor Byrne observed that mixed bathing had never been given a real chance at Oswestry. When it was previously tried ridiculous regulations were imposed. A woman was not allowed to enter the baths unless accompanied by a man, nor a man unless accompanied by a woman.

**(April 4)**

# GREAT NATIONAL SCHEME FOR UNEMPLOYED

**Earlier and Longer Benefit** | **Extension of Training Courses** | **Insurance Fund to be Made Solvent**

## STATE TO BE RESPONSIBLE FOR NEARLY 16,000,000 PERSONS

**By Our Political Correspondent**

Far-reaching measures for the reform of the Unemployment Insurance scheme are embodied in the Government's Unemployment Bill, which was formally introduced in the House of Commons yesterday.

Under the Bill the State will assume responsibility for the care of the whole of the able-bodied unemployed who are out of benefit or uninsured.

Other leading proposals are as follows:

**1. UNEMPLOYMENT INSURANCE**

Benefit – Rates of contribution and benefit will remain unchanged. But the period of benefit is to be extended from 26 up to a maximum of 52 weeks.

Juveniles – Will enter insurance immediately on leaving school. Insurance benefit will be payable after the age of 16. Up to that age dependants' benefit will be paid to parents of children unemployed or attending school or instruction courses.

Training – Workless juveniles under 18 will, in general, be compelled to attend instruction courses, which are to be widely extended.

The Minister of Labour is to be empowered to provide training courses for unemployed over 18 (attendance at which may be made a condition of benefit).

Finance – A Statutory Committee is to be set up to recommend any changes necessary to keep the Unemployment Insurance scheme solvent and self-supporting.

Agricultural Workers – The Statutory Committee is to draw up a scheme of agricultural insurance, but such a scheme will not come into force without further legislation.

**II. UNEMPLOYMENT ASSISTANCE**

New Central Authority – An Unemployment Assistance Board of five members is to take over from Public Assistance Committees the care of practically all the able-bodied unemployed out of benefit, whether insured or not. Its object will be to help them to re-enter employment.

National Finance – The cost of relief by the Board will be borne by the Exchequer, subject to contributions by local authorities of the amounts which the scheme will save them.

Training – The Board will be empowered to provide physical training courses for unemployed.

The effect of the measure is that the State assumes responsibility for about 4,000,000 persons at present outside insurance. With the 12,000,000 in the insurance scheme it thus undertakes the care, in the event of unemployment some 16,000,000 persons.

**(November 9)**

# PENNY A MILE FOR RAIL TRAVEL

Passenger fares on the railways will be reduced during the summer months to the pre-war rate of one penny per mile.

This is the effect of new travel facilities by "summer ticket" announced by the four main-line companies yesterday.

The reduced rate will apply from May 1 to tickets for return journeys. The tickets will be available for return within a month, and the following conditions will apply:

Tickets will be obtainable on any day of the week, and will be available, both forward and return, by any train on any day of the week.

They will be issued between all the principal towns and cities, seaside and inland resorts for return journeys with a minimum fare of 4s first-class and 2s 6d third-class. This means that the reductions in fares will operate between all places more than ten miles apart.

Summer tickets represent decreases of ½d a mile on existing third class ordinary return fares and of nearly 1d a mile on first-class returns. That is an approximate reduction of one-third on the present ordinary return tickets, which is about the reduction now made on week-end tickets.

The present ordinary third-class return fares work out at about 1 ½d a mile, and the new scheme, therefore, offers travel to the public at the average cost of 1d a mile.

**(March 11)**

# HYDE PARK CORNER TRAFFIC CONTROL

**By Our Motoring Correspondent**

Pedestrians are to be specially catered for by the automatic traffic signalling system at Hyde Park Corner – London's busiest traffic centre – work on which has just begun.

The installation, the first news of which was given in The Daily Telegraph on June 27, is to be of the traffic actuated type, like that in Trafalgar-Square, but it is intended to insert in the cycle of signals a 15-seconds pause, when the signals will show red to all vehicular traffic.

At present it is not intended to have special signals directing the pedestrian when and when not to cross, as the Ministry are still opposed to that in principle.

**(December 2)**

# BREACH OF OFFICIAL SECRETS ACT

## AUTHOR ORDERED TO PAY £200

Mr Compton Mackenzie, the author, of Beauly, Inverness, was at the Old Bailey yesterday ordered to pay a fine of £100 and a sum not exceeding £100 towards the costs for infringement of the Official Secrets Act.

The trial, which took place on a summons before Mr. Justice Hawke, was held largely in camera.

It was alleged that having obtained information as an Intelligence Staff officer serving in Gallipoli and Athens during the war years, Mr. Mackenzie communicated it to Cassell and Co., the publishers, in a book entitled "Greek Memories." The book was withdrawn from circulation almost as soon as it was published.

The Attorney-General (Sir Thomas Inskip, K.C.) and Mr. Eustace Fulton appeared to prosecute for the Crown, and Mr. Mackenzie was defended by Sir Henry Curtis Bennett, K.C., and Mr. St. John Hutchinson.

Mr. Mackenzie pleaded guilty.

**(January 13)**

# DENMARK WINS LAND OF ERIK THE RED

## GREENLAND DISPUTE ENDS

**From Our Own Correspondent**

THE HAGUE, Wednesday

By 13 votes to 1 the Permanent Court of International Justice to-day gave judgment in favour of Denmark in the territorial dispute with Norway over Greenland. The dissentient was the Norwegian judge appointed for the hearing.

The decision states that the whole of Greenland is Danish territory, and that the occupation by Norway on July 10, 1931, of part of eastern Greenland was illegal and invalid.

The disputed territory, known as "The Land of Erik the Red," comprises an area of 21,000 square miles free of ice. The entire continent of Greenland covers 800,000 square miles, of which 135,000 square miles is ice-free country.

**(April 6)**

# THE NEW ARMY UNIFORM

THE NEW UNIFORM – a photograph from Aldershot, where fifty men of the 2nd Batt. the Queen's Royal Regiment (West Surrey) took part in field training in the new service dress yesterday.

# OXFORD MEN AND PACIFIST MOTION

## PROTEST MOVEMENT ORGANISED

Determined efforts are to be made to secure the erasure from the minutes of the Oxford Union of the pacifist motion which was carried last Thursday.

Following the letter of protest published in THE DAILY TELEGRAPH on Saturday from a correspondent who signed himself "Sixty-Four," a movement has been organised to have the offending resolution expunged. Carried by 275 votes to 153, the resolution was:

"That this house will in no circumstances fight for its King and country."

Lord Stanley of Alderley, Mr. Randolph Churchill, and four other members of the Oxford Union Society yesterday sent out a circular letter to life members of the society appealing for support on Thursday, Mar. 2. They then propose to go to Oxford to move the adjournment of the Union, and, if possible, to expunge the motion from the records.

APPEAL TO MEMBERS

The circular letter is as follows:

"We, the undersigned life members of the Oxford Union Society, appeal to you to lend us your support in order that we may repair, as far as lies in our power, the damage that was done to its reputation last Thursday.

"We believe that, however expressive of modern Oxford thought may be the motion 'That this House will in no circumstances fight for its King and country,' it is totally unrepresentative of the Oxford Union as a whole.

"The ephemeral undergraduates who permitted this disgraceful motion to be carried constitute but a tithe of the Oxford Union: they are merely temporary trustees, and they have lamentably failed in their trusteeship. Consequently we propose to go down to Oxford on Thursday, Mar. 2, to move the adjournment of the Union and, if possible, to expunge this motion from the records of the House. We appeal to you to assist us in this project.

"If you are prepared to help us, please notify Mr. Randolph Churchill at the May Fair Hotel, Berkeley-street, W.1. as soon as possible."

| | |
|---|---|
| Randolph S. Churchill | Alan Lennox-Boyd |
| | Quintin Hogg |
| Stanley of Alderley | Edgar Lustgarten |
| | Frank Pakenham |

The Hon. Quintin Hogg (son of Viscount Hailsham, Secretary of State for War), who was president of the Oxford Union Society in 1929, told a representative of The Daily Telegraph that he had felt most humiliated by the motion.

"The authorities of the Union," he said, "have not given us a copy of the list of members, and so we have not been able to circularise them all. We consider it absolutely essential that all who regret the motion should come down to Oxford and protest against it."

**(February 15)**

# VITAMIN C

Dr. Fritz Michael, of Goettingen, according to a B.U.P. message, claims to have succeeded in making a synthetic preparation of Vitamin C – a most important discovery.

The great value to man of Vitamin C is that it prevents scurvy. It is present in the citrus fruits, the lemon, orange and grape fruit, in cabbages, and in most green salads.

Dr. H. Raistrick, Professor of Bio-chemistry, University of London, when the message from Goettingen was communicated to him by a representative of THE DAILY TELEGRAPH, said:

"If Vitamin C has been isolated in a pure condition and its chemical constitution worked out it would then be possible to manufacture it in adequate quantities."

**(March 3)**

# "IN ACTION" FOR THE FIRST TIME

## MEN APPROVE ITS COMFORT

**From Our Special Correspondent**

ALDERSHOT, Monday.

The new field service kit for British infantry, with "deer-stalker" cap and open-necked jacket, had its first thorough testing in the Aldershot Command to-day.

The experimental platoon of the 2nd Battalion the Queen's Royal Regiment (West Surreys) wore the newly-designed uniform and equipment in field operations in Long Valley. Half the platoon were wearing puttees and the other half gaiters, such as are worn by men of the Royal Navy when on shore duty.

The kit was planned with the object of providing as much comfort and as light a load as possible, and the exercises carried out were an excellent test. An attack on a strong point was carried out, the sections in their advance using the new entrenching tools (which are slung on the backs of the valises) to get head cover rapidly. A machine-gun section was seen in action, as well as signallers and other details.

DEERSTALKERS AND TIN HATS

The men expressed satisfaction at the ease and comfort of the jacket, and although, with the true instinct of the British Tommy they poked fun at the "deerstalker" head-dress, they, nevertheless, were of opinion that it was less troublesome in the field than the field service cap.

As they had not yet put the equipment to any lengthy test on the march, they could not give any opinion on other features of it. They found they could fit their steel helmets over the "deerstalkers" without any ill effects to the latter, while the entrenching tool gave them material for banter, on account of its small size.

Lt-Col. G.J. Giffard, D.S.O., commanding the battalion, who watched the operations, stated afterwards that the experimental uniform would be used solely for training work, and that members of the platoon would wear ordinary uniform for "walking out" and on parade. During the coming training season the kit will be subjected to extensive experimental work, both at Aldershot and Catterick.

**(January 10)**

# THE HOLY SHROUD EXHIBITED

## 25,000 KNEEL IN A TURIN SQUARE

**From Our Own Correspondent**

TURIN, Monday.

The focus of the Holy Year ceremonies was transferred to-day for a short period from Rome to Turin. Here, with elaborate and solemn ceremony, the Holy Shroud, in which, according to tradition, the body of Christ was wrapped, was taken from the cathedral treasury and exposed to the gaze of a great crowd.

To-day's ceremony was attended by Crown Prince Umberto and his wife, Princess Marie José. The presence of Italian Royalty was essential, for the precious relic of the Passion is the property of the House of Savoy. Every time that it is moved a solemn deed must be signed by both Royal and ecclesiastical authorities.

Should it require mending, either the Queen or one of her daughters goes to Turin to perform the task – and sews upon her knees.

The Holy Shroud is a long cloth of rough linen, 13 ½ft long by 4ft 3in wide. Dimly on both back and front can be seen the imprint of a human figure.

**(September 26)**

# TESTS FOR ALL MOTOR DRIVERS

## MINISTER'S HINT OF LEGISLATION

Two points of vital interest to the general public and to the motoring community are brought out in a debate on the Road and Rail Traffic Bill in the House of Lords last night and in a report of the Select Committee which has been considering the Road Traffic (Emergency Treatment) Bill.

The Marquis of Londonderry, the Government spokesman, foreshadowed the possibility of a driving test applicable to all motorists being included in legislation which is contemplated as soon as the official investigation into the causation of road accidents is completed.

The report of the Select Committee, which recommends the payment of 12s 6d for each case to doctors and hospitals for services rendered to persons injured in motor accidents, suggests that the money should be provided by motorists, who would have this further liability added to the compulsorily insurable third party risks.

**(November 14)**

# HINKLER'S BODY FOUND

The body of Sqdrn.-Ldr. Bert Hinkler, the Australian airman who had been missing since he left England on Jan 7 in an attempt to lower the record to Australia, was discovered near his wrecked machine in the mountain wilds of Tuscany, about 780 miles from his starting point.

A band of charcoal burners returning to Castel Franco di Sopra, near Arezzo, made the discovery as the result of a partial melting of the snows.

The body which bore marks of burns, was decomposed almost beyond recognition, and had been mutilated, probably by foxes or wolves. But it was identified by Hinkler's passport, which bore the name of his birthplace – Bundaberg, Australia.

The 'plane bore Hinkler's marks CF – APK. The body had a deep wound in the head, which the dead man probably received in a crash, and the left hand was missing. It lay about 100 yards from the 'plane, which appears to have caught fire after crashing, and of which the front part was embedded in the earth.

Watch at 3 o'clock.

Wreckage of the machine was strewn over a radius of nearly three-quarters of a mile. A pneumatic boat with oars was found in the cabin. Three petrol tanks were empty, and the fourth contained only the smallest quantity of fuel. The oil tank was dry.

A watch on the body had stopped at three o'clock. (Hinkler left England at dawn.)

**(April 24)**

# RADIO TIME "PIPS" TO BE CUT OUT

Radio "Pips" – the B.C.C. time signals from Greenwich – may be suppressed under a new system to be introduced in August. But the pips will still be heard at other times.

"Music-lovers have frequently complained of the jarring effect of the pips," says the Radio Times.

"Starting in August, a new system will be introduced. Except for the signals at 10.30 a.m. and 6 p.m. any signal which, superimposed on programmes, would have a definitely inartistic effect may be suppressed.

**(June 30)**

# THE HAPPIEST CHRISTMAS SINCE THE WAR

## MORE AT WORK THAN FOR OVER 3 ½ YEARS PAST

**All Britain is looking forward to the happiest Christmas since the war.**

**600,000 more people are at work than a year ago, and the total of employed is the highest for over 3 ½ years;**

**Shopkeepers report the best selling season they have ever known;**

**The Post Office and the railways are carrying more traffic than they have ever done before.**

**(December 23)**

# MAN WHO WANTED HIS PARCEL BACK

## POST OFFICE LOOKING FOR IT

**From A Special Representative**

A London man telephoned the Post Office yesterday asking them to return a Christmas parcel because he had omitted something from it. He added that it could be identified by the fact that it was wrapped in brown paper and had two lengths of string round it.

"Although we have not found the parcel yet, we are still living in hope," said Sir Kingsley Wood, the Postmaster-General, last night. Sir Kingsley was showing the Lord Mayor of London (Sir Charles Collett) and Lady Collett how the Post Office deals with the Christmas traffic at the Mount Pleasant sorting office.

In that office alone were 300,000 parcels – nearly all wrapped in brown paper and bound with double string.

**(December 23)**

# SPEED AGE GREETINGS

Apparently we are becoming more "telephone-minded," for this year shows a remarkable increase in the use of the telephone for exchanging Christmas greetings with friends and relatives overseas. "The number of radio telephone calls across the Atlantic has been increasing every year," Sir Kingsley told me. "On Christmas Day the Rugby wireless station and the Internal Telephone Exchange will be working at full pressure."

Telegrams, too, are being more widely used in this age of speed and last year a record of 30,000 Christmas greeting telegrams were sent from people in this country.

Another Speed Age manifestation is the increase in the volume of air mail traffic. The aggregate weight of the two Christmas air mails to India this year was 5,000lb compared with 4,000lb last year, and of the air mails to South and East Africa 2,000lb, compared with 1,500lb last year. Incoming air mails are expected to total 15,000lb – nearly seven tons.

**(December 23)**

# LAVISH SPENDING

## BRITISH TOY TRADE'S RECORD SEASON

More money has been spent this Christmas than in any year since before the war. This is the verdict of business men and shopkeepers throughout the country.

"We have had a record year" the head of a big London store told a representative of THE DAILY TELEGRAPH last night. "We have had far more customers than ever before. Sales have been extraordinarily large. There is a general feeling that times are better."

Similar reports come from other London stores, and from the provinces.

The British toy industry has enjoyed the most successful season in its history, in spite of large imports from abroad. So great have been the orders that toy factories have been working day and night.

**(December 23)**

# HUNDREDS OF EXTRA TRAINS

## RAILWAY PROPERITY

All the railway companies are experiencing the most prosperous Christmas season for years. Yesterday vast crowds thronged all the London termini, and hundreds of additional trains will be run to all parts of the country to-day.

The Southern Railway alone arranged for 140 extra expresses yesterday and to-day. The L.M.S. will run twenty-eight extra expresses to the North to-day, including some trains to Scotland composed entirely of sleeping-cars.

The Great Western Railway has planned to cope with 600,000 passengers between yesterday morning and this evening, and many extra trains are being run by the L.N.E.R.

Exceptionally heavy bookings have also been made for the air services to the Continent.

**(December 23)**

# A HOLBEIN OF HENRY VIII DISCOVERED

## "STRONG MAN" IN DISILLUSION

**By R.R. Tatlock**

A hitherto unknown portrait of Henry VIII has come to light at Castle Howard, near York, the seat of the Hon. Geoffrey Howard.

It will be universally allowed to be the finest and most intimate likeness of the King in existence. The picture is the work of Henry's Court Painter, Hans Holbein, and must be accounted one of the artist's greatest masterpieces.

In no case could there be any doubts as to authenticity, but if confirmation were needed the fact that the picture bears clear traces of Holbein's signature and of the date, 1542, would have put them at rest.

I have made the accompanying little drawing of this inscription, which appears on the staff in the King's left hand. It will be seen that the initial H (for Hans) has worn off and that the figure five is all but gone.

"IMPROVED" BY RESTORERS

It may well be asked how it comes about that a painting of such great aesthetic and historical importance should have hung unnoticed for so long in so well known a collection as that of Castle Howard.

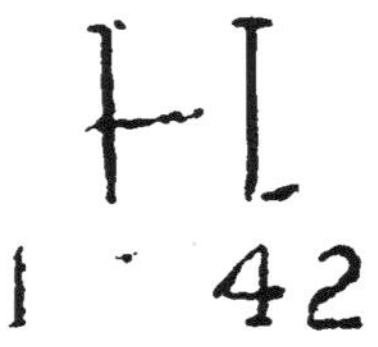


The answer is that, until a short time ago, it was hidden under four old but distinct coats of over-paint. These over-paints followed the main outline of Holbein's original figure and represent successive attempts on the part of later restorers to "improve" upon it. They have now been removed at the suggestion of Dr. Paul Ganz, to whom art historians already owe so much, with the brilliant result indicated.

The disillusionment of a strong man has perhaps never before or since been so subtly indicated in paint. We see him grown more corpulent, greyer, but still tight-lipped and tight-fisted.

The almost startlingly brilliant condition of the vivid colours must be seen to be believed. Messrs. Spink and Son, King-street, St. James's, have arranged to exhibit the portrait to the public from to-morrow.

**(October 2)**

# I.R.A. SPLIT WITH DE VALERA GOVERNMENT

A definite split between Mr. De Valera's Government and the Irish Republican Army is revealed in a remarkable statement issued early this morning, by the "Army Council" of the Irish Republican Army.

"That the Fianna Fail Government has adopted a policy of exercising coercion against Republicans is evidenced," the statement declares, "by the fact that a raid took place on the camp of well-known Republicans at Glendhu, co. Dublin, on Sunday, in which a large number of C.I.D. notorious in the Cosgrave regime took part.

"The Government functioning in the 26 counties has no more claim to the allegiance of the people than the Imperialist junta ruling in the six counties."

"The Army Council, in this situation, makes a strong and sincere plea to all Republicans to unite on the one and only basis upon which unity is possible – namely, the repudiation of the treaty of surrender of 1921 and the establishment of the Irish Republic.

**(August 31)**

# "JIGSOCRACY" SEIZES AMERICANS

## NEW NATIONAL PASTIME

**From Our Own Correspondent**

NEW YORK, Monday.

"Jigsocracy" – the jigsaw puzzle craze – is rapidly filling the place left by technocracy, mah-jong, and midget golf. Jigsocracy was almost unknown to Americans generally last autumn, but to-day its gentle smoke as an occasional hobby has roared up into a national blaze.

In New Jersey there is a jigsaw puzzle factory employing 250 men and women. The puzzles are stacked a yard high on newspaper stalls and the counters of popular stores, and comic artists of note are being engaged to design new victims for the busy fret-saw.

Things have reached such a pass in some places that the popularity of the new pastime has ruined the local cinemas.

**(February 7)**

# AMAZING WINTER SCENES IN EUROPE

**Wolves Raid a French Town** | **Ice Festival on German River** | **Blizzard Rescue in Morocco**

## THE THAMES FROZEN OVER FROM OXFORD TO SOURCE

## RHINE BLOCKED BY HUGE ICE-FLOES

### BATHERS COVERED WITH ICICLES

Further incidents of the great frost reported by representatives of The Daily Telegraph from all parts of Europe yesterday included the following:

People are travelling for miles to see the astonishing spectacle presented by the Rhine at the Lorelei narrows.

Huge ice-floes, some more than 100 square yards in area, are piled one upon the other, forming a jagged barrier across the river, across which the more adventurous pick their way from bank to bank. This Arctic landscape stretches for a distance of 6 or 7 miles.

In spite of yesterday's record frost in Berlin all-the-year-round bathers hacked a hole in the thick ice on the Wannsee in order to bathe. The water froze to icicles on their skin as they emerged.

French Villages Cut Off

Many roads in the Rhone valley are impassable with huge snowdrifts, and several villages are isolated from all supplies of food and other necessaries. Trains are reaching Marseilles considerably behind time, and in the South of France many high-tension electric cables have broken under the weight of snow. The River Saône is completely frozen over.

Owing to exceptionally heavy snowfalls in the Alps, the Riviera has been almost completely cut off from Paris and London by road.

Two of the main passes from Grenoble – known as the winter Alps route, since they are normally open all the year round – are closed. All traffic from the north must go by Lyons and Avignon.

In Paris the thermometer has not risen above freezing-point for ten days.

Winter Sports in Vienna

Four days' heavy snowfall in Vienna has transformed the capital into a winter sports paradise. Yesterday was a record for winter sports accidents – due not to any lack of skill but to the hundreds of thousands of skiers who crowded on to every possible slope in the hills of Vienna Forest. The scores of emergency firstaid stations established were kept busy until a late hour at night.

So serious was the toll of accidents that the authorities are proposing to limit the number of skiers in certain overcrowded areas. Other areas, with a particularly bad record for accidents, may be closed altogether.

Thousands of unemployed – unable to afford the trams – walked to the mountains, carrying borrowed or home-made skis.

**(December 14)**

# FROZEN THAMES

## WATER BOARD'S SUPPLY MAY BE RESTRICTED

**By A Special Correspondent.**

The combined effect of the frost and the drought has reduced the flow of the Thames at Teddington weir to 350,000,000 gallons a day – little more than one-sixth the average for December.

If the river falls any lower the Metropolitan Water Board is compelled by statute to restrict its normal supply of 180,000,000 gallons from the river. It must leave a flow of 170,000,000 gallons to the lower reaches.

This fact need cause no alarm, however, for if the board's replenishments were cut off entirely it would still have nearly 20,000 million gallons in storage – enough to meet London's average daily consumption of 280,000,000 gallons for about 75 days. In addition, in case of emergency, special powers can be invoked to enable the board to draw water from the Thames in excess of the statutory minimum.

Yesterday's flow was the lowest since the record year of 1921, when it fell below 300,000,000 gallons.

An official in the engineer's department of the Thames Conservancy Board told me that the Thames is frozen over from Oxford to its source, that many of the tributaries and feeders are also frozen and that the supply from the many springs supplying the river has been diminished by the frost.

"It is essential for the cleanliness of the river in the commercial area that the fresh water content should be well maintained," the official added. "If this were not done the condition of the river in the shipping area might become unbearable."

For the first eighteen days of this month the rainfall has been only .02in, compared with an average for December of 0.88in.

**(December 19)**

# 'ONE-WAY STREET' FOR 'NIPPIES'

## NEW CORNER HOUSE AT MARBLE ARCH

**By A Special Correspondent**

When "Maison Lyons," of Oxford-street, "moves" on Monday to Marble Arch, where a great new Corner House will open, there will be much for the public to see and admire; two cafés of impressive decor, striking equipment, excellent music, and room for 2,000 people at a time – 2,000 people who will expect and receive swift service.

Behind the scenes there will be a miracle of organisation. The kitchens are amazing. Leading from them, are "one-way streets" flanked by metal counters and tray rails.

When she has taken her orders the waitress – one of 500 – enters the "one-way street," places her tray on the rails, and moves along the counter, calling her wants to the service maids or helping herself from one of the many labour saving gadgets.

One side of the "street" has the hot dishes, the other the cold. Each section is neatly labelled, "fried fish," "hot sweets," "entrees," "soups," or "hors d'œuvres," "salads." One section ("dirties") is where the trayfuls of used things are deposited and left to the offices of endless chains and mechanical washers.

EVER-FRESH TEA

At the exit end of the "street" are several contrivances which the waitress manipulates herself. There is a "heavy soda arm," with which an ice-cream soda may be "topped off" with a last squirt, a big container of mayonnaise, and a row of squirters to project boiling water into teapots containing the dry leaves, so that the customer's tea is invariably fresh made.

Finally, at the door are checkers who take in at a glance the contents of a crowded tray, and check it with the amount on the waitress's slip.

More than 1,000 staff will be employed, the original Maison Lyons personnel having been increased by over 300 people. Yesterday little groups of waiters and waitresses were being conducted round the new quarters listening to lectures on variations in topography and improvements in equipment. By Monday, perfectly rehearsed, they will be playing their part in making a brand new restaurant behave as though it had been open for years.

**(October 21)**

# U.S. VOTES WORLD'S BEST-DRESSED MEN

## LORD WESTMORLAND FIRST

NEW YORK, Wednesday.

Who are the world's ten best-dressed men? This question has just been answered by the tailors of London, New York and Hollywood, regarded as the world's style centres for men. The list they have drawn up is:

1. Earl of Westmorland
2. Prince George of England
3. Mr. F. Frazier Jelke (New York)
4. Mr. William Goadby Loew (New York)
5. Mr. Michael Farmer (husband of Gloria Swanson)
6. M. Adolphe Menjou (the film star)
7. Sir Austen Chamberlain
8. Mr. Anthony J. Drexel Biddle (Philadelphia)
9. Marquis of Cholmondeley
10. Sir John W. Buchanan Jardine

Capt. Anthony Eden, British Under-Secretary for Foreign Affairs, was described in the Paris newspapers recently as the best-dressed man in Britain. – B.U.P.

**(December 28)**

# GIRL GOLFER IN MEN'S TROUSERS

Miss Pamela Shand, who is competing in the girls' golf championship at Stoke Poges, set a new fashion by appearing in a pair of men's mackintosh trousers during a stroke competition, held in heavy rain, yesterday.

"Trousers are better than skirts," she said, "because the rain does not drip into your shoes. I find them just the thing for golf.

**(September 13)**

# WHAT IS BEST FOR MUSIC'S FUTURE?

## SIR T. BEECHAM ON ITS NEEDS

**By H. E. Wortham**

Listen to Sir Thomas Beecham surveying the world from his armchair.

Hear the stream of anecdote and criticism, epigram and paradox, as it flows from lips round which the hint of a sardonic smile is always lurking, and you say to yourself that here is a conversationalist who has missed his vocation.

It would not be true.

For Sir Thomas Beecham's talk, salted as it is by the ironical insight of a first-class mind, and possessing also the urbanity of a man of the world, is at the same time inspired by the enthusiasm of the artist. Wit and humour with him are but the servants of his passion for the art to which he has devoted his life.

He was in the vein yesterday when he found an hour in which to talk of the things uppermost in his mind. A recent occassion at the Queen's Hall, at which many votaries of the Turf were present, reminded him of the strange creatures sometimes caught in the net of the symphony concert box-office.

A BARREN PERIOD

As Sir Thomas has just come back from Milan, it was natural that the younger generation of opera singers, whom he has just been "vetting," should pass across the conversational screen.

"At the moment we have struck a bad patch," he said. "There don't seem to be any young singers of quality. But, after all, what inducement have they? There is nothing being written for them to sing."

Looking critically at his unlighted cigar he added: "Coughing, barking, spitting aren't a substitute for the tunes that the public have always wanted and the great composers have always provided."

Sir Thomas Beecham, however, is no pessimist. There have been barren periods before now. It is true that to-day opera is living on its capital. Since Puccini and Strauss the strain has become exhausted. Of course there is "Wozzeck," but to give Berg's opera at Covent Garden would require twenty orchestra rehearsals, a prohibitive business.

BASTILLE OF MUSIC

"The best thing for the future of music in London," Sir Thomas throws out as an obiter dictum, "would be for bombs to be dropped on Covent Garden Opera House, the Albert Hall, and the Queen's Hall."

This tempestuously Shavian remark has only a suspicion of irony for seasoning. And as he develops it one's affection for the traditional home of opera in London ebbs away, while as for the Queen's Hall, that familiar and friendly spot becomes under Sir Thomas Beecham's indictment a new Bastille, the citadel of the ancien régime of music.

"What London wants," he declares, "is a new opera house which can also be used for symphony concerts. In England, where opera has never been regarded as anything except a commercial proposition, it is impossible to keep a theatre solely as an opera-house – as they do in Italy – which will be shut half the year."

What of the future? As Sir Thomas Beecham weighs the factors in the present situation of English music, he points out that the immediate task before the profession is to reorganise itself with a settled policy vis-á-vis the public and the B.B.C.

"The lives and careers of musicians," he says, "have been profoundly revolutionised by that powerful and monopolistic institution, and it is about time that they definitely made up their minds whether the change was for good or for ill. The surprising way in which practically the whole of the profession has accepted the B.B.C. as its lord and master is the most melancholy proof of its spiritlessness and complete brainlessness."

**(January 30)**

# THE FIRST QUARTO HAMLET

Shakespeare's birthday was comemorated in London last night with a very lively production by Sir Philip Ben Greet of the First Quarto Hamlet at the Arts Theatre Club.

No better tonic could be devised for all the people who suffer from jaded palates, excused by "too - much - Shakespeare - at - school." Cut to the bone for the sake of brisk action, and with quite half the favourite "set-pieces" omitted or maltreated, the 1603 unorthodox version administers a series of shocks to the memory.

The result is a complete freshening of the play – one feels inclined to cheer each time a familiar passage emerges safe and unharmed.

Still, there is plenty of good strong drama lying to the hand of a virile company, and not much of it was lost last night. In particular the prodigious energy of the duel scene threatened to overflow the tiny stage, and there was throughout an admirable atmosphere of bustle and business.

**(April 24)**

# THE AGONY OF THE HUMAN SOUL IN WAR

## MISS VERA BRITTAIN'S VIVID TESTIMONY

**By Rebbeca West**

**The Testament Of Youth, By Vera Brittain. (Gollancz. 12s 6d.)**

There is nothing harder in life than to verify fiction; to find out how far novels are truthful in their rendering of the day-to-day stream of consciousness in ordinary men and women.

For we do not know about the people next door, we hardly know about the people in the same house. The joys and sorrows of those not ourselves we can apprehend only as if they were beasts not of our kind in a jungle, by listening to whimpers and roars and the helter-skelter of unseen stampedes; and when it comes to ouselves, hardly any of us have the courage to face the ordeal of full memory. We gloss over the grimmer hours of our afflictions, for if the past was as horrible as that, so might the future be also, and that we could not face. Hence biography has in all ages made a profession of candour, but, with as few exceptions as can be told on the fingers, has as much right as a sundial to claim that it marks only the sunny hours.

It is because "TESTAMENT OF YOUTH" is among these exceptions that it has its special values. The author has a combination of qualities that are rare. She had a bland appearance – an Army sister was later to remark of her, "That V.A.D. of yours is a pretty little thing, but she's got a vacant face – very vacant!" – which enabled her to be accepted by ordinary people without a shadow of apprehension and to take a part in normal life. But she had a dogged intellectual quality that made her lay hold of the phenomena of life as they went past her, and a dogged moral quality that made her able, fifteen years later, to put herself through the agony of recalling the ghastly sum of those phenomena. Such hunger for reality, such stoicism, usually mark off their possessor from the beginning as the bearer of some special mission and restricts her experience; but the satisfying muliebrity of Vera Brittain gave her the general experience of ordinary women, and "TESTAMENT OF YOUTH" is a history of the normal.

When Vera Brittain, brought up in a house with three servants, became a V.A.D., she did not know how to boil an egg. There is some entertainment in the description of how, just before the war, she rebelled against this way of forcing women to make the worst of both worlds, and fought her way out of Buxton to a women's college at Oxford, where however, she was deeply shocked by the bad cooking and domestic sluttishness.

The particular form that interruption took in Vera Brittain's life gives one an eerie sense of passing into other people's lives, of discovering realities that lie behing more names. To middle-aged people the name of Mari Connor Leighton means a work named "Convict 99" which the young were not allowed to read, on the grounds of its sensationalism, but which fed their imagination by gorgeously lurid posters advertising it as a serial and a melodrama. One did not realise when one saw this name on the posters that it stood for a real woman, a woman who was the radiant centre of a group of human beings, and put into the world a son of fine quality. We know that many such died in the war, but we know it so well that our knowledge is atrophied and means nothing.

FROZEN AND REMOTE

Vera Brittain, with her bulldog tenacity, will not have it so, and out of the limbo of lost things she confronts us with the prize list of Uppingham, July 1914, with six out of the first seven prizes gained by one R.A.Leighton. That makes the sting smart as it should for wholesomeness; and so too, does her account of her courtship by this delightful youth, which is surely different from contemporary proceedings in the freedom of its proliferation, in the confidence with which it sent out all sorts of emotional and intellectual branches into the as yet undisturbed air.

Then the boy had to go to war, where, just before he should have gone on leave and been married, he ultimately met a totally unnecessary death, being killed because his regiment had taken over some trenches and the outgoing regiment had neglected to tell him that a certain area was regularly under the machine-gun fire of the enemy.

When he was killed it was found that he had been received into the Roman Catholic Church, but had excluded everyone from knowledge of this change. Though he was conscious some time after his injury and before his death, he left no message to his family or his betrothed, nor had he mentioned to any of his friends that he was going on leave and expected to see them.

And on examination there appeared to be a curious rashness, a cold and weary indifference to life and death, that had driven him out to the danger-point in bright moonlight.

THE PIT OF DESPAIR

Vera Brittain grasps the proportions of the event quite justly; she is no egotist, she sees that the person who came off worst in the tragedy was Roland and nobody else; but she does not disguise that this agonising death before death occurred, and that it was an agony and humiliation to the survivors.

Vera Brittain also lost her brother, a being fully as charming as Roland, who had kept his susceptibility at the front almost as tragically as her lover had lost his. She lost also a friend whom she had been about to marry as an act of devotion, since he had gone blind before his war malady declared itself as fatal. All this time she had been nursing in England, in Malta, in France, and her pictures of the hospitals would give the reader from another planet still further evidence of human infrangibility.

She lays before us more fairly and more vividly than any other writer on the war the vast and disgusting extent of its inefficiency. A thing so complicated and so immense and so ultimately dependent on human effort had to call into its service all the sub-men and sub-women, as well as the super-men and super-women, and the result was grimy and stupid and pain-dealing. Those abonimations Vera Brittain describes as she describes the pit of despair into which she fell when the war ended, and she found herself so geared to the abnormal that she had the greatest difficulty to adapt herself to the normal.

Whether such a book can do much to abolish war is doubtful; since if everyone in any given country saw war exactly as Vera Brittain did, that would avail them nothing in their desire for peace if some other country was still, owing to some temperamental defect, in love with war. But "Testament of Youth" adds immensely to the documentation of the human soul about which we understand so little, of which we are the tormentors and the victims until we fully understand it.

**(September 15)**

# 'TERRIFIC' FILM OF 50FT. APE

**By Our Film Correspondent**

In "King Kong," which I saw privately yesterday, Radio Pictures have produced what will almost certainly be one of the box-office sensations of the year.

It is not a picture for the fastidious. Its horrors are never far removed from laughter, the treatment is frequently banal and in places the machinery creaks badly. But as entertainment for the masses it is terrific.

Kong is an ape 50ft high, a survival from another age, with arms 23ft long, a mouth 6ft wide, a reach of 75ft, and hands so big that the heroine looks no bigger in one of them than a cigar.

The thrill begins with capture of the heroine by the ape, and ends with Kong carrying her to the top of the Empire State building, 1,200ft above the ground, where he is bombarded by a fleet of aeroplanes, one of which he plucks from the sky like a wasp and dashes to the street below.

TECHNICIANS' TRIUMPH

In between these episodes you see a fight to the death between Kong and a pterodactyl, whose jaw he breaks, Samson fashion, nightmare encounters with a tyrannosauraus (a huge dinosaur), and with a brontosaurus, and Kong wrecking elevated trains and houses, and crushing human beings beneath his feet like flies.

This fantastic stuff, obviously influenced by "The Lost World," was conceived by Merian Cooper, the Hollywood director, and partly written by Edgar Wallace just before his death. But the real heroes of the piece are the technicians who, by back projection, the use of miniatures and other processes, have worked a year giving the monsters sufficient illusion of reality to wring gasps from all but the most critical.

**(April 20)**

# FRED ASTAIRE RETURNS

## A DANCER OF REAL GENIUS

**By W. A. Darlington**

Fred Astaire and Claire Luce "stopped the show" last night at the Palace more completely than I have ever before seen that feat performed. At the end of their dance, "Night and day" – for which Cole Porter had provided a most luscious and haunting melody – a pandemonium of applause broke it.

Three times did Claude Allister, playing a silly-ass lawyer, emerge from the wings and try to get on with his part. Twice he had to retreat while Mr. Astaire and Miss Luce appeared again. The third time he was allowed to proceed – but only just.

In Act II much the same thing happened again. Indeed, the audience would clearly have liked Mr. Astaire to go on dancing for them till either his feet or their hands (and throats) wore out.

I don't wonder. Fred Astaire is, in his way, a genius. He has in a supreme degree that casual and lazy grace which conceals the hardest kind of efficiency. The simplest actions, done as he does them, have a rhythmic beauty which charms the senses like poetry.

AN IDEAL PARTNER

And Miss Luce makes him an ideal partner. She is as light as a feather, follows him like his shadow, and shares his happy sense of comedy.

I must not forget, by the way, that in between the dances a musical play went on. It was called "Gay Divorce," and the plot plumbed depths of imbecility not often sounded even in this kind of show.

Fortunately, however, the story does not matter and need not be told. The show exists chiefly to set off Mr. Astaire, and only when he or Miss Luce or Olive Blakeney – the gloriously definite personality – are on the stage does it come to life. At most other times it shows a woeful poverty of invention which good work by Eric Blore and Erik Rhodes, and top-speed callisthenics by the chorus, cannot disguise.

**(November 3)**

# BRITISH FILM TRIUMPH IN PARIS

## "PRIVATE LIFE OF HENRY VIII"

**By Campbell Dixon**

PARIS, Friday.

The first battle in the campaign to put British pictures on the world's screen was won this evening in Paris when London Film Production's "The Private Life of Henry VIII" had a triumphant première at the Cinema Lord Byron on the Avenue Champs Elysées.

It was the first time the picture had been shown in public anywhere. A touch of banality in the story, a little gaucherie in the execution, and the experiment of offering it first to the critical public of the Lord Byron, which specialises in the best American films, might easily have proved a fiasco.

MAGNIFICENT ACTING

But the producer's confidence was justified, Alexander Korda's direction, laying on the colour with bold, impressionist strokes, Charles Laughton's magnificent tour de force as Henry, Georges Perinal's glorious photography made it a triumphant success. "The Private Life of Henry VIII," stands out as perhaps the finest picture ever made in England, and a considerable achievement, judged even by the best world standards.

There might have been a little more depth in the story. It is slick and fast moving. It jumps from the tragedy of Anne Boleyn – quite admirably acted by Merle Oberson — to the bluff humour of the Tudor Court.

There is never a dull moment. Whether this is really Merrie England and this its fat and brutal and rather splendid king is a matter on which dons may differ. It is certainly first-rate cinema.

Charles Laughton, stepping straight out of Holbein's canvas, takes the eye on his first appearance and dominates every important scene – swaggering, bellowing, guzzling, shouting with laughter and weeping bitter tears, as intent on the swoop of a falcon as on the building of his navy, the very embodiment of his age. It is a remarkable performance, which no actor living could have bettered and few approached.

**(September 30)**

# VIVD PAGE OF HISTORY

**By W. A. Darlington**

"Richard of Bordeaux" was received at the New Theatre last night with a glorious full-throated roar such as the West-end seldom hears in these sophisticated days. Generally one has to travel to the Old Vic to hear the like, but this time the mountain (so to speak) decided to come to Mahomet.

But let us not go into the question whether the loud sounds were produced by a band of John Gielgud's and Gwen Ffrangcon-Davies's admirers from over the river, bent on giving their old favourites a send-off, or whether they were the spontaneous result of Gordon Daviot's admirable play. Whatever their cause and origin, they were sincere; and both the play and the actors deserved them.

The distinguished stage biography of Richard the Second has been much strengthened since it was first seen at a trial performance. The changes are subtle but important. They make much more dramatically plausible the author's explanation of Richard's change from an idealist with no thought but to govern strongly yet peaceably into a distrustful, vindictive ruler whom his subjects were glad to see deposed.

It now ranks as the best historical play that has been written of late years, after "Saint Joan."

It is brilliantly acted by Mr. Gielgud and Miss Ffrangcon-Davies (as Richard's queen and good angel).

**(February 3)**

# COUNTRY HOUSE OPERA

In a fold of the Downs a few miles east of Lewes lies a country house. Since it was first built by some Tudor gentleman the generations in their course have adapted it to their own ideas of comfort and culture. It has, however, remained for Mr. John Christie, the present owner of Glyndebourne, to do something that certainly never occurred to any of his predecessors of forebears.

This was to add a new wing, comprising an opera-house, complete to the last detail in every branch of operatic procedure as developed in Germany during the past decade. The last touches are now being given to what Mr. Christie claims is in many respects the most up-to-date opera house in existance. And as he shows you over it he explains with a proper pride how it embodies improvements which are so recent — particularly the system of dimming — that even the German theatres have not installed them.

He holds strongly to the opinion that to obtain festival spirit no concessions can be given to the world of affairs. Performances will begin at half-past five. There will be long entr'actes, during which the audience — the opera house, which consists only of stalls, holds 310 people — will have the run of the house and grounds.

An altogether delightful open-air beer garden is one of the theatre's adjuncts — and Mr. Christie hints at the possibility of free beer.

Apart from the festival performances, others will be given of a less ambitious nature. At these young English singers will be able to obtain valuable experience.

**(July 20)**

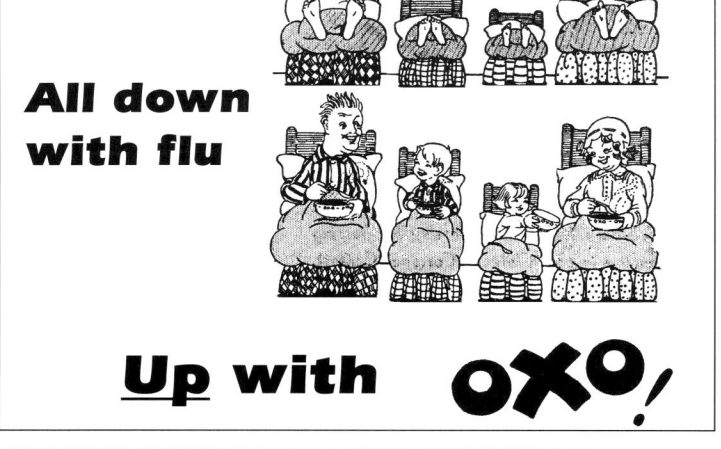

THE DAILY TELEGRAPH

135, FLEET STREET LONDON

Telephone: CENTRAL 4242

**TO-DAY'S WEATHER FORECAST**

LONDON & S.E. ENGLAND - Wind southerly, fresh, strong or gale locally, veering later; cloudy; rain, brighter later, but with showers; moderate temperature.

ENGLISH CHANNEL - Sea rough

## ROOSEVELT'S CALL TO ACTION

### Ready To Take War-Time Powers

If the promise of Mr. Franklin Roosevelt's Inaugural address is made good in the field of action, that utterance will certainly live in American history. It is a trumpet-call to the forces of national recovery. It is fitted exactly to the moral exigencies of the hour. Of the 22,000,000 citizens who put the new President in the White House, there can surely be none to-day to feel that his vote was not well bestowed. Emerson wrote of one whom many hold to be the greatest of Mr. Roosevelt's predecessors, that he "was sent to the helm in a tornado." If that could fitly be said of Abraham Lincoln, the words apply yet more closely to the President who took office on Saturday.

The American banking crisis, if not a thing without parallel in the distracted world of to-day, is quite beyond average American experience or imagination. The handling of it will be the first test of Mr. Roosevelt's statesmanship. But at the very outset he has appealed to the vast body of passionate public resentment over the financial misjudgement, and often worse, that has prepared the people of the United States so especially ill for the oncoming of the world depression. There are in Saturday's speech lashing phrases that might have been written by the President Roosevelt of twenty-five years ago in his long-sustained attack on "the Mammon of unrighteousness." Certainly no President since his day has dared to speak of business conduct "which too often has given to a sacred trust the likeness of callous and selfish wrongdoing"; to point to the "unscrupulous money-changers" defeated by their own "stubbornness and incompetence." These are among the flowers of invective in the new President's Inaugural.

**Immediate Action**

This is the note, recurring throughout the speech, which will have gone straight to the heart of a people reduced, in these latter days, to a complete collapse of all confidence. The President undertakes that there shall be action, immediate action. The very brevity of his Inaugural, which is unprecedented in this respect, was no doubt calculated to support his blunt intimation that there has been talking enough. He sketches rapidly a boldly ambitious programme. It is so "radical" as not to stop short – in the United States of all countries – of national planning and supervision for transport and all other utilities of a public character. It makes suggestive reference to the need of an "adequate and sound currency." Is there a shadow of controlled inflation here? It speaks of farmers' relief, land settlement, rigid retrenchment in every form of public administration.

**A Courageous Proposal**

Here is more than enough to strain the slow-moving machinery of the National Congress; and here comes in the astonishing climax of Mr. Roosevelt's appeal to his countrymen. Should Congress fail, he declares, he will demand the grant by that body to himself of "broad executive power to wage war against the emergency" – not merely such power as is by law the President's in time of war, but such as he would have the right to demand if the country were "invaded by a foreign foe." No President, until now, has ever hinted at the possibility of such a delegation of the sacred authority of the Legislature to the Executive. Constitutionally, indeed, it is not possible. But the mere proposal is the proof, not only of Mr. Roosevelt's grasp of the realities of the national danger, but of the singular courage which he brings to the gigantic task of coping with it.

**(March 6)**

## BESMIRCHING OXFORD'S FAIR FAME

Much feeling has been aroused, as the further letters we publish to-day indicate, by the recent vote of the Oxford Union Society, declaring that "in no circumstances would this House fight for its King and Country." The indignation is natural. The terms were needlessly, and it would seem, designedly provocative and offensive to what is still generally understood as loyal and patriotic sentiment. However uncompromising the pacifism of the motion, if it had been expressed in more abstract terms, it would not have excited the same reprobation, though it might have been no less heartily deplored. But the vote does not mean that Oxford has gone or is going Red, though it is notorious that among a certain not inconsiderable section of the undergraduate community extreme opinions are the vogue, and discretion in the method of their expression is taken for old-fashioned weakness of intellect and badness of heart.

We deplore this vote of the Oxford Union because of the bad impression which it is bound to create wherever it is read. Last Thursday's majority doubtless expected to be regarded as enlightened citizens of the better world which they are striving to create. Have they considered that their vote for pacifism in all conceivable circumstances will rather be taken as proof that the intelligentsia of Oxford are not so much Red as Yellow?

**(February 14)**

## THE NAZI POGROMS

The anti-Jewish campaign of the Nazis is being watched with disgust by all decent opinion outside Germany, and not least in this country. What most astonishes is the total lack of discrimination. The crime is to be a Jew, and for that no professional eminence, no degree of capacity in business, no public service, and no private virtue can atone. Professors are driven from their class-rooms, musical conductors from their concert-rooms, actors from the stage. Herr Feucht-wanger's Berlin home has just been invaded by Nazi rowdies, and his manuscripts destroyed.

To escape similar or worse indignities, Prof. Einstein, the most intellectually distinguished of living Germans, has exiled himself from Germany while such personal outrages are inflicted by Nazi Kultur. Violence, indeed, is officially deprecated; but the perpetrators go unpunished. Nor is it forgotten that Capt. Goehring himself declared last year that the Hitlerite policy was to expel all Jews who have come into Germany since 1914, and remove the rest from all public positions. Capt. Goehring cannot, it seems, forgive the Jewish race for having given birth to Marxism, and he attributes to the "Jewish vampire" all the manifold troubles from which Germany is now suffering. Such raving folly would be incredible were it not true. The more effectual a Jewish purge, the more irreparable would be Germany's loss, for she would lose at a stroke most of her best brains in the financial world and many of the best in commerce, medicine, the law and the arts.

**(May 18)**

## HIGHER TAXI FARES

On Aug. 1 and after the Londoner's taxi will cost him more. The Home Secretary, who made the announcement yesterday, has not come to this conclusion hastily, for as far back as last February it was confidently stated that an increase would shortly be authorised. Sir John Gilmour has added threepence to every taxi fare, and the minimum hiring fee will now be ninepence instead of sixpence. The view of the regular taxi-user will be that as this is virtually the least possible increase it must be endured philosophically. Certainly a sixpenny increase, which many of the drivers demanded, would have led to an immediate falling-off in public patronage.

**(July 20)**

## VIOLENCE & THE "CAT"

At the Old Bailey yesterday three prisoners were sentenced to terms of penal servitude and a flogging. Two had taken part in what was described as "the worst hold-up in London," for one threatened his pursuers with a sawn-off shot-gun, and the other slashed at the police with a dagger. The third was the miscreant who robbed with violence four defenceless women at Golders-green and Cricklewood and then violently assaulted a detective. All three used extreme violence, and not one of the three was more than twenty years of age.

In such cases as these there is no room for sentimentality. They will get their chance to reform while they are serving their sentences of penal servitude. But they will begin the course with a richly derserved flogging, and justly be made to suffer something of the pain which they have callously inflicted on others.

**(July 20)**

# GLARING EVILS OF OUR ILLOGICAL DIVORCE LAWS

By Sir Ellis Hume-Williams, K.C.

Year by year the lists of divorce cases for trial published at the beginning of each legal term seem to grow in length and prove how very nearly the Law of Divorce touches the lives of the people.

The law has grown up very gradually, inherited from the practice of the old Ecclesiastical Court, which with reluctance were sometimes persuaded to grant a separation "a mensa et thoro" from "bed and board," but exercised little further power.

And now the law of divorce, after much tinkering and many amendments, is probably harder and more illogical in this country than in any other country in the world.

To be honest about it, the law of divorce in this country is wholly illogical. Either we should say, as the Roman Catholics do, once married always married – marriage is a Sacrament, and if you have made a bad bargain you must nevertheless stick to it – or we should say that it is not in the interest of the community that people who have honestly tried to make marriage the successful companionship which it ought to be and have miserably failed – so much so that they are living separate and independent lives – should continue to be bound together.

"MANUFACTURED" EVIDENCE

In England cruelty, however brutal and sustained, even if it ruin the health and kill the happiness of the sufferer, is not ground for divorce. Neither is it if one of the parties becomes hopelessly insane or develops into a raving drunkard or a besotted drug maniac.

It is adultery, and adultery alone, which enables the marriage to be dissolved, however much and however fragrantly either party may have disregarded every honourable obligation which marriage entails.

Unless one party can prove the other to have been unfaithful, man and wife they must remain, although they may be living at opposite ends of the globe.

And so, as surely as you leave two people leading miserable lives no means of escape except proved adultery, human nature will prove stronger than any law, and collusive divorces will continue.

I have known more than one case in which those wishful to obtain a divorce have had some odd experiences. In one a friend of mine – who, however, had had the wisdom not to consult me – determined to give his wife the evidence upon which he could be divorced.

So he procured a lady (he informed me afterwards that she announced herself, as being, as usual, the daughter of a clergyman and the widow of an officer), who consented to spend the night with him at an hotel.

The hotel having been chosen and the time of meeting arranged, my friend arrived punctually at the tryst, and the lady duly turned up. She was quite pleasant, if a little prim, but looked, he thought, not in the best of health.

After a short and rather silent interval in the lounge of the hotel, the lady mounted, apparently with some difficulty, to the bedroom, the joint occupation of which was to provide the necessary evidence of a night of sin.

But no sooner did the lady arrive in the room than she was violently sick, and then lay down on the incriminating bed, and was seized with violent spasms.

My friend, a kind-hearted man, despite his matrimonial errors, at once sent for a doctor, who pronounced the lady to be suffering from a violent colic, which, unless promptly and continuously treated, might become exceedingly dangerous.

The lady dozed a little when daylight broke, and the man sat and watched in an armchair, where the waiter found him when he brought some tea in the morning. Fortunately the lady was able to return home with the help of some further soothing medicine. My friend duly paid her and the hotel bill, and was in due course properly divorced!

In another case a man, finding life with his wife very miserable, agreed with her to do the "gentlemanly thing" and give her the necessary evidence to divorce him. So he consulted two friends, not stodgy lawyers, but men of the world, who assured him that it was the easiest thing possible.

TRYING TO DECEIVE THE COURT

You had only to take a lady – any lady friend would do – to an hotel, spend the night in two rooms as far removed as the poles, but be careful to pay both bills yourself in the morning. And there you were! So this was done.

Later still following the same expert advice, he wrote a formal letter to his wife telling her that he had stayed the night at the hotel with a lady, and saying that she would find conclusive evidence of his adultery in the fact that he had paid the bill for both; and asking "would she please divorce him as soon as possible."

Then he went to a lawyer, and was told, of course, that his scheme was simply silly, and that a cat wouldn't be divorced because he and another cat had spent the night on neighbouring roofs."

"But," added the lawyer, "if your wife is so anxious to get a divorce, perhaps she has a reason; why not have her watched! This was done, and it was soon discovered that the wife was living in almost open adultery with another man, and the husband knew nothing.

So the husband thereupon presented a petition against the wife, instead of its being the other way round, and the case came on for trial.

But in England the law is that a man who has himself been guilty of adultery cannot obtain a divorce from his wife for her adultery, unless the judge exercises a discretion in his favour.

LUDICROUSLY WRONG

And here was a man who, with the intention of deceiving the Court, and in obvious collusion with his wife, had written to her saying that he had himself been guilty of the same offence! And that the letter was completely untrue made the matter, if anything, rather worse.

Fortunately, however, the case came before a kindly judge with a sense of humour, and by making some fun of the husband's amateur efforts at deception and proving the very bad and continuous adultery of the wife I got him through and he was given a decree.

It is true that if the complaining spouse, whether husband or wife, admits that he or she has been guilty of a similar offence the judge may, if he can find extenuating circumstances, nevertheless grant to him or her the desired divorce.

But surely the process should be reversed, and where both parties before the Court have been unfaithful the marriage should ipso facto be dissolved unless the judge finds the circumstances of the mutual unfaithfulness to be so scandalous that he must exercise the discretion with which he is vested against both or either applicant.

The bald statement to the effect that it is in the interests of the community that where one party has been unfaithful a marriage can be dissolved, but that where both have it must be maintained, seems to carry refutation on the face of it.

**(March 6)**

## LONDON DAY BY DAY: Royal Shot Duce at the Wheel

The King has not, I hear been shooting very constantly at Balmoral this season. It will be remembered that once or twice during the summer he was unable to wear uniform, as the result of rheumatism in the shoulder. For the same reason, he has found his freedom of movement with the gun a little cramped.

His Majesty's prowess as a crack shot, however, remains the talk of Deeside, where he has never looked better in general health, or seemed more the Laird of Balmoral.

**The Duce as Chauffeur**

I am not so certain that the further gesture, should it materialise, of the Duce acting as chauffeur to the party from Ostia to Rome will be so soothing as the flying boat trip.

Signor Mussolini is a somewhat awe-inspiring motorist, and has a nice taste in racing automobiles for private use. He put them to good advantage when he made a dramatic dash from Rome to Locarno in 1925.

But on this occasion, since the talks are the important feature of the visit, he may find it more economical of time to hand over control to a chauffeur and take a back seat.

**Changing Euston-road**

Going along the Euston-road, that erstwhile gloomy street, the Londoner cannot fail to be impressed by the great changes that have lately come about.

The dressing back of all the south side from St. Pancras Church to the Euston-square Metropolitan station with a frontage of new buildings has effected a wonderful improvement.

On the north side one is impressed by the progress towards erection of the new L.M.S. office block, which will accommodate 1,200 servants of the company, who, brought to London when the post-war railway grouping was done, have since been housed in scattered buildings.

**The New L.M.S. Block**

The demolition on this site is now completed, and I am informed the work of rebuilding will be starting immediately.

The St. Pancras Hotel, however, which many would gladly see demolished, is to stand in the meantime, despite the criticisms passed upon it from an aesthetic standpoint by the company's chairman, Sir Josiah Stamp, at a recent gathering of architects.

The company, I am told, is doing everything in its power to make it serve its purpose satisfactorily for some years to come.

**Delayed Enterprises**

Indeed, it is a bold company that is ready, at this moment, to embark on new London hotel construction. Overnight I had been listening to some big business men discussing the potentialities of the St. George's Hospital site.

One suggested the idea of a new hotel, and another was quick to recall the contention of the Grosvenor House company that there is not room even for two big hotels in Park-lane.

The Canadian Pacific Railway, too, has wisely deferred its big hotel project on the Berkeley-square Bruton-street site.

**The Prince's Service Ranks**

As the Prince of Wales has held for two years on the first of the month the ranks of Vice-Admiral, Lt.-Gen., and Air Marshal, there has been some expectation that he would be advanced a further step in rank in all three Services.

Though somewhat down the list of his rank in both the Navy and the Army, he is the senior of the Air Marshals, Sir Robert Brooke-Popham being next with seniority dating Jan. 1, 1931.

Sir Robert is now second in seniority on the Active List in the R.A.F., apart from Lord Trenchard, who is Marshal of the Royal Air Force. Sir Edward Ellington is the only Air Chief Marshal, and he is Chief of the Air Staff.

**In The House**

Prince Hubertus, the grandson of the ex-Kaiser, and the first Hohenzollern to visit this country since the war, was an interested spectator in the Distinguished Strangers' Gallery of the House of Commons yesterday.

The Prince, who was accompanied by Mecklenberg, listened intently to the questions and answers on the persecution of the Jews in Germany.

A representative of the Foreign Office sat with them and explained the procedure and pointed out certain prominent members. Before he left the Gallery Prince Hubertus plied the Foreign Office official with questions about all the Ministers and various members who were taking part in the Russian debate.

PETERBOROUGH

## THEATRE GUIDE

ALDWYCH – A BIT OF A TEST ........ 8.15
AMBASSADORS – THE STREETS OF LONDON . 8.20
APOLLO – DOUBLE HARNESS ........ 8.20
COMEDY– BALLYHOO ........ 2.30 & 8.20
CRITERION – FRESH FIELDS ........ 8.20
DALY'S – IT'S YOU I WANT ........ 8.30
DRURY LANE – WILD VIOLETS ........ 8.15
DUCHESS – CHILDREN IN UNIFORM ........ 8.30
EMBASSY – THE GLASS WALL ........ 8.15
GAIETY – MOTHER OF PEARL ........ 8.10
GARRICK – WHILE PARENTS SLEEP! ........ 8.40
HAYMARKET – TEN MINUTE ALIBI ........ 2.30 & 8.30
HIPPODROME – THE ONE GIRL ........ 8.15
HIS MAJESTY'S – THE DUBARRY ........ 8.15
LITTLE – COCK ROBIN ........ 8.30
NEW – RICHARD OF BORDEAUX ........ 8.15
OLD VIC – ROMEO AND JULIET ........ 8.00
PALACE – DINNER AT EIGHT ........ 8.30
PLAYHOUSE – FLIES IN THE SUN ........ 8.30
PRINCE OF WALES – TOUT-LE-TEMPS ........ 2-11.30
QUEEN'S – ONCE IN A LIFETIME ........ 8.30
SAVOY – JOLLY ROGER ........ 8.15
ST. MARTIN'S – THE GREEN BAY TREE ........ 8.30
STRAND – NIGHT OF THE GARTER ........ 8.30
VAUDEVILLE – Ballieff's Chauve Souris . 2.30 & 8.30
WHITEHALL – ROAD HOUSE ........ 8.30
WYNDHAM'S – SERVICE ........ 8.30

VARIETY ENTERTAINMENTS

HOLBORN EMPIRE ........ 6.30 & 9.00
PALLADIUM ........ 6.30 & 9.00
VICTORIA PALACE ........ 6.30 & 9.00

NON-STOP ENTERTAINMENTS

LEICESTER-SQ – NINA MAE MCKINNEY .. 2.30-11.30
LONDON PAVILION – NON-STOP VARIETY ... 2-11.30
MASKELYNE'S – NON STOP ........ 3-10.30
WINDMILL – REVUDEVILLE No. 21 ........ 1.30-11.30

PICTURE THEATRE

ACADEMY – 14 JUILLET (JULY 14th) ........ Cont.
ALHAMBRA – MOVIE CRAZY ........ 12 Cont.
ASTORIA – LOVE ME TO-NIGHT ........ Cont.
CAPITOL – THE GOOD COMPANIONS ........ Cont.
CARLTON – The Sign of the Cross . 2.45, 6.15 & 8.45
CINEMA HOUSE – KADETTEN ........ Cont.
COLISEUM – MOVIE CRAZY ........ 12 Cont.
EMPIRE – FAST LIFE ........ 10 Cont.
MARBLE ARCH PAV. – ENDURANCE ........ Cont.
NEW GALLERY – JUST MY LUCK ........ Cont.
NEW VICTORIA – LOVE ME TO-NIGHT ........ 12-11
PLAZA – BILLION DOLLAR SCANDAL .... 10.15 Cont.
POLYTECHNIC – Mr. Robinson Crusoe 2.30, 5.30 & 8.30
REGAL – A BILL OF DIVORCEMENT ........ Cont.
RIALTO – THE WHITE FLAME ........ 12-12
STOLL – MOVIE CRAZY ........ 12 Cont.
TIVOLI – CAVALCADE ........ 2.30, 6.15 & 8.45
TUSSAUD'S – MOVIE CRAZY ........ 1.30-11

# MAKING GOLF LESS EXPENSIVE

## SHOULD TIPS BE ABOLISHED?

**By George Greenwood**

The subject of tipping caddies, together with the amount of their fees, has lately been occupying the attention of the committee of one of the most important London golf clubs.

A suggestion was made that tipping should be strictly prohibited, and a fixed charge for each round be paid direct to the caddie-master, who would hand it to the caddie.

The committee agreed that the system was ideal if it could be worked, but it was asked: "Has any attempt at the abolition of tipping, either in this country or elsewhere, ever really succeeded?"

In my experience the answer is an emphatic negative. It was pointed out that the real responsibility for the excessive tip which the proposal attempted to deal with rested with the golfer himself. It is one thing making a rule prohibiting tipping, but quite another trying to enforce it.

£1 FOR ONE MATCH

I have in mind another well-known London club which fixed the sum of 2s as the limit of tipping for a day's golf. Although members were informed that the committee would take serious notice of any breach of the regulation, it was dead in a month.

I know of four-ball matches at some of the London clubs where the stake is £5 a corner and the tip to the caddies on the winning side is £1 each.

In the case of the London club mentioned above it was urged that while it was easy to deal with the caddie where tipping was detected, it was not so easy to take disciplinary action, such as dismissal from the club, against a member. What of the player, it was asked, who won a competition or match, and emerged richer by the sweep money or the stake involved. Would he not resent being debarred from giving the caddie something in addition to the fixed fee?

The committee finally decided that, while the usual procedure of a fee plus a tip should remain, members should be earnestly requested to limit the tip to a reasonable sum – 1s 6d per round in the case of first-class and 1s per round for second-class caddies, with a further request that in no case should a player give more than an additional 6d.

A first-class caddie will thus receive 4s fee plus 3s tip for two rounds, the charges to include lunch money and the cleaning of clubs.

**(March 1)**

# GAY CLOTHES FOR CRUISING

## WOMEN IN NAUTICAL AND MANLY STYLES

Divided skirts will share the honours with trousers as the smartest fashion for this year's holiday cruises.

The new skirts are trousers in disguise, very full and only coming to the middle of the leg, so that they have the appearance of skirts.

For deck sports it will be hard to distinguish between fashions for men and women. Both will wear white flannel trousers, with coloured blazers and caps. Women's flannels are cut on correct yachting lines, and one of the smartest outfits will be white trousers with scarlet blazer and cap.

The vogue of trousers for cruising is due to their being infinitely more practical than skirts for deck wear, where for one thing there is always a breeze to contend with. Coloured trousers will also be worn, and some are in the most vivid stripes.

For sun-bathing on deck there are entirely backless jumpers, tied on at the waist and neck, for wear with trousers.

TRANSPARENT HATS

Transparent sun-bathing hats and sun shades have been devised that keep out the red rays while admitting the ultra-violet ones. They are in a fireproof material similar to cellaphane; the hats are shaped on the lines of the national Welsh hat, with high crowns but wider brims.

Oblong sunshades, fitted at an angle to the handle, are being designed in cotton and towelling to enable one to read in comfort at any position on deck.

Vivid reds, brilliant oranges and yellows are the new cruising shades, borrowed from the South in order to give the wearers the tonic effect of sunshine.

For the afternoon promenade on deck there are tailored suits of uncrushable linen and silk, and women are taking half a dozen of these as a way of avoiding the high cost of laundering on board. Most of these suites are striped diagonally.

All cruising hats have a nautical air. Either they are versions of the "sailor" in straw or felt, or they are on the lines of a cap, in red, white and blue.

When evening comes the holiday-makers will become as feminine as they have been masculine for the earlier part of the day. Flowered cotton and silk frocks reaching to the ground will then fill the saloons of the holiday ship.

**(March 15)**

# IDEAL HOME EXHIBITION

## LAST FEW DAYS OF COMPREHENSIVE DISPLAY AT OLYMPIA

One of London's prime attractions during the past three weeks, and for many people one of the year's most interesting events, had but a few days more to run. The Ideal Home Exhibition at Olympia which is organised annually by the "Daily Mail" opened on March 29 and will close next Saturday.

The Ideal Home Exhibition is not so much a collection of merchandise – though even so it is probably unique – as a panoramic illustration testifying to the important part which home life plays in the lives of the British people.

### Progress of Designers

Every year there are such notable advances in designs and materials, so many new devices for the elimination of drudgery, and such manifold offerings at the twin altars of beauty and efficiency that one is tempted to believe that inventiveness can go no farther. The ideal home, one thinks, must surely now be attainable.

Ideality in domestic affairs is rarely interpretable in a few words, but from the housewife's point of view it centres in the smooth control of her practical responsibilities. This explains the interest displayed by women visitors in the "Commonsense Kitchens" designed by Mrs. Darcy Braddell. These five rooms are expressive of the modern woman's protest against kitchens and kitchenettes in which – as is often the case – there is hardly room to turn, much less to perform in reasonable comfort the all-important work transacted in this part of the house.

The Luxury Kitchen has a floor of rubber, double sinks and draining boards of rust-resisting metal, and a rubber-walled alcove in which is set an electric cooker with table tops of the same metal. The furniture is of chromium steel, whilst the cooking table has a top of armour-plated glass. Cupboards run from floor to ceiling, cheerfully varnished in white cellulose, which treatment has been applied to the cabinets, the electric refrigerator, and all the remaining wall surfaces.

Less ambitious but equally interesting is the dual purpose kitchen designed to serve as a maid's sitting-room. Between the windows is a specially designed folding table for meals which, when closed, conceals the wall-cupboard containing the maid's crockery. Curtains and rugs of fadeless material give an atmosphere of homeliness and warmth to the apartment. Other model rooms provide suggestions for kitchens of various sizes and dispositions.

### Home Management

Among the exhibits of practical character are many which offer increased efficiency in home management, and, in consequence, added comfort for the housewife.

An interesting display is that of Vac-Tric Ltd., who are the manufacturers of the well-known suction cleaner bearing that name. In addition to exhibiting their "Model H" and "De Luxe" models, this firm, who claim to be the first to manufacture an all-British suction cleaner, are also showing an entirely new and smaller machine, known as the "Popular."

On Stand No. 80 (ground floor, Grand Hall) Vac-Tric Ltd are showing their all-British refrigerator, which was first exhibited at last year's Ideal Home Exhibition. It is made with a pressed steel body, with white cellulose enamel finish and chromium-plated fittings.

The actual storage capacity is 5 cubic feet, the shelf area is 9 ¾ft, and the interior is finished in white vitreous enamel, making it easy to clean. Two ice-trays permit forty-two ice cubes to be made in one freezing, and a constant temperature of less than 59 deg. F. is maintained.

### Dry Cleaning

The "Spik" dry-cleaner shown on the stand of Messrs. Sankey Instone Ltd., is the result of many years of experimenting on the part of the scientists and engineers employed by this company. In order to perfect this machine, which enables dry-cleaning to be performed in the home, many obstacles had to be overcome. Not the least of them was the production of a fluid that would be perfectly safe from the point of view of inflammability.

Little labour is required for the operation of the "Spik" dry-cleaner. It is extremely simple in use, and the centrifugal action of the machine obviates any wringing of the garment after it has been removed from the machine – a definite advantage in the case of delicate fabrics.

It is claimed by the designers and builders of the "Spik" that it will effectively clean dresses, coats, hats, trousers, &c., and that it will not damage the daintiest materials.

One of the most interesting exhibits at this year's exhibition is that of "The Night Sky Telegram," which proposes to focus on the sky, by means of a battery of light projectors, news messages of important events which occur between 8p.m. and midnight.

The "Night Sky Telegram" will be shown in London from a battery of sky projectors installed on the roofs of buildings adjoining Trafalgar - square, Leicester - square, Tottenham - court - road, Marble Arch, and Piccadilly, and other batteries are to be installed in the suburbs and the provinces. Each projector is said to be of many hundred million candle power, and is designed to sweep the sky in all directions.

### Electrical Equipment

On the stand of the Hotpoint Electric Appliance Co. Ltd. is exhibited a wide range of kitchen equipment, including electric cookers, irons, washing machines, immersion heaters and suction cleaners.

The outstanding exhibit on this stand is the "Hotpoint-B.T.H." electric cooker, which is now being manufactured at the Rugby works of the British Thomson-Houston Co. In addition to having many new features, which include the "Hotpoint Torribar" boiling plates, the models shown are claimed to constitute a step forward in electric cooker design.

For many years the "Hotpoint" electric iron has been recognised as a product of high quality, and it is again well represented on the company's stand. A special feature is the patent flex support which is supplied free of charge with each 15s 6d iron. This support keeps the flexible cord out of the way of the operator when she is ironing.

Considerable reductions have been effected in the price of the "Hotpoint Super-Automatic" electric kettles, which are finished in either polished copper or nickel plate.

Other Hotpoint-B.T.H. products shown on this stand are an electric washing machine and an immersion heater. The former is finished in an attractive dove-grey enamel, has a large water capacity, yet occupies comparatively little space. The immersion heater can be fitted into any existing water tank, and with its aid hot water can be made available at any time.

The "Eco-Dry" cabinet is designed to afford quick and safe drying of household linen, wearing apparel, &c. Its use is not confined to the home, but extends to a wide range of public institutions, and it has been chosen for installation in the Commonsense Laundry at the exhibition, designed by Mrs. Darcy Braddell.

### Tonic Bath Salt

Although the invigorating properties of sea-water are well known, its benefits have only been available to the majority of people during holidays spent at the seaside. There is exhibited at Olympia a bath salt, sold under the trade name "Billowzone" which is not a "sea salt" as commonly sold, but which not only gives off the clean tonic scent of the sea but also oxygen compounds and organic iodine in a form of particular benefit to the human body.

"Billowzone" can be obtained in small cartons, boxes, or large drums.

A solution of the problem often presented by covering of a concrete floor is offered by "Expanco" cork flooring, which serves for this type of floor in the same way as linoleum does on wood.

Cork parquetry has many advantages. It is durable and (unless specially prepared for dancing) not slippery, although it can be highly polished. Moreover it is warm, and its appearance is attractive. "Expanco" flooring has one feature in particular to commend it; it is made in sections which fit closely together by virtue of a tongue-and-groove construction. Adhesive is unnecessary in laying the tiles, a task which is within the powers of an amateur.

Many hotels, clubs and similar large buildings have been laid with "Expanco," but it is, of course, equally suitable for dwelling houses of any size.

The ideal of using pure linen throughout a house appeals strongly to the housewife, and the Irish Linen Guild, on their stand at Olympia, demonstrate how pleasing an effect may be obtained by this material.

It is a fitting background — some would say the only appropriate setting — for fine china, cut glass, silver, and beautiful furniture. Irish linen needs no advocate, for its durable qualities, beautiful texture and appearance are generally known and appreciated. But it should not be forgotten that linen of good wearing qualities invariably proves economical.

**(April 25)**

# CAR WIRELESS ARRIVES

## BUILT-IN RECEIVER FOR MOTOR SHOW

**By L. Marsland Gander**

Car radio will be as common in Britain shortly as it is in the United States. This conclusion is irresistable afyter a tour of the Radio Exhibition at Olympia.

Reasons for the sudden crop of receivers of this type are clear. Automatic volume control eliminates sudden changes of signal strenghth as the car speeds along the road and swings round corners. Then, improvements in design have made sets more compact, and there are the all-metal Gatkin valves, smaller and more robust than any of their progenitors.

Car receivers fall into two classes those to be incorporated in a new purchase as an extra fitting, and those designed to be added to a car already on the road. In the first type comes the Elko set, which, I understand, will be built into 16h.p. and 20h.p. Austin models for the coming Motor Show, as an optional fitting, with an aerial in the roof.

DASHBOARD CONTROL

The set is Ekco's standard 7-stage superheterodyne. A neat feature is the oval illuminated dial, with stations by name, let into the dashboard. There are only two knobs to control everything. As with all car-receivers, the sparking-plugs have to be fitted with special suppressors. Passing cars may cause a little splutter in the loud-speaker, but is not serious.

Mr. W. I. G. Page, of Page Car Radio, showed me sets of the other type, to be fitted into existing cars. A five-valve all metal superheterodyne may be sunk into the floorboards and worked with remote control from the steering column, while a piece of "rabbit wire" in the roof is a first-class aerial. The speaker would be generally installed to the left of the clutch pedal. The amount of current used by this set is a little less than that taken by one headlamp.

**(August 22)**

# THE TOWN HOUSE PROBLEM

The next few years may see an exodus from Mayfair of both young and old owners of historic houses, flats and dwellings in fashionable mews to the ancient suburbs of Hampstead, Richmond, Wimbledon, Highgate and Roehampton. The main reason will be the ever-increasing noise of Central London, the ceaseless day and night traffic of the West-end.

Few Mayfair houses now possess gardens. Garage room for one or more cars belonging to each family is hard to come by, rents are still high, and many people who have had vistas of the cool, green parks find these blotted out by new mammoth blocks of flats.

One of the latest people to abandon the West-end for a suburb with an historic name is Sir Matthew "Scatters" Wilson, Bt., who has decided to leave his house in Cadogan-gardens for Forbes House, Ham Common. "I am getting to an age when I need peace and quiet in my own garden," Sir Matthew told me, "and at the same time," he added, "in thirty minutes by car I can be in Piccadilly."

**(August 11)**

# SELECTED FOODS FOR THE BREAKFAST AND TEA TABLES

To have one central thought and one fixed policy for over one hundred and fifty years is convincing evidence that some measure of success has been obtained. Over all this extensive period of time Messrs. Stephen Carwardine and Co. have continued to be exclusively Tea Blenders and Coffee Roasters. Their price list discloses the fact that Tea is sold by them at prices ranging from 1s per pound to 4s 6d.

The firm draw special attention to their X.L.N.T. 6lb post paid 10s. At a time when impositions of Tariffs tend to make some articles of foreign import dearer in price, it is refreshing to note that, owing to the Ottawa agreements, the price of Coffee has been reduced, and Stephen Carwardine and Co. quote the finest Coffee at 2s 6d per pound, and other varieties at 2s 2d, 1s 10d, all Empire grown.

A word must be given with reference to the Tea and Coffee Rooms opened by Carwardines at Victoria House, Southampton-row, where visitors can be quite sure of a delightful cup of Tea or Coffee, served amidst surroundings which are considered unique in London.

### Won the Confidence of the Public

With the opening of a small shop in Holborn sixty-four years ago, the House of Sainsbury erected its first sign. At that time provisions of first-class quality were to be obtained only by those who could pay the highest price and wait for the leisurely arrival of the uncertain carrier.

Now, half a million homes throughout the 70 square miles of Greater London, and in the adjacent counties from Cambridge to Bournemouth, and Brighton, depend upon Sainsbury for their daily supplies of fresh provisions, and Sainsbury's are ready to add the names of 100,000 new customers dwelling within reach of their service. Great care is taken to make the various branch establishments of this firm models of their kind. There are daily fresh supplies, and these can be purchased at the lowest market prices of the day.

Bermaline bread is real nourishment in a most attractive form, and in the maintenance of health the right diet and the right bread make all the difference. Bread is the staple food of millions of people, and when properly prepared and of the right quality well deserves the title of the Staff of Life.

The chief ingredients of "Bermaline" bread are flour and wheatmeal and "Bermaline" extract of malt. The flour and wheatmeal are made from selected wheats, specially milled to ensure purity and a fine dissection of the bran. The wheatmeal contains over 99 per cent of the wheat, its nutritive value represents the utmost food value of the wheat cereal, and the important accessory food factors are retained. This bread is a sound favourite with men and women of all ages and in all walks of life, be their occupation manual or sedentary.

### Efficiency in Fruit Transport

Fyffes's bananas are known all over the British Isles and they are one of the most popular energy-building fruits sought after by the public. The transport of these bananas is a work of art. Fyffes "Blue Label" Brand is seen in every city, town and village, and so complete are the transport arrangements that the fruit is delivered to the shops in perfect condition ready for the consumer.

### A Strengthening Breakfast Porridge

"Oatrex" is a pure oat food, prepared from the best of the Scottish oat crop, which has been subjected to a special process which partially cooks and sterilises and at the same time enhances the natural flavour of the meal. Medium ground "Oatrex" has been specially prepared in response to requests for a coarser cut meal for general use at the breakfast table, and it requires only a few minutes simmering to produce a most nourishing and strengthening breakfast porridge of characteristic flavour. It is packed in tins at 6½d, 1s, 1s 10d, and 3s 6d.

**(March 8)**

# SUDDEN DEATH OF "RANJITSINHJI"

Men in high places throughout the Empire have to mourn in the death of "Ranji" an enlightened ruler and a statesman of mark. Lt.-Col. his Highness Shri Sir Ranjitsinhji Vibhaji Maharaja Jamsaheb of Nawangar, G.C.S.I., G.B.E., twice representative of India in the League of Nations, and until a few days ago Chancellor of the Chamber of Indian Native Princes, commands respectful homage. His record in the War, when he not only served himself with distinction in our armies, but equipped a regiment and turned his English residence into a hospital, was of a piece with his statesmanship. He has deserved well of the commonwealth, which will not be slow to do him honour.

But amid all the pomp and circumstance of the Prince's passing, not the least splendid tribute to his memory will be the honest grief of the Englishman in the street that "Ranji" is dead. Ever since F.S. Jackson, captain of the Cambridge University Cricket Club, awarded him the first Blue ever given to an Indian, "Ranji" has been one of our popular idols. His personality, his supple grace, his lightning quickness of eye and wrist, made him a favourite with the sporting public; and when in due course he was chosen to play for England, nobody questioned his right. He was one of the greatest in an age of great batsmen, and his most characteristic feats on English playing fields will be remembered here with lively affection when his solider achievements as a potentate in a far land have faded into history.

**(April 3)**

# "ANTHONY HOPE"

## FAMOUS AUTHOR OF NOVELS OF RURITANIA

Sir Anthony Hope Hawkins ("Anthony Hope") who died on Saturday at the age of 70 at his home at Walton-on-the-Hill after a long illness, was less known to novel-readers and playgoers of the present day than to those of twenty years ago. His vogue had vanished with the years. He will be best remembered as the inventor of "Ruritania," a fanciful country in the Balkans, and for those two spirited Ruritanian stories, "The Prisoner of Zenda" and "Rupert of Hentzau." Perhaps "The Dolly Dialogues" will help with these to fix his fame.

The idea for "The Prisoner of Zenda" flashed across his mind while walking back to the Temple from Westminster County Court, where he had just won one of his rare cases. Before he reached his chambers the main theme of the romance had shaped itself. He sat down at once and wrote the first chapter, and within a month he had completed the book, enjoying, as he said, every word of it. The public shared his enjoyment. When it appeared it brought him fame and riches.

SIR ANTHONY HOPE HAWKINS.

The "Dolly Dialogues," a masterpiece of the comedy, of persiflage, and "The God in the Car" added to his reputation, and later he wrote the excellent Zenda sequel – "Rupert of Hentzau."

Anthony Hope made valiant efforts to be a novelist of character. he did not fail altogether. Once or twice he came near hitting off portraits which might live, with Quizanté the not altogether shady political adventurer, and again with the charming figure of his Bohemian heroine, Peggy Ryle.

### OXFORD AND FICTION

Anthony Hope Hawkins was the second son of the Rev. E. C. Hawkins, for many years vicar of St. Bride's, Fleet-street and a nephew of Lord Brampton (Mr. Justice Hawkins). From Marlborough he won a scholarship at Balliol, then at the height of its fame under Jowett's mastership. On leaving Oxford he was called to the Bar, and practised in London and on the Midland Circuit till 1894.

Anthony Hope was also a successful playwright, "The Prisoner of Zenda," dramatised by himself with Edward Rose, and "Rupert of Hentzau," by himself alone, give Sir George Alexander two plays of resounding success. A picturesque and witty eighteenth-century tale. "The Adventure of Lady Ursula," filled many a theatre. In a different vein as a satiric comedy of political life, "Pilkington's Peerage" had considerable vogue, and a film version of "Phroso" won great favour.

The novelist was knighted in 1918. He married, in 1903. Elizabeth Somerville, daughter of Mr. Charles J. Sheldon, of New York, and leaves two sons and a daughter.

**(July 10)**

# LORD GREY, THE MAN OF PEACE

## HIS GREAT ROLE IN AUGUST, 1914

## HIGH COURAGE AND CLEAR FORESIGHT

Viscount Grey of Fallodon, who died yesterday at the age of 71, was the man of peace who for eleven years directed the relations of his country with foreign Powers and who, with high courage and clear foresight, upheld her honour in the strenuous days, which preceded the declaration of war in August 1914.

When on June 28, 1914, the Archduke Franz Ferdinand was murdered, Grey was among the first to see that the ghastly crime was as a match that might light a huge European conflagration.

The Austrian Note to Serbia, with its most humiliating demands, allowed only forty-eight hours grace, but Grey put forward proposals for a conference which were immediately accepted by France and Italy, and approved by Russia, despite her sympathy with Serbia. Germany's refusal astounded him. He had not contemplated the eager encouragement which she gave to Austria in her impossible demands on Serbia, and the fruits of all his labours seemed to vanish in a few hours.

### MONDAY, AUG. 3, 1914

Never did Grey stand so high in the estimation of his countrymen as on the fateful Monday, Aug. 3, 1914, when he made a speech in the House of Commons which as he must have realised, might send millions of men to death on the battlefield.

He gave a masterly presentation of the situation, showing how "we worked for peace up to the last moment, and beyond the last moment. How hard, how persistently, and how earnestly we strove for peace the House will see from the papers that will be before it."

He spoke with absolute simplicity and a lack of rhetoric that made the speech all the more moving. For he built up his case with such stern logic that all were convinced that the case against Germany was unanswerable. The war was the only alternative to her acceptance of our conditions.

Above all, he impressed upon the House and the country "how vital is the consideration of the neutrality of Belgium."

On the following day he signed the famous declaration to Germany which brought Britain into the war. It ran:

"I have the honour to inform your Excellency (the German Ambassador) that, in accordance with the terms of the notification made to the German Government today, his Majesty's Government consider that a state of war exists between the two countries as from to-day at eleven o'clock p.m. – E. Grey."

With this declaration the conduct of affairs passed to the naval and military authorities, but the labours of the Foreign Secretary continued.

### IDEAL OF PUBLIC SERVICE HIS EARLY DAYS

Lord Grey came of a Northumberland house which had an instinctive leaning towards public service. It was under the influence of his grandfather, Sir George Grey, who was Home Secretary and Secretary of State for the Colonies, that the future Foreign Secretary grew to manhood (his own father died when he was twelve years of age) and his grandfather's home, Fallodon, became his before he inherited it. From Winchester, where fly-fishing, one of the master pleasures of his life, had interested him most he went to Balliol College, Oxford, where he took his degree.

He served as private secretary to Sir Evelyn Baring (the Earl of Cromer) then newly appointed British Agent in Egypt, and also to Mr. Hugh Childers, Chancellor of the Exchequer. At the general election of 1885 he defeated Earl Percy at Berwick-on-Tweed, a constituency which remained faithful to him until his elevation to the peerage as Viscount Grey of Fallodon in 1916.

### LONG TENURE AT FOREIGN OFFICE

When he had been in the House of Commons seven years, he was appointed Under-Secretary for Foreign Affairs in Mr. Gladstone's fourth and last administration. Young – he was only 30 – and untried, his appointment was not received with general approval, but he quickly justified it by his mastery of foreign questions, and the judicial manner in which he could state his case.

Although no lover of debate – indeed, he shunned unnecessary discussion – he was a highly effective speaker who commanded attention by the sincerity and directness of his utterances.

On the fall of the Government of Lord Rosebery, who had succeeded Mr. Gladstone, Grey passed into opposition.

On the return of the Liberals to power, under Sir Henry Campbell-Bannerman, Grey became Foreign Secretary and his tenure of that office was to last longer than that of any of his predecessors. He had already given his general adhesion to the foreign policy of Lord Lansdowne.

A more potent cause of his retirement perhaps was his impaired sight. He had to give up dry fly-fishing some years ago on that account, though he could still catch salmon and trout with the wet-fly, but this year he was forced to abandon even wet-fly fishing, and to confine his activities to the study of his beloved birds and to reading books in Braille, which he had learned at St. Dunstans. He was the only civilian who had been taught to read there.

VISCOUNT GREY

**(September 8)**

# "FATTY" ARBUCKLE DEAD

**By Our Film Correspondent**

Roscoe ("Fatty") Arbuckle died suddenly in New York yesterday, at the age of 52. He had been suffering from heart trouble.

To-day he will "lie in state" in the large funeral parlour on Broadway which, in 1926, was almost wrecked by the thousands who struggled to obtain a last view of the face of Rudolph Valentino.

A tremendous favourite in the silent "slap-stick" era, Arbuckle is remembered chiefly as the central figure in one of the most sensational scandals of the film colony. In 1921 Virginia Rappe, a minor actress, died after a drinking party, and Arbuckle was tried for manslaughter.

He was acquitted after three trials, which cost him £25,000. Adolph Zukor, president of the Famous Players Lasky Corporation, then announced that his latest film would be released immediately and that on its reception would depend Arbuckle's future.

What happened was that vehement protests were made by the Purity League and a number of other women's organisations, cowboys in Wyoming riddled the screen with bullets when Arbuckle's face appeared, and the film was hissed in Paris and London. Cancellation of the contracts involved a loss of £500,000.

**(June 30)**

# THE DALAI LAMA

## TIBET'S DIVINE RULER

His holiness Ngawang Lossang Thusten Gyatsho, the thirteenth Dalai Lama, who has died at Lhasa at the age of 60, was the temporal and spiritual head of Tibet. He was chosen for his high position at the age of 2 by the priesthood, proceeding according to the usual sacred formulae, and began his long period of 42 years' actual power at the age of 18.

The main article of the Lamaist creed is transmigration. A Lama does not die; his soul migrates, and is reborn in another human being. Certain physical signs are supposed to indicate the reborn saint; and it is the duty of the priests to find him, which they do according to an elaborate system of lot-drawing.

His first exercise of power was not happy. He chose, under the influence of Russian advisors, to ignore his treaty obligations with Britain. The outcome of the dispute was the British armed mission of 1904, which forced its way into the Forbidden City and compelled the signing of a new treaty by the Tibetan Ministers, The Dalai Lama himself had fled to Mongolia, and spend some years in exile there and in Peking.

### THREE YEARS IN INDIA

He returned to Lhasa in 1909, only to find that his Chinese hosts were now conspiring against him. He again fled, this time to British India, where he lived for three years at Darjeeling as the guest of the Government of India. At the end of that period the hold of China on Tibet was weakened by the Chinese revolution. The Tibetans then rose in insurrection, and the Dalai Lama was recalled.

**(December 10)**

# KING FEISAL'S GENIUS AS A RULER

## IRAK A NATION

## ARAB MONARCH WHO LOVED ENGLISH LIFE

**By H.E. Wortham**

The sudden death of King Feisal removes from the scene a personality who has played a prominent part in the history of the Middle East for nearly twenty years.

The drooping eye-lids, the black beard and the colourless face, which impressed Col. Lawrence at their first meeting, contributed to the air of distinction that no one who ever came into contact with Feisal failed to remark.

With his aloofness there went at the same time considerable personal charm. Though handicapped in his intercourse with Europeans by his indifferent French and still scantier English, it was remarkable how he managed to enjoy the pleasures which English society afforded. He was fond of London, its theatres , its restaurants, and not least its shops. But he admired English country life even more. On previous visits here he had stayed in many of our great houses, and he learnt at Hatfield, Longleat and Chatsworth to appreciate something of the traditions of English culture.

KING FEISAL

While King Feisel's partiality for the amenities of European, and particularly of English, life sometimes aroused criticism amongst his own subjects, there was never any question as to the earnestness with which he strove to realise the political aspirations of the Arabs.

### DESCENDANT OF THE PROPHET

It cannot be emphasised too strongly that these, while racial and, indeed, Imperial, were uncoloured by any religious prejudices. Though King Feisal was a descendant of the Prophet and belonged to the oldest and noblest family in Hejaz, he was able to divorce religion and politics in a way that showed real enlightenment. One of his most trusted advisers was a Christian. He had at least one Jewish Minister of Finance, and his principal private secretary belonged to the Shiite Sect. And while he observed the Islamic ordinances in the matter of attending prayer, he interpreted in a liberal sense the Koranic injunctions against forbidden meats and drinks.

From his earliest youth in Constantinople, where his father, afterwards to become King Hussein of the Hejaz, resided under the surveillance of the "Red Sultan," Abdul Hamid, he was brought into contact with the nationalist Arab movement. When the Great War broke out he was one of the Arab deputies in the Turkish Parliament. Djemal Pasha, the member of the Young Turk triumvirate who had assumed command in Syria, gave him a post upon his staff, so that he could watch him the more closely. Not until Emir Feisal escaped from this virtual captivity was his father in Mecca able to start the Arab revolt against the Turks. In this Feisal, with the help of Nari Pasha (who was with him when he died), Ja'far Pasha and of Colonel Lawrence, played a part that is familiar to all students of the Middle East campaigns.

### A VALUABLE ALLY

His exploits and adventures have been told by Col. Lawrence – Lawrence of Arabia – who was his liaison officer when the Arab army was organised to aid Lord Allenby.

The young Emir possessed the true Beduin instinct for a raid, and knew exactly when and where to strike at the Turkish left flank and at their communications with Damascus.

His proclamation as King of Syria in the spring of 1920 ended a month or two later in a clash with the French forces and in Feisal's enforced departure.

He came in the autumn of 1920 to London to plead the Arab cause, and it was no small tribute to his own personality and to the adroitness of his Arab advisers that, when he left London in 1921, his destination was Baghdad as the unacknowledged King-designate of Irak.

The decision of the British Government to support Feisal's candidature to the Iraki throne was largely due to Mr. Winston Churchill, the then Colonial Secretary. Towards the end of June 1921, Feisal reached Baghdad, and almost immediately he was declared King by the Council of Ministers.

Feisal's leadership was amply tested during the following years. He found Irak suffering from the effects of the very serious rebellion which had broken out during Sir Arnold Wilson's régime. His new subjects were inclined to regard him as a foreigner. The Moslem sect of Shias, who are very powerful in Irak, saw in him a representative of the greatest Sunni family. And to both Shias and Sunnis it was easy to represent him as subservient to the British.

Irak was also surrounded by hostile and powerful neighbours. The Turks claimed Mosul. The Persians, posing as the protectors of the Shias, refused to recognise him. In the western desert Ibn Saud was an enemy of the Sherifian family to which Feisal belonged. And the French could hardly be expected to regard Feisal's elevation with gratification.

During his reign King Feisal had the satisfaction of seeing these problems resolved one by one. The mandatory status of Irak – to which he was never a party – found a temporary solution in the British recognition of Iraki independence, our mutual relations being defined by treaty.

### IRAK JOINS THE LEAGUE

This was renewed in 1927 and continued in force until last year, when the mandate ceased altogether, and Irak became a member of the League of Nations. In turn relations with Turkey, Persia and King Ibn Saud were adjusted, though the recent Bassyrian imbroglio indicated that the relations between Baghdad and Damascus were still not so cordial as they might have been. In domestic politics King Feisal managed to make his influence felt through the somewhat ready-made machinery of the constitutional government, which was set in motion with his accession. He often found it convenient when mistakes in administration occurred to assume a strictly constitutional rôle. But there has never been any real question that Feisal once he had seated himself in the saddle, controlled his Ministers and not they him.

**(September 9)**

# PASSING OF A GREAT WRITER

MR. JOHN GALSWORTHY

## THE FORSYTE SAGA

MIRROR OF AN AGE

It has been said that sympathy made Mr. John Galsworthy, who died yesterday at the age of 65, a remarkable writer. More precisely it may be said that it was pity which made him write, and that the highest quality of what he wrote lies in its fineness and nobility of feeling. A sense of "the tears in human things" was keen in every line, it seldom or never led him astray into more sentimentality, it sometimes inspired work of rare and haunting beauty.

He was by instinct the champion of the unfortunate. Victrix causa Deis placuit, sed victa Cantoni. Always he spent his best skill on the broken men and women, the champions of lost causes, the miserable, sinners, the wastrels. He was never tired of telling us that, things being what they are, the

Mr. Galsworthy

noblest characters are most likely to be amongst those who lose everything; and even if the failure be a weakling, Galsworthy would have us believe that it is we and the system which we have established that drove him into disaster.

Yet he was zealous to be fair. When he wrote a play to convince – or convict – us of the cruelty of our criminal law and prison system the men who administered justice were honest, decent fellows. When he indicted class feeling his upper-class people were not brutes or fools, but just as much as their victims the creatures of circumstance. Nobody is to blame except the whole mass of us. If he had been asked what he wanted of us, he would have had to reply in the language of evangelical Christianity – conversion.

REFORMER AND ARTIST

There can be little doubt that Galsworthy's place in the future will depend upon how keenly the coming years feel this plea. The purely artistic quality of his work is secondary to and even dependent on its emotional and ethical force, and the beauty of its best things is essentially the beauty of a noble spirit rather than of a piece of well-wrought imagination.

As an artist his greatest power lay in the suggestion of a social circle, not an individual, of a family, not a man or a woman, of atmosphere, place, a way of life, a spiritual or mental attitude rather than character or action. His most successful dramatic persons tend to be types. But he has imagined some, the picturesque vagabond Ferrand in "The Pigeon," and in a quieter vain a number of motherly women scattered about the plays and novels who have life of their own.

He was a master of pathos, a fine restraint in style serving very happily his profound and subtle sympathy with humanity. He had at times a wistful, ironic humour of singular charm, but he was prone to let it degenerate into laboured triviality. He was fond of themes of passion, sometimes giving them the elaboration of a scientific treatise, sometimes introducing them into material with which they were discordant, but his treatment was curiously dry and cold, lucid enough, much wrought and recondite.

A LATE START

Galsworthy was born at Coombe, in Surrey, the son of a solicitor, and educated at Harrow and Oxford. At Oxford he was a "hunting blood." He was called to the Bar in 1890, but the profession had no claim on him, and has left no mark on his work. Shortly afterwards he travelled widely, visiting America, Egypt, Canada, the Cape, Australia, the Fiji Islands, and Russia. In the course of these wanderings he met – it was on a sailing ship voyage from Adelaide to the Cape – Joseph Conrad, then first mate, whose influence can be traced in his style and method of presenting character. His first four books were published under the pseudonym of "John Sinjohn." They did not receive, and there is no reason why they should have received, much attention.

Galsworthy was of the writers who develop slowly. His first important novel, "The Man of Property," was published when he was 39. In that and "The Country House," which followed next year, the power and scope of his talent – or shall we say his individuality – were fully displayed. These books have the appeal to pity and charity, the power of presenting the life of a family or class or castle, and that limited but subtle art of portraiture which we associate with his name, and with "Fraternity" they represent his best work as a novelist.

But after the war he made a great return. He wrote more Forsyte books – in those he had created a real family whom we know as our own families, and with whom he was still living till the end – and the earlier books about them were issued, in 1922, under the collective title of "The Forsyte Saga." With that Galsworthy swept the English-speaking world. He was not one of the great novelists, but it was evident, after hardy and Conrad died, that there was nobody better than he, except, possibly, Arnold Bennett.

A few years ago Galsworthy presented to the British Museum the original autograph manuscript of "The Forsyte Chronicles," a gift commercially estimated to be worth £10,000.

HIS PLAYS

It has been held, and the opinion has strong support, that he was most completely himself in his plays, which numbered more than a score. If to set people thinking and searching their consciences is the object of drama – and certainly it was one of Galsworthy's chief aims – no dramatist of his time or for many a year earlier is his equal. As a piece of craftsmanship he never did anything better than "The Silver Box" one of his first plays. It can be labelled as a propaganda play on the theme that there is one law for the rich and another for the poor. But it had a poignancy and force and touches of character which made it a true piece of art. "Strife," a thoughtful and deeply pathetic presentation of the misery and futility of the war between capital and labour, if technically less satisfactory, was even more impressive. But a later play may be ranked as the finest thing he ever did, the most affecting expression of that "sad nobility of soul," that wistful love of humanity which was his inspiration. "The Pigeon" produced in 1911, is anything you please except a well-made play, but it speaks to the heart.

Of a number of other ventures in the theatre the most striking were "Justice," a grim and harrowing indictment of criminal law and prison administration, and "The Fugitive," a painful study of the torture by our social system of a woman "too fine and not fine enough."

"Loyalties" and "Escape" each represented exceptionally hard cases: Galsworthy, facing the prison system and the desperate state of a convict escaping from it, had not quite the strength to pose his problem with a real tough criminal as central figure. He set out to be a realist, but his sentimentalism made him cheat.

**(February 1)**

# TEXAS GUINAN DEAD

"WHOOPEE QUEEN OF AMERICA"

**From Our Own Correspondent**

VANCOUVER, Sunday.

Texas Guinan, the most famous figure in the night life of New York, San Francisco, and other American cities, died in hospital here to-day.

Prohibition made her fortune, and she has died on the eve of its repeal.

"Texas" was appearing at a local theatre when she collapsed. She was at once rushed to hospital and operated on. Death was due to colitis (inflammation of the intestine).

Known as America's "Whoopee Queen" Texas Guinan was reported to have earned at the height of her career something like £25,000 a year.

She opened clubs in the bigger cities, acted as the hostess herself, and staffed the establishments with selected "whoopee girls." Her aim, she said, was to help people to get a "kick out of life."

"PUBLIC NUISANCE"

She figured in a number of trials, on one occasion being charged as a "public nuisance." On all occasions she succeeded in defeating the lawyers.

In 1931 she crossed the Atlantic with the avowed intention of "brightening up" Paris and killing Mrs. Grundy in London. Accompanying her were twenty of her "kids."

The French and British authorities, however, did not welcome her. They had heard of her plans to canter down the Champs Elysées and the Strand on a white charger and she was prevented from landing. On this venture she lost about £10,000.

**(November 6)**

# SUDDEN DEATH OF MR. COOLIDGE

"STRONG, SILENT" EX-PRESIDENT

**From Our Own Correspondent**

NEW YORK, Thursday.

Mr. Calvin Coolidge, President of the United States from 1923 to 1929, was found dead shortly after midday to-day, at his home in Northampton, Massachusetts.

Mrs. Coolidge, returning from shopping a little late, found her husband lying dead on the floor of his bedroom. He had taken off his coat and waistcoat, and there was evidence that he was about to shave.

His death is attributed to heart disease. He had complained of indigestion for the last two or three weeks, but had not consulted a doctor. He was 60 years of age.

PRESIDENT HOOVER'S TRIBUTE

President Hoover, in a proclamation announcing that Mr. Coolidge died at 12.25 p.m., eulogised his career and said: "His name became in his own lifetime a synonym for sagacity and wisdom. His temperateness in speech and orderly deliberation and action bespoke a profound sense of responsibility which guided his conduct of public business."

The President has ordered official flags to be flown at half-mast for thirty days. Naval and military honours will be paid at the funeral, which will take place on Saturday at Plymouth, Vermont.

Among the twenty-nine men who have been Presidents of the United States, Mr. Coolidge stood apart as an enigma. Praised by his supporters as "a strong silent man," he was ridiculed by his critics as "a very ordinary man with the mentality of a local politician."

One of his best-known utterances was made in 1928, when he handed to reporters a slip of paper with the words, "Do not choose to run." This was in answer to a question about Presidential candidates, and Mr. Coolidge refused to amplify it.

Another famous statement referred to war debts, when he said "They hired the money, didn't they?"

As he grew into public life he became known as "Honest Cal," and later as "Cautious Cal," but from first to last he was "Silent Cal."

During his Presidency, Prohibition was a big issue, but he took no part in the interminable discussions which divided Congress and the country beyond announcing that he stood simply for the enforcement of the law, so long as the Eighteenth Amendment and the Volstead Act were on the Statute Book.

After leaving the Presidency Mr. Coolidge wrote articles for American newspaper syndicates. These were always short and often wise in their comment upon men and things and institutions. He died as he lived, in an atmosphere of democratic simplicity true to his conviction that America is "God's own country."

**(January 6)**

# SIR HENRY ROYCE

Sir Frederick Henry Royce, the famous motor-car and aeroplane engine designer, died on Saturday at his home at West Wittering, near Chichester, aged 70 years.

Among his other triumphs he designed engines which gained for Britain the world's speed records on land, sea, and air, including those which enabled Flt.-Lt. Stainforth to set up the world's air speed record, Sir Malcolm Campbell to raise his own record on land, and Mr. Kaye Don to make a new water record.

He came of a family of millers in South Rutlandshire. The mechanical instinct was strong in his strain, for his grandfather was one of the first millers in the country to install steam engines in his water-mills.

Sir Henry himself started work as a telegraph boy, at a wage of a halfpenny a message, and after a spell at the City Guild Technical College, passed a few years of apprenticeship in the Great Northern Railway locomotive works at Peterborough, and then to employment as an engineering fitter in a machine tool works at Leeds.

His success was built on failures. It was the failure of a Liverpool electrical company which decided him to start in business for himself, and it was a slump in dynamos and electric cranes which turned his attention to motor-cars.

Having noticed the poor performance of a foreign automobile, he said: "I could make a better engine myself," and did so. He sent out a few 10 h.p. two-cylinder cars, which attracted the attention of the Hon. Charles Rolls, an enthusiastic motorist, who had long been planning to build and market a super-car.

In 1906 the firm of Rolls-Royce Ltd., with a capital of £200,000, came into being. Among the first productions was a 40.50 h.p. engined chassis called "the Silver Ghost," which was only replaced in 1925 when "the Phantom" overhead valved engine was introduced.

Mr. Rolls, who had also devoted himself to aviation, was killed in a flying accident at Bournemouth, and Sir Henry was left to carry on in the improvement of the motor-car to which his name is attached.

**(April 24)**

# "GENTLEMAN JIM" CORBETT

PICTURESQUE FIGURE OF PRIZE RING

**From Our Own Correspondent**

NEW YORK, Sunday.

James J. Corbett, heavy-weight champion of the world for five years, died on Saturday at his Long Island home at the age of 66.

"Gentleman Jim," or "Pompadour Jim," as he was variously known; retained his splendid physique to the end, and never let his muscles get soft and flabby. He was always to be seen at every great fight in the States, admired and respected by lovers of sport. Since last year, however, he had suffered from hardening of the arteries and occasional heart attacks, and a few months ago he had to take to his bed.

"I was forty years too soon," he said, recently, recalling his old days in the ring. "Now they invite fighters to Florida, and the authorities welcome them, bands play, and purses are fat. It was different in my day.

"I got £4,000 for my end in the Jacksonville fight, and I bet £2,000 myself. The money was in side bets, so I made £6,000 about the same amount I got when I won the title from John L. Sullivan two years previously. You never hear of fighters backing themselves with real money like that now. They get so much they don't need to gamble."

Corbett, who was born in San Francisco, the son of an Irish emigrant, was one of the most picturesque and commanding figures of the old Prize Ring days.

Like Gene Tunney, who retired the undefeated champion of the world a few years ago, Corbett began life as a clerk, in a bank, after passing through a convent school. Social distinctions are not so clearly cut today, where professional fighters are concerned, but when Corbett pursued the noble art for a livelihood, in order to keep himself and his young wife, they called him "Gentleman Jim." The name was both appreciative and suggestive of the rare phenomenon which had found its way into the pugilistic world.

Corbett was essentially a thinker. His slender physique did not match well with the big proportions of the fighters of his day. He developed his speed and his science to outwit his adversaries. When he fought John L. Sullivan, the famous Boston Boy with the mighty flat, Corbett bewildered the champion by the speed and variety of his methods. Sullivan, with his condition ruined by the wild excesses for which he was noted, was knocked out in the twenty-first round, and the world's title fell upon the slender young challenger.

A GREAT BLACK BOXER

The month before he met Sullivan, Corbett had fought a draw of sixty-one rounds with the great black boxer, Peter Jackson. Sullivan had drawn the colour line so far as Jackson was concerned, which was fortunate, perhaps, for Corbett, as the West Indian negro might otherwise have gained the title instead.

For three years Corbett maintained his position, and then on March 17, 1897, at Carson City, he was knocked out by the famous solar plexus punch in the 14th round by Bob Fitzsimmons. The latter who was barely a cruiser weight, was like Len Harvey, one of our present English champions, born at Helston in Cornwall. Later on Fitzsimmons was beaten by Jim Jefferies, and then Corbett endeavoured twice without success to regain his lost laurels.

**(February 20)**

# ARTHUR ROBERTS

GIFTED VETERAN OF THE HALLS

Old playgoers and habitués of "the halls" at the summit of their glory will be furbishing up their memories to-day, for they alone know the unique place that Arthur Roberts who died yesterday at his home in Westminster, in his 81st year, held so long in the world of entertainment. He linked back with a London of hansom cabs and feebly-flickering gas-lamps, when the dog-cart and its attendant "tiger" made a smart turn-out a town of night resorts and no licensing restrictions, and of practical jokes – a Bohemia that is as dead as Queen Anne.

At the top of his fame this ex-solicitor's clerk, and the son of a tailor's cutter, earned £200 a week, then by far the biggest income made in the stage.

Small and dapper, quick-eyed, mercurial, never wanting for an impromptu. Nature had equipped him well for his calling. He was rattling in his speech, always on the move, never solemn by any chance, and totally wanting in reverence. A gifted pantomimist, he had command of a hundred expressions, and in days when a quick-change artist was appreciated he would astonish his public by his facility in throwing off one part for another. The laughter had hardly died from the house at Roberts's masquerade as an irascible general when he stepped on from the wings as a cabman's wife.

GREAT LAUGHTER-RAISER

A Londoner born, he first appeared on Yarmouth sands, and made his bow to a London audience at the Old Mogul in Drury-lane in 1873. There he sang "If I was only long enough a soldier I would be," a song which brought him into prominence very quickly.

It has been said that the frowns of outraged authority led Roberts to migrate to the regular stage. After he had had a test at the Theatre Royal, Manchester, Sir Augustus Harris engaged him for his Christmas production at Drury Lane in 1880, and he played in three pantomimes there, winning golden opinions for his dash and humorous sprightliness.

It was while he and the sprightly little Vanoni were at the Avenue in the 'eighties that the theatre by the Embankment enjoyed its brightest phases. The success he obtained as Joe Taradiddle, the hotel tout, in a version of Offenbach's "La Vie Parisienne" was the precursor of much other smart work. The pompousness of Don Quixote, the humours of Varney, in the "Kenilworth" extravaganza, and "Gentleman Joe" in the play of that name, also gave him suitable openings for exercising that flood of humour which never gave signs of drying up.

At one epoch of his career at the Old Gaiety Arthur Roberts came in conflict with the censor. In the early 'nineties Stanley, the explorer, and Lord Randolph Churchill were very much in the public eye. The song introduced by Roberts as Arthur de Richemont – "I'm a Randy Pandy, oh!" – referred to the Conservative statesman, and the Lord Chamberlain's objection to "make-up" in reproduction of living personages came into force. The result was, as in the case of "The Happy Land," where three Liberal Ministers had been imitated, that the alteration became far more suggestive than the original drawing. Either as singing "I'm a regular jack the Dandy, oh" or "I went to find Emin" – a ballad dealing with Emin Pasha – Roberts scored immensely.

**(February 28)**

# TEST CRICKET SENSATION

## P.F. WARNER REBUKED

**By W.M. Woodfull**

ADELAIDE, Sunday.

England's leg theory tactics in the Test matches against Australia are causing friction between the two countries. Relations are now very strained.

The latest dramatic development in controversy was a rebuke administered by W.M. Woodfull, the Australian captain, to P.F. Warner, one of the joint managers of the English team, in the presence of several Australian cricketers.

It is revealed that after play on Saturday Warner went into the dressing-room of the Australian team to inquire after the wellbeing of Woodfull, who had been struck over the heart by a ball from Larwood.

He found the Australian captain on the massage table and went up to ask how he felt.

OBJECTION TO LEG THEORY

Woodfull replied that he did not want to talk to him as he considered that the leg theory was not "cricket." He did not approve of these tactics and never would, and he thought that England was not playing a sporting game.

Warner turned on his heel and left the dressing-room without reply. He refuses to comment on the incident, which is certain to have wide repercussions throughout Australia.

Feeling against the English tactics has been further aggravated because it is stated after Woodfull had been struck over the heart by Larwood when he was bowling to the off, the Notts bowler, after a consultation with his captain, Jardine, purposely changed his tactics and bowled to the leg.

"Old Boy," writing in the "Melbourne Argus," under a headline of "Body Bowling," declares that no one in close touch with the present Tests would think that cricket was a friendly game. The Warner-Woodfull incident has caused feeling which is far removed from the best sporting traditions of cricket.

**(January 16)**

# M.C.C.'S REPLY TO AUSTRALIA

The committee of the M.C.C. sent a dignified and firmly worded reply last night to the cabled protest of the Australian Board of Control against "body line" and "leg theory" bowling.

It was in the following terms:

"We Marylebone Cricket Club, deplore your cable.

"We deprecate your opinion that there has been unsportsmanlike play. We have the fullest confidence in the captain, team, and managers, and are convinced that they would do nothing to infringe either the laws of cricket or the spirit of the game.

"We have no evidence that our confidence has been misplaced. Much as we regret the accidents to Woodfull and Oldfield, we understand that in neither case was the bowler to blame.

"If the Australian Board of Control wish to propose a new law or rule, it shall receive our careful consideration in due course.

"We hope the situation is not now as serious as your cable would seem to indicate, but if it is such as to jeopardise the good relations between English and Australian cricketers, and you consider it desirable to cancel the remainder of the programme, we would consent, but with great reluctance."–

(Signed) Findlay, Secretary.

This reply was cabled to Australia last night.

The wording of the cable of protest sent by the Australian Board of Control to the M.C.C. on Wednesday last was:

"Body-line bowling has assumed such proportions as to become a menace to the best interests of the game. It is making protection of the body by batsmen the main consideration. It is causing intensely bitter feeling between players, as well as injury.

"In our opinion it is unsportsmanlike, and unless stopped at once it is likely to upset the friendly relations between Australia and England."

**(January 24)**

# TEST CRISIS OVER?

It is reliably reported from Australia that the word "unsportsmanlike" used by the Australian Board of Control in its cable of protest to the M.C.C. against "body-line bowling" is to be withdrawn.

Belief that a settlement of the dispute is impending is supported (says Reuter) by the speeches made at an official welcome to the M.C.C. players at Brisbane last night.

Mr. P.F. Warner, one of the managers of the England team asked everyone to do their utmost to "put things straight."

"Stretch out your right hand to us and we will grasp it eagerly, and not only we – the few representatives in Australia of the M.C.C. – but every cricketer in England, which means the world," he said.

The English captain, D.R. Jardine, said: "In the trials and tribulations of cricket I hold that the least said is the soonest mended, although there are times when it is not easy to remain silent."

**(February 4)**

# THIS "BODY-LINE BOWLING" IS NEW ONLY IN NAME

## FORM OF ATTACK AUSTRALIA'S BATSMEN SHOULD FACE WITHOUT RESENTMENT

**By P.G.H. Fender**

**The Former Surrey Captain and Test Player**

THE M.C.C. team's tour in Australia seems to have been more productive of controversy and acrimonious bickering than any other tour on record.

The main bone of contention, as officially noted in the cable from the Australian Board of Control yesterday, concerns what is described – whatever the term may mean – as "body-line bowling."

It is a pity that so much time and thought have been wasted in finding new and insinuating names for something which is as old as the hills.

Leg theory bowling, whether fast or slow, has been known and often used by the bowlers of both England and Australia. But never before has so much been made of it, and never has it been made the cause of such feeling.

JARDINE'S TACTICS

It would be ungenerous, and it is far from my mind, to allow that these repercussions are due to the success which has attended Jardine's way of handling leg theory methods of bowling. That his method is the only new thing about the employment of the theory is common knowledge in the cricket world.

The cricketing public usually are far more likely to admire than to denounce, in cases where novelty is the only point. These demonstrations and the uneasiness felt by many genuine lovers of the game in both countries, are due entirely to misapprehension.

For instance, the very words "body-line bowling" convey an entirely erroneous impression. Neither facts nor the imagination can substitute any charge that bowlers, either of yesterday or to-day, bowl with the intent to maim. The bowlers are men, and their captains cannot be charged with permitting such methods. Such inventions are mischievous.

The theory which words like "body bowling" purport to describe is a simple one, and the reasons for its employment are simple. Every cricketer knows that the majority of batsmen have their weak points. It is the business of the bowler to find out, as quickly as he can, what those weaknesses are, and to play on them to the batsman's discomfiture. Some are weak on the offside, others on the leg; some can hit and cannot defend, and others can defend and cannot hit.

"CAN'T COPE WITH IT?"

A Test bowler would not be worth his salt if he did not look for, and speedily direct his attack against, any such shortcomings. And I think that it is only fair comment at the moment to say that the Australian batsmen as a whole have a decided weakness on the leg stump.

Why Jardine's determination to play on this weakness should "cause intensely bitter feeling between the players" one can only guess. The complaint that it is dangerous and "makes protection of the body the main consideration" can surely not be sustained without coupling with it the admission that their batsmen are unable to cope with fast bowling on the leg stump.

The answer that one would expect from a Test batsman is that, if the ball is directed at the leg stump, he would naturally expect when he makes mistakes to be hit occasionally if, as is the tendency of some batsmen to-day, he moves in front of his wicket for every ball. If it is directed outside the leg stump there should be, on a good wicket, runs for the asking.

Unless the Australians take the line that they cannot cope with it, and for that reason want it stopped, and the M.C.C. agree to that for political reasons, there can be no ground for instructing our captain to discontinue this most successful form of attack.

It seems that Jardine has decided that the combination of fast bowling and the leg stump, with plenty of short legs to snap up the chances offered by batsmen who are not completely in control, is the recipe for the recovery of the "Ashes."

Without a doubt, any theory of bowling, properly bowled, and with a properly placed and packed field, cramps the batsman and forces him to try to find his remedy. It is also obvious that, because the fielders can stand much closer to the batsman on the leg side for a fast bowler than they can for a slow one, it is far more easy for a captain to pack a field and for the bowler to bowl to it than it is on the off side.

BATSMEN'S WICKETS

From time to time in the past the leg theory was exploited by such fast bowlers as Gregory and Macdonald, as well as Frank Foster, but the main difference between what they did and what Jardine is doing is that he has packed the field for that type of bowling in a manner which has seldom been done before. He has forced the batsmen to play on their weakest line, and used his troops so as to take the fullest possible advantage of any lapse on the batsman's part.

So far as the argument that leg theory bowling by a fast bowler is dangerous is concerned, it is possible that, if the series were played in England, a case of some sort could be made out. In Australia it is a very different matter.

When some of us murmured in 1920-21 at the bumpers of the two Australian fast bowlers, it was frequently pointed out to us that we had bats in our hands, and that the wickets were the best in the world. We need have no fear, we were told, about the ball doing odd things, as might be the case even on the best of English wickets. The Australian wickets were such that the ball always did the same thing, and we could depend that, given identical speed and length, the ball would always rise to exactly the same height.

WHAT "RANJI" LIKED

Again, we were told that, if we were good enough batsmen, leg theory bowling would only provide us with easy runs. We had it on the authority of H.H. the Jam Sahib that he and his fellows sometimes ran into it and welcomed it.

It is not as if the English bowlers were alone in bowling bumpers. Every Australian Test bowler knows that it is always worth while to bounce one at Herbert Sutcliffe when he is not expecting it. They give a little signal to the man on the deep square-leg boundary, and, in the expectation that Sutcliffe will hit the ball hard and well, they hope to get him caught on the leg boundary. During the last tour they brought it off with the last ball before lunch at Brisbane. They nearly did it at Manchester in 1930. They always have it up their sleeve.

Some people who happened to be at the Oval for the fifth Test in the 1930 series may remember that half-hour after rain when the ball was kicking. Jackson and Bradman were batting. Many, after watching the different methods with which the two men met the situation, came away with the impression that one at least of them did not like fast stuff at his leg stump. Bradman drew back and tried to cut it, while Jackson stood up and played it.

BRADMAN'S WEAKNESS

When the side was chosen for Australia this time, Bradman, and how to deal with him, seemed to be the big question. Some may have thought that they had discovered the leg stump to be the chink in his armour, and decided to attack him there, having men who specialised in that form of attack. If it was too much for Bradman, it might be for others.

There can be no question about the legality of attacking the leg stump, and if there were the slightest question of a bowler going out more for the body than the wicket, the umpires are there, on the spot, and would act without hesitation. They are the sole judges of fair and unfair play, and would act in respect of a bowler bowling, in their opinion, at the body, just as they would over a bowler running up the wicket after delivering the ball.

WHY THIS FRICTION?

The Press and the public, being 120 yards from the wicket, cannot see enough to warrant the belief that the success of our bowlers is due to anything more than that they have discovered a hole in the Australian batting, and are making full use of it.

In these circumstances there should be no question of the friendly relations between Australia and England being affected. All Tests have been won and lost as much through play on the weaknesses of one side or the other as they have been by outstanding ability.

**(January 19)**

# M.C.C. TEAM'S LOYALTY TO CAPTAIN

It was at Brisbane four years ago that England gained their biggest triumph of all – by 675 runs. Yesterday's figures are the next we have reached in the history of Test cricket between the two countries, and they come within 39 of Australia's record margin, established at Sydney in 1920.

To dwell on this proud aspect of the Adelaide achievement is useful; it helps to relieve, in our case, at all events, an atmosphere over there which has become in Reuter's words, "one of extreme bitterness, almost amounting to hysteria."

Both players and the public alike, the message continues, must have given a sigh of relief when the match ended. Indeed, so personal had the feeling become that before the final day's play began the England team thought fit to issue a statement which was published in the later editions of The Daily Telegraph yesterday as follows:

"Members of the M.C.C. and the England team do not desire to enter into public controversy, for they deplore the introduction of any personal feeling into the records of a great game.

"In view, however, of statements which have been given space in some sections of the Press, to the effect that there has been dissension and disloyalty in their team, they desire to deny this definitely and absolutely, while assuring the public of England and Australia that they are, and always have been, utterly loyal to their captain under whose leadership they hope to achieve an honourable victory."

Then, the game being the thing, they went on to the field and proceeded to make another step forwards towards that "honourable victory." The Australian batsmen were helpless against Allen and Larwood. Five wickets fell in a hundred minutes for 73 runs, and as Oldfield was unable to bat, the finish of the match came soon after lunch.

**(January 20)**

# ENGLAND'S OVERWHELMING TEST VICTORY

**By Thomas Moult ("White Willow")**

England gained an overwhelming victory by 338 runs at Adelaide yesterday in the third Test Match. The end came tamely, Australia being all out in their second innings for 193.

Only Woodfull, the captain, made any resistance, and he fought magnificently, carrying his bat for 73. England now lead 2-1 in the fight for the Ashes. Two Tests have still to be played, the next beginning at Brisbane on Feb. 10.

**(January 20)**

## BOAT RACE RECORD

Cambridge set up a new boat race record on Saturday by beating Oxford for the tenth year in succession. The Cambridge crew won by 2 ¼ lengths, in 20 minutes 57 seconds.

Huge crowds watched the race, and at night there were lively scenes in the West-end of London. Piccadilly-circus was impassable for an hour, and eventually mounted police had to be called out to disperse the crowds.

**(April 3)**

# HIGHEST SCORE IN ANY TEST

## BRADMAN'S 334 BEATEN

Everything else in the second Test between New Zealand and England, at Auckland on Saturday, was overshadowed by a magnificent innings of 336 not out by Hammond, which beat the previous record Test score of 334, by Don Bradman against England at Leeds in 1930.

England scored 548 for seven before declaring, and New Zealand replied with 8 for none in their second innings. They are now 382 runs behind with all their second innings wickets in hand.

Hammond hit with great power and precision to all parts of the field, says Reuter, pulling, cutting and driving in a manner which can seldom have been equalled. His footwork was also superb, and the way in which he pierced the field left the New Zealanders bewildered. The bowling, with the exception of the two Otago men, Badcock and Dunning, was however, generally very mediocre, while the fielding was deplorable.

HAMMOND

The chief features of Hammond's innings were: He hit ten 5's – three off successive balls from Newman – and thirty-three 4's, and his runs came at the rate of 50 in 76 min, 100 in 134 min, 150 in 172 min, 200 in 241 min, 250 in 268 min, 300 in 288 min, 336 in 318 min; he gave his first chance at 134; Dempster Badcock, and Dunning were injured in trying to stop some of his shots, Dempster, dropping a hot return and having to retire for a time; he was caught off a no-ball when 335.

It is a long time since the crowd had seen hitting to equal Hammond's and they gave the Englishman a wonderful ovation when he left the field still undefeated. The New Zealanders joined in the applause.

**(April 3)**

# THE FOOTBALL BALL-BOY

## FLOODLIT SOCCER LESSONS

**By Frank Coles**

Soccer football by floodlight was officially on trial last night at the White City. I am sure the verdict of the onlookers, was unanimously favourable.

The teams – Reds versus Whites – were drawn from the London professional clubs, and among the crowd of nearly 10,000 people, some critical, some merely curious, were Sir Frederick Wall, secretary of the Football Association, and half-a-dozen prominent members of the Council.

If Continental experience has not already done so, this test convinced them of the possibilities of floodlit football. Watching it for the first time, I found it a simple matter to follow every incident.

Indeed, when the strangeness of the first few minutes had been mastered I was at ease with the play. I saw much more of what was happening than I often do on an afternoon in midwinter.

GLEAMING WHITE BALL

The white ball and the relay of ball-boys were an object-lesson. A dozen balls were used. It was the duty of the ball-boys to capture them the instant they were sent into touch, plunge them into a pail of water, and produce a clean ball, gleaming white. Result: a definite speeding up of the game and an object which could be followed without trouble.

Floodlight or no floodlight, give me the white ball and the ball-boys in league football. That is one lasting impression of last night's game – and curiously one the promoters probably had no intention of conveying.

As for the players, it was obvious that they suffered no inconvenience in sighting the ball. The ground was muddy and treacherous, yet miskicks were few and far apart, and neither goalkeeper showed the slightest hesitation in fielding shots of high or low trajectory.

The winners were the Whites – players from Arsenal, Chelsea, Tottenham Hotspur, and West Ham clubs. They beat the Reds by 3 goals to nil.

**(January 5)**

# ARSENAL CHAMPIONS

With two weeks to spare, the Arsenal have, for the second time in three seasons, won the League championship. Success breeds envy. The Highbury club has its enemies, but the bitterest of them will concede the Arsenal's right to the title.

They have played football which has made them the greatest box-office attraction the game has ever known. On Saturday their crowning triumph at Stamford Bridge drew a crowd of 74,161, and their last four games have been watched by well over 200,000 spectators.

Their balance-sheet will be an amazing document, and I think it will reveal that, in spite of their dramatic Cup exit, their games have been watched by more people than last season, when all records for football were smashed.

**(April 24)**

# ROWDY FOOTBALL IN NICE

## "SLAUGHTER" OF THE"WOLVES"

NICE, Thursday

Extraordinary scenes marked the football match between the Wolverhampton Wanderers and the Olympic Gymnastic Club of Nice this afternoon.

The trouble began after half an hour's play, when the Wolves protested against the alleged kicking, tripping, and fouling of their opponents.

The two teams were separated by directors and officials who went on to the field.

After half-time the Wolves renewed their protests, and a force of police had to be brought on the field to maintain order.

Twenty minutes after the resumption the disorder became so great that Mr. Buckley, the manager of the Wolverhampton team, called his players off the field.

The directors of the Nice Club, fearing that the spectators might riot if the match were not continued, persuaded the Wolverhampton players to return, but there were further scenes, and Nelson, the Wolverhampton half-back, protested vigorously against the tactics of three of the Nice players.

Mr. Buckley, interviewed after the match, declared that he had been engaged in football for thirty years, but he had never seen such a "slaughter." He was emphatic that he would never bring his team to France again.

**(May 26)**

## NUMBERED PLAYERS AT WEMBLEY

It was officially announced yesterday that the players taking part in the F.A. Cup Final at Wembley, to-morrow week will, for the first time, be numbered.

The Everton players will be numbered from 1 to 11, in black on white shirts. Manchester City will wear white numbers, from 12 to 22, on scarlet shirts.

**(May 18)**

# RICHARDS GETS HIS RECORD

## 248TH WINNER AT LIVERPOOL

By winning the first race, on Golden King, at Liverpool, yesterday, Gordon Richards broke Fred Archer's 48-year-old record of 246 winners in a single season.

Richards's record-breaking winner was the 1,400th success of his career, and by riding Atwood to victory in the last race of the afternoon he brought his season's total 258.

News of the champion jockey's success on Golden King was telephoned to Buckingham Palace, and a few minutes later Richards received the following telegram from Sir Clive Wigram, the King's private secretary:

"I am commanded by the King to express to you His Majesty's hearty congratulations on winning your 247th race, and by this splendid achievement establishing a new record in the annals of racing in this country."

It was characteristic of the man that his first thought when he came into the weighing room with cheers of 15,000 people ringing in his ears, was for his wife at Marlborough.

He must have shaken hundreds of hands. Owners, trainers, jockeys, and unknown admirers all somehow reached him, while outside the weighing room the chorus of cheering continued with unabated enthusiasm.

He made perhaps one of the shortest speeches on record to the "talkie" camera. It was just this: "I am delighted to have broken the record and to know that it is all over."

**(November 9)**

# LORD DERBY WINS 150th DERBY

The King and Queen, most of the members of their family and hundreds of thousands of their subjects saw the Earl of Derby's horse, Hyperion, win the 150th Derby yesterday in the fastest time ever recorded.

Hyperion, who finished favourite at 6-1, completed the course in 2min 34sec – two-fifths of a second faster than the previous record, shared by Call Boy (1927) and Felstead (1928) and representing a speed of 35 miles an hour.

Sir Hugo Cunliffe-Owen's King Salmon was second, four lengths behind, and Mr. Victor Emanuel's Statesman was third, a length behind King Salmon.

Lord Derby's success, his second in the race founded by his ancestor in 1780 (he won with Sansovino in 1924) was most popular with the great crowd, which almost swept him from his feet as he entered the unsaddling enclosure.

### VETERAN TRAINER ABSENT

At his side was Mrs. George Lambton, wife of the Hon. George Lambton, his veteran trainer, who was unable to be present owing to an injury to his leg.

"I am delighted beyond measure," said Lord Derby. "It was a great victory and I have always had faith in the colt. Could there possibly be a greater tribute to a trainer than Hyperion was to Mr. Lambton to-day?"

Mr. Lambton had also trained Scarlet Tiger and Thrapston, who came in fourth and fifth respectively. He listened-in to the race on a wireless set at his bedside.

**(June 1)**

# RECORD TIME IN "NATIONAL"

## AMERICAN WOMAN WINS WITH £1 HORSE

1. **Kellsboro' Jack.........25-1**
2. **Really True................66-1**
3. **Slater..........................50-1**

Kellesboro' Jack, which is owned by an American woman, Mrs. Ambrose Clark, of New York, won the Grand National at Aintree yesterday in the record time of 9min 28 sec. The previous best was Grakle's 9min 32.4 sec in 1931. Mrs. Clark said that she had not backed the horse.

"Hotspur" on Page Seventeen, tells the story of how the winner was purchased for £1 by his present owner.

Slater was sold to Mr. Whitelaw, the Wantage owner-trainer, by the American, Mr. Whitney, just before the race.

No backer coupled Kellesboro' Jack with the Lincolnshire Handicap winner, Dorigen, in the Tote ante-post double, and the pool will be shared among those who nominated either horse.

Lord Dawson of Penn, speaking at a dinner at the May Fair Hotel last night to Sir Frederick Hobday, Principal of the Royal Veterinary College, disclosed that Sir Frederick had enabled a "roarer" to come in second in the Grand National.

Sir Frederick said that "Really True" had been one of his throat cases.

**(March 25)**

Fred Perry

# ENGLAND'S TENNIS TRIUMPH IN DAVIS CUP

## FIRST VICTORY FOR 21 YEARS

**By A. Wallis Myers**

PARIS, Sunday.

After twenty-one years England has regained the Davis Cup.

But it was a narrow victory. England had started splendidly by winning both singles matches on Friday. On Saturday, France won the doubles, to reduce our lead to two matches to one.

And yesterday, to the consternation of England, Austin lost to Cochet by 7-5, 4-6, 6-4, 4-6, 4-6.

Everything depended on the match between F. J. Perry and Andre Merlin. Perry beat his youthful opponent in four sets by 4-6, 8-6, 6-2, 7-5.

The Challenge Round of the Davis Cup will, therefore, be played at Wimbledon next year.

### A SPORTING FIGHT

England won the Davis Cup after five hours of tense and dramatic tennis. And as one leaves the Stade Roland Garros, the gates of which are jammed with thousands of heated partisans in swift reaction, all seeking transport to Paris at the same time, the final scenes persist.

The last rally is over, Perry has made the winning stroke, the last French urge to Merlin has been made, the last red cushion has been thrown on the court, the cheers have subsided, the famous trophy has been carried into the court, the teams are lined up for M. Pierre Gillou, the president of the French Federation, to present it to Mr. Roper Barrett, the British captain, and the strains of "God Save the King" float over the hushed stadium in the setting sun.

The "Marseillaise" follows, and so we remember that France is honouring the country which has beaten her in an honourable sporting fight, and that international games can promote the entente cordiale.

### PALPITATING MOMENTS

It proved to be the narrowest of victories for the challenging country. There were moments in the Austin-Cochet match when one thought the cup was already won; there were more palpitating moments in the succeeding Perry-Merlin match when the retention of the cup by France looked not only possible, but probable.

### HOW ENGLAND WON

First Round (European Zone)
England beat Spain, 4-1
Second Round (European Zone)
England beat Finland, 5-0
Third Round (European Zone)
England beat Italy, 4-1
Semi-final (European Zone)
England beat Czechoslovakia, 5-0
Final (European Zone)
England beat Australia, 3-2
Inter-Zone Final
England beat America, 4-1

### CHALLENGE ROUND

England beat France (holders) 3-2

**(July 31)**

# WIMBLEDON'S LAST THRILL

## UMPIRE WHO CHANGED HIS MIND

**From Our Special Representative**

The amazing Wimbledon of 1933, with its "best evers" in attendances, weather and thrills, ended in an appropriately sensational climax on Saturday.

In a packed centre court, with the King and Queen eagerly watching, Mrs. Wills Moody, the American woman champion, and Miss Dorothy Round, the gallant English challenger, found themselves involved in an extraordinary scene.

Through two sets so exciting that they might have served for fiction or scenario the two women had fought their way. Impassive Mrs. Moody had taken the first at 6-4. Miss Round had counter-attacked and, playing inspired tennis, reached 7-6 with her own service to follow.

The crowd was frantic; its applause hysterical. All through that grim second set the onlookers clapped loudly as Miss Round crossed over or as she walked back to serve.

The score is called – 7-6 to Miss Round and 30-40. A swift drive from the British player pitches near Mrs. Moody's baseline, "Game" calls the umpire, and the electric scoreboard flashes 7-7.

A linesman jumps up, approaches the umpire's chair, and says something to him. Pandemonium in the audience.

### EXCITED DISCUSSIONS

Again the umpire calls firmly, "Game, Seven-all." The balls are thrown across for Mrs. Moody to serve. Another linesman approaches the umpire. The audience is cheering and shouting, and excited discussions are going on everywhere.

"Seven-six and deuce," calls the umpire suddenly. There is a moment's silence, and then the babel of noise breaks out anew. Booing comes from several quarters, and someone calls from the covered stands, "Make up your mind, umpire!"

Miss Round stands there, the picture of distress. She appears to be appealing vehemently to the umpire to let the score stand; but now he is adamant.

She serves, and Mrs. Moody taps the next two points, lackadaisically into the net. Set to Miss Round, 8-6.

The last set was played in an atmosphere of strange anti-climax. Miss Round looked as shaken as her opponent by the episode, in which both players were, of course, equally the victims of circumstance. The end came when Mrs. Moody went out at 6-2.

**(June 10)**

# MISS SCRIVEN'S GREAT TENNIS TRIUMPH

## PLAYING A "LONE HAND"

Playing a "lone hand," Miss Peggy Scriven, the Yorkshire girl, whose home is at Byfleet, yesterday won the French Women's Singles tennis title at Auteuil, defeating Mme. Mathieu, the leading player of France.

Never before has an English player won the French women's championship, yet this gallant little lady:

Was ignored by the British team selectors and "unseeded" in the draw.

Went to Paris independently, finding her own hotel and paying her own expenses.

Received no moral support from the official team, the members of which had left Auteuil the day before the final round.

Miss Scriven's father stated last night that all through the tournament she had been handicapped by tonsil trouble, a complaint that has interfered with her play in the past.

**(June 6)**

# BRITAIN WINS RYDER CUP ON LAST GREEN

## HOW AMERICA WERE BEATEN BY ONE POINT

**By George Greenwood**

GREAT Britain won the Ryder Cup match, beating America by the narrow margin of one point on the Ainsdale course here to-day. The eight singles were halved, each side winning four, and the contest being decided on the foursomes, which Britain won by the odd match.

The Prince of Wales was an interested spectator. He saw the leading game, in which Sarazen defeated Padgham, and then crossed over to watch Hagen's great and successful fight with Lacey.

Finally, the Prince saw the game which settled the issue. It drew the entire crowd of 25,000 people, and provided the most thrilling episode yet associated with the Ryder Cup.

S. Easterbrook of Bristol, and Densmore Shute were the principals in the drama. Shute manoeuvred himself into the position of one up with four to play, but Easterbrook promptly squared by holing a putt of five yards for a 2. Then, amid great excitement, he holed a putt of six yards at the next for a half in 4.

### A CHARMED LIFE

Easterbrook had a providential escape at the seventeenth. He left himself two yards from the flag and half-stymied, but he managed to hole the putt for another half. He seemed to have a charmed life.

Now we come to the eighteenth, the hole which was to settle the contest and decide the destiny of the Cup. It was pardonable that in these exacting circumstances, with a vast horde of spectators rushing up the fairway to secure a place of vantage from which to see the last act of the drama, the players should feel the strain and the responsibility of their position.

Shute drove first and hooked into a bunker. This was Easterbrook's chance, but he also pulled into a bunker further up the course. Shute, with a mighty effort, played for the green, but was trapped in a bunker at the left-hand corner. Easterbrook dug his ball out, and each player arrived on the green with their third shot.

### SHUTE'S MISSED OPPORTUNITY

Easterbrook putted first and missed. Whereupon Shute said to himself, "Now is my opportunity," and quite properly, went for the hole. But it was a downhill putt and missing the hole, the ball ran six feet past. Shute studied the line from all angles, then putted – and missed.

Easterbrook, who was only about a couple of feet away, tapped the ball into the hole and a burst of tremendous cheering. The Cup had been won from America, and the Prince, in presenting the trophy, said that while he had to be impartial he was echoing the sentiments of all those present when saying that he was glad Britain has won.

**(June 28)**

# TWO AMERICANS TIE WITH 292

**From George Greenwood**

ST. ANDREWS, Friday.

Once again the British Open Golf Championship is destined for America.

Craig Wood and Densmore Shute, members of the United States Ryder Cup team, tie for first place with a total of 292. They will play off for the Championship over thirty-six holes to-morrow.

Craig Wood, a fair-haired, handsome looking man, is known throughout the States as golf's matinée idol. When play began to-day he was nine strokes behind the leaders.

It is significant that the aggregate of 292 is seven strokes more than that of Bobby Jones when he won the title six years ago.

Both Wood and Shute are 30 years of age, and both were competing for the British championship for the first time.

**(July 9)**

# DOYLE DISQUALIFIED

## PETERSEN KEEPS HIS TITLE IN AMAZING CONTEST

**By Our Boxing Correspondent**

"Back to your corner, Doyle!" That brief sentence brought disappointment to 70,000 people at the White City last night, when Jack Doyle, the young Irish giant, was disqualified for hitting low in the second round of his fight with Jack Petersen, the heavy-weight champion of Great Britain.

It was a miserable ending to an amazing fight. That Mr. G.H. Douglas's decision was correct there is no doubt whatever. To my mind he should have acted as he did more promptly and far sooner.

Three times in the first round, and once after the bell had gone, Doyle slung in low punches, but it was not until he had been warned on three occasions that he was finally disqualified.

The referee found it extremely hard to control the boxers at all; they took little notice of his orders, and more than once it seemed probable that the contest would develop into a fight to the finish, regardless of referee, rules, timekeepers, and stewards.

### "TAVERN BRAWL"

It is difficult to understand what caused Doyle to throw away his chance of a championship so recklessly. It is equally difficult to believe that he will ever become a champion while he is so lacking in self control.

Perhaps his Irish blood was too much for him; he fought, at any rate, as if he had suddenly been plunged into a tavern brawl, when his only concern was at all costs to hammer his man to the floor.

Yet Doyle, before the contest began, was the most self-possessed boxer I have ever seen. He waved gaily to his friends in the audience, preened himself in his green dressing gown, shook hands amiably with anyone who greeted him, and smiled affably at the world at large.

Petersen, on the contrary, seemed more determined and set than usual, as if he realised that there was stern business to come.

He had reason to be thoughtful, for when the two men stood together during the referee's homily, Doyle's height and breadth of shoulder and deep chest made it easy to realise that Petersen was giving away nearly two stones in weight. A superbly built fellow, this Doyle, and a cheerful one until the bell rang and the fight started.

### EYES BLAZING

Then we saw a different Doyle indeed. He came out of his corner, eyes blazing, teeth clenched, quick of foot, and at once hooked short punches to Petersen's head. Petersen was ready for him though, and met him with a left to the jaw and a right to the body which would have steadied most opponents.

It was then that we had a taste of Doyle's fighting fury; he crowded in battering Petersen to the ropes, and holding with his left.

Petersen swung away, catching Doyle with a right as they broke, and then came the first of the low punches, and a warning from the referee. More holding and clinching – Doyle's blows swinging dangerously low – another warning – a savage attack by Doyle, the bell, and a punch in the groin which obviously hurt Petersen though he made no sign.

### IRISHMAN CAUTIONED AGAIN

Before the men came out of their corners for the second round the referee cautioned Doyle once more, but after a minute of wild slogging Doyle threw restraint to the winds and Mr. Douglas ordered him back to his corner.

It was some time before the boxers realised the fight was over, but then Doyle sat down, apparently in stunned amazement, to hear the announcement of his disqualification.

What would have happened if the fight had not ended so wretchedly it is hard to say. Doyle was punishing Petersen severely without a doubt, and Petersen was swept out of his ordered plan of campaign.

Still, what science there was clearly belonged to Petersen, and he might well have landed the decisive punch. Anyway, both men live to fight again.

**(July 13)**

# SONJA HENIE'S GENIUS

## INCOMPARABLE STAR OF SKATING

**From Our Special Correspondent**

Poets are in the habit of complaining that nowadays there is nothing for them to write about. One would suggest that "To Sonja Henie on the Ice" is a tribute that, to be paid as it merits, deserves the pen of a poet, and is one which needs writing without delay – if indeed, it has not been already done.

Last night she was the incomparable star of the Ladies' Figure-Skating Championship for Europe, which was held at the Ice Club, Millbank. There were a number of magnificent lady skaters there who, in ordinary circumstances might have monopolised the spectators' stock of superlatives, but Frl. Henie stands far above them all, the reception she received was enthusiastic.

**(February 1)**

# STRIKING PICTURES FROM THE EVEREST EXPEDITION

EXCLUSIVE "DAILY TELEGRAPH" pictures from the Mount Everest Expedition on this page illustrate the ascent to the head of East Rongbuck Glacier.

(ABOVE) Everest from near Camp 2, at 19,500 feet. (RIGHT) Porters, one of whom is carrying the curved poles of an Arctic tent, are seen with their 40lb loads.

(LEFT) Glacier scenes at and near Camp 2 taken on the way to the trough which leads up the East Rongbuck Glacier towards Camp 3.

(ABOVE) PRINCESS ELIZABETH with her parents the Duke and Duchess of York watched the full-dress daylight rehearsal at Aldershot for the Aldershot Tattoo. Thousands of schoolchildren were guests at the rehearsal.

(ABOVE) MARLENE DIETRICH, who arrived in Paris from America yesterday, wearing trousers on board the liner Europa.

(LEFT) "ISOBEL", one of the bronzes in the exhibition of Jacob Epstein's work at the Leicester Galleries.

(LEFT) A POLICE CAR fitted with the new notice on the blind covering the rear window. Patrols are also to wear white gauntlets as shown.

In a wave of assassinations, King Alexander of Jugoslavia was shot in Marseilles and Chancellor Dolfuss of Austria was attacked by Nazi thugs and left to bleed to death in his own headquarters. Hitler, proclaiming a "1,000 Year Reich", invented a plot to rid himself of some of his early lieutenants like Captain Röhm. John Dillinger, called "Public Enemy No. 1", Babyface Nelson and the youthful bandits Clyde Barrow and Bonnie Parker were all eliminated by American law enforcement agencies.

Riots in Paris and the fall of a government followed the discovery of vast frauds perpetrated by the municipal bonds salesman, Stavitsky, who was officially stated to have committed suicide, though some thought that he had been murdered in order to prevent implicating people in high places. The Russian purges continued and there was further revolutionary activity in Spain. The United States devalued the dollar against gold in order to help the economy.

The pretence that the world might disarm mutually was becoming less and less plausible. The Japanese abrogated the naval treaty and the British government announced an end to cuts in armaments and outlined the expansion of the Royal Air Force.

The signs of recovery in Britain continued. Income Tax was cut by sixpence in the Budget and unemployment continued to fall, though the hunger marchers from the North of England, as well as Scotland and Wales, converged on London to demonstrate their plight. The Prime Minister, refusing to meet them, said that it was all "a communist plot". The clash between the communists and the increasingly high-profile British Union of Fascists, led by Oswald Mosley, came to a head at a turbulent meeting addressed by Mosley at Olympia in London. Hecklers were brutally ejected by male strong-arm squads and "ju-jitsu girls".

In the cinema the arrival of Shirley Temple was heralded while, rather prematurely, the death of the Western was forecast. Greta Garbo, when she was not gazing into the distance as Queen Christina, was thought to be speaking rather better English. Charles Laughton triumphed as Edward Moulton Barrett.

President Hindenburg, the former general and unwilling collaborator with Adolf Hitler, died, as did the much loved King of the Belgians. In the space of a few months, Britain lost its three leading composers: Edward Elgar, Gustav Holst and Frederick Delius.

Confidence in the future was demonstrated by the launch of the Queen Mary on Clydeside and the opening of the Mersey Tunnel. The increasing presence of the motor car was marked by new traffic signs and the introduction of pedestrian crossings. Two British pilots, flying a de Havilland Comet, won the London to Melbourne air race, chopping days off the previous record. They managed an average speed of 160 mph. For the first time for decades both the men's and the women's Wimbledon champions were British. Indeed, Fred Perry became a triple champion, winning in Paris and New York as well. The American hold on the golf Open Championship was broken by the success of Henry Cotton.

## WORKLESS RELIEF BOARD SURPRISE



# The Daily Telegraph



To-Days Weather : Unsettled; mainly fair in W. and N. Broadcasting: Page Five

No. 24,714 POSTAGE { INLAND, CANADA AND NEWFOUNDLAND, ONE PENNY / OTHER COLONIES AND PLACES ABROAD, THREE-HALFPENCE } LONDON, WEDNESDAY, AUGUST 8, 1934 ONE PENNY

*BIRTHS, MARRIAGES and DEATHS one guinea for three lines or less and 5s for each additional line. "IN MEMORIAM" notices is 12/6 for three lines or less and 3/6 for each additional line. (Special rate for five or ten years' automatic insertion on application.) Announcements authenticated by name and address of sender may be sent to The Daily Telegraph Fleet-street, E.C.4. or to 161 Piccadilly, W.1. or telephoned to Central 4242.*

## BIRTHS

BOYLE – On Aug. 4, 1934, at Danehurst, Sidcup, to Winifred (née Bacon), wife of Charles Harry Boyle, of 32, County-gate, S.E. 9, a daughter.

FARMER – On Aug. 5, 1934, to Isabel, wife of James A. Farmer, White Lodge, Leatherhead, Surrey, and Stumbleholme, Ifield, Sussex, a son.

FUDGER – On Aug. 3, 1934, at Stonefield, Blackheath, to Kathleen, wife of Thomas William Fudger, a son (Barry, John).

SAMWAYS – On Aug. 7, 1934, at 40, Belsize-grove, London N.W. 3. to Barbara (née Alderton), wife of G.S. Samways, a daughter.

## MARRIAGES

GRANT WATSON-McINERNY – On Aug. 7, 1934, Herbert Claude Grant Watson, elder son of Mr. H.A. Grant Watson, C.M.G., British Minister to Cuba, and Mrs Grant Watson of "Chat Parché" Le Touquet, to Aileen Marguerite Cady, only daughter of Mr. A.J. McInerny, of West Lodge, Pembroke-gardens, W.8., and of the late Mrs. McInerny

JAMES-EYRES – The wedding of Mr. L. Warwick James eldest son of Mrs. W. Warwick James, O.B.E., F.R.C.S., and Mrs. Warwick James of 2, Park-crescent, London W. 1. and Miss Margaret M. Eyres, elder daughter of Dr. Hugh M. Eyres and Mrs. Eyres, of Millgate House, Richmond, Yorkshire, took place at St. Agatha's Church, Easby, near Richmond, on Saturday, Aug. 4.

LAWRENCE-WICKSTEED – On Aug. 3, 1934, at Hampstead Town Hall, Walter Lawrence, son of the late Roger Bernard Lawrence, K.C. and Mrs. Lawrence, to Ursula, daughter of Joseph Hartley Wicksteed, M.A., and Mrs. Wicksteed.

McLELLAN-CARWARDINE – On Aug. 4, 1934, in London Dr. McLellan, Coatbridge, to Jean Carwardine, 7 West Lodge-avenue, London W.3.

ROYSTON-RIVERS – On Aug. 7, 1934, by the Archdeacon of Colombo, at St. Peter's Colombo, Reginald William, son of the late Mr. Percy Royston and Mrs. Royston of Muswell Hill, to Peggy Ethel, only daughter of Mr. and Mrs.A.T. Rivers, of Osterley, Middlesex.

### GOLDEN WEDDING

HARDING-DAY – On Aug. 8, 1884, at St. Leonard's Church, Streatham, John Harding to Amelia Day. Present address, 175, Mitcham-lane, Streatham.

## DEATHS

ALLEN – On Aug. 5, 1934, passed quietly Home, at her own nursing home , St. Michael's Upper Norwood. Mary Allen, friend and partner of Lillian G. Johns, both formerly of the Infant Welfare Centre, West Norwood.

BADCOCK – On Aug. 5, 1934, at Hillsboro. South church-road, Southend-on-Sea, Charles Alfred (late of Blackwall), aged 74, Funeral 2.30 to-morrow (Thursday) (not to-day as previously advised), at City of London Cemetery, Ilford. Memorial service to be announced later.

BOLDERO – On Aug. 5, 1934, at Blainslie, Hampden Park, Eastbourne, Clara, widow of John Boldero, of Frankham, and elder daughter of the late Thomas Bell Arnison,, aged 73. Funeral at Wadhurst Church to-day (Wednesday), at 12.15 p.m. No mourning. Flowers to Blainslie.

CHRISTIE – On Aug. 6, 1934, at 51a, Addison-gardens, W. 14, Gertrude, wife of Frank Christie, and mother of Kenneth Christie. Funeral service at St. John the Baptist, Holland-road, to-day (Wednesday), ten a.m.

DE BIERE – On Aug. 6, 1934, at 57 Beaumont-street, W. Arnold de Biere, aged 56, Burial to-day (Wednesday), at three o'clock. Willesden Jewish Cemetery.

de PLEDGE – On Aug. 4, 1934, in London, from pneumonia. Katherine Anne Douglas, widow of Frederic de Pledge, of Aban Court, Cheltenham, and daughter of the late Major John Gaspard Wright. Funeral at Charlton Kings, Cheltenham, to-day (Wednesday).

DIXON – On Aug. 5, 1934, Barbara Joan, elder daughter of Vivian and Doris Dixon, of Oaktree Cottage, Walton-on-Thames, after a short illness, aged 14 years. Service St. Peter's Hersham, to-day (Wednesday) at 11.30.

DRY – On Aug. 5, 1934 at Bournemouth, Flora Annie Mackenzie, widow of William Wakeling Dry. Funeral at Nunhead Cemetery to-day (Wednesday), at 2.30.

FITZGERALD – On Aug. 5, 1934, at Hastings, Robert John FitzGerald, J.P., D.L., of 40, Onslow-square, S.W.7. second son of the 19th Knight of Kerry, aged 82. Funeral, Putney Vale, one p.m., to-day (Wednesday). No flowers by request.

FRANCIS – On Aug. 5, 1934, at 22, Albany-road, St Leonards-on-Sea, the Rev. William Francis, formerly Vicar of Langley, Bucks, and of Wingrave, Bucks, aged 84.

GIBSON – On Aug. 5, 1934, at a nursing home in Norwich, Tom Gibson, M.R.C.S., (England), L.R.C.P. (London), of Shipham, Norfolk, aged 54 years, Cremation, Golders Green, to-morrow (Thursday), at 2.30.

GIFFORD – On Aug. 5, 1934, at The Croft, St. Just, Cornwall, Henry John of 9 Apsley-road, Clifton, Bristol. Funeral St. Just Church to-day (Wednesday), three p.m.

GRAY – On Aug. 4, 1934, in Paris, Helen Collins daughter of Travers Gray. Funeral Golders Green Crematory, Private.

HOOD – On Aug. 5, 1934, at 19 Downscourt-road, Purley, Jessie Beatrice, beloved wife of Geoffrey Hood. Service West Norwood Crematorium to-day (Wednesday), twelve o'clock. No mourning.

HULL – On Aug. 7, 1934, in London, twelve days after a serious operation. Thomas Halse Herbert Hull, for many years of the White Hart Hotel, Sonning-on-Thames. Funeral 2.30 Friday. Sonning Parish Church.

ISITT – On Aug.4, 1934, at 5, Queen's rd., Bradford, Yorks, Samuel Holmes, dear husband of Edith Isitt, in his 84th year.

## PERSONAL

*5s. per line (minimum 2 lines). Trade 12/6 per line. Lost And Found 2s 6d per line.*

HOME after 12th. Write. – A.M.L.W.Z.

KENTISH TOWN – Please SUPPLY NAME and ADDRESS. Strict confidence.

ALFRED, please ring Regent 6601.

WHATSOEVER IS BORN OF GOD overcometh the world: and this is the victory that overcometh the world, even our faith. – I. John iv., 4.

PLEASE SEND THEM

*One of the South London Mission Sisters-of-the Poor has appealed to me on behalf of twelve of her girls - members of her Club. They are from 14 to 16 years old, and not one of them has ever been to the Sea. All their lives have been spent in overcrowded houses in South London's worst Slums. They sleep night by night with 4 or 5 others in a stifling slum room. No wonder they are stunted and anæmic! One of them has just recovered from a long and serious illness. They are all so poor that they have no clothes fit to go away with. WILL YOU HELP US to send these unprivileged girls to Camp by the Sea with the Sister for one glorious week?*

THERE are also many Sick Children – their faces pitifully white and pinched, and their bodies wasted with illness – on our Waiting List to be sent to the Sea for a Red-Letter Fortnight that it may work its miracle of Healing.

Please send YOUR GIFT now to
REV. WALTER SPENCER,
3 Central Hall-buildings (Child Welfare),
TOWER BRIDGE-ROAD, London S.E. 1.
Inquiries and Visitors Welcomed. Clothing needed.

REQUIRED, UNFURNISHED FLAT, near Portland-place, 2 bed, 1 or 2 reception, bath room, kitchen. For middle-aged quiet professional man and wife. Highest credentials. Low rent, long tenancy. – 25 Park-lane, Beaconsfield.

OVAL TEST – FOUR SEATS for DISPOSAL. – Write O., Box 10,227, Daily Telegraph, 161, Piccadilly, W.

HAVE YOU HEARD that the terms at OATLANDS are now inclusive of Golf, Tennis, Swimming, Badminton, Billiards and Dancing? You can stay at this beautiful Mansion for as little as 5gns. per week, and enjoy all these amenities. There are 60 acres of glorious grounds and 150 attractive bed rooms and suites – 'Phone (Weybridge 1190), or write Oatlands Park Hotel, Weybridge, Surrey, for illustrated particulars. P.S. It's only 30 minutes from London.

GUY'S HOSPITAL S.E. 1.
URGENTLY NEEDS HELP.
Total annual expenditure £190,000.
Endowed income only £67,000.

L'INTEREST met en oeuvre toutes sortes de vertus et de vices. La Rochefoucauld.

IT IS IN YOUR POWER to bring health and happiness into a child's life. ONE GUINEA will send a poor or crippled kiddie to the sea or country for a fortnight's glorious holiday. – Please send your donation to-day to the SHAFTESBURY SOCIETY, John Kirk House, 32, John-street, W.C. 1.

AN ALTERNATIVE ROUTE? Of course there is! Consult the Autocar ROUTE-FINDER map, which gives correct routes and exits from London to any destination in Great Britain. OPENS LIKE A BOOK . Price 5s post free from Kelly's Directories Ltd., 186, Strand, London W.C. 2.

"ME GO? Naow, take the kiddies, it's them as needs a holiday." So says the self-sacrificing mother whose life in the slums is one long economic crisis. But what actually happens is this: The children go to the sea right enough, and so does mother – with them. It costs £5 for the fortnight, but it's worth it. don't you think? – Cheques &c., Preb. Carlisle. "Happy Holidays." Church Army, 55, Bryanston-st., W.1.

SMOKERS – You have missed a lot if you haven't yet tried that Grand Old Rich Tobacco called — TOM LONG.

SALE – Originial Model. £8 to £12. Day and Evening GOWNS, COATS, &c., reduced to £2 10s. – JEAN GASTON, 80 NEW BOND-STREET.

YOUNG Frenchman teaches French & Spanish, 2s hr. Write Y., Box 4,930. Daily Telegraph E.C. 4.

TRUSTEES have large funds available for MORTGAGE at 3 3/4 per cent. on first-class SHOP PROPERTY, or other securities 4-4 1/4 per cent. interest. – Write T., Box 8,476. Daily Telegraph. E.C.4.

"DISEASE IS NOT CURABLE: the Individual is curable" sums up findings of modern research. Send for free booklet "Health and Interest" which tells how a group of specialists in natural methods successfully treat illness on the principles of Individual Hygiene.
NATURAL THERAPY INSTITUTE
Dept. K2, 1B. Lancaster-gate, London, W.2.

BILL and LIZZIE calling! Please give these children a day at the seaside, 10s will send five. – R.S.V.P., John Pound's Mission, 24, Wellesley-street, Stepney.

THE CHILDREN'S COUNTRY HOLIDAYS FUND earnestly appeals for DONATIONS; £1 enables a poor, delicate London Child to enjoy a Fortnight's Summer Holiday in the Country. It is hoped to commemorate the Fund's Jubilee by sending away 36,000 children. Please send a gift to Hon. Treasurer (Room 4), 17 Buckingham-street, London, W.C. 2.

"BOB," – Norah and I staying as usual CROWN, and MITRE HOTEL, Carlisle. Join us there. – "JACK"

DO PLEASE SEND OLD CLOTHES, Toys, Books, Sports Gear, &c. Any description and condition. They are a tremendous help. Poorest district imaginable. Rev. S.G. Tinley, St. Luke's, Victoria Docks, E. 16.

BRITISH SAILORS' SOCIETY. – 116 years in Service for the Sailor. Gifts to help in relieving the appalling distress among British Merchant Seamen welcomed by Hon. Treas., Maj.-Gen. the Rt. Hon. Sir Frederick Sykes. P.C., G.C.S.I. &c., 680, Commercial-road, London E 14.

## PERSONAL (CONTINUED)

REDUCED FROM £3,500 TO £2,900. – Choice detached RESIDENCE, in the best part of BROMLEY, KENT (station 6 mins.). High altitude, excellent views. Near golf and open country, 3 reception rooms, 7 bed rooms, 2 baths, Garage, One-third acre. – Write R., Box 8,328. Daily Telegraph, E.C. 4.

CHOICE INDIAN and CEYLON BLEND "XLNT" 1s 8d per pound. 6lb post paid 10s. Every leaf guaranteed Empire. Purchase money returned in full if satisfaction not given. – STEPHEN CARWARDINE & CO., Tea Blenders, Dept. T., 4-5, Victoria House, Southampton-row, London, W.C.1. Established 1777.

£10 REWARD – LOST, on 17th July, between Chelsea, Pall-mall, and Covent Garden, ANTIQUE DIAMOND OVAL BROOCH. – Summers, Henderson & Co., 48, Lime-street, E.C. 3.

£3 REWARD – LOST, on 26th ulto., between Soho and Mayfair, DIAMOND and SAPPHIRE PLATINUM BRACELET. – Summers, Henderson & Co., 48, Lime-street, E.C. 3.

£2 REWARD – LOST, on 19th July, bet. Sussex-gardens, W. 2. and Savoy Hotel, W.C. 2. CRYSTAL, DIAMOND, and SAPPHIRE OCTAGONAL BROOCH, set plat. – Apply Frank Brown & Co., Palmerston House, Old Broad-street, E.C. 2.

I DON'T THINK much of a man who is not wiser to-day than he was yesterday.

IF YOU PAINT FLOWERS, make designs for machine-printed Cretonnes, &c. Postal Tuition and Sales Service. Day's sales exceed £200. – Write (D.T.) Textile Studio, 21 The Drive, Harrow Garden Village, Harrow.

CAREFUL TENANT WANTED, 18 months from October 1st. whilst owner abroad. COTTAGE 7 rooms, away from main road traffic. Company's water, telephone. – Rev. F. Dunnage, Kingsdown, Sevenoaks.

SHIPWRECKED MARINERS' SOCIETY. – Patron: H.M. the King. 1,000 Honorary Agents ALWAYS WATCHING, ready to give relief to survivors and to dependent relatives of those lost at sea. PLEASE HELP BY SENDING A CHEQUE. Bankers: Williams Deacon's Bank Ltd. Secretary: F.E. Thorn, Esq., 54 Carlton House, Regent-st., London S.W.1.

HAVE YOU HEARD that Harvey's of Bristol, the Wine people (shippers of the famous Bristol Milk Sherry), are now installed in London at 4a, King-street, St. James's? Ask them for a Price List.

FREE-EIGHT POUNDS WORTH OF DRY CLEANING. The purchase of a "SPIK" Home Dry Cleaning Machine will benefit your home more than any other household utility article. Its use is simple and "SPIK" Dry Cleaning Fluid is definitely non-inflammable, the safest on the market! A guinea a month will pay for the machine and save you pounds in dry cleaning bills. Write or visit our show rooms for free demonstration. – (SPIK) Sankey Instone Ltd., Dept. A, 37, South Molton-st., W.1.

LAST SUMMER REDUCTION

MARIE JOSE Ltd. is offering for one week only at reduced prices Day and Evening MATERNITY GOWNS. – 124, Regent-st., (2nd floor).

"I WOULD like to write a book about ..."
"Then you will need a Typewriter!"
ST. MARTIN'S TYPEWRITER CO. Ltd.,
92-93, St. Martin's-lane, W.C.2.
215 Tottenham Court-road, W. 1.
45 Tothill-street, Westminster.
DEFERRED TERMS FROM 10s MONTHLY.

ST. MARY'S GIRLS SCHOOL, Bungay, Norfolk. – We wish to put on record our deep appreciation of the care and attention given our daughter over her four years as border at this school. – Mr. and Mrs. French, Birdbrook, Essex.

2,000 DEAF MUTES were tested and only 2 failed to hear with the Multitone Deaf Aid. No matter what form of deafness you have, no matter how many deaf aids you have found useless, it would be unwise of you not to inquire further about the Multitone. The Multitone carries the sound direct to your aural nerve, so even if you were born deaf, or have nerve deafness, there is still hope. – Write for information to Multitone, 95, White Lion-street, London N.1.

STORAGE

MAPLES have the Finest Storage facilities at the Most Moderate Terms. Estimate free. Lowest Rates for Insurance. – Maple & Co. Ltd. The Largest Furnishing House in the World. Tottenham-court-road, W.1. 'Phone Mus 7000.

## CONCERTS, &C

QUEEN'S HALL
Sole Lessees – Chappell & Co. Ltd.,
**B.B.C. PROMENADE CONCERTS**
SAT. NEXT and NIGHTLY 20.00
FORTIETH SEASON, CONDUCTED BY
**SIR HENRY WOOD**
**B.B.C.**
**SYMPHONY ORCHESTRA**
OPENING NIGHT
SAT. NEXT, at 20.00

Prelude to The Kingdom ........ Elgar
(Two Preludes for Strings ........ Bach – Pick-Mangiagalli)
Mamie's Song (La Boheme) ........ Puccini
Symphonie Variations (Piano and Orch.) ........ Cesar Franck
Mercury – Saturn – Jupiter (The Planets) ........ Holst
"Largo al factotum" (Il Barbiere) ........ Rosini
Symphonie Poem. Till Eulenspiegel ........ Strause
Capriccio Espagnol ........ Rimsky-Korsakov
Mignon's Song "Knowest thou the land?" ........ Liszt
Joycuse Marche ........ Chabrier

MAGGIE TEYTZ. DENNIS NOBLE
Solo Pianoforte – IRENE KOHLER
FULL PROGRAMMES NOW READY
2s to 7s 6d. Season, 37s 6d, 21s (Promenade), at
B.B.C. BROADCASTING HOUSE, W.1.
Agents & Chappell's Box-office, Queen's Hall.

**CHAS. STILES & CO. EST 1853.**
GRANDS and UPRIGHTS by
**BECHSTEIN, BLUTHNER**
**CHALLEN, STEINWAY**
**CHAPPELL, BORD &c.**
New & Secondhand, Lowest Prices, Cash or Deferred terms, No deposit. – Write for lists 74-76, Southampton-row, W.C. 1. (1 min Holb. Tube).Holb. 0439.

## ARTICLES FOR SALE & WANTED

**FURNITURE**
**IMPORTANT**
**FURNITURE SALE**

FURNITURE. – An opportunity not to be missed. After prolonged legal formalities we have been directed by the Debenture Holders to dispose of the whole of the New Furniture made for a Super Hotel in the West Indies, not now required. These are of First-class workmanship, and being sold at Half Contract Price. Below only a few of the items, everything guaranteed.

25 Solid Oak Bed-room Suites, complete with wardrobe, beds and springs. £5 15s 0d. the set 15 Double-sized ditto. £7 15s 0d., 7 Very Elegant Italian Walnut Bedroom Suites in Dark and Light Grey Walnut, all Beautifully figured, with Beds complete, and springs £18 17s 6d., cost £30. Several others up to 80gns. 5 Complete Tudor-design Oak Dining Rooms, comprising Sideboard, Dining Table and chairs. 13gns. the set cost 20gns. Other complete Suites up to 50gns.5 only. Luxuriously sprung Lounge Suites of Modern Design, embodying the latest Dunlopillo cushioning and patent springing, upholstered in modern coverings. 22gns. Worth double. Gent's Fitted Robes £2 17s 6d. each. 75 Real Cowhide Lounge Chairs from 3gns. to 10gns Settees to match, Several odd easy chairs covered in tapestry and other coverings from 21s Chesterfields and Settees from 4gns. 250 Oak Dining Chairs 8s 6d. each. Bureaux, Bookcases, Cabinets and every item for complete furnishing. A GENUINE BARGAIN: Attractively designed, magnificently figured Burr Walnut Bed-room Suite, comprising Double Door Wardrobe. very elegant canted front Pedestal Dressing Table. triple Mirrors, Gentlemen's Wardrobe, Dressing Stool. and beautifully figured Double Bedstead to match complete with Staples Spring, Only 29gns., cost £50. Recently purchased, never used. Immediate inspection advised, any piece sold separately, stored and packed free for Country. – View at

**DAVIS'S**
**FURNITURE DEPOSITORIES**
Ltd, 83 and 85, St. John's-road, Clapham Junction, London S.W. 11, 6min. Waterloo and Victoria. Estab. 1880. 'Phone Battersea 4838. Open 9 to 8.

## EDUCATIONAL

**PITMAN'S COLLEGE**

Provides training for all branches of Commerce, Civil Service. London Matriculation, and all Professional Preliminary Examination.

Those who have undergone Commercial or Secretarial training are entitled to the lifelong use of the College Situations Bureau, from which leading employers regularly recruit their staff.

Advisory Governor: THE DUCHESS OF ATHOLL, D.B.E., D.C.L., LL.D., M.P.
Principal: R.W. HOLLAND, O.B.E., M.A., M.Sc., LL.D.
Write for
(a) "Day" Prospectus
(b) "Evening Study" booklet; or
(c) "Home Study handbook according to your requirements.
182 SOUTHAMPTON-ROW, W.C. 1.
Telephone: TERMINUS 4481
Branches at Brixton, Brondesbury, City Croydon, Ealing, Finsbury Park, Forest Gate, Lewisham, Maida Hill, North Finchley, Palmers Green, Wimbledon, Leeds, Manchester.

**KENSINGTON COLLEGE**
has the best
SECRETARIAL POSITIONS AT GOOD SALARIES
College Diploma
GUARANTEES REMUNERATIVE EMPLOYMENT
Individual treatment during and after training
Prospectus from Mr. L. E. Munford
34 Bishops-road, W.2. Telephone Paddington 9046

**BEDFORD SQUARE**
**SECRETARIAL COLLEGE**
(for educated ladies. Intensive and individual training. Moderate, inclusive fee to proficiency and a position. Frn. Languages. – 8 Bedford-sq., W.C.1. Tel. Museum 7323.

**LONDON COLLEGE OF SECRETARIES**
(Principal: Dr. E. Roberts)
Complete practical training for educated girls and women desiring to be PRIVATE SECRETARIES to professional men, politicians, or business men.
INDIVIDUAL TUITION
A suitable position found for every qualified student.
Special attention given to Foreign Shorthand.
Shorter courses in any secretarial subjects. – Apply 46, Grosvenor-place, S.W.1. (Tel. Sloane 2395.)

**SECRETARIAL COLLEGE**
Intensive Practical Training, with Modern Languages.
VACATION COURSES.
GOOD POSTS FOUND FOR ALL STUDENTS
Hostel, Lunch and Tea Canteen.
Write or Telephone for Free Prospectus
**MISS MILDRED RANSOM**
15, GREAT CUMBERLAND-PLACE, MARBLE ARCH, W.1.
Paddington 6302.

CUSACK'S COLLEGE enjoys a big reputation for preparing young people for business, banking, secretarial, and professional appointments. – Write to-day for Prospectus, SUN-STREET, Finsbury-sq., E.C.2.

**UNIVERSITY TUTORIAL COLLEGE**
SUMMER VACATION
A FOUR WEEKS' COURSE
**PRACTICAL SCIENCE**
for INTER. SC., B.Sc. FIRST MEDICAL, &c.
commences on
MONDAY, AUGUST 13th,
ALSO MATRICULATION REVISION CLASS
Full particulars from the Principal
UNIVERSITY TUTORIAL COLLEGE,
32 RED LION-SQUARE, HOLBORN, W.C. 1.

A TWENTY-GUINEA SCHOLARSHIP AT
**ST. JAMES'S**
**SECRETARIAL COLLEGE**
Awarded to students passing English Test.
Also Two Free Scholarships Annually.
34 and 35, GROSVENOR-PLACE, S.W. 1.

**MAYFAIR SECRETARIAL**
COLLEGE FOR GENTLEWOMEN,
25, BUCKINGHAM GATE, Vic. 4495.
Advanced training for the best posts found for students throughout their career. Three Scholarships. Own Hostel.

## EDUCATIONAL (CONTINUED)

HATS! Learn to make your own or as career – 12 Lessons 3gns – THE SCHOOL OF MILLINERY, 68, WIGMORE-STREET, Welbeck 9606.

THE ROSA BARRIE SCHOOL of BEAUTY CULTURE and HAIRDRESSING, 56, Baker-st., W., offers training to gentlewoman. – Write Secretary.

PUBLIC SPEAKING. – PRIVATE LESSONS given by Mr. C. SEYMOUR. Also Voice Breathing, Elocution. Confidence Prosp. for'd. – 401, Strand, W.C.2.

FOREIGN STUDENTS – Special holiday course now starting. Enrol at once. – London Schools of English, 319, Oxford-street, W.1.

FOREIGN GIRLS – Few received by University lady. Near London. Young society, Garden, Tennis, swimming, car, English lessons. – Rufford, Caterham, Surrey.

## PRIVATE SCHOOLS & COLLEGES

BOARDING SCHOOL AGENCY. – Full particulars (free) of all types of school, any district. – 93-94, Chancery-lane, W.C.2. HOLBORN 6105. SLOane 4554.

BRANKSOME GODALMING, SURREY. – A fine old PREP. SCHOOL, 50 BOYS fr. 6 yrs. Occasional vacs. 25gns. a term. Entire charge. – Pros. Headmaster.

## SHIPPING & MAILS

**P. & O. BRITISH INDIA & NEW ZEALAND**
**SHIPPING COMPANIES**
MAIL, PASSENGER and FREIGHT SERVICES
**P. & O. SAILINGS**
(Under Contract with His Majesty's Government.)
**BOMBAY, COLOMBO, AUSTRALIA.**

| | Ship | Tons | London | Mar's | Classes |
|---|---|---|---|---|---|
| 4, 5 | Mongolia | 17.,000 | Aug. 10 | Aug. 16 | T'st Class |
| 9, 5 | Mooltan | 21,000 | Aug. 24 | Aug. 31 | 1st & 2nd |
| 4, 5 | Moldavia | 17,000 | Sept. 7 | Sept. 13 | Tour. Cl. |

(and fortnightly thereafter)

**BOMBAY, COLOMBO, STRAITS, CHINA, JAPAN.**

| | | | | | |
|---|---|---|---|---|---|
| 3, 5 | Raw'pindi | 17,000 | – | Aug. 10 | 1st & 2nd |
| 1, 2, 3, 5 | Comorin | 15,000 | Aug. 17 | Aug. 24 | 1st & 2nd |
| 1, 2, 3, 5 | Ralputana | 17,000 | Aug. 31 | Sept. 7 | 1st & 2nd |
| 1, 2, 3, 5 | Chitral | 15,000 | Sept. 14 | Sept. 21 | 1st & 2nd |

(and fortnightly thereafter)

**SPECIAL SAILINGS TO BOMBAY**

| | | | | | |
|---|---|---|---|---|---|
| 2, 3, 5 | Kaisar-i-Hind | 11,500 | Aug. 10 | Aug. 17 | 1 class |
| 2, 3, 5 | Ranchi | 17,000 | Sept. 8 | Sept. 14 | 1st & 2nd |
| 5 | Viceroy of Ind. | 20,000 | Sept. 15 | Sept. 20 | 1st & 2nd |

Calling (1) Southampton, (2) Tangier, (3) Malta, (4) Port Sudan, (5) Tranship Bombay for Karachi.

**SPECIAL ROUND VOYAGE TICKETS**
AUSTRALIA £140 1st Class, £112 2nd Class.
CHINA and JAPAN £150 1st Class.
**P. & O. BRANCH SERVICE**
**FAST STEAMERS TO AUSTRALIA**
Via Malta Port Said, Suez, Aden and Colombo.
ONE CLASS ONLY. From £38 single, £68 return.

| | Tons | London | Plymouth | Liverpool |
|---|---|---|---|---|
| Ballarat | 13,000 | – | – | Aug. 18 |
| Barrabool | 13,000 | Sept. 14 | Sept. 15 | – |
| Bendigo | 13,000 | Sept. 28 | Sept. 29 | – |
| Balranald | 13,000 | Oct. 26 | Oct. 27 | – |

**BRITISH INDIA SAILINGS**
TO EAST AFRICAN PORTS

| Ship | Tons | Mid'sbro | London | Marseilles |
|---|---|---|---|---|
| §Malda | 9,066 | Aug. 18 | Aug. 24 | Sept. 1 |
| Madura | 9,077 | Sept. 15 | Sept. 21 | Sept. 29 |
| Matiana | 9,067 | Oct. 13 | Oct. 19 | Oct. 27 |
| Mantola | 9,066 | Nove. 10 | Nove. 16 | Nove. 24 |

§ Calls Tangier.

**P. & O. and B.I. JOINT SERVICE**
**COLOMBO, MADRAS AND CALCUTTA**

| Ship | Tons. | M'bro' | I'ham. | Antwp | London |
|---|---|---|---|---|---|
| †Domala | 8,441 | Aug. 11 | Aug. 13 | – | Aug. 18 |
| Nagpore | 5,283 | Aug. 23 | Aug. 25 | Aug. 27 | Sept. 1 |
| Modasa | 9,070 | Sept. 8 | Sept. 10 | – | Sept. 15 |
| Mulbera | 9,100 | Sept. 20 | Sept. 22 | Sept. 24 | Sept. 29 |

† Calls Tangier

**P. & O. and B.I.**
**PASSENGER OFFICES**
14, Cockspur-street, S.W. 1. (Whitehall 4444),
130, Leadenhall-street, E.C. 3 (Avenue 8000),
Australia House, W.C. 2. (Temple Bar 7924).
FREIGHT OR GENERAL BUSINESS.
P. & O. or B. I. Offices 122, LEADENHALL-ST., E.C. 3.
B. I. Agts. Gray, Dawes & Co. 122 Leadenhall-st., E.C. 3.

**NEW ZEALAND LINE**
To New Zealand and through bookings to Australia.
VIA PANAMA CANAL

| | | |
|---|---|---|
| ¶Remuera | 11,500 tons | London, Aug. 23 |
| †Rangitiki | 17,000 tons | London, Sept. 20 |
| *Ruahine | 11,000 tons | London, Oct. 4 |

and thereafter every 28 days.
* Tourist, one class only.
† First, Tourist, and 3rd Class, ¶ Cabin and Tourist Class.
Apply N.Z.S. Co. Ltd. Agents (J. B. Westray & Co. Ltd) 138, Leadenhall-street, E.C. 3 (Tel. Avenue 5220), or Trans-Pacific Psgr. Agcy. (W.L. James), 14, Cockspur-st., S.W. 1 (Tel. Whitehall 2953).

**CANADIAN AUSTRALASIAN LINE AND UNION ROYAL MAIL LINE**
to NEW ZEALAND and AUSTRALIA
By any Atlantic Line to Canada or U.S.A. Thence via VANCOUVER or SAN FRANCISCO.

| Ship | †From Vancouver | ¶From San Francisco |
|---|---|---|
| Maunganui | – | Aug. 29 |
| Aorangi | Sept. 12 | – |
| Makura | – | Sept. 26 |

†Canadian Australasian Line via Honolulu, Fiji, and Auckland to Sydney. ¶Union Royal Mail Line, via Tahiti, Rarotonga, Wellington to Sydney.
Apply the Trans-Pacific Passenger Agency Ltd.
(W.L. James, General Manager) 14, Cockspur-st. (1st floor), London S.W. 1 (Tel. Whitehall 2953) or for Vancouver Service any office of the Canadian Railways.

**ORIENT LINE to AUSTRALIA**
Through Tickets to NEW ZEALAND and TASMANIA.

| | London | Toulon | Naples |
|---|---|---|---|
| †Ormonde | Aug. 18 | Aug. 24 | Aug. 26 |
| Otranto | Sept. 1 | Sept. 7 | Sept. 9 |

Managers, Anderson, Green and Co., Ltd. 5, Fenchurch-avenue, E.C.3. West End Offices, 14, Cockspur-street, S.W.1.; No. 1, Australia House, Strand.

# KING ALEXANDER AND M. BARTHOU ASSASSINATED

## AT MOMENT OF WELCOME IN MARSEILLES

## 2 HIGH FRENCH OFFICERS WOUNDED

## CROAT'S SHOTS FROM CAR RUNNING-BOARD

## ALL EUROPE SHOCKED

**KING ALEXANDER OF JUGOSLAVIA AND M. BARTHOU, THE FRENCH FOREIGN MINISTER, WERE ASSASSINATED IN MARSEILLES SOON AFTER 4 P.M. YESTERDAY, ONLY A FEW MOMENTS AFTER THE JUGOSLAV MONARCH HAD LANDED ON FRENCH SOIL FOR AN OFFICIAL VISIT.**

**As King Alexander and M. Barthou were driving from the docks, a man ran from the crowds lining the pavement, jumped on to the running board of the closed car and fired a number of revolver shots at point-blank range.**

The assassin, who has been identified as a 34-year-old Croat, Petrus Keleman, was armed with a modern revolver holding 20 cartridges. He continued firing even after being struck down by the sabre of the chief of the mounted escort, who immediately spurred his horse forward.

The crowd, breaking through the police cordon, trampled him down, but he had already shot himself in the head.

Gen. Georges, of the French Supreme War Council, and the French Admiral Berthelot, who were riding in a second car, were critically wounded by shots. But it is unknown whether the latter were fired by the assassin or were stray police shots.

**M. BARTHOU ATTEMPTS TO SHIELD KING**

Despite his wounds, M. Barthou tried to shield King Alexander. But the latter, bleeding profusely, collapsed on the floor of the car and never regained consciousness. He was 46.

M. Barthou, who was 72, was rushed to hospital for an operation, and hemorrhage occurred while he was under the anaesthetic. A blood transfusion was instantly made, but he weakened rapidly, and died at 5.40 p.m.

Queen Marie of Jugoslavia would have been with the King, but owing to boisterous weather at sea and the state of her health she changed her plans at the last minute, and set out by train through Italy and Switzerland.

She collapsed, weeping, when the tragic news was broken to her on the train at Besançon. Later, while she was on her way to Marseilles, the train was stopped at a wayside station, and a doctor hurriedly summoned to attend her.

Her mother, Queen Marie of Roumania, is leaving London to-day to join her.

**REGENCY COUNCIL OF THREE**

The 11-year-old heir to the Jugoslav throne, Crown Prince Peter, is at Sandroyd School, Cobham, Surrey. The news of his father's death has so far been kept from him. Police were on duty at the school throughout last night.

It was officially stated at the Jugoslav Legation in London that Prince Peter has been proclaimed King. He must now return to Jugoslavia, where a Regency Council of three will reign during his minority.

It is not expected that the tragedy will affect the plans for the forthcoming marriage of Prince George and Princess Marina, which King Alexander was to have attended.

M. Lebrun, the French President, has left with M.M. Tardieu and Herriot for Marseilles. M. Doumergue, the Premier, will temporarily act as Foreign Minister.

THIS STRIKING PHOTOGRAPH was taken a moment after the assassination of King Alexander and M. Barthou. The smoke from the assassin's revolver is seen rising above the leading car, in which the King was driving with the French Foreign Minister and Gen. Georges.

## EYE-WITNESSES' STORIES

**From Our Special Correspondent**

MARSEILLES, Tuesday.

Eye-witnesses have told me to-night what they saw of the murder of King Alexander of Jugoslavia and M. Louis Barthou, the French Foreign Minister.

Gen. Georges, a member of the French Supreme War Council and Adml. Berthelot. The Maritime Prefect of Toulon, were wounded and are in a critical condition.

The King landed on the jetty of the Old Port at four o'clock, and having been welcomed by M. Barthou on behalf of the French Government set out in a procession in which the second car was occupied by the King and M. Barthou. This had not gone more than about sixty yards along the Cannebiere when a man stepped from a motor-car, and drawing a revolver fired six shots into the first and second cars.

King Alexander was hit by two bullets – one in the head and the other in the chest. He was immediately taken to the Prefecture to which several doctors had been urgently summoned, but was dead before the arrival of the car.

M. Barthou, who had been sitting on the left of the King, was shot in the right shoulder and the stomach. He died on the operating table in hospital in the middle of a blood transfusion operation.

Struck Down Assassin With Sabre

A graphic account of the assassination has been given by Col. Piolet, commander of the 115th Infantry Regiment. He himself struck down with his sabre the man he saw firing on the Royal car.

Col. Piolet, who rode at the side of the King's carriage, says:

"I had the mission of escorting the carriage in which were seated the King, and M. Barthou.

"The King was sitting on the right. My horse was at his side, but I held back sufficiently to allow his Majesty to salute the crowd.

"When we reached the Bourse-square, exactly opposite the police kiosk, a man forced his way through the line, ran forward a few steps, and before I could do anything, fired several shots point blank at the King.

"With two strokes of my sabre I felled the assassin to the ground. In spite of that he continued to fire, and I think he must have hit a General who was in the second carriage. The crowd flung itself on the perpetrator of this unspeakable deed, and he can hardly have escaped with his life.

"As the first shots were fired point blank nothing but a miracle could have saved the Sovereign."

Accomplices Escape

The police declared that Keleman, the dead assassin, carried a modern revolver which held twenty cartridges, and was in effect a "miniature machine-gun."

They said that first enquiries indicated that Keleman had accomplices. At the moment he was shooting several men rushed forward and began struggling with the police to frustrate any effort by them to stop Keleman.

Other evidence also suggests that the assassination had been carefully planned by a group of accomplices.

A witness on a balcony overlooking the Cannebiere, who saw every detail of the Royal arrival, has given the police the following account:

As the car in which the King and the Foreign Minister were riding passed under his balcony, he said, he saw a group of people suddenly surge out of the ranks of spectators and hang on to the footboard, while at the same time there was a fusillade.

"The Gardes Mobiles charged into the crowd, and several more shots were fired. I saw one man strike down another with his sword. The crowd broke through the barriers and fled in all directions."

It is believed that in the pandemonium the assassin's accomplices escaped.

A film of the actual assassination was secured by a news camera operator, but he immediately surrendered it to the police.

SILENCE, THEN UPROAR

Cavalry Charge on Mob

When the crowd heard the shots there was a second's dead silence, followed by indescribable uproar. For a moment King Alexander did not seem to be touched, but then he collapsed abruptly.

The vast crowd surged wildly forward, but the police and cavalry turned and started striking out indiscriminately at the mob with sabres and clearing a way.

There was a scene of wild disorder, and scores of people, including the assassin, were trampled on.

King Alexander fell to the floor of the car without speaking, bleeding profusely from the mouth. M. Barthou, despite being wounded, tried to shield the King, who had been sitting beside him.

ASSASSIN'S CRY

"Long Live the King!"

The chauffeur of the motor-car in which King Alexander and M. Barthou were riding, stated:

"I saw a man jump on the running board of the car, and heard him shout 'Long live the King.' I thought he was a supporter of the King, but he lifted his arm and began shooting with the pistol barely ten inches from the King.

"I struck him with my fist, but I was too late. The King never had a chance. The attacker was corpulent, bald, and well-dressed."

Another witness stated: "I was at the very edge of the pavement of the Bourse-square only a few steps from the spot whence the assassin hurled himself against the royal carriage.

"A fanfare of the Republican Guards had announced the approach of the King. Loud cheers were raised. The royal carriage advanced slowly, and the King raised his hand as a sign of acknowledgment.

"Suddenly hissing was heard on the right pavement. Another group of spectators in counter demonstration cheered loudly. Then there was a violent movement in the crowd, and a corpulent, bald-headed man burst through the cordon of police, sprang into the clear portion of the street, jumped on to the footboard of the carriage, and fired six shots from an enormous Parabellon pistol."

"Another car, in which the Jugoslav generals were seated, stopped in the middle of the road. Its occupants were weeping.

"The murderer was stretched out gasping on the roadway. He was literally torn to pieces by the furious witnesses of his outrage. Some paces distant several persons were bleeding from wounds they had received, and it was some time before the police could liberate them from the crowd.

## QUEEN MARIE'S GRIEF

### PATHOS OF JOURNEY INTO FRANCE

### HER LIFE SAVED BY CHANGED PLANS

PARIS, Tuesday.

Queen Marie, who had been unable to travel by sea with the King on account of the weather, was on her way by train to join the King when her train was specially stopped at Besançon to tell her of the assassination.

The telegrams sent to various stations in Italy and Switzerland had failed to reach her. When her train was stopped the Prefect of the Doubs Department, M. De La Roca, entered the Queen's private apartment, and told her first that the King had been wounded, and then broke the news of his death.

Queen Marie became prostrate with weeping. The blinds of her apartment were drawn, and M. De La Roca remained in the train to accompany her to Marseilles.

Later the train was stopped again at Lons le Saulner and a doctor hurriedly summoned to attend the Queen.

The train will arrive at Marseilles early to-morrow morning, and Queen Marie will go straight to the Prefecture, where the King's body lies.

When Queen Marie's train arrived at Lyons at 11.30 to-night, Mme. Herriot, wife of the ex-Premier, who is a member of the present National Government, joined the train to accompany Queen Marie to Marseilles.

In thanking Mme. Herriot for her expressions of condolence, Queen Marie said:

"My greatest consolation in this terrible misfortune is that the King died on French soil."

In thanking him Queen Marie said that her one desire was that the journey should be accomplished as quickly as possible. The station was packed with troops – Reuter and B.U.P.

## BOY HEIR TO LEAVE ENGLISH SCHOOL

### SLEEPS UNAWARE OF TRAGEDY

On the day of his father's assassination, the heir to the Jugoslav Throne, the 11-year-old Crown Prince Peter, was following the regular routine of his school at Cobham, Surrey.

He went to bed without knowing of his bereavement.

The news had been telephoned to Sandroyd School, Cobham, within a quarter of an hour of the assassinations. At the request of the Jugoslavian Legation, however, the headmaster of the school, Mr. Ozanne, did not tell the young Prince.

A body of police kept watch throughout the night outside the school at the request of the Jugoslav Legation. Six police officers, including two plain clothes men and a Special Branch officer from Scotland Yard were posted outside the school, and all the available Cobham police were brought in for duty.

The heir to the throne will, under the Constitution, be obliged to return to his native land to complete his education.

## BELGRADE FEARS CROAT RISING

### FORMER DICTATOR SUMMONED BY CABINET

**From Our Own Correspondent**

BELGRADE, Tuesday Night.

It is reported here that complete quiet prevails throughout the country.

The members of the Regency Council which is to be set up will be Prince Paul, Queen Marie, and the President of the Senate. The Cabinet is now in session.

Gen. Zhivkovitch has been summoned to return to Belgrade immediately by the Government, and will probably re-assume for the moment his old functions of dictator.

The news of the assassination of the King was withheld until about eight p.m., when the cinemas and cafés were crowded. Entertainment resorts were immediately closed and black flags hoisted on all public buildings, while the church bells tolled throughout the country.

NEWS BY WIRELESS

The tragedy was first made known to members of the public by broadcasts from German stations, and upon this the Government announcement was made.

Alarm is expressed unofficially lest the assassination be the prelude to a Croat rising.

The following official communiqué has been issued by the Government:

"The news of the dreadful deed has caused immense consternation and indignation throughout the country.

"The Government is fully aware of the difficult situation which has arisen from the death of our great King, and is taking into consideration the measures which are necessary in the interests of the State and of the people.

"In Jugoslavia the Royal power persists without interruption, as the King transferred his power, before his departure, into the hands of the Government.

"According to the constitution the heir to the throne will be proclaimed King, but as he is of minor age a regency will be nominated.

"The members shall consist of the men mentioned in the King's last will. Should these not be available, the members will be appointed in a full sitting of the State Council and of the Parliament.

"In all parts of the country law and order prevail."

The body of King Alexander will be brought back immediately on the Jugoslavian warship Dubrovnik, from which he landed in Marseilles to-day. There will be a French naval escort all the way. He will be buried in the mausoleum of the Karageorgevitch family at Topolaj.

The assassination of King Alexander adds one more to the long list of Serbian rulers who have come to a violent end.

As his enemies never ceased to remind King Alexander, no ruler of Serbian history has died in his bed while still in power. King Alexander's father, King Peter, died peacefully, but he was only nominally King, for Alexander was already Prince Regent.

All other Serbian rulers have either been assassinated, killed in battle, or been deposed before death. His fate is one which King Alexander has faced with open eyes for many years.

Certainly since 1928, when the Croatian patriot and leader, Stephen Raditch, was shot dead in the Belgrade Parliament by the Serbian deputy Punisha Ratchitch, he has been constantly menaced.

# HITLER'S EXECUTION OF HOSTILE NAZIS

## CAPT. ROHM DECLINES SUICIDE AND IS SHOT

**From Our Special Correspondent**

BERLIN, Sunday Night.

Capt. Ernst Röhm, leader of the Nazi Storm Troopers, was executed in the Stadelheim Prison, Munich, this evening.

This was the sequel to the most critical week-end for Herr Hitler since he assumed power seventeen months ago. Capt. Röhm's execution followed the shooting of the former Chancellor, Gen. von Schleicher, and the execution of a number of prominent Storm Troop leaders.

The official statement issued to-night says that Röhm, after being deposed from his leadership, was given a revolver to shoot himself. Until late this afternoon he had not done so. Police, therefore, went into his prison cell and shot him dead.

To-night, Dr. Goebbels, the German Minister of Propaganda, told the German nation that they owed a tremendous debt to Chancellor Hitler for his personal work in suppressing the attempted revolt by Röhm. He sternly warned other possible traitors that they would receive no mercy.

COUNTRY BEWILDERED

"Second Revolution"

Germany is dazed and bewildered by the dramatic, and in many ways inexplicable, events of this amazing week-end.

As the official communiqué of the Nazi party and the statements of Gen. Göring to the Press explain, a "second revolution" directed against Hitler and the Reichswehr, has been killed at birth. It has been killed by dramatic personal actions in the full limelight by Hitler in Munich and by Göring in Berlin.

What the alleged "second revolution" was to have been, against whom and by whom, is still a complete mystery. Many people think the events of the week-end were a purging of the Nazi party's discreditable elements and political suspects. What there could have been in common between Gen. Schleicher and Röhm, the two principal victims, it is difficult to imagine.

**(July 2)**

# HITLER TO RULE FOR LIFE

The general opinion held in Germany that Herr Hitler intends to retain his present powers indefinitely was authoritatively confirmed to-day.

Addressing the members of the German Academy of Public Administration, Dr. Lammers, permanent head of the Reich Chancellery, stated that Herr Hitler had assumed the offices of Reich President and Chancellor for life. The two functions could no longer be separated.

A subsidiary effect of their amalgamation, he pointed out, was that the responsibility of the Chancellor towards the Reichstag had no longer even a legal foundation, since it was obviously impossible for the head of the State to be answerable to Parliament.

At a sitting of the German Cabinet this evening a law was passed requiring Ministers of the Reich and members of the State Diets to take an oath of personal allegiance to Herr Hitler.

**(October 17)**

# ASTONISHING NUREMBERG SCENES

## LEADER'S SPECTACULAR ENTRY TO CONGRESS

**From Our Special Correspondent**

NUREMBERG, Wednesday.

A little auburn-haired woman, Fraulein Leni Riefenstahl – the cinema director and star – was the commander-in-chief of ceremonies at to-day's gigantic Nazi meeting in the Luipol arena.

For fourteen minutes 40,000 political leaders, S.S. (protective guards) and party dignitaries who filled the huge hall to-day, stood motionless in the stifling heat while she completed her preparations for the conducting of the Congress films.

Even Herr Hitler and his staff of party lieutenants were kept patiently waiting outside until the stage was set, and had to obey her orders.

Herr Hitler made his entrance when the powerful reflectors were lit and the camera men in position.

As he marched up the central aisle lined by two rows of S.S. guards, he was greeted with a roll of drums. Behind him came Herr Rudolf Hess, Herr Himmler, the head of the political police, Herr Lutze, chief of the Storm Troop staff, Dr. Goebbels, and Herr Frick.

The whole of the arena was beautifully decorated for to-day's festival. The walls were hung with fawn-grey drapery, and unbleached sailcloth covered the roof to keep out the sun's rays. The massive columns in the centre aisles were concealed behind red cardboard framework from which hung chains of brightly-coloured flowers.

These flowers were made by the tireless hands of thousands of Hitlerite girls. Embedded in the paper flowers were powerful reflectors, which, combined with the sun in adding to the stifling heat in the hall.

In a proclamation read by District Leader Adolf Wagner, Herr Hitler made the following assertion:

"By this revolution the German form of life is definitely settled for the next thousand years.

Other points from this proclamation, states the British United Press, were: "The will of the National Socialist Government leadership is unfaltering and unshakable.

**(September 6)**

# NAZI EXECUTIONER OVERWORKED

## A NERVOUS BREAKDOWN

BERLIN, Thursday.

The reason why Van der Lubbe was executed by Ahrhardt and not by the usual executioner, Groebler, a laundry owner, of Mecklenburg, is said to be that Groebler recently resigned his post of executioner for Prussia owing to a nervous breakdown due to overwork. This statement comes from a Socialist source at Prague.

Fifty executions with the axe have been carried out in Prussia since the Nazis came into power, says the Socialist statement. It adds that Groebler's nerves gave way after he had to behead three young workmen with the axe. Their screams as they were dragged to the block were heard all over the prison, and caused terrible scenes among the other inmates.

Groebler resigned and has been succeeded, so says the same Socialist source, by Bollmann, a horse slaughterer. – Reuter.

**(January 12)**



# A MILLION NEW HOUSES AT 10s A WEEK

## SCHEME TO COST £400,000,000

A £400,000,000 scheme for the provision of a million new houses at inclusive rentals of 10s a week and under within the next ten years is recommended in an interim report issued yesterday by the National Housing Committee, of which Lord Amulree is chairman.

The Committee's proposals may be summarised as follows:

The creation, under the Ministry of Health, of a national Housing Commission, comparable to the Central Electricity Board;

This Commission to be empowered to raise money to finance housing programmes, in particular by the issue of National Housing Stock;

All houses built under the scheme to be owned and managed, not by the Commission, but by local authorities or public utility societies.

The report emphasises that at least a million houses, at rentals of 10s a week and under, will be necessary in the next ten years, in addition to the Government's programme for slum clearance, reconditioning and overcrowding – the root cause of slums – be overcome.

LONG-TERM PLAN ESSENTIAL

For such a programme long-term planning on a national basis is essential. Experience has shown, it is claimed, that the need for cheap houses cannot be met by private enterprise, which, in any case, will be occupied for many years to come in supplying houses for those with larger incomes. Thus the scheme will not compete with private enterprise.

It is proposed that the National Housing stock should carry the full guarantee of the minimum. "If it can be issued on a 3 1/4 per cent. basis," the report adds, "the rents of minimum standard houses can be reduced to such a figure as to bring the economic rent within the ability to pay of the wage-earner in all but exceptional classes of cases."

In these exceptional cases it is recommended that financial assistance should take the form of allowances to bring down the rent.

It is estimated that an ample capital sum for 1,000,000 new houses would be £400,000,000. Not more than £60,000,000 would be required in any one year, and the charge for interest and sinking fund should not exceed £16,000,000 a year. It is considered unlikely that any part of this charge would fall on the Exchequer.

**(May 17)**

# THE LOCH NESS "MONSTER"

## 40 MINUTES VIEW OF STRANGE CREATURE

**From Our Own Correspondent**

INVERNESS, Sunday.

The most striking piece of evidence so far concerning the now famous Loch Ness "monster" was forthcoming to-day.

Mr. J. Goodbody, of Invergarry, a member and former chairman of the Ness District Fishery Board, stated that yesterday he and his two daughters had the "monster" under observation at a distance of 400 yards for fully forty minutes.

Mr. Goodbody, who has travelled all over the world, has hitherto been very sceptical.

"Indeed," he stated, "I thought it was just a cleverly worked piece of publicity. I have often been at the loch-side, but have never seen anything to warrant the belief that something unusual was in the loch.

"But to-day I can certainly state that there is an extraordinary creature in the loch, like nothing I have ever seen in my travels, which have been world-wide.

"My two daughters and I yesterday motored to about a mile east of Fort Augustus, on the north-east side of the loch.

"Shortly before 12 o'clock we were surprised to observe what we thought were the fins of some large fish moving slowly in the water. It was going in a north-easterly direction towards Inverness and coming near to the north shore.

"We had field-glasses, and when the object came within four or five hundred yards of the shore we clearly saw that what we took for fins were really humps. When the object turned we got a fine view of it.

"We saw the head twice. The creature had a long neck and a very small head, and there was a threshing movement under the water, which must have been made by the tail.

Mr. Goodbody stated that he was now quite satisfied that there was some abnormal and unknown creature in the loch. He said he watched the movements of the "monster" through field glasses for forty minutes, and at times had a very clear view of it.

**(January 1)**

# MR. BALDWIN'S ASSURANCE ON BRITAIN'S DEFENCE

## NO MENACE NOW: "WE SHALL NOT BE CAUGHT UNPREPARED"

Two important pronouncements were made by Mr. Baldwin last night during the debate, in a packed House of Commons, on Mr. Churchill's motion calling for an increase in our air defences.

He announced that a supplementary air estimate would be introduced in February. This is to meet an acceleration of the five-year air expansion programme which will secure the completion of "a substantial proportion" within two years.

He appealed to Germany to "tear away the veil of secrecy" from her armaments, which was responsible for Europe's fears, and resume conversations with her neighbours, so that the voice of wisdom and peace might again be heard.

Replying to Mr. Churchill, Mr. Baldwin said:

"There is no immediate menace confronting us or anyone in Europe. Should an emergency develop we shall not be caught unprepared.

"The Government are determined, in no condition, to accept any position of inferiority with regard to whatever force may be raised in Germany in the future."

Sir John Simon revealed that, before making his speech, Mr. Baldwin had taken the step of communicating it to the Governments of Germany, France, Italy and the United States. Points from other speeches included:

MR. CHURCHILL:

Germany had a well-equipped army with immense reserves; her munition factories are working under practically war conditions; by 1937 her military air force would be double the strength of ours.

Without powers of equivalent reprisal in the air – the only defence – we might be tortured into absolute subjection – with no opportunity for recovery.

MR. LLOYD GEORGE:

We are all united on the question of defending our shores.

But we must not try to arm against imaginary and exaggerated dangers.

Let us make it clear to Germany that we mean to give fair, impartial and judicial consideration to her grievance.

Mr. Baldwin's speech has aroused intense interest throughout the world. It is welcomed in France but has aroused disappointment in Germany, where Britain is accused of "sabotaging" the efforts to make effective the equality promised her.

**(November 29)**

# GIRL GANGSTER SHOT DEAD

## FORMER WAITRESS'S MAD CAREER

**From Our Own Correspondent**

SHREVEPORT (Louisiana), Wednesday.

The mad career of Clyde Barrow, a notorious gangster and outlaw of 23, and of "Bonnie" Parker, his 19-year-old girl companion famed for cigar-smoking, ended to-day.

For the past few months Barrow and his associates had terrorised the South-Western States with a series of murders and hold-ups.

To-day, after a sharp fight, detectives, led by a captain of the Texas Rangers, shot and killed him and the woman as they were returning to their secret and favourite rendezvous in a small town in Louisiana.

Barrow and Parker drove at 85 m.p.h. into a roadside trap which the police had prepared and kept ready every day for three weeks. Their bodies were riddled with shots from police machine-guns.

The car was overturned and completely wrecked, and Barrow was found dead under the steering wheel, while the girl's body was doubled over a portable machine-gun in her lap.

The car contained a miniature arsenal of shot-guns, revolvers and ammunition.

So bold and ruthless had been their crimes that the pair earned the sobriquet of "the wild human rats." Scores of police officers had been scouring the South-Western States for them for months past.

Only a month ago Barrow and his associates were within an ace of capture when they gained their freedom behind a fusilade of machine-gun bullets, which killed one officer. A week earlier the gang had murdered two highway patrolmen in cold blood.

"Bonnie" had been a waitress in a cheap coffee house before she joined Barrow. Previously she had been married to a murderer who is now serving a life sentence for killing a sheriff.

**(May 24)**

# VENICE SINKING

## TIDAL ACTION DANGER

**From Our Own Correspondent**

VENICE, Monday.

Alarm for the safety of many of the finest buildings in Venice is being expressed following the high tides which have flooded a greater part of the city.

There are no official records of the tides in Venice. In November, 1916, however, high-water mark reached 4ft 5in. The recent tides have been slightly below that figure.

It is believed that many of the buildings are in danger because the centuries-old wooden piles, sunk in the mud banks — upon which Venice is built — are gradually sinking owing to strong tidal action. This especially aplies to St. Mark's Cathedral.

**(November 13)**

# NEW HUNT FOR GIANT PANDA

**From Our Own Correspondent**

NEW YORK, Friday.

Seven young American sportsmen will leave for Tibet early in the autumn, on an adventurous search for the panda, a giant bear-like animal, specimens of which they hope to photograph and bring back alive.

The panda, which has thick, white fur, black legs and curious black-rimmed eyes, has puzzled scientists since it was first discovered sixty years ago by Père David, a French missionary, who bought skins from natives.

Living in small groups in barren foothills, remote from all human habitations, the animals can only be traced with great difficulty. Few white men have ever set eyes on them, and no living specimen has ever been captured.

The only specimen ever obtained is in the Chicago Field Museum. The animal was shot by the brothers Kermit and Theodore Roosevelt, at Yeli, in Szechuan Province, in 1929.

Months of arduous tracking through the wilderness will be necessary before the hunters reach the country where the animals are supposed to live. Even then signs of the elusive creatures may not be discovered. Mr. Lawrence Griswold, the noted explorer, will head the party, in which an ethnologist and a cinema-photographer will be included.

**(July 14)**

# 5d A DAY MORE FOR DOCKERS

## 150,000 TO BENEFIT

**By Our Industrial Correspondent**

The wage rates of 150,000 dock and riverside workers will be increased on Dec. 17 under an agreement concluded yesterday.

An offer by the Port employers to restore economy cut, was reported in The Daily Telegraph on Nov. 9. It was accepted by a conference of the Transport and General Workers Union on Wednesday, and confirmed by joint settlement yesterday.

A statement issued at the conclusion of the National Joint Council meeting stated that on and after Dec. 17 the minimum daily wage would be 11s 7d for the greater ports and 10s 7d for the smaller. Piecework earnings are to be increased by 2 1/2 per cent.

**(November 17)**

# NICARAGUAN REBEL LEADER SHOT

MANAGUA, Thursday.

A state of siege throughout Nicaragua has been proclaimed by Congress, on the request of the President (Dr. Juan Sacasa).

This follows the shooting by men of the National Guard of Gen. Augusto Sandino, who was the leader in a revolt last year. It is declared officially that this assassination was contrary to the President's instructions.

**(February 23)**

# DR. DOLLFUSS KILLED IN VIENNA REVOLT

## SHOT WHILE A NAZI PRISONER IN HIS OWN OFFICE

**DR. DOLLFUSS, THE AUSTRIAN CHANCELLOR, DIED YESTERDAY FROM WOUNDS RECEIVED IN AN ATTEMPTED NAZI RISING IN VIENNA**

He was shot when a party of 200 rebels, disguised in the uniform of the Heimwehr, captured the Chancellery.

Martial law has been declared throughout Austria. A provisional Government under Dr. Schuschnigg, Minister of Public Instruction, has been set up.

It is expected that Prince Starhemberg, the Heimwehr (Fascist) leader, will succeed to the Chancellorship when he returns by air from Venice to-day. Already by telephone he has ordered the mobilisation of the Heimwehr forces.

**(July 26)**

# GRAPHIC MESSAGE FROM OVER FRONTIER

## 1,000 TROOPS BATTLE FOR RADIO STATION

**From G.E.R. Gedye**
**Daily Telegraph Special Correspondent**

BRATISLAVA (Czechoslovakia), Wednesday Night.

I have had to cross the Austrian frontier because all telephone communication has been severed in Austria and telegrams severely censored.

Only by this means can I tell the astounding story of how under 200 Nazi rebels have held several members of the Austrian Cabinet prisoners all day in the Chancellor's office, following a daring coup de main.

Just as I left Vienna at 8 p.m., the Heimwehr were told officially that Dr. Dollfuss had been shot dead by the Nazi revolutionaries because he drew a revolver when they arrested him.

Life in Vienna seemed normal all to-day except for a desperate battle, at which I was present, for the building of the Ravag, the Austrian Broadcasting Co. I myself left this battle at 1.30 p.m. to follow a tank which drove to the Chancellor's department and stopped outside.

I assumed, as everyone else did, that this was a precautionary measure for the defence of the Chancellor.

Until late in the afternoon no one had an inkling that he and other members of his Cabinet, together with a great many civil servants, were all the time prisoners within looking down the muzzles of the revolvers of 150 desperate men.

The latter had gained entrance in military and police uniforms. In some quarters it is said that some of them are actual Nazi members of the Army and the police forces. They were aided by treachery from within.

### "I SAW IT ALL"
### Policeman Shot Dead

Shortly before 1 p.m. I was passing through Johannestrasse, a narrow side street in which the building of the Ravag is situated, when I heard a dozen shots fired. Three or four worried-looking policemen, revolvers in hand, were taking cover under the houses and occasionally firing desultory shots at the Ravag windows.

Within a few minutes some large motor-charabanes, packed with steel-helmeted police with rifles and bayonets, poured into the street and soon the crackle of rifle fire began. A woman, white and trembling came through the police cordon. She told me:

"I live just opposite and saw it all. A group of eight boys tried to enter the Ravag half an hour ago. When the policeman at the door challenged them they shot him dead.

"Inside the building they were resisted by one of the directors called Holt. Him they also shot dead.

"Entering the studio they placed their revolvers at the head of the announcer and forced him to broadcast the statement that the Dollfuss Cabinet had fallen and that Dr. Rintelen had become the Austrian Chancellor. Then the police alarm was given, fire was opened on the building and returned by the Nazis inside."

I was able to establish that it was correct that only eight desperate Nazi boys had carried out this daring coup, and subsequently held at bay for nearly three hours the biggest force the Vienna police could bring to bear on them, notwithstanding a terrific bombardment with machine-guns.

The cars halted, swinging their machine-guns towards the upper windows of the Ravag, and opened a furious bombardment while police battered in the doors and, throwing hand-grenades, charged into the building.

There were a few more bursts of firing and of hand grenade explosions and then silence. Ten minutes later I saw the first two prisoners brought out. They were respectable-looking boys who could not have been more than 20 years of age.

Surrounded by police they walked with white faces and hands above their heads. The face of one of them was streaming with blood, the other's shirt was blood-stained.

The fire brigade brought up ladders to enable the police to reach the remainder of the Nazis from the upper building. Three police were killed in this fighting and two Nazis. The number of wounded is not known.

**(July 26)**

# BRITISH FILM BANNED

## NAZIS & "CATHERINE THE GREAT"

**From Our Own Correspondent**

BERLIN, Thursday.

"We want no Jewish films," was roared by a cinema crowd gathered outside the Capitol Cinema in the heart of Berlin's West-end to-night. Inside, the British film "Catherine the Great," was being given its first performance. Miss Elizabeth Bergner, who acts the name part, is an Austrian Jewess by origin. Until a year ago she was one of the most popular actresses in Germany.

A small detachment of Storm Troopers, their leader brandishing a truncheon, restored order temporarily. But the cry "We want no Jewish film," was raised again, and for a moment it seemed that the cinema might be rushed.

Suddenly a cry of "Heil Hitler" was heard. Herr Ernst, the Storm Trooper leader for Berlin and Brandenberg, raised on the shoulders of his comrades was trying to address the crowd.

"This film has been banned," he shouted. "It will be shown no more after to-night. We want none of this Jewish stuff in the capital of National Socialism. I now call upon you to return quietly to your homes."

Satisfied by this assurance the crowd raised the cry of "Heil" six times and then dispersed quietly."

**(March 9)**

# FRANCE EXPELS TROTSKY

**From Our Own Correspondent**

PARIS, Tuesday.

Trotsky is to be expelled from France. This decision was taken at a Council of Ministers this morning under the Presidency of the President of the Republic.

As already stated in The Daily Telegraph, he was authorised when exiled from Russia to take up residence in Corsica, but last September took the Villa Kermonique, near Barbizon, at a rental of 1,000f a month.

The reason for his expulsion, it is understood, is that he has abused French hospitality by making his residence the centre of political activity.

Although he was obliged by the terms of his permit not to indulge in propaganda, he is said to have been busily engaged on a scheme for the foundation of a Fourth International and the restoration of Communism on the lines established by Lenin.

**(April 18)**

THE HULL OF THE MORRO CASTLE beached on the New Jersey coast. One of the buildings endangered may be seen on the right.

# COWARDICE CHARGE IN LINER DISASTER

**From Douglas Williams,**
**Daily Telegraph Special Correspondent**

ASBURY PARK, New Jersey, Sunday.

The Ward liner, Morro Castle, returning from a cruise from Havana to New York with 560 souls, of whom 318 were passengers, was destroyed by fire before dawn yesterday.

So far 171 are believed to be dead or missing.

Early this morning the smouldering hulk of the Morro Castle drifted ashore on the beach at Asbury Park, the popular New Jersey coast seaside resort, and, pounded by an angry surf, lay, still burning fiercely, within a few feet of the Convention Hall which extends out over the water.

All day yesterday tugs had tried to tow her to her berth on the Manhattan waterfront, but one after another the tow ropes snapped, and finally they left her to her fate. The huge vessel, swept by wind and tide, finally came ashore. Sparks and flames still shot out of her portholes, and a thick pall of gray smoke still eddied over the ghastly bulk.

Her whole super-structure was a mass of charred ruins, while here and there stretched on the deck could be glimpsed the vague outlines of bodies of unfortunate passengers burned to death as they strove to reach safety.

### MYSTERY OF CAUSE
### Lightning, Cigarette or Bomb?

The cause of the fire, which swept the doomed ship with incredible fierceness and rapidity, is still unknown. Three main suggestions are made:

(1) That it was started by a cigarette dropped by a passenger in the saloon during the gala evening celebrating the last night aboard.

(2) That it was due to lightning striking an oil tank, causing an explosion, just as happened to the giant airship Akron in the same vicinity a year or two ago.

(3) That it was caused by a time bomb placed in the oil tank before the ship left Havana by Cuban dock workers on strike wishing to avenge a grievance against the Ward Line because of alleged discrimination against them.

### Crew Save Own Lives

According to a report quoted by "The Daily News" there was fighting among members of the crew before the blaze was discovered.

The morning papers are filled with definite allegations that many members of the crew made off in the boats, leaving passengers to their fate, and members of the coastguard at New Jersey roundly declare that the disaster was one of the most cowardly in the history of the sea.

One burly coastguard, who spoke with special vehemence, illustrated his argument by pointing to a group of ninety-two survivors standing within a few feet of him awaiting a train to take them back to New York. Two of them were passengers and ninety were members of the crew.

A number of the lifeboats that reached the shore were only partly filled, several having only a few persons aboard. One contained four members of the crew – two Japanese and two Cubans – the only complement of the boat, which had capacity for fifty-eight.

All these boats must have traversed the rough sea in which people were still struggling.

A strange feature of the tragedy was the sudden death on the bridge from heart failure, seven hours before the fire was discovered, of Capt. Wilmott, the veteran commander of the Morro Castle. Capt. Wilmott was born in England, but had long been a naturalised American. Gossip aboard that he had been poisoned by Cuban Communists was discredited.

Chief Officer Warms, a native of New York City, took over the ship in his place, and high praise generally is extended to him for his magnificent conduct all through the desperate crisis with which he was suddenly faced. He stayed aboard the burning ship until he was removed by a coastguard cutter late yesterday afternoon.

### PANIC AND HEROISM
### Cut Off Without Hope

Survivors relating their experiences painted in broad strokes a story of mingled heroism and panic. Some told of jumping from the flame-swept decks and swimming eight miles to land. Others told how, after struggling in the water for an hour, they were finally picked up by rescuing craft.

Many were forced by the advancing wall of flame to jump 50ft into turbulent water, outlined blackly below them. Members of the crew related stories of groups of terrified passengers crowded aft and cut off without hope of rescue by the flames.

They told of women weeping and praying, and of other groups banding together and singing songs to bolster the courage of their more timid companions.

All agreed that the outstanding hero was Chief Officer Warms, who took charge of the vessel after the death of the captain. He remained on the bridge even after it was aflame, shouting orders to the crew in a voice hoarsened by smoke, and thinking only of the safety of his passengers.

The crew have insisted that their inability to do more to aid the passengers was because they were cut off from the aft section by the flames amidships. Stewards declare that part at lease of the death toll was due to some of the women passengers waiting too long in their cabins to dress.

**(September 10)**

# EGGS 6d A DOZEN

**From Our Own Correspondent**

PWLLHELI, Thursday.

Eggs were sold at 6d per dozen at Pwllheli market to-day – the lowest price on record for this time of year.

An article on a proposal to guarantee beef prices is on Page Nineteen.

**(March 6)**

# NOTABLE INVALIDS

CARDINAL BOURNE: Great Improvement.
LORD RIDDELL (a chill): About the same.
CONSTANCE, DUCHESS OF WESTMINSTER (influenza): Much better.
COUNTESS OF WARWICK (operation for appendicitis): Progressing very well.
MR. G. B. SHAW (a cold): Convalescing.
LT.-COL. JOHN WARD: Still seriously ill.

**(November 29)**

# SHILLING TRUNK CALLS

The Post Office was overwhelmed by the eagerness of people all over the British Isles to take advantage of the new flat rate of one shilling for long-distance telephone calls, which came into operation at 7 o'clock last night.

In some towns as many calls were put in between 7 p.m. and 7.10 as are normally dealt with in the whole twenty-four hours.

Aberdeen was the busiest exchange, followed by Edinburgh, Glasgow and Dumfries. Throughout the night "indefinite delay" was reported on calls to and from those towns.

But Scotland was not alone in taking advantage of the new telephone bargain. Thousands of people throughout England, Wales and Ireland made the most of this opportunity of talking to friends and relations far away.

"The results of the new rate have been far beyond our most optimistic expectations," said a Post Office official. "We were not prepared for such an avalanche of calls, and congestion was inevitable.

**(October 2)**

# WITCH-DOCTORS ROUNDED UP

## 700 TO BE REMOVED IN KENYA

NAIROBI (Kenya), Thursday.

Seven hundred witch doctors, members of an hereditary and powerful clan, are to be removed from the heart of the Lumbwa native reserve in Kenya. This step is being taken in consequence of the evil influence which they have long exerted.

Under special legislation introduced by the Government of Kenya it is proposed to remove the clan to a new area near Kisimu, on the shores of Victoria Nyanza. They will be compelled to stay there on pain of imprisonment.

The witch doctors are held responsible for increasing crime and unrest in the Lumbwa tribe, and it is expected that their removal will free the tribe from the fear they have exercised for at least half a century.

Under the influence of the witch-doctors it is alleged that the Lumbwas have been encouraged to thieve, especially cattle, and they are known to have made many murderous attacks on outlying farms and stores, particularly those controlled by Indians. The heads of the clan, known as Laibono, are called the "Big Eight."

When the witch-doctors are once established in the new reserve the Government will use all means in its power to change their outlook, and especially that of their sons, to whom, according to belief, the supernatural powers of the fathers are transmitted. – Reuter.

**(July 6)**

# PARIS CROWD'S FURY OVER STAVISKY SCANDAL

## 200 ARRESTS IN DEMONSTRATION LAST NIGHT

Hostility against the French Government over the Stavisky scandal culminated last night in a riotous demonstration in Paris. Over 200 arrests were made.

The verdict returned at Chamonix, in the French Alps, at the inquest on Stavisky, who died in hospital just before dawn, was one of suicide.

Despite the verdict and a definite statement by the three medical men in attendance, many Frenchmen are refusing to believe that Stavisky shot himself, and think the police killed him in case he should compromise persons in high circles.

This point of view was angrily voiced by the crowd outside the Chamber of Deputies last night, and exciting scenes are expected to take place in the Chamber tomorrow, when the Government faces the Opposition's allegations arising out of the bond frauds.

**(January 10)**

# STAVISKY THE IMPOSTOR

**From Our Own Correspondent**

PARIS, Monday.

Brief though Stavisky's career before the public eye has been, he will undoubtedly go down to history as one of the most audacious and imaginative impostors of our time.

The son of a petty merchant migrated to France from Russia, he began his career as a dealer in gems, and at one time had jewellery shops at Deauville and Le Touquet. Gradually he developed into a company promoter. Several undertakings which were founded by him – but with which he had severed his connection – seem to be still in existence.

Stavisky appears always to have sailed pretty close to the wind. After one or two minor conflicts with the authorities, which led to criminal charges though not to convictions, he was arrested in 1926 on a grave charge of swindling. For reasons which have not even yet been made quite clear – indeed, this is one of the chief points of the "affair" in so far as it constitutes a mystery – the hearing was adjourned again and again, and the fourteenth hearing was fixed for one day in the present month.

HUGE PROFIT DREAMS

With success Stavisky's ambitions expanded with ever accelerating speed.

There is a good deal of evidence to show that he actually regarded himself at times as a heaven-sent financial genius, who would eventually put straight all the economic complications from which the world is now suffering.

He looked round for suitable fields in which to exploit his talents. He caught a glimpse of the yet unsettled claims of dispossessed Hungarian owners of land which is now situated in other States formed out of the old Dual Monarchy.

The full story of his buying up of these claims has still to be told. But apparently if his gigantic scheme had been realised as he had planned it he would have been indeed one of the world's richest men.

But here Stavisky's fantasy evidently got the better of his judgment, and the prospects of selling at a huge profit the Hungarian claims which he had bought for an old song were dimmed by ominous clouds. An alternative plan was necessary, and the adventurer turned to the municipal pawnshops, beginning at Orleans.

His operation s here also ended with a scandal, which, however, aroused but faint echoes in public opinion.

There were doubts and questions, but Stavisky solved all problems by triumphantly redeeming his pledges with ready cash, which apparently was provided by Bayonne, where he had already become active.

Encouraged rather than deterred by his experiences at Orleans, Stavisky proceeded to develop his plans on a vast scale at Bayonne. He was well known as one of the most prodigal clients and benefactors of the fashionable watering-places in which the well-to-do citizens of Bayonne brush shoulders with leaders of society from half the capitals of Europe.

Thus Stavisky's nominee was gladly accepted as manager of the Credit. This was Tissier, whose full confession sealed the fate of his master and also led to the arrest of the Mayor of Bayonne.

HOW BONDS WERE FORGED

Tissier has made it quite clear how the frauds were carried out. Under a law passed in the middle of last century, French municipal pawnshops are allowed to raise capital by issuing bonds up to a certain proportion of the value of the pledges held by them.

It was known that Spanish refugees had pawned valuable jewellery at Bayonne, and at first the unusual quantity of Bayonne bonds which were put on the market excited no particular attention.

Municipal bonds are valid only with the signature of two responsible persons, so that Tissier was not able to act alone. He did, however, succeed in inducing his co-signer to put his name to blank forms, which Tissier could thus fill up with any sum required by Stavisky's financial exigencies.

In this way, bonds for hundreds of millions of francs were fabricated and hawked about among the insurance companies and other undertakings with large sums of money requiring temporary, investment. This brokers' work was carried out by Stavisky's agent.

PREFECT'S STATEMENT

The impunity with which Stavisky was able to carry out financial operations on a scale worthy of a Rothschild or a Pierpont Morgan, while still under remand on a very serious criminal charge, is rendered all the more mysterious by the statement made by the Police Prefect of Paris, M. Jean Chiappe, on his return to the city to-day.

M. Chiappe, who had been recalled from a short holiday at Florence in order to take over the direction of the Stavisky inquiry, was beset by journalists on alighting from the Rome express. He immediately replied to their questions with the assurance, "For ten years the judicial authorities have been on Stavisky's track."

"Did you ever meet him?" someone asked.

"Only once, in my office," replied M. Chiappe. "He had the impudence to complain that the judicial authorities were taking too great an interest in him and inquiring into his action and mode of living. I need hardly repeat the answer he got from me."

The Prefect added that reports that the police hospital had received benefactions from Stavisky were the very reverse of the truth.

**(January 9)**

# BABY SAVED BY "OXYGEN BED"

The life of an 18-month-old Greenwich boy, who accidentally swallowed some boiling water, has been saved by keeping him in an "oxygen bed" a recent American invention. There are at present only three such beds in this country.

The oxygen bed consists of a rubber tent, with mica windows, which is placed over the patient, and through which oxygen is constantly circulated. In nine-days 1,000 cubic feet of oxygen have been used to keep the baby alive.

The boy was admitted ten days ago to the Miller General Hospital at Greenwich in a critical condition. Ten hours after admission he was on the verge of suffocation, and a tracheotomy operation, which involves the opening of the windpipe, was performed. This gave some relief, but it was decided that the only way to save the baby's life was by keeping him in an oxygen bed.

One of the beds was obtained, and two hours after being placed in it the child's condition showed a marked improvement. Yesterday his name was taken off the danger list, and he is now regarded as being on the way to recovery.

**(October 27)**

# ARTIFICIAL RADIUM

## "IT MAY BECOME BETTER THAN THE REAL THING"

M. and Mme. Curie-Joliot were the joint authors of a long paper on "Artificially Produced Radio Elements," read at the International Conference on Physics at the Royal Institution in London yesterday.

Points from their paper, details of which were reported in THE DAILY TELEGRAPH yesterday, were:

"The energies and intensities at present obtained for producing accelerated particles allow us to hope that soon we shall be able to produce, by means of these particles, radio-elements with an intensity of radiation comparable, or even superior, to that of preparations of natural radio-elements now available.

"These radio-elements may be applied in medicine, and perhaps in other practical fields.

**(October 4)**

# BUDGET BENEFITS OF £29,000,000

**Income-Tax Down by 6d. | Half Pay-Cuts Restored | Pre-Crisis Rates for Workless**

Every man, woman and child in the country will benefit, directly or indirectly, from the Budget "opened" by Mr. Chamberlain, the Chancellor of the Exchequer, in the House of Commons yesterday.

He announced direct benefits to the following:

**Unemployed** – Full restoration of 1931 benefit cuts from July 1, with corresponding increases in transitional payments – to cost the Treasury £3,600,000 this year.

**Taxpayers** – Reduction of the standard rate of income-tax by sixpence – the cost £20,500,000 this year.

**Ministers, M.P.s, Judges, Civil Servants, Soldiers, Sailors, Airmen, Police, Teachers, and Insurance Doctors and Chemists** – Restoration of half the pay-cuts imposed in 1931 – to cost £4,000,000 this year.

**Motorists and Motor Trade** – Reduction from Jan. 1, of horse-power tax on motor-cars from £1 to 15s, with corresponding reductions in the duties on motor-cycles.

MOTOR-TAX REDUCTION

**Great Stimulus to Trade**

The reduction in motor taxation was the Chancellor's only big surprise. It is designed to stimulate the export trade, and has been warmly welcomed by leaders of the industry, who expect it to result in:

**More motoring;**
**Increased manufacture;**
**A reduction in unemployment;**
**The recovery of Britain's pre-eminence in the world market for motor vehicles.**

EFFECT OF INCOME TAX CONCESSION

**Equivalent to Ten Per Cent. Cut**

The income-tax concession works out as a cut of 10 per cent. in the tax on all earned and unearned incomes, whether the taxpayer is single, married, or married with children. To those who pay on the half rate (2s 6d) basis the relief amounts to 3d. The cut will first take effect on the income-tax payment due on Jan. 1, 1935.

The Chancellor, who announced a realised surplus of £31,000,000 for the past year, expressed an optimistic view of Britain's trade position:

"We have now finished the story of 'Bleak House'," he said, "and are sitting down this afternoon to enjoy the first chapter of 'Great Expectations.'"

**(April 18)**

# OGPU CEASES TO EXIST

**From Our Own Correspondent**

MOSCOW, Tuesday.

By a decree issued to-night the old "Cheka-Ogpu," Russia's dreaded secret police, is merged in the new "All-Union Peoples' Commissariat for Internal Affairs."

M. Henri Yagoda, who for long has been acting as chief of the Ogpu, stays on, however, as the new Commissary, with M. Agranoff and M. Prokovieff two veteran members of the old Ogpu Collegium, as his two Vice-Commissaries.

This "reform" has been expected since March, though it is much less wide than anticipated. The new Commissariat's powers will extend throughout the Soviet Union, but subsidiary Commissariats for local Soviet republics will be created.

The main real change is that the Ogpu's old unlimited powers of administrative sentence are not given to the new Commissariat, which does, however, retain the full right to pass sentences of condemnation to concentration camps or of exile up to five years.

The new Commissariat retains, moreover, the Ogpu's important function of investigating and preparing cases for courts. In future "crimes against the State" will be tried by a special triumvirate of the Supreme Court, and espionage and military cases by the military tribunal of the Supreme Court.

**(July 11)**

# FIRST AIR MAIL AT SYDNEY

## ONLY MINUTES LATE

SYDNEY, Friday.

Making an unexpected night flight from Narromine an Australian 'plane arrived here this morning with the first air mail from England only five minutes behind schedule.

The mails left Croydon on Dec. 9. At Port Darwin they were transferred to Australian machines for the last part of the journey.

**(December 22)**

# AUSTIN SEVEN IN NEW GUISE

**From Our Special Correspondent**

The Austin Seven, after twelve years of unbroken popularity and unchanged form, is to appear in a new guise. Its admirers will hardly recognise the 1935 "baby" in its new dress. But they will find behind the new radiator and new body lines the sturdy, reliable little engine practically unchanged, and prices, instead of being higher, are actually lower. There is also a two-seater Seven, known as the "Opal," at £100.

The new baby models and the rest of the comprehensive Austin range for 1935 were displayed at Longbridge to-day.

**(August 14)**

# WASHINGTON TREATY DENOUNCED

Mr. Hirota, the Foreign Minister, yesterday cabled to Mr. Saito, the Japanese Ambassador in Washington, the text of the notification of the termination of the Washington Naval Treaty. Mr. Saito afterwards handed it to the United States Secretary of State, Mr. Cordell Hull.

Simultaneously the spokesman of the Japanese Navy Office stated that the rapid progress in naval construction and armaments manufacture and the remarkable change in the international situation during the past 13 years, since the conclusion of the Washington Treaty, made the Treaty unsuitable for the new conditions, and caused a defect in Japan's national defence.

**(December 24)**

# HOW GOLD PRICE ROSE

## DOLLAR UNCHANGED

**By Our City Editor**

Mr. Roosevelt's proclamation was the dominating factor in City markets yesterday. Its first tangible effect was to raise the London gold price by 2s 5d to £6 15s 6d an ounce – a record high level.

Considerable excitement prevailed in the exchange markets. In the morning selling of dollars forced the value of the dollar down to $5.06 to the pound, on the initial assumption that Washington resources would be concentrated on depreciating the dollar.

A sharp recovery set in later, and the rate closed in London at $4.97 ½, or exactly the same as on the previous day.

The reason for this movement was chiefly a strong demand for dollars by speculators, American and otherwise, who were prompted by the recent strength in Wall-Street to believe that booming conditions are possible there in the near future.

Naturally enough great activity took place among gold shares, which showed sharp advances. Mr. Roosevelt has practically insured holders against a fall in the price of gold.

EXTENT OF RESTRICTIONS

Puzzling Features

The full implications of America's new policy are not yet clear. Apparently the regulations which are being issued contain certain restrictions on gold movements, the scope of which is not yet known. Upon the nature and severity of these restrictions must depend the solution of many present puzzles.

They are of profound interest in connection with the question of the extent of the gold drain that may develop upon the resources of the Bank of France. It was reported yesterday that shipments to America from Paris had already been arranged. Indeed a report from New York stated that the National City Bank was importing £700,000 in gold by the Berengaria.

Mr. Roosevelt's proclamation was welcomed in the City in so far as it restores the dollar to a more clearly-defined position. At the same time, it raises a new problem for the British financial authorities.

They will now probably be faced by the franc definitely on gold, and the dollar practically on gold, from the exchange point of view, while the pound is unfettered by any such condition. The Treasury will now have to decide whether it will follow the franc or the dollar, or compromise between those two courses.

The last named policy is thought to be the most likely to be adopted, if it becomes necessary to use the Exchange Equalisation Fund in the direction of conscious regulation over and above the purpose for which it has hitherto been used – namely, the obviation of unnecessarily sharp exchange fluctuations.

**(February 2)**

# SCOTT & BLACK WIN GREAT RACE

## ENGLAND TO AUSTRALIA IN 2 DAYS 4 ½ HOURS

**C.W.A. SCOTT AND CAMPBELL BLACK, IN THEIR BRITISH COMET 'PLANE, LANDED AT MELBOURNE AT 5.34 THIS MORNING (G.M.T.)**

**They left Mildenhall, Suffolk, at 6.35 a.m. on Saturday, and have thus covered the 11,300 miles of the Speed Race (Great Circle) course in**

**2 DAYS ... 23 HOURS ... 4 MINUTES**

**At an average speed, including five stops, of about**

**160 MILES AN HOUR**

The fliers reached the Australian coast, at Port Darwin, in 2 days, 4 hours, 34 minutes – less than a third of the 6 days 17 hours 45 minutes taken by Mr. Ulm, the previous record holder. The first flight to Australia, in 1919, took 30 days.

**By their magnificent flight, breaking all records, Scott and Black have won for England the greatest air race in history and for themselves the Trophy and prize of £10,000 offered by Sir Macpherson Robertson.**

**They flew the final stages – 400 miles over the shark-infested Timor Sea and the whole of the 2,200 miles across Australia – with only one engine running, the other having seized.**

At Charleville, their last stop before Melbourne, mechanics worked desperately to repair the engine, but when the airmen attempted to take off it failed again. After further delay they got away at 12.59 a.m. G.M.T., with the engine still giving trouble.

TWO HOURS' SLEEP SINCE LEAVING HOME

Before leaving Scott said that he had had only two hours' sleep since leaving England. His last food was the wing of a chicken at Port Darwin.

Since leaving England the airmen have only been on the ground for seven hours and eight minutes.

In hot pursuit this morning were their nearest rivals, the Dutchmen, Parmentier and Moll, carrying three passengers and a crew of four.

Although they took the handicap course, which is 1,000 miles longer, and stopped fourteen times, they reached Port Darwin only 12 hours after Scott and Black. They left again only 38 minutes later and passed over Cloncurry, Queensland, at 2.15 this morning.

**(October 23)**

# DRAMA OF THE KIDNAPPED LINDBERGH BABY

## ARREST 2 ½ YEARS AFTER OUTRAGE THAT SHOCKED WORLD

The kidnapping and murder of the baby son of Gol. Lindbergh – an event which shocked the civilised world two and a half years ago – was dramatically recalled to-day by the arrest of a former soldier of the German Army, Bernard Richard Hauptmann.

In the garden of his home at the Bronx, a New York suburb, detectives dug up the equivalent of £3,600 in ten and twenty dollar bills, which have been identified as part of the ransom paid over by one of Col. Lindbergh's negotiators, Dr. Condon, who figured in the negotiations as "Jafsie."

The charge against Hauptmann so far is merely that of "extorting money from Col. Lindbergh," but if police information is confirmed, he will be charged with the actual kidnapping of the baby.

The New York police Commissioner said to me to-night: "This arrest not only clears up the payment of the £10,000 ransom, but solves the whole mystery of the kidnapping."

To-night Dr. Condon ("Jafsie") definitely identified Hauptmann as the man he knew as "John" to whom he passed the £10,000, in a cemetery – the appointed meeting-place – on the night of April 2, 1932, following lengthy negotiations with the man as intermediary for Col. Lindbergh

Hauptmann is a sullen-faced man in his thirties. He was brought into the trial room of Greenwich-street police station with handcuffs on. Reporters shouted to him "Did you kidnap the Lindbergh baby?" In reply he shook his head.

**(September 21)**

# INLAND AIR MAIL BEGINS

**By Our Air Correspondent**

From to-day, letters posted in London before noon with an air mail label will be delivered in Glasgow or Belfast the same evening.

Britain's first regular inter-city air mail service, which is to be operated by Railway Air Services Ltd. on behalf of the L.M.S. Railway, will be inaugurated with suitable ceremony at Croydon this morning.

The service will link together three routes, all passing through Birmingham, of a total length of about 1,000 miles:

London, Birmingham, Manchester, Douglas, Belfast and Glasgow.

Liverpool, Bristol, Plymouth and Cardiff; and; Birmingham, Southampton and Cowes.

While it is in the experimental stage the service will be restricted to correspondence posted at the places mentioned for addresses in the town areas of the other places on the routes only. The postage rates for postcards and letters under 2oz weight will be the same as for the ordinary inland mail — 1d for postacrds and 1 ½d for letters.

**(August 20)**

## POLICE COLLEGE OPENS

The new police college at Hendon opened without formality. Two hours after the students arrived they were at work.

**(May 11)**



# PENNY A MILE ON RAILWAYS

## MONTHLY RETURNS TO BE PERMANENT

Details were announced yesterday of the decision of the railway companies (forecast in The Daily Telegraph) to reduce passenger fares.

The benefit of third-class penny-a-mile return tickets, available for a month, is to be permanent, the ticket previously known as "summer return" is to be called "monthly return."

First-class fares are to be reduced, and in the case of monthly returns will be 1 ½d per mile – the normal rate for third-class travel.

The monthly return ticket decision is the sequel to the success of the summer experiment.

EXCURSIONS AT ¼D A MILE

There is to be a great speeding-up of the railway services in the spring, for which the necessary arrangements are now being perfected. An official stated yesterday to a representative of The Daily Telegraph:

"Short excursion trips are to be a daily feature at rates which should meet coach competition. The cost of day excursion tickets will work out at less than ¾d per mile, half-day tickets at ½d per mile, and evening tickets at only ¼d per mile. Our programme is a very elaborate one."

The new fare arrangements will operate from Jan. 1.

First and third class monthly returns will be available for use on the outward and return journeys on any day within a month of issue. Hitherto it has been necessary to complete the outward journey in three days.

The minimum fares will be 3s 9d first-class and 2s 6d third-class on the Great Western, L.M.S., and L.N.E.R.; in the case of the Southern Railway the minimum will be 7s 6d and 5s respectively.

The reduction in first-class fares to 1 ½d per mile will, in addition to monthly returns, apply to cheap day, excursion and other reduced fares. This has been decided on as a method of inducing passengers to avail themselves to a greater extent of the extra comfort afforded by "first class" travel. To-day the compartments are often empty.

**(December 4)**

# MAN KILLED BY LIONS AT WHIPSNADE

**From Our Special Representative**

WHIPSNADE, Thursday.

A tragedy, without precedent in the history of the Zoological Society occurred at Whipsnade Zoo Park to-day, when Mr. Stanley Lewis Stenson, an employee of the catering department, was mauled by two lions, and was killed.

Stenson was attempting to recover a hat belonging to a visitor, which was at the bottom of the lion pit. He had walked along a parapet within the enclosure when one of the animals sprang at him, attempting to drag him down.

At first the beast clawed the man by the left arm. Then it grabbed him by the foot, pulling off one of his boots.

The visitor whose hat had been lost attempted to hold Stenson, who, however, ultimately fell into the pit.

Two of the four lions then dragged him across the enclosure, a distance of thirty or forty yards to a bush.

Keepers with poles attempted to beat off the beasts, and a number of blank cartridges were fired. Ultimately the animals were caged.

Stenson was found to be dead. He had been injured, probably rendered insensible, by his fall on to the concrete floor of the pit and had been badly mauled by the animals.

The lions had been fed only shortly before the incident.

**(June 8)**

# FOURTH LARGEST DIAMOND

## £60,000 GEM FOUND IN SOUTH AFRICA

Two remarkable diamonds have been found at Elandsfontein, 20 miles north of Pretoria. The first was unearthed by an alluvial digger named J.J. Jonkin.

The stone weighs 726 carats. It is two and a half inches in length, an inch and a half in height, and one inch in breadth. It is bigger than a matchbox. Its value is approximately £60,000.

The second, found on the same farm, weighs 500 carats.

Of the well-known diamonds, these are respectively the fourth and fifth largest in the world.

**(January 18)**

# THE QUEEN NAMES THE "QUEEN MARY'

## PERFECT LAUNCHING FOR THE GREATEST LINER

**By Rene McColl**

**Daily Telegraph Special Representative**

The great new British liner took to the waters of the Clyde yesterday under the title "Queen Mary" happily bestowed upon her by her Majesty the Queen – the well kept secret of the 534.

The Queen's words, "I am very happy to name this ship the Queen Mary" were greeted with a loud burst of cheering from the vast gathering at Clydebank. They were carried across the world by wireless, and were perfectly heard as far away as distant Australia.

For just under a minute – the unforgettable minute – the great ship slid suavely down the slipways while we clutched complete strangers by the arm, slapped each other on the back, and shouted, unheard, into each other's ears.

Behind the rain-blurred glass window the King, the Queen and the Prince stood side by side in a little group absolutely motionless. Behind them were officials of the Cunard and John Brown, their faces tense and still during these vital seconds.

As the great ship glided off the end of the slipway and took the water a crash of cheers arose. The strain had gone.

Beating Rain

The Royal trio, the officials and onlookers turned to one another, smiling amid congratulations.

The drama was staged in a beating downpour of rain. It soaked down without pause from half an hour before the ceremony. The huge crowd was wet through.

**(September 27)**

# £25,000 DAMAGES FOR FILM LIBEL

Princess Irma Alexandrovna Youssoupoff of Russia was yesterday awarded £25,000 damages in her libel action against Metro-Goldwyn-Mayer Pictures Ltd.

The action heard before Mr. Justice Avory and a special jury in the King's Bench Division was concerned with the film made by the defendants entitled, "Rasputin, the Mad Monk."

The Princess, who was both a niece and a cousin of the late Tsar, and whose husband, Prince Youssoupoff, killed Rasputin, complained that "Princess Natasha," in the film, a woman intimately associated with Rasputin, might be taken for herself, and that this was a reflection upon her chastity.

The defendants pleaded that "Natasha" was a fictional character, and in no way referred to the Princess.

After speeches by counsel, and the summing up by the judge, reported below, the jury retired for two hours. On their return they stated that they found a verdict for the plaintiff.

"For what amount?" the foreman was asked.

"We agree that persons ..." the foreman began, when Mr. Justice Avory interrupted. "I only want to know the amount," he said.

"For £25,000," said the foreman.

Sir Patrick Hastings, K.C. (for the plaintiff) asked for judgement for the Princess for that amount with costs.

NO STAY OF EXECUTION

Sir William Jowitt, K.C. (for the defendants) said, with reference to the costs of the amendment to the pleadings, he submitted that the amendment completely recast and reconstructed the action. It was plain that the action as originally constituted would fail, and he asked the judge to make an order about the costs of amendment.

"This is a matter," Sir William added, "in which we desire to consider the position with the view to taking it further, and I ask for a stay of execution on such terms as your lordship thinks proper."

Sir Patrick Hastings argued that the amendment was unnecessary. With reference to a stay of execution, Sir Patrick asked the judge to remember the position in which the Princess had been put, and to say that there was no reason why there should be a stay.

Mr. Justice Avory said in regard to the amendment, he considered the defendants had not been prejudiced, and he would not make any special order for costs. Nor did he see any reason to grant a stay of execution in this case.

His lordship gave instructions that the sum of £1,000 paid into court by the Princess as security for costs should be handed out to her solicitors on her behalf.

**(March 6)**

# NOBEL PEACE AWARDS

The Nobel Peace Prize for 1934 was to-day awarded to Mr. Arthur Henderson, president of the Disarmament Conference. That for 1933 was awarded to Sir Norman Angell, author of "The Great Illusion," "The Unseen Assassins," and other books.

At the Nobel Institute, before a distinguished audience, Mr. Hendersen was present to receive his prize. The British Minister in Oslo, Mr. C.F. Dormer, received Sir Norman Angell's, as he was unable to attend.

**(December 11)**

# PREMIER'S 'NO' TO 'MARCHERS'

## COMMUNIST AIMS WELL KNOWN

The Prime Minister has declined to receive a deputation representing the unemployed marchers who arrived in London yesterday, and who have announced their intention of holding a mass demonstration in Hyde Park to-morrow.

In a letter signed, amongst others, by Alex Gossip, Tom Mann, Harry Pollitt, and Wal Hannington, the request was made "that all members of the Government be present" to meet a deputation of the march council on Tuesday morning.

Through his principal private secretary, Mr. J. A. Barlow, the Premier has replied as follows:

"In reply to the letter sent through the National Congress and March Council asking the Government to receive a deputation from the unemployed marchers, I have been instructed to say that it is impossible to accede to your request.

"The deputation can do no service to the unemployed.

"The Communist purpose of these marches is common knowledge.

"The Government is responsible for a bill which, when in operation, will facilitate more satisfactory treatment of the whole question of unemployment, and that bill is now receiving consideration by a House of Commons composed of members whose knowledge and experience enable it to discuss the best way to achieve the objects of the Government.

"Individual members of the House are aware that Ministers are always desirous of helping them on any matter which they or their constituents wish to bring before the Government."

The Communist party, in a proclamation issued last night, announced that "The Marchers are here."

The Scottish contingent is quartered in Tottenham; Tyneside men are in Poplar; the Lancashire marchers are in Acton; the Yorkshires in Willesden; South Wales and Plymouth contingents have accommodation at Chiswick; the women's contingent is at Islington; Norfolk has marched into West Ham; the South Coast group is at Wimbledon, and the Kent contingent at Dartford.

The marchers intend to stay in London about ten days. This morning the Communist party, the Independent Labour party, the Unemployed Workers' Movement and representatives of all the marching contingents meet in a Congress of Action at Bermondsey Town Hall.

To-morrow afternoon the marchers, with as many London employed or unemployed as the Communists can muster, will march to Hyde Park.

**(February 24)**

# SUN-BATHING ON THE THAMES

## WHAT IS LIMIT OF "UNDRESS"?

The problem as to what costumes sunbathers on the river should wear has led to a difference of opinion between the Thames Conservancy and the Minister of Transport, Mr. Hore-Belisha.

A deadlock has been reached, and for the moment the sunbathers are free to please themselves, subject to the ordinary limitations imposed by law.

In response to complaints they had received the Conservancy made the following new by-law:

"No person while on board a vessel shall enter or be in any lock on the Thames wearing less than full rowing costume or full university bathing costume."

Any by-laws passed by the Thames Conservancy must receive the approval of the Ministry before they can be enforced, but Mr. Hore-Belisha has refused to pass this. It is the first time in the 77 years' existence of the Conservancy that a Minister has vetoed a by-law.

**(August 14)**

# WILD SCENES AT LONDON FASCIST MEETING

## FIERCE FIGHTING OUTSIDE AND INSIDE OLYMPIA

Wild scenes, such as have not been witnessed in London since the worst days of the Suffragist agitation, occurred both outside and inside Olympia last night at a meeting organised by Sir Oswald Mosley's British Union of Fascists.

Blackshirts and Communists – their leader claimed that 3,000 of the latter secured admission – fought fiercely both before and during the meeting.

Fifteen hundred police, both mounted and foot, were on duty, and on occasions had to draw their batons in an attempt to quell the disturbances. Twenty-three people, including two women, were arrested.

Chairs were smashed and boots used as weapons. Blackshirts – men and women – fought the gangs of interrupters with their bare fists, and there were numerous casualties.

There were early signs of trouble. An hour before the meeting two or three thousand people congregated outside the main gate of Olympia in Addison-road.

Just before eight o'clock, as a group of Fascists were standing lined up outside the entrance awaiting their turn for admission, about 100 Communists formed up in marching order, and walked down the road beside the Blackshirts, waving a red banner and singing the "Red Flag" and the "Internationale."

Having once marched past the Blackshirts, the Communists turned about and tried to break through their opponents' ranks, and in the ensuing struggle the Communist banner was torn.

A number of mounted policemen, with their batons drawn, appeared at the gallop and pushed their horses through the crowd.

Hundreds of extra police, both mounted and foot, were drafted from all parts of London. They were acting under the direction of a high police official, who was given a vantage point on the roof of Olympia, and who from time to time flashed messages by means of an electric torch to police Q vans and wireless vans which were stationed round Olympia.

Men and women in evening dress, who arrived in cars, were subjected to some abuse from rivals of the Blackshirts. One car drew the attention of several men who challenged the owner to come out and fight. The men tried to touch the windows, but a mounted police officer drove them away.

### INSIDE THE HALL
#### Fight in Gallery

Inside the hall it was not until a quarter to nine that the flags of the Blackshirts were brought in with arc-lights concentrated on them. A few minutes later Sir Oswald Mosley entered in a blaze of light.

When he began to speak a small body of opponents began to chant "Blackshirts mean blacklegs. Down with the Blackshirts." This was followed by interruptions in the balcony.

Voices in the gallery cried "Fascism means war" and "Blackshirts want war," and a number of Blackshirt defence corps immediately scrambled up the slope to the top tiers, and began to scuffle with the interrupters. After a fight which lasted for nearly a minute two men were thrown out of the meeting.

When the shouting had subsided Sir Oswald Mosley said, "It is customary at Fascist meetings for a very few people to try to prevent the audience from hearing the Fascist case. It is also customary for these few people to be unsuccessful in that attempt. Thousands have come to hear our case and thousands have joined the Fascist ranks."

A few minutes later another bout of shouting broke out in the gallery at the back of the hall. Sir Oswald appealed for silence and cried, "You must keep order or you will be thrown out." This was the signal for more concerted shouting, and a more serious scuffle started in the gallery. This lasted for several minutes, and broke out again only five minutes later.

After a fourth fight in a corner of the packed gallery Sir Oswald said: "We are very grateful to these few people for illustrating how very necessary the Blackshirt defence corps is to defend free speech in Great Britain."

#### SHOWER OF LEAFLETS
#### Thrown from Gallery

He had just said that he would carry on again with the meeting when renewed shouting drowned his voice, and other members of the defence corps ejected further interrupters.

After the first half hour the interruption became almost continuous, and people were being thrown out every few minutes.

During one of the few lulls Sir Oswald said: "These Reds have organised for weeks past not only this interruption in the hall, but they have attempted to intimidate those who have come to this meeting. We were informed that a few seat tickets had been forged for this meeting."

Someone shouted "Its a lie," and twelve Blackshirts ran to a block near the Press seats and pounced on the man who shouted. He was immediately thrown to the ground and flung down the stairs out of the arena.

#### "JU-JITSU GIRLS"
#### Woman Ejected

One of the most effective interrupters was a woman who screamed shrilly at the top of her voice, and she was dealt with by a member of Fascist "ju-jitsu" girls who have been specially trained for throwing out women interrupters.

A little later Sir Oswald Mosley said that it was a farce to speak of free speech in Great Britain to-day. and referred to Red agitators from the lowest ghettoes of the world using every kind of weapon.

**(June 8)**

# SOCIALIST RULE IN LONDON

## CONTROL OF 15 OUT OF 28 BOROUGHS

As a result of the municipal elections, polling for which took place on Thursday, the Socialists now control fifteen of the twenty-eight London boroughs. They have retained their hold on:

| | |
|---|---|
| *Bermondsey | Deptford |
| Greenwich | *Poplar |

and have gained majorities on councils previously held by anti-Socialists in the following boroughs:

| | |
|---|---|
| Fulham | *Stepney |
| Shoreditch | Islington |
| Battersea | Finsbury |
| Southwark | Hackney |
| Camberwell | Bethnal Green |
| Woolwich | |

In the Councils marked by an asterisk the socialists hold every seat.

The last occasion when the Socialists obtained control of a substantial number of London boroughs was in 1919, when they secured a majority on fourteen Councils. This was reduced to eight in 1922, and the number of Socialist boroughs remained at that figure until 1931, when four Socialist boroughs were lost to the Municipal Reform party.

**(November 3)**

# RUSSIA JOINS THE LEAGUE

Russia was elected to the League of Nations in the Assembly this evening by 39 votes to 3 negatives with 7 abstentions. Her opponents were Switzerland, Holland and Portugal.

M. Litvinoff, the Russian Foreign Commissar, in anticipation of the event, has been living just outside the Swiss frontier for several days. He came to Geneva this afternoon and entered the Electoral Building two minutes before his appointed time. The result was that the President and the officials of the Secretariat failed to notice his arrival.

He and his staff took the seats prepared for them before the actual voting had been concluded. Instead of the usual applause, silence greeted their arrival.

**(September 18)**

# PROF. BARTH DISMISSED
**From Our Own Correspondent**

BERLIN, Friday.
Prof. Karl Barth, the famous German theologian, has been dismissed from his post of Professor of Evangelical Theology at Bonn University. This drastic step follows his refusal to take without modification the oath of loyalty to Herr Hitler.

It is understood that the Professor, who has been one of the bulwarks of the opposition to Bishop Müller, the Nazi Primate, wished to insert in the oath a short phrase which would release him from responsibility to it should he be ordered to do anything which would offend his conscience as an Evangelical Christian.

**(December 22)**

# NOBEL PRIZE FOR PIRANDELLO
**From Our Own Correspondent**

STOCKHOLM, Thursday.
Signor Luigi Pirandello, the Italian author, has been awarded by the Swedish Academy this year's Nobel Prize for literature.

He is distinguished as dramatist, novelist and poet.

**(November 9)**

# 261 MINERS PERISH IN BLAZING PIT

## OFFICIAL STATEMENT LAST NIGHT:
## "NO PERSON CAN BE ALIVE"

## RESCUERS WITHDRAWN & SHAFT SEALED UP

| 3 Men Give Lives For Comrades | Boots Burned Off On Red-Hot Roads |
|---|---|

**By George Fyfe**
**The Daily Telegraph Special Correspondent**

After relays of rescuers had battled for forty hours against flame, at the Gresford Mine, near Wrexham, where an explosion occurred early on Saturday, all rescue work was abandoned at 6.30 last night. The rescuers were called to the surface and the shaft was sealed.

At 10.30 last night it was announced that the death-toll was believed to be 261. Only sixteen bodies have been recovered, and it will be some time before the names of all the victims are known.

The decision to abandon further rescue work and recall the rescuers to the surface of the burning Gresford Pit was reached at 6.30 this evening.

It followed a number of further explosions and the intolerable heat of the mine – which had become so great that the rescue workers were unable to work for more than three minutes at a time.

The news spread rapidly throughout the mining district, bringing its message of doom to the wives, mothers, sweethearts and children of the men who, since two o'clock yesterday morning, had been imprisoned in the underground inferno.

Some had already become reconciled to the probability, that their men were dead, but the majority found it impossible to believe that all hope had had to be abandoned.

Few relatives – and no women – were at the pit head when the last of the rescuers came up. It was in the home, away from the public gaze, that their sorrow expressed itself. The whole district was stunned.

Immediately after it came there was a scene of great activity at the mine. All men below were called at once to the surface and none could disagree with the wisdom of the official action.

### "A LIVING HELL"
### Risk of Further Catastrophe

"Down there it is a living hell," said one exhausted rescue worker to me when he came up. "The fire has spread with great rapidity and it is now raging furiously."

"Even with this short period of work the men were being affected so seriously by the heat that it was out of the question to ask them to continue further," an official told me.

The last living things to come up before the shaft was sealed at the top were the surviving ponies. Some had not been above ground for years. They stumbled along mystified.

The mine officials, many of whom have been at work for over 40 hours without sleep, received the news of the abandonment of rescue efforts with the quiet resignation that has been characteristic of this calamity. Doctors, ambulance men, police, and a host of other officials left the pit head.

### FIRST HINT OF DISASTER
#### Survivor's Three-Mile Run

The first hint of disaster to reach Wrexham shortly after two o'clock yesterday morning was the arrival of a naked man who ran three miles along a deserted road from the mine to his home.

His clothing had been torn from him by the explosion. As soon as he reached the top of the pit he ran, and ran, until, arriving at his home, he collapsed from exhaustion.

Throughout to-day, while rescuers battled with the flames below, relatives of the entombed men – mostly women and girls, many with babies – fought another battle against tragedy and despair at the pit head.

Dry-eyed and silent, they waited hour after hour for news of fathers, brothers, or sons. Long ago they had ceased to express their thoughts in speech. They stood motionless, daring neither to hope nor to fear.

A woman with a child a few months old in her arms sat hour after hour on a baulk of timber waiting for news. Mutely her eyes questioned the men of the rescue teams, but they shook their heads and passed on.

#### Silent Heroes

A line of young men moves forward in single file, equally silent. Only thin singlets cover the upper parts of their bodies.

Each carries a lamp and a fire extinguisher. On head and back hangs the 30lb oxygen apparatus. They move towards the cage, faces set. Each one is a hero – but he does not think of that.

Before entering the cage each man shakes hands with friends and relatives. He may never see them again. Already three of the rescuers have lost their lives.

As they reach the cage another party leaves it. They are the rescue party who went down, in just the same manner, two hours ago.

Now, with backs bent, faces and clothes black with coal dust, hair and eyebrows burned, and eyes reddened and bloodshot, they stagger, half-blinded, to where women have prepared food and coffee for them.

**(September 24)**

# ENDING STRIFE IN SOUTH AFRICA

PRETORIA, Tuesday.
There were published to-day the terms on which the Nationalist party, led by Gen. Hertzog, the Premier, and the South African party, led by Gen. Smuts, Minister of Justice, agree to amalgamate into one great party. Peace has thus been sealed after a quarter of a century of racial strife between Dutch and English in South Africa.

The New Party recognises the distinctive cultural-heritage of each section of the people.

It will aim at the realisation of the national aspirations and convictions of the people with the motto, "South Africa first."

Maintenance of the existing relationship between the Union and the British Commonwealth is affirmed. Co-operation with the other members of the Commonwealth is also affirmed. Subject, however, to there being no derogation from the status of the Union and no assumption of external obligations in conflict with the Union's interests.

The Party will make an earnest endeavour to reach a satisfactory solution of the native question along lines which, without depriving the native of his right of development, will recognise as paramount the essentials of European civilisation. The Party also stands for the protection of all sections of the population against Asiatic immigration of competition.

The Malanite section of the Nationalists have issued a counter programme. This includes a declaration that South Africa's loyalty to the Crown is voluntary and may be renounced whenever the South African nation so desires. – Reuter.

**(June 6)**

# LONDON'S CROSS ROAD PUZZLE

**From A Special Correspondent**

I spent a somewhat hazardous morning making a personal test of the new system of pedestrians' crossing places, which came into force yesterday.

I visited about a dozen of the busiest traffic junctions, and with the words of the regulation firmly impressed on my mind – "vehicle traffic turning at right angles must give way to pedestrians using the marked crossings" – I stepped boldly on to the white lines – but with a wary eye on the oncoming radiators. Briefly summarised, my conclusions are:

Improvements at isolated crossings, but generally no striking change in traffic conditions.

The most punctilious drivers to observe the safety zones were chauffeurs.

Next in order of merit were lorry drivers. About one in twenty private car drivers observed the regulations.

Taxi-drivers appeared to be completely oblivious of the existence of safety zones.

In fairness, however, I should record that one taxi-driver stopped with such suddenness to allow a pedestrian to cross that a bus bumped into the back of his cab.

### THE MOST SUCCESSFUL

For some unknown reason the most successful crossing was at the point where traffic turns from the Strand towards Waterloo Bridge. Here a large proportion of the vehicles courteously slowed down to allow pedestrians to pass.

This was not so at the Piccadilly-Haymarket junction. I attempted to exert my rights as a pedestrian several times at this crossing, but in every case I found that swiftness of foot availed me more than the edicts of Whitehall. Several taxi-drivers passed down Haymarket with, I fear, a not altogether complimentary opinion of my character.

**(June 12)**

# END OF £20,000 HUNT FOR DILLINGER

## PUBLIC ENEMY NO. 1 SHOT
### DEAD
**From Our Own Correspondent**

CHICAGO, Monday.
America's great hunt for John Dillinger, which ended late last night when Public Enemy No. 1 was shot dead on leaving a cheap Chicago cinema is estimated to have cost £20,000.

The sum of £3,000 in rewards will be paid to the woman who betrayed the 32-year-old gangster by telephoning to Federal officials the time when he would visit the cinema. Her identity is being kept secret, as the police fear Dillinger's friends may "take her for a ride."

It is said that she was persuaded to give the "tip" by a policeman whose friend was killed by Dillinger a month ago.

### RED HANDKERCHIEF SIGNAL

Mr. Malvin Purvis, of the Federal Department of Justice, was in charge of last night's operations. With him were fifteen picked officers, four of whom had seen Dillinger murder two of their lifelong friends a few months ago. For more than two hours they waited outside the Biograph cinema.

Inside the dimly-lighted hall John Dillinger was seeing a film called "Manhattan Melodrama." The end of this shows Clark Gable, impersonating a gangster, walking to the electric chair.

Dillinger left the hall with two women companions. He was turning into a lane where he had left his saloon car when one of the women dropped a red handkerchief. Two of the Federal officers immediately sidled up to Dillinger. "Hello Johnny!" one whispered in his ear.

Dillinger made an involuntary start. That was enough. A swarm of detectives surrounded him, a fusillade of shots was fired at close range, and the gangster, with bullets in his heart and two others in his back, staggered a few paces and crumpled up, face downwards, in the gutter.

The body was turned over and for a few moments the silent group stood in the dim light studying the changed appearance of the man for whom they had been intensively searching for months.

The formerly grey hair was dyed deep black. A small neatly-trimmed moustache masked the thin lips. The well-known scars on the cheeks had been removed. The large nose had been remodelled and straightened. One side of the face had been lifted.

Finger-print experts attach great importance to lack of success with which Dillinger had apparently tried to deface his skin with acid.

**(July 21)**

# NEW CIRCULAR ROAD COMPLETE

The Hon. Oliver Stanley's last public duty as Minister of Transport — he has been appointed Minister of Labour in succession to Sir Henry Betterton — was to open officially yesterday the now completed North Circular road. This road, which has cost £1,250,000, is 15 miles long and has been under construction since 1921, provides a great highway for East and West traffic, designed to relieve the streets of London.

**(July 3)**

# COVENT GARDEN IN SUSSEX

### IDEAL SETTING FOR "FIGARO"

**By Richard Capell**

LEWES, Monday.

The Glyndebourne opera house was opened to-night with a performance of Mozart's "Figaro."

This work, the most exquisite piece of entertainment ever devised by man, the most aristocratic, the most delicately gay and tender – the culmination of a whole civilisation, of which it is also a condemnation – finds in the new theatre which Mr. John Christie has attached to his house on the Downs an ideal setting.

Perfect weather favoured the opening day – and Glyndebourne needs good weather if all its possibilities are to be enjoyed. These include walks in the garden and the park in the generous intervals between the acts. Including one really long interval for dinner. "Figaro" to-night lasted close on five hours.

It may be said at once that the performance was delightful. The audience was entirely conquered. There is no doubt that many who came sceptically-minded went away marvelling at the achievement.

CHARMING STAGE-PICTURES

Fritz Busch's musical direction was vivid and purposeful; Carl Ebert's production abounded in good things; and Hamish Wilson's settings were both bright and elegant. Our one doubt in respect of Mr. Wilson's scenery is that of the second act, where it is essential to the action that we should appreciate the fact that the room is a room. At Glyndebourne there was an elegant rococo décor, but the solidity of real walls and ceiling was not suggested.

As for the singing, all of it was agreeable, and some of it more than that. It ranged from the lightest of girlish tones – tones that would have been really too light in a less intimate setting – to the sonority of a burly Figaro, who did not always appreciate the fact that he was not at Covent Garden. (The Glyndebourne Theatre is the size of a large drawing-room.)

**(May 20)**

# WILD WEST FILMS DEAD

### ONLY ONE 'COWBOY' LEFT

**By Campbell Dixon**

There is sad news for all who love clean romance, the lovely Western deserts and galloping horses.

The Western film is dead. Of the dozens of cowboy actors who took the world by storm only one, Ken Maynard, is still working in "horse opera." George O'Brien and Tim McCoy have just retired, Tom Mix has joined a circus, Hoot Gibson is in eclipse, and Buck Jones has retired into the obscurity that long since enveloped William S. Hart and "Bronco Billy" Anderson.

Other actors who have been seen in cowboy pictures, such as Randolph Scott and Tom Keene, will go on working, but only in straight roles. And to think that Scott works for Paramount, the company that made "The Covered Wagon" one of the greatest successes of all time – and a Western.

The Western slump has hit Hollywood hard. Scores of cowboy extras hang disconsolately around their "Water Hole" rendezvous, hundreds have drifted away, all, in the Western phrase, headed for the last round-up.

The modern boy, brought up on flying and motor-racing, regards the horse as too slow. But I believe boys of all ages will always like genuine dramas of the West, such as "The Covered Wagon" and "The Virginian" were, and such as (I hope) Gary Cooper's coming "Frontier Marshal," based on the life of Wyatt Earp, will prove to be.

**(February 1)**

Write to:
Hodder & Stoughton for a full list of Leslie Charteris' 'Saint,' books – 20 Warwick Square, London, E.C.4.

SHIRLEY TEMPLE, the new child prodigy.

# A FILM STAR OF FIVE

### AMAZING CHILD WHO HAS BEEN OFFERED £400 A WEEK

**By Campbell Dixon**

Another new film star has arisen. She is not a siren, she prefers sweets to diamonds, and she has no use for sables. Yet she gets away with every scene in which she appears, and Adolphe Menjou says she is the only actress in the world he cannot compete with.

Her name is Shirley Temple, and she was five years old on April 23, a date she shares with Shakespeare. She is paid £30 a week by Paramount, she has been offered £400 a week to make personal appearances at a New York cinema, and eight different agents are trying to induce her to go in for broadcasting.

Experts are of opinion that with luck she may have five or six active years still ahead of her.

Curls and Racketeers

Little Miss Temple may be seen this week in "Girl in Pawn," at the Plaza, and if you do not agree that she is bewitching, then I give you up as a surly curmudgeon and a very dull dog.

"Girl in Pawn" is frankly not a good picture. An affair of racketeers and gamblers redeemed by a little golden haired child, it is as sentimental an essay in hokum as the American screen can produce.

But it has its amusing moments, thanks to some shrewd touches of dialogue and direction, and the always expert acting of Adolphe Manjou; and Shirley is a prodigy of whom it is impossible to write without superlatives. At a sober, conservative estimate, she is the cleverest, most loveable, most mischievous, most amusing, most adorable, most –

What I mean is, the child is good.

**(June 25)**

# MLLE. PRINTEMPS' TRIUMPH

### THE NEW COWARD PLAY

**By W. A. Darlington**

Last night at His Majesty's was a great occasion. Even before we set out for the theatre we knew that Noel Coward's "Conversation Piece" – a successor to "Bitter Sweet" – was to have a first night in the grand style.

People had paid higher prices for the reserved seats, or waited longer hours for the unreserved, than ever before. The crowds of watchers outside the theatre as the audience went in formed a densely packed mass; and inside the theatre the air was electric with expectation.

Mlle. Printemps is no stranger to London audiences. Hitherto, however, she has been seen only in French plays, which necessarily have only a restricted appeal. Never before have she and the great London public met one another; and it was plain to be seen as the evening went on, that both had great joy of the meeting.

When the end came, and she took a call alone, the warmth and volume of applause moved her visibly to the verge of tears.

She is, indeed, an exquisite actress, with a bewitching personality. She sings, too with the unfettered ease of a bird. It was from the moment when she first sang the romantic theme-song "I'll follow my secret heart" (of which we shall hear more anon from all the gramophones in the world) that she had her audience in thrall last night.

Mr. Coward shares her triumph. Or rather, since he is author, composer, producer, and chief male actor, in this brilliant show, he enjoys a separate triumph all to himself.

The play has in a high degree most of the qualities which we have come to look for in his work.

It is a tale of Brighton in Regency days, slight in texture and artificial in manner. Yet the texture is so delicately woven, and the artifice handled with such complete certainly of touch, that its sheer skill makes it moving.

Mr. Cochran has staged the piece with his usual lavishness, and Mrs. Calthrop has excelled herself as designer. The result, combined with Mr. Coward's own sure pictorial sense as producer, is a continual delight to the eye. And the cunning devices by which Mr. Coward continually insists, without ever intruding himself, that his play is a piece of deliberate artifice, will be an added joy to the more sophisticated playgoers.

Cunning, also, is the way in which he has provided Mlle. Printemps with opportunities to be fluent in French as well as captivating in her limited English. Also, this seems the appropriate place in which to congratulate him on the fluency of his own French.

**(February 17)**

# ALBAN BERGS "WOZZECK"

### A MODERNIST ORGY

**By Richard Capell**

The B.B.C. must be thanked for giving Londoners the opportunity of hearing the music of Alban Berg's "Wozzeck" at Queen's Hall last night.

The work, though not seeming so novel in style as it would have done before so much of Schönberg's music had been heard here, remains excessively difficult, and the preparation of Adrian Boult's excellent performance must have entailed an enormous amount of work. As for the expense involved, only the B.B.C. could have faced it.

The performance was interesting, and it was not an experience one would willingly have missed. At the same time, however ungrateful it is to say so, the performance was radically an aesthetic mistake.

"Wozzeck" is an opera, an opera by a librettist of genius (Büchner), with music by a highly intelligent but academic composer, a composer of the utmost integrity, but theory-ridden and low-spirited.

Büchner drama – a drama of a bullied and somewhat sub-normal soldier, who is pitiably driven to murder and suicide – has, as everyone knows, at least by report, made the opera immensely effective on scores of Continental stages. A concert performance must depend wholly on the music, and Berg's music, so effective as a whispering, rustling, or sometimes horrified and stringent accompaniment, does not stand on its own feet.

No, not in spite of all the pedal-points to which he so freely resorts to hold his work together. Berg's apologists say that his use of old forms – passacaglia, sonata, fugue – gives coherence to Buchner's loosely constructed drama. One would have to be born with new ears to spot Berg's passacaglia as such.

The effect of the first act last night was, for all Berg's ingenuity, a monotony that promised in the long run to be deadly. But the second act developed more variety, and the scene in the beer garden made an undeniable effect of the brutality and distortions of intoxication. The famous orchestral crescendo on B natural, in the last act, expressing Wozzeck's horror at his crime, is not particularly striking in the concert room, and the wistful nature-music of the scene by the pond, after Wozzeck's death, seems to derive from Schönberg's "Gurrelieder."

**(March 15)**

# J.B. PRIESTLEY'S BEST PLAY

### "EDEN END" AT THE DUCHESS

**By W.A. Darlington**

"Eden End" at the Duchess is J.B. Priestley's best play. It is also one of the best three plays in London at present.

It has, in greater measure than his other dramatic work, that quality of human understanding, of grasp of realities, that is Mr. Priestley's finest gift as a writer. Every character lives. They are, all of them, people.

When Dr. Kirby comes in at dead of night, tired and hungry, he enters not from the wings of a little London theatre, but from the cold of autumn in the north, and from the cottage where he has been assisting a child into the world.

His two daughters, sitting up in their flannel dressing-gowns (the action happens in 1912, for some reason), are no dramatist's puppets, but two unhappy women caught in the perplexities of life, who only succeed in defining their antagonism as they try to talk things out.

THE MUDDLE OF LIFE

The theme of the play is gloomy enough. Dr. Kirby's elder daughter, an actress who has been touring the world for years, comes home to Eden End. Her family think of her as famous and happy; but she is only competent and discontented, and has come back to the peace and comfort of home as to a haven from the world's muddle. But home proves only a part of the muddle – and her return makes the muddle worse, for it spoils her sister's slender chance of marrying the man she loves. So she patches up a reconciliation with her shiftless actor husband, and goes away again for good.

The play is beautifully put together. Here, I think, is the place to record my enormous respect for Mr. Priestley, because coming from novels to plays, he had the wit to see that the two jobs are entirely different, and to learn the new one thoroughly.

The acting is as good as can be. Beatrix Lehmann, always one of our very cleverest players, gives a wonderfully quiet but moving performance as the actress. Ralph Richardson, as the actor, has a part more on the surface – but how brilliant is his detail. And how utterly right is every intonation and gesture in the scene where he gets philosophic drunk.

**(September 14)**

# FILM OF "SCARLET PIMPERNEL"

**By Campbell Dixon**

With "The Scarlet Pimpernel" which begins to-night what will undoubtedly be a very long run at the Leicester Square Theatre, Alexander Korda should repeat the world-wide success he had with "Henry VIII."

Indeed, I should not be surprised if "The Scarlet Pimpernel" does even better. What it lacks in the way of spice and sex is amply atoned for by the qualities – a good love story, quixotic bravery and exciting melodrama played out against a background of gay Regency England and Revolutionary France – that made Baroness Orczy's book one of the world's best sellers.

All the familiar ingredients have been preserved, and some new ones added. Tumbrels carrying the condemned to execution, the knife thudding down to screams of laughter and applause from women methodically knitting, aristocrats snatched away by a Scarlet Pimpernel in disguise – it is all there.

As Sir Percy Blakeney, Leslie Howard scores the greatest hit of his screen career. His amiable aristocrat, the embodiment of modish vacuity, is played with a distinction and style that make the portrait really memorable.

His scenes with the Prince Regent (Nigel Bruce) and Chauvelin (Raymond Massey) are in the great tradition of English high comedy, and it is hard to believe that any actor, past or present, could have bettered them.

Merle Oberon makes a lovely, appealing figure of Lady Blakeney.

**(December 21)**

## A GRETA GARBO TRIUMPH

**By Campbell Dixon**

It is eight years since Greta Garbo burst upon the English-speaking world in "The Torrent." That is a long time for a queen to reign in filmland. New stars have risen and shone brightly, and in the eighteen months since "Grand Hotel" some even among her most devoted followers must have had a secret fear that she was declining.

Their fears are groundless. Yesterday I saw "Queen Christina," which comes to the Empire Theatre to-morrow. I found her as lovely and glamorous, as exciting and as restful, as she was in the far-off days when she was just that Swedish girl supporting Antonio Moreno and the great John Gilbert. Her pure oval face is as unlined as ever; a little firmer, perhaps, when strength is called for; and she is definitely a better actress.

Her English is now good, and she has achieved a flexibility of voice which gives point to a satiric line, a new gaiety to a light one.

**(February 15)**

# "CLAUDIUS THE GOD"

### AN OUTSTANDING NOVEL

Claudius the God. By Robert Graves. (Arthur Barker. 10s 6d)

**By John Collier**

How the historical novel has altered! I think the change is vastly for the better, especially in those that deal with Greece or Rome.

I remember some well-known Roman novels that were still current when I began to read. There was always an early Christian maiden who inspired a flaming passion in a young patrician. To make the trouble worse, she inevitably had a fanatical uncle or grandpa, who could never be restrained from grinding his teeth, shaking his snowy locks, tossing up his arms, and crying "Woe! Woe!" or words to that effect, at the most important point of some sacred progress or other.

But Mr. Graves's novels on Claudius are a very different story. The new one is as good as the last, which is to say that it is a most absorbing, stimulating, and pleasurable book. It is necessary to say so very emphatically, for it stands so far above most novels of the season as to challenge judgement as a work of importance. At once a number of grave faults spring into view.

Judged purely as a novel, it is astonishingly ill-informed. It deals with Claudius's reluctant acceptance of power, his conscientious devotion to the Empire, the undermining of his position by what one character calls "his lustful girl-wife Messalina," and his spiritual collapse on discovering her iniquities.

Now, Mr. Graves builds up a most imposing edifice, a fine statesman at the head of an empire to which he is imparting new vigour. Moreover, he shows us, in this statesman, a very subtle and lucky man, modest, cynical, and whimsical, altogether a most sympathetic character, whose emotions interest us deeply. But all that we are made to feel about Claudius as an emotional man is in connection with the empire. We are told things now and then about his relation to Messalina, but are never made to feel that with her exposure Claudius will and must collapse. Consequently, what should be the greatest moment in the book is the weakest.

From the historical side, also, the book has, I think, a serious weakness. This has probably been fostered by the autobiographical method. Claudius, and all his associates and rivals, and even Messalina, are quite embarrassingly middle-class in their views and their motives.

A Modern Tendency

We are not shown the aristrocratic mind, that beautiful and blind monstrosity that was born of absolute power. This ancient monster, which can be reconstructed partly from vestiges in living organisms and partly from fossils embedded in the cliffy walls of libraries, has left its footprints on all the historical action of the book, but Mr. Graves shows us creatures of quite a different type in the very act of making these footprints. It is a common modern tendency, and a popular one, but it falsifies "the irregularities of vain glory and wild excesses of ancient magnanimity," and it robs the book of a chance of a true magnificence for the sake of a factitious intimacy.

**(November 6)**

# 'THE BARRETTS' AS A FILM

### CHARLES LAUGHTON & NORMA SHEARER

The love story of Robert Browning has already provided Mr. Rudolf Besier with a successful play, and "The Barretts of Wimpole Street," in the screen version presented at the Empire last night, looks as if it may achieve a greatly extended popularity.

Charles Laughton, with iron-grey hair and bushy side-whiskers, plays the original Hardwicke part of Edward Moulton-Barrett – archetype of the stern Victorian parent whose harsh autocracy threatens to wreck the lives of his children, and Miss Norma Shearer is Elizabeth.

Miss Shearer has never played better, and the conflicts between the two personalities, which end so happily for the poetess in her elopement with Browning, provide some brilliantly dramatic sequences.

Frederic March is rather less happily cast as the robust, tempestuous young man who bursts into the stuffy sick-room to bring health and hope to the languishing invalid. His accent is a trifle intrusive – that could hardly be helped. But beyond that he never quite convinces one that he has force of personality enough to sweep the Shearer-Elizabeth away into the strange outer world of which she knows so little.

It is, in fact, Laughton's evening, and he plays the ogre with all the force and insinuating cruelty which we know him to command – not shrinking from full implications of the old man's twisted, thwarted nature. A certain subtlety which belonged to the play is lost, but the resulting melodrama still makes ones of the best films that America has sent us for some time.

**(October 12)**

THE DAILY TELEGRAPH

135, FLEET STREET LONDON

Telephone: CENTRAL 4242

**TO-DAY'S WEATHER FORECAST**

LONDON & S.E. ENGLAND - Wind southerly, fresh, strong or gale locally, veering later; cloudy; rain, brighter later, but with showers; moderate temperature.

ENGLISH CHANNEL - Sea rough

## MR. CHURCHILL'S NEW DEMOCRACY

MR. CHURCHILL, in his uncensored broadcast speech last night, dealt with many vital matters of pressing national interest in his own peculiarly trenchant and stimulating way. Perhaps his most challenging argument was that Parliament requires to be restored to the high place in public estimation which it once held, but from which, unhappily, it has somewhat fallen in these latter days. As to why it has fallen opinions may differ. But, judging by the remedy he proposed, Mr. CHURCHILL would seem to consider that ROBERT LOWE was a true prophet when, in 1866, he observed: "As the polypus takes its colour from the rock to which it affixes itself, so do the members of this House take their character from their constituencies. If you lower the character of the constituencies, you lower that of the representatives, and you lower the character of this House.

It is not only because Parliament is held to be functioning indifferently or inadequately to some of the largest issues which confront it that its old authority might with great advantage be restored, if a feasible method can be found. An even more pressing reason is that Parliament is threatened by the Fascists, operating out on the Far Right, and by the Socialists who are vowing that they will overthrow the Constitution by Departmental Order and decree. Even moderate Socialists register their primary allegiance to the Labour party, and not to Parliament.

Mr. CHURCHILL, nothing if not inventive and original, proposes to overcome Parliament's present deficiencies by a scheme which is certainly provocative of thought. He would not disfranchise a single elector, but he would "give extra votes to millions of men and women, heads of households, and fathers of families, who are really bearing the burden of responsibility of our fortunes upon their shoulders, and are pushing and dragging our national barrow up the hill." If it were objected that this is not "democratic," Mr. CHURCHILL'S answer would probably be that only pedants or fanatics judge remedies by their labels.

At least it may be said that this is not one of those merely "fancy franchise" proposals which were common in Victorian days. It may prove, indeed, on examination, to have no more substance than some of the other bright bubbles which Mr. CHURCHILL is fond of blowing, but it is worth a place in any discussion of ways and means to produce a House of Commons that shall represent more faithfully the sober opinion of all classes of the community. "We need," said Mr. CHURCHILL, "more structure in our system. John Bull should have strong bones." If the latter are weak, steel supports may prove of advantage, and it is well worth arguing whether such a franchise reform for the Commons is not even more practical and therefore more urgent than that reconstitution of the House of Lords as "a strong and effective Second Chamber."

The best friends of Democracy are those who are prepared to accept reasonable safeguards against the follies and excesses which it may, in moments of passion, be tempted to commit. No one can truthfully say to-day that our Parliamentary institutions are safe beyond risk of assault and capture. Yet they are far better worth defending than any institutions yet invented by the painfully hived experience of man.

**(July 17)**

## GERMANY UNDER THE NEW TERROR

ONE can well believe the messages from Berlin which say that all is quiet in Germany. Where there is terror people move discreetly, and Herr HITLER and his henchman, Gen. GÖRING, by their swift and ruthless extirpation of the chief conspirators, have established a terror which will take time to subside, even if no further terroristic strokes are delivered. "Drastic action" GÖRING is reported to have said, "has come to an end." Nevertheless, some hundreds of arrests were made during Saturday and Sunday, and the fate of the arrested persons remains unknown. There is no suggestion, it may be observed, of anyone being put on trial. The method of June 30 was to make sure of silence either by shooting out of hand or by immediate execution after summary court-martial. If the Chancellor is at all susceptible to foreign opinion he can hardly fail to observe that the world which has no sympathy with traitors has still a very strong regard for the forms of law.

How far he has swung or means to swing to the Right cannot yet be estimated, but he has plainly identified the extreme Left with treason. So difficult is it to maintain in the face of obvious contradictions the façade of the Totalitarian State.

**(July 3)**

## 534 – A SYMBOL OF BRITAIN

NEVER within living memory has the building of a ship of peace excited such intense interest in this country as that of the great Cunarder which is to be launched in the Clyde to-day. Name for the moment she has none – only a number. Yet 534 is known in every household in the land. The QUEEN, who has chosen the name she is to bear, will keep the secret till the moment of naming her. May it be a name of good omen, and may this mighty ship fulfil the high hopes she has excited since first the idea of her was conceived and took shape. A variety of circumstances have combined to make this launch famous, and the whole people rejoice that the KING and QUEEN and the Prince of WALES are to take part in the ceremony. This new Cunarder is very much more than just another giant ship added to the word's Mercantile Marine, already far too vast for the shrunken volume of international trade. She stands as a symbol of Britain's shipbuilding skill, of her industrial energy, courage and faith. She stands, in a word, for Britain herself in a critical moment of her industrial history.

**(September 26)**

## AN ECCENTRIC WORLD

AMONG the many reasons which we have for envying our immediate ancestors is the lost security of science. The large scale universe has been made by the mathematicians notoriously incomprehensible. Lord RUTHERFORD, who has done as much as most men to disturb ideas once fixed, spoke last night upon a recent and particularly galling revelation of science. All of us, even those who had never held a test-tube, were aware of at least one chemical formula. We knew that water was H2O – two atoms of hydrogen to one of oxygen, and that water was a uniform substance, so simple that science used it as a constant measure for density and temperature and a dozen other properties.

Now we know better. There are at least two kinds of hydrogen which combine with oxygen to form water.

The common or garden hydrogen has a heavy-weight brother, who turns up about once in 35,000 times, and can then combine with oxygen to form a "heavy water," which is apparently different in many physical and chemical properties from ordinary water and less nourishing to some forms of life. Imagination can conjure up a pretty scientific "thriller," with a criminal who uses this stuff that looks like water and probably tastes like water to poison his innocent victim. Fortunately it is difficult to concentrate, and still more fortunately, there is no proof that it is disadvantageous to mankind. Every day, indeed, we are drinking minute quantities of it in our ordinary liquids, and absorbing it from the moist air. "Heavy water" is but one more example of the intransigence of the physical world to our old rules, an instance of eccentricity science will teach us to tolerate.

**(March 24)**

## SUNDAY RECREATION

To the office-bound the parks of London and many other cities have for some weeks offered the most obvious temptations to linger, as crocuses gave way to daffodils and daffodils found tulips for companions. Londoners take pleasure and pride not only in the Royal parks but in the L.C.C.'s many open spaces, and it is welcome news that additions may soon be made to these upon London's south-eastern side. It is apparently the intention of the new Committee dealing with these matters to survey also the provision of gymnasia and dressing-rooms attached to recreation grounds. More debatable proposals are being put forth to allow games in the L.C.C. parks on Sunday mornings as well as Sunday afternoons.

If the scheme bears fruit there will be an outcry from those who feel that a fresh temptation is being brought to the potential churchgoer, for Sunday morning games directly compete with Sunday morning service. But Sunday morning boating has already been permitted without, so far as is known, greatly decreasing the number of London churchgoers, and there seems no logical reason why Sunday morning bowls should have a more striking effect. For better or worse, this generation has a larger proportion than the last of young people who cannot be made to keep within doors, even within Church doors, during fine weather.

**(April 19)**

## OPERA MANNERS

SIR THOMAS BEECHAM is right in his protest against talking at the opera. His method of protest may be a little unorthodox, his language, as recorded by interviewers, somewhat vigorous, but he will have the music-loving public with him in his determination to have quiet while the story of the opera is unfolding. His demand for silence is less in the interest of singers, orchestra and conductor than of that public to whom the music is everything and without whose support opera could not be produced. The offenders are few; those who have their pleasure interfered with many. The issue is simply one of good manners.

Little by little there has grown up in this country a large body of lovers of music to whom a first night at the opera is something sacred. Conduct and understanding have become so immensely better that the breaking of silence at the wrong moment is an irritation to everybody.

**(May 2)**

## HIGH BUILDINGS AND THE BEAUTY OF LONDON

WHETHER the high buildings recently erected in London deserve censure as "a new and growing menace to the beauties of the metropolis" opinions will differ, despite the report of the Royal Fine Art Commission. That serious damage has been done must be admitted. Some of the finest prospects of St. Paul's from the bridges and the Surrey side have been grievously injured. Yet are we to say that rather than injure a view building owners must for ever acquiesce in great financial loss? For example, ought the buildings on the Embankment to have been governed absolutely by the elevation of 18th century Somerset House? Many of London's high buildings in the modern style have a massive grandeur of their own.

Leading factors in the problem are London's high ground rents and the huge fines exacted before new leases are granted. Increase of height is thus imperative in order to secure a return on outlay, if an old-fashioned town house in a London square is to be rebuilt as a block of offices or flats. On the other hand, the Comissioners do well to insist that as "every increase in height is a conession of which the money value is often great," exemptions from the restrictions of the Building Acts should be accompanied by some improvement, where desirable, in town-planning.

**(March 10)**

# WONDER CITY OF TEL-A-VIV

**By The Marquise de Verdieres**

THE majority of people in this country know little, if anything, of Tel-a-viv. Yet it is a centre of absorbing interest and conflicting passions in the Near East, and before long it is likely to loom large in the eyes of the world.

Tel-a-viv, the City of the Jews, is on the coast of Palestine, but a few minutes by 'bus from Jaffa, and about forty miles from Jerusalem.

I have heard it described as "a miniature Paris"; the most wonderful city on earth"; "an upstart town, too big for its boots"; "the most dangerous spot in present-day politics"; "the expression of a great ideal"; "a stunt exploited for financial purposes." I found it the most amazing place I have ever seen – and I have seen many.

But it is not like a miniature Paris. It is not like anything under the sun but Tel-a-viv. A city of youth, triumphant, eager youth, fulfilling the lifelong dream of age.

AN ORIENTAL SCENE

Twelve years ago there were sand hills and lonely sea-shore. Now there are wide streets, handsome shops, fine houses, schools and hotels, a hospital, a splendid synagogue and a beautiful up-to-date theatre, where artists of international repute give plays in Hebrew. It is the Children of Zion who have created all this in a dozen years. What other race could have accomplished as much?

It is a strange experience to walk their busy streets, where East and West meet and mingle. Motor-cars, 'buses, garries – there are horse-drawn carriages, mostly with Arab drivers – go side by side with a train of camels, their bells chiming, a couple of pack mules, or a man, looking like an illustration from the Bible, rising upon an ass – "the other animal," as it is polite to call it out there!

In the hot golden sunshine, on a summer afternoon, pass women of the West in Paris frocks; women of the East, veiled and inscrutable; Arabs, dignified in their picturesque draperies; Arabs not so dignified in European clothes; British officials; Palestinian police, Eastern children vivid as humming birds. Bedouins hasten along with their free, proud stride, the women a-glitter with coins and jewellery; beggars are seen in lovely rags; tourists of all nations, a motley of colour, a medley of types.

MENACE OF RACE HATRED

The languages spoken are Hebrew and Arabic. Signs over shops and offices are, as a rule, printed in both, but you hear many tongues when you go shopping in Tel-a-viv.

You see many incidents, too, trifles which set you wondering, and if you are at all observant you grow aware of hidden conflict and the menace of deep hatred.

There are two sources of hate and conflict in and around this spot. The first is between the Jews themselves, and is the outcome of religious differences. The trouble between the Zionists, Trumpledors, Revisionist Zionists, and revolutionary parties is extremely intricate.

Roughly speaking, the Zionists adhere rigidly to their ancient teaching, whereas the Revisionists desire certain modifications which they hold to be right. The feeling between the various sections is very bitter.

A few months back, on a starlit summer night, Arlosorow, leader of the Zionist party, was murdered while walking on the sea-shore with his wife, but a stones-throw from lighted cafés and promenade. This crime was apparently committed for a religious motive.

The second source of conflict and unrest is from the Arabs. They dislike the Jews and their prosperous, rapidly growing city.

When the Arabs owned the land it was uncultivated and yielded no profit. The Jews came and paid high prices for ground. They started irrigation and planted oranges. Now there are miles of orange gardens round Jaffa watered by pumps, each driven by its noisy little engine. The hideous sound, which never seems to cease, is a nightmare of the dry season.

The Arabs sold willingly and have reaped advantages from the Jewish settlers; but they are not pleased that such profit is being made from what was once theirs. They resent the exploitation of their country, and the utilisation of their labour to enrich others. They fear to be driven from their own land by peaceful invasion; they sense the might of brains and money.

Thus their dark eyes watch Tel-a-viv and the people who dwell there with dislike and distrust, and they mutter among themselves. When the East hates and whispers trouble is born.

Recently I talked with a Jew of strong personality – a Palestinian I should call him, for he is nationalised. He owns a fashionable café.

"I was here," he said, pointing to a vista of handsome buildings, "when they started to build our city," he added. "I saw it wrecked and built again.

"I shall see it wrecked in the future perhaps once, perhaps twice, perhaps a third time, who knows? May be one stone will not be found upon another. Yet we shall build anew. So long as any of our race endure so long lives Tel-a-viv.

From blood and ashes it shall rise again – to fulfil the dream – to prove our worth. This is our Holy Land. We have come home; and we have come to stay."

**(February 14)**

## COUNTRY CALENDAR

### GOLDEN PLOVER

In October the pretty liquid spring love-note of the golden plover is heard on moors or marshes, and sping-like courting displays and chases are evident. In exuberant spirits, the pack circles high into the clouds, then dashes headlong, shivering into atoms, to the ground.

White under-wings flash in a setting sun, murmuring chorus arises as the flock settles, and then the gold-spangled figures melt into their setting and are no more seen.

These are more typically plovers than the lapwings; and when the two kinds join forces in winter the sharply-pointed wings of the golden ones easily outdistance the others' round wings, and they prove themselves among our speediest birds.

M.W.

**(OCTOBER 10)**

## STREET MARKETS AND THE TRAFFIC PROBLEM

Charged as it is with the improvement of traffic facilities, the Ministry of Transport cannot be expected to take a favourable view of the street markets that obstruct many thoroughfares in London.

Its recommendation of the removal of the stalls from the Farringdon-road would certainly ease movement between north and south London. Apparently local sentiment is against the change, and the stallholders hope the market may yet be saved.

The street markets to be found in most districts of London are something more than a picturesque survival. They meet a real public need, and very few people have any desire that they should disappear. But London changes, and with every day the traffic problem becomes more difficult of solution. The street markets cannot remain as an obstacle to progress.

**(March 1)**

# LONDON DAY BY DAY:

**Realisitc Background**
**Honey for Tea**

DOZENS of aeroplanes droned over the Palace of Westminster last night while Lord Londonderry was replying in the House of Lords to the Socialist motion of censure on the Government's air programme.

Through the opened windows of the Chamber the aeroplanes could be distinctly heard as the imaginary attack on London developed.

It was a realistic accompaniment to the vindication by the Minister of the government's decision to strengthen our air defences.

Several Ministers came over from the House of Commons, and listened to the debate from the steps of the Throne. Among them were Mr. Chamberlain, Sir Kingsley Wood, Mr. Ormsby-Gore, and Mr. Anthony Eden.

An unexpected and particularly effective speech was that in which Lord Rennell interpreted the attitude of responsible Continental opinion to British policy.

### Mr. Lloyd George's Honey

MR. LLOYD GEORGE, whose honey won a prize at the Crystal Palace yesterday, is very proud of his apiary at Churt – proud enough to have had designed for its produce the special label which I reproduce to-day.

Bron-y-de is the name of the house, a corner of which can be seen on the label.

The label on Mr. Lloyd George's honey pots.

The breakfast table at Churt is never without its pot of home-produced honey. But most of the honey is sold in the shop on the estate, together with a variety of jams and other Churt produce.

To-day Mr. Lloyd George may expect a shower of congratulations from fellow-agriculturists; for he is giving a tea party at Churt to 400 potato growers.

### Judges' Legal Immunities

IN further reference to the hypothetical question asked by Sir Alfred Tobin, the Judge of the Westminster County Court – whether a judge could file a petition in bankruptcy and still remain on the bench – it might be remarked that County Court judges are in a much less favoured position than those of the High Court.

The judges of County Courts can be removed by the Lord Chancellor for incompetence or misconduct. It is probable that the Lord Chancellor might think a bankrupt judge unfit to administer justice.

A bad judge may be removed, but if he exceeds his powers he is liable to have an action brought against him by an injured party.

### Oil and Oratory

AN arduous fortnight is in store for those who attend the formal opening of the Irak pipe-lines.

These run through five countries – Irak, Transjordan, Palestine, Lebanon, and Syria. Each is to be visited in turn.

I reckon that at least 40 full-length speeches will be delivered in the course of the various ceremonies.

From my knowledge of the Arab world, I predict that those taking part in the ceremonies will also require gastronomical staying power.

I have known banquets in Baghdad extend to 12 courses. And the Irakis regretfully admit that as trenchermen the Syrians are their superiors.

PETERBOROUGH

# WHAT GOURMETS ATE

## DECEIVED BY THE HUMBLE HERRING

Members of the Wine and Food Society experts in the charms of the palate – net last night at the Savoy Hotel to bid farewell to their president, M. André L. Simon.

M. Simon, an acknowledged master of the delights of the table, is going to devote the next six months to educating the gastronomical tastes of America.

There were more than 450 guests at the farewell dinner last night. They agreed that it was a triumph in the career of the wonderful French chef. M. François Latry. Many French chefs in London get £3,000 a year for providing tasty dishes. Not even the most accomplished experts on the committee presumed to dictate, even to suggest shyly, to M. François Latry what he should provide.

**MENU**

Le Bortsch Koope aux Paillettes
La Matelotte de Harengs Savoy
La Fricassée de Volaille Vallée d'Auge
Les Petits Pois Frais
Les Pommes Berny
Le Nid de Foie Gras à la Gelée de Xèrès
Les Seuilles d'Autonne
Le Parfait Glacé Rothschild
Les Cerises Jubilée
Friandises
La Bonne Bouche Lucullus
Le Café

CHEF'S MASTERPIECE

What do you think was his triumph, his piece de résistance, his irresistible masterpiece? It astonished and delighted all.

It was the herring, the ordinary white herring, of which a hundred can be bought for the price of an oyster or two. It was honoured on the menu with the line:

La Matelotte de Harengs Savoy

M. Latry elevated the humble herring last night to the haute cuisine. Members were startled and delighted by the innovation.

Who knows but what it may now repeat the history of the salmon? Once fresh salmon was so cheap that servants made it a condition of service that they should not be required to eat it more than once a week. Nowadays, at expensive dinners, salmon is escorted into the dining room by pipers!

Ambassadors of several countries and some of London's most distinguished gourmets tasted the herring and asked, "What is this?" They were told, and they were astonished to hear of the troubles of the fishing fleet.

The herring had followed a delicious soup of the colour of port wine. It was honoured with the title "Le Bortsch Koop aux Paillettes," which, being interpreted, means a soup extracted from beetroot, a soup made by the peasants of Poland and Hungary.

**(November 14)**

# WHAT ENGLAND DRINKS

During the first nine months of this year 1,500,000 more bottles of sherry were consumed than during the same period last year. These figures, reflecting the popularity of the "Sherry Party" are revealed by the official statistics of consumption of wines in the United Kingdom just published from Stationery Office, for the period January-September.

The increase in sherry drinking has been almost spectacular in recent years, and the growth in consumption of this wine during the period under review represents an increase of over 2,500,000 bottles, as compared with 1932.

The next largest increase is in Champagne – 1,043,382 more bottles being drunk during the first three-quarters of the present year than in 1933. All champagne is imported to this country in bottle, and the increase is all the more remarkable in view of the fact that there has been a decline in other wines, both sparkling and still imported in bottles from France and Germany.

Wine merchants and restauranteurs attribute the fact that the most notable increases in wine-drinking have occurred in sherry and champagne, to the fact that both wines are known for their anti-fattening qualities, and are increasingly popular in their dryest types. The dryest Champagne produced in France is reserved for the English table.

"Our women clients are generally responsible for the selection of the wines at dinner and supper-parties," said the manager of a leading London restaurant yesterday, "and we find that, despite the slight curves which are now permitted to the feminine figure, ladies are still careful to inquire about the effect of both food and wines on the 'streamline.'

Port wine shows an increase of 4,686 gallons on the first nine months of last year, and Italian wines have also registered a slight increase.

**(November 20)**

# ROYAL WEDDING GROUP AT BUCKINGHAM PALACE

AN OFFICIAL PHOTOGRAPH OF THE ROYAL WEDDING GROUP TAKEN AT BUCKINGHAM PALACE YESTERDAY. It shows, (left to right): Princess Katherine of Greece, Lady Iris Mountbatten, the Prince of Wales, Princess Eugenie of Greece, the bride, formerly Princess Marina of Greece, the bridegroom, the Duke of Kent, Princess Kira of Russia, the Duke of York, Princess Irene of Greece, Queen Juliana of The Netherlands. In front: Lady Mary Cambridge and Princess Elizabeth.

# TRIUMPHAL DAY FOR DUKE OF KENT & HIS BRIDE

## PRINCESS'S FIRM "I WILL" HEARD WHOLE WORLD OVER

The romance of the English Prince and the Greek Princess reached its culminating point yesterday.

Amid scenes of the greatest popular enthusiasm the Duke of Kent and Princess Marina drove to Westminster Abbey to be made man and wife. Cheering crowds attended them throughout the day.

Complete success attended the admirable broadcasting arrangements. As a result, the firmly spoken "I will" of the bride was to be heard throughout the world.

Incident, unrehearsed but very charming, played its part amid the solemn beauty of the wedding ceremony in the Abbey

The main theme went its stately way, against a background of golden altar and dim, mysterious pillars. Kings, Queens, Princes and Princesses headed a brilliant congregation that included the greatest in the land.

And, against this crescendo of uniforms and sparkling orders ceremonial and hallowed tradition, a tiny child and a bridal bouquet provided between them the perfect counterpoint.

The ceremony had already begun; that ceremony which millions of people throughout the world were striving to imagine.

The two main figures stood side by side. With their simplicity, their faint hint of shyness, and their youthful good looks, they made it very hard for the onlooker to turn his eyes elsewhere.

Above them stood the Archbishop of Canterbury, speaking the words of the service. A few yards from the bride and groom at the side of the sanctuary, stood the King. Next to him was the Queen. Beyond her Majesty were the King and Queen of Norway, the Princess Royal, the Earl of Harewood, and the Duchess of York.

Behind the bridegroom, a little to one side, were the Prince of Wales and the Duke of York.

The congregation stood in dead silence listening to the Archbishop's solemn words. "I require and charge you both as ye will answer at the dreadful day of judgment...."

The Forgotten Bouquet

And then – a very human diversion. Princess Marina was still holding her large bouquet of lilies – she had forgotten to give it to the chief bridesmaid! In a few moments it would become a serious hindrance.

The Queen glanced down and saw what had happened. She touched the King on the arm and whispered. The King looked round quickly. Then he bent forward and gestured to the bridegroom.

The Duke of Kent looked at the King in astonishment. The King made a brief pantomime of picking up something. Then the Duke understood. He gently disembarrassed Princess Marina of the flowers.

The Prince of Wales stepped quickly forward, took the flowers from his brother, and laid them down on the floor near where he and the Duke of York were standing. The Queen nodded her head.

The whole episode was over in a few seconds, and the service was in no way interrupted. The Archbishop's voice continued without a break.

The other episode was provided by the innocently captivating behaviour of little Princess Margaret Rose.

While the grown-ups sat on their row of chairs in the sanctuary, she was accommodated on a tiny stool, only a few inches from the ground, that had been sent specially from Buckingham Palace.

Here, dressed in a little white coat and bonnet and a filmy blue dress, she perched herself at her mother's knee.

For some time, in the period of waiting before the ceremony, the Duchess of York kept the little Princess's hand in hers, but later on, in her anxiety to see who was coming down the Nave, the child broke away.

She appeared eager to exchange comment with her mother, but finding this discouraged, she pulled up her socks with great care. Then her mother whispered to her, and she tugged down her skirt to her ankles and hugged her knees with her arms.

Princess Elizabeth's Headshake

The first part of the ceremony held her attention, but later the charming little figure began to get a trifle restive. The crisis came when the bride and groom advanced and knelt at the altar steps.

The two dainty little bridesmaids, Princess Elizabeth and Lady Mary Cambridge, moved forward, too, and stood holding the bride's train only a few paces from the now intensely interested occupant of the stool.

Here was an unforeseen break in the monotony! For some moments there were obvious attempts to attract the attention of her sister. Then, seeing that there was no response, Princess Margaret Rose began stretching her arms out sideways and twiddling her fingers.

At this Princess Elizabeth glanced round and solemnly shook her head. Thenceforth, all exuberance was quelled.

**(November 30)**

# NEW HAT STYLES FOR EVERY MOOD

**By a Fashion Expert**

Madame 1934 changes her personality when she changes her hat. There are so many styles that one for every mood is a low estimate. The new slant, obvious in the sailor models, is rather less acute this season; 22 ½ degrees is about the angle. Rivals to straw for summer hats are found in Petersham ribbon, stitched taffeta, or material in strands,

**(March 8)**

# WHAT IS WRONG WITH THE MODERN HOUSE

**By Lady Kitty Vincent**

A Friend of mine has been looking for a house, and I have accompanied her on her wanderings. Her demands did not seem to be very extravagant, for she wants about four acres of ground and a medium-sized house – where, she does not much mind.

The agents sent her innumerable houses to see, mostly of the new type. Viewed from the outside, they are really charming, well proportioned, with sheer dignified lines, and no unnecessary decoration, but the interiors ...?

One wonders whether the modern architect has in his brain any idea of the functions of a home. Perhaps he is simply designing these houses as an expression of the modern trend of opinion. At any rate, quite a number of them are a cross between a cocktail bar, a swimming bath, and an Italian villa, with the faults of all of them, and few of their virtues.

TOO MANY DOORS

They are supposed to be designed on labour-saving lines, and in the matter of the height of sinks and the rounding-off of corners, this may be so, but they have a tendency to introduce any number of doors into the rooms, so that it is practically impossible to find a really "cosy" corner.

French windows crop up in the most unexpected places. A French window is very nice when the weather is fine and there are no draughts coming from under, but it is a veritable cold trap in the weather which we enjoy for so many months of the year in England.

The house agent usually informs would-be buyers that the house has five bedrooms, and so it has, but they are designed for people who come in late, tumble into bed and sleep till ten o'clock or so, and then go off again. There is no space, no cupboard room, and no feeling of restfulness. It would be depressing to be ill in such rooms. From every point of view, it would be far more satisfactory to have three good-sized rooms where there would be a place to have a little furniture and space to live one's life.

There is, as a rule, one servant's bedroom, which is so minute that it would be difficult to introduce a full-sized bed. I am certain that any maid would rather have a little extra sweeping to do and a room where she could put out a few of her pictures and belongings than these "cupboards." There is often not even a recess in the tiny kitchen where she can have an armchair, so that these modern houses are not calculated to solve the labour problem.

There is a smart little garage just big enough for a small car, but no crack or corner where boxes can be stored, and as there is certainly no room in any of the bedrooms the puzzle is, where are they expected to go.

Finally, my friend in despair decided that she would look at the older houses.

**(January 4)**

# FREDERICK DELIUS

## THE TRAGIC TWILIGHT OF HIS LIFE

The death of Frederick Delius at the age of 72 was far from being unexpected and, to music-lovers outside the circle of his personal acquaintance, it will come as a less severe blow than the tragic breakdown which, years ago, made the composer a helpless invalid.

Sticken with paralysis early in 1923, when engaged on the composition of the incidental music for the production of James Elroy Flecker's poetical drama, "Hassan," at His Majesty's Theatre, he struggled bravely on for some months, dictating the music note by note to his wife, until the additional calamity of blindness compelled him practically to abandon work. The last years of his life, however, were not wholly unproductive, thanks largely to the devotion of his amanuensis, Ette Fenby.

Delius was born at Bradford, Yorkshire, in 1862. The name Frederick was only adopted in later life, and some of his earlier compositions were published and performed under the name of Fritz Delius. Both parents were of German birth, but his father became a naturalised Englishman in 1850.

ON AN ORANGE PLANTATION

He entered his father's business in the wool trade in 1879, but from the first he showed neither liking nor aptitude for a commercial career.

In 1883 he resolved to abandon business and devote himself entirely to music. His father would not allow this, but as an alternative sent him to work on an orange plantation in Florida. Here he neglected the oranges to pursue his musical studies, at first alone, and later with T.F. Ward, an organist whom he met at Jacksonville.

But after a year his longing to enter the musical world proved too strong, and, after much parental opposition, he returned to Europe in 1886 and entered the Leipzig Conservatorium as a pupil of Reinecke, Hans Sitt, and Jadassohn.

His first composition to be performed in public was played at Monte Carlo in 1893. In 1897 he composed some incidental music for a play by Heiberg, which was produced in Christiania, where he met Ibsen; and in 1899 he gave a concert of his own works at St. James's Hall, London, with chorus and orchestra, under the direction of Alfred Hertz. This concert was favourably received by the critics, but eight years elapsed before another performance of any of his works was heard in England.

In the meanwhile Delius was winning recognition at important musical festivals in Germany. His opera, "Koanga," was staged at Elberfeld in 1904, with Clarence Whitehill in the title role "Appalachia" was given at the Lower Rhine Music Festival, Düsseldorf, in 1905; "Sea-Drift," at the festival of the United Musical Societies of Germany at Essen in 1906; the opera, "A Village Romeo and Juliet" at the Komische Oper, Berlin, in 1907, and "Brigg Fair," a rhapsody on an English folk-song, scored so great a success at the Zürich Festival in 1910 that within a year it was performed by thirty-six different orchestras in Germany. "Sea-Drift" was given at the Sheffield Festival in 1908.

In that year Sir Thomas Beecham began his great work of revealing Delius to his fellow-countrymen. No other conductor has done so much to popularise the work of Delius, and none has interpreted it with more sympathetic insight.

HIS PLACE IN MUSIC

Musical opinion is sharply divided on the merits of Delius's music. Certain of his admirers would accord him a place among the greatest composers of all time, while some critics point to his indifference to questions of craftsmanship and structural balance, and rank him as a sentimentalist with Spohr and Gounod. The truth seems to lie between these two extremes. That he has been over-praised is undeniable; he had neither the breadth of vision nor the sheer musical inspiration of Bach, Mozart, Beethoven, or Wagner. His very individual style, mature by 1900, developed no further; the idiom of "Appalachia" (1902) and "Sea-Drift" (1903) is essentially the same as that of the latest works.

His emotional range was not large, and as he abjured polyphony and rhythmic subtlety, relying wholly on harmonic resources, a certain monotony, both in mood and in the actual texture of the music, was inevitable.

**(June 11)**

# FRANCOIS DESCAMPS

Francois Descamps, well known as a boxing manager, and as the trainer of Georges Carpentier, died at his training camp at La Guerche on Thursday night.

He had a stroke on Sunday while watching a football match in which his son was playing, and his condition gradually became worse. He was 59 years of age.

Descamps' reputation was world-wide, and when Jack Doyle's backers recently sought a trainer of experience for him it was to Descamps they turned.

**(February 24)**

SIR EDWARD ELGAR

# SIR EDWARD ELGAR, O.M.

## A GREAT MUSICIAN AND A GREAT ENGLISHMAN

**By F. Bonavia**

When the "Enigma" Variations, which laid the foundation of Elgar's fame, were first given in Manchester under Richter, a critic describing the performance wrote that "the audience seemed rather astonished that a work by a British composer should have had other than a petrifying effect upon them." Those words described very fairly the then prevalent attitude of the public towards British music. The change which has taken place since, and which can be gauged by the interest aroused by a British programme at the Promenade concerts, is mainly, if not solely, due to Edward Elgar's influence and good work.

No other great composer was ever born into a world less prepared to foster musical genius. While the whole trend of music on the Continent during the last century had been towards greater orchestral developments such tradition as there was in England was essentially choral.

No other composer revolutionised more completely men's minds and general attitude by the confidence which his work inspired and the courage it put into the younger generation.

This is not to belittle the achievements of the musicians and scholars who preceded Elgar. They had the advantages of a continental education, but also its disadvantages. They were masters of an idiom which was common currency abroad, but they had to pay for it with the sacrifice of some degree of freshness and individuality. Elgar, who was born and died within sight of the Malvern hills, never lost touch with national thought; his instincts, influenced by contact with his countrymen, were quickened into activity by English life and art. When he had the means to measure his strength with foreign masters, his mind was already formed and could develop further only along its own lines.

Elgar always meant to write opera, in spite of the fact that of all musical forms it is the one which most Englishmen feel to be foreign to the national genius. We can only say that his music appears to us essentially English because it kindles in us feelings and emotions akin to those that are aroused only by English nature and English art.

But he was also one of that small band of Englishmen who discovered that a keen dramatic sense is no passport to public favour. The tragic tales of Thomas Hardy, like Masefield's "Nan," never found admirers in the mass, and it is probable that the early doubts aroused by the dramatic character of the Elgarian oratorio had their root in a prejudice against a tragic theme. But he fully shared the national dislike of rhetoric and popular demonstrations. The enthusiastic greeting he received whenever he appeared in public distressed him as much as it pleased him, and he jeopardised the immediate effect of more than one important composition because he could not bring himself to write a final flourish.

The "Enigma" Variations ended originally very quietly, and the remonstrances of a discriminating friend were needed to persuade him to add the present last section. The second movement of the cello concerto ends abruptly, and although in time that end appears perfect, at first its affect may appear somewhat strange and unsatisfying.

Elgar's genius was somewhat late in flowering. There are lovely things in his early works, and the fire and buoyancy of the "Froissart" Overture, which brought him into prominence when he was already 33 years old, are tokens of something greater than talent. Neither in these works nor in the lovely melodies of "Caractacus" is there anything like the ripe mastery of the Variations and "Gerontius." But when once maturity was reached he never faltered in his progress.

He had made English music admired on the Continent as it had not been since Dowland's time. At home, every festival courted his co-operation. Friendship with Richter provided a valuable link with both Manchester and the Continent; any work he chose to write was now sure of adequate study and performance.

The future, however, had still a few disappointments in store. Elgar had to discover that material remuneration is seldom proportionate to the merit of a musical composition. Not a few first performances in which his aim or his idiom seemed difficult to the larger public must have been at least disheartening. Both "The Apostles" and "The Kingdom" were at first misunderstood. That storehouse of orchestral wonders, "Falstaff," first heard at the Leeds festival of 1913, after a long and trying programme, did not reveal then half its wonders. Even the cello concerto, now most popular, failed at first to make the impression the composer had every right to expect.

If these disappointments were to some extend unavoidable and common enough when performers and public come in contact with a new and powerful individuality, others might have been avoided if our musical life had been better ordered. But no material consideration was allowed to stand in the way of composition, and from his pen poured those masterpieces which are for ever ours. Like all the greatest artists of the world his mind seemed to grow richer the more it gave. Two mighty symphonies followed the oratorios; he added a third to the two greatest violin concertos the world possesses; he gave artistic expression to the immeasurable sorrows of the war in the noble "Ode for the Fallen."

His place amongst the great composers of the world is assured. The generation of to-morrow will perhaps be better able to apportion praise and discover the secret of his greatness. But his contemporaries know how his battles were fought and won, how indifference turned to admiration, how doubts were solved and convictions formed. Nor are we likely to forget how a post-war audience was triumphantly won over again.

These were the events of our lifetime. Those who will succeed us can never imagine what a privilege it was to know the artist on whom pride of race sat so well, an artist so hospitable – so endeared by his very foibles – so frank in speech, so kind in deed, so great a lover of his country, so great a lover of his art.

**(February 24)**

# MRS. R.G. HARGREAVES

## INSPIRER OF "ALICE IN WONDERLAND"

Mrs. Reginald Hargreaves, who died late on Thursday night at her Westerham home at the age of 81, has been honoured in England and America, of recent years, because, as a little girl, she inspired the Rev. Charles Lutwidge Dodgson to write "Alice in Wonderland."

Alice Pleasance Liddell used to go boating with Dr. Dodgson and her two sisters, when she was about 10 years old. One hot summer afternoon in 1862, the party landed to sit in the shelter of a hayrick near Godstow, and Mr. Dodgson began the story of "Alice's Adventures Underground."

Alice, in her own words, "pestered him to write down the story" for her, and he did so. At the time when he presented it to Alice Liddell Mr. Dodgson had no thought of publication. But his friend, George Macdonald, the novelist, persuaded him to submit it to Messrs. Macmillan, who published it in 1865, with Tenniel's illustrations as "Alice in Wonderland" under Dodgson's pen name of "Lewis Carroll."

**(November 17)**

# GUSTAV HOLST: 1874-1934

## AVE ATQUE VALE

Gustav Holst's death means within the circle of his friends a loss which the world in general cannot be expected to understand. He was one of the most retiring of men. Fame came to him rather suddenly, after years of hard work in conditions of something like obscurity; and when it came Holst could not disguise the fact that he was rather more embarrassed than delighted.

To the public in general the composer of the magnificent and sometimes brazen "Planets" must have seemed a strangely elusive person. On rare occasions he conducted at Queen's Hall – and conducted in a thoroughly businesslike way – but the impression of him most concert-goers will retain is that of an obviously shy man acknowledging the applause after the performance of one of his works, and doing so with no enjoyment of the limelight.

The feeling Holst inspired in smaller circles was of a different intensity. The general public admired the boldness, originality and splendour of such music as "The Hymn of Jesus" "The Planets," and the "Perfect Fool" ballet. In the circle of his friends and pupils he was revered and beloved. His superb musicianship went with a nature in which was a vein of simplicity. He could be fierce in his hatred of shams. His humour could be naive.

Sometimes people said that Holst was "inarticulate," but his sometimes halting choice of words was surely one expression of his scrupulous integrity.

Holst's probity went with a great joy in life. A good walk in the Cotswolds or the Sussex Downs, or, failing them, along the Chelsea Embankment, was the remedy he would suggest for sophisticated pessimism. In his student days at the Royal College of Music he would walk home from Kensington to Cheltenham at the end of term. Not many years ago, when a work of his was to be performed in Canterbury Cathedral, he walked down through Kent along the old Pilgrims' Way.

Not that he was physically robust. As a child he was frail, and it was with a view to strengthening his health that he became a trombonist. This experience left a lasting stamp on his musical style. For some time he was a professional trombonist, and he only gave up the instrument when he found he could earn his living by teaching.

Gustav Holst

A teacher he remained all his life. He had a great gift for stimulating his pupils, and he enjoyed exerting it. After years of necessity he became, in 1923, independent, but he did not give up all his teaching then, and, so far as he gave up any of it, the reason was not his financial independence, but a failing of health, the immediate cause of which was an accident – a fall from a rostrum during a rehearsal at Reading.

That year, 1923, was a turning point in Holst's life. While he was being lionised in America his opera, "The Perfect Fool," was produced at Covent Garden with brilliant effect. "The Planets" and other works were being played all over Europe. Another man would have exploited this success, but Holst's "brilliant" period was, as it turned out, already almost over. The Choral Symphony, which was produced at the Leeds Festival in 1925, in part looked back to the brilliant period, and in part belonged to the group of severe works which Holst composed in his last years, a group that includes the concerto for two violins, "Egdon Heath," "Hammersmith," the set of Humbert Wolfe songs, and the Choral Fantasia. The Choral Symphony was revived a few weeks ago at Queen's Hall after long neglect.

The other works of the last period have each been performed once or twice only; the increasing bareness of the style, a sense of the composer's growing detachment, a feeling of frost in the air, all this disconcerted a public expectant of more gorgeous "Planets"; and the great musician has died at a moment of something like an eclipse, not certainly of his fame, but of his popularity. And still we believe that even the least expansive, the least glowing of Holst's last compositions will continue to command the engrossed interest of the few, if not of the many.

Holst's name – a foreign name, Swedish originally – has an unassailable place in the tale of English music. The family of Von Holsts came to England generations ago from the Russian Baltic provinces.

Gustav Holst was English of the English. When Elgar died we tried to define his art by likening it to the warm harmoniousness of Tennyson's verse. Holst's art, too has its kinship with English poetry, but not so much with the mellifluous as with the racy, hard-spoken poets, Hardy and Robert Bridges.

A great musician we maintain Holst to have been, while knowing that the whole claim is not everywhere allowed. The very slightest of his pages have just been turned to, and bring us the old conviction – our reference is to "Four Medieval Songs," for voice and violin, Op. 35. The slightest, the barest of pages! But all is pure music, with not a futile note; all is purpose, all is beauty. A thousand idle thoughts that another might have accepted have been eliminated before a result of such mastery as this is achieved.

**(May 26)**

# SIR GERALD DU MAURIER

## A GREAT MASTER OF HIS ART

By the death of Sir Gerald du Maurier at the age of 61 our Stage has lost one of its most prominent figures.

Although just recently his appearances had been regrettably rare, his was a name to conjure with for the past thirty years or more. A dramatic critic once complained that one of the chief disadvantages of his profession was that he so seldom saw du Maurier act, since all the plays he appeared in seemed to run for months or even years.

At the height of his powers he was one of the few actors who could draw the public even to a bad play. Partly this was due to his enormous personal charm, but still more to his amazing technical ability, both as player and as producer.

The sensitive skill which he brought to the producing of a play was the best refutation of the arguments of people – and they were surprisingly many – who maintained that he was not an actor, but only the projector of an attractive personality. Such people maintained that all du Maurier did on the stage was to "be himself."

Even if this were true, it showed ignorance of the fact that to be oneself on the stage is more difficult than to impersonate somebody else. It was not true, however, in the sense in which it was intended.

THE ACTOR'S PERSONALITY

Certainly, du Maurier, once he had risen to eminence in his profession, never disguised himself. True, also, he endowed most of the characters he played with his own tricks and mannerisms. But his skill in grasping and interpreting varying shades of character was none the less sure or delicate for that. He was, in fact, the most brilliant actor of the modern comedy of manners that we had.

Though he was not born to the stage, Sir Gerald had some theatrical associations, for his father was George du Maurier, the "Punch" artist, who was also famous as the author of "Trilby."

In the autumn of 1895 Tree produced "Trilby" at the Haymarket, and, with a very natural gesture, offered the author's actor son the important part of Little Billee. Young du Maurier, however, had the good sense and the modesty to plead inexperience, and instead played the small part of Dodor.

He was next engaged by Mrs. Patrick Campbell, and appeared with her at the Royalty in a succession of plays, which included "The Fantasticks" and revivals of "The Notorious Mrs. Ebbsmith" and "The Second Mrs. Tanqueray."

In 1902 he appeared in Barrie's "Admirable Crichton," in 1903 in the same author's "Little Mary," and in 1904 he created the parts of Captain Hook and Mr. Darling in "Peter Pan" – parts which he was to play for several succeeding years and again in 1929.

In 1906 he made his first big hit, as "Raffles," the cricketer-cracksman, at the Comedy; and he followed it with another success in the next year as Brewster in "Brewster's Millions."

ON THE SCREEN

In his later years he did a considerable amount of acting for the films. He never cared much for this kind of work; but in spite of his reluctance he brought to it the same brilliant technical skill that characterised his stage activities.

He was knighted in 1922. He took a very active part in the management of the great theatrical charities and was president of the Actors' Orphanage Fund and the Actors' Benevolent Fund.

**(April 12)**

# MME. CURIE

## THE DISCOVERER OF RADIUM

The name of Mme. Curie, who died yesterday at a sanitorium in Haute Savoie, at the age of 66, is for ever linked with the discover of radium. Her work on radium and radio-activity – both of which terms were her invention – marked the beginning of a new phase in human thought.

The fundamental theories of present-day physics are based upon it, and without it we should not possess the revolutionary and paradoxical conceptions of the universe with which Einstein, Eddington, and Jeans have dazzled the modern mind.

The genesis of the momentous discovery in 1898 may be told briefly. Three years earlier Röntgen had found the X-rays, the production of which, it was observed, was accompanied by phosphorescence of the glass tube. This led to experiments being made with phosphorescent substances and the discovery by Henri Becquerel, the French physicist, of the fact that uranium emits a radiation capable of passing through sheets of matter opaque to ordinary light.

Assisted by her husband, Mme. Curie began to search for other substances emitting these strange new radiations so closely akin to X-rays. The Austrian Government gave her a ton of the pitchblende residues from the State manufactory of uranium in Bohemia.

AN HISTORIC BURN

After infinite labour she succeeded in isolating a substance much more active than uranium. In honour of her native country, Poland, she named this polonium. Further investigation revealed yet another substance still more active, and this she called radium.

To-day we know that uranium, radium, and polonium are but three elements in a series of sixteen which are slowly transforming themselves from one into the other by a process of disintegration, until finally the inert element lead is reached.

The application of radium to the treatment of disease came about in a curious way. One day Mme. Curie presented M. Henri Becquerel with a small tube containing a few grains of the precious new element. He put it in his waistcoat pocket, and went about his affairs of the day.

That night when he went to bed he found on his skin, just underneath where the tube of radium had lain, a tiny sore. This, the famous "Becquerel burn," led to the discovery of the peculiar power of radium on living tissue.

SCIENTIST FROM CHILDHOOD

Mme. Curie was born in Warsaw on Nov. 7, 1867. Her father was a professor of physics, and she spent much of her childhood in his laboratory. When she grew old enough she became his assistant.

In 1891 she was compelled to flee to Paris for fear lest she should be forced to give evidence against some of her father's pupils whom the Tsarist Government had arrested. After much difficulty she obtained a post in the Sorbonne Research Laboratories.

There in 1895 she met her husband, Pierre Curie. The first occasion was at a gathering where he read a paper in which he declared: "Women of genius are very rare, and the average woman is a positive hindrance to a serious-minded scientist." A few months later they were married.

Pierre Curie was the son of a Parisian physician and professor at the municipal school of physics. They were close co-workers down to the day of his death in April 1906, the result of a street accident in Paris.

**(July 5)**

# MR. HERBERT CHAPMAN

## TRIBUTE TO A GREAT PERSONALITY

**By Frank Coles**

The world of Association football was shocked by the news of the death of Mr. Herbert Chapman, manager of the Arsenal Club. He died, aged 55, from pneumonia.

By his death Association football has lost its greatest official and its greatest personality. Wherever the game is played in this country the name of Herbert Chapman was known. He was the highest paid official in football. Quite recently he entered upon a new five-years' contract with a beginning salary of £2,200 a year. He was worth every penny of it.

Mr. Chapman lived for the Arsenal Club. He created the present wonderfully successful team – in the eight years of his managership they reached the Cup Final three times and won the Football League championship twice – and the magnificent new grandstand which was opened by the Prince of Wales a little more than a year ago is a lasting monument to his business sense and breadth of vision.

He was thorough to the core. He went into everything with sleeves rolled up and the light of battle in his eye. To him everything was worth doing well.

**(January 8)**

# HINDENBURG: THE MAN AND THE LEGEND

## PARADOX OF HIS POLITICAL CAREER

History presents no parallel to the career of Paul von Beneckendorf und von Hindenburg, whose death took place yesterday at the age of 86.

He became a legend in his lifetime – the legendary hero of a great victory, with which he had little more to do than watch the plans of others being put into execution. Nevertheless, a whole nation of 60,000,000 people believed – and still believes – in his military greatness.

After the war he was called into political life by the Monarchists to destroy the young German Republic, and in his first term of the Presidency he actually saved it for a time. Then, when in 1932 he was re-elected by an overwhelming Republican majority – by 19,300,000 votes, as against 13,400,000 cast for Adolf Hitler – his first step was to call a Monarchist Cabinet into office under Herr von Papen and set in operation the cataclysmic series of events which ended in the complete destruction of the constitution he had sworn to defend.

To complete the paradox in the last two months of German history which have witnessed the murderous Nazi "purge" and the serious crisis produced by the assassination of Chancellor Dollfuss, it was Hindenburg who proved the most marked – perhaps the only – steadying influence in the country.

PRESIDENT AND PEOPLE

It was much against his will that he was induced in 1925 to leave his quiet retirement and stand as candidate for the Presidency. His election produced a wave of uneasiness all over Europe; but a cynical German Parliamentarian remarked: "Hindenburg has always done what his Chief of Staff advised him to do, and he will go on doing so now that his Chief of Staff is the Chancellor."

This prediction was not quite justified. Hindenburg was by no means a subtle statesman, and could only grasp one idea at a time; but that idea, once grasped, he held very firmly, and was apt to embody it in action disconcerting to his colleagues.

Hindenburg's relations with von Papen are among the strangest episodes of his career. The ex-diplomat, who had no political following of any kind, was summoned from obscurity in 1932 as a kind of political gamble, in an effort to draw the teeth of the rising Nazi party, which the President always detested.

Ex-Chancellor Brüning had sought to outlaw the Nazis, and had failed. The idea underlying von Papen's experiment was that Hitler, who could not be suppressed, might be tamed by being induced to accept a share in the spoils of office.

THE NAZI REGIME

Hindenburg yielded, not willingly, to the Nazi demand for office; but he insisted on his nominee, von Papen, possessing the Vice-Chancellorship; and, as we have seen, to that nominee he remained faithful in all vicissitudes with the massive fidelity to a few simple ideas which was his chief characteristic.

Hindenburg as a politician will always be a puzzle to the student of history. How much of what he did or failed to do is to be set down to age, and how far he was allowed to know what the real political forces in Germany were, must long be a matter of dispute.

His military career was equally paradoxical. Probably no one was more astonished than Hindenburg himself by his abrupt leap to fame. In the middle of August, 1914, he was living at Hanover – a superannuated major-general. His career hitherto had been that of the average staff officer who rises to the command of an army corps in peacetime. Outside the army and landed gentry his name was quite unknown. Though Germany was engaged in a life-and-death struggle on two fronts his services had not been called for.

It was then that Hindenburg, who was in his 67th year, and Ludendorff were sent to take over the command.

The most important person in a German army command is the Chief of Staff, and Col. Ludendorff, who had distinguished himself by leading the night march through the belt of forts round Liége, was selected to play this part in the 8th Army. Hindenburg seems to have received his appointment merely because his name stood next on the roster of army commanders.

But when Hindenburg and Ludendorff reached the East Prussian headquarters on the afternoon of Aug. 23 they found that the situation had undergone a fundamental change. Yielding to the pleas of Grünert and Hoffmann, Prittwitz had revoked his order for the withdrawal behind the Vistula and sanctioned an attack on Samsonoff with the object of clearing the flank of the German force retiring before Rennenkampf.

A TREMENDOUS VICTORY

The Battle of Tannenberg was the result. Till Allenby's destruction of the Turkish army it was the heaviest individual blow struck during the war. The 13th and 15th Corps, which formed the bulk of Samsonoff's army, were wiped out. Hosts of Russians were killed and 92,000 were taken prisoners. Samsonoff himself stole away into the woods and shot himself. The tide of the war was turned on the Eastern Front, and Rennenkampf was compelled to retreat.

At the time, this looked to Germany and to the world like a miracle wrought by the genius of a single man. Now, however, we know that if there was anything miraculous about the battle it was the ineptitude and incompetence of the Russians.

Growth of a Myth

Whether the result of Tannenberg was chiefly due to German skill or Russian negligence, there is very little evidence that Hindenburg had anything to do with it. The literature on the subject does not attribute to him a decisive personal initiative at any stage of the operations. In Hoffmann's book, the standard work on the battle, he is hardly mentioned.

However, the immediate effect of the victory was to raise Hindenburg to a pinnacle much higher than that occupied by any of his contemporaries. It was universally believed that Germany had, in the hour of her need, produced one of history's great military geniuses, another Caesar or Napoleon.

PATRIOTIC INVENTIONS

He has indeed become a mythical figure, invested with a dazzling halo of legend. Throughout the world it was told that, as commander of an army corps in East Prussia, he had, with the prescience recorded of Napoleon, foreseen every detail of Tannenberg, and prevented the civilian authorities from draining the marshes into which he intended some day to drive multitudes of Russians.

This story, which was encouraged by the Government as a patriotic stimulant, was even farther from the truth than the fable of the Russian division being engulfed in the carp pond at Auterlitz.

In the autumn of 1916, when Falkenhayn's failures made a change in the Chief Command of the German land forces advisable, Hindenburg was called on to assume the grave responsibility.

The history of Hindenburg on the Western Front is the history of the crumbling of the German Army. It fell to him finally, after Ludendorff's retirement, to lead the beaten army home. But as long as the campaign is written about his name will live in the Hindenburg Line, that formidable defensive line which, constructed early in 1917, was not pierced until August, 1918.

It was a final paradox of his career that the only connection he had with the Hindenburg Line consisted in lending his name to it.

**(August 3)**

# SIR ALFRED GILBERT

## AN INSPIRED SCULPTOR

By the death of Sir Alfred Gilbert this country loses its most inspired sculptor. The loss is not only ours, but the world's for his achievement was of the supreme kind which belongs to universal art.

Rodin called him the "English Cellini." Comparisons help little in matters of art but it is a matter of general consent that Gilbert is fit to stand beside several of the great Italian masters.

He is best known to the British public by his famous statue of Eros in Piccadilly circus. It is strange to reflect now that when Eros was first produced it was the occasion of a storm of criticism – much of it from Gilbert's artistic fellows – and of a series of quarrels which came near to breaking its great creator's heart.

Gilbert's difficulties were due to his devotion to his art. He would not turn out second-rate work, and he would ruthlessly destroy over and over again work that seemed not quite good enough and begin anew. This led to delays. It also led to great expense, for the materials in which he wrought were costly, and his methods involved him in heavy losses.

He moved to Bruges, where he remained in silent exile, almost unheard of, for seventeen years, including the years of the German occupation. He did not cease work; but it was not until 1926 that he was persuaded by the King to return to England and complete the Clarence memorial which he had modelled twenty years before.

The welcome he received from all classes of his countrymen must have convinced him of the honour in which he was held and provided a balm for the wounds of earlier years.

It is not often that the nickname of an artist continues after the passage of years to mean much or anything. But when Rodin, in his merry way, called Gilbert "the English Cellini" he so aptly summed up the character and achievements of his English friend and fellow sculptor, that even now, when both are gone, the phrase echoes inevitably in the mind.

**(November 5)**

# MARIE DRESSLER

## FIFTY YEARS ON STAGE AND FILM

Filmland has lost its best-loved character. Other stars have their detractors. Nobody has ever been heard to speak of Marie Dressler except with love. She gave away most of the money that came to her late in life, and, often a sick woman herself, was never able to resist an appeal from those in trouble, even when they had not the slightest claim on her.

She was born in Coburg sixty-four years ago, her father being a retired army officer named Koerber. A German who fought on the British side in the Crimean War, he had a young English wife and a taste for music, which he tried to capitalise by teaching. Marie was christened Leila.

Little Leila Koerber's earliest memories were of wanderings. "Things went from bad to worse financially," she has recorded. "We continued to move around, but the pupils who came to my father for lessons grew fewer and fewer in each place.

Marie Dressler

"Finally mother and I realised that something must be done. I was the only one able to do anything, so I managed to get a job in a cheap little theatrical touring company. I was only 13 at that time, but I was so large that I easily passed for 18."

Success came to her early. She became a star in musical comedy, and was twice seen in London – in 1907 at the Palace, when she received what was then a record salary of £500 a week, and in 1909 in an unlucky managerial venture at the Aldwych. She tried the films, and in 1914 was starred in "Tilly's Punctured Romance," supported by a young newcomer from England, Charlie Chaplin.

The war came and Miss Dressler gave up film work to entertain soldiers. Her reward was that by 1919 she was almost forgotten.

The outlook for the elderly woman with the homely face and lumpy figure was black indeed when she was offered a part in a talkie "Anna Christie," supporting Greta Garbo. By her brilliant work as the drunken waterside drab she "stole" the picture, and the woman nobody wanted became the star every director must have.

After that Miss Dressler went from triumph to triumph, and became, in competition with Garbo, Dietrich, and other lovely sirens, perhaps the biggest box ffice draw in the world.

**(July 30)**

# ALBERT THE PATRIOT KING

Almost alone among the outstanding figures of the war, Albert, King of the Belgians, gained in stature by the lapse of time and the ebb of emotions and passion.

The slowly revealed truth of those years, which has tarnished and diminished so many dazzling reputations, left untouched the war legend of the hero Monarch.

It rather added to that legend the lustre of a degree of strategic generalship which entitles Albert to high rank as a military thinker. In the critical days at the beginning of the war he saw the realities of the situation much more clearly than any of the professional soldiers.

During the first few months of the war, when the wave of Germany's might swept over "gallant little Belgium," till all but a tiny strip of Flanders was under occupation, the picture that emerged of King Albert was of a young, handsome, determined leader of his people, whose fearless courage and unconquerable faith in idealism infused his nation with a will to fight against hopeless odds.

Like any simple soldier, he fought in the trenches. He moved from point to point of the battle front heedless of danger, clad in his general's uniform that made him a conspicuous mark for German sharpshooters. He shared all the privations of his troops, and radiated confidence and even light-heartedness wherever he went.

Occasions make the man. The immolation of Belgium called for a Galahad, a shining, knight-like figure – and it found King Albert.

A Great General

Now, since the publication a little over two years ago of a book by Gen. Galet, King Albert's wartime Chief of Staff, we know he was more than a leader in a national crisis, more than a comrade to his men, more than an inspirer of his people. He was a great general.

On his accession Albert was something of an unknown quantity. He had in youth no expectation of succeeding to the Throne. It was not until his elder brother, Prince Baldwin of Flanders, died tragically in 1891 that Prince Albert became heir to his uncle, Leopold II.

As Crown Prince he had been a quiet, rather shy man of a studious nature and fond of sport and engineering. The only other thing known about him was that he had shown aptitude in military theory at the Army Academy and during his period of service. Few could have imagined of what service to his country and the Allies this intellectual liking of his for strategy and tactics was one day destined to be.

He rapidly endeared himself to the people not only by his courtesy, devotion to duty, and encouragement of learning and the arts, but because of his simplicity of life and his democratic learnings. his first action which made Belgium realise that their new monarch was the son of an enlightened age was his clean-up of the Congo. This enabled him, too, to renew the ties of friendship between England and Belgium, which had been seriously frayed by Leopold II.'s methods of administration in Africa.

A Tactful Sovereign

The Belgian nation thus welcomed back from exile in November, 1918, a ruler who had proved himself both in peace and in war. During the difficult years that have followed he proved himself a wise and temperate monarch.

When in 1930 Belgium celebrated the centenary of her independence, the nationwide festivities were equally a tribute to King Albert's wise and beneficent reign. He will go down in history as a national hero, a good King, and a great man.

**(February 19)**

# ENGLAND LOSE THE ASHES BY 562 RUNS

By P.F. Warner

FIVE minutes to six at the Oval … Oldfield stumped Allen off Grimmett – and the "Ashes" went back to Australia.

So ended the final Test yesterday, with England beaten by 562 runs. Set the enormous number of 708 to make, England were dismissed for 145.

This is the heaviest defeat, with one exception, in the history of Test matches between the two countries. The exception was at Brisbane in 1928, when England gained the victory by 675.

We lost the match on the first day when some six or seven catches were dropped. This was followed by the withdrawal through illness, for part of the match of both Ames and Bowes.

But on the run of play Australia were the better team and deserved to win. Their fielding was markedly superior to ours; in Grimmett and O'Reilly they had a fine pair of spin bowlers, and the presence of Bradman, Ponsford, and McCabe made them a formidable betting side on the perfect wickets with which we have been favoured this summer.

Yesterday's play was in direct contrast to that of the previous three days, seventeen wickets falling for 286 runs. The pitch was worn, and the bowlers held the upper hand. Also England held on to their catches, as did the Australians – as usual.

It was not the fault of our bowlers that we lost. All of them – particularly Allen – were badly supported in the field, and it was the general opinion that our fielding, until yesterday, was probably the worst that has ever seen in a Test match.

The pitch yesterday suited Grimmett exactly. He could spin the ball so much from leg that he was able to place two men close up in the slips. At his age he has, perhaps, played his last Test match in this country.

To Woodfull, the Australian captain, I offer my congratulations. It is said that he is shortly to retire from cricket, and he does so with a great record both as a batsman and a captain. He has twice recovered the "Ashes" for Australia – in 1930 and now again this year.

Australia were 687 ahead and had made over 1,000 runs in their two innings. One's memory could not help dwelling on the long toll of dropped catches on Saturday, which contributed so largely to this mammoth score. The last wicket eventually added 55 runs before Ebeling, who had played an excellent innings in good style, was caught at short-leg by Allen off Bowes.

### THIRTY-SEVEN BYES

There were no less than 50 extras – 37 of them byes – but Woolley's was, of course, a thankless task.

The start of England's second innings could not have been more disastrous. Walters was completely beaten and Woolley caught by Ponsford running back from mid-off. Sutcliffe and Hammond – tremendous names in international cricket since the war – were now together. At 11 Grimmett came on at the Vauxhall end – the opposite to that from which he had bowled in the first innings – instead of McCabe, and Hammond, moving out of his ground, drove him on the full pitch past mid-off for 4.

For a long time little could be done with the bowling but suddenly there came a burst of fast scoring. Sutcliffe three times swept Grimmett to the long-leg boundary and cut him late for 4, while Hammond, on and off, drove O'Reilly and cut him square to the boundary. A magnificent on-drive for 6 off O'Reilly by Hammond brought the score to 55 in an hour.

When 29 Hammond jumped out of his ground to drive Grimmett, and missing the ball should have been stumped. He was very quiet for a time after this fortunate escape, but presently he hit O'Reilly to long leg for 4, and scored a 2 over deep mid-off's head.

A big stand seemed possible, but at 67 Sutcliffe was caught at second slip, off Grimmett.

The order altered, Leylands coming in next instead of Wyatt. He promptly hit Grimmett for two 4's on the leg side, the first a very hard-pulled drive. The tea score was 83 for three.

Immediately after tea Hammond was caught and bowled – O'Reilly holding the ball easily with his left hand.

Wyatt began with an on-drive for 6 off a no-ball of O'Reilly's followed by a beautiful straight drive for 4 off Grimmett. Then Leyland fell to a splendid catch at extra cover. He hit the ball hard and low, and Brown, making a lot of ground, caught it at the second attempt on his left side.

Wyatt, trying to pull, was nicely caught by Ponsford at mid-on. Allen drove to the on and hit well to leg, but the Grimmett-McCabe combination brought about Verity's dismissal and Bowes came in to be loudly applauded for his courage and his excellent bowling.

Bradman caught him at short leg at 141, and Allen, who had played an attractive and good innings, tried to hit Grimmett to Vauxhall Bridge; Oldfield did the rest.

There was a mad rush for the stumps and the ball. Allen, as he turned to leave, collared one stump with lightning rapidity, which he presented to McCabe on the way back to the pavilion.

## THE TEST SCORES

AUSTRALIA – First Innings

W.A.Brown, b Clark ....................................10
W.H. Ponsford, hit wkt, b Allen ..............266
D.G. Bradman, c Ames, b Bowes ............244
S.J. McCabe, b Allen ...................................19
W.M. Woodfull, b Bowes ............................49
A. F. Kippax, lbw, b Bowes .......................28
A.G. Chipperfield, b Bowes..........................3
W.A. Oldfield, not out .................................42
C.V. Grimmett, c Ames, b Allen .................7
H.I. Ebeling, b Allen.......................................2
W.J. O'Reilly, b Clark ....................................7
B 4, l-b 14, w 2, n-b 3...............................33
Total.....................................................701
Fall of Wickets: 1-21, 2-472, 3-488, 4-574, 5-626, 6-631, 7-638, 8-676, 9-682, 10-701.

Second Innings

W.A.Brown, c Allen b Clark .........................1
W.H. Ponsford, c Hammond, b Clark .......22
D.G. Bradman, b Bowes .............................77
S.J. McCabe, c Walters, b Clark ...............70
W.M. Woodfull, b Bowes ............................13
A. F. Kippax, c Walters, b Clark................8
A.G. Chipperfield, c Woolley, b Clark ......16
W.A. Oldfield, c Hammond, b Bowes..........0
C.V. Grimmett, c Hammond, b Bowes......14
H.I. Ebeling, c Allen, b Bowes ...................41
W.J. O'Reilly, not out..................................15
B 37, l-b 8, w 1, n-b 4..........................50
Total.....................................................327
Fall of Wickets: 1-13, 2-42, 3-192, 4-213, 5-224, 6-236, 7-236, 8-256, 9-272, 10-327.

ENGLAND – First Innings

C.F. Walters, c Kippax, b O'Reilly............64
Sutcliffe, c Oldfield, b Grimmett ................38
Woolley, c McCabe, b O'Reilly .....................4
Hammond, c Oldfield, b Ebeling................15
R.E.S. Wyatt, b Grimmett ...........................17
Leyland, b Grimmett .................................110
Ames, retired hurt.......................................33
G. O. Allen, b Ebeling.................................19
Verity, b Ebeling...........................................11
Clark, not out.................................................2
Bowes, absent ill ...........................................0
B r, l-b 3, n-b 1 .......................................8
Total.....................................................321
Fall of Wickets: 1-104, 2-108, 3-111, 4-136, 5-142, 6-263, 7-311, 8-321.

Second Innings

C.F. Walters, b McCabe ...............................1
Sutcliffe, c McCabe, b Grimmett................28
Woolley, c Ponsford, b McCabe ....................0
Hammond, c and b O'Reilly .......................43
R.E.S. Wyatt, c Ponsford, b Grimmett .....22
Leyland, c Brown, b Grimmett ..................17
Ames, absent ill .............................................0
G. O. Allen, st. Oldfield, b Grimmett........26
Verity, c McCabe, b Grimmett .....................1
Clark, not out.................................................2
Bowes, c Bradman, b O'Reilly .....................2
L-b 1, n-b 2..............................................3
Total.....................................................145
Fall of Wickets: 1-1, 2-3, 3-67, 4-89, 5-109, 6-122, 7-138, 8-141, 9-145.

**(August 23)**

# HOBBS' FAREWELL TO SURREY

Jack Hobbs, the famous Surrey and England batsman, has been reluctantly compelled to retire from county cricket.

The public, which has idolised him for thirty years, will receive Hobbs's decision with regret and disappointment, especially as it was hoped that the Surrey club would give him the chance of scoring three more centuries and bringing his total to 200, thus enhancing a record likely to remain unbeaten for many years.

Hobbs took part in Surrey matches with comparative regularity until the middle of June, scoring 544 runs in thirteen completed innings, his average being over 40.

He assures me that he is prepared to go on playing for the county, but that he has waited in vain for further invitations. "I have now given up the idea of playing again," he tells me, "until the Folkestone festival, when I am to appear in two matches against the Australians.

**(July 30)**

# GENTLEMEN'S VICTORY

For the first time since 1914, the Gentlemen beat the Players, at Lord's, Hendren, the Players' captain, declared his second innings closed with the score at 245 for five leaving the Gentlemen 232 runs to make to win in 172 minutes – a rate of approximately 84 runs an hour. And the Gentlemen won with seven wickets and twenty-five minutes to spare.

It was a remarkable performance, and the chief credit for it must be given to Wyatt and Walters. They scored 121 runs in an hour, and were not separated until they had put on 160 runs for the first wicket in 87 minutes.

This victory will give added stimulus and interest to a match which was in danger of losing popular support.

**(July 28)**

F. J. PERRY IN ACTION during his match with J. Crawford at Wimbledon yesterday.

# LARWOOD REFUSES TO PLAY AT LORD'S

## DECISION NEVER TO APPEAR AGAIN IN AUSTRALIAN TEST

Harold Larwood, the Notts and England cricketer, whose fast bowling contributed so largely to winning the Ashes in Australia, will not play at Lord's in the second game of the present matches, which opens on Friday.

He has definitely decided, he announced yesterday, never to play against Australia in a Test again. He complained of "political influence" to keep him out of the Tests.

Larwood, in his announcement, asserted that he was fit to play in the first Test, though he and his county captain, A.W. Carr, both stated at the time that he was not fit. He added that political influence had been brought to bear on the M.C.C. to keep him out of the Tests.

This was emphatically denied by Lord Hailsham, Secretary for War, the last president of the M.C.C., and by Mr. J. H. Thomas, Secretary for the Dominions.

"It is the most extraordinary moonshine I have ever heard of," said Lord Hailsham. "The only person who prevented Larwood from playing in the first Test match was Larwood himself. I am a member of the M.C.C. Committee and must have known had any influence, political or otherwise, been at work.

"I really cannot understand what Larwood means. Whose is the political influence supposed to be, and what is it supposed to do? When the first Test match team was chosen he said he was not fit, and that is the reason he was not chosen, so I always understood.

"I think it is a very great pity, when the Australians are over here, having a very pleasant time, and when there is no sort of unpleasantness or difficulty at all, that this sort of agitation should be worked up that can only do harm and spoil the tour. Good manners should have prevented this attack on the Australians, who, after all are our guests.

### Denial by Mr. Thomas

Mr. Thomas declared that there was not a vestige of truth in Larwood's statement. "Neither directly nor indirectly have any discussions taken place with politicians with regard to Larwood, either in Australia or here. It is rather unfortunate that Larwood, in his grievance against somebody, should have dragged in politicians."

The M.C.C. Selection Committee – Sir Stanley Jackson, the former England captain, Mr. Percy Perrin and Mr. T.A. Higson – meet to-day to select the English team.

Larwood is in wonderful form, as he showed by taking six wickets for 51 runs – at one stage he had six for 1 – against Lancashire on Saturday.

There is not the slightest doubt that the committee would have invited him to play, and Sir Stanley Jackson has stated that no conditions would have been imposed.

But, Sir Stanley added, Larwood would naturally be subject, like every other cricketer, to his captain's orders. Since R.E.S. Wyatt, who will probably lead England, is known to disapprove of fast leg-theory, this may be taken as an indication that "bodyline" is barred.

At all events it was so interpreted by Larwood. He declared yesterday that the M.C.C. were adopting a ruse to keep him out of the Tests. He added that from the first he had never intended to play against an Australian captain who regarded him as unsportsmanlike and unfair.

**(June 11)**

# NO RUGBY WITH FRANCE

## BRITISH UNIONS UNANIMOUS

PARIS, Thursday.

The four British Rugby Unions, in their reply to the French Federation, have decided that the time is not yet ripe for a resumption of international matches with France.

A translation of an extract of the letter, just received by the French Federation, reads: "If your federation has done much for the recovery of Rugby, we consider it has not yet done sufficient.

"As long as Rugby, as practised in France, is not played in the right spirit and in accordance with the traditions of the game long ago laid down by the home unions, and, above all, as long as the present system of competition exists in France, it will not be possible to consider the arranging of international or inter-club matches."

This negative reply has caused much disappointment in France.

"A masterly slap in the face," is the comment of the "Paris Soir."

M. Dantou, President of the French Federation, who was a member of the delegation who recently visited London, expressing his personal opinion said:

"I consider that we have no lessons or suggestions to receive from the British Unions. We have done without them for three years, and we shall continue to do without them in the future. As for suppressing competitions, like the French Championship, I reply, speaking for myself, that this is our business." – Reuter.

**(May 18)**

# BRITISH LIGHT CARS TRIUMPH

From Our Special Representative

MONTE CARLO, Thursday.

British light cars have beaten on their own ground most of the high-powered cars of Continental or American manufacture which opposed them in the Monte Carlo Rally.

Mr. Donald Healey, who has earned the nickname of "the Flying Cornishman," figured third in the general classification with his 12 h.p. Triumph car, being beaten only by Messrs. Gas and Trevoux on a big Hotchkiss and Messrs. Chauvierre and Lanciano, on an 8-cylinder Chenard-Walcker.

A little farther down the list comes Mr. Rupert Riley with his Riley Nine. Mr. Beck, who won through from Tallinn on another Triumph car, was beaten by two much larger cars of French manufacture. In the small car class Mr. Healey and Mr. Riley took first and second places respectively, while Mr. Ridley and Mr. Beck, both on Triumph cars, finished sixth and tenth.

The Hotchkiss car which won the rally as a whole is a fine French automobile, carefully prepared for the event, but in no sense freakish. The 8-cylinder Chenard-Walcker which took second place is a new model.

**(January 26)**

# TENNIS TITLE HOME AFTER 25 YEARS

## PERRY HOLDER OF TRIPLE CROWN

By A. Wallis Myers

"From wandering on a foreign strand" the lawn tennis championship has come back to England, its native place, after twenty-five years.

Yesterday, at Wimbledon, before an expectant throng, hoping, but not quite sure until the end, F.J. Perry defeated J.H. Crawford, the holder, in the final, and became the first home-grown champion since 1909. The score was 6-3, 6-0, 7-5.

Thus Perry became the holder of a notable triple crown. He is champion of Wimbledon, Australia, and America.

The result was epoch-making; the actual match was not an epic fight. It was, indeed, a hollow victory, only saved from becoming a debâcle by the Australian's plucky but fruitless effort to turn the tide in the third set.

Of Perry's fitness to hold the title by virtue of his play and resolution it gave open proof; as a spectacle and in relation to some much greater matches that had gone before this week it was almost an anti-climax.

For if the Perry enthroned yesterday was a better Perry than Wimbledon had ever seen – remorselessly accurate on the drive, very competent on the service, and brilliant on the few occasions when he ventured to the net – Crawford was certainly not the vibrant, resourceful, and calculating player who beat Vines in a classic match last year.

THE 1934 CHAMPIONS

MEN'S SINGLES – F.J. Perry (Great Britain)
WOMEN'S SINGLES – Miss D.E. Round (Great Britain)
MEN'S DOUBLES – G.M. Lott and L.R. Stoefen (U.S.A.)
WOMEN'S DOUBLES – Mme R. Mathieu (France) and Miss E. Ryan (U.S.A.)
MIXED DOUBLES – R. Miki (Japan) and Miss D.E. Round (Great Britain)

He only gave glimpses of the champion; for the rest he was like a man living under the shadow of defeat, his weapons blunted, his eye out of focus, and his enterprise gone.

The new champion is a native of Stockport. He is a Middlesex club player converted into a champion by his own volatile, sanguine character, by the confidence of his father, and by the facilities for "first ten" practice and experience all over the world provided by a discerning governing body.

### A 25 YEARS' MEMORY

As he was moving steadily but surely to his goal yesterday – an excitement he could hardly suppress only serving to increase the force of his inflexible pressure – my mind reverted back twenty-five years to the challenge round at the old Wimbledon, when A.W. Gore, the last English champion, won the title for the third time.

I have a vivid recollection of that encounter, because it produced one of the most surprising recoveries in the history of the championship. M.J.G. Ritchie was two sets up on the reigning champion, and held a winning lead in the third. The holder – we did not think of him as a veteran in those days, although he was 41 – was gasping for breath.

His passing seemed imminent, and probably Ritchie shared the opinion of the crowd. Gore's sound heart and the strength of his forehand drive turned the match completely round; he looked as if he could have played another set at the finish.

There was no similar denouement about yesterday's final – only a temporary interruption to Perry's progress in the third set. Before Crawford's belated stand came the challenger had created a new record for any men's Wimbledon final. He had won twelve games in succession – nominally two love sets. Such a break against a man of Crawford's class and experience suggests a brand of play unprecedented in its mastery and precision.

**(July 7)**

# "HE DIED LIKE THE SAMURAI"

"Haunted by fear that his illness would endanger Japan's chance of victory, Jiro removed himself, like the Samurai of old."

That is how Miss Sanae Okada thinks of the suicide of her fiance, Jiro Satoh, the world-famous tennis player, who threw himself overboard on the way to Europe.

[The Samurai, the members of the old military caste of Japan, never allowed themselves to survive disgrace.]

"But, oh," she said, as her eyes blurred, in telling me to-day of the tragedy, "if only he had patiently gone on I would still have him. How I hate them for obstinately forcing him to go against his will and driving him in desperation to death."

**(April 9)**

# MORE RECORDS AT THE EMPIRE GAMES

**By Bevil Rudd**

The Empire Games Athletics ended on a triumphant note at the White City yesterday. Three more British records were broken, and in the mile J.E. Lovelock, of New Zealand, failed by only 4-5th sec to beat his own figures of 4 min 12 sec.

G.L. Rampling, the Army and A.A.A. champion, was the hero of the day and indeed, of the Games. In winning the quarter-mile in 48 sec he beat by 2-5th sec the 26-year-old record set up by Lt. Halswelle at Glasgow in 1908.

Miss Eileen Hiscock, a London girl, won the women's 220 yds in 25 sec, and the third record of the afternoon was established by Miss Marjorie Clark, of South Africa, who won the 80 metres hurdles in 11 4-5th sec.

There was a big surprise in the Marathon, in which H. Webster, of Canada, defeated the favourite, D. McNab Robertson, of Scotland, by four and a half minutes.

It was the old Rampling we saw in the quarter-mile yesterday – strong and imperious. He drew the fourth lane and did not bother to race anybody. He concentrated on his own running.

For sheer speed and rhythmic power he was the best sight I have seen on a British track. Nor did he weaken as he swept into the straight with a commanding lead. He broke the tape in unimpaired form.

If Rampling's running suggested poetry – the dynamic energy of William Blake – we had melodious prose from J.E. Lovelock. He controlled the mile from the start. He tapped his resources with unerring discretion, and anticipated and dealt with the strenuous challenges of J.F. Cornes and S.C Wooderson with perfect serenity.

We were still to have two more records. Eileen Hiscock raced away from her field in the 220 yards. She was in an outside lane, but her amazing speed needed no competitive urge. She ran this distance in 25 seconds.

MISS CLARK'S GREAT WIN

The women's 80-metre hurdle race yielded not only a new record, but a brilliant race. Over the first five flights Betty Taylor, of Canada, showed incomparable form and celerity and looked a certain winner. But Marjorie Clark, of South Africa, buoyant after her high jump record on Saturday, and despite a bad start, seemed suddenly to remember all that S.J.M. Atkinson had taught her in Natal about hurdling.

Atkinson is an Olympic champion and holder of the British hurdle record. Marjorie Clark now holds an Empire hurdle title. She decided she was going to win, and she did; nor did her determination upset her style. Many who share with me a distaste for women's athletics were saying after that race: "Well, I'm not so sure."

An unnatural masculinity need not attach to women who excel. Betty Taylor's quiet eyes and gentle voice are an absolute denial of the dogmatic presumption that it does.

Miss Taylor's beautiful race was a signal for Canada to get going. At the moment she was hurdling so well H. Webster of Canada, was running into an unassailable lead in the Marathon.

LONG JUMP FOR RICHARDSON

Sam Richardson, the coloured, happy-faced, long jumper, then jumped 23ft 2in. This qualified him for the three final jumps, and at that juncture he was only 1 ½in behind John Luckhoff, of South Africa.

Being only 17 years old, Richardson revelled in the extra trial. He added a little of 4in to his qualifying jump and won the event. Luckhoff could not improve. In fairness to him it should be said that he only came to the long jump after a succession of highly creditable javelin throws, one of which gained him third place. The second was also won by a South African – the great H.B. Hart.

MARATHON FOR CANADA

D. McL. Wright, of Scotland, made a plucky attempt to hold the Empire Marathon, which he won in Canada. But his countryman, D. McNab Robertson, was too good for him. Better than both, however, was H. Webster, of Canada.

Tanned – with a face like granite – he imperturbably trotted the final two laps in the Stadium amid tumultuous applause, and when he had broken the tape there was still no sign of Robertson.

The new way of running this race at the White City – starting there with four laps and ending with two – is a good one. P. Kelly, of Newfoundland, led the field for the first four laps. He is a curious runner, with a short uneasy motion. Observing the runners separately, he appeared to be going slower than anyone, but there he was, definitely in the lead.

Kelly continued this defiant progress, and led the field towards Hayes and Southall.

### THE FINAL PLACINGS

| MEN | Firsts | Seconds | Thirds |
|---|---|---|---|
| England | 10 | 6 | 9 |
| Canada | 4 | 8 | 0 |
| South Africa | 3 | 5 | 1 |
| Scotland | 1 | 1 | 7 |
| Australia | 1 | 1 | 2 |
| British Guiana | 1 | 0 | 0 |
| New Zealand | 1 | 0 | 1 |
| Jamaica | 0 | 0 | 1 |
| **WOMEN** | | | |
| England | 6 | 3 | 6 |
| South Africa | 2 | 0 | 0 |
| Canada | 1 | 6 | 1 |
| Scotland | 0 | 0 | 1 |
| Rhodesia | 0 | 0 | 1 |

After 15 miles blistered feet forced him to retire, and Webster went strongly into the lead.

Robertson, the favourite, now moved up into second place, but although still in that position at 20 miles it was with consternation that we heard he was more than 2 ½ min behind the Canadian.

The Scot could not close the gap; Webster widened it instead, and won by 4 ½ min in the fine time of 2h 40min 36sec for the 26 miles 385 yards which constitute the Marathon.

**(August 8)**

# ANOTHER TRIUMPH FOR CAMBRIDGE

Cambridge on Saturday proved the quality of their crew by winning the boat race in record time of 18min. 3sec by 4 ¼ lengths. Their luck, which is becoming traditional, held at all points. It was the Light Blues' eleventh successive victory.

In spite of gale warning the weather conditions, if not perfect for fast time, were moderate, and at no stage of the course was the water rough enough to disturb a crew which must go down in history as one of the very best that has ever been seen on the tideway.

Oxford have no reason to be dissatisfied. Their crew had met with as much misfortune in the last weeks of practice as any crew could possibly sustain, and if they are accepted as the ideal pacemakers to a wonderful crew, that is a rôle it is no dishonour to fill. They were fast enough to make Cambridge give us of their best, and they rowed throughout the race with the greatest gallantry and persistence.

When they were beaten, as I feared they would be, just off Harrods – the point where Cambridge have in recent years made a habit of gaining their victories – they looked as if at any moment they might crack and go to pieces, but they never did, and the long spurt which Sutcliffe started at the bottom of the Duke's Meadows and maintained until the end of the course was one of the best feats of a beaten crew ever achieved in the long history of the race.

**(March 19)**

# WINDSOR LAD WINS THE DERBY

**Windsor Lad, the Maharaja of Rajpipla (15-2) ... ... 1**
**Easton, Lord Woolavington (100-9) 2**
**Colombo, Lord Glanely (11-8) ... 3**

The King and Queen were present at Epsom yesterday to see the Maharaja of Rajpipla's Windsor Lad win one of the most exciting Derbys of recent years. The time equalled the record set up last year.

The hot favourite, Lord Glanely's Colombo, finished third, a neck behind Easton, the mount of Gordon Richards.

After the long drought it was very disappointing to the great crowd that showers fell during the day, but fortunately the rain was not sufficient to interfere with the big race.

Their Majesties, with the Duke and Duchess of York, the Princess Royal and the Earl of Harewood, the Duke of Gloucester and King George of Greece, drove to the course in cars. They were received by the Earl of Lonsdale, the Earl of Rosebery and the Marquis of Crewe.

The Prince of Wales and Prince George arrived just before the second race.

The King sent for the Maharaja, who was conducted to the Royal box, congratulated him on his win, and chatted with him for several minutes.

The King gave his usual Derby Day dinner at Buckingham Palace last night to members of the Jockey Club. About fifty guests, including the Prince of Wales and other male members of the Royal Family, attended the dinner given in the State dining-room at the Palace.

THE ELEPHANT'S BOW

A young elephant wearing a garland in the purple and cream colours of Windsor Lad's owner played a prominent part in last night's festivities. Shortly after midnight the elephant and her trainer made their appearance on the floor of the Savoy Restaurant, where the Maharaja was entertaining forty guests to celebrate his horse's victory.

Proceeding in solemn measure round the floor, the elephant made obeisance opposite the table where the Maharaja was sitting, and then marched off amid rousing cheers. The elephant had been specially introduced into the cabaret as a compliment to the Maharaja.

**(June 7)**

GOLDEN MILLER being led in after winning the Grand National by five lengths, and setting a new time record.

# WOMAN WINS THE "NATIONAL"

## GOLDEN MILLER MAKES RACING HISTORY

**1 – GOLDEN MILLER (8-1)**
**2 – DELANEIGE (100-7)**
**2 – THOMOND II. (18-1)**

For the second year in succession victory in the Grand National Steeplechase, run at Aintree yesterday, has been won by a woman owner – Miss Dorothy Paget.

A year ago Mrs. Ambrose Clarke's Kellsboro' Jack made racing history by winning in record time.

Yesterday Golden Miller created a new time record for the race – 9min 20 2-5sec.

Miss Paget's victory was immensely popular amongst the crowd, and heartier cheers have not been heard at Aintree for many a day than those which went up as she proudly led her horse to the unsaddling enclosure.

There she was congratulated by the Earl of Lonsdale, and her father, Lord Queenborough, while police kept back the surging crowd.

CHEERS FOR MISS PAGET

"Three cheers for Miss Paget" shouted an onlooker, and cheers – an unusual gesture in the paddock – were given with great heartiness.

Miss Paget's rise to fame in the racing world has been almost meteoric. Five years ago her name was unknown as an owner. Then she began to get together the string which Mr. A.B. Briscoe now trains for her at Newmarket.

She has made many judicious purchases, but Golden Miller has been the most successful of them all. Miss Paget bought the horse three years ago from the late Mr. P.M. Carr – father of the Notts cricketer.

Miss Paget is one of the wealthiest women in England. Her grandfather was the late Mr. W.C. Whitney, the American millionaire, and her father, Lord Queenborough, is a director of several vast commercial concerns in the U.S.A.

# GOLDEN GRIST

## WHAT THE MILLER COST "THE BOOK"

The only people depressed by the results are the bookmakers. They claim to have been hit more heavily than by any important race in recent years.

Golden Miller was backed heavily all over the country, and, linked with Play On, the winner of the Lincolnshire, has brought fortune to many "doublers." Two recent doubles accepted by a big firm at Turf commission agents were £13,500 to £50 and £11,250 to £50.

Among the small backers Play On and Golden Miller was the popular doubles choice. "There have been more doubles won on these two horses than I can remember in the whole of my career as a bookmaker," said one of the fraternity after the race. "We have lost thousands of pounds."

**(March 24)**

# WORLD FOOTBALL TITLE FOR ITALY

ROME, Sunday.

Scenes of frenzied excitement were enacted here to-day when Italy won the world football championship, beating Czechoslovakia by 2 goals to 1.

The score was 1-1 at full time. In the sixth minute of extra time, which was punctuated by the shouts of 60,000 Italians and the cheers of 7,000 Czechs, Schiavio, the Italian, scored the decisive goal.

The Italian and the Fascist militia had hard work in keeping order, the Czechs protesting that it was an unfair goal and the Italians wildly cheering their side. Hand-to-hand fighting broke out all over the stadium.

**(June 11)**

# ARSENAL CHAMPION AND CHELSEA SAFE

## NEWCASTLE UNITED FALL

**By The Pivot**

NOT often does the curtain fall on a season's soccer with so many of its championship and relegation problems settled.

The most eventful of all post-war seasons comes to a close next Saturday, but already we know that Arsenal, Grimsby and Norwich City are champions of their divisions, and that Newcastle United and Sheffield United are relegated to the Second Division; that Lincoln go back to the Third Division, and Bournemouth, Cardiff City, Rotherham and Rochdale, if they wish to retain their Third Division membership, must apply for re-admission.

The excitement next Saturday is confined to the promotion and relegation question in the Second Division, and the championship of the Northern section of the Third Division.

ARSENAL'S "AWAY" RECORD

Arsenal are champions of the First Division because during the campaign they won 25 points on the grounds of opponents. They had their bad patches, but they pulled out that something extra which counts in the crisis of a race. No one will accuse them of being unworthy champions.

The writing has been on the wall for Sheffield United ever since they fell to the temptation to transfer Dunne to Arsenal. It is the irony of fate that the player whom the United missed so seriously, was not able to hold his place in Arsenal's League team.

Newcastle United's fall after 35 years in the First Division is a grim reminder of the changing fortunes of the game. Cup-winners two seasons ago, and the nucleus of that great team still in the field! A few weeks ago no one dreamed of associating them with relegation. There were at least six clubs in greater danger.

CHELSEA'S DRAMATIC RECOVERY

The point Chelsea gained from their draw with the Arsenal before a crowd of 65,000 at Stamford Bridge completed one of the most dramatic recoveries from a seemingly hopeless position at the foot of the table I can recall for many years. The club won thirteen of the last sixteen points played for.

As Arsenal also needed one point from Saturday's match to make sure of the championship, there will be the inevitable whispering – but not by those who witnessed a game fought out like a cup-tie between deadly rivals from beginning to end.

Chelsea have had many such narrow escapes without learning the obvious lesson. A club with their resources ought not to be eternally struggling to keep their First Division status.

**(April 30)**

# MR. S.F. ROUS APPOINTED F.A. SECRETARY

## STARTING SALARY OF £800

As forecast in The Daily Telegraph, Mr. S.F. Rous, the referee of last season's F.A. Cup final, has been appointed secretary of the Football Association in succession to Sir Frederick Wall.

The appointment was made at yesterday's meeting of the F.A.

Mr. Rous, whose salary will be £800 a year, rising to £1,500, is 39 years of age. Educated at Beccles School and University College, Exeter, he has been assistant master and games master at Watford Grammar School since 1921.

His wide knowledge of the game on the Continent – he has taken charge of many important games there – will assist in the maintenance of a good understanding between football in England and abroad.

Among the many offices held by Mr. Rous in English football are: President of the Referees' Association, representative of Hertfordshire on the F.A. Council, and honorary referees' secretary to the Isthmian League.

**(June 5)**

# COTTON NEARLY ROBBED OF GREAT TRIUMPH

**By George Greenwood**

SANDWICH, Friday.

Henry Cotton, Englishman, 27 years of age, professional at the Waterloo Club, Brussels, won the Open Golf Championship at Royal St. George's to-day with a score of 283, which equals the record established two years ago by Gene Sarazen.

Cotton has thus broken the American monopoly of the championship which has existed for eleven years.

Second was the South African champion, S.F. Brews, with 288. A.H. Padgham, of Sundridge Park, was third with 290, and then the Americans, Macdonald, Smith and Joe Kirkwood, tied for fourth place with the Frenchman, M. Dallemagne, at 292.

"I am thrilled that I have won, and delighted that I am the first British player to win after all these years." said Cotton to me on returning to the clubhouse.

He was obviously very exhausted, not so much because of the strain of playing six consecutive rounds in magical figures, but because of a temporary feeling of sickness.

After this morning's round he went back to his hotel and ate his lunch much too hurriedly. As the fatal last round progressed he was attacked by acute pains, and it was as much as he could do to keep going.

At one stage the prospect of disaster was imminent, but he took a grip of himself and the crisis was successfully surmounted.

PRACTICE IN A GARAGE

Cotton's career as a golfer is not without romance. Apart from a lesson and hints on essentials which I gave him as a boy, he is entirely self-taught. No man has ever worked harder to attain proficiency, and in his father's garage at Dulwich, with a mattress against the wall, he practised five hours every day hitting golf balls in the attempt to perfect the swing.

It can be said that no golfer, British or American, has a smoother, a more perfectly controlled, or a more beautifully timed movement. Success has at last come to a young man who once told me: "Some day I will win the championship. It is my dream to become as good as Bobby Jones, though that is asking a lot, I know." The future will decide this point.

It was intended that on leaving Alleyn's, Dulwich, Cotton should go into civil engineering, but golf had gripped him like a fever. He took the plunge into professionalism, first of all going as assistant to the Fulwell Club and then to Rye.

There have been occasions in Cotton's career when he has fallen foul of public opinion and of his brother professionals. This has been lived down, and his wonderful reception to-day when acclaimed the new champion shows that he is a popular figure in the game. He has cut his own path and has travelled it with courage.

Cotton will undoubtedly find a shower of money poured into his lap if the experience of former champions is any criterion. Bobby Jones is estimated to have realised nearly £100,000, having received at least £24,000 from Warner Brothers; of Hollywood, for his famous series of golfing shots. He received perhaps £5,000 a year from syndicated articles, and in addition has a five-year contract with a sports equipment firm at a salary believed to be at least £3,000 a year.

**(June 30)**

# £8,000,000 TRAFFIC TUNNEL UNDER THE RIVER MERSEY

(Above) ONE OF THE JUNCTIONS in the £8,000,000 Mersey Tunnel. The tunnel, which is to be known as Queensway, is 2.13 miles in length and wide enough to accomodate four lines of traffic. The road surface is of cast-iron setts and the lighting is specially designed to aviod glare.

(Left) THE OFFICIAL OPENING performed by the King.

THE CONSTRUCTION of a trans-oceanic seaplane (right) capable of carrying over 200 people, in addition to freight, at 187 m.p.h. is projected in Germany. This is a considerable advance on DO-x, hitherto the largest passenger carrying seaplane. DO-x carries 59 people and has a servicable speed of 115 m.p.h. The cross-section shown suggest the allocation of space. At 200 m.p.h. the machine would fly from Southampton to New York in under 15 hours!

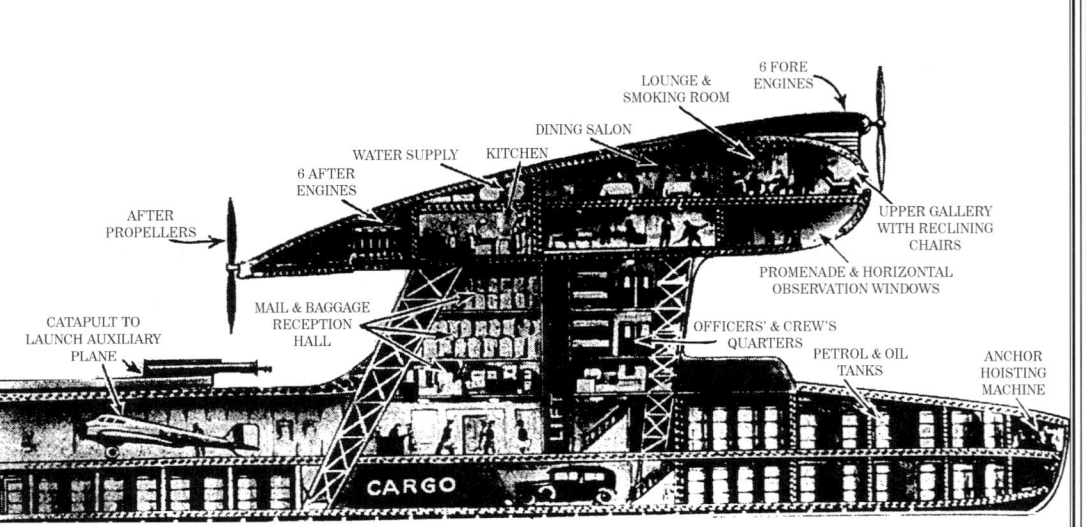

THE FIRST PICTURE wirelessed direct to London from Australia — a distance of 11,000 miles, which is 4,000 miles further than any previous telegraphed picture. It was printed in London 25 minutes after being handed in at Melbourne. The picture, which is reproduced exactly as received, shows the Duke of Gloucester, who is touring Australia, holding two bears.

PU YI AS EMPEROR of the puppey state of "Manchukuo".

## THE QUEEN MARY LAUNCHED

SEEN THROUGH THE RAIN, she made a splendid spectacle as she rode the water for the first time.

# 1935

After months of diplomatic manoeuvring, Italian troops finally crossed the Abyssinian borders, pitting their tanks against the spears of the tribesmen. This was the first of the Fascist aggressions and the first that tested the powers of the League of Nations as a peace-keeping force. Sanctions were imposed against Italy but they had little effect. The attempts of Sir Samuel Hoare and Pierre Laval, the foreign secretaries of Britain and France respectively, to end the war with a pact very much in Italy's favour caused dismay in both their countries. Sir Samuel Hoare was forced to resign as a result.

Germany re-occupied the Saar territories which had been taken from her at the end of the Great War after a plebiscite had shown an overwhelming desire by the people living there to return to their homeland. This, said Hitler, for the first time but by no means the last, was the end of his territorial ambitions.

The British rejoiced in their first state occasion since the Great War when, with due splendour, King George V celebrated his Silver Jubilee. The first test of the strength for the National Government came with an autumn general election called by Stanley Baldwin who had taken over as prime minister from the tired and ailing Ramsay MacDonald. The Government was returned with a substantial but reduced majority. Both MacDonald and his son, Malcolm, who was Colonial Secretary in the National Government, lost their parliamentary seats. Clement Attlee, the most moderate of the candidates, took over as leader of the Labour Party.

Millions of Britons took part in a "peace ballot" organised by the League of Nations Union which showed a huge majority in favour of disarmament. Despite this, the government announced plans for expanding the army and the R.A.F. The majority of the old cavalry regiments were to be mechanised.

In the United States, the opening of the Boulder Dam became a symbol of President Roosevelt's recovery programme. Huey Long, the demagogue state governor and, later, senator for Louisiana was shot dead. Three years after the crime, Bruno Hauptmann was found guilty of the kidnapping and murder of the Lindbergh baby.

T.E. Lawrence of Arabia was fatally injured in a motor-cycle accident. Queen Astrid of the Belgians died after she had been thrown out of a car being driven by her husband. Earl Jellicoe who had commanded the Royal Navy during much of the Great War died as did Lord Carson, the brilliant advocate and campaigner for Ulster's separate identity.

The cinema, visited by millions every week, showed another step forward when the first full-length colour film, *Becky Sharp*, was screened. The greatest theatre success was a performance of *Romeo and Juliet* in which John Gielguid and Laurence Olivier exchanged the roles of Romeo and Mercutio for different performances.

The continued failure of the English cricket team caused questions to be asked at Lord's but there were moments of triumph when the Welsh rugby team defeated the All Blacks and when the English football team beat a German team which, to the astonishment of the Wembley crowd, gave a Nazi salute before the match.

NEW CABINET TO-DAY



# The Daily Telegraph



To-Days Weather : Dull, Rain at times

Broadcasting: Page Eight

No. 24,971 POSTAGE { INLAND, CANADA AND NEWFOUNDLAND, THREE HALFPENCE; OTHER COLONIES AND PLACES ABROAD, TWOPENCE } LONDON, FRIDAY, JUNE 7, 1935 ONE PENNY

*BIRTHS, MARRIAGES and DEATHS as a line "IN MEMORIAM" notices 3s a line. (Special rate for five or ten years automatic insertion on application). Announcements authenticated by name and address of sender, may be sent to The Daily Telegraph, Fleet-st., E.C. 4 or 161 Piccadilly, E. 1 or telephoned to Central 4242.*

## BIRTHS

ALERS HANKEY – On June 4, 1935, at The Cottage, Castle Eden, to Penelope (née Longden), wife of Lieut. Com. C.B. Alers Hankey, R.N. a daughter.

BARLOW – On June 4, 1935, at Sherborne, to Margaret (née Carey), wife of Ralph M.M. Barlow, a son.

BRADFORD – On June 4, 1935, at Hendford Cottage, Yeovil, Somerset, to Christine Margaret (Peggy), wife of Philip R. Bradford, a daughter.

CURNOW – On June 5, 1935, at Crossway, Sapcote-road, Burbage, Leicestershire, to Doris (née Behr), wife of Cecil Curnow, a daughter (Ann Elizabeth Marguerite).

HALL – On June 4, 1935, at Courtlands, Walmer, to Cynthia, wife of James S. Hall, M.B., F.R.C.S.E. a daughter.

JACKSON – On June 5, 1935, to Mary (née Yates), wife of Arthur R. Jackson, of Rushton, Oaklands-avenue, Esher, a daughter (Susan Ann).

MILLS – On June 4, 1935, to Dr. and Mrs. J. Denholm-Mills, of Shortlands, Seaford, a son.

ORR – On June 4, 1935, at Redlands, Glasgow, to Rachel, wife of A.T. Orr, M.A., D.Sc., a son.

PUXON – On June 3, 1935, at Aldeby Lodge, West Bergholt, Essex, to Freda (née Atkinson), wife of F.E.M. Puxon, a daughter.

QUINN – On June 5, 1935, to Gladys, wife of Gerald Quinn, a son.

TERRY – On June 4, 1935, in Cyprus, to Leonie, wife of Lieutenant R.E. Terry, R.N., H.M.S. Ormonde, a daughter.

## MARRIAGES

CURTIS-ROSE – On June 6, 1935 Harold Curtis elder son of the late Mr. Siegmond Cohen and Mrs. Boss Price, to Katherine Rose, daughter of the late Mr. and Mrs. Samuel Rose of Philadelphia.

FERRO-O'HANLON – On June 4, 1935, at Nether Alderley Church, Cheshire Rolf Thornton Ferro, only son of Mr. and Mrs. W.K. Ferro, of Horsforth, Yorkshire, to Joan O'Hanlon, only daughter of Mr. and Mrs. H.D. O'Hanlon, of Alderley Edge, Cheshire.

FOX-FARQUHARSON – On June 4, 1935, at St. Peter's Church, Broadstairs, Captain Percy Russell Halton Fox. The Buffs, son of Sir Harry Fox, K.B.E., C.M.G., of Corlismore, Broadstairs, to Mary Jeannette, daughter of Mrs. Fahquharson, of Greenwood, Keith, Banffshire.

KITCHIN-POULTON – On June 5, 1935, at St. Michael's Church, Wandsworth Common, by the Rev. Kitchin, 4 Westcliffe-gardens, Westbrook, Margate, and the late Dr. E.S. Kitchin, to Marjorie Ada, only daughter of Mr. and Mrs. E.M. Poulton, 2A Broomwood-road, S.W.11.

STERN-GILDARD – On June 4, 1935, at St. Columba's, Pont-street, by the Rev. Archibald Fleming, D.D. David Michael Stern, F.R.C.S. elder son of Dr. and Mrs. A.L. Stern of 1 Dollis Hill-lane, N.W.2. to Eileen Freya Macleod, second daughter of the late Mr. J. Graham Gildard, of Glasgow, and Mrs. Gildard, of 17a Frognal, N.W.3.

ZWANENBERG-PYKE – On June 4, 1935, at Windlesham Parish Church, Jack Maurice Zwanenberg, younger son of Mr. and Mrs. F. Zwanenberg, of 38 Hanover Gate-mansions, N.W.1. to Rosemary Joyce Pyke, younger daughter of Mr. Arthur Pyke, of Westwoods, Windlesham.

## DEATHS

ALDRITT – On June 5, 1935, suddenly. William Bernard Aldritt of Highfields, Shanklin, aged 65. Funeral to-morrow (Saturday), 2.30. No mourning.

ANDERSON – On June 4, 1935, at The Spinney, Runfold, Elsie Ramsay, the dear wife of Alexander Anderson. Funeral private. No flowers.

BROWN – On June 5, 1935, William Brown, of 47 Klea-avenue, Clapham, and Robert Brown and Co. Engineers, 119 Oakley-street, S.E.1. aged 75 years. Funeral on Tuesday, at Church of Holy Spirit , Narbonne-avenue. Clapham at two p.m.

CANTER – On June 6, 1935, at 81 Newman-street, W.1. Sarah Pearl, the dearly loved wife of Lewis Canter. Funeral Sunday next at ten a.m. Willesden Cemetery.

CHIGNELL – On June 5, 1835, at Muswell Hill, Nella, widow of Harry Chignell. Madras papers please copy.

COURTAULD – On June 5, 1935, at Knights, Colne Engaine, Essex, Katherine Mina, eldest daughter of the late George Courtauld of Gosfield, in her 79th year. Service at Colne Engaine, to-morrow (Saturday, June 8), at eleven o'clock.

CROOCKEWIT – On June 5, 1935, at 32 Leyburne-road, Dover. John Henry Croockewit, aged 85.

CRUSOE – On June 6, 1935, Horatio Charles, dearly loved husband of Ethel Crusoe, Crafnant, Sidcup, and younger son of the late George Crusoe, formerly of Gibraltar, and Lucy Crusoe, of Bromley, Kent, aged 67 years. Dearly loved and deeply mourned by his wife, children, mother and brother. Chislehurst Cemetery 3.30 p.m. to-morrow (Saturday, June 8).

CUFF – On June 5, 1935 at Eltham, Anne H. Cuff, widow of Sidney H. Cuff. Funeral at Eltham Parish Church to-day (Friday), at 10.30 a.m. Will all except close personal friends please give a donation, instead of flowers, to the Woolwich War Memorial Hospital Extension Fund.

DIPNALL – On June 5, 1935, at 28, Cranes-drive, Surbiton, Edward Arthur Dipnall, beloved husband of Lily H. Dipnall, aged 77.

DRAPER – On June 5, 1935 at 30 Bramham-gardens, S.W.5. Ida, widow of Herbert Draper and beloved mother of Yvonne Draper. Funeral St. Stephen's Gloucester-road, to-day (Friday), 2.30.

GEE – On Wednesday, June 5, 1935, at 25, St. John's-road, Putney, the Rev. Richard Gee, dearly loved husband of Annie Rhoda Gee, and late Vicar of Olney and formerly Principal of Bishop's College, Calcutta. Funeral service at St. John's Church, Putney to-day (Friday), at four p.m. followed by burial at Putney Vale Cemetery, 4.45.

## PERSONAL

*5s. per line (minimum 2 lines). Trade 12/6 per line. Lost and Found 2s. 6d. per line.*

SIGNALS OF DISTRESS from sinking vessels are always answered swiftly. This is a signal of distress on behalf of British Sailors sinking into destination through compulsory unemployment. Will you come to their rescue? Enable us to supply shelter, food and clothing to such men, and to find them berths, by sending a contribution to THE DESTITUTE SAILORS FUND (founded 1827), Dock-street, London Docks, E.1. President: H.R.H. Duke of Kent K.G.

KING'S COLLEGE TAUNTON THE SCHOLARSHIP EXAMINATION this year will be held on JULY 4 and 5. Six scholarships, including one for Music, value £80 to £15. will be awarded. – Apply Secretary.

ALTHOUGH THE DERBY IS OVER, the "Whitsuntide Races" will to-day and to-morrow be in full swing. Across country Point to Point sort of affairs … plenty of hurdles and obstacles to be overcome in the shape of crowded trains, 30 mile limits … and then an hotel. "Sorry, but we're full up." The best chance of being sure of running in to "a place" is by ringing now. Worthing 2222.
WARNES, WORTHING,
The Hotel of Pleasant Surprises.
and say, "Any rooms left for Whitsun?" A.R.C.

THE Twenty-fourth Celebration of ALEXANDRA DAY will take place on Wednesday, 12th June. Will all helpers and those who can lend cars please communicate with Miss C. May Beeman, C.B.E., 33, The Grove, The Boltons, S.W.10.

VISCOUNTESS RIDLEY urgently appeals for your support of the work which the Babies' Hospital, Newcastle-on-Tyne, is doing for the Sick Babies in the areas of Tyneside and Durham – Please send a donation addressed to her at the Babies' Hospital, Newcastle-on-Tyne, 4.

"WHY YOU SHOULD NOT DYE GREY HAIR."Write for interesting free folder and learn how "Restorene" restores grey hair to natural colour, "Restorene" – month's treatment 8s post free. Also 4s 6d bottle. – THE RESTORENE CO., Dept. N., 23 Haymarket, London S.W.1.

FOURTEEN DAYS' HOLIDAY for ONE POUND seems absurd; but it is a fact that we can send a needy or ailing London child to seaside or country for a fortnight for this sum. Please help us.
THE CHILDREN'S FRESH AIR MISSION (Box 2).
75, Lamb's Conduit-street, W.C.1.
President: The Marquess of Northampton.
Treasurer: Ralph C. Hazell, Esq.

NATURAL HISTORY – Do you know that if you periodically send one of BURBERRYS' WEATHERPROOFS to be cleaned and renovated at their Reading Laboratories it has as many lives as a cat?

COVENT GARDEN. – One or two SEATS REQUIRED Saturday, June 8. – Purley 657.

WILL MEMBERS of the WINE and FOOD SOCIETY visiting the Hind's Head Hotel, Bray-on-Thames, please MAKE THEMSELVES KNOWN on arrival in order to obtain benefit of their membership. – Mine Host, Barry Neame, Maidenhead 567.

AMERICAN (cultured) undertakes private or business mission. – See Situations Wanted.

DON'T LET AGE BAFFLE YOU! Confidential home treatment for wrinkles and scientific rejuvenation without operation. – BM/MHTH, London W.C.1.

DAME CLARA BUTT writes, April 3rd. 1935: "Have received much comfort from the 'QRAY' Dry Compress " This Compress quickly relieves Rheumatism, Lumbago, Arthritis, and other painful disorders. Invaluable in any home. May be hired at nominal cost, and purchased only if completely satisfactory. – For Brochure, free demonstration, &c. write or call, Radium Electric Limited, 2, Stratford-place, Oxford-street, W.1.

DRAMATISTS COACHED and expert advice on all STAGE matters. – Louis Casson, 10, King-st., W.C.2.

UN HOMME QUI NEGLIGE SA REPUTATION est indigne d'en avoir.

PALACE HOTEL, Bloomsbury, W.C.1. Best 5-course Lunch, 2s 6d En Pension from 4 guineas weekly.

MAKE YOUR HOME for 3gns per week at Lexham Gardens Hotel, Kensington. See Page 22.

SOUTH CORNWALL – Spend your Jubilee Holiday at "Beach House," Portloe. On sea edge, bathing from house,farm produce, boating, fishing. June and Sept. 2gns. July and Aug. 2 1/2gns – Finnamore.

CONVALESCENCE. – We are faced with a grave problem down here in Stepney. Many children, in very poor homes, are weak and ailing. Will you aid us in this, our Golden Jubilee Year, to send at least 700 to a Convalescent Home for a fortnight? The cost is 30s for each boy or girl – Contributions to The Rev. Percy Ineson, East End Mission, 583, Commercial-road, Stepney, E.1.

FROM SORDID SLUM to SUN-LIT SEA. BILL and LIZZIE Calling! Please give us poor children a day at the Seaside. 10s will send five. R.S.V.P. – John Pound's Mission, 24, Wellesley-st., Stepney, E.1.

AT WINDSOR (adjoining Castle and Park) there is for SALE a tiny PERIOD HOUSE, combing real old-world charm with modern comfort. Newly built and most exquisitely appointed and furnished. Price, complete. £1,975. – To view, apply 28 Park-street.

PEGGY. – Can't think of dieting this holiday at The Headland Hotel, Newquay. Golf and surf-riding will look after the figure … not to mention dancing. – REX.

MODERN HOMES within EASY REACH of London. Illus. particulars appear on Page 25.

EVERY WOMAN will find a fund of ideas for menus in The Daily Telegraph Cookery Book. Price 1s., obtainable from any newsagent or bookseller.

MONEY! In PAINTING FLOWERS, for cretonnes. £7 7s course by post for £5 5s. Sale dept. – Write B & W Studios, 107, Fleet-st., E.C.4.

## PERSONAL (cont.)

GENTLEMAN well known in lawn tennis circles, would like to spend a week or two in a private house or houses away from London. Distance no object, coaching young players between the ages of 14-24. Twenty per cent. improvement in play guaranteed after a week. Very moderate terms. – Apply W.A., 66, Warminster-road, S.E. 25.

STAMMERING CURED by Mr. A.C. Schnelle, 119, Bedford Court Mansions, W.C.1. Established 1905.

BRILLIANT SALES MANAGER, organiser and profit-earner is available for appointment. – Write B. Box 3,908. Daily Telegraph E.C.4.

TENNIS, Golf, Badminton, Squash: lessons 5s. club 2gns. – Fulham-road and Marble Arch. – Put. 7654.

BRENT BRIDGE HOTEL, Golders Green, London. N.W.4. Tel. Hendon 8171. Lunch, 2s 6d; dinner 4s. Every Sat. dinner and dance, 5s; dancing only 3s. Best dance floor in London. Excellent cabaret 10 p.m.

A WELL-PREPARED MIND hopes in adversity and fears in prosperity. Horace.

NAVAL REVIEW – Following the success of the announcement of our De Luxe Day Cruise, we have arranged the additional charter of the Golden Arrow Cross Channel Steamer, T.S.S. Canterbury. – Apply at once, Hickie Borman Grant Ltd., 25 Cockspur-street, S.W.1. Whitehall 2094.

WHITSUN IN SUNNY CORNWALL. THE ideal Surroundings for a perfect week-end are to be found at KENEGIE HOTEL, GULVAL, PENZANCE.

A Tudor Mansion with modern equipment and comfort, overlooking Mount's Bay, 'Phone Park 2412, or write 112, Oxford-gardens, W.10. for particulars.

YOUR SON'S CAREER. – LET HIM FARM IN SOUTH AFRICA. Land and labour are cheap. Free training. Capital required only when settler is trained experienced and feels assured of his future prospects. – Write Dept. D.T.J. 7, 1820 Memorial Settlers' Association, 199, Piccadilly, London. W.1.

DOCTORS, Matrons, and Nurses interested in an effective, naturally-acting fruit laxative are asked to write to Prunol Produce Ltd., Dept. D.T. 2, 21, Cockspur-street, London S.W.1. for a free sample of PRUNOL CRYSTALLISED PASTILLES.

MONEY! IF YOU PAINT FLOWERS, make designs for machine-printed, cretonnes, &c. Postal tuition and sales service. 1 day's sales exceeded £200. – Write K. 38, The Textile Studio, 352a, Station-road, Harrow.

A BANKNOTE or CHEQUE for Whitsun, Sell your old Gold, Jewellery, Diamonds, Sovereigns, Silver Plate, &c. £1-£50,000. – HARRIS & CO., 37 Piccadilly, W.

ALL THINGS ARE FOR YOUR SAKES, that the abundant grace might through the thanksgiving of many redound to the glory of God. II. Corinthians iv. 15.

IF YOU FEEL that you cannot possible help now, will you not consider leaving a legacy for Brompton Hospital, to help it in its efforts to free the world from the scourge of tuberculosis? Will you think it over and write to the Secretary, Brompton Hospital, London, S.W.3?

DO YOU WANT to write to your M.P.? Where does he live? Who is he? This and many other questions are answered by KELLY'S HANDBOOK (price £2), which will also give you his biography, as well as about 30,000 others of the titled, landed and official classes. – Kelly's Directories Ltd., 2, Arundel-street, W.C.2.

GUY'S is on the Danger List. Please help by sending a Contribution to the Treasurer, Guy's Hospital, S.E.1.

JUST THE PRICE OF A NEW HAT will give a whole glorious fortnight of holiday to some poor or crippled child. ONE GUINEA from you means two weeks by the sea or in the country for a child who needs it badly. Send your donation to-day.

SHAFTESBURY SOCIETY and R.S.U. John Kirk House, 32, John-street, W.C.1.

WHAT'S NEW in Curtain Materials? EILEEN HUNTER FABRICS. 16, Grafton-street, W.1. REGent 1297. FROM ALL LEADING DECORATORS.

"WHY FIGHT SHY OF Sunbathing? A little hair is no excuse these days. This new Wax Treatment by Phyllis Earle fairly whisks it away – and it won't grow again for ages." Home outfit 5/6 – Phyllis Earle Ltd., 32, Dover-street, Mayfair. W.1. Regent 7541.

ECONOMISE LUXURIOUSLY by taking one of these Ultra-Modern FLATS at Fountain Court, Buckingham Palace-road, S.W.1. Inclusive rentals from £115 per annum. Restaurant and service optional. – Call, write, or 'phone (Sloane 0171).

*"O give me ears, that I may ever hear*
*The mystic melody, without, within:*
*Help me to trace the notes so sweet and clear*
*Of angel's song, 'mid earth's discordant din."*

THE above is an extract from "A Few Picked Gems," which contains delightful poems and other writings. Obtainable, price 1s. postage paid, from Eagle Press, 170, Church-rd., Hove, Sussex, or through the Eagle Press, from any bookseller. Open this little book where you will, and you will find something beautiful.

20, CHARLES-ST., MAYFAIR, – TWO FLATS, redecorated, Central heating. Rents £350 and £300 p.a. – Apply on premises.

GENTLEMEN, are you tired of so-called smart clothes that are as uncomfortable as they are shapeless – trousers that are murderous after an hour's motor-car ride; a coat collar that either knocks your hat off or wallows in waves and ridges. If so, give me a trial and experience the real lasting delight of a West End suit, and all for £6 6s 0d. cash – you don't even pay that unless I please you. – Major Daniell Ltd., 174, New Bond Street, W.1.

IT SHOULD NOT be a strange experience for mothers and children to enjoy the health-giving sea air, and yet it is. Do you realise that many poor slum-dwellers have never even seen the sea and the golden sands? Surely you will gladly make some little sacrifice to give a mother and her children two weeks at the sea. It will cost £5.

– Cheques, &c. Preb. Carlile,

"My Gift," Church Army, 55, Bryanston-street, W.1.

## PERSONAL (cont.)

AN opportunity offers for an Hotelier to secure an old established HOTEL, with wonderful connection, on the favourite Thanet Coast. Absolutely unique position in Cliftonville. 80 bed rooms and exceptional lounges, including ball room. Full residential hotel licence. Very favourable lease. Satisfactory figures for years. Family reasons for disposal. £6,000 or near offer for quick sale. – R. c.o. Hotels, 69, Fleet-street, London.

SMALL SELF-CONTAINED FLAT WANTED, furnished or unfurnished. Rent must be moderate. – Write S., Box 10,343. Daily Telegraph, 161 Piccadilly, W.1.

KEEP IN TOUCH when on the Continent. – Order The Daily Telegraph to be delivered to you each day. – Paris Office, 11, Rue Bolssy d'Anglas.

## FINANCIAL NOTICES

MEXICO TRAMWAYS COMPANY
(Incorporated in Canada with limited liability,)
NOTICE of ANNUAL GENERAL MEETING.

NOTICE IS HEREBY GIVEN that the ANNUAL GENERAL MEETING of the SHAREHOLDERS of Mexico Tramways Company will be held at the HEAD OFFICE of the Company, in the Canadian Bank of Commerce Building (20th Floor), 25, KING-STREET WEST, in the CITY of TORONTO, CANADA, on SATURDAY, the 29th day of June, 1935, at the hour of half-past eleven o'clock in the forenoon (daylight saving time), for the purpose of:

(1) Approving the consolidated balance-sheet as at the 31st December, 1934;
(2) Receiving and approving the report of the board of directors;
(3) The election of directors; and
(4) The transaction of such other business as may be transacted at a general meeting.

By Order of the Board,
R.H. MERRY, Secretary.
6th June, 1935.
25, King-street West, Toronto 2, Canada,

Copies of the accounts and annual report for the year 1934 can be obtained at the London agents of the company, Canadian and General Finance Company Limited, 3, London-wall buildings, London, E.C.2.

## CONCERTS, &C.

GLYNDEBOURNE FESTIVAL OPERA HOSUE,
Lewes, Sussex.
ORCHESTRAL CONCERT
SUNDAY NEXT, June 9th, at 3.30 p.m.
**SYMPHONY in E flat major (with Drum-roll), Haydn**
(1737-1809, Australian)
Adagio-Allegro con spirito.
Andante.
Menuetto.
Allegro con spirito.
**CONCERTO in G major, K.V. 453 for Pianoforte. Mozart (1756-1791, Austrian)**
with Orchestra.
Allegro.
Andante.
Allegretto
**SYMPHONY in D major, Op. 36 Beethoven (1770-1827**
German (Bonn))
Adagio molto-Allegro con brio
Larghetto.
Scherzo Allegro.
Allegro molto.
Conductor: FRITZ BUSCH Pianoforte: RUDOLF SERKIN
ORCHESTRA STALLS, 12s 6d. incl. Box Office: Ringmer 28 and North 1139.

**ROYAL ALBERT HALL**
JUNE 10th to 22nd inclusive.
EVENINGS at 8 p.m.
SATURDAY MATINEES, at 2.30 p.m.
**THE ROYAL CHORAL SOCIETY**
will present
**"HIAWATHA"**
A DRAMATIC VERSION with SCENERY and COSTUMES.
Arranged and produced by T.C. FAIRBAIRN.
1,000 PERFORMERS
Conductor: Dr. MALCOLM SARGENT.
PRICES: Stalls 10s 6d, Balcony 6s and 5s; Gallery 2s 6d. Boxes £4, £3 4s, and £2 Tickets at the Royal Albert Hall ('phone Kensington 3661) and Agents.

WIGMORE HALL. FRIDAY, JUNE 7, at 5.30.
**LA TOUR LOMAX**
**PIANOFORTE RECITAL.**
Bosendorier Piano. 9s., 6s., 3s. Box-office (Welbeck 2141).

AN ENGAGEMENT of a permanent character will shortly occur for a NOVELTY QUARTET, playing good-class programmes, at a well-known Midland café. – Write, giving full particulars, instruments, past engagements, fees, &c. A., Box 5,804, Daily Telegraph, E.C.4.

## MUSIC, SINGING, ELOCUTION, &C

REQUIRED, AMATEUR INSTRUMENTALISTS and VOCALISTS desiring public appearance. Also clever dancers, – Write R., Box 4,008, Daily Telegraph, E.C.4.

## DANCING

ALICE HALL SCHOOL (Wendy Pearson) – 5 private lessons £1 1s. Dance. TO-NIGHT, 8.30, 3s COURT CURTSEY. – 7, Hanover-st., W.1. May. 6319.

AT CASANI SCHOOL OF BALLROOM DANCING, 90, Regent-street, guarantees to teach you steps of any dance in three private lessons, £1 1s 0d; Court Curtsy, £1 1s 0d. 10 a.m. to 10 p.m. – Regent 4438.

COURT CURTSEY 7 Dancing Less. Expert tuition deportment, Mensendieck method. – RUBY PEELER, Eccleston Hotel, Eccleston-sq., S.W.1. Vic. 5770.

BARBARA DAVIDSON and BETTINA KENT, 83 BAKER-STREET, W.1. (Wel. 9415.) 5 PRIVATE LESSONS £1 1s. PRACTICE CLASSES.

GEM MOUFLET herself teaches 9-9 in PRIVACY, CURTSEY, TAP, Partner to Dances (Nr. Ritz.) – 11 ALBERMARLE-ST., PICCADILLY, REGent 4629.

## SHIPPING & MAINS

**ITALIAN LINES.**
**"ITALIA"**
**EXPRESS SERVICE TO S. AFRICA.**

| From – | Genoa | Marseilles | Gibraltar |
|---|---|---|---|
| s.s. "Giulio Cesare" | June 25 | June 26 | June 28 |
| s.s. "Duilio" | July 23 | July 24 | July 26 |

Sailings every 28 days. Calls: Dakar, Cape Town, Port Elizabeth, Durban, Reduced fares for Holiday Voyages.

**"ITALIA" – COSULICH**
**The SUNNY SOUTHERN ROUTE**
to
**NEW YORK, SOUTH and CENTRAL AMERICA and PACIFIC COAST.**

| To New York | Genoa | Nice | Gibraltar | New York |
|---|---|---|---|---|
| "Roma" | 10 June | 10 June | 13 June | 20 June |
| "Conte di Savoia" | 19 June | 19 June | 21 June | 27 June |
| "Rex" | 28 June | 28 June | 30 June | 6 July |
| "Conte di Savoia" | 12 July | 12 July | 14 July | 20 July |
| To South America | Trieste | Naples | Genoa | B. Aires |
| "Oceania" | 13 June | 15 June – | 1 June | |
| "Neptunia" | 10 July | 12 July | 13 July | 29 July |
| "Augustus" | – | – | 1 Aug. | 16 Aug. |
| "Neptunia" | 28 Aug. | 30 Aug. | 31 Aug. | 16 Sept. |

*Via Brazilian ports.
**REGULAR SAILINGS TO AUSTRALIA**
Particulars on application.

**P. & O. BRITISH INDIA & NEW ZEALAND SHIPPING COMPANIES.**
**MAIL PASSENGER and FREIGHT SERVICES.**
**P. & O. SAILINGS**
(Under Contract. with His Majesty's Government.)
**BOMBAY, COLOMBO, AUSTRALIA.**

| | Ship | Tons. | London | Mar's | Classes |
|---|---|---|---|---|---|
| 2.5 | Corfu | 15,000 | June 14 | June 21 | 1st & 2nd |
| 2.5 | Malola | 21,000 | June 28 | July 5 | 1st & Tourist |
| 2,4,5 | Strath'ird | 22,500 | July 12 | July 19 | 1st & Tourist |

(and fortnightly thereafter)

**BOMBAY, COLOMBO, STRAITS, CHINA, JAPAN.**

| | | | | | |
|---|---|---|---|---|---|
| 1,2,3,5 | Kaisar-i-Hind | 11,500 | June 7 | June 14 | 1st & 2nd |
| 1,2,3,5 | Ranchi | 17,000 | June 21 | June 28 | 1st & 2nd |
| 1,2,3,5 | Naldera | 16,000 | July 5 | July 12 | 1st & 2nd |
| 1,2,3,5 | Ranpura | 17,000 | July 19 | July 26 | 1st & 2nd |

(and fortnightly thereafter.)
Calling (1) Southampton (2) Tangier (3) Malta. (4) Port Sudan. (5) Tranship Bombay for Karachi.

**SPECIAL ROUND VOYAGE TICKETS.**
**AUSTRALIA £140 & £150 1st Class, £112 2nd Class.**
**CHINA and JAPAN £150 1st Class.**
**P. & O. BRANCH SERVICE**
**FAST STEAMERS TO AUSTRALIA.**
Via Malta, Port Said, Suez, Aden and Colombo.
ONE CLASS ONLY From £38 single. £68 return.

| | Tons | London | Plymouth |
|---|---|---|---|
| *BENDIGO | 13,000 | June 7 | June 8 |
| *Balranald | 13,000 | July 5 | July 6 |
| *Baradine | 13,000 | Aug. 2 | Aug. 3 |
| Barrabool | 13,000 | Aug. 30 | Aug. 31 |

*Carrying His Majesty's Mails.

BRITISH INDIA SAILINGS
TO EAST AFRICAN PORTS.

| Ship | Tons | Midsbro | London | Marseilles. |
|---|---|---|---|---|
| *MATIANA | 9,067 | – | – | June 9 |
| *MANTOLA | 9,066 | June 22 | June 29 | July 7 |
| *MALDA | 9,066 | July 20 | July 27 | Aug. 4 |
| *MADURA | 9,077 | Aug. 17 | Aug. 24 | Sept. 1 |

*Calls Tangier.

**P. & O. and B.I. JOINT SERVICE**
**COLOMBO, MADRAS AND CALCUTTA.**

| Ship. | Tons | M'bro. | I'ham | Antwp. | London |
|---|---|---|---|---|---|
| AUSTRALIA | 7,802 | – | – | – | June 8 |
| ✱†MULBERA | | 9,100 | June 15 | | June 17 |
| – | June 22 | | | | |
| LAHORE | 5,804 | June 28 | June 29 | | July 1 |
| July 6 | | | | | |
| †DOMALA | 8,441 | July 13 | July 15– | | July 20 |

† Calls Tangier. * Calls Cochin (passengers only).
P. & O. and B.I.

PASSENGER OFFICES
14, Cockspur-street, S.W.1. (Whitehall 4444).
130, Leadenhall-street, E.C. 3 (Avenue 8000).
Australia House, Strand, W.C.2. (Temple Bar 7924).
FREIGHT OR GENERAL BUSINESS
P. & O. or B.I. Offices, 122, LEADENHALL-ST., E.C.3.
B.I. Agts., Gray, Dawes & Co. 122, Leadenhall-st., E.C.3.

**NEW ZEALAND LINE**
To New Zealand and through bookings to Australia
**VIA PANAMA CANAL.**
†RANGITANE … 17,000 tons … London, June 27
†TANGITATA … 17,000 tons … London, July 25
and thereafter every 28 days.
† First, Tourist & 3rd Class.

Apply N.Z.S. Co. Ltd. Agents (J.B. Westray & Co. Ltd), 138, Leadenhall-street, E.C.3. (Tel. Avenue 5220). or Trans-Pacific Passenger Agency (W.L. James), 14, Cockspur-st., S.W.1. (Tel. Whitehall 2953).

CANADIAN AUSTRALASIAN LINE AND UNION ROYAL MAIL LINE
To NEW ZEALAND and AUSTRALIA.
By any Atlantic Line to Canada or U.S.A.
Thence via VANCOUVER or SAN FRANCISCO.

| Ship. | †From Vancouver. | *From San Francisco |
|---|---|---|
| AORANGI | June 19 | – |
| MAKURA | – | July 3 |
| NIAGARA | July 17 | – |
| MAUNGANUI | – | July 31 |

†Canadian Australasian Line. via Honolulu, Fiji and Auckland to Sydney. *Union Royal Mail Line, via Tahiti, Rarotonga, Wellington to Sydney.

Apply the Trans-Pacific Passenger Agency Ltd. (W.L. James General Manager), 14, Cockspur-st. (1st floor), London, S.W.1. (Tel. Whitehall 2953), or for Vancouver. Service any office of the Canadian Railways.

NEW ZEALAND Via Panama Canal.
THROUGH BOOKINGS TO AUSTRALIA.
CABIN CLASS and TOURIST CLASS Mail Steamers.
†TAMAROA … (Cabin Class), London, June 14
†MATAROA … (Cabin Class), Southampton, Aug. 10
†AKAROA … (Cabin Class), Southampton, Sept. 6
**SHAW, SAVILL & ALBION LINE**

# HEAVY GUNFIRE NEAR ADOWA LAST NIGHT

## ARTILLERY BOMBARDMENT FOLLOWS TWO ITALIAN AIR RAIDS

## ABYSSINIA REPORTS MANY CASUALTIES: BOMB HITS HOSPITAL

## COUNT VINCI EXPRESSES FEAR FOR HIS CONSULS

## IMPERIAL GUARD POSTED TO PROTECT THE LEGATION

**A prolonged artillery bombardment from the Italian lines north of Adowa was reported in an urgent message to the Emperor of Abyssinia by the Governor of the province late last night.**

**The campaign was opened yesterday with a bombing raid on Adowa, and the advance of infantry, artillery and native Italian troops across the Mareb River towards Adowa, 30 miles away.**

**Four bombers took part in the first raid at dawn. Two of the pilots, it is reported, were Mussolini's sons, Vittorio, 19, and Bruno, 18. Two other machines delivered a second attack at 10 o'clock.**

**Abyssinia asserts that 78 bombs were dropped, inflicting heavy casualties, and that one wrecked a Red Cross hospital.**

**After a strenuous denial the raid was officially admitted in Rome late last night, but it was declared that Abyssinian forts had first fired upon the machines.**

**It is reported that the Italian Minister, Count Vinci, who was startled by the suddenness of the advance, has been handed his passport by the Emperor.**

**When he heard of the attack he was pale and nervous, and expressed fears for the Italian Consuls who are travelling to the capital along the mule tracks from outlying parts.**

**The Emperor has demanded that safe conduct shall be accorded them, and he may send out military escorts to meet and accompany them to the capital. Last night a strong guard was thrown around the Italian Legation.**

## ABYSSINIA'S LEAGUE PROTEST AT ADOWA BOMBING

**From SIR PERCIVAL PHILLIPS, Daily Telegraph Special Correspondent.**

ADDIS ABABA, Thursday.

The Italian attacks which mark the opening of the war have been reported in two telegrams from the Abyssinian Government to the League of Nations. The first reads:

"Please communicate to Council and States members that a telegram was received this morning from Ras Seyum (governor) informing my Government that Italian military aeroplanes this morning bombed Adowa and Adigrat, killing and injuring a number of civilians, including women and children, and destroying numerous houses.

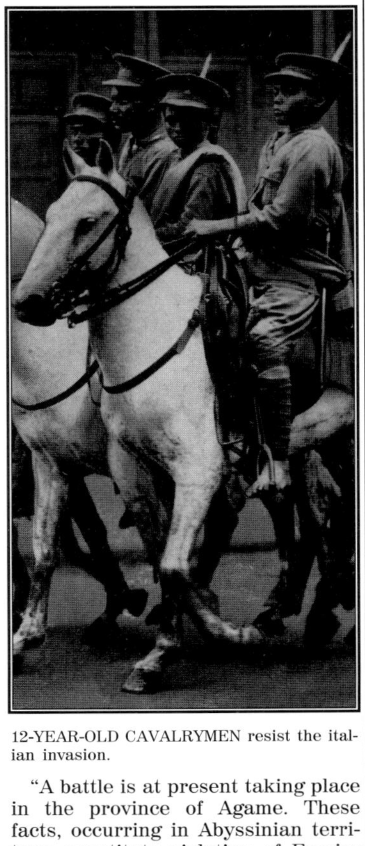

12-YEAR-OLD CAVALRYMEN resist the italian invasion.

"A battle is at present taking place in the province of Agame. These facts, occurring in Abyssinian territory, constitute violation of Empire frontier and a breach of the Covenant by Italian aggression.

"(Signed)

MINISTER FOR FOREIGN AFFAIRS."

This was followed by another telegram, which read:

"Continuation of previous telegram – Four Italian military aeroplanes this morning bombarded Adowa, an undefended town, dropping the first bomb on a hospital bearing the Red Cross emblem.

"Second bombardment was carried out at 10 o'clock by two aeroplanes. Up to the present 78 projectiles have been counted.

"(Signed)

MINISTER FOR FOREIGN AFFAIRS."

Abyssinians believe that the sudden Italian attack is intended to invite reprisals on Italians still in the country and give Italy justification for continuing her assault.

**Safe Conduct for Consuls**

It is clear that no such opportunity will be given. The Emperor is determined to provide the fullest protection for Count Vinci, the Italian Minister, and others, and it is probable that military escorts will leave here to-night to ensure safe conduct for the Italian Consuls now on their way here.

The Consul from Dessie is expected here to-morrow, and the party from Debra Markos perhaps on Saturday.

It was reported this afternoon that Count Vinci had received his passports from the Emperor. This has not been confirmed, and the Count stated this evening that, though he would not be surprised to receive them, he had not yet heard that he was to do so.

In the forenoon to-day Count Vinci was walking in the garden of the Legation when Commandant Dothee, of the Belgian Mission, went to him with the news of the bombing of Adowa.

The Count said he had just learned it, but could not confirm it. He seemed decidedly nervous.

### TROOPS SURROUND LEGATION

#### NO ONE ALLOWED OUT

Asked if his Consuls now en route to Addis Ababa were in danger, he replied, "I hope not."

Commandant Dothee then said: "Italians have been killing Abyssinian women and children. The people may take vengeance on your Consuls." Count Vinci, his lips twitching, repeated that he hoped not.

To the question whether he had taken measures for the protection of the Legation, he replied, "I am protected at this moment."

Twenty Abyssinian soldiers were on guard at the entrance to the compound. No other person could be seen.

At 1 o'clock the Emperor sent infantry and cavalry to protect the Italian Legation. They surrounded the grounds and allowed no Abyssinians to approach. Europeans are allowed to enter, but not to leave.

These measures are stated to be purely precautionary.

This evening Count Vinci was ordered by the Abyssinian Government to concentrate all Italians in the Legation for the night. But he protested that he was unable to communicate with them.

Italian shopkeepers and business men from the Dodecanese have closed down their premises and gone to the Legation.

### SHOCK FOR DUCE'S OFFICIALS

#### TWO PLAYING BILLIARDS

An ironical circumstance of the day's drama is that the Italians, who feel the most acute anxiety as to their position, showed, until they heard the news from Adowa, the greatest unconcern of all the foreigners here for the ceremony at the palace when the mobilisation order was proclaimed.

While Count Vinci was strolling in his garden, Major Calderini, the military attaché, was cashing a cheque at the Bank of Ethiopia, and two other officials were playing billiards at an hotel.

But since the news from the frontier began to trickle through none of the Italians have been visible in their usual haunts. Those staying in an hotel failed for the first time to appear at luncheon.

Wherever an Italian was encountered by a European or told what had happened he showed complete stupefaction. One who is employed here in a civil capacity was so taken aback as to reply helplessly: "I have always been a loyal supporter of Mussolini, but I cannot understand why he should expose us to such danger when our troops have not been attacked."

**All Quiet in the Capital**

No unusual activity was noticeable in the heart of the capital, which was as quiet as on a Sunday. It was a warm and sunny afternoon and fewer natives were in the streets. Melancholy Greek and Armenian traders stood disconsolately at the doors of their shops. A few were packing up their goods.

The only activity since the crowd dispersed from the proclamation ceremony was at the military depots, where munitions and equipment are issued all day long, and also at the barracks of the Imperial Guard, who were having target practice near the aerodrome, where aviators were tuning up and testing their machines. Not one hostile demonstration has taken place to-day.

## DAWN ADVANCE BY 'PLANES & INFANTRY

### SINGING BLACKSHIRTS AND SILENT NATIVES

### DUCE'S TWO SONS AS BOMBER PILOTS

WITH THE ITALIAN FORCES IN ERITREA, THURSDAY.

As dawn broke over the mountains to-day thousands of cheering young Italian infantrymen marched into Abyssinia.

As the infantrymen began their slow trek through the valleys the roar of Italian bombing 'planes, warming up in readiness for the first raid on Adowa, scene of the crushing Italian defeat by Menelik's troops 39 years ago, could be heard.

Before it was light the skirmishing parties, armed with machine guns, which preceeded the infantry, had crossed the Mareb river, making rapidly for their objectives. The infantry force crossed the Abyssinian frontier at widely separated points, converging on Adowa.

An hour after the infantry had left the base a number of squadrons of fast Italian bombing, fighting and scout 'planes roared overhead, crossed the frontier, and disappeared in the direction of Adowa, Adigat, and other points in the vicinity. Signor Mussolini's two sons, Bruno, 18, and Vittorio, 19, were among the pilots.

Count Ciano, Signor Mussolini's son-in-law, and Italy's youngest Cabinet Minister, led the famous Italian "Desperate" squadron. Before climbing into the cockpit he told me (wires a British United Press representative) that he knew that Adowa was defended with anti-aircraft guns.

### H.Q. MOVED NEAR FRONT

#### ASKARIS' MARCH

The heavily laden bombers had to climb 10,000 to 11,000 feet to cross the mountains encircling Adowa. Fifteen big Caproni bombers took off from one aerodrome alone.

It is not yet known whether any warning was given to the populations of the towns which were bombed.

Shortly after the 'planes left, Gen. de Bono, Commander-in-Chief of the Italian forces, moved the general staff headquarters nearer to the front.

Everything has moved with machine-like precision and according to plan.

The advance was preceeded by intense activity behind the Italian lines. Mechanics worked ceaselessly on the engines of the 'planes, and the roar of the motors could be heard intermittently while searchlights swept the skies.

The troops are composed of regulars, Blackshirt militia, and the Askaris (native troops). They formed the largest and best equipped army ever to advance on African soil.

## ROME ADMITS BOMBING AT ADOWA

### "PLANES FIRED AT BY FORTS"

**From Our Own Correspondent**

ROME, Midnight, Thursday.

A Government spokesman has officially admitted that Adowa was bombed by Italian 'planes. Earlier in the day this fact, announced from Addis Ababa, was strenuously denied.

It is declared that a bombing squadron, led by Count Ciano, Mussolini's son-in-law, left Eritrea on a reconnaissance flight. When near Adowa Abyssinian troops fired at the machines.

They flew on to Adowa, where one of the fortresses opened fire.at the machines.

None of the machines was hit, and bombs were dropped upon the guns.

The statement that a Red Cross hospital was struck is described as untrue.

It is also announced that Italian troops have advanced beyond the frontiers of Eritrea and are now occupying positions on the Abyssinian side. This move has been received here quite calmly.

Signor Mussolini's intentions not to stress the advance are proved by the complete absence of public demonstrations of any kind in Rome or in other cities.

The deserted streets and squares to-night contrast oddly with the marching and mobilisation of yesterday afternoon.

ABYSSINIA BLAMED

"Bloodthirsty Aggression"

Midday newspapers which announced the advance into Abyssinia found but few buyers. People went their way looking depressed. They have been keyed up for months., and now the moment for fighting is at hand they await the result with a sense of fatality.

The special communiqué announcing the military measures says:

"The order in Ethiopia for general mobilisation, under pressure of the warlike spirit and the aggressiveness fomented by chiefs and their followers, represents a direct and immediate threat for the Italian troops in our two colonies of East Africa.

"The threat is aggravated by the fact that the creation of a neutral zone announced from Addis Ababa with specious motives constitutes merely a strategem to help mobilisation and aggressive preparation on the Abyssinian side.

"SERIOUS PERILS"

Immediate Action Needed

"The continued and bloodthirsty aggression to which Italy has been subjected during the past decade is now entering a phase of greater proportions and of larger scope, of which the serious and immediate perils are evident. The elementary reason of security makes it necessary for us to react without delay.

"The supreme command in Eritrea has therefore received orders to act in consequence. The Italian troops are occupying certain advanced positions beyond our lines."

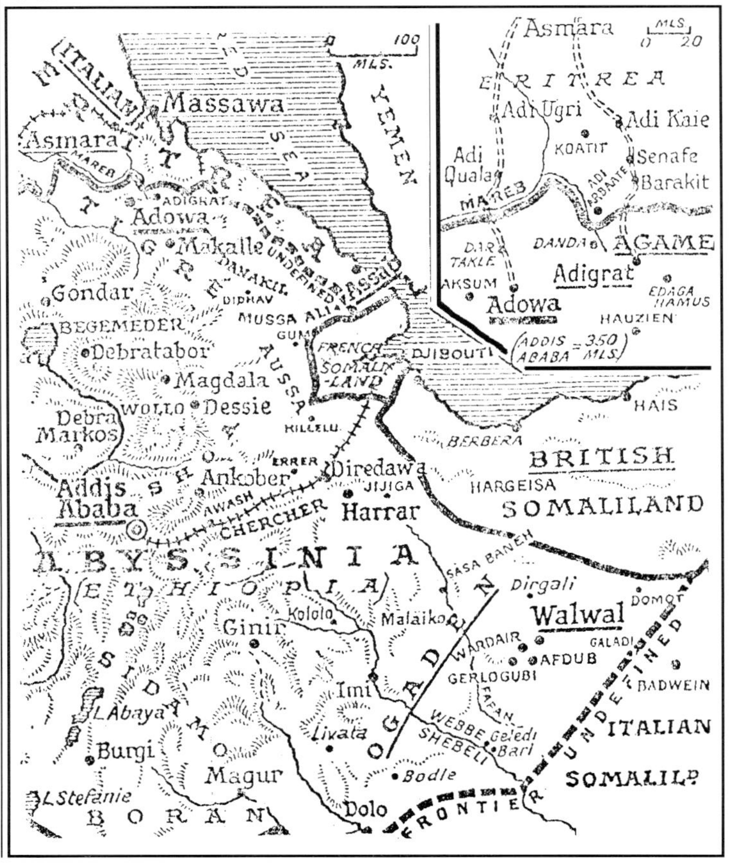

# THE KING THANKS HIS "VERY DEAR PEOPLE"

## "I DEDICATE MYSELF ANEW TO YOUR SERVICE"

## WEST END'S MERRIEST NIGHT SINCE ARMISTICE

**Floodlit Scene on Palace Balcony | London a City of Brilliant Light | Street Revels Continue Till Morning**

## 2,000 BEACONS BLAZE OUT ON BRITAIN'S HILLTOPS

**My very dear people ... The Queen and I thank you from the depth of our hearts for all the loyalty and – may I say? – the love with which this day and always you have surrounded us.**

**I dedicate myself anew to your service for the years that may still be given to me.**

**This moving message from the King, broadcast last night to the nation and the Empire, was the climax to a day of undimmed beauty and splendour which will live long in the memory of every Briton.**

**The stately Royal procession to the Thanksgiving Service at St. Paul's and back to the Palace after the ceremony was witnessed with delight by a great multitude of happy people, acclaiming with deep affection their beloved King and Queen.**

In London, the heart of the Empire's tribute, tens of thousands – many of whom had stood all night in the streets – acclaimed their Majesties with the greatest demonstration of love and loyalty the capital has ever known.

Royal weather graced their Majesties' progress. The day was the warmest of the year, with unbroken sunshine everywhere.

**MEMORABLE EVENING CELEBRATIONS**

**"For He's a Jolly Good Fellow"**

Vast crowds surrounded Buckingham Palace all day and until the early hours of this morning.

At 9.15 p.m. in response to repeated cries of "We want the King," their Majesties appeared – for the third time since their return to the Palace – on the balcony, to be acclaimed by a crowd of between 150,000 and 200,000.

The King commanded the floodlighting to be turned on, and for five minutes he stood with the Queen, waving to the throng.

The crowd cheered again and again and repeatedly sang "For He's a Jolly Good Fellow."

Shortly before ten his Majesty pressed a button in the Palace.

At once the great bonfire burst into flame – and a chain of 2,000 beacon fires blazed out on every hilltop in Britain.

Enormous crowds turned the West-end of London, brilliant with floodlighting into a carnival city. The revels in the streets continued until dawn and in some places later. It was the merriest London night since the Armistice.

**(May 7)**

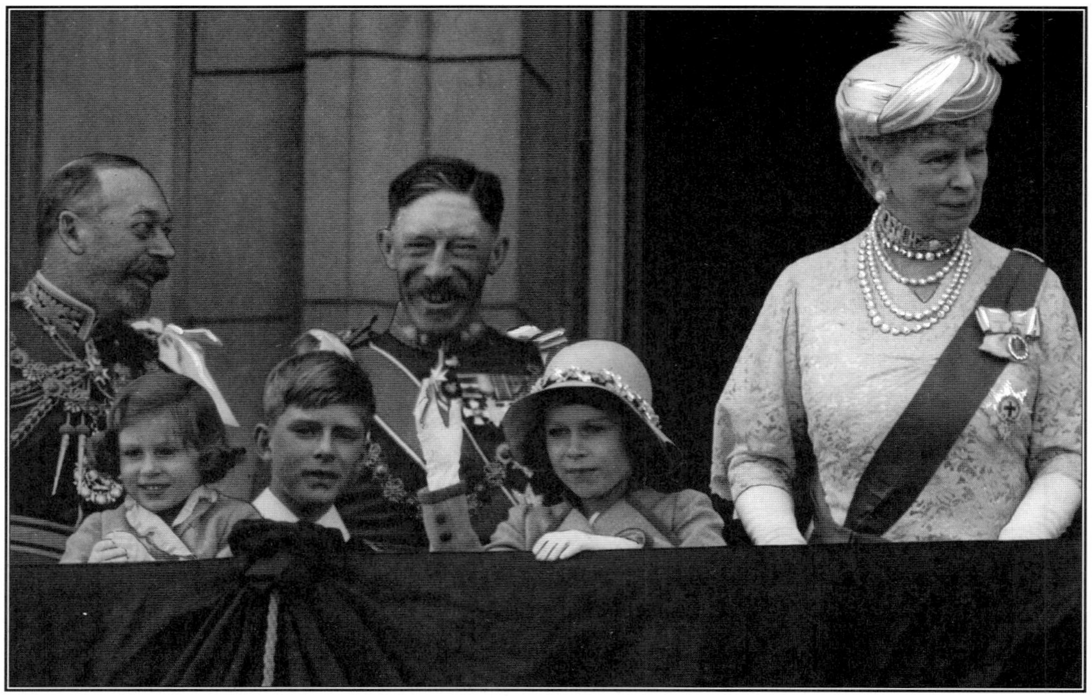

THE ROYAL GROUP smiles down from the balcony at Buckingham Palace while the vast crowd below cheers deafeningly. Left to right: The King, Princess Margaret Rose, the Hon. Gerald Lascelles, the Earl of Harewood, Princess Elizabeth, and the Queen.

## ANOTHER NIGHT OF CARNIVAL

There was another night of carnival in London last night. Until the early hours of this morning the streets of the West-end were packed with crowds dancing, singing, cheering and making a joyful noise. Many of them had not been to bed since Saturday.

For a long period the Strand, from Wellington-street to Charing Cross, was packed with dancers.

Trafalgar-square at midnight, one a.m., two a.m., and later, resembled a great pleasure garden of a seaside resort. Fairy lights twinkled in festoons from tall poles around the square and away in the distance down the Strand, Northumberland-avenue, and other approaches. The plinth of Nelson's Column was crowded with tiers of joyous folk – mostly young people – singing lustily.

**(May 7)**

## DOG HAS ITS DAY

This is the tale of the Jubilee Dog. It amused tens of thousands of spectators in Fleet-street and Ludgate-hill during the processions.

Shortly before the Royal family carriages were due to pass it darted from the crowd above Temple Bar and sped down the centre of Fleet-street. Three officers tried to stop it by holding out their swords; two police officers tried the same trick with their truncheons. But the dog sped on cheered lustily by the crowd, and disappeared up Ludgate-hill.

After the procession policemen and eyewitnesses along the route gave the following information: When it entered Fleet-street, it was a medium-sized brown mongrel with a trace of Alsatian in its pedigree; At the bottom of Fleet-street it was a large grey dog; At Ludgate Hill it had become a small black dog; At St. Paul's it was a very small grey dog

**(May 7)**

## "BIG BANG" BALL

### 1,000 "NIPPIES" IN FANCY COSTUMES

Hundreds of ingenious and pretty fancy dresses, every one of them home-made, were worn last night, by Lyons' waitresses at the annual "Big Bang" Ball at the Royal Opera House, Covent Garden.

The one thousand "Nippies" present had laid aside their black-and-white uniforms and appeared in such various characters as Cleopatra, Mme. Pompadour, and Miss Mae West. Some of the girls had spent months preparing their costumes.

"Chinese Screen" in which real faces looking through head holes completed a fascinating design, "Cameo Brooch," a Gainsborough picture receiving the finishing touches from the "artist" himself, and "Cocktails," modern and snappy, were the first three prize-winners in the special Decorations Department class. One of the "Mae Wests" who was attended by admirers, was first-prize winner among the remainder.

**(January 15)**

## WILLS OF THREE NOTED PEOPLE

The wills of three noted people have just been proved. They are those of -

Sir Albert Spicer, an ex-M.P., and formerly a director of Spicers Ltd., paper makers, who left ....................£74,590

Lady Lavery, wife of Sir John Lavery, R.A., the portrait painter....................£208

Mr. Cecil C. W. Aldin, the well-known painter of sporting subjects (estate in England) ....................£518

**(February 14)**

## GAY PAGEANT OF THE ROYAL PROCESSIONS

**By R. MacColl**

A proud and lovely piece of pageantry that went its way to a thunderous ovation of the people to their King and Queen – that was the great Jubilee Procession of yesterday.

Everywhere the massed onlookers gasped at the triumphantly effective panoply of uniform and weapon that glowed and twinkled in the sunshine of a perfect summer day.

But the climax to all its beauties was in the last half-mile, when the procession came along the Mall accompanied by a great crash of cheers.

Watchers at the Victoria Memorial gazing towards the distant Admiralty Arch saw a picture of which the frame alone was superb.

The line of tall masts swept, perspective-pulled, inwards to the distant Arch. Their banners, moving a little in the wind, glinted against the new green of the trees.

Lining the edges of London's noblest boulevard were the Guards. Never had their black and scarlet looked more magnificent. Behind were the eager people in all their thousands.

MASS OF MOVING COLOUR

Right away near the Arch were two blobs of white – the helmets of the Marines. And into this frame, glimpsed at first as a mass of moving colour and shifting pin-points of light in the heat haze, trotted the Cavalcade of Jubilee.

Whatever misgivings had at one time been voiced as to the scope of the procession, no carper in the world could have endured after one glance at that overwhelmingly fine sight.

Onward they came, with a swing and a flash, a jingle of harness, a proud tossing of pennant. Full-dress uniforms of the cavalry itself a survival from the age of chivalry.

Nearer yet, the dust rising lazily from the horses' hooves, the people cheering, the sun – most cunning, most grandiose of stage managers – flinging his beams off cuirass and helmet, sword and polished guns.

That was a sight to set one cheering even before the King and Queen could be seen, a sight to set the heart beating quicker. ... Lancers, with red and white pennons dancing, Carabiniers, Hussars, Dragoons, Royal Horse Artillery – a Royal show if ever there was one.

What a cheer the King and Queen had received when they left the Palace two hours before – first volley in a day's bombardment of cheers!

**(May 7)**

## The Daily Telegraph AND TELEVISION

The Daily Telegraph has installed a television receiving set in its offices.

Henceforth readers will be given the latest "first-view" information of all television developments.

The progress and reception of the B.B.C. transmissions will be described and commented upon in a regular weekly feature.

**(February 7)**

## POLICE MUST OBEY LIMIT

Sir John Gilmour, the Home Secretary, replying to questions in the House of Commons yesterday, said that the 30 m.p.h. speed limit would apply to the police as well as to the public.

**(March 14)**

## STREAMLINED TRAIN DOES 112 M.P.H.

### "SILVER JUBILEE'S" RECORD RUN

**From a Special Correspondent**

Yesterday afternoon, on its trial run, the London and North Eastern Railway's streamline train, "Silver Jubilee" reached a speed of 112 miles an hour. This is the fastest speed ever attained by a steam locomotive in this country.

But almost more astonishing than this sudden burst of speed was the average kept up for mile after mile. Typical averages included:

104.9 m.p.h. for 27 miles between Hitchin and Huntingdon.

96.9 m.p.h. for 55 miles between Hatfield and Yaxley.

92.1 m.p.h. for 70 miles from Wood Green to Fletton.

Even the 12 miles climb from King's Cross to Potters Bar was accomplished at a speed of 70 m.p.h. Before reaching Grantham the train was held up by the Harrogate express – which had left King's Cross 45 minutes before it!

COULD HAVE DONE 120 M.P.H.

It was rumoured that the "Silver Link" – that strange-looking engine which resembles, according to the mood, either a war tank coloured silver and black or a monster from the primeval age – could have drawn its load at a good 120 miles an hour.

At the highest speeds the sensation was exhilarating. The train seemed to skim over the rails rather than to run on wheels.

BEAUTY, COMFORT AND SAFETY

The train itself is 392 ft of beauty and ease. Even when it carries its full complement of 198 passengers every one will travel in luxury.

Its inauguration indicated the faith of the L.N.E.R. that better times are on the way for Tyneside. Sir Ralph Wedgwood, chief general manager of the company, expressed confidence that the train will run at a profit. "There is complete safety," he emphasised. "This is not an experiment.

"It is the fastest long-distance train in this country, and if you interpret the words 'long distance' to mean over 200 miles it is the fastest long-distance train in the world – oil, Diesel or steam."

**(September 28)**

## SKATING IN FULL SWING

### ICE CARNIVAL PLANS

Skating is in full swing in many parts of the country, and is likely to continue throughout the holiday. Special preparations have been made in several places for carnivals on the ice.

At Melton Mowbray to-night thousands will skate by the light of bonfires which have been built around the local lake.

Derwentwater, with its mountainous scenery, resembles a Swiss winter resort. Visitors are enjoying skating, curling, and ski-ing.

Skating began on many of the ponds in Windsor Great Park yesterday. Arrangements are being made for skating on the reservoirs of the Grand Union Canal Co. at Elstree and Ruislip.

**(December 24)**

## ALLOTMENTS FOR UNEMPLOYED

The first step in the Government's scheme for linking the unemployed with the land is the creation of another 10,000 allotment gardens this year in the special areas. There are at present about 76,000 allotments in these districts.

This step was announced yesterday by Mr. P Malcolm Stewart, Commissioner for the special areas, in a circular to all the local authorities in Durham and Tyneside, South Wales and Monmouth, and Cumberland. The circular sets forth the terms under which he is prepared to give financial assistance.

This is the first case in which grants from the Commissioner's funds are offered to local authorities.

The scheme is to help in the purchase or the rent of land in and around large centres of population where the expense could not possibly be met by the small rents paid by the allotment-holders. The Commissioner presumes that the allotments will be the usual plots of about 300 square yards.

This allotment scheme is not to be confused with that for smallholdings, which has been submitted to the Government and was outlined in The Daily Telegraph on Jan. 10. By that scheme, 18,000 workers would be settled in groups of 150 on 4-acre holdings for poultry, pigs and market gardening. Each man would build his own farm.

IMMEDIATE ACTION URGED

In his circular to the town or urban district councils, the Commissioner states that he is "anxious that the authorities responsible for the provision of allotments should make arrangements to meet any unsatisfied demand in their areas and should stimulate the interest of the unemployed or part-time employed in such occupation.

"It is important," he says, "that action should be taken at a very early date if it is to be in time for the 1935 season. Where it is not possible to hire land at a moderate rent, the Commissioner will be prepared to consider making a grant out of the Special Areas Fund towards the cost of purchasing the land.

"A fair rent for a 10-rod allotment (300 square yards) is reckoned to be in the neighbourhood of 8s to 10s. and in some localities may be higher, more especially if water supply is laid on.

**(January 15)**

## TWO ENGLISH SAINTS

### FIRST SINCE THE REFORMATION

VATICAN CITY, Wednesday.

The Congregation of Sacred Rites, it was learned at the Vatican to-day, will approve on Jan. 29, at a plenary session at which the Pope will preside the canonisation of the first English saints to be created since the breach between King Henry VIII. and the Holy See.

The Blessed Sir Thomas More, Chancellor to Henry VIII, and the Blessed John Fisher, Bishop of Rochester, will be the new saints.

Orders were given by the Pope for the canonisations to be expedited by special procedure as a token of his regard for Britain. It is thought that the ceremony of canonisation may take place on Easter Day. This is regarded as the Pope's response to the large number of British pilgrims who visited Rome during the Holy Year. – B.U.P.

**(January 10)**

# SIR SAMUEL HOARE RESIGNS

## LAST NIGHT'S DRAMATIC CLIMAX TO CONSULTATIONS

## CHOICE OF APOLOGY OR RESIGNATION

**By Our Diplomatic Correspondent**

Sir Samuel Hoare's resignation was tendered to the Prime Minister early yesterday afternoon, it followed a call on him at his home in Cadogan-gardens by Mr. Neville Chamberlain, one of Sir Samuel's oldest friends in the Cabinet and Mr. Baldwin's most intimate colleague.

Mr. Chamberlain had been requested by the Prime Minister to convey to Sir Samuel an expression of the strongly critical views voiced at the morning meeting of the Cabinet.

Ministers had had before them a statement from Sir Samuel, and a rough draft of the speech which he proposed to deliver in the House of Commons to-day. A considerable body of Ministerial opinion was opposed to the tenour of Sir Samuel's speech.

It was to have been a candid statement of the circumstances in which Sir Samuel agreed with M. Laval on the peace proposals.

SIR S. HOARE'S DEFENCE

What He Was to Reveal

Throughout the political storm which has been raging during the past week Sir Samuel has remained confident that he would be able to convince the House of Commons that there was full justification for his action in Paris.

He proposed to defend this action on bluntly realistic grounds, insisting that the future of the collective security system depends on frankly recognising its existent weaknesses.

It was his intention, as the first Government spokesman, to tell the House that the terms to which he and M. Laval set their names in Paris represented the maximum which would be likely to command the attention of the disputants.

He would have justified that statement by admitting that the League States are not at present able to apply the requisite further pressure to Italy which might compel Signor Mussolini to negotiate on some less favourable basis.

He would have shown that only Britain had taken any precautionary measures to resist retaliation to Sanctions. Had Sanctions led to war, Britain would have found herself standing alone among all the League States to meet the onslaught.

NO APOLOGY INTENDED

Younger Ministers' Threat

In these circumstances Sir Samuel proposed to make no apology for the initiative he had taken in Paris. A group of his Cabinet colleagues, however, felt that he should apologise to Parliament for an error.

The Ministers who have most strongly expressed that view are understood to be Mr. Duff Cooper, Major Ormsby-Gore, Mr. Oliver Stanley, Mr. Anthony Eden and Mr. Walter Elliot.

The real Ministerial struggle did not develop until yesterday morning, when a report was made on the line which Sir Samuel was determined to pursue.

It then became apparent that a number of the younger Ministers were prepared to resign if any attempt were made to justify the Paris decisions.

The position was one of extreme delicacy. The whole Cabinet was aware that Sir Samuel had referred back to London the text of the conciliation proposals. Their endorsement was recommended by the Foreign Secretary in the light of the information he had received.

CABINET APPROVAL

The Cabinet had considered the proposals on Monday evening and again on Tuesday, on which later day they had authorised Sir Robert Vansittart, Permanent Head of the Foreign Office, who remained in Paris after Sir Samuel's departure for Switzerland, to inform M. Laval that the British Government endorsed them.

The Cabinet, I learned, had also approved the text of the instructions sent to Sir Eric Drummond, British Ambassador in Rome, and to Sir Sidney Barton, British Minister in Addis Ababa, conveying the advice with which presentation of the proposals to the two Governments should be accompanied.

It was eventually decided yesterday that the only possible course was to request Sir Samuel to redraft the statement he had prepared for Parliament in different and more apologetic terms. This the Foreign Secretary was unwilling to do. Instead he preferred to tender his resignation.

**(December 19)**

# MR. EDEN SUCCEEDS SIR SAMUEL HOARE

## APPOINTMENT WELCOME ABROAD EXCEPT IN ROME

It was announced from 10, Downing-street, last night that the King had approved the appointment of Mr. Anthony Eden as Secretary of State for Foreign Affairs, in succession to Sir Samuel Hoare.

Our Political Correspondent states that Mr. Eden's former post of Minister for League Affairs is not to be filled. This decision means the end of dual responsibility at the Foreign Office.

The announcement of Mr. Eden's appointment was well received on the Continent, with the exception of Rome.

In France, during the week-end, the uncompromising attitude of Signor Mussolini led to a change of tone in the Press. The Duce was criticised in many quarters where, formerly, he had been defended.

**(December 23)**



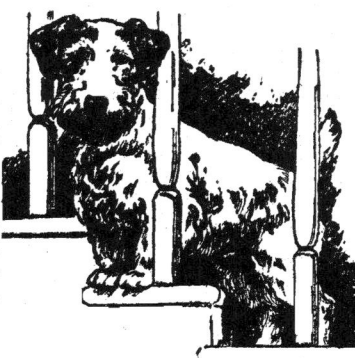

# FLIGHT OVER BATTLE LINES OF OGADEN

## BOMBING HAVOC

**From Our Special Correspondent**

ADDIS ABABA, Friday.

I have just completed a 700-miles flight over the Ogaden district, as far as the battle-lines south of Daggahbur.

On the way out and back my plane flew parallel with that of the Emperor for parts of the journey, while he was making his first visit to the war zone.

I left him at Diredawa, and reached Addis Ababa in time to welcome him on his arrival back.

Although I was warned by Gen. Nasibu, the Emperor's commander on the southern front, and by the Turkish officer, Wehib Pasha, who is acting in an advisory capacity, of the danger of being shot down by Italians, I flew over Gorahi, which the Italians occupy, sufficiently high to out-distance anti-aircraft and machine-guns.

From there I flew to Daggahbur, which is being daily bombed by Italian machines, and thence to Jijiga, the general headquarters of the southern armies.

The population of Daggahbur, mistaking my plane for an Italian fled in panic from the city. I learnt afterwards that two Italian planes had actually preceded mine on their way to Harrar and Diredawa. Their purpose was to observe the movements of the Emperor, who was preparing to return by air to Addis Ababa.

BOMB VICTIMS

HOSPITALS FULL

In warning me about the hazardous nature of the flight Gen. Nasibu urged that I should fly at a speed of 200 miles an hour, and maintain a great height.

"Yours," he said, " is the first foreign aeroplane, other than Italian, to enter this zone, which is far more dangerous than the north front. The Italians are bombing around here unceasingly and our hospitals are crowded with wounded."

When I took off from Jijiga for Daggahbur, Gen. Nasibu and Wehib Pasha both came to the aerodrome to deliver a final caution.

Within half an hour of leaving I was flying over Daggahbur, where Dr. Hockman, the American, has a field hospital. I could plainly see the Stars and Stripes flying above it.

The absence of an aerodrome and numerous anti-aircraft guns made it impossible to land. I could see stretcher-bearers carrying wounded to the hospital.

Flying on to Gorahi I could discern no large bodies, either of Abyssinian or Italian troops. This would seem to prove that Italian activities have thus far been confined to air bombing and tank attacks. Indeed, 90 per cent, of the wounded at Jijiga and Daggahbur are air-bomb cases – mostly civilians, including many women.

I found no gas cases whatever, which proves the reports that Italians were using gas to be entirely unfounded.

South of Daggahbur I was shown portions of several Italian tanks which the Abyssinians had captured.

The crews were killed by cutting off their heads, an example, they declared, of the fate awaiting other Italians.

The whole of the vast Ogaden war zone is a barren, desolate waste, with only scattered human habitations. There are frequent patches of cactus and brush, but no water is anywhere visible.

All the rivers have already dried up. Occasionally I saw small fungus-covered lakes in volcanic craters. Sun-scorched mountains are intersected by dried-up rivulets.

"WE WANT REAL FIGHTING"

Everywhere I landed during an eight hours' flight of the war zone I found unbounded enthusiasm among the natives for the Emperor. The magic name of Haile Selassie was on everybody's lips. One chief said to me:

"Now that he has seen the actual battle front, we know that he will be as great in war as in peace.

"We are tired of these silly air bombings by the Italians, which is not a real man's way of fighting. We want to fight the Italians hand to hand as real soldiers.

"That is why we tackled a half-dozen Italian tanks, armed with machine-guns, while we have only rifles and swords.

"We captured five of them, beheading the occupants and destroying the tanks."

**(November 23)**

# JEWS WANT TO JOIN THE LEAGUE

The Foundation Congress of the new Zionist organisation began last night in Vienna Concert House, Mr. Jacob de Kaaz, of New York, a pioneer of Zionism, presided.

Mr. Vladimir Jadotinsky, founder of this new Zionist movement, said that it aimed at securing for the Jews as a nation representation in the League of Nations. This would enable them to speak to the Governments of the world in the name of world Jewry, and to establish a Jewish State on both sides of the Jordan.

**(September 9)**

# SWEEPING CHANGES IN THE ARMY

**8 Cavalry Regiments To Be Mechanised** | **Mobile Division With Tanks To Be Formed**

## GUARDS AND LINE INFANTRY AS MACHINE-GUN BATTALIONS

**By Major-Gen. A.C. Temperley, Daily Telegraph Military Correspondent**

Sweeping changes in the reorganisation of the cavalry and infantry were announced by the War Office last night.

The existing Cavalry Division, of two horsed brigades and divisional troops, and the Tank Brigade are to be converted into a mechanised Mobile Division.

The Cavalry Brigade in Egypt is to be mechanised.

Two Foot Guards battalions and 13 line regiments are to be machine-gun battalions.

As to the cavalry, the changes are revolutionary. The total number of regiments affected is eight. This will leave six horsed cavalry regiments at home and six in India.

Any further step towards mechanisation will presumably depend upon the attitude of India, where conditions as regards the employment of cavalry are somewhat different.

The date of the conversion is not stated. It will probably depend upon the speed with which the new vehicle can be delivered.

The great gain from this reform will be the constitution of a mobile mechanised division which will consist of two mechanised cavalry brigades, a tank brigade and divisional units. The best methods of cooperation between tanks and mechanised cavalry will need careful study.

We can at any rate be satisfied that the new division will give to the cavalry mobility and power of surprise.

As regards the infantry, each regiment has one battalion at home and one abroad. This will therefore give 15 machine-gun battalions (including the two Guards battalions) for the 15 infantry brigades at home and 13 for service abroad.

The date of the conversion will be during 1936-37, but will not take place in India before 1939.

It is presumed that it will apply to the infantry of the Territorial Army, as the memorandum states that the "manner" of applying the policy to it is under consideration. No mention is made of the Yeomanry.

MACHINE-GUN BATTALION

The introduction of the machine-gun battalion is due to the previous tendency to overload the rifle battalion with too great a variety of weapons. Both the heavy machine-gun and the anti-tank weapons have now been transferred to the machine-gun battalion, which will also have a mechanised reconnaissance company.

The results of the experiments carried out by the 6th Infantry Brigade have therefore been considered satisfactory, and it may be deduced that further mechanisation of the first line transport will also be generally undertaken. To the infantry the reorganisation cannot fail to be satisfactory, and the brigade with its largely increased fire power and its more elastic organisation must become a more efficient fighting unit.

The memorandum gives shortly the reasons for the reorganisation of both arms which must meet with general approval.

NEW MODEL ARMY

This great scheme for the creation of a new model army must be welcomed by all thoughtful soldiers. It will no doubt be followed by a further mechanisation of the artillery, and it is to be hoped that the transport of the Territorial Army will soon be put upon a proper basis, for this is urgently needed.

The Army Council has shown itself able to take swift decisions as to reorganisation, and they must be accompanied by a relentless determination to ensure the provision of all the necessary weapons and vehicles without delay.

**(December 23)**

# STATE OF THE ARMIES

## GERMANY AND RUSSIA LARGEST

The strengths of the armies of the Great Powers are as follows:

BRITAIN:

Regular Army: 152,000.

Army Reserve: 111,500, rising to 113,000 by end of year.

Territorial Army: 7,030 officers, 123,458 other ranks.

FRANCE:

278,000 (figure given by M. Flandin).

237,000 in Colonial Army abroad

These figures do not include 72,000 Native Troops on French soil.

Reckoned in event of sudden attack France could put 225,000 men in line. Each battalion would have to absorb 75 to 90 per cent. reservists.

GERMANY:

Limited by Versailles Treaty to 100,000 officers and men, who must be voluntarily recruited.

Actual strength of Reichswehr in 1934 nearer 300,000; stated by French Premier M. Flandin, on Saturday to be 480,000.

ITALY:

Peace establishment is 254,000 men conscripted and serving 18 months.

Volunteer Militia for National Security: 430,000.

RUSSIA:

Red Army: 562,000 men.

Soviet Territorial Militia: 840,000 men trained annually.

BELGIUM:

94,000 men organised in 4 corps.

600,000 men could be mobilised.

AIR STRENGTHS

Germany's air strength is:

800 military aeroplanes last November;

1,000 to 1,100 to-day (estimate);

1,200 civil aeroplanes, including 180 airliners.

In the explanatory statement on the British Air Estimates which placed Britain fifth in the list of Great Powers and Russia first, the German Air Force was not taken into account. If the above estimate is approximately right, Germany at the present time is sixth.

Britain's air strength is:

1,020 first-line aeroplanes (not including training machines);

1,247 civil aircraft.

NAVAL STRENGTHS

Germany's naval strength, including ships under construction, comprises:

5 10,000-ton pocket battleships of high speed, great radius and heavy armament;

4 old battleships;

6 modern fast cruisers;

31 destroyers and torpedo-boats, and many smaller craft.

The following table shows the present strength of the British, French and Italian navies in vessels completed and building, but exclusive of those not yet laid down:

| | Britain | France | Italy |
|---|---|---|---|
| Capital ships | 15 | 11 | 6 |
| Aircraft carriers | 6 | 2 | 1 |
| Heavy 8in gun cruisers | 19 | 7 | 7 |
| Light 6in gun cruisers | 34 | 12 | 17 |
| Flotilla leaders | 16 | 32 | 16 |
| Destroyers | 258 | 50 | 78 |
| Submarines | 61 | 109 | 65 |

**(March 18)**

# BASHFUL LADY GODIVA

Owing to a girl's bashfulness, Brighton is without a Lady Godiva for its Jubilee Pageant to-day.

A last-minute effort is being made by the organisers to find a girl willing to take the part. Otherwise, the white horse will be ridden by a man wearing flesh-coloured tights and a wig of flowing golden hair.

**(May 6)**

# SIX MONTHS FOR GIRL OF 20

## FIRST CONVICTION

A sentence of six months' imprisonment was passed by Mr. Claude Mullins at Marylebone yesterday on a girl of 20 who had never been previously convicted.

Prisoner, who had given the name of Peggy Blonde, was Evelyn Gibbs, of Broadmore-avenue, Worley, Oldbury. She was accused of obtaining a meal to the extent of 1s 8d at an A.B.C. shop in Edgeware-road without having the means to pay for it.

Det. Berridge stated that her father described her as work-shy, lazy, and "a horrible liar to her mother."

"You want strong discipline. The best place for you is Holloway for six months," said the magistrate to the girl.

**(June 1)**

# COLLEGE P. C.S' FIRST DAY ON BEAT

The 31 students who passed out from Hendon Police College at the end of last term begin their duties on the streets to-day. Some have been posted to divisions in the West End and some to suburban stations. This will be the beginning of their year's practical training.

**(September 16)**

# COUNTRY GIVES THE GOVERNMENT 242 MAJORITY

## OPPOSITION OF 179: LIBERALS REDUCED TO 19

### Mr. MacDonald and His Son Defeated

### Narrow Wins For Mr. Elliot and Sir J. Simon

## NINE WOMEN AND ONE COMMUNIST IN NEW HOUSE

The General Election has resulted in a sweeping success for the National Government, surpassing the expectations of even its most optimistic supporters.

With fourteen results still to be declared, the Government has a majority of 242. The final figure is expected to reach 250. In the old House the majority was 411.

Socialists in the new House number no more than 155 – half of their 1929 strength and at least 60 below their confident predictions. Liberals in opposition are reduced to the mere handful of 19.

**(November 16)**

## MR. MacDONALD

### A PEERAGE UNLIKELY

With the election over, Mr. Baldwin must now devote attention to settling the question of changes that may be called for in the personnel of his Administration.

I learn that a wholesale reconstruction of the Cabinet is not in prospect. The Prime Minister does not consider it necessary.

Mr. Ramsay MacDonald's defeat at Seaham will it is anticipated, render vacant the office of Lord President of the Council. It has been freely prophesied that, in the event of an electoral reverse such as he has suffered, he would end his political career as a member of the House of Lords.

His friends say that this is unlikely. They foresee his retirement from active politics to devote his time to his books and to literary work.

His Ministerial colleagues would deeply regret a decision that would sever his connection with the Cabinet. It remains to be seen what effect their attempts at persuasion may have.

The defeat of Mr. Malcolm MacDonald at Bassetlaw, after putting up a splendid fight, is greatly deplored in Ministerial circles. The Colonial Secretary is thoroughly popular with his colleagues, and is held to have justified his promotion to Cabinet rank by the ability he has displayed as the head of an important department.

It may be that the loss of his seat will not mean even a temporary interruption of his Ministerial career.

The possibility of arranging for him to continue his duties as Colonial Secretary, though not a member of the House of Commons, until another constituency becomes available, will be considered.

Sir B. Eyres-Monsell, the First Lord of the Admiralty is no longer a member of Parliament. Until the Prime Minister announces his reconstruction plans it can only remain a matter of speculation as to whether there is to be a change in this connection or not.

It should not be forgotten that important negotiations with other naval Powers will begin in London early next month.

**(November 16)**

## SPECULATION OVER MR. CHURCHILL

### MAY RECEIVE OFFICE

There was speculation in political circles last night on the prospects of Mr. Churchill's inclusion in the Ministry.

The belief in informed quarters is that he may again be asked to take office.

Mr. Baldwin's intentions are, however, for the present his own secret.

When the National Ministry meets the new Parliament it will be confronted with an Opposition Front Bench much stronger in debating power than in the last Parliament. Ex-Cabinet Ministers who have won the right to resume championship of Socialist policy in the House of Commons are Mr. J.R. Clynes, Mr. Herbert Morrison, Mr. A.V. Alexander.

**(November 16)**

## MR. ATTLEE TO LEAD THE SOCIALISTS

Mr. C.R. Attlee, M.P. for Limehouse, was yesterday elected at a meeting of Socialist M.P.s as Leader of the party in the House of Commons for the remainder of the present Parliamentary session.

At the opening of a new session the party will choose its leader by ballot.

Mr. Attlee has been deputy-leader during the present Parliament.

The election followed the resignation of Mr. George Lansbury because of his differences with the party on the policy to be pursued regarding the Italian-Abyssinian war. When invited by a large majority to reconsider his decision, Mr. Lansbury declined to do so.

After the meeting Mr. Attlee said that he and Mr. Lansbury would be working together on all the main lines of the Socialist programme. It was only on the one issue – Sanctions – that there was any difference.

"LOVE NOT POISON GAS"

Mr. Lansbury, in an interview, said he hoped his colleagues would pin their faith not in poison gas or armaments, but in love and goodwill. Then, his voice trembling with emotion, added:

"I am very sad and sick at heart that I have been obliged to stick to my resolution resigning from my position as leader. My four years' work with my colleagues in the House of Commons have been harmonious. To break away now is one of the most distressing things that has ever happened to me, but the Socialist movement has the right to have as its leader one who whole-heartedly accepts the fundamentals of its policy.

"I shall work for Socialism with the Socialist party as long as my friends desire me to do so."

**(October 9)**

## THE VANISHING STRIKE

**By Our Industrial Correspondent**

Not since records were kept – and statistics have been compiled for more than forty years – has any year had so small a number of strikes in industry as 1934.

Nor has any year seen such a vast number of workers affected by collective agreements in reference to wages and conditions. Trade union leaders estimate that 10,000,000 workers – three times the membership of the Trades Union Congress – have hours and rates fixed by agreement with employers' associations.

The "Gazette" of the Ministry of Labour states that the total number of workpeople involved in all disputes in 1934 was approximately 134,000 and the working days lost number 960,000. Such figures are trifling by comparison with those of past years, and it is the first time the days lost have fallen below a million.

In 1921 nearly 86,000,000 days of useful work were lost, and 1926 gave the colossal total of 162,230,000 days. Then came reaction. The 1931 total was less than 7,000,000; 1932 was lower still, and 1933 only just exceeded a million.

**(January 19)**

### MR. BALDWIN LEAVES FOR CHEQUERS

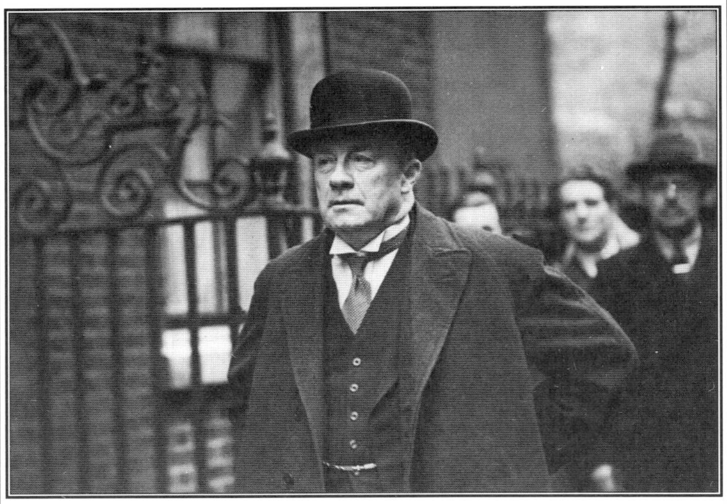

MR. BALDWIN ouside 10 Downing Street yesterday.

## MAJORITY OF 271 FOR THE INDIA BILL

### 83 OR 84 CONSERVATIVES OPPOSE

## MR. BALDWIN'S APPEAL TO A CROWDED HOUSE

### "NO HUCKSTERING SPIRIT" IN OFFER OF STEP TO PARTNERSHIP

| | |
|---|---|
| **FOR THE BILL** | **404** |
| **AGAINST** | **133** |
| **MAJORITY** | **271** |

This was the result of the historic division on the Second Reading of the Government of India Bill in the House of Commons last night. It compared with a vote of 410 to 127 for the Select Committee's Report – on which the bill was based – last December.

The minority against the bill included 79 or 80 Conservatives, in addition to four who were paired. This was a slight increase on the number – 80 – who voted against the Committee's Report.

Every part of the Chamber, including the public galleries, was crowded for the final scene, when Mr. Baldwin wound up the debate. This had been sustained on a high level by previous speakers, including Sir Thomas Inskip, Mr. Churchill, Mr. Isaac Foot, Lord Eustace Percy, and Mr. Lansbury.

"We are," said Mr. Baldwin, "offering India an opportunity of making a considerable step forward to the day when she will be a full partner with us in the Empire. Let us do it in no huckstering spirit, but willingly, generously, and with confidence."

**(February 12)**

## MR. A.P. HERBERT CELEBRATES HIS ELECTION AS M.P.

Mr. A.P. Herbert, novelist and humorist, who, with Lord Hugh Cecil, was elected M.P. for Oxford University, held a reception of his supporters yesterday at Hammersmith.

There was much enthusiasm yesterday. The doors of the crowded room where the reception was held bore the notice, "Private Bar." In addition to the habitués of this waterside meeting-place, "The Black Lion," there were present a film celebrity (Mr. Donald Calthrop), certain bearded personalities wearing black berets, and other residents of the sedate Bohemia close to the host's riverside abode.

Prominently exhibited was a "Sunday Times," poster, "A.P. Herbert, M.P.". Not all, of course, of those who voted for Mr. Herbert were able to be present. Mr. Herbert claimed that the clergy voters were among his staunchest adherents. He was particularly pleased, he said, with this, especially seeing that divorce reform was conspicuous in his programme. He remarked that their heavy responsibilities on a Sunday doubtless made it impossible for some of them to congratulate him in person.

Only a few score of the voters live in Oxford and the rest of the 20,418 electors are scattered far and wide. Twenty thousand letters, addressed by hand, 600 of them by Mrs. Herbert, were sent out from the Herbert headquarters. Mr. Herbert made one speech to the Union, and spent altogether one day and a half in his constituency.

Some of the recipients were so moved by his manifesto that they sent postal orders, and some cheques for as much as £5.

"But I little realised until the counting of votes how near I might come to forfeiting my deposit." said Mr. Herbert. "I escaped by over 1,400 votes. If I had known how great was the risk, if I had been aware that I might have been returned to Parliament and still forfeited my deposit, I would not have been a candidate.

"I did not know that unless you have one-eighth of the first preferences you forfeit your deposit. Although Mr. Cruttwell had a final total of 3,697 he polled only 1,803 votes in the first count, and therefore lost his deposit.

"If my first figures had been less than one-eighth I would have forfeited my deposit even if I had been elected on the third count."

**(November 19)**

## OPIUM FACTORY IN PARIS

### ALLEGED DRUG GANG LEADER ARRESTED

PARIS, Thursday.

The seizure of 300lb of opium at Moret, reported yesterday, was followed to-day by the arrest in a Paris hotel of a Pole named Alfred Rosenbaum, described as a notorious international drug smuggler.

Rosenbaum was arrested on a charge of travelling with a forged Canadian passport. He had travelled from Shanghai to Spain and come from Santander to Paris "to undergo treatment in a nursing home."

The police attach particular importance to yesterday's seizure, since the opium was in its raw state. This means that somewhere in or near Paris there is an opium-refining factory, which is probably doing a lively business.

**(March 1)**

## HAUPTMANN GUILTY OF MURDER

### SENTENCED TO DIE IN ELECTRIC CHAIR

**From Douglas Williams, Daily Telegraph Special Correspondent**

FLEMINGTON (New Jersey), Wednesday.

Late to-night, after many hours' absence, the jury returned the verdict that Bruno Hauptmann was guilty of murdering Col. Lindbergh's infant son.

He was found guilty of murder in the first degree.

He was sentenced to death – in the electric chair on March 18.

The jury had made a recommendation that a sentence of life imprisonment be inflicted.

The jury, eight men and four women, had retired shortly after 11.20 a.m. (4.20 p.m. G.M.T.), a few minutes after Judge Trenchard had finished his summing-up.

Two hours passed by, and the judge ordered food to be sent to the jury. Two more hours, and the jury sent for magnifying glasses the better to examine exhibits in the case. Still more hours, and it was learned that Judge Trenchard was prepared to remain until 11 p.m.

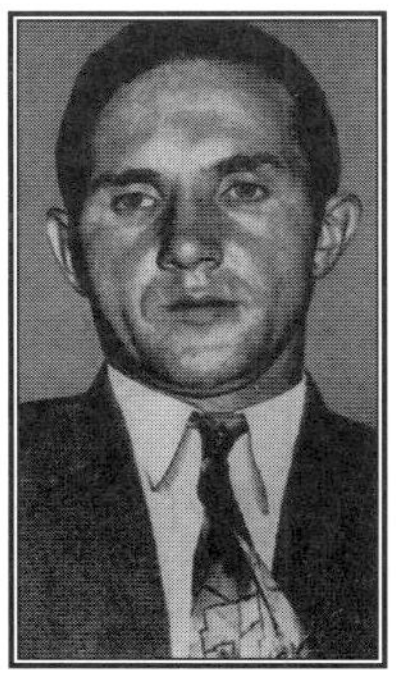

HAUPTMANN

Col. Lindbergh, whose infant son Bruno Hauptmann, a German carpenter, is charged with kidnapping, left the court shortly after the judge had concluded his summing-up. It was arranged that the result should be telephoned to him. Hauptmann remained in his cell reading the papers and smoking cigarettes. News-papermen awaiting the verdict were playing cards and munching apples.

Occasionally Judge Trenchard, smoking a large cigar, emerged from his private chambers and walked about the room exchanging remarks with counsel. There was an air of restless tension, and suppressed excitement.

Telegraph operators were remaining at their keys ready to flash the result to hundreds of newspapers throughout the world.

**(February 14)**

## OIL FLOWS ACROSS DESERT

### FROM IRAK TO THE MEDITERRANEAN

KIRKUK (Irak), Monday.

Two years of constant labour in stifling heat and bitter cold reached a successful conclusion to-day when the young King Ghazi of Irak, by simply turning a tap, caused oil to flow through 1,150 miles of steel pipe-lines from the Kirkuk oilfields to the Mediterranean sea.

Sixteen countries, including Great Britain, have been concerned in the construction of the great line built by the Irak Petroleum Company.

The pipe-line traverses Palestine, Transjordania, Syria, and Lebanon – across mountain, desert, river and basalt plain.

It will carry some 4,000,000 tons of oil a year from the heart of Irak to two points on the Mediterranean.

Starting at Kirkuk the pipe-line runs straight to Haditha, crossing the Tigris and Euphrates rivers. There it forks, one branch running across Syria to the port of Tripoli, and the other passing across the Syrian desert, through Transjordania, to the Palestinian port of Haifa.

In setting the seal on this great engineering triumph, which was sponsored by Sir John Cadman, of the Anglo-Persian Oil Company, King Ghazi made a speech stressing the importance of co-operation between the Irak petroleum company and the Irak Government. – Reuter and B.U.P.

**(January 15)**

## WAR THAT TURKEY FORGOT

**From Our Own Correspondent**

ISTANBUL, Sunday.

Turkey has just discovered that she is still in a state of war with a European republic.

This astonishing situation has been revealed, states the local Press, by a Turkish national having been refused permission to enter San Marino because he is a subject of a belligerent Power.

Investigation has disclosed that San Marino simultaneously with Italy declared war on Turkey during the Great War, and the treaties left this small State out of their calculations when their peace was concluded.

**(December 2)**

# GERMANY REJOICES OVER SAAR TRIUMPH

## World Welcomes The Verdict | Grave Menace To Peace Removed

### HITLER AND LAST TERRITORIAL DEMAND TO FRANCE

With wild rejoicing Germany yesterday welcomed home the Saar. Throughout the Reich there were amazing celebrations, culminating late last night with a great mass torchlight demonstration in Berlin.

The verdict of the plebiscite, announced in a special late edition of The Daily Telegraph yesterday, had shown a 90.08 per cent. vote in favour of a return to Germany. For the status quo 8.87 per cent. voted, and for union with France 04 per cent. The figures were:

| For Germany – | For Status Quo | For France – |
|---|---|---|
| 477,119 | 46,513 | 2,124 |

In the Saar the streets were thronged, a feature of the demonstrations being a mock funeral of the status quo.

**POLICE SENT ON LEAVE**

Last night, following a decision to send German "emigrant" members of the International police force on indefinite leave, a company of the East Lancashire Regiment was posted outside the police barracks at Saarbruecken.

Herr Hitler, in an address yesterday, said: "The German nation will make no further territorial claims on France," while M. Flandin, the French Prime Minister, referred to the problem of refugees from the Saar.

**(January 16)**

# PAGEANTRY OF BERLIN CELEBRATION

**From E.B.V. Wareing, Daily Telegraph Correspondent**

BERLIN, Tuesday.

The Minister of Propaganda has seldom staged a more picturesque scene than he did to-night.

The great glass dome of the Reichstag was illuminated from within and fires burned on its towers. On the steps, in the glare of a battery of arc lamps, the guard of khaki-clad storm troopers standing smartly to attention appeared like polished bronze statues.

The huge square was filled with detachments in all the countless uniforms of modern Germany, Reichswehr, Nazi Guards, Brownshirts, Stahlhelm, Air Sportsmen, and many others were all represented. All bore lighted torches.

Among them stood the general public, many of whom had marched in formation from their factory or business.

When Dr. Goebbels, shortly after eight p.m. mounted the Reichstag steps to speak, there were, he claimed, half a million people before him.

In short and impassioned address, which was amplified by loud-speakers on the square and broadcast all over Germany, he compared Jan. 15, 1935, with Jan. 30, 1933. the day on which Herr Hitler was called to power. He concluded by haranguing his hearers on the blessings of peace.

PAST KINGS' STATUES

Torchlight Procession

As Dr. Goebbels ceased, the uniformed contingents, torches in their hands, formed-up in columns in the light of the gigantic arc lamps which illuminated the front of the Reichstag. On a word of command from their leader they began to move, singing the "Horst Wessel Song," and thousands of the crowd, who had stood shivering in the cold, lined up behind them.

Headed by a Reichswehr guard of honour they marched past Dr. Goebbels and then, like a long serpent of flame crossed the great square and trailed away down the Siegesallee – the "Victory Avenue" – which is lined by the white statues of dead Kings of Prussia.

MUNICH'S 40,000 PINTS

Munich celebrated the news from the Saar with immense enthusiasm, with huge processions, thousands of flags, and well over 40,000 pints of beer in toasts.

Shops and streets were thronged, and the scene outside the station at noon, when the Saarlanders were returning by every train, resembled Trafalgar-square on Armistice Day.

The festivities reached their climax, however, at nightfall, when the Nazis began to assemble in the beer-halls. In the Hofbrau-House, Munich's largest beer-hall, to-night five bands were playing simultaneously, and every table and inch of standing room were taken.

**(January 16)**

# CUT OFF BY FALL OF ANCIENT BELFRY

COIMBRA, (Portugal), Thursday.

There were extraordinary scenes here this evening when the giant belfry of the 12th-century Cathedral of Santa Cruz was blown up and crashed across the principal thoroughfare, demolishing both the post-office and prison. The electricity, transport and telephone services are interrupted and the city is cut off from the rest of the country

The belfry was blown up to avert a major catastrophe, as it had tilted over dangerously and was expected to fall at any minute. Masses of masonry had already fallen. —Reuter.

**(January 4)**

# NORMANDIE'S NEW ATLANTIC RECORD

**From Our Own Correspondent**

PARIS, Wednesday.

When the Normandie reached Le Havre today on the completion of her maiden voyage from New York the giant French liner added another record to her achievement on the western run.

By her crossing of the Atlantic from the Ambrose Lightship to Bishop Rock, Scilly Isles, 3,015 miles, in 4 days 3 hours 25 minutes, at an average speed of 30.31 knots, she beat the Bremen's record, set up on June 15, 1933, as the following comparison shows:

| | TIME | SPEED |
|---|---|---|
| Normandie | 4 3 25 | 30.31 |
| Bremen | 4 16 15 | 28.51 |

The liner's time over the same distance on the outward run, when she captured the blue riband from the Italian liner Rex, was 4 days 3 hours 5 minutes, at an average speed of 30.1 knots.

The return voyage took 20 minutes longer, although the average speed – 30.31 knots – was faster. This is accounted for by the fact that wind and currents on the eastward run make deviations necessary. These added 35 miles to the distance.

CHEERED BY 100,000

A crowd of 100,000 cheered the Normandie's triumphant return, with the Blue Riband floating from her main mast. The world's largest seaplane, the 37-ton Lieutenant-de-Vaisseau-Paris, with 28 persons on board, flew out to meet her at Havre roads.

As the Normandie drew nearer a squadron of ten planes carried out formation flights around the seaplane, and the great vessel arrived in port amid the deafening sirens of a score of tugs and small craft.

**(June 13)**

# PEER'S DAUGHTER WHO "HATES JEWS"

### MISS MITFORD'S ATTACK

BERLIN, Friday.

The Hon. Unity Mitford, 21-year-old daughter of Lord Redesdale and sister of the Hon. Mrs Bryan Guiness, who was operated on yesterday in London following a car accident, announces that she is a "Jew hater" in an open letter to Herr Julius Streicher's notorious "Der Stuermer" paper.

"If we only had such a newspaper in England!" she writes. "The English have no notion of the Jewish danger. Our worst Jews only work behind the scenes.

"We hope, however, that you will soon see that we will soon win against the world enemy, in spite of all its cunning. We think with joy of the day when we will able to say with might and authority: England for the English! Out with the Jews! German greetings! Heil Hitler!"

In a postscript Miss Mitford says: "Please publish my whole name, I want everyone to know that I am a Jew hater." —Reuter.

**(July 27)**

# SIR M. CAMPBELL'S DISCLOSURE TO The Daily Telegraph

### HIS AVERAGE SPEED OVER 301 M.P.H.

**By Wireless Telephone to Salt Lake City, From a Special Correspondent**

Sir Malcolm Campbell revealed to me at 2.30 this morning that a revision of the official timing of his run on the salt lake at Bonneville Flats in his 2,350 horse-power car Bluebird, yesterday showed that his average speed was more than 301 miles per hour.

The revised figures are:

| | |
|---|---|
| First run | 304.331 m.p.h. |
| Second run | 298.013 m.p.h. |
| Average | 301.177 m.p.h. |

He thus broke his own world land speed record of 276.816 m.p.h. over the measured mile.

Sir Malcolm had just received the news when I spoke to him. From a crestfallen man, disappointed because the original official timing had given him an average speed of 299,875 m.p.h., he was transformed into a radiant, jubilant boy.

His joy was obvious. There was laughter in his voice as he spoke into the receiver.

"It's great news," he said. "Not long ago I was kicking myself because I had missed the 300 miles by an eighth of a mile. I should have had to try again in this terrific heat.

"Now there's no need to try again. I'm packing Bluebird up and coming home on the Majestic on Sept. 12.

"I was quite satisfied that the original timing was accurate, but the officials decided on a re-check which revealed the error.

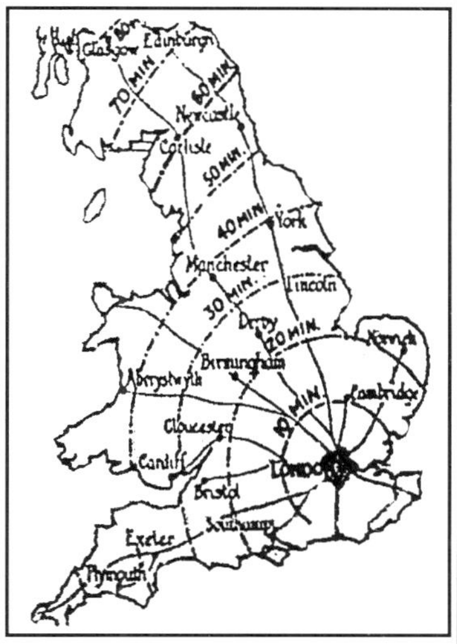


WHAT 300 M.P.H. MEANS. — A map showing how far along British roads a car running at Sir Malcom Campbell's speed could travel in the times indicated.

"These revised calculations mean everything in the world to me – and my boy, Donald, who is with me.

"I had set my heart on the 300 mark and I have to admit that I was down in the mouth after the first timing."

**(September 4)**

# POSTHUMOUS V.C.

### OFFICER'S GALLANTRY IN FRONTIER FIGHT

The posthumous award of the V.C. to Capt. Godfrey Maynell, M.C., who was mortally wounded in action against Mohmand tribesmen on the N.W. Frontier of India in September, was announced on Christmas Eve. It is just 14 years since the last V.C. was awarded, also for gallantry in India.

Sent forward for information, Capt. Meynell found the advanced troops engaged with an enemy greatly superior in number. He organised the defence, inflicting heavy casualties, until all his men were killed or wounded.

Capt. Meynell was a son of Brig.-Gen. Godfrey Meynell, of Meynell Langley, Derbyshire. He was educated at Eton and Sandhurst and won the M.C. in the Chitral expedition of 1932.

He had been in India 10 years. He was 31, and leaves a widow (formerly Miss Patricia Lewis, of Hampshire) and a son, who were out in India when he was killed.

The news was received during a family gathering on Christmas Eve, at which Capt. Maynell's baby son and widow were present. Brig.-Gen. Meynell, who was there, said: "I am proud of my boy. It is some recompense for his death."

**(December 27)**

# 30 M.P.H. LIMIT NOW IN FORCE

### GENERAL "SLOW-UP" AFTER MIDNIGHT

**From a Special Correspondent**

The 30 m.p.h., speed limit in built-up areas came into force at midnight. A few minutes before, in company with a commercial vehicle, a luxury car, and a motorcyclist, I was breaking what was soon to be "the law" along the Victoria Embankment. In fact a policeman seemed to look on us (at 40 m.p.h.) with approval, if not benevolence.

But as Big Ben completed the twelfth stroke of midnight traffic slowed down. Where, only a few minutes before, drivers had been speeding along merrily at anything up to 45, nearly all reduced speed to 25.

A tour of the West End – including thoroughfares where at that time of night a high speed might be expected – showed the same result. The exceptions – for example, the high-powered car which roared round Leicester-square at a speed which I should not like to estimate – merely served to accentuate the caution of the majority.

Officially, police cars were on the road from midnight onwards. But there was no indication of their presence. Nevertheless, motorists were on their guard, and I was amused to notice a procession of six or seven cars following a "baby" sports model containing two girls.

There was no evidence that the girls concealed gongs and uniforms beneath their coats. But the motorists following were determined to take no risks. It was to be observed, also, that most drivers had switched on their dashboard lamps, to enable them to watch their speedometers.

On the Hastings road, between Old Kent-road and Orpington. I recognised two unmistakable police cars on the prowl. They cannot have had a busy night.

**(March 18)**

# "GOLDEN-VOICED GIRL" CHOSEN

**By a Special Representative**

*"Then to come in spite of sorrow*
*And at my window bid good-morrow*
*Through the sweet-briar or the vine*
*Or the twisted eglantine ..."*

In the gilt telephones, the voice came through, cool, clear, delicately inflected, giving to Milton's lines their full rhythmic beauty. The judges listened and deliberated; and, a short time after, Miss Ethel Cain, aged 26, of Croydon, telephone operator at Victoria Exchange, was acclaimed the Girl With the Golden Voice, for whom the G.P.O. has been searching for weeks.

She will not – alas! – recite L'Allegro to subscribers. But one day in the not far distant future, if you are on a go-ahead exchange, you will be able to dial T-I-M and listen while a sound film of her voice tells you the time. And I, who have heard her speak, can recommend you to do so, as an aesthetic experience.

WINNER'S 10 GUINEA CHEQUE

The finals of the Post Office competition were held at St. Martin's le Grand yesterday morning. The judges were Mr. John Masefield, the Poet-Laureate, Dame Sybil Thorndike, Lord Iliffe, Mr. S. Hibberd (chief announcer of the B.B.C.), and Mrs. E.D. Atkinson, recently chosen as the perfect telephone subscriber.

The finalists spoke the passage from Milton, another from Stevenson's "Treasure Island," and a third test, giving nine different times.

Miss J. H. Dunn (Trunks, London) was runner-up. She receives 5 guineas, and the other finalists receive 2 guineas each.

Miss Cain was handed her cheque for 10 guineas by Major George Tryon, the new Postmaster-General. She will soon begin recording the 132 separate hours, minutes, and seconds which are required.

She told me yesterday that she had studied elocution for some years and was an enthusiastic amateur actress.

**(June 22)**

# BRITISH CULTURE ABROAD

### COUNCIL TO PROMOTE WIDER KNOWLEDGE

The formation of the British Council for Relations with Other Countries is announced to-day.

Its purpose is stated to be to promote abroad a wider knowledge of the English language, literature, art, music, science, educational institutions and other aspects of our national life, and thereby to encourage a better appreciation of Great Britain and to maintain closer relations between this and other countries.

British Ambassadors and Ministers abroad and special trade missions to various parts of the world have repeatedly recommended that some central body should be set up to undertake this work on a wider scale than hitherto, and to encourage and co-ordinate the activities of existing societies.

METHODS OF WORK

The following are stated to be illustrations of the means by which the Council intends to achieve its objects:

Encouraging the study of English in foreign schools, technical colleges and universities;

Extending a knowledge in other countries of English literature, both general and technical, through a wider distribution of English books in such centres as may be approved by the Council;

Assisting in the foundation of Chairs of English at foreign universities;

Arranging for a regular flow of carefully selected speakers for suitable societies and institutions abroad;

Arranging for the performance abroad of the works of British composers, and assisting in the organisation of exhibitions of British art, &c;

Arranging for courses of instruction in the United Kingdom for foreign teachers of English;

Founding general, technical, commercial or industrial scholarships or fellowships for students from overseas, and promoting in other ways the interchange of students between the United Kingdom and other countries.

The Government have expressed their willingness to propose to Parliament the grant of £6,000 from public funds for the financial year 1945-36, as a contribution towards the very much larger sum which will be required in order to perform effectively a task of urgent national importance.

Inquiries should be addressed to the Clerk to the Council, Lt.-Col. Charles Bridge, Shell-Mex House, Strand, London, W.C.2.

**(March 20)**

# WORLD'S LARGEST EXHIBITION FOR LONDON

Work will begin next month on the £1,250,000 scheme at Earl's Court which will give London, by Christmas, 1936 what is claimed to be the world's biggest permanent exhibition and large-scale entertainment centre. The building will house part of the British Industries Fair Exhibition in 1937, and later the Ideal Home Exhibition, and, as indicated in The Daily Telegraph on Tuesday, the Motor Show.

Arrangements are being made for a share issue next week. At the beginning of August the new company, Earl's Court Ltd. will take occupation of the old exhibition site of Transport Board. The work will employ 2,000 men.

Sir Ralph Glyn, M.P., chairman of the company, informed a Daily Telegraph representative yesterday that they hoped to provide good music, amusement and recreation on a scale which would be of real value for the physical development of the young.

Mr. Lewis, the managing director, describing the architectural features of the scheme, said a concrete building 80ft high would be built, providing over 12 acres of exhibition space on two floors and seats for 25,000 people for sporting events or large-scale entertainments. In addition, the existing Empress Hall would be reconditioned for ice-hockey, skating and other indoor sports.

**(July 18)**

# 53 BRITONS AMONG 20,000 DEAD AT QUETTA

## FAMOUS HILL STATION IN RUINS

Twenty thousand are dead in Quetta, the important military station in British Baluchistan, as a result of an earthquake which devastated the town and 100 miles of neighbouring country.

Forty-three British airmen, including one officer, who were stationed there, are among the victims. Between 20 and 30 others are missing, and believed dead.

About 10 other British residents have lost their lives.

The R.A.F. headquarters and the civil station are in ruins.

Towns and villages have been almost obliterated. Two relief trains are on the way from Karachi with doctors, nurses and medical supplies.

(June 1)

## TOWN COLLAPSES IN LESS THAN A MINUTE
### From Our Special Correspondent

KARACHI, Friday.

The Quetta wireless station is the only link between that stricken city and the outside world. Its messages, at first almost unintelligible, are now clearer.

They tell us that the earlier news of the great earthquake which shook British Baluchistan at 3.4 a.m. (10.34 p.m. Thursday, British Summer Time) had greatly underestimated its effects.

It is now declared that in the important military and railway centre of Quetta alone some 20,000 have lost their lives.

This famous hill station, 5,500 feet above sea level, favourite resort of British officers at this time of the year, was particularly interesting in ruins. The extensive and world-famous fruit gardens which surround the town have been entirely destroyed.

Dead are lying beneath debris piled high in the wrecked streets. The headquarters of the R.A.F., some little distance away from the military cantonment, have been razed to the ground.

We learn officially that 43 British airmen, including Flying Officer C.E. Paylor, of No. 5 Squadron, have been killed, and that 20 or 30 are missing. No names beyond that of Flying Officer Paylor have yet reached us, but there are growing fears for those reported missing.

### POLICE FORCE WIPED OUT
#### Entire Barracks Crumble

Fortunately the military station itself escaped serious damage, and the men of the garrison, few of whom suffered injury, have been at work all day extricating hundreds of injured. Native troops are assisting.

They have had to take the place of the police force, which was practically wiped out by the collapse of the police barracks. This fact helps one to realise the severe character of the shock, for the barracks were strongly constructed and substantial.

We shall not know for some time yet how many have been injured. It is certain, however, that the great majority of the victims were those sleeping in the congested part of the town.

Here houses crumbled at the first shock. Those who dashed in panic to the street were crushed by the falling structures.

In less than a minute the whole area was a huge pile of debris. There was no escape. The roads were blocked.

(June 1)

*Where good appearance counts ...*

The "Eclipse" Super Razor Blade (rendered 100% efficient by the "Eclipse" Razor) provides the clean-shaven appearance essential to every social activity.

**Razors 7'6    Blades 3 for 1'**

# TELEVISION IN ACTION

## FILM SHOWN AT DEMONSTRATION
### By Our Special Representative

London had its first demonstration yesterday of the new television service that is to be available to the public in a few months' time. As one of an audience of about 50 people, I sat in front of the new type of receiving set and was able to see and hear things that were happening at Crystal Palace.

The experience, coming so promptly after the announcement of the Postmaster-General that we can all become "lookers" before the end of the year, was particularly interesting. These televised effects were in every way superior to the efforts of the past.

Externally, the television set resembles a slightly larger edition of the ordinary broadcast receiver. In front, however, is a panel for a televised picture measuring 12 inches by 9. The picture, shown without any apparent noise and with practically no flicker, might have been likened to that obtained from a cinema film shown in miniature.

Miss Alma Taylor displaying one new hat after another and describing them at the same time, was also able to answer us back when we spoke to her by telephone in the studio. Then came an exterior scene. Horses were shown jumping in the grounds of the Crystal Palace, and the announcer – seen on the screen as clearly as he was heard explained that this was a scene comparable to that which might be seen in the future when the Derby is televised.

### A BOXING MATCH

Other scenes were of a boxing match in the studio (as if the fight were taking place at the Albert Hall); a lecture as from a school, with the lecturer drawing clear diagrams to illustrate his points; and portions of popular sound films.

Definition was extraordinarily good. Always, however, the best results were obtained when the human figures were shown only at half length. Details smaller than this were not very satisfactory. One was conscious after a while that the necessity for concentration was a little trying to the eyes.

In yesterday's demonstration, television was through the medium of a film. The scenes were photographed by a cinema camera at Crystal Palace and developed so rapidly that they were being televised within 30sec. while still partially wet. The time lag of 30sec did not in any way spoil the transmission.

(February 2)

## COLOUR BAR AT SWIMMING POOL

### INSTRUCTION TO RAILWAY

The Southern Railway is refusing to issue to coloured persons special tickets to include fare and admission to the Lagoon Swimming Pool, Orpington.

An official of the railway company stated to a representative of THE DAILY TELEGRAPH last night that the company was acting on the request of the proprietors of the swimming pool, with whom it had an arrangement for the issue of the tickets.

The manager of the Lagoon explained that ever since the pool was opened three years ago it had been the settled policy to refuse admission to coloured people. About a month ago some Indian students came from London and were turned away.

It was only right that coloured people should be told about the ban before they started on a 15-miles' journey. That was why the railway company had been requested to make it known that the special tickets would not be issued to them.

### PROPRIETOR'S VIEWS

At one or two other swimming pools in and around London the colour-bar question has been raised, but at the majority it is unknown.

The proprietor of one of the biggest open-air swimming pools north of London said: "The question has not arisen so far as we are concerned. If it did, however, I think I should do my best to keep coloured people out. I think their presence would be objectionable to many people."

The manager of another big swimming pool on the south side of the river said: "We feel it necessary to refuse admission to people of colour, because of the feelings of women using the pool. When it is a matter of using the same stretch of water for swimming in, the question becomes somewhat different from that of travelling in 'buses and tramcars with coloured people."

Surbiton, Wood Green, Hammersmith and Hornsey pools are among those where no colour ban is imposed.

"Why should we ban these people?" asked one manager. "We are not living in Germany."

At several pools it was stated that, while there was no official ban against the admission of coloured people, they were not encouraged to attend.

(August 17)

## 'PEACE BALLOT' RESULT

### 11,000,000 IN FAVOUR OF LEAGUE

The final figures of the votes cast in the National Peace Ballot, organised by the League of Nations Union, was announced by Viscount Cecil, president, at a mass meeting at the Albert Hall last night. The Archbishop of Canterbury was among those on the platform.

They showed that:

11,627,765 votes were cast in answer to questions asked.

Over 11,000,000 votes were in favour of Britain remaining a member of the League.

Nearly 10,500,000 favoured an all-round reduction of armaments, by international agreement, and the prohibition of the manufacture of armaments for private profit.

The questions were:

Should Britain remain a member of the League?

Are you in favour of an all-round reduction of armaments by international agreement?

Are you in favour of the all-round abolition of national, military and naval aircraft by international agreement?

Should the manufacture and sale of armaments for private profit be prohibited?

Do you consider that if a nation insists on attacking another the other nations should combine, to compel it to stop by:
(a) economic and non-military measures;
(b) if necessary, military measures?

The final figures were:

| Question | Yes | No | Doubtful | Abstentions |
|---|---|---|---|---|
| 1 | 11,000,387 | 355,883 | 10,470 | 102,425 |
| 2 | 10,470,489 | 862,775 | 12,062 | 213,839 |
| 3 | 9,533,558 | 1,089,786 | 10,976 | 318,845 |
| 4 | 10,417,329 | 775,415 | 15,076 | 351,345 |
| 5a | 10,027,608 | 635,074 | 27,255 | 855,107 |
| 5b | 6,784,368 | 2,351,981 | 40,893 | 2,364,441 |

The average poll for the whole country was 37.9 per cent.

Lord Cecil said that the number of votes cast varied – apart from London – from 12 per cent. of the possible total in King's Lynn to 86 per cent. in Montgomeryshire.

The latest electorate figures are: England, 24,799,619; Wales, 1,640,094; Scotland, 3,039,693.

### PRIMATE AND LEAGUE

The Archbishop of Canterbury, describing the results of the ballot as most remarkable, said they would do well to press home on the Government on M.P.'s and on their fellow citizens that these 12,000,000 people had recorded this decisive vote. It was the first time that, on a scale so large, the people of this country had been invited to express a free opinion. It was an intelligent opinion.

(June 28)

## KEW BREAKS 21-YR. SUNSHINE RECORD
### By Our Weather Expert

Apart from local thunderstorms, there is still no sign of rain to break the drought, which is now in its 23rd day in London and many parts of Southern England.

Rather cooler weather is likely to spread south to-day, but conditions will remain bright generally.

For most of England and Wales the week-end was exceptionally sunny and warm. At Kew, Saturday, with 13.5 hours of sunshine, was the sunniest day recorded so late in the year since 1914.

Many other places did even better, the highest figures being 14.8 hours at Ilfracombe, 14.3 in Jersey, and 14.2 at Lympne.

Both on Saturday and yesterday temperatures exceeded 80deg. in many places, and London had its seventh day this month in the eighties.

(Aug 12)

# QUEEN ASTRID KILLED IN LUCERNE MOTOR ACCIDENT

THE DAILY TELEGRAPH greatly regrets to announce the death of Queen Astrid, Queen of the Belgians, who was killed in a motor-car accident near the village of Juessnacht, on Lake Lucerne, Switzerland, yesterday morning.

King Leopold was himself driving the car when it mounted the kerbstone, swerved off the road, struck two trees and plunged into the lake fifty feet below.

The Queen was thrown out and her head came into violent contact with the first tree. She died in the King's arms without regaining consciousness.

The King received injuries to the face and arm. For a considerable time he was unable to speak.

They were going on a climbing expedition. It was while climbing in Belgium that King Albert, King Leopold's father, was killed eighteen months ago.

Queen Astrid was 29. As Princess Astrid of Sweden she married King Leopold on Nov. 4, 1926. She leaves three children.

(August 30)

## STONER FOUND GUILTY AND RECOMMENDED TO MERCY
### By Our Special Representative

In a crowded, hushed court, George Stoner, 18, a chauffeur, was at the Old Bailey yesterday found guilty of the murder of his employer, Mr. Francis Mawson Rattenbury, 67, at the Villa Madeira, Bournemouth.

He was recommended to mercy. The dead man's widow, Mrs. Alma Rattenbury, 38, was found not guilty.

After a 3½ hours' summing-up by Mr. Justice Humphreys, the jury were absent for about an hour.

When they came back to court Stoner leaned on the dock and looked fixedly at the solicitors' table. Mrs. Rattenbury, who carried long blue gloves, looked tired and worn.

The formal questions were asked. "Are the jury agreed?" "Do they find Alma Victoria Rattenbury guilty or not guilty?" "Not guilty," said the foreman.

Immediately Mrs. Rattenbury appeared to half turn and half stumble towards the side of the dock where Stoner was standing. Then two wardresses helped her hurriedly down the stairs.

"Do they find George Percy Stoner guilty or not guilty?"

"Guilty," replied the foreman.

Stoner came to attention again when he was asked if he had anything to say before sentence of death was passed?

"Nothing at all," he replied in a low firm voice.

Sentence of death was passed, but Stoner's expressionless features did not change. He stood erect to hear Mr. Justice Humphreys say:

"The jury have convicted you of the murder with a recommendation to mercy. That recommendation will be forwarded by me to the proper quarter, where it will receive consideration. My duty is to pass on you the only sentence that the law knows for the crime for which you have been convicted."

Then Stoner went below.

Mrs. Rattenbury was then called. She had been in a corridor below, and as wardresses assisted her towards the stairs leading back to the dock, she met Stoner. She looked hard at him as he was hurried past.

When Mrs. Rattenbury reached the dock she stood for a few minutes, while a second indictment was discussed. This charged her with being an accessory after the fact, knowing that George Stoner "had wounded with intent to murder."

It was announced that the prosecution would offer no evidence, and she was formally discharged.

(June 1)

## STALIN RIDES ON MOSCOW 'METRO'
### From Our Own Correspondent

MOSCOW, Tuesday.

M. Joseph Stalin, Dictator of Soviet Russia, has just taken his first journey by "tube."

Leaving the Kremlin after nightfall yesterday he drove with his three principal lieutenants, M. Molotoff, M. Orgonikidze and M. Kaganovich, to the Crimea Square terminal station, and from there travelled over the full eight miles of Moscow's new underground.

Properly to appreciate the wide interest this has caused here one must go back to the opening of the first steam railways in England.

Stalin, we are officially informed, was "wildly cheered" when he inspected the grandiose multi-coloured marble halls which, in Moscow, replace London's plain but practical Underground stations.

This new Tube, although virtually ready these last three months, has not yet begun selling tickets or conveying ordinary passengers to and from their work. It is hoped, however, to begin a regular service on Thursday.

Stalin closely inspected the new escalators. These moving stairs are the chief source of astonishment to Moscow residents. to-day a number of women and children who had been granted special "joy-riding tickets" could only be persuaded to scale the escalator when a policeman undertook to accompany them.

### SMALL BOYS BEG A RIDE

Yesterday and to-day queues of these privileged ticket-holders waited hours for their turn to have a free ride with more eagerness than any crowd ever waited for rides or a scenic railway at Wembley. Again, disconsolate youngsters loitered in the vain hope of begging or stealing a pass.

As expected, the gorgeous marble pillars, and the floodlit tiling in the stations, which would be worthy of a setting for grand opera, made a special appeal. As one of Moscow's oldest foreign inhabitants said to me, "This Metro is ultra-modern in its technique, but its gorgeous stations are the most characteristically Russian thing done here since the Revolution."

(April 24)

## NEW TELEPHONE BOOTHS

A new and more artistic telephone kiosk, to be know as the "Jubilee Design," has been designed for the Postmaster-General's department by Sir Giles Gilbert Scott. One of its internal amenities will be a small mirror.

(August 1)

# JEWS' STATUS IN GERMANY DEFINED
### From Our Own Correspondent

BERLIN, Friday.

After a delay of two months the executive regulations for the application of the anti-Jewish legislation passed by the Reichstag during the party congress at Nuremberg have now been published.

It is provided that "until further notice all German nationals of German or cognate blood who, at the time when the law came into effect, possessed the right to vote for the Reichstag shall be deemed citizens of the State." The law then defines the new category of persons who will in future be known as "Jewish crossbreeds."

These are persons descended from one or two racially "full Jewish" grandparents provided that they do not fall within the category of "Jews." A "Jew" is a person descended from three or more racially full Jewish grandparents.

"A Jewish crossbreed," it is added, "shall be considered to be a Jew if he is, or had been, a member of the Jewish religious community or married to a Jew or Jewess or descended from a Jewish parent as a result of a marriage contracted after Sept. 15, 1935.

Jewish officials who are still in office will be discharged at the end of the present year. Those who served during the war will be pensioned off at their present rates of pay.

### JEWISH FLAG

A slight alleviation has been made in respect of the employment of non-Jewish maidservants in Jewish homes. The age limit below which servants may be employed has been reduced from 45 to 35 in respect of those in employment when the Nuremberg laws were passed. Apart from this no maidservant under 45 may be engaged in any house where either the head or any male member of the family is a Jew.

(November 16)

## NAME SELECTED FOR BABY PRINCE

### TO BE A GEORGE

It is understood that George will be one of the names that will be given to the Duke and Duchess of Kent's infant son when he is christened. The other names have not yet been decided upon.

Last night it was stated at 3, Belgrave-square that the Duchess and her child were continuing to make very good progress.

(October 14)

# CINEMA-GOERS SPEND £40,000,000 IN A YEAR

## 18,000,000 TICKETS A WEEK SOLD

Some astonishing facts with regard to the cinema industry in Great Britain were revealed yesterday by Mr. S. Rowson, President of the British Cinematograph Society, in a statistical survey of the industry presented to the Royal Statistical Society. Mr. Rowson describes the cinema as "one of the sociological wonders of the century."

His paper is the first attempt made by the society to deal with facts and figures relative to the recreations and amusements of Great Britain. The figures given show that:

The people of Great Britain in 1934 spent £40,950,000 on going to the cinema;

They bought 957,000,000 tickets of admission and paid, on an average just over 10d for each ticket, and

Cinemas in Great Britain in that year totalled 4,305, 70 per cent. being smaller than the average London cinema, and seating 1,000 or under.

In the year ended March 31, 1935, 667 "subjects" for "long" films were registered, measuring 4,301,000 feet. Of these 119 were British, totally 1,186,000 feet, or 29 per cent. of the whole.

Each British film was screened on an average 7,420 times. The corresponding foreign film average was 6,900.

£6,800,000 DUTY

Of the £40,950,000 paid at the box-offices the Government claimed £6,800,000 in entertainment duty. Exclusive of duty, 42 per cent. of admissions were at prices not exceeding 6d. and another 36 1/2 per cent. cost not more than 10d.

In other words, four out of every five people visiting the cinema pay 1s or less for their seats.

The admission figure of 957,000,000 in the year gives an average of nearly 22 visits to the cinema a year by every man, woman and child in the country. Actually Mr. Rowson concludes that the figure is "very much higher" than 30 visits a year for each patron.

**(December 18)**

# FILM OF "DAVID COPPERFIELD"

**By Campbell Dixon**

The film business is full of ironies, but none more striking than this – that it has been left to Hollywood to turn out one of the most essentially British pictures ever made.

"David Copperfield" given an enthusiastic reception at the Palace Theatre last night, was produced and directed by Americans and perhaps half the cast is English. Yet nowhere is there a jarring note.

David Selznick, the producer, George Cukor, the director, and Mr. Hugh Walpole as adviser, spent the best part of a year and endless pains and money on making the picture as authentic as possible.

It is proof of their success that while all but the more rabid Dickensians will find it agreeably true to the original, the great majority who do not know the book will find it absorbing entertainment.

The picture, like the book, has almost everything, sound characterisation, sentiment, which only just fails to achieve the dignity of drama, and a deal of brilliant comedy – for which, of course, Mr. Micawber and Betsey Trotwood are mainly responsible.

While the whole production speaks eloquently of painstaking team-work, it is on the acting side a triumph for four people – W.C. Fields, whose Micawber is one of the richest bits of character-drawing the screen has ever given us; Edna May Oliver, whose Miss Trotwood runs him very close; Frank Lawton, the perfect choice for the adult Copperfield, charming, sensitive yet never mawkish; and little Freddie Bartholomew, who makes the sufferings of David as a boy very moving.

**(March 7)**

# GERSHWIN'S OPERA TRIUMPH

George Gershwin's musical adaptation of "Porgy," Du Bose Heyward's well-known drama of the Charleston waterfront, was produced in New York last night before an enthusiastic audience. It is expected to be the success of the season.

The opera is called "Porgy and Bess," and has been produced by the Theatre Guild.

A brilliant cast of negro singers, many of whom have never been on the stage before, reproduce against a background of mouldering tenements the tragedy of the negro cripple, with his goat-cart and his woman, Bess. There was great enthusiasm at the end of the second act as the curtain came down on a stage filled with terrified negroes, praying and shouting, their voices rising above the tumult of a gathering storm.

Critics agree that this is the most successful thing Gershwin has written since the "Rhapsody in Blue," and the best folk opera ever produced in New York.

**(October 12)**

# COLOUR STARTS NEW ERA FOR FILMS

**By Campbell Dixon**

Yesterday I saw film history made. "Becky Sharp," the first full-length feature in colour, is the greatest sensation since "The Jazz Singer" and "The Singing Fool."

The Technicolor process may not yet be perfect enough to satisfy academicians. Long shots and close-ups do not always match, and if life is to be exactly simulated it will be necessary to tone down the players' make-up and costumes and rely more on pastels and sepia.

But this hardly matters. What does matter is that "Becky Sharp" is brilliantly photographed in colours that will hit the public right in the eye – sky blue, brilliant yellow, dazzling scarlet.

For the first time in a full-length feature it is possible to see the heroine as she really is; the blue of Miriam Hopkins's eyes, the texture of her skin; the pale and shining gold of her hair.

Can it be doubted that the public will want to see Miss Garbo and Miss Dietrich, Miss Bergner and Miss Sten photographed with the same vividness and fidelity?

NO SUDDEN FLOOD

Naturally a sudden flood of colour pictures cannot be expected. Studios are not equipped to make them, and productions must generally be planned a year before exhibition.

But if colour does not kill black-and-white as quickly as talkies killed silents, I believe their victory is just as inevitable. The company that is not making colour pictures a year hence will probably be out of business.

"Becky Sharp" was made by a new concern in Hollywood, headed by the young millionaire, Mr. "Jock" Whitney, Rhuben Mamoulian, accustomed to using colour as a producer for the New York Theatre Guild, directed, and it is significant that another man of the theatre, Robert Edmond Jones, designed the colour settings.

They (particularly Mr. Jones) have done their job brilliantly. The characters move in authentic Regency costumes against rich and at times quite beautiful interiors, and again and again colour is cleverly used to suggest a mood and intensify emotion.

**(July 10)**

# HOLLYWOOD'S OWN SHAKESPEARE

## 'MIDSUMMER NIGHT'S DREAM' FILM

**By J.E. Sewell**

It can be done, and Max Reinhardt with the resources of Messrs. Warner Brothers at his disposal, has shown one way of doing it. Last night's world première of "A Midsummer Night's Dream" at the Adelphi Theatre (it was shown simultaneously in New York) may well place Shakespeare once more among the world's most popular entertainers.

The film is lavish as only Hollywood knows how. Dazzling, magnificent, over whelming, with moments of visionary beauty such as the screen has not seen before – it charmed and amused and astonished an audience by turns.

This is the general, the irresistible verdict. Yet I am bound to admit that even Reinhardt cannot keep the film alive for two and a half hours. One has a feeling that Hollywood, its heart in its mouth, has taken more of a chance than it needed, treating Shakespeare with a reverence which has no room for affection.

James Cagney gives a new, fresh, vivid interpretation of Bottom which deserves the attention of every Shakespearian. Nini Theilade's dancing provides some of the loveliest moments of the evening. Joe E. Brown's preposterous countenance makes even Flute funny, our own Ian Hunter speaks Theseus magnificently, and Mickey Rooney is a fascinatingly malicious little ruffian as Puck.

**(October 10)**

# B.B.C.S 'DONT'S' FOR COMEDIANS

A list of "don't's" for radio artists has been drawn up by the B.B.C.

The list, which will be given to artists when they receive their contracts for signature, reminds artists that they must not mention during their broadcast performance the name of any production in which they are appearing, the theatre in which they are performing, or the management to which they are under contract.

The banned subjects are:

Proprietary articles and business names;

Religion – including spiritualism;

Public personalities;

Marital infidelity;

Effeminacy in men;

Immorality of any kind;

Physical infirmities and deformities, including blindness, dumbness, stammering, loss of limbs, cross-eyes;

Painful or fatal diseases – including cancer, consumption, mental deficiency.

Reference to negroes as "niggers," and Chinese as "Chinks."

**(July 10)**

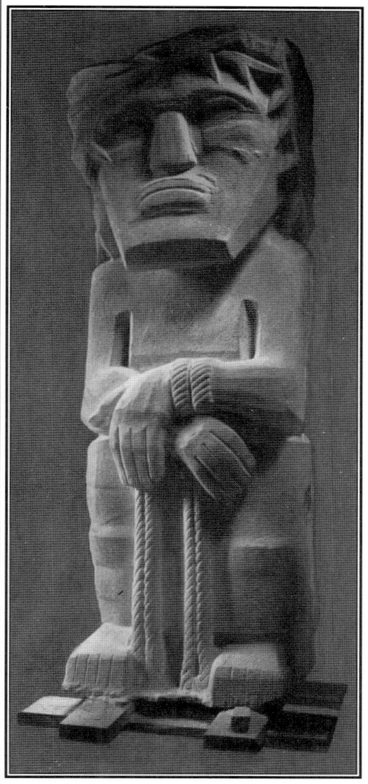

"BEHOLD THE MAN"

# BIG SUCCESS AT DRURY LANE

## "GLAMOROUS NIGHT"

**By W.A. Darlington**

There was wild enthusiasm at Drury-lane last night, to greet the production of Ivor Novello's big spectacular musical play, "Glamorous Night."

In contriving this show, Mr. Novello has brought off the biggest achievement of his career. It is not an easy task, now that the "talkies" have been brought to technical perfection, to invent a big-scale stage entertainment which will rival them in popular appeal. Only a superb theatrical craftsman could bring it off – and that is exactly what Mr. Novello is.

I have had hard things to say of him when he has tried to be serious and failed to be serious enough. Here, however, he is working well within the limits of his remarkable array of talents, and he commands my very profound respect.

Superior persons will no doubt scorn at the show, and dismiss it as a lot of nonsense. In fact, I heard one doing so in the interval last night – and very foolish I thought him. If it is nonsense, it is glamorous nonsense, and for those who are ready to be entertained, it is the best show of its kind that Drury Lane has had for years.

**(May 3)**

# A NEW KIND OF MURDER PLAY

**By W.A. Darlington**

In "Night Must Fall," Emlyn Williams has written the first murder play known to me in which the interest is concentrated not at all on the murderer's identity, but entirely on his psychology.

In a short prologue Mr. Williams tells us that a murder is to be committed, and by whom. For dramatic purposes he avoids telling us who is to be the victim – but that point is not allowed to take up much of our attention.

Mr. Williams is out to analyse a murderer's mind – the mixture of cunning, and vanity, and dementia which turns a pleasant youth into a dangerous criminal. He does it about as well as it could possibly be done, and his play is a brilliant success. It is also as grim a business as I have ever sat through.

Mr. Williams himself plays his murderer. His suggestion of Dan's mental kink is brought off with extraordinary sureness of touch – but then Mr. Williams has always been able to play these abnormal people rather better than anybody else.

**(June 1)**

# DAZZLING NEW STAR OF THE FUTURE

Last night's reopening of Sadler's Wells revealed a dazzling new star of the future.

Not since I first saw Tourmanova and Baronova have I been so impressed with any "child" as with Margot Fonteyn, and I am impressed now for very much the same reason.

In Ashton's sparkling "Rendezvous" she showed vitality, charm, lightness, and the suggestion of a virtuoso technique in the years to come. Rarest of all, her arms are full of expression.

**(September 28)**

# EPSTEIN'S 11ft CHRIST

## PRIMITIVE STYLE AND LITTLE DETAIL

The exhibition of recent sculpture by Jacob Epstein, which opens on Friday at the Leicester Galleries, is certain to rouse controversy. The sport of playing policeman to this artist has become an annual event for the more obstinate detractors of his work, and possibly they would be disappointed if he gave them no occasion for it.

Sometimes he has provided it in plenty, but such is not the case this year.

The chief feature of the show, a figure of Christ entitled "Behold the Man," offers fascinating opportunity for discussion from the point of view of aesthetics. Offence at it on other grounds suggests unreasonable haste in judgment, when it is not suspiciously artificial.

In any case, the qualities of the figure are so essentially sculpturesque that it must be seen in order to be praised or condemned. No adequate conception can be formed from photographic reproduction.

In Subiaco marble, weighing six tons and standing 11ft high, it represents Christ crowned with thorns and with bound hands. It follows closely, in its finished structure, the elongated cubic block from which it was carved.

"DWARFED" IN GALLERY

Even in the gallery it is not viewed at best advantage. The head is over-size in proportion to the rest of the body – as is proper for seeing it from below, on a tall pedestal or raised above the ground as part of a building. In the confines of a room it is unduly dwarfed.

But through all the mass there is a diffused energy inherent in its form and ordered by a discipline of pattern. This force of impulse radiates within the strictly-bounded shape. There is no violence of gesture, no sensational disturbance of the calm, straight pose. The effect is compelling and impressive.

The only strangeness in the work lies in the elimination of all but the barest detail and the broad lines on which the features of the face are indicated. But seen outside the limit of four walls, and at a greater height, the economy of detail would be a benefit. Also, closer facial likeness would be wasted, and the rudimentary, formal features would stand out more visibly.

**(March 7)**

# 2 1/2D "BEGGAR'S OPERA"

A concert performance of Kurt Weill's "Die Dreigroschenoper," the story of which is based on "The Beggar's Opera," was given under the title of "The Two-penny-halfpenny Opera" at Broadcasting House last night as the fifth of this season's concerts of contemporary music.

The work was described on the programme as "an experiment in Epic Theatre." It may be that; it is certainly not an opera. Like its eighteenth-century counterpart it consists of long stretches of dialogue, interspersed with songs. The period is supposed to be 1837, but apart from occasional references to "the coronation" the play seemed to be set in the twentieth century, to judge by Denis Freeman's idiomatic translation.

There is no mistake about the music, which has both its feet firmly planted in our own age. It is cinema music or perhaps rather revue music, no better and often slightly worse than the numerous popular successes which have adorned the London stage during the post-war years. To treat this hotch-potch of jazz seriously would be a waste of time.

**(February 9)**

# FINEST JULIET OF OUR TIME

## PEGGY ASHCROFT AT THE NEW

**By W.A. Darlington**

There were moments in "Romeo and Juliet" at the New Theatre last night when I felt myself moved as deeply as I ever remember to have been moved in the theatre. Some of the scenes, in the early part of the play particularly, had an almost intolerable beauty.

To Peggy Ashcroft for her exquisite Juliet, and to John Gielgud for his work as producer go the chief praises for this.

Between them they have captured the very ecstasy of young love and released it on the stage.

Miss Ashcroft's Juliet has been seen before. She played the part some years ago at Oxford. Then, she was utterly charming as the young girl newly in love, but she let the tragic Juliet evade her. Now, she gives us the whole portrait.

Of Laurence Olivier as Romeo there is much to be said in admiration. Unfortunately, there is this to be said on the other side, that he never once moved me at all.

Romeo hesitating in the garden when he might be climbing the balcony pillar; Romeo, in tears of despair in Friar Laurence's cell – these are aspects of the character which do not suit this actor's forthright personality.

Mr. Gielgud's Mercutio is a brilliant performance, executed with finish and power. No more gallant death has ever been died by this most gallant gentleman. Finally – leaving out, for lack of time and space, a dozen admirable performances – there is Edith Evans's grandly built-up character as the Nurse. There is the most real old woman you ever saw, earthy as a potato, slow as a carthorse, cunning as a badger.

It is with real joy that I reflect that I shall be seeing this production again in a few week's time, when Mr. Gielgud and Mr. Olivier change places. One visit is certainly not enough.

**(October 14)**

STEPHENSON'S
FLOOR POLISH
cleans, polishes and preserves stained floors; parquetry; old oak; painted or varnished woodwork; lino; trunks; brown footwear; and all leather goods, etc.
THE PUREST POLISH
3d., 6d., 1/-

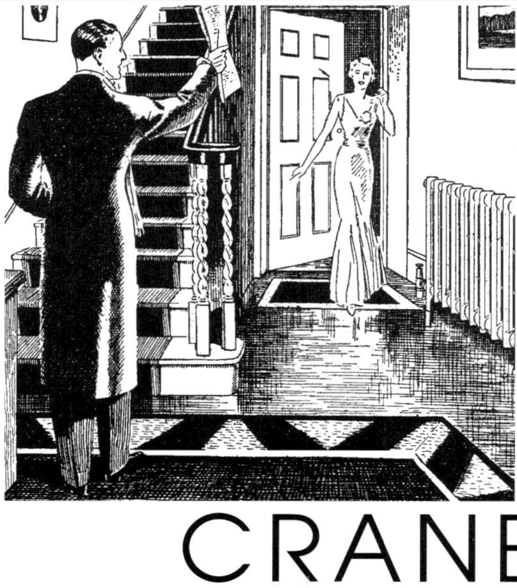

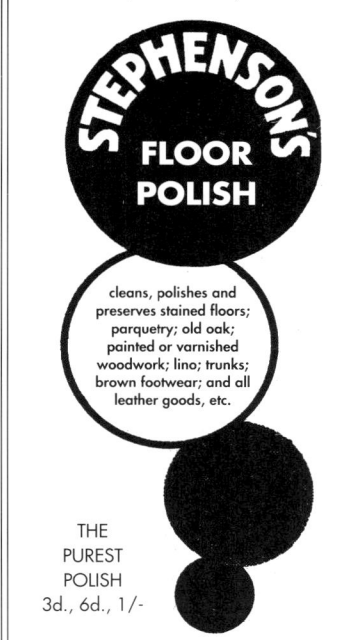

WARMTH EVERYWHERE
Nothing can keep your house so warm, cosy and comfortable from kitchen to attic as central heating. And there is no central heating equipment so economical, so efficient as Crane.
CRANE
RADIATORS & BOILERS

THE DAILY TELEGRAPH

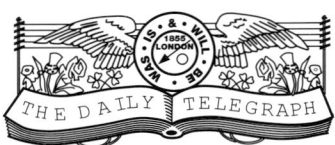

135, FLEET STREET LONDON

Telephone: CENTRAL 4242

**TO-DAY'S WEATHER FORECAST**

LONDON & S.E. ENGLAND - Wind southerly, fresh, strong or gale locally, veering later; cloudy; rain, brighter later, but with showers; moderate temperature.
ENGLISH CHANNEL - Sea rough

# GRAVE DECISIONS FOR THE LEAGUE

War has begun in Abyssinia. Denials were maintained in Rome throughout the day, but it was later admitted that Italian aeroplanes bombed Adowa early yesterday, though it was declared that the machines were fired on first. That served as Italy's actual declaration of war. In Rome the only official announcement was that the supreme command in Eritrea had been "authorised to take the necessary steps for defence" in view of the Abyssinian mobilisation and the aggressive spirit recently displayed.

Apparently it is still thought advisable to keep up the fiction that Italy has reluctantly been driven into a defensive war. Whether any serious Italian advance has begun or not, on one or two, or even on three fronts, as was variously reported yesterday, it is impossible to judge at the moment.

Much more vital to this country will be the grave decisions that must soon be taken at Geneva. The Council has been summoned for tomorrow, and in order to waste no time the Committee of Thirteen yesterday appointed a five-Power sub-committee to complete an analysis of the diplomatic history of the case. The Assembly is also expected to be called early next week.

British policy, as the whole world is aware, is firm for the application of Collective Sanctions on the declared aggressor. No doubt the Prime Minister will restate as plainly as possible the British case in his speech at Bournemouth tonight, and it will help to strengthen his hands that the leader of the Liberal Parliamentary party yesterday pledged his strong support of the Government position in a speech which contrasted agreeably in tone with those of most of the Labour spokesmen at Brighton, though they too endorse the Government's stand for the League.

The British Government will thus be able to speak at Geneva with an even firmer voice as representing virtually the whole country, except for the few dissentients who are opposed to the League itself and the extreme pacifists who were routed hip and thigh at Brighton. Mr. Lansbury has had the good sense to accept that overwhelming vote as final in regard to his own position as Leader of the party, and we are able to state that he has determined to resign without waiting for the unpleasantness of being superseded at the meeting which he himself called for Tuesday next. Sir Herbert Samuel declared that the duty of the initiative in challenging Italy's "scornful attempt to bring the League into futility and contempt plainly rested with the British Government." If the other members of the League accept the British initiative, then Great Britain's subsequent part will be, "as one among many," to solve the problems as they arise, as a loyal colleague with the other. Loyalty, perhaps, is even more essential than courage – loyalty, that is to say, to the basic principles of the League which, as the Liberal leader justly observed, it is "everybody's business" to uphold.

**(October 4)**

# THE AFTERMATH

It is perhaps too early yet to gauge the political effect at home of the crisis through which the Government has just passed. It was all the more disturbing because the storm sprang up so suddenly and beat violently down upon the ship when she had barely started on her new voyage. Damage has been done, and it would be futile to deny it, but it is reparable damage and it will speedily be repaired. Socialist taunts are but minor irritants.

Sober opinion will rather take note of the fact that, though the head of the Government made a mistake, he frankly admitted it in the House of Commons. The real gravamen of the charge against him was that the Paris Agreement which he too hurriedly endorsed violated the principles of the League to which he had sworn fidelity. Yet on Thursday the climax of his most explicit assertion was that his Government stood in relation to the League exactly where they had stood before, and that the League and the Covenant remain the keystone of British foreign policy.

A shrewd remark is made by a German newspaper in commenting upon the transaction. "The whole mentality of the British," says the "Lokal Anzeiger," "is expressed in this strange happening." It is this mentality which has so often puzzled foreigners before and will puzzle them again. Both Sir Samuel Hoare and Mr. Baldwin said that they had never been conscious at any moment of disloyalty to the League, either in drawing up or in endorsing the terms of this Agreement. That goes to the root of the matter. Yet to foreign commentators it merely seems a proof of British deceit, double-dealing, and hypocrisy. As bearing on that point, it may be observed that M. Laval, who also has no thought of resigning, has throughout declared himself a loyal supporter of the League, while at the same time the most insistent advocate of conciliation. What many home and foreign critics forget is that the League itself expressly authorised the British and French Governments to seek a settlement. It was to be submitted to the League for its criticism, and if not satisfactory for its amendment or rejection. How was this "going behind the League?"

As for the other foreign commentators who "heap scorn" on this failure of British diplomacy and the "abject scenes" in the House, they may fairly be asked to look in their own mirrors. If they are "observers" only and outside the League why do they remain for ever on the torrent's bank, too contemplative to throw even a line to those struggling in the raging waters?

**(December 21)**

# HORSELESS LONDON

Three years hence there may be no horse-drawn vehicles left in London streets – and only 30 years ago it was still impossible to cross London Bridge without meeting a white horse. The change in traffic conditions has come about gradually and its completion will be gradual too. The Minister of Transport proposes to get into touch with the owners of horse-drawn vehicles and arrange for the orderly elimination of that noble but now superfluous animal.

A horseless London will create new problems of traffic regulation. When horses were general it was possible for even an elderly pedestrian to cross the road when he chose by "slipping through" between the horses. To-day crossing is difficult, in spite of the beacons, unless the flow of traffic is intermittent. There is no natural place for the pedestrian in a stream of vehicles which is both fast and regular. There are three possible means of meeting the difficulty. The stream can be interrupted by policemen or traffic lights, or its speed can be reduced, or pedestrians can be provided with subways.

**(August 2)**

# JAPAN'S RUTHLESS GRIP ON CHINA

As our correspondent in Peking telegraphs this morning, the Japanese seizure of the railways in North China is a coup d'état that leaves the independence of the Northern Provinces only a matter for formal declaration. The Japanese military authorities have acted with ruthless promptitude once the provinces disclosed hesitation in their desire for autonomy. In taking possesion of the railway stations their announced intention is to prevent the removal of rolling stock. Quite obviously, their action must have the wider purpose of applying a pressure that China has no means of resisting in order to bring about the separation of the Northern Provinces from the Nanking Government's rule.

**(November 28)**

# SPEED LAW WEAKNESS

Law and administration are partners in government, and the Minister of Transport was justified in reminding a magistrates' conference of the part which its members should play in making the roads safe. We hear rather too much of technical offences against the traffic laws. These have been framed, as the Minister says, to protect the public, and it is undesirable that the Courts should encourage members of the public to regard them lightly.

On the other hand, so far as possible, Parliament should refrain from creating technical offences. They bring the law into ridicule. This is the weakness of the speed law.

**(July 10)**

# LONDON TEN-STOREY FLATS

## HIGH BUILDINGS AND LIFTS FOR TOWN DWELLERS WHO RESENT TRANSFERENCE

**By B.S. Townroe**
**A former Member of the Housing Committee of the London County Council**

At to-day's meeting of the London County Council Mr. W.H. Webbe, the leader of the Municipal Reformers, will move an amendment in the course of a debate on housing in London in favour of the erection of ten-storey flats in congested areas.

The battle of flats versus cottages is now raging in housing quarters. On the one side are many distinguished experts, including several of those who signed the report of the Marley Committee, issued last week. This report deprecated the present tendency towards higher buildings and greater density in central areas, and made suggestions to assist decentralisation.

On the other side are men and women who have found by experience that many families now living in our slums and overcrowded homes resent and oppose any transfer to suburban housing estates.

The opponents of high flats in the central areas point out the bad effects of many stairs upon mothers and small children; the dangers of making undesirable acquaintances on the communal staircases; the absence of gardens such as can be enjoyed on cottage estates; the absence of privacy. The critics emphasise these and many other defects, such as can be found in hundreds of Victorian and Edwardian tenements.

### THE THRILL OF TOWN LIFE

Nevertheless, many families taken from the most grim blocks in South London and given well-built and convenient cottages in Becontree or Downham have returned to their old haunts. The garden, the better air, the bathroom and all the other amenities have been counter-balanced by the fatigue and expense of the daily journey.

In considering the proposal – and to many it will at first sight seem monstrous – to build to the height of ten storeys, it is essential to bear in mind two fundamental facts:

1. Modern flats in design, planning and equipment are as much like Victorian tenements as a sports car is like a horse-drawn cab.

2. In housing we are dealing with human beings, and some families do not like the semi-rural life and prefer the thrill of the town, the familiar shop round the corner and the circle of old friends.

I know of dozens of families who have fought by every means in their power to avoid being moved even a mile or two from the district in which they were born and bred. We are reaching a deadlock, and many believe that the only solution is building upwards.

A modern working-class flat of the type built by progressive municipalities, like Liverpool and by courageous voluntary societies is usually in a block so sited as to obtain the maximum of sunshine. It is surrounded by playgrounds, and possibly with a day nursery in the basement.

In the latest type about to be erected in St. Pancras there are private staircases, spacious balconies and covered-in play-grounds, where the children and babies can enjoy themselves in bad weather. As a general rule these flats to-day are not higher than five storeys, and have no lifts.

It would, however, be out of the question to erect flats ten storeys high without installing lifts. These add to the capital cost and to the expense of maintenance. If they are automatic lifts they are easily put out of order, and are a possible source of danger to meddlesome children.

### TALL BLOCKS ON THE CONTINENT

I visited recently flats of ten storeys erected by the Socialist municipality of Villeorbanne, near Lyons, France. These were served by spacious lifts, were equipped with central heating and appeared to be very popular and well-managed. There are too, the Drancy Towers at Le Bourget, near Paris; the ten-storey block of flats without lifts at Pamphill in Rome, and a nine-storey block in Rotterdam.

On the Continent such experiments have gone much further than in this country, where we are conservative at heart and are rather slow to appreciate how modern science is revolutionising building.

Plans have been prepared in London for the erection of ten-storey tenements, giving 120 flats per acre, costing £402 for a flat with a living room and two bedrooms, to be let at an inclusive rent of 10s per week.

### ADVANCE IN DESIGN OF FLATS

The recent exhibition of drawings and models of working-class flats held at the Ministry of Health proved the advance that has been made in designing the interiors, in providing bathrooms, gas or electric cookers, balconies for babies, rooms for drying clothes, and new ways of disposal of refuse. The coming report of the Departmental Committee set up by Sir Hilton Young to advise on the technical questions involved will help still further to ensure that high flats can also be healthy homes.

Although any unprejudiced student of housing would without hesitation prefer cottages in semi-rural surroundings to high tenements, we must face realities. This country is far more overcrowded than either India or China, and the new legislation is at last giving an opportunity to clear slums and rebuild on a scale large enough to permit a thorough redevelopment of congested and ill-planned areas.

If we tried to rehouse, for example, the 70,000 persons now living in the one square mile of Shoreditch at the established standard of 12 cottages to the acre, we could only reaccommodate a fraction, and the others would have to move miles away to estates in Middlesex, Essex, or Kent. The ideal is removal to satellite towns, but without powers of industrial conscription so as to compel both people and industries to move at the will of a dictator this is Utopian.

### PROBLEMS OF THE DWELLERS IN MASS

For at least three years the Housing Committee of the London County Council has been considering the ten-storey flat solution. It is admittedly costly. It presents infinite conundrums of management. How for example, would 3,000 persons living in one block, possibly of varying nationalities, such as are found in Bethnal Green or Stepney, behave in the case of an air raid on London?

Nevertheless, in spite of all the admitted disadvantages no other constructive alternative has been put forward whereby thousands of London families can be housed within reasonable distance of their daily work. We may hope that as a result of to-day's discussion at the County Hall the London County Council will decide, without any partisan prejudices, to use the experience accumulated in France, Holland, Austria, and Italy.

**(April 9)**

# WORLD'S BIGGEST ARTIFICIAL LAKE

The Boulder Dam, in the Black Canyon on the Colorado River, where President Roosevelt spoke yesterday on his tour across the United States to California is the greatest of the many public works carried out in America during the depression period.

It is the latest, and perhaps the last, step in opening up the vast "untamed" country of western America. It has many purposes to fulfil: Irrigation, flood control, supply of domestic water and power generation.

When the lake which has been forming behind the dam, since early in February, reaches its full size it will be 115 miles long and 40 miles wide at the Virgin River, 30 miles upstream from the dam.

Already, though filled to only one-seventh of its capacity, it is the largest artificial lake in the world. Its capacity will be something like 10,000,000,000,000 gallons.

The Boulder Dam itself is one of the most wonderful feats of modern engineering. It rises to a height of 727st. and is 560ft thick at the base and 45ft. thick at the top, where the width is 1,180ft. Since work began in 1930, 5,000 men have been constantly employed and construction is 18 months ahead of schedule.

The cost of construction of the dam, estimated at £24,000,000 will be paid for in 50 years by selling electricity, already contracted for, from the power plant. Nearly a million acres of arid land and desert, "with only rainfall enough to make puddles," will be irrigated and supplied with electricity, and an aqueduct 250 miles long will carry some of the stored water as far as Southern California.

**(October 1)**

# NEW YEAR REVELS

Ravens of Cornish crags have been observed of late to be indulging in the fantastic flights which mark their nuptial season, soaring to a height, rolling as they fly, even turning on their backs, and shooting earthwards in the way of the rooks, with marvellous twists and turns.

In the days of White of Selbourne the courting of ravens must have been familiar in most countrysides when a New Year opened mildly. But the trees called "raven trees" have long been left to doves and starlings, as their old proprietors tended more and more to become cliff-dwellers, partly, no doubt, because of the ever-diminishing chance of earning a living inland as scavengers. On coasts they find food in plenty. And now, in some of their wild haunts where they they are prospering, there are signs of a return to a tree-nesting habit.

**(January 4)**

# LONDON DAY BY DAY:

**An Intimate Royal Address.**
**Uniforms in Procession.**

The King's speech in Westminster Hall at the meeting of the two Houses on Thursday will be very different from those he reads at the opening of Parliament.

On Thursday the King will make a more personal and intimate speech. He has devoted a great deal of care to its preparation.

The last of this kind that the King made was in November 1918, when in the Royal Gallery at the House of Lords he replied to Addresses from Parliament passed on the conclusion of the War.

Those of us who heard it will not soon forget the dignity of its language or the impressiveness of its delivery.

The conclusion of that speech is a passage which might well be repeated to-day: "For centuries Britain has led the world along the path of ordered freedom. Leadership may still be hers among the peoples who are seeking to follow that path. God grant to their efforts such wisdom and perseverance as shall ensure stability for the days to come."

### Cavalry Full Dress

While all will be familiar with the splendid regimentals of the Household Cavalry, the full-dress uniforms of the other cavalry regiments in to-day's procession will be new to the younger generation.

The Queen's Bays or 2nd Dragoon Guards will appear in all their pre-war splendour of scarlet tunics and black-plumed helmets. They were raised as the 3rd Regiment of Horse.

Their present title dates from Caroline. George II's Queen, when they were mounted by order on long-tailed bay horses. Hence their name, which is emphasised by the wreath of bay-leaves encircling the word "Bays" on one of their badges.

The revived title of 3rd Carabineers for the 3/6th Dragoon Guards was itself a battle-honour bestowed by William III. for gallantry, after the precedent of that famous French regiment, the Black Carabineers.

Their scarlet tunics have yellow facings and their helmets red and black plumes.

### French Best Seller

I believe that there is no intention of giving the circular now being prepared by the Air Raid Precaution Department the popular allure of "Paris under Gas."

This booklet, which is sold at the modest price of 50c, is enjoying a large sale. The cover shows an air raid in progress.

The artist presumably intends to show a direct hit on the Eiffel Tower. How far he has succeeded in this only the expert can decide.

The circular to be issued to our local authorities will, I understand, be brief; it will contain only short instructions for the public. A more elaborate document, however, is to be issued later by the Stationary Office.

This will contain full technical details of the various measures to be taken in case of "air" emergencies.

### Diplomats' Allowances

Though Sir Miles Lampson, as British High Commissioner in Egypt, occupies a position more exacting than many embassies, the pay attaching to the post is only that of a Minister.

He gets the same salary – £1,900 – as the British representatives in such comparatively unexacting countries as Sweden, Peru and Panama.

His unusual responsibilities, however, are compensated for in another way. Under the heading of frais de représentation he receives the annual sum of £8,100.

This entertaining allowance is far higher than that given to the majority of Ambassadors.

### D.H. Lawrence Semi-Centenary

The municipality of Vence on the Cote d'Azur is to celebrate the fiftieth anniversary of the birth of D.H. Lawrence, who died there in 1930.

It is proposed that there should be a lunch for prominent French and English writers, followed by a conference on the life and works of Lawrence.

The body of D.H. Lawrence is no longer at Vence. It was exhumed early this year, taken to Marseilles and after-cremation shipped to New Mexico. There the ashes are interred in a temple on Lawrence's ranch.

Vence is also to affix a plaque on the walls of the villa, where Lawrence lived – though a year or so ago there was a suggestion that his grave looked neglected.

**PETERBOROUGH**

# CRUISING TO ESCAPE INCOME TAX

## NEW GYPSIES OF THE SEAS WHO SAVE MONEY BY A WANDERING LIFE AFLOAT

### By Sir Percival Phillips

*Easter brings with it the start of the popular cruising season.*

*In this article the writer describes some unusual types who may on occasion be met with sailing out of the Mediterranean and Far Eastern ports.*

CAIRO, April.

A NEW type of tourist has appeared in the pleasure cities of the Mediterranean – the habitual cruiser who finds it cheaper to keep wandering in circles than to live ashore.

The Levant has seen much of them this winter. They are distinct from the amateur sightseer engaged in verifying Baedeker, and the refugee from winter who is only interested in changes of climate. You know them by their air of boredom, cautious avoidance of guides and curio shops, and the superior way they sheer off from the mobilisation centres for "doing" local sights in mass.

It was one of those keen students of humanity, a hotel-keeper, who first made me acquainted with the constant-cruiser, and put the creature under a microscope. This specimen was a portly woman – incidentally, a German – in a grim travelling suit apparently made of cast-iron, and a defensive hat of no recognisable vintage.

She climbed heavily to the hotel terrace, seated herself at an empty table for six, warned away the expectant Berber waiter with one fat hand, and deliberately ate sandwiches from a paper bag, utterly unmoved by the manager's malignant stare.

### NO COST BUT FARE

"Arnold friend," he said, bitterly, "This is the fourth time she has been here this winter. She comes up from Port Said by train, second-class, takes an omnibus to the hotel, and that is the last penny she will spend until she goes back by omnibus to take the night train back to the ship. Her winter home is a German cruising liner. She books for the round trip, spends from two to three weeks in the ports between Algiers, Istanbul, and the Canal, returns to Germany – and books for the next cruise, perhaps leaving again the day afterwards by the same ship.

"All it costs her is the fare. She does her own washing, and no steward could exist on the tips she almost gives them. Ashore she buys a few postcards, nothing else. Her expenditure is less per cruise than for the same period ashore."

The cruise-addict is for the most part a Continental product. I have seen none bearing a British stamp save a few doubtful specimens evicted by the gold Standard from pensions on the Riviera. These were tied to cruises covering the winter months and extending to the Far East in ships offering the simple comforts of a boarding house at 12 knots.

They can hardly be classed with the revolving pilgrims on the Mediterranean run. They get greater varieties of scene and climate and longer intervals in port.

### FULL YEAR AT SEA

I met a retired colonel and his wife this week who are cruising for a year to escape the income-tax. They spent two months pottering about the Mediterranean and Black Sea in a semi tramp steamer, and then joined a larger ship at Marseilles, which will make a leisurely voyage, lasting six weeks, to Dairen, in Southern Manchuria, after visiting eleven ports.

Just outside Dairen is a delightful little seaside resort, with family hotels run by Japanese in the European way. There they will spend the early summer. Living is cheap on the depreciated yen, and the total expenditure for two months' stay will be less than they would have to pay for as good accommodation at a coast resort in England – far less than in France or Belgium.

Their round-the-world ticket will enable them to move on to Japan after the hot weather. The next move will be by another slow ship, carrying a few passengers, across the Pacific and through the Panama Canal to the West Indies.

There they intend to remain until the late autumn. Then eastward again.

This nomadic life afloat would not appeal to every traveller, but it suits the colonel and his wife, and they are secure from the pressure of a surveyor of taxes.

Another variation of the cruise-addict crossed my path in Athens. An English novelist and his wife were on the third lap of a three months' tour by the same ship – what they called a "taxi voyage" of the Mediterranean. They left London on her first winter cruise, with a timetable adjusted to the ship's schedule for the season, and are being dropped at various ports to remain until she arrives next time round.

The same cabin is reserved for them and they keep part of their luggage on board. Thus they avoid the deadly monotony of living with the same people for weeks at a time, and are free to follow their own devices ashore. I imagine that their position as "permanent residents" has given them a slightly superior feeling.

As we sat over cocktails in the Grande Bretagne hotel three other obvious cruise passengers stopped for a moment at our table. I asked who they were. "I can't remember their names," said my friend indifferently, "they are only with us for this voyage."

It is a rather dismal sight when the cargo of a cruise-ship is decanted into a hotel on the circular route, and the diverse elements are herded by guides into groups for the usual intensive day's tour. They dash about from museums to ruined temples in a race against time. Nightfall finds them jaded and full of undigested history.

National characteristics reveal themselves unmistakably in these feverish attacks on the show places of a cruise itinerary. British sightseers are almost invariably cheerful, mildly conversational and interested in the day's work or pretending to play. They joke over minor mishaps, and refuse to be infuriated by delays or unforeseen discomforts.

The Americans plunge intensely into a set programme, tick it off item by item, make copious notes which they lose or forget and receive with cold cynicism the tall stories fed them by voluble touts. The French attack their ordered menu of "sights" with fierce energy, talking all the time at top speed, photographing everything in their path, and returning aboard to discard guide-book stuff for the interminable debate on the state of Europe.

### THE NEW GYPSIES

The Germans are different. They come ashore in any old clothes,with an air of being about to engage in a desperate adventure. The majority are middle-aged and of ample girth. I have seen very few young Germans addicted to cruising. They are disciplined beyond belief, and the most trivial movements overseen by their efficient leaders are executed with almost military precision.

If eight o'clock is the hour for mobilisation to see the Pyramids at 8.45, they are standing in line, punctual to the second, with their car numbers held aloft, cameras at the ready, and guide books in reserve. The hotels know them for their thriftiness. You never see half-a-dozen Prussian playboys ordering cocktails before the mess call is sounded. The servants know better than to linger with palms upwards when the food has vanished.

Amid this press of disciplined tourist traffic move the cruise-addicts, who are only ashore to stretch their legs. One port is to them as good as another. They drift about the Mediterranean rather like lost souls, indifferent to all impulses except hunger, hoping for a smooth sea to carry them to the next halt, but ready to accept any gale in preference to spending more money for a bed on firm ground. They are the new gypsies of our time.

(April 20)

## MAY THE MUFF BE WORN AT COURT?

### A CURTSEY PROBLEM FOR DEBUTANTES

#### By a Fashion Expert

Will the Lord Chamberlain permit debutantes to carry muffs at this year's Courts?

This is a question being asked anxiously not only by dressmakers and debutantes but by the dancing teachers who are holding curtsey classes now for the girls attending the March Courts.

If the new fashion of the evening muff receives official sanction, muffs will be used in place of bouquets at the West End department classes, so that debutantes may learn to handle their muffs gracefully.

Some of the new muffs are almost indistinguishable from shower bouquets of ethereal flowers. They are actually made of rows of shaded chiffon or velvet petals, stitched together, and in the same colour as the train. Floral trimmings and finishes of this kind are a great feature of the new evening modes being launched at the spring parades.

While the muffs look immense, some of them being more than two feet wide and over a foot deep, they are as light as thistledown, and for that reason easy to manipulate.

Although the Lord Chamberlain has applied the tape measure to the train, which "must not extend more than 18 in from the heel of the wearer when standing," he has never considered it necessary to limit the size of the fan or bouquet. The woman or girl attending Court is free to carry the most diminutive posy or the largest ostrich feather plumes.

(February 6)

---

# DOES A UNIVERSITY HELP A GIRL?

## EDUCATION THAT IS A BUSINESS AND SOCIAL ASSET

### By Helen Venner

IS it waste to send a daughter to the university, or is it time and money well spent? From the gabbled Latin of the matriculation ceremony to the last ordeal of "Schools," with all the lectures, tutorials, debates, coffee parties, river parties and other fun in between – is it worth while?

An authority at Cambridge said recently that if the University had room to increase the number of undergraduates by fifty per cent. every new place would be filled within a week from waiting applications. There is no doubt then of the widespread belief in the value of a university education. The fact that over half the students at the universities get there to-day only with the help of one or more scholarships, grants or loans is a further indication that large numbers of people believe a university education to be something for which a struggle is well worth while.

### THE SECRET

So, it is, if the individual knows how to use it and to be used by it, but some men and women alike "go up" and "come down" without learning the secret of the magic power of a university to develop personality and to turn brains into thinking instruments instead of mere memory tablets. That is where the value of university training lies; that is its power to make a girl's career more successful and her whole life more interesting and satisfying both as single woman and as wife and mother.

The university cannot increase ability if the ability is not there to draw upon; it cannot develop personality, nor force a girl to be more happy and effective in society, work and friendships, unless she responds to its influences. If she develops into a more or less automatic note-taking machine at lectures; if she avoids the main stream of university life; if she never ventures to cut a lecture in order to read desultorily or to have an afternoon for the river, walking or a theatre, she will no doubt obtain her degree but with very little else.

From a utilitarian point of view also a university education seems well worth while. Preference, in many posts, is often given to university women. Though this tendency is less active in the business world than elsewhere.

This tends to deprive her of one of the best delights of a university education, the freedom to sit up to what hour one pleases, eating indigestible but glorious suppers, and talking the meanwhile about everything under the sun.

### WHAT WILL IT COST?

Costs vary from university to university and from college to college. Oxford and Cambridge are hardly possible comfortably on less than about £200 to £230 a year for tuition fees, residence and personal expenses in term. Others may be managed on a little less or on much less, according to the university and the student's personal tastes.

Scholarships, grants, and loans are available in more generous degree for women than they were twenty years ago. Besides those awarded by college and university, there are State scholarships, others given by local education authorities, and several funds which now help women students. They are all rather less in number and quantity than the needs of women students who must have financial help to get to the universities, but all something to be grateful for as compared with the days, not so far away, when practically no scholarships at all were available for women.

(October 1)

## PLANTING THE WINDOW-BOX

A DRESS rehearsal for the Silver Jubilee window-box display in May is a good idea now that spring has arrived. All sorts of decorative bulbs and plants just coming into flower can now be bought. If carefully planted and looked after, they will make an attractive show for a fortnight or more.

Daffodils, if planted closely, are a splendid flower for a window-box. Most florists can supply them already in bud and ready to plant straight into boxes. Hyacinths are another good choice – or polyanthus, or smelling genistas and cinerarias.

Window-boxes will keep gay and fresh twice as long if they are kept well watered. Even in cold weather the soil quickly gets dry, and then the plants languish. It is a good plan to loosen the surface of the soil with a small fork now and then. C.H.B.K.

(March 23)

---

# TRADING STANDARDS TO PROTECT THE SHOPPER

## NEW BODY TO ENFORCE "TRUTH IN ADVERTISING"

A new organisation to protect the shopper and the fair trader, and to establish a precise standard of "truth in advertising" was inaugurated last night.

It is the Retail Trading Standards Association, founded by the heads of a number of large retail houses in the country, and launched at a dinner in London last night.

The object of the association is expressed in the adopted slogan "Straight-forward Shopkeeping." To secure this aim a set of standards has been drawn up, and will be adopted by the members of the association. Examples of the standards include the following:

"Sale price" really means a reduction from the normal price;

Merchandise displayed in the window is identical with similar articles sold in the shop;

A piece of furniture described as "antique" is at least 100 years old; and

"Woollen" is applied only to material made of wool. The men behind the new movement are leading figures in retail trading. Their names will give confidence to the public that the objects the association has set itself will be carried out. They are:

Sir. Woodman Burbidge (Harrods),
Sir Ambrose Heal (Heal and Son),
Mr. F. J. Marquis (Lewis's, of Liverpool),
Sir Frederick Richmond (Debenhams),
Mr. Snowden Schofield (Schofields of Leeds),
Mr. H. Gordon Selfridge (Selfridge's), and
Sir Sydney Skinner (Barkers).

### DEFINITION OF TERMS

The inaugural dinner, held at the Savoy Hotel, was attended by Sir Kingsley Wood, the Postmaster-General, and what is believed to be the biggest gathering of retail traders ever held in this country.

Mr. F.J. Marquis, chairman of the Incorporated Association of Retail Distributors, and one of the founders of the association, who presided, explained its object in the following terms:

"We are trying to bring into one of the oldest trades in this country a standard of trading practice. We are seeking to show the Government that we are anxious and willing to improve our trade, and to preserve the interests of the consumer.

"We are seeking to make advertising more effective as an instrument of trade by giving to advertisers and to the public an accepted meaning of words which, traders agree, properly describe the character of the goods.

"The other night I heard Mr. Baldwin say that in the future regardless of which party was in power, there would probably be an increase of Government intervention in business. We are very anxious that our trade should be left free.

"The public has become accustomed to Government departments undertaking the control of the marketing of various forms of agricultural produce, and is competent to judge how much they have gained as a result. It is our belief that distribution can best be controlled by the voluntary co-operation of those who have the technical knowledge and experience that befits them for the job.

Mr. H. Gordon Selfridge, toasting the guests, said that the association was the first their business of retailing had ever formed that faced fairly and squarely its duty to its customers. The people of the whole nation were customers of retail business, and they were, therefore, undertaking a work of national importance. They welcomed the support they had received from the Drapers' Chamber of Trade.

(March 28)

## A WEEK'S MEAL FOR 5/10 ½

### STUDENTS COOK B.M.A.

### MINIMUM DIET

#### From a Special Correspondent

The famous "B.M.A. minimum diet," materialised into meals, was on view at the Diamond Jubilee Exhibition of the National Training College of Domestic Subjects, Buckingham Palace-road, yesterday.

The B.M.A. diet, costing 5s 10 1/2d for an adult for one week, and the Ministry of Health's claim that a diet costing only 4s 10d weekly was sufficient, aroused great controversy last year.

The exhibit at the college, cooked by students, was drawn up in strict accordance with the B.M.A. dietary for two adults and three children, at an all-in cost of 22s 6 1/2d. These were some of the menus on view:

SUNDAY
DINNER
Roast pork and stuffing
Greens, potatoes
Apple pie
HIGH TEA
Bread and butter, Cake
Bread and cheese and cress
MONDAY
DINNER
Steak pie
Mashed potatoes
Hot beetroot
Steamed roly-poly
HIGH TEA
Pickled herrings
THURSDAY
DINNER
Sausage in batter
Carrots, gravy
Potatoes
Bird's nest pudding
HIGH TEA
Savoury beans

In addition there was a daily breakfast of bread and butter, tea and bacon.

An official of the College explained that the biggest difficulty at the cost was to obtain sufficient attractive vegetables and fruit.

(April 12)

"WHAT WOULD YOU DO WITH SUCH A NAUGHTY BOY, NURSE?"

"Don't scold him, Mrs Hardy. He doesn't look well. Are you sure he is not constipated? Whenever a child is cross and peevish, I look at the tongue. If it is coated or disagreeable, I know at once what is wrong. I always give 'California Syrup of Figs.' That moves the bowels in a few hours and cleanses the system.

Children don't understand the importance of regularity. They get absorbed in play and won't trouble. And it is only when they get thoroughly cross and miserable that you realise that they are constipated. I find it saves a world of sickness and worry to give them a regular weekly dose. I would do that if I were you. With a natural fruit laxative like 'California Syrup of Figs' you can't go wrong.

Doctors recommend it and give it to their own children, and we nurses swear by it. Get a bottle of 'California Syrup of Figs' from the chemist and give him a dose at bedtime. He'll be a shappy as a sandboy in the morning. There are two sizes; 1/3 and 2/6, you'll find the large bottle cheaper in the long run.

Never experiment with cheap and drastic preparations when buying children's laxatives. The safest plan is to do as I do, follow the example of the Doctors and give 'California Syrup of Figs' brand."

# COL. DREYFUS DEAD

## FAMOUS FIGURE OF SPY TRIAL

**From Our Own Correspondent**

PARIS, Friday.

Col. Alfred Dreyfus, the central figure of one of the greatest causes célèbres of all time, died at 5 o'clock this evening at his Paris home. He was 75.

The "Dreyfus case," which many Frenchmen regard as one of the most atrocious conspiracies in the history of their country, started in 1894. Col. Dreyfus, then a captain in the thirties, was sent to Devil's Island for selling military documents to Germany.

For many years the country was split into two camps, for or against Dreyfus. Emile Zola, with his "J'Accuse," attacking the French Ministry of War, was among those who took part in a great campaign for a revision of the sentence.

The campaign was encouraged by the confession – and suicide – of Lt.-Col. Henry, a leading witness for the prosecution who said he had forged some of the incriminating documents. Dreyfus was retried, again found guilty, but pardoned by the President.

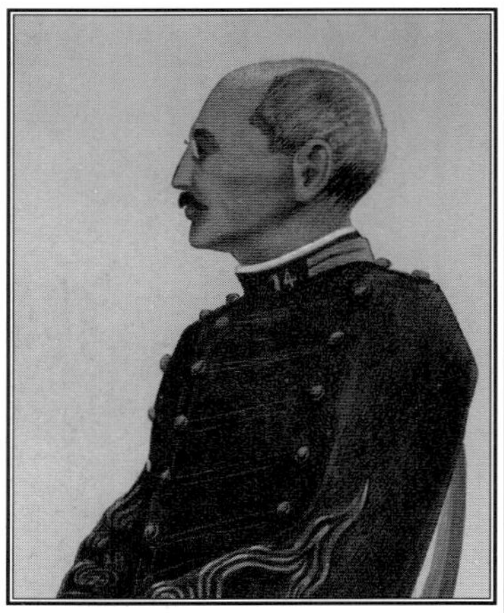

Col. Dreyfus

Finally, in 1906 the verdict of guilty was annulled. Dreyfus was reinstated in the Army, promoted, and awarded the Legion of Honour.

During the war – in which one of his sons was killed – Col. Dreyfus fought with the French army. Asked on one occasion why he never took cover, he replied: "When one bears a name like mine one does not take shelter."

After the war he retired to private life, practising, as he himself said, "the art of being a grandfather." It is believed that he wrote his memoirs with the provision that they were not to be published until after his death.

**(July 13)**

# ECONOMIST AND POET

## PARADOX OF GEORGE W. RUSSELL

Few living Irishmen have attained wider fame among English-speaking peoples than George W. Russell, who died last night at Bournemouth, aged 63. Brilliantly gifted, he was a paradox in intellect.

On the one hand he was an artist and a poet, who had become involved in the psychology of mystical consciousness. On the other, he was a practical man of affairs, an eloquent, hard-hitting economist, who with remarkable skill devoted his attention to stressing the merits of co-operative agriculture. His work in this respect led to his exerting a powerful influence.

He kept these two branches of activity severely apart, and for that reason was always George W. Russell when he was writing on economics and "A.E." when he was devoting himself to poetry.

It was as "A.E." he became best known not only in Ireland but in Britain and America. The pen-name was evolved accidentally.

He signed a poem "Æon," but wrote it so badly that the compositor could decipher only the diphthong. When he received the proofs the author adopted "Æ" as his signature, but later used "A.E." for convenience.

He edited for many years "The Irish Statesman," a noteworthy publication in which his articles were a regular feature.

Born on April 10, 1867, he became an accountant, and afterwards joined in Sir Horace Plunkett's efforts to improve conditions in Ireland and developed as an agricultural economist.

The author of many books, he went to America five years ago on a highly successful lecturing tour, and his hope in the later years of his life was to produce more poetry – for in that department of activity he felt that he was able to do his best work.

**(July 18)**

# "LAWRENCE OF ARABIA"

## A PERSONAL IMPRESSION OF A COMRADE IN THE GREAT WAR

**By Lt.-Col. W.F. Stirling, D.S.O.**
**Who Acted as Col. Lawrence's Chief Staff Officer in Arabia**

IT was my great good fortune to be appointed General Officer to the Arab Forces in the early part of 1918.

From then throughout the final phase of the Arab revolt on till the capture of Damascus, I worked, travelled, and fought alongside Lawrence. Night after night we lay wrapped in our blankets under the cold stars of the desert.

At these times one learns much of a man. Lawrence took the limelight from those of us professional soldiers who were fortunate enough to serve with him, but never once have I heard even a whisper of jealousy. We sensed that we were serving with a man immeasurably our superior.

As I see it, his outstanding characteristic was his clarity of vision and his power of shedding all unessentials from his thoughts, added to his uncanny knowledge of what the other man was thinking and doing.

### DARING COURAGE

Think of it! A young second lieutenant of the Egyptian Expeditionary Force goes down the Arabian coast to where a sporadic revolt of the Western Arabs had broken out against their Turkish masters. Then, with the help of a few British officers, all senior to himself and professional soldiers, who willingly placed themselves under his general guidance, he galvanises the Arab revolt into a coherent whole.

By his daring courage, his strategy, his novel tactics, he welds the turbulent Arab tribes into a fighting machine of such value that he is able to immobilise two Turkish divisions and provide a flank force for Lord Allenby's final advance through Palestine and Syria, the value of which that great general has acknowledged again and again.

No one, looking at Lawrence, would have considered him strong physically. The fact remains that this man, who was thought too delicate to play games at school, was to break all the records of Arabia for speed and endurance.

On one occasion he averaged 100 miles a day for three consecutive days. Such endurance as this is almost incredible. I myself have ridden 50 miles in a night, but never do I want to do it again.

What was it that enabled Lawrence to seize and hold the imagination of the Arabs? It is a difficult question to answer. The Arabs were noted individualists, intractable to a degree, and without any sense of discipline. Yet it was sufficient for almost any one of us to say that Lawrence wanted something done, and forthwith it was done.

How did he gain this power? The answer may partly be that he represented the heart of the Arab movement for freedom and the Arabs realised that he had vitalised their cause; that he could do everything and endure everything just a little better than the Arabs themselves.

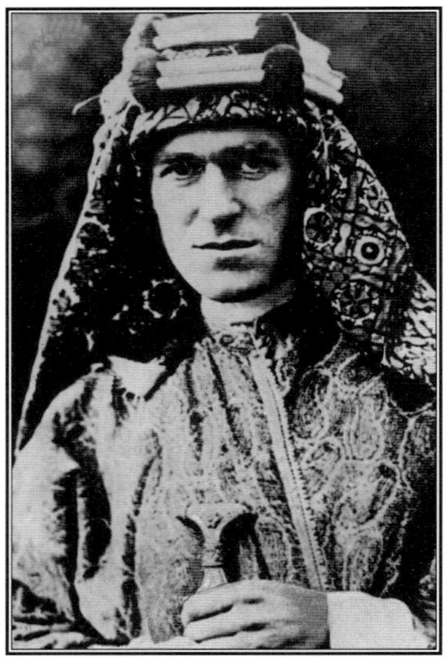

Lawrence in Arab costume.

But chiefly, I think, we must look for the answer in Lawrence's uncanny ability to sense the feelings of any group of men in whose company he found himself; his power to probe behind their minds and to uncover the well-springs of their actions.

Many stories have been told about Lawrence, most of them untrue. He was a good classical scholar, a military and political leader of worldwide renown, a writer of, perhaps, the greatest book of the century. After the peace he was offered a very high and responsible post under the British Government, and yet he cast everything aside and became a private in the Tank Corps and an aircraftman in the Air Force.

No one has yet been able to provide, even by conjecture, a satisfactory reason for his action.

I do not think that anyone ever will. The motives of his action came from within, and I doubt whether any of us living to-day would understand them even if he himself had cared to explain.

Lawrence was a man guided solely by his conscience. Had he accepted high office under the Government, he would never have carried out orders from Downing-street which conflicted in any way with what he thought was right. He knew this, and therefore refused. Further, he hated the petty trappings of officialdom, and the acceptance of any such post would have meant for him a life of continuous uneasiness.

"Ah yes," say some people, "but what of the man himself? Wasn't Lawrence just a poseur?"

Was he? Who are we going to take as arbiters of such a question? Are we to take obscure writers who have given their opinions or men like Field-Marshal Lord Allenby, Adm. Lord Wemyss, Mr. Winston Churchill, and the British officers who served with Lawrence throughout the campaign? There is not one of these I have mentioned but has admitted the genius and compelling power of Lawrence.

### A NEW LETTER

Turning to Lawrence's great book. "The Seven Pillars of Wisdom," which was published for private circulation, and of which only some 120 copies were printed, it is interesting to note the author's own feelings. He sent the book to me to review as to fact.

I made certain comments upon it, and in particular said that I thought he had laid insufficient stress upon the climax of the book – that is, the capture of and entry into Damascus. I said I thought that this was the goal of the whole Arab movement, which had been aimed at from the start. I also added that people who read the book would so understand it and enjoy it the more.

Lawrence's answers to my criticisms were quite definite. He said:

"I don't want readers to 'enjoy' the book. In girding at discipline and servitude, I seek mainly to condemn myself. My life has been service and I hate it. … Service to an ideal of scholarship, to the nation-building demand of nationality, and now service in the Ranks. As you say, in such surrender lies a happiness … but this seems to me an immoral feeling, like overdraft on our account of life. We should not be happy: and I think I've dodged that sin successfully! The Tank Corps is a happy penance for too rich and full a youth!"

Later, when discussing "The Seven Pillars of Wisdom" with Mr. H.G. Wells, who had also reviewed it. I asked him for his opinion. He said: "It is a wonderful book. In my opinion it is the finest piece of prose that has been written in the English language for 150 years."

I do not think anyone will accuse Mr. Wells of being the sort of man who throws bouquets around unnecessarily.

In my considered opinion, Lawrence was the greatest genius whom England has produced in the last two centuries, and I do not believe that there is anyone who had known him who will not agree with me. If ever a genius, a scholar, an artist, and an imp of Shaitan were rolled into one personality, it was Lawrence.

**(May 20)**

# THIRTY YEARS THE GUIDE OF BRITISH SOCIALISM

**By H.C. Bailey**

Though he was only its titular leader for short and widely-severed periods, Arthur Henderson exercised through 30 years a guiding influence on the Socialist party.

His power was not won by intellectual domination or masterful insistence on a policy of his own. As debater, platform orator, negotiator, or administrator, he made no figure. At best his performances were respectable.

Few men who have been Cabinet Ministers of importance have counted for so little in Parliament. He was capable of effective speech, but he seemed to shun the stricken fields of the House of Commons.

His record in office whether in the Coalition Government of Mr. Lloyd George or as Mr. Ramsay MacDonald's Foreign Secretary did not satisfy even his own party. And yet from first to last they trusted "Uncle Arthur" as a fount of pure wisdom.

There were two reasons for this unfaltering faith. First, Arthur Henderson was the perfect examplar of that from which the party drew the bulk of its strength, the earnest trade unionist who had adopted Socialism as the right political creed for a working man, just as, with no more exact understanding of what he meant by it, his father had sworn by Gladstonian Radicalism.

It was always long odds that what Henderson thought to-day the mass of the unions would think to-morrow.

### GOOD PARTY MANAGER

The second source of his power was in his ability as a party manager. Though himself an extraordinarily unfortunate candidate, he was a great organiser of elections, a master hand with a caucus.

Devoted friends and sneering enemies agree that the impressive growth of the Socialist party in the House of Commons between 1906 and 1929 was in large measure due to Henderson's work as its secretary.

That the shattering disaster of 1931 was also in part due to Henderson Socialists have done wisely to ignore. If in refusing to recognise the financial emergency and the necessity of economies he broke with Mr. Ramsey MacDonald and Lord Snowdon in order to lead the party into the wilderness, he was a faithful interpreter of the mind of the militant trade unionist.

Arthur Henderson was born in a working class region of Glasgow on Sept. 13, 1863. His father was a cotton spinner. When Arthur was some 10 years old the family moved to Newcastle, and as a boy of 12 he was apprenticed to that pioneer firm of locomotive engineers, Robert Stephenson and Co.

### LAY EVANGELIST

Still in his teens, he came under the influence of the evangelist, Gipsy Smith, then a captain in the Salvation Army. Arthur "gave his testimony" at an open air meeting and became a Wesleyan local preacher. He remained on the roll of that corps of lay evangelists till the end of life.

**(October 21)**

# CMDR. G.H. KELLETT

Cmdr. G.H. Kellett, R.N., retired, who died at Grimsby yesterday, was a distinguished officer of submarines both before and during the war. On one occasion he was the hero of a romantic adventure.

The engines of the S. I. which he commanded in the early days of the war, broke down in the Bight of Heligoland. He submerged the submarine and when at dusk he rose to the surface he found himself alongside a German trawler. He promptly captured this vessel, and made her tow the S.I. back to England.

Cmdr. Kellett, who took an important part in the taking over of 144 German submarines surrendered at Harwich at the end of the war, retired at his own request in 1922. He held the Humane Society's certificate for saving life.

**(February 7)**

# ALBAN BERG

## COMPOSER OF "WOZZECK"

Alban Berg, composer of "Wozzeck" and other works, died in Vienna on Tuesday from blood poisoning. He was born in Vienna 50 years ago.

The news of Alban Berg's premature death will have been received with regret in English musical circles. He was one of the representative musicians of his generation – an artist of narrow range but exquisite sensibility and the most refined technique. Of all Schonberg's pupils he was the one who most made his mark.

In point of fact not one of the master's works has ever won quite such wide acceptance as, for a time, did the pupil's opera "Wozzeck." Berg was not quite so energetic an experimenter as Schonberg. He concentrated on one of his master's styles and developed it with a delicate ingenuity.

The vagueness and elusiveness of Berg's music might never have won much of a hearing outside a small aesthetic circle if it had not been for his good fortune in alighting upon the effective subject afforded him by "Wozzeck."

The opera had an extraordinary vogue in Germany before the coming of the Hitler regime, but in 1933 Berg's name was relegated to obscurity, for both his choice of decadent subjects and the backboneless, dissolving style of his music were considered unworthy of the spirit of the new times.

**(December 27)**

# M. PAUL DUKAS

The death has occurred in Paris of the well-known French composer Paul Dukas.

Dukas was 69 years of age, and no work of his has appeared since 1911, when his ballet, "Le Peri," was produced. Even before that date his works were not numerous, as he gave most of his time to the composition of his great life work, "Arianne and Bluebeard," which is universally considered as one of the greatest of contemporary lyrical productions. In this three-act opera Dukas revealed himself at once to be not only a musician, but also a poet and a philosopher, a man of exquisite taste and sensitive nature.

**(March 20)**

# WILL ROGERS & WILEY POST KILLED

## AEROPLANE CRASH IN ALASKA

**From Our Own Correspondent**

NEW YORK, Friday.

All America is mourning to-day for Mr. Will Rogers, the famous comedian, described as the "best loved man in America" and Mr. Wiley Post, the one-eyed Oklahoma Indian air pilot who twice flew round the world.

The two men – old friends – were killed last night when the aeroplane in which they were making a pioneer flight to Moscow and back crashed in the icy wastes of Alaska, near Point Barrow, America's most northerly outpost.

The news of the tragedy has shocked America profoundly. From President Roosevelt downwards the whole nation feels that it has lost two of its heroes.

The President, when told the news at his summer residence at Hyde Park, New York, said:

"I was shocked to hear of the tragedy which has taken Rogers and Post from us. Will was an old friend of mine, humorist and philosopher, beloved by all.

"I had the pleasure of greeting Post on his return from his round-the-world flight. He leaves behind a splendid contribution to the science of aviation. Both were outstanding Americans who will be greatly missed."

### FROM OBSCURITY TO MILLIONS

Rogers had drawled his way from obscurity to millions and a position unique in American life.

His recent earnings are estimated at £100,000 a year. He made two or three pictures annually for Fox Films, receiving not less than £10,000 apiece, while he broadcast frequently for an oil company at a figure stated to be £2,000.

He was paid £3,000 for one stage appearance, and in 1930 received £15,000 for fourteen 15min broadcasts. He also did much newspaper work. He was insured for £200,000.

He is survived by a wife and three children – two sons and a daughter.

**(August 19)**

# "KING OF CHEFS"

## M. AUGUSTE ESCOFFIER

M. Auguste Escoffier, one of the greatest French chefs since Brillat-Savarin and the inventor of Péches Melba, whose death at the age of 88 is announced, was once described by M. Herriot as the most successful unofficial ambassador France has sent abroad for 100 years. It was true, for during his long life Escoffier carried the renown of French cooking to many parts of the world – England, America, Spain, Russia, Italy, India and Johannesburg.

The occasion of M. Herriot's tribute was the dinner which 400 of France's leading chefs and gourmets gave in March, 1928, in honour of M. Escoffier's nomination as Officer of the Legion of Honour. M. Herriot presided as head of the Department of Fine Arts.

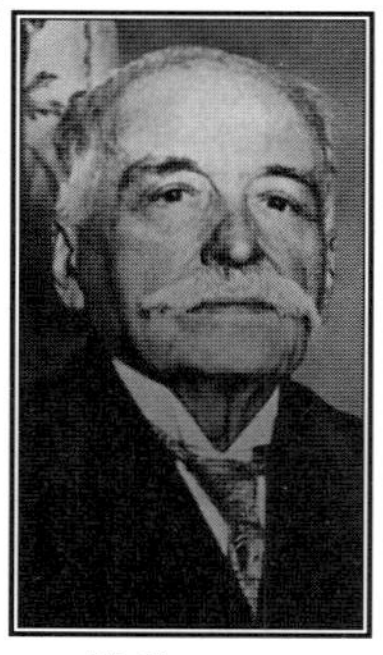

M. Escoffier

By that time M. Escoffier had earned by a lifetime of culinary creations in the world's most famous hotels and restaurants the title of the "King of Chefs and the Chef of Kings." It was in 1865, when he was not yet 20, that he came to Paris to the Petit Moulin Rouge, a fashionable resort of gourmets in the Avenue d'Antin, now the Avenue Victor Emmanuel III. One of the frequenters of this restaurant was King Edward VII., then Prince of Wales. Another of his Royal clients was Napoleon III.

By 1870 the young chef's reputation was established and during the Franco-Prussian War he had charge of the kitchen of the headquarters of the Army of the Rhine. After the Paris Exhibition of 1880 he became associated with M. Ritz, who brought him to London.

He was for many years chief chef at the Savoy and afterwards at the Carlton. It was while Melba was a guest at the latter hotel that Escoffier invented the famous sweet that bears her name. The story goes that Melba asked him if he could combine in perfect trinity the flavours of vanilla, the peach, and the raspberry. The result was Péches Melba.

M. Escoffier himself regarded his success in making frogs' legs acceptable when he was at the Savoy as his greatest English triumph. At a dinner for 700 he presented a new dish, "La Nymphe à La Rose." This was liked so much that it became a regular feature of the menu and one of the most popular dishes. It was long before it was discovered that the principal ingredient was frogs' legs with paprika sauce.

**(February 12)**

# LORD CARSON'S BRILLIANT CAREER IN LAW AND POLITICS

## SUPREME ADVOCATE AND FEARLESS CHAMPION OF ULSTER

There was no more outstanding figure in modern British legal and political history than Lord Carson. It may be difficult for those who did not meet him at the height of his brilliant career to realise adequately the magnificence of his all-compelling personality.

He stood alone. It was impossible to imitate one whose blend of striking qualities was unique. His grim Roman profile, utterly unlike that of his fellows, served to indicate at once his rare strength of character.

To some people whose political opinions were different from his that vigorous profile, allied with the fierce dominating characteristics of the man, seemed to suggest something sinister. Actually, his facial features were traceable to Italian ancestry. His eighteenth century forbears, when they settled in Ireland, were named Carsoni.

A tall man, black-browed, and with expressive eyes, he could pour out a torrent of passionate invective. Yet politicians who might writhe under his bitter jibes always paid tribute to his sterling honesty and resolute purpose.

### WILD ELOQUENCE

In public his emotionalism was such that he was often moved to tears.

This, far from being the cheap histrionic method his opponents sometimes represented it to be, was undoubtedly the product of his intense sincerity. With an impetuous eloquence to which it was fascinating to listen he roused his hearers to the greatest enthusiasm.

That he was no mere demagogue, however, was demonstrated by his brilliant successes at the Bar.

Irish politics claimed him at the outset of his career as a barrister. When Mr. (later the Earl of) Balfour was appointed Chief Secretary for Ireland in 1886, and got to grips with the Land League's campaign of violence, he took a warm liking to Carson, who became Crown Counsel to the Irish Attorney-General. It was a position of great unpopularity, and indeed of personal danger; but Carson carried out his duties so well that Balfour insisted he should enter Parliament.

The Unionist party went out of office almost immediately, and Carson then set himself to qualify for the English Bar. Here again he was exceedingly doubtful of his chances of making a living; but he found a backer in Mr. Charles (now Lord) Darling.

Darling insisted on putting Carson's name outside his own chambers, and bet a shilling that within a year the newcomer's practice would be larger than his own. The bet was amply justified, for Carson's rise to the leading position as an advocate, and still more as a cross-examiner, was very rapid.

The Unionists came back to power in 1895, but Carson was not included in the new Ministry. When, however, the Solicitor-Generalship fell vacant in May, 1900, it was offered to him by Lord Salisbury.

Five years later he was appointed Chief Secretary. He occupied the office for a single day and then resigned it for the rather Quixotic reason that he could not put his old friend, Lord Atkinson, then Irish Attorney-General, in the position of taking instructions from one who was very much his junior at the Irish Bar.

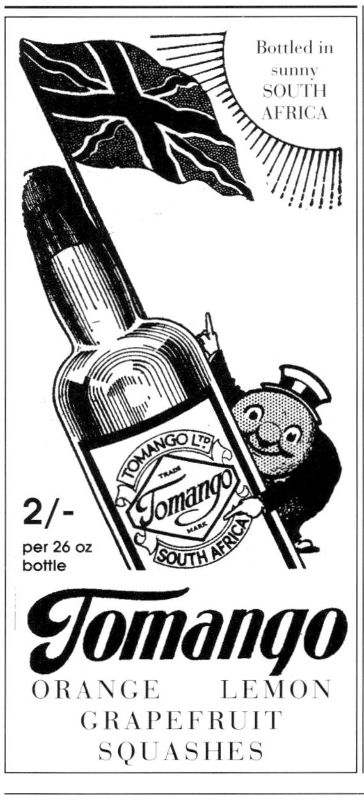


### THE IRISH CRISIS

Carson's real emergence into first-rate political importance dates from 1910, when the position of Ulster in regard to Home Rule became acute.

The Irish Nationalists in 1906 had acquiesced in the postponement of the Home Rule legislation to which the Liberal party were pledged. Now, in 1910, they claimed the fulfilment of these pledges. At once public opinion in Ulster became inflamed to fever heat at the prospect of compulsory inclusion in a Dublin Parliament with a permanent Nationalist majority. They regarded it as equivalent to exclusion from the United Kingdom.

At this juncture Carson stepped forward as the champion and leader of Ulster Unionism, and his accession was accepted with enthusiasm. For the next four years he devoted himself exclusively to this cause, and he was rewarded with a loyalty and implicit obedience such as no other British political leader has received in our day.

Whatever may be thought of Carson's policy, the sacrifices he made during these years for the cause of Ulster were very great. He gave up his legal practice and returned all his briefs, at a time when he was earning the largest income at the English Bar.

### ULSTER VOLUNTEERS

The bitter controversies of that time need not now be related in detail. It is sufficient to recall the signing of the famous covenant, the enroling of the Ulster Volunteers – a body which numbered some 90,000 men, organised and pledged to armed resistance if necessary – and the threat of establishing an Ulster Provisional Government in the last resort.

Finally, in April 1914, there came the landing of arms for the Volunteers at Larne, and the unfortunate orders for the redisposition of the military forces in Ireland which looked like the preliminary step towards at least a blockade of Ulster – a contingency so repugnant to the Army itself that it led to the so-called Curragh mutiny on the very eve of the war.

He openly invited prosecution as a rebel. If he had been prosecuted the result would probably have been very harmful to his own career; but he believed it would have so awakened the conscience of the nation that there could be no more talk of applying force to Ulster. The Liberal Government, however, after toying with the idea of prosecution, dropped it – on, it is said, the advice of Sir John Simon.

By far the most dramatic of his interventions was in December 1921, a few months after his appointment to the House of Lords, when the Irish Treaty was submitted for the approval of Parliament. It was his maiden speech in the House of Lords, and, regarded purely as oratory, it was probably the greatest effort of his career. But in its mordant invective and its concentrated bitterness it was unlike any speech heard in that august Chamber for generations. Every word was barbed; every sentence was a stab.

### THE OSCAR WILDE CASE

The greatness of Lord Carson as a politician, however, could never obscure his supreme gifts as a lawyer. The late Earl of Birkenhead described him once as the greatest advocate since Erskine.

Lord Carson's skill in appealing to juries was based on his almost uncanny estimates of human nature and his gift of eloquence. As a cross-examiner he was more feared than anyone at the Bar because of his deadliness. His memory was prodigious.

He achieved fame in the "Jack the Ripper" case, but it was his cross-examination of Oscar Wilde in the action for criminal libel against the Marquess of Queensberry, in 1895, that made him the acknowledged leader of the Bar. He was reluctant at first to accept a brief against his old schoolmate, and only consented when certain damming evidence had been shown to him, and further refusal would have been inconsistent with the duties of a lawyer.

### A DEADLY QUESTION

Wilde was not alarmed by this decision. His cross-examination was going to be a friendly scrap, with him as victor. In fact, the first day's conflict was flattering to Wilde, whose wit and brilliance had delighted the court.

But next morning the storm burst. Carson was calm. Before him lay the particulars which were completely to turn the tables. His questions, one after the other, came upon the poet and playwright quite obviously as a surprise.

Wilde's confidence deserted him. He was alternately indignant, hesitating, almost in tears. He could not shake off the relentless grip fastened upon him. To one deadly question he gave a fatal reply. It was the prelude to the subsequent criminal proceedings brought against him, and to his tragic end in Paris some years later.

Lord Carson appeared as counsel in the Jameson Raid trial, the details of which, in so far as they concerned the use of armed force against a Government were later to be compared with Lord Carson's own advocacy of armed force by Ulster.

**(October 23)**

# HUEY LONG'S RISE TO FAME

## FROM CHEAP JACK TO STATE GOVERNOR

The death of Huey Long – "Kingfish Long – Dictator of Louisiana State, removes one of the most extraordinary figures that has ever appeared in the politics of America.

Although only 42, for years his name had streamed across the front pages of the United States Press indicating some new stunt, escapade or political manoeuvre.

In the space of less than 15 years in politics, little more than three of them in the United States Senate, he had become one of the most hated politicians in all Congressional history. He had made himself nearly absolute in his native State. "Thrown spanners" into the works of Roosevelt's New Deal and was boasting that if not in 1936 then in 1940 he would be wearing the

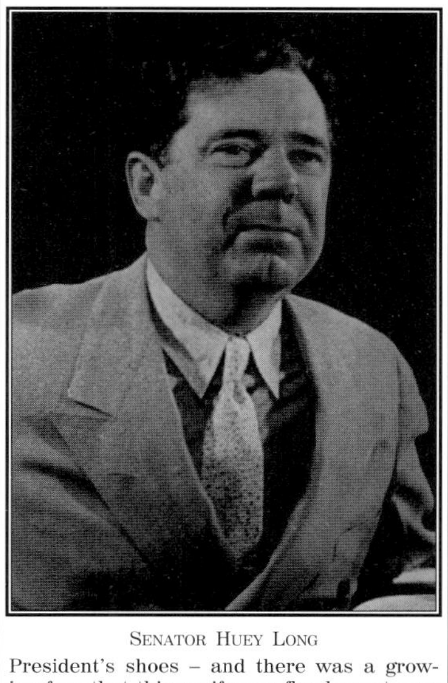
Senator Huey Long

President's shoes – and there was a growing fear that this vociferous flamboyant man might be able to contrive it.

Here is his strange history. The seventh son of nine children, born in the little town of Winnfield, Louisiana, he was taught to hoe cotton as soon as he could lift a hoe. He set out to see the world peddling soap, books, furniture — anything. From this he went on to patent medicines and the "hockum" of the cheap-jack on the corner of main street.

He made a little money, and after five months' law study in the University of Oklahoma there followed marriage at 19, a year at Tulane Law School, and at 21 he was back in his native town, the "shingle" up – a full-blown lawyer. In 1918 he turned politician, became Railroad Commissioner for North Louisiana, an unimportant post.

Four years of this and he decided to become Governor of the State. He knew the formula: get hold of the "outs and downs" the "under dog." He reckoned that, if promised the right things, 40 per cent. of the electors would vote for him and the remainder fight amongst themselves as to how best to fight him.

### BLACK EYES AND BRAWLS

He was "Kingfish" now, the King of Louisiana, and then came the regal manner. He received a formal visit from the gold-braided commander of the German Emden in blue and green pyjamas – the Louis Quatorze touch. He flouted every tradition of the Governor's office, and there followed brawls, black-eyes, scandals, arrests, bodyguards, even the "storm-troops" of the building dictator.

But things were done for (and to) the State. The roads were built and the schools were built, for this paradoxical Kingfish had faith in the power of education.

In 1932 he was elected Senator. They said this would be the end of this "political buffoon," that the "inflated frog" would burst in the rarer air of Washington. He became a thorn in the side of the Senate, a sort of burlesque Roosevelt, a noisy critic of the New Deal.

Meanwhile in Louisiana the "Kingfish" had consolidated his position as political Czar. Last November he passed 44 bills through the legislature in two hours. They made him master of everything. He met a minor revolt in January with his machine-guns and it faded away.

In the last session of the Senate he developed obstructionist tactics and carried them to fantastic lengths. His last great exploit was to speak for over 15 hours on end on any and every subject until exhausted. He became a music-hall turn in the Chamber, but yet could claim that his "share the wealth" scheme already had gained ten million adherents, and that he was well on the road to the Presidency.

He had enemies, of course, "I have been accused," he said once, "of every crime from stealing a quart of milk to murder." There was never a conviction. They could not catch him when he was impeached in his own State on 19 varied charges.

**(September 11)**

# HOW JELLICOE LED BIGGEST FLEET IN MODERN TIMES

**By Hector C. Bywater, Daily Telegraph Naval Correspondent.**

Admiral of the Fleet Earl Jellicoe of Scapa, who died yesterday at the age of 75, is assured of a niche in history as one of the outstanding figures of the Great War.

It fell to him to take command of the mightiest fleet ever assembled in modern times, to lead it into an action which the historian of later days may conceivably place among the decisive battles of the world and subsequently to bear the brunt of the German U-boat offensive, the deadliest and most insidious menace to which this country had been exposed for over a century.

No war leader on either side shouldered a heavier burden of responsibility than Jellicoe. He was, as Mr. Winston Churchill has put it so trenchantly, the only individual in either camp who could have lost the war in an hour.

On the day of the Battle of Jutland a single grievous error on his part might well have wrecked our naval fortunes, and with them the whole Allied cause.

Though the battle was indecisive in a material sense, Jellicoe himself never doubted the wisdom of his tactics. These, as is too often forgotten, were clearly foreshadowed in the memorandum which he addressed to the Admiralty in October, 1914 – 19 months before Jutland – the gist of which was that in no circumstances would he be lured into a close pursuit of the enemy fleet except on his own terms.

### GERMAN FLEET KEPT BACK

Strategically the battle was a decisive success for British arms. Save for the perfunctory sorties in August, 1916, and April, 1918, respectively, both of which were hurriedly abandoned at the first hint of interception, the German fleet remained quiescent for the rest of the war. Nevertheless, by almost universal consent, it was the rampart behind which the German submarine campaign, which so nearly proved fatal to Britain and her allies, was organised and waged.

### ADORED BY LOWER DECK

To no British naval leader since Nelson was greater affection given by his subordinates. It is not an exaggeration to say that he was adored by the lower deck, of whose welfare he was ever mindful.

Kindly and imperturbable in all circumstances, he rose to the level of greatness in the hour of crisis. His severest critics readily admit that Jellico's immense popularity was an asset of incalculable value to the Navy in the darkest hours of the war.

John Rushbrooke, first Earl Jellicoe of Scapa, G.C.B., O.M., G.C.V.O., who was born at Southampton, grew up in an atmosphere of the sea, for his father was commodore of the Royal Mail Steam Packet Co. and his great-grandfather, Adml. John Pattan, had been Second Sea Lord at the time of the Battle of Trafalgar.

Jellicoe joined the Navy in the early seventies and later became a gunnery specialist. He was executive officer of the Victoria in 1893 when that ship was rammed and sunk by Camperdown, with heavy loss of life. Jellicoe himself being saved with difficulty.

### ESCAPES FROM DEATH

This was not his only escape from death. In 1900, during the Boxer rebellion in China, he was flag captain to Adml. Sir Eduard Seymour, and took command of 2,000 seamen and Marines in a desperate attempt to relieve the Legation at Peking. The gallant effort failed, and in the fierce fighting during the march Jellicoe was severely wounded.

Admiral Jellicoe had for long been marked out for high command in war, but his sudden appointment, on Aug. 4, 1914, to take command of the Grand Fleet came as a surprise to navy and nation alike.

His deployment of the Grand Fleet though much criticised in later years, brought the enemy under devastating fire, and only the skilful manoeuvring of the German main body, covered by destroyer attacks and smoke-screens, saved Adml. Schoer from disaster.

### SUBMARINE MENACE

In December, 1916, Jellicoe left the Grand Fleet to become First Sea Lord. The submarine menace was already assuming grave proportions, and it was clear that upon its outcome would largely depend the issue of the war. Jellicoe applied himself to his new task with characteristic thoroughness and energy.

Almost the only criticism which has been directed against him in this oonnection concerns his lack of enthusiasm for the convoy system, which was to prove the real answer to the U-boat menace. It was not vouchsafed to him to reap the harvest he had sown, for

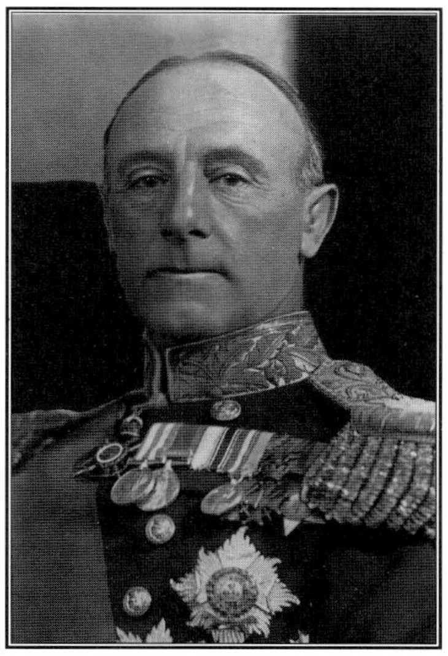
Earl Jellicoe

early in 1918 he was relieved of his post.

In 1919 Jellicoe was promoted to Admiral of the Fleet. At the request of the Admiralty he visited the Dominions to report on Imperial defence, and from 1920-1924 he served as Governor-General of New Zealand.

**(November 21)**

# FAMOUS MAKER OF CHEAP CARS

## M. ANDRE CITROEN

M. Andre Citroen has died in Paris at the age of 57. He was a man whose business achievements were astonishing.

By sheer ability he succeeded in making his previously unknown name almost as famous as any in Europe. Motor-cars were his medium.

When the war ended he began to produce them so cheaply and in such huge numbers that he dotted the roads of France with them. Then he extended his influence abroad. His operations in England, however, led him to protest in 1932, that he found the "Buy British" campaign tantamount to a boycott of his manufactures.

No enterprise was too great for Andre Citroen. To prove that his motor vehicles were good engineering propositions he sent them on a gruelling expedition across the Sahara that was reputed to have cost his company more than £200,000.

It was a first-class advertisement. So too was his costly acquisition of the Eiffel Tower for the Illuminated display of his name.

An active brain impelled him to carry out one great commercial adventure after another. The greater the risk the more the enterprise appealed to him.

Of Dutch-Jewish birth, he was the son of a diamond dealer, but had no liking for the business. He preferred engineering, and after leaving the Polytechnic College in Paris he opened a small factory employing 10 men for the production of helical gear wheels, an invention of his own which was destined to become famous throughout the world.

M. Citroen's gambling spirit, however, and his love of "taking chances" added to the effects of the world crisis, led to his downfall. At the end of last year the Citroen Motor Car Company filed its position in bankruptcy.

**(July 4)**

# SLEPT IN TOMB OF TUTANKHAMEN

## DEATH OF DR. J.H. BREASTED

Within two days of the 13th anniversary of the opening of the tomb of King Tutankhamen, in the Valley of the Kings, on the west bank of the Nile, on Nov. 30, 1922. Dr. James Henry Breasted, the distinguished Egyptologist, died in New York yesterday of streptococcus infection.

The doctor, states a Reuter message from New York, was reputed to have been the man who persuaded the Egyptian authorities to permit the excavation. His death has revived the story of the curse which was supposed to be associated with all those connected with the opening of Tutankhamen's tomb.

Two years ago when Dr. Breasted was discussing the curse, he said, "All Tommy-rot. I defy the curse. If anybody was exposed to it I was. I slept in the tomb for two weeks and even had my meals there. I never felt better in my life. He went on to point out that a number of scientists were then working in the tomb and said they were not afraid of the curse.

Among those connected with the excavation of the tomb of Tutankhamen who are popularly described as having been "victims of the curse" are:

Earl of Carnarvon, died 1923, aged 57.
Sir William Garstin died 1926, aged 77
Mr. Arthur C. Mace, died 1928, aged 54.
Mr. J.W.H. Carver, died 1929.
Mr. Mervyn Herbert, died 1930, aged 48.
Mr. Richard Bethell, died 1931, aged 48.
Sir Charles Cust, died 1932, aged 68.
Mr. Albert M. Lythgoe, died 1934.

**(December 3)**

# WALES' GREATEST WIN

## LATE TRY BEATS ALL BLACKS BY ONE POINT

**By Howard Marshall**

WALES ... 13 pts; ... NEW ZEALAND ... 12

WHEN New Zealand had made their last furious onslaught, and Wales had won by a single point at Cardiff, I saw a man part with his bowler hat for ever. He flung it far into the swirling crowd, and I was sorry to see it go.

That bowler had suitably punctuated a glorious game for me. When New Zealand scored in the first half it tilted lugubriously over its owner's nose. Then came that astonishing second half.

Two goals to Wales in six minutes, and the bowler was so prodigiously thumped that it became a billycock. A great dropped goal by Gilbert, another converted try which gave New Zealand the lead again, and the billycock swayed perilously upon its shattered brim.

The last Welsh try, three minutes before the end, and a hand like a ham descended from the row behind and turned the billycock into an opera-hat which would never open again.

What a game, what players, what prodigious excitement? They will still be telling the story of it all in 50 years' time.

Our grandchildren, I do not doubt, will hear of a giant Welsh centre three-quarter brushing the New Zealand backs made like flies.

This giant Wooller, their fathers will explain, was nearly seven feet high, and one of the greatest centres who ever smashed a desperate defence. And upon my word, where the question of Wooller's greatness is concerned I do not think they will be exaggerating unduly.

I grant you that I am in no mood for temperate criticism. As far as my judgement goes, all the Welsh players could with justice be given the freedom of Cardiff to-morrow and be made bards at the next Eisteddfod.

I only know that I never saw a more splendid match, fine in spirit and performance and strong endeavour.

An extraordinary match too, for all the Welsh tries followed punts ahead, and how often do we see the punt ahead which bounces kindly for the attacking team?

Then Gilbert dropped a goal from 40 yards' range and a wide angle with a low, raking shot which never seemed likely to carry the distance. Somehow, though, the ball bored its way through the air, and 50,000 Welshmen watched in horrified silence as it fell over the bar.

It was from another drop at goal, moreover, that Ball snatched an unexpectedly easy try after Wales had fumbled, so that opportunism was the order of the day.

That, I think is inevitable with modern defence in the highest class of football, and the course of the game may be simply stated. In the first half New Zealand monopolised the ball, and scored a try from short range, as we thought they would, a try which was the result of continuous pressure.

Then Davey brought Wooller into the centre instead of Idwal Rees, Wales began to heel, and no sooner did their backs have the ball than New Zealand were in trouble.

There is no doubt that the Welsh backs were far more menacing in attack; if only a scrummaging pack could be discovered, what a great team Wales would be!

The Welsh forwards, mind you, improved as the game went on, and always were mettlesome in the open. And young Tanner at scrum-half – how sensibly and proficiently he played in his first big match! Wales owed much to his stopping and saving and passing out.

**(December 23)**

# GERMAN WIN IN RACE OF 1,000 CORNERS

**From Our Special Correspondent**

MONTE CARLO, Monday.

A German car won the Grand Prix de Monaco – the race of 1,000 corners – run this afternoon through the streets of Monte Carlo. Fagioli, driving the successful Mercedes-Benz covered 198 miles in 3 hrs 23 min 49.8 sec, averaging 58.15 m.p.h.

This is the highest speed at which the race has ever been won. It was a very close thing. Dreyfus, who was second, was only 31 sec behind.

Despite his magnificent performance and the fact that he is an Italian, Fagioli received scarcely a cheer from the crowd. Dreyfus, a Frenchman, was greeted with prolonged applause.

The German cars did not by any means have things all their own way. Just before half-distance Etancelin, the French driver of a Maserati, overtook Caracciola, leader of the German team, and robbed him of second place. The German was then ordered to increase speed, and four laps later he easily overtook the Frenchman.

Their desperate duel played havoc with the engines of the Mercedes-Benz and Etancelin's Maserati.

FEELING RUNNING HIGH

Feeling ran very high. As the Frenchman caught up the German there were scenes of frantic enthusiasm. At the 40th lap Etancelin was 14secs behind the Mercedes-Benz. Next time round he was 11.2secs, and a lap later only 8secs separated the two cars.

While the Mercedes-Benz held superior speed and acceleration, the Maserati obviously had better brakes. Etancelin came through the "chicane" hard on the German's heels. Caracciola was repeatedly shown the blue flag as a signal to let Etancelin get by, but he did not give way until the display of a board bearing his number, which left him no alternative but to obey.

The other drivers showed great sportsmanship while this Franco-German duel was going on.

In a further ten laps Caracciola smashed a piston and came into the pits with smoke pouring from the bonnet of his car and retired. At that moment Dreyfus, on an Alfa-Romeo, took second place, and shortly afterwards Brivio, on another Alfa-Romeo, snatched third place from Etancelin.

**(April 23)**



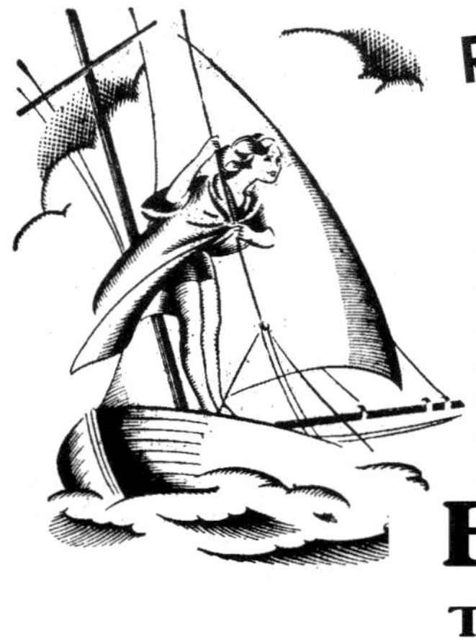



## LEADING IN THE GRAND NATIONAL WINNER

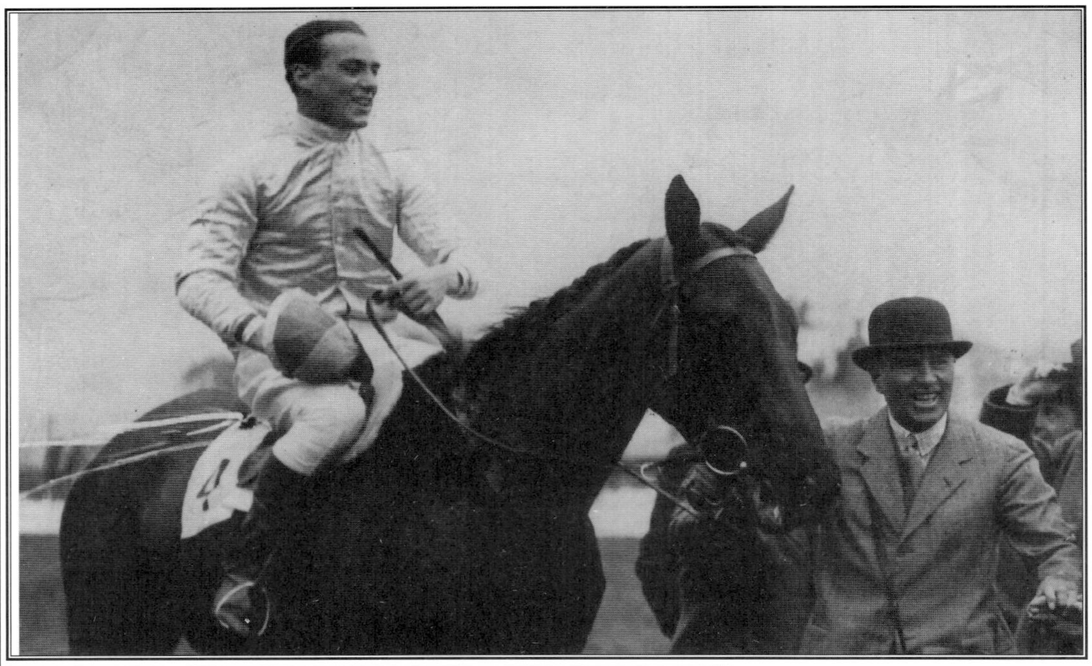

REYNOLDSTOWN, AN OUTSIDER, being led in through the crowd after winning the Grand National at Aintree yesterday.

# HOW LOVELOCK WON GREAT MILE RACE

## CUNNINGHAM FAILS TO STAY PACE

PRINCETON, Sunday.

JACK LOVELOCK, the New Zealand and Oxford University runner, gained a great triumph for the British Empire here yesterday by beating all the leading Americans in the "mile of the century."

He won by 10 yards from W.J. Bonthron, holder of the world's 1,500-metre record. Glen Cunningham, who holds the world's mile record of 4min 6 7-10sec, finished third, half-a-yard behind Bonthron. Gene Venzke, a former world's indoor mile record-holder, was fourth, Glenn Dawson fifth, and Joe Mangan, who recently broke the world's three-quarter mile record, last.

Lovelock's time of 4min 11 2-20sec, was well outside the world record, but the race, nevertheless, thrilled the 40,000 spectators.

After following at Cunningham's heels for most of the race, Lovelock challenged his rival on the last bend, and flashed past the post an easy winner.

"I enjoyed the race tremendously, but found the heat quite trying and the wind pretty solid," said Lovelock.

Mangan went into the lead at the start. Lovelock was lying fourth, but half-way round the first lap he went up to third place. Before the lap had been completed Cunningham had taken the lead, with Mangan second, Lovelock third and Bonthron fourth.

There was still no change in the third lap but it appeared that Bonthron was finished soon after the start of the final lap, as he began to drop back, and the race looked to be between Cunningham, who was still going easily in the lead, and Lovelock.

Then came the great thrill of the race. At the final bend into the straight Lovelock challenged Cunningham. He darted round the American on the right and made straight for the tape. Without looking to either side, he raced home an easy winner. Lovelock's famous final burst had again succeeded.

**(May 17)**

# "NO RISK TOO GREAT"

## NEW CHAMPION'S PLAY

**From George Greenwood**

MUIRFIELD, Friday.

Alfred Perry, of the Leatherhead Club (Surrey), won the open golf championship here to-day with a score of 283, equal to the world's record previously held jointly by Gene Sarazen, the American, and Henry Cotton.

Perry, who is 30, was born at Coulsdon, where as a boy he started to play on the Woodcote Park course. A purely self-taught player, his style is a little rugged according to modern standards, the right hand being held under the shaft. He has a fast, low swing, the club being whipped at the ball at a furious pace.

He is left-handed, and actually played left-handed as an assistant for some time, reaching a fair measure of skill. But recently he realised that as a left-hander he would never reach the top and decided to learn his golf all over again as a right-hander.

Throughout the week he never missed one short putt. In his record round of 67 he had only 28 putts.

**(June 29)**

# THE KING SEES BAHRAM WIN THE DERBY

## "BEST HORSE OF THE CENTURY"

**1. Bahram ... 5 to 4**
**2. Robin Goodfellow ... 50 to 1**
**3. Field Trial ... 9 to 1**

**From Our Special Representative**

EPSOM, Wednesday.

The Aga Khan has won the Derby a second time with the horse that everyone believed in. It was a splendid victory for Bahram, for Fox, his jockey, and for the trainer, Frank Butters. But the biggest cheer of all was given just after the horses had thundered past the post.

As they were disappearing, the Aga Khan himself stepped out on to the course from the owners enclosure, and half-walked, half-skipped along after them, twirling his umbrella vigorously and beaming with delight. It was the perfect picture of a happy man.

The crowd roared its satisfaction, and the King and Queen and other members of the Royal Family waved their congratulations from the Royal Box.

"He is a wonderful horse; the finest race-horse of modern times – of this century, anyhow," the Aga Khan remarked to the Marquess of Londonderry.

The huge crowd was agreeably surprised to see the King present, considering the unpleasant weather of the morning.

The cheers which greeted the Queen when she stepped from the Royal car on her arrival turned to a roar of gratified surprise when the King was seen to be with her.

This was the Duchess of Kent's first Derby and she backed the winner. She was obviously immensely interested in the vast panorama of cars and racegoers on "the Hill," and repeatedly asked questions of the Duchess of York. The King laughed and chatted with his sons.

BRILLIANT RACE

Bookmakers seemed to be less busy than one would have expected, but place-betting flourished, and the optimists with outsiders in mind caused one or two startling changes in the odds. But spectacle rather than speculation was the keynote, and the thousands of watchers were rewarded with as brilliant a race as Epsom has seen for years.

**(June 6)**

# FRED FOX BADLY HURT

**From Hotspur**

DONCASTER, Wednesday Night.

After Bahram's great victory in the St. Leger, I learned to-night that the condition of Fred Fox, the veteran jockey, who would have ridden the colt but for his accident there yesterday, was more serious than was at first thought.

Fox, who is 47, was injured in a fall during a race. He is now in a nursing home, and is suffering from a fractured skull. At present only his wife is allowed to see him.

His condition, however, is as well as can be expected. This afternoon he was able to listen-in to the broadcast of the race for the St. Leger.

It would have been a dull St. Leger this afternoon but for the brilliance of Bahram, who won it as easily as it has ever been won.

**(September 12)**

# FAMILY TRIUMPH IN THE GRAND NATIONAL

## OWNER'S AMATEUR SON RIDES WINNER

**From Our Special Representative**

LIVERPOOL, Friday.

Reynoldstown, an 8-year-old gelding owned and trained by Major Noel Furlong and ridden by his son, Mr. Frank Furlong, gained a great triumph in the Grand National here to-day.

Only six of the 27 starters completed the course, and Reynoldstown, a 22 to 1 outsider won by three lengths from Lady Lindsay's Blue Prince, a 40 to 1 chance, with Mr. J.H. Whitney's Thomond II, eight lengths further away third.

Golden Miller, the shortest-priced favourite in the history of the race – he started at 2 to 1 against – jumped only nine fences. At the tenth he tried to refuse, and Wilson, his jockey, was shot out of the saddle.

The Prince of Wales, who arrived on the course some time before the first race saw this misfortune from his box near Valentine's Brook.

As soon as Reynoldstown and his rider reached the paddock gate Major and Mrs. Furlong forced their way through the dense crowd to greet their son.

Mrs. Furlong, flushed with excitement, flung her arms round her son and kissed him. Then she kissed her husband, and friends insisted on kissing her.

"I am the proudest mother in England," said Mrs. Furlong. "My son might have chosen to ride our other horse, Really True. The result is a vindication of his judgment."

DID NOT MAKE A MISTAKE

Mr. Furlong, who is the first amateur rider to win the Grand National since Mr. W.P. Dutton was successful on Tipperary Tim in 1928, interviewed after the race, said:

"Thomond II. jumped across me once or twice. He struck into me when I was in the air at one of the fences during the second circuit. Reynoldstown did not make a single mistake, although he had further interference from a loose horse. He has not fallen for two years."

Reynoldstown, who has never before jumped the Grand National course, won in the last time of 9min 21sec. Last year Golden Miller won in 9min 20 2-5sec.

Reynoldstown's success has saved the bookmakers from very heavy losses.

"Had Golden Miller won to-day," said a well-known bookmaker, "half the starting price offices in the country would have been to let."

**(May 15)**

# ENDEAVOUR WINS KING'S CUP

The King's Cup, premier award in British yachting, was won to-day by Mr. T.O.M. Sopwith's Endeavour, which finished over 3min ahead of Velsheda.

Some disappointment was caused by the King's decision to withdraw Britannia from the contest. Even if Britannia had come home first, the King would not have claimed his own cup, but in former years he has competed. To-day, however, he stood aside, lest Britannia, in the conditions which prevailed should "blanket" a competitor.

**(August 7)**

# OVER 100,000 SPECTATORS AT NINE CRICKET MATCHES

OVER 100,000 people watched the nine first-class cricket matches yesterday, gate records being broken on several grounds.

The gates had to be closed at Bradford, where 27,000 spectators saw Bowes take six Lancashire wickets for 16 runs. The receipts amounted to £1,124.

Once again the attractive South African side proved a draw at Swansea. Fifteen thousand people paid for admission, and altogether 17,000 looked on. Even the football grandstand was packed, and only the Australian teams of 1921 and 1926 have drawn such a good crowd in Wales.

Derbyshire also did well, a record crowd of 7,000 paying to see the game with Warwickshire at Derby. These figures beat the previous record – 5,962; with Warwick, curiously enough, as the home county's opponents.

The Surrey v. Notts encounter drew nearly 15,000 people to the Oval; 12,000 watched Sussex and Middlesex at Hove and 12,000 were at Canterbury for the Kent-Gloucestershire match.

**(August 6)**

# ENGLAND BEATEN BY WEST INDIES

## SECOND INNINGS COLLAPSE

## CONSTANTINE BOWLS "BUMPERS"

PORT OF SPAIN, (Trinidad), Monday.

COLLAPSING badly after having a good chance of saving the game, England were beaten by West Indies in the second Test match here to-day by 217 runs.

The policy of George Grant, the West Indies captain, whose bold move had enabled England to win the first Test by four wickets, was to-day a success.

After Saturday's score of 150 for three had been taken to 280 for six at the luncheon interval, he declared, and England were thus left to score 325 to win.

If victory were, perhaps, beyond their compass, they had at least an excellent chance of forcing a draw. But the England batsmen were quite unable to cope with the brilliant bowling and keen fielding, and the side were all out for 107.

There was an incident during the closing stages in which Constantine was involved. His bowling was rather short, and two balls went right over Ames' head. The game was stopped while umpire Arthur Richardson, the old Australian Test cricketer, went over to George Grant and spoke to him about the bowling. The result was that Constantine was taken off amid loud barracking by the spectators.

England's chance of saving the game seemed to vanish when Wyatt was caught by Headley at slip off Constantine in the next over without addition to the tea score.

Hendren was easily run out at 79. He touched a ball to first slip and started to run, but Ames did not move, and before Hendren could get back the wicket had been broken.

**(January 29)**

# ENGLAND LOSE THIRD RUBBER IN 16 MONTHS

**By Thomas Moult**

England lost the rubber yesterday to South Africa for the first time in cricket history on English soil.

The final Test match ended in a draw at Kennington Oval, and the South African triumph is the result of their win at Lord's in the only game of the series to reach a definite conclusion.

Within the past 16 months the rubber has been lost three times by England – to Australia, the West Indies and South Africa.

R.E.S. Wyatt has been the captain throughout this humiliating experience, except when injury compelled him to stand down, and the latest Test series has ended in an atmosphere of unparalleled discontent, almost cynicism, behind the scenes of first-class cricket.

### RE-ELECTING WYATT

An increasing number of leading cricketers and personalities in the game view with apprehension the possibility that the existing Selection Committee may, if they wish, continue in office until the end of next summer, and, moreover, persist in re-electing Wyatt to the captaincy during the visit of the Indian cricketers next season, when three Test matches will be played.

I can reveal that a strong agitation is being fostered among M.C.C. members that may result in the whole position being re-considered as an emergency measure.

**(August 21)**

# 24 BATSMEN OUT L.B.W.

Twenty-four l.b.w. decisions were given in first-class cricket on Saturday. On the corresponding day last year there were only nine decisions of the kind.

The immediate effect of the ammended l.b.w. rule has, therefore, been remarkable. A batsman may now be out if a ball breaking from the off hits his pads, and no fewer than five were dismissed in this way at Lord's, where the M.C.C. are playing Yorkshire.

**(May 6)**

# UNKNOWN BATSMAN'S HUNDRED IN 63 MINUTES

## 18-YEAR-OLD SOMERSET DISCOVERY

ANOTHER Jessop looks on the western horizon. This time the 18-year-old son of a Somerset farmer – a youth unknown in big cricket – has taken a quick leap to fame with a whirlwind century in his first county match.

Harold Gimblett flashed across the Frome scene with a hundred in 63 minutes. Played by Somerset for his medium-pace bowling in this game with Essex, he smashed his way to three figures with a string of seventeen 4's and three 6's.

It is too early to know whether Gimblett can maintain this lightning-like cricket. Yet there is the authentic stamp about him; he played the Essex attack as if he had been facing county bowling all his life – and liked it.

Six Somerset men were out for 107 runs when Gimblett arrived. Things looked bad; but the youth, whose only previous experience had been for Watchet in club games settled down at once. He raced to fifty in 28 minutes, got his century in 63 minutes and reached 123 in 80 minutes.

There was nothing hit-or-miss about his display. It was fluent batsmanship – drives, cuts and leg hits came with style and certainty. In getting 123, he became the only Somerset player to equal B.L. Bisgood's 1907 record of a century in his first county game.

As it is, Gimblett has straightway put himself first favourite for the Lawrence Trophy for the season's quickest hundred.

He scored his runs out of 175 and, when ninth to leave at 282, he saw his county in a happy position. Andrews, the tall fast bowler and hard-hitting batsman, who has spent two seasons in Scottish cricket, followed Gimblett's example and trounced the Essex bowlers. His 71, including three 6's and five 4's in fifty minutes, was a brilliant effort.

With two hours left for play, Essex found Wellard working up to a good pace and keeping a fine length. Only Rist faced him with confidence, defying Somerset for an hour and a half, and hitting six 4's. Wellard, who got plenty of pace from the pitch, claimed all five wickets that fell for 36.

SOMERSET

| | |
|---|---|
| Lee (J.W.) c Eastman b Nichols | 3 |
| Lee (F.S.) lbw b Nichols | 41 |
| R.A. Ingle c Eastman, b Nichols | 12 |
| J.C. White c Eastman, b Nichols | 4 |
| C.C. Case, b Smith (P.) | 35 |
| H.D. Burrough b Nichols | 2 |
| Wellard, st Wade, b Evans | 21 |
| Gimblett c & b Eastman | 123 |
| Luckes, b Nichols | 7 |
| Andrews c O'Connor b Evans | 71 |
| Hazell, not out | 7 |
| B5 l-b 5 w 1 | 11 |
| Total | 337 |

ESSEX

| | |
|---|---|
| Cutmore, lbw b Wellard | 24 |
| Rist c Lee (J.W.) b Wellard | 41 |
| T.N. Pearce, b Wellard | 1 |
| O'Connor not out | 9 |
| Nichols c Lee (J.W.) b Wellard | 0 |
| T.P. Lawrence, b Wellard | 4 |
| Eastman, not out | 7 |
| L-b 1 | |
| Total (5 wkts.) | 87 |

Smith (P.), Wade, Evans and Smith (R.) to bat.

SOMERSET – First Innings

| | O. | M. | R. | W. |
|---|---|---|---|---|
| Nichols | 23 | 3 | 87 | 6 |
| Smith (R.) | 13 | 2 | 43 | 0 |
| Eastman | 13 | 4 | 38 | 1 |
| Evans | 14.5 | 1 | 69 | 2 |
| Smith (P.) | 13 | 1 | 89 | 1 |

Nichols bowled one wide

**(May 20)**

# WEDNESDAY'S THRILLING CUP WIN

## DRAMATIC GOALS BY RIMMER BEAT ALBION

**By Frank Coles**

SHEFFIELD WEDNESDAY... 4 ... WEST BROMWICH ALBION... 2

WEMBLEY'S thirteenth Cup Final was easily the best of all. For all time it will be remembered as the thrill-a-minute match.

I am sure no one in that vast 93,000-crowd had seen a big game so crowded with hot drama and tense excitement.

A goal in two minutes; two goals in the last four minutes; Albion twice equalising the scores; half a dozen easy scoring chances missed and – for the first time in more than 30 years – six goals that counted.

This 1935 Final began with a surprise and was a surprise to the very last kick. The form of Wednesday and Albion had suggested a dour battle, in which defence would be supreme. One goal, I thought would settle the issue.

Instead, we had the refreshing spectacle of both sides throwing their last ounce into attack. None of the "What we have we hold" business in this game. Hence the thrills and the 6 goals.

There were other surprises, too. Such as the sparkling form of Boyes, Albion's outside-left and the youngest and smallest player of the 22; the comparative failure of Albion's veteran right wing, Glidden and Carter, partners in over 300 matches; and the constant shuffling of Wednesday's attack.

### CARRYING THE BALL

Then there was the remarkable spectacle of the referee penalising both the goal keepers for carrying the ball. No decision of the sort had been made in any previous Wembley final.

I congratulate Sheffield Wednesday on their win. They deserve to hold the Cup because, late in the game with the score 2-2, they accepted their chances. Albion had had similar chances, easier, in fact, and missed them.

Yet I shall always regard Albion as the unlucky team. Certainly their courage was magnificent.

Remember that they recovered from the hammer-blow of being a goal down after two minutes, that they rallied again when Wednesday regained the lead midway through the second half and – most vital point – that they carried a semi-passenger for half the game.

Carter, key man of Albion's forward line, was hurt after 10 minutes. The ligament trouble that had kept him out of the team since the semi-final tie with Bolton returned and, as the game advanced, was aggravated.

With a half-speed inside right holding up his attack Glidden did the right thing, 20 minutes from the end, in sending Carter to outside-left and bringing Sandford over to inside-right.

And Carter, getting slower and slower because of his physical handicap, had the mortification of seeing a header of his strike the post when Albion were going all out for the winning goal 10 minutes from time.

**(April 29)**

# NEW SCORING RECORD

THE Christmas holiday football programme brought its usual crop of surprises – and a first-class scoring sensation.

R. Bell, the Tranmere Rovers centre-forward, scored 9 of his side's 13 goals against Oldham Athletic yesterday and beat the English League record by two.

Only a fortnight ago, Drake of the Arsenal, startled the football world by scoring seven against the Villa, equalling the record set up by James Ross, of Preston, in 1888. Six years ago, Whitehurst, of Bradford City, netted seven in a Third Northern match.

Bell, the new record-holder, joined Tranmere five seasons ago, and has been a much sought-after player.

His club, Tranmere Rovers, have an uncanny knack of discovering scoring centre forwards. Some years ago they "made" Dean, and transferred him to Everton, and a couple of seasons later were paid a big fee by Aston Villa for Waring.

Remarkable scenes followed yesterday's match at Tranmere, where, by the way, no fewer than 17 goals were netted in all. Spectators rushed on to the pitch and carried Bell shoulder high to the dressing room.

Tranmere's 13 goals equalled the League record which Stockport County set up in 1934, when in a Third Division match they beat Halifax Town at Stockport 13-0.

The break in the weather on Christmas Eve saved the Soccer programme. Only half a dozen fixtures were affected – five on Wednesday and one (Bradford v. Leicester) yesterday.

Though Sunderland played only one match – their Christmas Day game at Leeds was postponed – they maintained a five points' lead over all rivals. They are firmer favourites than ever for the championship which has eluded them since 1912-13.

Arsenal missed a golden chance of reducing the leaders' advantage. After beating Liverpool 1-0 at Anfield on Christmas morning, they lost the return game at Highbury yesterday by 2-1. A 60,000 crowd saw the champions fall at home for the second time this season.

**(December 27)**

# PERRY BEATS GERMAN

**By A. Wallis Myers**

F. J. PERRY is still champion, and the title which he regained for England last year remains at home.

In a match of super-speed, lasting 80 minutes and bristling with gorgeous shots, the holder resisted the German challenge of Baron G. Von Cramm without losing a set. His score was 6-2, 6-4, 6-4.

Wimbledon has yielded many closer and more fluctuating finals in the past. There have been matches in which net play has taken a more conspicuous part.

But for the sustained pace of the ground shots, for refined, accurate driving and for the thrusting power with which both men fought – Perry always a little quicker about the court than his rival – I cannot remember any contest quite like it.

Tilden and Johnston in their heyday used to whip the ball with dazzling pace from the baseline, and the first would carry his pugnacity into the service.

But they were neither as light-footed nor as quick in extracting the ball from the losing position as the champion and his challenger yesterday. They had caught the spirit of the time, which is speed.

Perry is not only the first "playing through" champion to keep his title; he properly reserved for the last round, when the opposition was strongest, his soundest and most concentrated display.

What a remarkable and romantic career Perry has had – the first "people's champion" we may call him.

A native of Stockport, Lancashire, he has just turned 26 – two months older than von Cramm. At Wallasey Grammar School and at Ealing County School he showed an aptitude for ball games, but it was not until he spent a family holiday at Eastbourne, and, as a boy of 15, watched the tournament in Devonshire Park, that his ambition to become a champion was fired.

### HIS FIRST VENTURE

A year later he turned up at the Middlesex junior championship with a racket that had two strings missing, and reached the final. Then he competed in the junior championship at Wimbledon, where his old racket collapsed in the middle of a game.

But, as his father said afterwards, he came home like the proverbial dog with two tails, for he had hung up his clothes in the pavilion of the All England Club in the locker used by Rene Lacoste, the reigning champion.

How Perry went to Budapest and became the first non-Hungarian competitor to win the world's table-tennis championship; of the table-tennis table, with the ball struck on the rise, to the tennis lawn, and came within a stroke of beating Austin at Queen's Club; how, given the opportunity to travel by his father and the Lawn Tennis Association, he subsequently won every important title open to competitors abroad, taking the crown at Wimbledon last year – that is only a bare outline of his upward flight.

### DISLIKES PRACTICE

His physical fitness is more a matter of instinct than rigourous training. He never touches alcohol, but is a moderate pipesmoker. He does not like practice games; he can never be quite serious at them. Keenly competitive on the court, he is the easiest fellow to get on with off it.

Incidentally, he can make a very neat after-dinner speech – and I've heard him tell an amusing story in more than one country.

**(July 6)**

# HOW LOUIS BEAT MAX BAER

## KNOCK-OUT IN FOURTH ROUND

**From Our Own Correspondent**

NEW YORK, Tuesday Night.

Joe Louis, the 21-year-old negro boxer, won the heavy-weight fight here to-night with Max Baer, the former world champion. He knocked Baer out in the fourth round.

Many of the crowd thought Baer could have gone on. When he left the ring with blood streaming down his face he was booed by many of the 100,000 spectators.

The huge open-air arena of the Yankee Stadium was filled with the din of tremendous applause when the opponents entered the ring. Louis began the fight as 2 to 1 favourite.

Round One – Baer tore into Louis but took a right on the jaw. This produced a savage expression on Baer's face. Then Louis got home a left-hook. Baer was bleeding from the nose badly, but laughed. Then he was battered into a corner, and covered up when in a helpless condition – Louis's round.

### BAER BLEEDING

Round Two. – Baer was watching for an opening to the stomach. After a little sparring Louis connected with a hard right hook to the nose, which was still bleeding.

Louis landed three more right hooks to the face. Baer covered up and replied with a left hook. The negro was deadly serious. He landed short, sharp blows, and Baer's nose was still bleeding badly. He seemed afraid to let himself go. Louis got home three more left jabs.

By this time Baer's face was a gory sight. He tried to keep in close and held on. Louis jabbed hard and Baer landed a left-right to the jaw at the bell, rocking Louis. Louis's round.

### REFEREE WARNS BAER

Round Three. – Baer began this round fighting with both fists to the head, but the negro backed and they fell into a clinch. The referee warned Baer to keep his punches up. Baer looked savage. Louis got in some left hooks and jabs. He was very cool.

Baer jabbed and then backed away repeatedly. With lefts and rights to the head, Louis battered Baer, who went down from one terrific left hook.

Baer waved to the crowd from a sitting position. He got up at the count of two. Louis landed a right to the head and a stinging left-hook again put Max on the floor, the bell saving him from a knock-out. Baer laughed while on the canvas.

Round Four. – Baer was still afraid to let himself go. The negro landed a hard blow to the stomach and then a left, right, and left to the head. He also scored to the body and worked Baer to the ropes, where he hammered away at him with both fists.

Louis continued to poke Baer's head back with left jabs. Then, another terrific right-hook floored Baer. This time he took the full count while kneeling on one knee. The blood was streaming down his face.

**(September 25)**

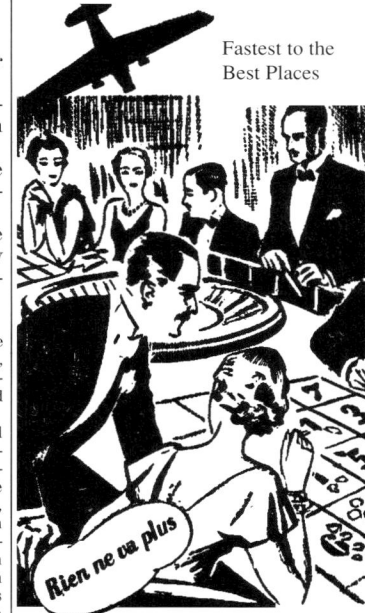

# QUETTA EARTHQUAKE DISASTER SCENES — PICTURES BY AIR

THE APPALLING EFFECT of the earthquake in British Baluchistan, India, is revealed by these pictures (received by air) from Quetta, where over 26,000 people perished and 3,250 were injured. The total for the whole area involved is expected to reach 65,000 dead.
Above: THE RUINS OF QUETTA RAILWAY STATION, where casualties were heavy. The shock lasted three minutes.
Left: A QUETTA STREET in ruins. In some districts 70per cent. of the native population were wiped out.

THE JUBILEE SPIRIT is as evident East as West — a snapshot of St. Leonard's-avenue, Poplar, yesterday.

## NATIONAL GOVERNMENT POSTERS

## THE JUBILEE CELEBRATIONS

# 1936

This was the Year of the Three Kings. Early in the year George V died, much loved and much missed. He was succeeded by Edward VIII who during his long years as Prince of Wales had earned the title "Prince Charming". He made his presence felt, ending some of the more antiquated procedures at court and touring the depressed areas. In South Wales, he told the unemployed that "Something must be done".

Papers in America and Europe were carrying stories of his love affair with Mrs Simpson. The British newspapers by mutual agreement reported nothing, apart from an obscurely placed paragraph announcing Mrs Simpson's divorce. The affair came to a head when the Bishop of Bradford made a reference to the King's conduct in a sermon reported in *The Daily Telegraph* under the anodyne headline. "A Bishop and the Meaning of the Coronation". For ten hectic days the Cabinet tried to find a way out of the Constitutional crisis but none was found, and the king abdicated, to be succeeded by his shy and stammering younger brother, who took the title George VI. *The Daily Telegraph* in a editorial cried loyally: "God Save King George and Queen Elizabeth".

The war in Abyssinia ended as the Emperor Haile Selassie was forced to flee after his troops and civilians had been subjected to gas attacks from the air by the Italians. The civil war in Spain began as General Franco arrived from Morocco, landing with a force of colonial troops, to lead a rebellion against the Socialist government. Both sides were ruthless with their enemies as the fighting intensified. Before the end of the year, German troops were fighting alongside Franco and Madrid was besieged.

The German forces marched into the de-militarised Rhineland in defiance of the Locarno Treaty to the dismay of France, and Hitler was steadily building up his armed forces. At the Olympic Games held in Berlin the German government produced a great display of Aryan might. To the disgust of Hitler, though, the principal figure of the games proved to be the Black athlete, Jesse Owens, who won four athletics gold medals. The success of the American runners led *The Daily Telegraph* athletics correspondent to speculate whether it was fair for black and white runners to compete in the same competitions.

In Britain, J.H. Thomas, a cabinet minister, was forced to resign when he was found guilty of leaking the contents of the budget to friends who made money out of the information. Income tax was raised to pay for the expansion of the armed forces. The Spitfire was seen for the first time at the Hendon Air Show as was an unnamed bomber, later to be known as the Wellington.

The liner *Queen Mary* sailed to new York on her maiden voyage and soon won the Blue Riband of the Atlantic from her rival the Normandie. The antics of a much smaller boat, *The Girl Pat*, fascinated the world as, instead of fishing in The North Sea, she sped off round the world, navigating by means of a sixpenny atlas, only to be impounded in British Guiana. The Crystal Palace was destroyed by fire.

As earlier in the decade one of the arts suffered a triple blow. This time it was literature: Rudyard Kipling, G.K. Chesterton and A.E. Houseman died within a few months of each other. The war leaders Allenby and Beatty also died.

## KING EDWARD ABDICATES



# The Daily Telegraph

To-Days Weather : Bright Periods; local fog

Broadcasting: Page TEN



No. 25,442 POSTAGE { INLAND, CANADA AND NEWFOUNDLAND, THREE HALFPENCE / OTHER COLONIES AND PLACES ABROAD, TWOPENCE

LONDON, FRIDAY DECEMBER 11, 1936

ONE PENNY

*BIRTHS, MARRIAGES and DEATHS in this column, one guinea for three lines or less and 5s for each additional line. "IN MEMORIAM" notices 12/6 for three lines or less and 3/6 for each additional line. (Special rate for five or ten years' automatic insertion on application.) Announcements, authenticated by name and address of sender may be sent to The Daily Telegraph, Fleet St., E.C.4. or 161, Piccadilly, W.1. or telephoned to Central 4242. Forthcoming Marriages in Court Page, 3 guineas for 3 lines or less, and 12/6 for each additional line.*

## BIRTHS

BOWIE – On Dec. 7, 1936, St. John's Birchington, Thanet, to Helen (née Fairweather), wife of Dr. A.M. Bowie, a son – New Zealand papers, please copy.

DYER – On Dec. 2. 1936, at Beechcroft, Alverstoke, to Elfreda (née Tuxford), wife of Lieut. Richard Dyer, R.N. a daughter. China papers, please copy.

FINLASON – On Dec. 9, 1936, to Norah (née Tutin), wife of Alan David Finlason, of 3, Dulwich Wood Park, a daughter.

WEBB – On Dec. 8, 1936, at Highmead, Lisvane, Cardiff to Kenneth and Anita Webb, a son.

WHYTE – On Dec. 8, 1936 to Mr. and Mrs. Frank Whyte (née Constance E. Appleton), "Strathmore" St. Margart-at-Cliffe, Kent, a son.

## MARRIAGES

BARTLETT-STANBURY – On Dec. 3, 1936, at St James's, Spanish-place, Henry David Hardington Bartlett to Kathlene Rosemond Stanbury.

JONES-NEISH – On Dec. 8, 1936, at Holy Trinity Episcopal Church, Monteith, Angus. Edward G. E. Jones, son of Mr. W. Jones, of Malvern, to Rachel Margery, second daughter of the late Mr. and Mrs. G.W. Neish, of Afflick, Menikie.

ROBERTS-JESSE – On Dec. 9, 1936 at the Parish Church, East Knoyle, Lieutenant E. H. Roberts, R.N.R. to Rosemary Joan Jesse.

VALENTIN-GEMMELL – On Dec. 5, 1936, at All Saints, Peterborough, SEYMOUR FAIRBRIDGE, son of Mr. and Mrs. G.S. Valentin, to Lisbeth, eldest daughter of Mr. and Mrs. D. Gemmell.

WEILL-CLAYTON – On Dec. 10, 1936, in London. Simon L. Weill, of 51 Lauderdale-mansions, W.9. to Beatrice, third daughter of Mr. and Mrs. E.E. Clayton, of Park-street, St. Albans, Herts.

## GOLDEN WEDDING

JOSLIN-SHERRELL – On Dec. 11, 1886, at the Parish Church, East Ham, Arthur Edward Joslin to Laura Mary Sherrell. Present address:- Brentwood.

## DEATHS

ARNELL – On Dec. 10, 1936, after a short illness, David Christopher Arnell, of V.T. Thompson & Arnell, 80 Bishopsgate, E.C.2. Funeral arrangements later.

BEABLE, Elizabeth (née Vaughan) for 55 years the beloved and devoted wife of W.H. Beable, passed peacefully away on Dec. 8, 1936, in her 78th year, at 38 Kirkstall-road, Streatham Hill, London S.W. 2. Interment Putney Vale Cemetery, noon, to-day.

BLOCH – On Dec. 10, 1936, at 47 Portman-square, W.1. Armand Gabriel Bloch, of Armand Bloch Ltd. Funeral 11.30 a.m. to-day, Dec. 11, at Willesden Cemetery.

DAVIS – On Dec. 10, 1936, at 40, Chatsworth-road, Brondesbury, N.W.2. Dora, wife of Lewis Davis, aged 68. Funeral at Willesdon, eleven a.m. Sunday.

DOWNING – On Dec. 10, 1936, at a nursing home, Miss Ellen Sylvania Downing, (of Australia), a lifelong friend of Mrs. E.B. Spooner and Mrs. A.J. Gordon. Particulars of funeral later.

FORSE – On Dec. 10, 1936, at Hollymount, Pepys-road, Wimbledon, S.W. William Arthur, beloved son of Mr. and Mrs. W.T. Forse, aged 23.

KERR – On Dec. 9, 1936, at St. Monclair, New Jersey, U.S.A. Janet Empsall, beloved wife of Robert C. Kerr formerly of Paisley, Scotland.

MELHUISH, Annie Bertha, on Dec. 8, 1936, at Ealing, Interment at Westminster Cemetery, Hanwell, to-morrow (Saturday), at eleven o'clock.

MEYERN-HOMENBERG – On Dec. 9, 1936, in an aeroplane accident, Baron Gottfried Meyern-Hoernberg, aged 36 years. Funeral service at St. Marylebone Cemetery, East End-road, Finchley, to-morrow (Saturday), at eleven a.m. Flowers may be sent to 5, Baker-street, W.1.

MILLER – On Dec. 9, 1936, at Falkland House, St. Austell, Julia Marion, the beloved wife of Sidney Miller. Funeral to-morrow (Saturday), leaving the house at eleven a.m. for Charlestown Cemetery.

MILNE – On Dec. 6, 1936, after a short illness, Arthur Kenyon Jolly (Jack) Milne, of Bays Hill Collage, Elstree, Herts. aged 25, Funeral private. No flowers please.

MUSTARD – On Thursday, Dec. 10, 1936, at 9, Makepeace-avenue, Highgate, Sarah, wife of J.T. Mustard.

NATHAN – On Dec. 9, 1936 David Lionel Nathan, of 39 Blomfield-road, W.9. Funeral 11.30 a.m. Sunday. Willesden United Synagogue Cemetery. No flowers.

PAGET – On Dec. 9, 1936 at Kings Newton Hall, near Derby, suddenly Sir Cecil Walters, C.M.G., D.S.O., the beloved husband of Florence Paget, in his 63rd year. Service at St. Andrew's Church (the Railway Church), London-road, Derby, at two p.m. Monday, Dec. 14; interment at Sutton Bonnington (station, Kegworth), at 3.30 p.m.

SASSE – On Wednesday, Dec. 9, 1936, Elizabeth Sasse, beloved wife of Ferdinand Sasse, 16, Stanley-gardens, Cricklewood, N.W. 2. Funeral Monday, 11.30 a.m. Golders Green Crematorium. No flowers, by request.

SMITH – ON DEC. 8, 1936, At Bournemouth , Edward Algernon, dearly loved husband of Jessie Louise Smith, after severe operation.

STEDMAN – On Dec. 9, 1936, at Leytonstone, Marguerite Adele, wife of James M. Stedman, in her 82nd year.

WRIGHT – On Dec. 9, 1936, at 3, Earlsfield-road, Wandsworth, J. Turton Wright, aged 81 years. Funeral service at East Hill Congregational Church at eleven on Monday, 14th followed by the interment at Putney Vale

## PERSONAL

*5s. per line (minimum 2 lines). Trade 12/6 per line. Lost and Found 2/6 per line.*

MONEY! IF YOU PAINT FLOWERS, earn at home making designs for machine-printed cretonnes, &c. Designs fetch from £6 6s to £21 each. Our unique postal method will teach you and a Sales service is provided through which we have sold hundreds of pounds worth of pupils' designs – For proof and free particulars write Q." The Textile Studio, 352a, Station-road, Harrow.

HOT TEA, bread and dripping at midnight is given free to hundreds of homeless and hungry men and women from THE SILVER LADY'S ALL-NIGHT TRAVELLING CAFE, which has never failed them yet, OVER 75,000 FREE MEALS AND 22,000 BED AND BREAKFAST TICKETS GIVEN THIS YEAR – Please help by sending a gift of money to Miss Betty Baxter, The Silver Lady Fund, 6, Tudor-street, London, E.C.4. Men's boots and clothing urgently needed, please.

MASSAGE & ELECTRICAL TREATMENT – Association of Certified Blind Masseurs (under Medical Direction) 204, Great Portland-street, W.1. Euston 1062. Blind Chartered Masseurs and Masseuses available on application to the Massage Secretary.

WINTER SPORTS FOR PUBLIC SCHOOLBOYS – Special Party to SWITZERLAND (Leukerbad), December 30th to January 13th. FEES NOW REDUCED. Reasonable inclusive rates (not run for profit). Excellent sport, experienced staff, good hotel, splendid opportunity. Separate party for Schoolgirls at adjacent hotel. A few vacancies – application urgent – For prospectuses apply Varsities and Public Schools Camps. 5, Wigmore-street, London W.1. (Langham 1774)

COOK: Cooks come. Cooks go, but be they long or short stayers, they are not easy to find. Running a house, keeping the staff on friendly terms, or keeping the staff at all make the labours of Hercules feeble in comparison! Leave the whole job to the Management of any of the "North" Hotels of London, where for one moderate inclusive sum per week you can enjoy a life of comfort freed from the worries of domesticity. For people say "There Is No Finer Hotel. Value. Anywhere.

*Stay, for instance, at*
ALWIN COURT HOTEL
2-5 Atherstone-terrace, South Kensington, S.W.7.

– the newest "North" Hotel. Completely redecorated. 50 bed rooms with running water, central heating and hand microphone telephone. Terms from 4gns., a week. Brochure on request. Telephone: Western 3274 (2 lines)
For descriptive folder of other "North Hotels, write Head Office, 14 Cromwell-place, S.W. 7. or telephone: Ken. 1212.

LET WHAT WILL be said or done, preserve your sangfroid immoveable, and to every obstacle oppose patience, perseverance and soothing language.

Thos. Jefferson.

HIS GRACE the ARCHBISHOP of CANTERBURY writes: "I cordially command this appeal. The Royal Cancer Hospital deserves all the help which can be given to it in its ceaseless endeavours to combat this scourge by patient research into its causes and by skilled and sympathetic treatment of those who suffer from it." Please send a Christmas Gift to the Earl of Granard, The Royal Cancer Hospital (Free), Fulham-road, London S.W.3.

"IF WINTER SUNSHINE is the QUEST, here is its achievement." So said one famous traveller speaking of Morocco. If you are seeking an inexpensive Winter holiday, why not follow his lead. – Full details from COOK'S, Berkeley-st., W.1. London & Branches.

GUY'S – A CITY OF HEALING, with an EMPTY TREASURE CHEST.
Help to fill it by sending a donation to the Treasurer, GUY'S HOSPITAL, S.E.1.

LA NATION, comme l'individu, est l'aboutissant d'un long passé d'efforts, de sacrifices et de dévouements.

E. Renan.

COUNTESS RECEIVES GUESTS for Winter Sports in her castle. Every modern comfort. Excellent table. 4 guineas weekly, inclusive afternoon tea. 50 Ski Tours, Skating, Dancing. 5 feet snow already. – Write C. Box 16,608, Daily Telegraph, 161 Piccadilly, W.1.

FLATS ANNOUNCEMENTS appear to-day on Pages 30 and 32.

JOURNALISM; STORY & PLAY WRITING Expert personal, postal tuition. Prospectus free. – Metropolitan College of Journalism, Dept. J5/6 St. Albans.

PRATTS HOTEL FOR COMFORT, AT BATH.

MODERN HOMES within EASY REACH of London. Illus. particulars appear Page 31.

FINE JEWELS precious stones, gold in any form, and sovereigns bought. We pay highest market prices. Please call or send by Registered Post. Cash or offer by return. LONDON JEWELLERY MART Ltd. 415, Oxford-st., W.1. (entr. in Duke-st.), op. Selfridges.

"THE NICEST HOTEL IN THE WORLD." See BRANKSOME DENE Advt., Page 28, Col. 2.

AT THE PRICE OF AN HOTEL BEDROOM a luxury service flat off Piccadilly. Any period. One or two bed rooms. Your own entrance hall and bath room. Expert valeting. Highest-class cuisine. Meals optional – a snack or a full course meal served in your own flat. Moderate inclusive rental. – Write, call or 'phone for descriptive illustrated brochure. Resident Manager, 20, Jermyn-street, S.W.1. 'Phone Regent 6651.

SUITABLE FOR A PRESENT. Many things of this kind are advertised in to-day's issue. See the column headed CHRISTMAS GIFTS on this Page.

SACKVILLE-STREET CLOTHES at City prices, Suit 8 1/2gns. Town O'ct. 7 1/2gns. Dress 11gns. Reg. 1095. J.W. Dore, 18 Sackville-street, W. Est. 60 years.

WESTCLIFFE-ON-SEA – Savoy Hotel, Charmingly appointed. Lift. Sea-front. New Year Eve festivities.

## PERSONAL

SAVOY TAILORS GUILD TAILORING SALE is now in progress. – 93,94,95, Strand. W.C.2.

UNWANTED – Artificial Teeth. Gratefully received. – Ivory Cross Dental Fund 67b, Welbeck-street, W.1.

THE quintessence of luxury and warmth found at SUNDRIDGE PARK HOTEL, BROMLEY, KENT. Centrally heated, 20 mins. Charing X., Cannon-street. In 2 18-HOLE FIRST-CLASS GOLF COURSES. Pension from 4gns and suites. Special Xmas Programme. 'Phone for Brochure. Ravensbourne 1172.

OLD SILVER, DIAMONDS & GOLD JEWELLERY WANTED. We offer big prices. – LONDON'S HIGHEST always HARRIS & CO. 37 Piccadilly, W.1.

MAKE A GRAMOPHONE RECORD OF YOURSELF AT LONDON GRAMOPHONE RECORDING COMPANY. 131-134, NEW BOND-ST., W.1. May. 0770.

WINTER SPORTS at sunny AROSA. Select party staying Hotel VALSANA has vacancies. Jan. 16th. 16 days 22 1/2gns., all inclusive. Leslie Ling. F.R.G.S.. 17, Philpot-lane, London. E.C. 3. Tel. Man. 2159.

JEWELS, DIAMONDS, Emeralds, Sapphires purchased at Highest Prices. Record Prices also for OLD GOLD, Gold Coins. Dentures, Sovs. Antique Silver, Plate, &c. BENTLEY & CO.

65 New Bond-st., (facing Brook-st.) W.1. Mayfair 0651.

BRITISH MALAYA – For information on all matters relating to trade, agriculture, mining, motoring, and travel attractions, you are invited to write for illustrated booklets, &c. to The Malayan Information Agency, Malaya House, Trafalgar-square, London W.C.2.

WE GLORY IN TRIBULATIONS: knowing that tribulation worketh patience: and patience experience; and experience hope. Romans v. 3, 4.

ELECTROLUX, very latest silent to 19 gn. model cleaner. Genuine sacrifice, 10 gns. – Write E.V., Box 4,178 Daily Telegraph E.C.4.

HERB FARM, Seal, Sevenoaks. Two vacancies for Women Students, January – Prospectus.

CHILDREN'S ENCYCLOPÆDIA WANTED, 10 vols. Write C.E., Box 11.312. Daily Telegraph E.C.4.

ECONOMIZE by sending your old "BURBERRY" Weatherproof to BURBERRYS' CLEANING WORKS, Reading, to be cleaned and reproofed by Burberrys' exclusive process.

FREE now, charming COTTAGE high up. Mod. conveniences, 4 bed. No children – Miss Wyatt, Corry Edge, Hindhead.

EASTERN or COLONIAL Handicrafts. – Will those with practical knowledge of above kindly write BM/NPOS, London W.C.1. No investment, but ready to join in scheme.

A SET OF STATIONS of the Cross wooden panels, 27in x 18in. oils, for SALE. – Write A. S. Box 11,378, Daily Telegraph, E.C.4.

AFTER the shops shut at 6, one can finish a Christmas shopping expedition by visiting Phyllis Earle. They are open until 7 o'clock between now and Christmas – 32, Dover-street, Piccadilly, W.1. Regent 7541.

SURGEON OFFERED FREE ROUND TRIP. Liverpool-Calcutta-Liverpool, in exchange for services. Sailing Jan. 2 – Write Box R., 465 c.o. Jackson's, 45, Fenchurch-st., E.C.3.

MANUFACTURERS, wishing to enter U.S. market, please communicate Agent in London till 21st December – Write M.W., Box 4,216, Daily Telegraph, E.C.4.

GOLFERS. MAYFAIR GOLF PRACTICE – Use that spare half hour to better your golf. Expert coaching. Practice nets. Spotlight golf. All golf requisites. – Particulars from 22, Brooks-mews, W.1. (Davis-st.) May, 3620.

HIS LAST TERM – and still uncertain what to be. The vigorous, open-air, type of boy might consider him on a farm of his own. For sound disinterested advice write to 1820 Memorial Settlers' Association (Dept. DTD11), 199, Piccadilly, London W.1.

DORIS – Meet me at National Institute for the Blind, 224, Great Portland-street, W.1. to choose Christmas presents for mother, dad and the others. – NIB.

A REAL HAPPY, HOLLY XMAS awaits you at Hotel Villa Belza, Torquay. Plenty of Good Cheer, and the Best of Everything. We hope you can join us. – 'Phone 2772.

PIANO WANTED. – Bechstein. Blüthner or Steinway pref. – Write P., Box 7,963. Daily Telegraph, E.C.4.

AXMAS HAMPER, with Turkey and Seasonable goods. An excellent present, 30s each, delivered free in the British Isles. Send for list of contents. Cheque or money order payable to H.G. Wheeler, Provision Store, Mount Royal, Oxford-street, W.1.

NERVOUS Disorders Successfully Treated. Consult Mr. J. Sparrow, Principal Institute of Psychotherapy, 107, Baker-st., W.1. WEL. 4233.

GENTLEMAN DESIRES to purchase OLD SILVER, SHEFFIELD PLATE & CHINA. High prices paid – Write G.D., Box 7,859, Daily Telegraph, E.C.4.

COPIES OF PHOTOGRAPHS APPEARING IN THE DAILY TELEGRAPH may be obtained at a small charge from The Daily Telegraph Photo. Sales Department, Fleet-street, E.C.4.

THE "DUNMORE," SHALDON, nr. TORQUAY – Join us for a real MERRY CHRISTMAS.

SUITE of OFFICES, about 150 yards from STOCK EXCHANGE, with area of 650 sq. ft. Unexpired lease of fifteen months. – Write S. Box 13,114, Daily Telegraph, E.C.4.

LIGHT OF ASIA – LA INSULAR, INDIA, & MANILA'S finest Cigars and Cheroots. Ill. Cats. free. – Spencers, 25, Victoria-street, S.W.1.

INTENDING ADVERTISERS can obtain help and advice in the compilation of their announcements at the West End Office of The Daily Telegraph, 161 Piccadilly, W.1.

THE LYGON ARMS, Broadway, Worcestershire. A Cotswold Inn famous for English cooking and comfort. Inclusive winter rates 12s. to 14s 6d. per day. – Booklet and tariff on request.

## MUSIC, SINGING, ELOCUTION, &C.

*2s. 6d. per line. Min. 2 lines.*

PROMISING SINGERS WANTED, to train for Musical Productions by Specialist Produce:- Write P., Box 17,211, Daily Telegraph, 161 Piccadilly, W.1.

## DANCING

*2s. per Line. Min. 3 Lines.*

AT CASANI'S SCHOOL OF BALLROOM DANCING. 90, Regent-street, guarantees to teach you steps of any dance in three private lessons £1 1s 6d. 10 a.m. to 8 p.m. – Regent 4438.

ADELE COLLIER, 124, New Bond-street, May. 6017.
SPECIALISTS in BALLROOM DANCING.
2 LESSONS FOR TEN SHILLINGS & SIXPENCE.

LONDON'S LARGEST DANCING CLASSES.
HEAD OFFICE: FIRS HALL, Winchmore Hill.
Write for parties, or 'phone Palmers Green 1908.

THE GOOD DANCER is always popular! Private lessons 5s 5 for 1gn. GLADYS JACKSON, 27, Eccleston-square S.W.1. Nr. Victoria Stn. VIC. 4592.

PARK SCHOOL (PATRICIA STILES). 4 Private Ballroom Lessons, 21s. Health Classes. 8 Tap Lessons 25s – 489, Oxford-st., Marble Arch. May. 6029.

HELEN WINGRAVE, A.T.R.G.D., M.I.S.T.D. gives PRIVATE LESSONS and CLASSES in greek and Ball Room Dancing – Inquiries to 33, Warwick-sq., S.W.1.

YOUNG LADY, I.S.T.D., M.A.O.D. (Adv.) GIVES private dancing lessons, £1 1s for 5. Studio near Victoria – 'Phone Renown 3824. 1-2.30 p.m.

RALPH MOODY – Course of PRIVATE Lessons, 1gn. Latest steps.. Cl. Tn. 7 p.m. Dance, Sat., dress – Palace Hotel, LANCASTER-GATE, W.2. Padd. 8281.

RUBY PEELER. Ballroom and Deportment lessons. Class Mon. 8-9 Dances Mon, 9-12 (dress) & Wed. 5.30 to 7. Partners. – Eccleston Hotel, S.W.1. Vic. 5770.

ALICE HALL SCHOOL (Wendy Pearson), All Dances, 5 private lessons £1 1s. DANCE TO-NIGHT, 8.30, 3s Partners. – 7, Hanover-street, W.1. May. 6319.

ALL DANCES quickly & patiently taught! Tap Dance, TO-NIGHT, 8.30 2/6 – JESSIE BROACKES 2, Jay-mews, Kensington Gore (nr. Albert Hall), Ken. 0492.

MAGDELEINE LEE, 1 S.T.D. will teach you to dance with ease and confidence (10 a.m.-10 p.m.), – HOTEL GREAT CENTRAL, N.W.1. Padd. 1220.

JOAN CARR. – Expert Tuition. 5 pte. lessons, 21s Dance to-night 8.30, 2s 6d XMAS GALA DANCE, Dec. 18. 3s – 2, Market-st., Haymarket. Whl. 8338.

LEARN CORRECTLY! HENRY JACQUES BRITAIN'S UNDEFEATED BALLROOM CHAMPION, and STAFF give private tuition daily. Beginners a speciality. – Imhof House, 112 New Oxford-st, Mus. 3270

DANCE in PRIVACY. – GEM MOUFLET gives 9.9, INDIVIDUAL tuition, PARTNER to Dances. TAP, 11, ALBEMARLE-ST., PICCADILLY. REGent 4629.

## LECTURES & MEETINGS

*4 Lines 11s 6d (Min.). 2s 6d. per Line after.*

ROYAL INSTITUTION, 21 Albemarle-street, W.1. TO-NIGHT at 9: The Astronomer Royal on LARGE TELESCOPES (Members and Friends).

Public lecture Courses SATURDAYS. Dec. 12, 19, at 3; Professor C.K. Webster, on BRITISH FOREIGN POLICY IN THE NINETEENTH AND TWENTIETH CENTURIES.

TUESDAY, Dec. 15, at 5.15; Professor E. Mellanby, on CHEMICAL, MESSENGERS OF THE BODY IN HEALTH AND DISEASE. SUBSCRIPTION: Single lecture, 3s.

## CONCERTS, &C

*3s per Line Min. 4 Lines.*

**QUEEN'S HALL,**
(Sole Lessees – Chappell & Co. Ltd.
**LONDON SYMPHONY ORCHESTRA**
**FIFTH CONCERT – 31st SERIES**
TO-NIGHT, at 8.15
Overture: "Midsummer Night's Dream" Mendelssohn
Violin Concerto Tchaikovsky
BUSTABO
Symphony No. 2 Sibelius
ALBERT COATES
Tickets. 10/-, 7/6, 6/-, 3/-, 2/-. Hall Agents and L.G. SHARPE, 1 & 3 Regent-st., S.W.1. WHI 1364.

**GROTRIAN HALL**
**ISOBEL & GEORGE**
**FORREST NEILLANDS**
RECITAL of SONATAS
for VIOLONCELLO and PIANOFORTE
TO-NIGHT, at 8.15
BECHSTEIN PIANO Tickets 12/-, 9/-, 6/-, 3/-.
WILFRID VAN WYCK, 170 Piccadilly, REG. 1136

WIGMORE HALL
**NORMAN TUCKER**
PIANOFORTE RECITAL
TO-NIGHT, at 8.30
STEINWAY PIANO, Tickets 9/-, 6/-, 3/-.
IBBS & TILLETT, 1 Wigmore-st., W.1. Welbeck 8418.

**JEAN NORRIS**
will BROADCAST to-morrow
on a BLUTHNER
**DOROTHY MANLEY**
will BROADCAST at noon to-morrow
on a BLUTHNER

THE POST of DIRECTOR of MUSIC at CHRISTS' HOSPITAL, HORSHAM, will be VACANT at the beginning of the Summer Term, 1937. Salary rising to £700 p.a. resident, or with allowances for non-residence. Applications should be sent to The Headmaster.

## CHRISTMAS GIFTS

*2s 6d. per Line, Min. 3 Lines.*

Floral Gifts Unrivalled selection of designs. GERARD LTD., Florist to H.M. Queen Mary,160 NEW BOND-STREET, W.1. Regent 1644/5.

GIVE YOURSELF this LUXURY CHRISTMAS PRESENT … useful too!

A Parcel containing 3lb. Chest Fine Tea.
2lb. Box Best Assorted Chocolates.
Drum Delicious Crystallised Fruits.
Large Jar High-grade Mincemeat.
Handsome 21-piece Tea Service.
… ALL for 21/-, carriage paid
Indian & Chinese Tea Co., (417), 36 Mincing-lane, E.C.3.

USEFUL, ORIGINAL, PERMANENT GIFTS. All the qualities of a good gift in an Atlas. – Write for free Illustrated List "B" of Atlases, from 1s 6d., G. Philip & Son Ltd., 32 Fleet-street, E.C.4.

JAMES LYLE'S FAMOUS CHRISTMAS HAMPERS – the finest present to give or receive. Brimful of choice, Christmas fare. From 10s 6d. to 5gns. delivered free England. – Obtainable from J. Lyle & Co., Saville-row, and 23, Bruton-street, Berkeley-square, W.1.. List on application. Regent 6331.

THREE NUNS FOR CHRISTMAS. Make a note of it now, and his present is as good as settled. A 1/4lb tin in its attractive greetings carton costs only 4s 10d., but it will give him pleasure out of all proportion to its cost.

AUTOMATIC FLOOR WAXER and POLISHER. Saves kneeling. Price 25s. Write for folder: DAZ POLISH & CO. Boscombe, Bournemouth.

COFFEE FOR XMAS – Save yourself trouble this year by instructing us to send your friends Guarantied "A" Grade KENYA MARK COFFEE in vacuum packed tens at 2s 4d/per lb or 3lb for 6s 6d. We pay postage and enclose card with Xmas Greetings. A. WARTNABY, Brook Cottage, Otford, Kent.

BOOKS are welcome gifts and the best books are at BUMPUS, 477, Oxford-street, W.1.

VIOLETS – Sweet scented blooms make a delightful gift. 5/-, 7/6, 10/-, 20/- – G. ZAMBRA. WINDWARD VIOLET NURSERIES. DAWLISH.

A ROCK GARDEN in the HOUSE. Miniature trees and Alpines growing midst moss and rocks. In two sizes. 12s and 7s. carriage paid. BROOKSIDE NURSERIES Ltd., Headington, Oxford.

VIOLET SCENTED GIFTS not seen elsewhere can be purchased from the Misses Allen-Brown. The Violet Nurseries, Henfield, Sussex. Write for illustrated catalogue.

GENUINE ELVAS PLUMS, Chocolate Coated, 5s 6d. lb. British PRESERVED APRICOTS, 4s 6d. lb., post free. Gifts which are always appreciated. A.T.K. LTD., 7, Byward-st., London, E.C. 3.

ELBOW PRESSURE RESTS and Bath Head Rests, 3s 6d each from the leading stores or ELBOEZE, 23, Gower-place, W.C.1.

"XMAS HAMPER." You must include YOUNG'S Morecombe Potted Shrimps.

Size 4/6 and 7/6 per basin. – YOUNG'S 1, Beauchamp-place, Brompton-road, S.W. 3. KENSINGTON 3736.

APPLES (selected), 10lb, 20lb, 40lb, boxes Cox: 5s., 10s., 20s. Allington: 3s., 5s., 10s. Bramley: 4s., 8s., Free Delivery England., Cash with order. – BAKER, Little Dale, Cranbrook, Kent.

DEVON VIOLET ESSENCE. The true fragrance of the violet, 3/-, 5/-, 8/6. Trial size 1/6 post free. Send for illustrated gift catalogue of Pot Pourri, Sachets, &c. – Lammas & Son, The Violet Farm, Dawlish, Devon.

BARR & STROUD BINOCULARS: entirely British; the ideal gift, a lasting source of interest. List D.T. and booklet. Choosing a Binocular, post free. – Barr & Stroud Ltd. 15, Victoria-street, London, S.W.1.

BINOCULARS for every purpose new, second-hand. All makes. Also Telescopes. Opera Glasses.
Lists free. – Cogswell & Harrison, 168, Piccadilly, W.1.

WINE. – 6 botts. Choice PORT, 25s.; 6 botts. Double Century SHERRY, 30s. GIFT CASE, 3 botts. Choice Port & 3 botts. Oloroso SHERRY 25s. Carr. paid. – SINCLAIR, BIRCH & CO., 33, St. Mary-at-Hill, E.C.3.

A WELCOME GIFT. – Choice blend Coffee 5lb, airtight tin, 10s., post paid in U.K. Whole or ground. – CITY OF LONDON COFFEE CO. Ltd., 49 Leadenhall-st., E.C.3.

A SACKVILLE-STREET SUIT as an Xmas gift at the mod. price of 8 1/2gns. Dinner Suit 11gns. Reg. 1095.
J.W. DORE, 18, Sackville-st., W.1. Est. 60 yrs.

PURE Digestive Keemin China Tea 5lb caddy in original Chinese chest. 15s 10d., post free. – ROWLAND STIMSON & CO., 28 Tower-hill, London, E.C.3.

CHRISTMAS BOXES of DAIRY PRODUCE, filled with Dorset Butter, Cream, and Cream Cheese, with miniature Cheddar Cheese, sent by post. – Price lists from WESSEX CHEDDS. Ltd. Sherborne, Dorset.

## SHIPPING & MAILS

*2s. per Line. Min. 4 Lines.*

**P. & O.**
**MAIL PASSENGERS AND FREIGHT SERVICES.**
(Under Contract with His Majesty's Government)
Mail steamer leaves Marseilles each Saturday at 4 a.m.
(All vessels may call at any Ports on or off the route – and the route and all sailings are subject to change or deviation with or without notice.)

BOMBAY, COLOMBO, AUSTRALIA, FORTNIGHTLY.

| Ship | Tons. | London | Mars. | Classes |
|---|---|---|---|---|
| 2,5 Mooltan | 21,000 | Dec. 11 | Dec. 19 | 1st & Tourist |
| 4,5 Moldavia | 17,000 | Dec. 24 | Dec. 31 | Tourist only |
| 2,5 Maloja | 21,000 | Jan. 8 | Jan. 16 | 1st & Tourist |

**BOMBAY, COLOMBO, STRAITS, CHINA, JAPAN – FORTNIGHTLY**

| | | | | |
|---|---|---|---|---|
| 1,2,3,5 Corfu | 15,000 | Dec. 18 | Dec. 26 | 1st & 2nd |
| 1,2,3,5 Carthage | 15,000 | Jan. 1 | Jan. 9 | 1st & 2nd |
| 1,2,3,5 Naldera | 16,000 | Jan. 15 | Jan. 23 | 1st & 2nd |
| 1,2,3,5 Ranchi | 17,000 | Jan. 29 | Feb. 6 | 1st & 2nd |

**SPECIAL SAILINGS TO BOMBAY**

Calling (1) Southampton, (2) Tangier and Gibraltar, (3) Malta, (4) Port Sudan, (5) Tranship Bombay for Karachi.

# ABDICATION OF KING EDWARD VIII

## PROCLAMATION OF THE DUKE OF YORK TO-MORROW

### TO REIGN AS KING GEORGE VI. WITH QUEEN ELIZABETH

### CORONATION STILL EXPECTED TO BE HELD ON MAY 12

### KING EDWARD TO BROADCAST TO-NIGHT BEFORE LEAVING FOR SWITZERLAND

KING EDWARD VIII. YESTERDAY ANNOUNCED HIS ABDICATION FROM THE THRONE, AFTER A REIGN OF ONLY 325 DAYS. HE WILL BE SUCCEEDED BY THE DUKE OF YORK, WHO WILL TAKE THE TITLE OF KING GEORGE VI.

HIS MAJESTY'S "FINAL AND IRREVOCABLE" DECISION WAS CONVEYED IN A MESSAGE TO PARLIAMENT AND TO THE GOVERNMENTS OF THE DOMINIONS AND OF INDIA. IN THIS MESSAGE HE DECLARED:

**"The burden which constantly rests upon the shoulders of a Sovereign is so heavy that it can only be borne in circumstances different from those in which I now find myself.**

**"I am conscious that I can no longer discharge this heavy task with efficiency or with satisfaction to myself.**

**"My mind is made up. Moreover, further delay cannot but be most injurious to the peoples whom I have tried to serve.**

**"I take my leave of them in the confident hope that the course which I have thought it right to follow is that which is best for the stability of the Throne and the Empire and the happiness of my peoples."**

#### ABDICATION BILL TO BE SIGNED TO-NIGHT

**Plans for King Edward's Departure Abroad**

King Edward will broadcast to the Empire to-night, probably at about ten o'clock, after the formalities of his Abdication have been completed.

He will make his broadcast in the capacity of a private citizen, owing allegiance to the new Sovereign, his brother.

He is expected to leave England to-morrow for Switzerland, possibly by air.

The Abdication Bill, to give effect to his Majesty's declaration, was given a first reading in the House of Commons last night, and will be passed through all its stages in both Houses of Parliament to-day.

**The bill, the text of which was issued last night, contains a clause providing that King Edward shall not be required to apply to the new Sovereign for permission to marry.**

King Edward will give formal assent to the measure this evening. It will be the last document to which he will attach the signature "Edward R.I."

The Governments of Canada, Australia, New Zealand and South Africa have already consented to the terms of the bill.

#### PROCLAMATION OF NEW SOVEREIGN TO-MORROW

**Special Session of Parliament**

The next stages after the Abdication has been completed, will be as follows:

**Accession Council at St. James's Palace at 11.0 a.m. to-morrow, at which the Duke of York will be proclaimed King and will take the Oath of Accession.**

**Proclamation of the Accession, with ancient ceremonial, at St. James's Palace at 2.30 p.m., at three other points in London and in the principal cities of the Nation and the Empire.**

**Special session of Parliament at 2.45 p.m. at which members of both Houses will take the Oath of Allegiance to the new King.**

**The Coronation. This, "THE DAILY TELEGRAPH" learns authoritatively, will take place on May 12 next year, the date originally fixed for the Coronation of King Edward.**

The new Sovereign will be 41 years old on Monday. His Consort will be the first Queen Elizabeth since Elizabeth Tudor, 1558 to 1603, and the first Scottish-born Queen of England since Matilda, who married King Henry I. in 1100.

Queen Mary will in future be known as the Queen Mother. Princess Elizabeth, who will be 11 years old on April 21, will be Heir Presumptive to the Throne.

#### MR. BALDWIN'S STATEMENT IN THE HOUSE

**"No More Grave Message Ever Received by Parliament"**

Immediately after the Speaker had read his Majesty's Message in the House of Commons, Mr. Baldwin rose to move that it be considered.

"No more grave message has ever been received by Parliament," he said, "and no more difficult and, I might almost say, more repugnant task has ever been imposed upon a Prime Minister."

At the conclusion of his speech Mr. Baldwin produced a pencilled note sent to him by the King that morning. In this his Majesty stated:

"The Duke of York and the King have always been on the best of terms as brothers, and the King is confident that the Duke deserves, and will receive, the support of the whole Empire."

The Duke of York dines with King Edward at Fort Belvedere last night, and at 12.15 this morning visited Queen Mary at Marlborough House. He was given a most enthusiastic ovation by a large crowd.

The end of the Constitutional crisis has been hailed with general relief throughout the world. On the London Stock Exchange there was a strong recovery in all sections, led by the market in gilt-edged securities.

## DUKE OF YORK'S CAR MOBBED

### 'LONG LIVE THE KING' CRY BY CROWD

### MIDNIGHT VISIT TO QUEEN MARY

**From a Special Correspondent**

Great crowds which had waited for hours outside the home of the Duke and Duchess of York, 145, Piccadilly, gave the new King an enthusiastic welcome when he returned there by car from Windsor 20 minutes before midnight.

The crowds continued to wait, and were again rewarded by a brief glimpse of the Duke as he came out shortly afterwards and drove first to Buckingham Palace and from there to Marlborough House to see Queen Mary. He spent an hour and 20 minutes with his mother, leaving at 1.25 a.m.

The Duke's return to 145 Piccadilly was signalled by a preliminary cheer raised a few hundred yards away, and this was immediately taken up by huge throngs which swept towards the Royal car.

"God Save the King!" shouted the people as they waved newspapers and umbrellas. "Long Live the King!" they roared again and again.

Dozens of police who had been drafted down to the Duke's house battled to clear a path for the car, but the wildly cheering crowd engulfed it and the chauffeur was compelled to stop.

TWO LITTLE FACES

Several minutes passed before the police cordons forced the people back and the car was able to proceed.

As he entered the house the crowd formed a great solid arc outside which held up traffic for a quarter of a mile, and started to sing the National Anthem.

Time and again the shouts, "We want the King" and "Long live the King" were raised.

Then from a lighted window at the top of the house a curtain was stealthily drawn aside, and two little faces peeped out on to the crowd. It was difficult to distinguish them, but the people, their imagination fired, cheered wildly and shouted, "Long live the Queen."

Earlier in the evening there had been enthusiastic scenes outside the house when Queen Mary – who was at 145, Piccadilly when King Edward's Message was read to Parliament – left to return to Marlborough House.

Police attempted to keep the people on the pavement, but they surged across the roadway, surrounding the Queen's car, holding up traffic.

Later when two small curly heads appeared silhouetted at a lighted window on the top floor, the crowd, recognising Princess Elizabeth and Princess Margaret Rose, raised cheers.

Until 8.30 p.m. the little Princesses, obviously too excited to sleep, were frequently seen peeping from under a blind over the window of a top storey room.

This caused people to congregate, and for a time the lights in the room were switched off.

Shortly before 1 p.m. yesterday Mr. Baldwin called to see Queen Mary at Marlborough House.

## THE KING HEARS BROADCAST

### PREPARES TO LEAVE

**From Our Special Correspondent**

FORT BELVEDERE, Thursday.

While millions of people this afternoon heard a B.B.C. announcer reading King Edward's message to Parliament renouncing the Throne, the King himself sat by a wireless set in the drawing room at Fort Belvedere and listened to his own fateful words.

His only companion was his youngest brother, the Duke of Kent.

Together they listened also to the broadcast of part of Mr. Baldwin's statement, and when that was concluded King Edward switched off the set.

Quietly the Duke of Kent left the room.

I learn that a few minutes later King Edward went to his study and put in a telephone call to the Continent.

To-day's events at Fort Belvedere began when the Duke of York, the Duke of Gloucester and the Duke of Kent arrived separately at about 10 a.m. They remained with their brother until Sir John Simon, the Home Secretary, came and the instrument of abdication was signed. Sir John stayed only an hour.

The Duke of York, who left Fort Belvedere during the afternoon for Royal Lodge, Windsor, returned to dine with King Edward.

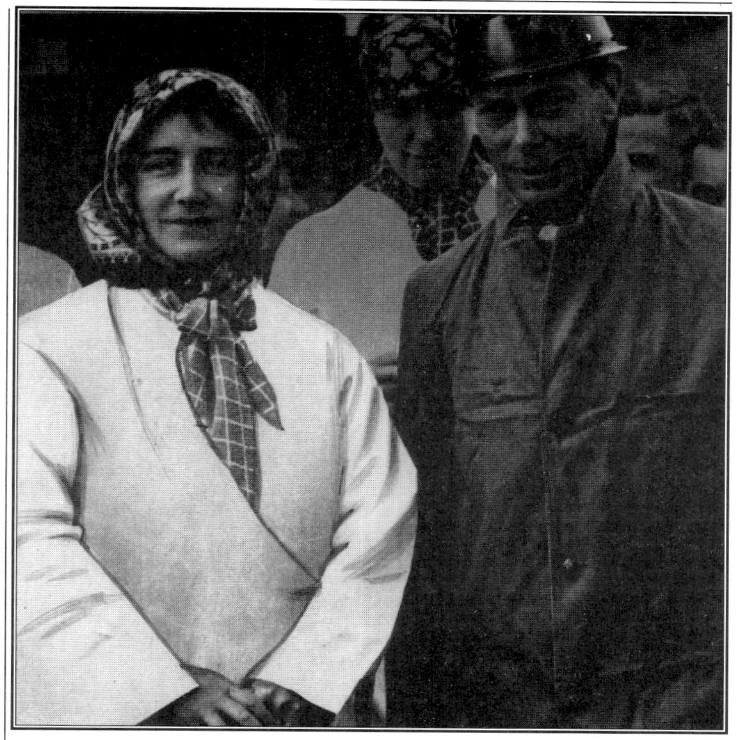

THE DUKE AND DUCHESS OF YORK

## PREMIER REVEALS TALKS WITH KING EDWARD

### LAST-MINUTE APPEAL: "HIS MIND WAS MADE UP"

Mr. Baldwin addressed the House of Commons yesterday as soon as the Speaker had read the King's message. In a voice shaken with emotion, which at times rendered him almost inaudible, he said:

"Sir I have to move that his Majesty's most gracious message be now considered.

"Sir, no more grave message has ever been received by Parliament. No more difficult – I may almost say repugnant – task has ever been imposed upon a Prime Minister."

There were low sympathetic murmurs of "Hear, hear," from all parts of the House. Mr. Baldwin paused for a moment, and then, in a broken voice, speaking with slow deliberation, he continued:

"I would ask the House, which I know will not be without sympathy for me in my position to-day (Hear, hear), to remember that in this last week I have had but little time in which to compose a speech for delivery to-day. So I must tell what I have to tell truthfully, sincerely and plainly, with no attempt to dress up or to adorn.

FRIENDSHIP WITH KING

"I shall have little or nothing to say in the way of comment, or of criticism, or of praise, or of blame. I think my best course to-day, and the one the House would desire is to tell them so far as I can of what has just passed between his Majesty and myself and what has led up to the present situation.

"I would like to say at the start that his Majesty, as Prince of Wales had honoured me for many years with a friendship which I valued, and I know that he would agree with me in saying to you that it was not only a friendship but, between man and man, a friendship of affection.

VAST CORRESPONDENCE

"As the House is aware, I had been ordered in August and September a complete rest, which, owing to the kindness of my staff and the consideration of all my colleagues, I was able to enjoy to the full.

"And, when October came, although I had been ordered to take a rest in that month, I felt I could not, in fairness to my work, take a further holiday, and I came, as it were, on half-time before the middle of October, and, for the first time since the beginning of August, was in a position to look into things.

"There were two things that disquieted me at that moment. There was coming into my office a vast volume of correspondence, mainly at that time from British origin in the United States of America, from some of the Dominions and from this country, all expressing perturbation, uneasiness, at what was then appearing in the American Press.

"I was aware also that there was, in the near future, a divorce case coming on, the results of which made me realise that possibly a difficult situation might arise later. I felt it was essential that someone should see his Majesty and warn him of the difficult situation that might arise later, if occasion was given for a continuation of this kind of gossip and criticism, and the danger that might come if that gossip and that criticism spread from the other side of the Atlantic to this country.

BOUND BY DUTY

"I felt that, in the circumstances, there was only one man who could speak to him and talk the matter over with him, and that man was the Prime Minister. And I felt doubly bound by my duty as I conceived it, to the country, and my duty to him not only as counsellor, but as a friend.

"I communicated with him through his Secretary, and stated that I desired to see him – that is the first and only occasion on which I was the one who asked for an interview – that I desired to see him, that the matter was urgent.

MUTUAL REGARD AND RESPECT

"I told him what it was. I expressed my willingness to go to Sandringham on Tuesday, the 20th, but I said I thought it wiser, if his Majesty thought fit, to see him at Fort Belvedere, because I was anxious at that time that no one should know of my visit, and that, at any rate, our first talk should be in complete privacy.

TWO GREAT ANXIETIES

"I told his Majesty that I had two great anxieties: one, the effect of a continuance of the kind of criticism that at that time was proceeding in the American Press, the effect it would have in the Dominions, and particularly in Canada, where it was wide spread, the effect it would have in this country.

"That was the first thing. And then I reminded him of what I had often told him and his brothers in years past.

"That is this: you take the British Monarchy – a unique institution. The Crown in this country, through the centuries, has been deprived of many of its prerogatives, but to-day, while that is true, it stands for far more than it ever has done in its history. (Loud cheers.)

"The importance of its integrity is, beyond all question, far greater than it has ever been, being, as it is, not only the last link of Empire that is left, but a guarantee in this country, so long as it exists in that integrity, against many evils that have affected and afflicted other countries.

"There is no man or woman in this country, to whatever party they belong, who would not subscribe to that. (Hear, hear.) But, while this feeling largely depends on the respect which has grown up in the last three generations for the Monarchy, it might not take so long, in the face of the kind of criticism to which it is being exposed, to lose that power far more rapidly than it was built up, and, once lost, I doubt if anything would restore it."

Mr. Baldwin paused. Then he continued:

"That was the basis of my talk on that aspect, and I expressed my anxiety, and then my desire, that such criticism should not have cause to go on."

# LAST SIMPLE RITES IN ST. GEORGE'S

ROYAL SORROW AT GRAVESIDE

## QUEEN'S COURAGE

**By Our Special Representative**

*In the courts at deep midnight the torches are gleaming,*
*In the proudly arched chapel the banners are beaming,*
*Far down the long aisle sacred music is streaming,*
*Lamenting a prince of the people should fall.*

George V., the King who said of himself, "I am only a very ordinary sort of fellow," but of whom the world thought differently, has reached his journey's end. In St. George's, the Chapel of England's chivalry, he was buried and there he will lie with his parents.

Only last month the King had stood sorrowing at the self-same grave-side, gazing down at the coffin of a loved sister. Now his own coffin lay there. His widow and his sons looked in mute anguish downward.

Kings and Queens, Princes and statesmen stood in mourning about the bier.

The simplicity of a straightforward man was with him to the end. One hymn, a brief service, no funeral hangings about the chapel, few flowers at the altar – such was the King's burial.

The new King laid a Regimental Colour of the King's Company, Grenadier Guards, on his father's coffin and scattered earth upon it as it sank into the vault.

To the last, the Queen maintained the unyielding courage she has shown all through the dark days. During the service she stood immobile, her gaze fixed upon the bier.

**(January 29)**

# A GREAT PERSONALITY

**By a Personal Friend.**

Never surely has a new King possessed so magnetic a personality.

The sincerity of his appeal, his tremendous energy, his sportsmanship and friendliness, his wide knowledge of affairs, and his untiring devotion to duty have endeared him to millions of people, not merely in his own country, but in every part of the world.

As the Prince of Wales he was unique. He is above all a man's man, yet to women he had made a wonderful appeal. Even when they smiled at his shyness as a youth their eyes grew misty.

His greatest characteristic has been a keen desire to do his best. The expertness and enthusiasm he has shown in regard to hunting, racing, golf, squash, flying, dancing, and other recreations have been no greater than the qualities which long ago made him a leader in all serious branches of activity.

His quick grasp of the complicated problems of government or industry, his unfailing tact and his keen desire to give aid where it was most needed, have supplied the moving force in one great national scheme after another.

It was the war that first revealed to any considerable extent his sterling worth. One saw him in France as a slim young officer, riding, rather awkwardly, at a smart trot by the side of the pavé road, or striding with youthful energy, head thrust forward, knees rather bent, across the shell-hole area where motor-cars and horses could not go. This close association with dirt and death, with disciplined life in its crudest form, affected the future King, but not at first in any visible way.

The war gave the Prince an opportunity of studying men " had there been no war the conditions of his study would have brought fewer good qualities to his notice – and incidentally it afforded a freer development to his character. He gained assurance, but he returned from the war with the same shyness, the same youthful appearance which made women smile and cry. He seemed so young that they were, perhaps, right to cry; it is certain that the weight of his position lay heavily on him at times.

Prince Charming he was called, and Prince Charming he remains – but his face has been hardened by the weather, and his character by experience. It is no longer an impression but a certainty that the man who sits and chats is a shrewd judge of character, very difficult to bluff or deceive. He has taken his life into his own hands, as far as the Prince of Wales can do so, and, like the boy at school, follows an interest he has made for himself with the same eager persistence and determination.

**(January 21)**

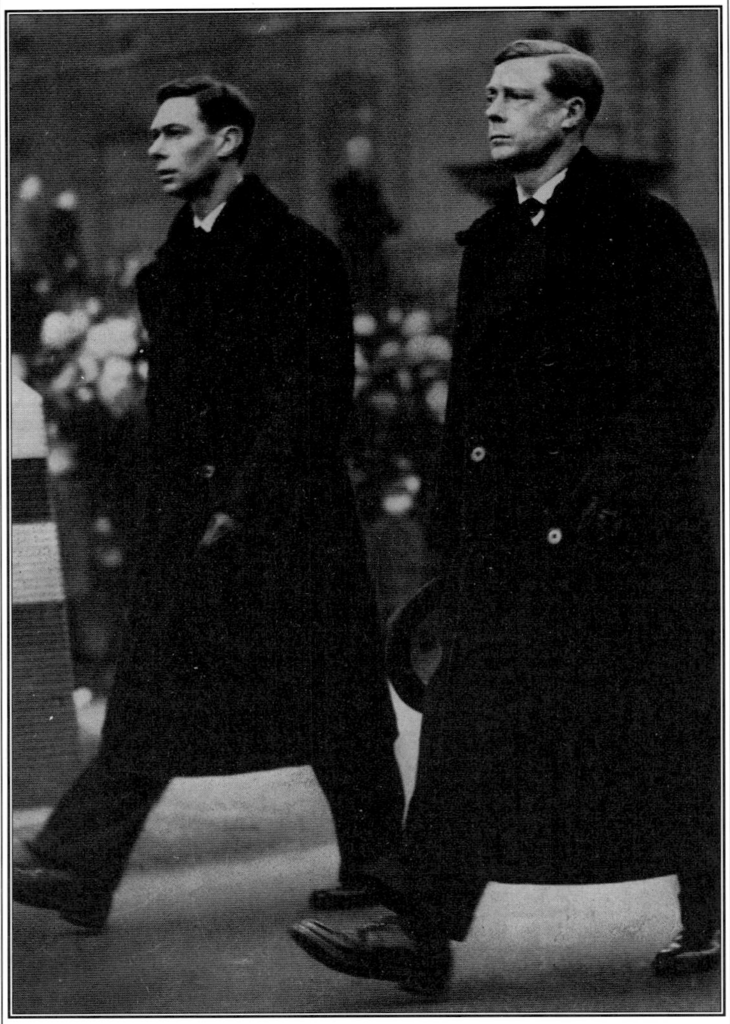

KING EDWARD VIII, with the Duke of York, the heir presumptive, on his right, following the coffin of King George in the Euston-road as the journey to Westminster-Hall began. The Queen, the Princess Royal, and the Duchesses of York, Gloucester and Kent did not take part in the cortège, but drove from King's Cross station in motor-cars, and awaited its arrival at Westminster.

# KING EDWARD'S ADMIRATION FOR SOUTH WALES

"SOMETHING WILL BE DONE"

**From Our Own Correspondent**

RHYMNEY, Thursday

With the fervent and grateful cheers of South Wales ringing in his cars, King Edward concluded his triumphal tour at Rhymney tonight and departed leaving behind a message of hope that has thrilled the people.

He declared to a group of unemployed men at Blaenavon: "Something will be done for South Wales in general."

Speaking earlier to an unemployed miner on the Pen-y-Garn estate at Pontypool, the King said: "I am here to help you all I can. You may be sure that all I can do shall be done. We certainly want better times brought to these valleys."

Just before this the King had seen a great banner across the road bearing the words: "We need your help."

As the King passed through Pontypool printed copies of "An Open Letter to his Majesty King Edward VIII." were being distributed in the streets. It was signed by men from the Monmouthshire Eastern Valley who took part in the recent march to London. The letter stated:

"To-day you will be visiting the towns and village in our valley – a valley blighted by the dead hand of poverty."It went on to declare that the King's tour had been so arranged that he would not see the real and terrible effects of poverty. After criticising the Means Test and "puny efforts of various voluntary social centres," it added:

"We, the unemployed, say, that our economic and social plight is the result of the policy pursued by your Ministers and Government."

When the King reached Blaenavon the chairman of the local Council mentioned this letter. The King said at once: "Where is it? I would like to read it."

**(November 30)**

# DIVORCE DECREE FOR MRS. WALLIS SIMPSON

A decree nisi, with costs, was granted by Mr. Justice Hawke, at Ipswich Assizes yesterday, to Mrs. Wallis Simpson, of the Beach House, Felixstowe, and of Cumberland-terrace, London, N.W., against Mr. Ernest Aldrich Simpson, of Bryanston-court, W. The petition was undefended.

**(October 28)**

# A BISHOP AND THE MEANING OF THE CORONATION

Alterations in the Coronation ceremony suggested by the Bishop of Birmingham, Dr. Barnes, were criticised yesterday by the Bishop of Bradford, Dr. A.W.F. Blunt, in his address to the Bradford Diocesan Conference.

"Let me emphasize," said Dr. Blunt, "one point which, I think, is very material for a proper understanding of the intention of the Coronation service.

"It is this: that on this occasion the King holds an avowedly representative position. His personal views and opinions are his own, and he has the right of us all to be keeper of his private conscience.

"But in his public capacity at his Coronation he stands for the English people's idea of kingship. It has for long centuries been, and I hope still is, an essential part of that idea that the King needs the Grace of God for his office.

"In the Coronation ceremony the nation definitely acknowledges that need. Whatever it may mean, much or little, to the individual who is crowned, to the people as a whole it means their dedication of the English Monarchy to the care of God, in whose rule and governance are the hearts of Kings."

Dr. Blunt said that suggestions made for inviting representatives of other denominations, in particular the Free Churches, to take part in the ceremony could only have been made by those who for the moment forgot what was the nature of the Coronation ceremony.

POSITION OF THE CHURCH

"If it were merely a service of prayer and aspiration," he said, "it would be natural and easy that representatives of other Christian bodies should have a share in it. But the service is not of such a character."

The whole service marked the position of the Church of England as an Established Church. The very idea of establishment was foreign and uncongenial to the Free Church system.

Speaking more directly of the Coronation itself, Dr. Blunt said: "The benefit of the King's Coronation depends under God upon two elements: one of which is on the faith, prayer and self-dedication of the King himself, and on that it would be improper for me to say anything except to commend him, and ask you to commend him, to God's grace which he will so abundantly need, as we all need it – for the King is a man like ourselves – if he is to do his duty faithfully. We hope that he is aware of his need. Some of us wish that he gave more positive signs of such awareness."

**(December 2)**

# MR BALDWIN'S VISIT TO THE KING

GRAVE CONSTITUTIONAL ISSUE

**By Our Political Correspondent**

At its usual weekly meeting yesterday the Cabinet was gravely concerned with a question of the highest national importance.

The greater part of the time spent in deliberation was devoted to discussing the relations of the King with his Ministers.

The Cabinet has been compelled to face a situation of extreme delicacy and difficulty in connection with the King's future domestic life.

It is the view of the Government that this problem, unless satisfactorily solved, must lead to a constitutional crisis of the gravest possible character, affecting not only this country, but the Empire as a whole.

Mr. Baldwin had an audience of the King last Wednesday evening. After yesterday's Cabinet meeting he again went to the Palace at six o'clock last night and left at a quarter-past seven.

CABINET TO-DAY

The advice which the Cabinet as a body has felt it necessary to tender to his Majesty formed, it may be assumed, the subject of the interview.

Mr. Baldwin returned from the Palace to the House of Commons and later he went to 10 Downing-street. At his request he was visited there by Sir John Simon, the Home Secretary. Sir John arrived by car at nine o'clock and left shortly before 10.30.

It is probable that a special meeting of the Cabinet will be held to-day.

The Government are sensible of the fact that statements published in American and some Dominion newspapers are being widely discussed in this country. A public announcement is likely at an early moment.

**(December 3)**

# MRS. SIMPSON'S NIGHT AND DAY JOURNEY

Mrs. Ernest Simpson was last night motoring swiftly across France in the direction of the Riviera. It was believed that she was making for Cannes, where she has friends.

Her departure from England was made with the greatest secrecy. She crossed by the Newhaven-Dieppe boat, leaving late on Thursday night.

Not even the harbourmaster at Newhaven was aware of her intended arrival. The only notification he received was a message from the R.A.C. which asked if he would allow a car to be shipped late at night. The car arrived shortly afterwards, driven by a chauffeur, and was embarked in the name of Simpson.

About half an hour later Mrs. Simpsor., heavily veiled and accompanied by two Scotland Yard detectives, arrived from London in another car. She boarded the boat a quarter of an hour before it was due to sail.

NO BERTH RESERVED

Her name did not appear on the passenger list and no berth was reserved for her.

Mrs Simpson was driven by a chauffeur and accompanied by the two detectives on her night and day journey through France. It was believed that she intended to meet Mr. and Mrs. Norman Rogers. American friends, who own a villa at Cannes. They were among the King's guests in the yacht Nahlin during his holiday cruise this year, and later they went to Balmoral.

Mr. Rogers has been a close personal friend of the King for some time, and has accompanied him on shooting expeditions.

The Court Circular of Sept. 23 stated:

Balmoral Castle

Mrs. Ernest A. Simpson and Mr. and Mrs. Herman L. Rogers have arrived at the Castle.

Their departure from the Castle was announced in the Court Circular on Sept. 30.

**(December 5)**

# STRANGE FOOTPRINTS IN HIMALAYAS

BOMBAY, Tuesday.

The old story that footprints of a strange shape are found at high altitudes in the Himalayas is revived by the report of Mr. Eric Shipton, the Everest climber, that he saw at a height of 16,000ft marks resembling elephant tracks, but the long stride suggested they were those of a biped.

**(December 9)**

# DEPARTURE IN SECRECY AT 1.45 A.M.

EDWARD VIII'S DRIVE TO DARKENED DOCK

Under conditions of great secrecy King Edward left England early this morning in a destroyer which sailed from Portsmouth dockyard at 1.45 with another destroyer as escort.

The two destroyers were Wolfhound and Fury.

The circumstances of the departure were as dramatic as any of the events which have marked the past ten days.

After his broadcast last night King Edward returned to Royal Lodge, Windsor, where he said farewell to King George VI, Queen Mary, the Princess Royal and the Duke of Gloucester.

These four drove off from the Lodge in a car, and a few minutes later King Edward himself left by the Englefield Green entrance and returned to Fort Belvedere.

King Edward left Fort Belvedere just before 11 o'clock, and his car covered the 65 miles to Portsmouth in about an hour and a half.

OFFICERS SALUTE CAR

It arrived at the Unicorn-street entrance to the dock-yard at 12.20 a.m. The blinds were closely drawn and it was impossible to see who was inside, but it is understood that King Edward was accompanied by his equerry, the Hon. Piers Legh.

The Royal car was escorted by a police car and accompanied by two yellow shooting brakes filled with luggage.

With its headlights on full it swept through the dockyard gates at about 30 m.p.h., but slowed down a second or two later as a sergeant of the dockyard police challenged it.

There was a muffled word from the car and the sergeant sprang to attention.

Two naval officers who had been pacing up and down saluted, and the royal car and its attendant vehicles proceeded towards the waterside.

King Edward first proceeded to the residence of the Commander-in-Chief at Portsmouth, Admiral Sir William Fisher, and spoke with him for some time before embarking.

HEAVY ULSTER COAT

The slight figure in a heavy ulster coat vanished in the shadows on the destroyer's deck, and shortly afterwards the vessel moved slowly from her berth.

She passed through the narrow strop of water leading past the Southern Railway jetty and out towards Spithead, with the other destroyer in attendance.

The Wolfhound, which is a vessel of 1,100 tons, belonging to the First Anti-Submarine Flotilla, had left Portland at five o'clock last night under sealed orders.

The Wolfhound crept into Portsmouth under cover of darkness in the early part of the night and slipped alongside the quay, where she waited with full steam up.

DESERTED ROADS

All was bustle and activity on board her. But ashore there was no sign of anything unusual until King Edward arrived.

The roads around the dockyards were silent and deserted. Only the usual number of police officers remained on duty at the gates, and even they had been kept in ignorance.

**(December 12)**

# 12 MONTHS' HARD LABOUR FOR McMAHON

George Andrew McMahon was sentenced at the Old Bailey yesterday to 12 months' hard labour on a charge of producing a pistol with intent to alarm the King.

The jury took only 10 minutes to reach their verdict of guilty.

The judge, Mr. Justice Greaves-Lord, said that the jury had arrived at the only possible verdict.

Dealing with a statement made in the witness-box by McMahon that he had been offered £150 by a foreign Power to kill the King, the Judge said to McMahon:

"I can well understand the jury not being misled by the story you told to-day."

He remarked that he was satisfied that at no time had McMahon any intention of harming his Majesty.

"MY ESCAPE REHEARSED"

"I do not want, and I am not going to make you into a sort of fancied hero," he continued. "No description would be further from the truth, and therefore I am not going to pass a sentence which would have any tendency to do that."

In low, halting tones, contrasting dramatically with his astonishing story, McMahon had stated that a foreign Power had offered him £150 to shoot the King.

He told how his escape was planned and rehearsed, and said that eventually he threw the pistol as "the only way to protect the King."

**(September 15)**

# MAIN STREETS OF MADRID BURNING THIS MORNING

## FAMOUS LANDMARKS STRUCK BY INCENDIARY BOMBS

**The centre of Madrid was early this morning in the grip of rapidly spreading fires, started by incendiary bombs dropped by Nationalist 'planes.**

The Duke of Alba and Berwick's palace, one of the most magnificent buildings in the city, was a mass of flames. Several other famous landmarks were blazing.

**The Gran Via and other main streets became rivers of fire as a ceaseless rain of bombs spread burning calcium. Heavy shells fell constantly among the militia fighting the fires.**

The Nationalists claimed last night that their tanks were penetrating the streets of the capital.

**(November 18)**

# HOUSE-TO-HOUSE BATTLE FOR BADAJOZ

## SPAIN'S 'KEY' CITY STORMED BY MOORS AND FOREIGN LEGIONARIES

**From Our Own Correspondent**

PARIS, Sunday.

The following telegram from Badajoz – the "key city" of Spain, captured by insurgent forces – was sent off from Elvas on the Portuguese frontier last night.

The troops which had surrounded Badajoz on Thursday evening and on Friday morning captured the fort of San Cristobal consisted of three columns under the supreme command of Lt.-Col. Yague.

They were composed, says the correspondent of "Le Temps" at Badajoz, of a bandera of the Tercio (Foreign Legionaires) of 800 men; of a Tabor of Regulares; of 600 Moroccan natives, and in addition some Micolets and numerous Phalangists who had been policing the villages.

After an artillery preparation, two columns attacked Badajoz at 4 o'clock on Friday afternoon. One of them, commanded by Major Castejon, penetrated without much difficulty into the Menach quarter, where there were no ramparts. The other, commanded by Lt. Ascensio, tried to force the Trinidad gate on the Merida road. But, taken in flank by Governmental machine guns, it had to retire.

The second assault, carried out with the bayonet and the poignard by the Tercio with their habitual courage, overcame the resistance of the Government forces, but only after a veritable butchery. The 15th Company of the Tercio had 30 dead and 50 wounded out of an effective of 120 men.

MASS EXECUTIONS

At 6 o'clock the town was taken, but a desperate struggle from house to house continued during a portion of the evening. The Government forces had two mortars, an armoured car, a certain number of machine guns, 800 Regular troops and about 4,000 militiamen armed with Mausers and sporting guns.

After the victory 380 political prisoners were liberated. They were all uninjured.

The militiamen and suspects arrested by the insurgents were at once shot. At the present moment about 1,200 have been shot on charges of resisting with arms in their hands or of serious crimes. I have seen the pavement of the military commandancia covered with the blood of the executed, in which their caps and other personal objects are still soaked.

AIR BOMBS WRECK HOSPITAL

A remarkable crowd is circulating feverishly in the town. It contains khaki uniforms mixed with the blue shirts of the Micolai. All of them bear on their chests a scapula and a model of the Sacred Heart of Jesus – not to mention the tarboosh of the Regulares and the white brassards of sympathisers of the Right.

In the course of the aerial bombardment of the three last days several bombs damaged or destroyed houses. In particular the infirmary of the provincial hospital has been destroyed.

Many insurgents fell when an attack on the ancient city wall was ordered with fixed bayonets, but the insurgents took the wall and poured into the city. There they found the Government forces scattering through the city to various strong-points, including the San Cristobal fort, where there was artillery and trench mortars that were used to fight off the insurgent advance.

Miners from the Rio Tinto mines manned the mortars. They fought to the death against the legionaries, who advanced through the streets with rifles in one hand and hand-grenades in the other.

One group of Government troops defended a bridge over the Guadiana River until the rebel command ordered a 'plane up to wipe them out.

The fighting was without mercy on both sides. In one street alone 80 members of the Workers' Militia were shot down after capture by the legionaries, who are taking no prisoners.

Lt.-Col. Yague, the chief commander of the nationalist troops, said: "It is a magnificent victory. We now intend, with the aid of the Phalangistes, to clean up Estremadura. The end of the campaign is only a question of days."

At midday on Saturday three Government 'planes dropped six bombs on Badajoz, but did not cause noteworthy harm.

**(August 17)**

# FRANCO INVESTED CHIEF OF STATE

## CEREMONY AT BURGOS

**From Valentine Williams**
**Daily Telegraph Special Correspondent**

BURGOS, Friday.

An historic event for Spain was signalised this morning at the insurgent headquarters here. Gen. Franco, fresh from the triumph at Toledo, was formally installed as chief of the new Government of the Spanish State proclaimed by the insurgents.

A crowd of many thousands gathered outside the military headquarters to await the appearance of Gen. Franco, who had arrived earlier from Valladolid.

The main square of the town was a mass of red, blue, and black berets in the bright sunshine and a forest of hands went up in the Fascist salute as Gen. Franco, Gen. Mola, the conqueror of Irun and San Sebastian, Gen. Cabanellas, and the Bishop of Burgos came out on to the balcony.

An impressive silence descended on the crowd as Gen. Franco, in ringing tones, spoke of his aspirations to create a true Spanish nation for all classes of Spaniards.

The formal investiture of the general with the powers of the head of the State followed in the ornate salon of the Town Hall. Gen. Cabanellas, who has acted as head of the Government, handed over the direction of the State to Gen. Franco, who accepted the charge in a speech that deeply stirred his military and civilian audience.

The first person whom he embraced after Gen. Cabanellas was Gen. Mola. As the two clasped hands the whole assembly broke into cheers.

**(October 3)**

# PRIMO DE RIVERA'S SON EXECUTED

## LEADER OF FASCISTS

ALICANTE, Friday.

Senor José Antonio Primo de Rivera, the Spanish Fascist leader, was executed by a firing squad in the prison yard here this morning before a few people.

Senor de Rivera was the 36-year-old son of the late Gen. Primo de Rivera, Spain's last "dictator." He was found guilty here on Wednesday of complicity in the insurrection.

He was a lawyer, and formed the Fascist party on a programme of national syndicalism and agrarian reform, a long way to the "Left" of the general programme that is now advanced by the insurgents.

With him were tried his brother, Miguel, who was sentenced to 30 years imprisonment and Miguel's wife, who was sentenced to imprisonment for six years and one day.

**(December 21)**

## SINGAPORE BASE

Mr. Kenneth Lindsy (Civil Lord of the Admiralty) stated, in reply to a question in the House of Commons last night, that it is anticipated the Singapore base will be ready for general use in the financial year 1939.

**(February 27)**

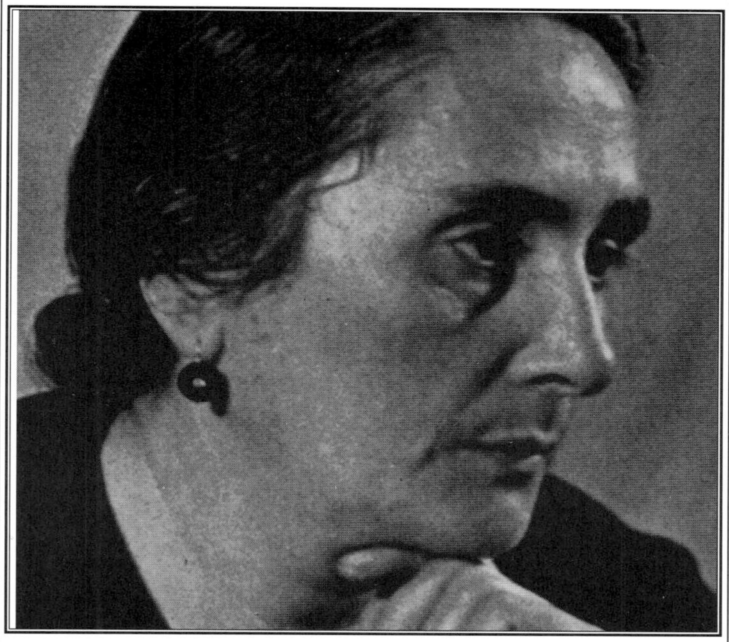

A SPANISH WOMAN Communist deputy, Dolores Barruri, addressing a massed meeting in the bull-fighting ring in Madrid. She is known as La Pasionaria (The Passion Flower) because of the vehemence of her oratory.

# CHINA'S PREMIER A PRISONER

## CAPTURE MAY LEAD TO CIVIL WAR

**From Our Own Correspondent**

NANKING, Sunday.

Civil war in China has come nearer with the announcement that the Government is preparing to launch punitive measures against Marshal Chang Hsuch-liang, who is holding prisoner the Premier, Marshal Chiang Kai-shek, in the north-western Province of Shensi.

War with Japan and an alliance with Russia are demanded as the price of the Premier's release.

It is believed that there is little chance of rescuing the Premier unless the rebels are placed at a military disadvantage. Government forces have advanced up the Lunghai railway to Hwayin, almost making contact with the mutineers.

Meanwhile the Australian adviser to Marshall Chiang Kai-shek, Mr. W. H. Donald, who was formerly adviser to the "Young Marshal," as Marshal Chang Hsueh-hang is called, has hurried to Loyano from Nanking to try to open negotiations with him.

The authorities here, however, doubt the possibility of a compromise because of the political considerations involved in the "Young Marshal's" alliance with the Reds.

LOYAL PROVINCES

Nanking's bewilderment at the shock of Marshal Chiang Kai-shek's capture was alleviated somewhat as it became evident that there would be no immediate break-up of the Government. Nobody is willing to predict the future, however, if the Premier is not rescued.

**(December 14)**

# WESTERN CANADA WANTS MEN

"Alberta and British Columbia have the room and the natural resources – agricultural, mineral, and timber – to support a population of 100,000,000."

Mr. G. G. McGeer, K.C., the Canadian M.P. and Mayor of Vancouver, who has come to London to return the visit of the Lord Mayor, Sir Percy Vincent to the Vancouver Jubilee celebrations, made this statement yesterday to a representative of The Daily Telegraph.

"We are on the verge of the greatest era of prosperity in our history." he said, "but at the moment it is being retarded by urgent financial problems.

"I hope to have during my stay an opportunity of conferring with the British bondholders who hold nearly £4,000,000 worth of Vancouver bonds. Vancouver is overburdened with high interest bearing debt. Something must be done to give prosperity a chance."

If these financial problems can be solved – and he is sure that they can – Mr. McGeer looks forward to an era of unparalleled prosperity on the Pacific Coast.

ALMOST ENTIRELY BRITISH

He pointed out that in the three Middle Western provinces of Canada 60 per cent. of the population was of European or American origin. British Columbia was almost entirely British and desired to remain so.

"Canada needs settlers as much to-day as she ever did not only on the farms but in the mines and in trade." declared Mr. McGeer, "Skilled labour is in demand, and any boom in the building trade will reveal a shortage."

**(October 5)**

# DEATH PENALTY FOR 16 MEN IN MOSCOW TRIAL

**From Our Own Correspondent**

MOSCOW, Monday Morning.

Zinovieff, Kameneff and 14 others accused of conspiring with Trotsky to murder Stalin and other key men in the Soviet Government were sentenced to death early this morning after a trial lasting five days.

The Court retired to consider the sentences at 7.30 last night after hearing the "last words" of the accused, who admitted their guilt.

When M. Ulrich, President of the Court, and the three other judges returned after six hours deliberations and announced the death penalty decision the spectators in the court applauded loudly.

The prisoners were sentenced to be shot, but sentence will not be carried out before 72 hours have elapsed. The sentenced men's only hope now lies in an appeal to the Central Executive Committee.

Under the new penal code no appeal is allowed, but in this case an exception has been made. The maximum period between sentence and execution under the code is 24 hours, but this has been extended.

Michael Tomsky, friend and co-worker with Lenin, committed suicide on Saturday afternoon, following disclosures at the trial alleged to implicate him in the plots.

His lonely death in his small country house near Moscow has made a tremendous impression in party circles here, because it is the first "new blood" to be drawn so far.

It is probable that he blew out his brains expecting that secret police agents were coming to arrest him. The official explanation is "Tomsky was too expressly compromised in the terrorist plot."

But it is fair to suppose that this proud old moderate Bolshevik and close personal friend of Lenin – who actually served 12 years in a Tsarist prison – preferred death by his own hand to being dragged through the interminable exhausting processes of secret interrogation, only to end like Zinovieff as a "political dupe" for future State trials."

**(August 24)**

# "KING EDWARD VIII. ISLAND"

AUCKLAND (New Zealand), Tuesday.

"This island belongs to King Edward VIII."

This proclamation, reaffirming Britain's title to a number of islands in the Phoenix group in the South Pacific, has been pasted

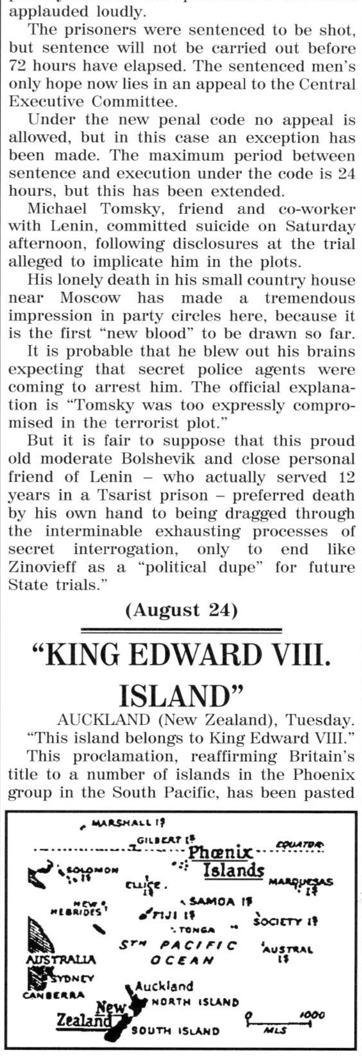


on notice boards attached to palm trees on the islands by H.M. patrol sloop Leith.

There is probably no other occasion on which the King's name has been used for such a purpose. The action taken by H.M.S. Leith follows the recent activity shown by the Americans and Japanese in the South Pacific. – Reuter.

**(October 2)**

# USE OF POISON GAS BY ITALY

## BRITISH NOTE AT GENEVA

GENEVA, Wednesday.

The British memorandum on the alleged use of poison gas by the Italian forces was distributed here this evening.

The memorandum is headed "Alleged Italian use of poison gas. Note communicated by the U.K. Delegation." It states:

1. On Dec. 30. 1935, an Abyssinian communiqué reproduced a report from Ras Imaru that Italian forces had used gas on Dec. 23.

2. On Dec. 30, 1935, also the Emperor, in a communication to the League of Nations, accused the Italian forces of using gas on the Takazze River on Dec. 23 (presumably the same attack).

3. On March 20 the Abyssinian Government addressed to the Powers represented at Addis Ababa and to the League of Nations a protest against the use of asphyxiating and other gases by the Italian forces, contrary to The Hague Convention and the Geneva Protocol.

4. Statements from non-Abyssinian sources: Dr. Melly, of the British Red Cross, testifies to having treated about 100 serious cases of mustard gas burning during the three days up to and including March 1. This is supported by photographs of British ambulances taken on March 4 and now in the possession of his Majesty's Minister at Addis Ababa, showing evidence of gas burns.

DOCTOR'S STATEMENT

5. A doctor of the British ambulance (Dr. J.W.C. MacFie) has made a signed declaration that between March 1 and March 18 he personally saw and treated "several hundreds of Abyssinian men, women and children suffering from burns caused by mustard gas."

6. It has been stated that a certified copy of a report by the Norwegian ambulance (Southern front) shows that 21 cases of mustard gas burns caused by one bomb occurred on March 19.

7. It has been stated that the Swedish ambulance reported gas cases treated by them on the Southern front in December.

8. Dr. Junod (International Red Cross) and Count von Rosen (Swedish Red Cross) saw gas used at Quoram on March 17, and were affected by it. Dr. Junod stated on March 24 that he had reported to Geneva.

A committee of jurists was appointed to examine the memorandum and report to the Committee of Thirteen.– Exchange.

**(April 9)**

# SWEDISH UNIT HAVOC

## LEADER'S ACCOUNT

**From Our Special Correspondent**

ADDIS ABABA, Sunday.

Before the wreckage of the Swedish Red Cross unit, bombed by Italian 'planes, had been cleared away another raid took place on an Egyptian ambulance near Daggahbur, in Ogaden.

News of this latest attack, only 19 miles from Dolo, where the Swedish unit suffered so badly, reached here to-day almost simultaneously with the arrival by aeroplane of Dr. Fritz Hylander, the Swedish Red Cross chief.

Dr. Hylander was himself wounded in the side and had to be lifted from the machine. He was driven to hospital in company with the Foreign Minister, M. Herouly.

M. Lundstrom, his engineer assistant, was so badly wounded that he died yesterday.

Dr. Hylander gave a graphic account of the raid. He stated that Red Cross emblems, signs and flags, 9ft cross, were clearly displayed, and there were no armed troops within three miles of the unit.

The first machines flew over on the morning of Dec. 22. They dropped bombs on the ambulance, and raked the lorries and Red Cross tents with machine-gun fire. No one was injured.

A telegram was immediately despatched to the Abyssinian Red Cross authorities, but this did not arrive.

On the morning of Dec. 30 six machines bombed the ambulance from a height of 650 feet, and were followed by four other planes which also dropped bombs.

One hundred bombs, incendiary, high explosive and shrapnel, were dropped, and fire was opened with machine-guns. All the tents were destroyed.

**(January 6)**

# £500 ON HEAD OF LT.-GEN. DILL

JERUSALEM, Friday.

Lt.-Gen. J.C. Dill, the British Commander-in-Chief in Palestine, has had a price put on his head by the self-styled "commander-in-chief" of the Arab rebels, El Kaukaji.

A reward of £500 is offered to anyone who will bring in to him Lt.-Gen. Dill, "dead or alive." – B.U.P.

**(October 3)**

# LEAGUE TO DISCUSS THE RHINELAND

## FRANCE DEMANDS GERMAN TROOPS WITHDRAWAL

**At the urgent request of France the League Council has been called for Friday to deal with Germany's rearming of the demilitarised Rhineland zone, and denunciation of the Locarno Pact.**

**Germany has been invited to attend.**

The British Cabinet will discuss the situation to-day and Mr. Eden will make a statement in the House of Commons this afternoon. Afterwards he will leave for Paris to attend a meeting of the Locarno Powers to-morrow.

At a meeting of the French Cabinet yesterday M. Flandin, the Foreign Minister, said that France would:

**Demand the complete evacuation of the demilitarised zone by German troops and failing this**

**Seek the imposition by the League of an embargo on the purchase of German goods.**

PEACE PACT OFFER REJECTED

**Britain's Aid to be Sought**

The Cabinet decided to:

**Reject Herr Hitler's offer to negotiate bilateral demilitarised zones and to conclude a 25-year non-aggression Pact with France and Belgium and a Western Air Pact:**

**Call for the assistance of the other signatories of Locarno – Britain, Italy and Belgium; and**

**Authorise the Ministers for War, Marine and Air to prepare such measures of defence as circumstances may require.**

In a broadcast announcing the Government's decision last night M. Sarraut, the Premier, said:

**We are faced with a most brutal fait accompli. There can be no more peace in Europe, no more international relations, if this method becomes general.**

**The bare fact that, in defiance of solemn engagements, the German soldier has established himself on the bank of the Rhine prohibits negotiation.**

**We mean to maintain the essential guarantees of French and Belgian security countersigned by the British and Italian Governments in the Pact of Locarno.**

**We are not ready to leave Strasbourg under the menace of German gunfire.**

Belgium has also decided to appeal to the League.

The British Government, it is understood, takes a serious view of the situation.

**Mr. Eden made it clear to the German Ambassador, Herr von Hoesch, on Saturday that Britain cannot overlook a gross violation of the Locarno Pact.**

**(March 9)**

# NEW GERMAN AMBASSADOR IN LONDON

## MAN WHO HELPED HITLER TO POWER

**From Our Own Correspondent**

BERLIN, Tuesday.

It was officially announced to-day that Herr Joachim von Ribbentrop has been appointed by Herr Hitler as German Ambassador in London.

The appointment comes exactly four months after the post became vacant by the sudden death in London or Herr von Hoesch.

It is not known on what date Herr von Ribbentrop will take up residence in Britain. It is understood, however, that he will do so as soon as his official duties in Berlin, as Herr Hitler's adviser on diplomatic matters, can be wound up.

The decision is regarded as a sign of Herr Hitler's anxiety to further good relations between Germany and Britain. Herr von Ribbentrop has himself stated that he regards this as his life's work.

The appointment of the new Ambassador was celebrated this evening by a huge dinner party in the gardens of Herr Von Ribbentrop's villa at Dahlem, five miles from Berlin. More than 500 guests were sumptuously entertained in a marquee especially erected for the occasion.

**(August 12)**

# CHANNEL FERRY OPENED

Describing it as a link which would strengthen the bonds between two great nations, the French Ambassador, M. Corbin, yesterday inaugurated the new train ferry service between Dover and Dunkirk. The service which has cost about £1,000,000, will enable passengers to travel from London to Paris by the same sleeping-car.

The inaugural ceremony took place in the Hampton ferry, one of the several vessels which will maintain the service. Among those present were Sir John Simon, the Home Secretary, who travelled in the vessel, and the Marquess of Willingdon, Lord Warden of the Cinque Ports.

The Hampton afterwards left for Calais.

**(October 13)**

# M. BLUM EXPLAINS HIS POLICY

**From Our Own Correspondent**

PARIS, Sunday.

M. Blum, the Socialist leader and presumptive Premier, spoke at the Socialist Party Congress here to-day amid scenes of almost extravagant enthusiasm. With regard to the foreign political situation he said:

"The voice of France will now be able to make itself heard throughout the world with increased force. We, international Socialists, will demonstrate that the peace which we desire to achieve is an absolute peace – indivisible, effective, disarmed.

"We shall do all in our power to remain worthy of the mandate with which we are entrusted, to elevate our courage and our will power to the same high level as the task before us. We shall do everything possible so that the victory of the Popular Front – Radicals, Socialists and Communists – may prove also a Socialist victory."

**(June 1)**

# MEXICAN OFFER TO TROTSKY

**From Our Own Correspondent**

OSLO, Monday.

Official information has been received from Mexico that Trotsky, the exiled Bolshevik leader, will be allowed to stay there. This solves a delicate problem for the Norwegian Government, which is eager to be rid of him when his permit to stay here expires on Dec. 18.

**(December 8)**

# "PIPS" WILL TIME TRUNK CALLS

Telephone trunk calls will be made after next Saturday without any interruption from the operator, for "thr-r-ee-minutes" is to be replaced by a mechanical device.

At present all trunk or toll calls to places over 15 miles away are timed, and every three minutes the operator has to announce "three minutes," "six minutes," and so on for the duration of the call.

In future all that will be heard will be four mechanical "pips" similar to the wireless time signal.

Business men on important calls have complained of the present system for some time, saying the intervention, sometimes in the midst of important matters, had a bad effect.

**(July 29)**

# TWO GIRLS TO BE TELEVISION ANNOUNCERS

## CHOSEN FROM 1,100 APPLICANTS

**By Our Television Correspondent**

Miss Jasmine Bligh, aged 22, and Miss Elizabeth Cowell, aged 23, were yesterday officially appointed the B.B.C.'s first announcers for the new television service.

They have been chosen out of 1,100 applicants, not only for beauty of face and voice but also for qualities which will enable them to act successfully as hostesses at the Alexandra Palace station.

Both join the B.B.C. staff on Monday. Until the opening of the television station they will announce frequently in the lighter sound programmes to familiarise themselves with the microphone. Neither has broadcast before. They will be heard for the first time in Geraldo's orchestral programme, "Romance in Rhythm" on Tuesday week.

LOW PITCHED VOICES

Both have low pitched and well modulated voices. Miss Cowell has the deeper and quieter voice. She speaks almost in a whisper.

They have the finely modelled features which make excellent television pictures. The television "make-up" which they will probably have to use comprises light yellow cheeks, dark yellow nose, brown lips and green eyelids.

Both have travelled extensively and speak French fluently, while Miss Cowell speaks German also.

Television announcements will have to be memorised. While one of the two is announcing the other will act as hostess to artists and speakers. There will also be a man announcer.

Miss Bligh and Miss Cowell have six months' trial contracts with the B.B.C. Their salaries are believed to be about £400 a year.

**(March 14)**

# MODEL FLATS FOR WORKERS

**From a Special Correspondent**

Model flats for working people, with labour-saving devices and garden surroundings, have been completed by London County Council in a square adjoining Holloway-road, N.

These flats, with their site, cost £100,000, cover five acres, and provide up-to-date accommodation for 1,500 people. They are a model for the dwellings which are gradually rising as a result of area clearance schemes in London. Their amenities include:

Children's playground.
Communal drying-rooms.
Gas and electric points.
Separate bathrooms.

The 321 flats which comprise the block are the forerunners of others, which will transform London's residential "black spots" into well-equipped estates for working people. Similar flats are being erected all over the Metropolis as the L.C.C.'s solution of the problem of housing workers within the "inner circle."

**(November 18)**

# 'OXFORD NO PLACE FOR WOMEN'

**From Our Own Correspondent**

OXFORD, Thursday.

That Oxford is no place for women is the contention of Miss Margharita Laski, herself an undergraduate member of the University.

Miss Laski, who is at Lady Margaret Hall, one of the Oxford colleges for women, is a daughter of Mr. Neville Laski, K.C., and a niece of Professor Harold Laski, of London University. She expressed her views in "Cherwell," the undergraduate journal.

"It is a bad thing for the university that Oxford has admitted women students," she writes. "Men are part of the tradition built up by men for hundreds of years. Educated women to-day, with their pitiable half-century of education behind them, cannot be absorbed into that tradition, cannot get anything save frustration from being surrounded by that tradition, and remain unassimilated, alien, and harmful.

"Men come up to imbibe that tradition, and if they feel it is becoming adulterated and distorted by the presence of women in the university then it is undesirable that women should intrude."

"There is no college life for women as for men," she continues. "There is only the life of the boarding school and that is not conductive to maturity.

"One never hears of young men being embroiled in a fast set of undergraduettes, yet the reverse is frequently the case. Probably the fast set consists in nothing more than a tendency to throw sherry parties and get a little drunk, but for women straight from a cloistered home or school it is debauchery unexampled."

Miss Laski suggests as remedy that boys and girls should be educated together from their earliest years, so that they can grow up together and accept each other naturally on an equal basis.

**(March 6)**

# DUCE DECLARES THE WAR ENDED

## "ABYSSINIA ITALIAN: WE WILL DEFEND VICTORY"

**"I announce to the Italian people and to the world that the war is finished. Peace is re-established, Abyssinia is Italian."**

Signor Mussolini made this declaration at eight o'clock last night from the balcony of the Palazzo Venezia in Rome.

**Four hours earlier Marshal Badoglio had entered Addis Ababa, riding a chestnut horse at the head of 25,000 men, with 50 aeroplanes flying overhead.**

The Duce's speech was broadcast to the world in Italian, English, French and German.

He declared that he had observed his undertaking to do everything possible to prevent the conflict spreading into a European war. "I am convinced ," he said, "that to disturb the peace of Europe would be to destroy Europe.

**"But I must add that we are ready to defend our victory with the same determination with which we won it."**

All Italy abandoned itself last night to rejoicing. Flags flew from every house, coloured lamps shone in the windows, and beacons blazed from the hilltops.

**(May 6)**

# "VICTORY ALMOST A LANDSLIDE"

**From Our Own Correspondent**

NEW YORK, Wednesday Morning.

Newspapers all over the country and of all parties concede that Mr. Roosevelt has been re-elected. Prominent among opposition newspapers which admit Mr. Landon's defeat is the "Kansas City Star," leading Republican organ in Mr. Landon's own State. It declares:

"The victory is of almost landslide proportions."

Mr. Roosevelt's victory became obvious when his big lead in such key States as Illinois, Pennsylvania, Ohio and even Connecticut was known. Mr. Landon's strength was confined to such traditionally Republican States as Maine, New Hampshire, Vermont, Massachusetts and Rhode Island.

As more and more returns came in it was realised that the only uncertainty was the size of the Democratic majority.

Mr. Roosevelt, who is 54, based his campaign on his New Deal. Mr. Landon, his 49-year-old rival, appealed to the more conservative elements.

Although only Mr. Roosevelt and Mr. Landon had any real chance of election three other candidates stood. They were:

Mr. Norman Thomas, Socialist.
Mr. Earl Browder, Communist.
Mr. William Leinke, Union party.

The weather was stormy, and in most parts of the country the electors had to fight their way through snow, rain and sleet to reach the polls.

**(November 12)**

# BRITAIN'S BIGGEST FILM STUDIO

**By Campbell Dixon**

To the accompaniment of popping corks, a witty speech by Dr. Burgin, Parliamentary Secretary to the Board of Trade, and applause from 1,200 guests, including 20 film stars, England's newest and most decorative film studios were declared open yesterday.

The function in itself suggested a scene from one of Mr. De Mille's more ambitious films. A special train had been engaged to take the guests to Iver, Bucks. A fleet of motor-coaches carried them from there to Pinewood.

A gigantic stage, equipped with loud speakers, lighted by arcs, and lined with sound-proof material like a padded cell, had been turned into a restaurant for the occasion. The 1,200 guests trooped in, Mr. J.A. Rank took the chair, a long line of waiters, standing three deep, charged across to the tables, and the most spectacular function in the history of British films was in full swing.

The eight stages, of which four are completed, have 7 1/2 acres of floor space and are equipped with every conceivable device, including compressed air, electrically-controlled doors 19ft. by 17ft. for facilitating the moving of scenery, and a tank 40ft. by 30ft. heated to any temperature desired and revealed by lifting a section of the floor.

The whole studios with Col. Grant Morden's former residence as a club-house and library, are set in lovely gardens and woods, and I could believe American visitors when they said that for combined efficiency and beauty Hollywood was beaten.

**(October 1)**

# HAUPTMANN PAYS THE PENALTY

**From Our Own Correspondent**

TRENTON (N.J.), Friday.

Bruno Hauptmann was electrocuted here at 8.47 p.m. to-day (1.47 a.m. Saturday G.M.T.) for the murder of the Lindbergh baby four years ago.

He was sentenced to death nearly 14 months ago, but the execution was postponed three times. Even to-night there was delay, as his death had been fixed for 8 o'clock.

Hauptmann made no confession. He went to his death courageously. When he entered the execution chamber at 8.41 he prayed aloud in German, repeating prayers muttered by the chaplain.

His eyes were dry and his chin held high. The guards on either side gripped his elbows, but he gave no sign of weakness.

After he had received three charges of electric current at minute intervals Dr. Weisler, a German physician, formally pronounced him dead.

DEATH CHAMBER WAIT

The doctors and witnesses had entered the execution chamber shortly before eight o'clock. When after 45 minutes no one had come out and no indication of whether the execution had been carried out was forthcoming the tension among the enormous crowd outside the prison became great.

At last Col. Kimberling, Governor of the prison, appeared. He walked across the street to the newspaper headquarters, where he told the reporters that Hauptmann at no time showed signs of distress. He had spent the day in fairly good spirits and had asked his spiritual adviser to express his gratitude to Governor Hoffman and the prison authorities.

So many dramatic events have been connected with the case that right up to the last moment few people believed that the execution would be carried out.

The condemned man's wife was among those who made the final efforts to save him. She heightened the drama by swearing a warrant charging Paul Wendel, the ex-lawyer, who last week was said to have confessed to the murder of the Lindbergh baby.

**(April 4)**

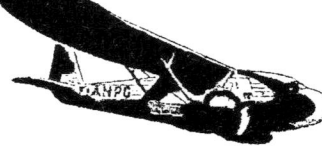

# MR. THOMAS BLAMED FOR BUDGET LEAK

## UNANIMOUS FINDING OF TRIBUNAL

### Divulged to Sir A. Butt and Mr. Bates

### "They Used It For Private Gain"

The Budget Inquiry Tribunal, in their report issued last night, unanimously found that Mr. J.H. Thomas revealed Budget secrets. The report states:

**There was an unauthorised disclosure of information relating to the Budget by Mr. J.H. Thomas to Mr. Alfred Bates and Sir Alfred Butt M.P. Both Mr. Bates and Sir Alfred Butt made use of that information for their private gain.**

The Tribunal further find that Mr. Leslie Thomas, son of Mr. Thomas, neither knew nor suspected that Mr. Bates had any improper information of Budget secrets.

They are satisfied that there was no disclosure of Budget secrets by any member of the Cabinet save Mr. Thomas, by any Civil Servant, nor by the Government printers.

**PURCHASE OF HOUSE**

**"No Connection With Leakage"**

The Tribunal report that they can see no connection between the Budget leakage and the purchase by Mr. Bates of a £15,300 house at Ferring for Mr. Thomas, "save that this accentuates the friendship between the two men and put Mr. Thomas under an obligation to Mr. Bates."

Mr. Thomas, after reading the report last night, said:

"It is a cruel verdict. I repeat what I stated on oath to the Tribunal, that I made no disclosure of Budget secrets."

**(June 3)**

# M.P.'s DEBATE WIDER GROUNDS FOR DIVORCE

**By Our Special Representative**

WESTMINSTER, Friday.

By a majority of 78 to 12 a private member's bill for the reform of the divorce law was given a second reading to-day.

This measure introduced by Mr. De la Bere with the short title of the Marriage Bill, is mainly based upon the old and familiar recommendations of the majority of the Commission of Divorce.

It would admit desertion, cruelty, incurable insanity, drunkenness and imprisonment under a death sentence as grounds for divorce, subject to the proviso that during the first five years of marriage no decree should be granted.

TREND OF OPINION

The proportions of the majority to-day and the trend of the debate, in which only one speaker declared fundamental opposition, would seem to indicate a movement of Parliamentary opinion in favour of divorce reform. But it should be observed that the attendance was small, and proceedings in Committee, to say nothing of the Upper House, offer large opportunities to opponents.

Mr. De La Bere, in moving the second reading, argued that the present system of divorce law was anomalous, ineffective, and far inferior to that of Scotland, the Dominions, and nearly every civilised country. It was impossible for a measure of reform to be non-controversial, but both the Archbishop of Canterbury and the Lord Chief Justice had admitted that reform must come.

Mr. A.P. Herbert argued for the bill in his most serious vein. Almost the only touch of humour in his speech was the opening protestation that he had been happily married, with the usual ups and downs, for 22 years, and possessed four children and a grandchild.

He thought it necessary to mention this because in discussion so many people interested in the sanctity of the home and the interests of the children turned out to be lifelong bachelors.

At present the state of the law, by the admission of the leaders of the Church, was conducive to immorality. The immoral people could get what they wanted, the right people could not. People were forced to choose between two abominations, either one of the parties must commit adultery, or one must commit perjury.

**(November 21)**

# A MIDWIFE FOR EVERY MOTHER

Important provisions intended to help the campaign to reduce the maternal mortality rate are contained in the Ministry of Health Midwives Bill, the text of which was issued last night.

The main features are:

A service of salaried midwives. Compensation for midwives who retire or are left out of the new service. Prohibition of maternity nursing by unqualified persons. Courses of instruction for all practising midwives.

Under the Bill, each local supervising authority — County Councils, borough councils, &c. — is required to secure the whole-time employment of a sufficient number of midwives for attendance on women in their own homes.

**(March 20)**

# LORD NUFFIELD'S NEW £750,000 GIFT TO OXFORD

**From Our Own Correspondent**

OXFORD, Tuesday.

There were unprecedented scenes when Lord Nuffield announced in Convocation at Oxford University to-day that he had decided to increase his gift of £1,250,000 for medical research at Oxford to £2,000,000.

The announcement, which was made as the meeting was about to end, came as a complete surprise even to Viscount Halifax, Chancellor of the University, and Mr. A.D. Lindsay, the Vice-Chancellor.

It was followed by a moment of dead silence in the assembly. Then doctors and dons, in their academic robes, rose to their feet with a burst of cheering which lasted five minutes.

The meeting was held to affix the seal of the University to a document establishing a trust to administer the original gift of £1,250,000 for the endowment of a post-graduate school of medicine at the University, made six weeks ago.

INCONSPICUOUS SEAT

Lord Nuffield, in his scarlet robe of Doctor of Civil Law – an honorary degree conferred on him by the University – took a comparatively inconspicuous seat in one corner near the Chancellor's dais. Lady Nuffield watched the proceedings from a seat in the body of the hall.

While the Vice-Chancellor and others made speeches, praising the munificence of the earlier gift, Lord Nuffield's features gave no indication of the decision he had taken.

Then, when the Chancellor was about to apply the closure to the ceremony, Lord Nuffield rose slowly to his feet and doffing his cap to the Chancellor, began his speech by thanking those who had spoken for their "kindly appreciation of my endeavours."

"I rise," he said, "by special leave of this house. I rise, in particular, for the reason that I understood through my secretary this morning that the money already subscribed as not sufficient to produce the effect I anticipate. I understand the amount necessary is £2,000,000, in lieu of £1,250,000.

"While I have been sitting here, I have been thinking that it would be a great pity if such a scheme should not be brought to fruition as soon as possible.

"I would not like to think that when all the work has been put into the scheme it should fail. I would hate to leave this building with the feeling that the scheme was not complete.

**(November 29)**

# HUEY LONG'S WIDOW

## APPOINTED TO SENATE

**From Our Own Correspondent**

NEW ORLEANS, Friday.

Mrs. Huey Long, whose husband, the Dictator of Louisiana, was assasinated last year, was to-day appointed to serve out the remainder of his term as United States Senator for Louisiana.

Mrs. Long will be the only woman in the Senate. There is one woman member of the House of Representatives.

**(February 1)**

# A GAS MASK FOR EVERYBODY

## PUBLIC TO BE ASKED TO TRY THEM

A further £850,000 to provide gas masks for the civilian population is included in Supplementary Estimates totalling £4,006,250 issued yesterday. The original estimate for masks was £390,000.

The masks will be mostly of a standard pattern, approved by the Government after careful research, giving complete protection to the eyes, nose and lungs against any known gas capable of use in warfare. They will be stored in convenient centres and issued free to the public if and when an emergency arises.

Meanwhile, arrangements will be made for the public to try the masks and become accustomed to their use. Facilities for this will be given, and it is hoped by the authorities that people will voluntarily take advantage of them.

The aim of the Air Raid Precautions Department is to be able to provide a mask for every member of the population; but this aim, it is understood, will not be realised this year, even with the additional expenditure.

Large numbers of specially durable masks for use by persons forced to work in the open during a gas attack are also being produced.

Other supplementary estimates for the Air Raid Precautions Department include £25,000 for the purchase and equipment of two factories in Manchester for the increased production of gas masks, and £7,000 for salaries of additional staff in the department.

**(July 15)**

# GAS ALARM TESTS

## SIRENS DROWNED BY CHILDREN'S VOICES

A "gas alarm test" was carried out by the Air Raid Precautions Department of the Home Office at Hendon yesterday morning.

Thirty-two observation posts were established 100, 200, 300 and 400 yards from the testing point. At 400 yards, only the warning police whistle, blown before each test, was regularly heard. This whistle is 53 years old, and has been in regular use since it was made.

Cmdr. I.B. Franks, who was in charge of the tests, said that the problem of alarms from small instruments had not been solved.

While sirens sounded a street musician played undisturbed a few hundred yards away. Shopkeepers almost opposite did not know that the tests were being made, and the noise of traffic drowned the sounds of the alarm signals.

Thirty-six devices were tested, ranging from a rattle, such as is used at football matches, to electric sirens worked from the battery of a car, ship's sirens, and iron bars beaten together.

**(March 11)**

# 4/- A WEEK FOR FOOD

Four and a half million people in this country spend on an average only 4s per head per week on food.

Sir John Orr, a member of the Diet of the People Committee, made this statement yesterday. He said that results of an investigation to be published shortly would show that:

The diets of the poorer classes were deficient in some substances required for health;

Disease, stunted growth in children and poor physique in adults, which one would expect to find in people on such diets, were prevalent in the poorer half of the population; and

When the diet of the ordinary school child was improved, growth was increased and health was improved.

**(April 7)**

"Wonderful stuff"

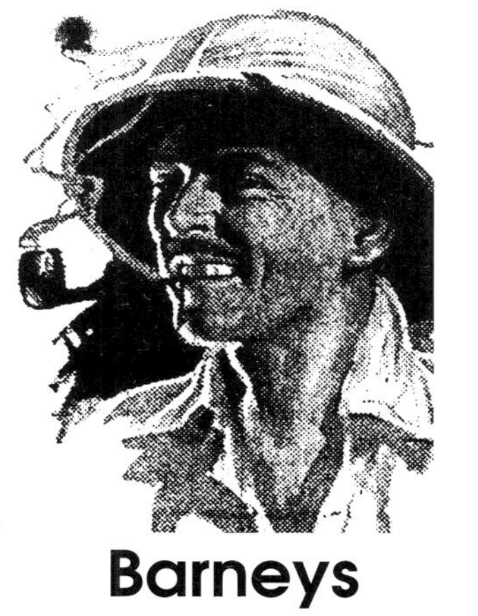

Barneys

Writes a Burma 'teak-wallah'

**Barneys** (medium), **Punchbowle** (full), **Parsons Pleasure** (mild), **1oz 1/2d.**

JOHN SINCLAIR LTD., NEWCASTLE-ON-TYNE

# R.A.F.'S SECRET MACHINES

## TO BE SEEN AT HENDON DISPLAY

**By Major C.C. Turner**

**Daily Telegraph Air Correspondent**

EASTLEIGH (Hants), Thursday.

Some of the new types of aeroplanes for the R.A.F. were demonstrated here to-day, among them the Supermarine – Vickers Supermarine "Spitfire I," and the Vickers twin-engined medium bomber, so far unnamed.

The "Spitfire" is a single-seater fighter which, it is understood, has attained a greater speed than any of its class anywhere in the world.

It will be shown in the machine park at the R.A.F. Display at Hendon on June 27, and will take part in the fly-past. The power of the Rolls-Royce "Merlin" engine, with which it is fitted, is not yet disclosed.

Another high-speed type, the Vickers bomber, is built on the geodetic system of construction, for which a great saving of weight is claimed. It is fitted with Bristol "Pegasus" engines.

This machine, the performance of which is a secret., has great range. In a demonstration flight it appeared to have a phenomenal range of speeds, a very steep climb, and a low landing speed. These qualities are attributed to a large extent to weight-saving construction.

SEA AIRCRAFT

One of the new "Wellesley" single-engined bombers, built on the geodetic principle, and fitted with a Bristol "Pegasus" engine, was flown, and a striking formation of three Vickers Supermarine sea aircraft individually displayed their flying qualities.

These were the big "Stranraer" flying boats with two Bristol "Pegasus" engines, a new type of high performance, now being supplied to the Air Force; the "Scapa," with two Rolls-Royce "Kestrel" engines, also in production; and the "Walrus" – Bristol "Pegasus" – an amphibian of remarkable adaptability.

Another Vickers fighter to be shown at the display will be a new and at present, unnamed, type fitted with a Bristol "Aquila" engine. Details and performance are still a secret.

**(June 19)**

# DEATH SENTENCE ON DR. RUXTON

**From Our Special Correspondent**

MANCHESTER, Friday.

Dr. Buck Ruxton, was, at Manchester Assizes this evening, found guilty of the murder of his wife Isabella Ruxton. He was sentenced to death.

The trial before Mr. Justice Singleton had lasted for 11 days. The jury took 64 minutes to decide on their verdict.

As they resumed their places in the box at 5.2 p.m. Ruxton was brought into the dock surrounded by four warders.

Twice he bowed to the judge. He did not look at the jury as the Clerk of Arraigns asked for the verdict.

At the word "guilty" he placed his right hand up to eye level with the open palm facing the judge.

As the black cap was placed on the judge's head Ruxton showed no sign of emotion, but when, in low, deep tones, the judge came to that part of the sentence referring to his being hanged by the neck Ruxton smilingly shook his head and his lips seemed to frame the world "No."

In passing his first death sentence since he became a judge in 1934, Mr. Justice Singleton showed signs of emotion, but kept his voice under control.

He said to Ruxton: "You have been convicted on evidence which can leave no doubt in the mind of anyone. The law knows but one sentence for the terrible crime which you committed."

"DON'T FUSS"

As Ruxton walked down the steps from the dock he said to the warders: "Don't fuss. I am all right. Don't fuss." Again he raised his right hand as if in salute to the judge.

Afterwards Mr. Slinger, his solicitor, said it was too early to say anything about the question of an appeal.

Dr. Ruxton was arrested on Oct. 13; he was sentenced on Friday, March 13. Since the committal from Lancaster he has been 13 weeks awaiting trial.

His name was originally Hakim Bakhtyar Rustoniji Ratanji. He is 36, and was a popular and successful doctor in Lancaster.

**(March 14)**

# "TERROR GANGS" IN HYDE PARK

Scenes at Marble Arch on Tuesday night when police officers had to use their truncheons were described at Marlborough-street police-court yesterday.

Charles McCann, 28, bar porter, of Chichester-road, Paddington, and Patrick Joseph Kearney, 22, boot repairer, were each sentenced to three months' hard labour for being armed with open razors with a felonious intent at Park-lane, W.

**(June 11)**

# HOOLIGANISM IN THE EAST END

## TERRORISING THE JEWS

**From a Special Correspondent**

Political antagonisms in the East End of London have led to a serious outbreak of hooliganism there.

In the past few weeks police in many districts have been on duty for more than 12 hours each day. At night almost double the usual number has been in the streets. More than 100 extra men have now been drafted into East End divisions.

Jewish householders living in quiet streets have been terrified of leaving their homes after dark, and the windows of a number of Jewish shops have been smashed.

Gangs of youths have been parading the streets and shouting Fascist and anti-Jewish slogans. In Stepney, where about a third of the population is Jewish, these youths, between the ages of 17 and 21, collect at street corners and, until they are moved on by the police, shout insults at and molest passing Jews.

According to police officials they have been stirred up by Fascist speakers, by slogans chalked on the streets and walls and by other methods of propaganda, until anti-Semitic feeling has reached a height unknown for generations in this country.

WEAPONS FOUND

I was shown yesterday weapons taken by the police from youths detained for minor crimes.

They included an inch-long cartridge containing about 20 small pellets, fired by placing it in a harmless-looking pair of paper perforators. The sharp end acted as a gun hammer.

The pellets, according to a police officer, were capable of blinding or inflicting other serious wounds up to a range of 10 yards, although they would not take life.

In one East End police-station over 500 marbles have been collected. These were taken from people who were about to throw them under the hoofs of police horses to prevent a charge of mounted police. Such charges are more terrifying to the East End hooligan than anything else.

Many catapults made of steel and heavy rubber have also been taken. They were used to fire dried beans and stones at shop windows and passers-by.

According to policemen who have been investigating the recent disorders, householders have been afraid to identify their assailants.

"Every time we call on someone who we know has been molested we hear the same tale," one of these policemen told me. "They say, 'I was struck by someone, but I don't know who did it,' Yet we have a collection of pieces of lead and iron with which these people were hit or which were thrown through windows.

"The truth is that the Jews fear reprisals should they attempt to identify their attackers. Usually they know very well who struck them. Often the offenders are boys from the same street."

"It is not really political. It is just that hooligans are taking advantage of the general unrest in this district to damage property and to loot when they have opportunity," a member of the C.I.D. said.

**(October 14)**

# UNIFORMS BAN TO-MORROW

To-morrow the ban on the wearing of political uniforms becomes enforceable.

Under the provisions of the Public Order Act, which was passed through Parliament in the autumn, quasi-military organisations also become illegal.

Increased powers are conferred on the police to regulate public processions which involve a risk of civil disorder, and if necessary to forbid them taking place in any given area.

A Home Office circular on the subject has been issued to magistrates and police authorities throughout the country. It is the Government's intention that the Act should be operated fully and effectively.

The red blouses and red shirts worn by members of the I.L.P. Guild of Youth are to come under the uniforms ban. This is indicated in a communication which the I.L.P. has received from the Commissioner of Police. The letter adds that if the police observe any person wearing in any public place or at any public meeting uniform denoting association with the I.L.P. Guild of Youth they will have no alternative but to take any steps necessary to secure compliance with the law.

The British Union of Fascists last night announced that it had taken counsel's opinion on the Public Order Act. In the opinion of counsel the Blackshirt uniform was illegal, but an ordinary shirt of black colour, with tie worn under an ordinary suit was legal.

"As it is the consistent policy of the movement to obey the law of the land," concluded the statement "the Blackshirt uniform will not be worn by members in any public place or at any public meeting."

**(December 31)**

# THE QUEEN MARY WINS ATLANTIC BLUE RIBAND

## NORMANDIE'S RECORD BEATEN BY 3 1/2 HOURS

**In spite of fog on her last lap, the Queen Mary, the 80,733-ton super liner, yesterday regained for Britain the Blue Riband of the Atlantic.**

**She passed the Bishop Rock, Scilly Isles, at 8.12 last night, having covered the 2,939 miles from the Ambrose Light, New York, in three days 23 hours 57 minutes.**

**This was 3 hours 31 minutes faster than the previous record, held by the French liner, Normandie.**

**The Queen Mary's average speed was 30.63 knots, compared with the Normandie's 30.31.**

**Only a week ago the Queen Mary broke the record for the westward crossing with a time of four days 27 minutes, beating the Normandie's best by two hours 38 minutes.**

**She was due at Cherbourg at 3.30 this morning and will dock at Southampton at one p.m.**

**The speed supremacy of the Atlantic is now held by Britain for the first time since the Mauretania lost it to the German liner Bremen in 1929.**

EXCITED PASSENGERS
"Record Parties" on Board.

There was great excitement among the passengers last night as the Queen Mary neared the Bishop Rock lighthouse and it was known that she had the record in her grasp.

They crowded the decks and many delayed their dinners until the ship had passed the lighthouse marking the end of the officially recognised "record course."

Mr. Roger Firestone, of the United States firm of Firestone Tyres, who was among the passengers, speaking to the representative of The Daily Telegraph by radio telephone, said: "We have done it, after a very enjoyable voyage. Everybody is delighted and 'record' parties are now in progress.

**(August 31)**

# YEOMEN SHAVE THEIR BEARDS

## 90 OF THE 100 MEN NOW CLEAN-SHAVEN

**From a Special Correspondent**

About 90 of the 100 men of the King's Bodyguard of the Yeomen of the Guard have availed themselves of the King's permission to shave their faces. Beards had been compulsory for 35 years, since the accession of Edward VII.

When next the Bodyguard appears on parade it is expected that practically all will be beardless.

At first there was some hesitancy, for custom dies hard. But as first one and then another began to shave, the others were ready to follow. The truth is that the men did not like their beards.

Sergt.-Major A. Lockyer, of the Bodyguard, and formerly of the 1st Royal Dragoon Guards, confessed to me yesterday: "We spend comparatively little of our time in uniform, and when we appeared in civilian dress our beards were frequently a source of annoyance to us.

"The Englishman will not believe that a fellow-Englishman of middle-age wears a beard. We were always being mistaken for foreigners

"I have been taken for a French gendarme, a Russian, a French Cabinet Minister, and an Italian officer."

Although Sergt.-Major Lockyer had his beard for 11 years, he told me that he felt very little different without it.

**(July 11)**

# "TIM'S" FIRST DAY AT WORK

"TIM," the new London telephone automatic time clock started work officially yesterday and had a busy day.

By midnight more than 5,000 London telephone subscribers had dialled T I M. Figures given to The Daily Telegraph for four of the London exchanges were: Museum, 93; Wimbledon, 18; Hop, 26; Kingston, 23.

The Postmaster-General, Major G. C. Tryon, said: "Here we have the latest and most wonderful of clocks. Every month 100,000 Londoners ring up their exchanges and ask the time. In future they will be able to get it with greater accuracy from the speaking clock.

**(July 25)**

# MOUNTING TOLL OF CASUALTIES ON ROADS

Nearly 3,000 more people were injured in road accidents in Great Britain during the first six months of this year than in the same period last year.

A total of 101,004 injuries is reported. The increase is 2.94 per cent.

**(July 3)**

# COMFORT IN THE HINDENBURG

## WOMEN PASSENGERS' IMPRESSIONS

**From Our Special Correspondent**

LAKEHURST, New Jersey, Sunday.

The 12 women passengers who have just crossed the Atlantic in the Hindenburg related to-day some of their impressions. Countess Rosie von Waldeck said:

"We had no room for clothes and no room to dress. The mirrors were so tiny that we could hardly see to put on rouge. The 'shower' in the bath-room was just a thin trickle of ice-cold water, and I think the cabins must have been designed by a woman-hater."

Mrs Clara Adams, an American who has made many trips in Zeppelins, disagreed with this view, and said the trip was the most wonderful she had ever had. "The ship was so steady," she said, "that filled glasses did not spill, while the food was wonderful and the beds very roomy."

Mme. Tatiana, a Frenchwoman, stepped off the ship clamouring for a hot bath. "During the day," she declared, "we were princesses, but at night we felt like paupers because our sleeping quarters were so cramped."

Mrs. Charles Parker, wife of a Cleveland business man, was so pleased with the trip that she threatened to stow away on the return voyage. "Travelling by airship," she said, "is a wonderful beauty secret. It is so absolutely calm and effortless that there is no nervous strain, and any woman knows what that does for her appearance."

Lady Drummond-Hay flatly contradicted critics of the Zeppelin's bathing arrangements. "There was plenty of hot water," she said, "and while the state-rooms, naturally, were not as large as in a steamer, they were fully as comfortable."

**(May 11)**

# TRAFFIC FUMES HARMLESS

## RESEARCH COUNCIL'S DISCOVERY

**From a Special Correspondent**

Experiments undertaken recently have proved that cigarette smoke and traffic fumes are not injurious to health.

The report of the Medical Research Council for 1934-35, now published, states that in the course of long range experiments mice were daily exposed to cigarette smoke and exhaust gases, the latter in a concentration likely to be encountered in a traffic block. No effect on the health or longevity of the mice resulted.

Summarising the experience of years of work on the subject of nutrition, the report states:

"In spite of the large number of new facts discovered in recent years, the essential teachings can be reduced to a few simple statements. The first is that, the younger the child, the more essential is correct feeding for proper growth and health. Natural feeding should be more extensively adopted and continued for longer periods.

"Much more milk, cheese, butter, eggs and vegetables (especially green vegetables) should be consumed. Milk should be the chief drink for children, especially in the first years. Bread and other cereals should be greatly reduced in these early years."

**(March 11)**

**BIG FIRE AFTERMATH**

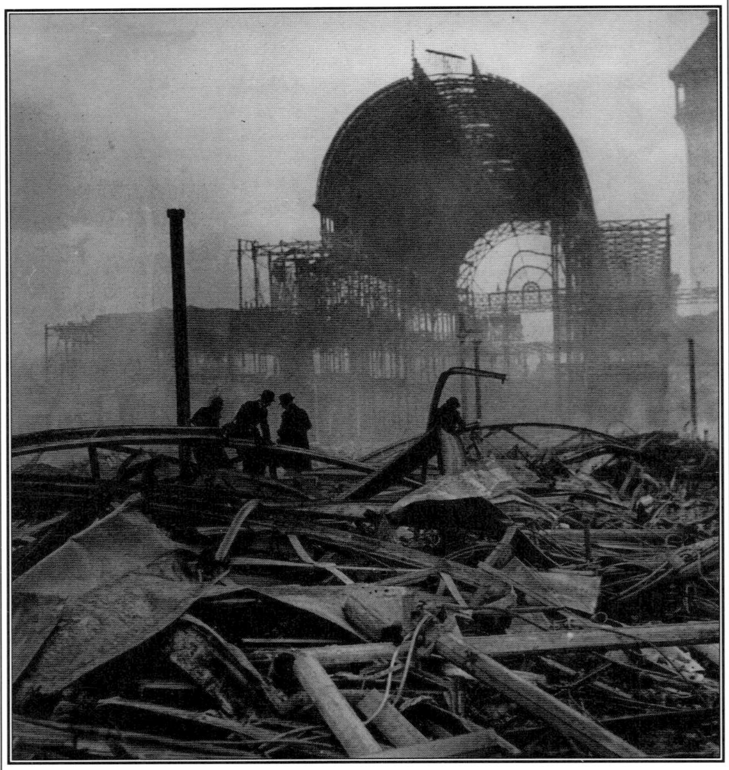

A VISTA OF DESOLATION — Twisted iron-work, broken glass and other debris, all that remains of the Crystal Palace.

# GREAT FIRE DESTROYS CRYSTAL PALACE

## ABLAZE FROM END TO END IN 20 MINUTES

## TELEVISION APPARATUS LOST: 3,000 POLICE CONTROL CROWDS

**The Crystal Palace, London's £1,500,000 amusement centre, on the top of Sydenham Hill, was destroyed last night in the most spectacular fire seen in Britain for many years.**

**The flames spread with amazing speed through the great halls. Within half an hour of the first alarm the building, 1,850ft long, and covering 25 acres was ablaze from end to end. Sparks were blown as far as Beckenham, two miles away.**

**Costly apparatus in the research laboratories of the Baird Television Co., the £9,000 organ and all the statuary, pictures and furnishings of the palace were destroyed.**

90 ENGINES AND 500 FIREMEN

**Flames Seen In Mid-Channel**

**Rising to a height of 300ft, the flames lit up the sky of South London. The glow was seen from an aeroplane in mid-Channel and from the Devil'd Dyke, near Brighton.**

**Hundreds of thousands of people flocked to the scene and fire engines (summoned from every station in the London area) had great difficulty in getting through the congested streets.**

**More than 90 fire appliances, with 500 firemen were engaged – a record for any London fire. Owing to the height of the Palace there was great difficulty in obtaining adequate water pressure, and domestic supplies were cut down over a wide area.**

HOTEL AND HOUSES EVACUATED

**Escape of Orchestra**

**Several of the men were injured by flying glass and others were overcome by the terrific heat.**

**Houses and an hotel near the tower were evacuated and buildings at the foot of the tower were blown up with dynamite.**

**An orchestra practising in the Palace had a narrow escape, leaving the building just before the great Centre Transept crashed, with a roar that was heard for miles, burying the cars of several members.**

**(December 1)**

# 'WOMAN' ATHLETE NOW A MAN

After living for 30 years as a woman Miss Mary Edith Louise Weston, an international athlete, has changed her sex and become a man. In 1934 she won the women's international championship for putting the shot and in 1927 secured the British women's championship for throwing the javelin.

Early this year she consulted a specialist and, after undergoing two operations in London, the first in April and the second early this month, she was released from hospital a few days ago. Yesterday she received the following certificate, signed by Mr. L. R. Broster, surgeon of Charing Cross Hospital:

"This is to certify that Mr. Mark Weston, who has always been brought up as a female, is a male and should continue as such."

**(May 28)**

# NO MORE DAZZLE HEADLIGHTS

Drastic anti-dazzle regulations for motor-cars are to be issued in the spring by the Minister of Transport, Mr. Hore-Belisha.

Thousands of motorists will be compelled to alter their headlights.

The regulations are substantially those circulated in draft form for criticism last July. They were then hotly criticised on many sides, and the R.A.C. told Mr. Hore-Belisha that the proposals were "undesirable and unworkable."

The regulations will make it compulsory for all headlamps to be either permanently dipped or capable of being dipped so that they will not dazzle a person 25 yards away with his eyes 3ft 6in or more above the ground.

Other rules are that side-lamps shall not exceed six watts in power and vehicles shall not be left stationary with lamps stronger than six watts in use.

**(February 2)**

# ALL HOPE FOR FAMOUS BARQUE ABANDONED

## HERZOGIN CECILIE TO BE DISMANTLED

**From Our Special Correspondent**

SALCOMBE (Devon), Monday

All hope of refloating the famous Finnish barque Herzogin Cecilie, which ran on the rocks in Sewer Mill Cove, near here, early on Saturday, has now been abandoned.

To-night I talked with the master, Capt. Sven Erikson, on board the vessel, and he told me that all was over with her. As we talked the waves rolled over her starboard rail.

"It is absolutely impossible to do anything for her now," said Capt. Erikson. "She is hard and fast on rock for most of her length, and nothing could get her off. It would be useless to try.

"We will save the grain from her after-holds , strip her of everything we can, and then leave her. We will probably start lifting the grain to-morrow."

To-day her mainsails were taken down and, together with her spare sails, carried into Salcombe by launch. The task of removing her remaining sails will be continued to-morrow. Capt. Erikson thinks it will take a little more than a week to dismantle the ship.

The captain, the first and second officers and eight men are remaining on board to-night. Mrs. Erikson, the captain's British bride, came ashore to-day to attend to some of the ship's business, and will not rejoin the ship till to-morrow.

At the first warning of bad weather, Capt. Erikson told me, he would send his wife and the men off. "I shall stay on as long as I can," he added, "I shall hate to leave.

"I have been in her eight years – seven of them as master. And now this is the end of her.

"In time she will break up and the Herzogin Cecilie will be no more. She was good for another 20 years too.

"I shall have to get another ship. It may be steam – I have to live – but I hope it will be sail. Yet there will be no ship for me like the Herzogin Cecilie."

**(April 28)**

# WEIGHT OF AGA KHAN IN GOLD

**From Our Own Correspondent**

BOMBAY, Sunday.

His Highness the Aga Khan was to-day weighed in the scales against a heap of gold. The treasure needed to balance him weighed 16 stone, worth about £25,000. Part of it will be distributed to the poor.

This ceremony was part of the celebration of his Highness's Golden Jubilee as head of the great seat of Ismaeli Mohammedans, of whom there are about 5,000,000 all over Asia.

The main celebrations were held in Bombay, where thousands of Khojas, as the Aga Khan's followers are known, assembled. Leading men and women of all communities were present.

The accession of the Aga Khan to the Imamate 50 years ago, at the age of nine, is being made the occasion of festivities in many parts of Asia, including the remotest districts. In the State of Hunza, beyond Gilgit in Kashmir, the ruler and his army and his chieftans have gathered to do honour to their spiritual leader, despite the snow blocked passes and bitter cold of the Himalayas.

**(January 20)**

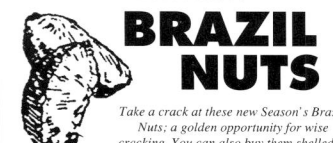

# CHAPLIN FILM PANDEMONIUM

## STARS MOBBED AT BROADWAY PREMIERE

## COMEDIAN'S FIRST WORDS ON SCREEN

**From Our Own Correspondent**

NEW YORK, Thursday.

There was pandemonium on Broadway last night when 1,800 people paid 30s each to see the world premiére of Charlie Chaplin's new film, "Modern Times."

Five thousand autograph-hunters collected outside the Rivoli Theatre and mobbed the celebrities – including Evelyn Laye, Tilly Losche, Gloria Swanson, Ginger Rogers and Eddie Cantor – who attended the performance.

A riot call was issued, but the crowd stoutly resisted the violent attempts of hundreds of policemen to drive them from the entrance of the theatre.

Many celebrities, endeavouring to run the gauntlet from their cars through the crowd, were badly manhandled as college students enthusiastically thrust autograph books under their noses and curious women fingered and clutched the dresses worn by famous actresses and screen stars.

Traffic was halted for more than a quarter of an hour. Many persons slipped on the icy pavements and received minor injuries.

FROM ALL OVER WORLD

People had come from all over the world to see the first Chaplin picture for nearly five years, and to hear Chaplin's voice on the screen for the first time.

The film was given an enthusiastic reception, and there was tremendous applause when Chaplin uttered his first words. This solitary breach of his silent tradition comes when Charlie sings a song in a night club and reveals that he possesses an unusually pleasant voice.

Losing the detachable linen cuff, on which he had carefully written the words of his song, he has to improvise, with the result that the song deteriorates into extraordinary gibberish reminiscent of the Jabberwock in "Alice in Wonderland."

We see the same old lovable clown, with the same cane, hat and oversize shoes, again cast as a brow-beaten tramp who, unable to find a niche for himself in modern society, is comforted by the companionship of an irrepressible girl waif, and pursued by the police as a vagrant. The same old "gags" that Chaplin has used for the last 20 years are brought out and surprisingly enough, they stand the test of time. Last night's audience showed their whole-hearted amusement by practically unceasing and vociferous mirth.

The picture ends, as do all Chaplin pictures, with a long shot showing the comedian walking down the highway. On this occasion, however, he is accompanied for the first time by a girl, his little gamin friend, attractively played by Paulette Goddard.

Neither Chaplin nor his leading lady was at the premiére.

**(February 7)**

# 'THINGS TO COME'

## MINOR FAULTS IN A MASTERLY PRODUCTION

**By Campbell Dixon**

FOR sheer immensity and daring "Things to Come" dwarfs all the pictures of the week. The average woman fan may find it a trifle cold and bloodless, for all its passionate argument and zeal for the betterment of the race.

Man, the more imaginative animal, cannot help being fascinated by the portentous visions of the future; the holocaust of another and greater world war; the swarms of strange-shaped planes stooping from the skies like disciplined birds of prey; the struggle between Liberalism (represented by the last surviving scientists and airmen) and the Dictators (some amusing satire here); and the attempt, when victory is won, to rebuild a world conceived in logic and conditioned by science.

OVERSHADOWED

Memorable, unforgettable, though it is, "Things to Come" is inevitably not without its flaws. The dialogue is a trifle literary, relying too much on direct statement instead of the implications of ordinary speech; and the characterisation in places is oddly flat. Ralph Richardson, as the Boss, shouts too much on the same key — after all, Herr Hitler and Signor Mussolini, whatever their other qualities, are both marvellous mob orators. Margaretta Scott plays the flashing-eyed cave-woman for all she is worth, and a bit more; and Ann Todd and Maurice Braddell both struck me as a trifle colourless and weak.

Indeed, looking back, I find only Raymond Massey, Sir Cedric Hardwicke, Pearl Argyle (for her looks rather than for any chance she gets to act) and John Clements, lingering in my mind.

**(February 24)**

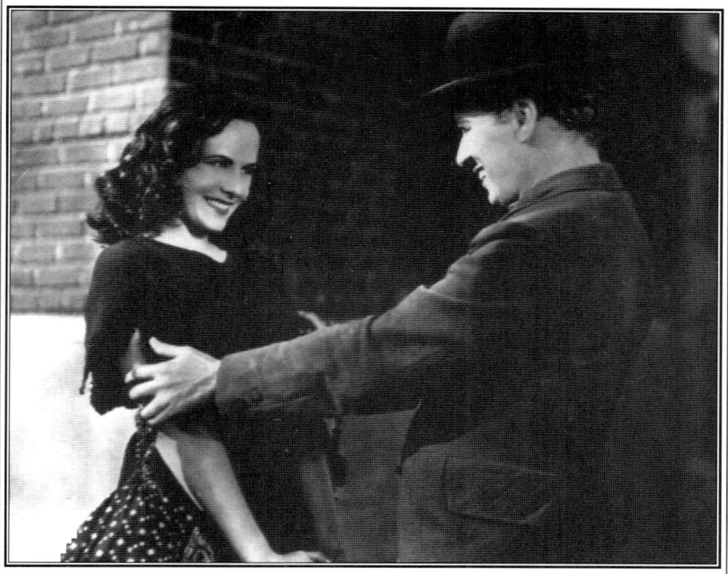

CHARLIE CHAPLIN with Paulette Goddard in his new film "Modern Times," which is to have its European première at the Tivoli Theatre next Tuesday.

# BIGGEST FILM MONEY-MAKERS

## SHIRLEY TEMPLE AT THE TOP

**By Campbell Dixon**

The biggest money-making star of 1934-5, so far as the American market is concerned, was Shirley Temple.

Reports from exhibitors all over the United States collected by the "Motion Picture Herald" place the six-year-old star at the top, with the late Will Rogers second, and Greta Garbo, Marlene Dietrich and Mae West nowhere in the first ten.

The list is:

| | |
|---|---|
| 1. Shirley Temple. | 6. Claudette Colbert |
| 2. Will Rogers | 7. Dick Powell |
| 3. Clark Gable | 8. Wallace Beery |
| 4. Fred Astaire and Ginger Rogers | 9. Joe E. Brown |
| 5. Joan Crawford | 10. James Cagney |

Little Miss Temple was born on April, 23, 1929, made her film début in 1932, and had her first role in an important feature in Paramount's "To the Last Man" (1933). Since then she has been employed so frequently that her employers have felt impelled to explain that every care is taken of her health and education.

Jackie Coogan was a dollar millionaire by the time he was ten. There is every chance that Shirley Temple will beat his record – providing, of course, that she is not discarded by that time as too old. Baby stars drop from favour even faster than their elders.

NOT A FAIR TEST

The exhibitors already quoted give "honourable mention" to:

| | |
|---|---|
| Mae West, | Katharine Hepburn, |
| Bing Crosby, | Buck Jones, |
| William Powell, | Fredric March, |
| Janet Gaynor, | Pat O'Brien, |
| Jean Harlow, | George O'Brien, |
| Norma Shearer, | Eddie Cantor, |
| W.C. Fields, | Robert Montgomery, |
| Ruby Keeler, | Wheeler & Woolsey, |
| Warner Baxter, | Gary Cooper, |
| Grace Moore, | and about 100 others. |

George Arliss is 36th, Charles Laughton 42nd, Greta Garbo 44th, Miss Dietrich does not even appear in the first hundred or the list of "Runner up," but is one of the players given a "blue ribbon," as being mentioned in one per cent. of the exhibitors' returns.

Quite obviously these figures do not represent the real drawing power of Miss Garbo, Miss Dietrich, Mr. Arliss and Mr. Laughton, whose "Mutiny on the Bounty" is now breaking all records at the Empire.

**(January 3)**

NEW FICTION

**Keep the Aspidistra Flying. By George Orwell. (Gollancz. 7s 6d)**

"KEEP THE ASPIDISTRA FLYING" is by the author of "Burmese Days," and is about that most harrowing of subjects – money. It really is about money, about those borderline cases where a sixpence more or less turns the scale between middle class and lower class, poverty or penury, and where the aspidistra, with its hint of luxury, of something that is not for use alone, is a class distinction.

It is a savage and bitter book, which the author's common sense carries to its inevitable conclusion, for the hero begins by defying society, by determining to be a martyr to his anti-money sense of values, to keep for ever out of the money world; and ends as any young man with a fiancée and a talent for copy-writing is bound to end. It is an anarchistic book: having demonstrated how the divinity in the shape of a shower of gold penetrates any defence and permeates every relationship, the author dismisses any political solution.

**(April 21)**

# SURREALISM IN ART

**By T.W. Earp**

Surrealism may be defined as serious nonsense. Its art portrays images conjured up in moments of dreaming, asleep or awake, when imagination is allowed its play, freed from the control of everyday reason and logic. It attempts to capture fantasy in its purest form, and Lewis Carroll has been hailed as its most typical exponent in literature.

The Surrealist Exhibition at the New Burlington Galleries, Burlington-gardens, is London's most sensational art-show for many years. Artists of 14 countries are represented, and the result is an astounding collection of work which ranges from rubbish to beauty. A display a quarter of its size would have been more effective.

A cash containing scraps of glass and scissor-blades, entitled "Objects made by a madman"; another "Object" consisting of a mirror and an egg; rows of half-empty liqueur-glasses attached to a waiter's jacket; a pair of white dancing-slippers with heels encased in paper cutlet-frills; a line of buttons; and a tree-trunk – these are specimens of too many exhibits which fail as humour and have nothing to do with art.

CHEAP HORROR

The pictures are often poor jokes, pointless indelicacies, or relics of an outworn romanticism. No extra significance, for instance, is given to the smidge called "Loplop introduces a young girl" by hanging an empty watch-case and a toy crab to it.

The picture, "Retrospective bust of a woman devoured by ants" is very cheap horror. The half-realised, shadowy human forms in the various canvasses like "Daily Torments" and "Archaic Fragments" are no improvement on the false mysticism of Böcklin and Doré.

For there are degrees of quality in fantasy as in other things, and a work is not justified merely because it comes under the surrealist category. It has to be good surrealism, and happily there is enough in the show to illustrate the movement's value as an effort to increase the sphere of imagination in art.

Chirico's white-robed figures in classic architectural settings, like "The Tower" and "The Square" have grace and a persuasive mystery. Dali in "The Dream" and "Daybreak," is a fine draughtsman of detail and a real inventor of landscape moods. Klee, a delicious colourist, shows a delightful innocence of whimsicality with "Garden Face" and "Mask of Fear," Joan Miro's alert grotesques share something with Bosch and the Flemish primitives.

And Picasso, taking in yet another-ism in his tireless stride, has found new colours and new harmonies of form in "The Studio." "Seated woman in red hat," and "Abstraction on a yellow ground." Yet these pictures, with their sternly intellectual construction, can hardly be considered as surrealist.

**(June 12)**

# FIRST WOMAN R.A. FOR 167 YEARS

At a general assembly of Academicians and Associates of the Royal Academy yesterday the following were elected Royal Academicians:

Mr. ARTHUR GEORGE WALKER, A.R.A. sculptor; Mr. HENRY RUSHBURY, A.R.A. engraver; and Dame LAURA KNIGHT, D.B.E., A.R.A., painter.

Dame Laura Knight is the first woman to be appointed an R.A. since 1769, the date of the foundation of the Academy. She is well known as a painter of scenes in the theatre dressing room, the ballet and the circus. Her husband is Mr. Harold Knight, the portrait painter, who was elected A.R.A. in 1928.

**(February 13)**

# THIS AUTUMN'S BEST PLAY

## "CHARLES THE KING" AT THE LYRIC

**By W.A. Darlington**

At last this undistinguished, autumn theatrical season has taken a real turn for the better. Hitherto its successes have either been revivals or plays of no special moment, and it had begun to seem that no really good new serious work would ever be seen again.

However, Maurice Colbourne's "Charles the King," staged last night at the Lyric, has ended that unhappy state of things.

Here is a piece of work that we can be proud of – one which we could show to foreigners.

Mr. Colbourne has set out to re-create for us the clash of ideas which rent seventeenth-century England and culminated in the execution of Charles I. in Whitehall. He does so with extraordinary fire and vividness.

Charles is throughout his hero, but though Charles carries our sympathy with him, he cannot win us to his side – so honourably has Mr. Colbourne held the balance true in the telling of his story. Cromwell is made an unattractive figure, and the ruthlessness of his methods condemned, and compared by implication with the methods of modern dictators. Yet we are not asked to call Cromwell's good faith in question.

A CLASH OR IDEALS

Charles and Cromwell, in fact, has each a different ideal for England. Only because those ideals are intensely felt and are irreconcilable does the quarrel end in war.

No doubt Mr. Colbourne, being a man of the theatre as well as a student of history, has whitewashed Charles a good deal in some respects. His turnings and twistings are never his fault but the fault of Henrietta Maria, or Strafford, or Laud. But nobody need quarrel with that since it gives Barry Jones so admirable a part to play, and enables him to paint with such deft strokes a man whose very faults proceed from his desire to be a good king according to his lights.

The Queen, Henrietta Maria, is made a very attractive figure both by Mr. Colbourne and by Gwen Ffrangeon-Davies, who combine to show why she was Charles's good angel in private and his evil genius in public.

**(October 10)**

# A GAY LIGHT COMEDY

**By W.A. Darlington**

The gift of real lightness is a rare one in the theatre, and Terence Rattigan is a lucky young man to have it. His "French Without Tears," at the Criterion last night, added a gay trifle to London's list of successful plays.

The chief ingredient in Mr. Rattigan's gift is good-temper. This band of young men, learning French in a villa in a small Riviera town, can be cynical, sophisticated, sentimental by turns. They can be witty – though wit is not really the name for their cheerful back-chat – and they can even turn serious for moments at a time. But collectively and individually, one feels that they all have perfect digestions, and that fate in consequence cannot harm them.

Their only trouble is a girl. One of their number otherwise negligible, has with him a sister who is a huntress of man. It does not satisfy her to have one man, or two, at call; she must have all the men in sight. So, what with one thing and another, this young woman gives Mr. Rattigan plenty of situations to keep his play going for three rapid and hilarious acts.

Especially since Kay Hammond plays the girl. Miss Hammond's particular method, which consists in concealing an exact comic technique under an appearance of attractive nitwittery, is quite perfectly suited to this part. And it provides, too, a perfect foil for the delicate, intelligent playing of Jessica Tandy, as the French girl whose pre-destined lover has gone straying with the rest after the siren.

The four young men could not possibly be better played than they are by Rex Harrison, Roland Culver, Robert Flemyng and Guy Middleton. Nor can I imagine any actor giving a better sketch of a pleasant, middle-aged Frenchman than Percy Walsh does here.

**(November 7)**

# DONALD WOLFIT AS HAMLET

**By W.A. Darlington**

To-night at the Shakespeare Memorial Theatre "Hamlet" was added to the repertory of the Festival Company. Donald Wolfit played the name part and gave one of the best individual performances I have ever seen in Stratford.

In Mr. Wolfit, however, the company has an actor who is not yet so well established in London that he dare not leave it, but is a player of a high and sensitive talent. His Hamlet has vigour, poetry and intelligence. His voice though low and rather high pitched, brings out the life, the meaning, and the variety of the verse. In fact, with this performance Mr. Wolfit makes a very big stride forward.

**(July 7)**

# B.B.C. TELEVISION STATION OPENED

## CEREMONY SEEN SIX MILES AWAY

**By L. Marsland Gander.**
**Our Television Correspondent**

The opening ceremony of the B.B.C. television station at Alexandra Palace was seen and heard in The Daily Telegraph office, Fleet-street, yesterday afternoon, while it was taking place six miles away. It was the first occasion in newspaper history on which transmission of moving pictures by wireless has supplemented other methods of collecting news.

Brilliant, sharply defined, and absolutely steady close-ups were seen of Major G. C. Tryon, the Postmaster-General, who performed the ceremony; Mr. R. C. Norman, chairman of the B.B.C.; Lord Selsdon, chairman of the Television Advisory Committee and other speakers.

The ceremony was first transmitted by the Baird system and then repeated for transmission by the Marconi-E.M.I. system. Both transmissions were picked up on a Cossor receiver

An interesting feature of the reception was that none of the electrical interference which makes reception of sound wireless programmes in Fleet-street difficult was experienced. Television is transmitted on ultra-short waves which are immune from the noisy interruptions caused on other wavelengths by tape-machines, lifts and electrical machinery.

A FAULTLESS TRANSMISSION

Some difficulty was experienced at times in getting the best reception of the Baird transmission. Adjustment of the set effected no improvement, but no doubt minor changes at the transmitting end will remedy the defects. The Marconi-E.M.I. transmission was faultless from beginning to end.

"At this moment," said Mr. Norman, "the British television service is undoubtedly ahead of the rest of the world. Long may that lead be held."

Roughly speaking, the television service would cover Greater London, with a population of 10,000,000. There might be surprising extensions. He would not lay heavy odds against a resident of Hindhead, 40 miles from London, viewing the Coronation procession.

**(November 3)**

## LONDON TELEVISION PROGRAMME

Alexandra Palace

Vision, 45 mc/s (6.67 m); Sound. 41.5 mc/s (7.23 m)

BY BAIRD SYSTEM

3. – Opening of B.B.C. Television Service by Major G.C. Tryon; Mr. R.C. Norman and Lord Selsdon will also speak.
3.15 – British Movietone News
3.20-3.30 – Variety: producer Dallas Bower; Adèle Dixon, Buck and Bubbles (comedians and dancers); B.B.C. Television Orchestra.

BY MARCONI-E.M.I. SYSTEM

1 – Programme Ceremony
1.15 – British Movietone News
1.20-1.30 – Variety

BY BAIRD SYSTEM

9 – Programme Summary
9.5 – Television comes to London. B.B.C. Film.
9.20 – Picture Page. Magazine of topical and general interest, devised and edited by Cecil Madden; producer G More O'Ferrall, with Joan Miller (the Switchboard Girl)
9.30-10– British Movietone News.

**(November 2)**

# LAVISHNESS OF ZIEGFELD FILM

**By Campbell Dixon**

"The Great Ziegfeld," launched by Metro-Goldwyn-Mayer at His Majesty's Theatre last night with all the pomp of a fashionable theatrical first night, is a film that can only be described in superlatives.

It may start another cycle of back-stage productions. Or its sheer length, opulence, massed stars and general lavishness, calculated to make the ordinary million-dollar production look a little niggardly, may discourage imitation.

"The Great Ziegfeld" is the longest talking picture ever made. Divided into two parts by an interval, it runs for three hours, and there were moments when I wished it had been shorter. Strange as Ziegfeld's career was, and brilliantly as his spectacles and the song hits of the last 30 years have been reproduced, the picture has too uniform a tempo and would be better for sharp cutting.

HUMOUR AND CHARM

The cast is extraordinarily strong. William Powell plays the showman with humour and nonchalant charm; Luise Rainer is his first wife, the French actress, Anna Held; Myrna Loy plays his second wife, Billie Burke – herself a popular screen actress still; Frank Morgan is a rival showman, not hard to identify; Nat Pendleton makes a credible Sandow; and a Chicago broker, hitherto an amateur actor, gives a lifelike impersonation of Will Rogers.

**(September 2)**

THE DAILY TELEGRAPH

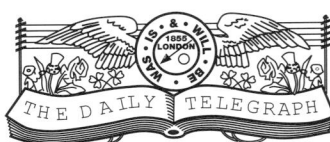

135, FLEET STREET LONDON

Telephone: CENTRAL 4242

**TO-DAY'S WEATHER FORECAST**

LONDON & S.E. ENGLAND - Wind southerly, fresh, veering later; sunny; but with showers later; moderate temperature.

ENGLISH CHANNEL - Calm

# A FAREWELL AND A WELCOME

## NATION'S UNSHAKEN FAITH IN KINGSHIP

Events moved as rapidly yesterday as in the last act of a Shakespearian tragedy. We saw the clearing of the stage after the great scenes had been played out and the emotions of the audience had been cleansed not by pity and fear but by pity and hope. Then late at night, after the new reign had already begun, King Edward VIII., who by his own volition has laid down the Crown and with it all its titles and dignities and honours, spoke on the wireless to a listening multitude of those who had been his loving subjects. It was the word of farewell and goodbye spoken with sincerity and emotion. Free as it was from the slightest trace of reproach, it must have reawakened in every feeling heart an acute sense of unavailing regret and brought a mist of tears to countless eyes. His general plea was that for him there could be no other way, that he had to judge entirely by himself, and that he had been influenced by the single thought of what would be best for the Empire. The most poignant passage in an earnest plea that the people should rally to the side of the new King was that in which he described him as enjoying "one matchless blessing not bestowed on me – a happy home with wife and children."

### Victory of Moral Sense

This distressing episode has ended in a resounding victory for the moral sense of the British people through-out the world. Those who would persuade themselves that it is merely a last belated triumph of Victorian morality utterly misread the underlying truths. Doubtless to many it seems only the triumph of moral conventions, but these moral conventions themselves are as broadly based upon the human experience of centuries as upon the categorical fiat of the Higher Law. Judgment is everywhere kindly and charitable. Even if there were any desire to be unduly censorious, the nature and degree of the self-imposed penalty would check the unspoken word. To lay down a Crown may be easy, to put off the crushing burdens and escape the exacting routine of Kingship may even seem a new-found liberty. But to abandon wholly and at once one's way of life, to put oneself outside the sphere of performing the welcome duties in which King Edward shone so brightly, to lose cherished opportunities of helping not merely individuals but whole classes of those sorely needing help and encouragement, and to leave the soil of his native land and become an exile – here is where the deepest hurt will be felt and, we fear, increasingly felt as the years pass by. Patriae quis exul se quoque fugit. The exile cannot escape from himself.

### "Embedded in Our Hearts"

During the discussion on the Abdication Bill the argument was advanced by an insignificant minority that it was "a retrograde step to set up again a governmental form which appertains to a class society." Could anything be more grotesquely remote from the truth? The democratic Dominions of Australia, New Zealand, Canada, and South Africa would not have agreed to concurrent legislation with Great Britain if the Crown during the recent episode had in any way challenged Constitutionalism or if they believed that the continuance of the Crown was incompatible with democratic government. They believe no such thing.

"Constitutional Kingship," said Sir John Simon – "is embedded in our hearts," Say rather that it is embedded in our convictions from a long experience – and the late short reign is no exception – that the constitutional Kings and Queens of England whom we have known for a century have deserved loyalty because they themselves have been loyal to their peoples and have sought to work their lasting good. This country, it has been said, has sometimes rebelled against Kings, but against Kingship never, and if times have changed, so have Kings. The idea that Parliament chose yesterday deliberately to "set the Monarchy up again" is nonsense. The succession passed from brother to brother with as natural a transition as day passes into night. Long live King George VI. and Queen Elizabeth!

**(December 12)**

# A DANGER AVERTED

London was spared yesterday what might have proved the most serious riot in its recent history by the wisdom with which the police handled a difficult situation, and, let it be added, by the readiness with which the followers of Sir Oswald Mosley conformed to police orders. As it was, the preparations made in the East End to resist any march of the Fascists resulted in disturbance which had to be quelled by police charges and ended in the arrest of more than 60 persons. Had the announced programme been carried out not the immense force of police on duty could have prevented serious disorder. The state of feeling that was revealed in the assembly of huge crowds, many members of which were prepared for mischief, is the justification for diverting the march and prohibiting the announced meetings.

Yesterday's challenge to the liberty of public speech was offered by those who are most interested to preserve that privilege, and who gravely threaten it by their action. Criticism has been made of the failure to prohibit the Fascist march in advance. It is stated to be debatable whether the police possess the power to prevent such a gathering, and in that respect the law may be unsatisfactory. But the Commissioner of Police was on this occasion on the side of freedom, though pushed to its extreme limits, and those who assembled to resist the march threatened it. Tact, combined with the minimum of force, saved London the experiences that make a tragic story from Paris this morning.

**(October 5)**

# A RUNAWAY OF THE SEA

"Her crew of four were taken to police headquarters in a closed police ambulance." So it ends, prosaically enough.

However commonplace the finish, the adventurers may feel that they added a final chapter of thrills to a mystery that the world has watched for weeks. How an unknown ship entered Georgetown Harbour, how the police launch that attempted to board her was threatened till she sheered off, and how a larger vessel carrying armed policemen chased and captured her and towed her into port — all this is of a piece with as strange a story as the sea has given us for years. In days when shipping movements are as regular as the running of trains we are transported back to the atmosphere of Marryat or Clarke Russell and catch a glimpse of the time when mariners left port on undisclosed missions.

Ten weeks have gone by since the Girl Pat, with her original crew of five, left Grimsby with no ostensible purpose but a fishing trip in the North Sea. Then she was heard of at Dover and next on the coast of Spain. Again she appeared at Dakar on the West African coast. Before that, rumour was busy. The vessel had been reported from half a dozen places so far apart that all the stories could not be true. Underwriters had been notified of a total loss. Questions were asked in Parliament. According to the story told by the mate, who had been left behind ill at Dakar, the trawler was being navigated by means of a sixpenny atlas. At whatever port she touched the Girl Pat quickly made off again to become the subject of fresh rumours and misleading reports.

**(June 20)**

# "NO SMOKING"

Though the world to-day is tolerant of smokers, some few restrictions remain upon the indulgence of their habit, as illustrated by the case of a member of Parliament who lighted a cigarette in Standing Committee, and of a young man fined for smoking in an air liner. The air passenger was a man of experience in flying, who claimed that he had always smoked, and it was pointed out that on another British air line, on the Continent, and in the American air liners smoking was permitted. The smoker at Westminster was the second offender within a few weeks; the previous case was that of a woman member.

It has been averred that the modern woman is more frequently to be found at fault with the light-hearted cigarette than is the man.

**(March 18)**

# KING GEORGE VI: A TRAINING IN IDEALS OF LEADERSHIP

**By Capt. Lionel Dawson, R.N. (Retd.)**

If the British public know less of the personal qualities of King George VI. than they did of those of his three predecessors at the time of their accession, that accords well with his Majesty's own desire. With fine loyalty to the English family determined while Duke of York to do nothing which might divert attention from his elder brother to himself.

In consequence there has almost been a risk of an inadequate appreciation of his real abilities and gifts of character in the minds of the people of the Empire. To discover the man himself has not been easy while he was bent on self-effacing rather than self-revealing lines of duty.

Now it is time that a fuller knowledge of his personality – the value of his many services to the State, his high sense of duty and of the fitness of things, and his capable and imaginative way of handling affairs – should be more widely shared.

### COURAGE AND RESOURCEFULNESS

To gain an effective background for a study of his career it is necessary to refer for a moment to one well remembered phase – his war service.

Entering the Navy as a cadet at the usual age, and passing through the preliminary stages of training as an ordinary cadet, the then Prince Albert heard the thunder of gunfire at Jutland, and shared in the events of that stupendous day as midshipman of a gun-turret in H.M.S. Collingwood. Passing on to the Malaya, in which he served as a junior commissioned officer, he was transferred to the Air Force not long afterwards and gained his wings as a pilot. The end of the war found him serving in the Independent Air Force as a flying officer.

From the day when he was first given charge of a picket-boat (he made her the apple of his eye), and throughout his service career afloat and in the air, his keenness and attention to duty and his courage and resourcefulness in its performance were outstanding. This devotion to duty and ideal of service he has since carried into his life as Duke of York and, in the last few months, as virtual Prince of Wales.

### STUDENT OF ALL SIDES OF SOCIOLOGY

There came a time when higher duties of State compelled cessation of service as an officer, and as a preparation for a new phase of activities he entered Cambridge University. There he was able to give full expression to the studious side of his nature. Like his great-grandfather and namesake, Albert the Prince Consort, his bent was towards philosophy. Albert of Saxe-Coburg at the University of Bonn and Prince Albert of England at Cambridge took similar courses. Both studied economics and sociology, to which the great-grandson added that modern branch of practical philosophy, civics.

The habits of learning and the love of philosophic statesmanship acquired in his student days have remained with his majesty ever since.

Good use, then, was made of the period of preparation for statesmanship. Indeed, on such occasions as have required him to represent his elder brother or play a larger part than usual upon the stage of affairs, those in contact with the King have been genuinely impressed with his knowledge, grip and capability.

His philosophic leanings are not towards metaphysics but to practical psychology, and his interest in sociology is more in the direction of actualities than of political theory. So is it that the subject nearest his heart has been that of industrial welfare, for which he has laboured harder than is known to any others than those of his immediate entourage.

His presidential speech read on his behalf on Wednesday at the annual meeting of the Industrial Welfare Society can be said to epitomise his outlook towards the objects of this society – the planned welfare of the worker. The tone of the speeches following that address emphasised the society's high appreciation of his services in that cause. Among other honorary positions he occupies is that of president and chairman of the King George Jubilee Trust – a responsibility hedged round with difficulties.

Something like fame – at least a great need of enthusiastic approval – has attached itself to him over the foundation of the scheme now so widely known as the Duke of York's Camps. It is in this connection, perhaps, that he has become best known to the people of the Empire, and even outside the Empire. The camps are entirely a product of his own. He conceived the first and set them going with triumphant success.

They go from strength to strength, becoming more popular every year. The social effects are marked; for the King's scheme proved the possibility of a complete mutual understanding between the public school boy and the boys of the Council schools. In the camps they live together cheek-by-jowl under informal conditions. The fact that the King foresaw the value of such association gives a very typical impression of the train of thought that is his and of the practical forms which his vision takes.

### FAMILY LIFE AND THE OPEN AIR

So much for the concern of a Royal Duke with his people's interests. What of the King himself. Ideally married and devoted to his wife and daughters, it is no mere fashion of speech to say that his happiest moments are those when he is able to be with them, undisturbed by the cares of his high station. To him family life is life at its best and sweetest.

Dogs come to him to make friends – a tribute to any man – and a dog is always at his feet when he works.

A good horseman, he gave up hunting at the time when economies were instituted in the Royal households during the economic crisis – just at the moment, indeed, when his stable had been constituted to his liking.

As a shot he is in the same category as his father – which is the highest econimium possible – and it may be mentioned that he has just the same stiff-armed action in bringing his gun up.

His golf handicap is lower than that of his elder brother, and he has all the same devotion to the open air and the normal life of an English country gentleman, in so far as it is possible for him to lead it.

Tradition and the value of it are very dear to him. It is said that his late Majesty King George V. was genuinely surprised by the depth of his subjects' devotion which the Jubilee celebrations revealed. The similar sentiments felt for King George VI. by his personal staff and by all who have come in contact with him at all intimately make it easy to prophesy that the new King will win for himself an Empire-wide love and admiration comparable to that felt for his father.

### HIS OWN DEFINITION OF A TRUE LEADER

The King is eminently fitted for the role of kingly leadership because he knows what good leadership should be. He once defined the true leader as a man with the gift of vision and the desire in his soul to leave the world a little better than he found it. Such a leader, he said, did not demand immediate results, but was willing to strive for what appeared to be unattainable, leaving it to his successors to gather the fruits, and content if he could feel that what he did made that ultimate harvest possible.

"It is England's mission, duty and interest to put herself at the head of the diffusion of civilisation and the attainment of liberty." So spoke the Prince Consort in 1850. The conception of leadership which his great-grandson holds, and the character and abilities which he has already shown himself.

**(December 12)**

# London Day by Day:

**Welcome for the Queen Mary.**
**Mr. Roosevelt's Radio Style.**

With loudspeakers booming congratulations from the sky and aeroplanes dropping flags and flowers on to her decks, the Queen Mary will receive a deafening welcome when she reaches New York to-day.

The harbour might have been planned for elaborate receptions, but the welcome will start when the Queen Mary reaches Nantucket lightship.

For the rest of the journey she will be accompanied by scores of aeroplanes, some filled with wireless commentators and reporters and others piloted by members of the National Guard.

By the time the passengers are within sight of New York the harbour will be a carefully organised bedlam.

Raucous voices from the clouds will be crying "Hats off to the Queen Mary." Dozens of fireboats will be spouting streams of water into the air and ships' sirens will join the chorus as she steams up the Hudson.

Battery Point, the south end of Manhattan Island, will be packed with people. Appropriately enough, the best "grandstand" overlooking the mouth of the river is the Cunard-White Star building at the lower end of Broadway.

## Mr. Well's Afterthoughts

Mr. H.G. Wells's "The Man Who Could Work Miracles," which will be shown as a film this week, has apparently undergone some drastic alterations since it left the library for the film studio.

The hero's miracles have been extended to include the materialisation of a tiger on a clergyman's hearthrug and a realistic view of Hades. The film will also contain a good many of Mr. Wells's propagandist afterthoughts, which were, perhaps fortunately, lacking from the story when it was written 30 years ago.

The autumn film season is incidentally starting earlier this year than usual.

Katherine Hepburn will be seen during the week as "Mary of Scotland." This, too, has suffered strange changes since it was first seen a year or two ago as a play in blank verse by Maxwell Anderson.

The verse has all been cut and so has every reference to Bothwell's surname. This was not done for historical reasons, but because it happened to be Hepburn.

## Dr. Goebbels's Persuasion

I have just been glancing through Dr. Goebbels's new book. It is called "Der Angriff" – "The Attack" – which is also the name of Dr Goebbels's paper.

The book consists of reprints of his old speeches. Whatever effect they may have on

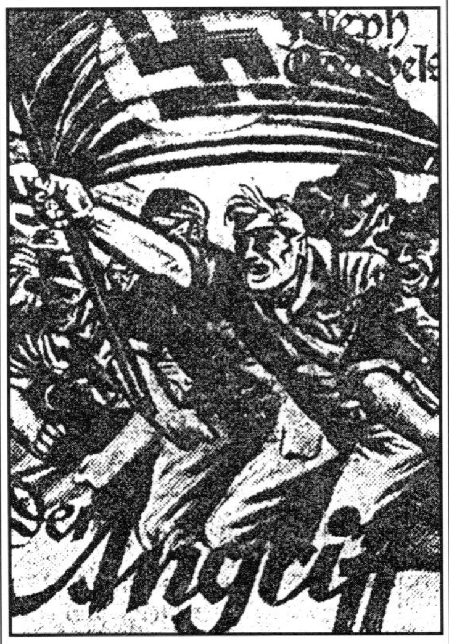

*Nazi Storm Troopers on the Offensive - from the jacket of Dr. Goebbel's New Book.*

the Nazi rank and file, it cannot be said that their mass appeal to an English reader is highly persuasive. The most notable thing about the book is the jacket.

## On the Air

Three years at the White House have not staled President Roosevelt's skill as a broadcaster.

In his speech at Quebec yesterday, which was relaid to London, his voice sounded as fresh and his delivery as conversational as in the broadcast "reports" on the New Deal which he gave to America soon after his inauguration.

These homely talks, in which the President explained his policy in simple language, added tremendously to his popularity among the people, whom he always addressed as "My friends."

Yesterday was a more formal occasion. But Mr. Roosevelt began his speech, "Your Excellency, Mr. Prime Minister" – a pause – "my friends and neighbours of Canada."

## The President's English

Mr. Roosevelt speaks English of a kind which still defeats Hollywood. His accent is midway between our own and that of most Americans. There was only one pronounced Americanism in his speech.

He said he hoped the King would one day go to Canada and afterwards "visit with" his neighbours in the United States.

Mr. Mackenzie King said it was significant that, whereas on Sunday King Edward received President Lebrun on Canadian soil, Lord Tweedsmuir was now welcoming President Roosevelt in Canada's ancient capital.

There was another noteworthy resemblance. Mr. Roosevelt followed the King's example by making part of his speech in French.

## Canting Arms

The partridges woven in the cope of the new Bishop of Portsmouth, in punning allusion to Dr. Partridge's name, represent a well-known device in heraldry.

At one time it used to be supposed that canting arms, or armes parlantes, belonged to the degenerate days of the heraldic art. The reverse is the case.

Most of the arms assumed in early days contained allusion to the name or office of the bearer.

An example of the former in present-day heraldry is the boar which is the crest of the Bacon family. The head of this family, Sir Hickman Bacon, is premier baronet of England.

A modern instance of a coat alluding to the office of the original grantee is to be found in Lord Tennyson's arms.

On his shield is a garland of laurel – a reference to the Poet Laureate founder of the family.

**PETERBOROUGH**

# NEW SEASIDE FASHIONS

## SHORTS, TROUSERS & "MONKEY JACKETS"

**By a Woman Representative**

A bewildering variety of choice is offered to women in their selection of holiday clothes this year.

"Monkey jackets," braided shorts and trousers, satin sun suits, and long rubber bathing capes are among the many new fashions which this season has produced.

The monkey jacket will replace the blazer this summer. It looks well worn over tailored frocks and skirts, and will add a finishing touch to trousers and shorts suits.

Scarlet flannel makes the monkey jacket I saw at Waring and Gillow. It is double-breasted, and fastens with chromium buttons stamped with anchors. The flap pockets can do handbag duty. This jacket is also made in navy flannel, and can be had in 34in to 42in sizes for 49s 6d.

A man's tailor has cut and made the shorts and trousers here. Linen trousers are cut on the best conservative lines, with slip pockets and a belt at the waist. They cost 21s in white and 23s 9d in colours.

SHOES FOR PEBBLY BEACHES

"Pneumatic soles" solve the question of shoes for pebbly beaches. At Waring and Gillow I was shown rubber sandals with thick sponge rubber soles and heels. They give you the feeling of "walking on air." The tops are in sandal shape, with wide rubber toe and ankle straps, and a cut-out heel. The sandals are made in white and pastel colours, and cost 6s 9d.

Gleaming satin sun suits will flatter newly achieved tan. They are made in white and pastel colours, among which I admired a suit in water blue. These suits are woven with an elastic thread, which achieves perfect fit. They are skirtless, and have narrow shoulder straps which cross over the sunbathing back.

Slip over your bathing suit one of the new rubber capes, and you will achieve the last word in beach smartness. A cape in pale green rubber that I saw buttons down the front and has arm slits. The price is 6s 11d.

Fine lace and flowered chiffons and crêpes make the dresses I saw at Woollands. Platinum lace is used for a graceful dress for the older woman. It is woven with a design of flowers, and worn over a black foundation. A bunch of parma violets is pinned at the V-neck. The dress has long sleeves, and a little cape swings from the shoulders at the back.

Bright colours strike an effective note on black and white ensembles. Scarlet tulips and white dahlias are printed on a black crêpe dress, which has a little tailored jacket, with long sleeves. The skirt is fitted at the hipline by three ruched panels, which flare out into the skirt. The back of the bodice is slit to the waist, and a bunch of pink tulips is poised on the shoulder of the coat.

**(May 19)**

# 1,250 FLATS IN ONE BLOCK

## £1,500,000 BUILDING BY THE THAMES

The first half of what is claimed to be the largest block of flats in Europe was opened yesterday at Dolphin-square, Grosvenor-road, Westminster, by Lord Amulree.

When it is completed there will be over 1,250 flats for a population of 3,000 built at a cost of about £1,500,000. The building will have a river frontage. Among its distinctive features are:

Dutch and Japanese gardens, in addition to the main open space;

Sports centre and swimming bath;

Pier for pleasure craft and river-taxis on the Thames;

Water supply from artesian wells, making the flats independent of London's supply; and

Children's nursery run on scientific lines, with a strict time-table and a carefully, supervised routine. A six-roomed dolls' house in the nursery was unveiled by Lady Diana Cooper.

REBUILDING LONDON

"Much of London will be rebuilt within the next 25 years," said Lord Amulree. "It will be a great loss, not only to the metropolis, but to the nation, if that rebuilding takes place without any coherent scheme dealing with the future development of London as a whole, but purely by piecemeal and unrelated efforts.

"For this purpose the present planning powers may from some points of view, be regarded as insufficient. The Government should in these circumstances consider the setting up of a Commission or other body to examine the problem of the planning of Greater London, including the re-development of central areas.

"The plan must essentially be a plan of action. Even Sir Christopher Wren, who planned London on paper, could not get the authorities of his time to implement his proposals, as the City has since found to its cost.

**(November 26)**

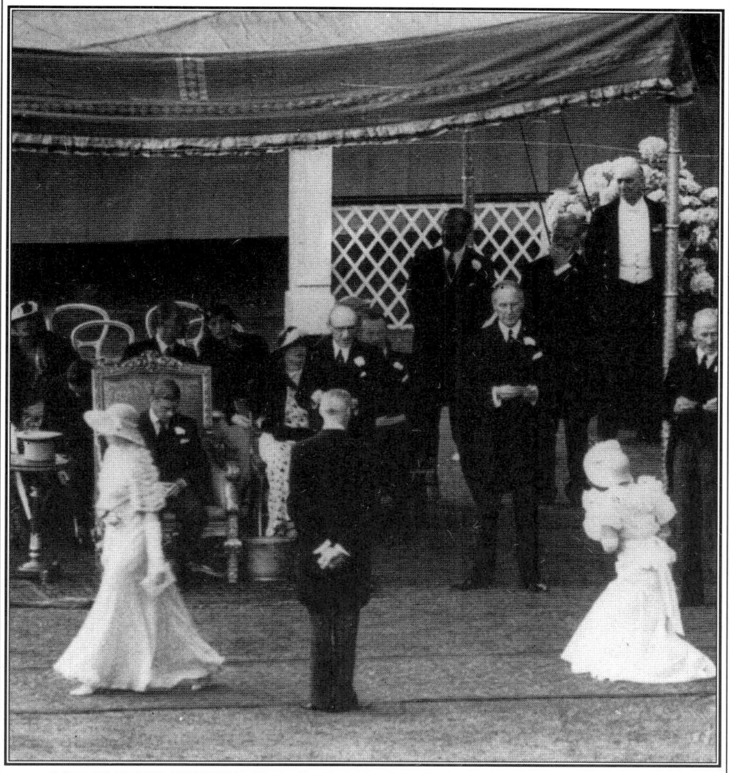

LADIES BEING PRESENTED to the Prince of Wales at Buckingham Palace to-day.

# SMOKING ACCESSORIES ENTER INTO THE ENSEMBLE

## CIGARETTE CASES AND HOLDERS MATCH GOWNS

**By Elizabeth Richmond**

THE importance of possessing small smoking accessories that harmonise with the rest of the toilette is emphasised this season in a particularly attractive manner.

When women buy new afternoon and evening frocks they give the order, too, for the cigarette case and holder that will match each gown. Withing 48 hours these can be supplied, an unusual finish to the ensemble, and as they are reasonable in price a woman can obtain a new set to tone with each new gown.

Material can be sent direct from the dressmakers or taken by the individual purchase to the tobacco firm specialising in this branch of work. The cases can be obtained to hold 10 or 15 cigarettes. The holders are finished with silver rims, so that they will not lose colour or be harmed by the smoke.

Some of these cases show an attractive contrast. They are in dark blue brocade and silver tissue, in rich coloured velvets and in delicate flowery crépe de Clune patterns. So comprehensive, indeed, is the range of materials and colours from which they have been made that the accessories themselves might inspire a woman in the choice of her new frocks.

The only materials which cannot be used are those which have a heavy, thick surface. Cigarette cases to harmonise with tweeds and morning frocks are, therefore, not to be seen at present. For those who wish to have a smoking accessory of some kind that will be a complement to their tweeds, there are appropriate lighters made from coloured leathers which can be selected to blend.

NOW that smoking has become such a regular habit among women, there is a tendency to carry massive cigarette cases that will hold an ample supply of cigarettes rather than the old-fashioned affair which contained a mere handful.

One new case has the merit of opening at any of its sides, and accommodates many layers; another has a small watch fitted outside. A cigarette case which has found great favour recently with American women who have been visiting England is of silver, with a map of Great Britain lacquered in blue on its surface. This blue map is dotted with red lines for the purchaser, so that when she has returned home she can show her friends, where she has been touring every time she produces her cigarette case.

CIGARETTES themselves are packed in many interesting and unusual ways. Containers can resemble small hat-boxes, boxes of powder or chocolates. There is the box which is like a bouquet of flowers, in which variegated coloured cigarettes are arranged.

Each hour of the day demands a special type of cigarette. For the cocktail party there are cigarettes with colourful, cheerful glasses stamped on them, and at bridge-time cigarettes used while play is in progress take their symbols from those on the cards.

**(November 2)**

# NO "HOSTESSES" IN BRITISH AIR LINERS

British air line operators have no intention of following the American and Continental system of employing "air hostesses" on their machines.

It has been found that the work required can be done as usefully by experienced male stewards.

"In all our air liners we employ two men to look after the needs of the passengers," said a representative of Imperial Airways yesterday. "They are fully-qualified stewards, with long experience in ships or trains.

"Sometimes we are asked why we do not have women stewards – or air hostesses, as the Americans call them – and the example of ships is quoted. Really, the situation is not the same.

"A ship may be at sea for weeks, and a woman needing feminine help in an emergency would be in a serious plight if no women stewards were employed.

"In an air liner, even on the long-distance Continental routes, the machine is never in the air for more than about three hours at a stretch, and on landing at the official stopping places women officials are available."

An official at Croydon aerodrome told me that the only lines employing "air hostesses" were the Dutch, Swiss and American.

It has been announced that the Royal Dutch Air Line has decided to augment its staff of "air hostesses." This is contrary to the growing practice in America, where women are gradually being displaced by male stewards.

**(December 24)**

# COLOUR AGAIN IN THE SHOPS

Colour is gradually returning to the West End dress shops.

Many people, both men and women, have chosen to follow the Court in continuing to observe mourning. Others still wear dark shades, such as navy blue and dark grey. But there is a growing tendency towards more colourful dress.

"There will be no sudden jump from black to brilliant colours," a leading dress designer said yesterday. "The first change from mourning has been a vogue for black-and-white and navy-and-white schemes.

"Now women are beginning to wear pastel shades and the more subdued colours.

"As summer approaches, soft blues, greens and beiges will become more and more popular, and brighter colours will probably begin to make their appearance."

QUEEN MARY'S FAVOURITE

Here are the colours that predominate among the spring models now being shown by one famous London fashion house:

| | |
|---|---|
| Lilac | Lily-of-the-Valley green |
| Violet | Delphinium blue |
| Heliotrope | Jewel blue |
| Petunia | A pink shade of buff |

Of these jewel blue is likely to be one of the most popular. It is Queen Mary's favourite colour.

Men's fashions, always tending to dark colours, are a less reliable index of change. It is noticeable, however, that many tailors now choose brown for their window displays.

**(March 3)**

# SCHOOLMASTERS URGE MANLY TRAINING FOR BOYS

## ALLEGED DELETERIOUS EFFECTS OF WOMEN'S TEACHING

The National Association of Schoolmasters' Conference at Sheffield yesterday unanimously demanded that all boys above infant school age should be taught by men teachers.

"The teaching of a boy is a man's job," declared Mr. F.A.Gibbs (London), moving a resolution demanding.

That in all boys' schools men teachers only should be appointed, and

That all mixed schools other than infants should be under a headmaster, with as many male assistants as would ensure that the boys came under the predominating influence of men.

Mr. K.B. Kaye (East Grinstead) said that, as a collier's son, he had gone through the elementary school and seen the process carried out by "Miss Teacher" of nipping out the shoots of young manhood among the boys.

This mental handling of boys in the crucial years of their lives by women had been one of the most pernicious things in elementary education. It had largely resulted in loss of stamina and calibre in boys.

Boys who had been under the control of women teachers were not so able to stand on their own feet, or to use a Yorkshire phrase, to be like a tub standing on its own bottom.

Was it right, he asked, that the education of boys should be left primarily to teachers who were "condemned to be maids – young maids, middling maids, or old maids"?

"THE MAN OF NINE"

One result of this was that boys were encouraged to think only of a collar and tie job and never of such a manly occupation as going down a pit and being a collier. They were encouraged to aim only at clean work and become, say, a clerk or a school teacher.

Mr. A.H. Russell (Bristol) said that the reactions of a little man of nine were vital to his whole life. He wanted at that age to get away from women's control.

If the State refused the demand of the boy's soul for the control of a man the State was definitely injuring the development of the boy.

"In schools where the headmistress inflicts corporal punishment on little boys of nine, ten, and eleven." said Mr. Russell, "they all go out laughing at the punishment they receive because not a single one of them dare acknowledge that a woman could hurt a man of nine. If he acknowledged that a woman could hurt him he would have lost dignity and the recognition of his own importance.

**(August 7)**

# WEEK-END FOOD PRICE GUIDE

Despite the Bank Holiday interlude housewives will find that prices this week have changed little. Had the weather been warmer there might have been a drop in the price of meat, but appetites have remained good, and in particular the small joints of the new season's New Zealand lamb have been in great demand.

Salmon and other game fish, as the season draws to close, are dearer. Chicken and other poultry remain at a rather high prices.

Approximate prices of good quality food include the following:

| | | | | | |
|---|---|---|---|---|---|
| Scotch beef: | | | Ducklings ......lb | 1/- | 1/2 |
| Sirloin....lb | 1/6 | 1/8 | Goslings | 1/2 | 1/4 |
| Topside | 1/4 | 1/8 | Ptarmigan | 1/2 | 1/4 |
| Top rump | 1/3 | 1/4 | Partridge......ea | 1/6 | 2/- |
| Silverside | 1/2 | 1/3 | Quail .........each | 2/9 | 3/- |
| Brisket | /8 | /11 | | | |
| Home lamb | | | Plums ..........lb | /6 | /8 |
| Legs | 1/6 | 1/7 | Black currants | /8 | /10 |
| Shoulders | 1/2 | 1/3 | Gooseberries | /3 | /5 |
| Loins | 1/8 | 1/9 | Eng. grapes | 1/9 | 6/- |
| Salmon ..lb | 2/8 | 3/2 | Bananas | 1/- | 2/- |
| Lobsters | 2/6 | 3/- | Beans ..........lb | /3 | /5 |
| Plaice | 1/- | 1/6 | Broad Beans | /3 | /4 |

**(August 7)**

# GERMANY'S £70 VOLKSWAGEN

**By A.G. Throssell**
**Daily Telegraph Motoring Correspondent**

For the motorist there is no country more interesting to-day than Germany, where, whatever the triumphs or failures of the Hitler Government in general, both the motor-maker and the motor-user are decidedly better off for it.

Just how ambitious is the Nazi motoring programme, now partly achieved, I had explained to me at length during my visit to the Berlin show by no less a person than the head of the Mercedes-Benz concern, much the largest and most powerful in the country.

There are now two million motor vehicles in use in Germany, and most of the cars are less than three years old, so that neither the trade nor the traffic is very much worried by old, out-of-date and unsafe machines. In 1933 the vehicle tax (it averaged £18 a year on an 18 h.p. car) was abolished entirely for all cars sold for the first time after April of that year. The result, of course, was a wholesale scrapping of old cars and soaring production. Last year Germany produced 180,000 cars, against 125,000 by France; in 1932 French production was five times Germany's.

The average German car is small. Eighty per cent. are under 1 $\frac{1}{2}$ litres, roughly 12-14 h.p., which is closely parallel to our own experience in spite of our much abused h.p. tax. With motor fuel at 2s per gallon, running costs are of first importance.

PRODUCTION-POOLING SCHEME

Now Herr Hitler will not be happy till Germany has four million car-owners. It is the volkswagen or popular car that is to create them. The volkswagen, as planned, must have a speed of 50 m.p.h., do 40 m.p.g., and be produced to sell at a price of about £70. The ideal is that everyone with an income of 3,000 marks a year (say, £200) should be able to own one.

All the manufactures are expected to combine for the joint production of this ideal cheap car, and in the strange new Germany this pooling scheme, impossible of attainment in France, where also they have been thinking of a "popular" car, and equally out of the question here, seems likely to be achieved.

**(February 20)**

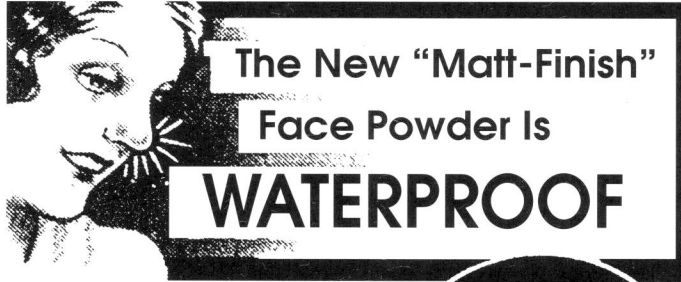

# GEORGE THE FIFTH: A TRUE LEADER OF THE NATION

## GREAT RECORD OF DUTY WELL DONE

**By Herbert Sidebotham**

King George is dead. The blow stuns with the suddenness of its fall for four days ago the King was about and apparently well. Yet it was not wholly unexpected, for his health was not robust and at seventy, after such an illness as not long ago carried him to the gates of death, life hangs by a thin-spun thread that is soon slit.

But the death of kings always finds us unprepared. If the suddenness of the shock makes it harder to realise what we have lost, it has the consolation that this is probably the death that a king tried so terribly by sickness as he has been would have chosen for himself. One's heart goes out in sympathy to Queen Mary who has been so good a wife and so devoted a nurse.

The King whom we mourn to-day was beloved of his people in a way that no king ever was before him. There have been monarchs with a stronger and more vivid personality, or with a wider range of intellectual gifts or a finer record of positive achievement and even, perhaps, more expressive of their people and their times.

When they learnt of Queen Victoria's death men burst into tears in the street not because they had any real idea of what the great lady was like, but because they felt as though something within them had snapped. So long had she reigned that they could hardly think of themselves as anything but strangers in a world without her.

HIS PEOPLE'S LOVE

The love that his subjects bore to King George was something quite different and more personal to himself. Partly, perhaps, it was because his broadcasting had made his rich voice and his beautiful enunciation familiar to millions. Partly, too, it was because he had accustomed us to think of all the Britons as one great family of which he was the head. And partly it may have been because he was not known to have peculiarities or eccentricities or even remarkable gifts that divided him from the rest of us, but was a King who might have been the head of any good British family. Certainly it is as revered relative and head of the family that millions are now mourning him.

Yet it would be easy to underestimate the element of greatness that was in him. It may not have been intellectual greatness, but it was certainly moral. No King has ever lived through times that were so testing of his quality. Only an intrinsic nobility of character and fine balance of mind could have carried him through without the suspicion of a slip.

He came to the Throne at a time when party strife was at its bitterest and both sides were striving for the possession of the King and his prerogative. King Edward died in May, 1910, five months after the Government of the day had announced that if the Parliament Bill were rejected by the Lords the Government would advise him to create a sufficient number of new peers to secure its passage.

King George had to decide one of the most difficult issues that have ever confronted a constitutional monarch. Not since the seventeenth century was the King's name brought into the turmoil of party politics so often as during the first year of his reign.

He must have surprised many by the promptness of his action. Queen Victoria would probably have remained at a distance and written letters. King Edward had given no indication of how he would solve the trouble. But the new King promptly suggested a Conference between the leaders on both sides, and came from Windsor to London so as to be in close touch.

His difficulties did not end there but continued till after his Coronation, more than a year later. A single slip, and the prestige of the Crown that had been rising since the declining years of Victoria might have suffered a check from which it would never have recovered. The King made no slip, and at the end of the first eighteen months of his reign he was revealed as a close student of Parliamentary politics and a master of the art of constitutional monarchy.

A CONCILIATOR

Nor was there ever any suspicion of timidity or pedantry in his interpretation of his duties as a constitutional monarch. Although the latter part of his reign has been much less stormy than its first half, there has never been a period in which there have been so many sweeping changes, and in many of them the King had the gift of combining with perfect constitutional propriety. Always his authority has been thrown on the side of compromise and moderate courses.

Whatever his personal views might be, he never allowed them to influence his strict impartiality in politics; indeed, he went out of his way to show the same personal friendliness to representatives of the Socialist Party as to those of any other party. At the same time his influence has been consistently exerted on the side of compromise and accommodation when the bitterness of party struggles threatened danger to the general well-being.

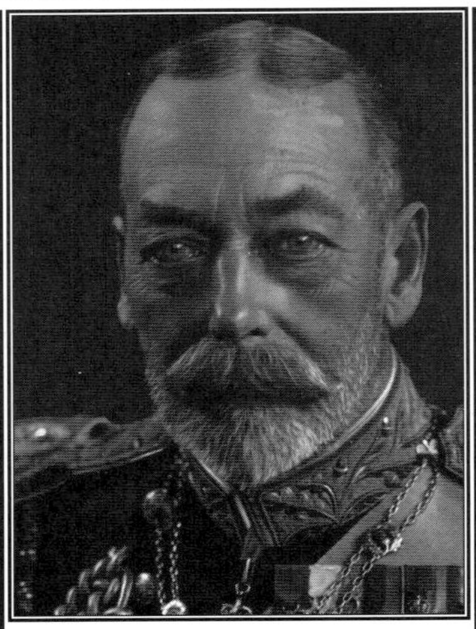

King George V

In 1931, because he believed there was national danger, he is known to have favoured a National Government in preference to a merely Conservative and party Government, which was the alternative. How far the King's mastery of the practice of constitutional monarchy – a mastery more complete than that of any of his predecessors has been – has helped to save our politics from the violent extremes to which the politics of other countries have run since the War it will be for history to decide.

But there have been times of great danger at which a single mistake by the Crown might have had grave consequences, and the influence of the King on the peaceful progress of our politics may have been greater than is generally realised. Certainly, his whole record in home politics refutes the idea which is common abroad that a king who is a constitutional monarch is only privileged to do no wrong by completely effacing himself as an influence for good in politics. King George has proved that there is far more truth in the contrary proposition: that the better a king understands constitutional practice the greater and more beneficial his influence in politics is likely to be.

THE SAILOR KING

King George was bred to the sea, and up to his twenty-seventh year was in the active service of the Navy. He never forgot the lessons that he learnt there: perhaps we are to find one secret of his success in the great political difficulties of his reign in the sailor's habit of not worrying about theories or forms but always asking what will work best and most smoothly.

To the end he retained his keen interest in the Navy; none was so quick at spotting a heresy in what he read about the Service or in letting it be known where the mistake was. Throughout the war he was a frequent visitor at the Admiralty which had no secrets from him. Yet it was characteristic of the King that he set himself to study the work of the Army in order that he might do equal justice to both Services. The war presents to the mind no picture so intimate and so endearing as that of him kneeling on the floor with Robertson or Maurice studying large-scale maps and moving pins backward and forward as the battlefront swayed and bent.

The trials of a war that toppled over most of the thrones of Europe confirmed King George as the symbol of his country's will and constancy. And that peace found the British monarch enthroned more firmly than ever in the people's love was due to the example of his character and to his gift of expressing a human sympathy in language of simple eloquence and dignity.

Some of his addresses to his people – that, for example, on his recovery from his illness in 1928, or his Christmas Day allocutions, notably that of 1933 – deserve to take rank with one or two of Elizabeth's speeches among the classics of our history. He had none of Elizabeth's subtlety or intellectuality, and certainly none of her passion for intrigue, but we should have to go back to Elizabeth for a monarch so completely and typically English as King George V.

The King was not a masterful personality, and though he had constancy and on many subjects strong views of his own, few would claim for him commanding scope or originality of mind. But he might have had these qualities and still have been far less successful as a King. His distinguishing intellectual gifts were patience, the power of detaching himself from theory and judging an old institution or a proposed change by the sole test of whether it had worked or would work smoothly, and sufficient imagination – all important in a constitutional monarch – to put himself at another point of view than his own.

A BROAD HUMANITY

For the rest, the qualities that made the King's success were moral qualities – a kindly and amiable nature and the graciousness that springs from it; a broad humanity; a complete sincerity and truthfulness which, when touched with emotion and warmed in the rich colours of his beautiful voice, had an abiding effect on the heart even more than on the mind of those who heard.

He always worked hard, but was said to read more for information or out of a sense of duty than from any aesthetic pleasure in literature. He is not known to have had any marked artistic tastes. His pleasures were always simple. The sea and shooting probably provided those that he liked best of all; in later life he became very fond of race meetings. Outside the range of his royal duties he was the typical English country gentleman, and if his reactions on many subjects were those of the plain man, it pleased him to be typical of his people rather than to be exceptional amongst them.

There are two tests of a successful king. One is to be beloved by his people, and of that King George received an assurance such as falls to the lot of few reigning monarchs. In November, 1928, he caught a chill at the Armistice Day ceremony which became a dangerous pleurisy that grew to its worst at Christmas time. Not until February was he able to leave the Palace for the South Coast.

"As month after month went by," he said in April in a message to the Empire, "I heard of the widespread and loving solicitude with which the Queen and I were surrounded. I was able to picture to myself the crowds of friends waiting and watching at my gates, and to think of the still greater number of those who, in every part of the Empire, were remembering me with prayers and good wishes. The realisation of this has been among the most vivid experiences of my life. It was an encouragement beyond description to find that my constant and earnest desire had been granted – the desire to gain the confidence of my people."

LEADERSHIP

The power to inspire so much affection among so many millions is a form of greatness and, in a monarch, the most desirable of all forms.

The other test of a King is leadership and, if the word be understood aright, King George, by reason of the terrible and anxious times in which the first part of his reign was cast, was a leader in a sense in which neither his father was nor even Queen Victoria herself – symbol as she was of the greatness that was ours in the nineteenth century.

"Leadership" Lord Tweedsmuir has written "does not consist only in a strong man imposing his will on a nation. In that sense it has no meaning for a British Sovereign. But in a far profounder sense, the King has shown himself a leader, since the true task of leadership is not to put greatness into humanity, but to elicit it, since the greatness is already there. That truth is the basis of all religion, it is the only justification for democracy. It is the chart and compass of our mortal life. The King has led his people, for he has evoked what is best in them.

**(January 21)**

# JOHN GILBERT, THE "IDEAL LOVER"

It is strange and saddening to think of John Gilbert being no longer with us. He was so full of fire, of burning vitality, and passionate zest for life.

The memories of "fans" are notoriously short. Only six years ago Gilbert was the biggest star in the whole film world. In 1927 he topped a voting competition, and in 1929 he was again an easy winner.

Those were the days when Gilbert's dark eyes and white teeth flashed through sensational drama after drama. As the "ideal lover" he was adored by the great film public, and in Miss Garbo they saw his perfect foil – blonde, mysterious and serene, where he was dark, dashing, and almost extravagantly exuberant.

Gilbert, as a great star, died when talk came in. His voice was high-pitched, and recorded badly. His salary of £30,000 a year went on for years after he had fallen, whether he worked or not; and eventually he remedied his diction sufficiently to attempt a come-back.

**(January 18)**

# EARL BEATTY AN ADMIRAL WITH NELSON TOUCH

**By Hector C. Bywater**

Admiral of the Fleet Earl Beatty, who died yesterday at the age of 65, shared with the late Earl Jellicoe the heavy responsibility of directing our major naval operations in the Great War.

His dashing exploits when in command of the Battle Cruiser Fleet for the first two years of the war brought his name prominently before the public, and were no doubt responsible for the popular conception of him as a sailor who was more of a fighter than a strategist.

His reputation has, in fact, suffered at the hands of admirers whose enthusiasm outruns their discretion. They have pictured their hero as always rushing, more or less blindly, towards "the sound of the guns." No portrait could be less faithful or more unjust.

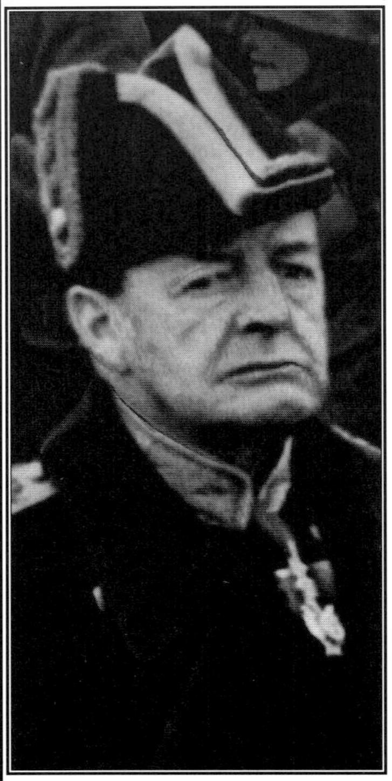

Earl Beatty

Beatty's actions were invariably controlled by a cool judgement that rarely proved at fault. There was nothing reckless or haphazard about his tactics during the three great encounters in the North Sea – Heligoland Blight, Dogger Bank, and Jutland.

That he happened to be in the thick of the fighting on all three occasions was due no more to his temperament than to the character of the force he commanded. It was essentially the mission of the battle cruisers to skirmish ahead of the main body, for which purpose they were endowed with a higher speed than that of the ordinary battleship. Naturally, therefore, they were always the first to make contact with enemy forces when the latter put to sea.

COOLNESS IN ACTION

There is abundant evidence that Beatty was never so tranquil, never so completely master of his faculties as in the turmoil of battle, when his own guns were thundering and enemy shells were exploding about the unprotected bridge of his flagship, from which exposed station he always commanded in action.

David Beatty was the son of Capt. D.L. Beatty, of Borodale, county Wexford, and entered the Navy as a cadet in 1884. His first active service was with the Nile gunboats in Kitchener's Sudan campaign of 1898, in which he gained the D.S.O. and promotion to commander.

Two years later he was distinguishing himself in China during the Boxer Rebellion. He was twice wounded when leading a most gallant attack on the Chinese guns at Tientain, and his conduct on this occasion brought him special promotion to the rank of captain in November, 1900. He was then the youngest post captain in the Royal Navy.

Advanced to flag rank in 1910, he hazarded his career by declining an appointment which, apparently, he did not think good enough, and was placed on half-pay. But Mr. Winston Churchill, newly-appointed First Lord, had his eye on this youthful and independent flag-officer, whom he promptly appointed his Naval Secretary.

On the outbreak of war Beatty was made an acting vice-admiral. In the Heligoland Bight action of Aug. 28, 1914, he had been ordered by Jellicoe to stand by to support, if necessary, the light forces detailed to carry out the raid. In due course he received an S.O.S. from Commodore Tyrwhitt, who was hard pressed by a concentration of German cruisers.

It was now that Beatty exhibited those qualities of cool judgment and rapid decision which are overlooked by his most fervent admirers. He revolved in his mind all the risks contingent on taking his valuable ships into waters which might be mined, and would certainly be alive with submarines, and in less than a minute had decided to accept them.

His decision transformed the Heligoland action from an indecisive skirmish into a resounding victory.

At the Battle of Jutland the brunt of the fighting fell on the Battle Cruiser Force. When Beatty first sighted his German "opposite numbers" from the Lion his total force consisted of six battle cruisers and four fast and powerful battleships of the Queen Elizabeth class (Fifth Battle Squadron).

He led into action at once, but for reasons too complicated and too controversial to be detailed here he was not at first supported by the Fifth Battle Squadron. On both sides the standard of gunnery was excellent, but our battle cruisers were defective in protection.

In a short time the Indefatigable and the Queen Mary had been destroyed by magazine explosions, and other ships, including the Lion, were damaged, but the enemy also had suffered. On learning that the whole German battle fleet had been sighted steering north, Beatty turned his force 16 points with the intention of leading Adm. Scheer into the jaws of the British Battle Fleet which Jellicoe was now bringing south at full speed.

Of the action that developed between the two main bodies little need be said here. Mutual errors in plotting their respective positions – natural enough in the case of Beatty's flagship, which had passed through a terrific ordeal by fire – handicapped the conjunction of the Battle Cruiser Force with the Grand Fleet, and inevitably delayed Jellicoe's deployment.

As we know, however, the latter was so well judged that the German fleet found itself ringed with fire and narrowly escaped destruction. Long after dusk had fallen on the troubled waters of the North Sea Beatty was still seeking the elusive enemy, and it was from his battered ships that the last heavy salvos were fired, as the first had been, in the greatest naval engagement of which history has to tell.

Towards the end of 1916 Beatty was appointed commander-in-chief, Grand Fleet, in succession to Jellicoe, who was recalled to the Admiralty as First Sea Lord. This change in command raised the hopes of those zealous but ill-informed partisans who still imagined Beatty to be a bull-headed fighter who rushed into battle blindfold.

To their disappointment the strategy of the Grand Fleet was in no way modified.

WISE CAUTION

Beatty, in short, observed the same wise caution that his predecessor had practised, and for precisely the like reason – that disaster to the Grand Fleet would have been immediately fatal to the Allied cause.

Both at the Dogger Bank and Jutland Beatty was condemned to fight with ships which were deficient in protection. Had the armour defence of his flagship, the Lion, been adequate there is little doubt that in the Dogger Bank fight he would have accounted for the greater part of the German battle cruiser squadron. As it was the Lion was disabled at the most critical phase of the action, and a misreading of Beatty's signals by his second-in-command resulted in the escape of the enemy.

At Jutland two of his battle cruisers, Indefatigable and Queen Mary, blew up in succession, yet he maintained an unruffled front and made no change in his dispositions. When, a little later, it was erroneously reported to him that a third ship, the Princess Royal, had gone the same way, he turned to his flag-captain (now Admiral of the Fleet Sir E. Chatfield) with the remark: "There's something wrong with our damned ships to-day, Chatfield!" and calmly ordered a change of helm which brought him still closer to the enemy.

JUTLAND CONTROVERSY
BEATTY'S BELIEF

In the controversy on Jutland which developed after the war Beatty was not entirely impartial. He never made any secret of his conviction that a more resolute handling of the battle fleet by Jellicoe would have brought about a great victory, and he inspired the publication of the official "Narrative of Jutland" in which, more by implication than direct statement, Jellicoe's tactics were censured.

Beatty's personal charm, unlike that of Jellicoe, was felt only by his immediate entourage. Yet his fiery courage, his indomitable will to win, was no less a national asset than Jellicoe's unsought-for popularity with the men of the Fleet.

A sidelight is thrown on Beatty's independence of mind by his refusal to conform to the regulations governing naval officers uniform. These prescribe four buttons on each side of the tunic, but Beatty wore only three.

**(March 11)**

# PHILOSOPHER OF LAUGHTER

## G.K. CHESTERTON'S GREAT VERSATILITY

Mr. Gilbert Keith Chesterton had many distinctions. None was greater than that he was known to the whole world as "G.K.C." He shared that unusual honour in regard to initials with George Bernard Shaw and Robert Louis Stevenson.

The versatility of Mr. Chesterton was astonishing, and few men have ever made so deep a personal mark on the literature of their time as he did. As if laughing philosopher and intellectual gymnast, whose overwhelming style was nevertheless employed with a passionate concern for the deepest things of life, he stood alone.

Mr. Bernard Shaw – from whom Chesterton differed on almost every matter that interested them both – has something of the same readiness to lay down the law on any and every question that may arise, and to do so in an unconventional and provocative way. But Shaw is without the imaginative rhetoric and the poetry that coloured Chesterton's writing, as he is without that all-embracing humanity, that profound sympathy with ordinary human tastes and pleasures that was an essential part of Chesterton.

Chesterton's range was of the broadest. In his lyrical poetry there is much that will certainly live. In political squibs and other verse of the lightest he was inexhaustible. He wrote plays that were full of matter. His novels and stories have been read all over the world. He made some notable excursions into biography and history. He was an admirable speaker.

Though his home for the last twenty years of his life was in Buckinghamshire, Chesterton was a Londoner by birth and allegiance, as so much of his best work in prose and verse proclaims. He was born at Campden Hill, the son of Mr. Edward Chesterton.

At St. Paul's School Chesterton's one scholastic success was the winning of the Milton poetry prize, the subject set being "St. Francis Xavier." He was the only Pauline ever to be officially designated as "ranking with the Eighth" without having been promoted to that form.

ARTIST AND CRITIC

Afterwards, for a short time, he improved at the Slade School that strikingly original talent for decorative and grotesque drawing that never left him but he was soon invited to try his hand at criticism of art and literature in the pages of the "Bookman" and the "Speaker." The vivid originality of his work quickly attracted attention. By the time the new century opened he had achieved, without a trace of ambition on his part, a place of his own among the rising generation of penmen, and from that time he made continual progress.

It was now, in 1901, that he married Miss Frances Blogg, herself a poet and in all ways a kindred spirit; and their mutual devotion realised thereafter one of the most firmly held of his ideals.

Before his name was known to all he had published his earliest book, a little volume of fantastic verses and sketches called "Greybeards at Play," now ranked as a classic of English nonsense.

This was in 1904, and the same year saw him break new ground in "The Napoleon of Notting Hill," his first novel, a story of the future, in which the sanctities of local patriotism were opposed to the rather overblown Imperialism of that day.

THE "FATHER BROWN" STORIES

In 1911, "The Innocence of Father Brown" opened the long series of short tales which carried their author's reputation to new heights by attaching the vast detective-story loving public to the body of his admirers. Chesterton's own passion for that kind of story was one of those innumerable links with everyday humanity that made him what he was.

He wrote books on Chaucer, Stevenson, Cobbett, St. Francis of Assisi, St. Thomas Aquinas, Bernard Shaw; and he wrote them, as he wrote everything; because he had things to say to a world that, in his conviction, had strayed from the right path – the path of firm and fixed belief, of the clear vision of right and wrong, of attachment to the fundamental sanities of existence.

**(June 15)**

# CREATOR OF FAMOUS STARS

The entire Hollywood film colony, from stars to office boys, expressed deep regret today at the sudden death yesterday, at the age of 36, of Mr. Irving Thalberg, the husband of Miss Norma Shearer, and "the boy genius of the film world." He rose from a £3 a week post as typist to be one of the six biggest men in the industry, earning £100,000 a year.

In his ten years in control of M.G.M., productions he created an era of magnificence in pictures which it will be difficult to maintain. He had a remarkable flair for visualising the finished film from a manuscript, and made a series of highly successful pictures.

**(September 16)**

# KIPLING, IMPERIAL POET THE WORLD ACCLAIMED

## MASTER INTERPRETER OF MEN OF THE SEVEN SEAS

**By H.C. Bailey**

At the faith that success is greatness no writer has scoffed with such fierce, persistent derision as Rudyard Kipling. Very few writers in all the world's history have won success so prolonged and abundant as his.

The brilliant precocity of genius which dazzled readers of English in the eighties developed a depth and a versatility of power beyond any estimated of its promise. Not only his own people but the whole world acclaimed him a master, an original force in literature.

Yet when he reviewed his career at 60 he said that he had been "extravagantly rewarded for having done what he could not help doing," and, in a sardonic glance at the possibility that it will endure, remarked that "quite a dozen authors had achieved immortality in the last 2,500 years."

Intensely individual, he conceded nothing to the changing fashions of literature and thought through 50 extraordinarily mutable years. He fascinated generation after generation, and with work immensely different.

Nobody ever wrote verse of more catchy, haunting jingle. With that from the first were mingled solemn drum-beating rhythms. As the years went by, there came a masterly elaboration of music charged with thought in organ melodies of sorrow and the majesty of life in deed and thought.

THE SOLDIER'S POET
INSPIRING HEROISM

No one has a better right to be the soldiers' poet. But his theme was not so much the splendour as the heroism and the endurance which war demands.

Its "iron sacrifice of body, will and soul" was always in his mind and its purpose, the reign of law. "By the peace among you peoples shall men know you serve the Lord."

He wrote as the prophet of Empire and his work was one of the great forces in arousing that new consciousness of the unity of the British dominions all over the world which has grown to strength in the last half-century.

Rudyard Kipling was born in Bombay – and he kept a memory of it as queen of cities – on the last day but one of 1865. By heredity he had a right to ability and character of distinction. His father, John Lockwood Kipling, whom he sketched, with affection that makes the portrait vivid, as the curator of the Lahore Museum, which Kim and the Lama visit, held that post for many years and was an artist of more than common skill.

According to the doom of English children born in India, Rudyard was sent home as a small boy. It may be safely conjectured that he knew from experience something of the miseries in such a separation, which he put into a poignant story. He was sent to school at the United Services College, Westward Ho! Contemporaries have declared that the description of this seminary in "Stalky and Co.," however horrifying to orthodox public school boys, is reasonably accurate.

MIRACLE OF GENIUS
KNOWLEDGE GAINED ON FIRST NEWSPAPER

Kipling was only 17 when he went back to India and became sub-editor of the Lahore "Civil and Military Gazette." It was a laborious job, and his absolute lack of experience must have made it harder.

For all his genius, for all the help which parents of ability and familiarity with India could give him, it is amazing that within a few years he contrived to obtain the consummate knowledge of Indian life on which his fame was founded.

He had only been sub-editing the Lahore paper for some years, he was not yet 21, when he published his first book, the volume of verse called "Departmental Ditties." Next year came prose, "Plain Tales from the Hills," and then in quick succession, "Soldiers Three," "The Story of the Gadsbys," "In Black and White," "Under the Deodars," "The Phantom Rickshaw," and "Wee Willie Winkie." "The Story of the Gadsbys" was actually written before he was 19.

He was not content to reveal India to the west, he travelled the world in search of facts and men, a determined Odysseus. It is a safe generalisation that no author has ever set himself to such a roaming of land and sea to find material for his art.

In one story told in the first person he said that he travelled thousands of miles to find a man who could tell him what the sea looked like as it came over the bulwarks of a sinking ship. What is put into fiction is not necessarily evidence, but this has the stamp of probability.

When "Barrack Room Ballads" appeared in 1892 even the scoffers recognised that he was a poet. The year before, he had attempted a full-length novel, and chose for his subject, perhaps to show that he would not be limited to India, or the exotic, the Bohemia of London journalism and art. His admirers cannot rank "The Light that Failed" high among his work, and, though there is grim realism in it which has power, he observed a significant reluctance to repeat the experiment.

About the same stage in his career he attempted collaboration, for the first and, apart from small things, the last time. With the American author, Wolcott Balestier, whose sister, Miss Caroline Starr Balestier, he married, he made a contrast of life in Western America and in a native Indian State. This book, "The Naulahka," has a clever vivacity, but more praise can hardly be given.

Versatility was developed as the years went by. Many a poet, since Homer brought their surge and thunder into the roll of his hexameter had sung. "The Seven Seas." Mr. Kipling found new rhythms for the zest of seamen and the prowess of ships and the might of wave and wind, and fashioned a tiny epic out of the live deep-sea fishermen in "Captains Courageous."

TRIUMPH OF "KIM"
INDIA'S EMOTIONS

Through all, his command of detail and the infinite care of his realism made his work brilliantly vivid. "For to admire and for to see, for to be old the world so wide," as he made his tramp declare, was a maxim of his own career, and he found "nought common on the earth." He could still return to his inexhaustible memories of India for some of his stories in "The Day's Work," and they provided him after many years with another masterpiece, his one completely successful long novel "Kim." Kipling's mind began to work forward into the future and back into the past. Meanwhile he made himself the poet of the nation and the Empire when he put into the volume of poems called "The Five Nations" the great and consummate "Recessional."

But the past had become as important to him as present or future. He played with queer vivid fancies of the life of primitive man in "Just So Stories." He devised a delightful reconstruction of the making of England in "Puck of Pook's Hill" and "Rewards and Fairies."

Through many a page may be read how much he lost when his only son was killed in Flanders. He wrote his "History of the Irish Guards in the War" as a labour of love for the regiment in which his dead son had served.

But his genius did not seek rest, and some of its latest fruits were of a subtle excellence. "In Debts and Credits," which came to us in 1926, and still more clearly in "Limits and Renewals," his last collection of stories to be published in 1932 came a maturity of thought, a sensitive delicacy of feeling for the secrets of emotion which passed into a strange power of suggestion. This minute knowledge of out-of-the-way things was as amazing as ever.

"DAILY TELEGRAPH" WRITINGS

Much of Mr. Kipling's work of later years, both prose and verse, appeared first in THE DAILY TELEGRAPH. In 1914 he contributed to a series of articles on "The New Armies in Training," and later a series on Italy's "War in the Mountains." In 1933 appeared also eight articles on his recollections of France.

Among the many honours conferred on him was his election as Lord Rector of St. Andrews University. In 1907 he was awarded the Nobel Prize for Literature, and in 1925 – a strangely belated recognition – the gold medal of the Royal Society of Literature. But he cared no more for such distinctions than for public applause, and when the highest of them all, the Order of Merit, was offered him he asked leave to decline the honour.

**(January 18)**

# DAME CLARA BUTT DEAD

Dame Clara Butt, whose death we announce with regret, was one of the most splendidly gifted singers England has ever produced.

It is sad that the closing years of a life which for so long was filled with private happiness and public triumphs should have been darkened by a long illness and that the last impressions Dame Clara's faithful public should retain are of a stricken woman.

To dwell overmuch on the years of decline would, however, be disproportionate. Clara Butt's life was over the greater part of its course one of triumph upon triumph.

The prodigious voice issued from a person who was handsome in the most commanding and imposing way. The splendour of her singing and her exceptional appearance only half accounted, however, for the vast popularity she enjoyed.

People also divined a kindly, generous, simple nature in Clara Butt, and the domestic happiness ensuing upon her marriage with the accomplished baritone singer, Kennerley Rumford, further enhanced her claims upon the hearts of a public far larger than the circle of the critically musical.

The latter circle was disposed at one time to find the worship of Clara Butt excessive, for she did not disdain to sing music that was rather trivial, and the resulting criticism unfortunately caused a thorn in the bed of roses of her happiest days.

**(January 24)**

# FAMOUS PIONEER OF AVIATION

## M. LOUIS BLERIOT

**By Major C.C. Turner**

M. Louis Blériot, whose death has occurred at the age of 64 will go down in history as the airman who made the first flight across the English Channel.

In that achievement the speed of his machine was between 40 and 45 miles per hour. Some years ago he predicted that speeds of over 750 miles per hour would be attained in the air.

None of the great flights of history has made a profounder impression on the world than did that achievement on Sunday, July 25, 1909. The first cross-Atlantic flight, 20 years afterwards, by the Englishmen Alcock and Whitten Brown was less surprising, and was hardly more perilous than Blériot's inspired feat.

Blériot himself was suffering from a very painful foot, damaged by a fire in one of his aeroplanes. He was only able to hop along, and had to be assisted into his little monoplane.

He had already established himself as a pioneer of flight, and had suffered innumerable mishaps; but nothing daunted him, and long after he had achieved the fame and the success upon which he might well have rested he carried on the dangerous work which flying was in those early days.

Blériot started from Barraques, a village west of Calais. Hubert Latham, on his Antoinette monoplane, had made a first attempt on July 19, but engine-failure caused him to return, and he came down in the sea close to shore without sustaining any serious damage.

START IN THE WEST

The morning was misty when Blériot set out at 4.30. A French torpedo-boat was on the way, in case its services should be needed. Very few people saw the airman's start. He circled around once or twice, and then headed out to sea. He said afterwards:

"I had no apprehension. The moment is supreme, yet I surprised myself by feeling no exultation. Below me is the sea, the surface disturbed by a breeze. Within a few minutes I have passed the torpedo-boat, and I turn my head to see in what direction I should go. But I see neither coast, nor any boat. For 10 minutes I am lost, unguided, and without compass."

As he knew very well, a slight change of wind would suffice to take him off his course, and in misty weather he would not be aware of this. He would probably have been lost as was the late Cecil Grace a few months afterwards.

Blériot says he let the aeroplane take its own course. When he sighted the British coast near Deal he saw some British destroyers. He flew along the cliffs westwards looking for a suitable landing place, and there is no doubt that had he exhausted his fuel he might not even have been able to get over the cliffs to land.

However, he found a place at Northfall meadow, close to Dover Castle, and there only one person met him, a French journalist. A policeman strolled up later. A stone monument in the form of an aeroplane now marks the spot.

Blériot landed at 5.12. His flight had lasted about 42 minutes.

Owing to his successful flights a great demand for Blériot monoplanes came from all countries, and he established a factory, which became famous even before the war. During that great struggle it produced thousands of machines, notably the Blériot Spad Fighter. Machines were turned out at the rate of 13 a day at one period.

Blériot had the ambition to design a great transatlantic passenger flying machine, but was unable to develop the idea. Two or three years ago he was faced with the necessity of closing his factory owing to lack of support.

**(August 3)**

# MR. FRANK HORNBY

## MAN WHO INVENTED MECCANO TOY

Mr. Frank Hornby, who introduced Meccano to the world, died yesterday in his native city of Liverpool at the age of 73.

Few men can have gained lasting fame so magically. And the whole secret was the appeal that his inventiveness made to boys in every country.

He saw their difficulty. They wanted to build things out of metal, and he showed them how to dispense with machinery or precision tools by the use of his ingeniously constructed parts.

That was 36 years ago, but his beginnings were so modest that his "works" consisted of a small room and his staff was one girl.

Slowly he progressed with what he called "Mechanics made easy," but real success did not come until 1908, when he adopted instead the word "Meccano." After that he found it difficult to keep pace with the demands.

Mr. Hornby died after a serious operation, and he leaves a widow and two sons.

**(September 22)**

# LYRIC POET OF STOICISM

## PROF. A. E. HOUSMAN'S "SHROPSHIRE LAD"

In the whole history of English letters there can be few instances of a poet who has achieved world-wide recognition with so restricted an output as that of Professor A. E. Housman.

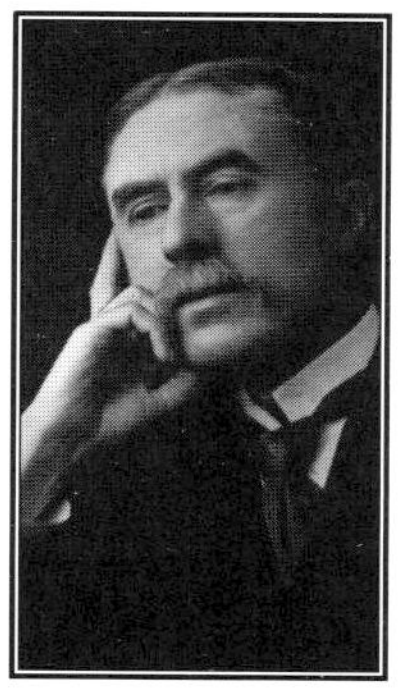
PROF. A.E.HOUSMAN

Two thin books contain the whole of his published verse — "The Shropshire Lad," published in 1896, and "Last Poems," published in 1922. There are in all 104 poems, most of them brief lyrics. Both books have achieved an enormous popularity, and Housman himself has exercised a strong influence, through them, not only on other poets, but on the day-to-day philosophy of the more cultured "man-in-the-street."

Housman's popularity owes nothing to any cheapness of standards. His philosophy was an austere stoicism in which only courage and comradeship remained as stand-bys in a world which

*"... has still*
*Much good, but much less good than ill."*

It is not, on the face of it, a popular doctrine. Its harshness, though, is mitigated in the exquisite, simple lyricism of Housman's style — a style which combines an intense feeling for the English countryside, with a fastidious, if narrow, perfection of metre and language, expressing the most subtle music in ordinary colloquial words.

TRANSCIENCE OF BEAUTY

"Last Poems" is actually a prolongation of the mood of "The Shropshire Lad," published 26 years earlier. Again, the "lads that shall die in their glory and never be old" face their disappointments with courage, and again the transcience of beauty haunts the verse. Perhaps the best known of the poems is the "Epitaph on an Army of Mercenaries," written in 1914.

Professor Housman declared in a preface that he felt it unlikely that he would be again "visited by those periods of continuous excitement" which made poetry possible.

Significantly, lecturing on "The name and nature of Poetry," at Cambridge in 1933, he described how, after drinking a pint of beer at luncheon, on occasions,

"There would flow into my mind, with sudden and unaccountable emotion, sometimes a line or two of verse, sometimes a whole stanza at once, accompanied, not preceded by a vague notion of the poem which they were destined to form part of ...Then there would usually be the lull of an hour or so, then perhaps the spring would bubble up again. I say bubble up, because, so far as I could make out, the source of the suggestions thus proffered to the brain was the pit of the stomach."

**(May 2)**

# NEGRO ATHLETE SMASHES MORE RECORDS

## LONG JUMP AND 200 METRES IN A DAY

**From Howard Marshall**

BERLIN, Tuesday.

This was another day of records in the Olympic Games. More world records have been beaten, subject to ratification, and six Olympic records have gone.

Without a doubt Jesse Owens, the American negro, is the outstanding personality of this Olympiad. Having already equalled the world record for the 100 metres with a time of 10.3 seconds, he to-day broke two more records.

His long jump of 26ft 61/4in beat the previous Olympic best by 1ft11/2in.

In two 200 metres heats, running well within himself, he beat the Olympic record of 21.2 sec by 1 sec.

Owens is extremely popular with his fellow-competitors, and his remarkable triumph has not in the least affected his modesty. Tall and perfectly built, he is one of the greatest athletes of history, and he may well break yet another world's record in the 200 metres final to-morrow.

Another outstanding personality is Miss Helen Stephens, the strapping 6ft American girl, who strode away with the women's 100 metres final in the record time of 11.5sec. She is a runner of remarkable power, and she won this race after hurling the discus prodigious distances for an hour previously.

QUEER CHARACTER

In one race we saw again the strange bearded Indian runner, who wears a little knot of blue ribbon tied on the top of his head and is content to trot along philosophically far behind the field. He did this in the 10,000 metres, a queer character indeed, tall, thin, melancholy and completely detached.

**(August 5)**

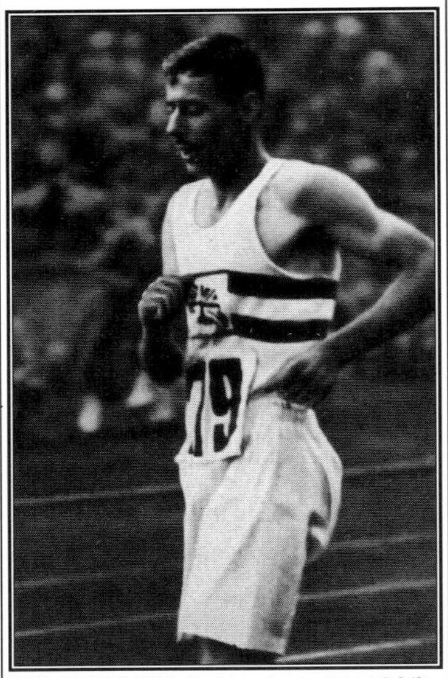

W.H. WHITLOCK (G.B.), winning the 50 kilometres walk at the Olympic Games yesterday. This was Britain's first athletic victory.

# LONDONER WINS IN RECORD TIME

Amid tremendous excitement Harold Whitlock, a 32-year-old London motor mechanic, scored Great Britain's first victory in the Olympic Games to-day. In a storm of rain and wind he emerged from the great Marathon gateway to win the 50 kilometres walk in the Olympic record time of 4hrs 30min 41sec.

Whitlock's fine performance was cheered by a huge crowd, and Herr Hitler and the Crown Prince of Italy sitting together in the seats of honour watched him break the tape.

Whitlock said afterwards: "It was the roughest going I have ever known. Part of the way was over cart tracks. But I feel fine and hope to compete in the next Olympiad."

**(August 6)**

# SHOULD BLACKS COMPETE IN OLYMPIC GAMES?

## THEIR GREAT PHYSICAL ADVANTAGE OVER WHITES

**By Bevil Rudd**

BERLIN, Tuesday.

The absence of any "incidents" in the athletic events during eight crowded days of international rivalry in the stadium here is a vindication of the Olympic ideal and a triumph of the sportsmanship, discipline and good sense of the athletes and of the predominating German crowd.

The vast and delicate organisation stood the strain without hitch or hiatus. The stage management was well nigh perfect and the actors were free to play their parts without worry or distraction.

The weather was not propitious and yet the majority of the records set up in 1932 under the ideal conditions of Los Angeles have been eclipsed in Berlin.

Man has not yet risen to the full height of his athletic ability; what that is we can only guess.

Perhaps in a decade or two we shall see man capable of running the 100 yards in under 9sec, the mile in under 4min, and capable of throwing a javelin 100 yards or high jumping 7 feet.

But the men who took the fantasy out of such figures are negroes or those of negroid extraction and we are forced to wonder whether the black man's physical make-up gives him a perpetual athletic advantage over the white man.

I have heard many theories advanced: the black has an elongated heel which gives him greater power of springing; he has longer arms, the correct use of which adds to his momentum; and a variety of other reasons have been given to explain his amazing ability.

Unfortunately the one female of the species — an American negress — fractured a small bone and was unable to compete.

But we are faced with the fact that barely one per cent. of the black races have athletic opportunities. If representatives of that one per cent. can win five Olympic events, what will happen when, say, 20 per cent. of the black population of the world adopt the white man's sport?

The Olympic Games may split into biological groupings; the White Olympiad in Europe or America, the Black in Africa, and the yellow in Asia.

For all their charming human attributes of keeness and sportsmanship, the black victors in this Olympiad were rightly or wrongly regarded as athletic abnormalities. These problems are for the future.

There are other considerations for the present, and if one day blacks do not compete against whites for reasons of muscular superiority I, personally, hope that, before then, women will be excluded for reasons of muscular inferiority.

To watch Jesse Owens run 100 metres in 10.3 sec and then to watch Helen Stephens run 100 metres in 11.5sec and to hear that both times are world's records is somewhat anomalous at an Olympiad.

I see no reason for admiring the developed masculinity of a woman even when it is accompanied by womanly grace.

Great Britain and the Empire were relatively successful with three wins, six seconds and four thirds. But we had several disappointments. Our sprinters lacked the necessary muscular preparation that continued competition gives, but in any case would have been no match for the American negroes.

J. V. Powell and S. C. Wooderson suffered one of those numbing gelatinous phases to which all runners are subject, and our quarter-milers just failed on the day by a small margin that a luckier draw for positions might easily have eliminated.

D. O. Finlay equalled the Olympic record in running second to the American hurdles genius, Forrest Towns.

Godfrey Brown was well inside 47secs when he was placed second in the 400 metres, and so was W. Roberts, not half a yard behind Brown, in fourth place, and E. Harper broke the Olympic record when he separated the two phenomenal Japs in the marathon and finished second.

Our two supreme moments last week were when J. E. Lovelock (who, though officially a New Zealander, is essentially one of us) raced off on the superb last lap of the 1,500 metres to shatter all opposition and a world's record, and when Godfrey Rampling restored our relay fortunes in the 1,600 metres by running with blended natural genius and high courage in perfect proportions.

Whether we should discipline ourselves more severely for Olympiads is a matter for later discussion; at least our opponents have not lost in sportsmanship what they gained in self knowledge by their patience and exacting preparation.

**(August 12)**

# HITLER CONSOLES GIRL

In the 400-metres women's relay race a German girl, Isle Doerffeldt dropped the baton at the final change-over, when Germany had a 10yds lead, and thus gave the victory to the United States team.

Later Fraulein Doerffeldt was presented to Herr Hitler. She was in tears, but he shook her by the hand and said: "Never mind. You did splendidly."

**(August 10)**

# ICE HOCKEY TRIUMPH OF BRITAIN

## SONIA HENJE KEEPS HE TITLE

**From Our Special Correspondent**

GARMISCH-PARTENKIRCHEN, Sunday.

For the first time in the history of the game Great Britain has won the Olympic ice hockey title, and with it the world and European championships.

Britain came near to winning another victory, for only a fall robbed Miss Cecilia Colledge, the 15-year-old English schoolgirl of the ladies figure-skating championship.

The triple crown in the ice-hockey championship came to Britain after a dramatic final game, in which Canada beat the United States by the only goal scored in a closely contested match.

Earlier, Britain had drawn with America after a teriffic struggle, in which three 15-minute periods and three overtime periods of 10 minutes each were played without a goal being scored.

It only remained for America to be beaten by Canada for Britain to win the championship on points.

Foster, the British goal-minder, had an unfortunate accident in the first period of the match with America, when the puck was driven hard into his face, but he carried on to give a masterly display.

A slip on the ice cost the 15-years-old English schoolgirl, Miss Cecilia Colledge, the ladies' figure-skating Olympic championship yesterday. The competition was one of the most exciting duels in personality and skill ever witnessed here.

Miss Sonia Henje, the Norwegian skater and Olympic winner of 1928 and 1932, won the gold medal with only six points more than her English competitor. Miss Colledge was awarded the silver medal for second place.

The cheering and applause which burst forth at the conclusion of Miss Colledge's performance demonstrated that she was the favourite.

Miss Henje undoubtedly gave the more finished performance. She followed the more conventional patterns on the ice, and her charm and graceful balance in pirouetting told heavily in her favour. But it was agreed unanimously that Miss Colledge gave the most original exhibition of figure skating.

**(February 17)**

# KENT "DISMISS" FREEMAN

## FAMOUS BOWLER WITH WORLD RECORD

Cricket-lovers everywhere will learn with regret that Freeman, the famous bowler, has made his last appearance for Kent.

It was announced last night by Mr. G. de L. Hough, manager of the county club, that his committee had decided not to re-engage Freeman for next season.

In recognition of the player's great services a gift of £250 will be made to him. His wages will be continued until the beginning of the season.

An official of the Kent club could give no explanation of the committee's decision, but said: "Of course, we have got to make room for our young players."

A BOWLING PROTEST

It will be recalled that the Kent committee recently dissociated the club from Freeman's protest in a newspaper against the bowling of K. Farnes in a match between Essex and Kent.

Freeman is now 48. His form last summer was disappointing.

**(November 21)**



# OBOLENSKY'S TWO HISTORIC TRIES

## ENGLAND'S FIRST TRIUMPH OVER ALL BLACKS

**By Howard Marshall**

ENGLAND … … … 13pts. NEW ZEALAND … … … 0

So England have beaten New Zealand at last! A clear-cut, decisive victory at Twickenham by a dropped goal and three tries to nil, and the 70,000 spectators will remember it for the rest of their lives.

Again and again this great match will be discussed. As we talk of it, smoking our pipes, we shall see once more the white figure of Obolensky, running gloriously, and Pete Cranmer, smashing his way through the centre, and the English forwards, solid as a wall against which the black waves of New Zealand broke in vain.

England played magnificently — let there be no mistake about that. The English selectors had summed up the New Zealand methods, and picked their men accordingly.

New Zealand would concentrate on midfield attack. Very well, Hamilton-Hill, Candler, Cranmer and Gerrard would be there to stop them, and stop them they did, with a vengeance.

Never has Caughey been so ruthlessly put down, and even Oliver, most dangerous of runners, was given short shrift.

England harried the New Zealand attack with merciless vigilance, with a proper bulldog tenacity which never lost its grip.

Then said our selectors these New Zealand forwards must be pounded and shaken — and pounded and shaken they were. The tight scrummaging ran fairly level, but the tearaway loose rushes of New Zealand were steadily controlled and held and worn down by the strength and weight of this grand English pack.

With the sting thus taken out of the New Zealand attack, the next problem was for England to score, and Cranmer was the man to find that gap in the New Zealand mid-field defence. Twice he found it, and went thundering up the centre to pave the way for tries, and once he checked suddenly and dropped a beautiful goal. The rest is Obolensky.

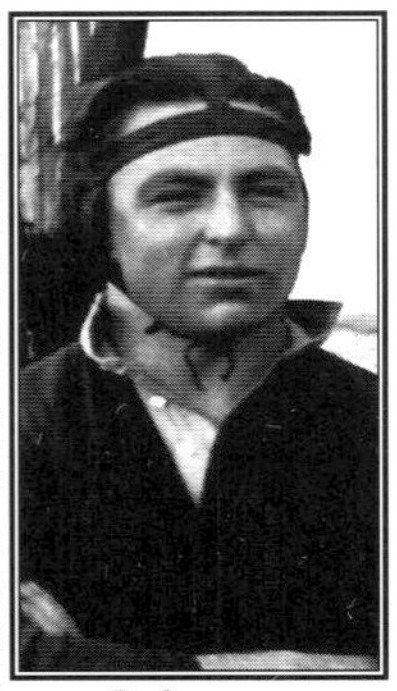

P. CRANMER

New Zealand must have been painfully surprised by the brilliance of Obolensky's running, though they had played against him on a miserable wet day at Oxford.

I shall never forget how Gilbert raised a hand helplessly, with a look of almost comical resignation on his face, as Obolensky lengthened his stride and raced round him to score England's first try.

Obolensky has a genius for the game, or I am much mistaken. The instinct which took him inwards from the right wing to run diagonally across the field and score his second try in the left corner showed the real player. Here is no mere sprinter, but a footballer who uses the weapon of exceptional speed with intelligence and precision.

DECEPTIVE CHANGE OF PACE

Obolensky has the most deceptive change of pace. He fades past his opponents like a ghost, and how refreshing it is to see a wing three-quarter in full cry for the line!

This has, indeed, been a rich season, and we must be grateful to New Zealand for the stimulus they have given to our game. They will not begrudge us our victory, I am sure, disappointed though they must have been. They had what they considered to be their strongest available team in the field, with the exception of J. R. Page, who has been out of action throughout the tour.

They ran up against an England side at the top of their form, that was all, and one little significant scene remains in my mind.

The very end of the game, a slight mist creeping across the ground, the little spurts of match flames pointing the gathering darkness in the stands, the players forming their swirling patterns on the green turf, the shrill final whistle, the deafening roar of the crowd — and then the New Zealanders rushing across to shake their victorious opponents by the hand.

From early morning the crowd had been assembling, and by one o'clock the road from the station was dense with hurrying enthusiasts. When I took my seat half an hour later the great terraces were packed, and a hum of conversation went round.

The ground was heavy and cutting up a bit, and Owen-Smith sent our hearts into our mouths when he ran and slipped and was caught in possession. A moment later he cleared perfectly, when Tindill punted ahead, and reassured us, and a determined dash by Ball was cut short by Obolensky.

The pace was tremendous, and the New Zealand pressure increased steadily. Cranmer kicked ahead; Gilbert took the ball on the run, burst through the centre, and set Reid, a grand forward, dashing along the touch-line. Owen-Smith put him down. Dunkley, playing splendidly, rushed the ball clear, Caughey kicked back, and New Zealand attacked again.

England were hard pressed indeed, but a penalty gave them relief, and then Obolensky struck his first blow.

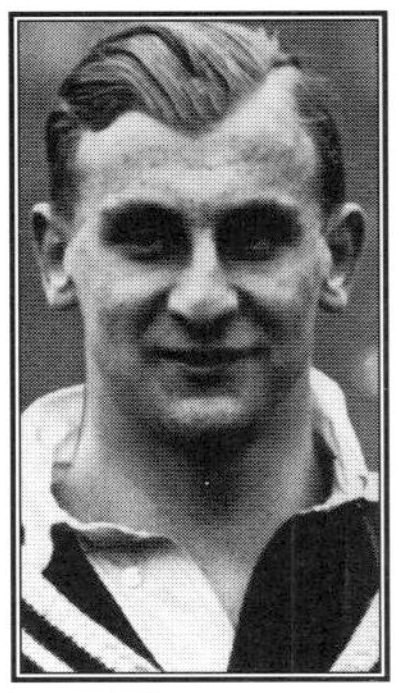

A. OBOLENSKY

England heeled from a loose scrum, Gadney whipped the ball across to Cranmer, and in short, sharp passes it went from Gerrard to Obolensky. Here was a chance surely, for Obolensky was 10 yards out from touch and near the half-way line.

He leapt into his stride, going right-handed as Gilbert raced in to cut him off. For a moment we thought he must be crowded into touch, but just as Gilbert shaped for his tackle Obolensky changed pace, swept past and was running like a hare clear for the line, with Gilbert watching him in sorrowful bewilderment.

That was beautiful running, and the crowd cheered as I never heard a Twickenham crowd cheer before, though a moment later New Zealand came perilously near to making the scores level. A knock-on by Owen-Smith, a scrummage in the England 25, Tindall cutting inwards and passing to his forwards, and Owen-Smith bundling McLean into touch only inches short of the England line.

AN INSPIRED MOVE

So 38 minutes passed, and then suddenly the ball came to Cranmer, who checked, shot swiftly through the centre for 30 yards, and passed to Candler, whose path was blocked by Ball and Gilbert. This was Obolensky's inspired moment, for he saw that there was no hope down his own wing, dashed inwards, took a pass from Candler, flashed through a barn-door gap, beat Mitchell by that subtle lengthening of stride and scored in the left corner.

A remarkable try which was not converted — our pace-kicking was lamentable — and at half-time England led by six points to nil.

A fine effort, but we wondered whether England could last the pace. We should have been happier if those tries had been turned into goals, and we shivered as New Zealand piled into a ferocious, roaring, headlong attack, with Hadley nearly over, and Mitchell swinging alarmingly through the defence, and Tindill and Gilbert both dropping at goal.

CRANMER'S DROP-GOAL

Anything might happen now, we thought, but there was plenty of resilience about the England team. A dash and a punt by Sever, some fine following by Dunkley and Longland, and once more New Zealand were driven back.

And then came Cranmer's chance, for the ball reached him quickly after a scrummage, and he checked, glanced at the posts, let fly, and that was another four points to England.

Fine work, and England kept at it, gradually taking control of line-outs and tight scrummages, packing 3-4-1, banging away at a brave defence. New Zealand did escape into the England half, but there the ball went loose, Candler picked it up, Cranmer broke through gloriously again, and Sever took an awkward pass, beat a couple of men, and raced round behind the posts.

ENGLAND — H. G. Owen-Smith (St. Mary's Hospital); A. Obolensky (Oxford University); P. Cranmer (Richmond); R. A. Gerrard (Bath); H. S. Sever (Sale); P. L. Candler (St. Bartholomew's Hospital); B. C. Gadney (capt.) (Leicester); D. A. Kendrew (Leicester); E.S. Nicholson (Leicester); R. J. Longland (Northampton); C. Webb ( Royal Navy and Devonport Services); A. Dunkley (Harlequins); W. H. Weston (Northampton).

NEW ZEALAND — G. Gilbert (West Coast); N. A. Mitchell (Southland); C. J. Oliver (Canterbury); N. J. Ball (Wellington); T. H. C. Caughey (Auckland); E. W. Tindill (Wellington); M. M. N. Corner (Auckland); A. Lambourn (Wellington); W. E. Hadley (Auckland); J. Hore (Otago); S. Reid (Hawke's Bay); R. R. King(West Coast); J. E. Manchester (capt.) (Canterbury); H. F. McLean (Auckland); A. Mahoney (Bush Districts).

Referee: J. W. Faull (Wales).

**(January 6)**

# HOW ENGLAND TRIUMPHED IN TEST

## AUSTRALIA ROUTED BY VOCE AND G. O. ALLEN

**By C. C. Macartney**

BRISBANE, Wednesday.

England triumphed in the first Test, which concluded here to-day, by 322 runs. Yesterday I cabled that only a miracle could save Australia, and that if rain fell their position was helpless.

There was heavy rain last night, followed by sunshine, and the batsmen were routed by Voce and Allen. The second innings total of 58 is Australia's fifth lowest score in the history of the Tests.

The batting failures on a difficult wicket were amazing. Allen and Voce bowled unchanged, and England's captain capped a great performance by dismissing both Badcock and Bradman before they had scored.

England's victory to-day was thoroughly deserved. It was regrettable that just enough rain fell to upset the wicket, but in any case Australia's task was too formidable.

An astonishing fact was that Australia were mown down without Verity handling the ball. There was never any doubt after Bradman had gone that Voce and Allen would finish off the side.

The bowlers' chief asset was good length. They allowed the wicket to do the rest. Only Oldfield and Chipperfield offered substantial resistance, and Oldfield defended soundly.

CHIPPERFIELD UNDAUNTED

Chipperfield made some delightful strokes, and was unbeaten. He adopted vigorous tactics, and while some of his shots were lucky, others were made with perfect timing and footwork.

His innings drives home the point I have made previously. Had more audacious measures been employed by recognised batsmen in Australia's first innings, there would not have been such mental strain to-day, despite the rain which played such a big part in the debacle.

Other batsmen were overawed by the conditions, which were not as bad as the final total would suggest. Nevertheless, the rain prevented the match from being fought out in conditions as nearly possible equal, allowing for the usual wear of the wicket.

Australia's batsmen seemed to have no knowledge of conditions prevailing after rain. This is not surprising, since Australians seldom have an opportunity of playing on this type of wicket.

In inter-State matches the pitches are covered, and bowlers cannot gain knowledge of what methods to employ in circumstances like to-day's. Consequently it is questionable whether Australia can produce a bowler capable of securing the results obtained by Allen and Voce.

One fact stands out prominently: Australia's failure in bowling and batting on the first three days was as much a cause of defeat as the rain.

ALLEN'S GREAT PART

From England's point of view, the victory is an achievement of which Allen and his team can be justly proud. The side was struggling to find true form right up to the beginning of the Test, and now has emerged with flying colours.

In every department, with the exception of wicket keeping, England were superior. Behind the stumps, however, Oldfield is still unchallenged.

While some of the tourists were below form, others fought splendidly. Allen never spared himself in bowling, batting and fielding. In several instances he displayed methods which others would be well paid to study. He is a tiger for work, supplying his side with the very best he can give.

England did well as a team. They achieved victory against odds. In contrast, Australia were never a team. The side did not wake up to the fact that it was necessary to fight as a whole until it was too late.

AUSTRALIA

| | |
|---|---|
| J. H. Fingleton, b Voce | 0 |
| C. L. Badcock, c Fagg, b Allen | 0 |
| M. Severs, c Voce, b Allen | 5 |
| W. A. Oldfield, b Voce | 10 |
| D. G. Bradman, c Fagg, b Allen | 0 |
| S. J. McCabe, c Leyland, b Allen | 7 |
| R. Robinson, c Hammond, b Voce | 3 |
| A. G. Chipperfield, not out | 26 |
| W. J. O'Reilly, b Allen | 0 |
| F. Ward, b Voce | 1 |
| E. L. McCormick, absent, ill | 0 |
| Extras | 6 |
| Total | 58 |

BOWLING
Second Innings

| | | | | |
|---|---|---|---|---|
| Allen | 6 | 0 | 36 | 5 |
| Voce | 6.3 | 0 | 16 | 4 |

No balls, 6.

ENGLAND WON BY 322 RUNS.

**(December 10)**

# BROKEN REINS ROB OUTSIDER OF NATIONAL

REYNOLDSTOWN, owner, Major N. Furlong, jockey Mr. F. Walwyn ........(10-1) 1
EGO, owner Sir David Llewellyn, jockey, Mr. H. llewellyn ..........(50-1) 2
BACHELOR PRINCE, owner Mr. James V. Rank, jockey J. Fawcus ........(66-1) 3

Yesterday's Grand National was one of the most dramatic in the 100-years' history of the race.

By winning it for the second year in succession, Reynoldstown equalled a record that has stood for 66 years.

Incidents in a race packed with sensations were:

Davy Jones, a 100 to 1 chance, was leading, and looked like a winner up to the last fence, when his reins broke and he ran wide;

Avenger, the favourite, broke his neck and died in a fall at one of the easiest jumps in the course, after completing the first circuit;

Golden Miller fell at the first fence, and after being remounted was baulked at the Canal turn.

Avenger, whose owner, Mrs Violet Mundy, is 76, was lying third when he fell. Three out of the first four horses past the post were ridden by amateurs.

**(March 28)**

# THIRD SUCCESS FOR THE AGA KHAN

For the second year in succession and for the third time in his career the Aga Khan won the Derby yesterday.

As though Mahmoud's victory — in the record time of 2 mins 33 4-5 secs— were not enough, he took second place as well.

The first four horses past the post were:

1. MAHMOUD (Aga Khan), ridden by C. Smirke ........100 to 8
2. TAJ AKBAR (Aga Khan), G. Richards ........6 to 1
3. THANKERTON ( Mrs J. Shand), T. Burns ........33 to 1
4. PAY UP (Lord Astor), R. Dick ........5 to 1

In the most open derby for several years, Mahmoud's prospects had been generally considered less favourable than those of Taj Akbar, the second favourite.

Charles Smirke, who rode the winner, is the Aga Khan's own jockey. He won in 1934 on Windsor Lad.

Gordon Richards rode Taj Akbar which was No. 13 on the card. Richards won the day's first two races, and the omens seemed to favour his at last achieving a Derby win, but he was beaten by three lengths.

Mrs. J. Shand's Thankerton won for her the honour of being the first woman to gain a place in any Derby run at Epsom. Lady J. Douglas's Gainsborough won the Derby in 1918, but, as in the other war-time meetings, this was at Newmarket.

**(May 28)**

# WELLARD'S FEAT FOR SOMERSET

## FIVE 6'S IN OVER

On the day in which they became champions Derbyshire suffered a remarkable defeat. Somerset began the day with 177 runs to make and two wickets down in their second innings.

Three more wickets fell — and 131 runs were still needed then came Wellard, famous for his hard hitting.

He maintained his reputation. He made 30 in one over by hitting five successive sixes, a feat believed to be unparalleled in first-class cricket.

He hit the ball out of the ground with three strokes in succession.

Wellard and R. A. Ingle, his partner, put on 77 for the sixth Somerset wicket. When Wellard was dismissed he had made 86 in 62 minutes.

When he left, Somerset wanted 29 to win, with three wickets left. Two more wickets fell and six runs were still needed. These were soon hit, leaving Somerset winners by one wicket.

**(August 29)**

# PERRY'S £20,000 CONTRACT

## PROFESSIONAL PLAY IN JANUARY

**From Our Own Correspondent**

NEW YORK, Monday.

F. J. Perry, three times Wimbledon champion, has at last turned professional.

It was announced to-day that he had signed a contract with a group of New York sportsmen.

Perry's contract should bring him a total exceeding £20,000. Francis T. Hunter, himself a former Wimbledon men's doubles champion, heads the syndicate which has secured his signature, and I understand that a large advance payment has already been made.

Perry's first professional appearance will be at Madison Square Garden early in January. After that he will make an extended tour of the United States, matched against Ellsworth Vines and possibly other well-known American players who have yielded to the blandishments of professionalism, such as W. T. Tilden, George Lott, Lester Stoefen, and Berkley Bell.

The present contract covers the United States and Canada only, and does not include Europe or the Dominions.

NEED TO MAKE MONEY

When the details of the contract had been made known Perry made this statement:

"After considering a number of attractive offers from various sources throughout the world, I am electing to accept the terms of a contract offered by Mr. Hunter, feeling that the conduct of this enterprise, which is backed by a group of well-known sportsmen, will do much to raise the level of professional competitive tennis in the eyes of the public, and place it on a sound basis, which it derserves for the future."

Discussing his plans with a few intimate friends during his stay here last Sunday week, Perry frankly admitted that he was reluctant to abandon his amateur status. He felt, however, that, being a married man — his wife is Helen Vinson, the film star — he was under the necessity to earn money.

**(November 10)**

# SUNDERLAND CHAMPIONS OF FIRST DIVISION

BIRMINGHAM ... 2 SUNDERLAND ... 7

Beating Birmingham at St. Andrew's, Sunderland are assured of the Football League Championship.

Sunderland did almost as they liked. The forwards, with Connor, Carter and Gurney at their best, often perplexed the home defence by their accuracy in passing.

Garney put Sunderland ahead 15 minutes after the start, and after Loughran equalised Carter restored the advantage. Clarke again put Birmingham on terms, but Hornby gave Sunderland an interval lead.

**(April 14)**

# DRAKE'S GOAL WINS CUP

**By Frank Coles**

ARSENAL ... ... ... 1 SHEFFIELD UNITED ... ... ... 0

Arsenal are Cupholders again for the second time in six-years. As expected they beat Sheffield United in Wembley's fourteenth Final Tie, but not as comfortably as 2 to 1 on favourites are supposed to win.

Actually Arsenal's form was a mixture of good and bad, and I am sure the players felt that they had failed to do themselves justice.

The honours of a match which rarely produced a high standard of play should go to Sheffield United, whose defence held out for an hour and a quarter, and who twice narrowly missed taking the lead before Drake scored.

In winning the cup for Arsenal at the 29th minute of the second half, Drake, recently recovered from a serious knee operation, accepted the only scoring chance that came his way.

The opening was made by Bastin, who tricked Hooper very cleverly before pushing the ball squarely across to his unmarked centre-forward.

It was the kind of opportunity Drake had been waiting for all the afternoon and, quick as thought, he swung his left leg at the ball. Before Smith, the goalkeeper, could move an inch a crashing drive had found the roof of the net.

Sheffield United, seeking for causes of their narrow defeat, could argue with justification that Bastin might not have put Drake through if Hooper had not been handicapped by a leg injury. They could also point to the fact that Jackson, playing immediately in front of Hooper, was also limping.

But injuries have to be accepted as the misfortunes of war.

Drake's goal gave new life to a game which, for the greater part of the second half, had lapsed into a dull, humdrum affair, so lacking in quality and thrills that the 93,000 crowd was almost silent. Even the partisans forgot to cheer.

**(April 27)**

# ROUGH PLAY AT FOOTBALL

## SEQUEL TO INQUEST ON GOALKEEPER

Sir Frederick Wall, former secretary of the Football Association, stated last night that in his view an inquiry should be held by the Association into the facts disclosed at yesterday's inquest on the Sunderland goalkeeper, James Horatio Thorpe.

The Sunderland jury found that Thorpe's death on Feb. 5, following the Roker Park match against Chelsea, refereed by Mr. warr of Bolton, was due to diabetes, accelerated by the rough usage he received in the game. They added:

"We are of the opinion that the referee was very lax in his control of the game, and as a rider we wish to add that we urge the Board of Management of the Football Association to instruct all referees that they must exercise stricter control over the players so as to eliminate as far as possible any future accidents."

"It is regrettable," Sir Frederick Wall said, "that the jury felt themselves compelled to come to such a decision about rough play, and doubtless the Football Association will give every consideration to the recommendations which they make in their rider.

"I feel that an inquiry should be held in order to take action upon their recommendations.

"In my opinion rough play has been developing in recent years. This has been the case more particularly during the past two or three seasons.

UNFAIR CHARGING

"One cause has been the introduction of the new system of re-arranging what one might call the field. I am thinking of the new formation which has introduced an attacking centre-forward and a defensive centre-half-back, commonly called the 'stopper'.

"That in my opinion, has completely changed the style of play and has been conducive to unfair charging — a dangerous practice.

"I think that the goalkeeper now has more protection than was given to him in my playing days, but, of course, that does not hold when incidents of rough play occur."

**(February 14)**

# BRITAIN'S FOUR TITLES AT WIMBLEDON

**By A. Wallis Myers**

Wimbledon, the "friendly war" of 30 nations, ended at sundown on Saturday with four-fifths of its spoils in British hands.

Home players had not only won the men's singles and doubles, the women's doubles and the mixed doubles, but a page of history that had stood since Perry's year of birth had been brightened. Not since 1909 had England claimed the two oldest championships at the same meeting.

The women's singles championship, the only title to go abroad, remained with California, which has held it for eight years out of the last ten.

Miss Helen Jacobs has been champion of America for the last four years. Her triumph on Saturday — and she had fallen so often from the heights of hope before — permits her to share an honour held only by Mrs. Moody in the past — to be champion of two hemispheres in the same year.

The Wimbledon just over may have lacked the continuous thrills of former years. Its threads were broken and its courts slowed down by fickle weather; accident and ailment took unusual toll among the champions, robbing relative form of its proper orientation.

But none will deny that Perry vindicated his right to hold the singles crown, or that three of the five finals yielded excitement, or that certain matches produced play worthy to be enshrined in memory.

One may name four in this category — the classic driving duel last Wednesday between Austin and Von Cramm; the brilliant, bustling fight between Perry and Budge which followed it on the same day; Senorita Lizana's set-and-a-half against Miss Jacobs, in which the Chilean champion revived the genius of Suzanne Langlen and looked, for that period, almost as invincible; and the great doubles match on Friday night between Allison and Van Ryn and Hughes and Tuckey, the strain of which was reflected in the British pair the next day.

PAID £20 FOR A SEAT

The curtain was lifted on the last day before another packed house, but I have seen the pressure in the standing space more irksome for those who have undergone an all-night vigil.

Indeed, some who had their normal sleep at home were able, by the irony of fate to get in. Yet seats in the stadium rose to a premium, and one Californian paid £20 to see his compatriot in her fifth final.

THE NEW CHAMPIONS

MEN'S SINGLES:F. J. Perry (G.B.), (holder).
WOMEN'S SINGLES: Miss H. Jacobs (U.S.A.)
MEN'S DOUBLES: G. P. Hughes and C. R. D. Tuckey (G.B.)
WOMEN'S DOUBLES: Miss F. James and Miss K. E. Stammers (G.B.), holders.
MIXED DOUBLES: F. J. Perry and Miss D. E. Round (G.B.), holders.

**(July 6)**

# FIRE HOSE TURNED ON CROWD

Fire hoses were turned on the crowd when an attempt was made to rush the barriers at Cardiff Arms Park, where the Wales v. Ireland Rugby match was played on Saturday.

Between 60,000 and 70,000 people were admitted, a record for the ground, but when the gates were closed, nearly two hours before the kick-off, thousands remained outside.

These made an effort to force their way in, and the police, finding themselves powerless, obtained fire hoses and directed streams of water on the crowd.

**(March 16)**

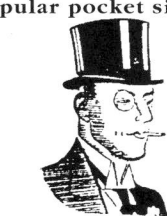

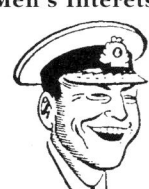

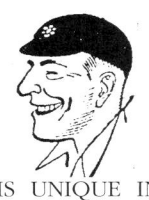

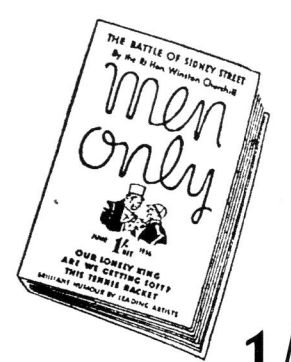

# SCENES OF PUBLIC DISORDER IN LONDON'S EAST-END.

(ABOVE) AN ARREST at Gardiner's Corner, Minories. About 10,000 police were on duty between Tower Hill and Whitechapel.

(BELOW) POLICE REMOVING A BARRIER erected in Cable-street, Stepney.

AT NEW YORK before the start of their Atlantic flight Mr. Richman (left) and Mr. Merrill, who landed in Wales. They are loading ping-pong balls into the tail to provide boyancy in case they had come down in the sea.

## ATLANTIC CROSSING

# EVEREST ASCENT ABANDONED

SPECIAL PICTURES taken by members of the Mount Everest expedition before the assault on the summit was abandoned.
(BELOW): Negotiating a crevasse on the East Rongbuk Glacier.

MR. WYN HARRIS testing the Oxygen apparatus, used at greater heights, at Tangu.

# 1937

The bombing of civilians from the air became a reality when, as the civil war in Spain continued, the town of Guernica was almost destroyed. On the other side of the world, the Japanese, in their relentless campaign against China, rained down bombs on the city of Canton. In the Western world, the provision of air raid precautions became a priority, even though the House of Commons could argue whether national or local government should pay for the necessary work. Big plans were made for the building of new warships and the construction of the defences of Singapore was hastened.

It became clear that the rebel forces of General Franco, now called the nationalists, were winning with the help of German and Italian air power. The screen the League of Nations attempted to put round the war area proved ineffective. Even so, the Communist government of Spain continued to fight on with the help of the International Brigades recruited from sympathisers on both sides of the Atlantic. The conflict, both in Spain and China, brought into prominence a new sort of war reporting — colourful, personal and exciting. It was dangerous too. Pembroke Stevens, *The Daily Telegraph*'s war correspondent, who had sent back vivid reports from Spain, was killed by a machine-gun bullet as he observed the fighting in China.

Adolf Hitler demanded the return of the German colonies, taken from his country after the First World War, so that his people might have more living space. At the same time as he was powerbroking the "axis" with Mussolini, Hitler was talking peace with the British cabinet minister, Lord Halifax. The pride of the new Germany, the airship *Hindenburg*, went up in flames soon after it had arrived in New Jersey on one of its regular Atlantic crossings. British flying boats had greater successes in their flights to New York.

In Britain, the memories of the year of the three kings were erased by the splendour of the Coronation of King George VI which was celebrated all over the country. For the first time, television covered the event. Ramsay MacDonald, the former prime minister who had headed the National Government of the early 1930s died, and his successor Stanley Baldwin resigned about the time of his 70th birthday, exhausted by the strain of his office. Neville Chamberlain took over and his shuffle of governmental posts moved the charismatic Minister of Transport, Leslie Hore-Belisha, to the War Office where he promptly reformed the senior command structure of the army.

During the year, another senior statesman, Sir Austen Chamberlain, died, as did the developer of wireless telegraphy and television, Marconi, and the atomic scientist, Professor Rutherford. Sir James Barrie, the author of *Peter Pan* and many other plays, died soon after his final work for the stage had proved to be a flop.

The British capacity for providing game losers was exemplified by the tenacity of the british heavyweight boxer, Tommy Farr, who stood up to the awesome power of the Champion of the World, Joe Louis, for 15 rounds and lost on points though some ringside observers thought that he had won.

In October, *The Daily Telegraph* announced that it had taken over the loss-making Conservative newspaper, *The Morning Post*. For the rest of the year, all the by-lines in the joint paper incorporated the ponderous phrase, "Daily Telegraph and Morning Post Special Correspondent".

To-Days Weather :
Thundery: Rather warm

# The Daily Telegraph
and
# Morning Post

Broadcasting:
Page Twelve



No. 25,691 POSTAGE { INLAND, CANADA AND NEWFOUNDLAND, THREE HALFPENCE / OTHER COLONIES AND PLACES ABROAD, THREEPENCE
LONDON, MONDAY, FRIDAY, OCTOBER 1, 1937
ONE PENNY

*BIRTHS, MARRIAGES and DEATHS in this column, one guinea for three lines or less and 5s for each additional line. "IN MEMORIAM" notices 12/6 for three lines or less and 3/6 for each additional line. (Special rate for five or ten years' automatic insertion on application.) Announcements, authenticated by name and address of sender, may be sent to The Daily Telegraph and Morning Post, Fleet St., E.C.4., or 161 Piccadilly, W.1. or telephoned to Central 4242. Forthcoming Marriages in Court Page 3 guineas for 5 lines or less and 12/6 for each additional line.*

## BIRTHS

BLAKE – On Sept. 28, 1937, to Greeba, wife of Arthur Speed Blake, Corwen, Bath-road, Worthing, a son.

CHAMBERLAYNE – On Sept. 28, 1937, at Maidenhead nursing home, to Frankie (née Reine Gray), wife of Lt-Comdr. Tankerville Chamberlayne (ref.), of 19, Bedford-gardens, Lutton, a daughter.

EVANS – On Sept. 29, 1937, at 27 Welbeck-street, to Doris Joan (née Vare), wife of Rupert E. Evans, of "The Culls," Stroud, Gloucestershire, a daughter.

FINCH – On Sept. 26, 1937, to "Fee" (née Blackstone), wife of E.J.B. Finch, of Dower Cottage, Chalfont St. Peter, a son.

GREENWOOD – On Sept. 29, 1937, at Wynniattes, Abberley, Worcester, to Violet Elizabeth, wife of Leonard Warwick Greenwood, a daughter.

FINZEL – On Sept. 27, 1937, to Mary Grace, wife of Harry F.M. Finzel, M.D., Nare House, St. Anne's Park, Bristol, a son

FLETCHER-BARRETT – On Sept. 29, 1937, at 3, Wilbraham-place, S.W.1. to Sheila Catherine Mackintosh, wife of Major K. Fletcher-Barrett, F.R.C.S., a son.

KEAST-BUTLER – On Sept. 26, 1937, at 19, Bentinck-street, W.1. to Marie Louise (née Brierley), wife of J.A. Keast-Butler, a son.

LOWDEN – On Sept. 27, 1937, to Peggy, wife of P.A.T. Lowden, of Winchester, a son.

RIDLEY – On Sept. 30, 1937, at 38, Inner Park-road, S.W. 19., to Joan Madelin Marling (née Roberts) wife of Keith Ridley, a daughter.

SARSON – On Sept. 29, 1937 at Kingslea Nursing Home, Sutton, Surrey, to Betty the wife of Wilfred Sarson, twin daughters (Patricia and Mary Elizabeth).

STOPFORD – On Sept. 27, 1937, at 39, Haymarket, St. Annes-on-the-Sea, to Mary, wife of John Stopford, a son.

SUNDERLAND – On Sept. 23, 1937, at Tree Tops, Sudbury Court-drive, Harrow-on-Hill, to Dorothy (née Campbell), wife of Arthur Grahame Sunderland, a daughter.

THOMPSON – On Sept. 27, 1937, at Canada House, Gillingham, to Florence May (née Walker) and Charles W.W. Thompson, F.R.I.B.A., F.S.I., Orchard Cottage, Rochester, a daughter.

WISEMAN-CLARKE – On Sept. 29, 1937, at Forest Lodge, Andover, to Cynthia (née Pemberton), wife of Lieutenant-Commander F.W. Wiseman-Clarke, a daughter.

## MARRIAGES

CAMBRIDGE-O'NEILL – On Wednesday, Sept. 29, 1937, before the British Consul-General at Marseilles, Reginald Newman Cambridge to Margaret O'Neill. African papers, please copy.

DAVIES-BURLTON-BENNETT – On Sept. 25, 1937, at St. Mary's, Beaminster, Dorset, by the Rev. Canon G.C. Hutchings and the Rev. J.G. Chambers, Flight-Lieut. Edward Basil Charles Davies, R.A.F., only son of Mr. E.A. Davies and the late Mrs. Davies, of Cape Town, S. Africa, to Elizabeth Mary, second daughter of the late Lieut.-Colonel J.A. Burlton-Bennett and Mrs. Burlton-Bennett, of The Grey Cottage, Beaminster.

WINTER-FROWD – On Sept. 30, 1937, at Holy Trinity, Kensington Grove, by the Rev. J.O. Hannay, John, only son of Mr. and Mrs. H Winter, to Norah Gwendoline, widow of the late Charles Frowd, of St. Leonards.

## GOLDEN WEDDING

BREWITT-FEARN. – On Oct. 1, 1887, at West Hackney Church, by the Rev. A.B. Hillard, Thomas Brewitt to Annie Fearn. Present address: The Moors, Royston, Essex.

## DEATHS

ALLPORT – On Sept. 29, 1937 at 103, Burbage-road, S.E. 24. Harriet Elizabeth, widow of Denison William Allport, of Dulwich. Service at Camberwell Green Church on Monday next, twelve noon.

BROWN – On Sept. 30, 1937, at a Bournemouth nursing home, Ernest Osman Brown, of the Homestead, Broadstone, Dorset. Service at Richmond-hill Congregational Church, Bournemouth, to-morrow (Saturday, Oct. 2), at 2.30 p.m. Interment private. Flowers to J.J. Allen Ltd., 3, Alum Chine-road, Bournemouth.

CHASE – On Sept. 29, 1937, at 7, Oakwood Park, Leeds, 8, aged 83 years, Elizabeth, the beloved widow of the late George Chase, Ashley, Market Harborough, Funeral at Ashley Church to-morrow, (Saturday, Oct. 2), at 2.30.

CHRISTIAN – On Sept. 30, 1937, at a London nursing home, following an operation and a very long illness most bravely borne, Ethel, beloved wife of Lt.-Col. J.B. Christian, I.M.S., (retired).

ELLERT – On Sept. 29, 1937, suddenly at a nursing home, Barbara Jean (née Havelock Allan), the dearly-loved wife of John Arnold Ellert, of Ractons, Henfield, Sussex. Service at Golders Green Crematorium to-morrow (Saturday), at 10.45. New York papers, please copy.

FEDDEN – On Sept. 29, 1937, Harry Vincent, of 37 Downleaze, Stoke Bishop, Bristol, husband of Ida Fedden and son of the late Mr. and Mrs. Henry Fedden of Henbury. Funeral at St. Mary's, Stoke Bishop, Bristol, to-morrow (Saturday, Oct. 2) at twelve o'clock, afterwards at Canford Cemetery. Flowers to Thomas Pakeman, 3, Whiteladies-gate, Bristol.

FENWICK – On Sept. 29, 1937, Major Stanley Fenwick, M.C. late Royal Army Medical Corps. aged 49, beloved husband of Rita Fenwick.

## PERSONAL

5S PER LINE (MINIMUM 2 LINES). TRADE 12/6 PER LINE. LOST AND FOUND 2/6 PER LINE.

R. – Pleased you are better. See me here before going anywhere. – B.

PROGRESSING SLOWLY. Very sorry your news. Suggest call box enquiries. LOVE.

S.O.S. JIMMY Return to Chapel-street. Only hope immediate return. Case desperate. S & R.

WILL No. 51 please write Ann, same address? Add opposite G.P.O.

MARGOT – Cannot persuade Uncle Eustace go Cannes. Insists on Wintering Bournemouth. His address, Prince's Hotel, Eastcliff. – ANN.

ROBERT. – Haven't found anyone nicer yet. Have you? – M

A. BACK at WORK, at L. All well. Miss you dreadfully and long for news. My thoughts and love, always the same. – C.

RENGEE – All my love as always. Still hoping to see you. – F.

ROSINE ELOISE HARPER, deceased., of Sutton Court, Chiswick, London, and some time resident at Worthing. – ANY PERSON having KNOWLEDGE of a WILL of the above-names, who died on 18th Sept., 1937, is REQUESTED to COMMUNICATE with BARRON & MORTON, Solicitors, 3, Gray's Inn-place, London, W.C.

OXFORD. A new HOTEL of charm, comfort and distinction. – Linton Lodge. 'Phone 5494.

A POOR WIDOW, 79 years, suffering from CANCER, and in a state of desperate poverty having unemployed son (no dole) and total income of only 15s per week out of which she must pay 7s rent. PLEASE HELP. – The National Society for Cancer Relief, 47, Victoria-street, S.W.1.

YOUNG GERMAN teaches German. 2s hour. Expert teaching. – Frey, 54, Manchester-st., W.1, Wel. 5351.

UNWANTED Artificial Teeth Gratefully Received. – Ivory Cross Dental Fund, 67b Welbeck-st., W.1.

ANTIQUE SILVER Plate, Jewels, Diamonds, Old GOLD Gold Dentures purchased, Highest prices. BENTLEY & CO. 65 New Bond-st., (facing Brook-st.), W.1. Mayfair 0651

AN ADVENTURE is only an inconvenience rightly considered. An inconvenience is only an adventure wrongly considered. G.K. Chesterton.

AUTUMN in New Forest. – From 3gns. weekly A.A., R.A.C., licensed. – Langdown Lawn, Hythe, Hants.

SACKVILLE-STREET CLOTHES at City prices, Suit 8 1/2gns. Town o'ct. 7 1/2gns Dress 11gns. Reg. 1095. J.W. Dore, 18 Sackville-street, W. Est. 60 years.

GRAFTON HOTEL, Tottenham Court-road, London, W.1. Central for everything, EUS. 3421. Telephones in rooms, Comfort without ostentation. 8/6.

THE DORMY HOUSE at Rock, Cornwall, provides all the amenities necessary for Autumn, Christmas, and Winter "change of air." Under the personal supervision of the owners, Commander and Mrs. Bannerman, Write for Booklet.

HINTON FIRS, at Bournemouth – The best food, beds and service. With modern comfort and the quiet distinction of a spacious country house in a sheltered garden by the sea. A delightful place for winter.

TORQUAY – PALM COURT HOTEL. On Promenade. Winter residential terms. 3 1/2-4gns. Tel. 2187.

RESIDENCE for ELDERLY GENTLEPEOPLE, "Dawn" Brooks Green, Horsham, Sussex, Extensive grounds. Sunny rooms, Every comfort. 3 guineas.

SIR REGINALD KENNEDY-COX will gratefully acknowledge jumble of all descriptions, especially frocks, overcoats, suits, boots and clothing for ANNUAL GIANT JUMBLE SALE – Dockland Settlements, Canning Town, E.16.

CONWAY N. WALES – OAKWOOD PARK HOTEL. Charming, first-class. Standing in 200 acres of glorious scenery. Own 18-hole golf course, close to sea. Beautiful ball room. Billiards , Tennis, Orchestra, Riding.

IN A FINE POSITION IN LONDON. HOTEL STRATHCONA, Lancaster Gate, Hyde Park. From 3gns per week. 12s daily, 7s 6d B.B.B.

IN the lea of the Leas … in the warmth of the Sun. In fact, a first-class situation for an autumn holiday or winter residence. – PRINCES HOTEL, FOLKESTONE. Write for tariff.

C'EST un poids bien pesant qu'on nom trop tot fameux. Voltaire.

EARN GOOD MONEY – Members of our organisation earn up to £3 a week. Spare time only – more for full time. Make confectionery for us at home. Experience unnecessary. Free outfit supplied. More members, wanted. – Full particulars, National Confectionery Industry, Dept. F.H. 87, Regent-st., W.1.

THE ALEXANDRA HOSPITAL for Children with Hip Disease, established in Bloomsbury, 1867. New Annual Subscriptions and Donations urgently wanted. – Any help to Offices, 117 Southampton-row, W.C.1. gratefully acknowledged.

BOTH HAIRDRESSING and BEAUTY CULTURE offer lucrative careers to-day. – See Durave's announcement in the Hairdressing Column, Page 26.

PLAITS made by Chaventre lend style and distinction to the most common-place coiffure. Prepared from best quality hair only, and made to fix firmly yet comfortably in place. – Write for illustrated plates. B. Chaventre. 289, Oxford-st. W.1.

2 GUINEAS a week, to Let, owing to owners leaving Island, from end of October, for winter months, a well-furnished HOUSE containing 2 sitting rooms, 7 bed rooms, 2 bath rooms, both with basins hot and cold water, sun lounge, kitchen, &c. Central heating in all rooms, electric light, gas, and company's water. All modern conveniences, including a lift and Frigidaire. Lovely garden of about 3 acres with view of sea. – Apply Mrs. Turner-Turner, La Favorita, Guernsey, C.I.

## PERSONAL (CONT.)

MODERN HOMES within EASY REACH of London. Illus. particulars appear on Page 31.

"IN THE STEPS OF MOSES, The Lawgiver," the great Travel-biography of the 20th century, from the pen of LOUIS GOLDING. Ask your librarian or bookseller.

VERSE WANTED. Must be inspired and sincere for well-known Book of Contemporary English Poetry. Arden-Godbold Press, 249 Shaftesbury-avenue, W.C. 2.

DO NOT MISS the Special Autocheque massage in last column on this page.

BOOKS – Will anyone possessing a copy of Priestley's "GOOD COMPANIONS" In which the third chapter commences: "We have left all the hills behind," write to Collector, Nightingale Cottage, Peppard Common, Oxon. Do not send actual book.

THE SOCIAL ROUND SIMPLIFIED – See the COUPE Advert, in the Motor Hire Column.

S.O.S. OCTOBER PLEASE START the month WELL – by assisting those to whom the coming winter must else bring disaster. The "Over 45's" Association have received: Previously acknowledged, £242; M.T.B., 10s; J.N.R., £1; L.G.W., £2 2s 6d; M.T., £10; E.L. 3s 6d; J.M., 10s; W.T., 10s 6d; Anon. £10; C.E., £10; C.A., 10s, D.V.S., £1. Please help us to reach the £1,000 required. – 2, Terminus-place, S.W.1.

A CHAUFFEUR-DRIVEN PACKARD of your own whenever you wish.– See "Motor Hire," Page 25.

LADY requires post TRAVELLING COMPANION, nursing, &c. – 151 Elm Park-mansions, S.W.10.

REVILLE SCHOOL OF FASHION – associated with the world-famous House of Court Dressmakers – gives thoroughly practical training in Dressmaking (including pattern drafting, cutting, fitting, &c), Fashion Creating, and Fashion Drawing. – Call or write for Brochure to The Director, 15, HANOVER-SQUARE, W.1. Mayfair 7068.

WHAT I SAY UNTO YOU i say unto all, Watch St. Mark XIII., 37.

THE SEAMAN'S CHRISTIAN FRIEND SOCIETY will carefully and prayerfully use GIFTS NOW of LEGACIES in the future in the best interests of seamen. – Secretary, 46, Denison House, Vauxhall Bridge-road. London. S.W. 1

HAPPY COUNTRY home for children whose parents are abroad. Good schools within easy reach. Excellent references. Pets welcomed. – Mrs. Evans, Gaskins, Stinfold, Horsham.

FINE JEWELS, ANTIQUE and MODERN SILVER. Sheffield Plate, also Coins and Medals, PURCHASED for cash at highest prices without deduction. – call or send Registered Post to SPINK & SON Ltd. (est'd. 1772), 5-7 King-st., St. James's, S.W.1. Whl. 5275.

6D A MILE from your door. Luxurious limousine cars, chauffeur driven. – Jepps, Mal. 2744.

REQUIRED IMMEDIATELY, young lady, 14-18, to take charge of two small boys. Good speaking voice essential. Nurse housemaid kept, Good home and allowance. – Write R.I., Box 5,612. Daily Telegraph, E.C.4.

MAKE YOUR LONDON HOME at PARK WEST, Marble Arch, W. Own swimming pool gymnasium, six squash courts, licensed restaurant, residents' club, &c. Flats from £95 p.a. inclusive – Call Letting Office or write for brochure, MP., Park West, Marble Arch, London. W.

LANGUAGES – Enjoy your holiday with a knowledge of the language. Learn and practise with native teachers at The Universal Language Club, 8, Southampton-row, W.C.1. Hol. 6241.

THE ONLY PLAYGROUND a back street, their homes a wretched hovel. Do please give these little mite's a fortnight's holiday (cost £1). Hundreds waiting. Alas no funds. Also clothing. – Rev. R. Jones, St. Paul's Bethnal Green, E.

GOLF AND LOVELY WOODLAND WALES. Quiet, comfortable GUEST HOUSE, adjoining golf course. Good cooking. Willing service. Bracing air. 3gns. – Cleburne, Liphook (Haslemere), Hants.

COPIES OF PHOTOGRAPHS APPEARING IN THE DAILY TELEGRAPH may be obtained at a small charge from The Daily Telegraph, Phone Sales Department, Fleet-street, E.C.4.

FROM 20GNS. A WEEK INCLUSIVE! WINTER RESIDENTIAL TERMS … and in a real hotel where for 20 years the resident proprietors have been purveyors of genuine comforts. Here is a price to suit those who are not as well off as they used to be. Here is an hotel, beautifully situated – many bed rooms with a southern aspect and a lovely view of Torbay. Two minutes town, four minutes sea. Hot and cold water, in all rooms; gas or electric fires; best English fare. – Write Miss I. Terry for brochure. SEASCAPE HOTEL, TORQUAY.

OCCUPATION WANTED by invalided naval officer, aged 37, Light sedentary work. Only nominal pay. To be of some use the chief end. Car and typewriter. – Write O. Box 5, 582, Daily Telegraph E.C.4.

BUDLEIGH SALTERTON – FURNISHED HOUSE. All modern conveniences E.1. gas Garage. Telephone. Adjoining golf links. Double drawing room, dining room, 4 bed rooms. 3gns. weekly for 6 months. Write Sercombe Smith, Belstone, Devon.

BOOKS WANTED by disabled ex-officer for bookshop. Immediate cash payments. – Letters first to B. Box 5,624. Daily Telegraph E.C.4.

OPENING OF PARLIAMENT, TIARAS and JEWELLED HEAD ORNAMENTS of every description in stock, or made to design. – CARRINGTON & CO. Ltd. Court Jewellers, 130 REGENT-STREET, W.1.

LADY WITH HOMELY COMFORTABLE FLAT near Wandsworth Common Stn. desires lady or married couple. Suit middle-aged people appreciating home. £2 5s weekly. – Write L. Box 5,622, Daily Telegraph E.C.4.

PEER;S DAUGHTER (married) would CHAPERONE girl this winter in London; references. – Box 5845, 12-14, Mayfair-place, W.1.

CASH IN PAYMENT for clothing and miscellaneous effects. Top prices given. – Send or call, Peter Dean, 151, 3 and 5. Edgware-road, W.2. Pad. 4320.

MISS ELSIE M. JACKSON Recommends study home in Paris. – Appointments 45 Berkeley-street, W.1.

JOURNALISM, STORY & PLAY WRITING Expert, personal, postal tuition. Prospectus free. – Metropolitan College of Journalism (15/6), St. Albans.

WINTER IN COMFORT THIS YEAR! COME TO LINCOMBE HALL HOTEL, TORQUAY, the Hotel with an all-the-year-round season. A full staff, Interesting and varied menus. Warmth, comfort and the free service of hotel bus to shops, theatres and golf. Beautiful grounds, and, above all – the certainty of meeting congenial people who appreciate the many amenities which Lincombe Hall provides from 4gns. a week. No extras. – Write for descriptive brochure, or 'phone 2302.

FOUND – An Hotel where guests STAY! Clive Hall, 27, Fellowes-road, Hampstead. Good food in plenty. 'Phone and heated bed rooms. Ample baths. Central heating. Garage. Partial board from 3gns. full from 3 1/2gns. – Write or 'phone PRImrose 6641, and ask for Miss Fisher.

LIGHT OF ASIA, BAHADUR, LOTUS LILY. India's finest Cigars. Illustrated Catalogue free from SPENCERS, 31, Victoria-st., London, S.W.1.

REQUIRED, tobacco trade, experienced SALESMAN. Must have qualification for position of trust. – Write R.T. Box 7,012, Daily Telegraph, E.C.4.

GENTLEMAN, wishes to purchase ANTIQUE SILVER, OLD CHINA, OLD GLASS. VERY HIGH PRICES PAID. No dealers. – Box 5825, 12-14 Mayfair-place, W.1.

SOUTH AFRICA. – The 1820 Memorial Settlers' Association is a patriotic organisation existing solely to advise and assist persons contemplating migration to South Africa – Write Dept. D.T.O.1. 199, Piccadilly, London, W.1.

PIANO WANTED, grand or good upright. – Write P. Box 6,351, Daily Telegraph. E.C.4.

SPEND WINTER in the SUNSHINE. Exquisitely furnished detached Houses TO LET. Every comfort. Divan beds. Beach hut. Garage. From 25s weekly – Saunders, Flansham-lane, Bognor.

EX-POLICE OFFICER (invalid), 26, urgently desires HOME for secretarial duties or other suitable work. Highest references. – Write E., Box 992, Daily Telegraph, E.C.4.

SEVERAL FRIENDS writing to Prebendary Carlisle ask if it is too late to send poor mothers and children from overcrowded slums to the sea. It is not, and when you realise that some have never seen the sea, or had a holiday, you will surely want to help. – £5 sends mother and children for a fortnight. – Cheques, &c. Preb. Carlisle, "Seaside Holidays," Church Army, 55, Bryanston-street, W.1.

MEMBERS OF THE PUBLIC ! !
DON'T MISS SEEING
THE HIGHLAND GAMES
TO-DAY and TO-MORROW (Oct. 1st and 2nd)
IN THE GROUNDS OF RANELAGH CLUB
150 BRAEMAR CHAMPIONS have come South and are displaying their prowess in Tossing the Caber, Throwing the Weight, Wrestling (Cumberland Style), Vaulting, &c. &c.
MASSED PIPE BANDS
FLOODLIT MARCH PAST
Fully licensed. Refreshments at Popular Prices.
ADMISSION (Rover ticket), 2s 6d Sessions, 3-5.30 p.m. and 8-10.30 p.m. (Evening Sessions Floodlit). Applications for Enclosures (prices 2s 6d., 5s 8s. and 21s) should be made to Mr. Ian Hay, Highland Gatherings (London) Ltd, c.o. Ranelagh Club, Barnes, S.W. 13. Putney 1417 and 6865. Public Entrances, Putney Gate, Lower Richmond-road, and Rocks-land, Barnes Common Corner. Station: Putney 'Buses 96, 22, 73 and 72. Barnes 5 minutes. (Car Park in Grounds.) (Proceeds to help the Scottish Boy Scouts.)

SIR REGINALD KENNEDY-COX will gratefully acknowledge jumble of all descriptions, especially frocks, overcoats, suits, boots and clothing for ANNUAL GIANT JUMBLE SALE – Dockland Settlements, Canning Town, E.16.

ON THE BRINK OF A PRECIPICE – That is the perilous position of little Doris, aged 9. Her mother is dead, and her father has just completed his second term of imprisonment for an unspeakable crime. Who will help us to rescue and bring back happiness again to this little child. 5s will keep her for a week. – Secretary, WAIFS AND STRAYS SOCIETY, Old Town Hall, Kennington, S.E.11.

RETREATS FOR AGED PEOPLE. Accommodation is available for Aged Men in well-equipped residences at "Sunbury Court," Sunbury-on-Thames; "Methland Park," Dumbarton; "Mowbray," Clevedon, Somerset, "Royal Soldiers Home," Edinburgh. Moderate weekly terms for board residence and laundry. Medical or Infirm cases not accepted. Applications invited. Applications from aged Married Couples considered. Write or call, The Secretary, 110-112, Middlesex-street, Bishopsgate, London E.1. Please mention "The Daily Telegraph and Morning Post."

OLD BRITISH WAR HORSES. IN BELGIUM 700 saved from indescribable misery, 1,500 yet to save. Old Army markings found on each horse. Please help their rescue. £10 will buy one, but any donation to this fund exclusively will be gratefully acknowledged by the Secretary. "Our Dumb Friends' League," 72, Victoria-st., S.W.1.

MAKE MONEY flower painting for cretonnes, &c. Earn £3 to £6 weekly. Write for prospectus of tuition and sales service. Only moderate ability necessary. – C. Queen's Studio, 100a, Queen's-rd., W.2.

FLATS OR ROOMS (Furnished or Unfurnished) to Let, in Residential Golf Club, situated in beautiful old park, 10 mins. G.W.R. main line station, 40 mins. Paddington. Excellent cooking. Hunting with two packs available in near neighbourhood. Good golf and comfortable accommodation. – For inclusive terms write F., Box 5,472, Daily Telegraph, E.C.4.

PARAPACK treatments for rheumatism, &c, Trained nurses. Free consultations and literature. – ib, Lancaster-gate, W.2. Pad. 0945 and 3960.

MISS ELSIE M. JACKSON, recently returned from the Continent, is now in London to interview parents with regard to schools in this country and abroad. – Appointments, Thos. Cook & Son Ltd., Berkeley-street, London, W.1.

## EDUCATIONAL

*2s per Line. Min. 3 Lines.*

UNIVERSITY
CORRESPONDENCE
COLLEGE
Founded 1887.
Founder: WM BRIGGS LL.D. D.C.L., M.A., B.Sc.
Principal: CECIL BRIGGS, M.A., M.C.
COURSES OF STUDY FOR
LONDON MATRICULATION
Intermediate and Degree Examinations. Also for School, Certificate, University Entrance, Civil Service, Bookkeeping, Accountancy, Royal Society of Arts Examination &c.
U.C.C. SUCCESSES – Above 1,000 U.C.C. students pass London University Examinations each year. 5,996 matriculated during the twelve years 1925-1936
PROSPECTUS and SPECIAL FREE GUIDE if exam. is mentioned may be had post free from the Registrar, 23, Burlington House, Cambridge.

**PITMAN'S COLLEGE**
Important posts in all branches of commerce, Civil Service and the professions are open to men and women who have benefited by the Pitman SPECIALISED TRAINING COURSES. Students receive the finest possible tuition for the best Secretarial and business appointments. The College Specialises in preparation for professional preliminary examinations and London Matriculation. Fees moderate.
Advisory Governor: THE DUCHESS OF ATHOLL, D.B.E., D.C.L., LL.D., M.P.
Principal: R.W. Holland, O.B.E., M.A., M.Sc., LL.D.
Write for (a) "Day" Prospectus.
or (b) "Evening Study" Booklet,
or (c) "Home Study" Handbook.
182, Southampton-row, W.C.1.
Telephone: TERMINUS 4481.
Branches at Brixton, Brondesbury, Croydon, Ealing, Finsbury Park, Forest Gate, Lewisham, Maida Hill, N. Finchley, Palmers Green, Wimbledon, Leeds, Manchester.

AN AUTHORITATIVE 132pp. "GUIDE TO CAREERS." is offered free by the Metropolitan College, the leading Commercial, Professional and University training Institution in the British Empire, Expert Coaching for all Accountancy, Secretarial, Banking, Legal and Insurance Exams., for Professional Preliminary Exams, Matriculation B.Com., B.A. and other London University Degrees, for Civil Service and Police Exams, &c. Also many Practical (non-exam) Courses in Accountancy, Secretarial and Commercial Subjects, Salesmanship. Foreign Languages, English, Public Speaking, &c. OVER 8,000 EXAM. SUCCESSES LAST YEAR. Specialised Postal Training taken at home in leisure time, also Intensive Private Oral Tuition in London. WRITE TO-DAY for free "Guide to Careers" to the METROPOLITAN COLLEGE, (G1/2a), ST. ALBANS (or call, 40-42, Queen Victoria-street, E.C. 4).

BUSINESS POSITIONS THE CIVIL SERVICE ALL EXAMINATIONS
Rapid & Economical Specialised Courses. A well-paid position guarantied for every proficient student. Prospectus and advice free.
Choose your Career and write, call or telephone for free particulars, Booklet and advice,
DAY, EVENING AND POSTAL TUITION
CLARK'S COLLEGE Ltd.
(Dept. 16), 126 Chancery-lane, London W.C.2.
'Phone: HOLBORN 5424.

**UNIVERSITY TUTORIAL COLLEGE**
Founder: WILLIAM BRIGGS, LL.D., D.C.L.
Principal: ADRIAN J.F. COLLINS, M.A.
LONDON MATRICULATION
CLASSES FOR THE EXAMINATIONS OF 1938 MAY BE TAKEN UP AT ANY TIME REDUCED FEES TO LATE ENTRANTS.
SPECIAL CLASSES FOR SPECIAL UNIVERSITY ENTRANCE
Write for Prospectus to the Principal
**UNIVERSITY TUTORIAL COLLEGE**
32 RED LION-SQUARE, HOLBORN, W.C.1.

A FREE SCHOLARSHIP.
**ST. JAMES'S SECRETARIAL COLLEGE**
AWARDED THRICE YEARLY
34 and 35, GROSVENOR-PLACE, S.W.1.

**LONDON COLLEGE OF SECRETARIES**
(Under Distinguished Patronage),
Complete and practical training for educated girls and women desiring to be PRIVATE SECRETARIES to professional men, politicians, or business men.

INDIVIDUAL TUITION. A suitable position is found for every qualified Student. Special attention given to foreign Shorthand. Shorter courses in any secretarial subject. Apply 46, Grosvenor-place, S.W.1. (Tel. Sloane 6151).

HOW TO PASS MATRIC. and all similar examinations. Be prepared by those who have had long experience of what the examiners require. Come to the STRAND TUTORIAL COLLEGE (late Preliminary Class, King's College, London). 353, Strand, London W.C.2. L. Hutchings, M.A. H.E. Weaver, B.Sc. Fees: 12 guineas a term. Next term begins 5th Oct. Pupils seen on Monday, 4th October, from 12.0 till 3.0. HIGH PERCENTAGE OF SUCCESSES.

**THE FINEST START**
FOR A SECRETARIAL CAREER IS TO GAIN A DIPLOMA
AT
KENSINGTON COLLEGE
Particulars from Mr. L.N. Munford, 34, Bishop's-road, W.2. Paddington 9046.

MRS. HOSTER'S SECRETARIAL TRAINING COLLEGE 29 Grosvenor Place, S.W.1. The appointments Bureau is available to all Pupils free of charge throughout their Secretarial career. For full prospectus, apply to Mrs. Hoster, F.C.I.S., St. Stephen's Chambers, Telegraph St. London E.C.2.

AERONAUTICAL ENGINEERING
The College of Aeronautical Engineering, Chelsea, S.W.3.
President: The VISCOUNT WAKEFIELD.
Next Probationary Term commences 5th October.
DAY and RESIDENTIAL Syllabus from the Registrar.

CUT, f.t, make your dress under expert tuition, 12 lessons, 3 gns. Also eveningg, Miss Morgan. 37 Marylebone High-street, W.1. Welbeck 5049.

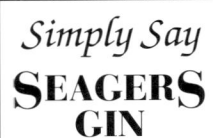

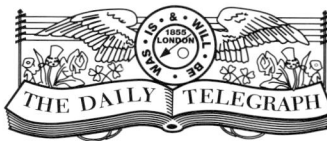

135, Fleet-st., London, E. C. 4.

THE DAILY TELEGRAPH

Telephone Central 4242

Thursday, May 13, 1937.

## GOD SAVE THE KING!

Another brilliant page was added yesterday to the story of the Kings and Queens of England. There is no other such Sovereignty among mankind. It was yesterday acclaimed in a great scene of loyal homage to which the world beyond the bounds of the King's realm can show nothing comparable. A whole Empire, girdling the earth with its unity of nations and peoples, honoured the King and crown, all proudly owning their allegiance. The glories of the Coronation day, as rapturously enjoyed as they had been excitedly anticipated, surpassed all expectation. On fears of the misty dawn followed a morning of silvery skies and, though heavy rain fell later, few would not count themselves fortunate in so much fair weather. The State procession was superbly marshalled. Military music enlivened the waiting hours. The steeples rocked with the frolic of the bells. Happiness was in the air. Mingled with happiness was sentiment and patriotic emotion, expectant of and responsive to the constantly awakening touch. All London seemed to be compacted along the processional way, but those multitudinous crowds, tense to the thrilling moment when the King and Queen should pass, were mustered from many a town and every shire in our Isles and from the Britains beyond the seas. So may be it for many centuries more, whoever may come swaying through the streets in the gold coach of State. To the Abbey to be anointed and crowned, at the Abbey to renew the sacred oath of obedience to the laws and service of God and the realm, from the Abbey to the Palace to be beheld by an "honest peaceable and obedient commonalty" wearing the Crown which from the dawn of history has symbolised government, majesty, authority and power — this it is to be crowned King of England.

To the signal and enduring significance of yesterday's act of fealty the Prime Ministers of Great Britain and the Empire bore witness in the broadcast speeches to which the King's was a moving climax. His message of thanks to his People declares in every word, as its tones brought home to those who listened, that he spoke "with a very full heart." The greatest orators are said to owe something to the inspiration of the audience about them. There is so keen a personal note in the King's phrases that he might seem to have been speaking from the balcony of the Palace to the vast and enthusiastic throng which greeted him on his return from the Abbey. But though it was clear that the great demonstrations of affectionate loyalty which he had seen and heard had touched him deeply, it was of "all his peoples" far and near that he thought, happy that on the day of his Coronation he could, the first of our Sovereigns, be heard in homes all over the Empire.

Neither in the Abbey nor outside was there the slightest interruption to the smooth sequence of events, upon which the Earl Marshal, the Lord Chamberlain and those in charge of the troops and the police deserve the warmest congratulations. An infinity of multitudinous detail in that marvellous procession took shape in perfect rhythm. What a tribute to our King and Queen was paid by the presence of those Royal Princes, special Envoys and Ambassadors! What a tribute also, we will not say to the Might of Britain – though we are proud of her might – but to her ancient and present prestige and to her lively sense of Justice, Law and Right! It was last paid in solemn silence amid the mourning of a mighty nation. Yesterday it saluted the radiance of the opening reign. In that radiance there also came from the depth of grateful hearts a reverent welcome to Queen Mary, which declared in the hour of her son's crowning, and as she came from it with his two fair children by her side, what the Crown and the realm have owed to her.

Eloquent of much was the presence in that procession of marching men from far distant lands proudly wearing the uniform of the King. Contingents from Canada,Australia, New Zealand and South Africa, young nations conscious of a splendid destiny; contingents representing the ancient chivalry of India, contingents from the smaller Colonial forces which help to preserve the British peace throughout the world. Outside observers keep trying to weigh the exact significance of it all in scales of their own. We who have our own tables of weights and measures prefer not to place such imponderables in the balance before sagacity urges or necessity compels. London loves to see these men from overseas march through the streets in step with British troops. This has been the first Coronation since the Statute of Westminster, and it confirms our polity. As long as the need of Imperial unity is thus felt and declared the British Commonwealth of Nations need not fear any future.

We have a King and Queen worth homage, worth respect, worth loyalty and worth love. As they acknowledged yesterday the salutations of the crowds they seemed to return smile for smile and blessing for blessing. Their personal devotion to one another as they rode side by side was delightful to witness, and as they both shared the triumph of the day so each for the other halved its burden. Any misgiving as to the future that may have lingered in nervous minds can now be regarded as effectually dispelled by yesterday's manifestation of joyous loyalty. Let us look before, not after! The King and Queen are still young enough to indulge the hope of a long reign. May it be a reign of unity and unbroken peace. We now know in our inmost souls that the King and Queen will never fail their peoples. Let us make it no less sure that we fail neither them nor ourselves.

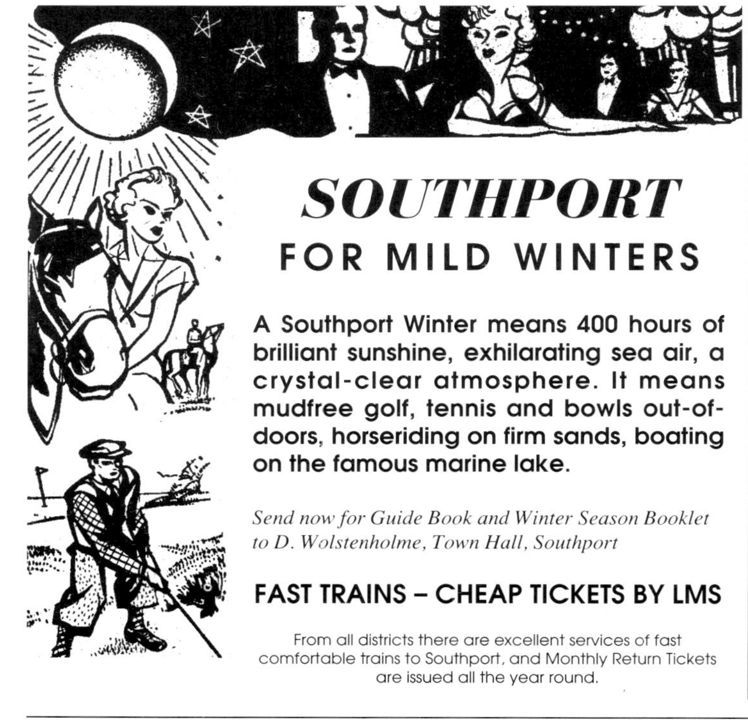


# KING GEORGE AND QUEEN ELIZABETH CROWNED AMID EMPIRE'S REJOICING

## ACCLAIM OF WESTMINSTER ABBEY GATHERING ECHOES AROUND THE WORLD

## 50,000 CHEER THEIR MAJESTIES ON PALACE BALCONY LAST NIGHT

## ROYAL BROADCAST: THE KING DEDICATES HIMSELF ANEW TO THE SERVICE OF HIS PEOPLES

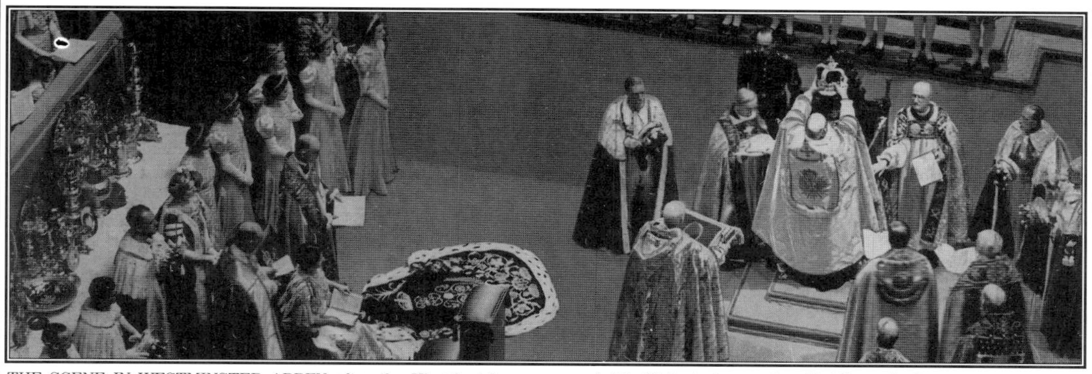

THE SCENE IN WESTMINSTER ABBEY after the King had been crowned. His Majesty is wearing St. Edward's Crown and is holding the Royal Sceptre in his right hand and the Sceptre with the Dove in his left. The Queen is seated, left centre, while in the middle of the box on the extreme left is Queen Mary.

**WITH ALL THE SPLENDOUR AND SOLEMNITY OF TRADITION, AND IN THE PRESENCE OF A DISTINGUISHED GATHERING REPRESENTING THE PEOPLES OF BRITAIN, THE EMPIRE AND THE WORLD, KING GEORGE VI. AND QUEEN ELIZABETH WERE CROWNED IN WESTMINSTER ABBEY YESTERDAY.**

Millions of his Majesty's subjects, massed in the streets of London and scattered throughout the length and breadth of his Dominions, heard him, in a strong, firm voice, solemnly promise to govern his Peoples according to their laws and customs, causing Law and Justice, in Mercy, to be executed in all his judgements.

**The triple acclaim of those in the Abbey, the crash of the bells and the united cry of "God Save the King!" which greeted the climax of his Crowning echoed around the world.**

After the ceremony their Majesties, wearing their robes of purple velvet and their jewel-encrusted crowns, passed, in the golden State coach, through the packed streets of their capital in a two-mile cavalcade rich in colour and pageantry. Three million people, many of whom had waited throughout the night, accompanied their passage with a mighty roar of cheering.

Rain, which had threatened throughout the morning, held off until their Majesties had almost reached the Palace. Here, after their return, took place one of the greatest demonstrations of popular enthusiasm ever witnessed.

**A vast crowd surged around the Palace, singing the National Anthem and maintaining a continuous cry of "We want the King and Queen!" until their Majesties appeared on the balcony, wearing their Robes and Crowns and accompanied by Queen Mary, Princess Elizabeth, Princess Margaret and other members of the Royal Family. The crowd increased throughout the evening, and twice more, at nine o' clock and 10.15, their Majesties appeared to be cheered by a multitude of more than 50,000**

In a moving broadcast to the Empire last night his Majesty dedicated himself anew to the Service of his Peoples.

## PEOPLE SHOUT THEIR "WILLINGNESS AND JOY"

**By R. MacColl, Daiy Telegraph Special Correspondent**

Before the Altar of Westminster Abbey King George VI., By that supreme act of dedication which has been forged in Britain's long history, was sacredly anointed and crowned, to rule and to serve the nation.

Joyously, full-throated, the people gathered in the Abbey acclaimed their King who bore himself throughout with simple dignity.

Queen Mary, watching her son "upon the threshold of a new life," was noticeably overcome with emotion on several occasions.

From the Nave the Royal procession moved in stately splendour. As it reached the Theatre, whereon soon history was to be made, it broke into its componenets, which grouped themselves to form the setting of the scene. Extra lights were turned on, and the whole Theatre was bathed in a sudden glow.

### THE QUEEN'S ENTRY
### Queen Mary's Curtsey

The Dean of Westminster, Dr. Foxley Norris, went to his place on the south side of the Altar. The Archbishop of York, Dr. Temple, and Dr. Ingram, Bishop of London, Dr. Garbett, Bishop of Winchester, and Dr. Pollock, Bishop of Norwich, went to the north of the Altar. At the Altar was the Archbishop of Canterbury, Dr. Lang.

The Queen, with her supporters and Bishops attendant, walked to her Chair of State, where she stood waiting. As she passed the Royal Box, Queen Mary dropped her a curtsey, with the other ladies.

Behind her were ranged her Mistress of the Robes, the ladies who had borne her train, her Lord Chamberlain and the Lords bearing her Regalia. At each elbow were her Bishops, Dr. Herbert, Bishop of Blackburn, and Dr. Furse, Bishop of St. Albans.

By the north-east pillar the Lord President of the Council, Mr. Ramsay MacDonald, stationed himself, Viscount Hailsham, the Lord High Chancellor, being by the south-east pillar, where were also the Lord Mayor of London, Sir George Broadbridge, Lyon and Ulster Kings of Arms and the Gentleman Usher of the Black Rod.

### PRINCESSES' INTEREST
### Scamper Upstairs

The King, grave and dignified, paced with his supporters and attendants to his Chair of State. At each side of his Majesty the attendant Bishops of Bath and Wells and Durham, Dr. Wilson and Dr. Henson, ranged themselves.

The Swords were on the King's right hand, with the Sword of State nearest him. The bearers of the King's Regalia stood near. Behind the King were the Groom of the Robes, the King's trainbearers, the Keeper of the Jewel House, and the Lord Chamberlain.

Looking out upon the Sacrarium from a box arranged on its south side – behind the Chairs of State — was Queen Mary, with Princess Elizabeth and Princess Margaret Rose, sitting between their grandmother and the Princess Royal, who occupied a seat at the western end of the front row.

The others in the front row were the Queen of Norway, the Duchess of Gloucester, the Duchess of Kent, the Countess of Strathmore, and the Earl of Strathmore, the parents of the Queen.

From the moment that they arrived at their places in the Royal Box after scampering up the stairs, the little Princesses showed a lively interest in all that passed.

Princess Elizabeth took the occasion with great decorum, turning to exchange comment with her grandmother, Queen Mary, and pointing out to her points of interest in the Order of Service Book.

Princess Margaret Rose was more exuberant. Not only the scene before her but the people behind and on either side of her attracted her excited attention.

The Princess Royal, sitting beside her small niece, was kept busy answering a stream of questions. Presently she drew the little girl's attention to the magnificent golden Altar plate, ranged just below the Royal Box

### WHISPERED QUERIES
### Round-Eyed Wonder

Princess Margaret Rose at once craned forward, her nose flattened on the ledge, and gazed in round-eyed wonder at the splendid vessels. Then she whispered volubly to the Princess Royal and finally succeeded in drawing her elder sister into the conversation.

When later she stood up with the rest of the Congregation her face only just cleared the top of the side of the box.

The appearance of her father and mother as the principals in the tremendous drama below her she at first found absorbing. But even this excitement did not contain her for very long, and soon she was plying her aunt with whispered queries once more.

The Queen had been awaiting her husband, standing at her Chair of State. The trains of both were arranged by their attendants in graceful folds over the left arms of the chairs. Together the King and Queen now knelt at their fald-stools offering their private prayers. Then they rose and sat upon their chairs.

The Archbishop of Canterbury came forward to present the King to his people for the Recognition.

Preceded by Garter King of Arms, the Archbishop, with the Lord Chamberlain, the Lord High Constable and the Earl Marshall, went to the east side of the Theatre, the Archbishop ahead of the others, his cope gleaming beneath the radiance of the lights.

The King rose and advanced to the front of the Sacrarium, where, standing beside St. Edward's Chair, he was visible to many in the Nave. Removing his cap he faced towards the east.

The Archbishop, in clear, strong tones, which he produced without apparent effort, cried: "Sirs, I here present unto you King George, your undoubted King; wherefore all you who are come this day to do your homage and service, are you willing to do the same?"

At once there came the answering shout from the thousands of men and women. "God Save King George."

# BASQUES FALL BACK ON NEW LINE OF DEFENCE

## PRIEST'S STORY OF DESTRUCTION OF GUERNICA

## GOING TO VATICAN TO APPEAL FOR INTERVENTION

The Basque forces fell back towards Bilbao yesterday. They are abandoning 10 miles of coast and taking up a new line of defence about two miles from the city.

**Their sacred city of Guernica, which was destroyed by fire on Monday and Tuesday, has now been occupied by the Nationalists.**

Canon Onaidnia, of Valladolid Cathedral, who was an eye-witness of the burning of Guernica, left for Rome yesterday on a mission from the Basque President.

**He is to ask the Vatican to intervene with the Nationalist authorities to try to prevent a repetition of the suffering in Guernica.**

The British Embassy at Hendaye is making inquiries about the city's destruction. In the House of Lords yesterday Viscount Cecil described the bombing as "one of the most horrible things that has ever been done."

**(April 30)**

# NATIONALISTS IN RUINED CITY

## SCENE OF DESOLATION

**From Pembroke Stevens, Daily Telegraph Special Correspondent with the Nationalist Forces**

GUERNICA, Thursday.

The still smoking ruins of Guernica, the ancient Basque capital, were occupied by the Nationalist forces to-day.

The Basque forces evacuated the town and withdrew in the direction of Bilbao an hour before the Nationalists entered the ruins. Guernica is just 15 miles north-east of Bilbao, just outside the second line of the city's defences. All the country behind Guernica – to the north and east of an estuary which joins Guernica to the sea – is being occupied by the Nationalists.

The importance of the advance along the coast is that it will enable the Nationalist artillery to dominate Bermeo, the port of Bilbao. This will strengthen the blockade. Ships will now find it more difficult to unload cargoes.

I entered Guernica with the Nationalist vanguard one hour after the departure of the Basque forces.

NO FOOD FOR THREE DAYS

Guernica presents an apalling spectacle of desolation. The destruction is even greater, even more complete than at Eibar.

Here and there a solitary wall of a house rears its gaunt and blackened silhouette against the blue sky. There is little else except wrecked houses blocking practically every street.

A group of excited and distracted women wearing a queer medley of garments – men's socks and shoes, ill-fitting blouses and skirts and overcoats too big for them – told me that they had lost everything in the fire. Their homes were destroyed at night. They had to flee in their night-dresses, grabbing clothes as they went from the wreckage of other houses that had not been destroyed by the flames.

The women hid in these ill-assorted garments in the woods until the arrival of the Nationalists. They had had nothing to eat for three days. I gave them what tinned food I had brought with me.

**(April 30)**

# MANY BRITONS KILLED IN SPAIN

**Daily Telegraph Special Correspondent with the Nationalist Forces**

SAN MARTIN DE LA VEGA, Tuesday.

Many English volunteers with the International Brigade in Madrid were killed or taken prisoner in the recent fighting south-east of the capital.

Sixteen English prisoners taken in the fighting at Arganda, on the Madrid-Valencia road, are now behind the lines at Navalcarnero. They have been set to work with pick and shovel on roads and bridges blown up by the Madrid troops.

Some of the men who perished before Arganda carried English letters, photographs of Englishwomen and men, and English banknotes.

The majority were youths with no previous experience of warfare.

The Legionaires who had fought them told me that the positions they held were usually captured by sunrise rushes. Those who survived the hand-grenades were usually so stunned by the explosions that they fell easy victims to an advance followed up by rifle, bayonet and knife.

The Legionaires tell me that the English were usually well supplied with food.

**(February 17)**

# BURNING OF CITY

## BRITISH INQUIRIES

**From Christopher Martin, Daily Telegraph Special Correspondent with the Basque Forces**

BILBAO FRONT, Thursday.

The British Embassy at Hendaye is seeking direct evidence definitely to fix the responsibility for the burning of Guernica.

The Nationalists advancing on Bilbao today menaced the port of Bermeo, and British destroyers evacuated refugees from there. The Basques have organised a last line of resistance about two miles east of Bilbao, running roughly through the outlying towns of Aldacano and Zamidio. This line might be compared to the line of the Manzanares river, outside Madrid.

The Basques claim to-day to be holding the enemy on the Durango to Bilbao road. Their munition works in Bilbao are working night and day, and shortage of munitions no longer is feared. Manpower also is ample and well disciplined.

Competent observers well acquainted with Spanish methods of warfare take the view to-night that the issue at Bilbao is likely to be in the nature of a long drawn out siege.

Bilbao now has food, thanks to the arrival of the British foodships. It is estimated that there are 350,000 people to feed in the town, with the influx of 50,000 refugees from the outlying districts.

**(April 30)**

# HOW SANTANDER SURRENDERED TO NATIONALISTS

**From Alan Dick, Daily Telegraph Special Correspondent with the Nationalist Forces.**

SANTANDER, Thursday.

Santander was occupied by Nationalist forces early to-day. The 12-day offensive ended in anti-climax.

The Nationalist troops were about two miles from the city, awaiting orders to advance, when at 8 a.m. two uniformed figures, carrying a large white flag, slowly walked up the hill from the city.

They announced themselves as Cmdr. Botilla, chief of the Santander militia, and Cmdr Vega, chief of police. They said: "We will give up the city if you will spare the women and children."

Then they were marched blindfolded to the Nationalist headquarters at Vargas, a short distance along the road. After a brief conference with the commanding officers there they posed for photographs and then entered a car with two majors of the Spanish Foreign Legion.

SOVIET SYMBOL

Cmdr. Vega, tall, thin and pale, was unshaven and obviously suffering from emotion. He was wearing the blue uniform of the shock police, and on his cap was the red Soviet five-point star and silver bars.

Botilla entered the car with the Nationalist officers while Vega sat with his legs straddled over a mudguard and bearing his white flag aloft. Troops cheered as the small grey car drove slowly down the winding slope to Santander, the white flag fluttering in the breeze.

The first Nationalist troops entered Santander at 11.15 a.m. The cavalcade into the city lasted more than two hours. Cars, tanks mules and men moved slowly along the dusty, winding road.

Many soldiers had decorated their rifles with flowers. Bouquets of carnations, roses and fuschias hung from machine-guns, while the tanks bore garlands of wild flowers gathered by village girls.

**(August 27)**

# DESTRUCTION OF ANCIENT BASQUE CAPITAL

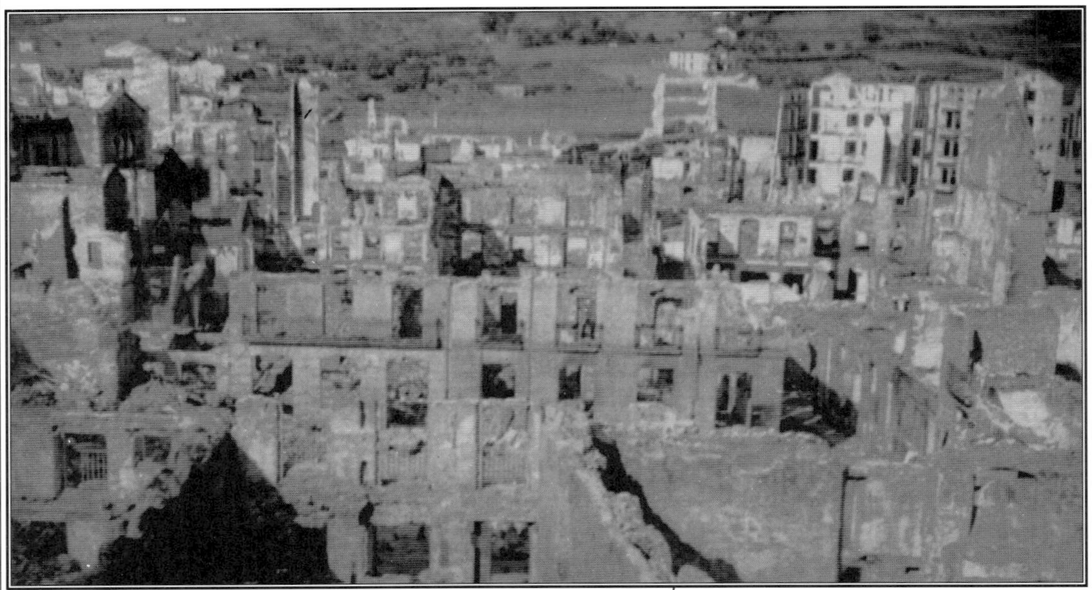

RUINED BUILDINGS IN GUERNICA, eight miles from Bilbao, after it had been devastated by the worst air-raid of the Spanish War.

# BRITISH WARSHIP HOLED OFF SPAIN

**The British destroyer Hunter, 1,340 tons, was badly damaged yesterday by an explosion while off Almeria, South-East Spain. According to the latest reports eight men were killed and 24 injured.**

An Admiralty announcement states that the cause was unknown, but it was reported from Valencia that the explosion was due to a floating mine. The destroyer's bows were holed and she was towed into Almeria by the Spanish destroyer Lazaga.

**The Hunter was one of the Navy's latest destroyers. She was patrolling the Mediterranean for non-intervention purposes with eight other British destroyers.**

**(May 14)**

# DEFENDERS OF MADRID HOLDING ON DOGGEDLY

**From Pembroke Stephens, Daily Telegraph Special Correspondent with the Nationalist Forces**

FRONT-LINE TRENCHES, SOUTH OF MADRID, Friday.

The morale of the defenders of Madrid remains unbroken. To-day they have counter-attacked without ceasing.

The resistance to the Nationalists has been of a savage intensity. In these attacks many of the Government troops have been killed and a large number of Russian tanks disabled or captured.

Nearly the whole of the International Brigade has been thrown into battle against the Nationalists in this southern sector.

The battalions are called after Communist leaders. There is the Thaelmann battalion, after the German leader; the Margarita Nelken battalion, and the Dimitroff battalion. A British battalion is called after Saklatvala.

An interesting method of testing the morale of the rival troops is to visit the front-line trenches at night and hear the two-sides, often separated only by 200 yards, shouting to each other through megaphones.

TRUCE AT SUNSET

By common consent rifle fire dies down as the sun sets, and then spokesmen on both sides shout news to each other from the newspapers. Political speeches follow, the soldiers shouting out slogans and points from the rival points of view.

"Hullo Fascists," cries a voice from the Government trenches," you have taken Malaga, we know. You may take Madrid, but we will be waiting for you at Valencia and Barcelona. You will never pass there."

"Bah!" replies a legionary. "You will run faster than ever when we reach the coast."

Government fighter: "We soldiers have nothing against each other. Why should we fight? Why can't we fraternise? Let us be brothers. Let us have an armistice."

A Moor: "The only thing I want to do is to fight and kill."

Government Fighter: "Desert to us."

Legionary: "But you have nothing to eat."

The voices in the trenches then begin to sing. The Legionaires join in their favourite anthem, "Fiancés of Death are we." The Government troops sing the Red Flag and the many French in their trenches sing the "Marseillaise."

Then gradually the sound of singing dies and the sentinels resume their watch beside the shining mortars and anti-tank guns.

**(February 20)**

# MEN TRAPPED IN ENGINE ROOM

## 14 PICKED UP

VALENCIA, Thursday.

It was officially announced in Valencia this evening that the British destroyer H35 – the Hunter, 1,340 tons – was badly damaged by an explosion, supposed to be due to a floating mine, five miles off the shore this afternoon. She was towed into port at Almeria.

Details received by the British representatives here to-night gave a casualty list of eight killed and 24 injured.

It was stated that the explosion was due to "some external agent, believed to have been a mine." It occurred at three p.m. today, and blew a hole in the bows of the destroyer.

The Valencia authorities hurried aeroplanes and ships to the scene for rescue operations. The Spanish ship Lazaga took the H35 in tow and brought her into Almeria Harbour.

A report by the captain of the Jaime Primero, issued by the Ministry of Air and Marine, says that the explosion occurred less than four miles from port.

The Hunter sank rapidly forward immediately after the explosion. Fourteen members of the crew were picked up by a Spanish launch.

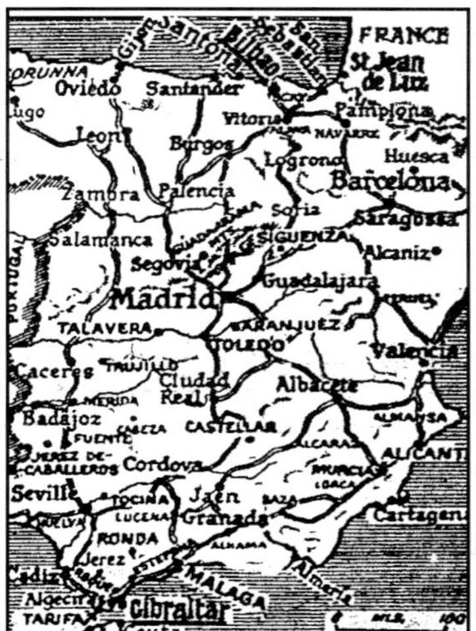


The captain adds that he immediately ordered several Spanish warships to the destroyer's assistance, including the Lazaga and a number of armed fishing boats.

**(May 14)**

# BRITISH PLAN TO DEFEND THE PACIFIC

## SINGAPORE BASE READY SOON

**By Hector C. Bywater, Daily Telegraph Naval Correspondent**

In July the huge graving dock at Seletar, the Singapore naval base, will be ready for occupation.

It has been designed to take ships up to 50,000 tons, though no warships of that size have been, or are likely to be built – at least for years to come.

For the past eight years a floating dock, able to house and lift ships up to 55,000 tons, has been moored at the Singapore base. By July, therefore, the new dockyard will be capable of docking and repairing simultaneously any two capital ships in the Navy.

The entire base, together with its fortifications, is due for completion at the end of 1939. By that date more than £10,000,000 will have been spent in making the Seletar the largest, best-equipped and probably the most strongly defended naval base east of Suez.

Its impending completion raises the question of the use to which it will be put. It is not improbable that Singapore will eventually become the headquarters of a new "Pacific Fleet," charged with the defence of our immense territories and interests within that ocean.

NEW SQUADRON POSSIBLE

It may not be a coincidence that the year which will witness the completion of the new base should also see the commissioning of our new battleships of the 1936-37 programme. Besides the King George V and Prince of Wales, begun on Jan 1, two or three additional ships are to be ordered as soon as the forthcoming Navy Estimates are passed.

Early in 1940, therefore, four or five battleships of the most powerful type will be ready for service. While it is improbable that they will be sent to the Pacific, their completion will release a corresponding number of older ships, whose presence at Singapore would be welcomed by the Dominions and colonies concerned.

**(January 19)**

# OUTRAGE BY I.R.A. IN DUBLIN

**From Our Own Correspondent**

DUBLIN, Thursday.

While a policeman stood by watching helplessly, a land mine destroyed the equestrian statue of King George II in St. Stephen's Green, Dublin, early to-day.

The mine exploded with a terrific roar. Windows in the vicinity were shattered; large pieces of masonary from the plinth of the statue were hurled high into the air.

The policeman and a number of people who had joined him had narrow escapes.

Just after daybreak the officer saw a number of young men running from the Green.

He went to the statue and discovered the mine – bags of high explosive forced into a hole which had been scooped at the base of the statue. From them came the ominous ticking of a clock which controlled the fuse.

The policeman was afraid to touch the mine. He sent for reinforcements and an explosives expert, but the mine exploded while he was awaiting their aid.

The explosion, which was heard all over the city, terrified the residents of the nearest houses. They believed that they were being bombed.

**(May 14)**

# FAIRYLAND SCENE ON THE PALACE BALCONY

## THEIR MAJESTIES & PRINCESSES IN ROBES AND CROWNS

By Herbert Ashley

**"WE WANT THE KING!" This cry, in increasing volume rose from the great crowd that surged forward up to the railings of Buckingham Palace almost as soon as the State Coach had disappeared into the Courtyard.**

**Part of the crowd broke through the police cordon before the Royal Coach had rounded the Victoria Memorial, but soldiers and police held back most of the people until the Guard of Honour of the three Services had marched away.**

**Then the crowd was a solid mass. Some climbed on the railings of the Palace; others on the lions and other figures of the Victoria Memorial. From all parts came the cry: "We want the King!"**

PRINCESSES DELIGHT
Smiling and Waving

Staid persons broke into song; some sang the National Anthem, others "For they are jolly good fellows!"

"We want the King!" The cry was now insistent.

Then at last, 26 minutes after they had returned to the Palace, their Majesties appeared. A great and memorable cry went up; a roar of over-whelming affection.

**To the delight and surprise of the crowd their Majesties were wearing the robes in which they had returned from the Abbey. They stood there, in their crowns, looking down on the great congregation of their subjects below them, smiling and obviously deeply moved by the warmth of the demonstration.**

Then the King, still pale and solemn from the experiences of the day, moved back and gently led forward his two children, Princess Elizabeth and Princess Margaret.

The children, also in their robes and with golden coronets on their heads, seemed to have stepped straight from fairyland.

Smiling happily they waved repeatedly to the cheering, singing, waving multitude. Princess Elizabeth bent down to whisper to her sister; Princess Margaret smiled back. Then both began to wave in unison.

Princess Margaret could be seen jumping up and down to get a better view.

QUEEN MARY'S EMOTION
A Scene of Memories

Then came an incident that touched all hearts.

**The King stepped back and gently led forward his mother, Queen Mary. The Queen Mother was obviously overcome by the spontaneous warmth which welcomed her.**

The crowd was instantly sensible of the memories that must have passed through her mind as again she stood where so often she has stood before – memories of her own Coronation, 26 years ago, of the great demonstrations at the outbreak and the end of the war, and of that unforgettable scene just two years ago when she stood there with King George V on the day of their Silver Jubilee.

Cheers were unrestrained and from the heart. Tears were in many eyes.

The King and Queen stood alone together for a moment longer. Then they, too, returned into the Palace. Many of the crowd were quietly singing "God Save the King."

For hours afterwards people continued to converge on the Palace. By six p.m. the sentries had to withdraw behind the railings into the forecourt.

At nine o'clock the Palace sprang into light as the floodlights were switched on. A few moments later, to the accompaniment of another great cheer, the King and Queen again appeared on the balcony.

**The King, bareheaded and in evening dress, and the Queen, in an evening gown of white and silver under an ermine cloak, her diamond tiara glittering in the floodlights, bowed and waved repeatedly in response to the tremendous acclamation of a crowd estimated at 50,000 people.**

After two minutes they turned to reenter the Palace, but another burst of cheering brought them back for a moment.

It was officially stated at Buckingham Palace that their Majesties were not unduly tired by their arduous day.

One who saw them said: "they seem to me to be just as fresh and in just as good spirits to-night as they were at the beginning of the day."

**(May 13)**

# KING INVITES 4 WORKERS TO CORONATION

The King has sent personal invitations to four working people – two men and two women –to attend the Coronation Service in Westminster Abbey on May 12.

The invitations were issued to mark his Majesty's interest in the industrial areas

The four working people from industrial centres who have received invitations from the King to attend the Coronation are:

Miss Lizzie McCulloch, 45, a weaver, of James Templeton and Co., Glasgow, who worked on the carpet made by the firm for the Abbey service;

Mr. Elfred Thomas, 34, a tinplate polisher at the works of W. Gilbertson and Company Ltd., Pontardawe, South Wales, who was one of the first boys to attend the Duke of York's camps;

Miss Doris Griffiths, 21, of Vicarage-road, Aston, Birmingham, employed by the General Electric Co. Ltd., and

Leslie Pollard, 20, employed in the Bolsover Colliery, near Chesterfield.

The industries and districts were selected by the Industrial Welfare Society and the representatives were chosen by the firms.

"What a grand piece of luck," exclaimed Miss McCulloch, when told of the invitation. "You can realise how proud I am to represent Scottish workpeople and the British textile industry at the Coronation.

"Little did I think when I was weaving the gold carpet for the Coronation that I would be present for the historic event, and see it in the Abbey."

Mr. Thomas has been closely associated with welfare movement activities at Gilbertson's works.

"It is all so sudden and wonderful," he said. "It will not be the first time I have seen the King, because I saw him in 1921. I was lucky enough to be at the very first of his boys' camps."

Miss Griffiths exclaimed: "I am so thrilled I hardly know what I am doing. I have never been to London before in my life – although I have always wanted to go.

"And think of it – I am going to see the Coronation at the invitation of the King. What an honour."

Leslie Pollard said: "I am very proud indeed. I do not know why I have been selected. I have never seen the King and Queen, and I have not been to London before."

**(April 6)**

# NAZI SALUTE FOR THE KING

## NOT WELCOME AT COURT

By Our Diplomatic Correspondent

Court circles have not been favourably impressed by the variation introduced on Thursday by Herr von Ribbentrop into the accepted ceremonial form of presenting diplomatic credentials to the King.

It is expected that each head of a diplomatic mission will halt three times and bow on his approach to the Sovereign, to whom he then hands his letters of credence. The German Ambassador, the last to deliver his papers as being the latest Ambassador accredited, replaced the first two bows with a click of the heels and a raising of the hand in the Nazi salute.

At the final halt before his Majesty, Herr von Ribbentrop conformed to the traditional etiquette of the Court. He bowed and presented his letters.

While there is no desire in official circles to magnify the incident, the introduction of national forms of salutation into a British Court ceremony is held to be one which cannot be welcomed.

It is understood that Herr von Ribbentrop will make an appointment to call in at the Foreign office next week. In the absence of Mr. Eden, who will be on holiday, he will presumably be received by Viscount Halifax.

**(February 6)**

# B.B.C. APOLOGISE FOR 'LAPSE OF TASTE'

The B.B.C. apologised last night for what it described as "an unfortunate lapse of taste."

During the broadcasting of a musical item in the National programme, entitled "Masculine fame on parade: a satirical revue of Yesterday's Heroes," there came, at the end of a song, an interjection – "Mrs. Simpson" clearly audible over the air.

Almost immediately after the conclusion of the revue an announcer made the following statement: "We apologise to all our listeners for an unfortunate lapse of taste which was interjected during the earlier part of the programme."

**(February 10)**

ROYAL FAMILY IN HAPPY BALCONY SCENE AFTER THEIR RETURN

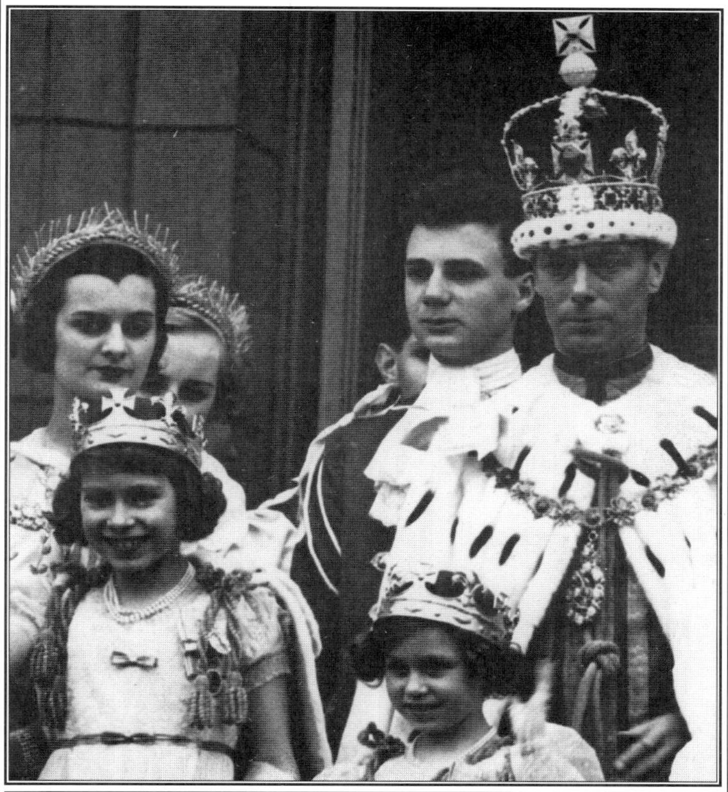

# PRINCESS ELIZABETH TO HAVE £6,000 A YEAR

## COMMITTEE'S PROPOSALS FOR NEW CIVIL LIST

An annuity for Princess Elizabeth and an additional £10,000 a year for the Duke of Gloucester are the principal recommendations in the report of the Select Committee of the House of Commons on the King's Civil List, issued yesterday.

It is proposed that in the event of the birth of a Duke of Cornwall, £25,000 should be paid from the revenues of the Duchy of Cornwall, partly for his maintenance and education and partly for the accumulation of funds to provide for a future Duchess.

The Committee recommends that Princess Elizabeth should receive £6,000 a year, rising to £15,000 when she is 21, in 1947, if there is then no Duke of Cornwall.

No provision is recommended for the Duke of Windsor.

The total of £140,000 allotted for a married King in the last civil list should, it is suggested, remain unchanged. This total is £60,000 less than that proposed for George V. in 1910.

DIGNITY OF CROWN
"Provision Adequate"

The Committee it is stated, finds that the total amount of the Civil List and its distribution were very carefully considered last year and sees no reason for recommending any alteration.

**"The provision then made," the report adds, "was adequate, but not more than adequate, for the proper maintenance of the dignity of the Crown."**

The extra £10,000 a year for the Duke of Gloucester, which will be added to his existing annuity of £25,000, is recommended in consideration of the fact that he will have additional duties to perform during the minority of Princess Elizabeth or of a future Duke of Cornwall. The annuity will be for life.

It is proposed that the existing provision of £70,000 a year for Queen Mary should remain unaltered. Similar provision should be made for Queen Elizabeth should she survive King George.

Should Princess Elizabeth pre-decease the King it is proposed that her annuity should be paid to the King's eldest surviving daughter.

PRINCESS'S MARRIAGE
No Provision Made

No special provision is proposed for Princess Elizabeth in the event of her marriage. The Committee considers that "it would be for Parliament to make such provision as may seem proper at that time, in the light of the circumstances then prevailing."

If the report is approved by Parliament the provision for the Royal family will be allocated between the Civil List, the Consolidated Fund and the revenues of the Duchy of Cornwall as follows:

Civil List

| | |
|---|---|
| His Majesty's Privy Purse | £110,000 |
| Salaries of his Majesty's household and retired allowances | £134,000 |
| Expenses of his Majesty's household | £152,000 |
| Royal bounty,alms, and special services | £13,200 |
| Total | £410,000 |

Consolidated Fund

| | |
|---|---|
| Queen Mary | £70,000 |
| Princess Louise, Duchess of Argyll | £6,000 |
| The Duke of Connaught | £25,000 |
| Princess Beatrice | £6,000 |
| Trustees for the daughters of King Edward VII | £6,000 |
| Trustees for the younger children of King George V | £56,000 |
| Total | £169,000 |

Duchy of Cornwall

| | |
|---|---|
| Princess Elizabeth | £6,000 |
| Duke of Gloucester | £10,000 |
| Total | £16,000 |

The revenues of the Duchy of Cornwall are estimated at £106,000 per annum. The £90,000 left after deducting the annuities to Princess Elizabeth and the Duke of Gloucester would be applied for the requirements of his Majesty's Privy Purse.

CIVIL LIST PENSIONS
Will Cost £50,000 a Year

Civil List pensions, the Report states, are nowadays granted only where there is both merit and hardship. Although the amount available for new pensions has been limited since 1837 to £1,200 a year, the total charge on the Consolidated Fund has averaged £23,000 a year during the last 25 years.

The proposed increase to £2,500 of the amount for new pensions will ultimately increase the total charge to about £50,000 a year. The Committee feels that this increase is justified by the changes in national conditions during the last 100 years.

An amendment moved by Mr. Attlee, leader of the Socialist party, urging greater simplicity in the state and ceremonial of the Court was defeated by 12 votes to three. Another, moved by Mr. Churchill, approving the present style and establishment of the Crown as "a bulwark against dictatorship and the symbol of the union of all the members of the British Commonwealth of Nations," was carried, also by 12 votes to three.

**(May 4)**

# NOTABLE INVALIDS

MARQUESS OF MILFORD HAVEN:
Fairly comfortable.
DOWAGER MARCHIONESS OF ZETLAND
Unchanged.
LORD MIDDLETON: Improving.
BISHOP OF WAKEFIELD: Improving
SIR E. KNAPP-FISHER: A little better.
MR. MATHESON LANG: Unchanged

**(December 18)**

# THE DUKE OF WINDSOR LEAVES FOR HONEYMOON

## QUIET WEDDING AT CHATEAU DE CANDE

From Our Own Correspondent

TOURS, Thursday.

The Duke and Duchess of Windsor, who were married at the Château de Candé, near here, this morning, are now on their way to Austria, where they will spend their honeymoon at Schloss Wasserleonburg, Carinthia. The Duke has rented the Schloss for three months.

They left here by car at 6.15 p.m. for Laroche-Migennes, near Paris, to join the Simplon express for Austria at midnight. Mobile Guards were posted along the route.

The Duke and Duchess are travelling in a special coach, and will leave the train at Arnoldstein, a little village station in Carinthia, to-morrow. From there they will drive to Schloss Wasserleonburg.

All day Tours has been in a state of excitement. Thousands of French sightseers, who arrived by charabanc and private car early this morning and late last night, gathered in the streets this morning outside the hotel to watch the guests departing for the Château.

MONEY FOR VILLAGERS

The villagers of Monts, to whom the Duke, in accordance with French custom, distributed a gift of money in honour of his wedding day, went out to the Château in a body.

The weather was brilliant, and the Duke was out early, walking in informal clothes on the terrace. The bride did not leave her room until just before the wedding.

There were two ceremonies – a civil service, conducted in French by Dr. Mercier, Mayor of Monts, and a religious ceremony conducted in accordance with the rites of the Church of England by the Rev. R. Anderson Jardine, Vicar of St. Paul's, Darlington.

The civil service, which preceded the religious ceremony, was brief and very informal. Only the two witnesses, Major E. D. Metcalfe, a former equerry to the Duke, and Mr. Herman Rogers, an American friend who has been acting as his host, and Mr. W. C. Graham, the British Consul-General at Monts, who represented the British Government, and five members of the press were present.

The Duke entered the room at 11.33, the bride some minutes later. The Duke was dressed in a black morning coat and striped trousers, and white and grey striped shirt and grey tie. A white carnation was pinned in his buttonhole.

The bride's wedding dress was a close-fitting, ankle-length, two-piece robe of powder blue crêpe. It was cut along very simple lines. Over it was a close-fitting short jacket of the same material as the dress. Her high-brimmed blue straw hat had a stiff veil turned upwards from the brim. Her only jewellery consisted of a pair of diamond and sapphire earrings and a bracelet of square-cut diamonds and sapphires, the gift of the Duke

RELIGIOUS CEREMONY

The religious ceremony in accordance with the rites of the Church of England followed 15 minutes later. This was held in the music room of the Château, which had been hastily converted into a chapel, with an old oak chest-of-drawers as an improvised altar.

The bridal couple entered the room by separate doors. The Duke was supported by Major Metcalfe. Mrs Warfield, leaning on the arm of Mr. Herman Rogers, who gave her away, carried a prayer book.

**(June 4)**

# DUKE OF WINDSOR SEES HITLER

## TEA AT BERCHTESGADEN

From Our Own Correspondent

MUNICH, Friday.

The Duke and Duchess of Windsor took tea to-day with Herr Hitler at his mountain villa, "Wachenfels," on the Obersalzberg, near Berchtesgaden. The visitors arrived at Berchtesgaden station at 1.20 p.m. in their special coach from Stuttgart and were immediately driven to the Koenigssee, Bavaria's most beautiful mountain lake.

An hour later they returned to Berchtesgaden and drove up the steep mountain road to Herr Hitler's home. The Fuehrer in his brown uniform welcomed them. The sun was shining all day and The Fuehrer could therefore show his guests the Alpine scenery to the best advantage.

The Duke's equerry, Mr. Dudley Forwood, Dr. Ley, leader of the German Labour front, and several Nazi officials were present.

The party returned to Berchtesgaden station at five o'clock. A small crowd of Bavarians and tourists had assembled to cheer them. A few minutes later the special train left, and at eight o'clock arrived in Munich, where a banquet in honour of the Duke and Duchess was given by Herr Hitler's deputy, Herr Rudolf Hess, and Frau Hess.

**(October 23)**

# DISASTER TO GIANT AIRSHIP: 50 DEAD

THE HINDENBURG leaving her base at Friedrichshafen on one of her Atlantic flights.

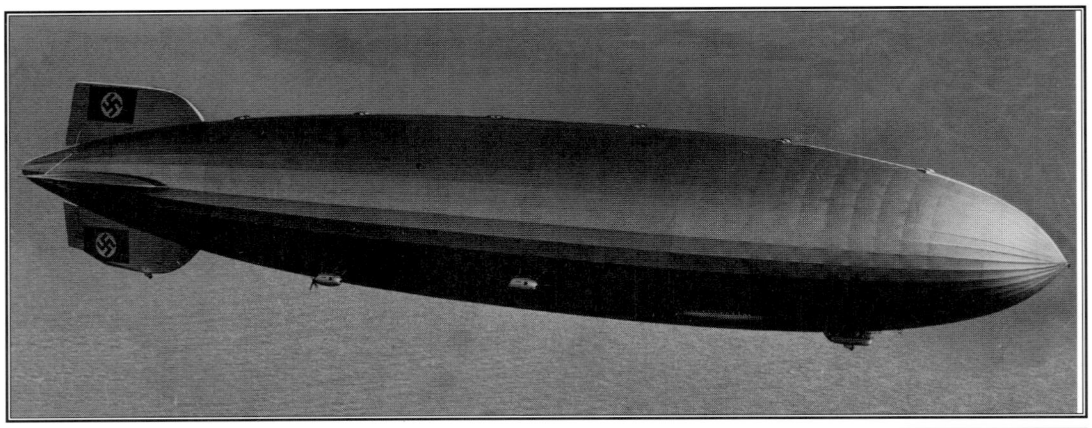

## HINDENBURG DESTROYED BY EXPLOSION

## HELD UP BY STORM: CRASH IN FLAMES

**DISASTER BEFELL THE GERMAN AIRSHIP HINDENBURG, WHEN SHE ARRIVED IN AMERICA YESTERDAY.**

**AN EXPLOSION OCCURRED AS SHE WAS MOORING, AND THE VESSEL WAS QUICKLY ENVELOPED IN FLAMES.**

**There were approximately 100 occupants on board, of whom about half perished.**

**The American Air Lines Company reported that 15 passengers and 35 members of the crew had survived.**

COMMANDER ESCAPES

Both the commander, Captain Max Preuss, and Captain Lehmann, who was acting in an advisory capacity, are among the survivors, although both are badly burned and in a critical condition.

A United States Navy report attributed the disaster to a hydrogen fire originating in the stern. This inflammable gas, and not helium, was used to inflate her.

The explosion occured as the Hindenburg was about to moor at Lakehurst, New Jersey, the landing ground for New York, from which it is 50 miles distant.

For an hour the Zeppelin had cruised around, a thunderstorm making it impossible for her to land.

SWIFT-SPREADING FLAMES

When the weather improved she approached the mooring mast. It was then that the explosion took place.

The flames spread with great rapidity. The airship collapsed to the earth, and was soon a mass of twisted wreckage.

Detachments of sailors were summoned to help in the rescue work. Roads near the airport were blocked with fire-engines, ambulances and the cars of police and doctors.

The ship cost £380,000 to build. Her insurance was largely covered in London.

**(May 7)**

## EYEWITNESS STORY OF THE DISASTER

### "ONLY MASS OF TWISTED STEEL IS LEFT"

"I am looking at the blazing wreck of the Hindenburg now. My impression is that many of the occupants have been trapped and burned to death.

"I can't tell you how many are dead. The airship crashed in a mass of flames, scattering hundreds of people near the mooring mast.

Shouting at the top of his voice, Commissioner of Police Deering told to a representative of THE DAILY TELEGRAPH on the Transatlantic 'phone from Lakehurst the story of the disaster.

"I was at the field when the giant came over. I was not there on business, but to meet a dear friend on board.

"Everything was O.K., and the wires were out for her at the mooring mast. Without warning there was a blast of fire, and the vast bulk just surged to the ground in a mass of flame.

"I don't know how many there were on board. As I speak to you I can see the rescue parties battling with the debris. In 30 years I have never seen such a sight ... it is terrible.

FLAMES TO GREAT HEIGHT

Heat Drives Back Crowd

"All I can say is that she just exploded and burned ... just flopped to the ground.

"I can't stay here any longer, I have to get to the ground again.

"As I talk to you I can see the crowds surging on the field. Police cars and ambulances are arriving amid a terrific roar of syrens and whistles.

"The flames leapt to a great height when she reached the ground, and then, in a terrific blast, myriads of sparks flew in the air, while the crowds fell back in a solid mass from the heat.

"There is nothing but a mass of twisted steel left."

Communication Officer Watson, speaking from Lakehurst early this morning said: "The airship is a total loss. There are some survivors.

"They are terribly injured, and have been taken to hospital. Police officers are at their bedsides.

"It is a terrible scene. The news has spread, and there are thousands of people here.

"Just as she reached the mast and the wires were out there was a terrific explosion, and I can only compare the explosion with a set scene on the talkies.

"She just went in the air in bits and pieces. I doubt whether we shall be able to identify anyone on board: they were just blown to bits."

**(May 7)**

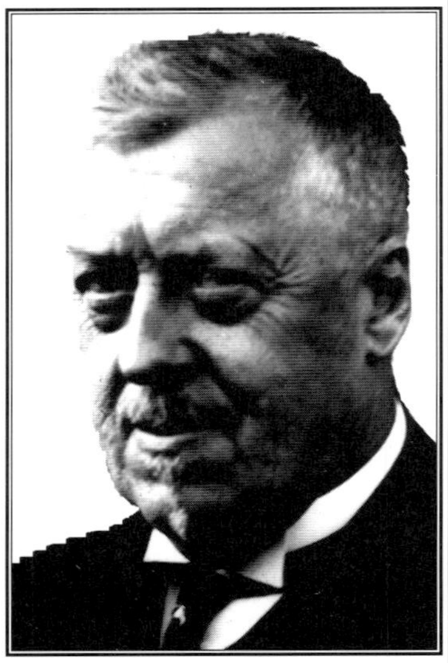

DR. ECKENER, designer and former commander of the Hindenburg.

## 197 ACRES ADDED TO "GREEN BELT"

Grimsdyke, the 110-acre Harrow Weald estate of the late Sir William and Lady Gilbert, is included in the 197 acres of land purchased as a public open space and part of London's Green Belt scheme by the Middlesex County Council.

This was reported at a meeting of the Harrow Urban District Council to-night.

At the time of the death of Lady Gilbert the hope was expressed that the house, which is of such great interest to lovers of Gilbert and Sullivan operas, would by some means be preserved, together with the beautiful grounds.

**(April 1)**

## BIG MAJORITY FOR AIR RAID PRECAUTIONS

**By Our Special Representative**

WESTMINSTER, Tuesday.

Earnest effort was concentrated to-day to obtain complete agreement on the Air Raid Precautions Bill. Appeals for unity were made from every side but the Socialist benches. Concession was offered by the Government.

All was in vain. The Socialists went into the lobby against the second reading of the bill and were defeated by 324 to 135.

Mr. Herbert Morrison was the director of this battle in his double capacity as a spokesman of the local authorities and as a Socialist leader.

He vowed that the authorities would accept nothing less than their claim that 100 per cent. of all local expenditure should be borne by the Treasury. He pledged the Socialists to fight for this claim as a principle of policy.

PLEA FOR UNITY

Mr. Churchill had opened the debate with a strong plea for unity on a question of national safety. The difference between the Government and the local authorities, he urged, had been reduced to microscopic dimensions.

Sir Percy Harris announced that the Independent Liberals would not vote against the bill, and supported Mr. Churchill's appeal for a united front on the defence of the civilian population.

Mr. Simmonds, from the Conservative benches, suggested that the Home Secretary might put into the bill an undertaking to review the financial arrangements after three years.

Sir SAMUEL HOARE agreed with Mr. Churchill that the margin of difference was very narrow and was anxious to eliminate it. But the Government could not recede from the position that there must be a local share in the expenditure to check extravagance in detailed administration on the spot.

Any expense more than a 2d. rate could only be properly incurred if the precautions were much greater than now contemplated.

COERCION BY MASS ATTACK

He was therefore prepared to accept Mr. Simmonds's suggestion of a time limit which should remove the last anxieties of the local authorities. A new clause would be moved by the Government providing for comprehensive revision of the financial scheme within three years.

Mr. Morrison promptly declared this of no use, and went on to offer the drastic alternative that the State should take over the whole charge, and put the local authorities under its orders.

Mr. Churchill's speech was quieter than his wont, but admirably argued.

He gave the bill wholehearted support, not without some sarcasm at the slowness of the Government in discovering the truth of what he said three years ago about the special danger of incendiary bombs and the general delays.

A model full scale of a London street was constructed with every underground service, such as electric mains, gas, hydrants and water mains.

Then semi-armour piercing bombs were dropped on it to discover exactly the type of damage they might expect in air raids.

They had decided to approve public shelters for congested areas, but in general it was better for people to stay in their own homes. For shelters, sandbags to the number of one or two million would be supplied to the local authorities free of charge.

**(November 17)**

## FAMOUS WAR CORRESPONDENT SHOT AT SHANGHAI

THE DAILY TELEGRAPH and MORNING POST deeply regrets to announce that its Special Correspondent on the Shanghai front Mr. Pembroke Stephens, was killed by machine-gun fire while observing Japanese troops attacking Nantao yesterday.

**(November 12)**

## LORD HALIFAX'S FIVE-HOUR TALKS WITH HITLER

### LOG FIRE IN STUDY

**From Our Special Correspondent**

BERCHTESGADEN, Friday.

Viscount Halifax had five hours' conversation with Herr Hitler at the Fuehrer's mountain chalet in Obersalzberg, near here, to-day.

He arrived here shortly before 10 a.m. by a train from Berlin, having travelled by special sleeping-coach which had been switched off at Regensburg to the Berchtesgaden line to avoid delay in Munich.

He was greeted at the station by Herr Brueckner, Herr Hitler's adjutant. They drove off immediately in the car which Herr Hitler had sent to the station to meet Lord Halifax.

The conversation began at 10 o'clock and continued, with only a short pause for luncheon, which Herr Hitler had served to his guests in the glass-enclosed balcony, until 3 O'clock.

INFORMAL TALK

In Hitler's Study

Besides Lord Halifax and Herr Hitler, there were present Baron von Neurath, the German Foreign Minister, who accompanied Lord Halifax from Berlin, Dr. Schmidt, a member of the German Foreign Office, who acted as interpreter, and Mr. I. A. Kirkpatrick, First Secretary of the British Embassy in Berlin. Mr. Kirkpatrick, I understand, merely acted as an observer and did not take part in the conference.

The conversations were of an exceedingly informal character. They took place in Herr Hitler's private study. His guests sat round the fireplace which, in honour of the English visitors, had a blazing wood fire.

Lord Halifax, accompanied by Baron von Neurath and Mr. Kirkpatrick, left Berchtesgaden for Munich shortly after 3 o'clock. Herr Hitler escorted his guests to their car, but did not accompany them to the station.

Late this afternoon the following short communiqué was issued from Berchtesgaden:

"Herr Hitler to-day received Lord Halifax, the British Lord President of the Council, and had a lengthy conversation with him, during which all problems relating to Anglo-German relations were discussed."

Herr Hitler left Berchtesgaden by private train for Munich half an hour after Lord Halifax's departure.

Lord Halifax spent two hours in Munich, during which he visited the Brown House, the Nazi party's headquarters. He left for Berlin with Baron von Neurath at 10.20 pm. and tomorrow will see Gen. Goering.

**(November 20)**

## NOBEL PRIZE FOR LORD CECIL

It is officially announced that Viscount Cecil of Chelwood has been awarded the Nobel Peace Prize for 1937. The prize is valued at £8,000.

Lord Cecil, who is in America to attend the World Alliance for International Friendship through the Churches, which is being held in Boston, said, when told that he had been awarded the prize, that he was most gratified and highly flattered.

He added that it was much too early to say what he would do with the £8,000.

Lord Cecil, who is 73, is the brother of the Marquess of Salisbury and of Lord Hugh Cecil. He is President of the League of Nations Union and has long been associated with peace movements. In 1934 he organised the Peace Ballot.

**(November 19)**

## SIR O. MOSLEY HIT BY STONE

### TAKEN UNCONSCIOUS TO HOSPITAL

A stone flung by a member of a crowd of 8,000 struck Sir Oswald Mosley on the head when he was about to address a meeting in Queens-drive, Liverpool, yesterday.

Sir Oswald, who was standing on the top of a loudspeaker van, fell unconscious. As members of the British Union of Fascists went to his aid, mounted police charged the crowd.

Hostile spectators were forced back, and first aid was given to Sir Oswald, whose temple was bleeding profusely. Bandages were fixed, and he was hurried to Walton infirmary.

There a minor operation was successfully performed. A bulletin issued last night said: "Sir Oswald Mosley is suffering from concussion and a punctured wound of the skull. His condition is giving no rise for anxiety at the moment."

VAN WINDOWS SHATTERED

A representative of THE DAILY TELEGRAPH and MORNING POST, was informed that Sir Oswald was unconscious when admitted, but that when he recovered he declared his intention of speaking at Birkenhead the same evening. He did not do so, however.

There was disorder in Queens-drive immediately the meeting began. As the loudspeaker van was driven on to a piece of waste land hundreds of missiles were thrown. The windows of the van were shattered.

Immediately Sir Oswald rose to speak he was struck, and a number of stones were also thrown at his bodyguard. Fifteen arrests were made by the police, and six people were treated for injuries, three being detained in hospital. The meeting was continued with a cordon of police around the loudspeaker van.

**(October 11)**

## NAZI ATTACK ON MR. CHURCHILL

**From Our Own Correspondent**

BERLIN, Thursday.

Under the heading "German Enemy No. 1," the "Angriff," the newspaper associated with Dr. Goebbels, to-day publishes on its front page a venomous attack on Mr. Winston Churchill.

The occasion for the attack is "an incendiary letter" said to have been written by Mr. Churchill on the danger to the British empire constituted by the foreign organisation of the National Socialist party.

"Mr. Winston Spencer Churchill," declares the writer, "has been everything already – journalist, officer, painter, poetaster, Chancellor of the Exchequer. First Lord of the Admiralty and globe trotter. His present occupation is German hater. For years now he has painted, not landscapes, but a picture of the German danger.

"But Mr. Churchill is the leader of the implacable haters of Germany in England, and even if he is somewhat less dangerous than those sinister wire pullers in the half darkness of the Secret Service and of many Ministerial quarters, yet nevertheless he sets in motion those waves of gall which are not to be taken too lightheartedly.

**(September 3)**

# 3,000 CIVILIANS DEAD IN CANTON AIR RAID

## BOMBS BEGIN FIRES IN PACKED CITY

## NOT ONE MILITARY STATION HIT

**From Our Own Correspondent.**

HONG KONG, Thursday.

Japanese bombers swooped on Canton to-day and, it is estimated, in 15 minutes killed 3,000 noncombatants.

It was at dawn that Japan's warplanes began what was to be the most devastating air raid of the Chinese-Japanese war. Ten bombers, escorted by fighting 'planes, took part.

Nearly all the bombs – explosive and incendiary – fell in the crowded poorer districts of the city; not one military station was hit.

Scores of bombs were dropped and within a few minutes many fires broke out.

Chinese fighter 'planes tried to keep the bombers away from the city, but they were hopelessly outnumbered and were engaged by the Japanese escort 'planes.

The Japanese 'planes did appalling damage; whole streets in the Chinese quarter of the city were demolished.

When the syrens shrieked their warning crowds of Chinese rushed for safety to the Bund, opposite the island-like Shameen, the foreign residential district. There they waited until, their mission of destruction ended, the Japanese war 'planes left.

CHILDREN TERRIFIED

It was only when the raiders had gone that any idea could be obtained of the fearful havoc that had been wrought. Buildings were reduced to little more than dust; their occupants were killed.

Rows of houses were demolished; in some places there were gaps 50 yards wide.

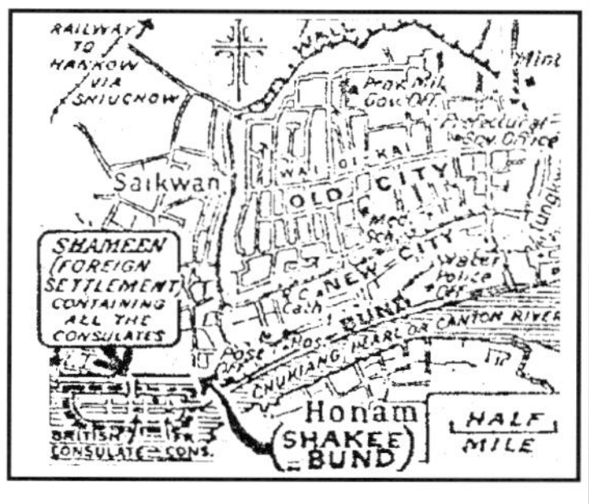


Bewildered people swarmed the streets searching for friends and relatives.

Terror-stricken children cried for their parents; women with torn hands pulled at piles of wreckage in attempts to find husbands and children.

Two hundred Chinese were killed near a school in the Tungshan area. The school building was destroyed, but, because of the holidays, it had only a few occupants.

Scores of people were buried alive in the ruins of their homes.

Now, however, the crowds are remarkably calm. And this in spite of repeated bombings during the last 48 hours.

Many people suspected of espionage have been executed without trial.

Thousands of refugees have left the city and are now pouring into Hong Kong.

**(September 24)**

# SCENES IN CITY OF TERROR

An eye-witness account of scenes in Canton is given by Reuter's Special Correspondent, who states:

The casualties were greater than in any other raid – worse even than in Shanghai's "Bloody Saturday."

After the raid I became caught up in the swirl of thousands of people who were roaming the streets terror-stricken and bewildered.

Many people have lost their reason.

I saw streets literally piled with dead; in one doorway there sat a Chinese woman, still and upright. She was dead.

In some places the dead lie as thick as flies on fly-paper in summer time.

I estimate that thousands of people have been maimed, but it will be days, perhaps weeks, before their number – and the number of dead – can be known with any accuracy.

EVERY MACHINE SEEN

The aerial battle and the fire of anti-aircraft guns was watched by the crowds of Chinese thronging the Shakee Bund, on the fringe of the European residential quarter.

The sky was cloudless and each machine was clearly visible. Bursting anti-aircraft shells showed brilliantly white against the blue sky. And, as an accompaniment to the spectacle, there was the splutter of machine-gun fire.

**(September 24)**

# YANGTSE GUNBOATS BRING BACK THE DEAD

## BRITISH OFFICERS GIVE FIRST FULL ACCOUNT OF ATTACKS

**From Ronald Monson**

**Special Correspondent of The Daily Telegraph and Morning Post.**

SHANGHAI, Friday Night.

Stirring accounts of British and American heroism as Japanese bombs and shells wrought destruction on shipping in the Yangtse were given me when the gunboats brought back their dead and wounded to-night.

They had returned from the Wuhu area, where British and American merchant ships and warships evacuating refugees from the war zone were systematically attacked by Japanese 'planes and artillery last Saturday and Sunday.

As the gallant little British gunboat, Ladybird, with her ensign at half-mast and holed below the waterline, limped ahead of the convoy up the Whangpoo, the bugles of the United States flagship, the cruiser Augusta, sounded "Attention" and "Hands, salute."

The United States gunboat Oahu followed the Ladybird, the Stars and Stripes draping the three coffins of those killed in the bombing of the Panay in her stern.

SUNSET SALUTE

Crew Stands Silent

The ratings and Marines in the Augusta stood in silence as the Panay's wounded were carried aboard her on stretchers. They came to the salute when "Evening Colours" rang out as the sun sank behind the Bund. Grim faces grew grimmer when survivors told their stories.

Standing in the shell-dented wardroom of the Ladybird, Lt. F. M. Crichton told me that the evening before the attack Lt.-Cmdr. H. D. Barlow, commander of the Ladybird, obtained permission from the Japanese commandant at Wuhu to bring a party of Britons from a concentration of refugees two miles below Wuhu to the town to inspect their properties.

The time of arrival was fixed for 9 a.m. on Sunday. At 8 a.m. the steamer Tsingtah arrived from a refugee concentration at Nanking and transhipped to the Ladybird Lt.-Col. W. A Lovat-Fraser, Military Attaché at the British Embassy Consul at Nanking, and Capt. G. E. O'Donnell, of the British gunboat Bee.

GUNBOAT UNDER FIRE

Hit Six Times

Suddenly machine-guns opened fire on a group of shipping carrying refugees. Lt.-Cmdr. Barlow decided to take the Ladybird alone to Wuhu to investigate this attack.

As the Ladybird was weighing anchor shells from a Japanese land battery on Wuhu Bund crashed among the refugees. With the object of drawing the fire from the refugees and investigating, the Ladybird was ordered to steam at full speed towards Wuhu. "For 20 minutes," said Lt. Crichton, "we steamed straight towards the Japanese battery, shells falling thick and fast round us. We were hit six times.

"One shell crashed down through the deck into the stokers' mess, where it burst deafeningly in the confined space. Tearing a coal-bin from the deck and ripping a hole four feet square in the planking, it filled the mess with a smother of steel and coal dust.

SAILOR KILLED

Miraculous Escapes

"Ten men were there. It was a miracle that any survived.

"A piece of flying steel decapitated T.N. Lonergan, but the others were unharmed. Another shell demolished a gun, wounding Petty Officer Smallwood in the head, and another struck near the bridge, wounding Capt. O'Donnell and Quartermaster Matthews.

"We did not reply. Even when the Japanese guns were firing at point-blank range they did not cease, and only when we were right under them and they could not lower sufficiently to hit us did they cease fire, still pointing in our direction.

"We bound up Capt. O'Donnell's wound, and Col. Lovat-Fraser went ashore to protest."

During the journey back to Shanghai a Japanese military motor-boat ran down a raft carrying Chinese refugees and machine-gunned them in the water. The Ladybird picked up some badly wounded men and women.

The Japanese cruiser with the convoy thereupon signalled. "If you do that again in front of our troops I will not be responsible if they fire on you."

Carrying 800 refugees, including 25 foreign women and children, and members of the German and British Embassy staffs, the river steamer Whangpoo was among British shipping bombed three times near Nanking on Sunday. Her master. Capt. W. G. Mackenzie, brought the Whangpoo to Shanghai in to-day's convoy.

JAPANESE VISIT

Still angry when speaking of the attacks, Capt. Mackenzie said that, but for the answering fire of the British gunboats Scarab and Cricket keeping the attacking 'planes high, there would have been a shambles that afternoon.

"I served in the world war," he said, "but I never experienced such horror, Bombs rained round us, missing by a miracle the panic-stricken women and children.

"Previously Japanese officers had visited our shipping concentration. They had been gone about an hour when three 'planes came over.

"We were astounded when we saw one detach itself from the others, hurtle down and loose a bomb. I shouted to the passengers to take cover as it burst near us with a shattering explosion, hurling water high in the air and throwing the ship almost on her side.

"Other 'planes power-dived, releasing more bombs and cascading us with splinters. The guns of the Scarab and the Cricket spoke and the 'planes were driven off.

"As I ran the Whangpoo towards the shore to beach her refugees from other steamers were being taken ashore in launches. Bombs fell round them.

"As we touched shore our passengers rushed madly inland and disappeared in the woods. We never saw more than 50 of them again. The steamer Whangtang was also beached.

"We went through two days of hell. It was wanton."

**(December 18)**

# JAPANESE TROOPS OCCUPY PEKING

## TANKS BROUGHT IN

PEKING, Sunday.

The last vestige of Chinese authority disappeared from Peking to-day. The city, which was the Chinese capital and a centre of Chinese life and culture for hundreds of years, is now securely under the control of the Japanese.

Thousands of Chinese lined the streets this morning to watch 4,000 Japanese troops, in full war equipment march into the city and occupy the main Chinese barracks in the "Temple of Heaven."

Besides the infantry there were 15 tanks. 10 heavy guns, other field artillery units. 80 supply lorries, and other auxiliary equipment.

The column was preceded by squadrons of cavalry, who examined every open shop in case of "surprises." – B.U.P.

**(August 9)**

# HITLER AGAIN MAKES DEMAND FOR COLONIES

Insistence on Germany's need for colonies was one of the main points of Herr Hitler's proclamation opening the Nazi Party Congress at Nuremberg yesterday. Points from the proclamation were:

Without colonies Germany's space is too small to guarantee that our people can be fed safely and continuously.

It is intolerable that year after year we should be dependent on the chance of a good harvest.

The attitude of other Powers to our demand is simply incomprehensible.

We can succeed only if the whole community displays the strictest discipline, putting blind trust in its leaders.

Germany is free and the guarantor of this freedom is our army.

We hope other Powers may understand the signs of the times and strengthen this front of reason – with Italy and Japan – to protect peace.

The work of the four-year self-sufficiency plan is going forward according to programme.

There are no genuine unemployed left in our country.

Germany, like present-day Italy, declared Herr Hitler, was a firm rock in the midst of unrest.

BUILDING FOR CENTURIES

Speaking last night, Herr Hitler said:

"We do not aim at the rude might of a Jenghiz Khan. We want to be the representatives of a higher culture."

Describing the building plans for German cities, he said that in the whole of German history no nobler buildings had been created than to-day. They were intended to last for centuries as tokens of National Socialist strength.

Herr Hitler spoke contemptuously of the German politicians before his time who, he said, wrote and talked for 15 years about international law, equality of rights, and the rights of man, without doing anything. It had, of course, been more difficult for him to occupy the Rhineland than to write articles about the true meaning of freedom.

**(September 8)**

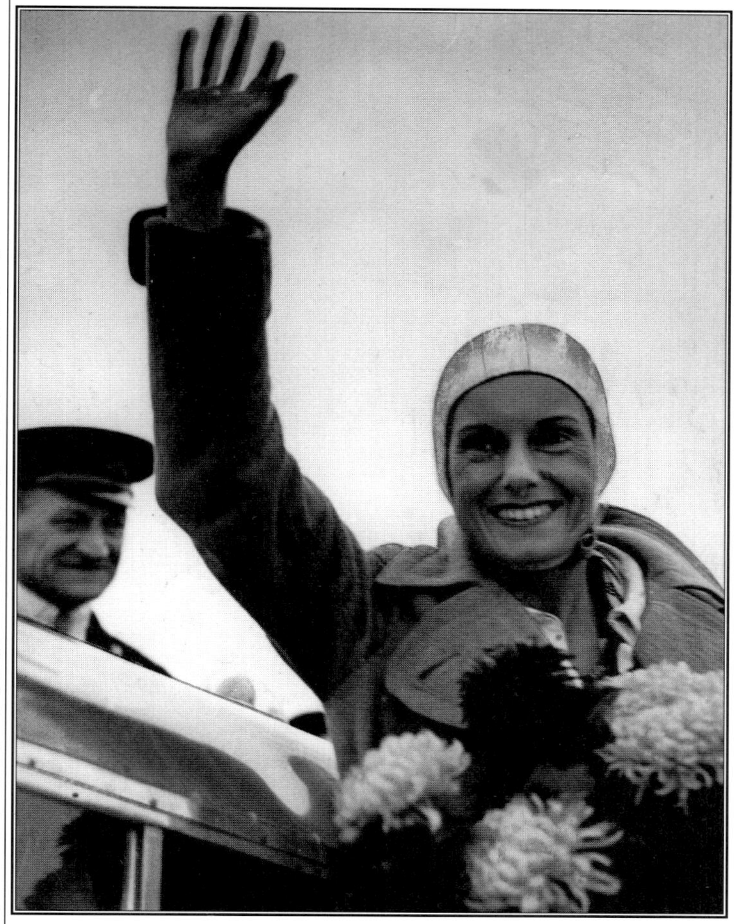

JEAN BATTEN

# JEAN BATTEN DESCRIBES HER RECORD FLIGHT

## APPALLING WEATHER MOST OF THE WAY

Miss Jean Batten, the 26-year-old New Zealand flier, had a great welcome from a crowd of 10,000 people when she landed at Croydon at 4.35 p.m. yesterday after breaking the Australia-England flight record.

"The weather most of the way to Marseilles was perfectly appalling," she said to a representative of THE DAILY TELEGRAPH and MORNING POST." "The machine at times was flung about with tremendous violence. I had lost count of time."

Miss Batten had come on to Croydon from Lympne, Kent, after beating by 14 hours 10 minutes the record of 6 days 8 hours 25 minutes put up in May by Mr. H.F. Broadbent.

She arrived at Lympne at 3.45 p.m. She took 5 days 18 hours 15 minutes for the 8,615-mile flight from Port Darwin, Northern Territory.

About 10,000 people were waiting to welcome Miss Batten when she arrived at Croydon at dusk yesterday. As she stepped from her aeroplane she was almost swept off her feet by the crowd.

Miss Batten, who flew a Perceval Gull monoplane fitted with a Gypsy 6 engine of 200 h.p. said:

"It has been the hardest flight so far as bad weather is concerned that I have ever made. The weather most of the way to Marseilles was perfectly appalling. The machine at times was flung about with tremendous violence. I had lost all count of time."

Miss Batten appeared dazed and deafened by the noise of the engines.

"All I know," she said, "is that I have arrived safely in England and that I am very happy to realise that I have broken the record. I feel dreadfully tired and I have got a great deal of sleep to make up. However, I feel quite fit physically except that my eyes seem very tired."

**(October 25)**

# EX-RECTOR OF STIFFKEY DEAD

Mr. Harold Davidson, the former Rector of Stiffkey, who was mauled by a lion in a Skegness amusement ground on Wednesday night, died in hospital at Skegness yesterday. He was 65.

In recent years he had been taking part in show-ground performances, including fasting in a barrel at Blackpool.

At Skegness he addressed crowds from inside a lion's cage, and on Wednesday one of the animals attacked him, inflicting severe injuries before being driven off by an attendant. The inquest will be opened at Skegness to-day.

Mr. Davidson, who was ordained 35 years ago, had previously been an actor, and he once said that he gave up an income of £1000 a year to become a curate of £3 a week.

SERIES OF CHARGES

He was rector of Stiffkey, in Norfolk, for 25 years, until, in March, 1932, a series of charges was preferred against him in the Norwich Consistory Court.

The proceedings lasted over several weeks, and ultimately five allegations of immoral conduct were found to have been proved.

The sentence of the bishop, Dr. Bertram Pollock, was that Mr. Davidson should be deprived of "all ecclesiastical dues and rights and emoluments belonging to the ecclesiastical promotions."

He embarked on a campaign against the Church of England hierarchy which he continued until his death. He adopted extraordinary methods to draw attention to his case, and thousands paid pennies "to see the ex-Rector of Stiffkey."

SAT IN A BARREL

He appeared on the stage in London and the provinces, and sat in a barrel at Blackpool until the police served a summons on him for obstruction. Crowds streamed past him as he read the summons in his barrel.

Prevented from continuing this exhibition he was shown to Blackpool crowds fasting in a glass cabinet. A further prosecution followed, and in 1935 he was sent for trial and acquitted on a charge of attempting to commit suicide by starving himself.

**(July 31)**

# BIG ARMY COUNCIL CHANGES

Important changes in the constitution of the Army Council were announced last night, involving the resignation of the occupants of the two chief posts in the Army and their replacement by men over ten years their junior. They are:

| | New holder | Former holder. |
|---|---|---|
| Chief of Imperial General Staff | Lt.-Gen. Viscount GORT, V.C. (aged 51) | Field-Marshal Sir CYRIL J. DEVERELL (aged 63) |
| Adjutant General of The Forces | Major-Gen. C. G. LIDDELL (aged 54) | General Sir HARRY KNOX (aged 64) |

**(December 3)**

# FRESH MINDS ON NEW WAR PROBLEMS

**By Major-Gen. A.C. Temperley**
**Daily Telegraph and Morning Post Military Correspondent**

The War Office announcement of an almost complete reconstitution of the Army Council cannot fail to be regarded as a step of considerable gravity.

Into the personal question there is no need to probe too deeply. Field-Marshal Sir Cyril Deverell, and Gen. Sir Harry Knox have both given great and devoted service to the State. Their records in the Great War had marked them out for the highest appointment.

It may be supposed that the governing reason in the mind of the War Minister, when he decided to make the change, was a feeling that younger men were required to face the stresses and strains of the present times. He was probably of the opinion that new methods in making war would require fresh minds.

It is understood that the general policy, which Mr. Hore-Belisha has initiated deals particularly with age limits. Generals in future are unlikely to be employed in important commands if they have reached the age of 60 or will do so during their tenure of the appointment.

No one can quarrel with such a decision on principle. Individuals will undoubtedly suffer as victims of stagnation in promotion which makes them unable to reach the rank and pension to which they are fully entitled on any reasonable calculation.

It may be hoped that hard cases in this respect will receive sympathetic consideration.

Yet it is not only that natural bias must be in favour of youth if united with reasonable experience, but also that modern war makes sterner demands than ever on mental and physical condition.

Movement throughout the Army is speeding up and a division which used to march a maximum of 15 miles a day can now cover 60 with ease.

The static conditions of the last war are not likely to be repeated. We must hope to produce a system of promotion and selection which will ensure that the right men reach the top when they are still in the absolute prime of life.

In the selection of the new Army Council to replace the old Mr. Hore-Belisha had had no hesitation in going far down the generals' lists to pick those whom he considers the most suitable men.

Lt.-Gen. Viscount Gort was specially promoted major-general on Nov. 25, 1935. He was given the local rank of lieutenant-general when he was appointed Military Secretary a few months ago.

At the age of 51 he becomes a full General and Chief of the Imperial General Staff.

The appointment is one of immense importance, as the holder is First Military Member of the Army Council. He has entire responsibility for training the Army and for all plans and military operations.

Lord Gort has a very distinguished war record. He won the V.C. as well as the D.S.O. with two bars and the Military Cross.

He commanded a brigade in the war. Since then Fortune has decreed that nearly all his time be spent on the Staff. This has certainly given him an insight into many sides of Army work.

Those who know him are well aware of his fine qualities as soldier and man. Perhaps most remarkable is his dynamic energy and vital force.

He has all the gifts required for the post except one and that is experience.

**(December 3)**



# MINERS EARN FROM £7 TO £10 A WEEK

## NOTTS COALFIELD PROSPERITY

**From Our Special Correspondent**

NEWSTEAD (Notts), Tuesday.

For Nottinghamshire miners this week is likely to prove the most prosperous since 1920. Colliery earnings are so much on the upgrade that the ascertainments for March involve an increase of wages of 12 1/2 per cent. on the "basic rate."

Last month there was an increase of 10 per cent, so that at present the current rate stands at 81.53 per cent. above the basis, the minimum percentage allowed by the agreement being 38.

The complications of the coal mining wage system may give at first glance no clear indication of the position of the miners.

In Newstead – a good but not the best example of a Nottinghamshire mining village in the full tide of employment – I found today that of the 1,400 men employed at the local colliery, 350 to 400 are now making more than £5 a week.

I was shown pay tickets of £7 and over and was assured that £9 and £10 were by no means uncommon. Wages of £13 a week had been known.

The village is prosperous, but not more prosperous than many others attached to collieries where natural conditions are even more propitious. I talked with miners who own their own cars, are accustomed to seek their relaxation and entertainment in Derby or Nottingham, and have substantial capital savings behind them.

From five to six shifts are worked each week at Newstead, and daily earnings at the coal face now range from 18s to 30s.

Sunday working is not uncommon. Thoresby, Crown Farm, Welbeck, Clipstone, Bolsover and Pinxton are other villages where a similar or even higher degree of prosperity is enjoyed.

MORE HOME COMFORTS

The larger towns within 'bus reach are participating in the new prosperity. Home comforts – especially radio sets of the better grade – are being bought at the big centres, and the entertainments provided by Nottingham and Derby are benefitting.

Newstead produces coal of all grades, but the bulk of Nottingham coal is used for household purposes. Mechanisation and rationalisation are well advanced in most of the pits. In 1931 13,321,453 tons of coal were produced in Nottinghamshire in 10,116,012 man-shifts. In 1936 14,060,653 tons were produced in 9,605,817 man-shifts.

**(March 3)**

# MR. BALDWIN'S REASONS FOR RETIREMENT

## BURDEN OF OFFICE TOO GREAT

**From Our Special Representative**

WORCESTER, Saturday.

Mr. Baldwin, speaking more slowly and deliberately than usual and with a sadness of voice and gesture, publicly confirmed here to-day the possibility of his early retirement.

He indicated to a large number of his constituents in the Bewdley Division, assembled in the Guildhall, that they would soon have to find another member.

The Premier, who will be 70 on Aug. 3, obviously found it an unwelcome task to tell these people, many of whom are his lifelong friends, of his impending retirement.

"Far better," he said, "to go when people may still think of you as perhaps not incompetent to do your work than to stay until perhaps they know before you do that you are becoming incompetent.

"My conscience in that matter is clear, and it may not be so very long before you will have to choose another member for West Worcestershire."

It was not the statement of a Prime Minister about to relinquish office so much as the homely regret of an M.P. who had represented his friends and neighbours in Parliament for nearly 30 years, and was loath to give up.

Another observation was that it was beyond human strength to carry the burden of his task many years after the age he had reached.

PERSONAL REGRETS

Two personal notes crept into his speech – his regret that Parliamentary duties had prevented him from making contact with the younger generation in the division, and that he would not be succeeded in West Worcestershire by another Baldwin, as he had followed his father.

In the small portion of his speech not devoted to his coming retirement the Premier warned the country against exotic and alien creeds which could do nothing to help us in solving our own constitutional problems.

"Look out for these people," he adjured, "who talk about sudden and violent changes. Let us keep this country secure from these strange creeds which to-day are rushing round the world."

**(April 12)**

# INVENTION TO DETECT 'PLANES IN DARKNESS

## "EYE" THAT PIERCES FOG AND CLOUDS

**By Major C.C. Turner**
**Daily Telegraph Air Correspondent**

A "Secret Eye" which will detect aircraft flying above clouds, in fog, or at night, has been produced by a British inventor.

By its use, also, sea collisions will be avoidable, for the "Eye" will give warning of unseen obstructions.

The "Eye" or "Detector," which is the invention of Mr. F. D. Aldridge, who is associated with Mr. T. Pollock-Brown in the production of automatic aircraft controls, uses wavelengths of light which are longer than those of the infra-red rays, but are shorter than the radio waves.

With the aid of the invention, approach to an obstacle may be indicated at a distance of many miles, and the inventor is confident of making refinements which will result in indication with no greater error than 100 feet.

In its present form it reveals the presence of an obstacle, and indicates its direction. This is sufficient for most practical purposes.

SPECIAL VALVES SECRET

The invention weighs only 40lb which is a small weight for ships, or for medium or big aeroplanes.

During a recent test in an aeroplane, the presence of hills five miles away was clearly indicated. St. Catherine's Light, Isle of Wight, 23 miles away, but invisible owing to mist, was not only indicated, but was identifiable.

This achievement impressed a firm of shipowners, who have given an initial order for two of the "Detectors."

The secret of the apparatus is the special valves, the design of which is Mr. Aldridge's invention. Power is supplied by three high-tension and two low-tension batteries. The instrument does not interfere with an aeroplane's or a ship's radio.

It is contained in a square box, about one foot in height, with two projecting tubes to protect the two "Eyes" which are merely holes. Control panel and indicator dial are contained in a second box, which is attached to the other.

**(August 19)**

# 10,000 MOTORISTS PARK IN WEST END STREETS

**From a Special Correspondent**

Ten thousand cars which are parked nightly in the West End will be affected by Mr. Hore-Belisha's plan to drive car parking from the streets of London.

This estimate was given to me by car park attendants, casual car watchers and policemen – during a tour last night of West End streets where pleasure-seeking motorists park their cars while they dine and dance or see a stage or film show.

Of these 10,000 about 2,000 are parked in authorised parking places, but these too, according to the statement of the Minister of Transport, are to be cut down.

During my tour I found every back street lined with cars. The owners were dining in the restaurants of Mayfair, Soho and Bloomsbury, watching stage and film shows, dancing in clubs, or attending parties in houses within a mile of Piccadilly Circus.

PACKED LIKE SARDINES

While I investigated the night car position in the West End I attempted to park my own car, imagining that the streets were already prohibited. Here are my experiences:

St. James's-square: More than 200 cars packed like sardines.

Hanover-square: Baulked at the last minute by a lucky driver who had found the last place of the night.

Golden-square: Cruised round with several other cars, none of us knowing which was coming or going; no room.

Soho-square: Found a space; told immediately that it was reserved for taxi-cabs. No other place available.

Side streets were almost as full. Eventually I parked my car in a garage, but only after two attempts. The first two, built to take some hundreds of cars, were full. I decided that the only alternative for the motorist bent on pleasure in the West End was to risk a summons for obstruction or pay anything from 6d for an authorised park, if he was lucky, to 1/6 or 2/- for a garage.

**(March 4)**

# BRITAIN'S 49 MORE MILLIONAIRES

There were 824 millionaires, or persons with incomes exceeding £30,000, in Great Britain and Ireland last year, compared with 775 the year before, an increase of 49.

There were 85,449 persons with incomes of £2,000 and upwards, an increase of 2,030. The aggregate income of all such persons was £424,339,484, an increase of £17,175,138.

These figures are revealed by the sur-tax assessments given in the report of the Commissioners of Inland Revenue for the year ended March 31 last, and are based on 1934-35 incomes.

The total number of persons assessed to sur-tax with incomes ranging from £75,000 to £100,000 was 60, compared with 50 the year before. The incomes of the latter class aggregated £11,485,300, compared with £10,878,605.

The number of persons who were charged with income-tax in the year ended March, 1936, was 3,350,000, compared with 3,500,000 in the previous 12 months.

The net receipts from death duties was £88,043,949, compared with £81,289,774.

**(March 12)**

# LAST OF TRAMS IN WEST LONDON

## 102 TROLLEY-BUSES START SERVICE

**From a Special Correspondent**

Shortly before three o'clock yesterday morning the last West London tramcar trundled into the Hammersmith depot and the area said good-bye to trams for ever. Two hours later the first trolley-bus of the five new services which came into operation in London during the day left Wandsworth for Battersea.

By midday 102 trolley-buses were in service on 24 ½ miles of routes, bringing the total length of trolley-bus services in London to 147 miles. When the changeover is complete there will be 330 miles of routes operated by 2,500 trolley-buses.

Most of the drivers are former tramdrivers who have learned to handle the trolley-buses at the London Passenger Transport Board's "school."

The obsequies of the last tramcars were uneventful. A few belated revellers cheered the Hammersmith car into its depot. Later it was driven off to Camberwell, where the majority of London's trams end their days – either to be broken up or reconditioned for service on other routes.

The number of passengers carried on the trolley buses during the day was above the average. Many of them " with the Londoner's zest for a novelty – were frankly out just for a ride on the new vehicles.

**(September 13)**

# 3,000 WOMEN WAIT FOR FILM STAR

## ROBERT TAYLOR'S ARRIVAL

**By Campbell Dixon, Daily Telegraph Film Correspondent**

Welcomed by a barrage of cameras and the shrill cries of thousands of excited girls. Robert Taylor, hailed as the greatest romantic favourite since Rudolph Valentino, arrived in England yesterday.

At Southampton Docks extra police protected the film actor while he faced the cameramen, professional and amateur, and signed scores of autographs.

At Southampton Central railway station he patiently signed an endless stream of autograph books, envelopes, film magazines, pages torn from notebooks, scraps of paper, a small boy's atlas and a passport. The train moved, the drawn blinds were raised, and Mr. Taylor sat back and breathed freely. But as the train steamed slowly out there came a high frequency screaming from the other side.

FRENZIED SCREAMS

At Waterloo the scenes have not been paralleled since the arrival of Valentino. Two or three thousand women had gathered an hour before the train arrived at nine o'clock, and Mr. Taylor's appearance was the signal for a scream which could have been heard a quarter of a mile away.

A squad of police kept the crowd back and advised against an attempt to pass through. In an instant Mr. Taylor had been hurried to a goods lift and had disappeared.

Amid frenzied screams a car presumed to be his was slowly driven off, but by this time Mr. Taylor had emerged in the street by an underground passage, had taken a taxi and was safely on the way to his hotel.

I had been led to believe that since the hysteria of New York, where two enthusiastic young women were found hiding under the twin beds in his cabin, Mr. Taylor was suffering from nerves.

PICTURE OF HEALTH

Actually I found him the picture of health and spirits. A certain complacency might be forgiven a man of 26 who is snatched away from a university, thrust into films without any effort on his part, paid £500 a week – with double as much to come – and assured weekly of the devotion of 6,000 or 8,000 admirers, Mr. Taylor has remained unspoiled.

"It is part of the job," he said to me philosophically. "I'll start worrying about the fans when the fans stop worrying about me."

Some film stars are disillusioning in the flesh. It may comfort his admirers if I say that Mr. Taylor, with his bright blue eyes and ruddy skin, is even handsomer then he looks on the screen. Technicolor should increase his following 25 per cent. and raise the approving chorus another octave.

Mr. Taylor has come to England to act in "A Yank at Oxford," the first picture which Metro-Goldwyn-Mayer's British studios are making in the best Hollywood style for world release. Jack Conway, the director, was also a passenger by the Berengaria.

**(August 28)**

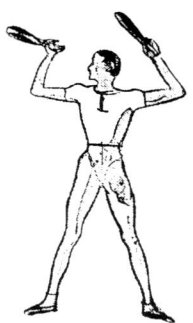

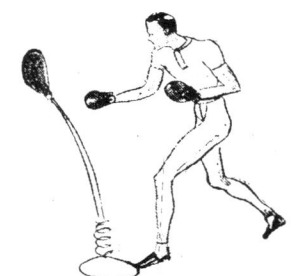

# NEW CHILD STAR IN A BRILLIANT COMEDY

**By Campbell Dixon**

HOLLYWOOD is lucky. Just think how much easier it is to make exciting or amusing pictures in a country where the wildest melodrama can really be happening, and probably is, where boys are full of wisecracks in their teens, and girls have poise and subtle charm at an age when, if they were English, they would be making a gauche entry into the breakfast-room or galumphing about the junior hockey field.

I won't go so far as to say that Deanna Durbin is typical. Good looks, acting ability, and a fine voice cannot be common at 14, even in America. But at least she is representative enough to be credible; whereas here she would be frankly a freak.

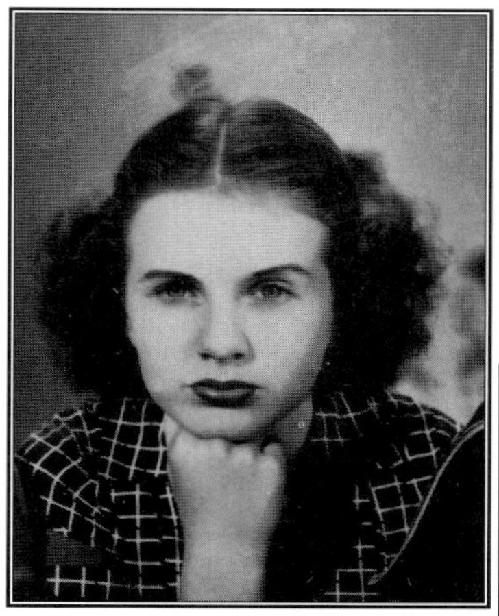

Deanna Durbin

Prophecy is as rash in the entertainment world as any other; but with "Three Smart Girls," I am ready to burn my boats. it is as brilliant a comedy, in its unpretentious way, as 1937 is likely to bring us; and I will eat my hat – the only grey hat left in the Critics' Circle – if it is not one of the most sensational successes. And this despite the fact that there is not one player in the cast who really means anything at the box-offices

The story, in one form or another, must have been used a hundred times. A gold-digger (Binnie Barnes) deludes an elderly millionaire (Charles Winninger) into proposing marriage; whereupon his three daughters, living with their mother in Europe, set out to dish the gold-digger and bring about a reconciliation between father and mother.

Witty Twists

They pull it off, but I will not say how. It might spoil the picture for you; and the stratagems they adopt, often with farcical results, would mean nothing in print anyway.

Everything depends, as it usually does, on the treatment. There is no attempt at a continuous stream of wisecracks, which I for one find dreadfully tedious; but again and again a familiar situation is given the wittiest of twists – all the funnier because they arise out of character and situation. Even the most eccentric figure, a Hungarian count, is a real human being: I personally know several of him.

The part is magnificently played by Micha Auer, the gentleman who ran up the curtains in "My Man Godfrey." Deanna Durbin sings sweetly and is a most winning little person altogether; but for me and a good many others Mr. Auer walks away with a picture really worth stealing.

**(March 14)**

# FILM OF "LOST HORIZON"

## £400,000 VERSION OF FAMOUS NOVEL

**By Campbell Dixon**

"Lost Horizon," which comes to the Tivoli on Monday, is in some ways one of the most remarkable pictures of the year.

No production directed by Frank Capra could be ordinary, and to "Lost Horizon" he has devoted all his talent and £400,000.

James Hilton's best-seller has been brought to the screen, with all the resources – a powerful cast, lovely sets and impressive photography – that Hollywood could lavish on it.

The results are as spectacular as anything the screen has ever given us. It may be that Shandri-la is a trifle too ornate – too like Utopia as conceived by an American town-planner.

The effects are lovely, nevertheless, and not since "Doomed Battalion" have I seen anything so remarkable as the scenes in the mountains of Tibet, as seen from an aeroplane, and the path along which the lost Europeans struggle through blizzards to the peace of Shandri-la.

Ronald Colman plays the hero. A strong supporting cast includes Edward Everett Horton, H.B. Warner, Margo, Jane Wyatt, Sam Jaffe and Isabel Jewell.

**(April 15)**

# END OF FAMOUS LIBRARY

In spite of last minute efforts to save the 95-year-old firm, Mudie's Library, an institution famous for many years among booklovers all over the English-speaking world, closed on Saturday.

Some hundreds of employees – men and girls – have been thrown out of work as a result.

To-day, only a skeleton staff will remain at the Southwark-street headquarters, to deal with correspondence.

Last July Mr. P. W. Strauss was appointed receiver and manager by a decision of Mr. Justice Farwell in the Chancery Division, following an application by a Debenture holder.

Subscribers to the library had already been notified by circular that the service would be discontinued, efforts for the re-organisation or sale of the business having failed.

Charles Edward Mudie, the founder, established his original library in 1842 in Chelsea, and moved to Bloomsbury in 1844. In 1864 a limited liability company was formed.

**(July 12)**

# A THEATRICAL EVENT

## "VICTORIAN REGINA" AT THE LYRIC

**By W.A. Darlington**

If ever a theatrical production was an assured success before the curtain rose on its first public performance, that production was "Victoria Regina" at the Lyric Theatre last night.

The lifting of the censor's ban might in itself have been enough to excite great public interest in the event; but the added facts that the piece had already had great success both at its private production at the Gate Theatre, and in New York gave a further guarantee that interest would not go unrewarded.

And so, rather late in this season, came its chief theatrical event, and some of its best acting. If one cannot go on to say its best play, that is merely because nobody could pretend that this collection of specimens from Laurence Housman's brilliant series of playlets about Queen Victoria really add up to a play at all.

VICTORIA THE GREAT

But it is not as a play that we must judge this production, but as a piece of popular history. Victoria, having spent much of her reign as a largely legendary figure – Victoria the Good – and having been distorted by her immediate posterity into Victoria the Absurd, is now coming back into perspective, and is emerging as the Great.

It is also very much of an opportunity for a stage tour-de-force. Pamela Stanley, having played the part brilliantly at the Gate, has very rightly been given the chance to do it again; and she is rewarded with a spectacular success.

REMARKABLE DISGUISES

"Spectacular" is, in fact, very much the right word, for Miss Stanley's success is due as much to a most remarkable set of disguises as to her excellent acting. The last three, showing the Queen at 42, at 58, and at her Diamond Jubilee, are striking in the extreme. Earlier, of course, only a slight modification of her own youth and good looks is necessary.

Dramatically, the most moving scene of all is one called "The Rose and the Thorn" where Victoria grows jealous of one of her ladies-in-waiting.

**(June 24)**

# MR. OLIVIER'S HENRY V.

The Old Vic is bringing its present season to a brilliant close with Tyrone Guthrie's production of "Henry V.," graced by the decorative settings of Motley and the music of Herbert Menges.

Since this comes so hard on the heels of the Stratford production of the same play a comparison between the two is not to be avoided. The conclusion to which I am forced is that in every way, except perhaps the acting of one or two not very important parts, the Old Vic does better.

Laurence Olivier's Henry is not the hearty young Rugby forward with a leaning for poetry that we usually get. He is a man conscious of destiny, sober under the weight of responsibility. Mr. Olivier has an extraordinary power these days of arriving at his top note early in a big speech, and maintaining it without effort to the end. It is a power that should be sparingly used, for if it develops into a mannerism it will be fatal. But it is most effective.

**(April 7)**

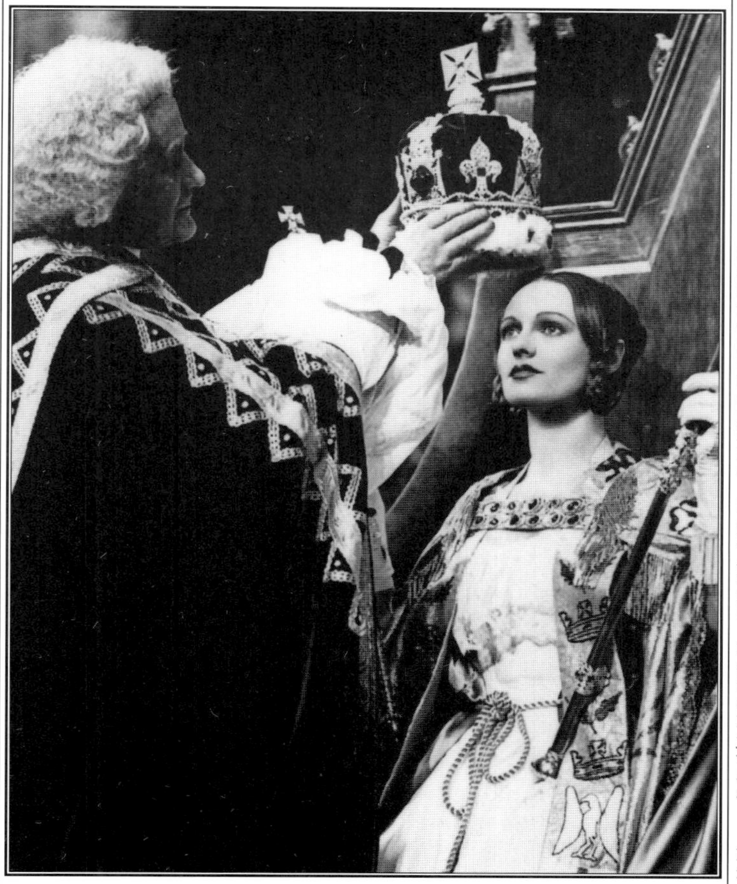

ANNA NEAGLE playing the role of Queen Victoria.

# FILM CROWNING OF A QUEEN

## ANNA NEAGLE PLAYS VICTORIA

**By Our Film Correspondent**

I saw a Queen crowned yesterday. It was only for a film, but the reconstructed Abbey was so convincing and the ceremonial so impressive that the many who see "Victoria the Great" will share to some extent in the experience of the few admitted to the Abbey on May 12 for the coronation of her great-grandson.

The set was as handsome as anything I have seen in a British film. The London Museum allowed Mr. Wilcox's designers to take Queen Victoria's actual Coronation robes from the cases and make copies. So exact is the workmanship that I doubt whether one person in a hundred would know which is which.

The present demand for peers' robes made it impossible to hire these costumes, so they had to be made for the occasion, at very heavy expense. It was surprising to learn that the black and gold peer's coat, by no means so magnificent as some of the glittering creations in velvet and ermine, costs over £100.

"Camera! Music! Action!" At Mr. Wilcox's command a still life became a moving picture. Three bishops solemnly advanced to the Altar bearing the great Bible, the Chalice and the Patina.

Miss Anna Neagle, with her hair in looped plaits, took her seat on St. Edward's Chair, with the Stone of Scone below. At her side were Lord Melbourne (H.B. Warner) and the Duke of Wellington (James Dale); behind them were the Royal Dukes and Princesses.

Some 20ft behind was the Chair of Homage, on the steps of which, in 1837, the aged Lord Rolle stumbled and fell and was assisted up by the young Queen – an incident reproduced in the film.

**(May 4)**

# TELEVISION AS A NEW ART

The television version of R.C. Sherriff's "Journey's End," broadcast last night, opened a wonderful vista of possibilities for a new form of dramatic art.

It was the first play to be televised at length, the transmission lasting an hour and 20 minutes. But the most interesting feature was the ingenious welding of film and studio presentation.

Thus, the skilful producer may in television use the best of two mediums. Viewers can see the realism of flesh-and-blood acting allied with the spectacular effects of the film. In this case the main scene was, as in the play, an officers' dugout. This was constructed in the studio, but viewers also saw the raiding party leaving the trench and going over the top besides pictures of no-man's-land and the inside of the German trenches.

**(November 12)**

# EDITH EVANS AS ROSALIND

## SUPERB ACTING AT THE NEW

**By George W. Bishop**

Edith Evans's Rosalind was noticed after the Old Vic production of "As You Like It" before Christmas. Last night at the New Theatre, where the play has been revived for a limited season. I realised again that the performance is one of the loveliest pieces of acting seen in London for years.

It is so gay, yet full of the tenderness of young love; so quick in its comedy and so richly in key with Shakespeare's glorious creation. Every now and then Miss Evans startles us with a brilliant and illuminating reading of a passage; often one feels that Shakespeare's wit has been matched for the first time.

Esme Church, the Old Vic producer, has kept the Watteau settings and costumes by Molly McArthur. Fortunately the lighting has been improved and the backgrounds are less subdued.

Michael Redgrave has come over from the Vic as Orlando, and a fine upstanding, crisply spoken performance he gives. There is a new Celia in Marie Ney, who enters with charm and high spirits into the scenes with Rosalind, and Frederick Lloyd's Touchstone is as interesting and amusing as it is original.

**(February 12)**

# MR. PRIESTLEY'S FINE PLAY

**By George W. Bishop**

A new play by J.B. Priestley is an exciting event, for here is an author who is brave enough to have something to say in the theatre. In "Time and the Conways" he reverts to the manner of "Dangerous Corner," but with a good deal of difference.

He shows us the Conways, a well-to-do provincial family, just at the end of the war. It is Kay's 21st birthday; there is a party and charades; Mrs. Conway sings a song in German; we wonder if Robin, just demobilised, will marry Joan; what will happen to the ridiculous little man who had been brought to the house by the family lawyer and to the other people Mr. Priestley has placed so vividly on the stage.

The second act is 19 years later – a picture of grim disillusionment. Things have gone wrong for most of the family. There is a conference, for stocks and property have fallen. Robin did marry Joan, but he drinks and is shiftless and they have parted. Kay is writing interviews with the "film stars who are always arriving at Southampton;" another daughter (so full of ideals) is now hard and pedantic; the gay youngest daughter is dead. The only really contented person is Alan. He has no ambitions – he is happy enough, jogging on, quoting the lines of Blake which form some sort of text to the play.

**(August 27)**

# Another Glorification of the Tough Guy

**To Have and Have Not.**
**By Ernest Hemingway. (Cape. 7s 6d)**
**The Citadel. By A. J. Cronin**

**By John Brophy**

THE Hemingway cult, it seems, is cracking and tottering, both here and across to any regrets, for from the first I have thought Mr. Hemingway's achievement over-estimated, and his influence on contemporary writers pernicious and tiresome. His scope has always been narrow, his inarticulate toughness an inverted sentimentality, his technique not always distinguishable from a stunt. There is little, if any, genuine novelty in his style, as nearly monosyllabic as may be. Its potentialities were discovered by Bunyan and Defoe two centuries ago, and I rather think they used it to better purpose

Ziegfeld "glorified" the American girl, and Mr. Hemingway "glorifies" the tough guy, as a bullfighter, as an ambulance driver at Caporetto, and now as a smuggler. "To HAVE AND HAVE NOT" is a short, brisk tale, lacking unity and needing a glossary, about Henry Morgan who runs guns and Chinamen across the Gulf of Florida in a small motor-boat.

The story has its excitements, for Mr. Hemingway possesses a boy's appreciation of adventure, and if he left sex and profanity and politics out of it, he might be taken seriously as an entertainer. But he doesn't leave them out, and he must therefore be judged by grown-up standards. His story is what the film trade calls "hokum," the recipe as before with inferior or stale ingredients, and his hero is just another Glamour Guy.

* * *

IN 1924 young Andrew Manson went to Blaenelly in South Wales and found himself in a strange situation. He was nominally assistant to a Dr. Page, but in fact all the work fell to him, for his chief was paralysed and bedridden. The little mining town was subject to epidemics of typhoid, and Manson, aiding and abetting another good-hearted though cynical assistant doctor, could remedy this state of affairs only by surreptitiously and illegally blowing up the main drain, thus forcing the authorities to provide another.

Manson soon quarrelled with his employers' miserly wife, and got another job, close at hand, on condition that he married. This enabled him to make a local school-mistress, originally from Yorkshire, his wife, and his practice among miners turned his mind to research into the lung diseases to which mine-workers are subject. Another quarrel took him to an office job in London, after he had risen in status by taking his M.R.C.P., but again he resigned, lapsed into a poor practice in the Paddington district, got involved with a fashionable "vamp" and thankfully restored himself in his wife's affections.

Fastidious readers will be repelled by the rough approximations of the writing – adjectives are too numerous and too vague, and almost every page is cluttered with clichés. The character drawing, too, though firm in outline, lacks both subtlety and profundity, and such theme as the book possesses is lost among the desultory sequence of incidents described apparently for their own sake. But if "The Citadel" falls short of the highest standards, and seems indeed to be unaware of their existence, it ought to succeed as entertainment: Dr. Cronin's sincerity makes him passionately interested in everything that happens to his naive hero, and such an interest emanating from the author almost invariably evokes a corresponding interest in the reader.

**(July 20)**

# B.B.C. IDEAL FOR CHILDREN'S HOUR

Mr. Val Gielgud, the B.B.C. Drama Director, who assumed control of the Children's Hour at the beginning of the year, described to me yesterday his conception of the children's ideal programme.

It should not, he said, be run on a mixed basis of "sentiment and soda water." He rejected the theory that the music children most appreciate is necessarily inferior. Classical composers should be strongly represented in the ideal programme.

Plays of many kinds should be included, Mr. Gielgud instanced "Treasure Island," plays of adventure generally, and of school life.

Broadcasting, he considered, ought also to show children "things as they are." They could learn, for example, how their daily milk reaches them and, through the microphone, visit a chocolate factory.

The Children's Hour should include, from time to time, all the best known international fairy tales. Instructive talks by broadcasters with marked microphone personality, such as the "Zoo Man" and the "Star Gazer," would always be popular.

Since January Mr. Gielgud has introduced a number of changes into the Children's Hour, which, however, continues under the personal supervision of Mr. Derek McCulloch.

**(March 3)**

THE DAILY TELEGRAPH

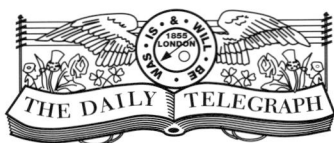

135, Fleet-st., London E. C. 4.

Telephone: Central 4242

TO-DAY'S WEATHER FORECAST

LONDON & S.E. ENGLAND - Wind westerly, heavy showers later; low temperature.

ENGLISH CHANNEL - Choppy

## MASS MURDER FROM THE AIR

UNLESS the conscience of civilisation is an idle phrase, it cannot fail to be deeply stirred by the appalling tales of death and devastation from Nanking and Canton. These two great Chinese cities, both well outside the actual war zone, have been ruthlessly bombed by Japanese aeroplanes. The civilian victims are counted in thousands. Moreover, a further systematic succession of raids is promised in order so to break the spirit of the Chinese people that they may force their Government to surrender abjectly to the will of Japan. Unless, therefore, the Governments of Europe and America protest to the Japanese Government in adequately impressive terms, Nanking and Canton are doomed to be the scenes of the most ruthless massacres of huge civilian populations on record. If sufficient foreign residents are among the victims the various Governments will be driven to protect their nationals by the irresistible force of public opinion. But it would be more to the honour of civilisation and humanity if, before that happened, the nations of the West and the United States entered a collective and effective protest.

"The results are before us. Large areas of Canton, a city as big as Birmingham, have been deliberately turned into a human shambles. So another ghastly epoch of "frightfulness" in war has been started and is even now in full career. Nor will those who started it stop it of their own volition. Even though the long term result must be to instil a deadly hatred of Japan into the hearts of the Chinese for a generation, those who direct this war from Tokyo are ready to sacrifice everything for a swift success. Canton's lurid fate should be taken to heart by the great capitals of Europe. This raid by heavy bombers is not aerial warfare: it is just promiscuous murder and massacre from the air. Nor are these the horrors of legitimate warfare. They are in flagrant violation of the spirit and – as far as there is a letter – of the letter of the rules of war.

Among the rules of The Hague Convention of Jurists appointed under the Washington Conference of 1922 is one which declared aerial bombardment to be legitimate only when directed at a military objective. There was no real military objective at Canton. Another expressly prohibited bombing when employed for the purpose of terrorising the civilian population. That was the sole object of the bombing of Nanking and Canton. One must admit that in the interval the exponents of these views have not gained but lost ground. Faith in the plighted word of nations has weakened. In a still well-remembered speech five years ago MR. BALDWIN declared his doubt whether any form of prohibition of the bombing aeroplane or of bombing would be effective in time of war. He was sharply taken to task in many quarters by optimists who said that "the breach of a solemn undertaking not to bomb great cities or use poison gas would go far to ensure ignominious defeat." Experience, unfortunately, has not upheld their prophecy. Yet only 18 months ago HERR HITLER'S Peace Plan proposed the prohibition of all bombing of "open localities" outside the range of the medium-heavy artillery of the fighting fronts and the bombardment of places outside the battle zone. That plan was never fully discussed.

If it is not raised, however, these bombing atrocities will continue and it will be said that, as civilisation has condoned the outrages committed in Spain and China, it is permissible to any other Power to repeat them. The nations have, in fact, been building up their aerial fleets on the assumption that there is and will be no effective ban on the bombing of crowded cities. The peoples of the world now know what heavy bombing means, and even the unquestioning obedience given to Dictators may yield to the horror and terror inspired by the fate of Canton.

**(September 24)**

## THE DAILY TELEGRAPH AND MORNING POST

TO-DAY the announcement is made that THE DAILY TELEGRAPH will henceforth add another and a famous name to its title and will become THE DAILY TELEGRAPH AND MORNING POST. That the "MORNING POST" will cease to have a separate existence will cause many and sincere regrets throughout the newspaper world, for it is impossible not to lament the passing of London's oldest daily paper after a continuous independent and honoured existence of more than a century and a half. English journalism at its best must be the poorer by its disappearance. But newspapers, like books, have their fates, and these are usually determined by a variety of factors which in combination are irresistible. These are times of very strenuous competition, from which the newspaper world is no more exempt than any other, and in the struggle the "MORNING POST" has for many years fought a losing battle. The paper could not go on by itself, so it starts a new phase of its long career in association with the journal which perhaps has stood closest to it in the broad issue of national policy.

Brief allusion may be made to the remarkable literary associations of the "MORNING POST" in the past. At one time in the opening years of the nineteenth century COLERIDGE, SOUTHEY, CHARLES LAMB, and WORDSWORTH were among its regular contributors, though – with the exception of SOUTHEY – they proved somewhat intractable in harness. Those literary associations were cherished and worthily maintained to the last. Again, the fashionable and society associations of the "MORNING POST" were of equally old standing, but that particular characteristic was perhaps much more valuable in Victorian days than now. Above all, politicians of every shade knew precisely where the paper would stand when it came to battle on any serious political and constitutional principle, and those who drew their weapons from a different armoury could still admire the unfailing dexterity with which those of the "MORNING POST" were used and the ringing blows they struck. THE DAILY TELEGRAPH is proud to take over a paper of such high traditions and associations, confident that the two will unite in a stable and durable harmony.

**(September 30)**

## THE DUKE'S MARRIAGE

CONTROVERSY raged round the Duke of WINDSOR'S marriage to the very last. With his marriage it should end. From now on, to quote the words of his own statement yesterday, he and his wife look forward to a "happy and useful private life." As they enter it they carry the good wishes of all with them. In the strenuous years when he served the country at his father's right hand the Duke deserved well of the British people, and millions remember him with gratitude. Now that he is, as he says, and as his conduct since his abdication has scrupulously indicated, a private citizen, he is entitled to his private happiness. May it be lasting and complete.

There are others besides himself for whose sake we would give him a word of greeting. His mother is a cherished figure in our national life; his brother is our Sovereign. We should like them, too, to know that we can think tenderly of the past and cordially of the future; and that, because of the intimacy which unites our people with its Royal House, we can in some measure enter into and sympathise with the feelings of its members. For them, even more than for us, no public change can break the private tie, and we share, so far as we may, the thoughts and hopes with which yesterday's news from France was read by those who in other circumstances would have stood by the bridegroom's side.

**(June 4)**

## FAREWELL, DALY'S

QUIETLY the last curtain will descend tonight at Daly's Theatre, and as fast as the house-breakers can work London will lose a focus of many memories of the stage. "Farewell, Leicester Square," the refrain to which the British troops marched in the war, will have acquired a new significance to the many thousands to whom "San Toy," "The Merry Widow" and "The Maid of the Mountain" embodied the spirit of the space that Baron GRANT embellished for Londoners.

**(September 25)**

# AMERICANISMS WHICH VULGARISE THE ENGLISH TONGUE

By J. B. Firth

ONE does not expect the sensational or the "tabloid" Press to be "a well of English pure and undefiled."

Indeed, it is a mistake to apply too exacting a standard of literary purism to any form of popular journalism, the practice of which is governed by certain inescapable conditions for which the literary purist makes quite inadequate allowance.

It is a matter of everyday observation that English "Journalese" is becoming Americanised. The worst faults of Victorian "Journalese" were directly derived from the tradition that the best literary models should be, as far as possible, laboriously copied. The result – in the hands of indifferent exponents – was long-windedness, rotundity of diction, redundancy, and an addiction to polysyllabic words which were supposed to smack of superior wisdom. To-day the opposite extreme is favoured and the exponents of the latest school of "snappiness" have gone to America for their models.

They imitate freely and borrow without a blush and in the American films they find their most potent ally. It is a combination dangerous to the English language, as it is spoken and written.

For nothing is sacred to them. The rules of grammar do not bind them. They have a contempt for established literary usage and convention. They mock at what is correct and academic. It is as if the aim of the writers were to jab the reader in the eye or the ear in order at any cost to attract attention.

Attempts are sometimes made to borrow together with the words the general style and atmosphere of the American paragraph. That, however, is more difficult, and success is rarely achieved. The results are bastard and mongrel.

### "No. 1 OFFICE BOY"

Reporters have suddenly become "newshawks" in certain English papers because they are so styled for the moment on the other side of the Atlantic. Members of the advertisement departments of newspapers have become "ad-men" a most hideous cacophony. London's most sought-after visitor, Mr. Robert Taylor, of Hollywood, is "Heart Throb No. 1." A boy-messenger who came to London on some trivial errand was thrust forward into the notice of the British public as "No 1 Office Boy of New York" – a grotesque hyperbole.

Sentences are made to open starkly without the customary article in order to supply the sought-for jolt. I do not mind saying a long farewell to that favourite old Victorian cliché "ladies of the ballet," but it is still pleasanter to the eye and ear than the new Americanism "a slick bunch of chorines."

It would be churlish, of course, to deny our manifold obligations to America for a host of valuable additions to the English vocabulary, especially in the way of racy and attractive slang. A country as big and as self-assured as the United States and composed of so many nationalities, was bound to develop a language of its own. It was no more likely to be tamely content with the language of King George III. than with his Constitution and his laws. Instead of chiding the Americans for evolving a language separate from English, we should rejoice that the connection between literary English and literary American is so intimate and fundamental that it is never likely to be broken.

### SOME USEFUL TERMS

The American language has many virtues. It economises words. It cuts out the dead wood. It trims the hedges of its sentences. it prefers the succinct to the ornate. It recoils from pedantic distinctions. Americans have shown a talent for inventing new and useful words, quite apart from their prolific generation of slang. Our English purists fought hard against the introduction of such words as "influential," "bogus," "reliable" – to which some English schoolmasters still object – and "stand-point," while words like "car," "stores," "interview," "wire" (for telegraph), and "cable" were still being denounced as monstrous excrescences within the present century, though well established in common use.

Slang belongs to a different category. The Oxford Dictionary censoriously defines it as "language of a low and vulgar type." That certainly is not applicable to such useful slang words as "joy-ride," "high-brow," "bootlegger," "speakeasy," "debunk," "has-been" and a hundred others.

On the other hand, the originators of "Oh, yea!" and "Sez you" and "swell" and "cutie" and "slobbered a bibful" and "going places" and almost every slang phrase associated with "eats" deserve to have such a punishment as being set to copy out "Paradise Lost" backwards as an addition to their purgatorial pains.

It is, of course, a mercy that slang is largely self-destructive. The mortality is great, and would be even greater were not many words kept alive by the talkies. But obsolete slang is as dead as obsolete theology, with as little chance of revival, The "Dame" of to-day becomes as the "Jane" or the "Baby" of yesterday, and it is already becoming "lousy" to mention the "swell guy" or the "Big Boy."

There are, however, morasses of American slang in which even the boldest English imitators have hitherto feared to tread. Let me give a single specimen as a cautionary example of the shameful indignities which may be heaped upon a language by scribes who have no respect for verbal decency and the honour of words. It comes from a critical "appreciation" of the "turn" of two American variety actresses which appeared a few weeks ago in the leading theatrical and film paper of New York:

"Jai Leta and Diane Johnson, both personable gals with plenty worth perusing, alternate in the strips, some under wraps, but mostly not. The ensemble numbers have plenty of chest undrapery. There are a coupla other specialities that smack of vaud, but don't get the proponents much attention, since there is neither programming, house billing nor mike announcement to give anybody an idea as to who's who or what's what. It is the old burley wheel argument that what's in a name so long as the epidermis is okay?"

### ROBBING THE DUST-BIN

For blatant vulgarity, that would be hard to beat. If it is English, alas! poor English; if it is American, it is a lurid commentary on Walt Whitman's contention that a man has a right to do what he likes with his own language.

It goes far to justify an outraged American professor's definition of slang half a century ago: "Slang is the speech of him who robs the literary garbage cans on the way to the dumps."

**(September 24)**

# LONDON DAY BY DAY:

**"Major" in Spain.**
**Mr. Joseph Kennedy**

SOME of my pacifist friends have been a little surprised at the action of the Spanish Government authorities in naming a unit of the International Brigade "the Major Attlee Company."

This restoration of his temporary wartime military title to the leader of his Majesty's Opposition cannot, they feel, but be distasteful to so good a pacifist.

They point to the fact that for some time now Mr. Attlee has dropped the title he bore as a temporary officer.

Neither in Hansard nor in the standard books of reference has he been called "Major" for the last two years – presumably at his own desire.

On his return it will be interesting to see whether Mr. Attlee gives effect to his regained military status by reorganising his followers into a British "Major Attlee Company."

### –And His Company

In this unit the C.S.M. would obviously be Mr. Herbert ("Carry on, Sergeant-Major") Morrison. Mr. Arthur Greenwood seems fitted for the post of Quartermaster-Sergeant. Their public-school origins would give Dr. Dalton and Mr. Noel Baker commissions as subalterns.

All pay would, of course, be handled by Mr. Ernest Bevin. Mr. Jack Jones would be put in charge of the canteen, and I appoint Mr. A. B. Swales, who is something of an epicure, Company Cook.

His stature would qualify Mr. Wedgwood Benn for the post of boy bugler, Sir Stafford Cripps would be an N.C.O.who is continually losing his stripes. Messrs. Maxton, Buchanan and Campbell Stephen, I suspect, would be permanently confined to barracks.

Mr. Harry Pollitt, the Communist leader, is obviously cast for the role of the rude little boy who makes remarks through the railings when the company is on parade.

Miss Ellen Wilkinson would make a high-spirited vivandiere who would never be found far behind the firing line.

### New U.S. Ambassador

MR. JOSEPH KENNEDY, the United States Ambassador-elect in succession to Mr. Bingham, is short, stocky, and red-haired. He has the great asset of personal magnetism and charm of manner.

He proved his talents as a negotiator when he was made chairman of the Securities and Exchange Commission. A prominent Wall Street broker himself, there was every reason why he should be anything but popular in his former milieu.

It says much for his natural talents for diplomacy that although the Commission's activities came in for much criticism, none was levelled at Mr. Kennedy himself.

Mr. Kennedy first met Mr. Roosevelt when he was Assistant Secretary of the Navy during the War. Mr. Kennedy, representing the Bethlehem Company, refused to hand over a ship they had built for a South American Government, and Mr. Roosevelt sent a naval party to seize it and remove it from the company's docks.

After the war Mr. Kennedy made a considerable fortune by consolidating cinema properties, and became known as the "boy wonder" of Wall Street.

He is a Boston Irishman, who married the daughter of a famous former mayor of Boston, John Fitzgerald. Fitzgerald was also a political figure and was better known by the sobriquet of "Honey Fitz." because of his excellent singing voice. He was credited with having sung himself into Boston Town Hall by countless renderings of "Sweet Adeline" during the mayoralty campaign.

### No "Stuffed Shirt"

Mr. Kennedy is an ardent Roman Catholic and has nine children.

I understand that Mr. Hearst did his utmost to persuade him to assume the management of his organisation.

A very American and forceful man of action, aggressive, temperamental, and with lots of go, he is the last person popularly thought of as likely to be selected as an ambassador. Yet he may be a great success. He is definitely the reverse of what Americans call a "stuffed shirt."

### Coronation Day Record

I MET at dinner yesterday a friend who lives in Hertfordshire whom I had not seen since the Coronation. He told me that he spent May 12 as follows:

10 a.m. – Went to the village and helped in the ex-Servicemen's rally.

11. – Returned home and listened-in to the Abbey ceremony.

12.15. – Fished his stream, caught a trout.

12.45. – More listening-in.

1.30. – Decided to go and see the procession.

2.20. – Reached the line of route north of Oxford-street. Was helped by other spectators to a post of vantage.

3.50. – Started home.

5. – Gave the children at the village tea an eye-witness account of the procession.

He thought this record sufficiently remarkable to write and congratulate his friend, Sir Philip Game, on the admirable police arrangements which made it possible.

### German Student Uniforms

YET another category of the German population, I hear, is to be provided with uniforms. This is the Heidelberg students, for whom a steel-grey dress of glossy cloth has now been devised.

It consists of a double-breasted jacket with dark grey buttons and flapless pockets. The trousers, which are of the same material, are not turned up and are sufficiently long to ride over the shoes. Above the left breast pocket is embroidered the German "symbol of sovereignty" – an eagle with outstretched wings bearing the swastika.

### Pro-Government Locomotives

THOUSANDS of Rumanian peasants recently gathered at Cluj Station, where Dr. Maniu, leader of the National Peasant party, had promised to address them during a half-hour halt of his train.

He was wildly acclaimed when he began his speech on an improvised platform before the station.

But at the first word of criticism of the Government the engine of his train emitted an ear-splitting blast. This was the prearranged signal for every other engine in Cluj Junction to blow its whistle.

PETERBOROUGH

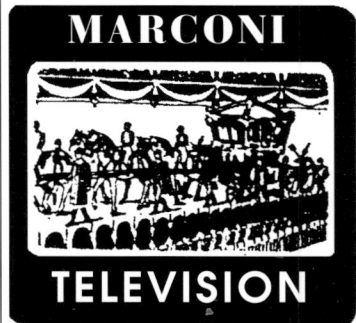

# CLOTHES THAT ROB THE ENGLISH WINTER OF ITS STING

## WARM FASHIONS FOR OUR COLD COUNTRY HOUSES

**By Jane Gordon, Daily Telegraph and Morning Post Fashion Expert**

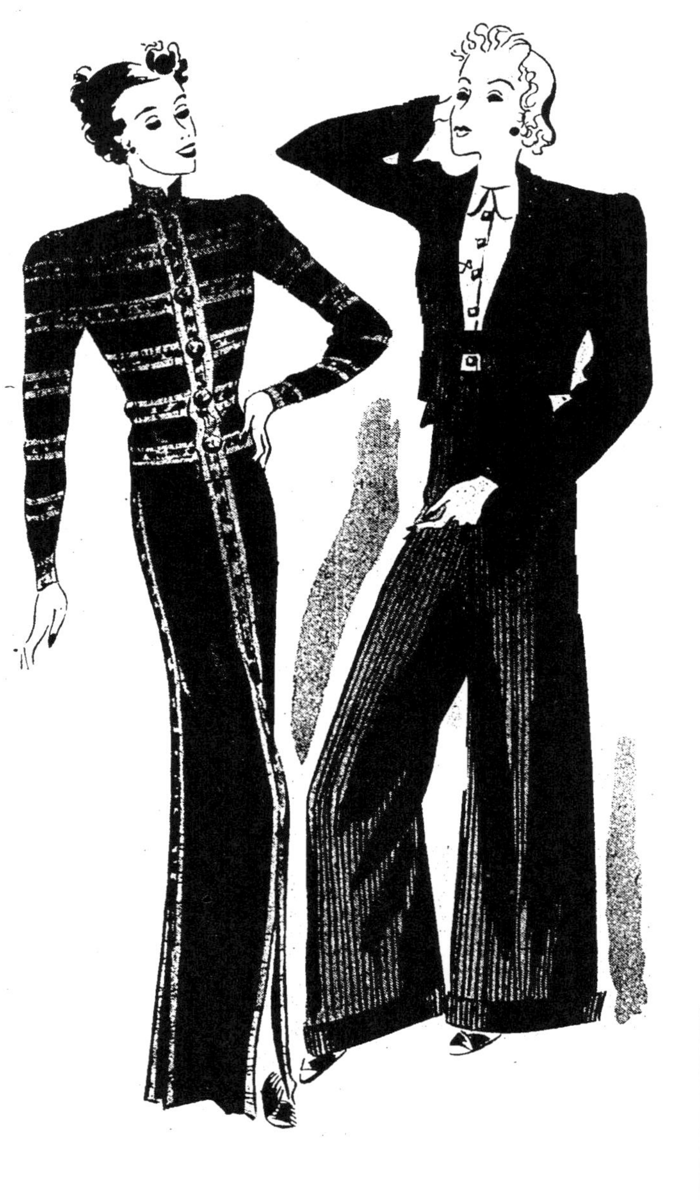

*Two examples of smart and cosy suits designed for cold country house wear. One is in flame-coloured crêpe with gold embroidery, and the second model is composed of leaf-green corduroy trousers, velvet jumper and short mess jacket.*

I AM sure it is not the roast beef of Old England that has made us the hardy nation that we are, but the coldness of our country houses and discomfort of our public schools.

If this supposition is correct, the two models sketched here should be viewed with alarm, for they infer that the blood of English women is running cold, and that such women are being mollycoddled by fashion.

Examine the girl wearing the leaf-green corduroy trousers suit. This is the model of a new housewear called Ships, and is designed to wear after hunting. The short mess jacket is lined with wadding and the slit pockets bound with braid. The long, well-tailored trousers are delightfully comfortable, and to ensure that the entire suit is draught-proof it is worn with a little velvet jumper in a lighter shade of green.

When you consider that the mother of the girl who wears this garment probably changed into a chiffon tea-gown after a hard day's hunting, and that she had never heard of central heating, you realise how pampered we are in these days.

A lapis-blue suit in hand-woven tweed has a plain blue skirt and a blue and black check jacket. A dark green suit, in a curious flat cloth rather like felt, has a divided skirt and very new V-shaped inverted pleats at the back of the jacket, which has stand-out pockets.

The belt of this suit is of leather, with a small white string ball bag at one side in which you can tuck two or three golf balls. Jade-green suede is used for a suit with a box jacket, slim-fitting skirt and suede hat to match.

IF you wish to continue this story of warm fashions for cold houses you have only to go on to the Echo de Paris and see the clothes designed by Princess Alfonse de Chimay, which are worn in many of the chilliest ancestral homes.

The "Band Master," suit sketched is a typical example of her evening suits. It is in flame-coloured crêpe with bands of gold-thread embroidery. The slim-fitting skirt, slit up the front, has bands of the embroidery down the side seams as well. Another suit of much the same cut is in deep night-blue with squares of blue sequins on the front of the jacket.

For hunt balls there is an evening dress in violet silk jersey, with the backless bodice cut to a deep V in the front and fulness at the front of the skirt. Round the high waist-line is tied a narrow rose-pink velvet ribbon.

**(November 22)**

# MODERN RADIO WONDERS

## CHEAPER & BETTER TELEVISION

**By L. Marsland Gander, Daily Telegraph Radio Correspondent**

The most interesting Radio Exhibition for many years opens at Olympia to-day. Owing chiefly to the wide variety of new television receivers the show will recapture the atmosphere of pioneer broadcasting days.

Several firms have produced television sets at prices below £50, hitherto deemed unattainable. At the other end of the scale are luxurious instruments combining in one cabinet television, all-wave radio and a gramophone.

The cheaper television receivers have been made possible chiefly by reduction in the number of valves and in the size of the principal component, the cathode ray tube. This tube normally resembles a glass flask in shape and the picture is seen on the base. Reduction of the size, therefore, has the effect of giving a slightly smaller picture than usual.

More expensive sets have been developed with double the average size of screen. The largest screen at Olympia will measure 22in. by 18in. the smallest 6in by 4 ½in.

### "BABY" SET AT £35

The small picture is on a G.E.C. "baby set" which costs only £35, the cheapest television receiver yet made. The set, which is in a cabinet measuring only 14in by 17in square and 21in deep, receives pictures only.

Its most ingenious feature is, however, that the sound accompanying the television transmission can be picked up by simply connecting the set to an ordinary broadcast receiver. When this is tuned to the wavelength of 550 metres it reproduces the 7-metre sound transmission from Alexandra Palace.

As an eve-of-the-show surprise the Marconiphone and H.M.V. companies announced that a new big screen E.M.I. receiver, showing a picture 22in by 18in, would be demonstrated.

Ekco have produced one of the table model television receivers, which will be sold at 45 guineas.

R.G.D. a firm whose name has always been associated with higher-priced quality sets, have for the first time produced an instrument which combines television, an all-wave radio receiver, and an automatic gramophone capable of playing eight records of mixed sizes. The picture size is 9 ½in by 7 1/2in. the range of the radio set 7 metres to 2,000 metres. and the instrument incorporates 37 valves. Its price is 170 guineas.

**(August 25)**

# NEW STANDARD OF ENGLISH COOKING

## MISTRESSES & MAIDS LEARN SIDE BY SIDE

**By A Special Representative**

One of the most practical and determined attempts to solve the domestic servant problem has taken form, and during the past few months has been growing apace, at Fareham, Hampshire.

Miss Florence White, founder of the English Folk Cookery Association and the guiding spirit of this enterprise, described it to me as the only satisfactory solution. In a 12-roomed house she is training at little cost, and in many cases entirely free: girls of elementary education and of school-leaving age to become good kitchen-maids and under-cooks.

The woman of some experience to become a cook worthy of an epicurean household;

The more highly educated girl and woman for posts as teachers, demonstrators, and lecturers.

First, students are taught to make wholemeal bread from equal quantities of wholemeal and white flour, and then the most perfect English puff pastry, of which the House of Studies is justly proud. The recipe for it was learnt by Miss White in Fareham, 54 years ago, when staying with two aunts.

### 65 LESSONS A WEEK

On an average 65 lessons are given each week in the two kitchens. The day is divided into three sessions – morning, afternoon and evening. Every day except Saturdays and Sundays lessons in cooking special dinners, luncheons, suppers and high teas are given, and instruction in house-keeping from the catering, buying and cooking standpoints.

The routine in the morning is that of a private house, and the work in the back kitchen is intended to train girls as kitchen-maids and single-handed cooks. A girl straight from school could be ready for a small post in a month; one not showing such aptitude might need two months' training.

### WHAT MISTRESSES LEARN

In the afternoons individual requirements are catered for. A mistress may send her maid to learn a new dish, or come herself to discover appetising, quickly-made supper dishes that she can prepare on the maid's night out. Cooking by gas and electricity is taught.

Nine girls were satisfactorily placed in domestic service positions recently in a week, although the House of Studies is not to be considered in the light of a registry office.

**(January 4)**

# LITTLE NOVELTIES FOR THE TRAVELLER

SINCE women showed their preference for travelling light all kinds of ingenious methods of saving space have made their appearance.

A bright new idea for a short journey is a three-decker cream container, which houses face cream, cold cream and skin-food in one single cylinder of washable composition. These containers are in white, striped with pastel colours, and will contain enough cream for a long week-end's use.

An outsize flapjack, which will hold enough face-powder to last for several days, is another novelty. It can be seen in different shapes. A large circular one, covered with petit point, will look well standing on the little dressing-table of a liner, train, or aeroplane. Others are semi-circular in shape and covered in suede.

Men and women alike will find a little leather case, holding mirror, shoe horn and button-hook, very useful. The whole outfit is small enough to be slipped into a handbag or pocket.

Double-sided hand mirrors for travellers are in polished metal and have folding handles.

The idea of well-cut pyjamas and tailored dressing gowns to wear when travelling has been adopted enthusiastically by women. Brown gabardine is the latest contribution to this fashion of travelling lingerie.

Smart dressing gowns seen in a shop in Regent-street, were of brown gabardine. One has wide revers bordered with brown petersham ribbon and another has straight lapels piped with pink, and the same piping round the cuffs. Both show a patterned foulard handkerchief tucked into the neckline, and have broad sashes of the same material.

**(September 14)**

# BEAUTY CULT NEED NOT BE EXPENSIVE

## WHERE WOMEN WORKERS HAVE THE ADVANTAGE

**By Jane Gordon**

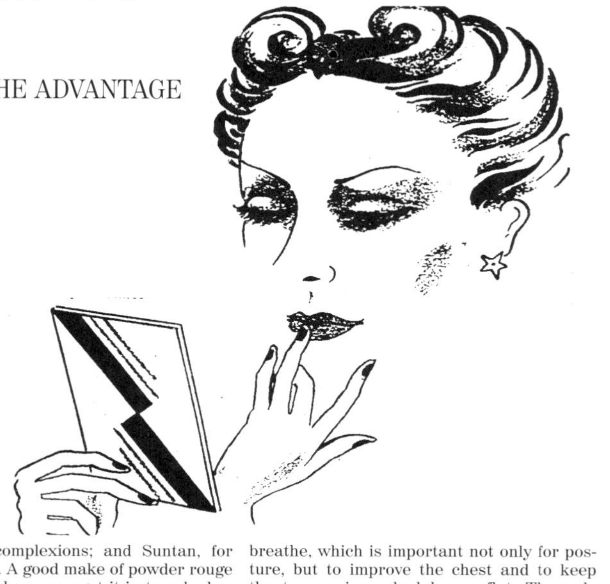

IT is believed generally that if a woman has plenty of money and leisure there is no excuse for her not being good to look at, simply because she can afford to spend a good deal of time and money in beauty parlours and on beauty preparations. I am inclined to think this is a fallacy. I believe it is far harder for the rich woman to keep her looks than it is for the poor.

If you take the trouble to inquire you will find that at a fashionable restaurant at least 60 per cent. of the women present are on a more or less strict diet. This would be quite unnecessary if they took an hour and a half's good walk every day. Compare their figures with those of the girls who work in shops all day and you will find the sales girl's figure in much better trim in spite of the fact that she probably pays no attention to her diet.

Look at the "frilly" jaw-line and slack contours of well-to-do women and compare them with women of the same age who are nursing many hours a day in hospitals. The amount of physical work that nurses do keeps their muscles braced as no beauty parlour can. An exception to this rule is the office worker who sits all day with her head bent. She needs to take special care of her figure, jaw-line and throat – but I will deal with this next week.

To-day I am writing for girls who are on a small allowance or earning their own living and are forced to be pennywise in their choice of beauty aids. As there are, literally, thousands of beauty aids on the market, women often feel that it is hopeless to try to search for exactly what they want. My work forces me to learn the merits of most of the better-known makes.

### A PURE CREAM

I know, for instance, of a cream costing 6d and 1s 3d a jar that is as pure and light as the most famous skin foods costing four times as much. Though this cream can be used for all purposes, I like it best as a cleansing cream and skin food. For 6d you can get a face powder which is as fine and pure as the most expensive face powder and only faintly scented. There are five shades: Natural, for ash blondes; Peach, for fair hair; Rachel 1 for pale skin or white hair; Rachel 2 for sallow complexions; and Suntan, for dark brunettes. A good make of powder rouge costs 1s 6d. and you can get it in ten shades.

You can get a lipstick with a famous name for 2s. This comes in five shades. Lavisible is a light shade suitable for blondes with blue or brown eyes; Capucine has an orange tone, suitable for auburn types or brunettes; Moyen is medium and suitable for grey hair or medium brunettes; Vif is a bright tone good for brunettes with blue-black hair blue eyes and fair skin; and Foncé is dark and suits medium brunettes with light eyes, or women with rather swarthy skins.

If the complexion is poor with spots enlarged pores and blackheads, the cure does not depend on expensive beauty parlours, but on a reformed diet and conscientious but inexpensive scalp and complexion treatment. I have a chart dealing with all this. You are welcome to it if you let me have a stamped addressed envelope.

### FIGURE CHART

Figure faults can usually be corrected by special exercises. Here again I have worked out a chart that gives you correct exercises for neck, arms, stomach, hips, legs, ankles and feet. It describes the correct way to breathe, which is important not only for posture, but to improve the chest and to keep the tummy in and abdomen flat. The only expense involved is a few minutes of your time before breakfast.

The expense of keeping your hands as fair and lovely as those of the leisured lady is not great. You can get a liquid polish in six clear or five smoky shades for 9d. a bottle of oil polish remover for 9d. cuticle remover 9d. emery boards 6d, orange sticks 6d, hand cream 2s a good hand lotion 9d. and a hand pack for 1s 6d.

### POWDER BLENDING SERVICE

As for beauty treatments, they are quite inexpensive if you know where to look for them. In the beauty parlour of a well-known Regent-street store you can have a 20 min clean up for 2s 6d. and a 15 min "Gin Kick" complexion treatment for 3s 6d. They also have a powder blending service here, where a specially trained blender will mix powders to suit your individual complexion.

In Knightsbridge you can get a manicure for 1s 6d. revarnish 1s. pedicure 2s 6d. and eyebrow tidy-up 1s 6d.

**(December 22)**

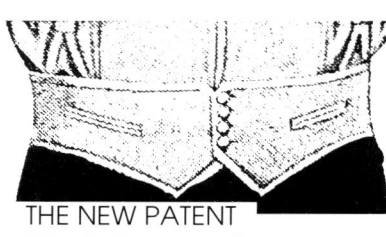

# A GREAT PATRIOT

## SIR AUSTEN'S SERVICES TO PEACE AND UNITY

SIR AUSTEN CHAMBERLAIN'S unexpected death comes with the shock of personal loss. All through his political life, which extended over more than 40 years and was rich in controversial matter, he never made an enemy; and in the last two Parliaments he had enjoyed that curious blend of respect and affection which the House of Commons reserves for elder statesmen whose reputation is finally secure. On what solid and eminently lovable qualities that reputation rested the public has lately been enabled to judge. Only last year Sir AUSTEN published the full text of the letters which he wrote to his father when illness had left him crippled in body but vigorous as ever in mind. In them a character of exceptional charm, sensitive, eager, generous and patient, reveals itself with a candour free from the least touch of self-consciousness.

A shrewd judgment of men, a large, and easy tolerance of outlook, and a modest sense of a growing personal hold over the House of Commons and the public, supply the essential human touch. It is hard to believe that the mind which could think so sanely and acutely has ceased to function and that the pen which wrote these genial, vivacious letters has been laid down for ever.

Though it is more than five years since Sir AUSTEN'S official life closed, he is still too near us for his achievement to be set in proper perspective. It may be that when the history of our century comes to be written his decision to remain in the BALFOUR Cabinet after his father resigned, and his quiet, persistent advocacy of the whole tariff policy, "food taxes" included, will be judged to have contributed decisively to that change in the current of economic thought which has turned the once unchallenged Free Trade doctrine into an historical curiosity.

But for us who mourn his loss the five years during which he held the seals of the Foreign Office stand out as the most memorable of his life. His services were not properly appreciated at the time and few things in his political life wounded him so much as the narrow margin by which he retained West Birmingham at the 1929 election. But in retrospect justice can be done to the contribution which he made to the appeasement of Europe. In a very real sense he was the author of Locarno.

Loyalty was the mainspring of his actions. Out of loyalty to his subordinates he insisted on resigning after the publication of the Mesopotamian Report. No one suggested that he was actually to blame for the medical shortcomings of the Indian Expeditionary Force. But he was Secretary of State, responsibility was technically his; and he found it intolerable that he should remain in office while others suffered in position and repute. A few years later he was confronted with a choice which any other man would have found difficult. The Coalition which Mr LLOYD GEORGE had headed was breaking up. The Conservative party was in full revolt. The Conservative leader who headed the rebellion had the reversion to the Premiership in his hands. All this mattered nothing to SIR AUSTEN. He had taken office as Mr. LLOYD GEORGE'S colleague and with him he was prepared to fall. Those who disagreed most strongly with his views approved of his motives, and there can be little doubt that the respect in which he was everywhere held helped towards that effective reunion of the Conservative forces which gave the country the strong Government it needed after the collapse of the first Labour Administration.

**(March 17)**

# IVOR GURNEY

## A MUSICIAN'S TRAGEDY

**By Richard Capell**

As a young student at the Royal College of Music, Ivor Gurney was recognised as a composer of the rarest talent. "Potentially the most gifted man that ever came into my care," said Stanford, "and the one who most fulfilled the accepted idea of genius," And Parry, who had been examining the young man's manuscripts with excitement, pointing out to his fellow-examiners the similarity in idiom and even in handwriting to Schubert, exclaimed on setting eyes on the composer, "By God! It is Schubert!"

Gurney was born at Gloucester in 1890. At 16 he became assistant to Brewer, the Cathedral organist, and at 20 he came up to the R.C.M. During the war he served in the 2/5 Gloucesters. In 1918 he was invalided out of the Army. His sufferings, mental and physical, were to prove beyond healing.

Still, for a few years he produced prolifically. Most of his 200 songs were written between 1917 and 1920. In 1917 there appeared his first book of poems, "Severn and Somme." and in 1919 another, "War's Embers." These pages speak of a passionate love of England and particularly of the poet's native county, and reveal a quivering sensibility as well as not a little of the heroic temper.

**(December 28)**

# DRAMATIC LIFE STORY OF MR. RAMSAY MACDONALD

## POOR BOY WHO BECAME PREMIER IN THREE GOVERNMENTS

The period after the Great War, which witnessed a number of amazing vicissitudes of fortune in the careers of our leading public men, saw nothing comparable to the case of Mr. Ramsay MacDonald.

Within the space of eight years he formed the first Socialist Government to be called to power in Great Britain; held the Premiership a second time as head of a far stronger Socialist Government; and thence passed directly to the headship of a National Government in which most of the Ministers were Conservatives, which was supported by the largest force of Conservatives ever returned to the House of Commons and which was bitterly opposed by all but a fraction of the Socialist party.

James Ramsay MacDonald was born in 1866, the son of a farm labourer, in the fishing village of Lossiemouth, Morayshire, which to the end of his life he felt to be his home. The family circumstances were those of the direst poverty. All the start in life that the young MacDonald had was the excellent grounding that has always been the glory of Scottish free education, and the interest taken in him by his schoolmaster, who made the boy a pupil teacher.

### FIRST EARNINGS

At the age of 18, with little more than enough to pay his railway fare he went to seek his fortune in London. He hoped to earn enough to support him while he studied science. For a time he knew destitution. He sought, and failed to get employment as an omnibus conductor. His first money, a few shillings a week, was earned by addressing envelopes for the Cyclists' Touring.

But it was the dawning cause of Socialism that more and more took possession of his mind. He was one of the earlier members of the Fabian Society, and he joined the London Trades Council at about the same time.

What he regarded as "fortune" came to him at last in the fourth year of his bitter experience in London. He attracted the notice of Thomas Lough, for many years a familiar figure in Radical politics.

That robust North Irishman wanted a private secretary; and when in 1888 he engaged the young Scots Socialist at a salary of £75, the whole prospect underwent for him a heartening change.

In 1895 MacDonald stood for Parliament for the first time as an I.L.P. candidate, and was soundly defeated by a "Lib-Lab" working-class opponent. It was not until 1900 that he won the first decisive success in his campaign to win over trade unionism. It was then that, by a decision of the Trades Union Congress, the Labour Representation Committee came into being, with MacDonald as secretary.

To the next House of Commons it secured the election of three members. At the election of 1906 it won 29 Independent Labour seats, and MacDonald was returned for Leicester.

Thus the Labour party, as it was thenceforward to be known, came fully into existence – virtually the creation of Ramsay MacDonald.

The opposition of a few obscure Socialists to the South African War had made no difference to anyone. The opposition of the Leader, as MacDonald now was of a rising party in Parliament to the intervention of his country in the Great War was another matter.

On the eve of the British declaration of War he was offered a place in the Government. He refused it, and announced in the House his own and his party's conviction that Great Britain should remain neutral. Two days later he was repudiated by his followers in Parliament and in the country. His name was execrated everywhere. Indignation and hatred pursued him throughout the war years; and when, in 1918, he lost his seat at Leicester by a margin of 14,000 votes, the seal seemed to be set upon his political extinction.

The fact that he came back to public life, with the full confidence of the Socialist movement behind him, was in part a tribute to courage and consistency in the urging of a generally detested pacifist policy while the war lasted.

### RETURN TO PARLIAMENT

It was at the General Election of 1922, after the break-up of the Coalition Government, that MacDonald was returned for the Welsh mining constituency of Aberavon. He came back as one of a party now more than 140 strong, animated by a new spirit of militant discontent, and his colleagues, first act was to elect him to the Parliamentary leadership.

This was to all appearance the summit of MacDonald's career. No one had reckoned with the possibility of the tragic death of Mr. Bonar Law soon after his notable triumph at the polls. Even more unforeseeable was

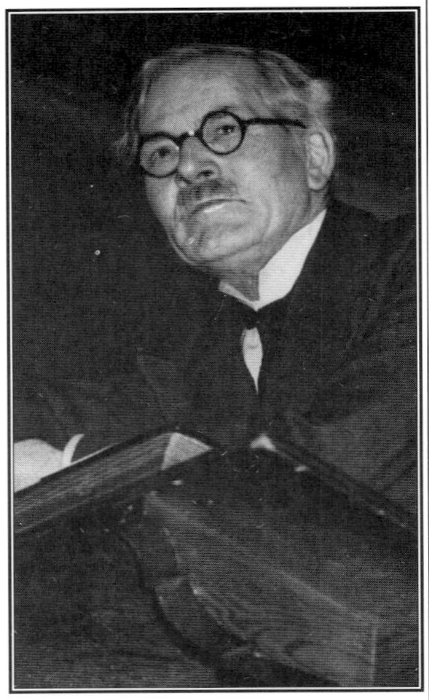

Mr. Ramsay MacDonald

the decision of the new Prime Minister, Mr. Baldwin, to appeal to the country – on the issue of Protection as the remedy for unemployment – within a year of his party's accession to well-established power.

### THE PREMIERSHIP

From the election of 1923 the Socialist party returned with 191 seats, virtually one-third of the House of Commons, and Mr. MacDonald unhesitatingly took office as Prime Minister, together with the Foreign Secretaryship in January, 1924.

The end came, however, over a secondary question – that of the prosecution for sedition of a Communist writer named Campbell. The action of the Attorney-General in dropping these proceedings was attributed to pressure privately exerted by the Government's Left-wing supporters. Mr. MacDonald, refusing all counsels of compromise, took up the somewhat half-hearted challenge of the now combined anti-Socialist parties, and on Oct. 8 the Government was defeated on a division by 166 votes. A dissolution and appeal to the country was announced next day.

### THE ZINOVIEV LETTER

The 1924 election, which was very bitterly contested, would probably have gone against Labour in any event; for the Government's Russian policy was deeply unpopular, and its failure to cope with unemployment was a fatal weakness. But the final blow came in the last days of the campaign, with one publication of the "Zinoviev Letter," an intercepted document, in which Zinoviev gave instructions to the British Communists for the furtherance of revolution. Together with this was published a Foreign Office Note to Moscow, signed, "In the absence of the Secretary of State," in which the "Red Letter" was sternly denounced and it could not be denied that MacDonald had completed the draft of this Note, although he had not formally signed it or authorised the publication of it.

The result of this departmental muddle was to sway a multitude of votes at the polls. Although Labour increased its national vote by upwards of 1,000,000 the Conservative poll was swelled by yet greater figures, and Mr. Baldwin came back with an enormous majority.

The years of Conservative administration that followed were not a period of promise for MacDonald's future. As the end of the Government's term drew near, however, MacDonald recovered all his tireless campaigning energy, and at the election of May, 1929, his party, for the first time, came back the strongest of the three parties with 290 seats; and he took office for the second time in June.

It was in August, 1931, that the most dramatic crisis of our modern political history arose. The report of the May Committee disclosed to all the world the desperate state of the national finances, with a £120,000,000 deficit in prospect. British credit the world over reeled under the shock, and the Cabinet set itself to devising a programme of bold and far-reaching retrenchment.

It was on the question of the reducing of unemployment benefit, among the other drastic "cuts" and economies proposed, that the majority of the Cabinet, with the trade unions' backing, renounced MacDonald's leadership. The die was cast on Aug. 23. On the next day the Labour Government resigned, to be replaced by a National Government under Mr. MacDonald's Premiership, with Mr. Baldwin and Sir Herbert Samuel as his principal anti-Socialist colleagues.

By the end of 1933 it was evident that Mr. MacDonald's strength had been over-taxed by the strain of four years of office, during which a tragic severance of lifelong political ties had been added to the shocks and anxieties of a profoundly unsettled time.

At the general election of November, 1935, he lost his seat for the Seaham Harbour division by a majority of 20,000. In February of 1936 he was re-elected to the House of Commons by a majority of over 7,000 as a representative of the Scottish Universities.

**(November 10)**

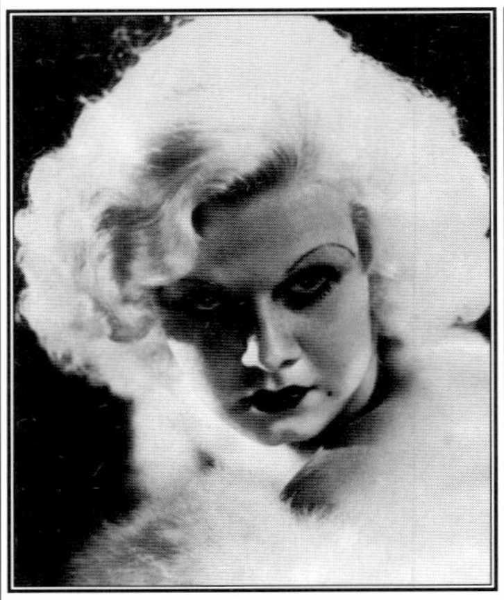

# JEAN HARLOW DIES AT 26

**From Our Own Correspondent**

HOLLYWOOD, Monday.

Miss Jean Harlow, the film actress, died here to-day after an illness of 10 days. She was 26.

Her death followed a sudden relapse. When she was first taken ill with uræmic poisoning her condition was not regarded as serious, and recent bulletins had announced considerable improvement.

Known as "the original platinum blonde," Miss Harlow, whose real name was Harlean Carpenter, was married three times. Her first husband was a wealthy young man whom she met at college, Mr. Charles F. Grew.

They eloped when she was 16, but the marriage had already failed by the time she reached Hollywood at the age of 17.

Her second husband was the film director, Mr. Paul Bern.

She married him in July, 1932. Two months later he committed suicide.

A year later she married Mr. Harold Rosson, a film photographer. There was a divorce in March, 1935.

Recently her name had been coupled with that of Mr. William Powell, the star with whom she appeared in one of her latest films, "Libelled Lady."

Mr. Powell was with her mother at her bedside during her last hours.

**(June 8)**

# FIRST PRESIDENT OF CZECHOSLOVAKIA

## DR. MASARYK'S UNIQUE PLACE IN HISTORY

Thomas Garrigue Masaryk, first President of the Czecholslovak Republic, occupied an almost unique position. Practically unknown to the vast majority of the British public until the time of the Armistice, by then he enjoyed a prestige upon which the future of his country was so largely to depend. Indeed, there is no single man more responsible for the present European structure that Masaryk, and the already 68-year-old professor elected to the Presidency of the new State in November, 1918, enjoyed the exceptional triumph of having won the day by many years of untiring labour and plain thinking.

The Armistice with Austria-Hungary was signed on Nov. 4th. Masaryk sailed from America on the 12th, and he was elected President of the new State for the first time on the 14th. He was re-elected to the Presidency in the years 1920 and 1927. In March, 1930, when the President celebrated his 80th birthday, he distributed the large monetary present received from the nation to various charitable organisations.

### RE-ELECTED AT 84

In May, 1934, when he was 84, he was re-elected for the third time as President of the Republic. In December, 1935 when his health was getting feebler, he resigned from the Presidency. His last act as President was to issue an amnesty granting freedom to hundreds of political prisoners. The Czechs awarded him the title of "President-Liberator."

**(September 14)**

# MRS. EDITH WHARTON

Mrs. Edith Wharton, the famous novelist, died yesterday at her home near Paris, at the age of 75.

In the 42 books she had written she gained a wide reputation in Europe and America for her scholarly and sincere style.

Although she worked energetically during the war for French and Belgian refugees, she published four books in that period. She was a life-long friend of Henry James.

In 1923 she became the first woman to receive from Yale University the honorary degree of LL.D.

**(August 13)**

# MARCHESE MARCONI

## HOW HE MADE WORLD RADIO POSSIBLE

Marchese Marconi – whose death occurred yesterday at the age of 63 – owed so much to the encouragement of England, where he made his home for 40 years, that there was little tendency except in Italy to associate his name very prominently with the country in which he was born and educated.

In recent years, however, his Fascist sympathies became more obvious, and they were emphasised by his championship of the war against Abyssinia.

For the greater part of his life he impressed most people by his outlook, his appearance, and even his speech, as typically British. It was not unnatural that this should be so.

His mother was an Irishwoman – Annie Jameson, daughter of Andrew Jameson, of Daphne Castle, county Wexford. It was while she was completing her musical education in Italy three-quarters of a century ago that she met and shortly afterwards married an Italian country gentleman, Giuseppe Marconi. They had two sons, of whom Guglielmo was the younger.

From an early age he was keenly interested in physical and electrical science, and in the cultivation of his gifts he was spared all the trials of the impecunious inventor. He was able to fit up a little laboratory in his home, and his mother gave him constant encouragement.

His father, however, was at times somewhat alarmed. When young Guglielmo, after ingeniously applying himself at a Leghorn shipyard to the perfecting of some delicate apparatus brought it home, his father regarded it as far too dangerous. He was "not going to have the house blown up," and he took drastic steps to avoid any such happening.

### CUSTOMS MEN'S FEAR

But Marconi survived the parental ban, and in the early summer of 1895, with crude and inefficient apparatus, was able to carry out many interesting experiments in the harnessing of electric waves.

It was in the following year he came to England, and there is a very amusing story on record that when his baggage was examined by the Customs authorities something like panic ensued over the discovery of his apparatus. The pale, slenderly-built young man who had brought it was suspected of carrying an infernal machine, and the story is that notwithstanding all his protests it was promptly dropped into a bucket of water for safety.

But very soon after his arrival in England to which he had been invited by the late Sir William Preece, Engineer-in-Chief to the Post Office. Marconi had embarked in earnest upon the great work that was to make him world-famous.

His triumph consisted in the practical application and commercial development of ideas which previously had been merely interesting experiments. By July, 1897, the Wireless Telegraph and Signal Co. Ltd. had been established. Three years later it became Marconi's Wireless Telegraph Co. Ltd.

His name before long had been flashed to every part of the world as that of a man who had performed one of the greatest miracles in history. His praises were sung everywhere; popular songs, laudatory addresses, books, and publicity of every kind appeared in embarrassing profusion.

Yet Marconi remained quite unperturbed. He went on adding to his achievements, working with great energy and attracting to himself a band of remarkably ingenious Englishmen.

Wireless developments came a little too late to be of any real service in the South African War, but in the Great War they were employed to remarkable effect. shortly afterwards Marconi acquired from the Admiralty his yacht Elettra in which he had been accustomed for many years past to carry out experiments.

**(July 21)**

# LT.-COL. C. McNEILE

## AUTHOR OF "BULLDOG DRUMMOND"

Lt.-Col. Cyril McNeile, who gained fame as "Sapper," the author of "Bulldog Drummond," died on Saturday at his home in Pulborough, Sussex, at the age of 49.

A genial man, of great personal charm and completely unspoilt by his great popularity as a writer, Col. McNeile was the son of the late Capt. Malcolm McNeile R.N. He was educated at Cheltenham, and after leaving the R.M.A. Woolwich, entered the Royal Engineers in 1907.

After the war he invented the character of "Bulldog Drummond" and it made a quick appeal. When dramatised it became, in the hands of the late Sir Gerald du Maurier, an extraordinarily successful play. Then came the film version, equally successful, with Ronald Coleman in the leading part.

"Sapper" was delighted with his successes to which he regularly added, but cheerfully denied that he possessed genius. In his modest way he attributed it to "luck."

**(August 16)**

# FOUNDER OF THE NEW "OLD VIC"

## MISS LILIAN BAYLIS'S GREAT WORK FOR STAGE

The stage suffered a great loss yesterday by the death at the age of 63 of Miss Lilian Baylis.

She was a woman of wonderful personality who possessed something like genius. Starting without any knowledge of Shakespeare she became so enthusiastic over his works that she produced them all. And at the same time she popularised grand opera in a manner that evoked national enthusiasm. To the end her indomitable spirit and untiring energy asserted itself.

She was born in London and her parents were concert singers. As a child she practised strenuously on the violin in the intervals of helping to look after younger members of the family. She had no other education beyond that devoted to music, and at an early age was appearing on the public platform.

In London she found her aunt, Miss Emma Cons, running the Royal Victoria Hall in Waterloo-road. It was a rather inferior type of music hall, and her aunt asked her to help. Miss Baylis agreed. her intention was to stay for only a brief period; instead she remained for the rest of her life and thus brought about her triumphs at "The Old Vic," of which she became manager on the death of her aunt.

START WITH FILMS

For some years she struggled to make the place pay as a music hall, but that form of entertainment did not appeal to her very much. "Animated pictures" were just being developed. She started to show them to audiences who paid a penny for admission. The quality of the films available proved unsatisfactory, and in her musical enthusiasm she decided to give symphony concerts instead. In that way she lost all of the £2,000 profit she had made out of films.

Then, in 1914, came her decision to produce Shakespearean plays. She knew nothing of Shakespeare, but went to men who did, and was convinced that poor people would be attracted if the prices were low enough. She fixed them at 2d, 4d and 6d.

The audience sat on bare wooden seats; the scenery was cheap; only the acting mattered. Men and women who played for her have since become famous actors and actresses.

**(November 26)**

# MR. GEORGE GERSHWIN

Mr. George Gershwin, the American composer, died yesterday at Hollywood, aged 38.

Within the past 12 years his compositions had become familiar all over the world. Born in New York, he was a pianist who began as a prolific writer of popular songs.

His gifts in producing striking melodies were undoubted, and in this respect he was at his best in "Lady Be Good," one of the large number of musical comedies for which he was responsible.

In the same year, 1924, came his "Rhapsody in Blue." It was written for Paul Whiteman's band, and behind it lay the ambition to produce serious work without abandoning the vigour and popular appeal inherent to his songs.

Gershwin followed this with a concerto in F. written for the New York Symphony Society in 1925; a second rhapsody, "An American in Paris," and in 1935 the opera "Porgy and Bess."

**(July 12)**



# SIR JAMES BARRIE AS GENIUS, MAN AND FRIEND

## MASTER OF FANTASY AND MAGIC

**By H.C. Bailey**

Since Robert Louis Stevenson passed away no man of letters has won such general affection as Sir James Matthew Barrie, who died on Saturday at the age of 77.

Though few famous men of our own or any other time have more shyly avoided the public eye, no one ever thought of Barrie's work apart from the man, no one could keep out of admiration a feeling of personal kindliness. It is not difficult to discover the reasons. In all his later work for the stage there was an eager cry of the heart. The familiar appeal of his Peter Pan, "say you believe in fairies," was no mere adroit stroke of stagecraft, but typical and characteristic. Barrie seemed always asking us to "say we believed" in his people, in his fun and his pathos, to say we were friends and liked him and his work.

Something childish in this there is as dull people did not fail to complain. But it is of the essence of Barrie's art that he kept always the spirit of a child, the eternal child whose charm he loved to celebrate.

A romantic, indeed, he never was, Barrie would have liked to give us romance, but somehow, even in "Peter Pan," there always crept in mockery and whim. It made at its best work of singular charm. We have had many greater novelists, and playwrights. We have never had one like him. He stands alone, and from generation to generation children will love him and keep their love to the end.

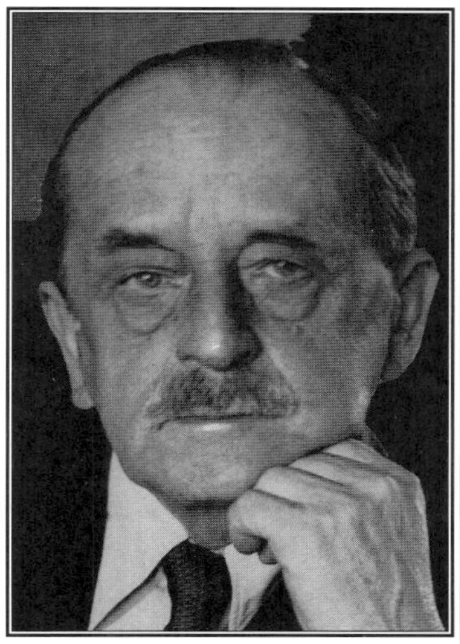

Sir James Barrie

EARLY YEARS

BARRIE'S TRIBUTE TO HIS MOTHER

Barrie was born on May 9, 1860, at Kirriemuir, in Fife. Kirriemuir is Thrums, "a handful of houses jumbled together in a cup," with a background of grey hills. In his youth "its every other room, earthen-floored and showing the rafters overhead, had a handloom," and the weavers led the hard life which never knew respite. Of his home in those early days he has told us in "Margaret Ogilvy," a book which, if it sometimes troubles us by the intimacy of its revelations, has a haunting pathos and beauty, a son's tribute to a mother unmatched in literature.

Barrie was educated at Dumfries Academy – his brother was inspector of schools at Dumfries – and at Edinburgh University, which afterwards called him to be its Chancellor. He took his M.A. in 1882, and next year accepted a post as leader-writer on the "Nottingham Journal." As a journalist he wrote much and wrote well, but his first book was still some years off, nor was it a masterpiece when it came. "Better Dead" has the marks of a clever and humourous mind, but no very distinctive quality.

"AULD LICHT IDYLLS"

"Auld Licht Idylls," which followed in 1888, is a very different matter. Cautious critics could say that Galt, the Scottish Balzac had found a new and perhaps a greater successor. Enthusiasts talked (rather wildly) about a blend of Dickens and Richardson. What was certain was that a novelist who could use the methods of realism with uncommon delicacy and grace, a master in miniature of pathos and humour had arisen. And the promise of "Auld Licht Idylls" was amply fulfilled by "A Window in Thrums." "Barrie is a beauty!" said Stevenson and pronounced the best of the new book "true as death and judgment."

THE NOVELIST'S MASTERPIECE

But his finest work as a novelist was still to come, the character of Grizel of the Crooked Smile, the heroine of the two fine novels "Sentimental Tommy" and "Tommy and Grizel". In her all the beauty of Barrie's imagination, with his subtlety and delicacy of insight, find worthy expression. With "Tommy and Grizel," published when he was 40, his career as a novelist closed.

From the first play to the last, one was never quite sure that an exquisite piece of fancy or pathos would not end in contortions of triviality. But the best things were exquisite from "Quality Street" to "Dear Brutus," and when one was under their spell, whether it was in the sisters of "Quality Street" or the artist and his dream daughter in "Dear Brutus" all faults and flaws were forgotten, and the theatre of Barrie became a treasury of the subtlest and most delicate pleasure.

The first great display of the power to which he owed his unique position came in the brilliant fantastics of "The Admirable Crichton." A trial piece it may have been in so far as it relied on powers which he had not used before, but if it was a coup d'essai it was also acoup de maitre. The man whom critics had likened to Galt or Jane Austen, or even Richardson, stood out a master of fantasy, a playwright of genius who, whether one liked his work or not, owed nothing to anybody or any school.

But "The Admirable Crichton" was ironic comedy rather than fantasy. The fantasy was almost pure in the masterpiece which came in 1904, "Peter Pan."

Its first state differed a good deal from that which children see now. Barrie worked over it with loving care, and always for the better. As it stands, it is for the critic, as for the child, not flawless, indeed, but almost pure delight, a possession for ever; one of those fables in which genius touched to inspiration, creates a piece of folk-lore for his race.

The fantastic vein thus triumphantly worked was laid under contribution again and again. Hardly any succeeding play, though some were essentially pure comedy, had no element of fantasy, and it is possible that Barrie would have been wiser to avoid these difficult harmonies.

A PLAY FOR ELLEN TERRY

"Alice Sit by the Fire," written for Ellen Terry in 1905, was followed by "What Every Woman Knows" in 1908. The character of the scotsman intent on rising in the world was a mordantly brilliant satiric portrait and the figure of his shrewd, self-sacrificing wife was fashioned with keen insight and sympathy, and gave Hilda Trevelyan the chance for a piece of acting that haunts the memory.

"The Adored One" (1913) and "A Kiss for Cinderella" (1916) rank as minor pieces, but "Dear Brutus" (1917), in spite of some laboured humour, contains some of the best work he ever did for the stage; and "Mary Rose" (1920) is to some a pure and rare delight.

He broke his long silence last year with "The Boy David," but the piece was a failure. It was as if he had recognised in Elizabeth Bergner the actress who was his ideal Peter Pan; and because she had come too late to play Peter himself, Barrie had tried to provide her with another part in exactly the same vein. The biblical hero proved too big for such treatment, and refused to dwindle into a dream-child.

Barrie was made a baronet in 1913, and created O.M. in 1922. He was married in 1894 to Miss Mary Ansell, from whom he obtained a divorce in 1909. There were no children of the marriage.

**(June 21)**

# MAURICE RAVEL

**By J.A. Westrup**

Maurice Ravel, who died in a Paris nursing home yesterday morning at the age of 62, was one of the most distinguished French composers of our time, and certainly the best known outside his native country.

Regarded in his youth as a wild revolutionary, he lived to see his music take a permanent place in the concert repertory, and even gained a reputation in circles where serious composition is generally ignored.

He was born at Ciboure, near St. Jean de Luz, in the Basses-Pyrénées, on March 7, 1875. While he was still a boy the family moved to Paris, and at the age of 12 he entered the Conservatoire. Here he studied the piano, harmony, counterpoint and composition, his master for the latter being Gabriel Faure.

Works for piano were published as early as 1895. Two celebrated pieces – the "Pavane pour une Infante défunte" and "Jeux d'eaux" – appeared in 1899 and 1901 respectively. In 1901 Ravel was awarded the second Grand Prix de Rome for a cantata, "Myrrha," but he was unsuccessful in obtaining the Premier Prix in 1902 and 1903, and in 1905 he was disqualified on the results of the preliminary competition.

The judges' decision aroused a storm of indignation, as the composer was by this time well known, and his String Quartet (1903) had established his reputation.

From the first his music was stamped with his own individuality. In the early days of the century he was mistakenly regarded as a follower of Débussy, his senior by 13 years, but it was not long before his personal qualities were recognised.

**(December 29)**

# INVESTIGATOR OF THE ATOM

## SCIENCE'S DEBT TO LORD RUTHERFORD

Lord Rutherford, O.M., F.R.S., died yesterday at the age of 66. His achievements have not only made him one of the greatest scientific figures of our time, but have assured him a permanent and illustrious place in the annals of science.

Ernest Rutherford was born at Nelson, New Zealand, and was the son of the late James Rutherford, of New Plymouth, Taranaki, New Zealand. After a brilliant career at New Zealand University he was elected in 1894 to an 1851 Exhibition Science Scholarship; he proceeded to Cambridge and entered Trinity College. Here he worked with Sir J.J. Thomson on the subject of the conduction of electricity through charged atoms or molecules.

These early researches, which were of great importance, though somewhat eclipsed by his later towering discoveries, led to his appointment in 1898 as Professor of Physics at the McGill University, Montreal, where his encounter with Frederick Soddy, who was a demonstrator at that university from 1900-1902, led to a most fruitful collaboration.

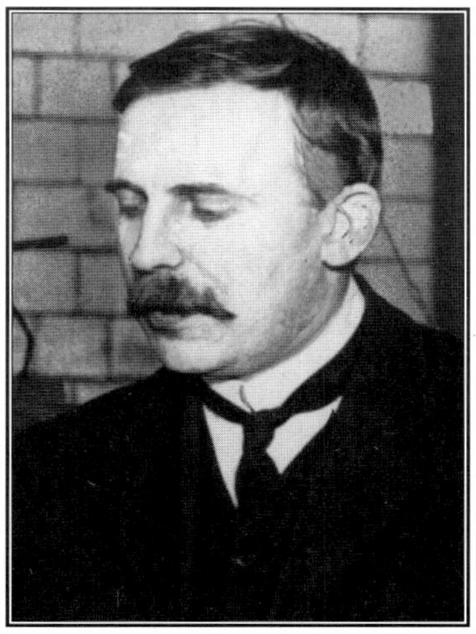

Lord Rutherford

Rutherford's name will be remembered as that of the maker of three closely connected fundamental discoveries namely, the nature of radioactivity, the nuclear structure of the atom, and the electrical nature of matter.

Before the year 1900 there was little indication that the atom – the smallest possible portion of any element – had any structure or was other than a hard, massive and unalterable particle. Radioactivity the continuous emission of rays by certain elements such as uranium, was discovered by Becquerel in 1896, and Mme. Curie and others soon succeeded in isolating radium, polonium and other elements, which displayed an intense degree of radioactivity.

The work of Rutherford and Soddy from 1900 onwards demonstrated that radio-activity was the explosive disintegration of the individual atoms of an element. They showed that the atoms broke up, expelling with enormous velocity X-particles, which were later shown to be electrically-charged helium atoms; B-particles, which were shown to be electrons, and J-rays, which were shown to be radiation of a type similar to X-rays. By this process the atom became converted into the atom of a different element.

TRANSMUTATION OF ELEMENTS

They thus demonstrated that the transmutation of elements, the impossibility of which was in the Nineteenth Century almost an article of faith, was continually taking place. Rutherford and Soddy worked out genealogical trees showing how the parent elements, uranium and thorium, broke down and after giving rise to a dozen or more different elements ended up as the homely and inactive substance, lead. In studying these changes Rutherford discovered the relatively vast quantity of energy evolved from a minute weight of radium or other such element – a first hint of the huge store of power locked up in the atom.

In 1911 he put forward his theory of atomic structure. It had been found that if the high-speed particles expelled by a radioactive substance were caused to pass through a thin sheet of matter – e.g. goldleaf – most of them passed right through the atoms of gold and were but little deflected, while a definite but very small proportion were sharply deflected through a large angle, or even forced back.

From these facts, mathematically analysed, Rutherford deduced that the atom consisted of a loose cloud of very light electrons (incapable of seriously deflecting an X-particle) surrounding a very minute, heavy, positively charged nucleus, the size of which was very small in comparison to the minute atom itself, while its mass and charge were large enough to deflect an X-particle through a large angle.

**(October 20)**

# MISS AMELIA EARHART

## FIRST WOMAN TO FLY ATLANTIC

**By George Fyfe**

The real significance of Amelia Earhart's achievement lay in the whole-hearted enthusiasm she evoked among women all over the world. No one within the past few days could have remained oblivious to the tremendous hold she had gained in this respect.

Miss Earhart certainly attracted the hero-worshippers to a very marked extent, and much of the glamour was probably due to her dash of masculinity. When I met her nine years ago, shortly after her first flight across the Atlantic, she suggested by her demeanour a very likeable tomboy with a pronounced sense of humour.

The fact that she made this flight only as a passenger did not detract, in the opinion of the public, from the interest of the performance, for it enabled her to become the first woman to fly the Atlantic.

Actually she was well able at that time to handle a machine in the air, but circumstances compelled her to depend on the great skill of a male pilot, Wilbur Stultz.

NON-STOP ACROSS U.S.

The Atlantic crossing was accomplished in 20hrs 40mins, and for 1,900 miles out of 2,100 the machine was in fog.

Three years later she married Mr. George Palmer Putnam, the American publisher, but stated that for her business purposes she would continue to use her maiden name. In 1932 she determined to fly the Atlantic herself, and after a thrilling journey as the first woman to cross that ocean alone by air she arrived in England on the fifth anniversary of Col. Lindbergh's feat.

Later that year Miss Earhart flew non-stop across the United States from Los Angeles to Newark New Jersey, a distance of more than 2,500 miles, in 19 hours.

But although her long-distance flights evoked so much enthusiasm an undercurrent of criticism asserted itself. There were people who wished she would remain content with what she had done.

This feeling led to protests in America against Miss Earhart's decision in 1934 to fly from Honolulu to the American mainland. It was pointed out that to do so in a single-engined land machine was foolhardy and would mean nothing if she succeeded.

Miss Earhart declined to listen to protests of this kind, and in January 1935 flew the 2,400 miles from Honolulu to Oakland, California, in 18 1/4 hours.

Then, several months later, came her preparations to fly round the world, a distance of 27,000 miles. Last March she and her navigator, Capt. Noonan, flew the first stage across the Pacific, from Oakland to Honolulu, but when Miss Earhart was attempting to take off again the machine crashed through a burst tyre.

After repairs had been effected a fresh start was made on the round-the-world slight at the beginning of last month. On this occasion, however, it was decided to attempt the flight in the reverse direction.

Everything went well for 20,000 miles. Then on the final portion of the trip came the flight from Lae, New Guinea, which led to disaster.

**(July 20)**

# THE DUCHESS OF BEDFORD

## FIRST SOLO FLIGHT WHEN AGED 64

The death has now been regretfully presumed of the Duchess of Bedford at the age of 71. All trace of her was lost a week ago when she set out alone in her aeroplane for what was to have been a short flight.

Her achievements as a pilot may be best appreciated by reflecting that next year she would have celebrated her golden wedding.

Forty-four years have passed since her husband succeeded to the dukedom of Bedford, and he had married the Duchess five years before. She was then Miss Mary du Caurroy Tribe, daughter of the Archdeacon of Lahore, the Ven. Walter Harry Tribe, who died in 1909.

Fishing, hunting, big game shooting, and skating were other sports she enjoyed. She purchased Prince's skating rink at the beginning of the century. Among her other interests were nursing – she built a hospital – radiography, ornithology, and the keeping of animals.

But nothing in her later years made so tremendous an appeal to her as flying. She took it up when she was 61.

In 1930 she set up a record in air touring, covering 19,000 miles from England to South Africa and back in 20 days. In 1934, during a flight over North Africa, her machine was fired on by natives. In 1935 she made a long trip over the Sahara to Central Africa and back.

**(March 30)**

# COTTON WINS GOLF OPEN IN DELUGE

## GREENS TURNED INTO LAKES

**By George Greenwood, Daily Telegraph Golf Correspondent.**

CARNOUSTIE, Friday.

Henry Cotton, aged 30, of the Ashridge Club, Herts, scored a great victory for Britain by winning the open golf championship here to-day.

His score was 290, six strokes less than T.D. Armour's total in 1931, when the course was shorter and easier.

Reginald Whitcombe, of Parkstone, Dorset, was second, two strokes behind, after leading with one round to play.

A torrential rainstorm swept the course and turned several of the greens into miniature lakes. Indeed, so bad did conditions become that play was almost on the point of being abandoned. No championship of recent years has been played in such atrocious weather.

Nearly 20,000 people, most of them drenched to the skin, watched the play.

The famous American players were completely eclipsed and the Ryder Cup defeat was amply avenged. The first member of the American team, Byron Nelson, United States Metropolitan champion, could do no better than finish with an aggregate of 296 for fifth place. Alfred Padgham, the holder, shared seventh place with two others.

Calm and deliberate in his play, Cotton gave a masterly display in defeating the elements. He is the first British player to win the title twice since the days of the late Harry Vardon.

When it was all over Cotton said to me: "I am thrilled not only to have won, but to have kept the British flag flying. And don't forget the Whitcombe brothers, for they played a great part in a British golf revival."

Walter Hagen, non-playing captain of the U.S. Ryder Cup team, said: "It's no good blaming the weather. Golf is an all-weather game, and if you cannot play in the rain you do not deserve to be champion. Henry has done well. In fact, so has Great Britain as a whole."

**(July 10)**

# THE KING SEES ROYAL MAIL WIN NATIONAL

Though Golden Miller once again disappointed thousands of his supporters in the Centenary Grand National at Aintree yesterday, the victory of Royal Mail – forecast by "Hotspur" in The Daily Telegraph yesterday – was tremendously popular.

The King and Queen, witnessing their first Grand National, were spectators of a thrilling contest.

The first four horses, with their jockeys and starting prices were:

1. Royal Mail (E. Williams) 100-6
2. Cooleen (J. Faweus) 33-1
3. Pucka Belle (Mr. E. Bailey) 100-6
4. Ego (Mr. H. Llewellyn) 10-1

There was a great demonstration of enthusiasm when Royal Mail flashed past the post.

It was redoubled when the King and Queen sent for owner, trainer and jockey to congratulate them.

Mr. H. Lloyd Thomas, owner of Royal Mail, is the British Minister in Paris, and was formerly Assistant Private Secretary to King Edward VIII, when he was Prince of Wales. He himself was one of the best amateur riders in the country, having won the Grand Sefton Steeplechase at Liverpool on his own horse Destiny Bay.

"I was never confident about Royal Mail's chance," he said to a representative of The Daily Telegraph after the race. "You cannot be in races like this. But I always was hopeful. Williams rode a magnificent race, and I am delighted."

"JUMPED PERFECTLY"

Evan Williams said "Royal Mail" jumped perfectly. He made one or two slight mistakes but nothing serious. I was blocked a bit by the loose horses, so I decided to go to the front soon after the start of the second round. Royal Mail was as steady as a rock."

In addition to being owned and ridden by Welshmen, Royal Mail was trained by a Welshman, Mr. Ivor Anthony. The trainer is the eldest of the three trainer brothers who were formerly successful amateur riders. He was the leading amateur rider in 1909 and 1910, and after becoming a professional he headed the list of winning jockeys in 1912.

Of the 33 runners in yesterday's race seven completed the course. There were many falls, but only three jockeys were injured, and these but slightly.

The much fancied Don Bradman was remounted after falling at the first fence. Golden Miller, the 1934 winner, who fell last year and unseated his rider in 1935, again displayed a dislike of the course. He refused on the first circuit at the same open ditch which he would not jump two years ago.

**(March 20)**

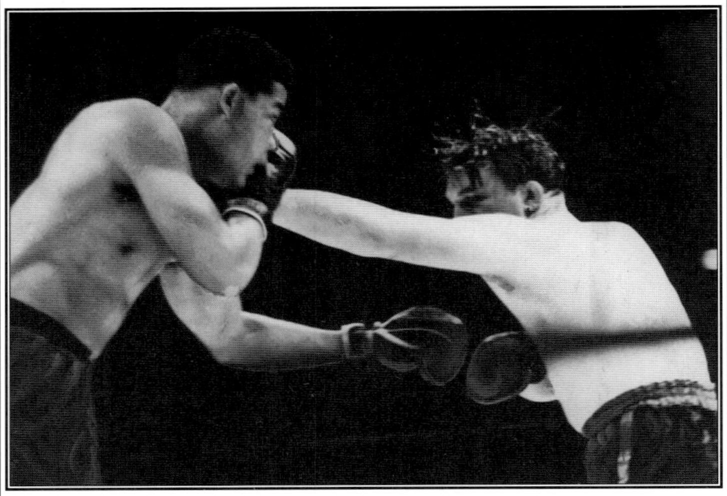

LOUIS DUCKING AS FARR attacks in the seventh round.

# FARR'S GLORIOUS FAILURE IN FIGHT WITH LOUIS

## A SCIENTIFIC BOXER WHO MAY YET WIN WORLD TITLE

**By Harold Lewis**

Tommy Farr is an amazing fellow, but he has amazed us so many times during the past twelve or eighteen months that his magnificent feat in staying with ease through 15 rounds with Joe Louis on Monday night should not have caused any real surprise to those who knew and studied him in this country.

Fortunately, I have no words to eat over this fight. I gave Farr a chance, though not a big one. I knew, as others should have known, that he has an extraordinary fighting mentality.

The bigger the task before him, the greater the weight of public opinion against him, the more coolly his fighting brain operates.

His courage has never been doubted, but what was not sufficiently appreciated was a spirit not quite the same – that peculiar quality which possesses some men when the odds are against them, a grim, bitter determination to prove to the world that it is wrong. It is the spirit that enables a man to produce a superhuman effort, and that is what Farr did.

LACK OF PUNCH

To be honest and frank, nothing in Farr's career or boxing form suggested that he could hold a man of the reputation of Louis.

Some of his recent victories were accomplished by a level of skill which would have taken him nowhere against Louis – and these were victories which were in doubt until the referee held up Farr's glove.

Farr's American critics, having recovered from their welter of praise, are fairly certain to damn it later with jibes that Farr still has to prove that he has a punch, and that, also, is true. But it has been true of many of the world's greatest boxers.

Farr is not a bone-crusher, he is a scientific boxer – an extreme rarity among heavyweights. If he were also a hitter, no man living would stand against him. But if you go through the history of world champions you will find very few who were scientific boxers and also possessed a terrific punch.

His manager believes that Farr will yet be a heavy hitter because the Welshman has developed late and is still developing.

Farr has made his effort and failed gloriously but others before him failed ignominiously, yet were afterwards world champions. We have every right to hope for even better things from the man from Tonypandy.

## "A MORAL VICTORY"

### U.S. CRITICS TRIBUTE

NEW YORK, Tuesday.

Tommy Farr's plucky defence against Louis last night has won him the unstinted admiration of all American boxing enthusiasts. The Press, which before the fight was filled with scathing comments on the Welsh challenge, has to-day completely reversed its tone to one of glowing praise.

"Louis lost everything but the title," declares the New York "Herald Tribune." His thunderous punch was absorbed as easily as if it were a sofa cushion. Farr showed not the slightest respect for his blows. Whenever Schmelling catches the negro the German will be favourite ."

Other typical comments include:

NEW YORK TIMES – "Farr stood up to Louis battering blows. He fought back savagely, furiously and contemptuously at times in a glorious offensive against tremendous odds, and ended by going a longer distance with the 'Bomber' than has anybody else.

"The champion has retained the title but has suffered a loss of prestige. Louis was harassed at every turn, even when he had Farr jarred and staggering."

ASSOCIATED PRESS – "Farr, who was not supposed to have a chance, took everything but the decision.

"Farr not only stunned the experts, but he thrilled the comparatively small crowd by the game, determined fashion in which he repeatedly carried the fight to the hard hitting champion."

NEW YORK DAILY MIRROR – "Tommy Farr scored a moral victory by staying the full 15 rounds, but official victory was Joe's by decision."

Farr's bearing after the fight has won him as much praise as his courage during the contest.

"Louis is the best and cleanest fighter I ever met," he said, "and he hits harder than all of them put together. But I would like to fight him again. And I would like to meet Schmeling, too."

Louis described Farr as "a great opponent," but declared that he could not hit hard. "If we meet again," he added, "I shall knock him out. I might have done it to-night if I had not bruised my left hand.

"Farr was hard to hit because he kept pulling away constantly. After the third round all I could do was a jab." – Reuter and B.U.P.

**(September 1)**

# FASTEST RACE AT BROOKLANDS

**From Our Motoring Correspondent**

BROOKLANDS, Monday.

The fastest race at Brooklands since the famous track was opened in 1907 thrilled a great crowd of spectators at the first meeting of the season this afternoon.

It was the chief event of the day, the Broadcast Trophy Handicap, over 29 miles. John Cobb, superbly driving his huge silver record-breaker, won it at 136.03 m.p.h. from a standing start.

Cobb had to give starts to nine other competitors, but he won with ease. His car, which is capable of 170 m.p.h., and has maintained 150 m.p.h. for 24 hours, holds the Brooklands lap record at 143 m.p.h.

It is probable that to-day's figures represent the highest speed at which any race of more than sprint distance can be won at Brooklands.

"B. Bira," Prince Birabongse, the brilliant young Siamese driver, made a good beginning to the season's racing. Besides taking second and third prizes in his two "mountain" races, he twice successfully avoided collisions among a press of cars fighting for the turn under the members' bridge.

His skill and daring got him out of tight corners on successive laps when he was within inches of collision.

**(March 30)**

# PERRY'S TENNIS TOUR SUCCESS

NEW YORK, Tuesday.

According to reports reaching New York, Fred Perry, who plays his 25th match against Ellsworth Vines in Salt Lake City, Utah, to-night, is more than satisfied with the financial results of his decision to join the ranks of professional lawn-tennis players.

Excluding taxes, the receipts during his tour have already reached the impressive total of £34,800. Of this sum Perry receives 37 1/2 per cent. which means that he has earned approximately £13,000.

The tour, which has so far carried Perry and Ellsworth Vines into 17 states in the East, South Middle-West and Far West, is only one-third complete.

**(March 3)**

# OXFORD'S THRILLING VICTORY IN BOAT RACE

## THREE-LENGTHS WIN ENDS SEQUENCE OF THIRTEEN FAILURES

**By G.C. Drinkwater**

AFTER thirteen, as it seemed, never ending years of bitter defeat, the little Dark Blue flag which flies in front of the bow oarsman was pushed first past the post yesterday morning at Mortlake when Oxford, as I anticipated in yesterday's DAILY TELEGRAPH, won the Boat Race. The margin in their favour was three lengths.

The time – 22min. 39sec. – was the slowest since the dead-heat race of 1877. This fact, I must say at once, is no reflection on the quality of the crews engaged. It is due entirely to the slackness of the neap tide pushed back by the huge quantity of land water coming down from the upper reaches.

I do not think that it is solely because I am an Oxford man myself that I can describe the race as one of the most thrilling I have ever seen. Even Cambridge men must agree in this, and must admire, as much as I do, the magnificent fighting race which Perfitt, the Cambridge stroke, put up.

Until they were definitely beaten off Duke's Meadows, Cambridge rowed at the top of their form, but nothing that Perfitt could do – and he piled in spurt after spurt where the run of the course assisted his crew – could shake the steady, quiet determination of Hodgson, who not only won his spurs but covered himself with glory.

Incident after incident added thrills to the race. A false start to begin with – the first I have ever seen, and I have seen more Boat Races than I like to remember, Stewart, in the Oxford boat, was not ready. His heels were out of the heel traps. Wisely he shouted "No!" and held up his hand.

The Umpire neither heard nor saw him, though his shout travelled right across the river to my launch, which was lying on the Surrey shore. Cambridge rowed a stroke on the word "Go," held her, and then backed down to the stake boat again. It was lucky there was no tide to speak of.

But the thrills that were to follow, from fear of a foul, were much worse. Twice, indeed, there were clashes, just below Hammersmith Bridge and again at the crossing where Chiswick Reach merges into Corney.

CAMBRIDGE COX AT FAULT

The Cambridge cox was very much at fault. He steered in such a way as to force a foul if the Oxford cox, Merifield, did give way when, within his rights, he had no need to do so. Luckily, as things turned out, Merifield did the sporting thing, but in each case had to lose his crew some distance.

In the Oxford crew, after giving Hodgson his full meed of praise, it is hard to divide Sturrock from Cherry. Both rowed magnificently from start to finish, with perfect steadiness and splendid drive. Burrough also rowed with great consistency. I had been afraid that he might lose his steadiness in so gruelling a race, but he never faltered.

OXFORD

| | St. | lb |
|---|---|---|
| *M.G.C. Ashby (Oundle & N. Coll.) bow | 12 | 4 |
| 2* D.M. de R. Winser (Winchester & Corpus) | 12 | 0 |
| 3 R.R. Stewart (Eton & Magdalen) | 13 | 0 |
| 4 R.G. Rowe (Eton & Univ.) | 12 | 11 |
| 5 J.P. Burrough (St. Edward's & St. Edmund H.) | 13 | 7 |
| 6* J.D. Sturrock (Winchester & Magdalen) | 14 | 4 |
| 7*J.G. Cherry (Westminster & B.N.C.) | 13 | 11 |
| A.B. Hodgson (Eton & Oriel), stroke | 12 | 2 |
| G.J.P. Merifield (King Edward VI. & St. Edmund Hall), cox | 7 | 11 |
| Total weight (excluding cox) | 103 | 11 |
| Average | 12 | 13½ |

CAMBRIDGE

| | St. | lb |
|---|---|---|
| *T.S. Cree (Geelong & Jesus), bow | 11 | 6 |
| 2*H.W. Mason (Clifton & Trinity Hall) | 11 | 8 |
| 3 M. Bradley (Monckton Combe & Pembroke) | 13 | 2 |
| 4 D.M.W. Napier (Eton & Magdalene) | 12 | 9 |
| 5* M.P. Lonnon (Westminster & Third Trinity) | 12 | 11 |
| 6 T.B. Langton (Radley & Jesus) | 13 | 11½ |
| 7 A. Burrough (St. Paul's & Jesus) | 12 | 3 |
| R.J.L. Perfitt (K.C.S., Wimbledon, Trinity Hall), stroke | 12 | 0½ |
| T.H. Hunter (Harvard & Trinity Hall), cox | 8 | 0 |
| Total weight (excluding cox) | 99 | 9 |
| Average | 12 | 5½ |

* Old Blue.

**(March 25)**

# STEVE CHOSE THE WRONG HORSE

## LAST RACE DRAMA AT MANCHESTER

**By Watchman**

STEVE DONOGHUE had set his heart on winding up his career as a jockey with a winning ride.

In the Final Plate at Manchester he had been offered the mount on Pegomas. That gelding won the corresponding race last season, when Highlander had been a bad third. On that occasion the two horses were at even weights, whereas Highlander was receiving 10lb on Saturday.

This caused Steve to suppose that Lord Derby's gelding had the better chance of success. Lord Derby's jockey, Dick Perryman, kindly soul that he is said he would gladly stand aside to help Donoghue ride his last winner.

C. Leader, the trainer, thought that a change of jockeys would make no difference to Highlander. There remained the owner of the gelding. Lord Derby promptly agreed with Steve's suggestion that he might ride his horse.

And so all was fixed up. Donoghue rode out happily. The bookmakers asked odds about his mount, and the great crowd prepared itself to give Steve a tumultuous reception.

Then came the anti-climax. Highlander was again beaten into third place.

Gordon Richards' View

Gordon Richards who rode in the race told me that Highlander was unlucky, the Irish horse, Spot Barred, having cut across him. Even so, the old horse has such a good turn of speed that he was still reckoned to have a prospect of winning, despite being several lengths behind the pacemaker, Pegomas, two furlongs from the end.

Donoghue had him beautifully balanced for his culminating run, and the familiar shout "Come on Steve!" went up from all the enclosures. Highlander's effort did not suffice to get him on terms with the leader, and a few yards from the post, perceiving that it was impossible to win, the jockey drew rein, the result being that his mount finished 3 1/2 lengths behind Pegomas, who beat Domaha by half a length.

It was characteristic of Donoghue that while intensely anxious to win he refrained from giving Highlander a punishing race. He will always be remembered as a great jockey who was never hard on his horses. It was the irony of fate that he should have chosen the wrong horse for his last mount, and his face was a study in seriousness as he rode into the unsaddling enclosure.

**(November 29)**

# AUSTRALIA WIN BY INNINGS & 200 RUNS

## ENGLAND'S FAILURE TO RECOVER 'ASHES'

MELBOURNE, Wednesday.

Australia won the final Test by an innings and 200 runs, and retain the Ashes by three matches to two.

England won the first two Tests at Brisbane and Sydney, and Australia replied by winning the third at Melbourne, the fourth at Adelaide, and the fifth and decisive game here to-day.

Altogether, in the history of Test cricket, Australia have won 56 Tests and England 54, with 29 drawn.

To-day England faced a hopeless task when Verity and Voce resumed batting. With two wickets in hand 200 runs were needed to avoid defeat by an innings.

A surprisingly large crowd was eager to see the end, and by 11.30 am, there were 10,000 people present in cool, sunny weather.

England failed to add to their total. The first ball of the day from Fleetwood-Smith, dismissed Voce, who swung it hard to long-~~on~~, where he was caught by Badcock. Next ball Fleetwood-Smith dismissed Farnes, who made a wild swipe and was caught by Nash at deep mid-on.

BRADMAN TAKES A STUMP

Bradman grabbed a stump and raced to the pavilion, while thousands jumped the fences and swarmed on to the ground. Some got out pen knives and cut pieces out of the wicket for souvenirs, and others ran to gain the best places in front of the pavilion.

The players had to fight their way through the excited spectators to get to the dressing room. Nash, the fast bowler, held on to the ball.

Eventually Bradman appeared on the balcony and spoke through a loudspeaker.

Every mention of Allen was greeted with cheers, "Rain dealt England a very cruel blow," said Bradman, "but I yet have to hear one single word of complaint from any one of the players.

"I should like to thank my team mates for their support right through the series. Without this we could not have won," Bradman added: "It will only be another year before another Australian team goes to England. I hope I shall be with that team and renew my acquaintanceship with friends I have made during this tour."

ALLEN'S TRIBUTE

In reply Allen said: "If I were in Bradman's position and had his ability I should be very glad to be standing here. I make no bones about it, I am a very disappointed man. Australia owes a great deal to a captain who has shown magnificent form, first with the bat and then with that infernal coin."

Allen continued: "Bradman says none of the England team has complained about our luck in this game. I am not complaining, but I think you will agree that we shall not go down in history as the luckiest team ever to tour Australia.

"Australia played wonderful cricket, and fought out of difficult positions. This is probably my last appearance at Melbourne. It has been a sad one for me but never mind."

**(March 3)**

# HENDREN'S 100 IN LAST MATCH

There was an unprecedented scene at Lord's yesterday, when Hendren, the Middlesex and England batsman, completed a century in what is the last match of his career in county cricket.

It was the 170th century innings he has played.

The crowd of 13,000 watching the game between Middlesex and Surrey, gave Hendren an ovation which has had no parallel since Hobbs played his final innings at the Oval against the Australians six years ago.

For the space of several minutes, Hendren had to remain at the wicket lifting his cap in acknowledgment of the cheers that were raised from all quarters of the ground. An umpire took out his watch to time the cheering.

**(August 31)**

# FROM CRICKET TO SOCCER FIELD

Denis Compton, the cricketing-footballer, played his dual role yesterday, when, after hitting 50 runs for the M.C.C. against Yorkshire at Lord's, he was in the Arsenal side against the Spurs in the final of the London Challenge Cup Soccer final at White Hart-lane.

Compton's innings at Lord's finished at 4.30, and he was driven in a car by Hulme, a team-mate, to Tottenham, where he arrived three-quarters of an hour before the kick-off.

Mr. George Allison, the Arsenal manager, explained why Compton made the hurried journey from the cricket to Soccer field. "He had played in all the previous rounds of the Challenge Cup," he said, "and I wanted to give him every opportunity of winning a medal."

**(May 4)**

# SCOTS AGAIN SUPREME AT HAMPDEN

## ENGLAND PLAYERS SHOWED GREATER TALENT

## Should Have Won In First Half: Two Fine Centre-Forwards

**By Frank Coles**

SCOTLAND................................3 ENGLAND................................................1

SOCCER'S world record crowd of 149,407 – the receipts were £22,000 – were rewarded with the finest display seen in an international match at Hampden Park, Glasgow, since the War.

Over 100,000 of this immense gathering were packed like sardines on the steeply banked terraces an hour before the start. They had responded faithfully to the get-there-early appeal, and got a drenching from the heavy rain for their pains.

But the discomfort was worth while. The 61st meeting of Scotland and England will live in the memory not so much for its many thrills as for the rare quality of the football.

That England lost 3-1 does not matter a deal. In any case they did not deserve to be beaten by a margin of two goals.

Most pleasing to English ears was the genuine Scottish praise poured on the England players. Glasgow's unanimous opinion was that the more talented team lost. And Scotland is the home of the purists.

The first half was England's by the length of a street. Mastering the slithery, skidding ball sooner than the Scots, our fellows settled down to play football that was an eye opener to the crowd.

With the Scottish forwards firmly held for half an hour, England concentrated on attack, and the Stoke City players, Matthews and Johnson, thrilled the crowd with brilliant wing-forward raids.

MATTHEWS-BEATTIE DUEL

Matthews, conscious of the fact that Scotland's left back, Beattie, was having his international baptism, struck again and again on this flank in the hope of unsettling the newcomer. By taking the ball boldly up to the back he won the admiration of every lover of artistry in a winger.

But though Beattie was beaten a number of times (he came into full bloom later) greater danger to Scotland threatened from the other wing, where Johnson repeatedly outwitted Anderson.

So much so that Massie had to go to Anderson's aid to check England's flying left-winger. Incidentally, Massie was very lucky not to have a penalty given against him midway through the opening half, when he caught Johnson by the legs as he was in the act of shooting from an ideal scoring position.

STOKE TRIO TRIUMPH

We lost, yet there were more successes than failures in this latest England team. If I were choosing the side anew I would certainly stick to the Stoke City three – Matthews, Johnson and Steele. All are accomplished players, and I predict a brilliant future for young Steele, especially.

| INTERNATIONAL TABLE | | | | | Goals | | |
|---|---|---|---|---|---|---|---|
| | P | W | D | L | For | Agst | Pts |
| Wales | 3 | 3 | 0 | 0 | 8 | 3 | 6 |
| Scotland | 3 | 2 | 0 | 1 | 7 | 4 | 4 |
| England | 3 | 1 | 0 | 2 | 5 | 6 | 2 |
| Ireland | 3 | 0 | 0 | 3 | 3 | 10 | 0 |

Male and Barkas could not have been improved upon as a full-back partnership, and Woodley was a confident goalkeeper. Young, too, lived up to his big reputation as a defensive centre-half. I do not know of another England third-back who would have tackled the problem of holding O'Donnell in check more effectively.

The wing halves and inside wing forwards were not so uniformly good. Britton and Bray needed to be that important fraction quicker in tackling, and Britton held the ball far too long. He should have given Matthews a faster service, particularly when the Scottish hurricane died down in the second half.

SCOTLAND– Dawson (Glasgow Rangers); Anderson (Heart of Midlothian); Beattie (Preston North End); Massie (Aston Villa); Simpson (Glasgow Rangers) (captain); Brown (Glasgow Rangers); Delaney (Celtic); Walker (Heart of Midlothian); O'Donnell (Preston North End); McPhall (Glasgow Rangers); Duncan (Derby County).

ENGLAND – Woodley (Chelsea); Male (Arsenal) (captain); Barkas (Manchester City); Britton (Everton); Young (Huddersfield Town); Bray (Manchester City); Matthews (Stoke City); Carter (Sunderland); Steele (Stoke City); Starling (Aston Villa); Johnson (Stoke City).

**(April 19)**

# FOOTBALLERS TO BE RICHER NEXT YEAR

## BONUS PROPOSALS

**From Our Own Correspondent**

WELCOME evidence of the improving financial outlook of Soccer clubs is provided by the proposals to come before to-day's annual meeting of the Football League in London. The Management Committee will propose increases in pay for the players both in the League and Cup competitions.

In the First and Second Divisions, talent money will be payable to the top four clubs from £275 downwards. These sums will be distributed amongst the players principally concerned in winning these positions.

In the Cup it is proposed to increase the bonus for winning a round, the amount for the final being £12, and to introduce talent money for each of the clubs reaching the last eight, the sum to be divided amongst the actual Cup winners being £275.

Talent money on a similar but smaller basis is to be paid to the top three teams in each section of the Third Division. These increases which are expected to be carried, will raise the earnings of players in teams winning the League or Cup to roughly £500 a year, and next Saturday, at the International Board meeting at Llandudno, an increase will also be made in the amounts to be paid to players in international games, probably to £8 per match.

INCREASE FOR REFEREES

Derby County also desire to-day to double referees fees, and to pay them six guineas for First and Second Division matches, and four guineas in the Third Division. In order to help the Third Division clubs, Derby propose that the First and Second Division members shall pay this two guineas increase.

As the full scheme means that First and Second Division clubs will have to pay a total of 16 guineas a match for the referee and linesmen, plus expenses, it is questionable whether this scheme will go through. Derby are to the fore again with the proposal that four instead of two clubs shall be promoted and relegated each season. last year the voting was 33-15 so that three more votes would give the agitators the necessary three-fourths majority.

**(June 7)**

# DAVIS V. LINDRUM

Joe Davis and Horace Lindrum each won three frames at the opening session in their match at Thurston's, London, yesterday. The game is of 143 frames, and Davis concedes 7 points in each frame. Interval score Lindrum, 42 frames; Davis, 36.

**(February 4)**

# RANGER WINS FOURTH RACE & RETAINS CUP

## NEW RECORD SET UP FOR THE COURSE

**From Major B. Heckstall-Smith, Daily Telegraph Yachting Correspondent**

NEWPORT (Rhode Island), Thursday.

Mr. Vanderbilt's yacht Ranger to-day won her fourth consecutive race, and as a result the America's Cup remains in America's possession.

Ranger to-day sailed the 30-mile triangular course in the fastest time ever recorded in the history of the America's Cup. The previous fastest time was made by Endeavour I, on Sept. 18, 1934 – 3hrs 9mins 1sec – but to-day I made Ranger's time for completing the course to be 3hrs 8mins.

Mr. Sopwith's Endeavour II, the Royal Yacht Squadron's representative, has been severely defeated by a yacht of unquestionably faster design, but the decreasing margins show that superior handling and steering has in this series counted for a maximum proportion of the defeat.

For instance, to-day, boat for boat, Endeavour sailed faster when reaching and probably was as good as Ranger to windward in a smart breeze without much real strength or weight. The wind gauges gave a wind speed of 15, increasing to 16 miles an hour.

From the starting signal, however, Endeavour's chance was lost. She misjudged her start, was over the line too soon and was recalled.

Owing to this error she not only lost 1min. 10sec, but began the windward work with an opponent able to place herself leisurely upon her weather bow and thus backwind her mile after mile exactly as she pleased. I consider that in this unfortunate start Mr. Sopwith gave Mr. Vanderbilt three minutes, if not four.

For the remainder of the race there was little or nothing to indicate that Ranger was any better a boat than Endeavour.

CREW'S GOOD WORK

The English crew of paid hands deserve the greatest credit. They have not been beaten or outclassed by Mr. Vanderbilt's men. Our fellows were just as smart.

To-day and yesterday, as the times show, Endeavour was a greatly improved boat. If this is accounted for by the removal of two or three tons of lumber and ballast out of the vessel, the obvious question is: Why was not this corrected during the tuning-up trials instead of after two races had been lost?

Whatever the causes, no challenger for the cup has suffered such a crushing defeat for half a century.

**(August 6)**

# HOW CITY BECAME CHAMPIONS

## DOHERTY INSPIRES WIN OVER WEDNESDAY

**By Our Special Representative**

Manchester C 4 Sheffield Wed. 1

IN beating Sheffield Wednesday at Maine-road, Manchester City set the seal on a non-stop run of 21 matches without defeat, which has won them the First Division championship for the first time in their 43 years' history as a League club.

There were enthusiastic scenes at the end when the crowd surged over the ground, though they were prevented from carrying off the players in their delight by a strong force of police.

Lining up in front of the stands, they would not disperse until Mr. "Bob" Smith, the chairman of the club, and Barkas, the captain of the team, had acknowledged their greetings and that they had come prepared to cheer exultantly was proved during the match itself.

Every goal the City scored was received by tumultuous applause and a fanfare of trumpets, and though the game had run almost 20 minutes before the first arrived the match was in their safe keeping before the interval.

It was not until a minute from the end that Brook obtained the fourth goal, but the first three, scored during a spell of 13 minutes in the first half, knocked the bottom out of the Wednesday's hopes, practically doomed them to relegation, and served as another reminder of the magnificent part Doherty has played in Manchester City's triumphant march.

Every one was the result of the Irishman's genius. He continued the spadework done by Percival to leave Brook with a clear field for the first, gave Tilson a simple chance, the second by a dazzling run, and not to be outdone, scored the third himself after a delightful exchange of passes with Tilson.

The Wednesday were simply run off their feet during this brilliant phase, but they obtained a consolation goal a quarter of an hour from the end, when Rimmer netted after Swift had parried a point-blank drive by Luke.

**(April 26)**

# BUDGE'S TRIPLE CROWN AT WIMBLEDON

**By A. Wallis Myers**

WIMBLEDON is over, its prizes won and lost. The Americans among them have won six firsts, England three firsts, France one.

But this total of 10 includes the two consolation Plate events. The fate of the five championships, by which international prestige is rated, do not reveal home players in the same ratio.

Last year Great Britain held four titles. This year we hold only one and have a half-share in another. The United States have captured the two senior events, and produced in J.D. Budge a player who has established a record by winning three.

It has been America's Wimbledon, yet the victory of Miss Dorothy Round, on Saturday, by which she regained the women's singles championship, after the closest final against Mlle. Jedrzejowska, champion of Poland, proves that talent and tenacity can still prevail in the home of lawn tennis.

Miss Round had not given herself much of a thought this year, nor had the popular publicists. Perhaps this is why, moving in "the unpierc'd shade," and seeded No. 7 in the official list, though she was No. 3 in the world's "First Ten," her mind was less diverted and her chance, by sound judges of her game and character, deemed the stronger.

She had not gone great guns this year. Senorita Lizana had beaten her at Bournemouth and Brighton. Miss McOstrich at Melbury. She had got her own back on the Chilean champion at Birmingham, but she came to Wimbledon without any blare of trumpets.

RELATIVE VALUES COUNTED

Yet, if relative values count at all, the player who had defeated the holder conclusively in their Wightman Cup match at Wimbledon a year ago, and on the same court had confirmed this verdict at the Wimbledon just over, was at least a likely champion; and when her passage to the final without a vantage set in her five rounds was recorded, she herself might justly think her big chance had come again.

But Miss Round did not play in the final on Saturday – save in sections – with the confidence or consistency of earlier engagements. For this decline there were reasons. The day was sultry, hot pockets of air, influencing the ball flight, had invaded the centre court; the top-spin attack of her opponent, who had been unbeaten in three successive tournaments in England, was encountered for the first time.

THE NEW CHAMPIONS
Men's Singles: J.D. BUDGE (U.S.A.)
Women's Singles: Miss D.E. Round (G.B.)
Men's Doubles: J.B. BUDGE and G. MAKO (U.S.A.)
Women's Doubles: Mme. R. MATHIEU (France) and Miss A.M. YORKE (G.B.)
Mixed Doubles: J.D. BUDGE and Miss A. MARBLE (U.S.A.)

HIGH HEART IN CRISIS

I believe that Miss Round's strokes and heart – for the latter was sorely needed in the third set crisis – alone among those in competition at Wimbledon this year, could have survived the sterling, fast-footed challenge which the Polish champion offered in the last round.

I pass to less pleasant things for England. The doubles between the champions of Great Britain and the United States was except in one set, a one-sided affair. Hughes and Tuckey were outplayed by Budge and Mako; the title changed hands with emphasis.

Perhaps Friday's almost epic doubles match, in which the American's survived against the Germans, affected spectators and competitors alike. The Californians played on Saturday as if they knew their greatest danger had passed; the British came into court with the memory of Budge's disintegrating blows at Eastbourne last year.

**(July 5)**

# 4 Min 6.6 Sec FOR ONE MILE

## CUNNINGHAM'S TIME BEATEN BY 1.5SEC

S. C. WOODERSON, the British one-mile champion and successor to Jack Lovelock as Britain's greatest miler, beat the world's mile record with 4min 6.6sec. at Motspur Park on Saturday.

This time is one-fifth of a second better than the world record set up by Glenn Cunningham. Lovelock's old rival, at Princeton, New Jersey, three years ago. Wooderson also lowered his own British record made at Chelmsford last year by more than four seconds.

Wooderson made his new record in a specially framed handicap, in which he started from scratch. Four A.A.A. timekeepers held watches, and the track was remeasured. The quarter-mile circuit was found to be two inches and a fraction short of 440 yards, but this had been anticipated by the officials, and they had arranged for Wooderson to start 10 inches behind the starting line.

**(August 30)**

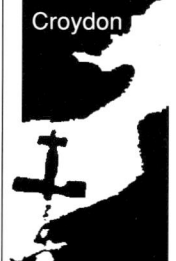

## SIGNOR MUSSOLINI AND HERR HITLER MEET

(ABOVE): SENOR MUSSOLINI, who is visiting Germany, being greeted by Herr Hitler on his arrival at Munich railway station.

(LEFT)" A STRIKING POSE by Senor Mussolini as he waved aloft the two-handed sword of Islam presented to him by chieftains during a spectacular ceremony near Tripoli on his Libyan tour.

## NEW EPSTEIN EXHIBITION

(ABOVE): EPSTEIN with his statue, Consummatum Est, a recumbent figure of Christ, uncovered yesterday at the Leicester Galleries, W.C., where an exhibition of the sculptor's work opens to the public on Saturday.

## INDIAN FRONTIER FIGHTING

TWO BRITISH OFFICERS and 15 Indian Scouts have been killed and two British Officers and 75 Indians wounded when the coloumns were trapped in an ambush during frontier fighting in the Khatsora Valley near the Khyber Pass. They had been sent into Waziristan on account of disaffection among the Khaisora and Khel tribesmen.
(BELOW): INDIAN ARTILLERYMEN on the North West Frontier.

A VERTICAL PARKING GARAGE, known in America as the Autostack, seen in a Chicago street. The Westminster City Council has refused an application for permission to erect garages of this type in Chandos-street, Covent Garden. The Autostack, which has the advantage of using up little ground space, provides a cage for each car. The cages are hauled up one side of the lift system and go down the other.

# 1938

It was the time when the word on most people's lips was appeasement. Hitler, ever conscious of the increasing power of his armed forces and the constraints of his frontiers, looked for *Lebensraum*. In the spring he calmly annexed his own native country, Austria, declaring it to be a German province. As the year wore on, he began to look hungrily towards Czechoslovakia. His first demands seemed modest: he claimed the Sudeten territories where the links with Germany were close.

Britain and France had guaranteed the Czech frontiers and it seemed in August that war must be inevitable. Neville Chamberlain, the British prime minister, who had earlier in the year made a pact with Mussolini and, in the process, had to accept the resignation of his foreign minister, Anthony Eden, sought a solution that would appease the situation. With the like-minded French premier, Daladier, he went twice, his umbrella in his hand, to see the German leader and brokered a deal which gave Hitler most of what he immediately wanted.

As he landed from his aircraft, bringing home the terms of the agreement that had been signed in Munich, Chamberlain declared that what had been achieved was "Peace in Our Time". As the four-day debate in the House of Commons showed, the country was deeply divided over the rightness of appeasement. *The Daily Telegraph*, after initially welcoming the end of the immediate crisis, began increasingly to echo one of its leading contributors, Winston Churchill, in wanting to stand up to Hitler.

With hindsight, many have argued that it would have been disastrous to have gone to war in the state of unpreparedness existing in 1938. Even so, it was the failure to prepare for the inevitable conflict, apart from some hastily prepared civil defence plans, that caused the greatest divisions in the country.

Throughout the year, it was the events in and around Germany that dominated the news. The growing realisation by Hitler that any of his intentions would not be immediately challenged led to his stepping up his campaign against Jews. This reached a climax when, as a reprisal against the shooting of a German diplomat by a Polish youth, there were bloody anti-Jewish riots in Berlin and elsewhere. Step by step, all Jewish rights were forfeited. The earlier trickle of refugees became a flood. Britain not only received hundreds of Jewish children but also Sigmund Freud.

Meanwhile the civil war continued in Spain with the Franco forces, aided by their German and Italian allies, driving back the Republican armies on every front. Both in Spain and in China, where the Japanese continued their advances, the use of aerial bombardment of cities increased.

Indeed, there was not much time for levity during the year. There were, however, brighter moments. Len Hutton hit 364 runs against Australia in a timeless test. Howard Hughes flew round the world in just over three days, and one of his fellow countrymen managed, according to his story, to misread his compass so that he flew to Ireland when he thought he was flying to California. Perhaps this was symbolic in a year when the whole world seemed to be turned upside down.

CABINET CALLED FOR MONDAY



# The Daily Telegraph and Morning Post



To-Days Weather : Mainly Fair

Broadcasting: Page Eight

No. 22,982 POSTAGE { INLAND, CANADA AND NEWFOUNDLAND, THREE HALFPENCE; OTHER COLONIES AND PLACES ABROAD, TWOPENCE } LONDON, FRIDAY, SEPTEMBER 9, 1938 ONE PENNY

*BIRTHS, MARRIAGES and DEATHS in this column, one guinea for three lines or less and 5s for each additional line. "IN MEMORIAM" notices 12/6 for three lines or less and 3/6 for each additional line. (Special rate for five or ten years' automatic insertion on application.) Announcements, authenticated by name and address of sender, may be sent to The Daily Telegraph and Morning Post, Fleet St., E.C.4., or 161 Piccadilly, W.1. or telephoned to Central 4242. Forthcoming Marriages in Court Page 3 guineas for 5 lines or less and 12/6 for each additional line.*

## BIRTHS

AUSTIN – On Sept. 7, 1938, to Eileen, wife of Geoffrey Austin, of "Gables" Manor-drive, Friern Barnet, a son.

BLAKEY – On Sept. 6, 1938, at Eastbourne, to Edna (née Hodsoll), wife of James W. Blakey, a daughter.

FARRANT – On Sept. 7, 1938, at Grove House, Lymington, Hants to Bonella, wife of Captain R.H. Farrant, Royal Artillery, a daughter.

HULKES – On Sept. 7, 1938, at Romney Chase, Hornchurch, to May, wife of Arthur Sackville Hulkes, a daughter.

JEFFREE – On Sept. 8, 1938, at Croydon, to Madaleine (née Tredgett), wife of John Leslie Jeffree, a son.

LIDDELL – On Sept. 8, 1938, at Mardale, Watford, to Peggy (née Fulton), wife of A.O. Crawford Liddell, a son.

McINTYRE – On Sept. 6, 1938, at Sunnyfield House, Guisborough, Yorks, to Silvia (née Stainthorpe), wife of Squadron Leader R.V. McIntyre, a daughter.

ORMEROD – On Sept. 7, 1938, at Poona, India, to Barbara (née Cuff), wife of Arthur Ormerod, a son.

PUDDEPHATT – On Sept. 6, 1938, to Marjory May (née Bone), wife of Noel Puddephatt, of Shaldon, Watchetts-drive, Camberley, a daughter.

THOMPSON – On Sept. 6, 1938, at the Manor House, Studley, War, to Doreen (née Farr), wife of Richard W. Thompson, a son.

## MARRIAGES

ALLEN-GELL – On Sept. 7, 1938, at St. Anne's Soho, by the Rev. R. Webb Odell, Derek Fortrose Allen, second son of Mr. and Mrs. E. Stirling Allen, to Godythe Winifred Gell, only daughter of Mrs. S.M. Lewis-Hall and of Major P.F. Gell, D.S.O.

BEARD-MARSHALL – On Sept. 6, 1938, at St. Lawrence's Church, Appleby, Stanley, son of the late Mr. Walter Beard and Mrs. Beard, Truro, to Betty Margaret, elder daughter of Mr. and Mrs. J.C. Marshall, Appleby.

BROOMHALL-ALLEN – On Sept. 7, 1938, quietly, at St. Paul's, Portman-square, by the Rev. Colin C. Kerr, M.A. Paul John, elder son of Dr. and Mrs. B.C. Broomhall, to Rosalind Mary, eldest daughter of the late Mr. H.D. Allen and of Mrs. Allen.

CHESTER-WILLIAMS-DEERY – On Sept., 8, 1938, at St Jude's Church, Plymouth, Trevor L. Chester-Williams, M.R.C.S. L.R.C.P., to Gwyneth, elder daughter of Dr. and Mrs. George Deery, of Greenbank-avenue, Plymouth.

CRAGGS-FOSTER – On Sept. 7, 1938, at All Soul's Church, Langham-place, W.1. Stanley Foxton Craggs, third son of Mr. and Mrs. H.F. Craggs, of Brough, E. Yorks, to Bessie only daughter of the late Mr. Charles Foster and Mrs. Foster, of Brough, E. Yorks.

GRILLO-GRANT – On Sept. 6, 1938, at St. Mary's Guildford by the Rev. M. Tobias, of Shalford, Bernard Francis, only son of Professor E. Grillo of Glasgow University, and Mrs. Grillo, of Guildford, to Priscilla Mary Sturge, only daughter of Mrs. Grant, of Guildford, and the late A.S. Grant, of Hillside, Reigate.

KEMM-THOMAS – ON Sept. 8, 1938, at Christ Church, Barnet, Dr. Rupert St. John Kemm, of Cheddar, younger son of the later Dr. and Mrs. F. St John Kemm, of Worle, Somerset to Kathleen Morva, second daughter of Mr. and Mrs. J. Llewellyn-Thomas, of Barnet, Herts.

LAMPE-ROBERTS – On Sept. 7, 1938, at Widcombe Old Church, Bath, by the Rev. H.L. Franklin, assisted by the Rev. W.E. Purcell and the Rev. L.J. McKay, the Rev. G.W.H. Lampe to Miss E.E. Roberts.

MACMILLAN-CALVERT – On Sept. 6, 1938, at the Church of St. John the Baptist, West Wickham, Kent, by the Rev. W.H. Gregory, assisted by the Rev. C. Windsor Richards, M.A., Colin Herdman, youngest son of Mr. and Mrs. Thos. F. MacMillan, Innerwick, Murrayfield, Edinburgh to Wilhelmina, youngest daughter of the late William John Calvert of Ballymacrandle, Portadown, and Mrs. Calvert, Belfast.

MOGER-HEALY – On Sept. 6, 1938, at the Church of Our Lady of Good Counsel, Hythe, H.J. Moger of Uplands, Hillcrest-road, Hythe, Kent, formerly of Pulborough to Nora Healy, daughter of the late David D. Healy, J.P. and Mrs. Healy, Clash House, Kilcummin Kilarney.

PROCTOR-CARDALE – On Sept. 8, 1938, at St. Paul's Church, Camberley, John Tyndale Proctor, son of the late Tyndale, Procter and of Mrs. Procter, Cherry Hill House, York, to Helen Mary, only daughter of the Reverend and Mrs. R.F. Cardale, St. Paul's Vicarage, Camberley.

THOMPSON-MEESON – On Sept. 8, 1938, at St. Phillip's Church, Hove, Percy Thompson, of Calcutta, to Margot Joy Meeson, of Hove, Sussex. Indian papers, please copy.

## DEATHS

ADDINGTON – On Sept. 7, 1938, at Wyboston, Sophia Ann, widow of William Addington, in her 104th year. Funeral at Roxton Church 3.30p.m., to-morrow (Saturday, Sept. 10).

ALDRIDGE – On Sept. 7, 1938, at 68, Ashworth-mansions, W.9., Estelle Cordeliam beloved wife of S.C. Aldridge, M.V.O. Indian Police (retired). Funeral service at St. Peter's Church, Elgin-avenue, to-day, three p.m. afterwards at Kensal Green Cemetery. Indian papers, please copy.

ASTINS – On Sept. 6, 1938, at 77, Lyncombe-hill, Bath, Som., Louisa Astins, youngest daughter of the late Alfred Parker, of the Strand, London.

BISHOP – On Sept. 7, 1938 at "Kingsmead," 39 Arthur-road, Wimbledon Park, S.W. 19 (late of 9 Glenalmond, Manor Fields, Putney Heath), Francis Leonard Bishop, beloved husband of Evelyn M. Bishop. Service as Golders Green Crematorium to-morrow (Saturday, 10th) at eleven a.m. Australian and New Zealand papers, please copy.

## PERSONAL

*5s per line (minimum 2 lines). Trade 12/6 per line. Lost and found 5s per line.*

ROBERT. – PLEASE TELEPHONE. – JOSE.

DICKOO – Meet me London or elsewhere. Leaving here in few days. – JOAN.

EMSLEY – THE KIN of OSCAR HAIGH EMSLEY, late of 3, Hope-street, Milnsbridge, Huddersfield, Yorks, who died there on 27th January, 1938, are REQUESTED to APPLY to the Treasury Solicitor, (B.V.) Storey's Gate, London, S.W.1. (Estate about £450).

WEST – THE KIN of ELIZABETH WEST, Spinster, late of Bunbury-lane, Spurslow, Nantwich, Cheshire, who died there on 27th June, 1938, are REQUESTED to APPLY to the Treasury Solicitor, (B.V.) Storey's Gate, London, S.W.1. (Estate about £700).

NORMAN BIRKETT, K.C., ON LONELINESS! – Listen in to the London Regional Appeal on Sunday evening, September 11th, at 8.45 p.m.

VOLUNTARY HELPERS required to make known showings of "MANAGER TO CROSS" film at Grotrian Hall. – Those willing assist, even small way, please attend meetings Monday next, 6.30 or 8.30, 115, Wigmore-street.

IF YOU PAINT FLOWERS! Earn at home designing Printed Textiles. A PUPIL MADE £90 AFTER THREE CORRESPONDENCE LESSONS. As long established designers to the Textile Trade, we can offer the finest Postal Tuition and market for your work. OUR TOTAL SALES OF PUPILS' WORK ARE UNEQUALLED – For free details of the ORIGINAL Textile Course and Sales Service, write "W" TEXTILE STUDIO, 352a Station-rd, Harrow.

BEFORE IT IS TOO LATE! MUST the summer pass without a glimpse of the Country or the Sea? This will be the sad lot of a number of the poorest children in Central South London unless friends send their GIFT without delay. Our children live right at the heart of crowded London, Hemmed in by miles of dangerous traffic-filled streets, they are farther away from Country scenes than any other London children. These are wistfully hoping that their turn will come before it is too late, but that depends upon the response to this appeal.

£5 WILL SEND A TIRED OVER-BURDENED MOTHER and 3 CHILDREN TO THE SEA FOR A "RED-LETTER" FORTNIGHT.

£1 WILL SEND 10 CHILDREN FOR A "RED-LETTER" DAY TO THE COUNTRY – THEIR ONLY DAY THE WHOLE YEAR ROUND.

2s WILL SEND ONE CHILD.

Please give happiness to others by sending your Gift to: Rev. WALTER SPENCER, THE SOUTH LONDON MISSION, TOWER BRIDGE-ROAD, London S.E.1.

INCORPORATED ACCOUNTANTS. – For particulars of next Examination see Page 19.

FRENCH – Frey 54, Manchester-st., W.1. Wel. 5351. GERMAN – Young expert teachers. Low fees.

GOLD urgently wtd. Highest prices. Also Sovs., Diamonds, Pearls, Jewellery, Silver, Plate, &c. BENTLEY & CO. 65 New Bond-st., (facing Brook-st) W.1. Mayfair 0651.

A FURNISHED FLAT FOR TWO from 21/2gns. per week. Every modern luxury. Roland House, Roland-gardens, South Kensington. – Call, write or 'phone Kensington 8676.

UNWANTED Artificial Teeth Gratefully Received. – Ivory Cross Dental Fund, 67b Welbeck-st., W.1.

MODERN HOMES within EASY REACH OF LONDON. Illus. particulars appear on Page 23.

LANGUAGES 2/6 WEEKLY. EXPERT TUITION. NATIVE TEACHERS – UNIVERSAL LANGUAGES, 8 SOUTHAMPTON-ROW, W.C.1. HO. 6241.

WHEN IN LONDON stay at 1, DUCHESS-STREET, W.1. LUXURY SERVICE SUITES. Day and Night Restaurant service. Lift to all floors. PERSONAL ATTENTION. Three, four and five-room suites with private bath rooms from 8 guineas. – LANGHAM 2030.

LADY CRIPPLED with arthritis, dependent on devoted sister whose health is now failing. PLEASE HELP, Treasurer, Distressed Gentlefolks' Aid Association, 74, Brook Green, W.6.

"DRESS DESIGNING AS A CAREER." A free booklet giving all information regarding prospects remuneration, training, &c. is offered by the BRITISH INSTITUTE OF DRESS DESIGNERS, 210 Piccadilly, W.

SI l'order domine dans le genre humain, c'est une preuve que la raison et la vertu y sont plus forces. Vauvenargues.

OH! FOR A BREATH OF SEA AIR. – The poor families who have to live in Hoxton's unhealthy and overcrowded slums can never afford a holiday, although they need one more than most of us. We have been able to send away for a week or a fortnight a large number of them, but there are still some more who ought to be included. Will you please help by sending a gift of £1 to pay for a week for a father or mother, or 10/- for one of the children? – F.L. Jerman, Supt., Hoxton Market Christian Mission, Hoxton Market, London N.1.

A CHAUFFEUR-DRIVEN PACKARD of your own whenever you wish. – "Motor Hire," Page 19.

SPITE OF ALL MODESTY, a man must own a pleasure in the hearing of his praise. Farquhar.

PARENTS and GUARDIANS should consult the "Educational" Columns, on This Page, where they will find particulars of SCHOOLS and other EDUCATIONAL INSTITUTIONS.

ST. JOHN'S WOOD – Attractive modern, NON-BASEMENT HOUSE in Queen Ann style, lovely LARGE GARDEN with flagged terrace. Countrified atmosphere. 7 bed rooms, 3 tiled bath rooms, 3 reception rooms. GARAGE, C.H., C.H.W. Large rooms, splendid fitted cupboards, concealed lighting. PRICE £8,250; 80 years £75 p.a. – REGENT 0041, or write W. Box 24,464, Daily Telegraph E.C.4.

## PERSONAL (CONT.)

FRESH INTERESTS, CHEAPER LIVING, South Africa is the wisest choice for your retirement. Thousands of English people of moderate means are enjoying low taxation, glorious sunshine and untroubled conditions. What better place for you and your family? Write 1820 Memorial, Settlers' Association (Dept. D.T.S.9.) 199, Piccadilly, London, W.1.

HOTEL ACCOMMODATION APARTMENTS and BOARD-RESIDENCE, at home and abroad, may be secured readily and quickly by consulting the advertisements under these headings on Page 19.

INTENDING ADVERTISERS can obtain help and advice in the compilation of their announcements at the West End Office of "The Daily Telegraph and Morning Post" 161, Piccadilly, W.1.

PIANO – Weber Duo-Art Pianola, little used, perfect condition. Cost £257, accept £100 or near offer. Going abroad – A.E.B., West Smithfield, London, E.C.1. 'Phone City 4466.

£75 REWARD. – LOST, at the Victoria Palace Theatre or between there and Pall Mall, S.W., 19th Aug., a GOLD WEDDING RING, inscribed "D.I. and J.S.S., 24th Jan., 1894," together with a single stone, a 2-stone crossover, and a 3-stone diamond ring, all set platinum, contained in a white satin purse. Apply Daniel Smith & Co., 4, Tokenhouse-bldgs., E.C.2.

£5 REWARD – LOST, on 3rd Sept., between Cowes Pier and Hythe Pier, SAPPHIRE, EMERALD AND DIAMOND PLATINUM SET CLIP ORNAMENT – Summers, Henderson & Co., 48 Lime-st., E.C.3.

LOST. – ALSATIAN DOG Answers to name "Tony." Name and address on collar. Reward. 78 Hemingford-rd., N.1.

YES! YOUR SKIN COULD BE LOVELY if you gave it a chance. Why not arrange a full consultation with Mrs. Pomeroy, the Bond-street specialist, who can banish those blemishes, blackheads and skin troubles which are spoiling your charm? - 'Phone for an appointment at 29, Old Bond-street, London W.1. Tel. No: FULHAM 1381.

OMY FATHER, if this cup may not pass away from me, except I drink it, thy will be done.

St. Matthew xxvi., 42

"MERCIFUL RELEASE" – Have you ever thought what it means to watch by the bedside of a loved one slowly but surely dying from some agonising disease – waiting for the inevitable end to bring release from almost constant suffering? The Voluntary Euthanasia Legalisation Society is working to amend the law so that such sufferers, if they so desire, may legally and honourably substitute a quick and painless end for a slow and painful one. – Literature free from Hon. Sec., V.E.L.S., The Gilroes, Leicester.

STAMMERING and SPEECH DEFECTS. _ A FREE LECTURE by W.A. CAROT, the Eminent Specialist, explaining psychological causes and correct cure, Caxton Hall, Westminster, Wed., Sept. 14, at 7.30 p.m.

REVILLE SCHOOL OF FASHION. Associated with the world-famous House of Reville – gives expert individual training in Creative Designing, Fashion Drawing, and Dressmaking. All Professional methods taught with view to career. Courses of varying length to suit personal needs may be started at any time. Call, write or telephone now for descriptive Brochure.
15, HANOVER-SQUARE, W.1. MAYFAIR 7608.

A TONIC BEYOND COMPARE. CHANGE OF SCENERY AND FRESH AIR. TRY GLENROYD PRIVATE HOTEL. PALMEIRA-AVENUE, WESTCLIFF-ON-SEA H & C and SEA VIEW all bed rooms. English meat only served. 12/6 day. Wkly. fr. 3gns. – Southend 3243.

NO MORE HEAT RINGS on polished table tops. Unique heat-and-water-proof pad positively prevents all disfigurements. Fits table open or closed. Folds away. - Write Unique Table Pad Co. Cardiff.

LADY offers very comfortable home (Surrey) in her well-appointed house to delicate elderly or old lady with maid (Oct.), appreciating home comforts. Good cooking. Car. Good terms. References essential. Old gentleman not objected to. – Write L. Box 5,466. Daily Telegraph, E.C.4.

SACKVILLE-STREET CLOTHES at City prices. Suit 8 1/2gns. Town Overcoats 7 1/2gns. Dress 11gns. Reg. 1095. – J.W. Dore, 18 Sackville-st., W. Est. 60 years.

ECONOMIZE LUXURIOUSLY by living at OVINGTON COURT, Brompton-road, KNIGHTSBRIDGE. MODERN FLATS, only £150-£240 p.a. absolutely inclusive. Constant hot water, central heating, lift, &c. – Call, write, or 'phone Ken. 8234.

SHE KNOWS THEM BY THEIR VOICES, her two sons Terence and James, for she is now quite blind. Every since their father was killed in an accident six years ago, she has supported them, but now, her sight gone and her savings spent, she has asked us for help. Will you give a hand to these boys and send us a gift towards their keep? 5s very welcome. – WAIFS AND STRAYS SOCIETY, Old Town Hall, Kennington, S.E.11.

ST. JAMES'S – Convenient self-contained MAISONETTE, on two floors. Two bed rooms, sitting room, dining room, kitchen and bath room. Constant hot water. To let furnished or unfurnished. Reasonable rent. – Bryant, 41 St. James's-place, S.W.1. (Reg. 0054).

A POOR MAN SUFFERING FROM CANCER, and distraught with worry, having wife and 4 young children to support and only 19/- per week total income after paying rent. PLEASE make it possible for us to provide funds for special nourishment and fares to hospital for treatment. (Case 281/38) – National Society for Cancer Relief, 47, Victoria-street, S.W.1.

WHEN IN LONDON stay at 5, PORTLAND-PLACE, W.1. LUXURY SERVICE SUITES. Day and Night Restaurant service. Lift to all floors. PERSONAL ATTENTION. Three, four and five-room suites with private bath rooms from 9 guineas. – LANGHAM 2030.

LAUNDRY – Well-known laundry can accept a few additional private accounts. First-class work and service assured. – Write L. Box 7,761. Daily Telegraph, E.C.4.

MONEY saved is money earned. – For a few weeks I am offering a reduction of a guinea off my usual prices. Suit to measure from 5 guineas cash now, prices reduced but quality of workmanship as usual. – Major Daniell Ltd., Gentlemen's Tailor, 174, New Bond Street.

EARN £3 to £6 weekly flower-painting for textiles. Only moderate drawing ability necessary. Prospectus of individual postal tuition and sales service – Write Queen's Studios C, 100a Queensway, W.2.

WELL-KNOWN South Coast GIRLS SCHOOL offers vacancy. Riding, dancing, gymnasium, swimming, games, elocution, included in ordinary fees. – Write Box U. 608 c o Shelley s, 11, Crooked-lane, E.C.4.

BILL AND LIZZIE CALLING! It is not too late to send a slum child to the seaside for a day. 10s will send 5 – R.S.V.P. John Pounds Mission, Wellesley-street, Stepney, E.1.

TO LET FURNISHED, AT UNFURNISHED RENT, SUSSEX. Charming country HOUSE, easily run. Main electric, 6 bed rooms, 3 reception. Near golf, fishing and hunting. Suit officer home on leave. 4gns. – Bay. 5661.

THANK-OFFERINGS for FREEDOM from PHYSICAL DISABILITIES are invited by this Society. It provides 500 surgical appliances each week to sufferes who NEED THEM but CANNOT PAY the cost. Four letters of recommendation for your allocation will be sent for each guinea you subscribe. Address Sec., ROYAL SURGICAL AID SOCIETY, Salisbury-square, London, E.C.4.

GENTLEMAN wished to purchase ANTIQUE SILVER, old CHINA, Furniture, Very HIGH prices paid. No dealers. – Write G., Box 11,048, Daily Telegraph, E.C.

A MOTHER wishes to RECOMMEND a SCHOOL on South Coast, specially suitable for delicate or only girls. Good education. Great care paid to health and general culture. – D.617, Shelley's Crooked-land, E.C.4.

BAKER-ST STATION – Attractively furnished flat to let. 3 bed rooms, 1 reception, dining recess, kitchen and bath. Constant hot water. Lift. Porters. 6 1/2gns weekly. – 'Phone PAD. 2060.

SCARS, facial blemishes eradicated one treatment. – Abbott-Brown Ltd., 49, South Molton-street, W.1.

D.E.F. – AM WRITING PALM COURT HOTEL, Torquay, for brochure. Everybody tells me it's wonderful – S.T.D.

THERE IS STILL TIME for you to provide a holiday for some poor soul from one of the slum homes which abound in Clerkenwell. £2 will give a fortnight to a poor man or woman, or £1 for a boy or girl. I appeal to you to help to brighten the drab lives of these unfortunate ones. – Rev. F. Norman, Charley, London Central Mission, 3, St. John's-square, London, E.C.1.

SPLENDID OPPORTUNITIES FOR BOYS (10-18) in ideal school in Switzerland. Limited number of bursaries now available. – Interviews Cook's Scholastic Service, Berkeley-st., London, W.1.

COPIES OF PHOTOGRAPHS APPEARING IN "THE DAILY TELEGRAPH AND MORNING POST" may be obtained at a small charge from "The Daily Telegraph and Morning Post," Photo Sales Department, Fleet-street, E.C.4.

THE HALL Uppingham – Old Boys of The Hall, HOUSE DINNER will be held on Friday, 23rd Sept., at 7.30 for 8, at May Fair Hotel, Berkeley-st., W.1. Tickets 12s 6d – Apply Secretary E York, Winchester House, Old Broad-st., E.C.2.

GRAFTON HOTEL, Tottenham Court-road, London, W.1. Central for everything, telephones in bed rooms. EUSton3421. Charges moderate. First-class cuisine.

RETREAT FOR AGED COUPLES. A Home in attractive surroundings will be opened this month at "Oakfield," Radcliffe-on-Trent, near Nottingham. It will provide warmth, comfort, friendship, good table and Christian "atmosphere," Aged Couples who can contribute towards the cost of their maintenance and who do not need nursing gladly received. – Please write at once to or call upon, the Secretary, 110 Middlesex-street, London E.1.

MORE THAN THEY CAN PAY. DID YOU NOTICE our request, headed "Whatever shall we do?" In this column last week? Our Mission comes to the rescue of ailing children who must have a fortnight in a Convalescent Home if they are to recover health and strength. The cost is more than the parents can pay. It is 30s. We give this benefit to 800 each year. May we welcome your kind gift, if you have not responded already? – The Rev. Percy Ineson, EAST END MISSION, 583, Commercial-road, Stepney, E.1.

OLD GOLD AND SILVER – Harrods pay the best prices for OLD GOLD and Diamond JEWELLERY, PRECIOUS STONES, ANTIQUE SILVER, SHEFFIELD PLATE and SECOND-HAND SILVER IN ANY CONDITION. Offer or cheque by return. Call, or send jewellery registered. Silver and plate COLLECTED FREE in our delivery area. – HARRODS LTD., LONDON S.W.1.

SEVERAL FRIENDS writing to Prebendary Carlile ask if it is too late to send poor mothers and children from overcrowded slums to the sea. It is not, and when you realise that some have never seen the sea, or had a holiday, you will surely want to help. £5 sends mother and children for fortnight. – Cheques, &c. Preb. Carlile, "Seaside Holidays," Church Army, 55, Bryanston-st., W.1.

CAN STRONGLY RECOMMEND first-class NURSE-GOVERNESS who has looked after my child from birth to 5 years and is now seeking situation in London. Cannot speak too highly of her qualities. – Write C.S. Box 12, 674, Daily Telegraph, E.C.4.

OXFORD GRADUATE aged 29, holding responsible merchandise position with well-known London store, 6 years' experience, seeks change, preferably outside retail trade, where greater scope for individual ability and enterprise can be used. – Write O.G. Box 12,662, Daily Telegraph, E.C.4.

WHY NOT TAKE A COLLECTING BOX if unable to send a donation to GUYS? Particulars of boxes gladly sent. – Appeal Secretary, GUY'S HOSPITAL, London-Bridge, S.E.1.

HEREFORDSHIRE – FOR SALE. perfect small county property, 2 miles from a town 3 reception rooms, 6 bedrooms (4 with H & C basins),modern bath room. Acme of ease of upkeep. Main electric light and water. Garages, Stabling. Very pretty garden, paddock, 4 1/2 acres. Price £3,300 or offer. – Write H. Box 12,678 Daily Telegraph, E.C.4.

A LADY (L.R.A.M.) offers accommodation to foreign young lady, in musical family – Write L. V., c/o Vickers, 24, Austin Friars, E.C.2.

TO LET – Suite of Offices on First Floor of Modern Buildings close to Mansion House, E.C. for two or four years. Rent £1,100 per annum, including Rates. Heating and Cleaning. – Write T. Box 10,758. Daily Telegraph, E.C.4.

PEERESS WILL CHAPERON a girl or entertain for married lady Autumn Season in London. References and remuneration essential. – Write P., Box 5,432, Daily Telegraph, E.C.4.

SAVE WEEKS OF FLAT-HUNTING! – Read about a short cut to the flat you are seeking. – in the "Bell" Modern Flat announcements on Page 24.

TO Professional or Literary Persons – WANTED by lady, sole PAYING GUEST, Small house, 28 miles London; 1/2-mile from station. Garage available. Every modern convenience. Warm. 3 1/2gns per week. – Address K.G. Lloyds Bank, Brackness, Berks.

MISS OLIVER, Colonic Irrigation, Constipation, Rheumatism, Obesity, Arthritis. – LAN. 2651.

MODERN YOUTH seeks situation in London. – Write M., Box 5,562, Daily Telegraph, E.C.4.

REQUIRED IN SWEDEN. Young Englishwoman (under 30) as friend and companion to well-to-do Swedish girl of 19 returning shortly to Stockholm. Must be well-educated, good family, accustomed to travel and keen outdoor sports. First-class references and personal interview essential. Apply in writing, stating age, full particulars, to Box No. 2,135, Joshua B. Powers Ltd., 14, Cockspur-street, S.W.1.

HAMPSTEAD GARDEN SUBURB – Paying Guests. Delightful private house. – Speedwell 9975.

JOURNALIST (29) seven years editor London suburban newspaper, seeks responsible post on London weekly. – Write J. Box 5,580, Daily Telegraph, E.C.4.

RARE PLATYPUS RUG (50 skins), AUCTION SALE WEDY. NEXT. – WATTS, Auctioneers, Wokingham.

WHEN IN LONDON stay at 11 PORTLAND-PLACE, W.1. LUXURY SERVICE SUITES. Day and Night Restaurant service. Lift to all floors. PERSONAL ATTENTION. Three, four and five-room suites with private bath rooms from 8 guineas – LANGHAM 2030.

LEARNERS! Pass your trial motoring test with honours. Every "L" Driver should read "36 QUESTIONS AND ANSWERS." These have been prepared in pocket-book size to enable every learner to memorise and pass his oral test with confidence. – Obtain your copy now from "The Daily Telegraph and Morning Post," (Book Department), 135 Fleet-street, E.C.4. price 3d. post paid 3 1/2d.

ALCOHOLISM. – Interesting Brochure No. 2 on medical treatment free. – Secy., 40, Marsham-st., S.W.

## CONCERTS, &C.

*4s per Line. Min. 4 Lines.*

**QUEEN'S HALL,**
(Sole Lessees – Chappell & Co. Ltd.)
B.B.C.
PROMENADE CONCERTS
NIGHTLY, at 8, UNTIL OCT. 1st.
**SIR HENRY J. WOOD**
**B.B.C. SYMPHONY ORCHESTRA**
TO-NIGHT, at 8
Overture: Fidelio Beethoven
Concerto in C (Piano, Violin, Violoncello) Beethoven
Symphony No. 7 in A Beethoven
Symphonic Variations: Islar d'Indy
Theme, Variations and Rondo (K 361) Mozart
**JOHN McKENNA**
**THE GRINKE TRIO.**
**GEOFFREY PHILIPPE**
will BROADCAST TO-DAY on a
CHAPPELL
WEST OF ENGLAND PROGRAMME.

## MUSIC, SINGING, ELOCUTION, &C.

3s per Line. Min. 2 Lines.
TRINITY COLLEGE OF MUSIC
(Instituted 1872)
MANDEVILLE-PLACE, WIGMORE-STREET, W.1.
Principal:
E. STANLEY ROPER, M.V.O., M.A., Mus.B.

## EDUCATIONAL

*2s per Line. Min. 3 Lines.*

CLARK'S COLLEGE LTD (Dept. 116) 126 CHANCERY-LANE, W.C.2. 'Phone HOLborn 5424 UNIVERSITY CORRESPONDENCE COLLEGE. Founded 1887. Founder: WM. BRIGGS, LL.D., D.C.L. M.A. B.Sc. Principal: CECIL BRIGGS, M.A., MC. COURSES OF STUDY FOR LONDON MATRICULATION INTERMEDIATE & DEGREE EXAMINATIONS U.C.C. offers instruction by a resident staff of specialist tutors. Fees are extremely low, and may be paid by instalments. SUCCESSES – More than 1,000 U.C.C. Students pass London University Examinations each year. 5,029 matriculated during the ten years 1928-1937. PROSPECTUS giving particulars of U.C.C. Courses, and SPECIAL GUIDE if exam, is mentioned, may be obtained post free from the Registrar, 23 BURLINGTON HOUSE, CAMBRIDGE.

UNIVERSITY TUTORIAL COLLEGE Founder: WILLIAM BRIGGS, LL.D., D.C.L. Principal: ADRIAN J.F. COLLINS, M.A. CLASSES FOR PRE-MEDICAL, 1st M.B. INTER. SCIENCE commence MONDAY, SEPTEMBER 19, DAY & EVENING CLASSES for LONDON MATRICULATION may be taken up at any time. Full particulars from the Principal, UNIVERSITY TUTORIAL COLLEGE, 32, RED LION-SQUARE, HOLBORN, W.C.1. ST. GEORGE'S COLLEGE Founded by W. BRAGINTON, M.A. Educational Adviser, MISS S. BRAGINTON, M.A. CIVIL SERVICE Girls and women are prepared for Civil Service Examinations, including the Executive Class, Clerical Classes, Clerical Assistants, Typists, Telegraphists, &c. Numerous vacancies are open to girls in the Civil Service, and St. George's College students have been particularly successful in securing appointments.

**SECRETARIAL TRAINING**
Educated girls trained for
Secretarial and Business Posts.
FOR PROSPECTUS AND INTERVIEWS
Apply to the Head Mistress, Miss J. LAURISTON, B.A., St. George's College, Red Lion-square, W.C.1.

**PITMAN'S COLLEGE**
Important posts in all branches of Commerce, Civil Service and the professions are open to men and women who have benefitted by the Pitman SPECIALISED TRAINING COURSES, Students receive the finest possible tuition for the best Secretarial and Business appointments.

# PREMIER'S TUMULTUOUS WELCOME HOME

## CHEERED FOR FIVE MINUTES ON PALACE BALCONY

## "I BELIEVE IT IS PEACE FOR OUR TIME"

## REJOICING IN PARIS, ROME AND BERLIN

## BRITISH TROOPS GOING TO CZECHOSLOVAKIA

The Prime Minister was given one of the greatest ovations ever accorded to a British statesman when he arrived in London last night from Munich.

**He was greeted by vast, cheering crowds at Heston aerodrome, where he broadcast the declaration renouncing war signed by Herr Hitler and himself yesterday morning.**

From there he drove to Buckingham Palace, where his appearance for five minutes on the balcony with the King and Queen and Mrs. Chamberlain was the occasion of a memorable demonstration.

**On arrival at No. 10 Downing-street Mr. Chamberlain made a short address to the great throng, in which he said that his mission to Germany had resulted in peace with honour. "I believe it is peace for our time," he added.**

Similar welcomes were received yesterday by M. Daladier, the French Premier, and Signor Mussolini when they returned to their capitals. A tremendous reception is being organised for Herr Hitler when he enters Berlin this morning as a peacemaker.

**Britain is to send a brigade of infantry, including, it is expected, battalions of Foot Guards, to assist in maintaining order in Sudeten areas during the period of transition.**

German troops will enter a limited zone of the ceded Czechoslovak territory to-day. Last night it was reported from Warsaw that simultaneous occupation of Teschen-Silesia by Polish troops was contemplated.

A further meeting in the near future, possibly at Rome, between Mr. Chamberlain, Signor Mussolini and M. Daladier is hinted at in Italian political quarters. It is thought that such a conference might attempt to reach a settlement on Spain.

# PREMIER READS AGREEMENT TO CROWD

Scenes reminiscent of Armistice night in November, 1918, marked Mr. Chamberlain's return to London from Munich last night.

The enthusiasm of the huge crowds which greeted him everywhere reached its greatest pitch when Mr. Chamberlain, accompanied by his wife, appeared with the King and Queen on the balcony of Buckingham Palace.

After five minutes of unbroken cheering, during which the Premier stood in the glare of a searchlight, waving to a huge throng, the crowd began spontaneously to sing the National Anthem.

Again, when he returned to Downing-street there was a great demonstration and the Prime Minister had to appear at a window and make a brief speech before the crowd could be persuaded to disperse.

### THOUSANDS WAIT IN RAIN

### 'Plane's Arrival

Mr. Chamberlain had driven to Buckingham Palace from Heston airport, where he landed in the 'plane which brought him from Munich.

Heavy rain failed to damp the enthusiasm of the thousands of people who had waited hours to greet him. Many had no protection from the downpour, yet so determined were they to be among the first to welcome the Prime Minister that all kept their places.

At 5.30 the Prime Minister's 'plane was seen circling over the aerodrome. As soon as it touched the ground and began to taxi across to the tarmac a roar of cheers broke out.

These were redoubled when it came to a stop and the Prime Minister was seen looking out of the window. He looked tired after his exertions, but he immediately gave a broad smile.

### MINISTERS CHEER

### Count Grandi's "Viva'

Viscount Halifax, Foreign Secretary, was cheering loudly. Mr. Malcolm MacDonald, Colonial Secretary, waved his hat. Mr. Hore-Belisha, War Minister, Mr. Geoffrey Lloyd, Minister in charge of A.R.P. and Capt. David Margesson, the Chief Whip laughed and cheered together.

Cheers came from Mr. Vincent Massey, Mr. S.M. Bruce, Mr. T. Water and Mr. Dulanty, the High Commissioners for Canada, Australia, South Africa and Eire. Count Grandi the Italian Ambassador, clapping his hands cried "Viva!"

As Mr. Chamberlain appeared on the steps of the 'plane, he hesitated momentarily and looked as though he was about to fall. He immediately recovered himself and with a smile and wide wave of his hat, he stepped to the ground.

The first man to meet him was the representative of the King, the Earl of Clarendon, Lord Chamberlain. He handed the Prime Minister a letter in the handwriting of the King. Mr. Chamberlain carefully placed this in his pocket to read at a quieter moment.

Then, Lord Halifax stepped forward, grasped Mr. Chamberlain's hand in both of his and shook it with great warmth while he congratulated him.

M. Corbin, the French Ambassador, Count Grandi, and Dr. Kordt, the German Chargé d'Affaires, next shook hands.

### SPEECH TO CROWD

### Thanks for Support

Next it was the turn of the Lord Mayor of London, Sir Harry Twyford, to offer the gratitude of Londoners, and then the Prime Minister looking a happy man, walked over to the microphone. Addressing the crowd, he said:

"There are only two things I want to say. First of all I received an immense number of letters during all these anxious times. So has my wife – letters of support and approval and gratitude, and I cannot tell you what an encouragement that has been to me.

"I want to thank the British people for what they have done, and next I want to say that the settlement of the Czechoslovakian problem, which has now been achieved, is in my view only a prelude to a larger settlement in which all Europe may find peace."

# BRITAIN SENDS A BRIGADE TO SUDETEN AREAS

## GUARDS LIKELY TO BE INCLUDED

## BRIGADIER THORNE IN COMMAND

**From A Special Correspondent**

The War Office has decided to send a brigade of infantry to Czechoslovakia under conditions similar to those of the Saar plebiscite.

I understand that a composite brigade of Foot Guards and Infantry of the Line, comprising four or five battalions, is likely to be sent.

The brigade will probably be composed of London and Aldershot units of the Brigade of Guards and one or two line battalions.

Commanders of certain battalions of Foot Guards have already been informed that the services of their units may be required for the duty.

### PROBABLE COMMANDER

The composite brigade will, it is understood, be commanded by Brig. A.F.A.N. Thorne, who commands the 1st (Guards) Infantry Brigade, 1st Division, Aldershot Command.

This brigade consists of the 3rd Bn. Grenadier Guards stationed at Windsor, the 1st Bn. Scots Guards and the 1st Bn. Welsh Guards.

The order to the Guards to stand by is apparently in pursuance of the clause in the Four-Power agreement which states that while plebiscites are being completed in certain territories they will be occupied by international bodies.

Presumably troops from France and Italy would also take part in these police duties.

# PARLIAMENT ON MONDAY

## 3-DAY DEBATE POSSIBLE

**By Our Political Correspondent**

A full statement on the Munich agreement was made to the Cabinet by Mr. Chamberlain immediately on his return to London last night.

The meeting lasted slightly over half an hour. All members of the Cabinet were present except Lord Stanley, the Dominions Secretary, who is in hospital.

A further meeting will be held this morning. Some members of the Cabinet are awaiting with great anxiety what the Prime Minister has to say about the possibilities of a general appeasement in Europe.

It is at present expected that, immediately after the House meets, there will be a motion for the adjournment. The Premier will then make a full statement on the Munich discussions and subsequent events, including his private talk with Herr Hitler.

A debate will probably follow. This will almost certainly extend throughout Monday's sitting and may continue over three Parliamentary days.

Present indications are that the Prime Minister will meet with considerable criticism from the Opposition benches and from some Government backbenchers.

Mr. L.S. Amery, Conservative M.P. for Sparkbrook and a former Colonial Secretary, hinted in a speech last night that Germany would be likely to draw the conclusion that a victory had been achieved by fear and force. The same view will find expression with considerable vigour from a number of backbenchers.

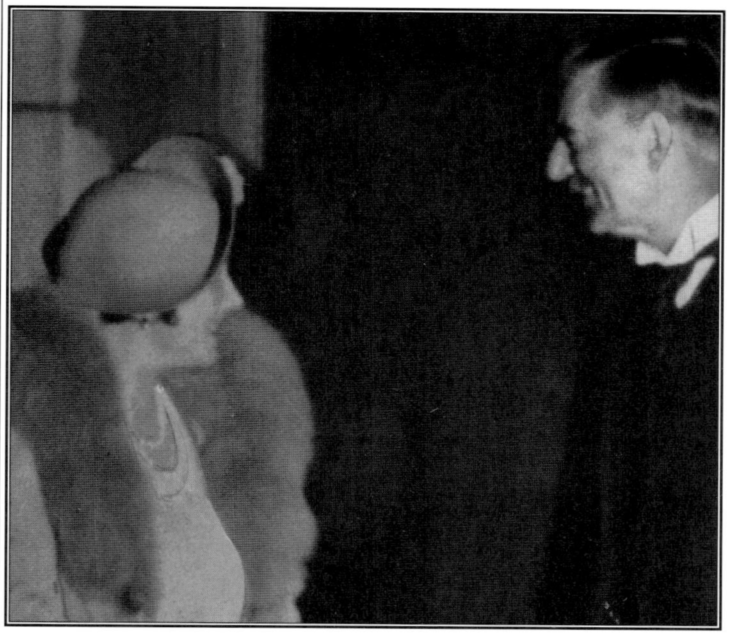

THE KING AND QUEEN WITH MR. CHAMBERLAIN on the floodlit balcony of Buckingham Palace last night receiving the acclamation of a vast crowd

# MR. CHAMBERLAIN'S PLANS FOR LASTING PEACE

## WIDE SURVEY WITH FUEHRER OF WORLD SITUATION

**From Our Diplomatic Correspondent**

MUNICH, Friday.

When the terms of the four-Power agreement were given out shortly before two o'clock this morning there were many of us who asked ourselves what else Mr. Chamberlain would take back with him to London. It seemed clear that this could not be all.

So important a pact would certainly be used to seek some more far-reaching Anglo-German understanding by which the peace of Europe, snatched at the last moment from the flames, might be secured on a lasting basis.

It was known that Mr. Chamberlain's policy was founded on the conviction that Britain and Germany must somehow find the means of pursuing their respective destinies without clashing at any vital point.

When the Prime Minister left his hotel this morning for a further call on Herr Hitler it was not known whether the two leaders would meet purely for formal leave-taking, whether the Fuehrer would take his guest on a sightseeing tour of Munich, or whether they would sit down to a further serious discussion.

Mr. Chamberlain was prepared to fall in with the mood of his host. As soon as he arrived at the Fuehrerhaus it was clear that Herr Hitler was in the mood for talking.

The joint statement issued at the close of their conversation, which lasted for an hour and a half and was conducted alone except for the presence of Herr Hitler's personal interpreter, Dr. Schmidt. speaks for itself.

### REMOVING DIFFERENCES

This declaration states:

"We the German Fuehrer and the British Prime Minister, have had a further meeting to-day and are agreed in recognising that the question of Anglo-German relations is of the first importance for the future of our countries and of Europe.

"We regard the agreement signed last night and the Anglo-German naval agreement as symbolic of the decision of our two peoples never to go to war with one another again.

"We are resolved that the method of consultation shall be the method adopted to deal with any other questions that may concern our two countries, and we are determined to continue our efforts to remove possible sources of difference and thus, to contribute to assure the peace of Europe."

This statement may mean much or little, according to the depth of the convictions which have made it possible to avert the war which, 48 hours ago, appeared almost inevitable.

For dictators it is a necessary qualification that they should sense the will of the people over whom they rule. To-day I am profoundly convinced that it would be impossible, even for Herr Hitler to lead the German people into any general war– least of all a war against Britain.

The spontaneous public demonstrations which we have witnessed in Munich, the astonishing display of grateful affection for Mr. Chamberlain, have a single, simple explanation. The German people believes that he has saved it from being led into a devastating war. The atmosphere is one of profound relief.

Possibly there may have been some element of the same emotion in Herr Hitler's own mind when he received Mr. Chamberlain this morning, obviously in happy mood.

Unquestionably Field-Marshal Goering has played an important and useful role in the discussions of the four Powers on the immediate issue. His contacts with M. Daladier, the French Premier, resumed this morning for a short time, have been of a realistic character, and seem to have shown a sense of moderation and proportion.

### HITLER'S CONVICTION

It was said to me this morning by a diplomat of long standing and experience in Berlin that, on this issue of the Sudetenland, Herr Hitler was alone in Germany in believing that the issues justified a world war. It is known that in his recent conversations, he has said bluntly that if Britain and France offered armed opposition to him, he would meet their challenge with complete confidence.

He has also explained his view that not even the combined forces of France and Britain can prevent him from establishing a predominant position in Europe, which he conceives to be necessary for German safety and dignity.

Admitting frankly that it is an inconvenient geographic fact for Germany that Britain is situated athwart his sea communications, he says, I gather, that it is foolish for Britain to complain against the geographic facts of Central Europe.

In his talk with Mr. Chamberlain this morning, I believe discussion proceeded along such general lines as these rather than on the details of questions awaiting specific solution. There appears to have been no attempt to secure an agreement for general demobilisation in Europe.

### COMPREHENSIVE SURVEY

No agenda has been drafted for a future talk and no date for a new meeting has been contemplated. I gained the impression from Mr. Chamberlain that, first, it was necessary to concentrate on the practical evolution of the Czechoslovak reform scheme, and next to note developments in the general situation.

Apparently, however, Mr. Chamberlain and Herr Hitler made a comprehensive general examination of the questions which primarily interest the two countries.

First impressions on the terms of settlement for transfer of the German-speaking Czechoslovak territories to Germany have been somewhat modified to-day since it has been possible to study on a map what has exactly been conceded.

The area to be handed over progressively during the first seven days, starting with a first march by German troops into the extreme South-Western point of Czechoslovakia late tomorrow, are relatively small.

They comprise only areas containing on the admission of Czechoslovakia, some 90 to 100 per cent. of Germans. By comparison with the demand put forward by Herr Hitler at Godesberg they are insignificant.

### SHORT TIME-LIMIT

The real difficulties will be encountered by the International Commission which is to determine which other areas may be occupied by German forces before Oct. 10. There is a strong feeling here that this date has been fixed too early for practical purposes.

It is pointed out that the lot of Czech minorities and anti-Nazi Germans remaining in those areas when they are handed over may be hard in the extreme. Insufficient time will be allowed to them for evacuation of their homes should they elect not to be transferred to German sovereignty.

Although the plan allows the population to choose on which side of the frontier it will live and cross over within a stated period, fears are expressed lest oppression be employed by the forces against political opponents.

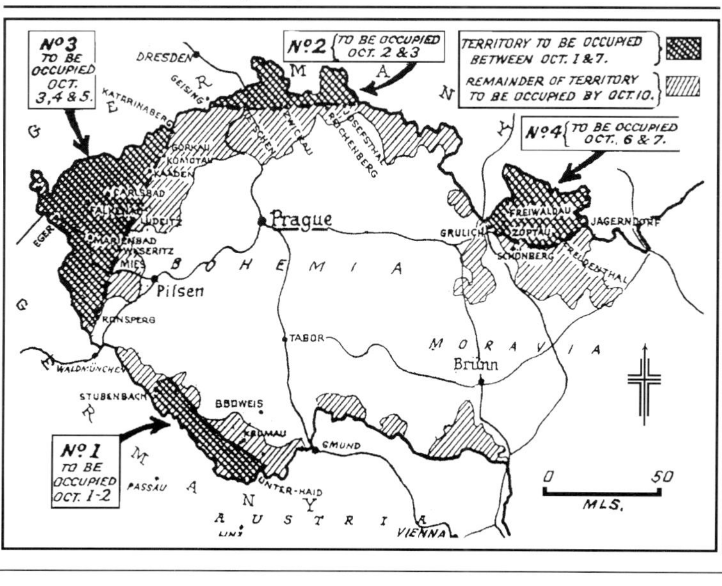

# AUSTRIA DECREED A GERMAN PROVINCE

## DIPLOMATS RECALLED FROM FOREIGN CAPITALS

**The existence of Austria as an independent State was brought to an end at eight o'clock last night, when her incorporation as part of Germany was officially decreed in Vienna and Berlin.**

Austria now becomes a province, with the same status as Bavaria and other provinces. She will probably have a Governor appointed from Berlin, while Dr. Seyss-Inquart, Chancellor for two days, will be Prime Minister.

**The President, Dr. Miklas, resigned last night at the request of Dr. Seyss-Inquart, to whom he had recently administered the oath of office. Dr. Miklas, the last head of a Sovereign Austrian State, held the position for 10 years.**

The Austrian Army and Air Force have been incorporated in the German Army and Air Force, under Herr Hitler's command.

BRITISH MINISTER RECALLED

Austrian Ministers in foreign capitals have been recalled and the Powers are to be asked to withdraw their Ministers from Vienna.

**The British Minister in Vienna, Mr. C.M. Palairet, has already been instructed to return. He will leave to-day for London, where he will report to the Cabinet on the situation.**

TELEGRAM FROM MUSSOLINI

Herr Hitler will fly to Vienna to-day. Yesterday he remained at Linz, where he received from Signor Mussolini a telegram stating:

**"I congratulate you on the way you have solved the Austrian problem. I had already warned Schuschnigg."**

The following reply was sent by Herr Hitler:

**"Mussolini, I shall never forget this."**

60,000 ARMY OF OCCUPATION

More than 200 'planes and the main body of the German Army of Occupation, which is estimated at 60,000 troops, arrived in Vienna yesterday. German troops are stationed on the Italian frontier at the Brenner Pass.

French troops manning the Maginot Line are confined to their quarters. All leave has been cancelled.

The British Cabinet is meeting this morning at No. 10, Downing-street, and this afternoon the Prime Minister will make a long statement in the House of Commons.

**(March 14)**

# EVERY JEW IN VIENNA TO LOSE HIS JOB

**From Our Own Correspondent**

VIENNA, Sunday.

Every Jewish employee in Vienna who has not already been warned to leave office, factory or shop will to-morrow be given 14 days notice of dismissal.

Germany evidently means to clear Vienna of its Jewish population with the utmost rapidity, and it appears that it will now be impossible for a Jew to retain any sort of employment.

Many Aryan masters who were notified of the new order by the Nazi party last week protested that their trained Jewish servants would seek employment with Jewish competitors. Jewish employers have now been told to dismiss Jewish servants and engage no more.

This affects many thousands of men and women in greater Vienna, where Jews number nearly 300,000 in a population of just over 2,000,000.

The only Jews whose employers will be allowed to pay them compensation will be men who served in the war or many years with the same firm, and the maximum is three months' salary.

**(July 27)**

# 12,000 COLONISTS FOR LIBYA

The nine steamers conveying the 12,000 peasant settlers from Northern Italy to Libya sailed from Genoa yesterday afternoon. Marshal Balbo accompanied the convoy on board the liner Vulcania, 24,469 tons, which was the last to sail.

The quays were crowded with people, who gave the peasants an enthusiastic send-off. Bands played, flags waved, and the peasants who crowded the decks, sang patriotic songs and cheered back, repeatedly shouting "Duce, Duce."

When Marshall Balbo embarked he was informed of the birth of another baby, this being the fourth since the settlers arrived in Genoa. He decided to stand godfather to the new arrival, who will be christened at sea.

Two steamers bearing the 225 peasant families from Calabria, the Abruzzi and Apulia, sailed at noon to-day from Naples.

**(October 31)**

## NAZIS TAKE OVER A ROTHSCHILD BANK

**From Our Own Correspondent**

It is officially announced to-night that the S.M. Rothschild Bank in Vienna has been taken over by a public body, the Austrian Credit Institute for Public Works.

The proprietor, Baron Louis Rothschild, is under arrest, and the other partners have been suspended.

**(April 8)**

# NILE IN FLOOD CAUSES ALARM

**From Our Own Correspondent**

CAIRO, Thursday.

The Nile is in flood and the waters, which have been swollen by the recent rains in the Sudan, have reached a dangerously high level.

In an attempt to ease the strain on the river banks, the Government to-day ordered the opening of canals in Upper Egypt to allow the water to flow into irrigation basins and thus flood the countryside, ruining thousands of acres of unpicked cotton and causing extensive losses to landowners.

All available men have been marshalled to keep a constant watch on weak places along the river banks, but if the waters continue to rise, as at present seems certain, breaches will occur, with attendant dangers of flooding of fields and towns.

Particular care is being taken in the vicinity of low-lying Cairo, because the last time a heavy flood occurred many parts of the capital were under water, while the drainage system, which is rarely called on to cope with more than a day's rain in the year, broke down completely, and there was a grave danger of an outbreak of epidemics.

**(August 26)**

# 23 FIRMS MAKING SPITFIRES

## FASTEST R.A.F. PLANES

**By Group Capt. L. G. S. Payne**

Twenty-three firms are now assisting in the manufacture of Supermarine Spitfire eight-gun fighters, which have a maximum speed of more than 355 m.p.h. and are the fastest military aircraft yet in service.

The acceleration in the rate of production that has resulted affords a convincing proof of the success of the Air Ministry's policy of extending the system of sub-contracting. The output of Spitfires will be further increased when Lord Nuffield's new factory at Birmingham, which has been given an order for 1,000 of these machines, is in full operation.

**(November 24)**

# BEST FED ARMY

Sir Isidore Salmon, M.P., honorary catering adviser to the Army, speaking at a Greenford, Middlesex, luncheon yesterday, said it was his aim that all soliders engaged in cookery should pass through the School of Cookery at Aldershot.

"The cookhouse has hitherto been treated somewhat as a Cinderella," said Sir Isidore, "but I hope that those days will soon pass, and that the British Army will become the best fed in the world."

**(May 10)**

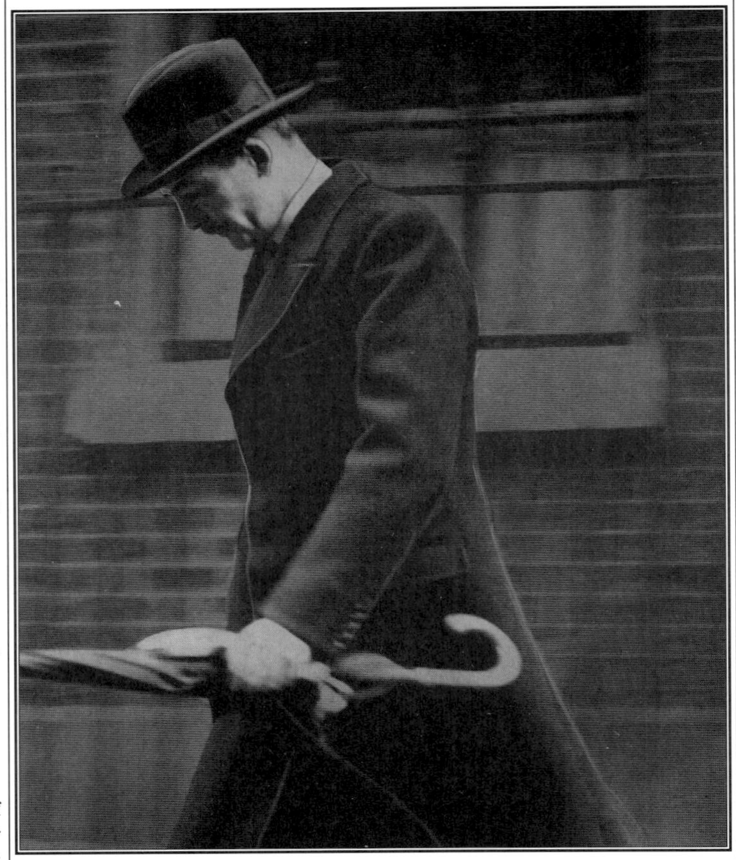

MR. EDEN LEAVING 10, DOWNING-STREET for the second and last time yesterday. He went to the Foreign Office when the special Cabinet meeting adjourned, and returned to convey to the Ministerial conference his decision to resign.

# MR. EDEN RESIGNS FROM CABINET

Mr. Anthony Eden last night resigned from the post of Foreign Secretary in the National Government, following differences of opinion with the Prime Minister on the question of negotiating a settlement with Italy.

Viscount Cranborne, Foreign Under-Secretary, also resigned.

It is understood that Mr. Chamberlain has invited Viscount Halifax, Lord President of the Council, to succeed Mr. Eden as Foreign Secretary.

**(February 21)**

# DEBATE TO-DAY IN THE COMMONS

**By Our Political Correspondent**

As the outcome of Mr. Eden's resignation from the Cabinet last night the House of Commons will to-day witness a momentous scene.

In accordance with precedent, Mr. Eden, who will sit on the back benches, probably in a corner seat below the gangway, will ask leave of Mr. Speaker after questions to make a personal statement.

In this he will outline to the House why he has considered it imperative to resign.

He will, I understand, say that during all the negotiations with Italy he has always considered that a settlement of the intervention issue in the Spanish war is an essential preliminary to any further understanding between this country and Italy.

Further, he is expected to point out that he has always held that the question of unfriendly propaganda should be satisfactorily settled, and that recognition of Italy's conquest of Abyssinia is not a matter for negotiation between the two countries but for the League to decide.

LOYAL SUPPORT

Future Attitude

Since Mr. Chamberlain and he cannot see eye to eye on the method of negotiation he will declare he feels that if any other policy is to be pursued, he is not the man to undertake the new negotiations.

He will make it clear that for this reason, and for this alone, he has tendered his resignation.

This does not mean, he will point out, that he has any intention of giving anything but loyal support to the Government on other questions of public policy, on which he is as much in agreement with the Government as ever.

The Prime Minister will emphasise I gather, that it is on a question of method rather than principle, that he differs from Mr. Eden. He will state that although he deeply regrets the loss of a valued colleague, he reluctantly accepted the resignation because be realised that he could not expect Mr. Eden to carry out a policy, passed by the Cabinet, with which he felt himself in disagreement.

When he makes this statement, Mr. Chamberlain will move the adjournment of the House. This will leave members free in the debate that follows to say anything they choose on the subject of the resignation and foreign affairs in general.

Great excitement prevailed in political circles last night. Speculation was rife on the question of the attitude which members of Parliament would adopt.

Great interest was taken in the part likely to be played in the debate by Mr. Churchill.

It seems probable that the situation will, in the end, be accepted by the majority of Government supporters.

**(February 21)**

# ROOSEVELT ON SPY MENACE

**From Our Own Correspondent**

HYDE PARK, NEW YORK, Friday.

President Roosevelt to-day stated that he was considerably concerned over the activities of foreign spies in the United States, and indicated that he was taking a close personal interest in the spy trial which starts in New York next Friday.

Espionage, he told newspaper correspondents, was much commoner in this country to-day than 10 years ago. The Government's object was to separate propaganda by foreign Governments from military and naval spying.

He declared that the present Federal machinery for dealing with the latter evil was not in his opinion sufficiently compact. The creation of a special agency to combat spies was apparently desirable.

Spy cases are at present handled by the Federal Bureau of Investigation, the Army and Navy Intelligence Service, and special units of the Treasury and State Departments.

Mr. Roosevelt, I learn, has discussed the spy situation with Mr. Lamar Hardy, the Federal District Attorney, who will play a leading part in the forthcoming trial.

At this trial four of the 18 persons indicted by a grand jury last June will appear on charges of conspiring to steal American military secrets. Fourteen persons against whom accusations have been made including several high officials of the German Intelligence Service, are in Germany.

**(October 8)**

# MAN DIES AGED 117

**From Our Own Correspondent**

JERUSALEM, Wednesday.

A man 117 years old, Meyer Dickstein, who came to Palestine at the age of 82 "to spend his last years in the Holy Land and to be buried in the land of his forefathers," died last night in a nursing home at Tel Aviv.

He is survived by a son aged 90 and five generations of descendants, who are scattered throughout the world.

**(November 3)**

# JEWISH CHILD REFUGEES REACH ENGLAND

## FIRST CONTINGENT FROM GERMANY

**From Our Special Correspondent**

HARWICH, Friday.

The first 206 Jewish refugee children from Germany to be brought to Britain were landed here early to-day.

Next Friday a further contingent of 300 will arrive and thereafter said Major G.H. Langdon, of the British Committee for the Care of Children from Germany, who received them, "as many will be brought over, and as quickly, as the big-hearted British public will allow us to do through their hospitality."

Unlike the Basque children, who returned to their own country at the end of a few months, most, if not all, of these Jewish boys and girls will become British citizens.

Many of them are now orphans, others know that their parents are in concentration camps, and all who have mothers and fathers living fear that they will never see them again.

Among those who went on board with me was a German Jew, who obtained refuge in this country awhile ago. He was there to meet his son, a boy of about 13 or 14. Father and son wept tears of gratitude as they embraced.

A PARTING GIFT

One little girl, deprived of her parents, hugged a doll which had been their parting gift, and an officer of the L.N.E.R. steamer Prague in which the children travelled said that she had not allowed it out of her arms throughout the crossing.

The ages of the children range from 5 to 17. There were about 160 boys and 40 girls. They were all well clothed and well nourished, and quite a fair proportion of the older lads appeared to be of good physique.

Many spoke English, and some had brought with them violins and other musical instruments. Each child had been allowed to bring out of Germany one mark, as well as clothes and other personal possessions.

There had been a medical examination on the other side, but another examination was carried out on board. Not a single child was turned back.

All had to pass before the Immigration Officer. Some produced passports, but the necessity had been waived by the authorities, who had issued a special form bearing photograph, name and name of parents, as identity papers.

FROM MIDDLE-CLASS HOMES

The children came from either the Berlin, Hamburg, Leipzig or Breslau areas, and are from middle-class homes. They were brought over under the charge of an English woman, Mrs. Nankivell and Mrs. De Bussy, from Holland and with them were eight school teachers, who will return to Germany.

**(December 3)**

# SECRET POLICE TO RE-EDUCATE NIEMOELLER

**From Our Own Correspondent**

BERLIN, Friday.

Pastor Niemoeller, leader of the Confessional section of the Evangelical Church in Germany, and former submarine commander, who was re-arrested at the conclusion of his trial on Wednesday, has now, I understand, been sent to the concentration camp for "enemies of the State" at Sachsenhausen, near Oranienburg, about 18 miles north of Berlin.

He is thus now entirely in the hands of the secret police, who can detain him at their discretion and subject him to the treatment normally accorded to inmates of concentration camps.

It is believed that some of the prominent witnesses who testified in the Pastor Niemoeller's defence will endeavour to intercede for him with the German Government. There is little reason to hope that any such attempt will be successful in view of the strong opposition of the more active section of the Nazi party.

"DEATH'S HEAD" BATTALION

The Pastor, an ex-officer, whom the court treated as an honourable man, and who had only a £120 fine to pay, will now be subject to the orders of a camp commandant who is a member of the S.S. – black-uniformed Protective Guards – and is assisted by a battalion belonging to the "Death's Head" section of that body. These men, drawn from the peasantry, have control over 3,000 persons detained in the camp.

It is impossible to forecast for how long the Pastor will be kept there. This is a matter for the secret police to decide, in consultation with the camp commandant, who has to take into consideration the extent to which each inmate responds to the Nazi "re-education" process to which all are subjected.

**(March 5)**

# HITLER DELIVERS ULTIMATUM

## "DR. BENES MUST CHOOSE PEACE OR WAR"

**Herr Hitler declared last night that, unless by Saturday Prague had ceded the territory demanded in his final memorandum, Germany would march against Czechoslovakia.**

This ultimatum, delivered to Dr. Benes, the Czech President, by name, was made in a speech at a mass demonstration in Berlin, in which the Fuehrer said:

**"I wish to declare before the German people that, where the Sudeten German problem is concerned, my patience is at an end. I have made Benes an offer.**

**"It is nothing more than the realisation of what he has promised already. The decision between peace and war is in his hands.**

**"Either he will accept this offer and at last give the Germans their freedom or we shall secure this freedom for them ourselves."**

The Fuehrer asserted that Dr. Benes had never in his life kept his word. Now, for the first time, he was going to be made to keep it.

Appealing to the nation to stand united behind him, he declared:

**"I go now in front of my people as its first soldier, and behind me, the world should realise, marches a united people and a different one to that of 1918.**

**"I call on the German people to march behind me. At this hour we wish to join in one sacred resolution which will be stronger than any test or danger. We have made up our minds. Let Benes choose."**

**A TRIPLE ACCORD**

It was authoritatively stated in London last night that, should Germany in spite of all efforts made by the British Prime Minister, attack Czechoslovakia, France would be compelled immediately to go to the Czech's assistance and Britain and Russia would certainly stand by France.

A final message from Mr. Chamberlain to Herr Hitler, urging him to refrain from aggression was taken to Berlin by air yesterday by Sir Horace Wilson, the Prime Minister's personal assistant.

The Prime Minister will make a full statement to-morrow in the House of Commons, which has been specially recalled. He is expected to announce that everything is ready to place Britain on a war basis at a moment's notice.

**TERRITORIALS CALLED UP**

The following units of the British Armed Forces were called up yesterday:

Anti-aircraft and coast-defence units of the Territorial Army;

Balloon Barrage, Fighter Squadrons of Auxiliary Air Force and Observer Corps.

All R.A.F. personnel on leave was recalled, and the air-raid warning system was instituted.

The King held a Privy Council at 10 o'clock last night. His Majesty has, at Mr. Chamberlain's request, cancelled his engagement to accompany the Queen when she launches the new liner, Queen Elizabeth, at Clydebank to-day.

**(September 27)**

# KING'S MESSAGE

## "KEEP COOL HEADS & BRAVE HEARTS"

A message to the nation from the King was delivered by the Queen in the course of her speech when she launched the new Cunard White Star liner Queen Elizabeth at Clydebank yesterday.

Her Majesty said:

"The King bids the people of this country to be of good cheer, in spite of the dark clouds hanging over them, and, indeed, over the whole world.

"He knows well that, as ever before in critical times, they will keep cool heads and brave hearts.

"He knows, too, that they will place entire confidence in their leaders, who, under God's providence, are striving their utmost to find a just and peaceful solution of the grave problems which confront them."

**(September 29)**

# DAWN-TO-DAWN REJOICINGS IN AUSTRALIA

**From Our Own Correspondent**

SYDNEY, Thursday Morning.

Celebrations of the 150th anniversary of Australia's first white settlement, which opened here yesterday, continued into the early hours of this morning.

Great crowds thronged the streets all night. The city and the water front of the packed harbour were brilliantly floodlit until daybreak.

From dawn to dawn the city was astir. Thousands of people had slept in the open on Tuesday night to secure good places for yesterday's pageantry.

The festivities, which will last for three months, began early in the morning with a realistic re-enactment of the landing of Adml. Arthur Phillip, the first Governor, in 1788.

Afterwards the pageant of Australia's "March to Nationhood" proceeded for three miles through the lavishly decorated streets. It was witnessed by 1,000,000 people, the largest crowd ever seen in Australia.

U.S. WARSHIPS' VISIT

The pageant reproduced the chief events in the Dominion's history, from Adml. Phillip's landing among hostile aborigines through the pioneering stages and the gold-prospecting days, down to the present, with Sydney as one of the largest cities in the Empire. More than 1,500 amateur actors and actresses took part.

Mr. J.A. Lyons, the Commonwealth Prime Minister, was the chief speaker at a luncheon given on board the Orient liner Ormonde, and attended by the Governor-General, Lord Gowrie, State Governors, diplomatic representatives, and officers from United States, Italian, Dutch and French warships.

The visit of four United States warships as described by the Press as highly significant and a welcome indication of Anglo-American co-operation.

**(January 27)**

# POLICE DOGS FOR LONDON

## FIRST TWO ON DUTY THIS WEEK

**From A Special Correspondent**

A London police constable who has been specially detailed from his beat in a southern suburb to become accustomed to police dog work will return this week from the Home Office dog training school at Washwater, near Newbury, Berks, with two animals of a Labrador type. They are to form the nucleus of a new branch of the Metropolitan Police.

London's first police dogs have been appointed to No. 4 District, with headquarters at Peckham and covering many countrified districts such as Chislehurst, Banstead, Wallington, Kenley, Sidcup, Bromley, St. Mary Cray and Farnborough. They will accompany officers on lonely beats.

The dogs are two of a number of various breeds, which have been under training for some time in the kennels of Mr. H.S. Lloyd, breeder of sporting dogs and Liaison Instructor of British Army dogs in France during the Great War.

Some county constabularies have used dogs for many years, particularly in murder hunts. Bloodhounds have been used more than any others for tracking down criminals, but a type of Labrador has been chosen by the Metropolitan Force for its first experiment in canine police work, for several reasons. The Labrador of this type

Is easily trained

Will take a message back to its local station on a word of command

Is a first-class retriever of burglar's kit or stolen goods, which have been hidden.

Is a good tracker of a human quarry.

It is expected that the first two London police dogs will be housed in a suburban station where there is stabling for the horses of the mounted branch.

**(May 9)**

# CZECH-GERMAN CRISIS — SPECIAL MAP

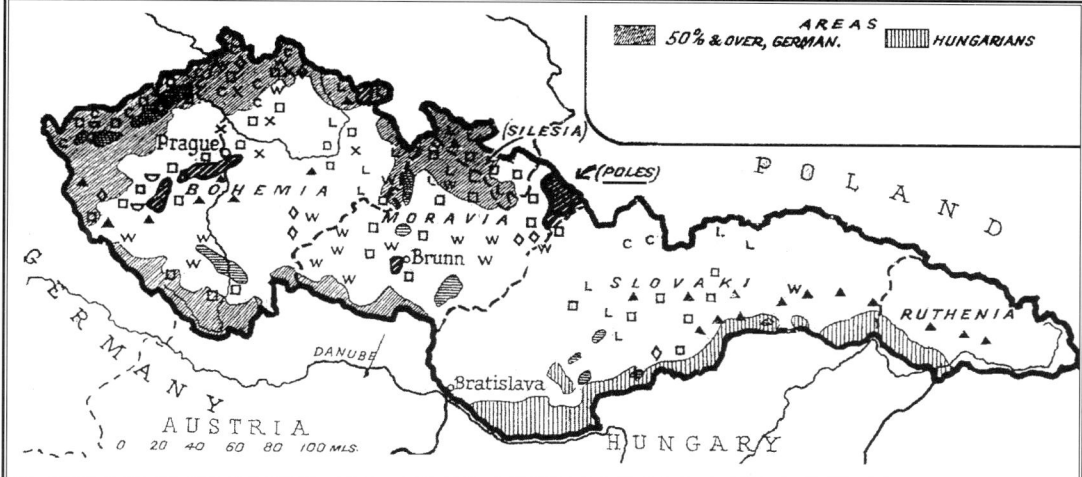

A MAP OF CZECHOSLOVAKIA, SPECIALLY DRAWN FOR THE DAILY TELEGRAPH AND MORNING POST, to show at a glance the distribution of the various industries and main industrial resources of the country. The position of the areas inhabited by the minorities, and the provincial boundaries, are also indicated. From this map it is possible to form an idea of the general effects of the proposed cession to Germany of the areas in which Germans preponderate.

# 4 POWERS AGREE ON CZECHOSLOVAKIA

## GERMAN OCCUPATION TO START TO-MORROW

**It was officially announced at Munich at 1.45 this morning that agreement on a peaceful solution of the Czech crisis had been reached following a conference lasting 12 hours, with brief intervals, between Mr. Chamberlain, M. Daladier, the French Premier, Herr Hitler and Signor Mussolini.**

The following is the official text of the four-Power communiqué:

"Agreement between Germany, Great Britain, France and Italy, concluded in Munich on Sept 29, 1938.

"The conversations which the chiefs of the Governments of Germany, Italy, France and Great Britain began on Thursday noon have found their conclusion in the late evening.

"The agreements, which were reached, which are laid down in the following documents, have been immediately transmitted to the Czech Government.

"Germany, the United Kingdom, France and Italy have agreed, taking into consideration the settlement already agreed upon in principle concerning the cession of the Sudeten German districts, on the following conditions and procedure and the measures to be taken, and declare themselves individually held responsible by this agreement for guaranteeing the steps necessary for its fulfilment:

"1. The evacuation begins on Oct. 1.

"2. The United Kingdom of Great Britain, France and Italy agree that the evacuation of the region shall be completed by Oct. 10, without destruction of any of the existing installations, and that the Czechoslovak Government bears the responsibility for seeing that the evacuation is carried out without damaging the aforesaid installations.

**INTERNATIONAL COMMISSION**

"3. The conditions governing the evacuation will be laid down in detail by an International Commission composed of representatives of Germany, the United Kingdom, France, Italy and Czechoslovakia.

"4. The occupation by stages of the predominantly German territories by German troops will begin on Oct. 1."

[Four territories marked on an attached map will be occupied by German troops in stages, to be completed by next Wednesday.]

"The remaining territories of predominantly German character will be ascertained by the aforesaid International Commission forthwith and be occupied by German troops by Oct. 10.

"5. The International Commission referred to in paragraph 3 will determine the territories in which a plebescite is to be held. These territories will be occupied by international bodies until the plebescite has been completed.

"The same Commission will fix the conditions in which the plebiscite is to be held, taking as a basis the conditions of the Saar plebiscite.

"The Commission will also fix the date at the end of November on which the plebiscite will be held.

**POPULATION TRANSFER**

"6. The final determination of the frontiers will be carried out by the International Commission.

The Commission will also recommend to the four Powers, Germany, The United Kingdom, France and Italy, in certain exceptional circumstances, minor modifications in the strictly ethnographical determination of the zones which are to be transferred without plebiscite.

**(September 30)**

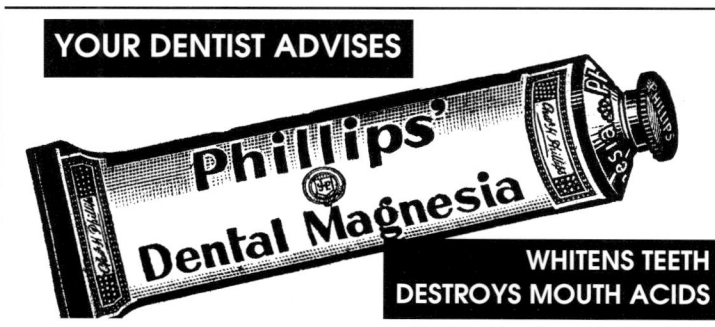

# WOMEN TO BE ENROLLED FOR DEFENCE

**From A Special Correspondent**

Enrolment of at least 500,000 women between the ages of 17 and 65 in the country's passive defence services is to be undertaken immediately by a new national organisation called Women's Voluntary Services.

Under the direction of the Dowager Marchioness of Reading and with the co-operation of all the existing women's voluntary organisations concerned, Women's Voluntary Services has been formed, at the request of the Government, to assist local authorities in finding and instructing women urgently required for A.R.P. and other defence duties.

These plans for the formation of the biggest women's movement ever attempted in this country during peace-time were announced last night by the Home Secretary, Sir Samuel Hoare, under whose department the new organisation will function.

The movement it is emphasised, has no military significance. It is essentially civilian. No uniforms will be worn, but at a later stage badges will be available.

TASKS FOR ALL

It is stated that at least 50 branches of work are available.

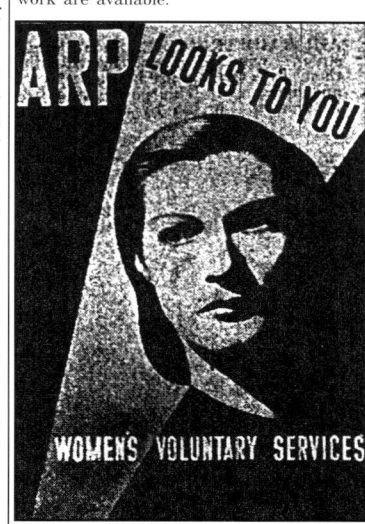

NEW A.R.P. POSTER, in which a "typically English" portrait is used in place of the original portrait, photographed yesterday. It is one of ten posters for an A.R.P. recruiting campaign.

Women of all ages, married or single, and in every walk of life are needed not only for A.R.P. duties performed by air-raid wardens, nurses, voluntary aid detachments, and lorry drivers, but as cooks, typists, clerks, lecturers, instructors, advisers and canvassers.

It will be the aim of the Women's Voluntary Services to ensure that every woman who enrols is given a job to which she is suited – a task hitherto beyond harassed and over-worked local authorities.

Flexibility will be the keynote of the organisation. It is recognised that every local authority in the country has different problems, which must be met by different methods.

At present organisation is confined to broad outline. More details will be completed as experience indicates.

Primarily W.V.S. will endeavour to stimulate women's interest in and obtain volunteers for all air raid precautions work.

**(June 7)**

# PREMIER ON LESSONS OF THE CRISIS

## CALL FOR ACTIVE EFFORT TO MAKE PEACE ENDURE

## NO RELAXING OF REARMAMENT:"WE MUST BE ON GUARD"

## TRIBUTE TO CZECHS: £10,000,000 IMMEDIATE LOAN

Opening in a packed House of Commons yesterday a debate which will continue to-day, and to-morrow, the Prime Minister explained the policy which resulted in the Munich agreement on Czechoslovakia and through which he hopes to achieve the general appeasement of Europe.

**It could not be expected, he said, that paradise could be achieved in a day. "The path to appeasement bristles with obstacles."**

**Lasting peace was not to be obtained by sitting still. There must be active, positive effort.**

In the meantime, accelerated progress in rearmament was necessary. "We must remain on guard."

**(October 4)**

# OBSTACLES ON PATH TO PEACE

**By Our Special Representative**

WESTMINSTER, Monday.

Once again the great majority of a crowded House started up and waved their order papers and cheered long as the Prime Minister came to his place on the Treasury Bench.

But to-day there was none of the excitement, none of the surging emotion of last week's historic debate.

Members thronged every bench and corner and packed the galleries. All the famous veterans sat on the alert, Mr. Lloyd George and Mr. Churchill in their keenest mood.

There was the thrill of personal drama foreshadowed by Mr. Duff Cooper in the corner seat sacred to Ministers who have to tell why they left office and by the presence of Mr. Eden close beside him.

Speeches did not answer each other, they were separate statements of policy. But to-day we had from the Socialists vehement outbursts of party feeling.

Mr. Attlee was himself careful to be moderate in personal attack while he repeated the whole party case and in his conclusion something like a development of the Prime Minister's general purpose was confessed.

Mr. Eden, critical of the course and result of the negotiations did not stint praise of Mr. Chamberlain. His call for a new national effort in rearmament and in the organisation of civil effort amplified what the Prime Minister had already said.

DIFFERENCES EXPLAINED

No Personal Triumph

Mr. Duff Cooper's exposition of his reasons for resignation which preceded the debate was severely critical of the policy of the Prime Minister and Cabinet.

The Prime Minister spoke in one quiet sentence of the joy and thankfulness that since last week the prayers of millions had been answered and the cloud of anxiety lifted from their hearts.

Then slowly he expounded the difference between Herr Hitler's ultimatum at Godesberg and the agreement at Munich.

Every fair-minded man Mr. Chamberlain declared, must agree that the alterations were of considerable extent. No longer was the method of transfer to be ultimatum, supervision by an international body was substituted. That was not a personal or a national triumph.

It had been shown that representatives of four great Powers in discussion could avert a catastrophe which would have ended civilisation.

Relief at escape from the great peril of war, he went on, was everywhere mingled with profound sympathy for Czechoslovakia. "Shame," cried the Socialists. "I have nothing to be ashamed of," Mr. Chamberlain cried, and long and loud cheers supported him. "Let those who have hang their heads.

"I say in the name of this House and the people of this country," his voice rose again, "Czechoslovakia has earned their admiration by the restraint and dignity and discipline with which her people have faced a trial such as few nations have endured."

The strongest force of all, Mr. Chamberlain declared was the sense of unanimity among the people of the world that war must somehow be averted. Those of the British Empire were at one with those of Germany, France and Italy, and their desire for peace pervaded the whole atmosphere of the Munich conference and made possible concessions.

"Ever since I took my present office," Mr. Chamberlain went on, "my main purpose has been to work for the pacification of Europe.

"The path of appeasement is long and bristles with obstacles. Czechoslovakia was perhaps the most dangerous. Now further progress may be possible."

He had made no pact, no new commitment, no secret understanding, with Herr Hitler. Everything depended on the sincerity and goodwill of both sides. But the significance of the published declaration went far beyond the words.

One lesson the events of the last few weeks had taught. Lasting peace was not to be obtained by sitting still and waiting for it to come. There must be active positive effort.

Our rearmament was increasing daily in pace and volume. We could not afford to relax our efforts. At this the Socialists broke out in roars of exultant laughter.

Disarmament could never be unilateral again, Mr. Chamberlain retorted, and there was great cheering. We had tried that once, and it nearly brought disaster. Disarmament must come by steps, by agreement by active co-operation with other countries. Meanwhile, we must stand on guard.

Determination must be renewed to fill up the deficiencies which yet remained in armament and defence precautions. With an equal sense of reality he saw fresh opportunities of approach to disarmament at least as hopeful to-day as they had ever been.

"To the gradual removal of hostility between nations," Mr. Chamberlain concluded "till we can safely discard our weapons I wish to devote whatever time is left me before I lay down office."

MR. ATTLEE'S SORROW

Unavailing Sacrifice

Mr. ATTLEE declared that this speech would need a reply, and proceeded to remark that the Prime Minister's insistence on the need for continuing to arm was incompatible with his other statement that peace was assured "for a generation."

They were all full of relief war had not come this time, but we had only an armistice. There could be no carefree rejoicing but a sense of humiliation and foreboding.

He felt, as he felt on the night of the evacuation of Gallipoli, sorrow for unavailing sacrifice, for a great chance passed away, satisfaction at being a short time out of the firing line, certainty before long of being in it again.

[Mr Attlee served at Gallipoli with the South Lancashire Regt.]

Herr Hitler, without a shot, had won the dominating position which Germany vainly sought in four years of war.

Mr. Attlee thought a Four-Power Pact "enormously dangerous" but allowed that the "great defeat" of Britain and France was not all due to the Prime Minister. He put the chief responsibility for the "débacle" on France and attacked Sir John Simon and Sir Samuel Hoare.

SIR ARCHIBALD SINCLAIR, the Opposition Liberal leader, said that the policy which brought us to the edge of war, and from which we were extricated only through immense sacrifices by a small and weak nation, was the policy of successive retreats in the face of aggressive dictatorships. Abyssinia, Spain, Austria and now Czechoslovakia were examples of that policy, which imposed injustice on small and weak nations and tyranny on free men and women, and which could never be a foundation for a lasting peace.

We should live to rue the day when the Government sold the pass in Central Europe and laid open to Hitler the resources of Eastern Europe.

MR. EDEN'S PLEA

Mr. EDEN'S rising filled the House again. After a tribute to Mr. Duff Cooper's stocktaking, he proceeded to declare that in the respite now won there must be a great national effort.

The warmth of the Prime Minister's reception in Germany showed the deep desire of the German people for peace. We must not overlook the significance of the moral forces of the last few days in resisting the march to war. To them President Roosevelt gave admirable expression.

Another influence was the Prime Minister's refusal to abandon hope. Another, the announcement on Tuesday that France would go to the assistance of Czechoslovakia and that Great Britain and Russia would stand by France. Mr. Eden agreed with Mr. Duff Cooper that "some such step" as the mobilisation of the British Fleet should have been taken earlier.

No one contended that the latest agreement was just. We were immensely grateful that it had averted war, but the cost was the gravest injury to a small and friendly nation.

The time was cruelly short for the movement, while boundaries were still uncertain, of people from the areas to be annexed. There would be a panic flight from a dread rule.

Mr. Eden was glad to hear of the loan, but we should not be the only nation to assist. There ought to be compensation for individuals and public services.

Reciprocity in release of prisoners ought to be assured. The Daily Telegraph and Morning Post stated that there were 800 Czechs in German prisons. Would Germany bear part of the existing Czechoslovak loan or would all be a burden on the truncate State?

The Munich agreement was an improvement on Godesberg, but he must reserve judgment till the Commission reported.

It was impossible not to feel grave anxiety for the economic stability and political life of the truncated State and therefore anxiety over our guarantee, an important departure from the traditions of British policy.

Mr. Eden announced three conclusions. Speed of rearmament must be accelerated by every means. Scope and character of rearmament must be re-examined. On the civil side the nation must be so encouraged and organised as to meet any future menace under fairer conditions.

However the immediate issues were resolved, dangers would endure for some time. They would not be conjured by words or good will, only by a revival of national spirit and by a foreign policy on which the nation could unite."Such a policy," Mr. Eden declared, "can be found. If ever there was a time for the effort of a united nation it is now. That would not only save peace this year and next, but for a generation."

After a fervent plea for world conference from Mr. LANSBURY, Mr. CULVERWELL, Sir LAMBERT WARD, Mr. H. RAIKES, and later Sir A. SOUTHBY warmly supported the Prime Minister.

A "QUEER TRIUMPH"

Mr. RICHARD LAW, in a speech of remarkable force, while praising Mr. Chamberlain's efforts, was critical of the results. We were told, he said, to welcome the Munich agreement as a triumph for the Prime Minister.

It might have been prudent, but it was a queer kind of triumph. Could they believe that 3,500,000 Sudetens, or for that matter 3,500,000 human beings anywhere would willingly want to put themselves under Nazi brutality.

They were also told that they had obtained "peace with honour" and "peace for our time," but he wished he could see strong grounds for these claims. Herr Hitler had given a pledge that his territorial ambitions in Europe were now satisfied, but we had heard that before.

Mr. HUGH DALTON observed that Signor Mussolini took with him to Munich his Foreign Secretary, Count Ciano. The Prime Minister did not think fit to take Lord Halifax. Instead of Foreign Office advisers he was accompanied by a Labour Ministry official.

He believed that the Prime Minister submitted to a brutal and calculated impatience on Herr Hitler's part, which had succeeded in attaining its object. In his opinion the Prime Minister was unduly hustled and intimidated and, he regretted to say, outmanœuvred by Herr Hitler.

CZECHOSLOVAKIA SAVED

Sir Samuel Hoare winding up the debate for the Government, remarked that some believed that no peace was possible in Europe so long as dictatorships existed. The Prime Minister had been the spokesman of millions of men and women who insisted that we should try to control events and avert a catastrophe which would end civilisation as we knew it.

**(October 4)**

# BRITAIN BUYS BREN GUNS FROM CANADA

The Canadian Government has placed an order with the Toronto plant of the John Inglis Company for 12,000 Bren machine-guns, 5,000 of which are for the British Government.

The Bren gun, which is a Czechoslovak patent, has been adopted by the British Army after exhaustive tests of many light machine-guns. Some machines formerly used for the production of Ross rifles and still owned by the Canadian Government are being utilised for the production of the new equipment.

**(May 6)**

# GERMAN MOBS' VENGEANCE ON JEWS

## NATION-WIDE POGROM FOLLOWS DEATH OF DIPLOMAT

**From Our Own Correspondent**

BERLIN, Thursday Night.

An officially countenanced pogrom of unparalleled brutality and ferocity swept Germany to-day. Beginning in the early hours of this morning and continuing far into to-night, it puts the final seal to the outlawry of German Jewry.

Mob law ruled in Berlin throughout this afternoon and evening and hordes of hooligans indulged in an orgy of destruction. I have seen several anti-Jewish outbreaks in Germany during the last five years, but never anything as nauseating as this.

Racial hatred and hysteria seemed to have taken complete hold of otherwise decent people. I saw fashionably dressed women clapping their hands and screaming with glee, while respectable middle-class mothers held up their babies to see the "fun."

Women who remonstrated with children who were running away with toys from a wrecked Jewish shop were spat on and attacked by the mob.

The fashionable shopping centre of the capital has been reduced to a shambles, with the streets littered with the wreckage of sacked Jewish shops and offices. No attempt was made by the police to restrain the rioters.

JEWS SHOT DEAD

The attacks on Jews and their property started all over Germany, as if by a concerted signal, soon after midnight, when the beer halls closed. In the course of the night two Jews were shot dead by armed mobs, one of them being an inmate of a camp for training Jewish emigrants at Bomsdorf.

The caretaker of the synagogue in the Prinzregentenstrasse is reported to have been burnt to death together with his family. It is learned on good authority that two Jews were lynched in Berlin's East End early this morning and two more in the West End. Numbers of further deaths were reported from other parts of the country.

A Rumanian Jew in Dortmund was made to crawl a distance of 2 1/2 miles this morning, beaten continuously by hooligans.

Two Jews who were pursued by hooligans into a second storey of a Berlin house were seen to jump from a window to the pavement below. They suffered severe injuries.

All important synagogues throughout the country have been burnt out or wrecked and between 2 a.m. and 6 a.m. the windows of every Jewish shop in Berlin and in all important provincial towns were smashed to atoms by organised bands and the contents of the windows looted or destroyed.

APPLAUDING CROWDS

The pavements of entire streets in Berlin were covered with broken glass this morning, while the windows were surrounded by crowds who applauded the gangs of rowdies who were completing the work of destruction inside the stores.

Throughout the day fashionable streets, such as the Kurfurstendamm as well as the poorer quarters of Berlin's East End, were filled with dense crowds, mad with excitement and eager to share in the loot from Jewish business houses.

A movement which began in early business hours with women helping themselves to stockings and underwear which lay among the broken glass of wrecked shop fronts developed later into an insane pandemonium, in the course of which articles of value were thrown from upper windows of Jewish stores on the heads of the crowds below, where the booty was eagerly disputed.

CITROEN SHOW ROOMS

Among the thousands of businesses which have been completely wrecked are the Berlin showrooms of the Citroen motor company and all branches of Etam, the well-known firm of silk mercers.

Smart milliners' and dress shops, such as Altaba and Rosner, and the premises of Manfield, the shoe firm, were this evening nothing but a mass of torn materials, hats and other articles of clothing trodden underfoot with frenzied delight by the crowd.

I watched a gang of small boys, led by a member of the Hitler Youth in uniform, demolishing a corset shop in the Wielandstrasse. They then ran round the corner into the Kurfurstendamm, where they undressed the dummies in a women's dress shop, and tore them limb from limb amid roars of laughter from the excited crowd.

In the Tauentzienstrasse, one of the smartest shopping streets in Berlin, no fewer than 24 shops were demolished. They included jewellers', stationers' and dress shops.

In Dobrin, a fashionable Jewish café, the mob smashed the counter and the tables and chairs, and stamped cream cakes and confectionery into the floor. Weisz Czarda, a restaurant owned by a Hungarian Jew, was invaded by another horde, which cast chairs and tables out on to the streets.

Early this evening the official German News Agency issued a proclamation by Dr. Goebbels, Reich Minister for Public Enlightenment and Propaganda, describing the mob's outrages as the "justified and comprehensible indignation of the German people at the cowardly assassination of a German diplomat."

Dozens of foreigners, including a Cuban diplomat, who attempted to take photographs of ruined shops and burning synagogues were arrested. They were taken to police stations, where their films and cameras were confiscated without any receipt or compensation being given.

A woman member of the staff of THE DAILY TELEGRAPH AND MORNING POST, who was arrested in this manner, was detained for some time in a public street, surrounded by a curious crowd, and afterwards in a police station. Her camera has not been returned.

A state of hopeless panic reigns to-night throughout German Jewish circles. Hundreds of Jews have gone into hiding, and many business men and financial experts of international repute have not dared to sleep in their own homes.

**(November 12)**

# THE PREMIER RESUMES HIS HOLIDAY

## VOTE OF CONFIDENCE IN THE COMMONS

**By Our Political Correspondent**

Six hours after Parliament had adjourned, Mr. Chamberlain left King's Cross by the 10.35 p.m. train last night to resume his holiday in Scotland, which was interrupted by the crisis.

He will be the guest of the Earl of Home at The Hirsel, Coldstream, Berwickshire. The Earl is the father of Lord Dunglass, Mr. Chamberlain's Parliamentary private secretary.

COMMONS VOTE

The Government Whips claim that the majority of 222 by which the motion of confidence was carried yesterday is two above the normal Government majority.

The vote on the motion, moved on Wednesday, brought to an end four days' debate in the House of Commons on the international situation.

The following members, apart from the Socialist and Liberal Opposition who voted against the Government, abstained from voting:

| | |
|---|---|
| Sir D. Gunston | Mr. Amery |
| Mr. Emrys-Evans | Mr. Eden |
| Mr. A Crossley | Viscount Wolmer |
| Mr. S.V.T. Adams | Mr. H. Macmillan |
| Mr. Richard Law | Mr. H Nicolson |
| Mr. D. Sandys | Mr. J.P.L. Thomas |
| Cmdr. Bower | Mr. J. R. H. Cartland |
| Brig.-Gen. Spears | Sir Roger Keyes |
| Mr. R. Boothby | Sir Sidney Herbert |
| Mr. Churchill | Mr. B Bracken |

Of these 20 members all are Conservatives except Mr. Nicolson, who is National Labour.

**(October 7)**

# GOVERNMENT HOLD OXFORD

The result of the Oxford by-election was declared late last night as follows:

| | | |
|---|---|---|
| **Mr. Quintin Hogg** | **(Nat. Con.)** | **15,797** |
| **Mr. A. D. Lindsay** | **(Ind. Prog.)** | **12,363** |
| | **Majority** | **3,434** |

The Government have therefore, held the seat. At the last election the figures were:

| | | |
|---|---|---|
| Capt. R. C. Bourne | (Con.) | 16,306; |
| Mr. P Gordon-Walker | (Soc.) | 9,660; |
| | Majority | 6,645. |

The by-election was the first to be held since the Munich agreement, and Mr. Quintin Hogg, commenting on the result said: "It is not my victory. It is Mr. Chamberlain's victory. It is a victory for democracy, for peace by negotiation; and it is a victory for a united Britain."

"SHOCK OF CRISIS"

Mr. Lindsay said: "All we want is a little more time to get people to recover from the shock of the crisis. I do feel that there is a spirit in Oxford which nothing will stop."

Mr. Hogg, who is 31, is the elder son and heir of Viscount Hailsham, Lord President of the Council. He is a barrister.

**(October 28)**

# 30 HOURS OF AIR ATTACKS ON BARCELONA

## BOMBS WRECK BLOCKS OF FLATS

**From Our Own Correspondent**

BARCELONA, Friday Morning

Barcelona which has experienced the most disastrous series of air attacks ever made on a civilian centre, was again raided early to-day.

It had suffered 11 devastating attacks in 24 hours and had hardly begun to take stock of the position when Franco bombers again appeared over the city.

Once more the people had to crowd into underground railway stations and other refuges.

Tens of thousands slept all night in underground tunnels.

It is known that over 600 people have been killed and 1,500 wounded. Already 330 bodies have been recovered. Numbers still lie beneath the great piles of smouldering ruins.

The centre of the town presents a scene of desolation. Broken glass and debris litter the streets. Lovely avenues in what was one of Europe's finest cities are now battered and desolate.

CROSS-ROADS BOMBED

Tramcars Wrecked

Sirens screamed a warning at 10.30 a.m. yesterday as four gleaming Italian 'planes roared across the city in the spring sunshine. Wheeling swiftly, the 'planes discharged their bombs. A second later a big cross-roads in the Barcelona district which is its amusement and pleasure centre was turned into a shambles.

When I arrived 20 minutes later, more than 200 casualties had already been loaded into the ambulances and trucks. Probably 100 were already dead and many others would not live long.

The high explosives did their work thoroughly. What was left of the two tramcars, which a few minutes earlier were each crowded with 70 or 80 people, all going about their daily business, does not bear description.

While rescue workers sought the dead and injured, market women, only 100 yards away from the debris, went on calmly selling carnations, daffodils and other flowers piled high on their stalls.

The city's ordeal grew worse as the day wore on. In the morning it was just a matter of 100lb bombs. But the luncheon hour was rudely disturbed by great 1,000lb missiles, which tore down 10-storey buildings and blew a motor-bus across the street.

This was the 11th raid since 10 o'clock the night before. It was also the worst.

It will be hours – perhaps days – before the gangs can clear away the huge piles of debris and find out what happened to the hundreds of occupants of four big blocks of flats.

Many bodies must be in the basements, for there was about a one-minute interval between the alarm and the release of the bombs from five silver Italian 'planes.

CINEMA SHATTERED

Great Craters in Road

Four or five lighter bombs and two or three heavy ones fell. These were sufficient to wreck a whole district of Barcelona. The 1,000lb bombs blew out windows a mile away.

No sight in Madrid during the worst bombardments there was so terrifying. Imagine a broad, spacious avenue, at least 80ft across, with wide footpaths and trees down the middle.

At one side stood the largest cinema in Barcelona, with one of the most popular cafés of the city at its side. All around were huge blocks of flats.

Now this is all wreckage. It is as if a great battle had been fought. There are great craters in the roadway with water gurgling in them. A twisted bundle of steel rods was all that was left of a motor 'bus. Battered piles of matchwood were tramcars.

Early to-day the Government announced its decision to continue the fight and to take measures to end air attacks on civilian populations.

**(March 11)**

# PROF. FREUD TO REMAIN IN ENGLAND

**From A Special Correspondent**

Prof. Sigmund Freud, the pioneer of psycho-analysis, accompanied by his wife and other members of his family arrived in London yesterday morning from Vienna.

The Home Office has given him an unrestricted permit to live in this country.

Prof. Freud, who was 82 last month, has taken up residence in a house in Ellesworthy-road, St. John's Wood.

As soon as he arrived at the house, which has been rented for him by his younger son, Prof. Freud went to bed. The doctor who had travelled with him from Vienna forbade him to see any visitors.

His daughter Dr. Anna Freud told me last night of her father's plans to spend the remainder of his days in study and research in England.

The interview took place in a room filled with flowers, sent by admirers of the aged professor's work.

BUSINESS CLOSED

"My father," the daughter said, "is overjoyed to have received news that the German authorities have consented to allow his library and personal effects to be sent after him.

"His publishing business in Vienna has been closed. Now we are hoping to be able to make a living in England.

"All that my father asks is peace to devote himself to his analytical study of the Bible. Possibly he may also see a few patients. I myself am a psychoanalyst and hope to get permission to practise here."

Her father, she added, wished to deny rumours that he had been under arrest in Vienna. Neither he nor any other member of his family had been arrested. They were, she said, treated with consideration when leaving.

**(June 7)**

# 5 HURT IN HYDE PARK DISORDERS

## FASCIST BADGES AT SOCIALIST RALLY

At least five people were injured when disorder broke out yesterday afternoon at an "Arms for Spain" demonstration held in Hyde Park by the Socialist party.

Sir Stafford Cripps, M.P., was addressing one of four meetings attended by about 50,000 people, when sections of his audience saw a woman who was wearing a swastika badge.

The crowd demonstrated against her and police formed a cordon for her protection.

With a crowd following the woman was escorted across the park, and in Park-lane the police put her into a 'bus.

Last night Miss Unity Mitford, daughter of Lord Redesdale, in answer to an inquiry, disclosed that she was the woman who figured in the incident.

BADGE LOST

Miss Mitford who is 24, is a supporter of Herr Hitler and is anxious to take up German nationality. She is in the habit of wearing a swastika badge given her by the Fuehrer.

"Some of the crowd saw the badge," said Miss Mitford "and someone snatched if off and threw it to the ground.

"I tried to get it, and then the crowd surged round and went for me. I was kicked and hit. Fortunately, police came to my rescue.

"My badge was trampled underfoot, and I am afraid I have lost it for good. I do not think it can be said that I did anything to incite people.

"Fortunately, I was not seriously hurt, only a few kicks and bruises."

After another outbreak at the meeting five men, one of whom appeared to be unconscious, were carried away in an ambulance, and two other men were taken away by police officers.

**(April 11)**

# JAPAN'S REIGN OF TERROR IN CHINA

## FIRST AUTHENTIC DESCRIPTION

**From Our Special Correspondent**

HONG KONG, Thursday.

From reports and letters sent by professors at the University of Nanking and by American missionaries to the Japanese Embassy and to the missionary headquarters, I am now able to reveal for the first time the full extent of the atrocities carried out by Japanese soldiers at Nanking and Hangchow.

These reports describe wholesale executions, rape and looting. One missionary estimates the number of Chinese slaughtered at Nanking as 20,000 while thousands of women, including young girls, have, it is stated, been outraged.

The writers do not wish their names to be revealed, but I have seen all the documents. There can be no doubt of their complete authenticity.

Repeated complaints are made that the Japanese authorities have done nothing to curb the troops. Unspeakable crimes, it is declared, have been committed in full view of the Japanese Embassy staff.

BOY'S SEVEN WOUNDS

One missionary, writing from Nanking on Jan. 11, says that while walking with the Japanese Consul-General, he saw bodies in every street. This was four weeks after the occupation of the city on Dec. 13. The letter declares:

"A little boy died in hospital here this morning from seven bayonet wounds in the stomach. I saw a woman yesterday in hospital who had been raped 20 times, after which the soldiers had tried to cut off her head with a bayonet., but had inflicted only a bad throat wound.

"I was told by the Buddhist nun that soldiers rushed into the temple, killed the Mother Superior and an apprentice nun eight years old, and bayoneted another apprentice aged 12.

One American missionary writing on Dec 19, says that Chinese were marched off and shot in droves. Some 300 were taken in one batch to a pond and shot as they stood in the icy water. This letter adds:

"Another big batch was forced into a mat shed ringed by machine-guns. The shed was then set on fire, all inside being burnt to death.

"The soldiers have been looting to their hearts' content. All property Chinese and foreign has been sacked" Another missionary's report states: "Last night they violated two Buddhist nuns who crossed the street from my house for food." Another recounts how a crowd of Chinese men was mustered by the Japanese and given 20 minutes to confess if they had borne arms. They were promised their lives if they confessed, but 200 who stepped forward were all shot.

APPEAL TO EMBASSY

Writing to the Japanese Embassy at Nanking on Dec. 14, the American chairman of the Emergency Committee of Nanking University complains that soldiers have torn down the American flag and Embassy notices from the gates of the university agricultural compound adjoining the Japanese Embassy, have smashed the doors and robbed the teachers.

The following day the looters returned, stole money and abducted women.

In the library building where 1,500 refugees were being sheltered, four women were outraged. Six others were carried off and only three returned.

The writer says that 100 more cases of rape were reported to him the same night from other parts of the city. He adds:

"The fear is so great that people are afraid to venture abroad for food, the soldiers stealing all their money and food in repeated raids.

"We urge you, for the sake of the reputation of the Japanese Army and Empire, and for the sake of your own wives, daughters and sisters, to protect the families of Nanking from the violence of your soldiers."

In spite of this appeal the atrocities continued unchecked.

**(January 28)**

# BRITONS FREED BY GEN. FRANCO RETURN HOME

**From A Special Correspondent**

Forty Britons released from Gen. Franco's prisons in Spain returned to London yesterday. They represented the vanguard of 100 members of the International Brigade who have been exchanged for Italians held by the Spanish Government.

The remaining 60 are expected to return in a few days' time.

Many of the men were still suffering from the after-effects of the wounds they received in the fighting on the Aragon front in late March and early April, in which most of them were captured.

Coming up with the men on the boat train to Victoria I heard many tales of grim experiences on Spanish soil.

"BETTER TREATED BY ITALIANS"

Wolf Nathan of London, who showed me marks on his wrist which he alleged had been caused by having being hand-cuffed to barbed wire by the Italians at Palencia prison camp, said for all that he had been better treated by the Italians than the Spanish.

"I was taken to a prison in Bilbao," he said. "When they learned that I was English they told me that as 'Potato' Jones had held up the insurgent capture of Bilbao three months by bringing food into the besieged city, they intended to 'take it out of all Englishmen.'

"Like all the rest of us, I was sentenced to death after capture. Three times I and several others were lined up before a firing squad, who fired over our heads to unnerve us. We were beaten every day for six weeks.

"Tommy Pecton, a Welsh ex-Navy boxer, was one of a batch of prisoners brought into Bilbao. He was told to stand aside when he said he was British, and he was shot dead on the spot.

**(October 26)**

# POPE'S BLESSING FOR GEN. FRANCO

Pope Pius XI, in reply to a telegram from the Nationalist leader has sent his apostolic blessing to Gen. Franco and to the Spanish people. The Papal message says:

"Happy to hear in your Excellency's message of the living faith of Catholic Spain, the crown of whose saints has been enriched by a new hero of Christian fortitude; we send you and them the apostolic blessing from the bottom of our hearts."

The new hero to whom the Pope refers is St. Salvador de Horta, whom the Pope canonised in St. Peter's yesterday.

Gen. Franco sent a message of devotion to the Pope and to express his own and the Catholic Spaniards' gratitude for the canonisation.

**(April 19)**



# FIRST MAN IN ENGLAND SAVED BY "IRON LUNG"

**From A Special Correspondent**

Mr. Cecil Cooper, who has spent five weeks in a Drinker "iron lung" apparatus, was taken out yesterday for just long enough to tell me how it felt to be the first man in England to be saved by the "iron lung."

Mr. Cooper, who is 28 and lives in Ealing, W. was ill with infantile paralysis, when he was taken to the London Fever Hospital, Islington, on Aug. 8. For five weeks he has been lying on his back, unable to read, scarcely able to sleep and, all the time, under the watch of doctors and nurses.

"I was dying – completely paralysed and unable to breathe – when I came here," he said to me.

"My greatest impression has been the kindness of the doctors, sisters and nurses.

"I have not been left alone for a minute, and now for the last few days, although I am still kept in the apparatus, I can breathe freely without it.

CONSTANTLY IN PAIN

"Proper sleep has been impossible, for I have been constantly in pain. The greatest relief is to have the pumping apparatus turned off and to have a few hours of comfortable sleep.

"At times I listened to the wireless, but I do not like the promenade concerts; in hospital one wants something lighter and more cheerful.

"I have eaten because I had to. Food is uninteresting when one is lying still all the time."

A doctor who attended Mr. Cooper told me that this was, to his knowledge, the first time that the "iron lung" had been used in England to save a man when there were no other means.

The "lung" which is now on the electric mains was worked at first from the hospital's own plant. An extra ton of coal was used daily to keep it going.

**(September 14)**

# SIR OSWALD MOSLEY MARRIED

## HERR HITLER AS WITNESS

**From Our Own Correspondent**

BERLIN, Sunday.

It is learned that Sir Oswald Mosley and Mrs. Diana Guinness, formerly Miss Diana Freeman-Mitford, were married on Dec. 4 1937 in the Fuehrerhaus in Munich.

The witnesses were Herr Hitler and Herr Lammers, chief of the Reich Chancellery. The ceremony was performed by the Lord Mayor of Munich, who took charge of the marriage certificate.

The wedding was followed by a breakfast at which Herr Hitler was present.

The report of the marriage has been current in Berlin ever since, but confirmation could not be obtained, as the official record was inaccessible.

**(November 28)**

# PREMIER SEES DUKE OF WINDSOR

PARIS, Thursday.

Mr. Chamberlain and Lord Halifax paid a courtesy visit this evening to the Duke of Windsor at the Hotel Meurice. They arrived at 20 minutes to eight and were greeted by the Duke and Duchess.

The Duchess then withdrew, and Mr. Chamberlain and Lord Halifax remained in conversation with the Duke for 35 minutes. They were in consequence late for the British Embassy dinner, which was timed for eight o'clock.

The entourage of the Duke and Duchess of Windsor is extremely interested in the meeting between the Ministers and the Duke. They regard it as the prelude to the return of the Duke and Duchess to England at an early date.

**(November 25)**

# TWO NON-STOP BOMBERS LAND IN AUSTRALIA

## 7160 MILES FLOWN FROM EGYPT IN TWO DAYS

Early this morning two of the three R.A.F. Vickers Wellesley bombers landed at Port Darwin, Australia, after a non-stop flight of 7,160 miles from Ismailia, Egypt. The third, No. 2 machine, had landed at Koepang. Timor, 500 miles from Darwin, owing to petrol shortage.

**All three had broken the world's long-distance record of 6,306 miles, when they passed the Island of Celebes, east of Borneo, and 6,368 miles from their starting point.**

Though it was decided that the three planes should fly independently, they had kept remarkably close together on the long flight.

**Their flight over desert, jungle and ocean must rank as one of the most spectacular even attempted.**

The machines left Ismailia at 3.55 a.m. Greenwich time on Saturday morning. Despite tropic storms in the Dutch East Indies, they arrived ahead of schedule, having covered the distance in approximately two days.

STANDARD MACHINES
"Automatic Pilots"

The three 'planes are standard Vickers Wellesleys as supplied to R.A.F. squadrons modified for long-distance work.

They are cantilever monoplanes with retractable undercarriages and totally enclosed cabins, so arranged that one pilot can sleep in a bunk while others are on duty.

With its enlarged fuel tanks and other modifications, each machine weighs approximately 19,000lb fully loaded compared with 11,000lb for the standard Service machine. Each is fitted with a single Bristol Pegasus XXII engine, which gives the standard machine a maximum speed of 210 m.p.h. and a cruising speed of 180 m.p.h.

In addition, each machine is fitted with an "automatic pilot" which relieves the pilot of much of the strain which arises from flying for long periods on a fixed course. The automatic control mechanism is so sensitive that any deviation from the set course is instantly detected and corrected.

The signals officer of No. 1 Aircraft and the wireless operator mechanic in the other machines are also qualified pilots.

HEATED SUITS
Leader Aged 33

The men were supplied with heated suits with a satin-covered lining of kapok to give extra warmth.

The crews of the three machines are:

Aircraft No. 1: Sqdn.-Ldr. R. Kellett, aged 33, pilot and leader of the flight. He was born at East Stonehouse, Devon. Flt.-Lt. R. T. Gething, second pilot and navigator. Pilot-Offr. M.L. Gaine, signals officer of the unit.

Aircraft No. 2: Flt.-Lt. H.A.V. Hogan, first pilot. Flt.-Lt. R.G. Musson, second pilot and navigator. Sgt. T.D. Dixon, wireless operator and mechanic.

Aircraft No. 3: Flt.-Lt. A.N. Combe, first pilot. Flt.-Lt. B.K. Burnett, second pilot and navigator. Sgt. H.B. Gray, wireless operator and mechanic.

**(November 7)**

# FLEW ACROSS ATLANTIC "BY MISTAKE"

**From Our Own Correspondent**

DUBLIN, Monday.

Appearing literally "out-of-the-blue," Douglas Corrigan, the 31 year-old Californian airman, landed at Baldonnel Aerodrome near Dublin at 2.30 p.m. to-day. He had accomplished in 28hr 13min the first surprise crossing of the Atlantic.

Without official permission, without passport or visa, with no radio and no parachute, he had flown the ocean alone in a nine-year-old 'plane which American authorities had described as "not airworthy."

His second-hand 'plane cost £225 and much of its simple equipment was home-made. The cost of the flight is estimated at less than 2d a mile. Mr. Howard Hughes and his four companions spent £4 a mile on their record world flight last week.

Nine days ago Corrigan flew 3,200 miles non-stop from Long Beach, California, to New York. When he took-off from the Floyd Bennett airfield yesterday at 10.15a.m. B.S.T. it was believed that he would fly back to Long Beach.

To the astonishment of the airport officials he headed east instead of west. Until his 'plane appeared over Belfast, to-day nothing more was heard of him.

"THAT'S CALIFORNIA"

When I met Corrigan here this evening he told me that his arrival was "all a mistake." He should have been "in California instead of Dublin."

"Before I took off from New York," he said, "I set the compass properly as I thought, but here is where it brought me! Having flown for 35 hours above the clouds I decided to come down to find out where I was.

"I saw mountains and said: 'Good! That's California.' But some time later on I saw the sea and thought I was over Hudson's Bay. I struck land again sand saw that the mountains were not rugged enough for any Californian range that I knew. I realised then that I was over Ireland, and that the old compass had let me down – or rather, that I had done it by making that initial mistake.

"I followed the coastline, then cut inwards to the east and found myself over Baldonnel where I brought the 'bus down."

"HAVE TO WALK HOME"

The flight, he said was uneventful all the way. He just gauged how high he was flying and kept above a few rainstorms which he encountered.

When I put it to Corrigan that he was almost as famous as Col. Lindbergh, he replied in his Californian drawl: "Well I guess I'll have to walk home to Los Angeles. That old 'bus would not do the Atlantic the other way, and I have only 11 dollars – £2 – on me now."

For more than two hours Corrigan was in the airport offices explaining why he had no papers. The American Minister in Dublin helped him to straighten out matters and to-night he rested at the Legation.

When I left Corrigan he was telephoning to New York and giving a description of his flight. His last words were: "It beats me to know just how I came to Ireland!"

**(July 19)**

# MAIDEN FLIGHT OF GIANT LINER

**From Our Special Correspondent**

PARIS, Thursday.

Ensign, first of a fleet of 14 Imperial Airways liners, made her first passenger flight from Croydon to Le Bourget to-day in 1hr 19min at an average speed of 158 miles and hour.

From the moment of leaving Croydon a few minutes after noon to landing at Le Bourget, the liner, which is virtually a flying hotel behaved perfectly.

Luncheon was taken in the smoking saloon, forward of the promenade deck and of the 123ft silver wings with their four Armstrong Siddeley Tiger engines, capable of 3,400h.p. Glasses of wine on the tables scarcely registered a tremor.

From the window I looked back and saw the six-feet landing wheels, retracted into the wings, being slowly turned by the rush of air. That was the only sensible evidence of movement I experienced beyond the sensation of slowly crawling past landscapes and sea 4,000ft below with sunshine and clear crisp air sharply defining every detail.

I understand that the whole fleet of 14 liners, each with room for 42 passengers, and each a colossus of the air by present world standards, will soon be in commission. But for the priority demands of national defence on time and material they would have been in regular service on Empire and Continental routes long ago.

**(November 21)**

## TELEVISION CAR FOR B.B.C.

A complete mobile film unit has been purchased by the B.B.C. for television purposes. It consists of a saloon car, equipped with a camera and sound head and with a specially reinforced roof on which the camera tripod can be mounted.

This outfit resembles the "trucks" used by news-reel companies, but the B.B.C. disclaims any intention of competing with them in the production of topical films.

**(August 12)**

# MENINGITIS CURE

## NEW DRUG AVAILABLE IN HOSPITALS

Following two remarkables cures, the new drug of the sulphanilamide group, known for short as M and B 693, is to be available generally to hospitals and doctors for the treatment of pneumococcal meningitis, a disease from which few have recovered in the past. It will also be available for the treatment of other diseases.

A seven-year-old girl, desperately ill with the disease was admitted to the Royal Hospital, Wolverhampton, in July, and after eleven days' treatment with M and B 693 she had partially recovered

**(September 19)**

ROUND-THE-WORLD AIRCRAFT IN NEW YORK - WIRELESSED PICTURE

A WIRELESSED PHOTOGRAPH of the Lockheed monoplane carrying Mr. Howard Hughes and his companions just after it had landed at the Floyd Bennett Field, New York.

# FIRE DESTROYS BLACKPOOL PIER PAVILION

**From Our Own Correspondent.**

BLACKPOOL, Monday Morning.

Thousands of holiday makers lined the promenade and beach here last night to watch a great fire which destroyed the theatre pavilion at the end of the North Pier.

At one time the flames from the blazing building reached a height of 100ft and dense clouds of smoke rolled two miles inland. For three hours 80 firemen fought the outbreak and prevented the flames from spreading to the rest of the pier, which is one of three at Blackpool and is a quarter of a mile long.

Early this morning the under-structure of the pavilion was still smouldering with occasional bursts of flame. Firemen were still playing water on the burnt-out building.

The fire broke out shortly before six o'clock, an hour and a quarter after an orchestral concert in the pavilion had ended.

ANGLERS AS FIREMEN

Anglers who had been taking part in a festival from the pier jetty entered the building with buckets of water. With attendants they fought the flames until the pier fire brigade arrived. Emergency hose was then brought into play and a score of men, forming a human chain, drenched the planking round the building with buckets of sea-water.

The main body of the Blackpool Fire Brigade was on the scene within a few minutes of the alarm.

Artists appearing in Lawrence Wright's production, "On With the Show," at the pavilion, who happened to be on the pier at the time, ran into the burning building to rescue personal property from the dressing-rooms. Among them was Miss Tessie O'Shea, who stars in the show, and Mr. Sam Sherry, one of the two Sherry Brothers, who also feature prominently.

**(June 20)**

# STROMBOLI IN SPECTACULAR ERUPTION

**From Our own Correspondent**

MESSINA, Sicily, Wednesday.

Stromboli, the island volcano between Messina and the mainland, has been in full eruption all day and has made an impressive sight.

The eruption began late on Sunday afternoon, but only the staff of the Geophysical Institute in Messina were aware of the fact.

The Italian Government has offered to take the inhabitants, numbering about 1,800 fishermen and their families, off the island, but they refuse to move.

The volcano to-night gave the impression that the whole cone of Stromboli mountain was on fire, and that the inhabitants must be swallowed up. But as the track of the fire is one side and the eruption is confined to the slope that runs into the sea, visitors who are watching from all kinds of craft can enjoy one of the greatest thrills of the world in perfect safety. The lava, bright red to-night, but merely peat colour, with patches of fire, in daytime, creeps slowly down to the sea.

It looks like a prehistoric monster with its tail endlessly emerging from the top of the mountain. Its long, serpentine body is occasionally severed by deafening explosions. These are frequently followed by the throwing up of black blocks of lava the size of cottages.

**(May 26)**

# HUGHES HALVES RECORD FOR WORLD FLIGHT

**From Our Own Correspondent**

NEW YORK, Thursday.

Greeted by a wildly enthusiastic crowd of about 40,000 people, Mr. Howard Hughes and his four companions landed at the Floyd Bennett airport here to-day at 2.37 p.m. local time, 7.37 B.S.T., after flying 14,874 miles round the world in 3 days 19 hours 17 minutes.

They had thus more than halved the time of 7 days 18 hours 50 minutes taken by the late Mr. Wiley Post when he did the same flight solo in 1933.

To achieve their remarkable record the five Americans averaged 163 m.p.h., including six stops totalling just over 20 hours. Their actual flying time was 71 hours 4 minutes, at an average speed of 209 m.p.h.

As the great 14-seater Lockheed air liner touched the ground at almost the exact spot from which it had taken off on Monday morning the great crowd threatened to become out of hand, and police had to use their truncheons.

More than 1,000 police and detachments of troops and marines had been drafted to the airport. It was all they could do to prevent the weary fliers from being mobbed.

Car horns, sirens, bells, whistles and rattles set up a deafening noise. There have been no scenes like this demonstration since Col. Lindbergh's return from his Atlantic flight in 1927.

The arrival of the 'plane although eagerly awaited for several hours, was curiously startling in its suddenness. Lowering clouds lay over the airport, making visibility poor. All of a sudden the silver machine broke through the mist and appeared apparently right overhead.

"Here he is," shouted the crowd with one immense voice, and there was a great surge forward.

Mr. Hughes was at the controls of the great monoplane as it swooped over the heads of the spectators. He made a perfect landing.

As the 'plane came to rest after its stupendous flight over oceans, deserts and mountains, the crowd forgot the rain and suffocating heat in the exhilaration of the historic moment.

Hats, newspapers and handkerchiefs fluttered in a wild demonstration of public joy at the fliers' safe return.

Hughes looked tired but wore a wide grin as he stepped towards the dozen radio microphones to greet his welcomers.

"I am glad to be back," he said. Then he added. "I believe this crowd frightens me more than anything that has happened in the past three days."

In the background stood the amazing product of the engineers' skill which had made the historic achievement possible.

Its wings were damp with rain and there were a few steaks of oil on the metal surface. It could have gone straight into the Lockheed showroom with nothing more than a wipe with a damp rag.

**(July 15)**

## "CAT" MAY BE ABOLISHED

No wrong-doer will ever again be sentenced to the "cat" or the birch in a Court of Law in Great Britain if the recommendations of the Departmental Committee on Corporal Punishment, whose report was published yesterday, are accepted by the Government. The Committee do not think that corporal punishment has the deterrent effect claimed for it, or that it exercises positive reformative influence.

**(March 15)**

# BRITISH TRAIN SPEED RECORD

## 125 M.P.H. ATTAINED ON TEST RUN

A speed of 125 miles an hour – 11 m.p.h. more than the previous British record for steam locomotives – was attained yesterday by an L.N.E.R. streamlined engine, the Mallard, on a test run between Grantham and Peterborough.

The Mallard, with tender, was drawing a streamline train of seven coaches, to which was attached a dynamometer car with instruments to confirm the speeds. The train carried only engineers and staff.

The speed of 125 m.p.h. registered when the train was approaching Peterborough, was maintained for 306 yards.

Previously 120 m.p.h. had been kept up for three miles beyond Little Bytham station.

The engine was driven by Driver J. Duddington and Fireman T.H. Bray of Doncaster. Locomotive Inspr. J. Jenkins, of London, was also on the footplate.

The previous British record was held by the L.M.S. whose locomotive Coronation Scot attained 114 m.p.h. on a stretch near Crewe on June 29, 1937, while the L.N.E.R. Silver Jubilee train registered 113 m.p.h. on August 27, 1936.

The world record for steam locomotives is claimed by the United States with 127 m.p.h. Britain holds the record for the highest sustained speed an average of 100 m.p.h. for nearly 43 miles, set up by the engine Silver Link, drawing the Silver Jubilee train, on a test run in 1935.

"These tests are made to discover what locomotives are capable of doing," Mr. W. Whitelaw, chairman of the L.N.E.R. said to a DAILY TELEGRAPH AND MORNING POST representative last night.

"Such a test as to-day's shows how much power is held in reserve. I think the travelling public has the right to know how much there is in hand."

**(July 4)**

## SOVIET TROOPS IN MANCHUKUO

The Japanese Foreign Office spokesman stated to-day that the Government of Manchukuo had made a strong protest to the Russian authorities against an "invasion" of Manchukuo by Soviet troops. The immediate withdrawal of the troops and a guarantee against a recurrence of similar incidents have been demanded.

**(July 16)**

# New Fiction

## AN OLD PLOT IN A MODERN DRESS

**Rebecca By Daphne du Maurier, (Gollancz 8s 6d)**
**Brighton Rock By Graham Greene (Heinemann 7s 6d)**
**Scoop. By Evelyn Waugh. (Chapman and Hall. 7s 6d)**
**By John Brophy**

WHEN that I was and a little tiny boy, and the wind and the rain kept me indoors, I would sometimes steal from the kitchen a popular magazine called, I think, "The Young Lady's Journal." Of the many stories I read in it I remember only one highest common factor of a plot – the governess or companion, ill-treated by her employer, invariably married a handsome aristocrat in the end.

I did not know then that this plot had a Brontë origin, nor could I foresee that in 1938 Miss du Maurier would take it and twist it and develop it into a clever story full of an atmosphere of foreboding and mystification.

The young woman narrator of "REBECCA" is companion to a snobbish harridan on the Riviera, when Maxim de Winter, widowed, wealthy and blue-blooded, sweeps her away to be his wife and mistress of the great house Manderley.

Manderley with its legend of de Winter's first wife, the lovely and gracious Rebecca, is too much for her. She cannot feel adequate to it, she cannot feel that de Winter has ceased to love Rebecca. And then she begins to stumble on secrets, which, like old Russian toys, open only to disclose further secrets.

"Rebecca" will, I am sure, be popular, but not with the discriminating. Miss du Maurier performs the task she has set herself with great skill, but her appeal is to emotions which seem to me spurious. The atmosphere of the story is produced largely by writing full of archaic-poetic touches. The characters are hardly real, and in-so-far as they are real, I repudiate the valuation set upon them here.

**(August 5)**

* * *

"BRIGHTON ROCK" reads like a collaboration. Mr. Graham Greene, the novelist, tells a story of murder, and treachery and mystification altogether excellent, one of the very best. But every now and again he is elbowed away from the writing desk by Mr. Graham Greene, the theologian, who can see in these desperate, vulgar but convincing characters no more than manifestations of abstract forces, evil which must seek goodness as its complement, a physical joy in life which harms no one but must be regarded as the enemy of the spiritual.

I advise readers to concentrate on the story, which is superbly told, for the passages which undertake to explain motives, whatever their subtlety, seem to me irrelevant. A journalist employed by a popular newspaper to show himself in various parts of Brighton, at stated times, in order that readers may have an opportunity of challenging him by name and claiming a reward, is murdered on Bank Holiday in broad daylight.

We know that a youngster named Pinkie, who has just succeeded to the leadership of a Brighton gang battening on bookmakers, is the murderer. We know the false alibi Pinkie has made for himself, and we know that its one weak link is a waitress, Rose.

The excitement – and it is genuine, tense and maintained to the end – arises from the indignant curiosity of a jolly woman, goodhearted but no better than she ought to be, named Ida. Ida was with the murdered journalist just before he died. She disbelieves the verdict of natural death and goes round asking awkward questions.

**(July 22)**

* * *

THE News is Good, for Mr. Evelyn Waugh continues his ribald, fantastic and unpredictable way. This time he turns on the newspaper world, and, as a hard-working novelist who has lately seen much money and fame cornered by war correspondents turned author, let me confess that I enjoyed nothing in "SCOOP" more than those interludes in which we glimpse Mr. Wenlock Jakes tapping out fatuous passages from his forthcoming reminiscences for which he is to receive an advance of 20,000 dollars.

"Scoop" is about the Boots, three of them. One is a novelist in need of money – Mr. Waugh never disdains realism in its due place. A society hostess uses her influence with the newspaper proprietor, Lord Copper, to secure for this John Boot the post of special correspondent in Ishmailia, where civil war is expected to break out.

Lord Copper's staff have never heard of this highbrow novelist (more grim realism!), and when they discover that the man who sends in Nature Notes from the depths of the country is a William Boot, they promptly pack him off to Ishmailia.

Mr. Waugh is not a satirist, for indignation founded on some belief is necessary to satire and I have never been able from his books to discover what Mr. Waugh believes in. His job is to provide laughter without tendenciousness, and how well he does it.

**(May 13)**

DETAIL FROM A PORTRAIT of Mr. T. S. Eliot by Mr. Wyndham Lewis which was rejected by the Royal Academy.

# MR. AUGUSTUS JOHN RESIGNS FROM ACADEMY

## PROTEST AT "INEPT REJECTION"

Mr. Augustus John announced yesterday that he had resigned from the Royal Academy.

The resignation, foreshadowed in The Daily Telegraph and Morning Post, was a protest against the rejection of the portrait of Mr. T.S. Eliot, the poet, painted by Mr. Wyndham Lewis.

Mr. Augustus John is to meet Mr. Wyndham Lewis to-day. They will discuss the possibility of taking further measures to register their disapproval of certain aspects of the Academy's policy. It is possible that questions may be put down for answer in the House of Commons by the Prime Minister.

Outlining the reasons why he had resigned, Mr. Augustus John said last night, "I very much regret to make a sensation, but it cannot be helped.

"Nothing that Mr. Wyndham Lewis paints is negligible or to be condemned lightly. I strongly disagree with the rejection. I think it is an inept act on the part of the Academy."

### "WHERE I BELONG"

"The rejection of Mr. Wyndham Lewis's portrait by the Academy has determined my decision to resign from that body.

"I do so with much reluctance for I have made among my colleagues numerous personal friends for whom I have the highest regard and who, I fear, will greet this step with some resentment.

"If however, I remain, I shall be doing an injustice to myself, if not to the Academy, for I shall henceforth experience no longer the uncomfortable feeling of being in a false position as a member of an institution with whose general policy I am constantly in disagreement. I shall be happier and more honest in rejoining the ranks of those outside, where I naturally belong.

"In so doing I shall of course, cease to benefit by the widely spread superstition that R.A. stands for 'real artists' I shall again have to submit to criticism on my merits alone, but of that I am not afraid.

"But in leaving the R.A. I am entering no other opposing camp, for I shall be alone and completely unattached, except to the interests of all I take to be vital and enduring in art, wherever I meet with it. That I consider to be the greater loyalty."

**(April 26)**

# TELEVISION OPERA EXPERIMENT

The B.B.C. embarked on a bold experiment yesterday, when two television performances of the second act of "Tristan" were given. The rôles were doubled; the singers were merely heard, while the action was performed on the screen by other persons.

The intention behind this division of labour was good but its execution was far from happy. For one thing we were treated to scenes which Wagner preferred to leave to the imagination – rolling breakers during the introduction and a hunting party when the horns are heard, to say nothing of occasional reminiscences of Act. 1.

Most of the action – or "miming" as it was called – was unsuited to the music. There was too much vague undulation of arms and far too much restlessness in the movements.

**(January 25)**

# A PLAY OF REAL QUALITY

## INDICTMENT OF WAR

**By W.A. Darlington**

Many plays have been written in the past few years in indictment of war. Most of these plays, though they have commanded our sympathy, have failed to stir our feelings because – for one reason or another – they were bad plays.

In "Idiot's Delight," by Robert E. Sherwood, produced at the Apollo last night and received with the utmost enthusiasm, we have something of an altogether different order. Mr. Sherwood feels as passionately as anybody can that a great international war is an insanity that might destroy our civilisation. But because he is playwright before propagandist, he uses those feelings to make a background, against which his characters play out their personal story.

The result is a play of enormous drive and compelling power, which seems likely to repeat here the great success it had in New York.

Its people are a group of oddly-assorted characters, assembled by chance at a hotel outside Switzerland at the moment a war of appalling proportions is about to break out. Chief among these are Harry Van an American tap-dancer who is touring Europe in company with a team of hard-bitten blondes, and Achille Weber, an armament-maker whose travelling companion is a mysterious Russian aristocrat named Irene.

### AN UNUSUAL PERSONALITY

Harry and Irene make two brilliantly effective acting parts, and Raymond Massey's nervous intensity and sardonic humour make him the perfect actor for Harry. Incidentally, he brought the house down by his performance of Harry's turn with the blondes. Irene is Tamara Geva a young lady who has come from Russia via the United States, and has the charm of the unusual.

**(March 23)**

# MODERN ART OF GERMANY

**By T.W.Earp**

The exhibition of 20th Century German Art, which Mr. Augustus John will open at three o'clock to-day at the New Burlington Galleries, Burlington-gardens, W., is a voluntary companion to that of "Degenerate Art" now taking place in Berlin.

All the 54 artists represented in London figure in the official German show, and those still living are either in exile or forbidden to exhibit.

They have come under Herr Hitler's ban on both aesthetic and political grounds. In opening the Berlin exhibition he said:

"Futurism, Impressionism, Cubism and the rest have nothing in common with the German people. I wish, in the name of the German race, to forbid such lamentable unfortunates, who plainly suffer from defective sight, to try to talk the world into accepting their false observations of reality."

It is nothing new to raise such a cry against new movements in the arts. The epithet of degeneracy is a burr which time has frequently brushed from the vesture of art.

Its application to the Burlington Galleries exhibition can only disappoint seekers for excitement though the London show is presumably chosen from the artists' best output as the Berlin one from their worst.

**(July 7)**

# U.S. "INVASION" PANIC: INQUIRY ORDERED

## TERROR SPREAD BY RADIO PLAY

**From Our Own Correspondent.**

NEW YORK, Monday.

The Federal authorities to-day began investigation of the most amazing episode in the history of broadcasting, the dramatisation of H.G. Wells's novel "The War of the Worlds," which last night flung thousands into a state of panic, and convinced them that the United States was being invaded by a host of supermen from Mars.

The names of American cities were substituted for the original placenames, and Mr. Wells to-day cabled his American representative, Mr. Jacques Chambrun, stating that "totally unwarranted" liberties had been taken. He also expressed deep concern at the effect of the broadcast.

Mr. Chambrun has placed the matter in the hands of his lawyers.

He said to me: "At no time was it explained that this dramatisation would take liberties that amounted to complete rewriting of the novel, rendering it an entirely different story.

"Mr Wells and I consider that in doing this the Columbia Broadcasting System and Mr. Orson Welles – the producer and principal actor in the play – far overstepped their rights. I believe that the Columbia Broadcasting System should make a full retractation."

### DEATH RAYS

The play was presented as a series of news bulletins and commentaries. Monsters as tall as skyscrapers and armed with death rays were described by the announcer.

"One of the gigantic creatures," he said, "is straddling the Pulaski skyway. (The road carried on a viaduct out of Jersey City.) We warn the people to evacuate New York City as the Martians approach."

Fantastic as it may seem, scores of reports from every part of the country bear witness to the fact that the wildest fear took hold of hundreds of households from Rhode Island to California.

Mr. Welles was stunned by the results of his efforts, because, he said this afternoon, he hesitated to put the show on thinking "it might bore people."

The Columbia Broadcasting System no less perturbed, points out that the programme was interrupted four times with reminders to listeners that it was all just a play from the New York studio.

### WAVE OF TERROR

The panic was caused by the fact that many persons who tuned in casually became convinced that they were listening to authentic news bulletins describing the wholesale destruction of cities in Eastern America. A wave of terror swept the nation from coast to coast and produced results without precedent.

Thousands of people in New York and New Jersey fled into the streets. Scores were treated in the hospitals for shock and many suffered heart attacks.

When the truth became known the victims of this mass hysteria were naturally highly indignant, and typical expressions of opinion to-day were, "rotten," "asinine," "criminal," "disgraceful," and "a public outrage."

Never has an authentic news announcement brought such startling reaction. Some people ran about affirming that they had actually seen the invading Martians and heard terrific explosions.

People who believed these strange events had come to pass had only one thought – to escape. They snatched a few belongings, packed their families into their cars, and started driving wildly towards the open spaces. Policemen on traffic duty were dumbfounded by the spectacle of cars rushing past, well in excess of the speed limit.

### PRAYERS IN CHURCHES

Terror took hold of certain districts in Harlem, New York's great negro quarter, where people either fled or crowded into the churches to pray. Residents of many Southern cities gathered in the streets to pray. At Indianapolis a woman ran screaming into a church where evening service was being held and shouted: "New York has been destroyed. It's the end of the world. Go home and prepare to die."

Police stations and newspaper offices were swamped by telephone calls. Philadelphia police received 3,000 calls in an hour, and the Philadelphia radio station, which relayed the programme, received 4,000. New York police sent a motor-cyclist to find out what was happening.

At Newark New Jersey, all the occupants of blocks of flats left their homes with wet towels round their heads as improvised gas masks.

Men of the National Guard of New Jersey, started reporting for mobilisation, and a man at San Francisco telephoned the police, saying: "Where can I volunteer? We've got to stop this awful thing."

Throughout the night all broadcasting stations made announcements intended to allay these astonishing fears, and the panic subsided as quickly as it spread.

**(November 1)**

# FAULTS IN "SNOW WHITE" FILM

## FANTASY SPOILED BY SLAPSTICK

**By Campbell Dixon**

If you go to the seven-reel "Snow White and the Seven Dwarfs" expecting it to be seven times as good as "The Three Little Pigs" or "The Little Brown Hen" or as good as seven Disney one-reelers laid end-to-end, you may be disappointed.

It is not in the nature of things that it should be. Mr. Disney's art, as a private view yesterday of "Snow White" reminded one, is the art of the miniature. An extension to a full-sized canvas has involved a certain amount of repetition and padding that slow down the tempo and dilute the wit.

There is too much knockabout. The dwarfs are continually running into things in the manner of the Keystone cops. The sneezing, the grimacing, the comic business, are all a little obvious, judging by Mr. Disney's own standards.

### ILLUSION BROKEN

Pictorially, Mr. Disney is a poet, as anyone who sets out to tell fairy tales must be. The slapstick of his earlier grotesques is out of place in a delicate fantasy of childish dreams, acted by creatures that simulate real life.

Above all, like the film men first confronted with the problem of speech, he must learn to make more effective use of sound. "Snow White" expresses herself in verse, like the fairy queen in a pantomime, but the dwarfs talk commonplace Americanese. Every time this happens the illusion is broken, the story drops into another key.

If I have dwelt on the film's faults rather than its countless felicities and charming humour, it is because I feel Mr. Disney is an artist, and "Snow White" a production worth taking seriously.

"Snow White" may even be a portent Its success – and I have no doubt its reception here will be as warm as in America – opens up possibilities of synthetic stars one day, rivalling Garbo and Gary Cooper, Mae West and Shirley Temple.

### FRIGHTENING EPISODE

The story begins enchantingly, with the kitchen princess, singing, very sweetly, into the wishing well while the birds gather round her and the Queen watches jealously from a window.

The attempt of the Queen's fierce Hunter to kill her, and the girl's headlong flight through the forest, with trees clutching at her with spiny hands, owls screaming and crocodiles snapping might well frighten a nervous child out of seven years' growth.

So might the Queen's transformation into a hideous witch, the great raven that perches on a skull, the vultures that follow her on her murderous errand and the witch's spectacular fall into the abyss.

It is true that such things have always been part of the Grimms' nursery tale. On the screen however, they acquire a nightmarish power which explains the Censor's view that "Snow White" is not a film for the unaccompanied child.

**(February 21)**

# DRAMA & HUMOUR IN "THE LADY VANISHES"

**By Campbell Dixon**

"The Lady Vanishes," is a story of espionage – fast-moving, exciting and very funny. None of Mr. Hitchcock's other pictures has hung together so coherently. None has achieved its effects with so little strain.

The working out of a melodramatic story to a chorus of two pukka Englishmen intensely concerned with a crises at home, which turns out to be a Test match, is immensely diverting. For the first time in my recollection a British thriller has steered a successful course between schoolboyish heroism and irritating facetiousness in the face of danger.

**(October 6)**

and
MORNING POST
DAILY TELEGRAPH - 29th June 1855.
MORNING POST - 2nd November 1772.

135, Fleet-st., London E. C. 4.
Telephone: Central 4242

## WHAT SORT OF PEACE?

### GAINS FROM THE MUNICH SETTLEMENT

PEACE, even at a price, is a blessing so inestimable that the first and predominant reaction to our release from the torturing fears of the past few days is necessarily one of profound thankfulness. In all parts of the world yesterday there were the most impressive demonstrations of relief and satisfaction that war no longer threatens. Before we take stock of all that has befallen, it becomes us to acknowledge the enormous debt we owe to the lofty and indefatigable endeavour of a single man. Never for a moment has Mr. CHAMBERLAIN spared himself in the pursuit of his mission for peace. He stood on no ceremony; he never lost his courage or faltered in his resource even at the darkest hour; and it is already a matter of history that war would have been loosed upon us but for the dramatic initiative of his flight to Berchtesgaden. No one can deny him the honours of a noble battle nobly won.

#### The Evacuation Terms

Now that peace is assured we are bound to ask, what sort of peace? That a price has had to be paid for it is clear to all. Is it too high a price? In answering this question the first test that may be applied is to consider how much is conceded in the Munich agreement beyond what was already conceded in the Anglo-French plan. In certain main essentials it seems that the Czechs lose no more under the agreement than the plan had granted. They are to evacuate in the first instance only that territory where the Sudeten Germans are definitely established to be in a majority. Where doubt exists a plebiscite is to precede the final delimitation of the frontier by an international commission on which the Czechs are represented together with the four Powers. That is a reasonable provision which in no way exceeds the implications of the Anglo-French plan. It is altogether a different matter from the demands of the Godesberg memorandum, which insisted on the occupation by German troops not only of the Sudeten areas, but of districts containing Czech majorities. In this and other respects the agreement removes some of the most objectionable features of the memorandum. Moreover, not only is the evacuation restricted to a smaller area, but the time-limit is spread over 10 days instead of being confined to a single day. To the new and extended time-limit little exception can be taken; Lord RUNCIMAN himself had recommended that evacuation should be prompt and expeditious in order to avoid the exacerbation of tension before and during the process. Finally, the Munich agreement restores with immediate application the Anglo-French guarantee which had been excluded from the memorandum.

#### Hungarians and Poles

Where the agreement goes beyond the Anglo-French plan is chiefly in disallowing the destruction of existing "installations" during evacuation. What exactly is meant by "installations" is not yet clear, but they seem to include the military and other equipment referred to in the appendix to the Godesberg memorandum. In that event, the Czechs would have to abandon, for example, the guns fixed in emplacements on their frontier fortifications, and this must be accounted an undoubted hardship. There is also the question, for example, of industrial machinery belonging to Czech firms, for which compensation will apparently have to be paid to Germany in the case of firms desiring to transfer their location into Czech territory. Moreover, the Munich agreement unlike the plan, envisages the amputation of the Hungarian and Polish frontier areas. This amputation however, had become inevitable and it is perhaps some gain to have provided for its orderly execution within a reasonable time, especially as the completion is to bring the addition of an Italo-German to the Anglo-French guarantee of the new Czechoslovak frontiers. Another consideration is that the

idea of detaching the Slovaks, with which Herr HITLER seems to have been playing, is now definitely ruled out. Altogether, therefore, the Munich agreement appears not unfavourable from the Czech point of view as compared with the earlier plan. It certainly eliminates the feature of arrogant dictation, backed with the threat of force, against which Mr. CHAMBERLAIN had taken his stand at Godesberg.

#### Czech Sacrifices

Where the agreement is chiefly open to criticism is not so much in its contents as in the manner in which it was negotiated over the heads of the Czechs. If the Czechs could not be a party to the discussions, there seems no good reason why they could not have been privy to them and have been permitted to represent their point of view. When it is recalled that they had been forced to accept the Anglo-French plan unconditionally, the least they might have expected was the right of being consulted in its execution. If this right had been granted, they might for example have warned the Munich conference of the difficulties that are presently going to face the frontier delimitation commission.

#### A Broader Appeasement?

It was generally hoped that Mr. CHAMBERLAIN would find the means of securing through any Czechoslovak settlement the foundation of a broader appeasement of the kind which is well known to have been one of the major objectives of his foreign policy ever since his succession to the Premiership. The still ratified Anglo-Italian agreement was a first step in this direction, and the joint Anglo-German declaration signed yesterday morning is no doubt intended as a second. But prudence compels us as yet to refrain from setting undue store by it. If we could accept at its face value Herr HITLER's latest assurance that territorial demands in Europe are now at an end, the hopes that could be reposed in the declaration would be considerably enhanced. But it is impossible to forget that after the retrocession of the Saar and the reoccupation of the Rhineland he gave similar pledges, the practical outcome of which has been vividly impressed on our minds during the current year. Certain it is that the declaration would not survive a repetition of the policy of threats and "surprise" which has just brought all Europe to the verge of a general conflagration.

(October 1)

## SNOW WHITE AND THE CENSOR

By withholding from "Snow White and the Seven Dwarfs" the certificate of "universal" release the British Board of Film Censors appear at first sight to have established a paradox. Here, it will be said, is a film made for children by that children's laureate, Mr. WALT DISNEY – made, moreover, from the inspiration of those fairy tales compiled by the Brothers GRIMM on which the censors' own childhood must surely have been nurtured – and now the film is adjudged unsuitable for children to see.

We believe, however, that Snow White's character remains spotless, and we doubt if Lord TYRRELL and his Board of Censors have exposed themselves to any counter-attack by the nursery battalions. For by all accounts Mr. DISNEY, in this £300,000 saga, his first full-length film, has aimed as much at adults as at children, and has enhanced the already melodramatic story of Snow White with incidents visually horrific. Fairy tales have, as it happens, usually a touch of the macabre and the horrible, which the teller in modern times glosses over. The film lends something of its hypnotic realism to these blood-curdling fantasies. If some of the terrors are snipped from "Snow White and the Seven Dwarfs" we may catch our breath less often than Mr. DISNEY intended, but we are more likely to take our children with us.

(February 7)

## FRANCE'S JOYOUS WELCOME

PARIS yesterday gave to KING GEORGE and QUEEN ELIZABETH more than the promised cordiality of welcome. In the descriptions of French enthusiasm that we publish to-day the formal note of such an occasion is eclipsed by the unrestrained delight of the populace. All that pomp and pageantry can give of magnificence to the celebrations was apparent in the Royal progress, but their Majesties will have even been more deeply touched by the spontaneous evidence that they hold a place in the hearts of the French people, to whom they have chosen to make their first journey abroad.

(July 20)

# HOW STAND BRITAIN AND FRANCE SINCE MUNICH?

◆

## Democracies Take Stock in a Changed Europe

## Peril From Any Manoeuvre For Separating Them

### By the Right Hon. Winston Churchill, M.P.

SPECULATION has been rife about the purpose and the results of the visit of the Prime Minister and Lord Halifax to Paris last week. In the grey aftermath of Munich, it was certainly necessary that the Ministers at the head of both countries should take stock of their position and of their mutual relations.

An immense change has occurred in the balances of Europe; and far-reaching reactions are also in progress in the public minds of both the Western democracies.

Great Britain is divided upon foreign policy as she has never been for fifty years. Political controversy is lively and will become more severe. In France the impact of September's grim event has struck all the more deeply because it has been borne in silence. The Chamber endorsed Messieurs Daladier and Bonnet's action almost unanimously, one single member of the Right, Monsieur de Kerilis, alone voting with the Communists against it. But every section of French society has been shaken to its foundations.

#### Collapse of France's System of Alliances

The bloodless conquest and virtual absorption of Czechoslovakia by Nazi Germany has transformed the military position of France. All her system of Alliances in Eastern Europe has collapsed and can never be reconstituted, except, perhaps, after a lapse of years and in an entirely different form. Hitherto France and Great Britain have had the feeling that they were stronger than Germany. Henceforward a different order prevails.

We have seen what Herr Hitler has been able to accomplish in spite of his weakness. We have now to learn how he will use his strength. If Munich and other triumphs were gained in the green wood, what will be done in the dry?

The statesmen of Great Britain and France have written, or will write, their names upon pieces of paper which Hitler willingly signs; but no one in either country feels any more security from such pious and vague affirmations of good will than the nations of the world felt about the Kellog Pact, to which all subscribed.

#### Not Resigned to Minor Power's Role

It must be frankly admitted that the friends of France in England have sustained an impression of bewilderment. Even I, who for thirty years have steadfastly pursued in peace, in war, in after-war, the cause of Anglo-French solidarity, am now somewhat baffled.

One does not know what the new France stands for, or amounts to, at the present time, or what infernal changes lie ahead of the Third Republic. These changes may be drastic.

I have no doubt that by one road or another they will end in a reassertion of the French will-to-live. No one who knows the

inherent strength of France can believe the defeatist tales, which are spread so eagerly, that that great nation is willing to resign itself to the rôle of a minor Power. There must be and there will be, a vehement revival on both sides of the Channel. But how it will come in France, and in what form, is a mystery of the future.

The outbreak of strikes and disorders fomented by the parties of the Left, may have the effect of momentarily weakening France; but it would be a great mistake to regard them as a sign of morbid weakness.

The principle which united the mass of the French people in resistance to the dictatorships of the totalitarian Powers has been rudely shaken. The Socialist and Communist workmen who obeyed a few weeks ago the mobilisation orders with devotion and punctuality, are no longer held to their duty by the theme of resistance to foreign tyranny. They do not quite understand what high world-object they are now to toil for. If it is merely to be an appeasement of Nazi and Fascist Dictators by concessions to their demands and submission to their wills, why should the hours of work be lengthened?

#### Parable of Optimist and Pessimist

The sunshines on a fair land; leisure is sweet to the working masses. Undoubtedly science and machinery could to-day give an easier and broader life for all but for this external menace which casts its shadow across so many lands.

Is Nazi aggression to be resisted, or are the Western democracies to sit by with folded hands and watch resignedly the formidable events which impend in the centre and east of Europe? We remember the sardonic war-time joke about the optimist and the pessimist. The optimist was the man who did not mind what happened, so long as it did not happen to him. The pessimist was the man who lived with the optimist. Is this, then, to describe our joint or respective futures?

#### France's Unaltered Military Advantages

It is now known that, during the late crisis, Herr Hitler concentrated three-quarters of his armies against Czechoslovakia, and left on the French frontier, to guard his uncompleted defences, a force far inferior to the French army. Everything we have learned of those days shows the solid strength and quality of the French army. The sober confidence expressed in it by its chiefs was confirmed by everything that happened in the mobilisation.

Although the German army is growing stronger month by month, and although Germany possesses double the man-power of France, if must not be forgotten that the French reserves of trained soldiers are at present far larger than those of Germany.

It is only three years since conscription was reintroduced in breach of Treaty engagements, throughout Germany. There are, therefore, only three annual quotas of trained Reservists. These quotas are no doubt numerically equal to five or six annual quotas of French Reservists. But France has twenty quotas of men who have been trained, and for all of these there are well-established and matured formations. Besides this, the shortage of officers in Germany is grievous and cannot be speedily repaired.

#### Cause of Weakness Not Among Workers

Either Herr Hitler must be a desperate gambler, or he must have felt pretty sure that he would be let alone to work his will on the Czech Republic.

As these facts soak into the French nation, they are bound to stir deep feelings. No one who has studied the history of France since 1870 can doubt that a fire is smouldering; but no one can say how and where it will manifest itself.

Too little attention has been paid to the remarkable speech of the Comte de Paris, in which he condemned the capitulation of Munich. This speech should recall to their duty certain elements of the Right who have allowed their alienation from the Republic to lead them to take a poorer view of the strength of their country than is warranted by the circumstances. The reasons why France does not present herself in her full strength at the present time are not to be found among the working masses, who are also the soldiers of France, but in certain strata of the middle-class and the well-to-do. Something of this kind can also be seen in Great Britain.

#### Power to Protect Political Liberties

The two great peoples whose fortunes are interwoven should search their hearts. It is certain that they have only to rouse themselves in their true strength, and in the spirit of old days, to put themselves in a position of security amid present dangers. They still have the power to command and safeguard their future, with which are intertwined the liberties gained for all the world by the long forging of the British Parliamentary system and the swift hard lessons of the French Revolution.

Above all, it is indispensable that renewed exertions and sacrifices should be made by the British and French peoples, and that they should repel as a mortal thrust any manoeuvre to separate them from each other.

*World copyright wholly reserved by* THE DAILY TELEGRAPH AND MORNING POST *and Co-operation.*

(December 1)

## LONDON DAY BY DAY:

MR. CHAMBERLAIN'S umbrella has now been included in the repertory of German cartoonists. The artist who has drawn the cartoon which I reproduce from "Brennessel" ("Stinging Nettle") has also managed to make a pun out of "mein gampf."

He heads his cartoon "The Patron (Schirmherr) of British Foreign Policy." Schirmherr can also be read to mean umbrella-gentleman (schirm-Herr).

The cartoon is more notable for being the first satirising Mr. Chamberlain published in Germany for many months. The caption runs: "We rely on other ideals than those of the authoritarian States."

Why the Prime Minister is shown gazing at the Tower Bridge is a mystery I cannot explain.

#### "Devolution" at the B.B.C.

An inkling of Sir John Reith's coming departure from Broadcasting House was given just over a fortnight ago by the Radio Correspondent of The Daily Telegraph and Morning Post.

He described after a talk with the Director-General how Sir John had completed a devolution of authority so that he could at any time relinquish the controls. He had already handed over many of his former duties to Mr. Cecil Graves.

Sir John was then joking about the slippered case of retirement. Evidently, however, he was quite ready to plunge into a new sphere of activity.

#### Privacy Afloat

One of Sir John Reith's closest friends is Mr. Montagu Norman. They have a com-

*The Umbrella Reaches Germany*

mon dislike of personal publicity.

Last winter Sir John and Lady Reith and Mr. and Mrs. Norman went on a cruise to the West Indies and South America. They travelled, literally, in a class by themselves. The liner's tourist class accommodation had been closed for this "all-first" cruise.

Sir John and Mr. Norman asked to have the tourist saloon opened for their benefit so that they might take their meals in privacy.

#### Premier Caricatured by Nazis. Wightman Cup Captaincy.

#### Inconsiderate Petrol Thief

LAST night I was dining with some friends in Kensington who have a private drive to their house. After dinner I went out to fetch some papers which I had left in the car and found a strong smell of petrol.

The cap of the petrol tank had been removed and a rubber tube inserted. Through this the petrol was being run off into a tin.

Either the thief had been disturbed or inconsiderately had left, meaning to return later. In any case his two-gallon tin had been full for some time, and the rest of my petrol supply had run out on the ground.

A policeman whom I called in said it was the first time he had come across this particularly irritating kind of theft perpetrated on private property.

#### Words Cannot Express ...

THIS is how the overwrought tape machine announced Mr. Chamberlain's departure from Munich:

```
CHAMBERLAIN LEAVES MUNICH, FRI-
DAY.
 .4 :£-.?34)-8, )3%5 ?6 -84 x94
)9, 9, -5 2.20 P.M.
 - - BRITISH UNITED PRESS.
C.2.57 P.M.
```

To make it still more emphatic the message was labelled "Confirmation."

PETERBOROUGH

# AIR RAID PRECAUTIONS

## PROTECTING THE CIVILIAN AGAINST ATTACK

MENTAL and moral preparedness, the first elements of our national defence, depend upon the realisation by the public of the grim fact that a number of air raids will doubtless coincide with the outbreak of hostilities in a new war. It is more than ever essential to our safety that the perilous factor of surprise be mitigated by cool-headedness and calm judgment at such a time; and this state of readiness can only be ours when adequate defence measures can be put into immediate operation at the moment of danger.

### Guarding the Home Front

For more than three years the reconstruction of the nation's naval, military and air defence has been a paramount consideration of the Government. Protection of the civilian population has been termed the fourth line of defence, and much valuable preparatory work has been done in this connection. Unfortunately, however, a number of factors – not the least of which has been the indifference of a greater part of the public – has tended seriously to retard progress in this field. In so far as it has aroused apprehension sufficient to bring about a far greater degree of response of the individual citizen to the educational efforts of the authorities, the recent crisis may therefore be said to have proved a blessing in disguise.

The technique of civilian defence may be simple enough in itself, but it must be thoroughly understood and mastered by every householder if the maximum degree of protection is to be obtained from the measures recommended. For this reason a careful study of the published information made available by the Government should by no means be postponed. It cannot be too much stressed that the whole population of these islands is exposed to the air danger, and that workers and dwellers in large cities and industrial areas are likely to find themselves at a moment's notice in the front line of defence. It may not be realised that the latter constitute about nine-tenths of the total inhabitants of Great Britain, in itself the third most densely populated country in Europe. During the last war, when aerial bombardment was in its infancy, over 8,000 bombs were dropped on England, involving some 1,400 deaths and more than 3,000 other casualties. In a future war we may expect an attack on this scale in a single day.

Air-raid precaution measures, whether public or private, fall under three main categories. These are: gas protection devices, air-raid shelters, and fire-fighting equipment. To these must be added the provision of appropriate sanitation equipment – a most important point which should not be overlooked.

Gas protection devices take the form both of individual respirators and of special filtering devices for changing the air in gas-proof rooms and shelters. In both cases – whether respirators or ventilation apparatus – activated carbon forms the filter substance which removes even the most minute trace of deadly poison gas from the air. In view of the vital importance of this filter material, upon whose perfect functioning our lives may depend, it may well be asked what is the nature of this substance?

Activated carbon is produced from carefully selected coals, carbonised and activated under a special process by which extraordinary powers of rapid and complete absorption of noxious vapours are given to the material. Being itself derived from coal, it is, however, no protection against coal gas; but this form of gas is, of course, never present in bombs.

### Scientifically Built Shelters

In the building of air-raid shelters strength based on scientific design and the use of appropriate materials, is the primary requisite. It cannot be too strongly emphasised, that expert supervision is essential to really reliable construction; and this holds equally true whether the shelter be designed to serve as protection against the effects of explosion or against the effects of incendiary bombs and gas. Experts agree that the high-explosive bomb represents indubitably the chief source of danger to be apprehended from an enemy air attack. Thus there is sound reason for primary concentration upon the splinter and bullet-proof shelter, although the ordinary type of shelter cannot be expected to withstand a direct hit. While it is always preferable, especially for the householder, to incorporate gas-proofing features into the construction, the difference in cost between an efficient splinter-proof shelter and a properly equipped anti-gas chamber is considerable. Where economy is essential it is, there-fore advisable to concentrate upon a strongly constructed shelter of the simplest splinter-proof type, although this should be designed in such a manner that effective gas precautions can be added at any time without serious structural alterations.

### Steel or Concrete-Lined Trenches

For the accommodation of larger numbers of people, a well-thought-out trench system

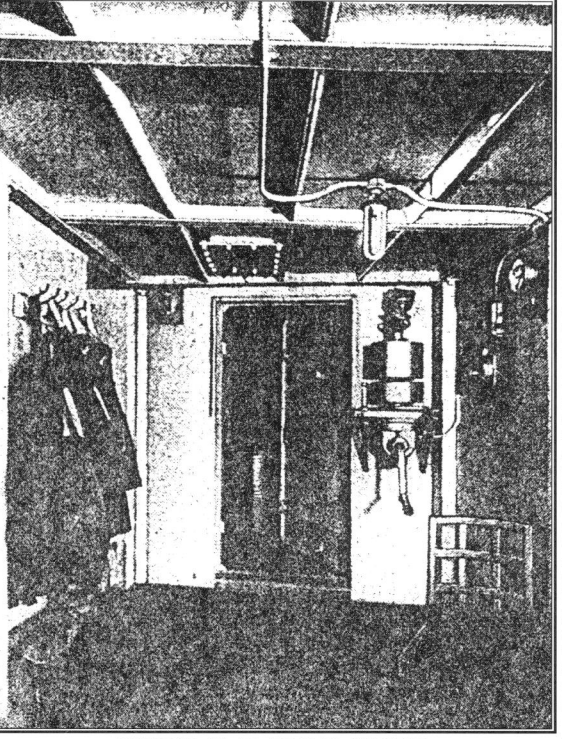

INTERIOR OF AN AIR RAID SHELTER

incorporating a strong steel or concrete lining is on all counts, including that of cost, generally the best solution to the problem. However, the trench system is precluded wherever there is danger from flooding, either from an adjoining river or canal or from burst water mains, or where there is water in the subsoil. In such cases shelters would have to be erected on the ground level, the frame being of steel or concrete, covered as thickly as possible with earth or sandbags.

### Convenient Portable Apparatus

A point to be borne in mind considering the question of the incorporation of sanitary equipment is the probability that existing sanitary surfaces may be out of commission through the disruptive action of high-explo-sive bombs. In this event the use of ordinary domestic equipment between air raids may not be possible, and the presence of alternative arrangements will be found not only a convenience but a definite aid to the maintenance of health.

The provision of suitable closets of the type recommended by the authorities enables the disposal of sewage to be deferred until convenient opportunities present themselves. In the case of an air-raid shelter this would, in all probability, be undertaken during the day time, and the portable nature of the closet enables the sewage to be transported readily.

### Quick-Built Family Shelters

Another type of shelter, which offers the advantage of minimum cost, consists of corrugated steel sheets, 20 gauge thick, made and curved in one length to suit the height and capacity of the chamber to be built. Since the arch is composed of a single piece, the use of bolts, screws, or fitments of any kind is entirely obviated, and erection thus involves the minimum amount of skill. The length of the shelter is determined by the number of corrugated arches used. The shelters can be supplied with a plain end frame with door of gas-proof construction, or, where additional protection against gas is required, with both an air lock and door. After erection the shelter can be covered with earth or sandbags, the right-angle entrance affording complete protection from shell blast. The same kind of corrugated sheeting is used for circular designed family shelters covered with a conical roof, and these can be erected entirely by unskilled labour, no tools other than a shovel being required.

The advantages of concrete construction are utilised in a special design of shelter assembled of precast reinforced concrete ribs, made to form an arch with a joint in the apex.

### Useful Fire-Fighting Equipment

The call for additional fire-fighting equipment to cope with the varied needs of A.R.P. work has been answered by the development of a special type of small, highly mobile fire pumps and engines. One of these designs, eminently suitable for hospitals, villages, factories, country houses and farms, is built on the trailer principle; but its mobility is carried even farther by the fact that the pump unit can be instantly withdrawn from the trailer by one man and wheeled on its pneumatic tyres to a source of water inaccessible even to the small trailer.

(December 3)

# MLLE. SUZANNE LENGLEN

## TENNIS CHAMPION OF WORLD AT 15

**By A. Wallis Myers**

Mlle. Suzanne Lenglen, whose death has occurred in Paris at the age of 39, was not the youngest champion Wimbledon knew – that distinction was held in 1887 by an English girl of 15, Miss Lottie Dod – but she was its greatest artist and its most magnetic personality. By her prowess and publicity she was to prove the unconscious author of a revolution in the physical development of her sex.

Before the French girl's reign began, talented players, many of them perhaps steadier in execution and shrewder in tactics than those who keep Press photographers busy to-day, was subordinate in public interest to the men's game. It was Suzanne's grace and genius, her complete control of the ball in motion, the effortless ease with which she dominated all her opponents, reducing them to impotency, that not only brought fame to this young girl from Picardy, but fired an athletic trail among her sex throughout the world.

Suzanne Lenglen

Born in Complègne on May 24, 1899, she was a delicate only child, and if her father M. Charles Lenglen had not been himself a keen athlete, showing his stamina on the cycle track, his theory that strength can be invoked by methodical training would never have been illustrated in his own daughter.

There were Lenglen legends even in those early days. One of them concerned the iron discipline to which she was subjected in training. The stories were exaggerated. M. Lenglen was not a martinet, but he was a clever and practical coach and determined that his daughter should not defy the laws of physical mechanics and play lawn tennis as so many girls do to the detriment of success, with anatomical strain.

Mlle. Lenglen's first prize was won in the handicap singles at Cannes, when she was 12 years old, and the fact that two years later, when she was only 14, she carried off the championship of Picardy and won the open singles at Lille, reveals the measure of her father's training and her own instinctive skill.

In May, 1914 she celebrated her 15th birthday by winning the world's hard court championship at St. Cloud, an event open to all comers.

Mlle. Lenglen won her first championship at Wimbledon in 1919, after a dramatic challenge round against Mrs. Lambert Chambers, at which King George V. and Queen Mary, watched.

Before she came within a stroke of defeat in a contest indelibly marked in the annals of the Old Wimbledon – for there was never a loose shot in it and both competitors were as level as could be – the French girl had shown signs of physical collapse. From the covered stand her agitated father admonished her to go on, throwing down a brandy ball on to the court to sustain his daughter.

For five successive years she was invincible at Wimbledon, until in 1924, she was forced by illness to retire when playing in the semi-final against Miss McKane – who went on to become the holder. In 1925, however, Suzanne returned, to defeat Miss McKane in two love sets. That was her year of zenith, for she won all three championships both at Wimbledon and St. Cloud.

**(July 5)**

# HOW KEMAL ATATURK CREATED MODERN TURKEY

## GREAT EFFORTS FOR BALKAN PEACE

Kemal Ataturk, President of the Turkish Republic will go down to history as the man who rid Turkey of her Greek invaders in 1922, who won for his country a position of moral and diplomatic equality with the Great Powers, and who expelled the Christian subjects of the former Sultans from the present-day State.

He will also be remembered as the leader or dictator who completely modified social and religious conditions in an area where the people always have been and still are conservative at heart.

Yet at the time of the Armistice he was hardly known abroad. Within his own country the position was different. The reputation he gained during the war had given him the support of a strong party in Turkey, and he showed that their faith in him was not misplaced when in May, 1919, he was given an important post as Inspector-General of the Turkish Forces in Anatolia.

His choice by the Constantinople Government was approved by the Allies and from the moment of his arrival in Anatolia he devoted himself to the organisation of forces that would protect Turkish rights.

Some alarm in Constantinople over his rapidly increasing influence led to his being ordered to return to the capital. He bluntly refused, and was outlawed, whereupon he drew up the famous National Pact which formed the battle cry of the Turks for the next few years.

ELECTED PRESIDENT

In 1920 the first Grand National Assembly met at Angora, and Kemal was elected President. He saw to it that the former irregular bands were replaced by a regular army, and he drew up a military convention with Soviet Russia, which supplied him in return with financial assistance and arms. Almost concurrently public opinion was inflamed by the signature of the Treaty of Sèvres by the Constantinople Government and by the renewed Greek advance in Asia Minor.

In 1921 and 1922 things moved apace. The battle of the Sakaria (August-September, 1921) in which Kemal himself took the command, saw the end of Hellenic military successes. Kemal's prestige rose more and more rapidly, and in September 1922, the Greeks had fled from Asia Minor, the Turks had occupied Smyrna and the late President had been made a Ghazi – an honour reserved for those who have won a striking victory over a Christian enemy.

The Hellenic débâcle marked the completion of the Nationalist military victory. The Western Powers were thereby brought face to face with the necessity of either meeting the Turks on the field of battle or of negotiating with them, and, when France had openly stated her pacific attitude, and the British people had shown their opposition to further fighting, the armistice signed at Mudania in October, recognised Eastern Thrace and Asia Minor as Turkish.

Very shortly after Mr. Lloyd George had retired from the Premiership, the Grand National Assembly proclaimed the end of the Constantinople Government, and the Sultan fled to a British warship. His office was abolished and a cousin of the former ruler elected Khalif. After a conference lasting for many months, the Treaty of Lausanne, signed in July 1923, gave to Turkey practically, if not absolutely, the whole of the conditions claimed in the National Pact.

This, in conjunction with the Allied evacuation of Constantinople, made Mustapha Kemal the creator of modern Turkey.

The Ghazi's régime was a dictatorship; it was supernationalistic and anti-clerical in the extreme. He secured the passage of legislation at will. Ministers depended upon his favour. If Kemal was not himself an actual free thinker, he did everything within his power to decrease the influence of the Moslem imam, and in April 1928, he completely laicized the State by bringing about the repeal of the clauses of the Constitution dealing with religion.

Nothing was more characteristic of Kemal Ataturk than his refusal to exploit his magnificent career as a soldier. He put away his uniforms as soon as his task as soldier was finished. After becoming President of Turkey he never wore uniform. Peace within his frontiers and abroad was his unswerving policy, and he maintained that for him to continue to wear uniform was undesirable, misplaced.

NEVER AT A LOSS IN CONVERSATION

While he rigidly exercised supreme power himself, he would not permit any misuse of authority by subordinates, however highly placed. If he discovered that some modest employee was being harshly treated he would severely chastise those responsible.

A man of great ability, he was never at a loss for a subject of conversation, and within the space of two hours he once gave the foreign diplomats a sample of his knowledge by discussing grammar, politics, history, Darwin, Napoleon, and Lloyd George.

EXPERT POKER-PLAYER

At the annual State ball in Angora it was quite common for him to invite diplomatic representatives of countries of diametrically opposed politics into a corner of the ballroom and draw them into discussion on a subject which afforded him great delight, but which to them meant great discomfort.

He could play as hard as he could work, and one of his favourite games was poker. Games with distinguished and expert players often continued through the night and the President almost always won. But if the differences were too great, and he was winning, he had the habit of pushing his counters into the middle of the table and stating that the game had been played only for fun.

Kemal Ataturk

His generosity became a by-word in Turkey, though he never advertised his gifts. Many orphans of brother officers owe to him their education and secure positions in life. Kemal Ataturk had no thought for personal gain, and he was the enemy of anyone who tried to make unreasonable gain to the detriment of the country or the people. He was undeniably the greatest factor for peace that his part of the world has ever known, and he was the only dictator who had been able fully to realise his goal and pass on without ruining his work.

He used the mailed fist to set Turkey on its feet again, but once he accomplished his aim no former animosity obscured his vision. He made peace with his greatest enemies – the Greeks – and he would tolerate no persecution of the Jews in Turkey. He determined that Turkey should be made strong for the enforcement of peace, and he succeeded in attaining his goal.

**(November 11)**

# HEAD OF MOSCOW ART THEATRE

Constantin Stanislavsky, perhaps the greatest figure in the modern history of the stage, died suddenly yesterday in Moscow at the age of 76. He was director of the Moscow Art Theatre, which he founded with Nemirovitch-Dantchenko 40 years ago.

It has become almost a commonplace in recent years to hear of his being described as towering above all others in the theatre, a genius with supreme gifts in relation not merely to acting but to production.

In every country eager disciples have paid tribute to his remarkable work in Moscow, which has profoundly affected all stage productions.

A man of great driving power, and intensely earnest, he always insisted that actors must show they were actually living their parts and not merely repeating the words; that "personality actors" were unworthy of attention if their technique was defective; and that craftsmanship must assert itself unerringly in the slightest details of production.

A dozen years ago he wrote 'My life in art,' a work that was immediately hailed as a classic, and last year appeared another volume which also attracted great attention, "An actor prepares."

**(August 8)**

# DEATH OF ABBOT OF BUCKFAST

The Right Rev. Dom. Anscar Vonier, Abbot of Buckfast, Devon, died yesterday. He was 63.

He appeared to be in good health at 6.30 last evening when an Abbey attendant visited his room. An hour later he was found dead in his bed, having apparently had a heart attack.

He succeeded the first Abbot in 1906, after escaping death in a shipwreck in which his predecessor lost his life. He was the moving spirit in the rebuilding of the Abbey Church, a task which took 25 years.

**(December 27)**

# REVIVED GLORIES OF THE CIRCUS

## MR. BERTRAM MILLS

## GENIUS AS SHOWMAN

Mr. Bertram Mills, who with something like genius brought back the glory of the circus in its most spectacular form, died on Saturday at Chalfont St. Giles at the age of 65.

His remarkable imagination, his energy and his great organising ability made him a very popular public figure.

When he was 15 he entered his father's coachmaking business at Paddington. Throughout his life he had an extraordinary affection for horses.

At 16 he often travelled on the driver's box of the London to Oxford coach, and was frequently allowed to take the reins. In 1936 he acted as coachman to "Mr. Pickwick" on the run from Charing Cross to Rochester.

In his young days he travelled frequently on the Continent to attend shows at which his father was exhibiting carriages, and in that way made a point of visiting any circus he could find.

At the end of the Great War – during which he was in the R.A.S.C. – he was pondering over future activities when he went to a circus at Olympia. "I'd eat my hat" he remarked to the late Lord Woolavington "if I couldn't put on a better show than that." Thereupon he was challenged to do so in a year's time.

Mr. Bertram Mills

WORLD TOURS FOR TALENT

Thus began a great annual venture which led to his touring the world in search of new acts. He journeyed for thousands of miles each year and spent large sums in securing novelties. The big organisation he developed attracted many well-known people, and no one was more fascinated by the circus folk he assembled than writers and artists. Mr. Mills gave them every facility.

Dame Laura Knight, who toured with the circus on several occasions and spent much time at Olympia during the annual performances, painted several well-known Academy pictures with the circus as their theme. Lady Eleanor Smith also found inspiration as a writer in the same surroundings.

**(April 18)**

# MR. CHARLES CRUFT

## FOUNDER OF FAMOUS DOG SHOW

Mr. Charles Cruft, founder and organiser of Cruft's Dog Show died on Saturday in London, aged 86.

He first thought of starting his show, now the greatest annual event of its kind in the world, 50 years ago. He was then in business as a maker of dog foods in a firm in which he started as a messenger. The first Cruft's Show had only 500 entries; in recent years the total has reached nearly 10,000.

It was thought that the Agricultural Hall, in Islington, would be too large for a dog show, but the first entries included dogs belonging to Queen Victoria and the Prince of Wales. Queen Victoria sent a collie and three pomeranians. The Prince showed an arctic dog and four bassett hounds.

Under such Royal approval and support, Cruft's Show prospered. The Royal family has continued to send dogs. King George V. regularly sent his retrievers and spaniels, King Edward VIII., when Prince of Wales, entered an alsatian, and the Duke of Gloucester a mastiff.

He did not keep a dog. A Londoner, living in London, he said that a dog needed room and air. In his home he had a cat.

**(September 12)**

# DEATH OF LORD HAWKE

## ONE OF CRICKET'S GREATEST CAPTAINS

No one in the history of cricket bore a more honoured name than Lord Hawke, whose death occurred yesterday in an Edinburgh nursing home at the age of 78.

He had been president of the Yorkshire County Cricket since 1898, was a former president of the M.C.C. and from 1932 until last April was treasurer of the M.C.C.

In his day he was perhaps the greatest personality in the cricket world; to the Yorkshire eleven, which he captained for 28 seasons, he was an inspiration.

The barony he held was created in 1776, and his father, a Lincolnshire rector, succeeded to it on the death of his cousin. Martin Bladen Hawke was 10 at that time, and seven years later went to Eton. There he was a splendid athlete. He became captain of the football team, and as a runner his success may be judged from the fact that he won the quarter mile, the mile, the hurdles, and the steeplechases. But his outstanding interest was in cricket, and it was with an excellent reputation he went to Magdalene College, Cambridge.

Very quickly he became a Blue. He was not a great batsman, but a good one. He did not bowl, and as a fieldsman he was active rather than superb. Yet from the outset he dominated his fellows by his inherent qualities of leadership and his high sense of values.

HIS TEAM FIRST

To him it was not the individual but the game that mattered. Throughout his long career he condemned anything that savoured of playing for averages; he was always annoyed when individual performances were made to the detriment of a team's play. At all times he played for his side and not for himself. His personal performances neither elated nor depressed him. If he had scored 90 and thought it better for the match he should get out than reach the hundred, he would do so without the slightest regret.

He became a member of the Yorkshire team in 1882, and in the following year, when he was 22, began his great period of captaincy which was to last until the end of the 1910 season. It included one remarkable spell in which the Yorkshire side went for nearly three years, without losing a match.

He formed the opinion that the professionals had been "doing themselves too well." During a county match he noted with displeasure that one player, for whom he had a great liking, was a little tipsy. That sort of thing, he announced, must stop. He sent the man off the field and told him that if such conduct occurred again he would be dismissed from the Yorkshire eleven.

SENT PLAYER OFF

Shortly afterwards the offence was repeated, and Lord Hawke at once adopted the disciplinary measures he had threatened.

He established a real bond of affection with all members of the team, achieving a spirit of camaraderie that was in every way noteworthy. Yet in his staunch and consistent support of the professional he held tenaciously to the belief that the captain must always be an amateur, and long-remembered was his exclamation of a few years ago, in relation to Test matches: "Pray God no professional may ever captain England."

A remark of this kind came characteristically from one who never hesitated when discussing cricket, to give blunt expression to his opinion.

**(October 11)**

# MISS PEARL WHITE

Miss Pearl White, who became famous in the days of silent films, died yesterday in Paris.

She was a beautiful American actress who had played for some time in small touring companies, when she was attracted to Hollywood, then in the early stages of its development. By exploiting her skill as an acrobat and her liking for daring feats, she became the central figure in films depicting all kinds of thrilling adventure.

They were of the "to be continued in our next" variety, and the heroine was always left in a position of such startling peril that filmgoers were supposed to wait with some anxiety for the showing of the following week's instalment.

In 1914 her "Perils of Pauline" appeared and "The Adventures of Elaine" followed. The success was such that Pearl White was credited with receiving a salary of £1,000 per week. Dizzy adventures on the brink of a precipice, on railway lines in front of an approaching train, or in a cellar containing slowly rising water were among the many scenes she depicted.

There were occasions when she was responsible for some extremely hazardous feats, and she had more than one accident.

Shortly after the novelty of such films had worn off she retired, and for some years past she had lived in France on the fortune she amassed. She attributed her ill-health to the after-effects of one of her accidents, and her failing eyesight to the powerful glare of the old film studio lights.

**(August 5)**

# D'ANNUNZIO, ONCE ITALY'S IDOL

## FIUME'S POET-DICTATOR

**By George Fyfe**

There was probably no more picturesque personality in the world than Gabriele d'Annunzio – poet, novelist, dramatist, and passionate patriot of Italy. He has died at the age of 74.

He reconciled qualities that were full of contradictions. He wrote poems and threw bombs. He was an exquisite who revelled in luxury yet cheerfully endured hardships.

He was accused of being a decadent dilettante, yet astonished everyone by his bravery. He liked seclusion and became for 12 months the noisy despot of a city.

An incurable romanticist, he was able to frame in the most practical way the complete constitution of a new country.

A fine writer who could also be a man of action, d'Annunzio was a remarkable mixture of arrogance, egotism, theatricality, idealism, fanaticism, courage, and oratory. He could not say anything simply; he must always act with a flourish.

GABRIELE D'ANNUNZIO

When he was dropping mines he became a technical expert, but at the same time he was talking about the darkened sea with its "innumerable pulsations," and its "nocturnal phosphorescence." The new moon was like "a burning hand full of sulphur," the long torpedo tubes "beasts in ambuscade."

Yet he roused the enthusiasm of millions of his fellow-countrymen and never to such telling effect as in the most remarkable adventure of his exciting career – his seizure of Fiume.

The war had been over for some months and d'Annunzio had gone into retirement as a national hero. Then, in September, 1919, the inhabitants of Fiume found that their city was to be given to the newly-created kingdom of Jugoslavia; that the Italian troops were to be reduced to a handful; that the National Council was to be dissolved, and that English and Americans were to come in to preserve order.

### HOW HE SEIZED FIUME

The Italians of Fiume demanded that they should be left in what they described as their mother country of Italy. Help was asked from d'Annunzio.

He promptly responded. At the head of a small army he marched into Fiume. He was the liberator.

A startled Italian Government took action against him. The members of it, relying for food supplies on the Allies, did not want international complications, and demanded that d'Annunzio should give up Fiume.

He replied by annexing it. The nation supported him; the Army and the Navy and the Air Force provided him with determined support.

The Government replied with a blockade, but for a year d'Annunzio held out. He developed ideas of conquest. He felt that Fiume should be capital of some kind of Dalmatian Empire and that he should be its chief. He established a Regency and drew up a remarkable constitution.

### HIS PALACE SHELLED

The Italian Government, however, was determined to carry out the Treaty of Rapallo and, to show they were in earnest, directed a few shells from a warship at d'Annunzio's palace.

The population decided to submit. Large numbers of people had become tired of the poet dictator; moreover, they could see that they no longer enjoyed outside support.

He had handed over his authority to the municipal council, and the demands of the Government were obeyed. Then d'Annunzio retired to private life and was not heard of for a long time.

There was general agreement that d'Annunzio's actions were ill-advised and might have had very serious effects for his country, but there was no tendency in Italy to condemn him unduly. His war exploits were remembered. They were certainly remarkable.

**(May 2)**

# Sir HENRY NEWBOLT

## POET OF PATRIOTISM AND CHIVALRY

Sir Henry Newbolt, the poet, who practised as a barrister for 12 years and also became the official Naval Historian of the Great War, has died in London at the age of 75.

His fame was such that an unusual honour was paid him in 1927, a tablet being erected at Bilston, Staffordshire, to mark the vicarage in which he was born. He jokingly remarked that as the first Englishman to see a memorial unveiled to him in his lifetime, he feared there be some chagrin elsewhere, and he would take care to acquaint his friend Mr. G. B. Shaw with what had happened.

Sir Henry, who was knighted in 1915 and became a Companion of Honour in 1922, was the elder son of the late Rev. H.F. Newbolt. He was educated at Clifton, where he had as a great friend Sir Arthur Quiller-Couch, and at Corpus Christi College, Oxford, where another distinguished poet, Robert Bridges, had been nearly 20 years earlier.

### "ADMIRALS ALL"

On leaving Oxford he entered Lincoln's Inn and was called in 1887, but while still practising at the Bar, began to write. In 1897 he suddenly became famous with the publication of "Admirals All" a volume which included not only the spirited ballad from which it took its name, but "Drake's Drum," "The Guides at Cabul" and "Ionicus."

The wave of national pride which rose high with Queen Victoria's Diamond Jubilee, no doubt had its part in carrying the gallant sea songs to success. The new poet was very much the man of the hour.

But every critic who knew his business and read "The Guides at Cabul" knew that there was nothing "momentary" about Newbolt. He was plainly a poet of the right royal line. Limited he might be – the future would show – but the authentic virtue was in him.

Next year came "The Island Race," and his position was defined. His later poems, "The Sailing of the Long Ships," in 1902, and some others neither added to nor diminished his reputation. There were among them some exquisite things, but of the same kind as "The Island Race."

Limited he was, or chose to be, till the end; love he left severely alone, the "obstinate questionings" of many a great poet did not trouble him, he had no new revelations of Nature to reveal to us – so one may labour out a catalogue. But patriotism no one has ever sung more nobly, no one has expressed with more beauty the faith of chivalry.

The same sort of judgment may be passed on his technical accomplishment. He did not attempt more than a small part of the music of poetry. The ringing ballad, the stately anthem manner, the subtle and elaborate harmonies, of slow lyric measures, to these he confined himself. But his use of them was consummate. Whatever he did was an exemplar of its kind.

In all his magnificent music about "the sound and splendour of England's war" there is nothing flamboyant or strained. We have no verses in our language which breathe a more eager patriotism than Newbolt's. There is no patriotic poetry in our language or any other cleaner of violence or hate or the baseness of pride in conquest.

**(April 22)**

# M. KAREL CAPEK

## CZECHOSLOVAK AUTHOR AND PLAYWRIGHT

M. Karel Capek the Czechoslovak author, who died of pneumonia in Prague on Christmas Day, had not quite reached the age of 49. His health was not robust, but he had never let that fact subdue his spirit.

He was a prolific, author, and, in the main, a cheerful one, who saw humanity with a satirical but not a jaundiced eye. His early death is a great misfortune.

His work took many forms. He began by writing short stories with his brother Josef, and when he turned his attention to the theatre he still had his collaborator with him in "The Insect Play." In "R.U.R." however, he tackled the subject of man and the machine alone.

Both these plays were produced with success in London in 1923, and made Karel Capek's name famous. Neither play has dropped out of remembrance.

Meanwhile, M. Capek had become director of the National Theatre in Prague, and later became a journalist. During the recent political crisis his voice was heard from Prague frequently on the wireless appealing for calm and confidence.

In spite of his full and busy public life he found time to write more plays, many novels and a series of books of travel essays, of which "Letters From England" had, naturally enough, a special vogue in this country. Apart from one or two big political figures he had probably the greatest international reputation of any Czech of his time.

**(December 27)**

# CHALIAPIN'S MANY GIFTS

## GREAT ACTOR AS WELL AS SINGER

**By Richard Capell**

Feodor Chaliapin more properly Sheliapin, died yesterday at the age of 65.

Most musical executants, however brilliant pass away and are as though they had never been, but the name and reputation of this extraordinary man – of his kind the greatest artist, with his combination of vocal and histrionic genius of the lyric stage of his time, and possibly in the whole history of music – will never be forgotten.

Purely as a singer he was supremely gifted, with a basso-cantant voice of a range, power, flexibility, expressiveness and technical accomplishment that to-day has not its like in the world.

But Chaliapin, if he had not been a singer at all, might have been equally famous as the greatest actor in the Europe of his time. And those who saw him at work at rehearsal at Covent Garden or at Sir Thomas Beecham's season of Russian opera at the Lyceum Theatre in 1931 realised that his instinct for mise-en-scéne and theatrical effect would have made of him a supreme producer or stage regisseur, if some misfortune had rendered him incapable of singing or acting.

### OF HUMBLE BIRTH

Added to the prestige of his genius and his person – he was physically a giant – was the romance of a life-story that reads like a novel.

Chaliapin was born at Kazan on the Volga in 1873. He was of the humblest birth, and as a child and youth suffered extremes of privation. He himself gave in his autobiography an unvarnished tale of his childhood in the underworld. His father drank, as did nearly everyone else in their unlovely slum, and beat his wife sometimes to unconsciousness. Chaliapin says:

"One day I felt sure she was dead, and I howled with despair. As soon as she came to she caressed me, saying stoically, "It is nothing'."

As a lad Chaliapin worked for a time as a stevedore on the Volga, and he tells us:

"We unloaded flour. The five-pood (180lb) sacks wore me out till I almost lost consciousness. At night I felt stinging pains in the neck; and in legs and loins the bones might have been broken. ... My mother began to make and sell patties of fish and berries. She did washing on board the boats. And still hunger gripped our entrails."

It was not many years before Chaliapin was singing at a grand duke's house at a party given in honour of the Tsar, and he describes how:

"The Grand Duke Sergei Mikhailovitch brought me some champagne in a Venetian goblet on a silver salver. Drawing himself to his full height, he said, still holding the tray, "Chaliapin, the Tsar has asked me to offer you a glass of champagne to thank you for your singing, and so that you may drink his Majesty's health'."

Between his stevedore days and this brilliant scene Chaliapin had sung with a touring opera, had been given serious tuition by Oussatoff at Tiflis, and after appearing at St. Petersburg had made his name at Moscow at the age of 23.

Two motives inspired his art – a passion for national Russian music and his faith, as an actor, in the force of words. He once said: "It is a small thing to sing a song or ballad. What is indispensible is to understand the sense of the words one utters and the feelings that dictated the choice of those words." And again: "In opera one should sing as one speaks."

### FIRST LONDON APPEARANCE

When Chaliapin first sang in London, at the season of Russian opera at Drury Lane in 1913, sponsored by Sir Joseph Beecham, he was at the same time at the height of his powers and already an almost legendary figure. In 1913 and 1914 he appeared as Boris Godounoff, as Ivan the Terrible in "The Maid of Pskoff," and in "Prince Igor," "Khovanstchina," and other works. To Londoners of the time it was the revelation of a new music and a new art.

Never afterwards was Chaliapin heard to such advantage, for in his post-war appearances at Covent Garden in 1928 and 1929 in Boito's "Mefistofele," in Gounod's "Faust" and in Rossini's "Barber" the company surrounding him had other traditions, and he seemed to belong to a different world, while the Russian company at the Lyceum in 1931 was a mere ghost of that of 1913-14.

During the war Chaliapin was in Russia, and at the time of the Revolution he took up the democratic cause, delighting in the power which his gift of oratory exerted over the masses. But he seized the earliest opportunity of escaping from Leninism.

He reappeared in London in 1921 as a concert singer, and for years his appearances at the Albert Hall were enormously popular, although his histrionic impulse led him more and more to exaggeration, and, indeed, to paraphrases of the music in hand.

In private life Chaliapin was a man of infinite vitality. he was as proud as Lucifer, but could exert an irresistible charm. Along with egotistic, shrewd and simple elements, characteristics of the Volga peasant, went an unmistakable greatness. There was no possible company in which he was not the dominating figure.

**(April 15)**

# LADY OTTOLINE MORRELL

The death occurred yesterday at Tunbridge Wells of Lady Ottoline Morrell, wife of Mr. Philip Morrell. She was half-sister of the Duke of Portland and sister of Lord Charles Cavendish-Bentinck.

Lady Ottoline Morrell, who was 64, possessed pronounced literary and artistic tastes which brought her the friendship of many distinguished writers and painters. Her collection of contemporary pictures was a noteworthy one, which included a celebrated portrait of herself by Augustus John, and another by James Pryde.

She married Mr. Philip Morrell in 1902. He was formerly Liberal M.P. for Henley and Burnley. There is one daughter, Mrs. Victor Goodman.

The funeral takes place at Welbeck on Monday, and there is to be a memorial service on Tuesday at 2.30 p.m. at St. Martin-in-the Fields.

**(April 22)**

# THE COUNTESS OF STRATHMORE

## MOTHER OF THE QUEEN

The Countess of Strathmore, mother of the Queen, whose death was reported in the later editions of The Daily Telegraph and Morning Post yesterday, was 75 years of age. She died at her London home, Cumberland-mansions, Portman-square, W.

Nina Cecilia, Countess of Strathmore and Kinghorne, Dame Grand Cross of the Victorian Order, and Dame of the Order of St. John of Jerusalem, was the eldest and only surviving daughter of the late Rev. Charles W.F. Cavendish-Bentinck, who was a grandson of the third Duke of Portland.

She married the Earl of Strathmore and Kinghorne in 1881, and the union was an extremely happy one. When they celebrated their golden wedding in Glamis Castle, more than 1,500 people attended the garden party, including the King and Queen, Princess Elizabeth and Princess Margaret. King George V. and Queen Mary sent a magnificent gold cup.

Among the presents was a picture in tapestry and framed in gold, bearing the words, "Designed and embroidered by Cecilia, Countess of Strathmore, and presented to her husband on the occasion of their golden wedding."

### PRIDE IN HER GARDEN

This little gift provided evidence of the great skill Lady Strathmore had always possessed as a needlewoman. On the valance of the canopy of a four-poster at Glamis, she worked the names of her children and the dates of their births. The great four-poster in the room of the castle in which Prince Charlie slept has hangings and a coverlet of brilliant gold silk embroidered by Lady Strathmore. They are exact copies of the originals preserved in another part of the castle.

But as a gardener she was also active, and the famous herb garden at Glamis was her particular pride. A book, kept in the library, contains a list of all the herbs in the different beds. Lady Strathmore discovered how to preserve rose petals in their original colour, and only the wife of one of her gardeners shared the secret.

At charity bazaars she sold the rose petals for use in place of lavender, Orchids from the hothouse at Glamis, pot-plants and pottery figurines of old Scottish soldiers collected by Lady Strathmore were also sold by her for charity.

**(June 24)**

# BIGGEST TEST VICTORY

## AUSTRALIANS COLLAPSE ON PERFECT WICKET

**By Howard Marshall**

ENGLAND won the final Test match at the Oval by the immense margin of an innings and 579 runs. This is by far the most decisive victory ever recorded, and it is the first time England have beaten Australia at the Oval since 1926.

With Bradman and Fingleton so unluckily out of action, Australia had no chance whatever, and they made very little real attempt to prolong the agony. Their last wicket fell at 20 mins to four, and we were left to ponder the lessons of this extraordinary game.

One thing is surely certain. There will never again be a timeless Test match in this country. We may be glad that England shared the honours of the series, and it is extremely satisfactory that in Hutton we have found a batsman who can rival the Australians in concentration, endurance and skill.

The match, indeed, became a trial of endurance. All the real cricket was knocked out of it by a wicket so unhelpful to the bowlers that batting was largely a matter of patience and physical stamina.

This brings us to our second lesson. The authorities must inevitably be forced to take drastic action about the over-preparation of wickets.

The turf at the Oval was as perfect yesterday, so several of the players assured me, as it was on the first morning of the match. Tuesday's hot sun had perhaps given it a little more pace, but that, if anything, was in favour of the stroke player.

BALANCE DESTROYED

Even if we admit that Australia took the field with an exceptionally weak opening attack, it remains manifestly ridiculous that the balance between bowler and batsman should be deliberately destroyed.

The conditions in which this match was played were, therefore, totally unfitted for a fair test of cricketing ability. The toss became decisive, and Australia, but for the uncetainty about the weather, might as well have ceded the match to England as soon as Bradman had called incorrectly.

Test matches should show us cricket at its best, which means that they must be played upon wickets which give the bowler a reasonable chance. If such wickets are unobtainable at the Oval, Test matches should be played elsewhere, and if this is the view taken by those in authority, England's prodigious total will have served the cause of cricket very handsomely.

MACABRE INTEREST

I will not deny that the match has had a macabre interest of its own. We shall long remember the cumulative tension in Hutton's innings, and Bradman, with his own great record in jeopardy, crouching desperately at silly mid-off, hoping against hope for the catch which never came.

We shall remember too, the brilliant Australian fielding, sustained for 15 hours without a moment's flagging, and in face of that crushing total and that constant battering. In this phase of the game Bradman won for himself fresh renown, and it was bitterly ironical that he should fracture a shinbone when in despair he tried to rest his weary bowlers by going on himself.

If we accept the conditions in which the match was played, as, obviously, we must, it is at least highly encouraging that England rose so magnificently to the occasion.

HUTTON'S MATCH

It was, beyond question, Hutton's match, and never will a young player have a greater or more thoroughly deserved triumph. Leyland and Hardstaff played their parts finely, and yesterday Bowes, bowling splendidly, completed the Australian rout. Yorkshire's share in England's victory has been a noble one, and the greatest of competing counties has just cause for pride.

We may reasonably argue that the match vindicates our belief that English cricket is in the ascendant, and when we next meet Australia it will be with considerably augmented confidence in our own strength.

COMPLETE SCORE

ENGLAND

| | |
|---|---|
| Hutton c. Hassett, b. O'Reilly | 364 |
| Edrich, lbw b. O'Reilly | 12 |
| Leyland run out | 187 |
| †W.R. Hammond lbw, b. F. Smith | 59 |
| Paynter, lbw, b. O'Reilly | 0 |
| Compton, b. Waite | 1 |
| Hardstaff, not out | 169 |
| *Wood, c and b. Barnes | 53 |
| Verity, not out | 8 |
| B22, l-b 19, w 1, n-b 8 | 50 |
| Total (7 wkts dec) | 903 |

K. Farnes, Bowes did not bat.

AUSTRALIA

| | |
|---|---|
| C.L.Badcock, c Hardstaff, b Bowes | 0 |
| W.A. Brown, c Hammond, b Leyland | 69 |
| S.J. McCabe c Edrich, b Farnes | 14 |
| A.L.Hassett, c Compton, b Edrich | 42 |
| S. Barnes, b Bowes | 41 |
| B.A. Barnett,c Wood, b Bowes | 2 |
| M.G. Waite, b Bowes | 8 |
| W.J. O'Reilly, c. Wood, b Bowes | 0 |
| L. O'B. Fleetwood-Smith, not out | 16 |
| †D.G. Bradman, absent hurt | 0 |
| J.H. Fingleton, absent hurt | 0 |
| B 4, l-b 2, n-b 3 | 9 |
| Total | 201 |

Second Innings

| | |
|---|---|
| C.L. Badcock, b. Bowes | 9 |
| W.A. Brown, c. Edrich, b Farnes | 15 |
| S.J. McCabe, c. Wood b Farnes | 2 |
| A.L. Hassett, lbw b Bowes | 10 |
| S. Barnes, lbw, b Verity | 33 |
| B.A. Barnett, b Farnes | 46 |
| M.G. Waite, c. Edrich, b Verity | 0 |
| W.J. O'Reilly, not out | 7 |
| L. O'B. Fleetwood-Smith, c. Leyland, b Farnes | 0 |
| D.G. Bradman, absent hurt | 0 |
| J.H. Fingleton, absent hurt | 0 |
| B 1 | 1 |
| Total | 123 |

FALL OF THE WICKETS

| 1 | 2 | 3 | 4 | 5 | 6 | 7 | 8 |
|---|---|---|---|---|---|---|---|
| 15 | 18 | 35 | 41 | 115 | 115 | 117 | 123 |

BOWLING

ENGLAND – First Innings

| | O. | M. | R. | W. |
|---|---|---|---|---|
| Waite | 72 | 16 | 150 | 1 |
| McCabe | 38 | 8 | 85 | 0 |
| O'Reilly | 85 | 26 | 178 | 3 |
| F-Smith | 87 | 11 | 298 | 1 |
| Barnes | 38 | 3 | 84 | 1 |
| Hassett | 13 | 2 | 52 | 0 |
| Bradman | 3 | 2 | 6 | 0 |

O'Reilly bowled 7 no-balls, Fleetwood-Smith 1 no-ball, and Waite 1 wide.

AUSTRALIA – First Innings

| | O. | M. | R. | W. |
|---|---|---|---|---|
| Farnes | 13 | 2 | 54 | 1 |
| Bowes | 19 | 3 | 49 | 5 |
| Edrich | 10 | 2 | 55 | 1 |
| Verity | 5 | 1 | 15 | 0 |
| Leyland | 3.1 | 0 | 11 | 1 |
| Hammond | 2 | 0 | 8 | 0 |

Edrich bowled 2 no-balls, Hammond 1.

Second Innings

| | O. | M. | R. | W. |
|---|---|---|---|---|
| Farnes | 12.1 | 1 | 63 | 4 |
| Bowes | 10 | 3 | 25 | 2 |
| Leyland | 5 | 0 | 19 | 0 |
| Verity | 7 | 3 | 15 | 2 |

Umpires: Chester, Walden

**(August 25)**

## RECORD-SMASHING TEST

Hutton established a world's "endurance" record for the longest individual innings – 13 hours 20 minutes.

His 364 beat Bradman's 334 at Leeds in 1930, the previous highest in an England-Australia Test; passed Hammond's 336 not out against New Zealand at Auckland in 1933 (formerly the biggest innings in any Test), and made a record for the Oval, exceeding Bobby Abel's 357 for Surrey v. Somerset in 1899.

Hutton and Leyland, by putting on 382 set up a record for the second England wicket in a Test against Australia. They beat the 188 by Sutcliffe and Hammond at Sydney in 1932.

Hardstaff, who scored his first Test century against Australia, and Hutton, in adding 215, created a new record for the sixth England wicket, beating the 186 by Hammond and Ames at Lord's this season.

England's total of 903 for seven (declared), exceeding their 658 for eight (declared) at Nottingham in June, was not only their highest against Australia, but the biggest in any Test. Australia's highest is 729 for six (declared) at Lord's in 1930.

The England total is also the biggest made in a first-class match in this country, beating Yorkshire's 887 v. Warwickshire at Edgbaston in 1896.

Three Yorkshiremen (Hutton 364; Leyland, 187, and Wood, 53) obtained 604 of the score in an innings lasting 15 hours and a quarter – the longest in Test history.

# TIMELESS TESTS TO END

If Australia accepts a proposal passed by the Advisory County Cricket Committee, in London yesterday, there will be no more timeless Test matches.

The recommendation, which is fully expected to be confirmed by the M.C.C., is that future Tests in both countries should be limited to 30 hours' play – five days of six hours each in England and six days of five hours each in Australia.

Last summer the first four Tests between the countries were limited to four days of six hours each and the fifth Test was played to the finish.

It was in the fifth Test that Hutton made the record score of 364, and the match won by England by an innings and 579 runs, lasted four days.

In Australia, under the present rules, every Test is played to a finish.

**(November 23)**

THE HIGHEST INDIVIDUAL SCORE in a Test match was made yesterday at the Oval by Hutton, with 364. Above, he is being congratulated by D. G. Bradman, who with 334 previously held the record for the England-Australia series. On the right, Hardstaff is offering his hand.

# BRITAIN'S EMPHATIC WALKER CUP WIN

**By George Greenwood**

AFTER 16 years of untiring effort, Britain has beaten the United States in the Walker Cup contest. The victory gained at St. Andrews – 7 matches to 4, with one halved – admits of no equivocation; it is both emphatic and decisive. Thus has the spell cast by America over Britain's amateur golfers at last been broken.

This was the tenth contest between the two countries, the previous nine having been won by the United States. While failing to make it "ten straight" – their battle cry – the visit of the American players has not been barren of results, for they take back with them the Amateur Championship.

This, no doubt, is some consolation for their loss of the Walker Cup, which, I strongly suspect, was wholly unexpected. Britain's success greeted with frantic delight by 15,000 spectators scampering hither and thither in the rain, has shown conclusively that by intelligent captaincy, and the encouragement of the young players – a lesson I have been preaching for years – we have nothing to fear from America's so-called super-golfers.

Having taken possession of the Cup, there is no reason why we should not hold it for just as long a period as the United States. They will probably have different ideas on the subject. In any event, we must expect a strong and determined challenge when the next match comes to be played in America, two years hence.

But there will be no cause for alarm if Britain pursues the same policy which produced so unqualified a triumph as on this occasion. In a chat which I had with my old friend Frances Ouimet, the American captain, after the excitement of the match had died down, I gathered that he was not altogether displeased at Britain's victory.

While it is only human to desire success. Ouimet is shrewd enough to know that it is possible to have too much of a good thing, and in all conscience America has had a surfeit in this respect.

"All good things must come to an end some time or other, and speaking for my boys and the American people at large, we are delighted you have won," said Ouimet.

He added: "We did our best, but that wasn't good enough. In the British players we have faced one of the greatest golf teams that has ever been assembled."

That is true enough, but success would not have attended their efforts unless the players themselves were inspired with the feeling that they could break down the American monopoly.

While in no sense attempting to minimise Britain's triumph, I feel bound to say that, in my opinion, the American team, both in strength and personalities, was not comparable to those which have previously visited this country.

I am prepared to wager that when the next Walker Cup match is played the American team is constituted far differently from the one that has met its first defeat.

**(June 7)**

# HON. P. BEATTY'S DERBY VICTORY

**From A Special Correspondent**

The Hon. Peter Beatty, whose horse, Bois Roussel, gained a thrilling victory at Epsom yesterday, is one of the youngest owners ever to have won the Derby. He is the brother of Earl Beatty, and is 28

The result of the race, with owners, jockeys, and starting prices, was:

1. – Bois Roussel (Hon. P Beatty), ridden by E.C. Elliott, 20 to 1

2. – Scottish Union (Mr. James V. Rank), B. Carslake, 8 to 1.

3. – Pasch (Mr. H.E. Morriss), G. Richards, 9 to 4.

A record for any single race in England was made by the Totalisor, the turnover being £53,081. The previous record was £42,150 on the Royal Hunt Cup at Ascot last year. The odds paid by the Tote on Bois Roussel were 44 to 1.

Mr. Beatty paid £8,000 for his horse. His winnings in stake money on the Derby were £9,228. When he led the horse into the unsaddling enclosure, the first person to greet him was the Aga Khan, who wrung his hand and said: "I offered to go halves with you, didn't I?"

LITTLE BACKING IN FRANCE

It was the Aga Khan's son, Prince Aly Khan, who bought Bois Roussel for Mr. Beatty after the horse had won his only race at Longchamp. Although the horse came from France very little money was staked on him there for the Derby.

It was not until some weeks after Bois Roussel's arrival at Beckhampton that Fred Darling, the trainer realised that the colt was fully up to the high standard demanded in the Derby.

**(June 2)**

# LOUIS BEATS SCHMELING IN FIRST ROUND

## FIGHT OVER IN TWO MINUTES

**From A Special Correspondent**

YANKEE STADIUM, New York City,
Wednesday Night.

Eighty thousand spectators paid nearly $1,000,000 for one of the shortest, most one-sided fights on record here to-night when they watched with incredible eyes, Joe Louis the Alabama negro, knock out Max Schmeling for the heavyweight championship of the world in 2 min 18 sec.

Louis, the champion, thus avenged the knock-out he himself suffered at the hands of Schmeling in 12 rounds two years ago.

The dramatic suddenness of it bewildered everyone. People had hardly begun to shout when it was all over.

Louis had said: "I will come out fighting. I will never give Schmeling a chance to settle down this time. His famous right hand will never come into action."

Brave words, they seemed, but never were words more truly spoken. Louis did indeed come out fighting to-night. As soon as Referee Donovan had finished his lecture to them on clean breaks and the like they retired to their corners. They turned as the gong was struck, and the negro walked straight into the German with his soft, swift tread.

DOWN AFTER 50 SECONDS

Hardly had the fight begun – after 50 sec. to be precise – than Schmeling was down. It seemed impossible, Schmeling rose almost at once, and spectators thought it was merely a slip. It was something far worse than that.

Just before he fell he had received a terrific short right-hand punch in the middle of the stomach. Only those at the ring-side could have realised the force of that perfectly timed punch. It was followed at once by upward hooks, left and right.

Louis knew what had happened. He saw the hazy look in Schmeling's eyes, and coolly, but with relentless speed, stepped in close and chopped his opponent to either side of the jaw.

Down went the German a second time. This time for a slightly longer count.

When Schmeling rose again, Louis went in for the finish. Vainly did Schmeling put up his hands, endeavouring to guard his jaw.

A dig to the stomach forced him instinctively to lower his right elbow, and over shot the famous Louis left hook. We at the ringside heard the crack of that blow plainly. It was the punch that won, though followed in the same smooth action by a right.

TOWEL THROWN IN

Schmeling tumbled backwards, turned as he fell, and was finished. His seconds threw in the towel, and the referee signalled the fight over. Even at the count of ten Schmeling was still unconscious, and several minutes elapsed before he was able to get off his stool and congratulate the negro.

Louis was 6lb the heavier, and 8 1/2 years the younger. The difference in age counted most, for Schmeling fit though he looked, was plainly slower than he used to be.

Never a speedy heavyweight, always a slow starter, the ex-champion to-night was so slow that he never started at all. I cannot recall that he struck a punch worthy of the name.

**(June 23)**

# MEGAN TAYLOR'S WORLD SKATING TITLE

**From Our Own Correspondent**

STOCKHOLM, Sunday.

Miss Megan Taylor, the 17-year-old Manchester girl, to-day wrested the women's world amateur skating championship from Miss Cecilia Colledge, also aged 17. Miss Colledge won the title last year – the first after Miss Sonja Henie, the Norwegian, had turned professional.

Miss Taylor's victory came after a keen fight and was greeted with thunderous applause.

In yesterday's obligatory figure-skating contest she was leading after five figures, but was passed by Miss Colledge in the seventh figure.

More than 10,000 tickets were sold in advance for to-day's fancy-skating contest due to be held in the Stockholm open-air stadium.

A thaw overnight caused the competition to be transferred to an indoor rink accommodating only 2,000 spectators.

Every seat and square inch of standing room was filled, and thousands of people were turned back at the gates, where mounted police controlled the crowds.

**(February 7)**

# ALL WIMBLEDON TITLES FOR AMERICA

## MRS. MOODY'S RECORD FEAT IN WOMEN'S CHAMPIONSHIP

**By A. Wallis Myers**

IT was America's Wimbledon. In 1930 the invading players from the States won four championships and shared a fifth with Australia. This year they carried away all five. Three, as last year, were captured by Donald Budge, who, giant that he is, maintained his unbeaten record and only sacrificed one set in repeating a triple triumph.

To Mrs Moody the Wimbledon which closed on Saturday brought a unique honour. By defeating Miss Helen Jacobs in the final she claimed the women's singles for the eighth time, eclipsing the record established by Mrs. Lambert Chambers, who was champion seven times.

The story of Mrs. Moody's career at Wimbledon is worth its epitome. In 1924, when she first came over at the age of 18, she reached the final with conspicuous ease and appeared to have the title in her grasp when she led Miss McKane 6-4, 4-1. A lack of match-play experience and the courage of the English girl thwarted her.

| THE NEW CHAMPIONS |
|---|
| Men's Singles: J.D. BUDGE (U.S.A.) |
| Women's Singles: MRS. H. WILLS MOODY (U.S.A.) |
| Men's Doubles: J.D. BUDGE and G. MAKO (U.S.A.) |
| Women's Doubles: MRS. S.P. FABYANA and MISS A. MARBLE (U.S.A.) |
| Mixed Doubles: J.D. BUDGE and MISS A. MARBLE (U.S.A.) |

In 1926, the year of her famous contest with Mlle. Lenglen at Cannes, Miss Wills had been forced to retire from the French championship in Paris, a victim of appendicitis.

Recovering from her operation, she came to Wimbledon as a spectator, but in 1927 she began her championship reign, losing a set to Miss G. Sterry in the first round, but defeating Senorita de Alvarez in the final after a most exhilarating display.

She competed in 1928, 1929, 1930 (when she appeared as Mrs. Moody) and 1932 without losing a set. The next year she was harried by Miss Dorothy Round in the final, but survived with the loss of the middle set.

Returning after two years' absence she was nearly beaten in the fourth round by a courageous Czech girl, Mlle. Cepkova, who won the first set and had a point for a 4-1 lead in the second; and in the subsequent final, after an hour and 40 minutes' breathless play, she was within a stroke of losing the championship to Miss Jacobs.

### 111 SETS TO 6 AT WIMBLEDON

Since she first competed at Wimbledon 14 years ago, Mrs. Moody has won 111 sets and lost only six – four to English players, one to Mlle. Cepkova and one to Miss Jacobs. In that period she has collected 22 love sets. Her total number of games won is 701; she has lost 263.

She came to her last final on Saturday before a stadium packed to its utmost limits, a crowd many of whom had queued up outside the ground overnight and who waited, eagerly and expectantly, for this fourth centre court final between two of the keenest rivals the game has known.

At the head of this concentrating gallery was Queen Mary, who arrived in the committee box just before the start of the final, and who had been present with King George V. at Mlle. Lenglen's first championship final 19 years earlier.

Her Majesty remained at Wimbledon for nearly four hours, coming back after the rain had interrupted play during the doubles to see the giant tarpaulin in mechanical action shedding its containing water. Queen Mary gave a gracious bow to every finalist, and during one of the intervals she conversed with W.T. Tilden, who was presented to her by Sir Louis Greig, the All England Club chairman.

The Helens might come from the same Californian town – their families indeed, actually occupied the same house in turn – have gone to the same college, and graduated in tennis at the same club; but this neighbourly propinquity only added to ambitious zest and made competition all the stronger. And the incentive on the day was absorbing.

If Helen I. triumphed, she would claim a record reign. If Helen II. succeeded, she would, as an unseeded player – "the forgotten woman" so to speak – have come through the most talented field ever assembled at Wimbledon, including her famous rival from her home town.

### HISTORY REPEATED

But history repeated itself, and Mrs. Moody prevailed again. Her score was 6-4, 6-0, but the figures, standing alone, do not tell the story of Miss Jacobs's defiant fight in the first set; nor of Mrs. Moody's tranquil resistance, founded on a superiority of stroke technique; nor of the untimely accident to Miss Jacobs which rendered her virtually hors de combat and suddenly changed the contest from a speculative and exciting struggle into a rapidly deflating encounter which could have only one ending.

Miss Jacobs was forced to withdraw her resistance after straining her Achilles tendon in the ninth game of the first set. She had her right ankle tightly bound up when she came into court, having damaged it in her hectic struggle against Miss Marble two days earlier.

(July 4)

# BUDGE BECOMES A PROFESSIONAL

**From Our Own Correspondent**

NEW YORK, Thursday.

Donald Budge, the United States holder of the Wimbledon lawn tennis championship, entered the ranks of professional players today.

Budge has signed an agreement with the sports promoter, Mr. Jack Harris, of Chicago, under which he will receive a guarantee of £15,000 and a percentage of the gate receipts for a year's play.

The first match will take place with Ellsworth Vines, a former Wimbledon champion, at Madison Square Garden on Jan. 3 next year, and will be followed by a tour of leading cities in the United States, with Vines, Bruce Barnes and Richard Skeen.

Mr. Pate informed me that in the latter part of 1939 Budge hoped to visit England, probably with F.J. Perry.

**(November 11)**

# NECK AND NECK FINISH TO GRAND NATIONAL

**From Watchman**

LIVERPOOL, Friday.

After one of the most thrilling finishes ever seen in the great steeplechase, the Grand National ended this afternoon in a triumph for America, for a 17-year-old boy jockey, and for a woman owner, who is the wife of a well-known film actor.

Battleship, an American horse owned by Mrs. Marion Scott, won by a head from Mr. H.C. McNally's Irish-trained Royal Danieli, with another Irish horse, Sir Alexander Maguire's Workman, a poor third.

Mrs. Scott is the wife of Mr. Randolph Scott, once a noted American footballer and now a film star.

All the placed horses were outsiders. The betting was 40 to 1 against Battleship, 18 to 1 Royal Danieli, and 28 to 1 Workman.

In winning to-day's race, as well as the American Grand National, Battleship set up a record which may never be equalled.

Bruce Hobbs, the successful jockey, is the youngest rider to win the National. He was 17 on Dec. 27 last, and not long ago he was at Newbury Grammar School.

Hobbs rode one of the grandest races I have ever seen at Aintree. It was with uncanny skill that he gave his horse an easy time until about five furlongs from home. At this point the finish seemed certain to be fought out by Royal Danieli and Workman.

However, the complexion of the race changed when Battleship made his finishing effort. Workman died away, but Royal Danieli fought on with the utmost resolution.

**(March 26)**

# RUGBY PLAYER EXPELLED

Alban Davies, the Cardiff Rugby Union full-back, has been expelled from the game owing to an alleged contravention of the laws on professionalism.

This announcement was made yesterday by Capt. Walter E. Rees, secretary of the Welsh Union, who stated that Davies had been informed of his expulsion.

"When sending in his expenses for the match at Oxford, in which he assisted Major R.V. Stanley's team on Nov. 23, he included the sum of £3 for the loss of work," said Capt. Rees. "A claim for such an item is a contravention of the laws and sufficient to bring about his expulsion from the game."

**(December 23)**

# HUDDERSFIELD UNLUCKY

## DRAMA OF PENALTY GOAL IN LAST 30 SECONDS

**By Frank Coles**

**PRESTON NORTH END ... 1 HUDDERSFIELD TOWN ... 0**

FORBIDDING Wembley has relented again. Preston North End, beaten in last year's Cup Final by Sunderland, won the precious prize on their second appearance there by defeating Huddersfield Town, after the most dramatic finish of all time.

Ninety minutes – no goals. An extra half-hour ordered (the first time this has happened in 18 years), and – with less than a minute left – still no goals. Our thoughts were on a replayed final on Aston Villa's ground next Wednesday when, suddenly, Mutch, Preston's raven-haired inside-right, went darting through like a snipe.

He reached the penalty area, chasing the ball full tilt. A breathtaking moment, and it ended in stark tragedy for Huddersfield. Their captain, Young, brought the Preston flier to earth with a mistimed and technically unfair tackle. The extreme penalty was inevitable, and Much, taking the kick himself, won the Cup for Lancashire with 30 secs to spare.

There you have the plain story of how, fifty years after their first triumph, North End recaptured their glory. They richly deserve the honour because of the high standard they have set this season. However, I cannot go so far as to say that they deserved to beat Huddersfield in the final.

Huddersfield were unlucky losers. To be beaten with practically the last kick of the match after two hours' gallant endeavour – and a penalty kick at that – is as near heartbreak as anything I can think of, and it is a fine tribute to their players that not one with whom I talked after the match disputed the justice of the referee's decision in awarding the penalty.

Actually, Mr. Jewell had no option in the matter; he had to penalise Huddersfield to the extreme limit. It may have become an unwritten law among referees on Cup Final day to turn a blind eye on offences committed in the "fatal area," but this was a foul that could not possibly be overlooked.

### YOUNG'S PREMATURE TACKLE

When Young ran across Mutch to check his dash through I am certain he had thought of stopping his man at any price, but instinctively his left leg went right across the oncoming forward's legs two yards before he reached the ball.

Mutch off his balance, took a headlong dive and, hitting the ground hard, lay sprawling face down, arms and legs outstretched. He must have been only one among 93,000 people at Wembley who did not hear the blast of the referee's whistle or see that pointing finger.

Poor Alfred Young. He had played magnificently for two hours, holding up the Preston forwards and marshalling his forces with rare generalship. A captain courageous. And now there he stood, in mute appeal.

My eyes turned to the crowd of players clustering round Mutch, slowly recovering his senses with the aid of the trainer's magic sponge. Who would take this fateful penalty kick? And, as I wondered, Mutch, of all people, placed the ball on the 12-yards' spot, shook himself like a sleepy dog, stepped back a few paces, and hit the roof of the net with a shot which no goalkeeper could have saved.

### AN UNBELIEVABLE BLOW

The whole Preston team took one joyous leap at their hero. The Huddersfield players stood there, dazed and dejected. The ball was kicked off again, and then, in a few seconds, the last whistle. Never has a Cup Final ended in such a tense, highly-charged atmosphere.

To most of the Huddersfield team the dramatic climax was an unbelievable blow between the eyes. I saw Hesford, the goalkeeper, reel in his walk to the centre of the field, and other wearers of the blue and white stripes suddenly grew leg-weary. But I also noticed Young running with outstretched hands to congratulate Smith, the Preston captain.

That last minute of the 1938 Cup Final will remain an indelible memory. And the amazing contradiction is that for nearly two hours the crowd had been bored by the low standard of the football and the lack of thrills.

### PRESTON FORWARDS HELD

Apart from the drama at the finish this was indeed a dull Final. On both sides the forward play was dreadfully poor, and I must say I did not recognise the Preston forwards as the clever, quickwitted fellows whom I saw bewilder both Brentford and the Villa.

**(May 2)**

# YORK WEATHER THE STORM

## GRAND DEFENCE FOILS 'BORO' IN GALE

**By Our Special Representative**

York City ... 1 Middlesbrough ... 0

WHEN the lugger overhauls the schooner in a squall there is only one reason for it – better navigation. Middlesbrough very much resembled a schooner, her rigging torn to shreds, in the squall that blew up on York City's ground, and so much better did the humble little Third Division (North) team weather the conditions that the romance of modern football occurred.

A team which cost only £50 to build up entered the charmed circle of the last eight of the Cup.

The wind, strong enough on the ground to blow the ball off the spot where it was placed for a free-kick, blew from end to end. Middlesbrough won the toss and decided to let their opponents battle against it first.

So heartily did the York men battle, even when their own kicks turned in mid-air and floated back to meet them, that the Boro' could claim little advantage from this blustering opening half, and it would not be far short of the mark to say they were outclassed in the second, when York faced a blinding setting sun.

At half-time it was a question of how much their grand fight against the gale had taken out of the gallant York team. Their answer soon came in the second half, when they simply stormed the Middlesbrough goal, tore into the fray, with the wing-halves close up in support of the forwards, and forced corner after corner.

In this period of stress the Middlesbrough defence behaved well, and especial praise is reserved for Baxter, the centre-half, for his great coolness.

**(February 14)**

# RECORD FEE OF £13,000

## PLAYER'S SHARE OF DEAL IS £10

**By Frank Coles**

BRYN JONES, the brilliant Wolverhampton Wanderers and Welsh international inside forward, has, at last, joined the Arsenal. The very much discussed transfer was completed at Wolverhampton yesterday.

The transfer fee of £13,000 is a record, easily passing the £10,890 paid by the Arsenal to Bolton Wanderers for the services of David Jack ten years ago.

Another five-figure fee was paid by Aston Villa in 1934 when they parted with a cheque for £10,775 to Portsmouth for James Allen, their centre-half. Both Hugh Gallacher (signed by Chelsea from Newcastle United in 1930) and F. Doherty (bought by Manchester City from Blackpool in 1936) were also £10,000 men.

It is more than two years since Mr. George Allison, Arsenal's manager began his quest for Bryn Jones' transfer, and the Welshman would have been at Highbury 12 months ago if he had then passed a physical fitness test. As it was feared he was suffering from knee trouble, the proposed deal was postponed.

All Jones receives from the record deal is the £10 signing-on fee permitted by the rules of the Football League. He will of course, be paid the maximum wage of £8 per week during the playing season and £6 per week in the summer months.

The transfer fee of £13,000 may look a fantastic figure, but I should say the Arsenal will soon see their money back for everybody in Soccer football agrees that Bryn Jones is by far the biggest box-office draw since Alex James was at the height of his prowess. I do not know another player who has his gift of turning the fortunes of a game so swiftly. A great deal of the remarkable success of Wolverhampton Wanderers has been due to the inspiring influence of this little Welsh wizard, who stands 5ft 6in and weighs only 10st.

**(August 5)**

## BARRAGE BALLOONS ON THE MOVE

(ABOVE): THE BARRAGE BALLOONS, a feature of which is their mobility, moving across country. The tender is a motor chassis carrying a wire winch behind the driver's cabin.

## AN AIR-RAID SQUAD

(BELOW): EQUIPPED FOR DECONTAMINATION duty, seen during training in London yesterday. The squad had been "summoned" from the Westminster centre in Monck-st.

## BRITAIN'S FIRST GAS-PROOF HOUSE

GAS-PROOF ROOM in a London house. The entrance to a room in Warwick-gardens, Kensington, which can be transformed in five minutes into a shelter for eight people. Entrance is made through an air-lock tunnel protected by a thick blanket, as shown above.

## THE FINISH OF THE 1938 EPSOM DERBY

2—SCOTTISH UNION
(B. Carslake)
8-1

1—BOIS ROUSSEL
(C. Elliott)
20-1

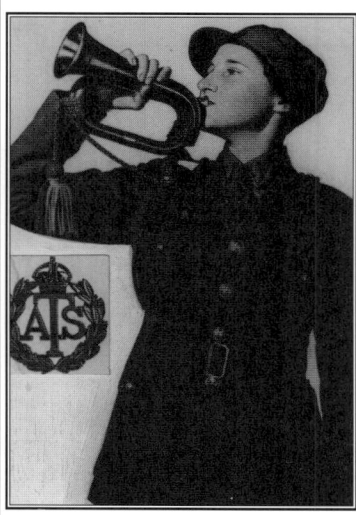

BADGE AND UNIFORM of the new Auxiliary Territorial Service, an organisation of women for non-combattant duties with the Regular and Territorial Armies and Royal Air Force.

The march towards war was inexorable. It did not come until German troops marched into Poland on September 1, an action to be followed by the British and French declaration of war on September 3 in fulfilment of the allied pact to preserve Polish frontiers. The inevitability of conflict was clear in the spring when Hitler ordered his troops to occupy the whole of Czechoslovakia and soon after began to apply pressure on Poland. For good measure, Mussolini occupied Albania.

Neville Chamberlain's policy of appeasement, despite his frenzied efforts to make it work, came to nothing. A pact with Italy served little purpose and the Anglo/French to achieve some common front with the Russians against Hitler was abortive. Indeed, just before the war came, Hitler secured his Eastern front by signing a pact with Stalin. The Daily Telegraph predicted that this alliance was bound to founder.

The whole year was dominated by the coming war. For the first time conscription was introduced into Britain, more air raid shelters were dug, plans for the building of both bombers and fighters were put into operation and the schemes for the evacuation of children from the big cities were brought up to date. The main fear was the use of poison gas and respirators, including all-enclosing ones for babies, were issued.

After Poland was overrun by both German and Russian troops, the land war paused, apart from a few skirmishes in the territory between the two great fortified lines of defence, the Maginot and the Siegfried. At sea the rapidly deployed U-boats took an immediate toll of the allied shipping. A British battleship and an aircraft carrier were sunk as were a number of merchant ships.

The lightly armed merchant cruiser, Rawalpindi, bravely turned to face the pocket battleship, Deutschland, and was destroyed protecting the convoy she was guarding. It was not until December that the first large-scale naval engagement took place. Three British cruisers, Exeter, Ajax and Achilles, closed in on the Graf Spee which was harrying merchant shipping in the South Atlantic and after a running battle forced the German pocket battleship to seek shelter in Monte Video. There it was scuttled.

Air activity was limited. The RAF dropped leaflets over Germany and occasional dog fights took place over France. The Luftwaffe, in small numbers, raided the dockyards on the Forth and the naval base in Scapa Flow.

At the beginning of December, Russian armies, without any warning, marched into Finland and were faced with far stronger opposition than they expected. By the end of the year, the Finnish armies were, for the time being at least, beating back the vastly superior Russian forces.

On the home front in Britain, the first plans to ration foodstuffs and petrol were brought into force and the blackout was imposed throughout the country. The most popular song was "We're going to hang out the washing on the Siegfried Line". The Christmas Day royal broadcast contained a poem beginning "I said to the man who stood at the gate of the year" which brought comfort to many and instant fame for a hitherto unknown poet who had written the work before the First World War.

# The Daily Telegraph

No. 26,554     LONDON, MONDAY, SEPTEMBER 4, 1939     Broadcasting: Page Four     ONE PENNY

# GREAT BRITAIN AT WAR

## THE KING'S MESSAGE TO THE EMPIRE

## MR. CHURCHILL FIRST LORD: POST FOR MR. EDEN

### PREMIER SETS UP WAR CABINET

### VISCOUNT GORT TO COMMAND FIELD FORCE

The Prime Minister announced yesterday in a message broadcast to the Empire, that as from 11 o'clock in the morning, Great Britain was at war with Germany.

The Commonwealth of Australia proclaimed a state of war three hours later, New Zealand followed and France was at war from 5 o'clock in the afternoon. Canada has given an assurance of effective co-operation.

The House of Commons met at noon to hear from Mr. Chamberlain the declaration that Britain was at war.

In the Lords a similar announcement was made by Lord Halifax. M.P.s will meet again to-day at 3 o'clock.

PREMIER SEES THE KING

At 6 o'clock in the evening the King broadcast a rallying call to the Empire. An hour later Mr. Chamberlain had an audience of his Majesty.

It was later announced that the Prime Minister has established a War Cabinet, consisting of eight members in addition to himself.

It includes Mr. Winston Churchill, who has joined the Government as First Lord of the Admiralty, the post he held at the outbreak of war in 1914.

Mr. Eden returns to the Government as Dominions Secretary, without a seat in the War Cabinet, to which he will have special access.

NEW CHIEF OF STAFF

It was also announced that the King has appointed:

Gen. Viscount Gort, V.C., Chief of the Imperial General Staff, to be Commander-in-Chief of British Field Forces;

Gen. Sir Edmund Ironside to succeed as Chief of the Imperial General Staff; and

Gen. Sir Walter Kirke to be Commander-in-Chief of Home Forces.

FALSE RAID ALARM

Half an hour after Britain entered the war there was an air raid warning. It proved to be a false alarm, but it provided a test for the machinery.

An Order in Council makes to-day a banking holiday and no savings bank business will be transacted.

New regulations for motorists provide that the running boards and bumpers of cars must be painted white. Petrol to be rationed from Sept. 16.

The Admiralty announced that all British merchant ships are liable to be examined for contraband. The Navy is at its war stations in full strength, supplemented by armed merchant ships as auxiliary cruisers. The naval convoy system has already been reintroduced.

Hitler is to take over supreme command of the German forces on the Eastern front. In a proclamation to the German people he found it necessary to state that whoever offended against national unity "need expect nothing other than annihilation as an enemy of the nation."

## PREMIER'S HISTORIC DECLARATION

**By Our Own Representative**

WESTMINSTER, Sunday.

"This country is now at war with Germany."

The sentence came from the Prime Minister's lips in tones of sharp precision.

A profound silence fell upon the House, not of surprise or anxiety as the calm, stern faces testified, but of grim satisfaction.

Hundreds of men on the crowded green benches drew a long breath of relief that the issue was declared and joined beyond a peradventure.

Conditions, circumstance and chance united to invest the Prime Minister's declaration with arresting dramatic force.

As dusk gathered the night before he had made a provisional, ad interim statement which, the words are not too strong, bewildered and shocked the House by its vagueness.

He told members then that he was waiting for the result of consultations with France, but his promise to be definite to-day did not allay the anxieties in which they went home.

Definite he was this Sunday morning. The tragic irony that a proclamation of war which will convulse the world and determine its destinies should be made in the sunshine of a Sunday struck home to every heart.

### DUKE OF KENT

The Admiralty announces that Rear Admiral the Duke of Kent has taken up his war appointment. His Royal Highness was to have assumed the position of Governor-General of Australia in the autumn.

### BANKS SHUT TO-DAY

Banks including the Post Office Savings Bank and other savings banks, will be closed to-day. They will reopen to-morrow.

### SIR A.W. LAWRENCE DEAD

Sir Alexander W. Lawrence, a grandson of Lawrence of Lucknow, has died in London at the age of 65.

---

## WAR CABINET OF NINE

### MR. CHURCHILL BACK AT ADMIRALTY

### MINISTER OF HOME SECURITY

A War Cabinet of nine has been set up on the lines of that established in December, 1916. It was announced from No. 10, Downing-street, last night that the King had approved its constitution as follows:

PRIME MINISTER AND FIRST LORD OF THE TREASURY: Mr. Neville Chamberlain.
CHANCELLOR OF THE EXCHEQUER: Sir John Simon.
SECRETARY OF STATE FOR FOREIGN AFFAIRS: Viscount Halifax.
MINISTER FOR CO-ORDINATION OF DEFENCE: Adml. of the Fleet Lord Chatfield.
FIRST LORD OF THE ADMIRALTY: Mr. Winston Churchill.
SECRETARY OF STATE FOR WAR: Mr. Leslie Hore-Belisha.
SECRETARY OF STATE FOR AIR: Sir Kingsley Wood.
LORD PRIVY SEAL: Sir Samuel Hoare.
MINISTER WITHOUT PORTFOLIO: Lord Hankey.

Mr. Churchill replaces Earl Stanhope as First Lord of the Admiralty and Sir Samuel Hoare replaces Sir John Anderson as Lord Privy Seal.

OUTSIDE THE CABINET

Later it was announced from Downing-street, that the King's approval had also been given to the following appointments of Ministers not in the War Cabinet:

LORD PRESIDENT OF THE COUNCIL: Earl Stanhope (formerly First Lord of the Admiralty).
LORD CHANCELLOR: Sir Thomas Inskip (formerly Dominion Secretary).
SECRETARY OF STATE FOR THE HOME DEPARTMENT AND MINISTER OF HOME SECURITY: Sir John Anderson. (formerly Lord Privy Seal).
SECRETARY OF STATE FOR DOMINION AFFAIRS: Mr. Anthony Eden.

Mr. Eden is to have special access to the Cabinet in order to be in the best position to maintain contact between it and the Dominions.

Lord Hankey, who is 62, was better known as Sir Maurice Hankey, until he retired from the Secretaryship of the Cabinet last year, after holding that position since 1919. During the last war he was Secretary of the War Cabinet and later of the Imperial War Cabinet.

## BRITISH ARMY LEADERS

### SIR E. IRONSIDE'S POST

It was announced last night that the King, on the advice of the Government, had approved the following appointments:

Commander-in-Chief, British Field Forces: Gen. VISCOUNT GORT, V.C.
Chief of Imperial General Staff: Gen. Sir EDMUND IRONSIDE.
Commander-in-Chief, Home Forces: Gen. Sir WALTER KIRKE.

Lord Gort, who is 53, a captain in the Grenadier Guards in 1914, won the M.C. in 1915, the D.S.O. to which he added two bars, in 1917 and in 1918 the V.C. – the latter, when commanding his battalion, by forcing the crossing of the Canal du Nord though three times wounded.

He became Commandant Staff College, Camberley, 1936, Military Secretary, Secretary for War, 1937 and Chief of the Imperial General Staff later in the same year.

Sir Edmund Ironside, who is 59, commanded a brigade in France during the war, was Commander-in-Chief Allied troops, Archangel, Oct. 1918-Oct., 1919, and has since commanded the 2nd Division, Aldershot Bn., Quarter-Master-General in India.

## JAPAN TO BE NEUTRAL

### PLEDGE TO BRITAIN

It is reliably learned that the Japanese Government is to remain neutral in the present European war.

Assurances to this effect are stated to have been given to the British Government.

---

## HIS MAJESTY'S BROADCAST

The following message was broadcast by the King from Buckingham Palace throughout the Empire at 6 o'clock last evening:

In this grave hour, perhaps the most fateful in our history, I send to every household of my people, both at home and overseas, this message, spoken with the same depth of feeling for each one of you as if I were able to cross your threshold and speak to you myself.

For the second time in the lives of most of us we are at war. Over and over again we have tried to find a peaceful way out of the differences between ourselves and those who are now our enemies. But it has been in vain.

We have been forced into a conflict. For we are called, with our Allies, to meet the challenge of a principle which, if it were to prevail, would be fatal to any civilised order in the world.

It is the principle which permits a State, in the selfish pursuit of power, to disregard its treaties and its solemn pledges; which sanctions the use of force, or threat of force, against the Sovereignty and independence of other States.

Such a principle, stripped of all disguise, is surely the mere primitive doctrine that might is right; and if this principle were established throughout the world, the freedom of our own country and of the whole British Commonwealth of Nations would be in danger.

But far more than this – the peoples of the world would be kept in the bondage of fear, and all hopes of settled peace and of the security of justice and liberty among nations would be ended.

This is the ultimate issue which confronts us. For the sake of all that we ourselves hold dear, and of the world's order and peace, it is unthinkable that we should refuse to meet the challenge.

It is to this high purpose that I now call my people at home and my peoples across the Seas, who will make our cause their own.

I ask them to stand calm, firm and united in this time of trial. The task will be hard. There may be dark days ahead, and war can no longer be confined to the battlefield. But we can only do the right as we see the right, and reverently commit our cause to God.

If one and all we keep resolutely faithful to it, ready for whatever service or sacrifice it may demand, then, with God's help, we shall prevail.

May He bless and keep us all.

---

SPECIAL EDITION

## BIG BRITISH LINER TORPEDOED

### 1,400 PASSENGERS ON BOARD.

### 'SINKING RAPIDLY' MESSAGE

The Ministry of Information announced early this morning that the Glasgow liner Athenia, with 1,400 passengers on board, had reported to the Admiralty that she had been torpedoed 200 miles west of the Hebrides.

At 5 a.m. it was stated that "the last official information received by the Admiralty was that the ship was sinking rapidly."

A previous announcement had stated that the liner had sunk.

The Athenia, which was owned by Donaldson Atlantic Line Ltd., was of 13,581 tons. She was built by Fairfield Co., Glasgow, in 1923.

Recently she was reconditioned on a large scale involving reconstruction throughout in passenger quarters.

## HITLER GOES TO POLISH FRONT

### TO COMMAND ARMIES

BERLIN, Sunday.

Hitler left the Chancellery in Berlin this evening for the eastern front, where he is to assume command of the German Armies. Four bodyguards were on the running-board of his car.

Earlier in the day he had announced his intention to go east in a message to the German Army on the western front, which, with others, was broadcast.

To the German people he declared: "If the soldier is fighting at the front no one shall profit by the war. If the soldier falls at the front no one at home shall evade his duty.

"It was the lack of unity in 1918 that led to collapse. Whoever offends against this unity need expect nothing else than annihilation as an enemy of the nation." – British United Press and Reuter.

### DOMINIONS AT WAR

Australia and New Zealand yesterday declared war on Germany in support of the action of Great Britain.

The Canadian Cabinet met for two hours and it was stated afterwards that an announcement would be issued later.

### THE BOMBING OF KATOWICE

At 8.45 this morning I was awakened by the sound of gun-fire and I saw 40 German bombers dropping incendiary bombs. The Poles brought their anti-aircraft batteries into action, but none was shot down

Some time later there was an outburst of firing from the frontier, eight miles away. The population had been warned by radio to expect an A.R.P. practice, so were indisturbe

---

## FLEET BEGINS BLOCKADE

### SHIPPING LIABLE TO EXAMINATION

### SYSTEM OF CONVOYS REINTRODUCED

An Admiralty announcement last night, that all British merchant vessels are liable to examination by the British Naval Contraband Control Service, indicated that the blockade of Germany had begun.

Ships will not normally be detained on interception longer than is necessary to establish their identity if they are:

Ships on Government charter.

Ships bound direct for British or allied ports and which will discharge all their cargo and passengers in such ports.

Ships whose last port of call was British or allied and which have a special war clearance therefrom.

THREE CONTROL BASES

Other British ships may on interception on certain routes be required to put into a contraband control base for more detailed examination. They are, therefore, advised to call at contraband control bases as follows:

Ships proceeding eastward through the English Channel with the intention of passing the Downs, if not calling at any other Channel port, should call at Weymouth for contraband control examination.

Ships bound for European ports on routes to the North of Scotland should call at Kirkwall.

Ships bound eastward through the Straits of Gibraltar should call at Gibraltar.

The Royal Navy is fully mobilised and at its war stations in full strength, supplemented by a number of duly commissioned armed merchant ships as auxiliary cruisers.

The Admiralty, profiting by past experience, has already taken certain measures which were developed only slowly during the last war. Among these is the reintroduction of the convoy system for merchant shipping to assist the Merchant Navy in its vital duty of ensuring the overseas traffic of the British Commonwealth and its Allies.

## FIERCE FIGHTING ON TWO POLISH SECTORS

Fighting on a more extensive scale is developing on both the main fronts in Poland.

The German attempt to cut the Corridor between Chojnice and Graudenz was reported in Warsaw last night to have failed. At the same time it was stated that the Poles have recovered certain of their towns in this zone and had penetrated across the border into East Prussia.

Further raids were made on Polish towns over the week-end. A Polish Foreign Office statement estimates that 1,500, including women and children, have been killed and wounded by bombing since Friday. The Germans occupied Rybnik, Teschen, Frystat, and have reached the suburbs of Katowice.

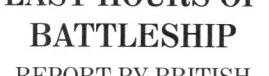

# The Daily Telegraph
### *and Morning Post*

No. 26,378 — LONDON, MONDAY, DECEMBER 18, 1939 — Broadcasting: Page Four — ONE PENNY

# GRAF SPEE GOES DOWN IN FLAMES

## EXPLOSIONS END DRAMA OF 70-MINUTE VOYAGE

### SCUTTLED BY BOMBS: CREW ESCAPE

### BRITISH 'PLANES FLY OVER SINKING WARSHIP

### CRUISER CUMBERLAND ASSISTS & RESCUES BY SEARCHLIGHT

**From Our Special Correspondent**

MONTE VIDEO, Sunday Night.

ONE OF THE MOST AMAZING CHAPTERS IN NAVAL HISTORY WAS ENDED TO-NIGHT AT 7.25 (10.55 G.M.T.) BY A TERRIFIC EXPLOSION, WHICH SENT GERMANY'S NEWEST POCKET-BATTLESHIP, THE £3,750,000, 10,000-TON ADMIRAL GRAF SPEE TO THE BOTTOM OF THE PLATE RIVER.

This deliberate act of self-destruction was ordered by Hitler personally. Capt. Hans Lansdorf, the commander, was rescued and is being taken to Buenos Aires. All the crew aboard, numbering 180, are reported to be saved.

The battleship, which the Nazis did not want interned and which they did not want the British to sink in battle, was about five miles off Monte Video harbour when the first blast occurred. It shook the harbour.

A great column of smoke rose and flames quickly began to spread the entire length of the ship. Five minutes later there was another explosion. This must have been the magazine.

The ship was sunk, it is stated, by the exploding of a number of large bombs placed in the hull, fore and aft.

Standing at the waterside, jostled by crowds of people who in awed silence watched this fearful scene, I could now see the Admiral Graf Spee sinking fast.

Much of her superstructure was blown away, but the funnel and control tower could still be seen outlined against the sky.

After a time she seemed to come to rest on the bottom of the river. There, it was said, she would be a danger to navigation as the wreck obstructed the anchorage off the harbour.

Only a little of the ship showed above water which at this point is about 26ft deep; the battleship's draught was 21 2-3ft.

Near at hand was the German cargo boat Tacoma which had followed the battleship out of harbour. The Tacoma, itself loaded with fuel oil, was in great danger of catching fire.

It looked as though attempts were being made to pick up members of the crew in boats.

### LAUNCHES TO RESCUE
#### Search for Survivors

When the port authorities realised what had happened a fleet of motor launches hurried out to search for survivors.

The British cruiser Cumberland and an unidentified British destroyer also raced to the scene and turned their searchlights on the sea to facilitate rescue operations.

The flames licking the super-structure lit up the swirling waters round the wreck of the battleship that was one of the proudest possessions of the German people.

Late to-night it was still impossible to discover how many men sailed out into the river aboard the Admiral Graf Spee to blow her up. It was stated in some quarters that a skeleton crew of 186 remained on board.

The Admiral Graf Spee transferred between 850 and 900 officers and men, including all the married men, to the merchantman Tacoma this afternoon.

There is also some uncertainty as to whether 31 or 22 wounded sailors were sent ashore this afternoon. Both reports are current.

The sinking of the Admiral Graf Spee took place only 70 minutes after she had sailed.

### CAPTAIN STAYS ON BOARD
#### Handful Of Men With Him

Most of the men remaining on board the battleship when she sailed were put into lifeboats before the explosion.

After the explosion five British 'planes flew over the sinking battleship.

The Monte Video newspaper "El Pueblo" reports that the captain said before leaving: "If I cannot get through the blockade I will sink my ship at 8 o'clock."

When she steamed from Monte Video harbour early this evening the Uruguayan authorities declined to say whether they knew where she was going.

### THE RIVER PLATE ZONE

A big proportion of Monte Video's population of 600,000 gathered at the waterside and other points of vantage to see the beginning of the drama. They caught a last glimpse of the Admiral Graf Spee as she rounded the breakwater and, rapidly gathering speed, disappeared in a southerly direction.

### BRITISH WARSHIP SEEN
#### Tug Leads the Admiral Graf Spee

A tug preceded the Admiral Graf Spee from the harbour, and the battleship was followed by the Tacoma and half a dozen launches.

In the river, just beyond the three-mile limit of Uruguayan territorial waters, an unidentified British warship and an Argentine patrol boat had earlier been seen waiting.

For some time after leaving Monte Video the battleship seemed to be making towards Buenos Aires. Then she turned back along the Uruguayan coast in the direction of the river mouth. She appeared to be merely playing for time, giving rise to a belief that she was waiting for complete darkness.

Monte Video broadcasting station predicted that shortly after the battleship left her crew would scuttle her in the estuary.

German official sources here also asserted that the commander, Capt. Langsdorf, would sink his ship at 8 p.m. – 11.30 p.m. G.M.T. – and that the crew would take to the boats.

## LAST HOURS OF BATTLESHIP
### REPORT BY BRITISH MINISTER

Following is a time-table of the Graf Spee's last movements from Monte Video, the times being local times, which are about 3 1/2 hours behind G.M.T.:

**5.10 p.m.** – Graf Spee weighs one anchor.
**5.25** – Second anchor up.
**5.55** – Signals exchanged with German freighter Tacoma in harbour.
**6.0** – Bulk of crew transferred to Tacoma.
**6.19** – Graf Spee sails from inner harbour.
**6.40** – Ship turns west, followed by six launches.
**6.53** – Moving south-west.
**7.0** – Graf Spee halts in middle of estuary.
**7.25** – Graf Spee scuttled by her crew

Early this morning the following announcement was made in London by the Foreign Office:

"Mr. E. Millington Drake, H.M. Minister at Monte Video, reported to London by telegram that he had watched the Graf Spee blow herself up at 7.55 p.m. local time, just at sunset, some miles out, after a skeleton crew had left her in boats.

"Later Mr. Millington Drake reported that the Graf Spee was still burning fiercely at 8.45 watched by the whole town."

A few minutes before 7.30 p.m. – 11 p.m. G.M.T. – the crowds standing in the gathering twilight saw a flash and heard an explosion in a position towards which the Admiral Graf Spee was last seen moving.

The scuttling ended a day of tense drama in Monte Video. As daylight dawned over the beautiful harbour the great grey hulk of Germany's pocket-battleship Admiral Graf Spee began to take shape against the dark background of Cerro Hill. Thousands of sleepy, disappointed men, women and children of all nationalities started returning to their homes.

Most of them had stood about the docks all through the chilly night, hoping to see history in the making as the battleship slipped out to sea to meet her fate.

### PLAN FORESTALLED
#### British Convoy Put to Sea

Many believed that she would make her dash last night before the Allied fleet was fully prepared for action.

If this move were indeed contemplated, it was forestalled by British officials, who sent five Allied merchantmen to sea in convoy. Under international law, an enemy warship cannot leave within 24 hours of the departure of ships belonging to the other side.

This meant that the Admiral Graf Spee had to stay until to-day, whether she wanted to or not.

This afternoon 31 of the Admiral Graf Spee's wounded were transferred to hospital in Monte Video. This was more than half the total of wounded, which was officially placed at 59 to-day.

### MANY CONFERENCES
#### Sailors Polish Guns

All day launches continued to shuttle backwards and forwards between the battleship and the shore, while officers repeatedly disembarked to confer with German consular officials.

While work on repairs continued some of the sailors were busy polishing her guns.

The difficulties facing the Admiral Graf Spee in a break for sea include the low water of the River Plate, which was three feet below the normal level. On the other hand the weather was overcast.

The battleship's departure spoilt the plans of seven American business men who had subscribed £1,250 apiece to charter a 'plane which, leaving New York to-morrow morning, was to have flown them to Monte Video in the hope of catching a glimpse of the anticipated battle.

### DIPLOMATIC ACTIVITY

American radio programmes were dramatically interrupted a few minutes before five o'clock this evening for a special broadcast from Monte Video, where the announcer described the Admiral Graf Spee moving out of the harbour.

There was much diplomatic activity here before the sailing of the battleship.

While the Uruguayan authorities insisted that the 72-hour period of grace considered necessary to make the Admiral Graf Spee seaworthy expired at 8 p.m. to-night – 11.30 p.m. British time – Mr. Millington-Drake, British Minister in Uruguay, told newspaper correspondents that the hour fixed for the battleship's departure was 6 p.m.

## SUNK ON ORDER FROM HITLER

### PROTEST AT ACTION BY URUGUAY

### DECISION TO INTERN
#### THE CREW

It was announced in Berlin early this morning that Herr Hitler had himself ordered the Graf Spee to be scuttled.

An official German News Agency's announcement stated:

"Regarding the sinking of the armoured cruiser Graf Spee, it is made known that the Fuehrer and supreme commander gave the order to Capt. Langsdorf to destroy the ship by blowing it up, inasmuch as the Uruguayan Government declined to allow the time necessary to make the ship seaworthy."

Following conflicting reports about the fate of Capt. Langsdorf and some of his crew, it appeared early this morning that all were saved.

It was learned in Monte Video, says the B.U.P., that the crew left behind there and survivors of the sinking would be interned.

According to the Buenos Aires wireless Capt. Langsford was the last man to leave the warship.

It was confirmed in Buenos Aires that he was aboard a launch near the Graf Spee on the way to Buenos Aires.

#### HINDRANCE TO SHIPPING

General indignation was expressed in Monte Video that the place chosen for the blowing-up of the Graf Spee was in the main anchorage. The wreck will be a serious hindrance to port traffic, and it is probable that it will only be removable by dynamite.

The Uruguayan Government is regarded as having given the battleship considerate treatment. Many people think that an "incident" between the two countries may result.

As the Graf Spee settled down, escaping fuel oil caught fire and enveloped the superstructure in flames. For a time an immense surface of the sea was illuminated.

The fire burnt out at 9.28 p.m., when very little of the battleship was showing above the water, though the depth at this spot is only 26ft.

The dramatic effect of the flames was enhanced by constant explosions as the fire, which was also burning under water, reached the shells.

#### CAPTAIN'S LETTER

In a letter left at the German Legation in Monte Video Capt. Langsdorf protested bitterly against the Uruguayan Government's refusal to allow more time for repairs to his ship.

The letter stated that it was impossible to effect repairs within 72 hours, not only for combatant purposes but also for facing the normal perils of navigation and the sea.

In view of the attitude of the Uruguayan authorities and his responsibility for the lives of 1,000 men, the only course left was to prepare to save the crew and blow up the vessel in the vicinity of the port of Monte Video as a protest, the latter added.

Capt. Langsdorf disclosed that he asked for 15 days as the necessary time to repair his ship.

## EMPIRE AIR PLAN

### TO COST £120,000,000 FOR 3 1/2 YEARS

OTTAWA, Sunday.

Mr. Mackenzie King, the Canadian Prime Minister, in a broadcast to-night on the Empire Air Training Scheme, said that for the period of 3 1/2 years agreed upon it would cost the Governments participating approximately 600,000,000 dollars (£120,000,000).

He said that 40,000 men would be required immediately to supply the ground personnel of Canadian training stations. It was estimated that the schools will have in training at their peak 4,000 pilots, wireless operators, gunners and air observers.

## WARSHIP SAVES NAZIS' PETS

CAPE TOWN, Sunday.

How a British warship, twice stopped shelling an abandoned German merchant vessel to rescue pets left aboard her was revealed to-day.

The warship was shelling the Adolf Leonhardt, 2,989 tons, to prevent her becoming a danger to navigation, when it was discovered that a dog had been left behind. The warship ceased fire and lowered a boat, which brought the dog across.

## FINNS SMASH TWO SOVIET DIVISIONS

### 36,000 MEN CAPTURED OR CASUALTIES

**From Our Special Correspondent**

ROVANIEMI, Sunday.

The Finnish counter-attack which has followed the Russian push on the northern and central front in Finland has had an astonishing success.

The Finnish G.H.Q. informed me this afternoon that two Russian divisions, totalling 36,000 men, had been smashed. Nearly all the men are either prisoners or casualties.

Finnish tactics all along, a highly-placed staff officer told me, have been to retreat slowly, luring more and more Russians to the attack.

The High Command gave strict instructions that the Finns were not to cross the Russian frontier, so that it was necessary for them to retreat to allow the Russians to advance on to Finnish soil. The counter-attack was then launched with outstanding success.

There is an air of tremendous optimism at Rovaniemi to-day. On the northern front the Finns have not yet withdrawn to their prepared and fortified line, now termed "the Mannerhelm Line of Lapland." They are still holding the Russians back with comparative ease in the icy waste of the central tundra.

The main scenes of the successful Finnish counter-drive were Suomossalmi and the area immediately north of Lake Ladoga.

To-day heavy snow is reported on the Petsamo front – conditions which make life intolerable for the Russian attackers.

The Finns are now holding the district round Pitkajaervi against Russian troops of somewhat poor quality. It was in this district that I saw two Russian tanks in use, the first to be seen on the northern front.

#### ILL-CLAD HUNGRY RUSSIANS

This afternoon I interviewed a Russian prisoner, aged 27. He was terribly emaciated and ill-clad.

The Russian prisoner said: "I was called up seven months before we came to Finland and sent to Brest Litovsk, in Poland. Before we were transferred here we were weeded out by political commissars, who told us we should have to fight only for a fortnight against England and France, who were backing Finland in her attack on Russia.

"We had no hot food at all," he said, "and no tents to shelter in. When we tried to dry our boots, which were of bad quality, they cracked and fell to pieces. We nearly all have skin diseases and frostbite."

As I write a battalion of Finnish pioneers is exercising outside. Their morale could not be better.

To-day's official Finnish communiqué says:

"Land army: In the Karelian Isthmus Soviet attacks have continued, several of them being supported by artillery. They have all been repulsed.

"During the fighting on Friday and Saturday a total of 30 enemy tanks has been destroyed. The enemy tried to cross the River Suvanto, but was repulsed.

"In the west of the Karelian Isthmus local Russian attacks have been repulsed. At the moment there is only artillery fire in this district. Three 30-ton tanks have been destroyed by the Finns.

#### "HEAVY RUSSIAN LOSSES"

"On the eastern front enemy attacks, which continue near Lake Ladoga, have been repulsed. In the district of Loimala two Russian battalions have suffered heavy losses.

"On the Tolvajaervi front the Finnish advance continues slowly. Near Aglaejaervi, 12 miles north-east of Tolvajaervi, violent fighting has taken place.

"Navy Coastal batteries on Lake Ladoga have destroyed three out of a column of Russian armoured cars. Elsewhere on the sea there has only been reconnaissance.

"Air: During the day there has been some Russian aerial activity. At Petsamo and in Northern Lapland there have been Soviet bombardments of slight importance. The Finnish Air Force has been very active in the course of the day. Near the front Finnish aircraft have bombarded a column of armoured cars."

It is semi-officially announced that since the beginning of hostilities the Finns have destroyed or captured 250 Russian tanks. The Red Army are now using 30-ton tanks in their desperate attempts to pierce the Mannerheim Line.

Moscow wireless claims advances in the Murmansk district yesterday to points 47 miles south of Petsamo. In the direction of Uhta Soviet troops are stated to have occupied the village of Kurso, which is 83 miles west from the frontier.

# HITLER TO TAKE PRAGUE

## PRESIDENT HACHA'S ORDERS TO PEOPLE NOT TO RESIST

**German troops and aircraft were ordered by Herr Hitler to begin the complete occupation of Czechoslovakia at six o'clock this morning.**

**At five a.m. an official statement from the Czech President, Dr. Hacha, who had just concluded talks with the Fuehrer in Berlin, was broadcast from Prague.**

**This declared that German forces would enter Prague at 6.30 a.m. and ordered that there should be no resistance.**

**The slightest opposition, it was stated, would lead to the intervention becoming utterly brutal. The entire Czech Army was to be disarmed and no 'planes must take the air.**

**(March 15)**

# TOWNS OCCUPIED LAST NIGHT

## CURFEW IMPOSED

**From Our Own Correspondent**

PRAGUE, Tuesday.

German troops to-night occupied Maehrisch-Ostrau, Vitkovice, Frydek and Mistek, in the Czech province of Moravia. They then advanced to Petrocovice and Koblowo, after entering which they moved, it is stated, eastwards toward Slovakia.

There are 100 tanks in Koblowo. The motorised troops continued to pour in until a late hour.

They immediately occupied the banks, public buildings and railway stations. No resistance was offered and no casualties are reported.

The commander of the German troops in Maehrisch-Ostrau to-night issued a proclamation, which is affixed on notice boards and in public places, requesting the public to maintain order. No cafés or restaurants are authorised to remain open after 8 o'clock.

A curfew is imposed from 9 p.m. to 6 a.m. All public meetings and processions are prohibited.

All arms, including explosive materials, are to be delivered to the German authorities and also all radio sets. Infringement will meet with heavy punishment.

The Moravian towns to-night occupied by German troops were the last important centres of the Czech iron, steel and coal industries.

### 14 DIVISIONS

### Polish Town Occupied

Fourteen German divisions are reported to be approaching the Czech and Slovak frontiers.

Other reports received here late to-night just before telephonic communication was interrupted, state that German troops have occupied Bohomin, Carvin and Polish, as well as Czech, Teschen – that is to say, part of the areas ceded to Poland under the Munich agreement have been occupied by German troops if this true.

The official German reason given for this move is, apparently, that, to aid Slovakia, it is necessary to obtain control of the railways. Bohomin is an important railroad centre for lines leading to Slovakia.

There are rumours here that in Poland nine classes of reservists have been called to the colours.

This invasion began while the 67-year-old Czech President, Dr. Hacha, and his Foreign Minister, M. Chvalkovsky, were on their way from Prague to Berlin to offer terms to Herr Hitler in an attempt to avert large-scale military action against their country.

The former Czecho-Slovak Republic had already been dismembered earlier in the day by the proclamation of the independence of Slovakia. Later, Ruthenia also broke away.

**(March 15)**

# BRITISH AIRWAYS MERGER

## CORPORATION OF THREE

The Air Ministry last night announced the establishment of the British Overseas Airways Corporation which will take over Imperial Airways and British Airways in accordance with the British Overseas Airways Act. 1939.

There are only three members – Sir John Reith, chairman, Mr. Clive Pearson, formerly chairman of British Airways, deputy chairman, and Mr. Leslie Runciman, formerly on the board of Imperial Airways.

Sir John Reith, hitherto chairman of Imperial Airways, was formerly director-general of the B.B.C. Mr. Runciman is the elder son of Viscount Runciman.

**(November 27)**

# FIFTY PRINCES AT CORONATION OF THE POPE

## CEREMONIES LAST FIVE HOURS

**From Our Own Correspondent**

VATICAN CITY, Sunday.

Amid all the splendour of Roman ritual, in the sunlight of a glorious Roman morning with a background of priceless works of art, Pope Pius XII. was crowned to-day on the open loggia above St. Peter's, to the cheers of more than half a million people.

Not within the memory of the oldest Roman had there been such a coronation. For enthusiasm and the multitudes, for the number of Royal Princes present – more than 50 – the ceremony has had no equal in the annals of the Church.

Pius XII. is a Roman of the Romans. All Rome, its city and its province, sent somebody to applaud him and to receive his blessing.

He was worn and pale before the long ceremony was over, but his voice rang out clear and steady as he gave his Pontifical Benediction from the open loggia surrounded by his court of Cardinals, his Swiss and Noble Guards, and near by were the Princes who had come from all parts of the earth to honour him.

### THE POPE'S MASS

Thousands of people had waited in the cold early morning wind from before dawn, and the Pope finally turned from the open loggia at 1.7 p.m. He was up before 6 a.m. and spent some time in private devotions.

The ceremony of the Coronation is the most solemn and longest of all functions of the Church. To-day it lasted for more than five hours. It consisted of:

The Pontifical procession and entry into St. Peter's Basilica;

Pontifical High Mass, celebrated by the Pope;

Procession to the Hall of Benedictions, which ends in the great open loggia;

The Coronation itself and the Pope's Benediction to the crowd and to the world.

**(March 13)**

# GIGANTIC ATOMIC "CANNON BALL"

## ENERGY FROM MASS

**From Our Own Correspondent**

NEW YORK, Tuesday.

The production of a gigantic atomic "cannon ball" generating energy of 100,000,000 electron volts was announced yesterday by the Department of Physics, Columbia University.

The new process, which results from splitting a uranium atom into two parts, is stated to yield the largest conversion of mass into energy that has yet been obtained by terrestrial methods.

An interesting point in the new process is the fact that neutron bullets used to split the atom travel with an energy of only one-thirtieth of a volt, to produce two cannon balls generating an energy 6,000,000,000 times greater.

Two European Nobel prize winners, the Physics Professor, Signor Enrico Fermi, Rome, and Prof. Niels Bohr, Copenhagen, both of whom are working in the United States, have been pursuing similar lines of investigation and took a prominent part in the work.

**(February 1)**

# NOTABLE INVALIDS

PRINCESS ANDREW OF RUSSIA: Much better.
MR. C. R. ATTLEE: Very much better.
MISS GRACIE FIELDS:
Improvement continues
BRIG.-GEN. SIR R. G. GILMOUR: Very low.

**(June 24)**

COUNT CIANO, the Italian Foreign Minister, in Tirana. He is seen with officers and Albanians during the reception organised for him on his arrival by air.

# ITALIANS INVADE ALBANIA

Italian troops invaded Albania yesterday and occupied the ports of Durazzo, Valona, Santi Quaranta and San Giovanni di Medua.

Twenty thousand men are stated to have been landed, while 400 warplanes dropped leaflets advising the Albanians not to resist. Other 'planes bombed the ports, which were also bombarded by warships.

The invaders met with fierce resistance, which, late last night, according to a telegram received by the Albanian Legation in London, was becoming more extensively organised.

King Zog is reported to be planning to retreat into the mountains to organise guerilla warfare. Queen Geraldine left Albania yesterday with her two-day old son and arrived by car in Greece last night after a 14-hour journey.

It was stated in Rome that 140 Albanians had been killed and several hundred wounded in the fighting. Italian casualties were estimated at 25 killed and 60 wounded.

**(April 8)**

# 400 'PLANES A MONTH FOR ROYAL AIR FORCE

## NEW PURSUIT 'PLANES ORDERED

**By Group Capt. L.G.S. Payne**

Britain's air rearmament is now proceeding at a greatly accelerated rate. Output of military aeroplanes has been nearly quadrupled in the past 12 months and now exceeds 400 machines a month.

Official reticence about the progress of British rearmament has led foreign observers to under-estimate the great strides made in this country during 1938.

The Prime Minister declared in his speech at Birmingham on Saturday that we had doubled the rate of aircraft production "in the last few months." After careful consideration of such evidence as is available, I have no hesitation in saying that British output of military aeroplanes was nearly quadrupled in the past 12 months and now exceeds 400 machines per month.

This, it is true, compares with a German output assessed by experts as between 500 and 600 monthly. Nevertheless, we are within measurable distance, for the first time for several years, of equalising the rate of aircraft production in Britain and Germany.

### GERMANY'S STRENGTH

### Fewer 'Planes for Navy

Germany to-day is estimated to possess between 4,000 and 4,500 firstline machines, of which only an insignificant proportion are allocated for naval operations. Between 600 and 700 are, however, detailed for army co-operation duties. I believe the strength of Germany's bomber force to be approximately 1,400 long-range aircraft.

The five bomber groups in Britain contain 57 regular bomber squadrons, or a total of, probably, about 650 aircraft.

The powers of invasion possessed by modern high-speed aeroplanes make it impracticable to stand on the defensive in air warfare; and the most effective method of defence is a counter-offensive bombing force strong enough to break down the enemy's scale of attack.

I understand that the Air Ministry has placed a large order for high performance, long range, twin-engine pursuit aeroplanes of an entirely new type. These, it is considered, will be a most important addition to our fighter strength.

It has been said that the war in Spain has proved the necessity for escorting bombers with fighters. The provision of such escorts in Spain is however, largely due to the inferior defensive armament of many types of European bombers.

### RECRUITING PROGRESS

### 5,800 Trained R.A.F. Pilots

Spitfires and Hurricanes both carry eight fixed guns firing forward. Their fire-power is greatly superior to that of the two machine-guns carried in the rear turret of the average Continental bomber.

Recruiting for the R.A.F. has been most satisfactory. I am able to reveal that the Regular Air Force now has approximately 5,800 trained pilots and 1,830 under instruction.

There are 3,800 pilots trained and under training in the various R.A.F. reserves, excluding the Civil Air Guard, which has 1,400 qualified "A" licence pilots and 3,800 pupils undergoing flying instruction.

**(January 30)**

# SURREALIST IN STORE SCENE

**From Our Own Correspondent**

NEW YORK, Friday.

Salvador Dali, the Catalonian surrealist artist, found himself unexpectedly in a New York police station last night after falling through a display window at a Fifth Avenue department store.

Dali had accepted a commission from the store to execute some special windowdressing based on his own ideas of surrealism.

Aided by his wife he worked all night, finally producing two masterpeices – one labelled "day" and the other "night."

The central motif of one window was an old-fashioned zinc bath-tub filled with water and covered with narcissi, from which emerged ghostly wax hands holding mirrors. The figure of a woman with floating red hair gazed languidly into the water.

### SHOCK FOR ARTIST

The night tableau showed another woman, apparently asleep, on a bed of red hot coals, with the head of a huge buffalo leering over her.

The management of the store decided that Dali's work was a little too exotic for their clientèle and made certain changes.

Later in the afternoon Dali sauntered down Fifth Avenue to inspect his work, and as soon as he discovered the changes he rushed into the shop and protested.

Not satisfied with the explanations made by the harassed manager, he burst into the display window and started to overturn the bath-tub, which crashed through the window on to the pavement, carrying Dali with it.

When the circumstances were described at court the magistrate dismissed the case.

**(March 18)**

# GEN. FRANCO MASTER OF WHOLE OF SPAIN

**From R. MacColl, Daily Telegraph Special Correspondent with the Nationalist Forces.**

MADRID, Wednesday.

The end of the Spanish civil war was announced by the nationalists' wireless station at Burgos to-day.

It was the 985th day since the Franco rising on the night of July 17-18, 1936.

Valencia surrendered about 1 p.m. and the other provincial centres followed in quick succession.

To-day Madrid settled down to the new régime after the city's surrender yesterday. Falangist youths were on guard outside all Madrid's main buildings, banks and big offices.

These youths, who have been in Madrid throughout the war, have emerged dressed in Franco uniforms, which they had kept hidden, and carrying automatic rifles. To-day they questioned everybody entering the buildings and carried out police duties.

### GIRLS IN UNIFORM

Falangist girls wearing blue Franco uniforms paraded the streets. Columns of food lorries lined the city squares and boulevards.

The inhabitants do not look starved or hungry. They seem vigorous, well-groomed and cheerful, but complain of the short rations they have had.

Madrid undoubtedly is giving a spontaneous demonstration of joy and relief. One would not guess that this was the defeated side.

The city was handed over without the loss of a single life on either side. Although the Republican lines were immensely strong, from what I saw, the troops left them and dispersed.

Nationalists have captured many important Republican leaders here. One of them is the Lord Mayor of Madrid, Rafael Henche. He wanted to leave, but could not find any chauffeur willing to take him.

### VETERAN SOCIALIST STAYS

Don Julian Besteiro, the veteran Socialist leader, who was President of the National Council of Defence until the surrender of Madrid, is still in the city. He chose to stay in the Ministry of Finance building, where he is being treated with every consideration.

Special food is sent in to him. The Nationalist authorities stress that he is not under arrest. He is still in the suite of rooms he occupied as President of the Republican Junta.

During the past three weeks he has greatly aged. He took office only so that he could help to bring the war to an end and hand Madrid over without bloodshed.

**(March 30)**

# 5-YEAR-OLD BOY AS RULER OF TIBET

**From Our Own Correspondent**

SHANGHAI, Thursday.

A five-year-old boy, discovered living in a cave in Kokonor Province, on the borders of Tibet and Kansu, China, has been accepted by Tibetan Lama, the Supreme Pontiff and Ruler of Tibet.

The boy is described as bright and intelligent, fulfilling the prophecy made by the Fifth Dalai Lama. He accords with the conditions outlined in the will of the last Dalai Lama.

He is therefore being escorted to Lhassa, the capital of Tibet, for installation at Potala, the Dalai Lama's palace, as the 14th Dalai Lama.

Lama disciples say that a dream, declaring that the new Lama would be found among a mixed race dressed in strange apparel, led them to the vicinity of Tar temple, 500 miles from Lhassa in Kokonor Province, where the boy was found living in a tribesman's cave. He speaks perfect mandarin language. His brother is a Lama in a neighbouring temple.

### THREE-YEAR SEARCH

The 13th Dalai Lama died in December, 1933. His successor had to be found among children born at the time of his death, one of whom is held to reincarnate him.

The search took three years. When found the boy was put under examination. At the end of two years he showed true reincarnation, possessing dignity and serenity. It was therefore decided to take him to Lhassa.

He will rule the monastic kingdom of Tibet after the customary rites, under the guidance of the Lama Council.

This will end the strange situation which has left Tibet without a ruler owing to the death of the Dalai Lama five years ago and that of the Panchan, or Tashi Lama two years later.

The last Lama reached the Biblical span of life, as his mother prepared his food and examined everything reaching him, thereby checkmating the intrigues of the other Lamas.

The 13th Dalai Lama was pro-British, in contrast to the last Panchan Lama, who was pro-Chinese. He left Tibet in 1924 for China and never returned.

Recent political conditions have placed Tibet in an unusual position between India and China, resulting in the formation of a powerful young Tibetan Nationalist party, opposing Lama rule in the country, where one-fifth of the men are Lamas. This party is working to transform Tibet into a modern State.

**(July 21)**

# BRITAIN'S PLEDGE TO POLAND

## "ALL SUPPORT AT ONCE" IF SHE IS ATTACKED

The Prime Minister announced in the House of Commons yesterday that Britain had pledged herself to defend Poland against attack. He declared that Warsaw had been assured that:

In the event of any action which clearly threatened Polish independence, and which the Polish Government accordingly considered it vital to resist with their national forces, his Majesty's Government would feel themselves bound at once to lend the Polish Government all support in their power.

The French Government, he added, had authorised him to make it plain that they stood in the same position on the matter as his Majesty's Government. Later, in answer to the question, he said that there were no ideological impediments between Britain and the Soviet, which was included in consultations on the formation of a group of States determined to end aggression.

Final details of an Anglo-Polish military alliance of mutual assistance, which is now understood to be in preparation, will be settled when Col. Beck, Polish Foreign Minister, reaches London next week.

**(April 1)**

# GERMAN PACT WITH SOVIET SIGNED

It was officially announced in Berlin early to-day that the Russo-German Non-Aggression Pact was signed in Moscow last night by Herr von Ribbentrop and M. Molotoff in the presence of M. Stalin and Count von der Schulenberg, the German Ambassador.

The Pact was signed at the second meeting which Herr von Ribbentrop and Count von der Schulenberg had with Stalin and Molotoff in the Kremlin. Herr von Ribbentrop reported to Herr Hitler the conclusion of the Pact by telephone at 1 a.m. He is to fly to Berchtesgaden this afternoon.

**GERMANY'S "VITAL INTERESTS"**

Germany's reply to the British declaration, renewing the pledge of support for Poland, was announced last night in an official communiqué issued at Berchtesgaden following a brief interview between Herr Hitler and Sir Nevile Henderson, the British Ambassador.

The Ambassador, who flew to Berchtesgaden from Berlin, conveyed a Note from the British Government repeated the statement of policy made by the Cabinet on Tuesday, in the light of the announcement of the intention of Germany and Russia to negotiate a non-aggression pact. The German communiqué stated:

"The Fuehrer left no doubt in the British Ambassador's mind that the obligations undertaken by the British Government could not move Germany to renounce her national, vital interests."

It is understood that Sir Nevile was later given a memorandum written by Herr Hitler, for transmission to London, emphasising Germany's determination to follow her own course "without interference."

**PRECAUTIONARY MEASURES**

Mr. Chamberlain will make a further important declaration when the House of Commons meets at 2.45 this afternoon.

A bill conferring extensive emergency powers on the Government will then be passed through both Houses, and is expected to receive the Royal Assent to-night.

**(August 24)**

KHAKI UNIFORMS are now being issued to the Women's Auxiliary Territorial Service. Above: Members wearing the new kit at the Duke of York's headquarters, Chelsea.

# BRITAIN TO INTRODUCE CONSCRIPTION

## 450,000 MEN OF 18 TO 20 MAY BE CALLED UP

**By Our Political Correspondent**

After a two-hour meeting of the full Cabinet in the Prime Minister's room in the House of Commons, Mr. Chamberlain was received in audience by the King at 9.30 last night at Buckingham Palace, and remained for an hour.

It is confidently expected in well-informed political circles that the Government will announce in both Houses of Parliament to-day that it has decided on a measure of compulsory military service.

Last night Ministers continued a discussion of the subject which had lasted for some time after the Budget proposals had been revealed to his colleagues by Sir John Simon on Monday evening.

The meeting was concerned with the method of making public Monday's decision in principle, and deciding how far the proposals should go at this stage.

I understand that Viscount Buckmaster, who tabled a motion on the subject in the Lords, has been asked to raise the matter in the form of a question. This procedure is thought to be due to the desirability of making simultaneous announcements in both Houses.

The exact nature of the statement to be made to-day was last night kept a close secret. It is believed that a period of compulsory, military training for men in the age groups from 18 to 20 has been decided on.

450,000 AFFECTED

According to Ministry of Labour calculations approximately 300,000 men are included in each age group. After deductions for reserved occupations and those already serving in the Forces, it is calculated that about 150,000 recruits from each group will be called to the Colours, making a total of 450,000 men.

It is not expected that all these would be called up simultaneously.

The proposition before the Cabinet last night was that men from these three age groups should undergo compulsory military training of three to four months this summer in camps with Regulars. After that they would be transferred to the Territorial Field Force.

AGE FOR EXEMPTION

The Schedule of Reserved Occupations was already in process of being overhauled by the Ministry of Labour after consultation with the War Office. The age for exemption and in a number of occupations will be raised.

Presumably, further modifications will be made in the light of the decision to call up the 18-20 age groups.

**(April 26)**

# BERLIN EXPELS SIX BRITONS

**From Our Own Correspondent**

BERLIN, Wednesday.

The British Embassy in Berlin was informed to-night that six British subjects resident in Germany must leave the territories of the Reich by May 24 as a reprisal for the expulsion from Britain of six agents of National Socialist organisations.

Mr. Hugh Carleton Greene, chief Berlin correspondent of The Daily Telegraph, is the first of the expelled Britons.

It was made clear to the British Embassy to-night that Mr. Greene's expulsion indicated no criticism of his journalistic work, nor did it imply any dissatisfaction with the editorial policy of The Daily Telegraph.

DUESSELDORF RESIDENTS

The full list of the expelled Britons is as follows:

Mr. H.C. Greene, a member of The Daily Telegraph Berlin staff since February, 1934, and chief correspondent since October, 1938.

Mr. W.L. Dickinson, a business man resident in Duesseldorf.

Mr. H. Pink, a Duesseldorf teacher.

Mr. R.P. Smith, a Duesseldorf engineer.

Mr. H. Large, director of a boot polish factory at Cologne.

Mr. Parnell, director of the firm of Weddel and Company, Hamburg.

**(May 4)**

# MAN WITH PIERCING EYES SOUGHT

## ATTACKS ON WOMEN

**From Our Own Correspondent**

ETON, FRIDAY.

A man with dark, piercing eyes who has attacked a number of women in the Eton district is being sought by the Buckinghamshire police.

Several women using the footpath across the Eton College playing fields close to the river have been molested, and special watch is being kept.

Yesterday a young married woman living at Slough was walking through the playing fields with her baby daughter when a man sprang from behind a tree and put his arms round her neck. Her screams were heard by groundsmen, and when they appeared the man ran off. He climbed a fence and got away on a bicycle.

**(May 6)**

# DUKE OF NORFOLK SELLS A TOWN

Property which comprises almost the whole of Littlehampton has been disposed of by the Duke of Norfolk for the development of the resort, it was announced to-day.

The estate has been in the possession of the family for centuries and includes more than 1,100 acres of open land.

Of these 850 acres are suitable for building. Hundreds of leaseholds and general house properties are in the deal.

The Duke, it was stated, has for some time been interested in projects for the development of Littlehampton.

**(June 17)**

# PALESTINE TALKS ENDED

## BRITISH PROPOSALS REJECTED

It was announced officially last night that both the Arab and Jewish delegations have rejected the British Government's proposals for future policy in Palestine. The Palestine Conferences which were opened by the Prime Minister on Feb. 7, have thus ended unfruitfully.

The British Government's policy will be considered over the week-end and announced in a White Paper some time next week.

The Arabs made known their decision to reject the proposals at a two-hour meeting in St. James's Palace yesterday afternoon.

The Jewish refusal was conveyed to Mr. Malcolm MacDonald, the Colonial Secretary in a letter from Dr. Weizmann.

"INSUPERABLE OBSTACLE"

A "statement on behalf of Arab delegations" was issued last night by the Egyptian Embassy. It contained the following passage:

"We have realised with regret that, through pressure from one quarter or another, the Arabs are being asked to surrender any hope there may be in the future of any Independent Palestine State, it being clear that under present conditions of continued immigration the majority position now held by the Arabs in Palestine will be revised in favour of the Jews.

"It is with profound regret that we have been forced to realise that the apparent impossibility of securing the slightest reduction of the Zionist claims has placed at any rate for the moment, an insuperable obstacle in the way of agreement.

"We feel, too, that although the Conference has made quite clear the essentials of the Arab case, it has been less successful in securing any final definition of the British point of view, either as to what the British Government considers to be its obligations to the Jews or as to what is its conception of a Jewish National Home in Palestine."

**(March 18)**

# GOLD & SILVER RELICS OF SAXON ENGLAND

## TREASURE TROVE IN FUNERAL SHIP

Experts in laboratories in the British Museum are giving appropriate treatment to relics of Saxon England unearthed in the grave of a warrior Prince at Sutton Hoo, near Woodbridge, Suffolk.

This warrior, who was given a ceremonial burial in a ship, lived about the year A.D. 600, and was probably a member of the family of the great East Anglian King, Redwald.

The relics, which were brought to light in what is one of the most important archæological discoveries ever made in England, include:

A set of armour;
Gold coins of the Franks;
Gold ingots;
A bronze bowl from Egypt;
A great silver dish made in Constantinople.

The public will not yet have an opportunity of seeing the treasures.

"They are not in a fit condition to be exposed," said Sir John Forsdyke, director of the British Museum, yesterday.

Sir John said that it was not certain where the treasures would find a permanent home. In the case of an archæological discovery of this kind the material found is controlled by the excavator until after a "treasure trove" inquest.

BURIED BY SAND

A statement issued yesterday by C.W. Phillips, who acted on behalf of the Office of Works, described how the finds were made.

In the course of digging in the late spring, he stated, it became apparent to Mr. Basil Brown, who was in charge of the excavation, that a large ship had been buried in a trench some 10ft deep and 20ft wide, dug in the old ground surface.

It was found that a large equal-ended vessel 82ft in length and some 16ft in beam, had been interred, covered amidships by a wooden structure to accommodate the burial and the objects deposited with the dead man for use in a future life.

The burial chamber had ultimately collapsed, throwing hundreds of tons of sand and soil on to the burial. No surviving trace of the body of the man buried was found.

BODY FULLY ARMED

The body was buried with a full equipment of arms, including a large iron sword, with pommel and hand-grip enriched with gold and garnet cloisonné work and gold filigree. The sheath, completely decayed, may have been covered with ivory and it was decorated with similar pieces of gold work and two beautiful cloisonné studs.

**(August 5)**

# B.E.F. OF 158,000 MEN NOW IN FRANCE

## CORPS COMMANDERS: SIR J. DILL AND LT.-GEN. BROOKE

## ARMY VOLUNTEERS AGAIN: HOME DEFENCE BATTALIONS

Mr. Hore-Belisha, Secretary for War, made a statement in the House of Commons yesterday on the situation of the Army. He announced that:

By the end of last week 158,000 men of the Expeditionary Force had been transported to France;

This involved the transport of 25,000 vehicles;

Volunteers for the Army will again be accepted;

Home Defence Battalions and Auxiliary Military Pioneer Corps are to be formed, giving opportunities for elder men.

Mr. Hore-Belisha also stated that under the Commander-in-Chief of the B.E.F., Gen. Viscount Gort, V.C., there are two Corps Commanders – Lt.-Gen. Sir John Dill and Lt.-Gen. Alan F. Brooke.

**(October 12)**

Lt-Gen. Sir J. Dill, Commanding the 1st Corps.

Lt-Gen. A. F. Brooke, in Command of the 2nd.

# LONDON'S FIRST RAID WARNING

Half-an-hour after Britain's declaration of war, London had its first air-raid warning. There was no panic, and people responded calmly.

A crowd assembled outside Buckingham Palace heard the blasts of the sirens and within two minutes the great circular space around the Queen Victoria Memorial was completely empty. Air raid wardens and policemen had shepherded the people into the nearest shelters and trenches.

Almost before the all-clear signal had died away, the people had congregated again near the palace, to which an unfamiliar air was given by the sentries in Khaki service kit and the policemen at the gates in blue steel helmets.

The warning came at a time when a large number of Peers and M.P.s were in the Houses of Parliament, awaiting the sitting which was to begin at noon. They were scattered through the building when the first notes of the siren were heard.

All proceeded to the shelter which has been provided for them. Many had their gas-masks slung over their shoulders.

MR. LLOYD GEORGE'S COMMENT

There were no distinctions of class or function. Tea-room girls and barmaids found themselves standing next to famous politicians.

No signs even of uneasiness were to be seen. Mr. Lloyd George, as he descended the stairs, remarked cheerfully that there was "nothing new in all this" for him.

The "all-clear" signals were still sounding when the Houses assembled.

The reactions of people living in a certain large block of flats may be taken as typical of many similar communities. Five minutes after the warning went everyone was safely in the basement shelter, and the gas-tight doors were closed.

There was no haste – men and women walked quietly down the many flights of stairs. Lifts were reserved for invalids.

As soon as the "all clear" sounded, the return journey to empty flats began by lifts and stairs.

Later in the day the Air Ministry announced: "At 11.30 a.m. an aircraft was observed approaching the South Coast. As its identity could not be readily determined, an air-raid warning was given. It was shortly afterwards identified as a friendly aircraft and the all-clear signal was given."

**(September 4)**

# THE CHILDREN'S ZOO

## OPENING NEXT MONDAY

The opening of the Children's Zoo at the Regent's Park Zoo has been postponed until next Monday.

There will be an official opening and private view at 11.30 a.m. and it will be open to the public in the afternoon. By then it is hoped that the new exhibition cage for Ming, the baby giant panda – a bandstand erected near the Lion House – will be ready for her, and that the male adult giant panda Tang, will make his long-delayed debut in the cage Ming now occupies.

**(May 15)**

## MILK PLAN FOR BABIES

The Minister of Agriculture, Sir Reginald Dorman-Smith, disclosed in the House of Commons last night that fresh milk is to be made available henceforth for all infants and nursing mothers either free, if conditions make this desirable, or at a maximum charge of 2d a pint.

Experiments in trial areas for this cheap milk scheme have proved successful in Yorkshire.

**(June 15)**

# EYE-WITNESS'S ACCOUNT OF CAMPAIGN

## EIGHT-SIDED GERMAN ONSLAUGHT

Below is printed an eye-witness account of the Polish campaign from our Warsaw correspondent, who vividly describes the events of the first week of the war.

**From Hugh Carleton Greene**

CZERNOWITZ,
Rumano-Polish Frontier, Sunday.

The military position at the end of the first week of war finds the Germans in occupation of the following big towns – Grudziadz, Bydgoszcz, Torun, Poznan, Lodz, Piotrkow, Kielce, Wielun, Czestochowa, Random, Katowice, Cracow, Tarnow, Mlawa, and Przasnysz.

The whole of the Silesian industrial area is lost. The fall of Warsaw can hardly be long delayed. Nevertheless, the spirit of Poland is unbreakable, and the real war on the Polish front has still yet to begin.

The civil population shows no signs of nervousness or panic. I spent two hours in a cellar under the bank of the Stanislowow, near the Rumanian frontier, during a heavy air raid, and saw elderly women with their shopping baskets gossiping as if they were quite accustomed to seek sudden refuge from German attacks.

The rolling countryside in the south-east of Poland is as peaceful as ever. Here the peasants in their picturesque costumes are ploughing and working the land, quite oblivious of the strife going on elsewhere.

Tactics of "Lightning War"

I was a member of the last party of British journalists on the frontier late last night to leave Poland by way of the Rumanian frontier. From Warsaw we travelled for nearly 500 miles over rough roads that were constantly menaced by German aeroplanes, and we were also severely handicapped by a shortage of petrol, which is now reserved for military purposes.

Our only halt was at a quiet country resort in the Lublin district, where the Foreign Ministry and the British, French and American Embassies made a 24 hours' stay in the hope that the Government would be established there. The rapidity of the German advance, however, caused a further Government withdrawal eastwards into the marshy districts.

So far the war has gone according to plan. The Polish General Staff never envisaged the possibility of a prolonged defence of the western provinces, and contemplated that its main resistance would be opened on the line of the rivers Bug and Vistula, thus leaving a third of Poland in German hands. This stage has now been reached.

**(September 11)**

# ATLANTIC MAIL ARRIVES BY AIR

## CLIPPER OPENS SERVICE

**From Our Own Correspondent**

Yankee Clipper, the Pan-American Airways flying-boat which left Port Washington, Long Island, U. S. A., at 6-7 p.m. (B. S. T.) on Saturday, reached here this evening at 8.49 (B. S. T.) after a stop of 3hr 10min at Horta in the Azores.

Including the stop, she flew the 3,800 miles in 26 hours 42 minutes, maintaining a speed between 160 and 170 m.p.h.

The importance of the trip is that she is opening a regular Transatlantic mail service, and on this first service flight she is carrying 100,00 letters for Briatin.

**(May 22)**

# U.S. PROCLAIMS NEUTRALITY

**From Our Own Correspondent**

WASHINGTON, Tuesday.

President Roosevelt, at 1 p.m. Washington time to-day, signed a proclamation of United States neutrality. It became effective a few minutes later when it was signed by Mr. Cordell Hull, Secretary of State, and carried from the White House to the State Department, where the seal of the United States was affixed to the document.

The proclamation names Germany, France, Poland, the United Kingdom, India, Australia, and New Zealand as the seven belligerents involved in war.

It declares that whereas war exists between these nations , the United States is "on terms of friendship and amity with the contending Powers and with persons inhabiting their several Dominions."

It asserts that nationals of the United States should observe strict neutrality towards all nations involved in the European War.

**(September 6)**

# MR. CHURCHILL & MAGINOT LINE

## ABSOLUTE SECURITY AGAINST INVASION

BELFORT, Wednesday.

Mr. Winston Churchill, who is making a tour of the Maginot Line at the invitation of Gen. Gamelin, General Officer Commanding the French Army, arrived here to-night. For 12 hours to-day he had visited various sections of the Maginot defences.

Giving his first impressions, he said:

"My first impression, the strongest, is that France is protected by a shield of material and, above all, by a shield of men who should assure you of absolute security in this region and defend you against the horrors of invasion.

"As a former officer of the British Army," said Mr. Churchill, "I have been particularly struck by the alert mien and intelligence of the troops. Each rank and each N.C.O. can immediately explain his role with precision.

"ONE MAN'S RESPONSIBILITY"

"I have appreciated the happy comradeship which binds men and ranks in their idea of duty. That more than guns and concrete, gives me absolute confidence in the maintenance of French security."

Passing to the international situation, Mr. Churchill said that if war occurred "two-thirds of the human race would be at our side."

"But no one can guarantee the future," he added. "It depends upon the good will and whim of a single man.

"If this man is reasonable, all can breathe freely. If he attacks us, or if he attacks our allies, he assumes a heavy responsibility to history." – Reuter.

**(August 17)**

# FIRST R.A.F. ATTACK OF THE WAR

## 6,000,000 LEAFLETS SHOWERED ON GERMANY IN NIGHT FLIGHT

**It was officially announced last night that a successful attack was carried out yesterday afternoon by units of the R.A.F. on vessels of the German fleet at Wilhelmshaven and Brunsbuttel, at the entrance of Kiel Canal.**

**Several direct hits with heavy bombs were registered on a German battleship in Schilling Roads, off Wilhelmshaven, which resulted in severe damage.**

At Brunsbuttel an attack was carried out on a battleship lying alongside the mole, causing heavy damage. During the operation, which was carried out in very unfavourable weather conditions, our aircraft encountered air attack and anti-aircraft fire, resulting in some casualties.

Another successful British air operation was carried out in the night of Sept. 3-4, the first night of the war, when aircraft of the Royal Air Force carried out extensive reconnaissance over Northern and Western Germany.

**They were not engaged by enemy aircraft. More than 6,000,000 copies of a note to the German people were dropped over a wide area.**

The Admiralty announced that naval activity continues on all seas, but as yet there are no major operations to report. The port of Dover is closed to commercial shipping.

**(September 5)**

# RUSSIAN INVADERS IN POLAND

## SEQUEL TO SWIFT GERMAN ADVANCE

**From Our Own Correspondent**

MOSCOW, Sunday.

At four o'clock this morning the Red Army began its invasion of Poland along the entire frontier from Polotsk on the north to Kamenetz-Podolsk on the south.

A few minutes earlier M. Potemkin, Vice-Commissar for Foreign Affairs, had handed a Note to the Polish Ambassador here, M. Grzybowski, seeking to justify this military operation.

The Ambassador indignantly refused to accept the Note, but said he would inform his Government about it.

Identical Notes were delivered to all the other diplomatic missions here with an assurance of the Soviet's intention to pursue a policy of neutrality "towards all Governments with which she has diplomatic relations."

Evidently this did not include Poland, since the Note asserted that the "Polish State and its Government have ceased to exist."

There has recently been a steady trend here towards a policy of occupying Polish "White Russia" and as much of the Polish Ukraine as the Germans will let the Kremlin take.

Four or five days ago opinion in the highest Kremlin circles was sharply divided on this issue. Several members of the supreme party "Polit-bureau" were strongly in favour of biding their time.

M. Stalin, on the other hand, and some other of the more energetic members were in favour of immediate action but no decision was then reached.

Since then, however, the rapid German progress eastwards across Poland, in all probability going beyond the limit presumably fixed in the Soviet-German pact, has precipitated Soviet intervention in Poland.

It is quite possible that Berlin warned Moscow that if it did not occupy whatever zone was earmarked for Russia, German troops would have to do so in pursuit of Polish armies.

On their side the Kremlin's perturbation over the German's swift eastward drive is only too apparent in M. Molotoff's statement this morning that "Poland has become a suitable field for all manner of hazards and surprises which may constitute a threat to the U.S.S.R."

To-morrow we shall witness the strange spectacle of Red Army forces approaching the German lines in Poland in open country, far outside Russia's fortified western frontier.

However much the Berlin and Moscow Governments now understand each other, such a situation is ultimately, if not immediately, precarious.

Both know that whatever commercial agreements may exist between them, Russia has little or no surplus in foodstuffs or raw materials to cede to Germany whatever efforts Soviet State institutions may have to make to fulfil eventual German demands.

Thus Soviet-German relations may not be so happy in the future as they appear on the surface to be at present. In fact, Russia's invasion of Poland may in the long run embarrass Germany more than Britain, although its immediate object and the hope lying behind it is to see as many German divisions as possible removed from Poland and Eastern Europe to a safe distance from the Soviet Union, that is, to the Western Front.

**(September 18)**

# DEUTSCHLAND SANK THE RAWALPINDI

## 40 MINUTES' FIGHT AGAINST HUGE ODDS

**In tempestuous weather, and both by night and in the brief hours of daylight, the British Navy is searching for the German pocket-battleship Deutschland and another enemy warship which, it is now revealed, sank the armed merchant cruiser Rawalpindi, 16,697 tons.**

**Details of the Rawalpindi's gallant fight against overwhelming odds were given in the following statement issued by the Admiralty last night:**

**"The armed merchant cruiser Rawalpindi was forming a part of the Northern Patrol, by which the contraband control of German trade is enforced.**

**"This duty is particularly arduous on account of the long, dark nights, and severe cold, and required for its performance large vessels of good sea-keeping qualities, capable of enduring the frequent storms.**

**"At 3.30 p.m. on the afternoon of Thursday, Nov. 23, when cruising to the south-east of Iceland, she sighted an enemy ship.**

**"Capt. Kennedy, having examined this vessel through his glasses, said: 'It's the Deutschland all right.' and the crew were immediately ordered to action stations.**

**"Course was altered to bring the enemy on the starboard quarter. Smoke-floats were lit and cast into the water to enable the Rawalpindi to escape. However, a second enemy ship was soon seen to starboard.**

SALVO AT 10,000 YARDS

**"The Deutschland, approaching, signalled to the Rawalpindi to stop, and when she continued her course fired a shot across her bows.**

**"As this warning was rejected, the first salvo was fired by the 11in guns of the Deutschland a little after 3.45 p.m. at a range of 11,000 yards. The Rawalpindi replied with all her four starboard 6in guns.**

**"The third salvo from the Deutschland put out all the lights and broke the electric winches of the ammunition supply. The fourth salvo shot away the whole of the bridge and wireless room.**

**"Both the German ships were now closing rapidly, and by this time the second had gone round the Rawalpindi's stern and was firing from the port side. The Rawalpindi maintained the fight until every gun was put out of action and the whole ship ablaze except the forecastle and the poop.**

30 MEN BELIEVED PRISONERS

**"After about 30 to 40 minutes of this unequal combat, about 4.15 to 4.25 p.m., the enemy ceased firing, and three boats which were not shattered by shell-fire, one of which became water-logged, were lowered. Two of these boats, containing over 30 men, were, it is believed, picked up by one of the German ships.**

**"The 11 survivors, who have been brought in by the Chitral, swam to the waterlogged lifeboat, and would probably have been picked up, but for the fact that at about 6.15 p.m. the approach of a British cruiser caused the enemy immediately to withdraw.**

**"The Rawalpindi continued to burn amidships until 8 o'clock, when she turned turtle to starboard and foundered with all remaining hands.**

**The Rawalpindi was manned by merchant seamen, reservists and pensioners of the Royal Navy, and by men of the Royal Naval Reserve and Royal Naval Volunteer Reserve.**

**(November 28)**

# LEGLESS PILOT BACK IN THE R.A.F.

## TO FLY SINGLE SEATERS

Flying-Officer Douglas Robert Stewart Bader, who is legless as the result of a flying accident eight years ago, is once more an R.A.F. pilot, somewhere in England.

Within nine months of the accident Flying-Officer Bader was equipped with two artificial legs and again passed as a first-class pilot.

He took a course in civil aviation and piloted a 'plane operating the rudder controls with his false limbs. He applied to be taken back into the Service, but as it was peace time the Air Ministry refused.

On the outbreak of war he renewed his application to the Air Ministry, asking to be allowed to fly single-seater machines. This time he was accepted

Before his crash Flying-Officer Bader was a Hendon aerobatic pilot. He played Rugby for Surrey, the Harlequins and the R.A.F.

He is a short handicap man at golf, dances, and drives his own motor-car.

**(October 27)**

# REVIVAL OF THE "WRENS"

**By a Naval Correspondent**

The King has given permission for the formation of a corps to be known as the Women's Royal Naval Service, who will replace naval officers and ratings in war time on certain duties, in naval shore establishments. Training for some of these duties is to be given during peace.

Mrs. Laughton Mathews, née Vera Laughton, has been appointed Director of the W.R.N.S., and will take up her duties immediately. She served during the Great War as an officer of the W.R.N.S. formed at the beginning of 1918 and demobilised in the autumn of 1919. She is one of the pioneers of the Sea Ranger branch of the Girl Guides movement and a Divisional Commissioner of Girl Guides.

Intending volunteers for the W.R.N.S. are asked to await the publication of a booklet, to be issued shortly, giving the conditions of service and informing candidates how they can join.

**(April 14)**

THE GERMAN POCKET BATTLESHIP DEUTSCHLAND

# HEROISM AT SINKING OF THE COURAGEOUS

## U-BOAT BLOWN TO PIECES

Many of the survivors of the aircraft-carrier Courageous, sunk on Sunday night by a German submarine, brought to their homes in Britain yesterday stories of the heroism shown by men of the Royal Navy as their ship sank.

They gave accounts of:

A boy seaman who waited on deck and smoked a cigarette until the cry went up. "Every man for himself."

A petty officer who dived 10 times from a destroyer into the sea to rescue exhausted men.

A badly-burned stoker, whose first words were, "What about the lads down below?" and

The captain, who issued orders until the last minute, standing at the salute on his bridge as the ship took her final plunge.

ADMIRALTY STATEMENTS

Official announcements by the Admiralty yesterday showed that there are 712 known survivors, but 548 men still unaccounted for.

A German official statement broadcast yesterday said: "The announcement of the British Admiralty regarding the sinking of the aircraft-carrier Courageous has been confirmed by the attacking U-boat."

Doubt is cast on the authenticity of this communiqué by the British Admiralty's statement that "the submarine was immediately heavily attacked by destroyers and is believed to have been sunk."

**(September 20)**

# MYSTERY OF LOSS OF ROYAL OAK

**By A Naval Correspondent**

It is expected that Mr. Winston Churchill. First Lord of the Admiralty, will make a statement in the House of Commons on the loss of the Royal Oak, possibly when the House meets to-morrow.

The Admiralty lists issued yesterday give the names of 414 survivors, but it was stated that the hope of others being saved is now remote.

In the meantime and in the absence of details from official sources, the circumstances in which the battleship came to be sunk must be a matter of conjecture. There is good reason to suppose that she was torpedoed either during Friday night or about daybreak on Saturday.

Experience proves that dawn is always a dangerous time in war at sea. Presumably the Royal Oak was being screened by destroyers, but this protection is not absolutely proof against a lucky shot.

It may be suggested that a big ship such as the Royal Oak, fitted with anti-torpedo bulges, should have been able to survive the effects of one or two torpedo hits.

A great deal must obviously depend on the particular spot in which a torpedo hits. Bulges do not cover the extreme ends of a ship.

One theory advanced at the time of the loss of H.M.S. Courageous was that she was sunk by a torpedo set to run immediately beneath her and exploded there by a special electrical device without any contact being made with the hull. There appears to be no evidence to support this.

The suggestion that a mine may have been responsible for the loss of the Royal Oak is discounted by the official statement that the sinking is believed to have been due to U-boat action.

**(October 16)**

# STRONG REINFORCEMENTS SENT TO MONTE VIDEO

## BRITISH CRUISERS' BRILLIANT TACTICS

**From Our Special Correspondent**

MONTE VIDEO, Thursday.

One of the 10,000-ton £3,750,000 pocket battleships, on which Germany had staked such high hopes, to-day swung at anchor in Monte Video harbour, crippled by at least 13 hits from the smaller guns of three British cruisers.

She had suffered disastrous defeat in the first serious naval engagement of the war and one of the most thrilling fights in the annals of the sea.

Her opponents were the Ajax, 6,985 tons; Achilles, 7,030 tons, and Exeter, 8,390 tons.

Bigger and stronger than the British vessels that pursued her like terriers in an all-day running fight along the Uruguayan coast, the German ship had been forced to turn tail and seek refuge in this neutral port with 36 dead and 60 seriously wounded and with 30 or 40 minor casualties.

EXPERTS AMAZED

First Real Test

Naval experts here are amazed at the success of the three small British cruisers in forcing the pocket battleship, in her first real test, to run away from her far less formidable pursuers at the utmost speed.

The fight began soon after dawn yesterday when the German ship encountered the French steamer Formose, 9,975 tons en route from Rio de Janeiro to Monte Video. She promptly attacked the British cruiser, Ajax, convoying the Formose.

Commodore Harwood commanded the British squadron from the bridge of the Ajax. She returned the fire while calling for help.

Before Cmdre, Harwood went into action, newspapers here state that he hoisted Nelson's famous signal: "England expects every man this day will do his duty."

Very soon two other cruisers of the British South Atlantic Squadron, the Exeter and the Achilles, appeared on the horizon and an intense gunnery duel began.

The Achilles was the first to arrive, and passengers in the Formose saw the opening round of the fight.

While the Formose departed safely from the scene, the cruisers threw a heavy smoke screen around the battleship. They took up positions on each side and in the rear and poured shells into her.

BRITISH SKILL

Enemy Silhouetted

The Exeter's eight-inch shells wrecked the battleship's forward turret and control tower almost immediately. The German commander, realising the danger from this cruiser, which is larger and more heavily gunned than the other two, concentrated his fire on her.

As a result the Exeter was severely damaged and forced out of the fight.

All the time the four ships were running in a southerly direction. When the Exeter had to drop out, the pocket battleship herself was so badly damaged that it was obvious she would have to seek refuge in the River Plate.

The Ajax and the Achilles were still on her heels, blazing away with their 6in guns, and they continued in pursuit throughout the afternoon.

Soon after the warships passed Punta del Este, which projects far into the sea, the two cruisers turned westward towards the shore to take full advantage of the setting sun. The German battleship was silhouetted on the sky while the cruisers were protected by the shadow of the land.

This forced the battleship to change her course to the south-east. Firing was renewed and continued until well after sunset. Darkness enabled the battleship to change her course again and make for Monte Video.

The German raider entered the difficult port towards midnight with all lights extinguished and without the aid of a local pilot.

Expert eye-witnesses of the action paid tribute to the magnificent seamanship displayed by the British in manoeuvring their ships in such a way as to avoid salvoes from the battleship's bigger and longer range guns, while repeatedly darting in to fire their own shells.

Utilising smoke screens to conceal their precise positions, they twisted and turned continually, never letting the quarry get away from them.

**(December 15)**

# WORLD HORROR AT SINKING OF BRITISH LINER

The world was horrified yesterday by the first German Sea atrocity of the war – the torpedoing of the British liner Athenia, 13,581 tons, 200 miles north-west of Ireland, at 8.59 p.m. on Sunday. No warning was given by the German submarine which fired the torpedo.

The Athenia carried 1,400 passengers, 311 of whom are Americans, and 630 of these are believed to have been saved by two Scandinavian ships. Another 500, including 10 injured, are in two unknown vessels expected in the Clyde this morning.

The liner belonged to the Donaldson Atlantic Line, and the following notice was posted in the window of the offices in Glasgow:

"Passengers and crew, except those killed by explosion, taken to boats and picked up by various ships.

(Signed) Cook, Master."

The Athenia had lifeboats to carry 1,830 passengers. Friends of those on board received picture postcards from her yesterday, saying that the vessel had sailed under wartime conditions, with her portholes blackened and passengers wearing lifebelts.

It is understood that 75 per cent. of them were women and children.

"DIRECT CONTRAVENTION"

The Ministry of Information issued a statement that the sinking "is in direct contravention of the rules regarding submarine warfare by which Germany is bound.

"These rules, to which Germany agreed to adhere, laid down clearly that no merchant ship may be sunk without warning, and that in any case no merchant ship is to be sunk until the safety of all passengers and crew has been assured.

"The rules further state that ships' boats are not to be considered a place of safety unless within half an hour's pulling distance of land under favourable conditions."

The Athenia was 200 miles from land at the time.

**(September 5)**

# FASTEST BOMBER PASSES TEST

**From Our Industrial Correspondent**

GEODETICS TOWN, Wednesday.

Two fearsome-looking, camouflaged Wellington long-range bombers roared a few feet above my head to-day.

They were identical. Both were fully loaded – five members of the crew, six machine-guns and bombs.

The performance possibilities of both machines are the same. Yet one tore through the air at a speed faster than that of any other type of bomber owned by the belligerents. The other moved, relatively, at a snail's pace.

It was a demonstration of the versatility and manoeuvring capability of the world's best bomber, which is being produced here at a rate unimagined but a few months ago.

Geodetic construction, reduced to simple language, means perfect streamlining of wings and bodies, built from a "meccano" of two-dimensional cylindrically curved parts. The results is a machine, which can fly further and faster and carry more bombs than any aeroplane possessed by the enemy.

Two of the machine-guns carried by the Wellington are operated from a contraption from which the fire of the guns can be directed at almost any angle.

**(December 7)**

# FINNISH CABINET RESIGNS AT MIDNIGHT

## BID FOR PEACE AFTER DAY OF FIGHTING

Following a day of air, land and sea attacks on Finland by Soviet forces, the Finnish Government resigned at midnight, despite a unanimous vote of confidence given to the Cabinet by Parliament.

It was hoped in Helsinki (Helsingfors) that a new Government would be formed which would be able to negotiate with Russia and come to terms with that country.

Four bombing raids – one late last night – were made on Helsinki. Latest reports state that 80 people were killed, mostly women and children.

During the day it was reported that Russian troops had advanced ten miles beyond the frontier. Soviet warships shelled the Finnish coast and strategic islands were seized.

(December 1)

## 'PLANES RAIN DEATH ON HELSINKI

### From Herbert Beck, Daily Telegraph Correspondent

HELSINKI, Thursday.

At 9.15 this morning the inhabitants of Helsinki heard their first air raid warning. Children at once returned to their homes from school, and all traffic was suspended with the exception of official vehicles. The people displayed wonderful coolness.

Catching the last tramcar to the Post Office I found the personnel of the telegraph office marshalled in air raid shelters. Police cycled along the middle of the streets warning pedestrians to return home or seek shelter.

First reports stated that three Soviet 'planes had been seen flying high over Kallio, the industrial quarter. Later, it was reported that the 'planes had actually flown over Paasila, a suburb, where five incendiary bombs were dropped without causing any damage.

### 'PLANES FIRED ON
### Russians in Finnish Territory

At 9.45 a large Soviet bomber flew low over Helsinki and went out to sea without dropping any bombs. Anti-aircraft guns fired upon it, but apparently it was not hit.

The excitement caused by these incidents had scarcely died down when at 11 o'clock four more Russian 'planes were sighted. They flew over Helsinki Harbour and were fired upon without success.

On the Karelian isthmus heavy artillery fire is reported to have occurred at the village of Kivinebb, and at Suojaervi, 70 miles north of Lake Ladoga, the Russians are reported to be in occupation of a small strip of Finnish territory. The Finns are stated to be offering strong resistance to the Russian advance. It is reported that they have captured or destroyed eight Soviet tanks. Two Soviet 'planes are reported to have been brought down on the isthmus. These attacks occurred at the same time as the first air-raid on Helsinki.

Russians are also stated to have occupied the Finnish part of the Ribach Peninsular the "Fisherman's Peninsular" at the northern end of the Finnish frontier.

### NAVAL BOMBARDMENT
### From Base and Ships

From the sea Russians bombarded Vammelsu on the Karelian Isthmus. The firing is believed to have come from Kronstadt, the Soviet naval base in the Gulf of Finland. One report states that ships at sea also shelled the town.

Unconfirmed reports state that Soviet troops have landed at Hangoe, at the entrance to the Gulf of Finland, after the port had been bombarded.

At 11 o'clock this morning the industrial quarter of the town of Enso was bombed, and an hospital was set on fire. Otherwise the damage was only slight. Many cellulose plants are situated in the vicinity. The town of Imtrata was also bombed, but no serious damage was caused.

### BUILDINGS ON FIRE
### Bombs to Put Our Fires

About a quarter to three several Soviet 'planes raided Helsinki.

Many bombs were dropped, most of them being incendiary. The number of casualties is very great, the dead whose number was at one time estimated at 200, was last night declared in a Helsinki radio announcement to be 80. Some buildings are still in flames, and powerful bombs are being used in an effort to put out the fires. Streets are strewn with shattered glass.

All the windows of the Soviet Legation were broken by bombs dropped by the raiders. The raid lasted an hour and 40 minutes. One Soviet 'plane was brought down.

As I sat at a window writing raiding 'planes were reported over the fortress of Suomenlinna, Helsinki. It was clear, sunny weather, and people were walking calmly about the streets. During the bombardment of Suomenlinna one soldier was killed.

Leaflets dropped from Soviet 'planes over the Soernaes workers' quarter of Helsinki called on soldiers and workers to throw down their arms in a hopeless struggle and save their wives and children from the horrors and sufferings of war.

At nine o'clock to-night Soviet aircraft again approached Helsinki. One raider was shot down in flames.

President Kallio to-day proclaimed the country as being in a state of war, and at a council meeting, 72-year-old Field-Marshal Baron C.G. Mannerheim was appointed Commander-in-Chief of the Finn forces. To-night the Finnish Cabinet was in session.

(December 1)

## NEW EINSTEIN THEORY

### SOLVING GRAVITATION
### From Our Own Correspondent

PRINCETOWN, Monday.

A new theory which he believes may solve the riddle of gravitation is announced in a birthday interview to-day by Prof. Albert Einstein, who will be 60 to-morrow.

Einstein declined to divulge details of what he thinks may prove the clue to the long-sought single law explaining the structure of the entire universe and all the mysteries of matter and radiation.

"The layman," he said, "can at least realise one thing – that the pursuit of such a goal requires almost unlimited patience. Since the formulation of the general theory of relativity there has existed the problem of bringing under one unifying mathematical concept the gravitational field, the electro-magnetic field and material particles.

"Mathematical construction for the unified field theory devised by me heretofore have not stood the test of experience. A year ago I discovered a new solution, and I am now engaged with two collaborators developing the results to a point where they could be checked by experimental facts."

(March 14)

## GERMANY CLAIMS AIR SPEED RECORD

### 470 MILES AN HOUR

The absolute world speed record of 464 m.p.h. claimed by Germany with a Heinkel pursuit plane less than a month ago is claimed again at approximately 470 m.p.h. by a German Messerschmidt pursuit plane piloted by Herr Fritz Wendel, aged 24, at Augsberg, Bavaria. The plane was powered by a Mercedes benz engine developing 1,175 h.p. This engine was also fitted to the Heinkel machine. .

(April 28)

## £150 A YEAR PENSIONS FOR M.P.S IN NEED

By a majority of 204 to 103 the House approved to-night the scheme of contributory pensions for its necessitous members recently drawn up by a departmental committee. It was a free vote. The Prime Minister took pains to emphasise that the Government as a Government had no opinion, and that he would not reproach any member for voting against the scheme.

(February 3)

## LEAGUE OF NATIONS EXPELS RUSSIA
### From Our Own Correspondent

GENEVA, Thursday.

At precisely six o'clock this evening the President of the League Council, M. Costa de Rels, Bolivia, tapped the bronze-topped marble council table with his chairman's wooden hammer and pronounced the one word "Adopted."

From that moment Soviet Russia ceased to be a member of the League of Nations, having been expelled for violating the Covenant.

The resolution thus passed stated that "by its act the Union of Soviet Socialist Republics has placed itself outside the League of Nations. It follows that the Union of Soviet Socialist Republics is no longer a member of the League."

This final meeting of the Council at which the historic decision was taken marked the end of much longer discussions in the Assembly and in the committees.

### 45 MINUTES TO DECIDE

It took the 11 members of the Council, the delegates for Soviet Russia and Iran being absent and Peru no longer being a member of the League, only three-quarters of an hour to lead up to the final act.

The discussion in the marble Council hall was dignified as always. The speeches were delivered as usual by each member seated.

The meeting opened at two minutes to five o'clock. Mr. Wellington Koo, the Chinese delegate, a past president of the Council, remained immersed in a manuscript. This led many to believe that he would make a prolonged speech. In fact when his turn came he merely intimated that his Government would abstain from voting.

M. Holsti the Finnish delegate, drew a piece of paper from his pocket and, speaking in English with a pleasant deep-voiced accent, briefly thanked the President for his words of sympathy and encouragement. Though not bound to do so by the rules of the Covenant he declared that he would abstain from voting on the motion to expel Russia "so that the Council's resolution shall have a character of greater impartiality."

The delegates of Greece and Jugoslavia also expressed their decision to abstain.

(December 15)

## FIRST CASUALTIES OF B.E.F.

### VICTIMS OF NIGHT PATROL
### From Douglas Williams, Daily Telegraph War Correspondent
### With the British Forces in the Maginot Line, Sunday.

The first casualties of the B.E.F. since they took over a sector of the Maginot Line some weeks ago are announced officially in one laconic sentence: "The British now have their wounded and even their dead on French soil once again."

In the whitewashed ward of a French hospital lent to us by the French authorities in a town behind the Maginot Line I talked with the first soldier of the British Army to be a battlefield casualty since the war started more than three months ago. The casualty occurred in the course of a night reconnaissance in no man's land separating the British and German lines.

My casualty had both his arms seriously but not dangerously wounded and bandaged to the elbows with splints and cotton wool. His head and shoulders had been scarred by innumerable small splinters of metal. He was happy and cheerful, however, and sat up in bed as he recounted his adventure.

### CRAWL IN SNOW AND DARKNESS

A platoon sergeant-major of 16 years' Army service, he had been instructed on the night in question to take a small party from a well-known Midland country regiment out on patrol in the sector it had just taken over. The night was bitterly cold with occasional flurries of snow, and pitch dark.

Wearing warm leather jerkins over their battle dress and high rubber boots and carrying rifles and hand grenades, the little band started out on its mission of reconnaissance. They wormed their way over rough ground, sometimes having to crawl through holes half filled with water or having to cut their way through old rusty wire, against which they bumped in the darkness.

Their course had to be taken largely by radium-illuminated compass. All went well until they approached a gully.

All of a sudden a mine went up seemingly under their very feet, wounding several of the party, including the sergeant-major. A corporal suffered severe wounds to the feet, and others less dangerous injuries.

The sergeant-major, although bleeding profusely from his arm wounds, rallied his party and pushed forward.

(December 18)

# ATTACK ON WARSHIPS IN FIRTH OF FORTH

## R.A.F. & A.A. GUNS BRING DOWN FOUR 'PLANES

An air raid on the East Coast of Scotland, in which from 12 to 14 German 'planes took part, was carried out in the Firth of Forth yesterday. It was the first time in the present war enemy 'planes have reached Britain.

Four of the enemy 'planes were brought down. There were 35 casualties among crews of British warships during the raid, of which no A.R.P. warning was given to the public.

Three of the crew of one of the raiders, brought down in the sea by a Fighter, were rescued by a fishing boat and brought to land.

The following communiqué was issued by the Admiralty, Air Ministry and Ministry for Home Security through the Press Bureau last night:

"To-day, Oct. 16, between 9 a.m. and 1.30 p.m., several German aircraft reconnoitred Rosyth. This afternoon, at about half-past two, a series of bombing raids began.

"These were directed at the ships lying in the Forth and were conducted by about a dozen machines. All the batteries opened fire upon the raiders, and the Royal Air Force, fighter squadron ascended to engage them.

"No serious damage was done to any of his Majesty's ships. One bomb glanced off the cruiser Southampton, causing slight damage near her bow, and sank the Admiral's barge and a pinnace which were moored empty alongside.

"This was the first hit which German aircraft have made during the war upon a British ship.

"There were three casualties on board the Southampton and seven on board the cruiser Edinburgh from splinters.

"Another bomb fell near the destroyer Mohawk, which was returning to harbour from convoy escort. This bomb burst on the water, and its splinters caused 25 casualties to the men on the deck of the destroyer.

"Only superficial damage was caused to the vessel, which, like the others, is ready for sea.

"On the other hand, four bombers at least out of 12 or 14 were brought down, three of them by fighters of the Royal Air Force.

"The first contact between Royal Air Force aircraft and the enemy raiders took place off May Island at the entrance to the Firth of Forth at 2.35 p.m. when two enemy aircraft were intercepted. They were driven down by our aircraft from 4,000 feet to within a few feet of the water and chased out to sea.

"Another enemy aircraft was engaged ten minutes later over Dalkeith. It fell in flames into the sea.

"Within a quarter of an hour a sharp combat took place off Crail, and a second raider crashed into the sea.

"A third German aircraft was destroyed in the pursuit.

"Two German aviators have been rescued by one of our destroyers, of whom one has since died.

"No civilian casualties have been reported, and none occurred in the Royal Air Force."

(October 12)

## R.A.F. AGAIN OVER GERMANY

### ONE MACHINE MISSING

The Air Ministry announced yesterday that R.A.F. aircraft carried out a successful reconnaissance of North-West Germany on Wednesday. One of the aircraft failed to return.

Yesterday's German communiqué attempted to minimise the success of the flight, saying that the British 'planes were repulsed by anti-aircraft fire.

They admitted that two British 'planes reached the coast and that one was shot down by a German fighter.

(December 29)

# MR. WODEHOUSE, D.LITT.

## OXFORD HONOUR FOR "MAGIC WRITER"

**From Our Own Correspondent**

OXFORD, Wednesday.

Mr. Cyril Bailey, Fellow of Balliol College, made his last appearance at the Encaenia at Oxford to-day as Public Orator, when Mr. P.G. Wodehouse was among those receiving honorary degrees.

He introduced Mr. Wodehouse for his D.Litt. in Latin verse as "a magic writer, than whom none more skilled, to charm men's minds and raise a ready laugh." The Latin text appears below with a free translation of some of its delightfully expressed sentiments.

JEEVES AND MULLINERS'

The Public Orator, who is to be succeeded next month by Mr. T.F. Higham, Fellow of Trinity College, introduced Mr. Wodehouse as follows:

*Ecce auctor magicus, quo non expertior alter*
*delectare animos hominum risusque movere.*
*namque novas scaenae personas intulit et res*
*ridiculas cuique adiunxit, Cui non bene notus*
*dives opum iuvenis, comisque animique benigni,*
*nec quod vult fecisse capax, nisi fidus Achates*
*ipse doli fabricator adest vestisque decentis*
*arbiter? aut comes ille loquax et ventre rotundo*
*cui patruusque neposque agnatorum et domus omnis*
*miranda in vita - sic narrat - fata obierunt?*
*Nobilis est etiam Clarens, fundique paterni*
*et suis eximiae dominus, Psmintheusque relicta*
*cui fac cuncta, Augustus item qui novit amores*
*ranicularum, aliusque alio sub sidere natus.*
*non vitia autem hominum naso suspendit adunco*
*sed tenera pietate notat, peccataque ridet.*
*Hoc quoque, lingua etsi repleat plebeia chartas,*
*non incomposito patitur pede currere verba,*
*concinnus, lepidus, puri sermonis amator.*
*(Who does not know the rich youth, mild and kind.*
*Unable to do what he would, unless*
*Jeeves "rallies round" to make the plan for him*
*And choose his socks? Or Mulliner, our friend*
*With wagging tongue and portly shape, who tells*
*How cousins, uncles, aunts and all his house*
*Have met with strange adventures in their lives ...*
*Nor does he scorn the weaknesses of men*
*But marks them lovingly and smiles at faults.*
*And though the common speech fills every page.*
*No careless words, no hasty writing mars them*
*He's neat and smart, a lover of pure style.)*

**(June 22)**

# R.A.F. PROVIDE FILM THRILLS

"The Lion Has Wings," Alexander Korda's film of the Royal Air Force began its run at the Leicester Square Theatre yesterday. Within the next 48 hours it will be flying to all parts of the world.

Vividly, with magnificent flying shots, moving sentiment and some nice touches of humour, the film tell the story of the R.A.F.'s part in the war.

Flag-wagging has been avoided. Britain's devotion to the pursuits of peace up to the very last is emphasised, and when war does come we see the Air Force going about its business with a single-mindedness all the more effective for its freedom from hysteria.

Some 300ft were cut by the Censor at the request of the Air Ministry, and one can well believe that some shots must have demanded careful thought.

Even as the film stands, the scenes showing the interior of a Wellington bomber (a trifle obsolescent, no doubt), and the fascinating glimpses of the Air staff following operations on a map running the whole length of the floor below, seem remarkably convincing and complete.

The flying shots, made with the co-operation of the R.A.F., have uncanny precision and rare beauty; and the reconstruction of the raid on a German battleship at Wilhelmshaven is a marvel of realism.

**(October 31)**

ROBERT DONAT AND Ronald Ward in "Goodbye Mr. Chips!"

# IS MR. CHIPS A MYTH?

## A MAN – OR AN IDEALISED MEMORY?

**By A Film Correspondent**

THE event of the week is "Goodbye Mr. Chips!" at the Empire. It is the third successful film, made by M.G.M. in Great Britain, and America has already begun to call it a masterpiece.

I saw it at the height of a heatwave, in a private theatre, which is not air-conditioned. And it really is so good that I could not forbear, in all my limp deliquescence, from wanting to get my teeth into it.

If you think that is a paradox, cast your mind back to the last 10 films you have seen. Some you enjoyed, some you found exciting, some irritating, some dull. I doubt if you feel like arguing about any of them now. They are just so many vague impressions of entertainment.

"Goodbye, Mr. Chips!" will outlast them in your mind, and probably the next 10 pictures which you see after it; and because it has such a compelling quality, it must be measured, not by other films and plays, but by life itself.

### A "Real" Character

IT has set me arguing, but not about its charm, its appeal, its entertainment value. They are all beyond question. Rather I want to argue about Mr. Chips himself, as if he were as real and as important as Mr. Chamberlain.

Is he the hero of the British public-school system, or its chief victim? That life of selfless devotion to generation after generation of schoolboys, that monastic absorption in the narrow world of elementary Latin and Greek and schoolboys' games – are they quaintly magnificent, as every celluloid inch of this film suggests? Or are they the result of some interior flinching, a refusal to face the wider world?

Is Mr. Chips quite a good thing for our growing boys? Might not somebody a little less sympathetic, less devoted to tradition, but more like the kind of person they will meet when they step off into the cruel, hard world, do them more good?

### Memory of Boyhood?

FINALLY, does Mr. Chips, did Mr. Chips, ever exist? Is he, perhaps, the projection of a boyhood memory on the mind of middle-age – a well-loved master, still seen through the eyes of immaturity, his schoolmasterly faults tenderly caricatured, his schoolmasterly virtues made dazzlingly effulgent, while his faults and virtues as a man, being unknown, are reconstructed on insufficient evidence?

Whatever your own particular answers to these questions, you will not be disappointed in the film. It has an artistic harmony of its own, and the doubts and questionings come later.

Mr. Sam Woods's direction is simple.

### Triumph of Developing Character

ROBERT DONAT'S performance is the tour-de-force I expected of him. The youthful diffidence, the single-minded devotion to his job and to the woman who has the understanding to identify herself with it, and then the gradual expansion of the character into the benignant symbol of Brookfields' continuity are all delicately presented.

In his moments of drama and pathos he suggests the emotions which Mr. Chipps would never have known how to express. The gentleness, courtesy and spiritual endurance are there, and the whimsicality of great age, at which only the austerest of critics could cavil.

Whether the fans, who have learnt to love Donat in more dashing guise, will be so pleased is another matter. But perhaps we need not bother too much about them.

### Charm of "Mrs. Chips"

GREER GARSON scores magnificently as Katherine, who, having persuaded Mr. Chips to marry her, breeds in him some hesitant belief in himself and then dies. What a deathbed scene we were mercifully spared! ... and how marvellously she suggested by a sort of quiet, happy charm, the sincerity of her love for the gauche, middle-aged schoolmaster.

## JOHN FORD GOES WESTERN

BACK in the realms of entertainment, pure and simple in the Wildean sense of the words, let me commend "Stagecoach" at the Odeon. This is just another film which leads one to suppose – erroneously, I admit, except now and again – that the less money spent on a production the better it is likely to be.

"Stagecoach" was made for a Hollywood song, or maybe aria of £50,000, by John Ford. The only visible economy is the absence of a star; but in dramatic force, scenic impressiveness and neat small-scale character-drawing it comes near to challenging the best of the year.

The main drama obviously concerns the passengers as a group. There are half a dozen subordinate dramas of individuals – the absconding bank manager, the bad girl thrown out of town, the officer's wife who wants to have her baby near her husband, the Southern ne'er-do-well who travels with her from motives of chivalry, the outlaw with a grudge to settle in Lordsville, the drunken doctor and the whisky salesman who looks like a parson.

There is, in fact, nothing new in "Stagecoach" and yet it is all as fresh as the dawn, thanks to really intelligent direction and some acting with real heart in it from Thomas Mitchell, Claire Trevor, Berton Churchill, John Wayne, John Carradine, Donald Meek and Tom Tyler – not especially in that order.

If I were a producer, I should also like to put under contract the mesas (huge rock-formations) of the Monument Valley, Arizona. I calculate their moral value at about £10,000 in this film.

**(June 12)**

# MUSIC AT NATIONAL GALLERY

## MIDDAY CONCERTS

Though the National Gallery has been stripped of all its pictures for the duration of the war, it will soon be attracting again a multitude of quiet visitors.

From Tuesday daily concerts by distinguished artists will be given from 1 p.m. to 2 p.m. in the Dome and adjacent rooms of the Gallery. Admission will be 1s.

There will be no concerts on Saturdays and Sundays, but on Tuesdays and Fridays there will be additional concerts from 4.30 to 5.30 p.m., admission 2s 6d. At these the midday programmes will be repeated.

The first two concerts will be given on Tuesday by Miss Myra Hess, the well-known pianist, who is one of the originators of the scheme. Other artists who have promised their services are Roy Henderson, Moiseiwitsch, Catherine Long, Gerald Moore, Orloff, Lisa Perli, Joan Cross, Isolde Menges, and the Griller String Quartet.

**(October 7)**

# FILM OF "WUTHERING HEIGHTS"

**By Campbell Dixon**

Rarely have so many members of the Diplomatic Corps, politicians, distinguished writers and actors been seen at a first night as at the premiere of "Wuthering Heights" at the Gaumont Cinema, Haymarket, last night.

They saw a production given rare distinction by its fidelity to the original, the fine integrity of William Wyler's direction, and the acting of Merle Oberon and Laurence Olivier.

Mr. Olivier is, of course, a tragedian of great experience and power. Miss Oberon's performance will surprise those who know her only for her work in comedy and light romance. The scene where Heathcliff carries the dying girl to the window for her last glimpse of the moors she loved moved many of last night's audience to tears.

**(April 26)**

New Fiction

# MR. JOHN STEINBECK'S EPIC STORY

**The Grapes of Wrath. By John Steinbeck. (Heinemann. 8s 6d.)**
**How Green Was My Valley, By Richard Llewellyn. (Michael Joseph. 8s 6d.)**
**By John Brophy**

LOTS of people settling down to an amended routine of life should be glad to know that at the nearest bookshop or library they will find an attractive choice of novels both new and good. First place undoubtedly belongs to "The Grapes of Wrath," by Mr. John Steinbeck, who wrote "Of Mice and Men." It is a long story and for all its detailed realism, deliberately epical in scope and style.

The Joads are a family of Oklahoma sharecroppers typical of thousands of others who find they can no longer wrest even a poor living out of soil breaking up into dust. They collect a little money and an old lorry and take to the road, heading for California, the promised land full of oranges and grapes. Tom just released from prison for manslaughter, shares the driving with young Al, a born mechanic. Father and mother depart more reluctantly. The grandfather and grandmother die on the road.

Their progress is makeshift, adventurous, and they are often in danger of starvation. But unsophisticated as they are, mingling ribaldry with an elementary piety, they are all alive. Mr. Steinbeck is an authentic creator of human beings.

The villains of this large, swift, crowded and moving story are not so much the banks and the deputy sheriffs as impalpable forces; and in his generalisations on this theme Mr. Steinbeck is not so successful. Sometimes he has the blandly ludicrous air of a film travelogue commentator. But he has written what is in every sense a "big" book. It carries its few faults easily, and is guaranteed to absorb the reader's attention away from present-day worries.

**(September 22)**

## IN A WELSH VALLEY

Reading this first novel, one has the impression of living in a backwater of time, to be sitting quietly by the side of an old man as he looks back over 50 years and wonders at the strange trend of civilisation. For, sharply down the vista of a half-century, existence in the little Welsh valley stands out as a goodly thing.

Money was plentiful, men and children well fed and clothed, and kindliness prevailed.

Huw, the narrator, tells of the meeting of his father, at 20, with a girl of 16, of the simplicity and courage of their life together. Justice was elemental, men took the law into their own hands yet decency and order reigned. But the world outside was to penetrate that green valley. The younger men became infected with the new ideas, strikes were organised among the colliers, and the old father stands aloof, finely indomitable, preaching his direct doctrine of clean living and high thinking.

It is an absorbing narrative, the style, with its crisp staccato sentences, almost Biblical, and rising at times – in the descriptions of the strike meetings and the father's death in the mine – to whiteheat intensity.

**(October 6)**

# FILM DEMANDED 116 MIDGETS

**By Our Film Correspondent**

The oddest scenes ever witnessed even in Hollywood followed Mervyn Le Roy's request to the casting department to supply 116 midgets to play in his film, "The Wizard of Oz."

Leo Singer, tersely described as midget-monger, already had a company of 28 performers in Hollywood. With two 'buses he set out, and in due course returned with the other 88 travelling four to a seat.

In Hollywood the 116 formed a colony in a large apartment house.

At 6.30 they were all awakened by an alarm bell and ate a hearty breakfast – for it seems that, contrary to the general impression, the midgets have full-sized appetites.

The little people are of many nationalities and have followed all sorts of callings.

One Billy Curtis, studied law at the University of Iowa, but decided that a yard-high barrister would have little chance in court. He went into vaudeville.

Another, Leo Robbe, is a chef.

CARRIED TO SAVE TIME

To save time, midget-lifters, six tall men, were employed on the set to carry the players up stairs. Studio drinking fountains were too high for them, and special children's chairs were scattered about the set so that they might rest.

To conform with the law, the studio had to engage teachers for the children, and this led to embarrassing mistakes. The midget children, discovering that in make-up they were indistinguishable from the others, played truant, and wrathful teachers would seize an adult like Carl Becker, to be informed, with some annoyance, that he was already an engineer of the University of Hamburg.

"The Wizard of OZ," long a favourite of American children, is directed by Victor Fleming, with Frank Morgan as the Wizard and Judy Garland as the girl dropped by a cyclone in the midgets' city.

**(March 15)**

# A BIG SUCCESS AT DRURY LANE

**By W.A. Darlington**

Ivor Novello certainly has the Drury Lane touch. Almost alone among our theatre men he is able to devise shows that will fill that enormous playhouse, and he seems to be able to do it at will. "The Dancing Years," which began its run last night, is likely to be even more successful than its predecessors.

Every ingredient of a big romantic musical play has been poured into this show. Its setting is Vienna, the Vienna – except for the final scenes – of the old days, which stands on the stage for song and laughter and youthful passion.

Mr. Novello plays a young composer. Mary Ellis is the girl who sings the leading part in his first opera, and loses her heart to him. They are separated in the end by a Great Misunderstanding, which depends on the most stagey of coincidences – but that is Mr. Novello's secret; he knows that with this kind of show real life has nothing whatever to do.

The more trifle and obvious the story, the more surely he gets it across. Criticism is disarmed and is content to be so; for competence on this great scale amounts to something like genius.

**(March 24)**

**FOR A.R.P.**

Wardens who have to face weather most testing it is imperative to wear the best weatherproof.

The Burberry, The World's Best Weatherproof, preserves good health and provides the greatest security and comfort under the most testing conditions

**ORDER BY POST**

**The Burberry sent on approval on receipt of cheque covering. Measurements required: Size of linen collar; height; inches round chest.**
**Price list and patterns by post.**

*Burberrys have decided, as in the last war, to clean and re-proof free of charge all Burberry Service Weatherproofs worn by men and women Officers on active service in His Majesty's Forces.*

*BUSINESS HOURS AT PRESENT: 9 A.M. UNTIL 5.30P.M.*

BURBERRYS LTD., HAYMARKET, LONDON, S.W.1.

THE DAILY TELEGRAPH

and

MORNING POST

Daily Telegraph - 29th June 1855.
Morning Post - 2nd November 1772.
[Amalgamated 1st October, 1937]

135, Fleet-st., London E. C. 4.
Telephone: Central 4242
Net Daily Sales Over 750,000

# BRITAIN TAKES UP THE NAZI CHALLENGE

## TO SAVE LIBERTY ITSELF

With conscience clear, with no purpose to serve but the saving of liberty itself, Great Britain and France are at war with Germany. In the King's noble broadcast to the Empire, as in the message in which the Prime Minister yesterday announced that the last bid for honourable peace had failed, the ends for which we have taken up the Nazi challenge are put beyond the question of history. We have entered upon a conflict that may well call for such sacrifices as the nation has never before made in the single belief that the Nazi creed and the existence of freedom for the weaker peoples of the earth cannot exist together; that the one must be stamped out if the other is to survive. At this moment our people put aside every unnerving thought. Though civilisation itself may be in jeopardy, we are confident that after the trial to which it will be subjected it will emerge freed from the threat that Hitlerism holds to everything that makes life worth while to those who have not accepted its creed of violence. The things against which we fight are, as the Prime Minister has summed them up "brute force, bad faith, injustice, oppression and persecution." We enter the battle in no spirit of vainglory – never was a nation more calm, less exuberant, more resolved, at the beginning of war – but with the unshakable conviction that right must ultimately prevail.

All delay all suggestion of hesitation is ended. Without a dissenting voice our people have pledged themselves to help Poland to the very limit of national endeavour. From the first moment that Poland was assailed there has been no doubt in the mind of all our citizens what our response must be, what honour and sacred obligations and even the safety of civilisation itself required. Hence the pained surprise on Saturday when Mr. Chamberlain had to announce to an astonished House of Commons that a declaration of war awaited the outcome of Signor Mussolini's last effort for peace, and that no time limit had been fixed for the German reply. Had the mood of our people been the overriding factor in the situation, the first shot across the Polish frontier would have been the signal for British intervention.

In entering upon war to root out "the plague and scourge of mankind," there has already been the fullest response to his Majesty's appeal that his peoples should "stand calm, firm and united." Never was there the least doubt that the Empire would share the sentiments and be prepared for the sacrifices of the Motherland. Their instant association of themselves with the cause that the democracies have sworn to protect is already assured. They have recognised with ourselves, that we fight to save the whole world from the pestilence of Nazi-ism. Two other things we may feel as we enter upon the highest trial to which the nation has been subjected. In the last few days the crisis has produced such evidence of preparedness as has never before been attained at the commencement of war. The fine organisation of the protective services, the smoothness with which the evacuation of 3,000,000 women and children has been carried through, the calm with which precautionary measures were taken in the first air-raid warning yesterday, provide convincing evidence that our people will remain unshaken by the experiences they must face. Secondly, there is, as Mr. Churchill said in the House of Commons yesterday, a generation ready to prove itself not unworthy of those who laid the foundations of the land, and not unworthy as we may add, of the magnificent Allied armies which in the years of the Great War checked the German ambition at domination now revived under Herr Hitler.

**(September 4)**

# ERSATZ

Just as few of the last war's songs went quite so well with bored British troops as the Hymn of Hate, so many English people now rely on Zeesen, the Nazi short-wave station, for entertainment on dull Sunday afternoons. Without wishing to carp, they feel the commentator in English is letting them down. Yesterday he returned to the attack on "We're Gonna Hang out the Washing on the Siegfried Line." It may comfort him to know that many Britons, of undoubted loyalty, feel about it as he does. A lyric may have the magic of Herrick, the tuneful wit of Sullivan, and still pall after a time.

**(October 30)**

# 119TH DAY OF WAR

## A MOMENTOUS YEAR

We stand at the end of the year looking back upon four months of war. Their events have been very different from what we expected on that brilliant Sunday in September when the country heard "with composure and resolution" that it was at war with Germany, still more different from the anticipations of the Fuehrer and his deluded people. Before long we may be fighting a strenuous air campaign, but four months' testing time has given us no reason to fear the quality of the German machines or pilots, and each day that passes brings us nearer the attainment of power to command the air. Hitler boasted that Britain was no longer an island, yet his navy has been as impotent as his air force to close our seaways. In a campaign of reckless brutality against British and neutral shipping the German submarine service has again earned the detestation of the world, but its power of destruction has been so checked by the Allied navies that the tide of the U-boat war "flows steadily and strongly in our favour."

A battleship and a large aircraft carrier have been actually sunk by Nazi torpedoes and many more capital ships by the mouth of Dr. Goebbels. The Deutschland's big guns sank an armed merchant cruiser. But the one naval action, the running fight of the other "pocket battleship" Graf Spee with Adml. Harwood's three light cruisers, brought no renown to the Nazi navy, and its issue saw the Fuehrer wrapping himself in ignominy. The disappointments and humiliations of the naval war appear to have made Hitlerism hopeless of any future on the seas. No other explanation accounts for the policy of destruction by scuttling of German ships safe in neutral harbours. On land the war has been static as regards movement, but active in the strengthening of defences.

Mr. Churchill predicted that if we came through the winter without any serious blow we should have "gained the first campaign of the war." At the outset Poland was overrun and shamelessly partitioned between Hitlerism and the Soviet. Then the Fuehrer thought fit to talk peace. The reply from the Allies was concentration of all their resources "for the effective prosecution of the war." From the neutral States Hitler received no encouragement. Italy and Japan made it plain that the alliance of Nazi with Bolshevik lacked any charm for them. Soon enough the enormous price which the Fuehrer had promised for the pleasure of wreaking his spite on Poland was exacted and startled the world. Stalin advanced from establishing his control of the Eastern Baltic to devour Finland. Not a tongue might wag in comment so that it could be heard in Germany, though all the Teutonic traditions and the Nazi racial creed, the old Germany policy and Hitler's most precious purposes, were alike abandoned. But the rest of the world knew that the Fuehrer had lost the initiative, that what happened on his eastern frontier and round the Baltic would be determined in his despite, while he could find no means to break through the grip of the blockade in the West. It must be dawning on him that Britain has never in her history taken up arms with unity so complete. The Empire has rallied to a common effort with more than loyalty, with a conviction that liberty in every Dominion and Colony is threatened by Hitlerism. We have worked out such close concord with France as to multiply the strength of each country. Yet the power of the enemy must not be underrated. Efforts of some hundred million people driven on under a desperate régime will only be overcome by tenacity. But we are assured of the issue of a fight. For all men's native land and worth the price of all men's service and their sacrifice.

**(December 30)**

# THE WEATHER

Owing to the outbreak of war, no weather forecast is being issued by the Air Ministry.

# GERMANY HAS IMPOSED A BARBAROUS RULE ON POLAND

**By Dorothy Thompson**

*In the following striking article Dorothy Thompson, one of the best-known commentators on world affairs in the United States, sets forth the terms of bondage which Germany has imposed on conquered Poland.*

*The article is a reply to those who have professed to see iniquity in the Treaty of Versailles. As first published in the New York "Herald Tribune" it bore the title "This is Iniquitous."*

IT is perhaps inevitable that there should have been only meagre reporting regarding the condition of Poland since the partition. Neutral journalists cannot get into Poland. No one can enter without a special permit, and permits have been refused to reporters.

The terms imposed upon Poland are, nevertheless, of the first importance in arriving at an objective judgment regarding the aims of the war and the effect upon Europe of a possible German victory.

The facts about Poland are vastly more important than the propaganda of any of the belligerants. From them one can derive a picture of what Europe might be like under Nazi domination.

KNELL OF SMALL NATIONS

Such information as we possess has come to us from American and other neutral journalists, either gleaned from émigrés or from official German sources. If we confine ourselves exclusively to the latter reports from Berlin we shall hardly get an impression that errs on the side of unfairness to the Nazis.

From these reports, one must conclude that continued fulminations against the "Versailles system" can come with good grace only from those responsible for it – from the Allies.

In the Allied journals there is, indeed, much discussion regarding the future of Europe and much searching analysis and criticism of the European system erected after the last war. But it must categorically be stated that the "Versailles Peace" compared with the Nazi peace, the outlines of which are indisputable, emerges in retrospect as enlightened, humane and progressive.

The Nazi peace for Europe – basing one's judgment upon the official facts regarding Czechoslovakia and Poland – means the end of all small nations, not by absorbing them as equal individual citizens into larger political and economic units, but by their subjection as nations into colonial "protectorates," and by the subjection of their peoples into serfs of the German master race.

DRAGOONING THE PEOPLE

The conquered are to be permanent slaves to the conquerors. They are to have no full citizenship at all. They are to be hewers of wood and drawers of water; soldiers, workmen and peasants engaged in organised production for their masters, under the masters' orders.

In this article I shall deal wholly with the Nazi "peace" for Poland. The Sovietisation of Poland is a chapter in itself, and the facts are even more obscure.

But that part of Poland annexed by the Germans has been divided into purely German territory and into a colonial territory, a protectorate, along the model of the division of Czechoslovakia into purely German (Sudetenland) and a colonial protectorate (Moravia-Bohemia).

Poland, at the time of Hitler's conquest, was inhabited by Poles in the relation of eighteen Poles to one German, and in the annexed territory, in the proportion of eight to one. These Poles are being removed from the annexed territory into the Governement General, the rump-Poland occupied by Germany, ruled and directed by Germany, but not admitted to the Reich.

Into this same territory, but on special reservations are being moved all the Jews of Poland, Czechoslovakia, former Austria, and the Reich proper.– some 440,000 souls – to swell the population of a territory already overcrowded. The Jews are permitted to carry with them only the equivalent of 300 marks and such personal belongings as they can carry in a suitcase.

The deportation orders apply to adults. Many have been unable to take their children and must leave them behind to the care of international Jewish charity or to orphan asylums.

Germans, then, from the Baltic States and from the rest of Poland and former Czechoslovakia are to be moved into the Polish territory definitely annexed to the Reich.

The serf-population left in the Gouvernement General are to live in vastly greater numbers on radically diminished territory, at a social, economic and cultural level to be systematically kept below that of Germany.

The official German newspaper in Warsaw says "There can be no thought of sentimental fraternisation between Germans and Poles." The West German "Beobachter" sums up the position in the words "A strong, thoroughly German peasantry, thoroughly conscious of its rights as masters, shall find a permanent home in this land."

The property of the Polish State has been confiscated by Germany. The Polish port of Gdynia, built by Polish labour and Polish money, has been taken over by the Germans and all Poles driven out of it.

The German Labour Service has been sent into the Gouvernement General to organise the Polish workers and speed them up. Drilled like soldiers, these youths are apparently ruthless foremen.

And, of course, the Secret Police, the Gestapo, is ubiquitous.

To find parallels one must go to the old imperial conquests of African and Asiatic tribes, back to a form of imperialism which the modern world has long since rejected, or back beyond that to the enslavement of the "barbarians" by the Romans – though even they admitted to Roman citizenship the peoples living in territory annexed by the Empire.

The citizens of the Allied countries may therefore demand that their Governments indicate peace terms in case of their own victory. But no terms conceivable to the civilised mind can be as bad as the terms Nazi Germany has already imposed where she is victorious. They are of a cruelty and a barbarism – made more horrible by modern efficiency – which baffle analogy.

So let us at least hear no more about the iniquity of the Treaty of Versailles. It belongs to an imperfect but still moral humane epoch. It was at least a treaty. There is no Treaty of Warsaw. For a treaty implies legal rights to both signers.

# NEIGHBOURLINESS TO THE TROOPS

## A WAY FOR CIVILIANS TO BE USEFUL

**By Our Military Correspondent**

THROUGHOUT the winter, and perhaps for many months to come, there will be a small detachment of soldiers scattered all over the country – air defence groups, parties from home defence battalions and similar groups – guarding vulnerable points or on duties of that kind.

It is not easy in these days of the war to ensure that such parties should have well-found accommodation, and their duties are often far from exciting though they necessitate constant vigilance. Anti-aircraft and other defence groups have to wait for the enemy to come along; they cannot have the interest of hunting for him. In short, the duties may become boring, and the men will have few opportunities for recreation or relaxation.

They will often be strangers to the district and will be without friends to visit them or to take an interest in them; that is to say, so long as neighbouring residents adopt the attitude that these are soldiers who have "nothing to do with them," I do not imply that that attitude is often adopted, but at times there is hesitation to make the first move, and ignorance of the way assistance can be given.

Recreation and Comforts

It was recently announced that an Army social welfare organisation had been started, which I have no doubt will be able to do a great deal to improve conditions under which troops are living. Where large numbers of troops are concerned, the organisation is essential. It may take time, however, for it to embrace scattered detachments, and I think something more than organisation is required in their case.

What I would appeal for is the display of individual neighbourliness and friendship towards them, and I think there are many who would gladly show that form of interest who might fight shy of "organisations," which so often mean committees, begging and making up of parcels.

The sort of things a neighbour can do is to find out if all the men have a chance of getting a hot bath, of getting their clothes washed, of getting a hot cup of tea or cocoa when they come off duty on cold, damp winter nights. Again, a neighbour might find out if the men are short of books and papers, if they have cards or games of any sort to pass the time in long evenings? Have they a football and a field in which to kick it about? Where there is lack of space they might be introduced to deck tennis, which takes little room and gives plenty of exercise in a short time.

A little friendly conversation with someone from outside may be what is chiefly wanted, for subjects of conversation are apt to run dry when a small party is isolated, and it is easy enough for men to get on each others' nerves.

Again, it may be thought that everyone may be trusted to do what they can for these little parties without exhortation. I cannot forget, however, my own experience in the winter of 1914. In one town where troops with whom I was concerned were quartered, nothing could exceed the kindness shown to officers and men. In two others, the attitude of the local residents was purely negative.

**(November 30)**

# LONDON DAY BY DAY:

THE House of Commons yesterday cheered Mr. Churchill's tribute to "the remarkable exploit of professional skill and daring" of the German U-boat that sank the Royal Oak. It heard the news that the Scapa Flow defences had been penetrated with a surprised silence.

Mr. Churchill was more formal than usual. He read his statement at a fast pace and with none of the emphasis the House has come to expect from him.

### Parliament's Dinners Cut Down

CMDR. OLIVER LOCKER-LAMPSON will suggest to Mr. W.S. Morrison to-day that menus in all public dining places should be reduced to two or three courses. Parliament has already set a good example in this respect. Full-course dinners disappeared when the war started.

In spite of the number of extra sittings, all of them well attended, the war is doing little to ease Mr. Bracewell Smith's perennial burden of balancing the Parliamentary domestic budget. Most M.P.s do not arrive until after lunch, and frequently the House has risen before dinner.

So far August and September sittings have tended to diminish rather than increase profits in the kitchen department.

### It Might Have Been Worse

Many different messages to the German people have now been scattered by the R.A.F.

One statement, however, is common to them all.

Prominently displayed are the words: "THIS MIGHT HAVE BEEN A BOMB."

### Spendthrift Motorist

FROM "Punch" this week I reproduce a cartoon which deals not with the Fuehrer, but with a problem nearer home – that of the motorist's units.

*"I can't move on - I've used up all my units," [Reproduced by permission of "Punch"]*

The artist, Mr. Wallis Mills, used his wit and his pencil to some purpose in the last war. It is pleasant to see that the humour of this veteran runs as fresh as it did 25 years ago.

### Oxford Union Makes History

TO-DAY the Oxford Union ends the first term of the war with a gesture. It is holding a "soirée dansante" in the dining room – the first of its kind, I believe, that the Union has ever held.

### Formal First Lord. Restricted Menus

This is not to imply that the society has lost any of the intellectual fibre which at one time brought it such prominence in the Press. There have been nearly the normal number of debates this term. Before the last the house adjourned for one minute as a mark of sympathy with the Czechoslovak students whose universities have been closed.

While the Oxford Union dances, that at Cambridge is holding a meeting to-night to express sympathy with Finland. It has been organised by Mr. Francis Noel Baker, secretary of the University Finnish Independence Day Committee. He is a son of Mr. Noel Baker, the Socialist M.P.

### Killed Rescuing a Kitten

COL. J.P. SHELLEY, Passport Control Officer at Warsaw, arrived here yesterday with all the members of his staff. He immediately placed his services at the disposal of the War Office.

As I stated a fortnight ago, Mrs. Shelley was killed by a German bomb. She had gone to the village of Lukow, an evacuation centre about 20 miles from Warsaw.

During an air raid Mrs. Shelley went out to rescue a terrified kitten standing in the middle of the street. A bomb fell almost on the very spot, and Mrs. Shelley, with 29 other victims, was blown to pieces.

### Cockney Comment

OVERHEARD in the Strand: "Why didn't they sound the sirens for the air raid on the Forth?"

"Oh, Scotsmen don't care. The only time they take cover is on a flag day."

**PETERBOROUGH**

# COUNTRY LIFE AS SEEN BY NEWCOMERS FROM LONDON

## YOUTH ADAPTS ITSELF TO SOME SURPRISING "MANNERS AND CUSTOMS"

By W.A. Darlington

IN our village a good many people hardly noticed the outbreak of war. They were too busy. For our village stands in a reception area, and all through Saturday and Sunday it was so deeply occupied in welcoming its guests and settling them in that it had no attention to spare for larger but more distant events.

Our village really consists of little more than a church, a farm, and the buildings connected with one or other. Nearly all the cottages are occupied by the farm people. There are half a dozen middling-sized houses of which the oldest and largest was once the Manor House and is now a school. The place stands back from the stream of life, which flows past it along the main road to a seaside resort near by; and it is guarded by a sign which says "No Through Road."

### Small, Bewildered Strangers

But on Saturday strangers arrived – small, bewildered strangers, transported from the town by the Vicar and one or two volunteers, and dumped on the Manor House lawn to be distributed. They were homesick and lost and desperately shy, but they responded bravely to their hosts' advances and were easy to convince that at least we meant to be kind.

The work of distribution was not difficult. Most of the cottagers gallantly took a child apiece – many proceeding, it seemed, on the theory that in a large family one more makes no odds – and the larger houses according to capacity.

Almost the youngest of the party were Kitty and Jacqueline, sisters aged six and five respectively, who were watched over by a care-worn and anxious-eyed brother named Henry, aged 12. One of the Vicar's helpers, who frankly admitted that she had had her eye on Kitty and Jacqueline from the first, bore them off to her home; and these two inhabitants of a mean street in the East End found themselves taken in charge by a small, excited girl of eight and a kind but firm nanny, and were introduced to a way of living which must have been not only new but profoundly mystifying.

Manners, for instance. Kitty and Jacqueline had obviously been very carefully brought up; and the anxious-eyed Henry, himself billeted next door, accompanied his sisters to their new home to see that they behaved.

"Now mind, Kitty," he said at the garden gate, "don't walk on the grass," and was quite confounded when "the lidy" said she might walk on the grass as much as she likes – it was there to be walked on.

But if "the lidy" was lax about grass, she had several nonsensical notions upon which she was strangely insistent. Why, for instance, was Jacqueline not allowed to run into the street, her natural playground? Why all this fuss about washing? And why spoil your beautiful clean handkerchief, ordered by the evacuation authorities, when you have a couple of handy and unspoilable thumbs.

### Even Villages have "Gangs"

Henry shook down less easily. Once his sisters were off his hands (he was much shocked by the way, to discover that they had forgotten to say "Thank you" for their car ride) he had fallen from his high, grown-up estate. On Sunday morning it was reported that he had cried all night and was talking wildly of running away. This phase soon passed, however. When last I saw him Henry had ceased to be either an anxious elder or a lonely alien. Somebody had given him a pair of shorts, and he had joined a gang of small village boys and was looking incredibly juvenile.

On the whole, it is wonderful how these visitors from another world have merged into our little community. Each of us, however, has a tale to tell of the strangeness of their ways – how this child cannot sleep in the dark, or that one hates having a room to itself.

The most revealing of all these tales is told by the cowman's wife. Her guest could by no means be persuaded at first to sit up to the dinner table; never in her life had she eaten her meals anywhere but on the door-step.

On the Sunday morning there arrived a consignment of elders – invalids, and mothers with young babies. These were not so easy to cope with. They did their best, poor ladies, and so did we; but your dyed-in-the-wool Cockney does not transplant very easily.

From the moment when I took the Gosling family aboard my car, for instance, I knew that they were never going to find our village their spiritual home.

There were five Goslings in all. Granny Gosling, fat and lame; her daughter, her daughter-in-law, and their respective offsprings. Collected on the Manor House lawn, they looked about them with a dawning hopelessness while the Vicar tried to find them billets near to one another.

The Goslings were polite and appreciative of our efforts, but sank moment by moment into deeper gloom. Somewhere in their peregrinations they had learnt that we had no pub and that in our one little general shop you could not even get yourself a nice cup of tea.

Some cheerful lady helper, thinking how lucky they were to escape into clean Sussex air, said brightly, "You'll be new beings by the time you leave here." But the Goslings had no sort of desire to be new beings. They wanted to go on being their comfortable stuffy selves. They wanted a public bar, and quick Cockney jokes, and loud rude Cockney laughter, and two bottles of stout and a drop of port for Granny.

I wish I could tell you where the Goslings are now, but I have come up to their beloved London and have lost touch with them. Undoubtedly they are very lucky to have got away, and it ought to do them a great deal of good; but I doubt very much whether they will ever see it in that light.

READY FOR THE FIRST TEA-PARTY

**(September 7)**

# BUTTER AND BACON TO BE RATIONED

**Mr. W.S. Morrison, Minister of Food, in the House of Commons yesterday, stated that food rationing, to begin in mid-December, will be necessary only in the case of two commodities – butter and bacon.**

**Ration cards are to be issued within the next fortnight, and although they include coupons for other foods, these will not be operative.**

**The ration of butter and bacon, which includes ham, will probably be of four ounces each per person per week, the exact amount depending on the available supplies when the scheme starts.**

**The position of other main foods was outlined by the Minister as follows:**

**SUGAR – Supplies available for months provided that each person only buys 1lb a week.**

**MEAT — Ample supplies in sight.**

**MARGARINE – Manufacture has been greatly increased since the war.**

**COOKING FATS – Normal supplies available.**

**Though sugar will not be rationed as yet, consumers are asked to register to provide the authorities with an indication of what is needed in each district.**

**(November 2)**

# FOOD FROM THE ALLOTMENT

By H.H. Thomas

Soon there will be half a million new allotment holders in this country, and the crops they will produce next year are expected to add considerably to the national food supply.

They will welcome the extension of summer time, for the extra daylight will enable them to push on with the preparation of the land for planting fruit trees and bushes in autumn and sowing and planting vegetables in spring.

A 10-rod allotment – i.e. an area of approximately 300 square yards – will supply a family of five with fresh vegetables for the greater part of the year. Their cash value is estimated by the Ministry of Agriculture to be about £6 10s in normal times, but as it is likely that vegetables will be dearer if the war continues the allotment holder's crops will be worth more. The great benefit of having freshly gathered vegetables cannot be expressed in terms of cash.

### THE MOST PROFITABLE CROPS

The most profitable crops are potato, carrot, onion, runner bean, broad bean, parsnip, turnip, spinach, leek, peas, cabbage and winter greens. Lettuce can be grown as a catch crop between the rows of other vegetables.

If the allotment holder devotes half his plot to potatoes he will have enough for the needs of an average family for the whole year.

Many of the new allotments will consist of neglected ground that has become rough and weedy. Coarse grass and weeds should be taken off and burnt before the ground is trenched. If the turf is good it should be stripped off and stacked. Land cultivated now will be in first-rate condition for sowing and planting in spring if the surface is left rough or ridged up to expose it fully to wind, rain and frost.

The allotment holder should lime his land after it has been trenched and then plant part of it with cabbage. He may sow broad beans and peas and plant shallots in autumn. Crops that may still be sown are onion, winter lettuce, cauliflower and spinach.

### WHEN TO PLANT BUSH FRUITS

Only extensive cultivation will yield the maximum amount of food. Fruit trees trained on trellis by the sides of the path will yield satisfactory crops. Blackberry and loganberry will thrive on arches, a rough support of poles or a fence.

The bush and cane fruits – gooseberry, currant and raspberry – are very profitable and well suited to allotments. November is the best month for planting. No time should be lost in preparing the land by digging it about two feet deep. It is necessary also to order the bushes so that they will arrive in time for planting in autumn.

First-rate sorts are the raspberries Norfolk Giant and Lloyd George; black currants September Black and Davidson's Eight; red currants Laxton's Perfection; gooseberries Lancer and Whinham's Industry; blackberries Bedford Giant and John Innes.

**(September 23)**

# POEM THE KING QUOTED

## LINES WRITTEN BY AN ENGLISHWOMAN

Daily Telegraph Reporter

I am able to reveal the authorship of the quotation with which the King ended his Christmas Day broadcast to the Empire.

Literary experts throughout the world sought in vain to discover the origin of the lines. The King himself, it is understood, did not know whence they were derived.

He came across them recently, not in a book, and was so struck by them that he decided to incorporate them in his broadcast.

The lines I can state, were written by Miss M.L. Haskins, of Crowborough, Sussex, novelist and poet, who, until the beginning of the war, was employed as a tutor in the Social Science Department of the London School of Economics.

"The quotation by the King in his broadcast," Miss Haskins said to me last night, "occurs in a collection of short poems called 'The Desert,' which I wrote before the war of 1914-18, and which printed privately in aid of an Indian charity. The poem containing the quotation is called "God Knows."'

### AUTHOR RECOGNISED WORDS

The lines quoted by the King and those following were:

And I said to the man who stood at the gate of the year: "Give me a light that I may tread safely into the unknown!"

And he replied:

"Go out into the darkness and put thine hand into the Hand of God. That shall be to thee better than light and safer than a known way."

So I went forth and finding the Hand of God trod gladly into the night. And He led me towards the hills and the breaking of day in the lone East.

So heart be still:<br>What need our little life<br>Our human life to know,<br>If God hath comprehension?

Miss Haskins told me how she, with a family party at Crowborough, listened to the King's broadcast.

"When I heard the quotation," she said, "it sounded familiar, and I thought I recognised the words. Then I realised that the quotation was from my own poem.

"My recollection of the circumstances in which the lines were written is vague. I know it was shortly before the war of 1914-18 and I believe I was in the West of England at the time the inspiration came to me."

Eleven years ago Miss Haskins published her first novel, "Through Beds of Stone," which has also been published in America. It was followed by another, "A Few People."

### QUERY FROM AMERICA

The world-wide interest in the mystery of the quotation is shown by the fact that a cable from the New York Office of The Daily Telegraph seeking enlightenment, admitted that the American Press had hunted in vain for the source of the quotation.

The New York Public Library and the British Library of Information, it was stated, had consulted scores of reference books without success.

**(December 27)**

# KING AND QUEEN REGISTERED

## CALLING ROLL OF THE NATION

The King and Queen like every one of their subjects in England, Wales and Scotland, were included in the national registration last night.

The necessary details affecting their Majesties were recorded on appropriate forms in London, at the time when millions of householders were completing a similar record.

This morning 65,000 enumerators will start collecting forms from every dwelling in the country. It is hoped that the collection will be completed by next Friday.

The Register will contain the names and particulars of 46,000,000 people. Not a man, woman or child in the country will have been omitted from the roll-call. Registration is compulsory.

So essential is it that the householder should have received a schedule that instructions have been issued for those who may have missed the enumerator.

Vagrants and temporary homeless in London numbering several thousand were all included in the registration.

At midnight police specially detailed to deal with tramps and others who prefer to sleep in West End doorways and alleys or under railway arches had reported well over 100 persons sleeping out of doors.

The majority of the casuals, however, were registered at the eight L.C.C. casual wards or at the Salvation Army and Church Army hostels and at the Rowton houses.

The enumerators' tasks were simplified by the black-out, which took most of the casuals to their beds long before midnight.

**(September 30)**

# PETROL FOR 200 MILES A MONTH

## EXTRA RATIONS IN CERTAIN CASES

By Our Motoring Correspondent

Owners of private cars must not expect that the petrol ration books they are to receive on or after Sept. 16 will enable them to purchase motor fuel in large quantities.

The books will contain coupons, each representing one gallon, and the number of coupons will vary according to the rated horse-power of the car as shown in the registration book, which must be produced when application is made.

I understand that the books are being made up on a basis of about 200 miles a month so that the owner of an "Eight" would get each month a book of five coupons (reckoning 40 miles to the gallon), and of a "Twelve" a book of eight coupons (reckoning 25 miles to the gallon), and so on in proportion to the average petrol consumption for the different sizes of engine.

This it should be noted, will be the basic rate of rationing. All private-car drivers will have to start with that, and anyone who wants more will have to apply to the Divisional Petroleum Officer in his area, and produce acceptable reasons why he should be granted extra rations.

Lists of the names and addresses of the divisional officers will be published shortly. Meanwhile there is no need for any rush to secure either the basic or extra rations.

Until Sept. 16 it will be possible to buy petrol as in peace time at peace prices, the only restriction being that car tanks only can be filled. After that date, as already announced, "pool petrol" will be sold against ration coupons at 1s 6d per gallon.

**(September 6)**

# BLACK-OUT IN FORCE FOR ALL BRITAIN

Black-out regulations came into force at sunset last night. An official notice issued from the Lord Privy Seal's office stated:

"A lighting order has been made under Defence Regulation. No. 24 and comes into operation at sunset to-night as a further measure of precaution.

"The effect of the order is that every night from sunset to sunrise all lights inside buildings must be obscured, and lights outside buildings must be extinguished, subject to certain exceptions in the case of external lighting where it is essential for the conduct of work of vital national importance. Such lights must be adequately shaded."

Drivers who had been unable to take the full measures prescribed under the Lighting Restriction Order were allowed to employ the following improvised methods for one night only:

Sidelamps: Covered by two thicknesses of newspaper, with side, rear or top panels completely obscured;

Headlamps: Thick cardboard disc behind the glass, with a semi-circular hole not more than two inches wide, the straight side uppermost and not above the centre line of the lamp; and

Rear Lamps: All glass panels other than the obligatory red lamps completely obscured, and the red light covered with two thicknesses of newspaper.

**(September 2)**

Every section of the Government's plan for Civil Defence, from the Administration itself, down to Lighting and Food Storage, is covered in

**A.R.P.**

**A COMPLETE GUIDE**

by

**William F. Deedes**

*"Daily Telegraph"*

*A.R.P. Correspondent*

The interest aroused since this book was published on Monday of this week has created such a demand that the first and second impressions have been exhausted, and the third is now on sale.

An indispensable possesion for every householder.

*Obtainable from Bookstalls and Newsagents, 1/-, or 1/2 post free from Book Department, Daily Telegraph, 135, Fleet Street, E.C.4.*

### BE WARY IN TALK

Always be on your guard in conversation, not only when talking to strangers but also when meeting friends and relatives. A casual remark may give valuable information to the enemy. This applies particularly to war workers. Thousands of people are occupying responsible posts for the first time. They should never talk about their work.

**(September 20)**

# PIONEER OF BRAIN SURGERY

## PROF. HARVEY CUSHING

**By Our Medical Correspondent**

By the death of Prof. Harvey Cushing at Newhaven, Connecticut, at the age of 70, not only America but the world at large has lost one of the greatest figures in modern surgery. Indeed, the surgery of the brain, as we know it to-day, probably owes more to Harvey Cushing than to any other man.

By his long and patient researches, by the amazingly efficient technique he adopted and taught to other surgeons who came to learn from him, he was directly and indirectly the means of saving many thousands of lives that, but for him, must have been lost.

Probably his chief work was in the unravelling of the secrets of the pituitary gland in the base of the skull – a gland that is now recognised as mainly responsible for many if not most of our instinctive reactions and the adjustment of our physical processes to such emotions as anger, fear and anxiety, and that may well be described as a primitive brain in itself.

### LENGTHY OPERATIONS

It was largely as the result of close observation of the changes wrought by diseases and tumours of this gland that Harvey Cushing brought into light many of its hitherto unsuspected functions.

And it was his deft and patient surgery – some of his operations lasted for as long as seven or eight hours – that showed how such tumours, in what had been believed to be a quite inaccessible position, could be successfully removed.

In the history of medicine his place and name are secure. But to all who had the privilege of his friendship he was modesty itself, the finest type of broad-minded, enthusiastic, scholarly and practical American education.

He had hosts of English and European friends. He served in France during the last two years of the Great War, receiving the C.B. and Legion of Honour. He was, in addition, the author of the classical biography of his great friend, the late Sir William Osler, many of whose characteristics he shared.

### BRITISH HONOURS

He was a lover, like Osler, of old medical books and first editions. He was, in England at least, also a lover of the theatre; and in addition to being awarded the Lister Medal in London in 1930 he was given honorary degrees by Oxford, Cambridge and a large number of universities.

One of his daughters is the wife of Mr. James Roosevelt, the son of President Roosevelt. No less in England than at Harvard, and indeed, wherever medicine and surgery are studied, he will be missed as a great and lovable man and one of the foremost surgeons of his age.

**(October 9)**

# GREAT PIONEER OF 'PLANE DESIGN

## GERMANY'S DEBT TO ANTHONY FOKKER

**By George Fyfe**

Mr. Anthony Fokker, the aviation pioneer who proved to be one of Germany's greatest assets in the last war, has died in New York during the Christmas holidays at the age of 49. He was not only a clever designer but a remarkably able pilot.

Son of a Dutch coffee planter, he was a brilliant inventor who, at the age of 18, became wildly excited over human flight. Long before he had seen a machine in the air he was busily designing one. Then he taught himself to fly. In an attic at home he rigged up an imitation cockpit. It consisted of an old wooden chair, on each side of which a moveable stick was fitted.

One stick represented the elevator; the other was for wing warping, after the manner introduced by the brothers Wright. For hours he would sit on this chair, laboriously familiarising himself with the controls. Then he made his first flight. For the next 20 years he made a point of testing each of his new types himself.

Ill-luck attended his efforts to sell his machines. Holland, Italy, Russia and England were not interested in the work of the smiling but somewhat gawky youth, and he went to Germany. There, in 1913 he obtained all the encouragement he needed.

When the war broke out in the following year he devoted himself to the design of a single-seat fighter. Its worth was beyond all doubt.

### INTERRUPTER GEAR IN 3 DAYS

The German High Command asked him if he could add to its merits by evolving a method of sending bullets through the whirring airscrew. He had never seen a machine-gun before, but within three days he had produced his interrupter gear.

Thus equipped in the autumn of 1915, the Fokker fighter went on to inflict heavy casualties on Allied machines. Its speed was no more than 70 m.p.h. and its ceiling 6,000ft, but its great manoeuvrability and its synchronised fire left Britain's slower B.E. 2c's at its mercy.

Britain lost large numbers of fine pilots until the Fokker scourge was ended in 1916 by two "pusher" machines, the F E 2b and the D H 2.

In an attempt to regain supremacy Fokker designed many new aeroplanes, the most notable being his triplane, which was extraordinarily successful until it was realised that in attaining fine climbing powers and manoeuvrability there had been a sacrifice of speed.

**(December 27)**

HIS HOLINESS wearing the triple crown of the Papacy during the celebration of his tenth anniversary of his coronation, in 1932.

# PIUS XI'S CAREER AS SCHOLAR, DIPLOMAT & REFORMER

His Holiness Pope Pius XI, who died this morning at the age of 81, was born at Desio, a little town in the plains of Lombardy. He was not of noble birth, and in that respect was unlike many of his predecessors, for he came of a family of weavers, who had carried on that occupation from father to son for hundreds of years.

Achille Ambrogio Damiano Ratti was the son of Francisco Ratti and his wife Teresa, and his early education, like that, of all the other children in a district that was without a school, was given him by the parish priest.

It was not long, however, before his vocation became clear, and he travelled to Milan, where, at the College of St. Carlo, he presently took his degree as Bachelor of Philosophy. Then he went to Rome, where he continued his studies at the Collegio Lombardo.

When he was 22 he was received into the priesthood, and the first to be given his blessing were his father and one of his brothers. In the next few years he graduated as Doctor of Canon Law, of Theology, and of Philosophy.

His fame as a scholarly librarian led Pius X. to install him in 1912 as vice-prefect of the Vatican Library and Canon of St. Peter's while, three years later Benedict XV, insisted on his becoming Librarian of the Vatican despite his desire to devote himself to his beloved Ambrosiana Library. By a compromise he was to stay for alternate periods of two months in Rome and Milan, but ultimately he was constrained to remain in Rome.

But although he had many duties, and attended to them assiduously, he had one absorbing recreation. He was fascinated by mountaineering.

So energetically had he pursued his studies, however, that he was 28 before he found it possible to make any spectacular ascents. By the time he was 31 he had been on numerous climbs that included Mont Blanc.

### SWEEPING REFORMS
### PRONOUNCEMENTS ON POLITICS

His Pontificate may be described as the most notable of modern times. Its outstanding event was the recovery in 1929 of temporal sovereignty and the creation of Vatican City as an independent State, but it was also marked by many reforms which were directly due to the Pope's forceful character. By the conclusion of concordats, by unequivocal pronouncements on political and social matters, and by the encouragement of scientific and learned research and their practical application, Pius XI, has stamped both his character and his personality on the Vatican.

In 1918 Benedict XV, suddenly removed Mgr. Ratti from his books and manuscripts and launched him on a diplomatic mission for which his abilities seemed in no way fitted. Amid all the difficulty and confusion of the world war he was despatched as apostolic delegate to the newly created Republic of Poland. On this delicate mission he had only the rank of priest, but so disarmingly successful was the bookworm in his strange role that his sphere was extended, he became nuncio and was consecrated in Warsaw as titular Archbishop of Lepanto.

It was in recompense for his noble labours in Poland during the whole of the time that it was menaced by the Bolshevik occupation that Benedict XV raised him in 1921 to the Sacred College and appointed him to succeed Cardinal Ferrari as archbishop of his native diocese of Milan.

In less than a year he had been chosen to succeed his patron as Pope. The Consistory concluded on Feb. 6, 1922, with the election of the junior Cardinal Priest, then a man of 64.

As the youngest among the Princes of the Church Cardinal Ratti was hailed as scholar and diplomat. He could speak 24 languages and had a modest reputation both as author and athlete.

On the very day of his election he created a precedent which seized the popular imagination and was counted as an omen in the solution of the "Roman question." For the first time since 1870, when the Pope became a voluntary "prisoner of the Vatican," the new Pope appeared before the crowd in St. Peter's Square on the outside loggia of the basilica and there — instead of within St. Peter's – imparted the traditional blessing urbi et orbi.

### FIRST ENCYCLICAL

Within the first year of his pontificate the Pope issued the first of the several encyclicals which were to command the interest and respect of countless persons outside his obedience It was concerned with the peace of the world and the foundations on which the post-war world must rebuild if its foundations were to be durable. Chief among them he placed the sanctity of family life, a theme to which his subsequent utterances frequently recurred.

In another encyclical denouncing "the lust of earthly possession" as the fundamental cause of world confusion, the Pope exhorted the faithful against the growing strength of atheistic and subversive forces which were taking advantage of world-wide misery. The evils of atheism and Communism were ever-present in the mind of Pius XI, and in 1931 he unequivocally denounced Socialism.

One great event of Pius XI's pontificate was the conclusion in February, 1929, of a treaty between the Italian Government and the Vatican by which the Pope was established as an independent sovereign with his own territory. The Pope was assured of an indemnity of £22,000,000 for losses sustained in 1870, and the control of the clergy over marriage law and education was restored. The Concordat virtually restored in Italy the medieval relations of Church and State.

Trouble arose within two years of the signing of the treaty, but the quarrel was ultimately settled and honour appeased on both sides.

**(February 10)**

# PROF. SIGMUND FREUD

## PSYCHO-ANALYSIS AND ITS EVOLUTION

Professor Sigmund Freud, who died in London on Saturday, aged 83, completely revolutionised the world's attitude towards problems of psychology.

He was born at Freiburg, Moravia, of Jewish parentage, and was taken to Vienna at the age of four. He became a medical student and obtained his degree in 1881.

His psychological theories were revolutionary, and embraced the conclusion that there was generally a sexual basis to mental disorders. In developing these ideas in 1895-96 he evoked angry dissent. Although in 1902 he was appointed Professor of Neurology at Vienna University, he remained to a large extent ostracised.

Suddenly, however, the world began to take notice, and in 1910 the International Psycho-Analytical Association was formed. His teachings spread rapidly.

Tirelessly Freud devoted himself to his practice and his writings. He saw his books translated into many languages, and nothing was more noteworthy than his refusal to interrupt his activities when he was attacked by a malignant disease.

By 1923 he had finished his decisive contribution to psycho-analysis. He applied himself now to cultural problems, and from his pen came books such as "The future of an illusion" in 1927, and "Civilisation and its discontents" in 1930. In 1939, "Moses and Monotheism" appeared. In this he suggested that Moses was not the child of Hebrew parents, but of Egyptian, and that he was murdered during a rising of his followers.

**(September 25)**

# SCREEN'S GREAT ATHLETE HERO

## DOUGLAS FAIRBANKS, SENIOR

Just a quarter of a century ago a young man in a silk hat, with the broad shoulders and slim hips of a middle-weight boxer, an acrobat's agility, and a grin that would not come off, laughed and leapt his way through "The Lamb."

That was the debut of Douglas Fairbanks – one did not need to add the "senior" then, and it seemed incredible that we ever should – and the beginning of one of the greatest careers the screen has known.

Born at Denver, Colorado, 56 years ago, Mr. Fairbanks started as a Shakespearian actor, playing Cassio. "Mr. Warde's supporting company was bad," wrote a critic, "but worst of all was Fairbanks."

But Fairbanks could not be stopped. He brought to Broadway the novelty of the athletic hero. In "Hawthorne, U.S.A." he made his entrance by jumping a wall and ended the third act by leaping from a balcony at the villain's throat. Audiences were enchanted.

D.W. Griffith made him an offer. "The Lamb," made by the famous Triangle company, was followed by "Reggie Mixes In" and "The American," both exploiting the same mixture of fast action, acrobatics and laughing gallantry.

### "THREE MUSKETEERS"

They carried Fairbanks to success, and with the later "Mark of Zorro," "Three Musketeers," "Black Pirate," "Robin Hood" and "Thief of Bagdad," he achieved a fame equalled only by his partners in United Artists, Mary Pickford and Chaplin.

Mr. Fairbank's first wife was Miss Beth Sully. His second marriage to Mary Pickford in 1920, ended by divorce 15 years later, and his third marriage to Lady Ashley are too familiar to need retelling. No stars have ever had quite the frenzied reception given to Mr. Fairbanks and Miss Pickford in London.

**(December 13)**

# MR. FORD MADOX FORD

Mr. Ford Madox Ford, the author and critic, died in a nursing home at Deauville yesterday, aged 66. He changed his name from Hueffer to Ford shortly after the war, in which he served in a Welsh regiment.

The son of the late Dr. Hueffer, the music critic, and grandson of Ford Madox Brown, the painter, he was brought up under the influence of the Pre-Raphaelites, and hated them.

He once said: "To me life was simply not worth living, because of the existence of Carlyle, of Mr. Ruskin, of Mr. Holman Hunt, of Mr. Browning, or of the gentleman who built the Crystal Palace.

"These people were perpetually held up to me as standing upon unattainable heights and, at the same time, I was perpetually being told that if I could not attain to these heights, I might just as well not encumber the earth."

**(June 27)**

MR. W. B. YEATS

# MR. HOWARD CARTER

## MAN WHO FOUND TOMB OF TUTANKHAMEN

Mr. Howard Carter, the famous archaeologist, who died in London yesterday, at the age of 65, caused a world sensation when 17 years ago, he discovered the tomb of Tutankhamen in conjunction with the late Earl of Carnarvon.

The triumph was the result of patient laborious work over a period of many years. The general assumption of experts in Egypt was that the Valley of the Tombs of the Kings had been cleared.

Tirelessly excavators had applied themselves before this to work which in its main aim proved profitless. Mr. Carter and Lord Carnarvon refused to be discouraged and in their thoroughness decided that their excavations, instead of being confined to the surface, must go down to bedrock.

The great dumps left by earlier excavators had to be cleared, and this task systematically carried out, entailed the removal of between 150,000 and 200,000 tons of earth.

STEPS CUT IN ROCKS

But the rewards were slow in coming. Small discoveries of interesting objects were made, but only by the greatest patience was victory attained.

In November, 1922, Mr. Carter suddenly came on steps that had been cut ages before in the rock. They led to a wall bearing an ancient Royal seal, and before long a sealed doorway was revealed.

Beyond this lay another door which when broken open showed the wonderful treasures of a tomb that had been concealed in the rock for more than 3,000 years.

The statues, representations of animals in gold, chairs, chariots, vases and the great wealth of picturesque ornaments that were exposed to view left the explorers dazzled and spellbound.

In the weeks that followed Mr. Carter directed activities of an important kind. Electric light was introduced, precautions were taken to guard against the decay of any of the ancient treasures, catalogues were prepared. And throughout this lengthy task Mr. Carter knew that other secrets lay beyond. For a further door had still to be opened that led to an annexe.

CURIOSITY STIFLED

It was in every way characteristic of Howard Carter that the remaining secret should be disregarded, and all curiosity stifled, until the first discovery had been dealt with.

Not until nearly three months had elapsed was everything cleared, and then, while the world waited excitedly for news, an entrance was affected. The new discoveries were even more wonderful. One chamber after another contained treasures of exquisite craftsmanship and fabulous value, with a wall of solid gold, shrines, and the great sarcophagus.

Several years were devoted to the recovery of the treasures, which were accommodated in the Cairo Museum.

The discoveries provided abundant material for the study of the customs of ancient Egypt and people from every country flocked to the scene, paying a heavy fee for the privilege of visiting the tomb.

He was only 17 when he went to Egypt as a member of the staff engaged on the Egyptian Exploration Fund's archaeological survey, and in the years that followed the work became with him a passion. He learned eagerly from all the great archaeologists he met and devoted himself to excavations with enthusiasm.

In 1892, on behalf of Lord Amherst of Hackney, he assisted Sir Flinders Petrie at his work at Tal-el-Amarna and in the following year became a draughtsman in the six years Deiz-el Bahari campaign.

**(March 3)**

# W.B. YEATS

## POET, PLAYWRIGHT AND POLITICIAN

English literature suffers a heavy loss in the death on Saturday at Mentone, on the French Riviera, of William Butler Yeats, the famous Irishman, who was the greatest living English poet. He was 73, English, because while he was Irish by birth and a passionate patriot, his language was English and as poet and artist he was the heir of a great English tradition.

Yeats's art was deeply coloured by Ireland and Irish folklore. But while he had spiritual ancestors in the minstrels of his own island, he had them also in the English Pre-Raphaelites, in Coleridge and Keats and Blake, and before them in the Elizabethans.

Yeats possessed the magical gift of the great poets in restoring to hackneyed words new-born freshness and an original tune. He could write of the rose and of the moon and it was as though they were new symbols. His early lyrics with their irresistible sweet tunefulness – for instance, the songs, "All the words that I utter," "I will arise and go now," and so many others – and his later writings, less decorative, but more intense and deep-searching, will always be cherished by those with a care for the finest flavours of literature.

A FAMILY OF ARTISTS

Yeats was born in Dublin in 1865, the same year as Rudyard Kipling. He came of Cornish and Irish stock. His great-grandfather and grandfather were Protestant clergymen and his father a painter, John Butler Yeats. Like his younger brother Jack, who was to make a considerable name, W.B. Yeats for a time thought of painting as a career after his schooldays (in London and Dublin), but at 21 decided for literature. "I was" wrote Yeats of himself at this period, "in all things Pre-Raphaelite."

In 1887 the Yeats family returned from Ireland to settle in London, at Bedford Park, W.B. Yeats now wrote reviews for the "Bookman," and W.E. Henley published his first lyrics in the "National Observer." Lionel Johnson, Ernest Dowson and John Davidson were his friends, fellow-members of the Rhymers' Club.

The nineties were the time of, among other things, Kipling and Imperialism on the one hand and Yeats and Celtic Twilight on the other. Scoffers said that Maeterlinck, the Fleming, was the inventor of Celtic Twilight, but what might have been a mere fashion was given substance by Yeats's genius. It was the period of his "Countess Kathleen," "The Shadowy Waters," "The Secret Rose," and the marvellous love-poems of "The Wind Among the Reeds."

YEATS THE SENATOR

The next phase was that of the Irish theatre – an heroic period and a picturesque one, celebrated in countless memoirs. Miss Horniman, of Manchester, financed the Dublin Abbey Theatre, and chief of the dramatists were Yeats for poetic drama and Lady Gregory for racy peasant plays. And, of course, there were others. The poet turned administrator, and anyone who expected to find in him an ineffectual dreamer met with the surprise of his life.

A hint has been given of the modified style of the ageing, disillusioned Yeats. Personally the lank, abstracted aesthete of the nineties became robust and almost hearty in appearance – almost a country squire. In 1917 he married and had a son and a daughter. A Cosgrave man in politics, he was elected to the Irish Senate in 1922, and a year later received the Nobel Prize for literature. In 1931 Oxford awarded him a doctorate.

Not all the developments in the new Ireland were to his taste. He seems to have been unprepared for the clerical power in Free State politics, and was keenly disappointed by the imposition of a literary censorship. In religion he was far from orthodox, and, while a Nationalist, a romantic one.

**(January 30)**

# HERR ERNST TOLLER

Herr Ernst Toller, the German playwright and novelist who has committed suicide in New York at the age of 46, made many friends in London, where, in his exile, he spent a considerable amount of time.

The interest taken in him by extremists was added to generally by his eloquent descriptions of life in German captivity.

A pacifist who was born on the Polish border, he served in the German army, fierce revolutionary. He took part in the Bavarian rising in 1919 and after being captured was sentenced to five years' imprisonment.

In that period he occupied himself with the writing of books and plays in which he gave full vent to his Communist doctrines. His works included "Masses and Man," "Machine Wreckers," "I Was a German" and "Letters From Prison." But nothing Toller wrote attracted more attention than a book of poems which included one about swallows which made a nest in his cell. He lamented bitterly that the prison governor, not content with destroying the manuscript because it was "propagandist," destroyed the nest and others which the swallows later endeavoured to make.

**(May 23)**

# DR. HAVELOCK ELLIS

## MANY CONTRIBUTIONS TO LITERATURE

Dr. Henry Havelock Ellis, one of the most vital personalities of his time, has died at Hintlesham, Suffolk, at the age of 80.

A man of extraordinary erudition, he produced imposing, and to many people repellent, scientific works that were marked by deep research and originality of outlook. He was at the same time a writer who, by his diversified gifts and literary craftsmanship, attracted the attention of readers all over the world.

Havelock Ellis has been described more than once, as a man who for the greater part of his life was always ahead of his age, and nothing was more noteworthy than the change of attitude which in recent years had greeted his labours.

OUTLIVED OBLOQUY

Forty years ago he was being widely condemned because of his writings on sexual problems, yet he outlived obloquy and became instead the subject of extravagant eulogy.

DR. HAVELOCK ELLIS

Born at Croydon he was the son of a ship's captain. His childhood was spent on long sea voyages and eventually he lived in the Australian bush. At 16 he became a teacher in New South Wales and returned to England at 22 to study medicine at St. Thomas's Hospital.

When he gained his degree he did not practise very much; one of his few patients was his friend, Olive Schreiner, the once famous author of "The Story of an African Farm".

MADE IBSEN KNOWN

Havelock Ellis went on to write for the magazines, to translate Heine, and to edit the valuable Mermaid series of old English dramatists. This was followed by the "Contemporary Science" series – to which he contributed his own volume on "The Criminal" – "Man and Woman," "A Study of British Genius," "The Explanation of Dreams."

He also helped to introduce to the British public the works of Ibsen, Nietzsche and other Continental writers who were then little known in England.

His greatest interest, however, expressed itself in "Studies in the Psychology of Sex.." This monumental work, which was to occupy him for some 30 years and to consist of seven volumes, caused a sensation with the appearance of the first volumes.

A PROSECUTION

A prosecution for "obscene libel" was instituted against the vendor in 1897. In consequence the rest of the books were published in the United States and directed to scientific readers. Only in recent years have they been issued in this country as standard works.

Apart altogether from "Studies in the Psychology of Sex" and inter-related books, Havelock Ellis has left a very rich general literary treasure in his "New Spirit," "Affirmations," "The Soul of Spain," "Little Essays in Love and Virtue," three books of "Impressions and Comments," and numerous other volumes in which his great culture is displayed.

**(July 11)**

# MRS. RUDYARD KIPLING

Of Mrs. Rudyard Kipling, whose death occurred yesterday at the age of 73, the world learned very little. This was certainly not because of a lack of interest, for it was inevitable that there should be a certain amount of curiosity concerning the wife of so world famous a man.

The reason lay in her desire to escape the limelight. The public platform and social happenings were shunned. She confined her activities to a very much secluded home. It always seemed that for a great deal of her life her aim was to guard it from any intrusion, however friendly the intention.

Mrs. Kipling was of American birth. She was Caroline Starr Balestier, and her brother, Wolcott Balestier, collaborated with Kipling in the writing of "The Naulhakha."

**(December 20)**

# KING GHAZI OF IRAK

King Ghazi of Irak, who has been killed at the age of 27, in a motoring accident at Baghdad, had an interesting association with this country for he was educated at Harrow.

He was the only son of the late King Feisal, and his boyhood in the desert was spent at a time when his father was fighting desperately to secure his country's freedom from Turkish rule. At the age of 14 he was sent to England, and after being with a tutor in the South of England for a few months went to Harrow in 1927. There he made many friends through his pleasant demeanour and took some interest in sport, favouring cricket and tennis but relishing most of all the skiing he was able to practise during a holiday visit to Switzerland.

In 1928 he returned to Irak, and shortly afterwards was enrolled as a cadet in the military school at Baghdad. On the completion of his training there he became A.D.C. to his father.

The sudden death of his father while on holiday in Switzerland led to Prince Ghazi succeeding him in September, 1933.

He was just 21, and no longer the rather weakly-looking boy who had gone to Harrow. He was now well built and handsome, and in his uniform as a second lieutenant he took the oath of accession at a special session of Parliament in Irak.

Violently antagonistic political opinions in Irak led to more than one crisis in his short kingship. A revolt last month was quickly suppressed.

MODERN IDEAS

He had no doubt of the value of modern ideas, and it was natural for him, after his English experiences, to acquire not only powerful cars and to drive them, but to purchase aeroplanes for his own use. Similarly he became greatly interested in radio.

**(April 5)**

# MR. MARK GERTLER

## WELL-KNOWN BRITISH ARTIST

Mr. Mark Gertler, the artist, who has died at his Highgate studio, aged 46, was born in Spitalfields in December, 1892. As a child he revealed an exceptional gift for drawing, and after he had entered a stained-glass window factory in Bloomsbury at 14, his work came to the notice of the Jewish Educational Aid Society.

With its support he was sent to the Slade School of Art at London University, where he became one of its most brilliant students, winning a Slade scholarship and, later, one from the British Institute.

Before he was 20 he had won a reputation, receiving the encouragement of many connoisseurs of contemporary art. His pictures found ready acceptance at exhibitions of the New English Art Club, of which he was elected a member in 1912, and of the London Group.

Though visiting Paris and eagerly investigating the production of the modern French School, he painted chiefly in London, until a serious illness made him move to the country.

After 1920 he held one-man shows at the leading London galleries, of which the most recent was at the Lefevre Gallery last month. He was one of the representative British artists invited to show extensively at the Biennale Exhibition in Venice. The Tate Gallery possesses his "Agapanthus," and the National Portrait Gallery his portrait of Sir George Darwin, while others of his pictures have been acquired by the foremost provincial galleries and the Contemporary Art Society.

He was one of the first introducers of the methods of Post-Impressionism into British painting.

**(June 26)**

# R. BURTON NEW OPEN GOLF CHAMPION

## BRILLIANT LAST ROUND OF 71 BEATS AMERICAN

## FIVE TIE FOR THIRD PLACE

**By George Greenwood**

ST. ANDREWS, Friday.

RICHARD BURTON 31, of Sale, Cheshire, Ryder Cup player, is the new Open champion. With an aggregate of 290 he won the title here to-day by 2 strokes from John Bulla, of Chicago, at the end of a thrilling pursuit. Burton, whose 4 scores were 70, 72, 77 and 71, appeared to have thrown his chances away with his third round, but making a supreme effort he forced his way back into the running.

Following a brilliant patch in which he accomplished 8 holes, starting at the sixth in 5 under 4's, he learned when on the 14th green what it was necessary to do in order to overhaul Bulla. The remaining 4 holes had to be done in 18 strokes to win. Burton did them in 17, finishing with a glorious 3 – a superb drive of nearly 350 yards, a mashie-niblick 12 feet past the pin, and the putt holed amid deafening cheers.

It was a magnificent finish to a courageous round of fighting golf. For two hours Bulla, sitting in the smoking room of the Royal and Ancient Club, had been hailed and congratulated as the champion, for it was thought to be impossible for anyone to catch him after he had shaken off Perry and Shankland.

Doubts arose , however, when the news filtered back that Burton, after dropping two strokes in the first five holes, had reached the turn in 36. This was true enough, and what was more from the 6th to the 13th his figures were 4, 3, 3, 3, 4, 2, 4, 4 – a memorable display of opportunist golf.

A tall, powerful man, Burton slogged the ball enormous distances, and moreover holed some vital putts, though even in his invaluable run in the middle of the round he failed surprisingly with a couple of "sitters." Burton played the dreaded 14th safely in five, taking no risks but the next two holes were somewhat adventurous.

At the 15th he pulled his 2nd, and left himself with a putt of enormous length, only to hole one of 7ft for a four. Then at the 16th a hooked drive brought a five in its train, but he finished superbly.

Twice within a month Bulla, the giant American, has been robbed of victory, first in the U.S. Open, in which he was leading after three rounds, and now in the British Open.

Armed with still another new putter, he shook it destructively when the ball failed to drop, but actually kissed it when it brought him success, one occasion being when he holed from 16 feet for a 3 at the 18th, to round off a grand day's golf with a 73, following his 71 in the morning.

Bulla who is 25, and the son of a retired Methodist minister, need have no regrets, for to finish second in the Open at his first attempt, is no mean achievement. "I shall come again and perhaps next time I shall be more fortunate," said Bulla cheerfully.

"A new personality established himself in the front rank in W. Shankland, an Australian and an old Rugby-League player, who is now professional at Temple Newsam, Leeds. Splendidly endowed physically, he is a great attacking player, quite unperturbed and tireless.

With Alfred Perry as his partner a tremendous three-cornered fight developed, with Bulla as the third party. Shankland eventually found himself with a putt for a 3 to tie with the American, who had finished immediately ahead. He went boldly for the hole, but unsuccessfully, and failed with the return.

All the favourite – Cotton, Bobby Locke, Bruen, Pose, the Argentinian, and the deposed champion, Reginald Whitcombe – flattered only to deceive, but of them Whitcombe went nearest. Only his ineradicable weakness on the green prevented him from making a bolder bid to retain the title.

Cotton lost heart at the sixth, where he sliced into the gorse and, finding an unplayable lie, had to go back, the hole costing him a 6. It is a long time since he has played so consistently below his form, his two 76's to-day being totally unrepresentative of his powers.

Equally disappointing were Locke and Bruen, though Bruen had the distinction of finishing first amateur. The high wind cheated Locke, while the magic of the boy Bruen had lost something of its potency.

Five players shared third place, and of these King had a great chance, only putting errors at the sixth, seventh and eighth, which cost him in all 10 putts, turning the scale against him, for he came home in the amazing score of 33 – the best inward half accomplished during the championship. The other four players were Fallon, Shankland, Perry and Whitcombe.

**(July 8)**

# PLAY-TO-FINISH TEST NOT FINISHED

DURBAN, Tuesday.

THE play-to-a-finish Test farce played itself out appropriately here today. It was abandoned to enable the England team to catch the homeward-bound ship in which their passages had been booked.

England, having won the third Test, the only one of the five to be finished, thus won the rubber and avenged South Africa's victory in England in 1935.

After 10 days of record breaking, heart-breaking cricket, it was agreed between the two captains and the South African Board of Control that the final Test should be abandoned, even though England required only 42 runs to beat South Africa, with five wickets still to fall. All were agreed that, so far as it lay in their power, no such uncricketlike contest would ever be waged between the two countries again.

Rain had the final say. It came on so hard during the tea interval that a postponement until to-morrow was inevitable if the match was to be finished. A special train, then, for the long journey to Cape Town would have left the players with bare time to catch the ship.

There were records galore. Here are some of them:

World's Record Fourth Innings Total – England's 654 for five wickets beats New South Wales' 572 against South Australia (Sydney, 1907-8).

World's Record Aggregate – The 1,981 runs scored in this match beat the record aggregate of 1,919, scored in the New South Wales v. South Australia match (Sydney, 1925-6), and the Test record of 1,815 in the West Indies v. England match (Kingston, 1930).

Longest Match – The nine-day match between West Indies and England (Kingston, 1930), was the longest in first-class cricket history until this one.

Record Stand – The partnership of 280 by P.A. Gibb and Edrich was a record for any wicket in Anglo-South African Tests, beating the 268 by Hobbs and Sutcliffe (Lord's, 1924).

Record Innings – England's second innings total was their highest in Tests against South Africa; South Africa's first innings their highest against England.

W.R. Hammond and Paynter made a wonderful effort to force a win when they saw the change in the weather, and the England captain's innings of 140 was one of the finest of his career. With Paynter he set up a new record stand of 164 for the fourth wicket, beating the 151 made by Leyland and himself at the Oval in 1935.

England went so near to winning that it seems difficult to understand why it was so necessary for them to catch a particular ship home. When, after 10 days, there was so much to gain it would surely not have been out of place to catch another ship for England.

All through this longest-ever match, one factor stood out above everything else – the wicket. In the words of a South African critic, the wicket, not the cricket, killed the timeless Test in South Africa and put the game back 10 years.

**(March 15)**

COMPLETE SCORE

SOUTH AFRICA

| | |
|---|---|
| P.G. Van Der Byl, b. Perks | 123 |
| A. Melville, hit wkt, b Wright | 78 |
| F.A. Rowan lbw b Perks | 33 |
| B.Mitchell b Wright | 11 |
| A.D. Nourse b Perks | 103 |
| K. Vitjoen c Ames, b Perks | 0 |
| E.L. Dalton c Ames, b Perks | 57 |
| R.E. Grieveson b Perks | 73 |
| A.B.C. Langton, c Paynter, b Verity | 27 |
| A.S. Newson c and b Verity | 1 |
| N. Gordon not out | 0 |
| Extras | 20 |
| Total | 330 |

Second Innings

| | |
|---|---|
| P.G. Van Der Byl c Paynton, b Wright | 97 |
| A. Melville, b Farnes | 103 |
| F.A. Rowan c Edrich, b Verity | 0 |
| B.Mitchell hit wkt b Verity | 89 |
| A.D. Nourse c Hutton b Farnes | 25 |
| K. Vitjoen b Perks | 74 |
| E.L. Dalton c and b Wright | 21 |
| R.E. Grieveson b Farnes | 39 |
| A.B.C. Langton, c Hammond, b Farnes | 6 |
| A.S. Newson b Wright | 3 |
| N. Gordon not out | 7 |
| Extras | 17 |
| Total | 481 |

ENGLAND

| | |
|---|---|
| Hutton run out | 38 |
| P.A. Gibb c Grieveson, b Newson | 4 |
| Paynter, lbw b Langton | 63 |
| W.R. Hammond st Grieveson, b Dalton | 24 |
| Ames, c Dalton b Langton | 84 |
| Edrich c Rowan, b Langton | 1 |
| B.H. Valentine st Grieveson b Dalton | 26 |
| Verity, b Dalton | 3 |
| Wright, c Langton b Dalton | 26 |
| K. Farnes, b Newson | 20 |
| Perks, not out | 1 |
| Extras | 26 |
| Total | 316 |

# OLYMPIC GAMES FOR LONDON

## FIRST TIME IN 36 YEARS

**By Bevil Rudd**

The International Olympic Committee, meeting in London yesterday, decided to hold the 1944 Olympic Games in London.

This the 13th Olympiad will be the second held in Great Britain. The first was in 1908.

Lord Burghley a delegate on the committee, told a representative of The Daily Telegraph that the British Olympic Committee has already laid the foundations of the financial and administrative structure of the 1944 Games.

Accusations of ill-feeling had been made about previous Games, said Lord Burghley, and Britain's main object in 1944 will be to try to regain the real Olympic spirit.

It is understood that, although the Government is keeping in the background, it is anxious to do all it can for the success of the Games and especially to make the year 1944 an historic one in the campaign for physical fitness.

FINANCIAL NEEDS

The Games will not, it is expected, need Government financial support. The British Olympic Committee has already received generous offers of support even for such a gigantic undertaking.

The amount of guarantees needed is not yet fixed, but Lord Burghley pointed out that it will be a very large sum and will have to come from the pockets of British sportsmen.

**(June 10)**

# FOOTBALLERS WANT HIGHER WAGES

Threat of strike action, if other methods fail to give them better conditions, was made by Football League players at a private meeting of the Players' Union in London last night. Those present included many of the most famous men in the game, including a number of Internationals.

Demands made by the meeting, which will go forward to an extra-ordinary meeting of delegates, included the following:

Raising of the maximum wage to £9 per week;

Minimum of £4 per week throughout the year;

More compensation for injured players;

Doubling of bonuses in Cup-ties and talent money payable to clubs finishing at the head of their divisions; and

Representation on the Football League Jubilee Fund.

The meeting which was presided over by "Sammy" Crooks, International and Derby County forward, represented about 75 per cent. of the first-class players in the country. It was stated that the union's membership was nearly 2,000.

**(February 28)**



# WORKMAN SCORES ALL-IRISH TRIUMPH

**By Hotspur**

LIVERPOOL, Friday.

WORKMAN, an Irish nine-year-old horse belonging to Sir Alexander Maguire, a wealthy Dublin and Belfast match manufacturer, won the Grand National here to-day. His starting price was 100-8. Capt. L. Scott Brigg's MacMoffat, (25-1) was second, beaten by three lengths and Miss Dorothy Paget's Kilstar, the 8 to 1 favourite, third a further 15 lengths behind. Eleven of the 37 starters finished.

The Irish triumph was complete, for Workman, in addition to being trained and ridden by an Irishman, was backed by practically everyone in Navan, the home of Sir Alexander Maguire in County Meath, with a population of about 10,000.

"I persuaded everyone to support Workman last year when he finished third" the owner told me, "and this time I begged them to back him again. I do not think there is a man or woman in Navan who is not on him."

Sir Alexander Maguire is a Native of Liverpool and has a seaside home at Eastbourne. He bought Workman three years ago for 1,500 guineas from Capt. Stedman after the horse had won a race at Punchestown Ireland.

"I liked him because he was a remarkable jumper and very speedy," he said. "Later I found out that he had the other necessary attribute of an Aintree horse – stamina – and I was then convinced that I had got a Grand National winner."

The trainer of Workman, John Ruttle, is an ex-cross-country jockey who has ridden at Aintree, but not in the Grand National. When Workman was led into the unsaddling enclosure Ruttle dived a hand into his pocket and produced two boxes of matches. "I carry them for luck," he told me.

The jockey, T. Hyde, won the Irish Grand National last year on Clare County.

Workman, who is the first Irish horse to win the Grand National since Troytown in 1920, was bought as a two-year-old for 40 guineas. He has already won more than £10,000 in prize money.

The owner was mobbed when he led in his horse, for the victory was tremendously popular and prominent bookmakers declared that Workman was the best-backed runner on the day of the race.

The success was well merited, but the hard luck story of the race comes from Jack Moloncy, the veteran rider of Mrs. C. Jones' Black Hawk. He said: "Black Hawk was travelling so well that I felt certain my turn to win had come at last.

"Three fences out Workman collided with him. My horse 'lost' his hind legs and tossed me out of the saddle, I think I must have won."

Hyde, rider of the winner, told me: "My only anxious moments were when I could not shake off a loose horse for two or three fences before Becher's the second time round."

Coming on to the racecourse, Under Bld and Kilstar moved up and were just in front of 'Dominick's Cross, Red Hillman, and Black Hawk over the water.

Dirthgift ran across the second fence in the country and caused Blue Shirt and Tuckmill to refuse as well, but they were a considerable way behind the leaders at the time. Sporting Piper fell at Becher's and Kilstar would have done so had he not made a wonderful recovery.

Black Hawk and Workman had now more or less sorted themselves out from the rest, of whom I noticed Royal Mail going well, and I thought Black Hawk looked a likely winner, barring accidents. Unhappily, Workman gave him a bump in mid-air at the fence after Valentine's, and Moloney was unseated.

That left Workman in front, with MacMoffat rapidly making up ground, only to find himself baulked by Black Hawk, who was running on riderless.

When the racecourse was reached the second time it was obvious that Workman or MacMoffat would win, as Kilstar had taken too much out of himself when he blundered, and had no steam left. The weight also began to tell on Royal Mail, and he faded out, and Inversible came down at the last fence when lying fourth.

Workman had a lead of a couple of lengths from MacMoffat at the final obstacle and not only held on to his advantage, but slightly increased it in the long run-in to the accompaniment of tremendous cheering from his host of backers.

**(March 25)**

# CROWD OF 100,000 SEE HARVEY WIN WORLD TITLE

**By Harold Lewis**

LEN HARVEY, once again beating Jock McAvoy in a very hard and close battle over the full 15 rounds at the White City last night, earned for himself the right to be described in this country at any rate, as world champion – champion at light-heavyweight.

By way of contrast, this fight was followed by the eclipse of Jack Doyle at the hands of Eddie Philips, who accomplished his task with a single punch in the first round.

All the fights between Harvey and McAvoy have been close, have lasted the full fifteen rounds, and have been moderate stuff to watch as regards spectators who like thrills. This one was nearly all close-quarter fighting – boring, holding, hitting on the break, bustling, pushing, and numerous little tricks which are not entertaining.

There is no love lost between these two when they are opposed in the ring. Two aspects of it deserve to remain in the memory – the marvellous courage and skill of Harvey in a crisis in the 14th round, when he was on the verge of being knocked out, and his remarkable stamina through the second half of the fifteen rounds.

QUESTION OF AGE

Obviously Harvey was not strong at the weight, despite the stories of the ease with which he had removed half a stone. Equally obvious was the fact that Harvey is 32 today; hence the strain, the necessity for conserving energy with the utmost care, against this powerful, aggressive man from Rochdale.

In the matter of points the fight wavered. First came Harvey, with fine pounding on McAvoy's nose. Then came McAvoy, incessantly boring in, savagely jabbing away at the body, cuffing the back of Harvey's head.

At times Harvey looked desperately tired. His eyes were sunken and lined, his face white, his mouth open. By sheer will power he seemed to pull himself together, and would surprise McAvoy with an occasional rally and some tremendous hooks to the stomach.

The crowd in the distant stands began booing in the seventh round. They wanted more action. The in-fighting meant nothing more to them than a hugging match. From the ringside one could see how bitter this struggle was, but as seen from 50 yards or more away it must have been sorry stuff.

After 13 rounds there was very little in it. Perhaps Harvey led by an odd point or two. And quite probably McAvoy realised it. At any rate he then decided to stake all he had on one great effort.

That effort nearly won him the fight. A fierce left-hook to the jaw unsettled Harvey. He ducked away, left himself open in retreat, and was hit again and again.

The crowd began to roar for a knockout, and Harvey staggered across the ring, his eyes glazed and his arms falling to his sides. But McAvoy himself had shot his bolt. He had not the energy left to follow up with his customary "devil."

Mechanically, Harvey fenced for a while, and gradually recovered. And when the gong went for the last round, this man of 32, haggard, both eyes bruised, came from his corner like a greyhound and with an overpowering attack swept McAvoy to the ropes. That last round was Harvey all the way – an amazing Harvey, astonishing his own seconds by his vitality.

Harvey won that fifteenth round by a wide margin. Even so, Mr. C.B. Thomas, the referee, retired to a neutral corner and added up the points of his card carefully, checking and double-checking while each man and his seconds waited expectantly with the smile of victory hovering on their lips.

**(July 11)**

# R.L. RIGGS TRIUMPHS AT WIMBLEDON

**By Our Special Representative**

ROBERT L. RIGGS, of America, yesterday joined the select band of those who have conquered Wimbledon at the first attempt. he beat his compatriot, E.T. Cooke, by 2-6, 8-6, 3-6, 6-3, 6-2, in the final of the men's singles.

G.L. Patterson, W.T. Tilden and Ellsworth Vines are the only other players who have done it. Riggs therefore, joins high company – but how vastly different his methods from those of the redoubtable hitters with whom his name is not linked.

And what a strange sight to see empty benches and walking-room on the terraces on a Wimbledon Finals day! Hundreds of the open stand seats – available only at the turnstiles – for which the midnight queues once formed, were unsold. And after two sets the vast arena half-emptied and the tea marquee filled.

Indeed, I heard one man who can remember Wimbledon in its pre-war setting, describe this Riggs-Cooke final as an anachronism.

If that is true, and the Renshaws, the Baddeleys, and the Doherty's match their wits as Riggs matched his against the speed and force which Cooke attempted to impose, the game itself will not suffer by a retrogressive step.

The athletic prowess of a Borotra and the controlled hitting of a Johnston or a Vines are not given to all of us, and if a few club players were made to realise, watching Riggs, that science can still achieve much on the tennis court, their enjoyment of the game will increase.

FINE DETERMINATION

Primarily though, Riggs is to be praised for the fact that he won when below his best form. The effort to raise his game to its highest level was at times obvious. The strokes did not flow with the same spontaneity and sparkle as they had against Puncec, for example, but his will and determination were rigid, and even when everything appeared to be going against him he never lost sight of the ultimate goal.

There were many rallies that, frankly, were boring, long back-hand exchanges that cried out for a stroke of enterprise. But there were many just as enthralling, and the fluctuations of the score should have been enough to keep interest alive.

To the young and once promising competitor sitting in front of me whose promise is so much greater than his ambition that he buried his nose in a novel, I would suggest that he failed to observe something that all young English players could usefully have absorbed – the immense concentration of the two men on the court.

American dominance perforce imposed a tremendous strain on their players, and after the strenuous singles battle and all the physical and mental strain it involved, Riggs had to wade through another six sets before he piloted Miss Marble into her third final. He too, appears in two more finals to-day, the men's and mixed doubles.

There was no other way out of it if the meeting was to be completed to-day, and Riggs, tired though he was, took his full share in his side's victory over C.M. Jones and Miss E.H. Harvey by 5-7, 6-1, 6-3; and then over C.E. Malfroy and Miss Nuthall by 3-6, 6-2, 6-4 in the semi-final.

There is, however, still a British interest in all four events to be finished to-day. Miss Marble beat her singles opponent, Miss Katherine Stammers, in a women's doubles semi-final – the first match on the centre court yesterday. Miss Marble and Mrs. Fabyan won 8-6, 6-3 against Miss Stammers and Mrs. S.H. Hammersley.

THE 1939 CHAMPIONS

Men's Singles: R.L. Riggs (U.S.A.)
Women's Singles`: Miss A. Marble (U.S.A.)
Men's Doubles: RIGGS and E.T. COOKE (U.S.A.)
Women's Doubles: MRS. S.P. FABYAN and MISS MARBLE (U.S.A.)
Mixed Doubles: RIGGS and MISS MARBLE (U.S.A.)

**(July 8)**

ALL ENGLAND LAWN TENNIS Championships at Wimbledon. R.L. Riggs (US), versus Ghaus Mohammed (India).

# BIG SURPRISE IN ASHTON CUP

## EDMUNDSBURY PARK BEAT COWDRAY PARK

The first tie in the Ashton Cup high handicap tournament at Hurlingham resulted in a surprise win for Edmundsbury, who, with half a goal to start, defeated Cowdray Park by 111/2 goals to 2.

Edmundsbury were much the better team. Major Harrison made some good clearances for Cowdray Park, and Keith Rous worked hard, but his side were soundly outplayed.

At half-time, despite a goalless first period, Edmundsbury were leading by 31/2-0, and their five further goals in the fourth period settled matters. It was not until half-way through the concluding period that Rous got Cowdray's first goal, and with the last shot in the match Major Harrison credited them with their second from a free hit wide out.

Edmundsbury are a hard side to beat from their 15 points rating.

**(July 11)**

# MATTHEWS STAR FORWARD IN HAMPDEN BATTLE

## GREAT RALLY FOLLOWS DEPRESSING START:

## LAWTON'S LATE GOAL

**By Frank Coles**

SCOTLAND 1; ENGLAND 2

HISTORIC Hampden Park, scene of many a grim fight between the countries in the last 30 odd years, has never staged quite such a dramatic finish as when Lawton won Saturday's match for England with a magnificent goal two minutes from time.

And if ever a team deserved to snatch victory spoils from the dying embers of a game it was those 11 gallant Englishmen who showed their grit by rallying from a depressing start – they were a goal down after 21 minutes – and, long before the winning point was scored, had the Scotsmen on the run.

Scotland on the run at Hampden! A rare and refreshing sight for English eyes – and the more remarkable because, for the greater part of the first half, the Scots, playing in traditional style, seemed to be moving calmly and confidently to success, according to custom.

On a miserably wet day, and with a strong wind blowing from goal to goal – it was raining hard when the Duke and Duchess of Gloucester arrived – I estimated the worth of winning the toss at one goal start.

Scotland had the luck to name the coin right, and might have been in an impregnable position by half-time. They certainly would have been if the finishing had equalled the approach work, and Milne of Middlesbrough, must shoulder most of the responsibility for the missed opportunities. He seemed afraid to put his shooting luck to the test.

I confess that England's defenders gave me more shivers in the first half-hour than the cold wind. Woodley was uneasy in goal. After taking a divot nearly the size of a ball when kicking clear, he misjudged the pace of a corner-kick. Luckily, it flashed across his front and out of play.

Morris and Cullis, young men of iron nerve when in the uniform of the Wolves, made the most elementary mistakes, too. Cullis, of all people, nearly gave two goals away, and while the defence was in this panicky state Hall and Goulden simply had to remain in their own half.

MORRIS BLUNDERED

With Scotland so obviously the dictators, I started to count the corner-kicks. They had forced six when, at the 21st minute, England's unhappy defence fell. It was a gift goal, due to a first-class blunder by Morris.

All Dougal, the scorer, had to do was to tap the ball through a vacant goal. Woodley had gone out to field a back-pass from Morris, but, to the goalkeeper's dismay Morris carelessly put the ball 10 yards away from him, towards the left post.

Poor Woodley, taken by surprise and his boots stuck in the mud, never had a hope of getting back to avert the impending tragedy. Almost before the goalkeeper could turn Dougal had the ball in the net.

BEASLEY'S GREAT SHOT

Matthews, a starved winger in more senses than one for half an hour, took the ball up to and past Cummings in his best style, and Beasley, who had been out of it, crashed in a wonderful shot which would have beaten nine goalkeepers out of ten.

My half-time impression was that if England could keep their attack going the game was a long way from lost. Well, with the wind at their backs, they at once pegged their rivals down to defence and even when the 150,000 crowd let themselves go with the deafening Hampden roar the Scots had as much chance of turning the tide as King Canute.

But they were stubborn. Indeed, the match was an hour old before a corner-kick was conceded. It did seem inevitable though, that England's persistent pressure would be rewarded and when the equalising goal came it was a replica of Scotland's point.

Again a right back blundered, Carabine being the offender this time. When there was no obvious danger, he missed his kick and let through Beasley, who accepted the gift of the gods by blazing the ball into the roof of the net without hesitating a second.

England had earned the goal all right. Could they go on and smash through to the first English triumph at Hampden in 12 years? The golden opportunity seemed to have been thrown away when Lawton, given a perfect opening by Goulden, put the ball wide. And Scotland looked safe after Dawson had turned aside a great shot by Matthews, only three minutes from the end.

But it was to be England's day after all. With two minutes to go they made a last desperate throw. Goulden, darting across-field like a snipe, slipped the ball out to Matthews and back it came plumb right for Lawton. Up went the centre-forward for a header and with fine judgment, the ball was steered safely home. He had beaten Baxter to the jump.

Very fitting that Matthews should have made the winning opening. Once he began to receive an adequate service, he gave a display comparable with the old masters and every Scotsman I spoke to after the match agreed that Matthews was a handsome winner of his duel with Cummings.

While, however, Matthews was head and shoulders above every other forward on the field, he does not get the title of Man of The Match. I award that honour, without a moment's reflection, to Mercer, a left-half with the heart of a lion.

If ever a player inspired his side to victory, Mercer did on this his first appearance at Hampden Park. When England were in trouble he was a dour tackler, and when, in the last 25 minutes, he realised that the enemy were tiring under the strain he was up with the forwards, collecting every loose ball and setting up the wings going again and again.

**(April 17)**

# DERBY WON BY FOUR LENGTHS FROM FOX CUB

**By Hotspur**

EPSOM, Wednesday.

BLUE PETER, 7 to 2 favourite, gained a most spectacular triumph in the Derby this afternoon, drawing away from his rivals a couple of furlongs from home and going on to win easily by four lengths from Fox Cub, who beat Heliopolis by three lengths for second place.

Lord Rosebery, Blue Peter's owner, was overwhelmed with congratulations on achieving his first success in the great race, as were Jack Jarvis who had not previously trained the winner, and E. Smith, whose first classic victory was on Blue Peter in the Two Thousand Guineas a month ago.

Smith wore a set of racing colours that had been made years ago for Lord Rosebery's father, but had never been used. Lord Rosebery recently found the jacket at his London house. Smith doubtless will wear the lucky set of colours in the St. Leger.

When I congratulated Lord Rosebery he said: "Of one thing I was sure, and that was that Blue Peter would stay. We had tried him with Challenge, who was second in last year's St. Leger, and as a result of the gallop I was sorely tempted to double my bet."Smith took his triumph very calmly, as did Jarvis, who said to me: "I told you he was the best horse I had ever trained. now he has proved it." Blue Peter's success was especially gratifying to me as I have insisted for many weeks that he is the best three-year-old in training.

The result was one of the most popular in the history of the race, and never has a Derby winner been more loudly cheered than Blue Peter was. All the way back to the unsaddling enclosure, and for some time after Lord Rosebery had led his colt in, the cheering went on.

Lord Rosebery has been racing for more than 30 years and has been a member of the Jockey Club since 1924. No one has worked harder than he in the best interests of the Turf. His father won the Derby three times, with Ladas, St Visto and Cicero.

In the midst of Blue Peter's great triumph I felt real sympathy for Gordon Richards, who rode Fox Cub. The champion jockey, who has now been runner-up in the Derby three times, has yet to record his first success in the race.

There was the usual huge crowd in the paddock before the race. I thought Blue Peter, who was sweating considerably, looked grand, and Heliopolis, Fox Cub and Admiral's Walk were all obviously perfectly trained. The parade passed off without incident, and in a surprisingly short space of time the field of 27 were lined up at the gate.

Capt. Allison sent them off to a perfect start. Bellman and Fairchance being rivals, and, as I had anticipated, the moment Blue Peter was asked for his effort his stride lengthened with devastating effect, and he strolled away from the opposition.

Fox Cub, who was nearly last after they had gone half a mile, passed Heliopolis, but could make no impression on Blue Peter, who passed the post with his ears pricked, four lengths ahead. Fox Cub was three lengths in front of Heliopolis, and then came Casanova, Buxton, Admiral's Walk and Hypnotist, the French colt, Salford II, being last of all.

And so ended one of the best Derbys of my time, and so also was exploded the myth that the stock of Fairway cannot stay, a view that I personally have never held.

**(May 25)**

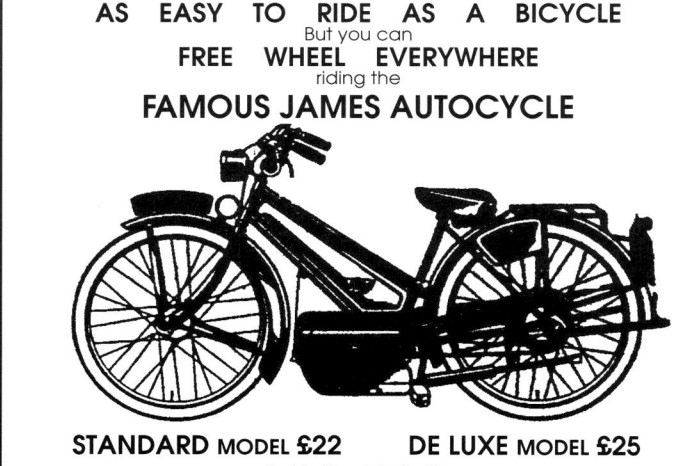

# 186,000 ATTEND REGIONAL SOCCER GAMES

**By Frank Coles**

THE 40 matches played in the eight regional competitions on Saturday – the first day of competitive football since the war started – were watched altogether by 186,000 spectators and although there were many fixtures between great local rivals, not one five-figure "gate" was recorded.

Fears of crowds swarming to football grounds in peace-time numbers having proved unfounded, these regional tournaments should proceed smoothly, and even with a 4,000 crowd, representing about £200 in receipts, clubs will be able to pay their way.

With points at stake, the play was much keener and more penalty kicks were awarded than on any afternoon I can recall. No fewer than four penalties were given, for technical offences, in the match between Arsenal and Charlton Athletic, at White Hart-lane, and Leslie Compton converted three of them.

The Compton brothers, both Middlesex cricketers, again played a leading part in Arsenal's latest spectacular scoring feat. Leslie, who had twice before registered a hat-trick of goals, scored four times and Denis twice. Charlton's 8-4 defeat was not so overwhelming as it looks, as at one point in the second half they rallied from 1-4 to 4-5.

EVERTON IN 4-4 DRAW

Everton, the champions were also in a free-scoring game. Shortly after half-time they led Stoke 4-1, but, thanks to Sale, who got three goals, Stoke forced a 4-4 draw.

One centre, where a maximum crowd was anticipated, was Wolverhampton, where the Wanderers met Birmingham, who had the assistance of several Aston Villa stars. But only 3,500 were present. Birmingham's 3-2 win was also a surprise.

Arsenal's 8,931 was the largest "gate." At Fulham 8,000 saw the local team defeat Portsmouth, the Cupholders, by 2-1, and 6,700 were at West Ham, where Crystal Palace gained a most unexpected 6-2 success. There were approximately the same number of onlookers at Brentford, where Chelsea drew 2-2.

**(October 23)**

# RECORD CROWD FOR LEAGUE MATCH

**By Our Special Representative**

Rangers 2 Celtic 1

BEFORE a crowd of 120,000 people – a record for any League game in the world – Glasgow Rangers triumphed over their traditional Celtic rivals at Ibrox Stadium yesterday and thus practically assured themselves of the Scottish League championship.

More than 25,000 were unable to gain admission and thus missed one of the best and fastest matches in the long history of thrilling encounters between the clubs.

The record attendance for a League match in England is 82,905, set up when Chelsea and Arsenal met at Stamford Bridge in 1935. All attendance records for any game in Great Britain were broken in April, 1937, when 149,547 spectators saw the Scotland-England international match at Hampden Park, Glasgow.

Celtic were unfortunate in that they had to take the field without Paterson, Crum and Divers, all injured in Saturday's game against Hearts, Lynch, Carruth and Birrell filled the vacancies. Rangers reintroduced MacKillop in the half-back line and had Harrison at inside-right in place of the injured Fiddes.

Victory went to the better side. Throughout the game Rangers were the sweeter moving team. They were always striving for smoothness and cohesion in attack and were generally successful. Kinnear and Waddell on the wings were both tremendously fast and full of cunning.

**(January 3)**

# EVACUATION REHEARSALS

(ABOVE): CHILDREN REHEARSING FOR EVACUATION – Ready for everything, these little ones were well prepared for a possible threat.

## TROOPS ON THE MOVE

(ABOVE): THESE TROOPS, Seen before leaving for active service, were in good spirits, as evidenced by the characteristic comments in chalk.

(BELOW): FAREWELL CHEERS by a party of British troops before they left England for active service in France.

## THE A.T.S. AT WORK

(RIGHT): KEEPING THE country moving.

(BELOW): ARRANGING KIT in the store at a military camp.

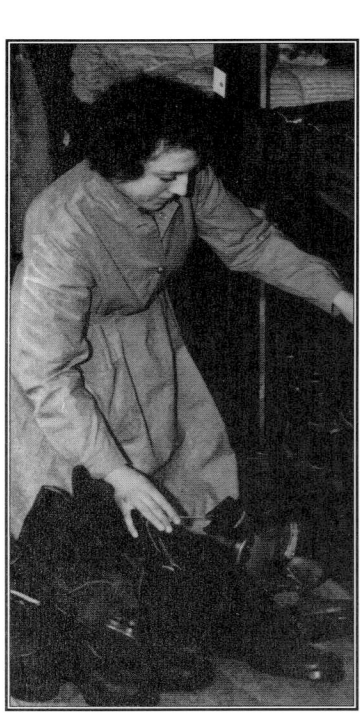

# INDEX

a = column 1    b = column 2    c = column 3    d = column 4    e = column 5    f = column 6